Street by Street

CN00664734

GREATER MANCHESTER

Enlarged areas BOLTON, BURY, OLDHAM, ROCHDALE, STOCKPORT, WIGAN

Plus Altrincham, Ashton-under-Lyne, Glossop, Hazel Grove, Leigh, Middleton, Sale, Salford, Stalybridge, Stretford, Wilmslow

3rd edition October 2007
© Automobile Association Developments Limited 2007

Original edition printed May 2001

Enabled by Ordnance Survey This product includes map data licensed from Ordnance Survey® with the permission of the Controller of Her Majesty's Stationery Office. © Crown copyright 2007. All rights reserved. Licence number: 100021153.

The copyright in all PAF is owned by Royal Mail Group plc.

Published by AA Publishing (a trading name of Automobile Association Developments Limited, whose registered office is Fanum House, Basing View, Basingstoke, Hampshire RG21 4EA. Registered number 1878835).

Produced by the Mapping Services Department of The Automobile Association. (A03490)

A CIP Catalogue record for this book is available from the British Library.

Printed by Oriental Press in Dubai

The contents of this atlas are believed to be correct at the time of the latest revision. However, the publishers cannot be held responsible or liable for any loss or damage occasioned to any person acting or refraining from action as a result of any use or reliance on any material in this atlas, nor for any errors, omissions or changes in such material. This does not affect your statutory rights. The publishers would welcome information to correct any errors or omissions and to keep this atlas up to date. Please write to Publishing, The Automobile Association, Fanum House (FH12), Basing View, Basingstoke, Hampshire, RG21 4EA. E-mail: streetbystreet@theaa.com

Ref: MX044y

Key to map pages	ii-iii
Key to map symbols	iv–1
Enlarged map pages	2-15
Main map pages	16-131
Index – towns & villages	132-133
Index – streets	133-196
Index – featured places	196-204
Acknowledgements	204

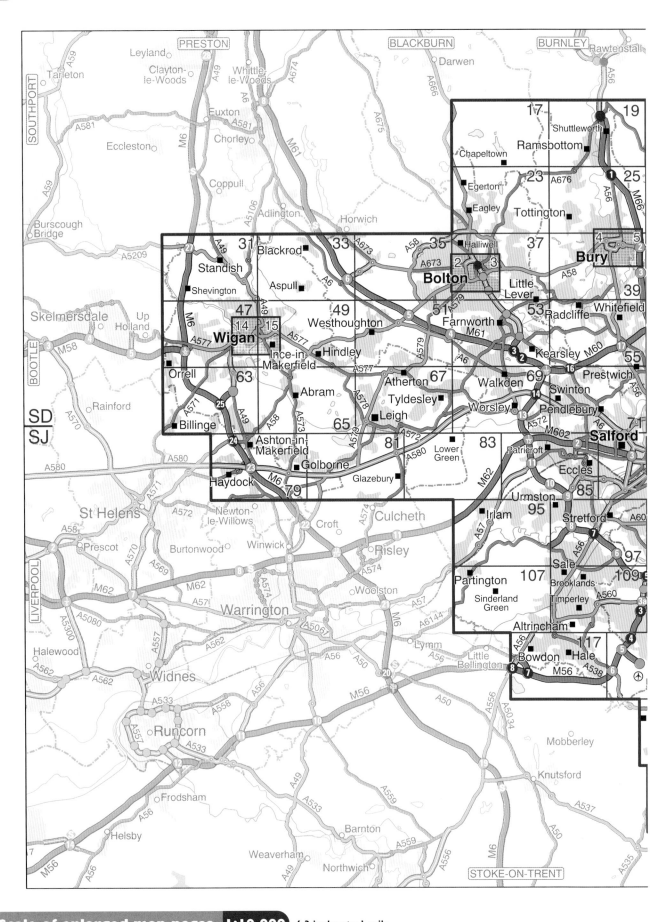

Scale of enlarged map pages `1:10,000` 6.3 inches to 1 mile

National Grid references are shown on the map frame of each page.
Red figures denote the 100 km square and blue figures the 1 km square.
Example, page 6 : Manchester Victoria Station 384 399

The reference can also be written using the National Grid two-letter prefix shown on this page, where 3 and 3 are replaced by SJ to give SJ8499.

3.6 inches to 1 mile **Scale of main map pages 1:17,500**

Junction 9	Motorway & junction	*LC*	Level crossing
Services	Motorway service area		Tramway
	Primary road single/dual carriageway		Ferry route
Services	Primary road service area		Airport runway
	A road single/dual carriageway		County, administrative boundary
	B road single/dual carriageway		Mounds
	Other road single/dual carriageway	93	Page continuation 1:17,500
	Minor/private road, access may be restricted	7	Page continuation to enlarged scale 1:10,000
	One-way street		River/canal, lake
	Pedestrian area		Aqueduct, lock, weir
	Track or footpath	465 ▲ Winter Hill	Peak (with height in metres)
	Road under construction		Beach
	Road tunnel		Woodland
P	Parking		Park
P+	Park & Ride		Cemetery
	Bus/coach station		Built-up area
	Railway & main railway station		Industrial/business building
	Railway & minor railway station		Leisure building
⊖	Underground station		Retail building
⊖	Light railway & station		Other building
	Preserved private railway	IKEA	IKEA store

⌐⌐⌐⌐⌐⌐⌐	City wall	✗	Castle
A&E	Hospital with 24-hour A&E department	🏛	Historic house or building
PO	Post Office	Wakehurst Place (NT)	National Trust property
📖	Public library	M	Museum or art gallery
i	Tourist Information Centre	🐎	Roman antiquity
i	Seasonal Tourist Information Centre	⊥	Ancient site, battlefield or monument
⛽⛽	Petrol station, 24 hour Major suppliers only	🏭	Industrial interest
†	Church/chapel	✽	Garden
🚻	Public toilets	⚙	Garden Centre Garden Centre Association Member
♿	Toilet with disabled facilities	💐	Garden Centre Wyevale Garden Centre
PH	Public house AA recommended	♣	Arboretum
🍴	Restaurant AA inspected	🛒	Farm or animal centre
Madeira Hotel	Hotel AA inspected	🦌	Zoological or wildlife collection
🎭	Theatre or performing arts centre	🐦	Bird collection
🎬	Cinema	🍃	Nature reserve
⚑	Golf course	◀🐟▶	Aquarium
▲	Camping AA inspected	V	Visitor or heritage centre
🚐	Caravan site AA inspected	♔	Country park
▲🚐	Camping & caravan site AA inspected	◠	Cave
🎢	Theme park	✗	Windmill
🏛	Abbey, cathedral or priory	🛢	Distillery, brewery or vineyard

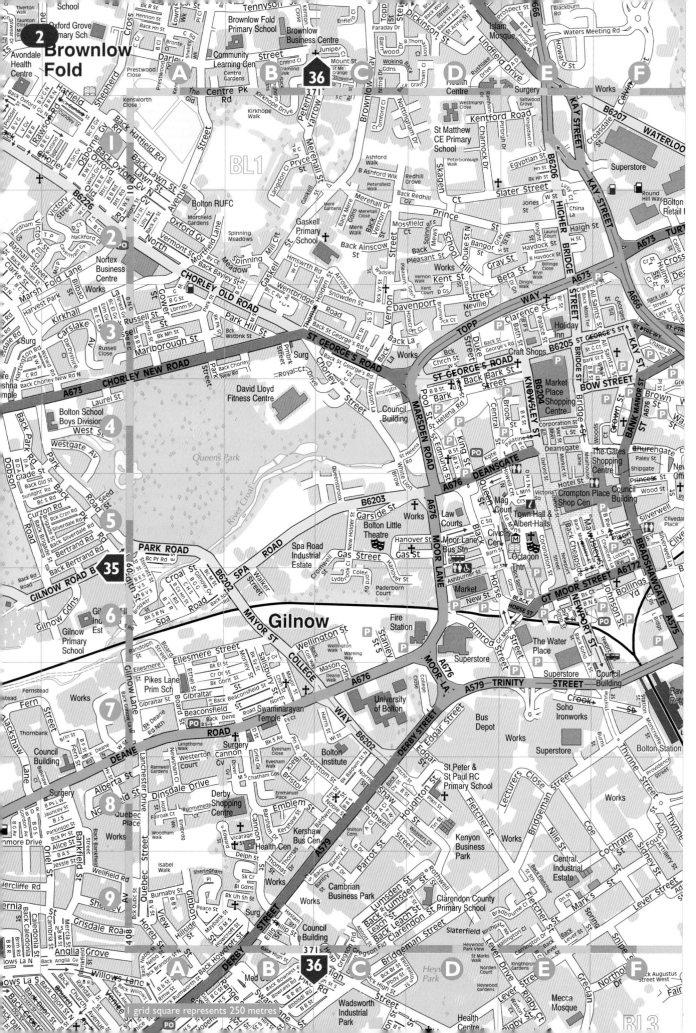

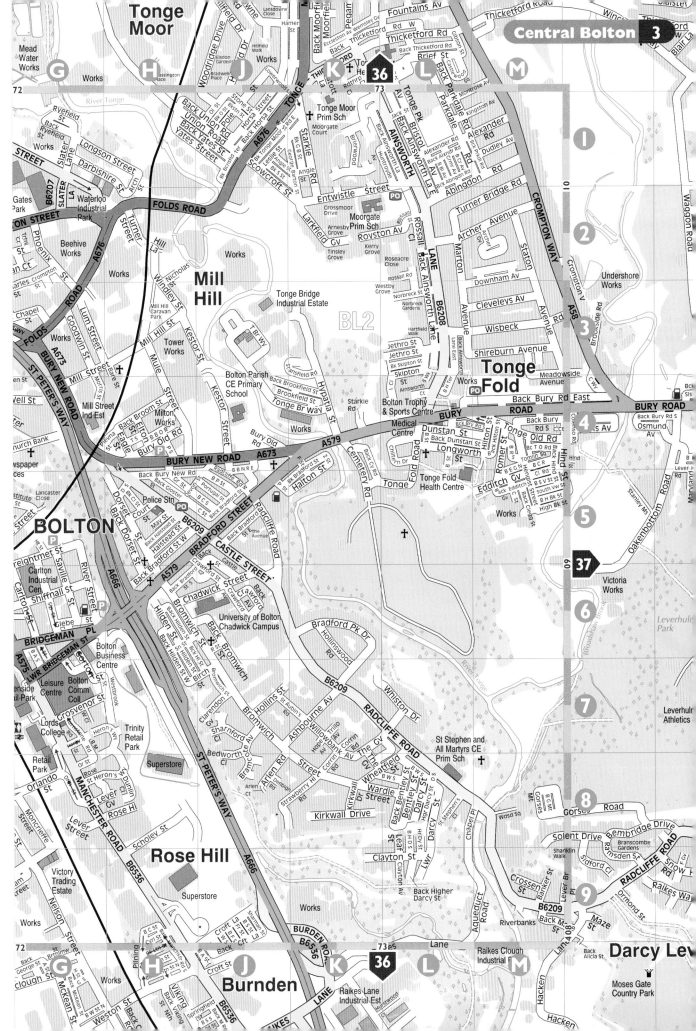

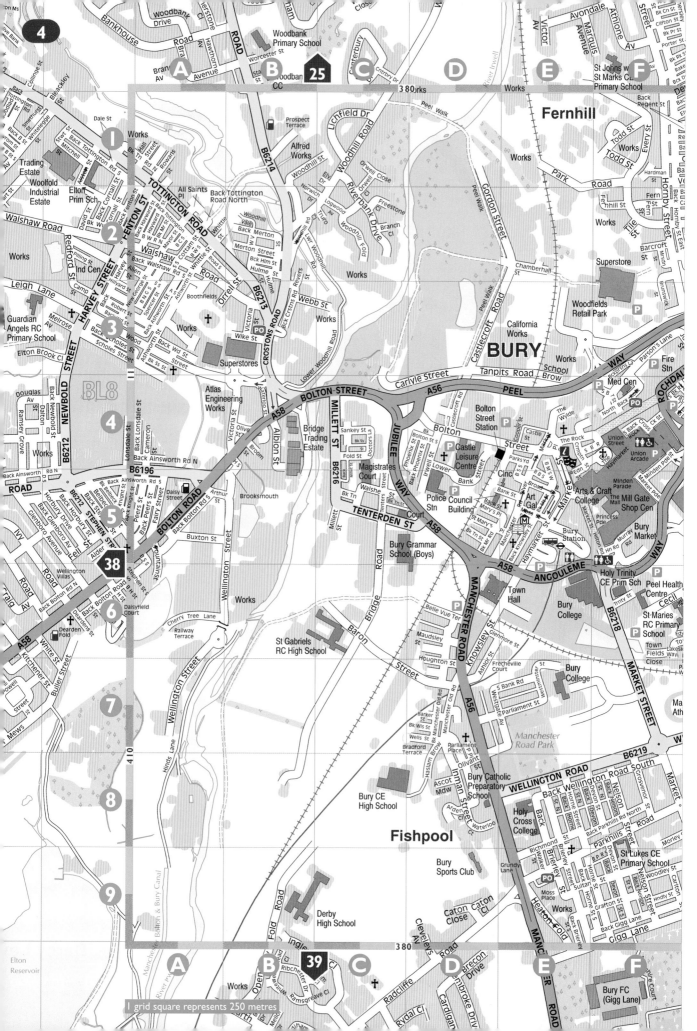

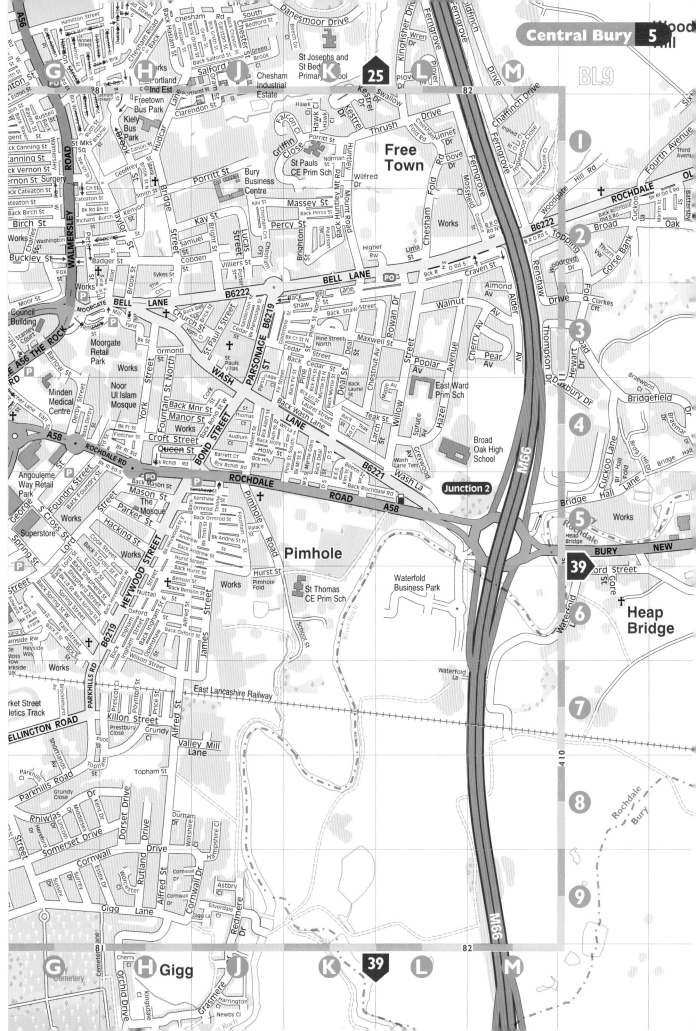

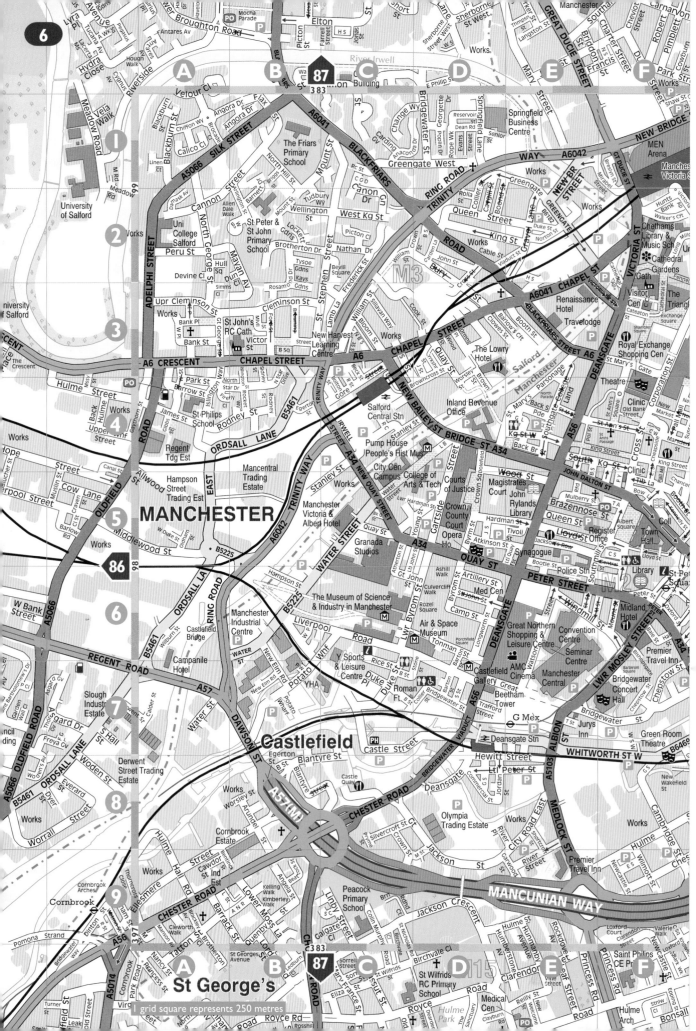

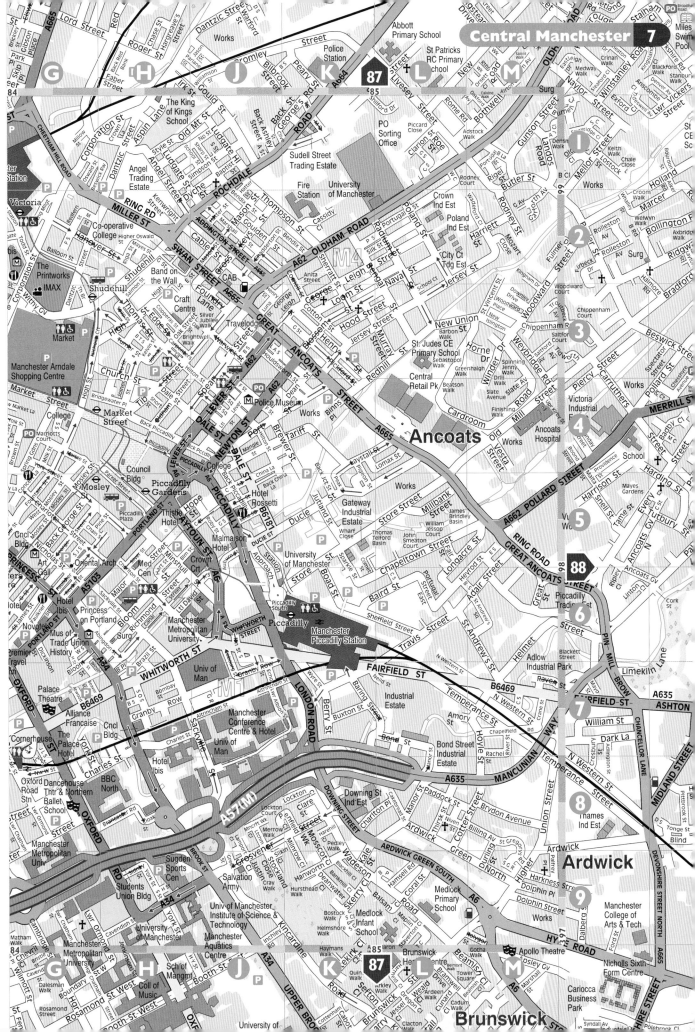

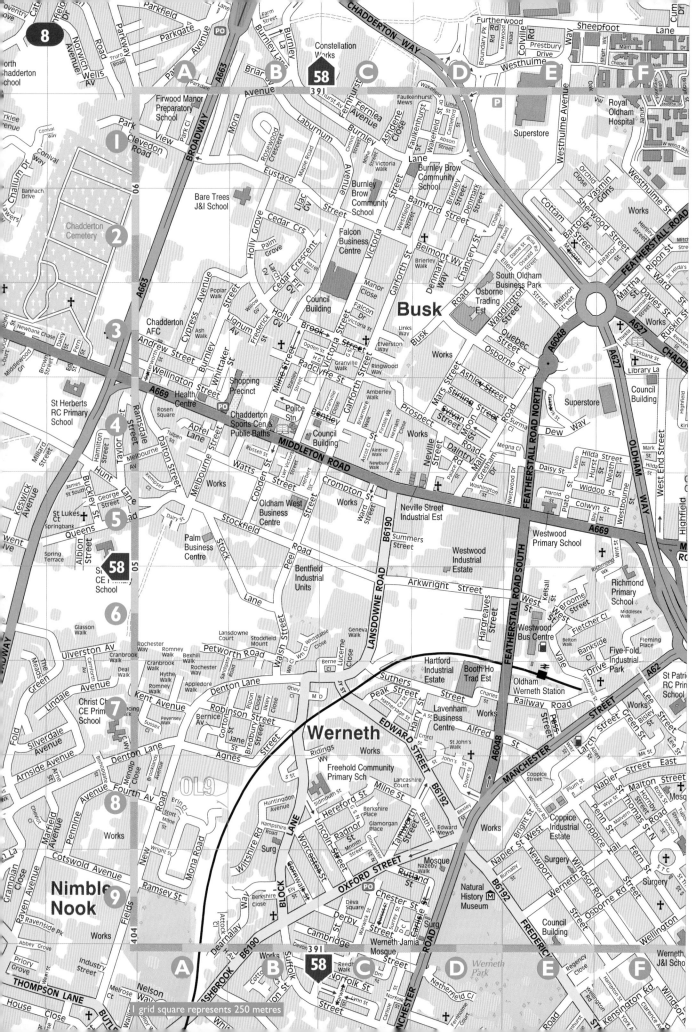

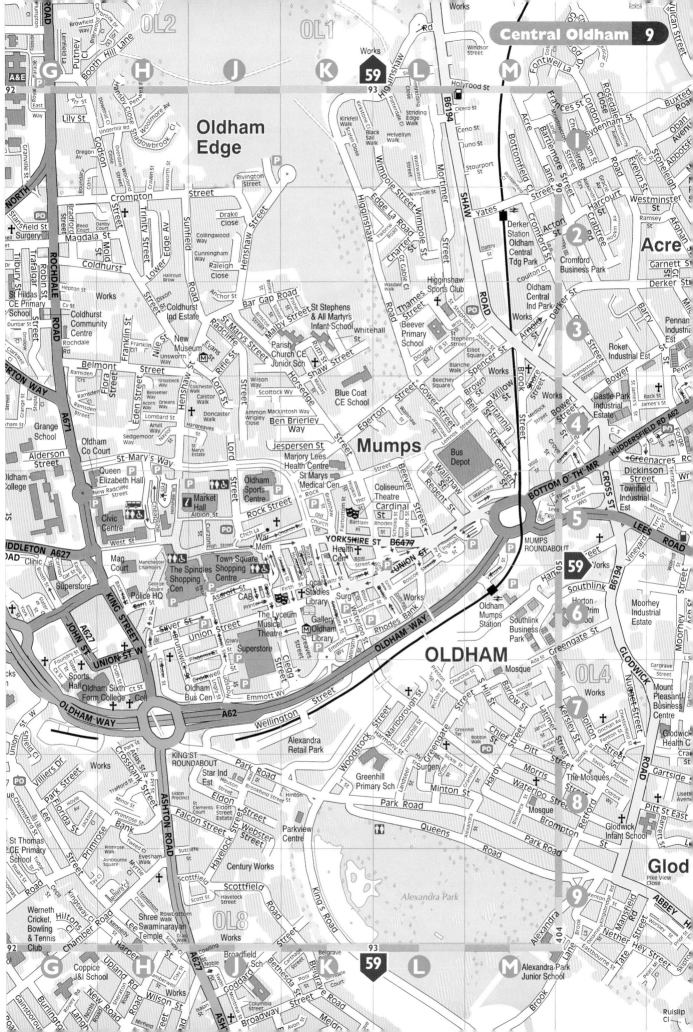

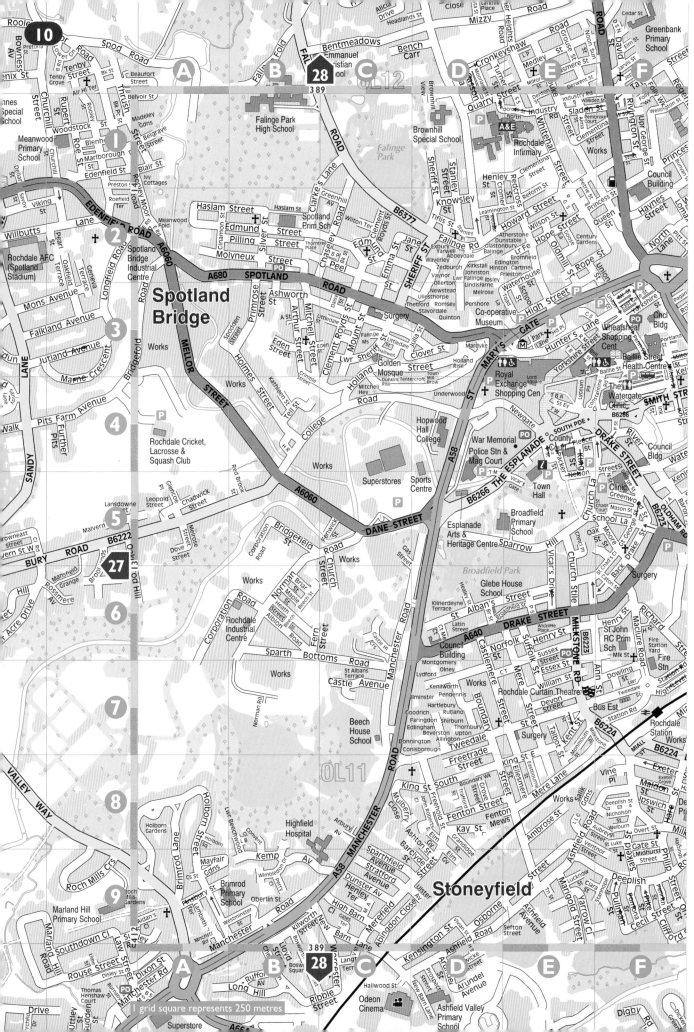

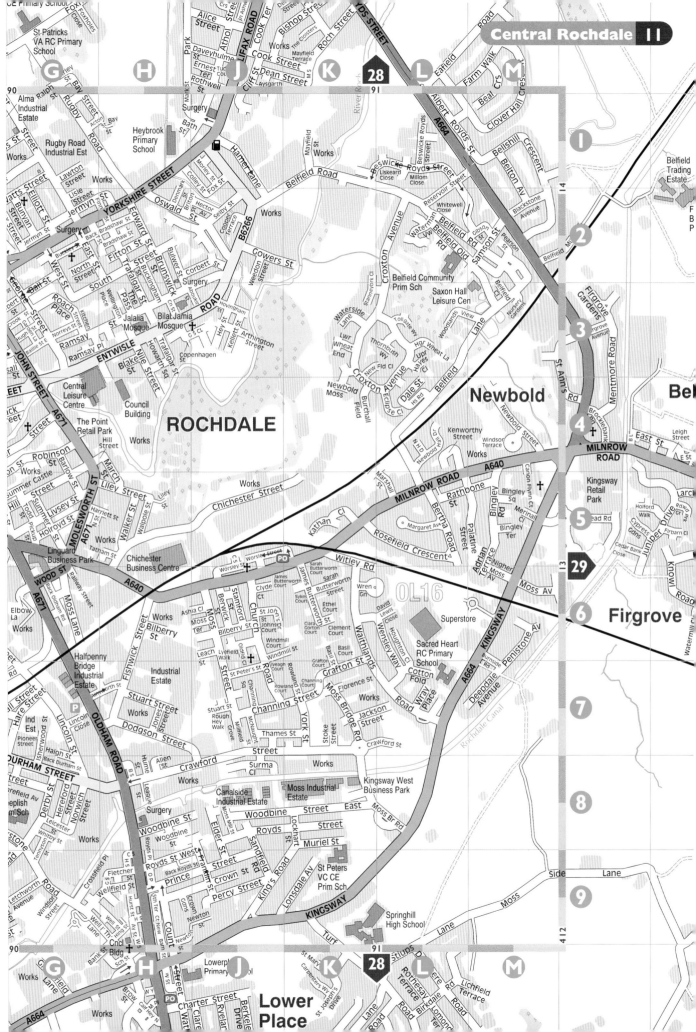

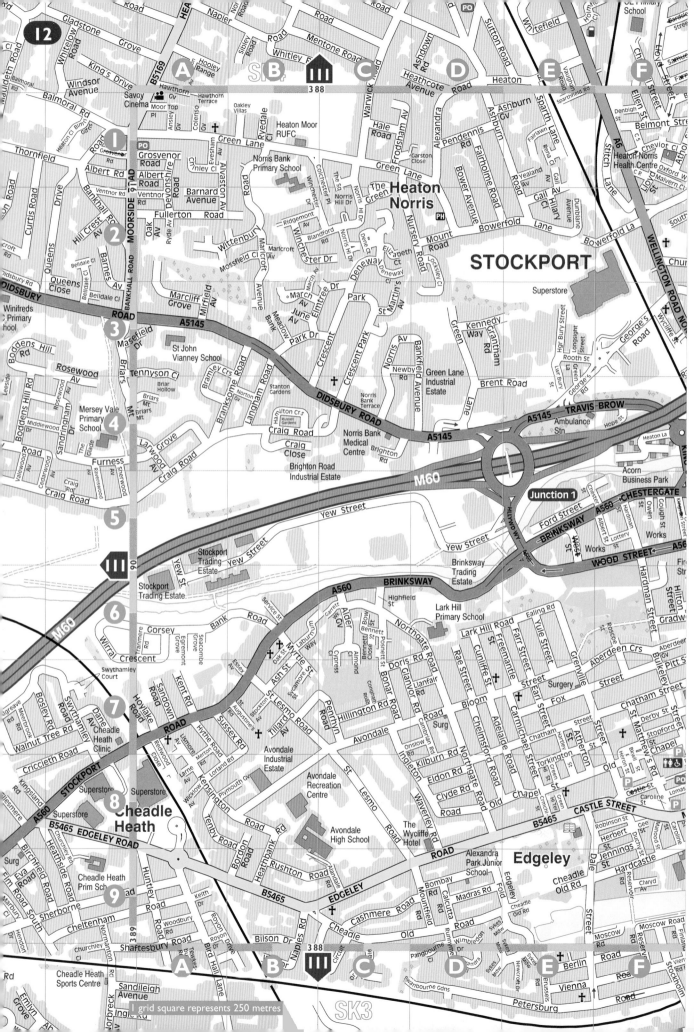

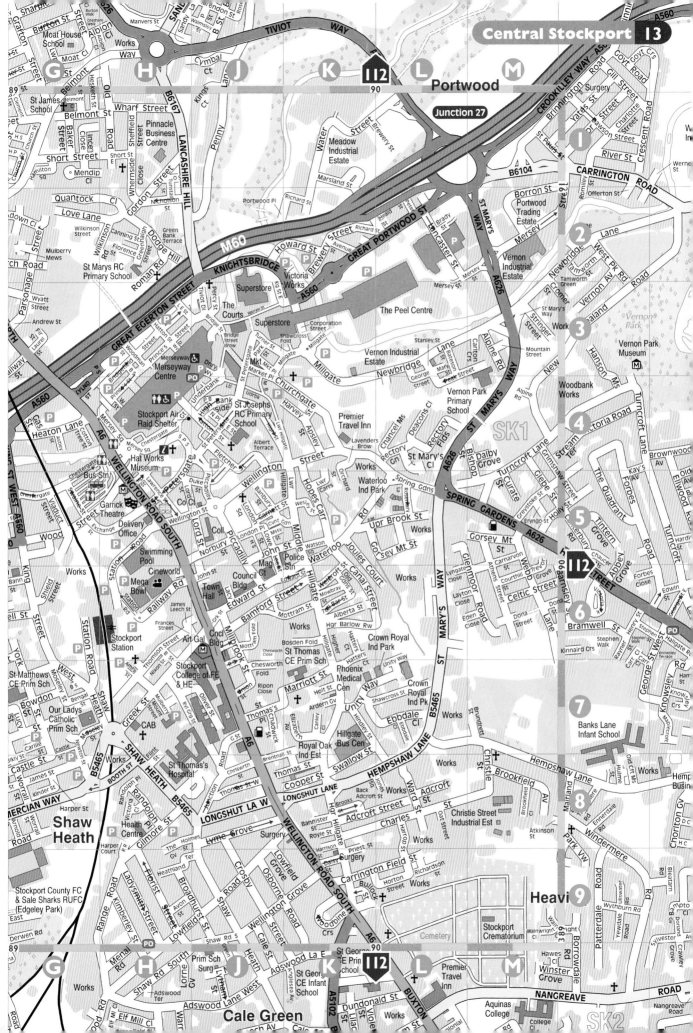

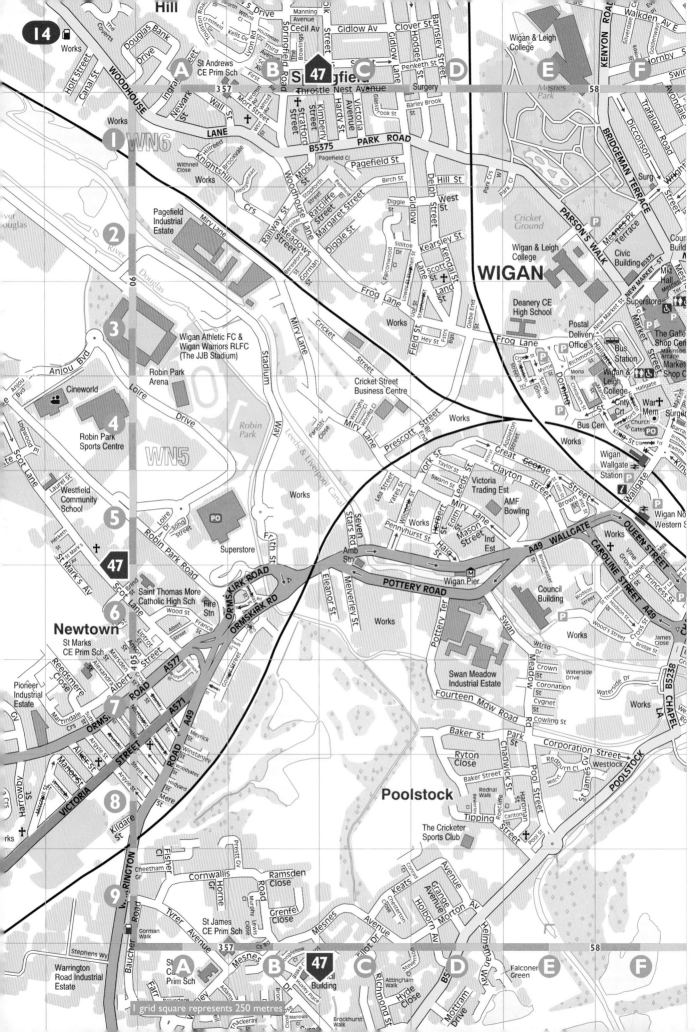

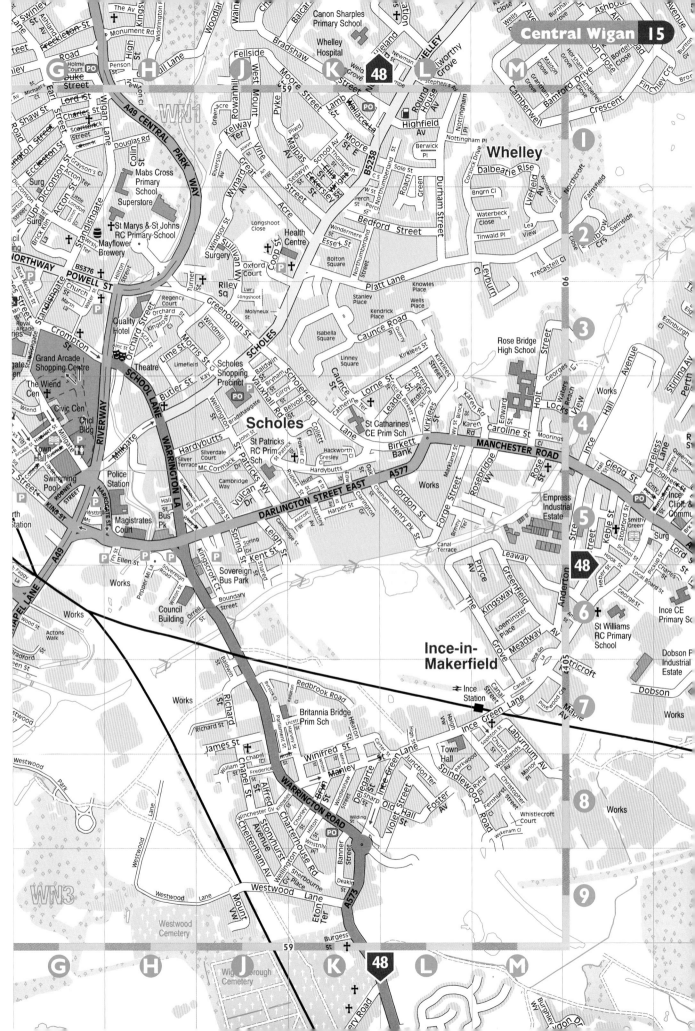

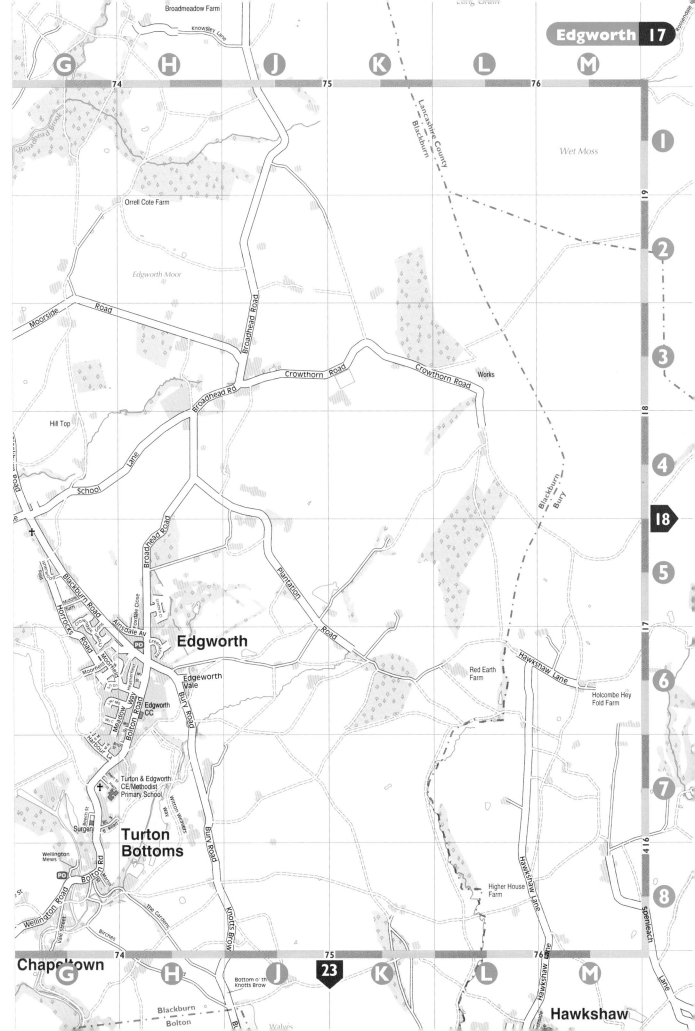

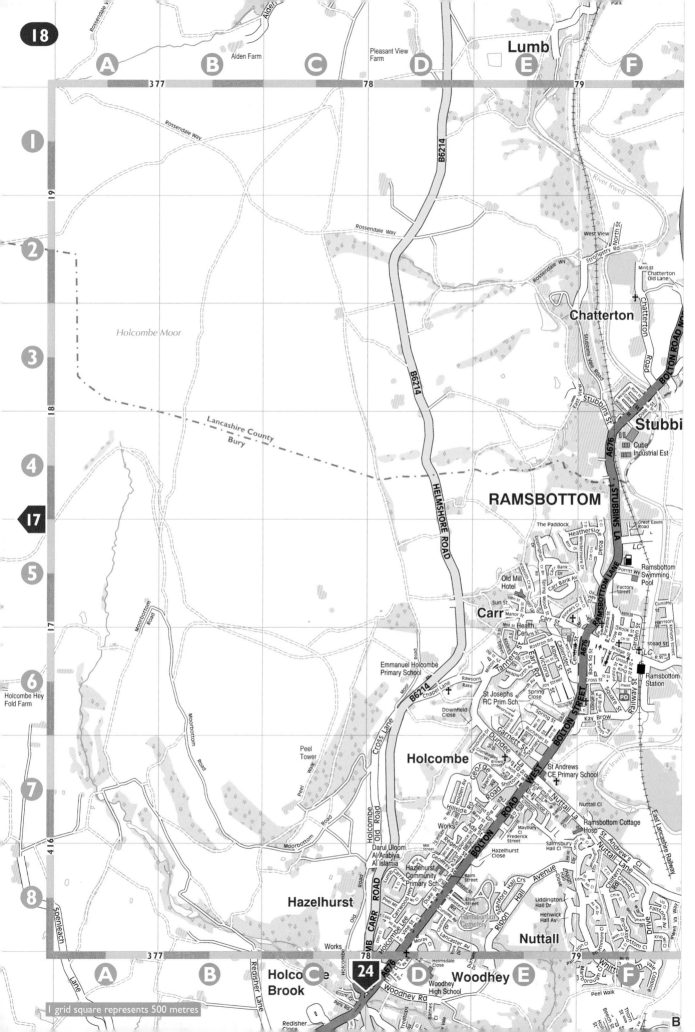

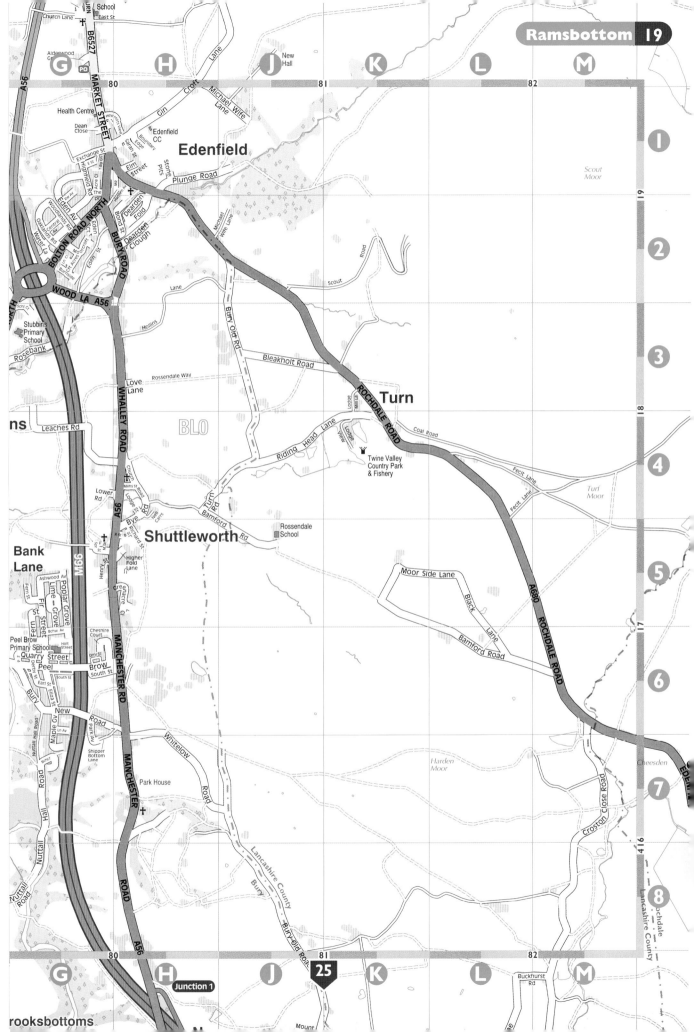

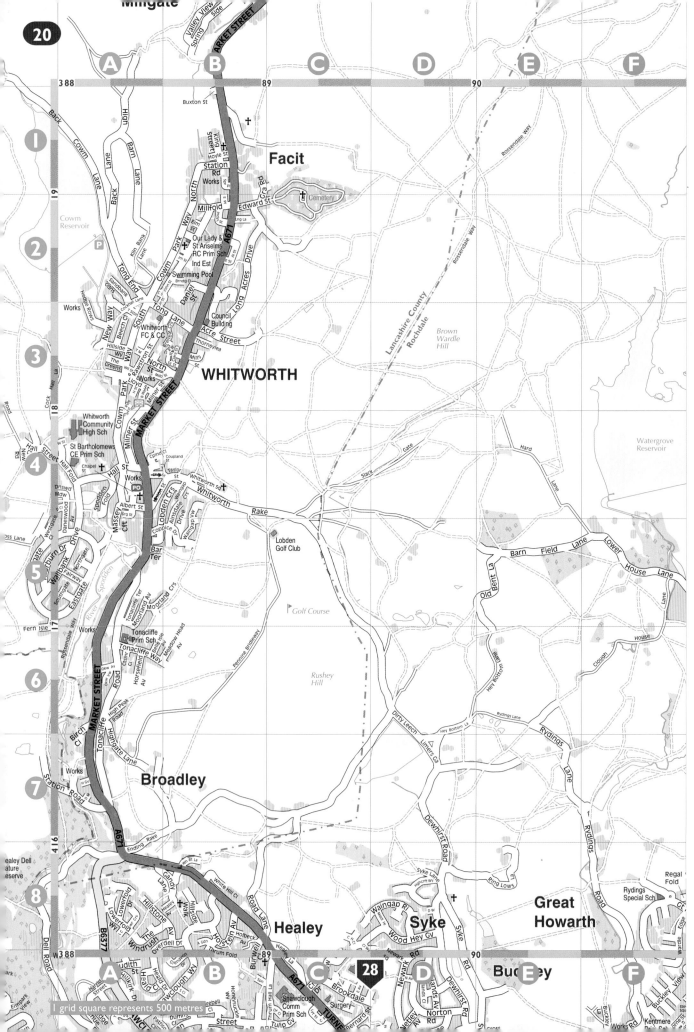

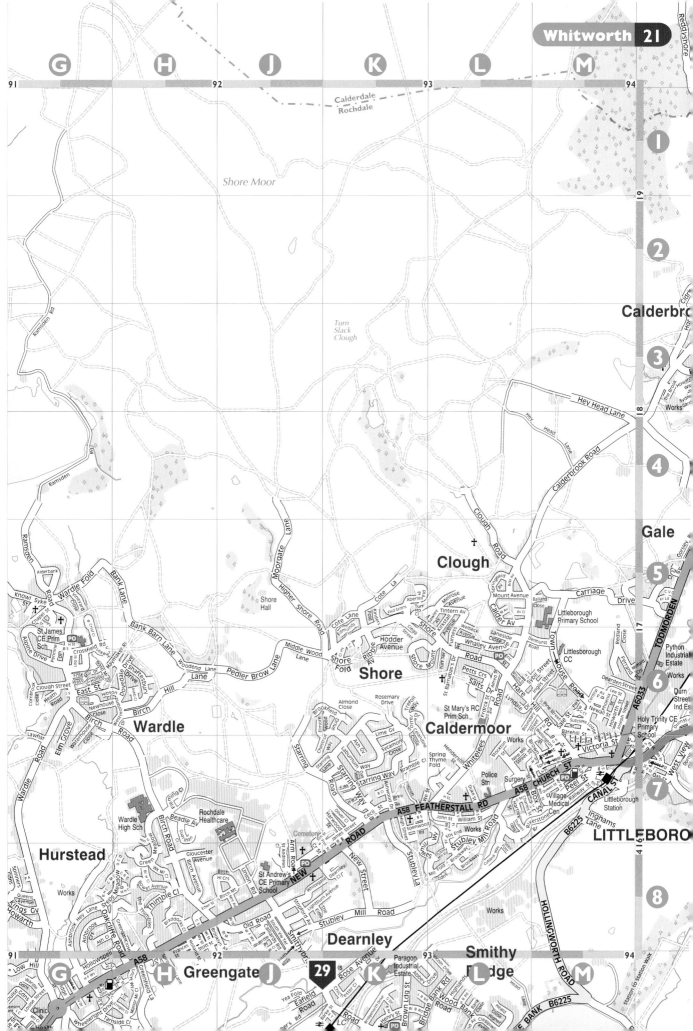

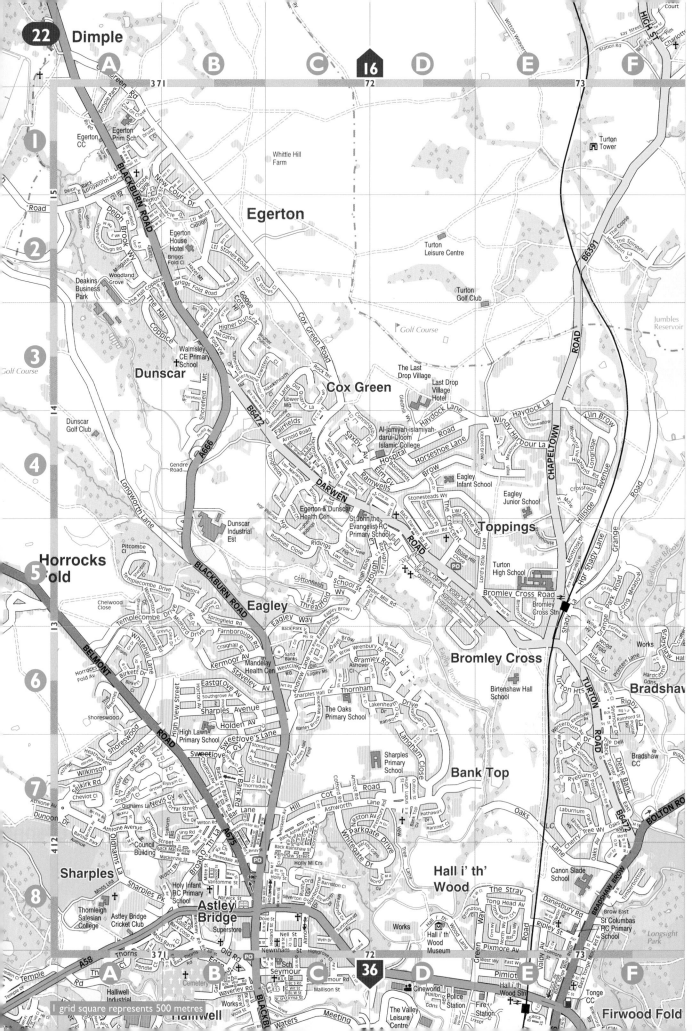

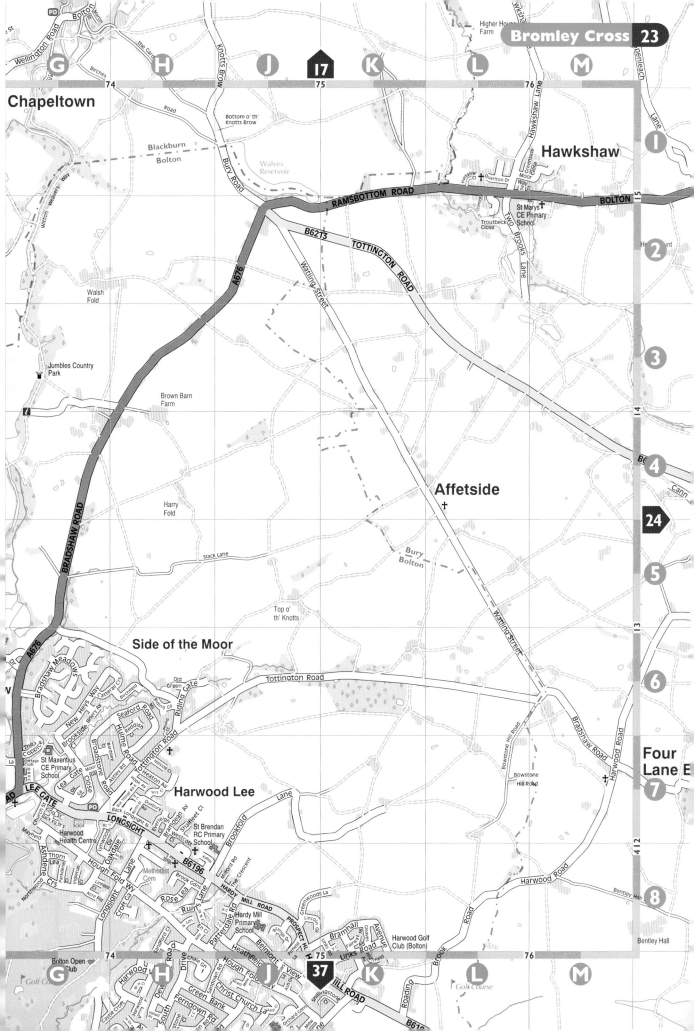

Chapeltown

Hawkshaw

Higher House Farm

Blackburn
Bolton

Bottom o' th' Knotts Brow

Walves Reservoir

RAMSBOTTOM ROAD

St Marys CE Primary School

Troutbeck Close

BOLTON

B6213

TOTTINGTON ROAD

Watling Street

Bury Road

A676

Walsh Fold

Jumbles Country Park

Brown Barn Farm

Affetside

Harry Fold

Bradshaw Road

Slack Lane

Bury Bolton

Top o' th' Knotts

Watling Street

Side of the Moor

Tottington Road

Bradshaw Road

Harwood Road

Four Lane E

A676

Bradshaw Meadows

New Heys Way

Catterall Crt

Old Green Gate

Riding Gate

Bowstone Hill Road

Bowstone Hill Road

Seaford Road

Hulme Road

Brookside

Broadstone Road

Tottington Road

St Maxentius CE Primary School

The Coppice

Cottage Croft

Lea Gate

Moor Close

Wheaton Av

Harwood Lee

Lane

LEE GATE

LONGSIGHT

St Brendan RC Primary School

Harwood Health Centre

Brookfold

Brook

Harwood Road

Bentley Hall

B6196

Methodist Cem

Hardy Mill Road

HARDY MILL ROAD

PROSPECT HL

Hough Fold Lane

Rose Lane

Hardy Mill Primary School

Greenwoods La

Bramhall

Harwood Golf Club (Bolton)

Links Road

Avenue

Reading

Bentley Hall

Bolton Open Club

Golf Course

Golf Course

Christ Church La

Green Bank

Ferndown Rd

Hough Fold

ILL ROAD

37

B616

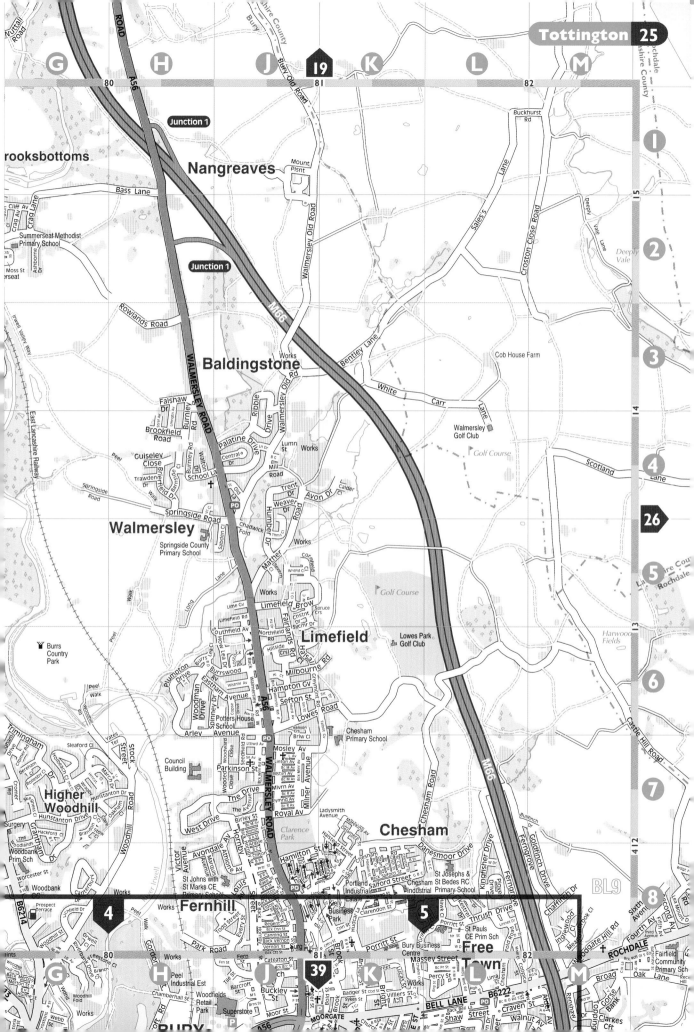

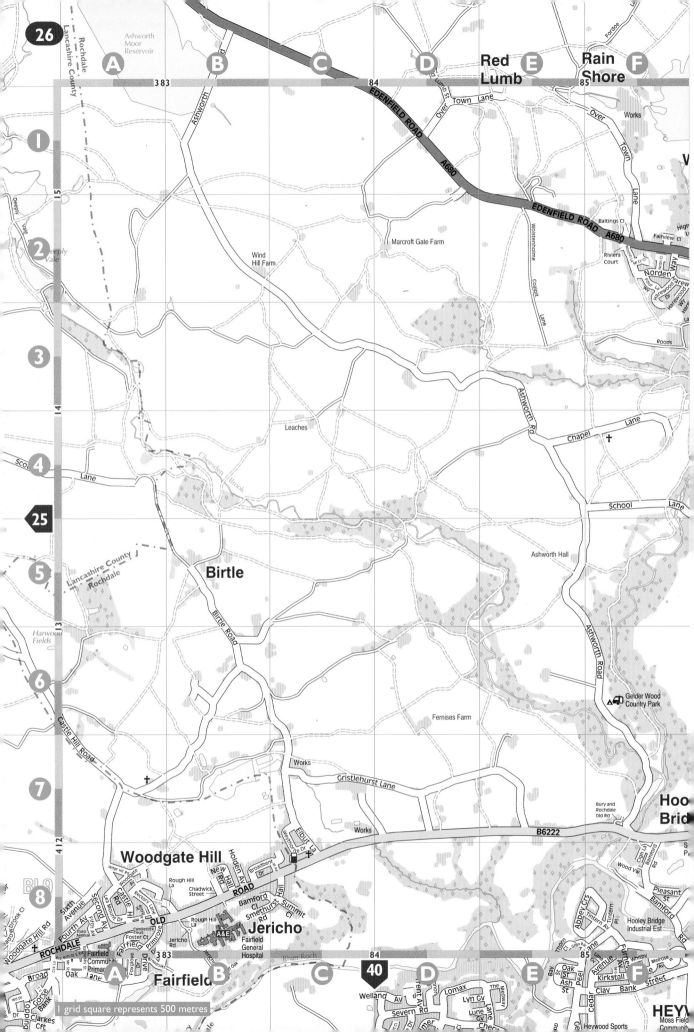

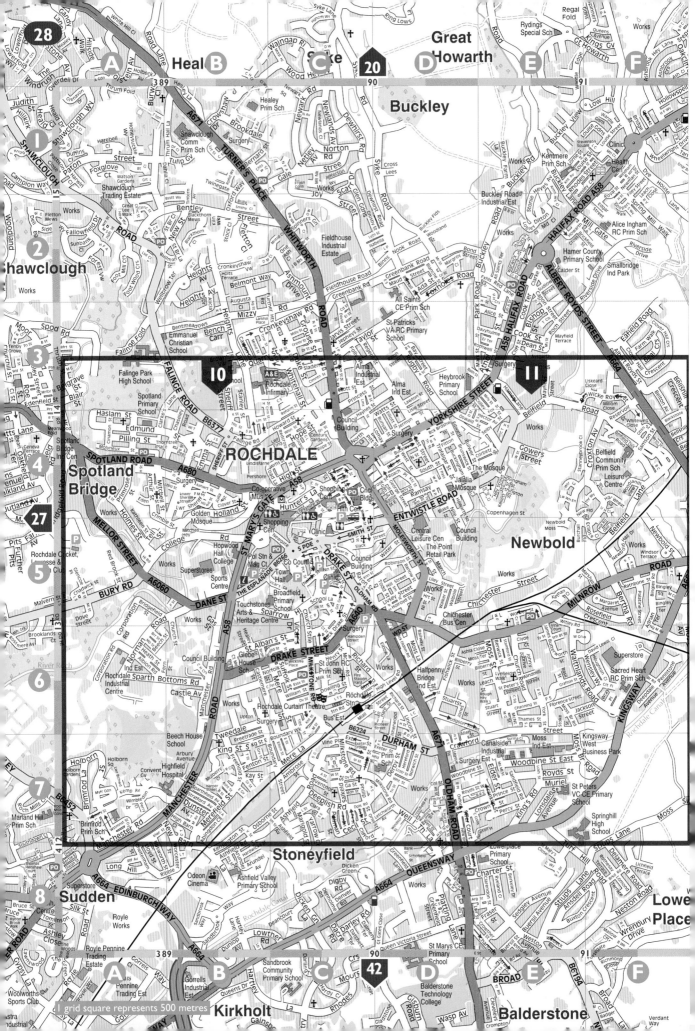

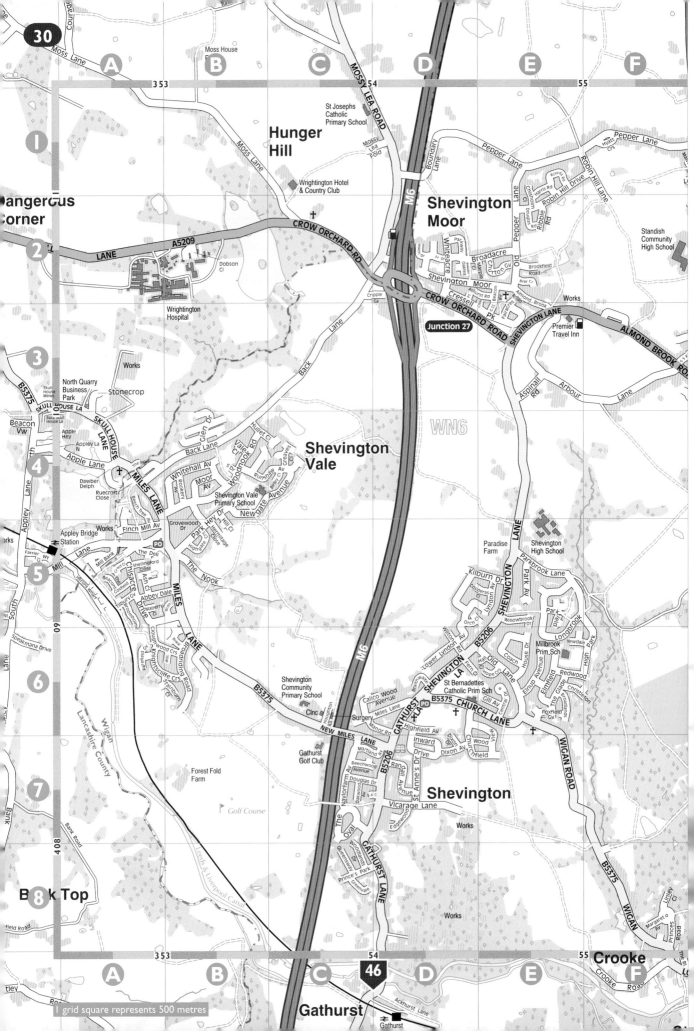

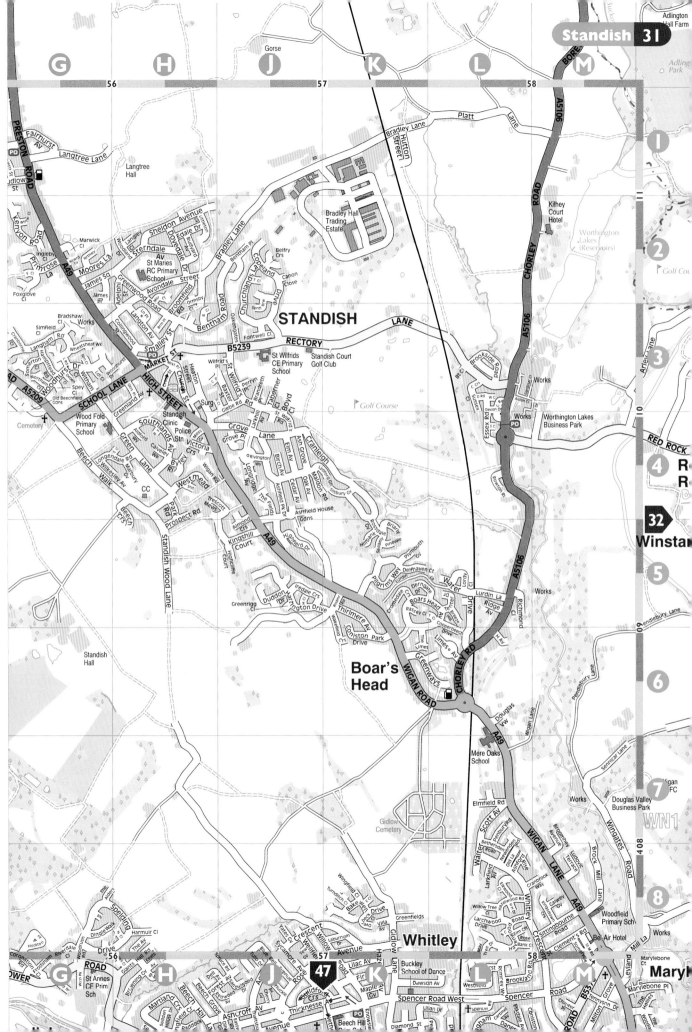

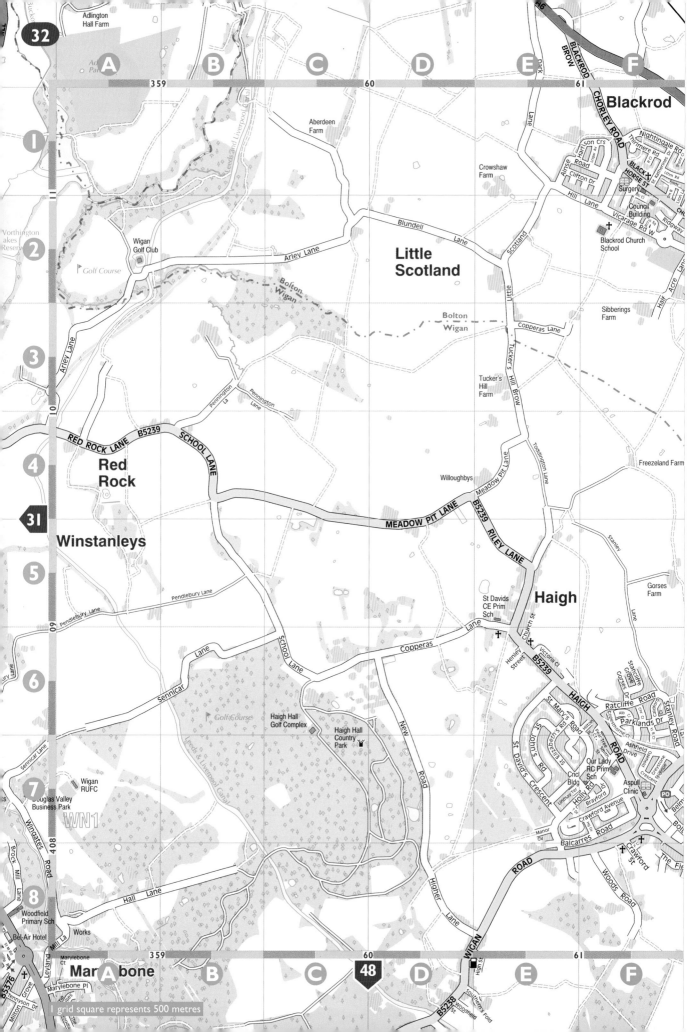

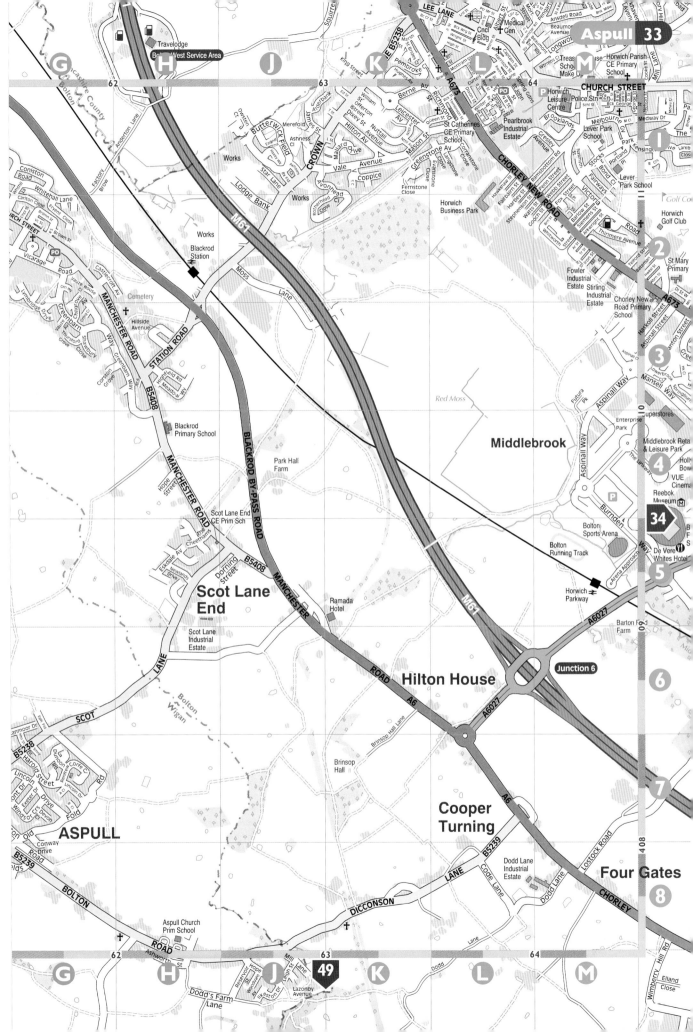

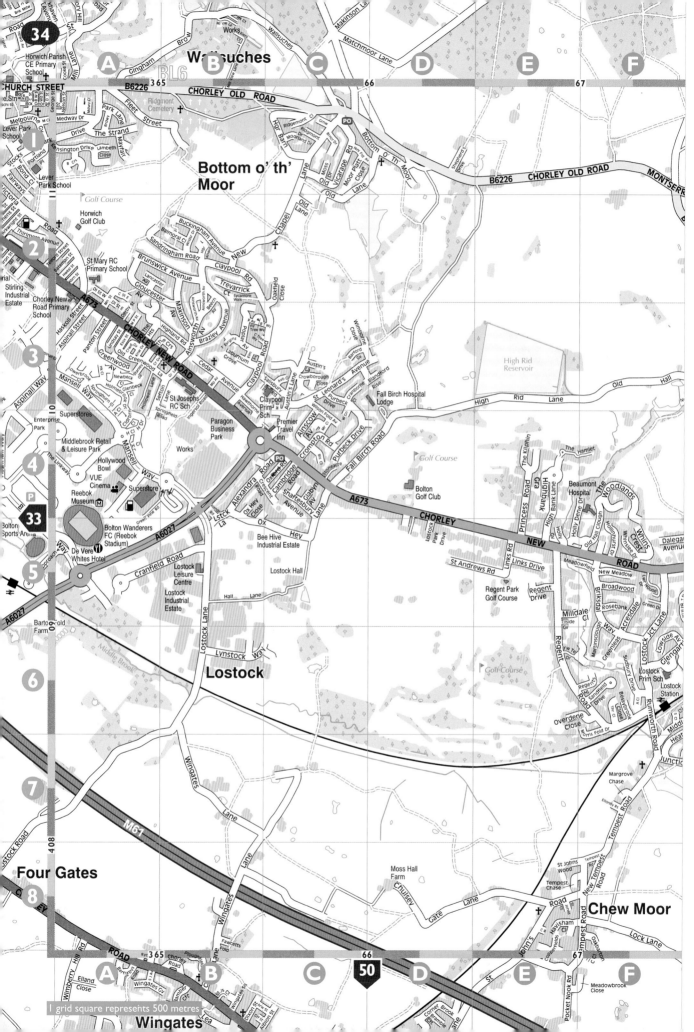

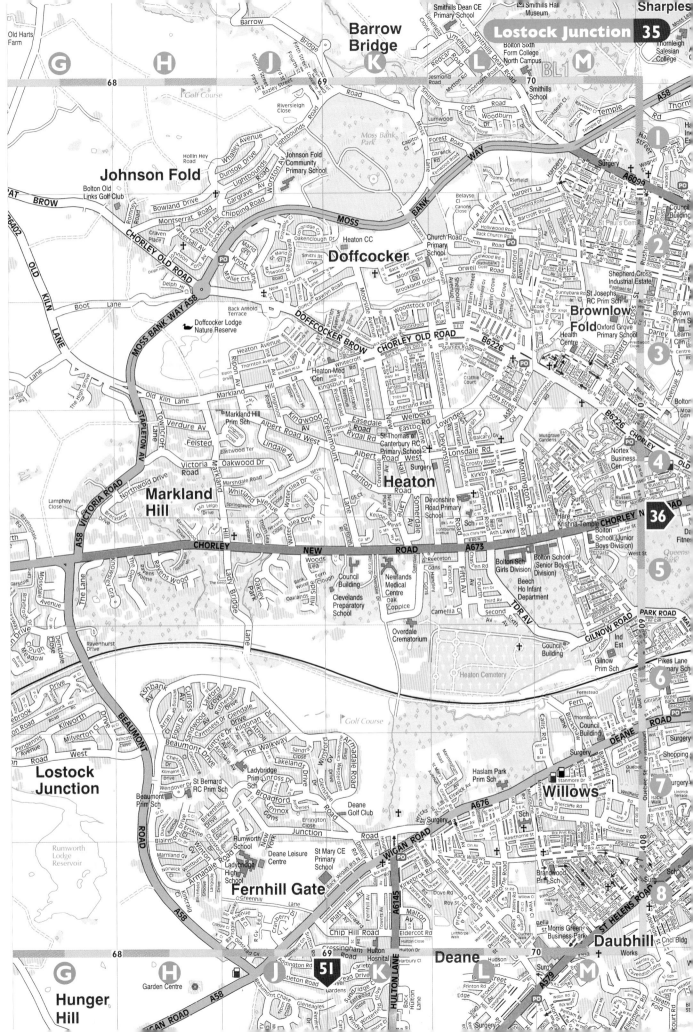

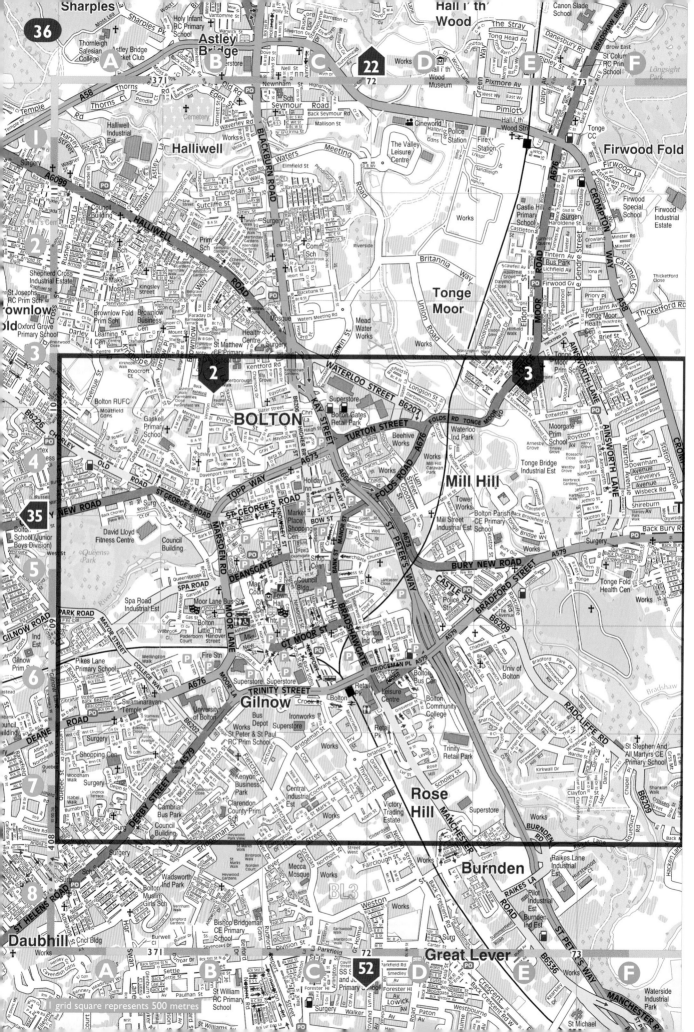

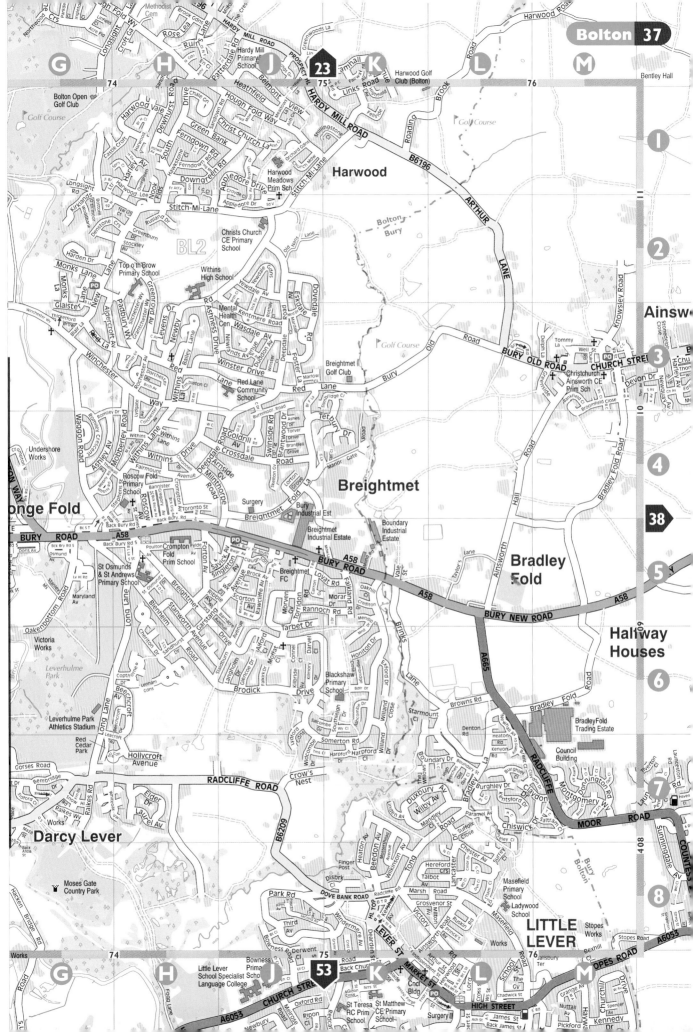

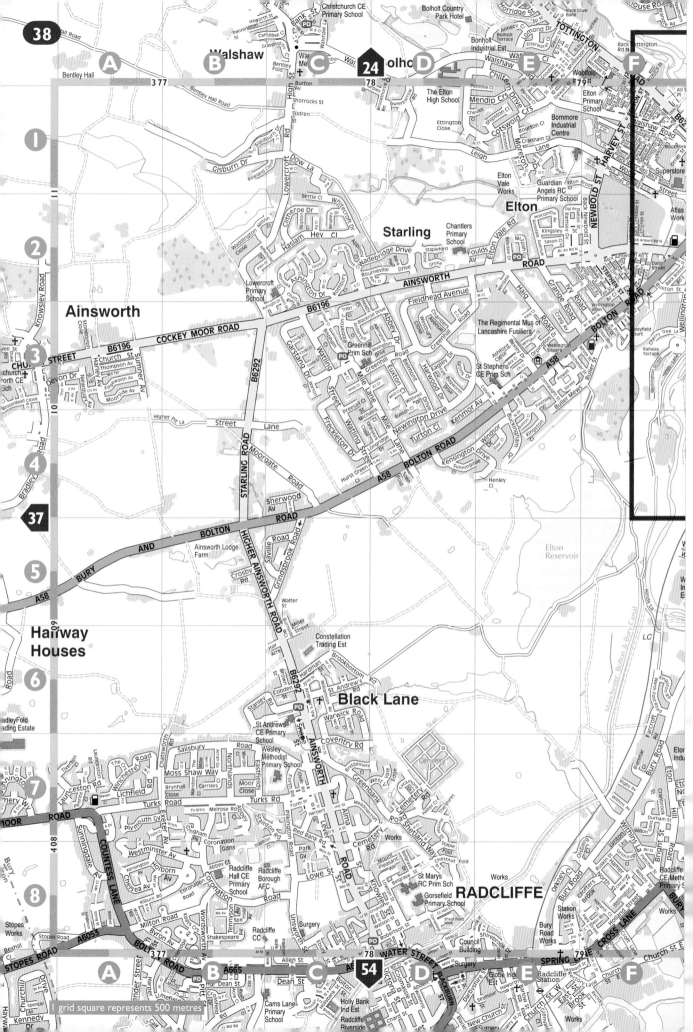

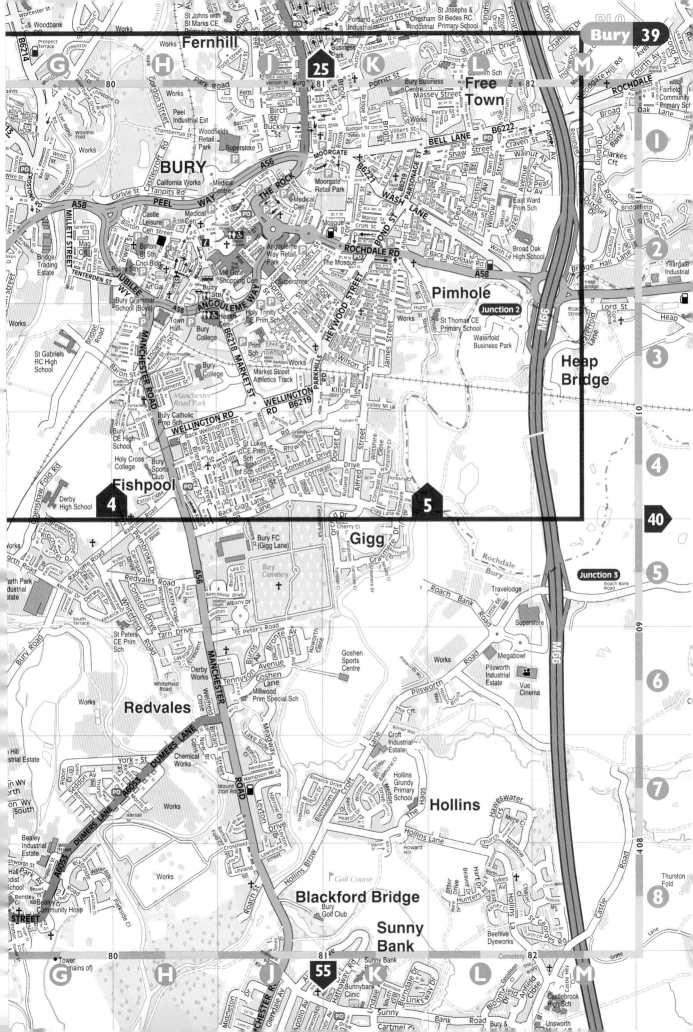

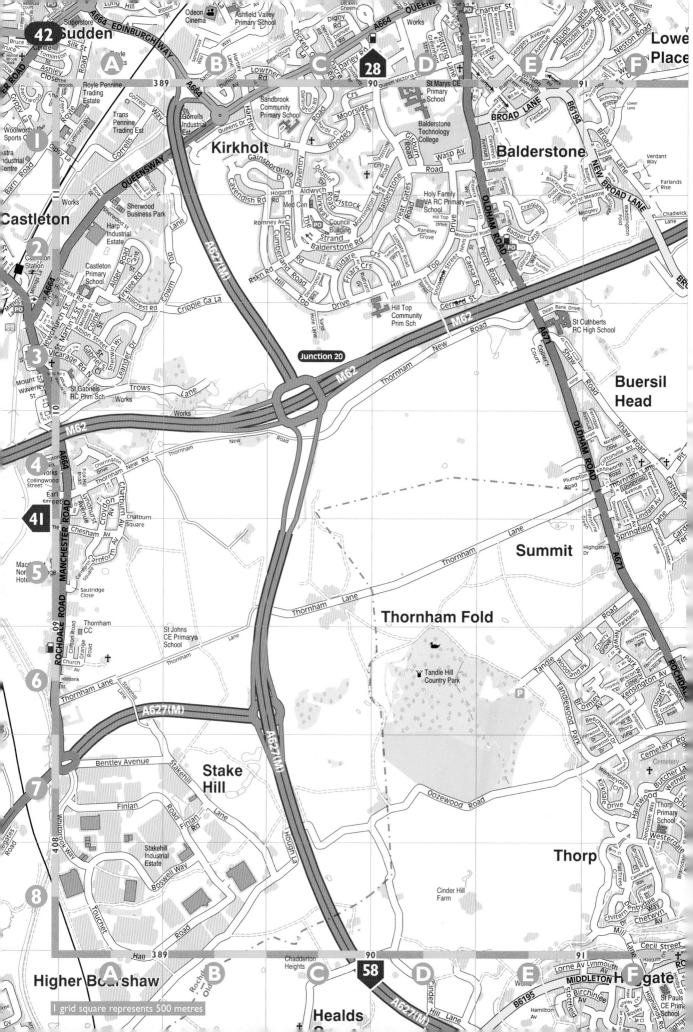

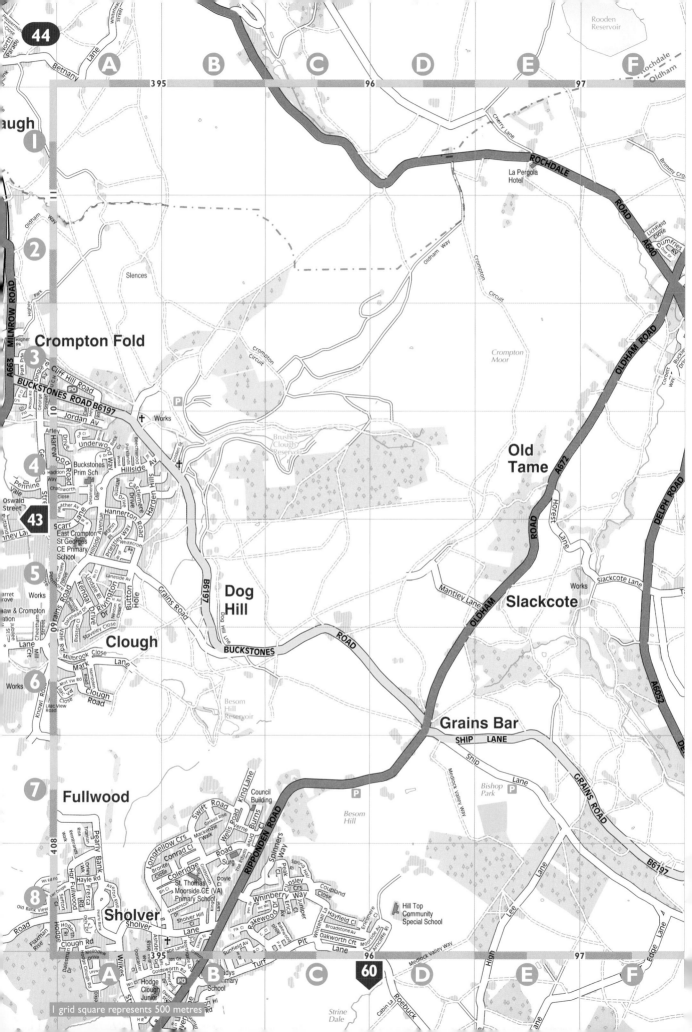

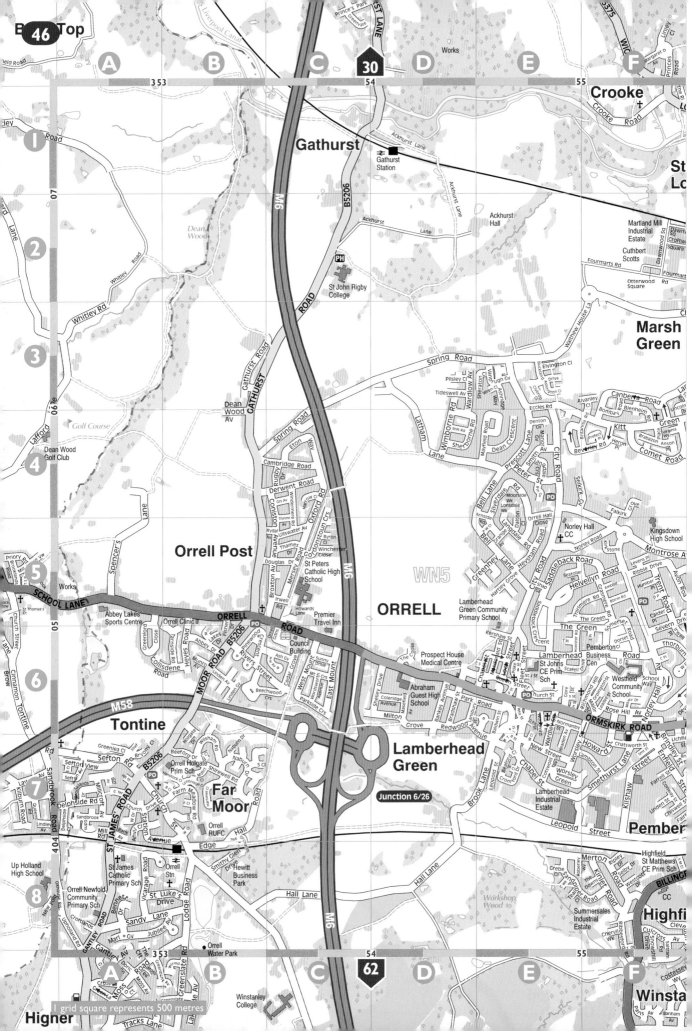

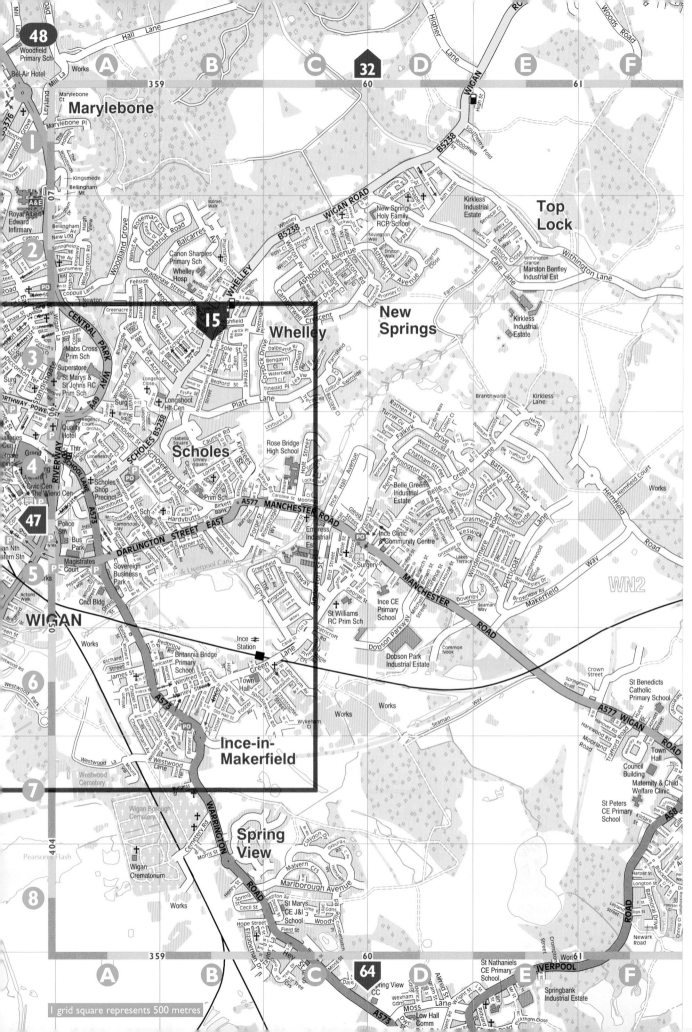

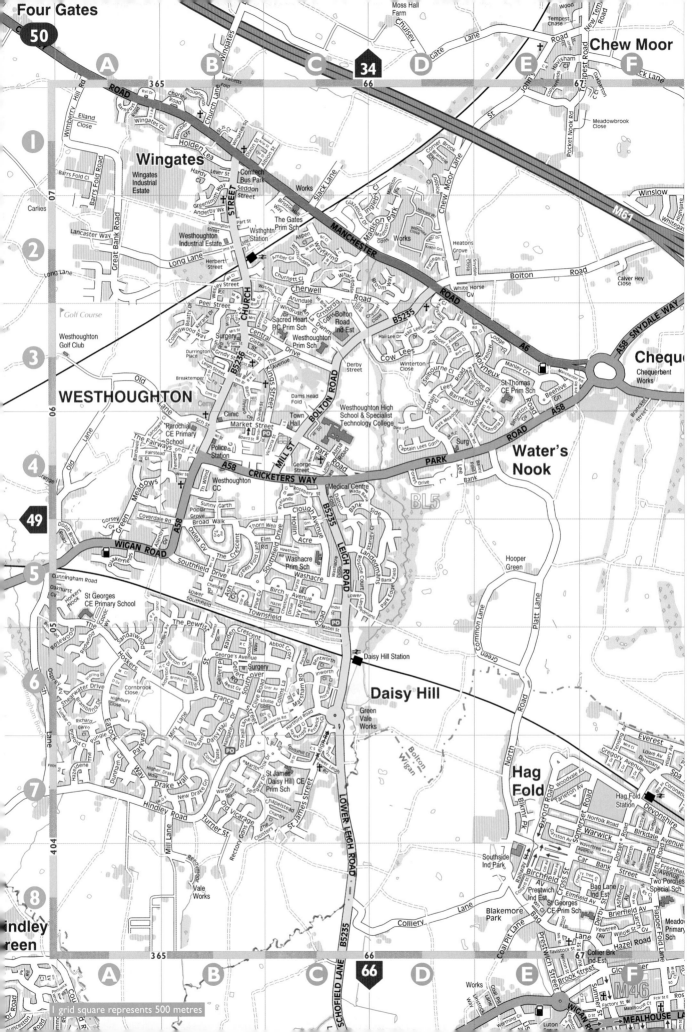

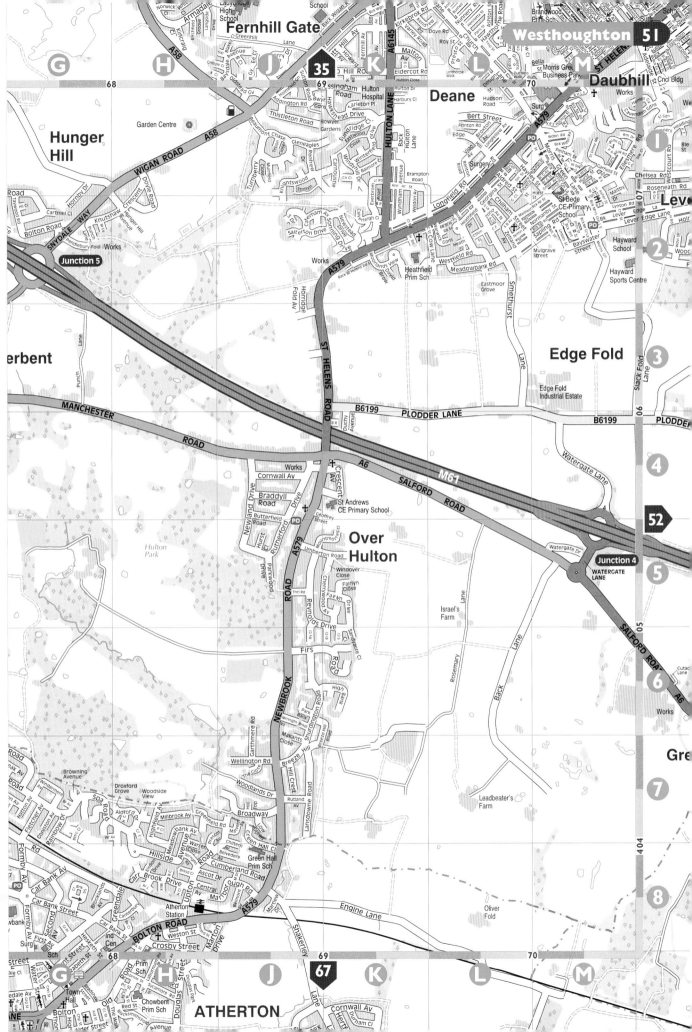

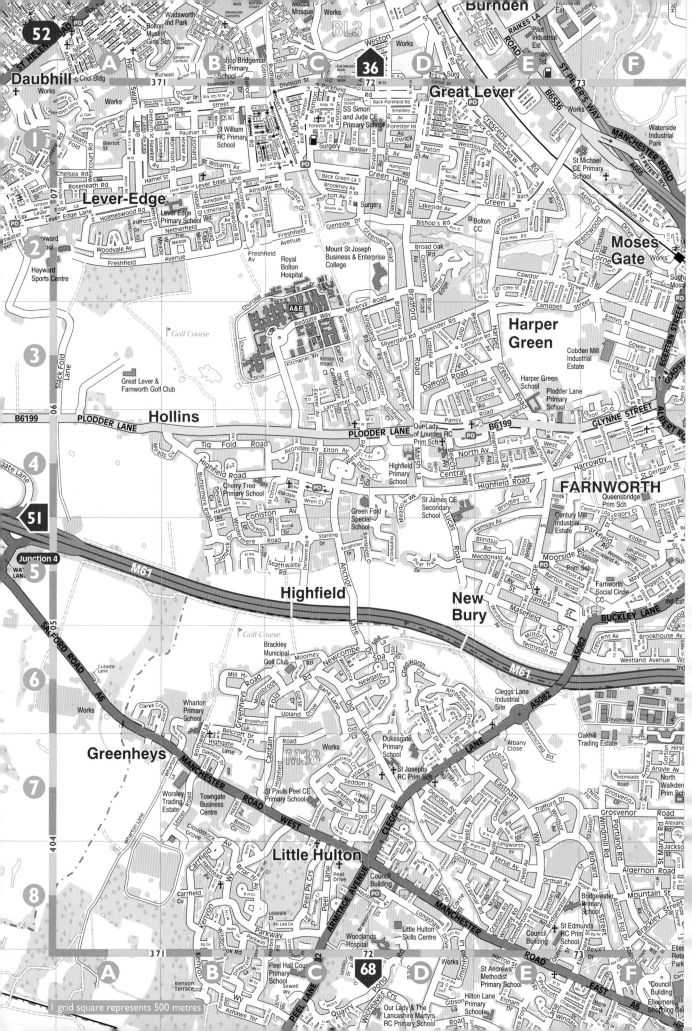

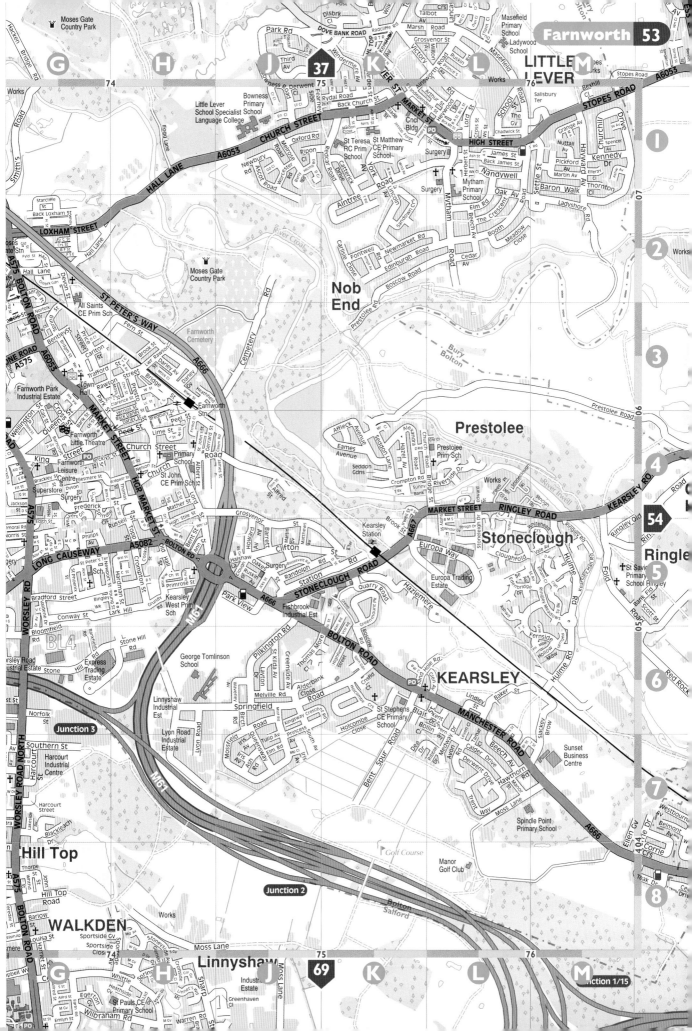

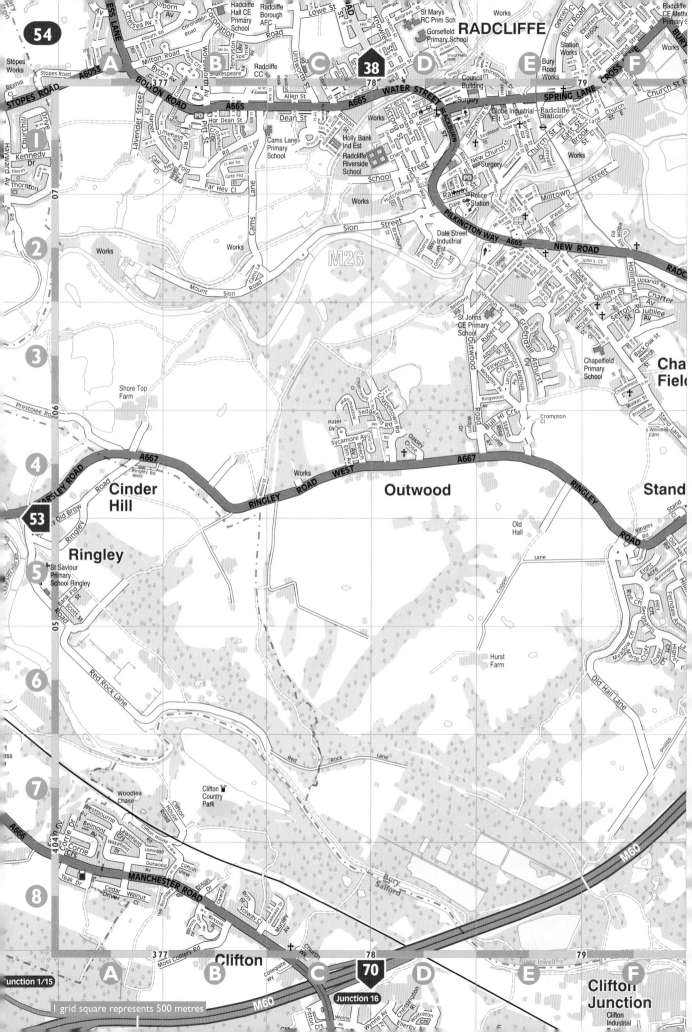

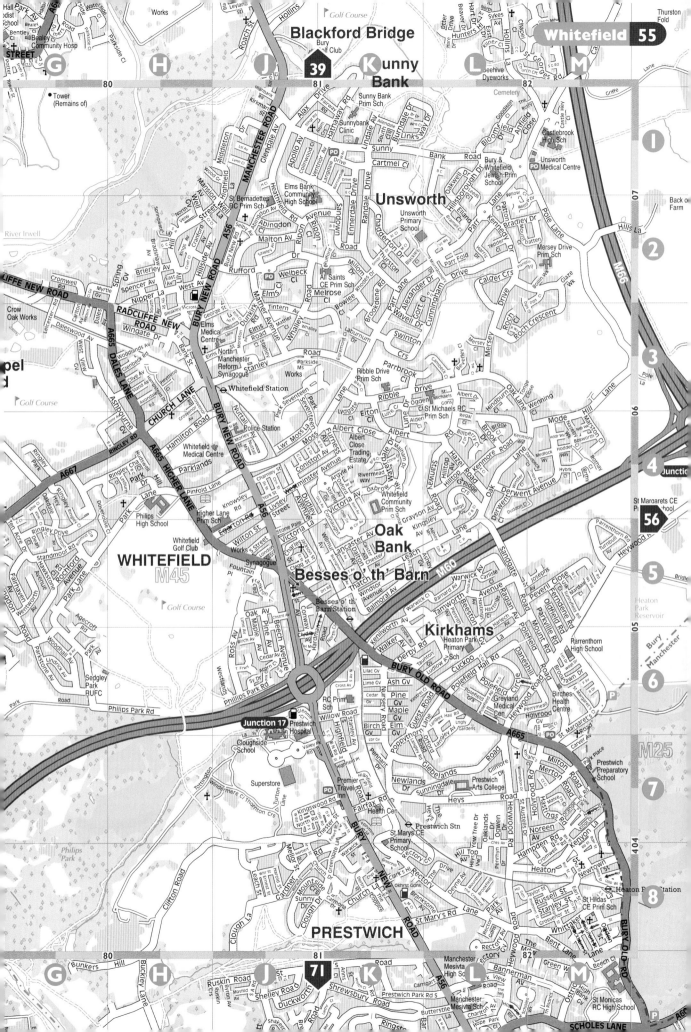

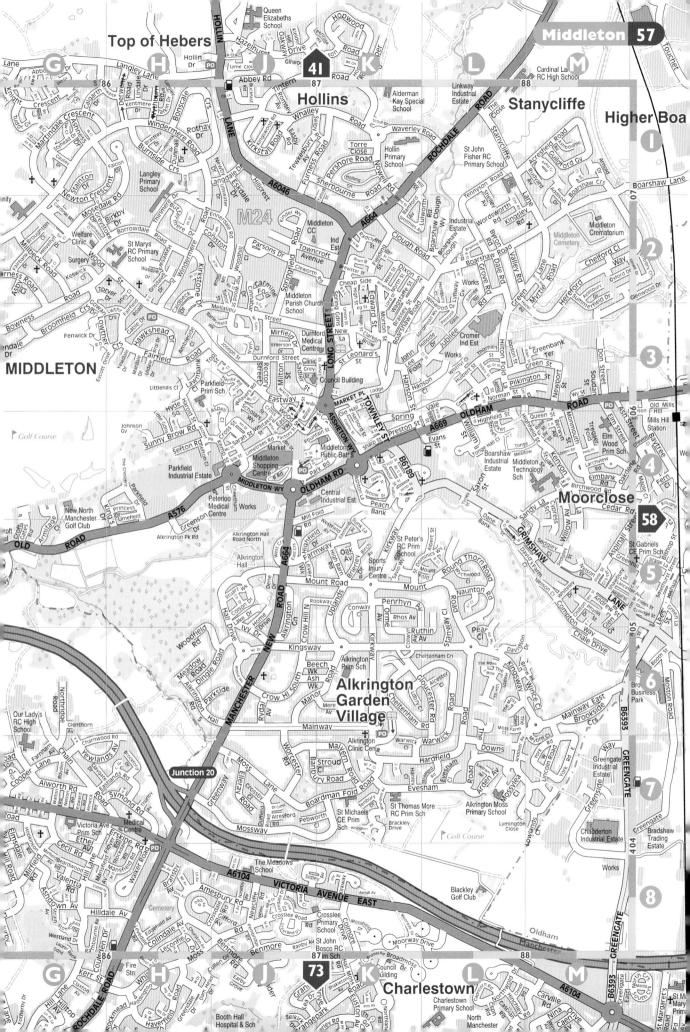

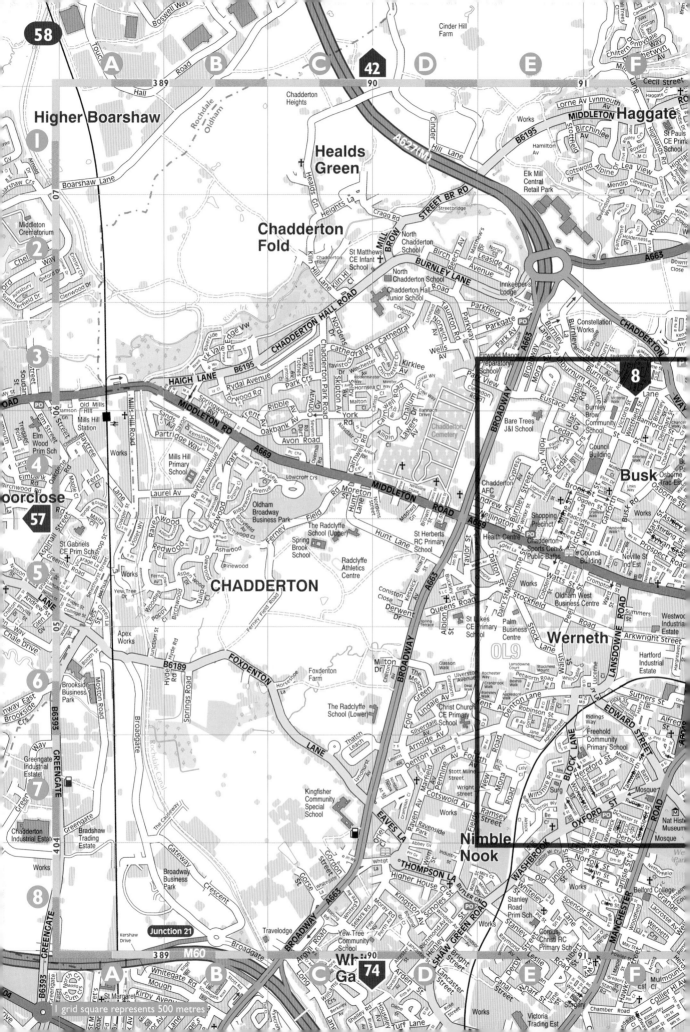

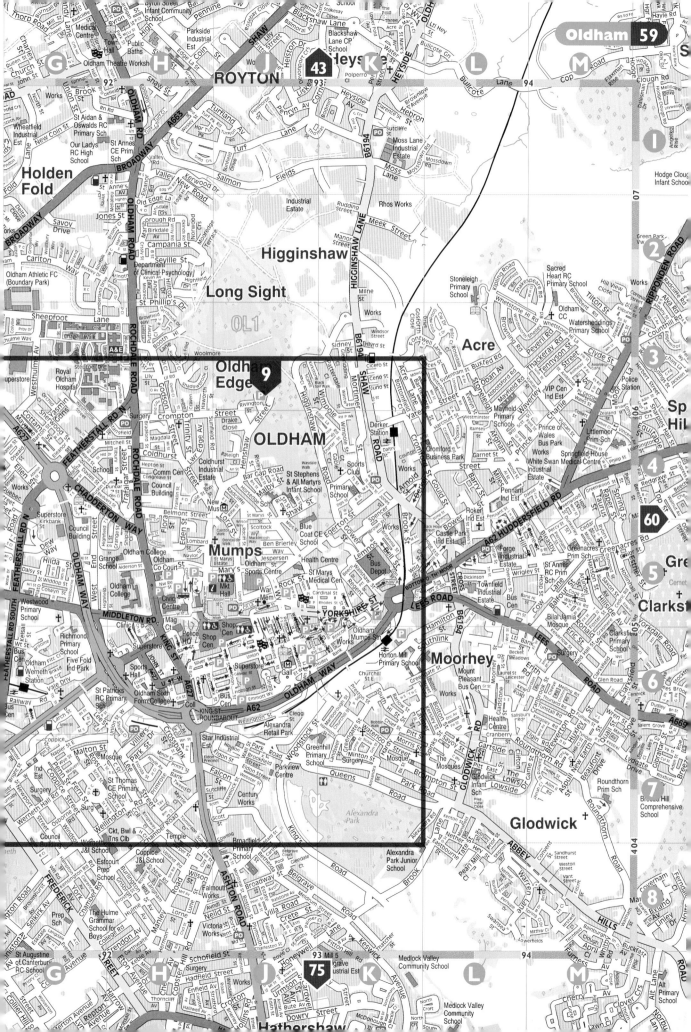

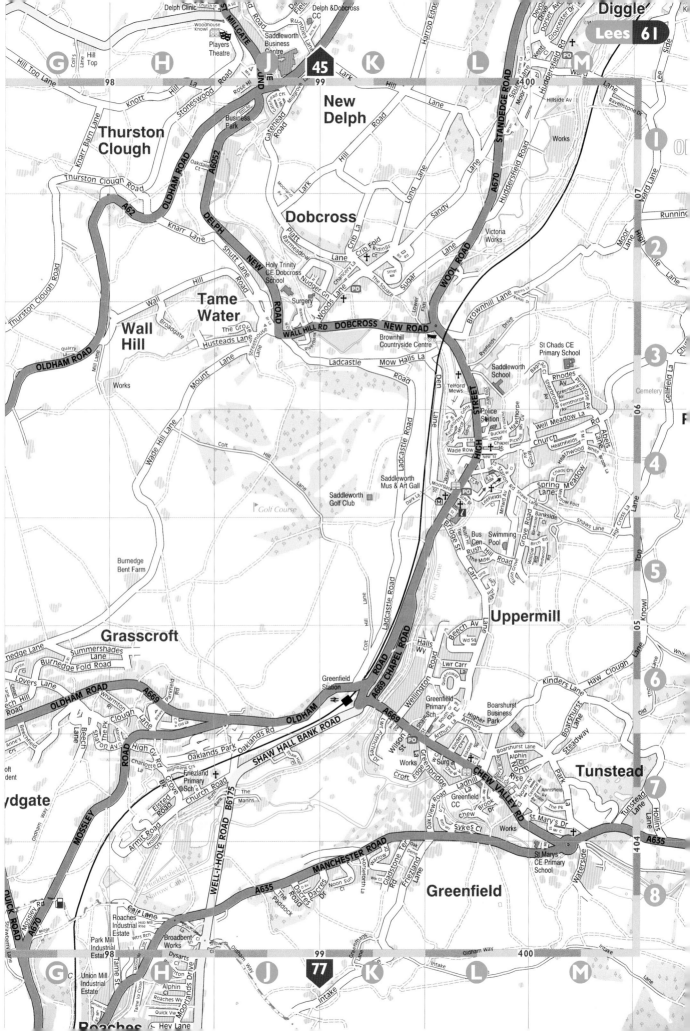

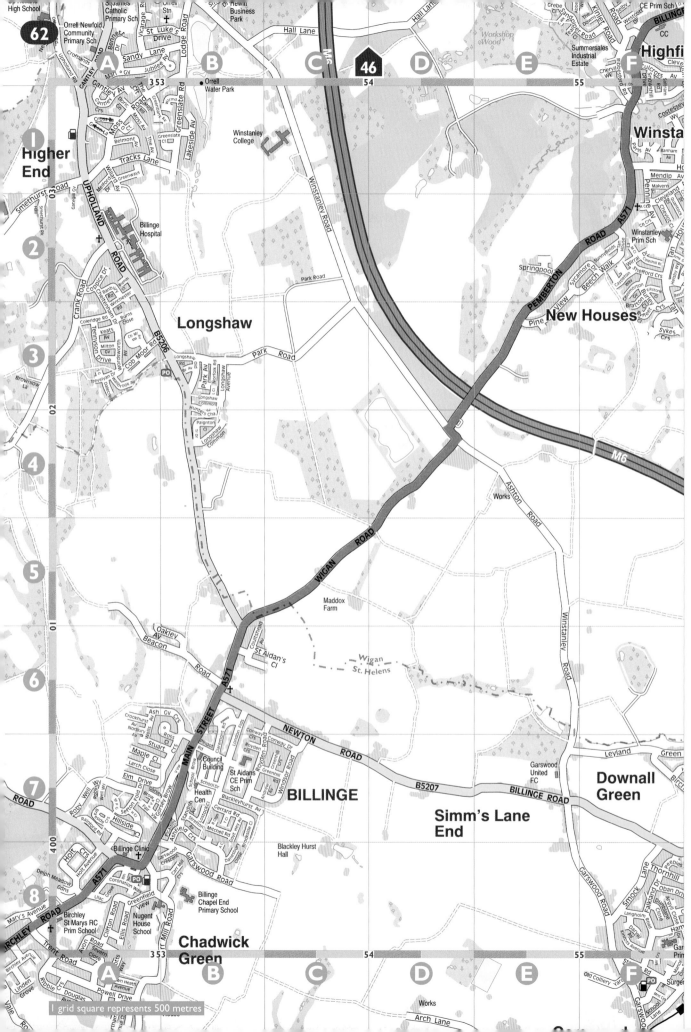

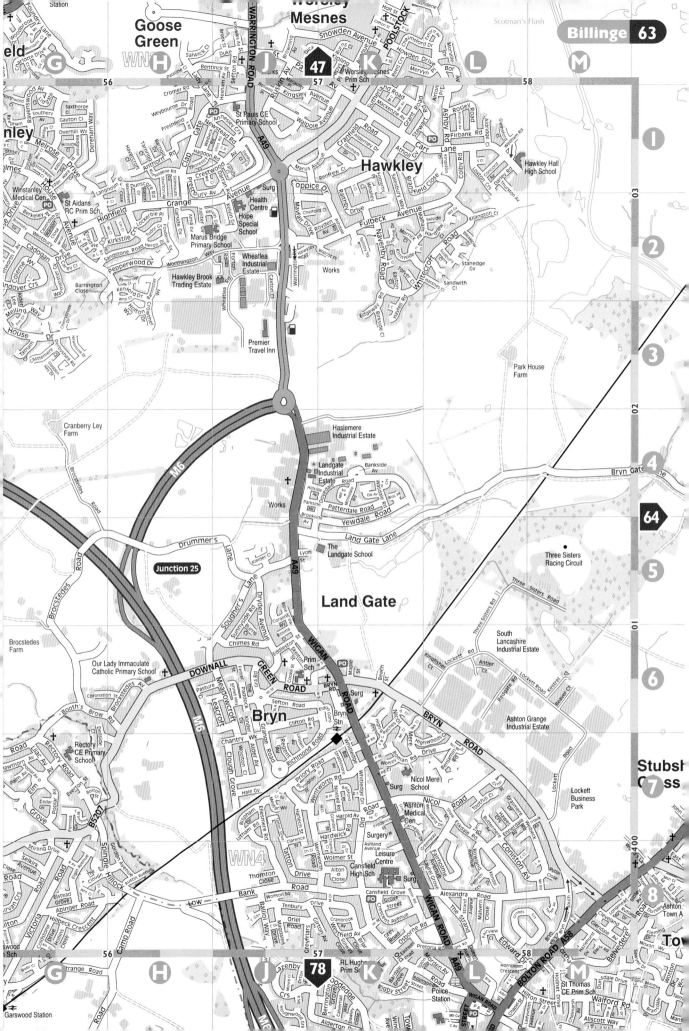

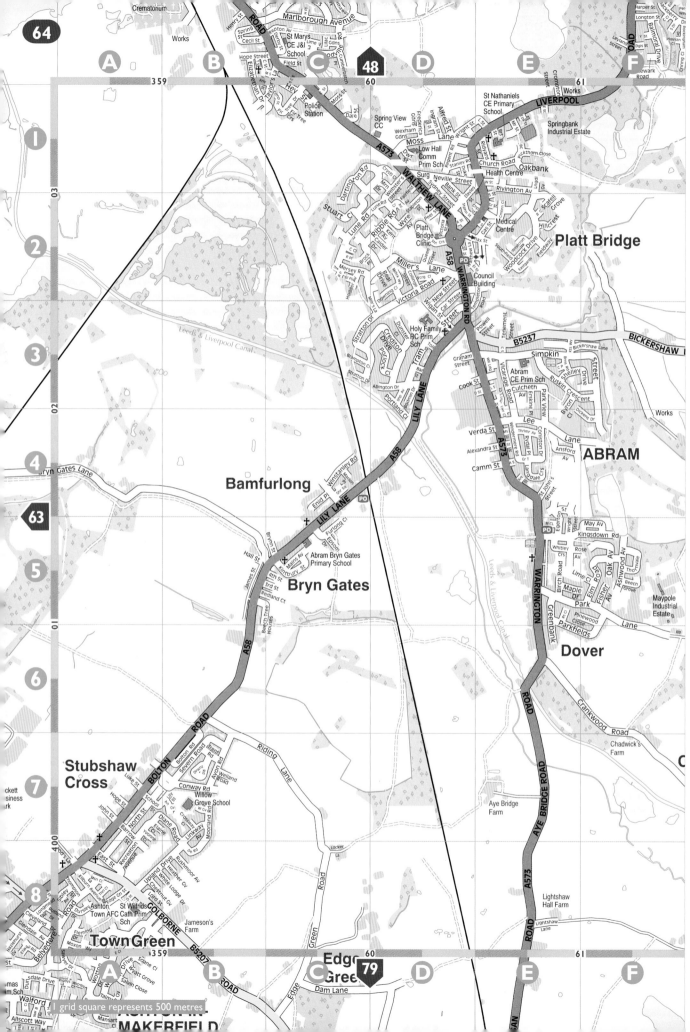

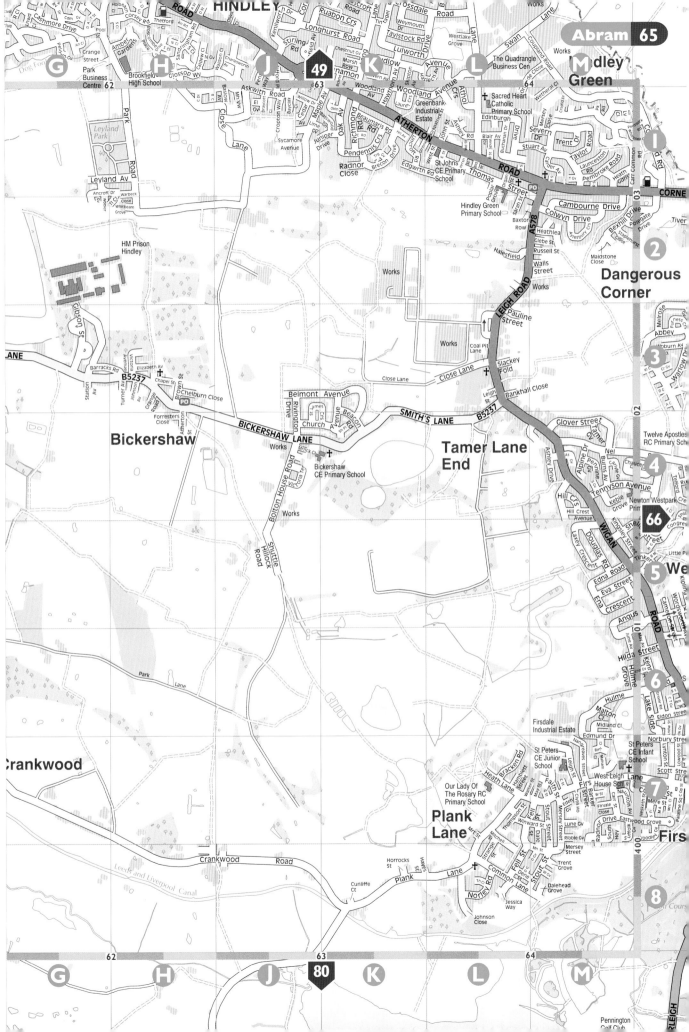

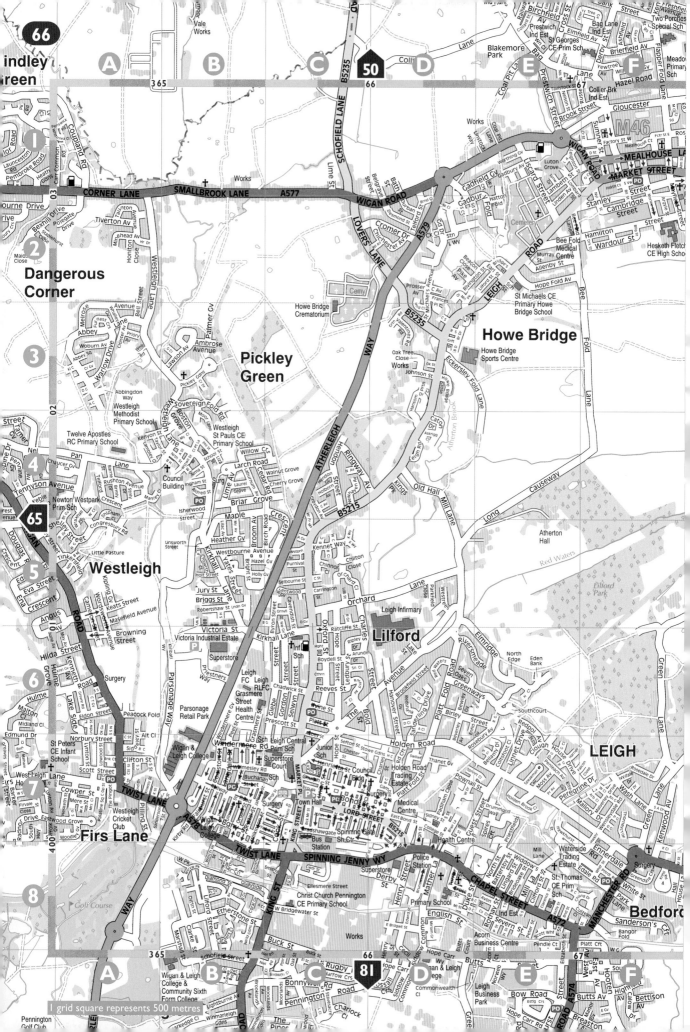

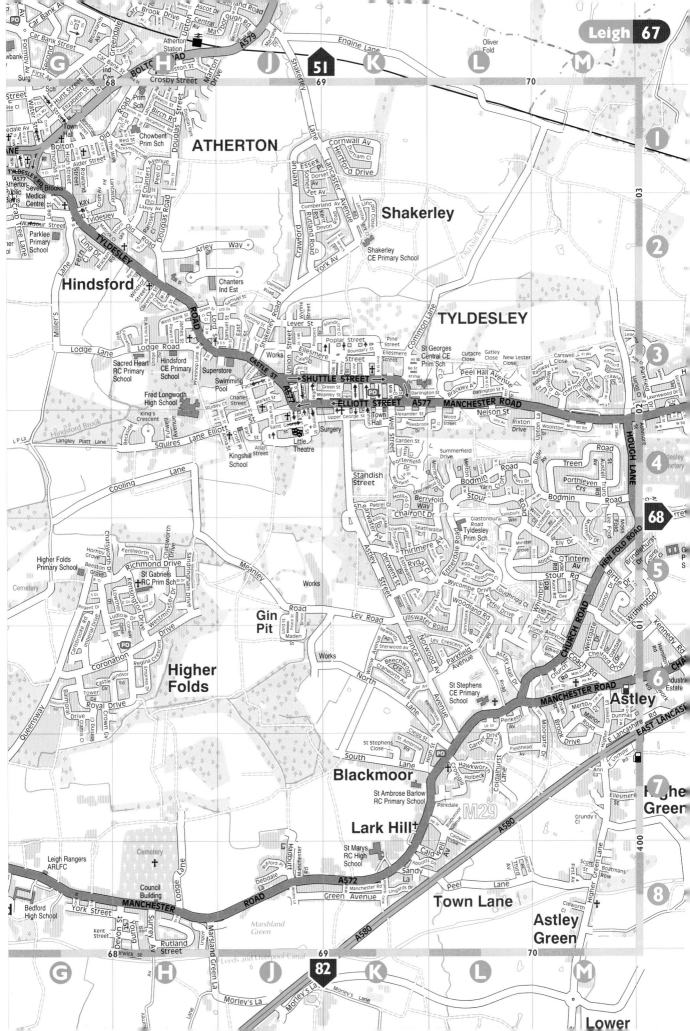

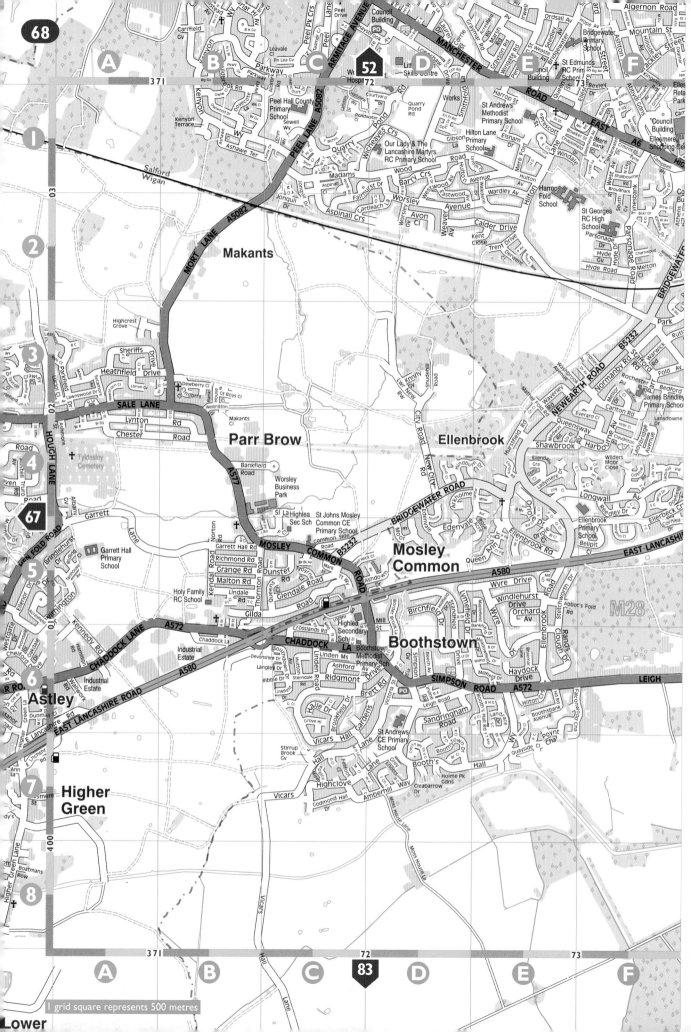

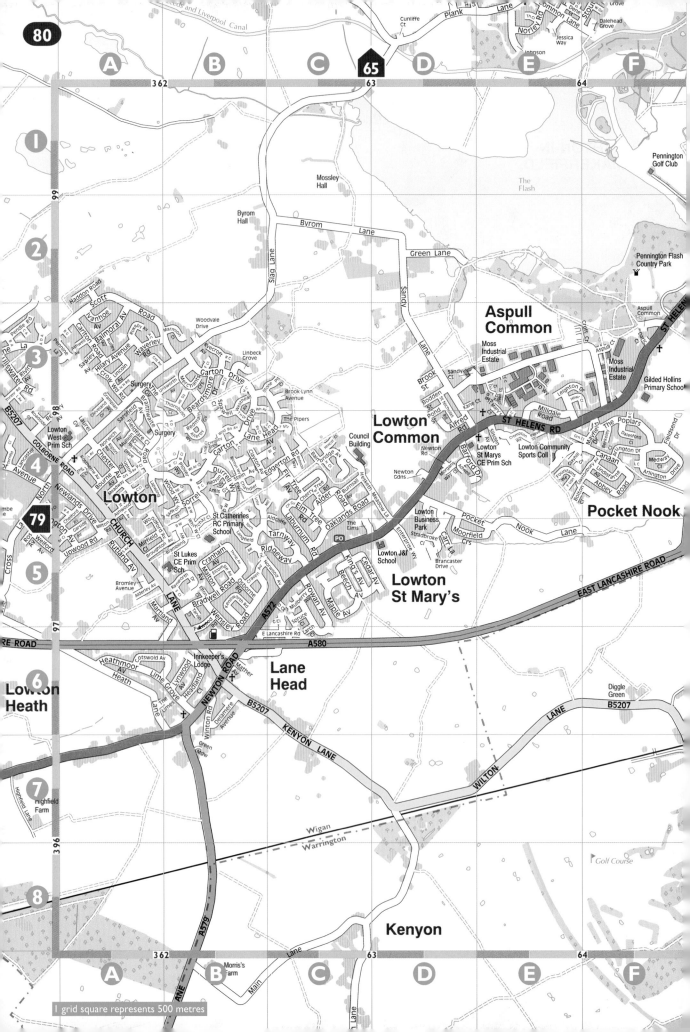

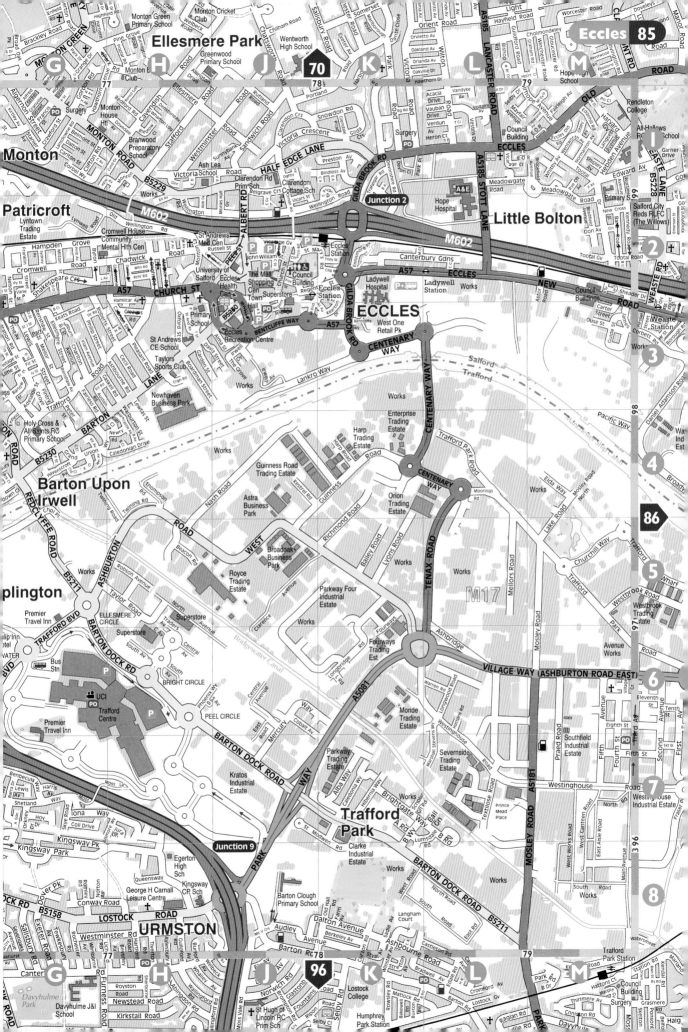

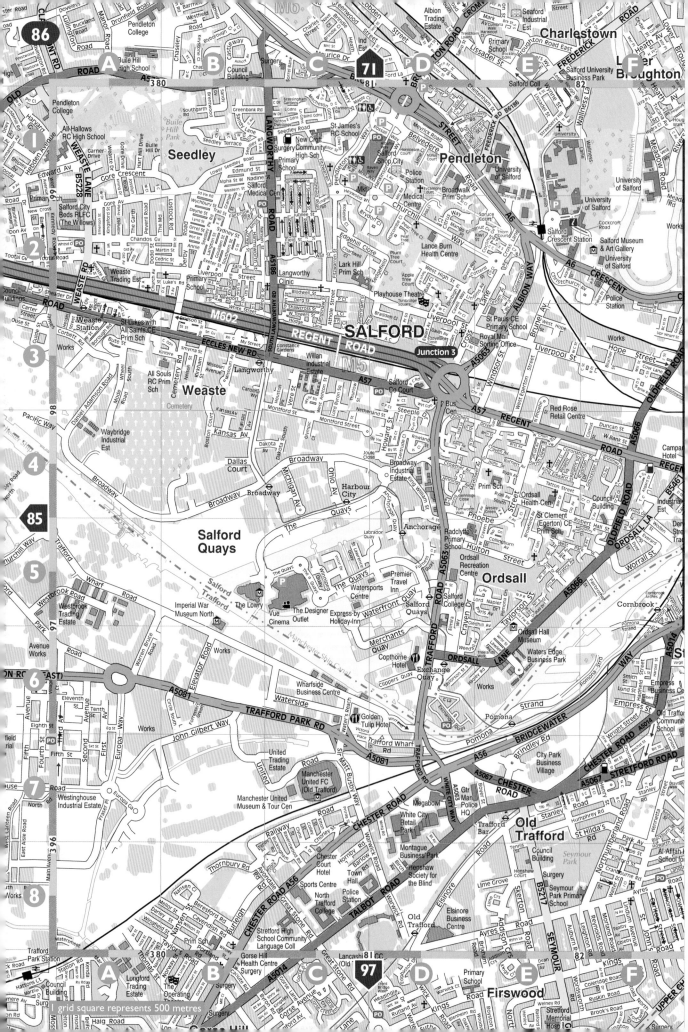

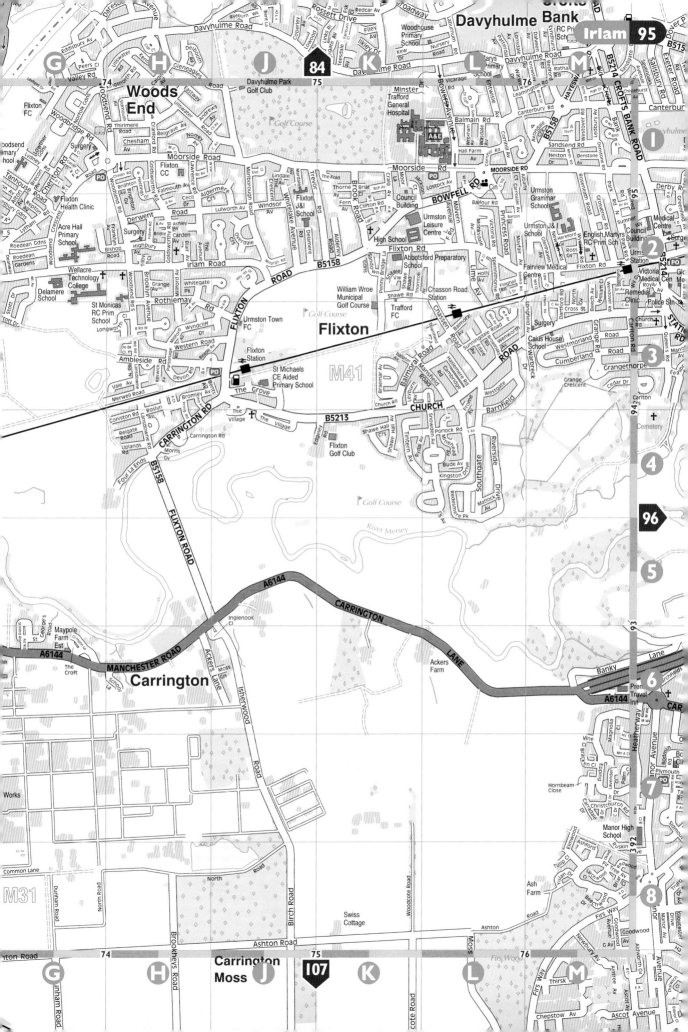

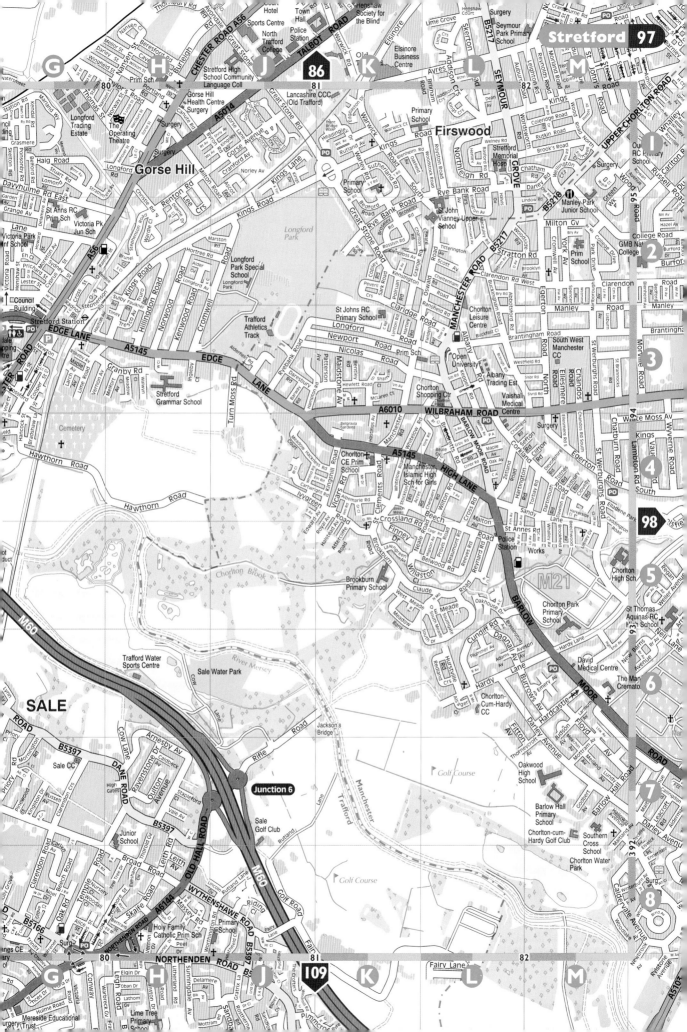

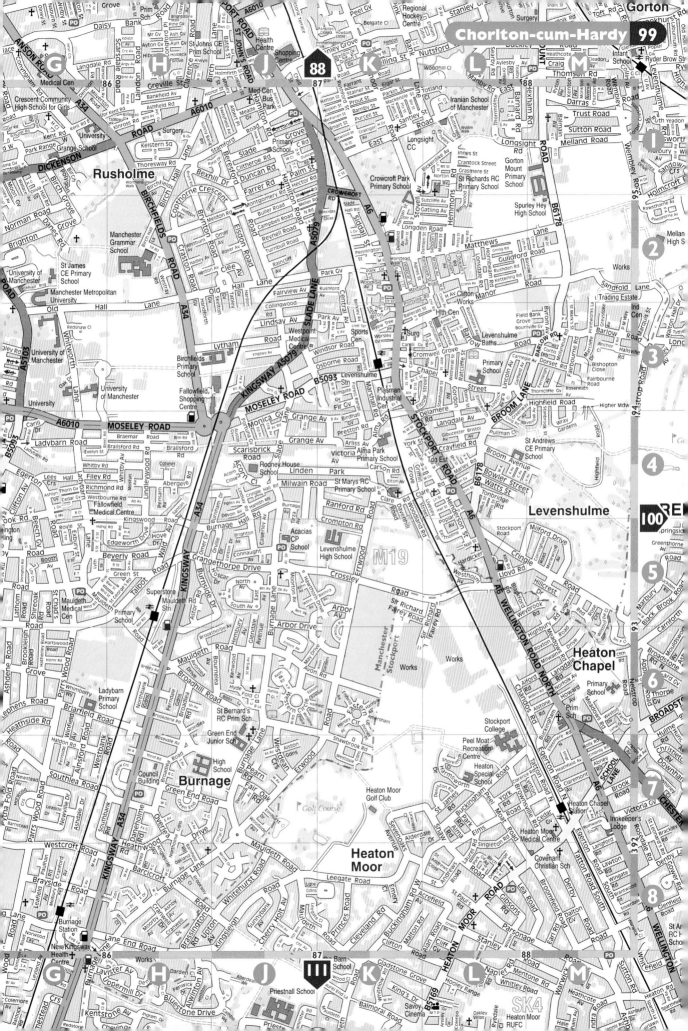

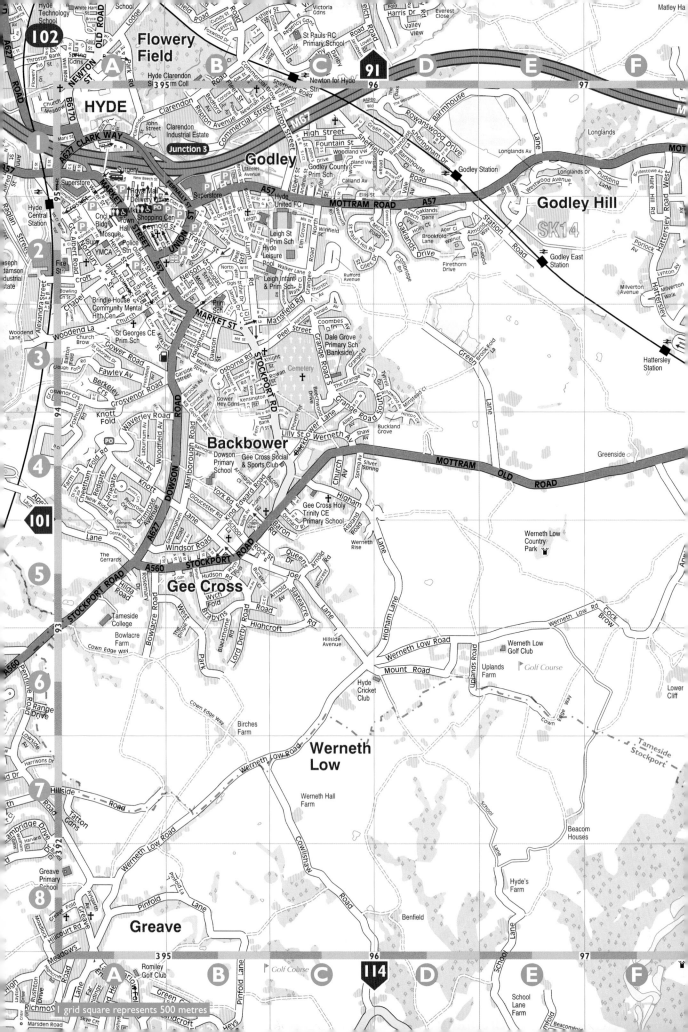

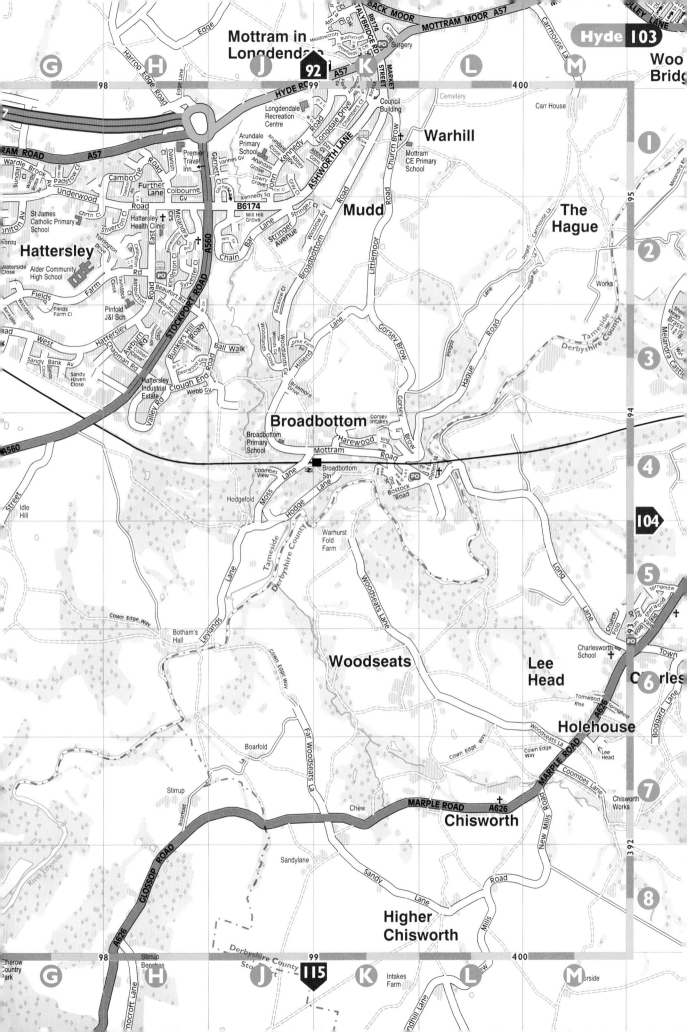

Mottram in Longdendale

92

Warhill

Mudd

The Hague

Hattersley

Broadbottom

104

Woodseats

Lee Head

Holehouse

Chisworth

Higher Chisworth

115

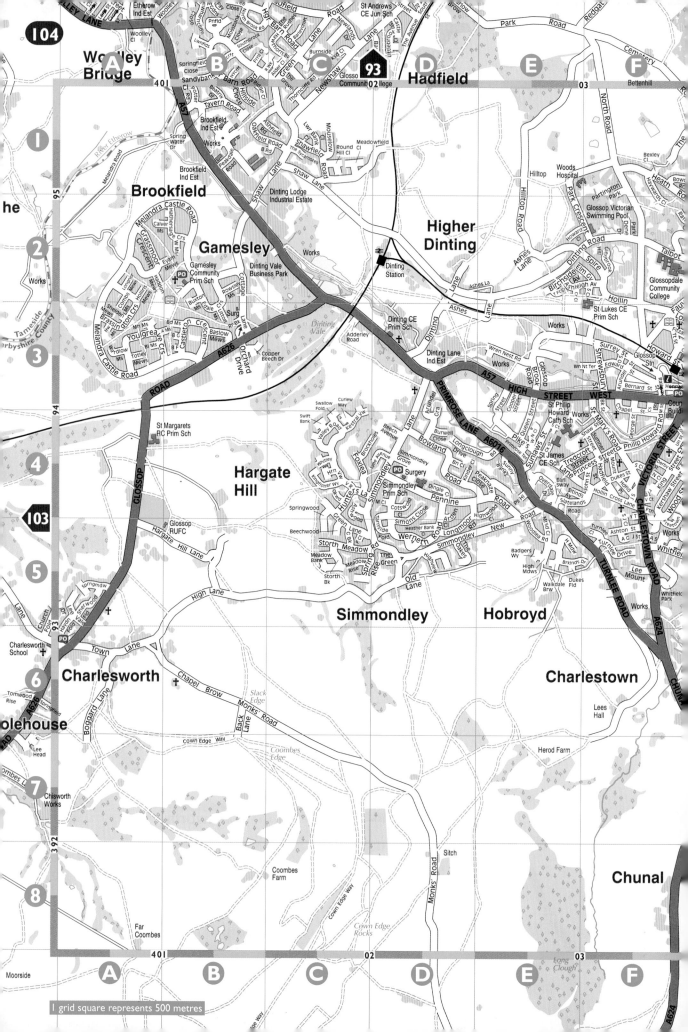

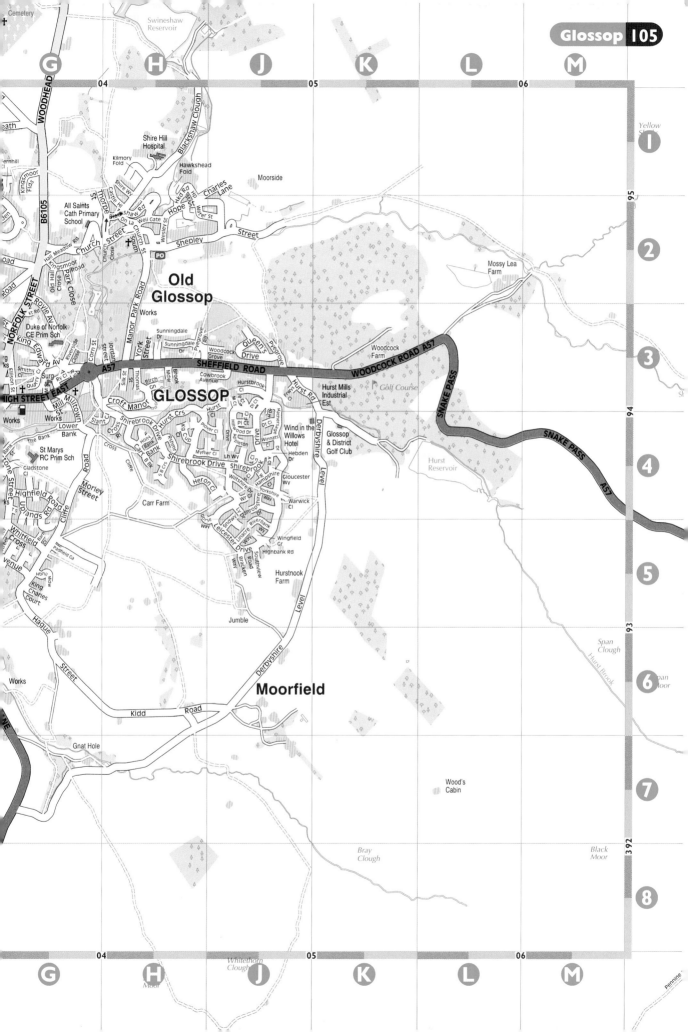

Cemetery

Swineshaw Reservoir

G H J K L M

04 WOODHEAD 05 06

95

Shire Hill Hospital

Kilmory Fold

Hawkshead Fold

Moorside

Blackshaw Clough

All Saints Cath Primary School

Hope St

Charles Lane

Water St

Shepley Street

94

Mossy Lea Farm

Old Glossop

PO

Works

Sunningdale Dr

Queen's Drive

Woodcock Grove

Sunningdale Dr

Woodcock Farm

Cowbrook Avenue

Hurst Rd

WOODCOCK ROAD A57

Golf Course

Norfolk St

Duke of Norfolk CE Prim Sch

King Edward Av

SHEFFIELD ROAD A57

SNAKE PASS

GLOSSOP

Hurstbrook

Hurst Crs

SNAKE PASS A57

HIGH STREET EAST

Croft Manor

Shirebrook Drive

Hurst Cl

Wind in the Willows Hotel

Hurst Mills Industrial Est

St Marys RC Prim Sch

Gladstone Cl

Shirebrook Drive

Shirebrook

Heron Cl

Hampshire Way

Gloucester Wy

Glossop & District Golf Club

Hurst Reservoir

Highfield Road

Morley Street

Carr Farm

Wiltshire Cl

Yorkshire Cl

Warwick Cl

Whitfield Cross Avenue

King Charles Court

Leicester Drive

Wingfield Gr

Highbank Rd

Hurstnook Farm

Snake Pass A57

Hague Street

Jumble

Derbyshire Level

Span Clough

Hurst Brook

Moorfield

Derbyshire Level

Kidd Road

Gnat Hole

Wood's Cabin

Bray Clough

Black Moor

Span Moor

93

92

G H J K L M

04 05 06

Whitethorn Clough

Pennine

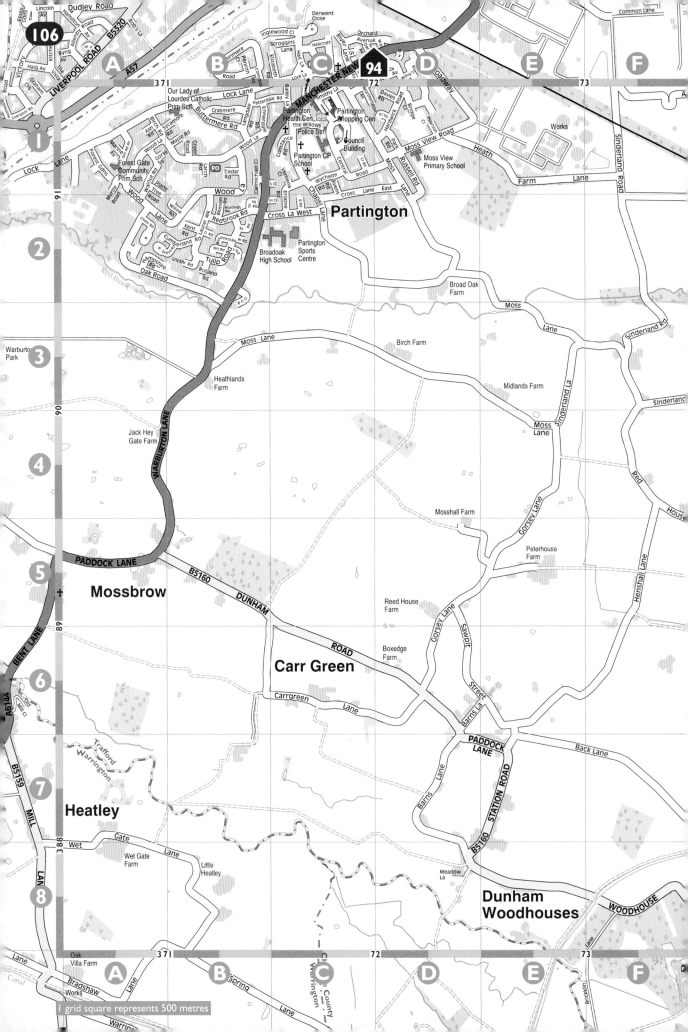

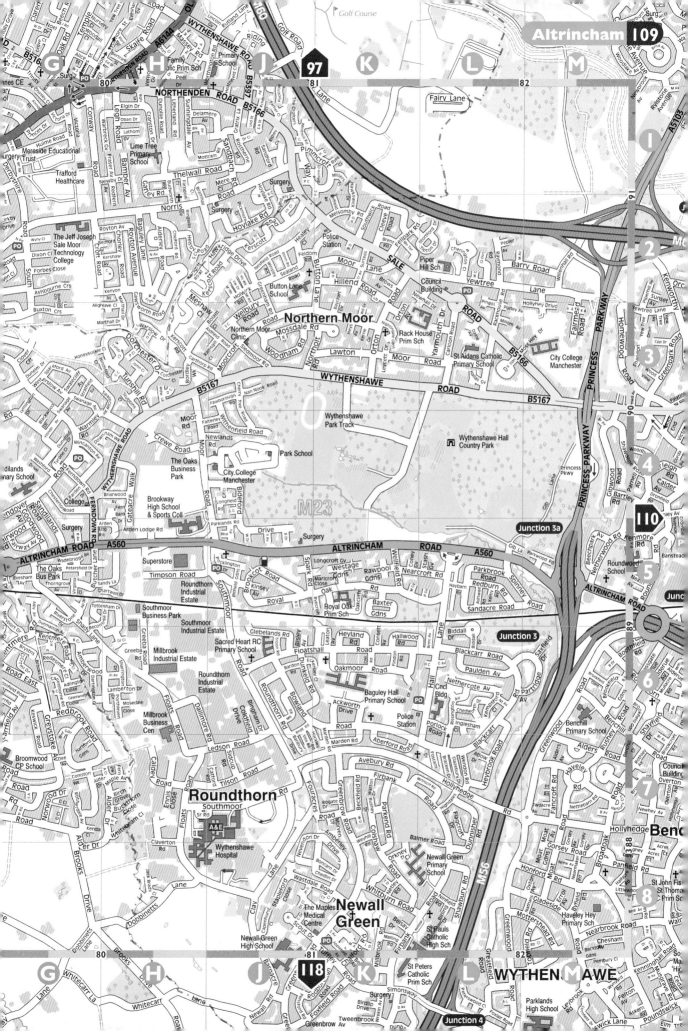

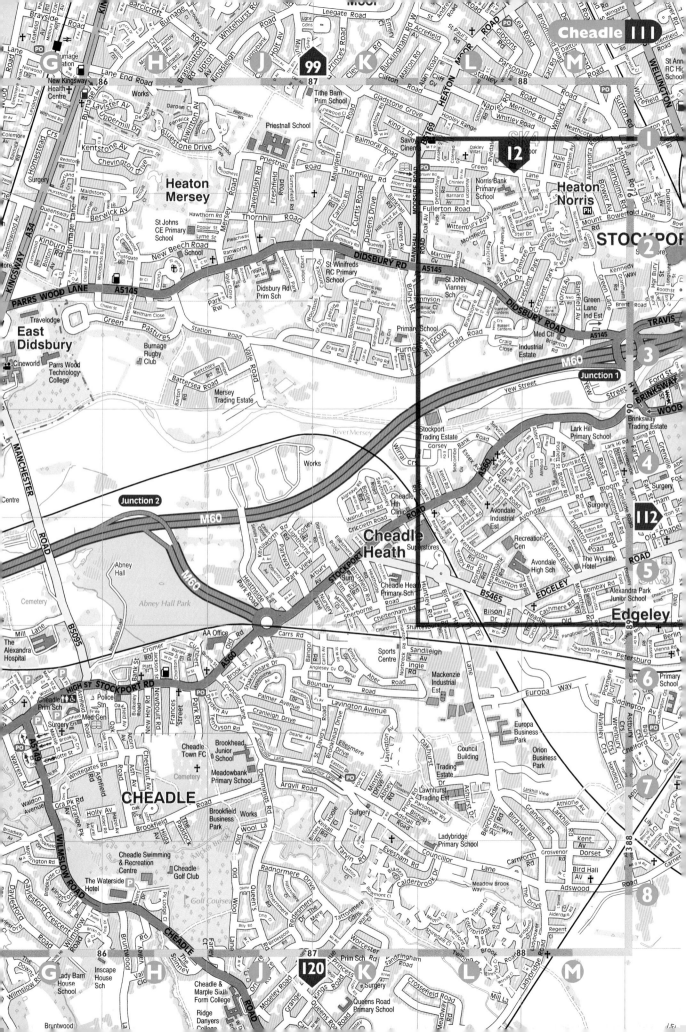

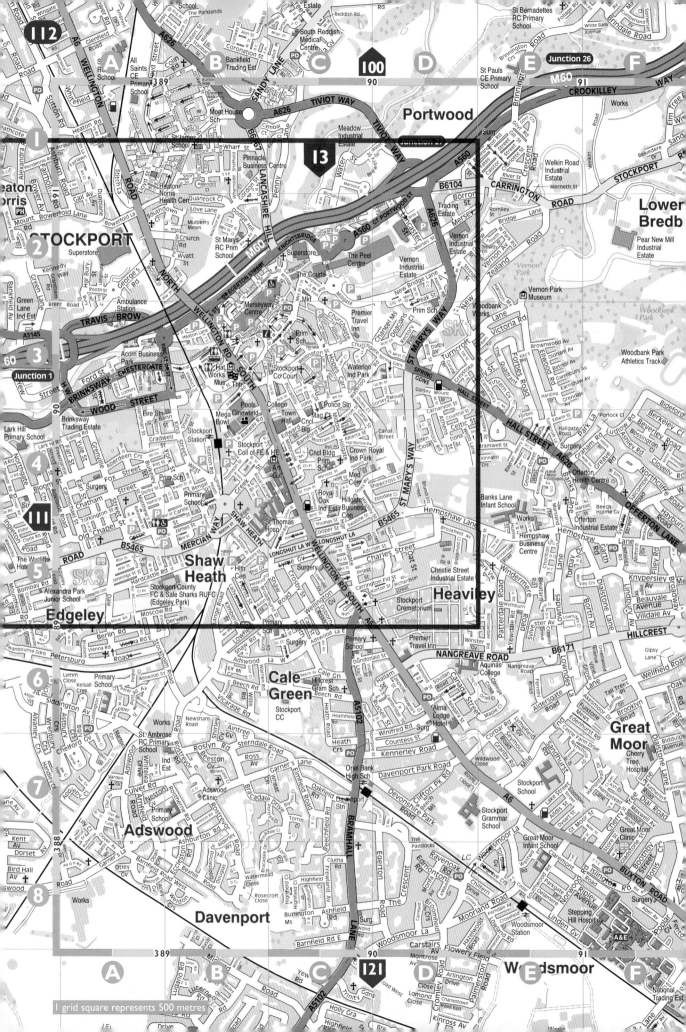

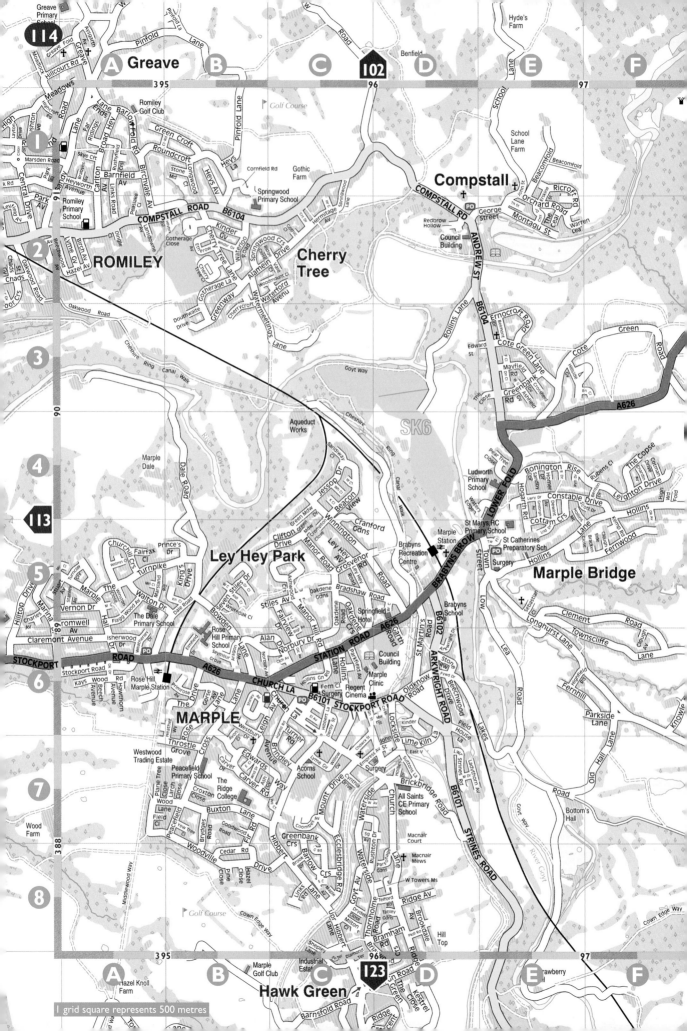

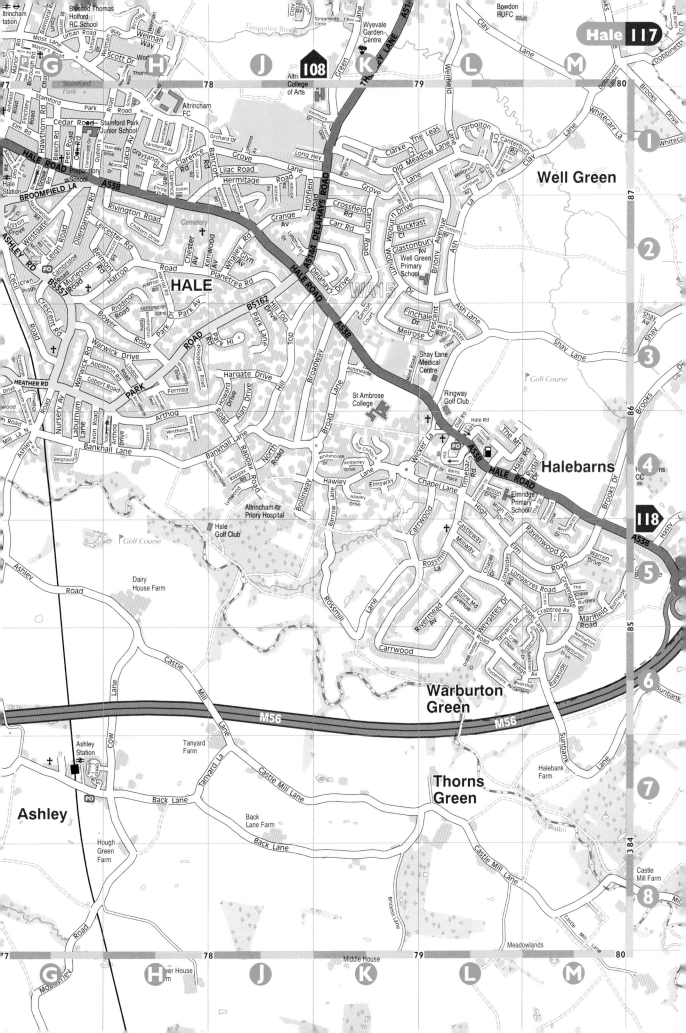

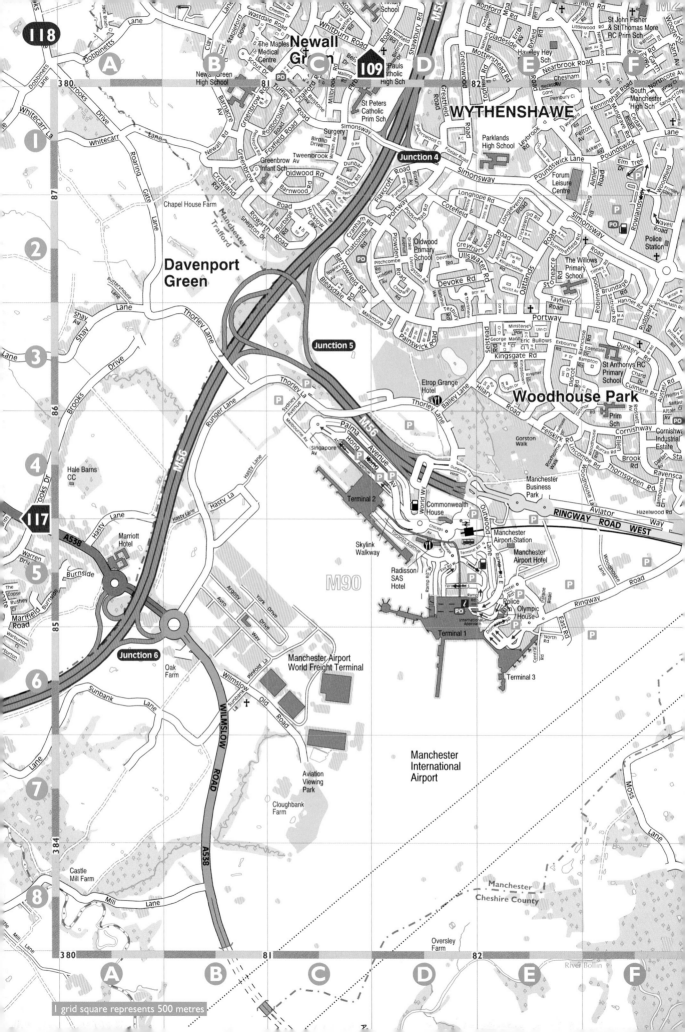

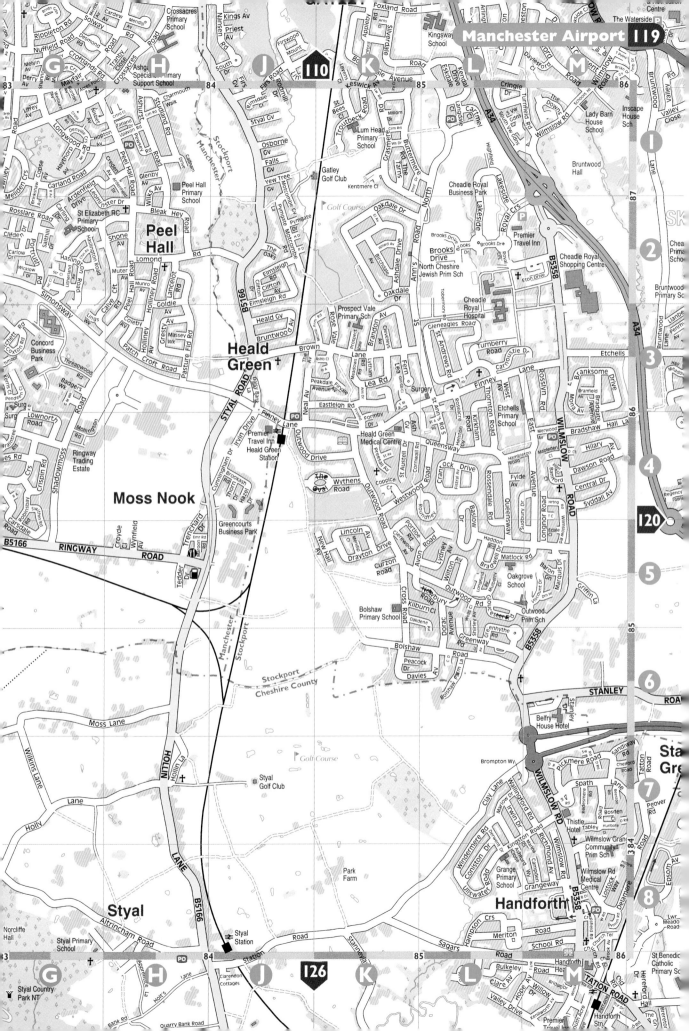

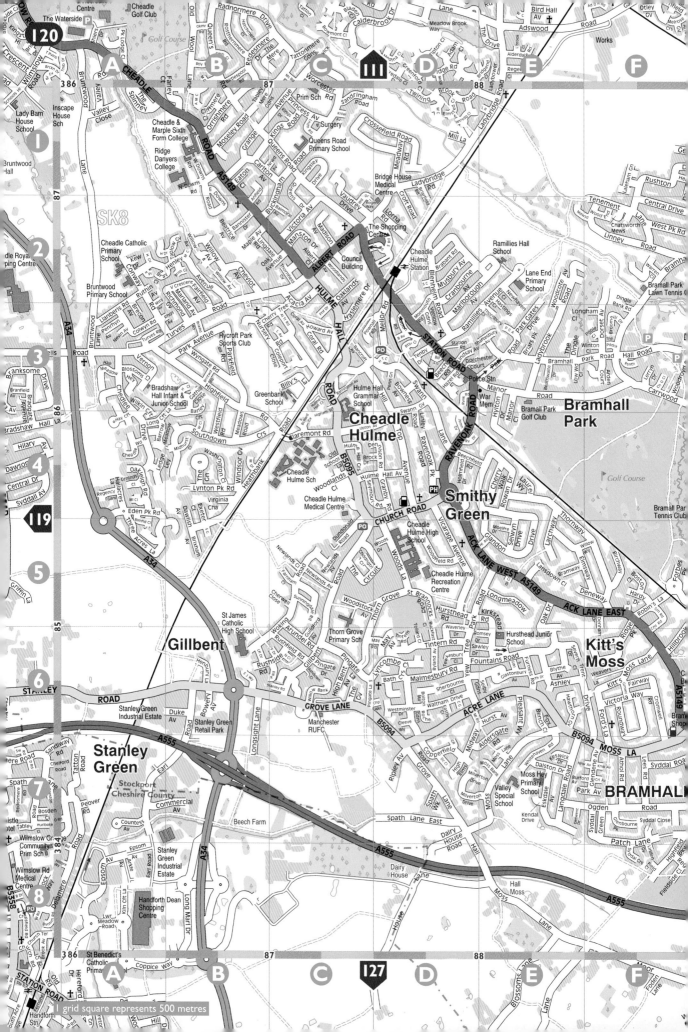

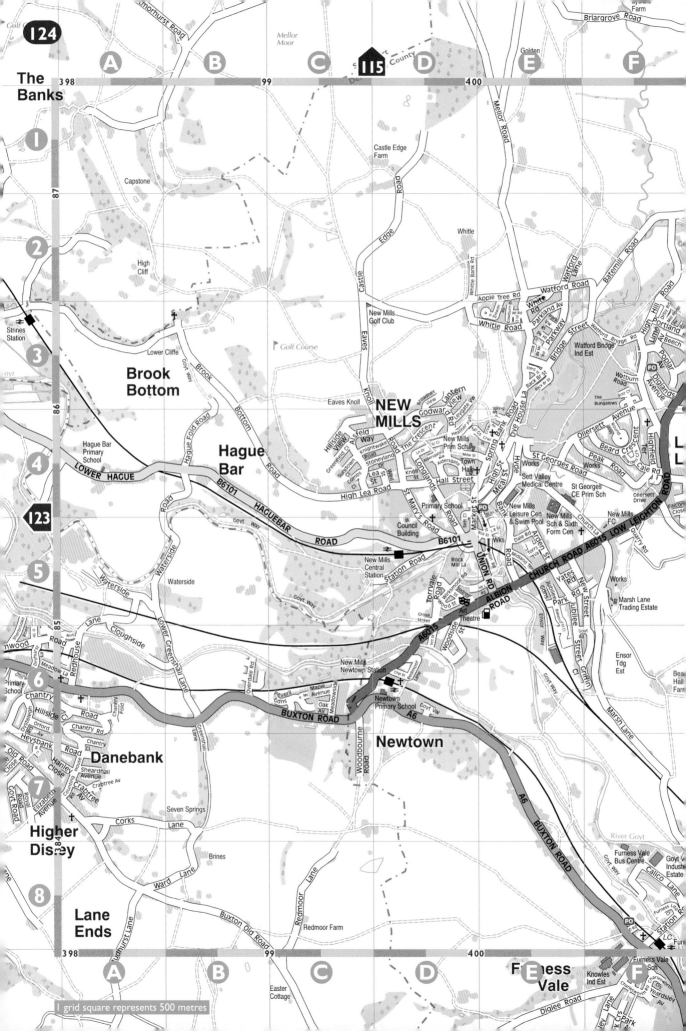

G H J K L M

02 03 04

Aspenshaw Hall

Wethercotes

Cliff

Swallow

House

River Sett

Pike Cl

Bank Vale Road

Lea Rd

Fairy Bank

Highgate Rd

Kinder Rd

Cote Lane

Hayfield Primary School

Wood Gdns

Chander

Bowden Cl

Wood La

PO

Council Building

Surg

Hayfield Site

Market Street

Snudhill Rd

Bank

Vicarage

Thornsett Primary School

Sycamore Road

Quarry Road

Spinnerbottom

Station Rd

PO

Birch Vale Industrial Estate

Works

Birch Hall Cl

NEW MILLS ROAD

PH

A6015

Surg

Station Rd

Church St

St John's Street

Mudhole

Fr Br

PH

Thornsett

Thornsett Trading Estate

Works

Works

Lantern Pike View

Hayfield Road

Sett Valley Trail

Morland Road

The Birches

The Oaks

Ridge Top Lane

Hayfield

Valley Road

87

I

2

Highgate Road

A6

3

CHAPEL

HAYFIELD ROAD

Ridge Top

Over Lee Farm

Barnsfold Farm

86

W ighton

ngot oad

Works

Cold Harbour Farm

Over Hill Road

Ollersett

Far Phoside

4

Moor Lodge

5

Piece Farm

Hills Farm

85

Laneside Road

6

Shedyard Farm

Over Hill Road

New Allotments

7

Beardwood Farm

3 84

8

Gowhole

Vale Station

Ladypit Road

The Haugh

Cloughhead

Throstle

Cracken Edge

G H J K L M

02 03 04

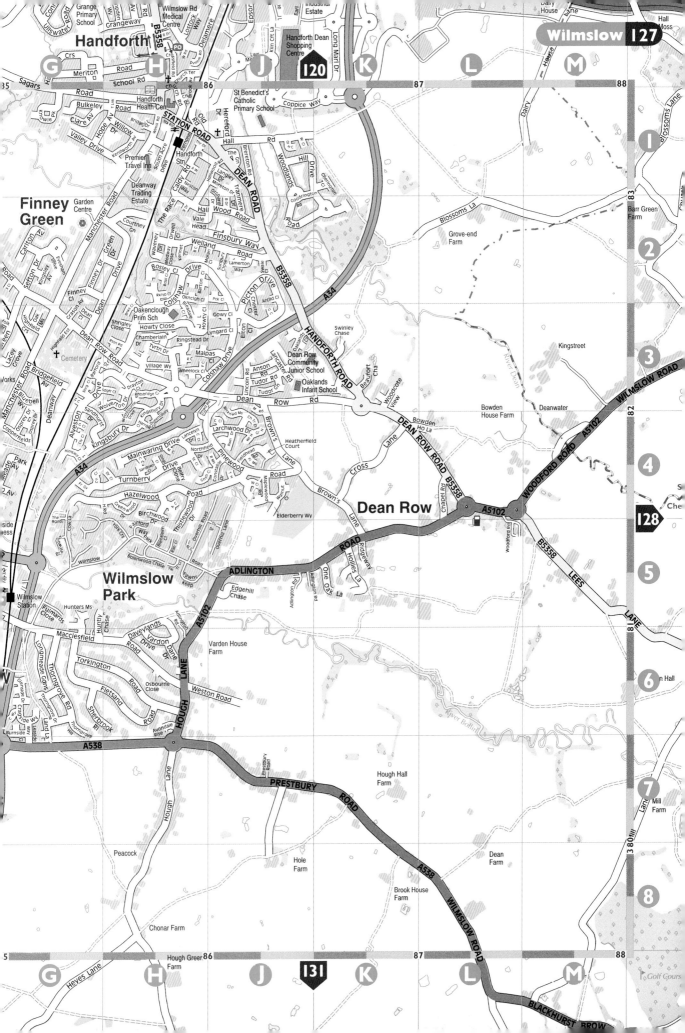

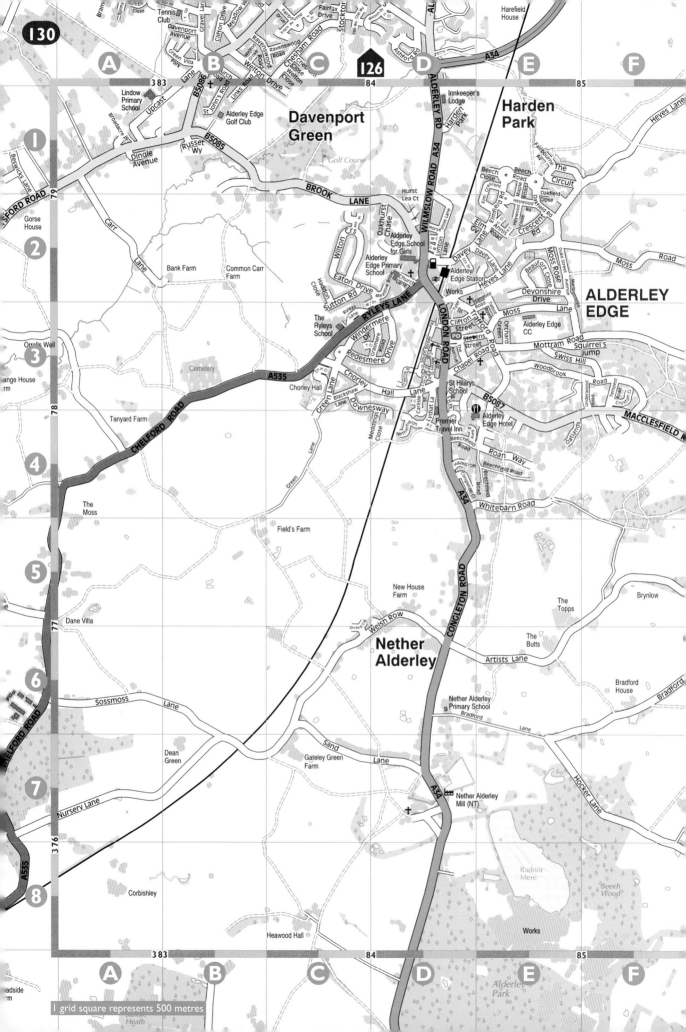

Abbey Hey ... 89 J7
Abram ... 64 F4
Acre ... 59 L3
Adlington ... 128 F7
Adswood ... 112 A7
Affetside ... 23 L4
Ainsworth ... 38 A3
Alder Forest ... 69 J8
Alderley Edge ... 130 F2
Alkrington Garden Village ... 57 K6
Alt ... 76 A1
Alt Hill ... 75 M4
Altrincham ... 108 C7
Ancoats ... 7 L4
Arden Park ... 101 G8
Ardwick ... 7 M9
Ashley ... 117 G7
Ashley Heath ... 116 F4
Ashton-in-Makerfield ... 79 G1
Ashton-under-Lyne ... 90 B1
Ashton Upon Mersey ... 96 C6
Aspull ... 33 G7
Aspull Common ... 80 E3
Astley ... 67 M6
Astley Bridge ... 22 B8
Astley Green ... 67 M8
Atherton ... 67 H1
Audenshaw ... 90 B5
Austerlands ... 60 E4
Backbower ... 102 B4
Bagslate Moor ... 27 J4
Balderstone ... 42 E1
Baldingstone ... 25 H3
Bamford ... 27 G5
Bamfurlong ... 64 B4
Bank Lane ... 19 G5
Bank Top ... 22 D7
Bardsley ... 75 K3
Barton Upon Irwell ... 85 G4
Bedford ... 66 F8
Beech Hill ... 47 J2
Belfield ... 29 G5
Belle Vue ... 88 E7
Benchill ... 110 A7
Bentgate ... 43 J1
Besses o' th' Barn ... 55 J5
Beswick ... 88 C3
Bickershaw ... 65 H4
Billinge ... 62 C7
Birch ... 40 F8
Birtle ... 26 B5
Blackford Bridge ... 39 J8
Black Lane ... 38 C6
Blackley ... 73 H3
Blackmoor ... 67 K7
Blackrod ... 32 F1
Bleak Hey Nook ... 45 M5
Boar's Head ... 31 K6
Bolholt ... 24 D8
Bolton ... 3 G5
Booth Green ... 129 J5
Boothstown ... 68 D6
Bottom o' th' Moor ... 34 B1
Bowdon ... 116 B3
Bowgreen ... 116 C3
Bowlee ... 56 D3
Bradford ... 88 C2
Bradley Fold ... 37 L5
Bradshaw ... 22 F6
Bramhall ... 120 F7
Bramhall Moor ... 121 K2
Bramhall Park ... 120 E3
Bredbury ... 113 H1
Bredbury Green ... 113 K2
Breightmet ... 37 K4
Brinnington ... 100 E7
Broadbottom ... 103 J4
Broadfield ... 40 E3
Broadhalgh ... 27 J5
Broadheath ... 107 M5
Broadley ... 20 A7
Broadoak Park ... 69 M7
Bromley Cross ... 22 D6
Brook Bottom ... 76 D2
Brook Bottom ... 124 A3
Brookfield ... 104 A2
Brooklands ... 108 E2
Brooksbottoms ... 24 F1
Broughton Park ... 72 A3
Brownlow Fold ... 35 M3
Brunswick ... 87 L6
Brushes ... 92 B1
Bryn ... 63 J6
Bryn Gates ... 64 C5
Buckley ... 28 D1
Buckton Vale ... 77 H7
Buersil Head ... 42 F3
Burnage ... 99 H7
Burnden ... 36 D8
Burnedge ... 43 H3
Bury ... 4 D3
Busk ... 8 C3
Calderbrook ... 21 M3
Caldermoor ... 21 K6
Cale Green ... 112 C6
Captain Fold ... 41 H1
Carr ... 18 E5
Carrbrook ... 77 K5
Carr Green ... 106 C6
Carrington ... 95 H6
Carrington Moss ... 107 J1
Castlefield ... 6 B7
Castle Hill ... 101 H5
Castleton ... 41 M2
Chadderton ... 58 B5
Chadderton Fold ... 58 C2
Chadkirk ... 113 L4
Chadwick Green ... 62 B8
Chapel Field ... 54 F3
Chapeltown ... 23 G1
Charlestown ... 71 L8
Charlestown ... 73 K1
Charlestown ... 104 E6
Charlesworth ... 104 A6
Chatterton ... 18 E3
Cheadle ... 111 H7
Cheadle Heath ... 111 K5
Cheadle Hulme ... 120 C4
Cheetham Hill ... 72 E6
Chequerbent ... 51 C2
Cherry Tree ... 114 C2
Chesham ... 25 K7
Chew Moor ... 34 F8
Chisworth ... 103 L7
Chorlton-cum-Hardy ... 98 A5
Chunal ... 104 F8
Cinder Hill ... 54 A4
Clarksfield ... 60 A5
Clayton ... 88 F1
Cliff ... 125 K1

Clifton ... 70 B1
Clifton Green ... 70 E2
Clifton Junction ... 70 F1
Clough ... 21 L3
Clough ... 44 A6
Collyhurst ... 73 G6
Compstall ... 114 D1
Cooper Turning ... 33 L7
Copley ... 91 M2
Copster Hill ... 75 H2
Cox Green ... 22 C5
Crankwood ... 64 F7
Crimble ... 27 J8
Crofts Bank ... 84 F8
Crompton Fold ... 43 M3
Crooke ... 46 F1
Crowhill ... 75 J8
Crumpsall ... 72 C3
Cutgate ... 27 K4
Daisy Hill ... 50 D6
Daisy Nook ... 74 F7
Dale ... 45 J7
Dales Brow ... 70 A6
Dane Bank ... 100 E2
Danebank ... 124 A7
Dangerous Corner ... 65 M2
Darcy Lever ... 37 G7
Darn Hill ... 40 C5
Daubhill ... 35 M8
Davenport ... 112 B8
Davenport Green ... 118 B2
Davenport Green ... 130 C1
Davyhulme ... 84 E8
Deane ... 51 L1
Dean Row ... 127 K4
Dearnley ... 21 K8
Debdale ... 89 J8
Delph ... 45 H8
Denshaw ... 45 G2
Denton ... 101 J4
Didsbury ... 110 E1
Diggle ... 45 M1
Dimple ... 16 A8
Disley ... 123 K6
Dobcross ... 61 J2
Doffcocker ... 35 K2
Dog Hill ... 44 B5
Dover ... 64 E6
Downall Green ... 62 F7
Droylsden ... 89 H3
Dukinfield ... 90 F5
Dumplington ... 84 F5
Dunham Town ... 107 G8
Dunham Woodhouses ... 106 B8
Dunscar ... 22 A3
Eagley ... 22 B5
East Didsbury ... 111 G3
Eccles ... 85 K3
Edenfield ... 19 H1
Edge Fold ... 16 D3
Edge Fold ... 51 M3
Edge Green ... 79 J1
Edgeley ... 112 E8
Edgworth ... 17 H6
Egerton ... 22 B2
Ellenbrook ... 68 D4
Ellesmere Park ... 70 B8
Elton ... 38 E2
Facit ... 20 C1
Failsworth ... 74 B5
Fairfield ... 40 A1
Fairfield ... 89 K5
Fallowfield ... 98 E4
Far Moor ... 46 B7
Farnworth ... 52 E4
Fern Bank ... 91 L3
Fernhill ... 23 J4
Fernhill Gate ... 35 J8
Finney Green ... 127 G2
Firgrove ... 29 H6
Firs Lane ... 66 A7
Firswood ... 97 L1
Firwood Fold ... 36 F1
Fishpool ... 4 C8
Fitton Hill ... 75 K2
Flixton ... 95 K3
Flowery Field ... 91 G8
Foggbrook ... 113 J5
Four Gates ... 33 M8
Four Lane Ends ... 24 A7
Fowley Common ... 81 L7
Free Town ... 5 L1
Fullwood ... 44 A7
Fulshaw Park ... 126 E7
Gamesley ... 104 B2
Gathurst ... 46 C1
Gatley ... 110 D8
Gee Cross ... 102 B5
Gigg ... 39 K5
Gillbent ... 120 D6
Gilnow ... 2 B6
Gin Pit ... 67 J5
Glazebury ... 81 L6
Glodwick ... 59 L7
Glossop ... 105 H3
Godley ... 102 B1
Godley Hill ... 102 E2
Golborne ... 79 L5
Goose Green ... 47 H8
Gorse Hill ... 97 H1
Gorton ... 88 F8
Gowhole ... 125 G6
Grains Bar ... 44 D6
Grasscroft ... 61 G6
Gravel Hole ... 43 G5
Great Howarth ... 20 E8
Great Lever ... 52 D1
Great Moor ... 112 F6
Greave ... 102 A8
Greenacres ... 60 A5
Greendale ... 131 M5
Greenfield ... 61 L8
Greengate ... 29 G1
Greenheys ... 52 A7
Greenmount ... 24 B2
Greenside ... 89 L1
Grotton ... 60 E6
Guide Bridge ... 90 B3
Hadfield ... 93 K8
Hag Fold ... 50 F7
Haggate ... 58 F7
Hague Bar ... 124 B4
Haigh ... 32 E5
Hale ... 117 H2
Halebarns ... 117 M4
Halfway Houses ... 37 M6
Hall i' th' Wood ... 22 D8
Halliwell ... 36 B1
Handforth ... 119 L8
Harden Park ... 130 E1

Hargate Hill ... 104 B4
Harper Green ... 52 E3
Harpurhey ... 73 H5
Hart Common ... 49 L5
Hartshead Green ... 76 D4
Hartshead Pike ... 76 C3
Harwood ... 37 K1
Harwood Lee ... 23 H7
Hathershaw ... 75 J1
Hattersley ... 103 G2
Haugh ... 43 M1
Haughton Green ... 101 K4
Hawk Green ... 123 G1
Hawkley ... 63 K1
Hawkshaw ... 23 M1
Haydock ... 78 A6
Hayfield ... 125 L2
Hazel Grove ... 122 C3
Hazelhurst ... 18 C8
Hazelhurst ... 69 L6
Hazelhurst ... 76 D7
Heady Hill ... 40 D2
Heald Green ... 119 J3
Healds Green ... 58 C1
Healey ... 20 C8
Heap Bridge ... 39 M3
Heatley ... 106 A7
Heaton ... 35 K4
Heaton Chapel ... 99 M6
Heaton Mersey ... 111 H1
Heaton Moor ... 99
Heaton Norris ... 12 C2
Heaviley ... 13 M9
Heights ... 45 G6
Heyheads ... 77 G5
Heyrod ... 76 E8
Heyside ... 43 K8
Heywood ... 40 F1
Higginshaw ... 59 J2
High Crompton ... 43 K4
Higher Blackley ... 56 F8
Higher Boarshaw ... 57 M1
Higher Broughton ... 72 A6
Higher Chisworth ... 103 K3
Higher Dinting ... 104 D2
Higher Disley ... 123 M7
Higher Folds ... 67 H6
Higher Green ... 68 A7
Higher Poynton ... 129 M2
Higher Woodhill ... 25 G7
Highfield ... 46 F3
Highfield ... 52 C5
High Lane ... 123 C5
Hill Top ... 53 C8
Hilton House ... 33 K6
Hilton Park ... 71 K2
Hindley ... 49 H8
Hindley Green ... 49 M8
Hindsford ... 67 G2
Hobroyd ... 104 E5
Hockley ... 129 L1
Holcombe ... 18 D7
Holcombe Brook ... 24 C1
Holden Fold ... 59 G1
Holehouse ... 103 M6
Hollingworth ... 92 F6
Hollins ... 57 J8
Hollins ... 52 A4
Hollins ... 57 J1
Hollinwood ... 74 D3
Holts ... 60 B8
Hooley Bridge ... 26 F7
Hooley Brow ... 27 G8
Hooley Hill ... 90 B5
Hope Green ... 129 H3
Hough ... 131 G3
Howe Bridge ... 66 E3
Hulme ... 87 H6
Hunger Hill ... 30 C1
Hunger Hill ... 51 G1
Hurst ... 76 A7
Hurstead ... 21 G8
Hyde ... 102 A1
Ince-in-Makerfield ... 15 L6
Irlam ... 94 C3
Irlams o' th' Height ... 70 F7
Jericho ... 26 B8
Johnson Fold ... 35 G1
Jubilee ... 43 L2
Kearsley ... 53 L6
Kenyon ... 80 D8
Kersal ... 71 L3
Kingston ... 101 L1
Kirkhams ... 55 L6
Kirkholt ... 42 B1
Kirklees ... 24 E5
Kitt Green ... 47 H5
Kitt's Moss ... 120 F6
Knott Lanes ... 75 J5
Lacey Green ... 126 F3
Lady House ... 29 H8
Lambehead Green ... 46 D7
Land Gate ... 63 K5
Landslow Green ... 92 E5
Lane Ends ... 115 G3
Lane Ends ... 124 A8
Lane Head ... 80 C6
Langley ... 56 F1
Lark Hill ... 67 K7
Lately Common ... 81 M3
Lee Head ... 103 M6
Lees ... 60 B6
Leigh ... 66 F7
Levenshulme ... 99 M4
Lever-Edge ... 52 A2
Ley Hey Park ... 114 B5
Lilford ... 66 D6
Limefield ... 25 J6
Limehurst ... 75 K6
Lime Side ... 75 G3
Linfitts ... 45 G7
Linnyshaw ... 69 H1
Little Bolton ... 85 L2
Littleborough ... 21 M7
Little Clegg ... 29 H2
Little Hulton ... 52 C8
Little Lever ... 37 L8
Little Moor ... 113 G4
Littlemoss ... 74 F8
Little Scotland ... 32 D2
Longshaw ... 62 B3
Long Sight ... 59 H2
Longsight ... 88 C7
Lostock ... 34 B6
Lostock Junction ... 35 G7
Low Compton ... 43 H6
Lower Bredbury ... 112 F2
Lower Broughton ... 71 M8
Lower Green ... 82 F1
Lower Kersal ... 71 K6

Lower Place ... 28 F8
Low Leighton ... 124 F4
Lowton ... 80 A4
Lowton Common ... 80 D4
Lowton Heath ... 79 M6
Lowton St Mary's ... 80 D5
Luzley ... 76 E5
Luzley Brook ... 43 J7
Lydgate ... 60 F7
Makants ... 68 B2
Manchester ... 6 A5
Markland Hill ... 35 H4
Marland ... 27 L7
Marple ... 114 B6
Marple Bridge ... 114 E5
Marpleridge ... 123 H2
Marsh Green ... 46 F3
Marylebone ... 48 A1
Matley ... 92 C6
Mellor ... 115 H6
Micklehurst ... 77 H3
Middlebrook ... 33 L4
Middleton ... 57 G3
Middlewood ... 122 D7
Midway ... 129 H2
Miles Platting ... 88 A1
Millbrook ... 77 G8
Mill Brow ... 115 H4
Mill Hill ... 3 H3
Milnrow ... 29 K6
Monton ... 85 G1
Moorclose ... 57 M4
Moorend ... 115 K6
Moorfield ... 105 J6
Moorhey ... 59 L6
Moorside ... 60 E1
Moorside ... 70 A5
Morley ... 126 A3
Mosley Common ... 68 C5
Moss Gate ... 52 F2
Mossbrow ... 106 A5
Mossley ... 77 G2
Mossley Brow ... 76 F3
Moss Nook ... 119 H4
Moss Side ... 87 J8
Moston ... 73 L3
Mottram in Longdendale ... 92 C8
Mottram Rise ... 92 B5
Mottram St Andrew ... 131 K3
Mudd ... 103 K2
Mumps ... 9 K4
Nangreaves ... 25 H1
Nether Alderley ... 130 D6
Newall Green ... 109 K8
Newbold ... 11 M4
New Boston ... 78 C6
New Bury ... 52 D5
New Delph ... 61 K1
Newhey ... 29 K8
New Houses ... 62 E3
New Mills ... 124 D4
New Moston ... 73 M4
New Springs ... 48 D3
Newton ... 91 K7
Newton Heath ... 73 K7
Newton-le-Willows ... 79 G7
Newton Wood ... 90 D6
Newtown ... 47 H6
Newtown ... 70 B3
Newtown ... 128 D7
Nimble Nook ... 58 D7
Nob End ... 53 K2
Norbury Moor ... 122 A3
Norden ... 27 G3
Northenden ... 110 A4
Northern Moor ... 109 J3
North Reddish ... 100 B3
Nuttall ... 18 E8
Oak Bank ... 55 K5
Offerton ... 113 H5
Offerton Green ... 113 K6
Old Boston ... 78 E5
Oldfield Brow ... 107 L7
Old Glossop ... 105 H2
Oldham ... 9 L7
Oldham Edge ... 9 J1
Old Tame ... 44 E4
Old Trafford ... 86 E7
Openshaw ... 88 F4
Ordsall ... 86 E5
Orrell ... 46 D5
Orrell Post ... 46 B5
Outwood ... 54 D4
Over Hulton ... 51 K5
Padfield ... 93 M7
Park Bridge ... 75 M2
Parr Brow ... 68 B4
Partington ... 106 C2
Patricroft ... 84 F2
Peel Green ... 84 C4
Peel Hall ... 119 H2
Pemberton ... 46 F7
Pendlebury ... 70 F5
Pendleton ... 86 B2
Pennington ... 81 G1
Pennington Green ... 49 H2
Pickley Green ... 66 B3
Pimhole ... 5 K5
Pitses ... 60 A8
Plank Lane ... 65 L7
Platt Bridge ... 64 E2
Pocket Nook ... 80 F4
Poolstock ... 14 C8
Portwood ... 112 D1
Pownall Park ... 126 D4
Poynton ... 122 B8
Prestolee ... 53 L4
Prestwich ... 55 J8
Quick ... 60 F8
Quick Edge ... 76 E1
Radcliffe ... 38 D8
Rainsough ... 71 K3
Rakewood ... 29 M3
Ramsbottom ... 18 E4
Reddish ... 100 A4
Red Rock ... 32 A4
Redvales ... 39 H6
Rhodes ... 56 E5
Ridge Hill ... 76 D3
Ringley ... 54 A3
Roaches ... 77 G1
Rochdale ... 11 H4
Roebuck Low ... 60 D2
Roe Cross ... 92 C7
Roe Green ... 69 J4
Romiley ... 114 A2
Rose Hill ... 3 H9
Rosehill ... 116 E3
Roundthorn ... 109 H7
Royton ... 43 J2

Rusholme ... 99 G1
St George's ... 86 F6
Sale ... 96 C6
Salford ... 6 C3
Salford Quays ... 86 B5
Scholes ... 15 J4
Scot Lane End ... 33 H5
Scouthead ... 60 E3
Sedgley Park ... 71 M2
Seedley ... 86 B1
Shakerley ... 67 K2
Sharples ... 22 A4
Sharston ... 110 C7
Shaw ... 43 M6
Shawclough ... 27 M2
Shawfield ... 27 J3
Shaw Heath ... 13 G8
Shaw Side ... 43 L7
Shevington ... 30 D7
Shevington Moor ... 30 D3
Shevington Vale ... 30 C4
Sholver ... 44 A8
Shore ... 21 K6
Shuttleworth ... 19 H5
Side of the Moor ... 23 H6
Simister ... 56 B4
Simmondley ... 104 C5
Simm's Lane End ... 62 D7
Sinderland Green ... 107 G3
Skellorn Green ... 129 H1
Slackcote ... 44 E5
Slattocks ... 41 M6
Smallbridge ... 29 G1
Smallshaw ... 75 L6
Smithy Bridge ... 29 K1
Smithy Green ... 120 D4
South Reddish ... 100 B2
Spotland Bridge ... 10 A3
Springfield ... 47 J3
Springhead ... 60 C7
Spring Hill ... 60 C7
Spring View ... 48 B3
Stake Hill ... 42 B7
Stalybridge ... 91 J3
Stand ... 54 F4
Standish ... 31 J3
Standish Lower Ground ... 46 F5
Stanley Green ... 120 M4
Stancycliffe ... 57 L7
Starling ... 38 D2
Stepping Hill ... 113 G8
Stockport ... 12 D2
Stoneclough ... 53 L5
Stoneyfield ... 10 D9
Stoneyfield ... 28 C8
Strangeways ... 72 C8
Stretford ... 96 E3
Strines ... 123 L3
Stubbins ... 18 F4
Stubshaw Cross ... 64 A7
Styal ... 119 G3
Sudden ... 27 M8
Summerseat ... 24 E3
Summit ... 40 C2
Summit ... 42 E5
Sun Green ... 77 H8
Sunny Bank ... 39 K8
Swinton ... 70 A4
Swinton Park ... 70 E6
Syke ... 20 D8
Tamer Lane End ... 65 L7
Tame Water ... 61 H5
Taunton ... 75 H7
The Banks ... 115 G8
The Hague ... 103 M4
Thornham Fold ... 42 D5
Thornsett ... 125 G2
Thorns Green ... 117 L7
Thorp ... 42 E8
Thurston Clough ... 61 G1
Timperley ... 108 D5
Tintwistle ... 93 L3
Tonge Fold ... 3 M3
Tonge Moor ... 36 D2
Tontine ... 48 A6
Top Lock ... 48 E2
Top of Hebers ... 41 H8
Top o' th' Meadows ... 60 C4
Toppings ... 22 E5
Torkington ... 122 D2
Tottington ... 24 B6
Town Green ... 64 B4
Town Lane ... 67 L8
Town of Lowton ... 79 K7
Trafford Park ... 85 K7
Trub ... 41 M5
Tunshill ... 29 M5
Tunstead ... 61 M7
Turf Hill ... 29 G8
Turn ... 19 K3
Turton Bottoms ... 17 H7
Twiss Green ... 81 H7
Tyldesley ... 67 L3
Unsworth ... 55 K2
Uppermill ... 61 L5
Urmston ... 85 H8
Walkden ... 53 G8
Wall Hill ... 61 H7
Walmersley ... 25 H5
Walshaw ... 24 B8
Warburton Green ... 117 L6
Wardle ... 21 L6
Wardley ... 69 M3
Wardsend ... 129 L3
Warhill ... 103 L1
Waterloo ... 75 J7
Watersheddings ... 60 A3
Water's Nook ... 50 A3
Weaste ... 86 B3
Well Green ... 117 M1
Werneth ... 8 B7
Werneth Low ... 102 C7
West Didsbury ... 98 B7
Westhoughton ... 50 A3
Westleigh ... 66 A5
Westwood Park ... 69 K8
Whalley Range ... 98 B2
Whelley ... 15 M5
Whitefield ... 55 H5
White Gate ... 58 B5
Whitley ... 31 K8
Whitworth ... 20 B3
Wigan ... 14 D2
Willows ... 35 M7
Wilmslow ... 126 F6
Wilmslow Park ... 127 G5
Windlehurst ... 123 G3
Wingates ... 50 A1
Winstanley ... 62 F1
Winstanleys ... 31 M5

Winton 84 F1
Withington 98 F6
Wolstenholme 26 F1
Woodend 77 H2
Woodend 123 L4

Woodford 128 B2
Woodgate Hill 26 A8
Woodhey 24 D1
Woodhouse Park 118 E3
Woodhouses 74 D6

Woodhouses 107 L2
Woodlands 91 L5
Wood Lanes 129 L4
Woodley 101 M7
Wood Road 24 F3

Woodseats 103 K6
Woods End 95 H1
Woodsmoor 121 K1
Woolfold 24 D8
Woolley Bridge 93 G8

Worsley 69 J5
Worsley Hall 46 F6
Worsley Mesnes 47 J8
Wythenshawe 118 D3
Yew Tree 91 H5

USING THE STREET INDEX

Street names are listed alphabetically. Each street name is followed by its postal town or area locality, the Postcode District, the page number, and the reference to the square in which the name is found.

Standard index entries are shown as follows:

Abberley Dr *NEWH/MOS* M40 ....**74** A2

Street names and selected addresses not shown on the map due to scale restrictions are shown in the index with an asterisk:

Abbeyfield Sq *OP/CLY* M11* ...**88** E4

GENERAL ABBREVIATIONS

ACC...................ACCESS	CUTT...................CUTTINGS	HOL...................HOLLOW	NW...................NORTH WEST
ALY...................ALLEY	CV...................COVE	HOSP...................HOSPITAL	O/P...................OVERPASS
AP...................APPROACH	CYN...................CANYON	HRB...................HARBOUR	OFF...................OFFICE
AR...................ARCADE	DEPT...................DEPARTMENT	HTH...................HEATH	ORCH...................ORCHARD
ASS...................ASSOCIATION	DL...................DALE	HTS...................HEIGHTS	OV...................OVAL
AV...................AVENUE	DM...................DAM	HVN...................HAVEN	PAL...................PALACE
BCH...................BEACH	DR...................DRIVE	HWY...................HIGHWAY	PAS...................PASSAGE
BLDS...................BUILDINGS	DRO...................DROVE	IMP...................IMPERIAL	PAV...................PAVILION
BND...................BEND	DWGS...................DWELLINGS	INF...................INFIRMARY	PDE...................PARADE
BNK...................BANK	E...................EAST	IND EST...................INDUSTRIAL ESTATE	PH...................PUBLIC HOUSE
BR...................BRIDGE	EMB...................EMBANKMENT	INF...................INFIRMARY	PK...................PARK
BRK...................BROOK	EMBY...................EMBASSY	INFO...................INFORMATION	PKWY...................PARKWAY
BTM...................BOTTOM	ESP...................ESPLANADE	INT...................INTERCHANGE	PL...................PLACE
BUS...................BUSINESS	EST...................ESTATE	IS...................ISLAND	PLN...................PLAIN
BVD...................BOULEVARD	EX...................EXCHANGE	JCT...................JUNCTION	PLNS...................PLAINS
BY...................BYPASS	EXPY...................EXPRESSWAY	JTY...................JETTY	PLZ...................PLAZA
CATH...................CATHEDRAL	EXT...................EXTENSION	KG...................KING	POL...................POLICE STATION
CEM...................CEMETERY	F/O...................FLYOVER	KNL...................KNOLL	PR...................PRINCE
CEN...................CENTRE	FC...................FOOTBALL CLUB	L...................LAKE	PREC...................PRECINCT
CFT...................CROFT	FK...................FORK	LA...................LANE	PREP...................PREPARATORY
CH...................CHURCH	FLD...................FIELD	LDG...................LODGE	PRIM...................PRIMARY
CHA...................CHASE	FLDS...................FIELDS	LGT...................LIGHT	PROM...................PROMENADE
CHYD...................CHURCHYARD	FLS...................FALLS	LK...................LOCK	PRS...................PRINCESS
CIR...................CIRCLE	FM...................FARM	LKS...................LAKES	PRT...................PORT
CIRC...................CIRCUS	FT...................FORT	LNDG...................LANDING	PT...................POINT
CL...................CLOSE	FTS...................FLATS	LTL...................LITTLE	PTH...................PATH
CLFS...................CLIFFS	FWY...................FREEWAY	LWR...................LOWER	PZ...................PIAZZA
CMP...................CAMP	FY...................FERRY	MAG...................MAGISTRATE	QD...................QUADRANT
CNR...................CORNER	GA...................GATE	MAN...................MANSIONS	QU...................QUEEN
CO...................COUNTY	GAL...................GALLERY	MD...................MEAD	QY...................QUAY
COLL...................COLLEGE	GDN...................GARDEN	MDW...................MEADOWS	R...................RIVER
COM...................COMMON	GDNS...................GARDENS	MEM...................MEMORIAL	RBT...................ROUNDABOUT
COMM...................COMMISSION	GLD...................GLADE	MI...................MILL	RD...................ROAD
CON...................CONVENT	GLN...................GLEN	MKT...................MARKET	RDG...................RIDGE
COT...................COTTAGE	GN...................GREEN	MKTS...................MARKETS	REP...................REPUBLIC
COTS...................COTTAGES	GND...................GROUND	ML...................MALL	RES...................RESERVOIR
CP...................CAPE	GRA...................GRANGE	MNR...................MANOR	RFC...................RUGBY FOOTBALL CLUB
CPS...................COPSE	GRG...................GARAGE	MS...................MEWS	RI...................RISE
CR...................CREEK	GT...................GREAT	MSN...................MISSION	RP...................RAMP
CREM...................CREMATORIUM	GTWY...................GATEWAY	MT...................MOUNT	RW...................ROW
CRS...................CRESCENT	GV...................GROVE	MTN...................MOUNTAIN	S...................SOUTH
CSWY...................CAUSEWAY	HGR...................HIGHER	MTS...................MOUNTAINS	SCH...................SCHOOL
CT...................COURT	HL...................HILL	MUS...................MUSEUM	SE...................SOUTH EAST
CTRL...................CENTRAL	HLS...................HILLS	MWY...................MOTORWAY	SER...................SERVICE AREA
CTS...................COURTS	HO...................HOUSE	N...................NORTH	SH...................SHORE
CTYD...................COURTYARD		NE...................NORTH EAST	SHOP...................SHOPPING

SKWY...................SKYWAY	
SMT...................SUMMIT	
SOC...................SOCIETY	
SP...................SPUR	
SPR...................SPRING	
SQ...................SQUARE	
ST...................STREET	
STN...................STATION	
STR...................STREAM	
STRD...................STRAND	
SW...................SOUTH WEST	
TDG...................TRADING	
TER...................TERRACE	
THWY...................THROUGHWAY	
TNL...................TUNNEL	
TOLL...................TOLLWAY	
TPK...................TURNPIKE	
TR...................TRACK	
TRL...................TRAIL	
TWR...................TOWER	
U/P...................UNDERPASS	
UNI...................UNIVERSITY	
UPR...................UPPER	
V...................VALE	
VA...................VALLEY	
VIAD...................VIADUCT	
VIL...................VILLA	
VIS...................VISTA	
VLG...................VILLAGE	
VLS...................VILLAS	
VW...................VIEW	
W...................WEST	
WD...................WOOD	
WHF...................WHARF	
WK...................WALK	
WKS...................WALKS	
WLS...................WELLS	
WY...................WAY	
YD...................YARD	
YHA...................YOUTH HOSTEL	

POSTCODE TOWNS AND AREA ABBREVIATIONS

ALT...................Altrincham	CCHDY...................Chorlton-cum-Hardy	LIT...................Littleborough
ANC...................Ancoats	DWN...................Darwen	LYMM...................Lymm
AIMK...................Ashton-in-Makerfield	DTN/ASHW...................Denton/Audenshaw	MCFLDN...................Macclesfield north
AUL...................Ashton-under-Lyne	DID/WITH...................Didsbury/Withington	MCFLDS...................Macclesfield south
AULW...................Ashton-under-Lyne west	DROY...................Droylsden	MANAIR...................Manchester Airport
ATH...................Atherton	DUK...................Dukinfield	MPL/ROM...................Marple/Romiley
BKLY...................Blackley	ECC...................Eccles	MDTN...................Middleton (Gtr. Man)
BOL...................Bolton	EDGY/DAV...................Edgeley/Davenport	MILN...................Milnrow
BOLE...................Bolton east	EDGW/EG...................Edgeworth/Egerton	MOSL...................Mossley
BOLS/LL...................Bolton south/Little Lever	FAIL...................Failsworth	NM/HAY...................New Mills/Hayfield
BRAM/HZG...................Bramhall/Hazel Grove	FWTH...................Farnworth	NEWH/MOS...................Newton Heath/
BRO...................Broughton	GLSP...................Glossop	Moston
BRUN/LGST...................Brunswick/Longsight	GOL/RIS/CUL...................Golborne/	NEWLW...................Newton-le-Willows
BNG/LEV...................Burnage/Levenshulme	Risley/Culcheth	NTHM/RTH...................Northern
BURY...................Bury	GTN...................Gorton	Moor/Roundthorn
CMANE...................Central Manchester east	HALE/TIMP...................Hale/Timperley	OFTN...................Offerton
CMANW...................Central Manchester west	HTNM...................Heaton Moor	OLDTF/WHR...................Old Trafford/
CSLFD...................Central Salford	HEY...................Heywood	Whalley Range
CHAD...................Chadderton	HOR/BR...................Horwich/Blackrod	OLD...................Oldham
CHF/WBR...................Chapel-en-le- Frith/	HULME...................Hulme	OLDE...................Oldham east
Whalley Bridge	HYDE...................Hyde	OLDS...................Oldham south
CHD/CHDH...................Cheadle (Gtr. Man)/	IRL...................Irlam	OP/CLY...................Openshaw/Clayton
Cheadle Hulme	KNUT...................Knutsford	ORD...................Ordsall
CHH...................Cheetham Hill	LEIGH...................Leigh	PART...................Partington
CHLY/EC...................Chorley/Eccleston	LHULT...................Little Hulton	POY/DIS...................Poynton/Disley

PWCH...................Prestwich	WALK...................Walkden
RAD...................Radcliffe	WARRN/WOL...................Warrington north/
RNFD/HAY...................Rainford/Haydock	Woolston
RAMS...................Ramsbottom	WGTN/LGST...................West Gorton/
RAW/HAS...................Rawtenstall/Haslingden	Longsight
RDSH...................Reddish	WHTN...................Westhoughton
ROCH...................Rochdale	WHTF...................Whitefield
ROY/SHW...................Royton/Shaw	WHIT...................Whitworth
RUSH/FAL...................Rusholme/Fallowfield	WGN...................Wigan
SALE...................Sale	WGNE/HIN...................Wigan east/Hindley
SLFD...................Salford	WGNNW/ST...................Wigan northwest/
SALQ...................Salford Quays	Standish
SKEL...................Skelmersdale	WGNS/IIMK...................Wigan south/
STLY...................Stalybridge	Ince-in-Makerfield
STKP...................Stockport	WGNW/BIL/OR...................Wigan west/
STRET...................Stretford	Billinge/Orrell
SWIN...................Swinton	WILM/AE...................Wilmslow/
TOD...................Todmorden	Alderley Edge
TOT/BURYW...................Tottington/	WYTH/NTH...................Wythenshawe/
Bury west	Northenden
TRPK...................Trafford Park	
TRPK...................Trafford Park	
TYLD...................Tyldesley	
UPML...................Uppermill	
URM...................Urmston	

1

3rd St *WGNE/HIN* WN2 .... 64 B5	
4th St *WGNE/HIN* WN2 .... 64 C5	

A

Abberley Dr *NEWH/MOS* M40...... 74 A2	
Abberley Wy *WGNS/IIMK* WN3.... 46 E8	
Abberton Rd *DID/WITH* M20 ...... 98 D6	
Abbey Cl *ALT* WA14 .... 116 C3	
BOLS/LL BL3 .... 51 L2	
RAD M26 .... 38 B7	
STRET M32 .... 96 C1	
Abbey Ct *POY/DIS* SK12 .... 129 H1	
RAD M26 .... 38 B8	
WGNNW/ST WN6 .... 47 H2	
Abbeycroft Cl *TYLD* M29 .... 67 M6	
Abbey Dl *WGNNW/ST* WN6 ...... 30 A5	

Abbeydale *WHIT* OL12 .... 10 D2	
Abbeydale Cl *AUL* OL6 .... 76 C6	
Abbeydale Gdns *WALK* M28 ..... 52 F8	
Abbeydale Rd *NEWH/MOS* M40.... 73 M4	
Abbey Dr *LIT* OL15 .... 29 J1	
SWIN M27 .... 70 B4	
TOT/BURYW BL8 .... 38 D3	
WGNW/BIL/OR WN5 .... 46 B6	
Abbeyfields *WGNNW/ST* WN6.... 47 J2	
Abbeyfield Sq *OP/CLY* M11 * 88 E4	
Abbey Gdns *HYDE* SK14 .... 103 J1	
Abbey Gv *CHAD* OL9 .... 58 D8	
ECC M30 .... 85 H2	
HYDE SK14 .... 103 J1	
STKP SK1 .... 112 E4	
Abbey Hey La *GTN* M18........... 89 H6	
Abbey Hills Rd *OLDS* OL8 .... 59 M8	
Abbey La *LEIGH* WN7............... 66 A3	
Abbey Lawn *OLDTF/WHR* M16... 97 L1	
Abbeylea Dr *WHTN* BL5 .... 50 D2	
Abbey Rd *CHD/CHDH* SK8........ 111 K7	
DROY M43 .... 89 J1	
FAIL M35 .... 74 E4	
GOL/RIS/CUL WA3 .... 80 F4	

MDTN M24 .... 41 J8	
RNFD/HAY WA11 .... 78 B3	
SALE M33 .... 96 D6	
SWIN M27 .... 67 M5	
UPML OL3 .... 45 H7	
Abbey Sq *LEIGH* WN7 .... 66 A3	
Abbey St *LEIGH* WN7 .... 66 C6	
Abbeyville Wk *HULME* M15 * 87 H7	
Abbeyway North	
RNFD/HAY WA11 .... 78 D5	
Abbeyway South	
RNFD/HAY WA11 .... 78 D6	
Abbeywood Av *GTN* M18 * 89 H8	
Abbingdon Wy *LEIGH* WN7 .... 66 A3	
Abbot Cft *WHTN* BL5 .... 50 C6	
Abbotsbury Cl *POY/DIS* SK12 ... 121 M7	
Abbots Cl *SALE* M33 .... 97 G7	
Abbotsfield Cl *URM* M41 * 95 G1	
Abbotsford Dr *MDTN* M24 .... 41 G8	
Abbotsford Gv *ALT* WA14 .... 108 B4	
Abbotsford Rd *BOL* BL1 .... 35 K3	
CCHDY M21 .... 97 L3	

CHAD OL9 * 58 B4	
OLD OL1 .... 59 L3	
Abbotside Cl *OLDTF/WHR* M16 ... 98 A1	
Abbotsleigh Dr	
BRAM/HZG SK7 .... 121 H2	
Abbotts Gn *TYLD* M29............. 67 K8	
Abbott St *BOLS/LL* BL3 .... 2 C9	
ROCH OL11 .... 41 L1	
WGNE/HIN WN2 .... 48 F6	
Abden St *RAD* M26 .... 54 D1	
Abels La *UPML* OL3 .... 61 M4	
Aber Av *OFTN* SK2 .... 112 F8	
Abercarn Cl *CHH* M8 .... 72 D5	
Abercorn Rd *BOL* BL1 .... 35 L1	
Abercorn St *OLDE* OL4 * 60 A6	
Abercrombie Ct *SALE* M33........ 97 G7	
Aberdeen Gdns *WHIT* OL12....... 20 B8	
Aberdeen Gv *EDGY/DAV* SK3 ... 12 F6	
Aberdeen St *BRUN/LGST* M13 ... 87 L7	
Aberford Rd *NTHM/RTH* M23 .... 109 K7	
Abergele Rd *RUSH/FAL* M14 ...... 99 H4	
Abergele St *OFTN* SK2 .... 112 C6	
Aberley Fold *LIT* OL15 .... 21 K5	

Abernant Cl *OP/CLY* M11 .... 88 C3	
Abernethy St *HOR/BR* BL6 .... 34 A2	
Aber Rd *CHD/CHDH* SK8.......... 111 K6	
Abersoch Av *RUSH/FAL* M14 ..... 99 H4	
Abingdon Av *WHTF* M45 .... 55 L3	
Abingdon Cl *CHAD* OL9 * 58 E8	
ROCH OL11 .... 28 B8	
WHTF M45 .... 55 J2	
Abingdon Rd *BOLE* BL2 .... 3 L2	
BRAM/HZG SK7 .... 121 G2	
RDSH SK5 .... 100 C3	
URM M41 .... 96 B1	
Abingdon St *AUL* OL6 .... 91 G2	
M1 .... 7 C6	
Abinger Rd *AIMK* WN4 .... 63 G3	
Abington Dr *WGNE/HIN* WN2 .... 64 D3	
Abington Rd *SALE* M33 .... 108 F1	
Abney Gra *MOSL* OL5............... 77 H4	
Abney Rd *HTNM* SK4 .... 99 M7	
MOSL OL5 .... 76 F4	
Aboukir St *MILN* OL16 .... 11 H3	
Abram Cl *RUSH/FAL* M14 .... 99 H4	
Abram St *SLFD* M6 .... 71 J6	
Absalom Dr *CHH* M8 .... 72 C5	

Abson St OLD OL1 .... 8 D1
Acacia Av CHD/CHDH SK8 ...... 120 C2
  DTN/ASHW M34 .... 101 K1
  HALE/TIMP WA15 .... 117 K1
  SWIN M27 .... 70 B6
  WILM/AE SK9 .... 126 D5
Acacia Crs WGNNW/ST WN6 ..... 47 J1
Acacia Dr HALE/TIMP WA15 .... 117 K1
  SLFD M6 .... 85 L1
Acacia Rd RDSH SK5 .... 100 C3
  OLDS OL8 .... 75 G3
The Acacias URM M41 .... 96 B2
Acacia St NEWLW WA12 .... 78 C8
Academy Wk HULME M15 * 87 H7
Ace MI CHAD OL9 * 58 C8
Acer CI HYDE SK14 .... 102 D2
  ROCH OL11 .... 27 C3
Acer Gv BRO M7 .... 72 A5
Acheson St GTN M18 .... 89 G7
Ackers La PART M31 .... 95 H6
Ackers St BRUN/LGST M13 .... 87 L1
Acker St MILN OL16 .... 10 F3
Ackhurst La
  WGNNW/BIL/OR WN5 .... 46 D1
Ack La East BRAM/HZG SK7 .... 120 E5
Ack La West CHD/CHDH SK8 .... 120 D5
Ackroyd Av GTN M18 .... 89 K6
Ackroyd St OP/CLY M11 .... 89 H5
Ackworth Dr
  NTHM/RTH M23 .... 109 K6
Ackworth Rd SWIN M27 .... 70 B3
Acme Dr SWIN M27 .... 70 E4
Acomb St HULME M15 .... 87 L7
  RUSH/FAL M14 .... 98 E1
Acorn Av CHD/CHDH SK8 .... 111 H7
  HYDE SK14 .... 102 B4
Acorn CI BNG/LEV M19 .... 81 J1
  LEIGH WN7 .... 81 J1
  WHTF M45 .... 55 J6
Acorn Ct LEIGH WN7 .... 81 L1
Acorn St OLDE OL4 .... 60 B6
Acorn Wy OLD OL1 .... 9 H4
A Ct AIMK WN4 .... 78 E1
Acre Barn ROY/SHW OL2 .... 43 H4
Acre CI RAMS BL0 .... 19 C1
Acre Fld BOLE BL2 .... 23 C8
Acrefield SALE M33 .... 108 D1
  URM M41 .... 96 C3
Acrefield Av HTNM SK4 .... 99 K8
  OLD OL1 .... 9 M1
Acresbrook STLY SK15 .... 91 M5
Acres Ct WYTH/NTH M22 .... 110 A8
Acresdale HOR/BR BL6 .... 34 F6
Acresfield TYLD M29 .... 67 J3
Acresfield Av DTN/ASHW M34 ... 89 L3
Acresfield CI HOR/BR BL6 * 34 F2
  SWIN M27 .... 70 D6
Acresfield Rd
  HALE/TIMP WA15 .... 108 D4
  HYDE SK14 .... 91 J7
  LHULT M38 .... 52 E8
  MDTN M24 .... 57 K4
  SLFD M6 .... 71 G7
Acres Fold Av WYTH/NTH M22 . 110 B8
Acres La STLY SK15 .... 91 L3
Acres Rd CCHDY M21 .... 97 K4
  CHD/CHDH SK8 .... 110 D7
Acres St TOT/BURYW BL8 .... 24 C7
  DTN/ASHW M34 .... 101 H1
  GLSP SK13 .... 104 F5
  RAD M26 .... 54 B1
  WHIT OL12 .... 20 D3
Acreswood Av WGNE/HIN WN2 .. 49 K8
Acre Top Rd BKLY M9 .... 56 E7
Acreville Gv GOL/RIS/CUL WA3 .. 81 M5
Acton Av NEWH/MOS M40 .... 73 L8
Acton St OLD OL1 .... 9 M2
  WGN WN1 .... 15 G1
  WHIT OL12 .... 11 G1
Actons Wk WGNS/IIMK WN3 ..... 15 G6
Acton Ter WGN WN1 .... 15 G3
Actonville Av WYTH/NTH M22 .. 118 F1
Adair St CMANE M1 .... 7 M6
  ROCH OL11 .... 41 L2
Adam CI CHD/CHDH SK8 .... 111 L8
Adams Av CCHDY M21 .... 97 L6
Adams CI POY/DIS SK12 .... 129 J2
Adams Dr WGNS/IIMK WN3 ...... 47 J7
Adamson Gdns
  DID/WITH M20 .... 110 C1
Adamson Rd ECC M30 .... 84 F4
Adamson St AIMK WN4 .... 78 D1
Adamson Wk RUSH/FAL M14 * .. 98 E1
Adam St AUL OL6 .... 90 F1
  BOLS/LL BL3 .... 2 F9
  OLDS OL8 .... 75 J2
Ada St BKLY M9 .... 73 G3
  OLDE OL4 .... 9 M1
  RAMS BL0 .... 18 D7
  WHIT OL12 .... 28 D2
Adbaston Rd STRET M32 .... 85 K7
Adcroft St STKP SK1 .... 13 L8
Addenbrook Rd CHH M8 .... 72 B7
Adderley Rd GLSP SK13 .... 104 C3
Addingham CI BKLY M9 .... 56 F8
Addington CI WGNE/HIN WN2 .... 49 G8
Addington Rd BOLS/LL BL3 .... 51 J1
Addington St ANC M4 .... 7 J2
Addison Av AUL OL6 .... 91 G1
Addison CI BRUN/LGST M13 ...... 87 M6
Addison Crs OLDTF/WHR M16 .... 97 L1
Addison Dr MDTN M24 .... 57 J5
Addison Rd HALE/TIMP WA15 ... 117 M2
  IRL M44 .... 83 M8
  PART M31 .... 95 G6
  STRET M32 .... 96 E2
  URM M41 .... 96 A3
Adelaide Rd BRAM/HZG SK7 .... 121 G6
  EDGY/DAV SK3 .... 12 D7
Adelaide St BOLS/LL BL3 .... 36 A8
  CHH M8 .... 72 C7
  ECC M30 .... 85 G3
  HEY OL10 .... 41 H2
  MDTN M24 .... 57 K4
  RAMS BL0 .... 18 D8
  SWIN M27 .... 70 A5
Adelaide St East HEY OL10 .... 41 H2
Adelphi Dr LHULT M38 .... 52 E7
Adelphi Gv LHULT M38 .... 52 E7
Adelphi St CSLFD M3 .... 6 A3
  RAD M26 .... 38 D3
  WGNNW/ST WN6 .... 31 H3
Aden CI WGTN/LGST M12 .... 88 A4
Aden St OLDE OL4 .... 60 A7
Adisham Dr BOL BL1 .... 36 C3
Adlington CI HALE/TIMP WA15 .. 109 G6
  POY/DIS SK12 .... 129 K2
  TOT/BURYW BL8 .... 38 D3
Adlington Dr STRET M32 .... 96 B1
Adlington Pk MCFLDN SK10 ..... 129 G3
Adlington Rd WILM/AE SK9 ..... 127 J5

Adlington St BOLS/LL BL3 .... 52 A1
  OLDE OL4 .... 60 A3
  WGTN/LGST M12 .... 88 A4
Adrian Rd BOL BL1 .... 35 M2
Adrian St NEWH/MOS M40 .... 73 K5
Adrian Ter MILN OL16 .... 11 M6
Adscombe St OLDTF/WHR M16 ... 87 H8
Adshall Rd CHD/CHDH SK8 ...... 111 K7
Adshead Cl WYTH/NTH M22 ..... 118 D1
Adstock Wk NEWH/MOS M40 ..... 7 L1
Adstone Cl ANC M4 .... 88 A3
Adswood Cl OLDE OL4 .... 60 A3
Adswood Gv EDGY/DAV SK3 .... 112 A6
Adswood La East OFTN SK2 ..... 112 C6
Adswood La West
  EDGY/DAV SK3 .... 112 B6
Adswood Old Hall Rd
  CHD/CHDH SK8 .... 112 A8
  EDGY/DAV SK3 .... 112 A7
Adswood Rd CHD/CHDH SK8 .... 111 M8
  EDGY/DAV SK3 .... 112 B6
Adswood St NEWH/MOS M40 .... 88 D2
Adswood Ter EDGY/DAV SK3 ... 112 B6
Adwell Cl GOL/RIS/CUL WA3 ..... 80 D4
Aegean Cl BRO M7 .... 71 M7
Aegean Rd ALT WA14 .... 107 K6
Affetside Dr TOT/BURYW BL8 .... 38 E2
Affleck Av RAD M26 .... 53 K4
Afghan St OLD OL1 .... 59 L4
Age Cft OLDS OL8 * 75 M1
Agecroft Enterprise Pk
  SWIN M27 .... 71 H5
Agecroft Rd MPL/ROM SK6 ..... 113 K3
  SWIN M27 .... 71 H4
  WHTF M45 .... 55 C6
Agecroft Rd East PWCH M25 .... 71 K2
Agecroft Rd West PWCH M25 .... 71 K2
Agincourt St HEY OL10 * 40 E2
Agnes Cl CHAD OL9 .... 58 F8
Agnes St BNG/LEV M19 .... 99 K2
  BRO M7 .... 72 C5
  CHAD OL9 .... 8 B8
Agnew Pl SLFD M6 .... 71 K8
Agnew Rd GTN M18 .... 88 F7
Aigburth Gv RDSH SK5 .... 100 B2
Ailsa Cl NEWH/MOS M40 .... 73 C7
Aimson Rd East
  HALE/TIMP WA15 .... 108 F6
Aimson Rd West
  HALE/TIMP WA15 .... 108 F6
Ainley Cl WYTH/NTH M22 ...... 118 F1
Ainley Wd DUK SK16 .... 91 G5
  UPML OL3 .... 45 H7
Ainsbrook Av BKLY M9 .... 73 L1
  UPML OL3 .... 45 J8
Ainscoughs Ct LEIGH WN7 ...... 66 B8
Ainscow Av HOR/BR BL6 .... 34 C4
Ainsdale Av ATH M46 .... 50 F8
  BRO M7 .... 72 A3
  EDGW/EG BL7 .... 17 C5
  TOT/BURYW BL8 .... 38 D2
Ainsdale Cl BRAM/HZG SK7 .... 121 J5
  OLDS OL8 .... 59 C8
Ainsdale Crs ROY/SHW OL2 .... 59 H2
Ainsdale Dr CHD/CHDH SK8 .... 108 B2
  SALE M33 .... 108 K3
  WHIT OL12 .... 20 B5
Ainsdale Gv RDSH SK5 .... 100 C3
Ainsdale Rd BOLS/LL BL3 .... 52 B2
Ainsdale St WGTN/LGST M12 ... 88 C6
Ainsford Rd DID/WITH M20 ..... 99 C7
Ainsley Gv WALK M28 .... 69 C6
Ainslie Rd BOL BL1 .... 35 K3
Ainsty Rd RUSH/FAL M14 .... 87 K8
Ainsworth Av HOR/BR BL6 ...... 34 B3
Ainsworth Cl DTN/ASHW M34 .. 100 E1
Ainsworth Ct BOLE BL2 * 3 L4
Ainsworth Hall Rd BOLE BL2 ... 37 L5
Ainsworth La BOLE BL2 .... 3 L1
Ainsworth St BOLS/LL BL3 .... 53 K1
  RAD M26 .... 38 C7
  TOT/BURYW BL8 .... 38 D2
Ainsworth St BOL BL1 .... 35 M2
  MILN OL16 .... 11 C7
Aintree Av SALE M33 .... 107 M1
Aintree Cl BRAM/HZG SK7 ...... 122 B2
Aintree Dr ROCH OL11 .... 27 H4
Aintree Gv EDGY/DAV SK3 ..... 112 B7
Aintree Rd BOLS/LL BL3 .... 53 K2
Aintree St OP/CLY M11 .... 88 E3
Aintree Wk CHAD OL9 .... 8 B8
Airedale Cl CHD/CHDH SK8 ..... 110 F6
Airedale Ct ALT WA14 .... 108 B7
Aire Dr BOLE BL2 .... 22 E7
Aireworth St WHTN BL5 .... 50 B1
Air Hill Ter WHIT OL12 * 27 M3
Airton Cl NEWH/MOS M40 .... 87 M1
Airton Pl WGNS/IIMK WN3 ...... 63 L1
Aitken Cl RAMS BL0 .... 18 E7
Aitken St BNG/LEV M19 * 99 M3
Ajax Dr BURY BL9 .... 55 J1
Ajax St RAMS BL0 .... 18 E7
  ROCH OL11 .... 41 L1
Aked Cl WGTN/LGST M12 .... 88 A6
Akesmoor Dr OFTN SK2 .... 112 E6
Alameda Dr MPL/ROM SK6 ..... 114 B2
Alan Av FAIL M35 .... 74 C7
Alanbrooke Wk HULME M15 * .. 87 H7
Alandale Av DTN/ASHW M34 ... 90 B5
Alandale Rd EDGY/DAV SK3 .... 12 C9
Alan Dr HALE/TIMP WA15 .... 117 J4
  MPL/ROM SK6 .... 114 B6
Alan Rd DID/WITH M20 .... 98 F6
  HTNM SK4 .... 111 L1
Alan St BOL BL1 .... 36 A1
Alan Turing Wy
  NEWH/MOS M40 .... 88 B1
Alasdair Cl CHAD OL9 .... 58 C4
Alba Cl ECC M30 .... 85 C3
Alban St BRO M7 .... 72 A7
Albany Cl OP/CLY M11 .... 89 J5
Albany Ct LHULT M38 .... 52 E7
  Albany St URM M41 .... 95 L1
Albany Dr BURY BL9 .... 39 J5
Albany Gv TYLD M29 .... 68 A4
Albany Rd BRAM/HZG SK7 ..... 121 G8
  CCHDY M21 .... 97 L3
  ECC M30 .... 85 H3
  WILM/AE SK9 .... 126 D7
Albany Wy SLFD M6 .... 86 D1
Alba Wy STRET M32 .... 85 K7
Albemarle Av DID/WITH M20 ... 98 D6
Albemarle Rd CCHDY M21 .... 97 K4
Albemarle St AUL OL6 .... 90 F1
  RUSH/FAL M14 .... 98 C1
Albemarle Ter AUL OL6 * 90 F1
Alberbury Av
  HALE/TIMP WA15 .... 109 G5
Albermarle Rd SWIN M27 .... 70 B5

Alberta St BOLS/LL BL3 .... 35 M7
  STKP SK1 .... 13 K6
Albert Av DUK SK16 .... 90 F6
  GTN M18 .... 89 H8
  PWCH M25 .... 71 M3
  ROY/SHW OL2 .... 43 K7
  URM M41 .... 96 B2
  WALK M28 .... 53 C7
Albert Cl CHD/CHDH SK8 .... 120 C2
  WHTF M45 .... 55 K4
Albert Colliery Est
  WGNE/HIN WN2 * 65 J4
Albert Ct ALT WA14 .... 108 A8
Albert Dr WHTF M45 .... 55 L3
Albert Gdns
  NEWH/MOS M40 .... 74 A7
Albert Gv FWTH BL4 .... 53 C4
  WGTN/LGST M12 .... 88 D8
Albert Hill St DID/WITH M20 * .. 110 E1
Alberton Cl WGNE/HIN WN2 .... 32 F6
Albert Park Rd BRO M7 .... 71 M7
Albert Pl ALT WA14 .... 108 A7
  BRUN/LGST M13 .... 99 J1
Albert Rd CHD/CHDH SK8 ...... 120 C2
  ECC M30 .... 85 J3
  FWTH BL4 .... 53 G4
  HALE/TIMP WA15 .... 117 G1
  HTNM SK4 .... 12 A1
  HYDE SK14 .... 102 A1
  SALE M33 .... 96 F8
  WHTF M45 .... 55 K4
  WILM/AE SK9 .... 126 E6
Albert Rd East
  HALE/TIMP WA15 .... 117 G1
Albert Rd West BOL BL1 .... 35 K4
Albert Royds St MILN OL16 ...... 11 L1
Albert Sq ALT WA14 .... 116 F1
  CMANW M2 .... 6 F5
  STLY SK15 .... 91 J3
Albert St AIMK WN4 .... 78 E1
  BOLS/LL BL3 .... 53 L1
  BRAM/HZG SK7 .... 121 M1
  BURY BL9 .... 5 J4
  CHAD OL9 .... 74 E1
  DROY M43 .... 89 L3
  DTN/ASHW M34 * 101 J1
  EDGW/EG BL7 .... 22 A1
  EDGY/DAV SK3 .... 12 F5
  FWTH BL4 .... 53 H4
  GLSP SK13 .... 93 K7
  HEY OL10 .... 40 E2
  HYDE SK14 .... 102 C1
  IRL M44 .... 94 B6
  LIT OL15 .... 21 L6
  MDTN M24 .... 57 L5
  MILN OL16 .... 29 J7
  OLDE OL4 .... 60 B7
  OLDS OL8 .... 74 E3
  OLDTF/WHR M16 .... 86 F6
  OP/CLY M11 .... 88 C3
  PWCH M25 * 55 M7
  RAMS BL0 .... 18 E6
  ROY/SHW OL2 .... 43 G8
  ROY/SHW OL2 .... 43 K5
  WGNE/HIN WN2 .... 49 G7
  WGNW/BIL/OR WN5 .... 14 A6
  WHIT OL12 .... 20 A4
Albert St West FAIL M35 .... 74 A6
Albert Ter STKP SK1 .... 13 J4
Albine St NEWH/MOS M40 ...... 73 J4
Albion Cl HTNM SK4 .... 112 B1
  WGNE/HIN WN2 .... 48 E2
Albion Dr DROY M43 .... 89 K2
Albion Fold DROY M43 .... 89 K2
Albion Gdns STLY SK15 .... 91 L2
Albion Gardens Cl
  ROY/SHW OL2 .... 43 J8
Albion Gv SALE M33 .... 96 D8
Albion Pk
  GOL/RIS/CUL WA3 * 81 M6
Albion Pl BRAM/HZG SK7 * 121 M1
  BRO M7 * 71 M7
  ORD M5 .... 86 F2
  PWCH M25 .... 55 K8
Albion Rd NM/HAY SK22 .... 124 E5
  ROCH OL11 .... 10 B6
  RUSH/FAL M14 .... 98 F3
Albion St AUL OL6 .... 90 F1
  BOLS/LL BL3 .... 2 E7
  CHAD OL9 .... 58 D6
  CMANE M1 .... 6 F7
  FAIL M35 .... 74 B5
  FWTH BL4 .... 53 K6
  LEIGH WN7 * 66 C8
  LIT OL15 .... 21 L7
  OLD OL1 .... 9 J5
  OLDTF/WHR M16 .... 87 G8
  RAD M26 .... 54 E3
  ROCH OL11 .... 42 A3
  SALE M33 .... 96 E8
  STLY SK15 .... 91 L2
  SWIN M27 .... 70 D4
  TOT/BURYW BL8 .... 4 E3
  WGNE/HIN WN2 .... 48 E2
  WGNE/HIN WN2 .... 64 D2
  WGNE/HIN WN2 .... 50 B1
Albion Wy ORD M5 .... 86 E3
Albury Dr BNG/LEV M19 .... 111 G1
  WHIT OL12 * 27 J4
Albury Wy WGNE/HIN WN2 ..... 48 C2
Albyns Av CHH M8 .... 72 D5
Alcester Av EDGY/DAV SK3 ..... 111 J5
Alcester Cl MDTN M24 .... 57 L6
  TOT/BURYW BL8 .... 38 E1
Alcester Rd CHD/CHDH SK8 .... 110 E8
  SALE M33 .... 108 A2
Alcester St CHAD OL9 .... 74 D1
Aldborough Cl
  DID/WITH M20 .... 98 E6
Aldbourne Cl
  NEWH/MOS M40 .... 73 G7
Aldbury Ter BOL BL1 * 36 A3
Aldcliffe GOL/RIS/CUL WA3 ..... 80 C5
Aldcroft St GTN M18 .... 89 K6
Alden Cl WGN WN1 .... 31 L3
  WHTF M45 .... 55 K4
Alder Av AIMK WN4 .... 63 J7
  BURY BL9 .... 5 M3
  POY/DIS SK12 .... 129 K1
  WGNW/BIL/OR WN5 .... 47 G6
  WGNW/BIL/OR WN5 * 62 A7
Alderbank HOR/BR BL6 .... 33 C7
  WHIT OL12 .... 21 C5
Alderbank Cl FWTH BL4 .... 53 C7
Alderbrook Rd LHULT M38 ...... 68 C1
Alder Cl AUL OL6 .... 75 L5
  CHD/CHDH SK8 .... 119 M4
  GLSP SK13 .... 93 J8
  LEIGH WN7 .... 81 J2
  TOT/BURYW BL8 .... 38 F2
Alder Ct CHH M8 * 72 C3
Aldercroft Av BOLE BL2 .... 37 G5
  WYTH/NTH M22 .... 118 E2

Alderdale Dr DROY M43 .... 89 G2
  HTNM SK4 .... 99 K7
  MPL/ROM SK6 .... 123 G5
Alderdale Gv WILM/AE SK9 .... 126 C5
Alderdale Rd
  CHD/CHDH SK8 .... 111 M8
Alder Dr HALE/TIMP WA15 ..... 109 H7
  SWIN M27 .... 69 M3
Alderfield Rd STRET M32 .... 97 J3
Alderfold St ATH M46 .... 67 G1
Alder Forest Av ECC M30 .... 69 K8
Aldergate Gv AUL OL6 .... 76 C7
Alderglen Rd CHH M8 .... 72 C6
Alder Gv DTN/ASHW M34 .... 101 K1
  EDGW/EG BL7 .... 22 F6
  EDGY/DAV SK3 .... 12 C6
  STRET M32 .... 97 H2
Alder La OLDS OL8 .... 75 G2
  WGNE/HIN WN2 .... 68 C1
Alder Lee Cl WGNS/IIMK WN3 .. 63 L7
Alderley Av BOL BL1 .... 22 B7
  GOL/RIS/CUL WA3 .... 80 A5
Alderley Cl BRAM/HZG SK7 .... 122 B4
  POY/DIS SK12 .... 129 K2
Alderley Dr MPL/ROM SK6 ...... 101 M8
Alderley La LEIGH WN7 .... 81 L2
Alderley Ldg MCFLDN SK10 .... 131 J2
  RDSH SK5 .... 100 C2
  URM M41 .... 95 K2
  WGNE/HIN WN2 .... 49 K7
  WILM/AE SK9 .... 126 E6
Alderley Rd AUL OL6 .... 76 A7
Aldermary Rd CCHDY M21 ...... 97 J4
Aldermaston Gv BKLY M9 .... 56 E6
Alder Meadow Cl WHIT OL12 ... 27 K3
Aldermere Crs URM M41 .... 95 H3
Alderminster Av LHULT M38 .... 52 D2
Alderney Dr WGNS/IIMK WN3 .. 63 K1
Alder Rd CHD/CHDH SK8 .... 111 G1
  FAIL M35 .... 74 D6
  GOL/RIS/CUL WA3 .... 80 C4
  MDTN M24 * 57 M2
  ROCH OL11 .... 42 A2
Alders Av WYTH/NTH M22 ..... 109 M7
Alders Ct OLDS OL8 .... 75 K4
Aldersgate NM/HAY SK22 ...... 124 D4
Aldersgate Rd
  CHD/CHDH SK8 .... 120 E7
  OFTN SK2 .... 112 E6
Aldersgreen Av
  MPL/ROM SK6 .... 123 H5
Alders Green Rd
  WGNE/HIN WN2 .... 49 K7
Alderside Rd BKLY M9 .... 73 G4
Aldersley Av BKLY M9 .... 56 E8
Alderson St SLFD M6 .... 9 G4
  SLFD M6 .... 71 K8
Alders Rd POY/DIS SK12 .... 123 J5
  WYTH/NTH M22 .... 109 M7
The Alders WGNNW/ST WN6 ... 31 G8
Alder St ATH M46 .... 67 G1
  BOLS/LL BL3 .... 52 C1
  ECC M30 .... 69 K8
  FAIL M35 .... 74 B5
  LEIGH WN7 .... 66 B4
  ORD M5 .... 86 E2
  WGNE/HIN WN2 .... 49 G8
Aldersyde St BOLS/LL BL3 .... 52 A1
Alderton Dr WHTN BL5 .... 50 B6
Alderue Av WYTH/NTH M22 .... 110 A6
Alderwood Fold OLDE OL4 .... 60 E4
Aldfield Rd NTHM/RTH M23 .... 109 J3
Aldford Cl DID/WITH M20 * 110 F1
Aldford Dr ATH M46 .... 51 H7
Aldford Gv BOLE BL2 .... 37 L7
Aldford Pl WILM/AE SK9 .... 130 C2
Aldford Wy WGNNW/ST WN6 ... 31 H4
Aldham Av NEWH/MOS M40 .... 73 M8
Aldon St BOLS/LL BL3 .... 51 L1
Aldred Cl CHH M8 .... 72 E6
Aldred St BOLS/LL BL3 .... 51 L1
  ECC M30 .... 84 F3
  FAIL M35 .... 74 B5
  LEIGH WN7 .... 66 B4
  ORD M5 .... 86 E2
  WGNE/HIN WN2 .... 49 G8
Aldridge Cl
  WGNS/IIMK WN3 .... 63 L1
Aldsworth Dr BOLS/LL BL3 ...... 36 B8
  NEWH/MOS M40 .... 73 H7
Aldwick Av DID/WITH M20 ..... 110 F1
Aldwinians Cl
  DTN/ASHW M34 .... 90 B7
Aldworth Gv SALE M33 .... 96 A8
Aldwych ROCH OL11 .... 42 C1
Aldwych Av RUSH/FAL M14 .... 98 E1
Aldwyn Cl DTN/ASHW M34 ..... 90 B7
  RAD M26 .... 54 E3
Aldwyn Crs BRAM/HZG SK7 .... 121 L2
Aldwyn Park Rd
  DTN/ASHW M34 .... 89 M5
Aldwyn Av FAIL M35 .... 74 D4
Alexander Briant Ct
  FWTH BL4 * 52 F5
Alexander Dr BURY BL9 .... 55 K3
  HALE/TIMP WA15 .... 108 D6
  MILN OL16 .... 29 J6
Alexander Gdns BRO M7 .... 72 A8
Alexander Rd BOLE BL2 .... 3 M1
Alexander St ROCH OL11 .... 41 L2
  SLFD M6 * 86 D2
  TYLD M29 .... 67 J4
Alexandra Av HYDE SK14 .... 101 M2
  RUSH/FAL M14 .... 98 C2
  WHTF M45 .... 55 K4
Alexandra Cl EDGY/DAV SK3 ... 111 M6
Alexandra Crs OLD OL1 .... 59 L4
  WGNW/BIL/OR WN5 .... 47 H6
Alexandra Dr BNG/LEV M19 .... 99 K3
Alexandra Gv IRL M44 .... 94 C4
Alexandra Ms OLDS OL8 * 9 M9
Alexandra Rd
  AIMK WN4 .... 63 L8
  AUL OL6 .... 75 L8
  DTN/ASHW M34 .... 90 D8
  ECC M30 .... 84 E3
  FWTH BL4 .... 53 K6
  HOR/BR BL6 .... 34 B4
  OLDTF/WHR M16 .... 87 H8
  RAD M26 .... 38 D5
  SALE M33 .... 109 G1
  STLY SK15 .... 91 L2
  TYLD M29 .... 67 J4
  WHIT OL12 .... 10 L5
Alexandra Rd South
  OLDTF/WHR M16 .... 98 B1
Alexandra St AUL OL6 .... 76 A8
  BOLS/LL BL3 * 36 A8
  BRO M7 * 53 G5
  FWTH BL4 .... 53 C5
  HEY OL10 .... 41 H4
  HYDE SK14 .... 101 M3
  OLDS OL8 .... 9 M8
  WGNE/HIN WN2 .... 64 D4
  WGNW/BIL/OR WN5 .... 47 J6
Alexandria Dr AULW OL7 .... 90 B3
  WHTN BL5 .... 50 A4
Alford Av DID/WITH M20 .... 98 D4
Alford Cl BOLE BL2 .... 37 J6
Alford Rd HTNM SK4 .... 99 L6
Alford St CHAD OL9 .... 74 E2
Alfred Av WALK M28 .... 69 L5
Alfred James Cl
  NEWH/MOS M40 .... 7 M1
Alfred Rd GOL/RIS/CUL WA3 ... 80 D4
  RNFD/HAY WA11 .... 78 B5
Alfred St AUL OL6 * 76 A8
  BKLY M9 .... 73 C4
  BURY BL9 .... 5 H9
  CHAD OL9 .... 8 D7
  ECC M30 .... 85 G1
  EDGW/EG BL7 .... 22 A1
  FWTH BL4 .... 53 G2
  FWTH BL4 .... 53 H4
  HYDE SK14 .... 101 M1
  IRL M44 .... 94 B6
  LIT OL15 .... 21 L6
  RAMS BL0 .... 18 E7
  ROY/SHW OL2 .... 43 K5
  TYLD M29 .... 67 J3
  WALK M28 .... 69 G1
  WGN WN1 .... 47 L2
  WGNE/HIN WN2 .... 15 J3
  WGNS/IIMK WN3 .... 15 J3
  WHIT OL12 .... 20 B2
Alfreton Av DTN/ASHW M34 ... 101 K4
Alfreton Rd OFTN SK2 .... 113 C6
Alfriston Dr NTHM/RTH M23 .... 109 K2
Alger Ms AUL OL6 .... 76 A8
Algernon Rd WALK M28 .... 52 F8
Algernon St ECC M30 .... 85 G1
  SWIN M27 .... 70 A4
  WGNE/HIN WN2 .... 49 G7
  WGNS/IIMK WN3 .... 47 K6
Alger St AUL OL6 .... 76 A8
Algreave Rd EDGY/DAV SK3 .... 111 K4
Alice Ingham Ct ROCH OL11 .... 27 L3
Alice St BOLS/LL BL3 .... 35 M7
  HYDE SK14 .... 102 B5
  SALE M33 .... 97 G8
  SWIN M27 .... 70 E4
  WHIT OL12 .... 28 E3
Alicia Dr WHIT OL12 .... 28 B2
Alison Kelly Cl BKLY M9 .... 73 J4
Alison St ROY/SHW OL2 .... 43 K4
  RUSH/FAL M14 .... 98 C1
Alker Rd NEWH/MOS M40 * 88 A1
Alker St WGNW/BIL/OR WN5 ... 47 J6
Alkrington Cl BURY BL9 .... 55 K2
Alkrington Gn MDTN M24 .... 57 J6
Alkrington Hall Rd North
  MDTN M24 .... 57 J5
Alkrington Hall Rd South
  MDTN M24 .... 57 H6
Alkrington Park Rd MDTN M24 . 57 H5
Allama Iqbal Rd OLDE OL8 * 59 M7
Allandale ALT WA14 .... 107 L8
Allandale Dr ROY/SHW OL2 .... 42 F7
Allandale Rd BNG/LEV M19 .... 99 J3
Allan Roberts Cl BKLY M9 ...... 73 C3
Allanson Rd WYTH/NTH M23 ... 110 B3
Allan St TYLD M29 .... 67 J4
Alldis Cl WGTN/LGST M12 ...... 88 D7
Alldis St OFTN SK2 .... 112 E7
Allen Av GOL/RIS/CUL WA3 .... 81 M4
  HYDE SK14 .... 102 C4
Allenby Gv WHTN BL5 .... 50 B5
Allenby Rd IRL M44 .... 94 A8
  SWIN M27 .... 69 M6
Allenby St ATH M46 .... 66 E2
  ROY/SHW OL2 .... 43 L5
Allen Cl ROY/SHW OL2 .... 43 K6
Allendale Dr BURY BL9 .... 55 K1
Allendale Gdns BOL BL1 .... 36 B2
Allen Dale Wk CSLFD M3 .... 6 A2
Allen Rd URM M41 .... 96 C3
Allen St BOLS/LL BL3 .... 53 K1
  MILN OL16 .... 11 H8
  OLDS OL8 .... 8 E7
  RAD M26 .... 54 C1
  TOT/BURYW BL8 .... 4 A3
Allerby Wy GOL/RIS/CUL WA3 . 80 B4
Allerdean Wk HTNM SK4 .... 111 J1
Allerford St OLDTF/WHR M16 .. 87 H8
Allerton Cl WHTN BL5 .... 50 D3
Allerton Wk BRUN/LGST M13 * . 87 L6
Allesley Cl WHTN BL5 .... 50 D3
Allesley Dr BRO M7 .... 72 B5
Allgreave Cl SALE M33 .... 109 H3
Alliance St WGN WN1 .... 15 H5
Alligin Cl CHAD OL9 .... 58 D4
Allingham St BRUN/LGST M13 .. 88 B8
Allington ROCH OL11 .... 10 D7
Allington Dr ECC M30 .... 70 B8
Alliott Wk HULME M15 .... 87 H7
Allison St CHH M8 .... 72 C7
Allotment Rd IRL M44 .... 94 A6
All Saint's Cl ROY/SHW OL2 .... 43 G7
All Saints Gv WGNE/HIN WN2 .. 49 H7
All Saints Pl TOT/BURYW BL8 ... 4 E2
All Saints' Rd HTNM SK4 .... 112 A1
All Saints St BOL BL1 .... 2 E3
  NEWH/MOS M40 .... 73 M7
All Saints Ter WHIT OL12 .... 28 E2
Allscott Wy AIMK WN4 .... 78 F1
Allsopp St BOLS/LL BL3 .... 2 E7
Alma La WILM/AE SK9 .... 126 C6
Alma Rd BNG/LEV M19 .... 99 K4
  BRAM/HZG SK7 .... 122 C4
  HTNM SK4 .... 108 A2
  SALE M33 .... 108 D2
Alma St ATH M46 .... 66 F1
  BOLS/LL BL3 .... 35 M8
  BOLS/LL BL3 .... 53 L1
  ECC M30 .... 85 J3
  FWTH BL4 .... 53 L7
  LEIGH WN7 .... 66 B4
  RAD M26 .... 38 D5
  STLY SK15 .... 91 L2
  TYLD M29 .... 67 J3
  WGNE/HIN WN2 .... 49 G7
  WHIT OL12 .... 10 E5
Alminstone Cl
  NEWH/MOS M40 .... 74 A8

Almond Av BURY BL9 ....5 M3
Almond Brook Rd
  WGNNW/ST WN6 ....30 F3
Almond Cl EDGY/DAV SK3 ....12 C6
  FAIL M35 ....74 C6
  LIT OL15 ....21 K6
  SLFD M6 ....86 D2
Almond Crs WGNNW/ST WN6 .....31 K3
Almond Dr SALE M33 ....96 C6
Almond Gv BOL BL1 * 36 C1
  WGNW/BIL/OR WN5 ....47 H6
Almond Rd OLDE OL4 ....60 A3
Almond St BOL BL1 ....22 C8
  FWTH BL4 ....52 F4
  NEWH/MOS M40 * 72 E8
Almond Tree Rd
  CHD/CHDH SK8 ....120 C5
Almond Wy HYDE SK14 ....102 E2
Alms Hill Rd CHH M8 ....72 D5
Alness Rd OLDTF/WHR M16 ....98 B2
Alnwick Cl WGNE/HIN WN2 ....33 G7
Alnwick Dr BURY BL9 ....39 K7
Alnwick Rd BKLY M9 ....57 G2
Alpha Ct DTN/ASHW M34 ....100 F1
Alpha Pl HULME M15 * 6 D8
Alpha Rd STRET M32 ....96 F3
Alpha St OP/CLY M11 ....89 H5
  SLFD M6 ....86 C1
Alpha St West SLFD M6 ....86 B1
Alphin Cl MOSL OL5 ....77 H1
  UPML OL3 ....61 L7
Alphingate Cl STLY SK15 ....77 G8
Alphin Sq MOSL OL5 ....77 G8
Alphonsus St OLDTF/WHR M16 ....86 F8
Alpine Dr LEIGH WN7 ....65 M4
  MILN OL16 ....29 K5
  ROY/SHW OL2 ....58 F1
  WHIT OL12 ....21 G3
Alpine Rd STKP SK1 ....13 M4
Alpine St OP/CLY M11 ....88 E2
Alport Av OLDTF/WHR M16 * 97 M2
Alresford Rd MDTN M24 ....57 J7
  SLFD M6 ....71 G7
Alsager Cl CCHDY M21 ....97 L6
Alsfeld Wy NM/HAY SK22 ....124 C4
Alsop Av BRO M7 * 71 L5
Alstead Av HALE/TIMP WA15 .....117 J1
Alston Av ROY/SHW OL2 ....43 L5
  SALE M33 ....108 C1
  STRET M32 ....96 F1
Alston Cl BRAM/HZG SK7 * 121 J3
Alstone Dr ALT WA14 ....107 K6
Alstone Rd HTNM SK4 ....99 M6
Alston Gdns BNG/LEV M19 ....99 J7
Alston Lea ATH M46 ....51 H8
Alston Rd GTN M18 ....89 H7
  WGNE/HIN WN2 ....48 C2
Alston St BOLS/LL BL3 * 52 B1
  TOT/BURYW BL8 * 24 F8
Altair Av WYTH/NTH M22 ....118 F4
Altair Pl BRO M7 ....71 M8
Altcar Gv RDSH SK5 ....100 B3
Altcar Wk WYTH/NTH M22 ....118 E2
Alt Cl LEIGH WN7 ....66 A7
Alt Fold Dr OLDS OL8 ....75 M1
Alt Gv AUL OL6 ....75 L6
Altham Cl BURY BL9 ....39 G5
Alt Hill La AUL OL6 ....75 M4
Alt La OLDS OL8 ....75 M2
Alton Av URM M41 ....95 C2
Alton Cl AIMK WN4 ....63 K8
  AUL OL6 ....75 M5
  BURY BL9 ....39 G4
Alton Rd WILM/AE SK9 ....126 D4
Alton Sq OP/CLY M11 ....89 H5
Alton St OLDS OL8 ....75 J1
Altrincham Rd
  NTHM/RTH M23 ....109 G5
  WILM/AE SK9 ....119 G3
  WYTH/NTH M22 ....109 M5
Altrincham St CMANE M1 ....7 J7
Alum Crs BURY BL9 ....55 K1
Alvanley Cl SALE M33 ....108 E3
  WGNW/BIL/OR WN5 ....46 E3
Alvanley Crs EDGY/DAV SK3 ....111 M4
Alvan Sq OP/CLY M11 * 89 H1
Alva Rd OLDE OL4 ....60 A2
Alvaston Av HTNM SK4 ....12 A1
Alvaston Rd GTN M18 ....89 H8
Alveley Av DID/WITH M20 ....98 F7
Alverstone Rd DID/WITH M20 ......98 F6
Alveston Dr WILM/AE SK9 ....127 K5
Alvington Gv BRAM/HZG SK7 ....121 J3
Alwin Rd ROY/SHW OL2 ....43 K4
Alwinton Av HTNM SK4 ....111 H1
Alworth Rd BKLY M9 ....57 G2
Alwyn Cl LEIGH WN7 ....81 J3
Alwyn Dr BRUN/LGST M13 ....88 B8
Alwyn St WGN WN1 ....15 J1
Alwyn Ter WGN WN1 ....15 J1
Amar St WGNE/HIN WN2 * 48 C5
Amathyst Cl WGNE/HIN WN2 .....48 D3
Ambassador Pl
  HALE/TIMP WA15 * 108 B7
Amber Gdns DUK SK16 * 90 E4
  WGNE/HIN WN2 ....49 H8
Ambergate ATH M46 ....67 G2
Amber Gv WHTN BL5 ....50 C2
Amberhill Wy WALK M28 ....68 D7
Amberley Cl BOLS/LL BL3 ....35 J7
  WGNE/HIN WN2 ....48 C2
Amberley Dr HALE/TIMP WA15 ...117 K4
  IRL M44 ....94 D3
  NTHM/RTH M23 ....109 K8
Amberley Rd SALE M33 ....96 B7
Amberley Wk CHAD OL9 ....8 C4
Amberswood Cl
  WGNE/HIN WN2 ....48 E5
Amberwood CHAD OL9 ....58 B4
Amberwood Dr
  NTHM/RTH M23 ....109 G6
Amblecote Dr East LHULT M38 ....52 D6
Amblecote Dr West LHULT M38 ....52 D6
Ambleside STLY SK15 ....91 K1
  WGNE/HIN WN2 ....48 C4
  WGNW/BIL/OR WN5 ....46 F5
Ambleside Av AULW OL7 ....75 J4
  HALE/TIMP WA15 ....108 F7
Ambleside Cl BOLE BL2 ....23 J8
  MDTN M24 ....57 H3
Ambleside Rd RDSH SK5 ....100 C6
  URM M41 ....95 H3
Ambrose Av LEIGH WN7 ....66 B3
Ambrose Ct WYTH/NTH M22 * ...110 A3
Ambrose Dr DID/WITH M20 ....98 B8
Ambrose St ROCH OL11 ....10 E8
  WGTN/LGST M12 ....88 D3
Ambush St OP/CLY M11 ....89 J3
Amelia St DTN/ASHW M34 ....90 D8
  HYDE SK14 ....102 E2
Amersham Cl URM M41 ....84 E7

Amersham Pl BNG/LEV M19 ....99 K6
Amersham St ORD M5 ....86 C3
Amesbury Dr WGNS/IIMK WN3 ....62 F2
Amesbury Gv RDSH SK5 ....100 C7
Amesbury Rd BKLY M9 ....57 H8
Amherst Rd DID/WITH M20 ....98 F5
Amis Gv GOL/RIS/CUL WA3 ....80 B4
Amlwch Av OFTN SK2 ....113 G6
Ammons Wy OLDS OL8 ....45 J7
Ammon Wrigley Cl OLD OL1 ....9 J4
Amory St WGTN/LGST M12 ....7 L7
Amos Av NEWH/MOS M40 ....73 M8
Amos St BKLY M9 ....73 J5
  SLFD M6 ....86 B2
Ampney Cl ECC M30 ....84 E3
Amwell St CHH M8 ....72 E5
Amy St MDTN M24 ....57 L3
  WHIT OL12 ....27 L3
Anaconda Dr CSLFD M3 ....6 C1
Anchorage Quay SALQ M50 ....86 E4
Anchorage Rd URM M41 ....96 D3
Anchor Ct BNG/LEV M19 ....99 M3
Anchor Ct CHH M8 * 72 C3
Anchor La FWTH BL4 ....52 C5
Anchorside Cl CCHDY M21 ....97 L5
Anchor St OLD OL1 ....9 J3
Ancoats Gv ANC M4 ....88 A3
Ancoats Gv North ANC M4 ....88 A3
Ancoats St OLDE OL4 ....60 B6
Ancroft Dr WGNE/HIN WN2 ....65 H1
Ancroft St HULME M15 ....7 H6
Anderby Wk WHTN BL5 ....50 B2
Anderton Cl BURY BL9 ....55 J4
Anderton Gv AUL OL6 ....76 B7
Anderton La HOR/BR BL6 ....33 H1
Anderton St WGNE/HIN WN2 ....48 C5
Anderton Wy WGNE/HIN WN2 .....48 C5
  WILM/AE SK9 ....127 H1
Andoc Av ECC M30 ....85 J3
Andover Av MDTN M24 ....57 L7
Andover Crs WGNS/IIMK WN3 .....62 F2
Andover Rd RNFD/HAY WA11 ......78 B4
Andover St ECC M30 ....84 F5
Andre St OP/CLY M11 * 88 F2
Andrew Av
  WGNW/BIL/OR WN5 ....62 C7
Andrew Cl RAD M26 ....54 F3
  TOT/BURYW BL8 ....24 C3
Andrew La BOL BL1 ....22 C6
Andrew Rd BKLY M9 ....73 G3
Andrews Av URM M41 ....95 H1
Andrew St AUL OL6 * 76 A7
  BURY BL9 ....55 H5
  CHAD OL9 ....58 D4
  DROY M43 ....74 D4
  FAIL M35 ....74 D7
  HTNM SK4 ....13 G3
  HYDE SK14 ....102 C1
  MDTN M24 ....57 M5
  MOSL OL5 ....77 J1
  MPL/ROM SK6 ....114 D2
Anerley Rd DID/WITH M20 ....98 E8
Anfield Cl BURY BL9 ....55 L1
Anfield Rd BOLS/LL BL3 ....52 B2
  CHD/CHDH SK8 ....120 B2
  NEWH/MOS M40 ....74 A3
  SALE M33 ....96 F7
Angela Av ROY/SHW OL2 ....59 H2
Angela St HULME M15 ....6 B9
Angel Cl DUK SK16 ....90 E5
Angelko Ri OLD OL1 ....60 A1
Angelo St BOL BL1 ....36 A1
Angel St ANC M4 ....7 H1
  BRAM/HZG SK7 ....121 M1
  DTN/ASHW M34 ....90 D8
  HYDE SK14 ....102 C1
  MDTN M24 ....57 M5
  MOSL OL5 ....77 J1
  MPL/ROM SK6 ....114 D2
Anglers Rest IRL M44 ....94 B7
Anglesea Av OFTN SK2 ....112 C6
Anglesey Cl AULW OL7 ....75 J6
Anglesey Dr POY/DIS SK12 ....122 A6
Anglesey Gv CHD/CHDH SK8 .....111 J6
Anglesey Rd AULW OL7 ....75 J6
Anglesey Water
  POY/DIS SK12 ....122 A6
Angleside Av BNG/LEV M19 ....99 H8
Angle St BOLE BL2 ....3 K1
Anglia Gv BOLS/LL BL3 ....35 M8
Angora Dr CSLFD M3 ....6 A1
Angouleme Wy BURY BL9 ....4 E6
  LEIGH WN7 ....65 M6
Angus Av HEY OL10 ....40 D3
Anita St ANC M4 ....7 K2
Anjou Bvd WGNW/BIL/OR WN5 ...47 H4
Annable Rd DROY M43 ....89 L3
  GTN M18 ....89 H6
  IRL M44 ....94 C4
  MPL/ROM SK6 ....113 G1
Annald Sq DROY M43 ....89 K4
Annan Gv AIMK WN4 ....64 B7
Annan St DTN/ASHW M34 * 90 D8
Anne Cl AULW OL7 ....75 K6
Annecy Cl TOT/BURYW BL8 ....24 F8
Anne Line Cl ROCH OL11 * 11 G9
Anne Nuttall Rd HULME M15 ....6 B9
Annersley Av ROY/SHW OL2 ....43 K6
Annersley Rd WGNS/IIMK WN3 ...63 J1
Annesley Rd NEWH/MOS M40 ....74 B3
Anne St DUK SK16 ....91 G4
Annette Av NEWLW WA12 ....78 D7
Annie St ORD M5 ....86 B2
  RAMS BL0 ....18 D8
Annis Cl WILM/AE SK9 ....130 E2
Annisdale Cl ECC M30 ....84 E2
Annisfield Av UPML OL3 ....61 M7
Annis Rd BOLS/LL BL3 ....35 L8
  WILM/AE SK9 ....130 E2
Annis St BKLY M9 ....73 H5
Ann La TYLD M29 ....67 M7
Ann Sq OLDE OL4 ....60 A4
Ann St AULW OL7 ....75 K6
  DTN/ASHW M34 ....101 H1
  FWTH BL4 ....53 H5
  HEY OL10 ....41 C1
  HYDE SK14 ....101 M1
  LEIGH WN7 ....66 B4
  RDSH SK5 ....100 B8
  ROCH OL11 ....11 G8
Anscombe Cl NEWH/MOS M40 ...88 A1
Ansdell Av CCHDY M21 ....97 L5
Ansdell Dr DROY M43 ....89 K3
Ansdell Rd MILN OL16 ....28 E8
  RDSH SK5 ....100 D3
  WGNW/BIL/OR WN5 ....45 J6
Ansdell St CHH M8 ....72 D5
Ansell Cl GTN M18 ....89 G6
Anselms Ct OLDS OL8 ....58 F8
Ansford Av WGNE/HIN WN2 ....48 E3
Ansleigh Av CHH M8 ....72 C3
Ansley Gv HTNM SK4 ....12 A1
Anslow Cl NEWH/MOS M40 * 73 L7
Anson Av SWIN M27 ....70 B6
Anson Cl BRAM/HZG SK7 ....121 H1

Anson Pl WGNW/BIL/OR WN5 .....46 F4
Anson Rd DTN/ASHW M34 ....100 D2
  POY/DIS SK12 ....129 M1
  RUSH/FAL M14 ....88 A3
  SWIN M27 ....70 B6
  WILM/AE SK9 ....127 J3
Anson St BOL BL1 ....36 C1
  ECC M30 ....84 E1
  WGNW/BIL/OR WN5 ....47 J5
Answell Av CHH M8 ....72 D2
Antares Av BRO M7 ....87 C1
Anthony Cl WGTN/LGST M12 ......88 B5
Anthony St MOSL OL5 ....76 E7
Anthorn Rd WGNS/IIMK WN3 ....63 H1
Antilles Cl WGTN/LGST M12 ....88 D8
Antler Ct AIMK WN4 ....63 L6
Antrim Cl BNG/LEV M19 ....111 C2
  WGNS/IIMK WN3 ....62 F2
Anvil Cl WGNW/BIL/OR WN5 ....46 A7
Anvil Wy OLD OL1 ....9 H4
Apethorn La HYDE SK14 ....101 M4
Apfel La CHAD OL9 ....8 A4
Apollo Av BURY BL9 ....55 J1
Apperley Gra ECC M30 ....70 B8
Appian Wy BRO M7 ....72 B7
Appleby Av HALE/TIMP WA15 ....108 F7
  HYDE SK14 ....90 F7
Appleby Cl EDGY/DAV SK3 ....112 A7
  TOT/BURYW BL8 ....38 C2
Appleby Gdns BOLE BL2 * 3 H1
Appleby Rd CHD/CHDH SK8 ......110 E8
Applecross Dr OLDS OL8 ....75 M1
Apple Dell Av
  GOL/RIS/CUL WA3 ....79 M3
Appledore Dr BOLE BL2 ....37 J2
  NTHM/RTH M23 ....109 C5
Appledore Wk CHAD OL9 ....8 A7
Appleford Av
  NTHM/RTH M23 ....109 K8
Appleford Dr CHH M8 ....72 E6
Apple Hey WGNNW/ST WN6 ....30 A4
Apple La WGNNW/ST WN6 ....30 A4
Apple St HYDE SK14 ....102 F5
Applethwaite
  WGNE/HIN WN2 ....48 E4
Appleton Dr GLSP SK13 ....105 J4
Appleton Gv SALE M33 ....108 B2
Appleton La WHTN BL5 ....50 C3
Appleton Rd
  HALE/TIMP WA15 ....117 C3
  HTNM SK4 ....100 A6
Appleton St
  WGNS/IIMK WN3 ....14 C4
  PWCH M25 ....71 L2
  SWIN M27 ....70 A6
Apple Tree Ct ORD M5 ....86 D2
Apple Tree Rd NM/HAY SK22 .....124 E3
Apple Wy MDTN M24 ....57 L6
Applewood CHAD OL9 ....58 A5
Appleyard Cl SWIN M27 ....71 G4
Appley La North
  WGNNW/ST WN6 ....30 A4
Apprentice La WILM/AE SK9 ....126 D1
April Cl OLDS OL8 ....59 M8
Apsley Cl ALT WA14 ....116 D3
Apsley Gv ALT WA14 ....116 D3
  WGTN/LGST M12 ....87 M6
Apsley Rd DTN/ASHW M34 ....90 C8
Apsley St STKP SK1 ....13 K4
Aquarius La SLFD M6 * 71 M8
Aquarius St HULME M15 ....87 K7
Aqueduct Rd BOLS/LL BL3 ....3 M8
Aragon Dr HEY OL10 ....40 F2
Aragon Wy MPL/ROM SK6 ....114 B6
Arbor Av BNG/LEV M19 ....99 K5
Arbor Dr BNG/LEV M19 ....99 J5
Arbor Gv DROY M43 ....89 J1
  LHULT M38 ....52 B8
Arbory Av NEWH/MOS M40 * 73 L7
Arbour Cl BURY BL9 ....25 H6
Arbour Cl LEIGH WN7 ....66 F7
  SLFD M6 ....86 C1
Arbour La WGNNW/ST WN6 ....30 E3
Arbour Rd OLDE OL4 ....60 B8
Arbroath St DROY M43 ....89 H3
Arbury Av EDGY/DAV SK3 ....111 J5
  ROCH OL11 ....10 C8
The Arcades AULW OL6 * 90 C1
Arcade St WGN WN1 ....15 C4
Arcadia Av SALE M33 ....108 D3
Archer Av BOLE BL2 ....3 L2
Archer Gv BOLE BL2 ....3 M2
Archer Pk MDTN M24 ....57 H4
Archer Pl STRET M32 ....96 C2
Archer St LEIGH WN7 ....81 L2
  MOSL OL5 ....76 F2
  OP/CLY M11 ....88 D2
  WALK M28 ....68 B6
Archie St ORD M5 ....86 D5
Arch St BOL BL1 ....3 H2
Archway WHIT M12 ....87 J7
Arclid Cl WILM/AE SK9 ....127 J2
Arcon Cl MILN OL16 ....29 H6
Arcon Dr OLDTF/WHR M16 ....98 B1
Arcon Pl ALT WA14 ....107 K6
Ardale Av NEWH/MOS M40 ....73 M1
Ardcombe Av BKLY M9 ....56 F7
Ardeen Wk BRUN/LGST M13 * 87 M4
Arden Av MDTN M24 ....57 L7
Arden Cl AUL OL6 ....76 C6
  BURY BL9 ....40 D5
  GLSP SK13 ....104 D5
Arden Ct BRAM/HZG SK7 ....120 F3
  DTN/ASHW M34 ....101 K5
Ardenfield Dr
  WYTH/NTH M22 ....119 H1
Arden Gv NEWH/MOS M40 ....73 M3
Arden Lodge Rd
  NTHM/RTH M23 ....109 M3
Arden Rd MPL/ROM SK6 ....101 H5
Ardens Cl SWIN M27 ....70 A2
Ardent St CHAD OL9 ....74 D1
  NM/HAY SK22 ....124 E5
Ardent Wy PWCH M25 ....71 L3
Arderne Pl WILM/AE SK9 ....130 D3
Arderne Rd
  HALE/TIMP WA15 ....108 D4
Ardern Gv STKP SK1 ....13 K7
Ardern Rd CHH M8 ....72 C3
Ardwick Gn North
  WGTN/LGST M12 ....7 M9
Ardwick Gn South
  BRUN/LGST M13 ....7 L9
Ardwick Ter WGTN/LGST M12 ......88 C4
Arena Ap HOR/BR BL6 ....33 H1
Argo St BOLS/LL BL3 ....36 A8
Argosy Dr ECC M30 ....84 C5
  MANAIR M90 ....118 B5
Argus St OLDS OL8 ....74 F2
Argyle Av RUSH/FAL M14 ....88 B8
  WALK M28 ....52 F7
  WHTF M45 ....55 K5
Argyle Crs HEY OL10 ....40 E3

Argyle St ATH M46 ....66 F2
  BRAM/HZG SK7 ....121 M2
  BURY BL9 ....25 J3
  DROY M43 ....89 K3
  GTN M18 ....89 G7
  HEY OL10 ....40 C3
  HYDE SK14 ....101 M3
  LEIGH WN7 ....66 B8
  PWCH M25 ....55 J8
  RDSH SK5 ....100 B5
  ROY/SHW OL2 ....43 K5
  SWIN M27 ....70 A5
  TOT/BURYW BL8 ....38 C2
  WALK M28 ....69 G3
  WALK M28 ....68 B8
  WGNE/HIN WN2 ....49 H7
Artillery Pl WYTH/NTH M22 * 110 C8
Artillery St BOLS/LL BL3 ....2 F8
  CSLFD M3 ....6 D6
Artists La MCFLDN SK10 ....130 E6
Arundale Av OLDTF/WHR M16 .....98 B3
Arundale Cl HYDE SK14 ....103 J1
Arundale Gv HYDE SK14 ....103 J1
Arundel Av BRAM/HZG SK7 ......121 M4
  ROCH OL11 ....28 B8
  URM M41 ....95 L5
  WHTF M45 ....55 L5
Arundel Cl HALE/TIMP WA15 .....117 L3
  STLY SK15 ....77 J6
  TOT/BURYW BL8 ....24 C6
Arundel Dr LEIGH WN7 ....66 C6
Arundel Gra GLSP SK13 ....104 E8
Arundel Gv OFTN SK2 ....112 E8
Arundel Rd CHD/CHDH SK8 ......120 C6
Arundel St AUL OL6 ....91 H1
  BOL BL1 ....22 B7
  GLSP SK13 ....104 F3
  HULME M15 ....6 B8
  MOSL OL5 ....76 F3
  OLDE OL4 ....59 M5
  ROCH OL11 ....28 B8
  SWIN M27 ....70 A7
  WGNE/HIN WN2 ....49 H7
  WGNW/BIL/OR WN5 ....47 J6
Asby Cl MDTN M24 ....57 G2
Ascension Rd BRO M7 ....87 J4
Ascot Av SALE M33 ....107 M1
  STRET M32 ....97 J1
Ascot Cl CHAD OL9 ....8 C4
  ROCH OL11 ....27 H4
Ascot Dr ATH M46 ....51 H8
  BRAM/HZG SK7 ....122 C2
  URM M41 ....94 F2
Ascot Mdw BURY BL9 ....4 D6
Ascot Pde BNG/LEV M19 ....99 J6
Ascot Rd BOLS/LL BL3 ....53 J1
  NEWH/MOS M40 ....73 L8
Ascroft St OLD OL1 ....9 J6
  WGN WN1 ....15 K5
Asgard Dr ORD M5 ....86 E4
Asgard Gv ORD M5 ....86 F4
Ash Av ALT WA14 ....107 K7
  CHD/CHDH SK8 ....111 H7
  IRL M44 ....94 A7
Ashawe Cl LHULT M38 ....68 B1
Ashawe Gv LHULT M38 ....68 C1
Ashawe Ter LHULT M38 ....68 B1
Ashbank Av BOLS/LL BL3 ....35 H6
Ashbee St BOL BL1 ....36 B1
Ashberry Cl WILM/AE SK9 ....127 H4
Ashborne Dr BURY BL9 ....57 K8
Ashbourne Av BOLE BL2 ....3 K7
  CHD/CHDH SK8 ....111 J6
  MDTN M24 ....57 M1
  URM M41 ....95 M1
  WGNE/HIN WN2 ....48 D2
  WGNE/HIN WN2 ....49 J7
Ashbourne Cl LEIGH WN7 ....66 A3
  WHIT OL12 ....21 G8
Ashbourne Ct GLSP SK13 ....105 J4
Ashbourne Crs SALE M33 ....109 G2
Ashbourne Dr AUL OL6 ....76 D6
  MPL/ROM SK6 ....123 G6
Ashbourne Gv BRO M7 ....72 B5
  WALK M28 ....55 H4
  WHTF M45 ....55 H4
Ashbourne Rd BRAM/HZG SK7 ...122 B2
  DTN/ASHW M34 ....101 H3
  ECC M30 ....85 H3
  SLFD M6 ....70 F7
  STRET M32 ....85 K8
Ashbourne Sq OLDS OL8 ....9 H9
Ashbourne St ROCH OL11 ....27 H3
Ashbridge TRPK M17 ....85 H5
Ashbridge Rd FAIL M35 ....74 E6
Ashbrook Av DTN/ASHW M34 ....100 E1
Ashbrook Cl CHD/CHDH SK8 .....119 K3
  DTN/ASHW M34 ....100 E1
Ashbrook Crs WHIT OL12 ....21 G8
Ashbrook Farm Cl RDSH SK5 .....100 C2
Ashbrook Hey La WHIT OL12 ....21 G8
Ashbrook La RDSH SK5 ....100 C2
Ashbrook Rd MCFLDN SK10 ....131 J6
  OLDE OL4 ....60 C7
Ashbrook St OP/CLY M11 ....89 K5
Ashburn Av BNG/LEV M19 ....99 H8
Ashburn Cl HOR/BR BL6 ....34 A4
Ashburner St BOL BL1 ....2 E6
Ashburn Gv HTNM SK4 ....12 D1
Ashburn Rd HTNM SK4 ....12 D1
Ashburton Cl HYDE SK14 ....103 H2
Ashburton Rd EDGY/DAV SK3 ....112 B8
Ashburton Rd West
  TRPK M17 ....85 H5

Arrowfield Rd CCHDY M21 ....98 A6
Arrowhill Rd RAD M26 ....38 C4
Arrowsmith Rd
  RNFD/HAY WA11 ....78 C5
Arrow St BOL BL1 ....2 C2
  BRO M7 ....87 J1
  LEIGH WN7 ....81 L1
Arthington St MILN OL16 ....11 J3
Arthog Dr HALE/TIMP WA15 ......117 H4
Arthog Rd DID/WITH M20 ....110 F2
  HALE/TIMP WA15 ....117 H4
Arthur Av WALK M28 ....52 F7
Arthur La BOLE BL2 ....37 L2
Arthur Rd OLDTF/WHR M16 ....97 M1
Arthurs La UPML OL3 ....61 L7
Arthur St BOLS/LL BL3 ....53 K1
  ECC M30 ....84 F3
  FWTH BL4 ....52 E1
  HEY OL10 * 41 C2
  HYDE SK14 ....101 M3
  LEIGH WN7 ....66 B8
  PWCH M25 ....55 J8
  RDSH SK5 ....100 B5
  ROY/SHW OL2 ....43 K5
  SWIN M27 ....70 A5
  TOT/BURYW BL8 ....38 C2
  WALK M28 ....69 G3
  WALK M28 ....68 B8
  WGNE/HIN WN2 ....49 H7
Artillery Pl WYTH/NTH M22 * 110 C8
Artillery St BOLS/LL BL3 ....2 F8
  CSLFD M3 ....6 D6
Artists La MCFLDN SK10 ....130 E6
Arundale Av OLDTF/WHR M16 .....98 B3
Arundale Cl HYDE SK14 ....103 J1
Arundale Gv HYDE SK14 ....103 J1
Arundel Av BRAM/HZG SK7 ......121 M4
  ROCH OL11 ....28 B8
  URM M41 ....95 L5
  WHTF M45 ....55 L5
Arundel Cl HALE/TIMP WA15 .....117 L3
  STLY SK15 ....77 J6
  TOT/BURYW BL8 ....24 C6
Arundel Dr LEIGH WN7 ....66 C6
Arundel Gra GLSP SK13 ....104 E8
Arundel Gv OFTN SK2 ....112 E8
Arundel Rd CHD/CHDH SK8 ......120 C6
Arundel St AUL OL6 ....91 H1
  BOL BL1 ....22 B7
  GLSP SK13 ....104 F3
  HULME M15 ....6 B8
  MOSL OL5 ....76 F3
  OLDE OL4 ....59 M5
  ROCH OL11 ....28 B8
  SWIN M27 ....70 A7
  WGNE/HIN WN2 ....49 H7
  WGNW/BIL/OR WN5 ....47 J6
Asby Cl MDTN M24 ....57 G2
Ascension Rd BRO M7 ....87 J4
Ascot Av SALE M33 ....107 M1
  STRET M32 ....97 J1
Ascot Cl CHAD OL9 ....8 C4
  ROCH OL11 ....27 H4
Ascot Dr ATH M46 ....51 H8
  BRAM/HZG SK7 ....122 C2
  URM M41 ....94 F2
Ascot Mdw BURY BL9 ....4 D6
Ascot Pde BNG/LEV M19 ....99 J6
Ascot Rd BOLS/LL BL3 ....53 J1
  NEWH/MOS M40 ....73 L8
Ascroft St OLD OL1 ....9 J6
  WGN WN1 ....15 K5
Asgard Dr ORD M5 ....86 E4
Asgard Gv ORD M5 ....86 F4
Ash Av ALT WA14 ....107 K7
  CHD/CHDH SK8 ....111 H7
  IRL M44 ....94 A7
Ashawe Cl LHULT M38 ....68 B1
Ashawe Gv LHULT M38 ....68 C1
Ashawe Ter LHULT M38 ....68 B1
Ashbank Av BOLS/LL BL3 ....35 H6
Ashbee St BOL BL1 ....36 B1
Ashberry Cl WILM/AE SK9 ....127 H4
Ashborne Dr BURY BL9 ....57 K8
Ashbourne Av BOLE BL2 ....3 K7
  CHD/CHDH SK8 ....111 J6
  MDTN M24 ....57 M1
  URM M41 ....95 M1
  WGNE/HIN WN2 ....48 D2
  WGNE/HIN WN2 ....49 J7
Ashbourne Cl LEIGH WN7 ....66 A3
  WHIT OL12 ....21 G8
Ashbourne Ct GLSP SK13 ....105 J4
Ashbourne Crs SALE M33 ....109 G2
Ashbourne Dr AUL OL6 ....76 D6
  MPL/ROM SK6 ....123 G6
Ashbourne Gv BRO M7 ....72 B5
  WALK M28 ....55 H4
  WHTF M45 ....55 H4
Ashbourne Rd BRAM/HZG SK7 ...122 B2
  DTN/ASHW M34 ....101 H3
  ECC M30 ....85 H3
  SLFD M6 ....70 F7
  STRET M32 ....85 K8
Ashbourne Sq OLDS OL8 ....9 H9
Ashbourne St ROCH OL11 ....27 H3
Ashbridge TRPK M17 ....85 H5
Ashbridge Rd FAIL M35 ....74 E6
Ashbrook Av DTN/ASHW M34 ....100 E1
Ashbrook Cl CHD/CHDH SK8 .....119 K3
  DTN/ASHW M34 ....100 E1
Ashbrook Crs WHIT OL12 ....21 G8
Ashbrook Farm Cl RDSH SK5 .....100 C2
Ashbrook Hey La WHIT OL12 ....21 G8
Ashbrook La RDSH SK5 ....100 C2
Ashbrook Rd MCFLDN SK10 ....131 J6
  OLDE OL4 ....60 C7
Ashbrook St OP/CLY M11 ....89 K5
Ashburn Av BNG/LEV M19 ....99 H8
Ashburn Cl HOR/BR BL6 ....34 A4
Ashburner St BOL BL1 ....2 E6
Ashburn Gv HTNM SK4 ....12 D1
Ashburn Rd HTNM SK4 ....12 D1
Ashburton Cl HYDE SK14 ....103 H2
Ashburton Rd EDGY/DAV SK3 ....112 B8
Ashburton Rd West
  TRPK M17 ....85 H5

Ashcombe Dr BOLE BL2 ....37 K6
RAD M26 ....38 A7
Ashcott Av WYTH/NTH M22 .....110 A9
Ashcroft Cl HOR/BR BL6 ....35 G7
Ashcroft WILM/AE SK9 ....126 D7
Ashcroft Av SLFD M6 ....71 H4
WGNNW/ST WN6 ....47 J1
Ashcroft St CHAD OL9 ....49 H8
Ashdale Av BOLS/LL BL3 ....35 H7
Ashdale Cl RDSH SK5 ....100 C3
Ashdale Crs DROY M43 ....89 J3
Ashdale Dr CHD/CHDH SK8 .....119 K2
DID/WITH M20 ....99 G7
Ashdale Rd WGNE/HIN WN2 .....49 J7
WGNS/IIMK WN3 ....47 J7
Ashdene AUL OL6 ....90 F2
Ashdene Cl OLD OL1 ....8 C1
OLDE OL4 ....60 C5
Ashdene Crs BOLE BL2 ....23 G8
Ashdene Ri OLD OL1 ....44 A8
Ashdene Rd BNG/LEV M19 .....111 G2
DID/WITH M20 ....99 G6
WILM/AE SK9 ....126 D7
Ashdown Av BKLY M9 ....57 G8
MPL/ROM SK6 ....101 M7
Ashdown Cl CHD/CHDH SK8 .....120 C6
Ashdown Dr BOLE BL2 ....36 F1
SWIN M27 ....70 D6
WALK M28 ....68 C5
Ashdowne Lawns STLY SK15 .....92 A1
Ashdown Gv BKLY M9 ....57 G8
Ashdown Rd HTNM SK4 ....111 M1
Ashdown Ter BKLY M9 ....57 G8
Ash Dr SWIN M27 ....69 M2
Asher St BOLS/LL BL3 ....51 M1
Ashes Cl STLY SK15 ....91 M4
Ashes Dr BOLE BL2 ....37 L4
Ashes La GLSP SK13 ....104 E2
MILN OL16 ....29 H5
OLDE OL4 ....60 C6
STLY SK15 ....91 M4
Ashfield DTN/ASHW M34 ....90 D7
Ashfield Av ATH M46 ....50 F8
ROCH OL11 ....10 E9
WGNE/HIN WN2 ....49 J8
Ashfield Cl SLFD M6 ....86 B1
Ashfield Crs CHD/CHDH SK8 .....111 G6
OLDE OL4 ....60 C6
WGNNW/BIL/OR WN5 ....62 B7
Ashfield Dr NEWH/MOS M40 .....74 A8
WGNE/HIN WN2 ....32 F7
Ashfield Gv BOL BL1 ....22 D6
EDGY/DAV SK3 * 112 C8
GTN M18 ....89 J3
IRL M44 ....94 B6
MPL/ROM SK6 ....114 E3
Ashfield House Gdns
WGNNW/ST WN6 ....31 J5
Ashfield La MILN OL16 ....29 J8
Ashfield Park Dr
WGNNW/ST WN6 ....31 J4
Ashfield Rd BRUN/LGST M13 .....99 H1
CHD/CHDH SK8 ....111 G6
EDGY/DAV SK3 ....112 C8
GLSP SK13 ....104 B1
HALE/TIMP WA15 ....117 G1
ROCH OL11 ....10 E9
SALE M33 ....96 F2
URM M41 ....96 A2
Ashfield Sq DROY M43 ....89 J3
Ashford SALE M33 ....95 M8
Ashford Av ECC M30 ....84 F4
RDSH SK5 * 69 M6
SWIN M27 ....69 M6
WALK M28 ....68 C6
Ashford Cl BOLE BL2 ....23 H8
TOT/BURYW BL8 ....38 E3
WILM/AE SK9 ....119 L8
Ashford Ct OLDE OL4 ....60 A4
Ashford Gv WALK M28 ....69 J4
Ashford Ms GLSP SK13 ....104 A3
Ashford Ri WGN WN1 ....31 L8
Ashford Rd DID/WITH M20 ....98 D5
HTNM SK4 ....100 A6
WILM/AE SK9 ....126 E8
Ashford St HEY OL10 ....40 C2
CHAD OL9 * 58 D8
Ashford Wk BOL BL1 ....2 C1
Ashgate Av WYTH/NTH M22 .....118 D6
Ash Gv ALT WA14 ....116 E3
BOL BL1 ....35 L4
BOLE BL2 ....37 J1
CHD/CHDH SK8 ....119 K4
DROY M43 ....89 K4
GOL/RIS/CUL WA3 * 79 M4
HALE/TIMP WA15 ....117 H4
HTNM SK4 ....100 A7
LIT OL15 ....21 K7
MILN OL16 ....43 K1
MPL/ROM SK6 ....114 B7
OLDE OL4 ....60 D5
PWCH M25 ....55 K6
RAMS BL0 ....24 C1
ROY/SHW OL2 ....43 G6
RUSH/FAL M14 ....88 B3
STLY SK15 ....91 J2
STRET M32 ....96 F4
SWIN M27 ....70 A7
TOT/BURYW BL8 ....24 D7
WALK M28 ....69 H3
WGNNW/ST WN6 ....31 J4
WGNW/BIL/OR WN5 ....46 C6
WHTF M45 ....55 J5
Ashgrove MILN OL16 ....42 E3
Ash Grove Crs
WGNW/BIL/OR WN5 ....62 B6
Ash Hill Dr MOSL OL5 ....77 H4
Ashia Cl MILN OL16 ....11 H6
Ashill Wk CSLFD M3 ....6 D6
Ashington Cl BOL BL1 ....35 L1
WGNW/BIL/OR WN5 ....46 E3
Ashington Dr TOT/BURYW BL8 ...38 D3
Ashkirk St GTN M18 ....89 G7
Ashland Av AIMK WN4 ....63 K8
WGN WN1 ....47 M2
Ashlands SALE M33 ....96 D3
Ashlands Av NEWH/MOS M40 ...73 M3
WALK M28 ....68 C3
Ashlands Dr DTN/ASHW M34 .....90 B6
Ashlands Rd HALE/TIMP WA15 ...108 C3
Ash La HALE/TIMP WA15 ....117 J3
WGNE/HIN WN2 ....48 D2
Ash Lawns OLDE OL4 ....60 E6
Ashleigh Av GOL/RIS/CUL WA3 ..104 E2
Ashleigh Cl ROY/SHW OL2 ....59 H2
Ash Leigh Dr BOL BL1 ....35 H4
Ashleigh Rd HALE/TIMP WA15 ..108 E4

Ashley Av BOLE BL2 ....37 G4
OLDTF/WHR M16 ....87 G8
SWIN M27 ....70 A6
URM M41 ....95 H2
Ashley Cl ROCH OL11 ....27 M8
Ashley Court Dr
NEWH/MOS M40 ....74 C3
Ashley Crs SWIN M27 ....70 A5
Ashley Dr BRAM/HZG SK7 .....120 E6
LEIGH WN7 ....65 M4
SALE M33 ....108 B2
SWIN M27 ....70 A6
Ashley Gdns HYDE SK14 ....102 B3
MPL/ROM SK6 ....122 F4
Ashley La BKLY M9 ....73 J4
Ashley Ms HYDE SK14 ....102 B3
WHTF M45 ....55 L5
Ashleymill La ALT WA14 ....116 F4
Ashley Mill La North
ALT WA14 ....116 F4
Ashley Rd ALT WA14 ....116 F4
DROY M43 ....89 H2
OFTN SK2 ....112 F4
WGNE/HIN WN2 ....65 L1
WILM/AE SK9 ....126 F3
Ashley St ANC M4 ....7 J1
CHAD OL9 ....8 D3
HYDE SK14 ....91 H8
SLFD M6 ....86 B2
Ashling Ct TYLD M29 ....67 M3
Ashlor St BURY BL9 ....4 F7
Ashlyn Gv RUSH/FAL M14 ....99 G4
Ashlynne AUL OL6 ....90 F1
Ashmeade HALE/TIMP WA15 ....117 K3
Ashmond Rd OLDE OL4 ....60 C6
Ashmoor Rd WYTH/NTH M22 ....118 F3
Ashmore Av EDGY/DAV SK3 .....111 J5
Ashmore St TYLD M29 ....68 A4
Ashton Dr WHIT OL12 ....28 A2
Ashness Cl HOR/BR BL6 ....33 J1
Ashness Dr BOLE BL2 ....37 H5
BRAM/HZG SK7 ....121 H4
MDTN M24 ....57 G1
Ashover Av WGTN/LGST M12 * ..88 C3
Ashover Cl BOL BL1 ....22 C6
Ashover St STRET M32 ....97 H1
Ashridge Cl HOR/BR BL6 ....34 F6
Ashridge Dr DUK SK16 ....90 E5
ECC M30 ....84 F4
Ashridge Wy
WGNW/BIL/OR WN5 ....46 E3
Ash Rd DROY M43 ....89 J2
DTN/ASHW M34 ....89 K8
FWTH BL4 ....53 J7
PART M31 ....106 A1
POY/DIS SK12 ....129 K1
RNFD/HAY WA11 ....78 B3
Ash Sq OLDE OL4 ....60 A4
Ashstead Rd SALE M33 ....108 C3
Ash St BKLY M9 ....73 G5
BOLE BL2 ....3 G6
BRAM/HZG SK7 ....121 M1
BURY BL9 ....5 J4
DTN/ASHW M34 ....90 A5
EDGY/DAV SK3 ....12 B7
FAIL M35 ....74 B4
GOL/RIS/CUL WA3 ....79 L2
HEY OL10 ....40 E1
MDTN M24 ....57 M3
OLDE OL4 ....59 L6
ROCH OL11 ....41 M2
SLFD M6 ....86 C2
TYLD M29 ....67 K3
Ashton Av ALT WA14 ....108 B6
Ashton Crs CHAD OL9 ....74 D1
Ashton Field Dr WALK M28 ....52 F8
Ashton Gallery WGN WN1 * 14 F3
Ashton Gdns GLSP SK13 ....104 F5
Ashton Heath AIMK WN4 ....78 F2
Ashton Hill La DROY M43 ....89 K4
Ashton La MDTN M24 ....57 K4
SALE M33 ....96 C7
Ashton New Rd OP/CLY M11 .....88 C3
Ashton Old Rd OP/CLY M11 ....88 B4
Ashton Pl BRAM/HZG SK7 ....122 C3
Ashton Rd BKLY M9 ....57 G7
DROY M43 ....89 K3
DTN/ASHW M34 ....90 B7
FAIL M35 ....74 F6
GOL/RIS/CUL WA3 ....79 J2
HYDE SK14 ....91 H7
MPL/ROM SK6 ....101 M6
NEWLW WA12 ....78 F6
OLDS OL8 ....9 H8
PART M31 ....106 F1
SALE M33 ....95 M8
WGNW/BIL/OR WN5 ....62 E4
Ashton Rd East FAIL M35 ....74 D5
Ashton Rd West FAIL M35 ....74 B5
Ashton St BOLS/LL BL3 ....35 L8
BOLS/LL BL3 ....53 L1
CHAD OL9 ....74 C1
DUK SK16 ....90 D6
GLSP SK13 ....104 F5
HEY OL10 ....40 F7
MPL/ROM SK6 ....101 M6
ROCH OL11 ....10 C8
Ash Tree Av DROY M43 ....89 J2
Ash Tree Dr DUK SK16 ....91 J5
Ash Tree Rd CHH M8 ....72 D3
HYDE SK14 ....91 L7
Ashurst Av OP/CLY M11 ....88 E2
Ashurst Cl BOLE BL2 ....37 J1
HYDE SK14 ....102 D3
Ashurst Dr EDGY/DAV SK3 .....111 L7
Ashurst Gv RAD M26 ....54 E3
Ashurst Rd WGNNW/ST WN6 ....30 D2
WYTH/NTH M22 ....119 H1
Ashville Ter NEWH/MOS M40 ....73 J3
MDTN M24 ....57 J6
Ashway AUL OL6 * 90 D1
Ashwell Av GOL/RIS/CUL WA3 ...80 A3
Ashwell Rd NTHM/RTH M23 ....109 L1
Ashwell St BOLE BL2 * 36 E1
Ashwood ALT WA14 ....116 D4
CHAD OL9 ....58 B5
GLSP SK13 ....104 C4
RAD M26 ....53 G5
Ashwood Av AIMK WN4 ....78 D2
DID/WITH M20 ....98 B8
DTN/ASHW M34 ....100 D1
GOL/RIS/CUL WA3 ....80 A5
RAMS BL0 ....19 G5
SALE M33 ....108 B1
WALK M28 ....52 F7
WGNE/HIN WN2 ....64 D3

Ashwood Crs MPL/ROM SK6 ....114 C5
Ashwood Dr LIT OL15 ....21 K7
ROY/SHW OL2 ....42 F7
TOT/BURYW BL8 ....24 E6
Ashwood Rd POY/DIS SK12 * ...123 H6
Ashworth Av BOLS/LL BL3 ....53 M1
DTN/ASHW M34 ....95 M1
Ashworth Cl ALT WA14 ....116 D3
CHAD OL9 ....58 E8
LIT OL15 ....21 L5
Ashworth La BOL BL1 ....22 C7
HYDE SK14 ....103 J1
Ashworth Ms HEY OL10 ....40 D2
Ashworth Rd ROCH OL11 ....26 E3
Ashworth St CHH M8 ....72 B7
DTN/ASHW M34 ....90 B8
FAIL M35 ....74 A4
FWTH BL4 ....52 F4
HEY OL10 ....41 G4
RAD M26 ....38 F8
TOT/BURYW BL8 ....4 A3
WHIT OL12 ....10 B3
Asia St BOLS/LL BL3 ....52 D1
Askern Av WYTH/NTH M22 .....118 F1
Askett Cl NEWH/MOS M40 ....74 A6
Askrigg Ct ATH M46 ....66 D4
Askwith Rd WGNE/HIN WN2 .....65 J1
Aspell Cl MDTN M24 ....57 J4
Aspen Cl HALE/TIMP WA15 .....109 H7
WHTN BL5 ....50 C2
Aspen Gn DTN/ASHW M34 .....101 K2
Aspenshaw Rd NM/HAY SK22 ..125 G1
Aspen Wy CHD/CHDH SK8 * ...110 B6
Aspen Wk WGNNW/ST WN6 .....47 K1
Aspenwood AIMK WN4 ....78 D2
Aspenwood Cl MPL/ROM SK6 ..114 B3
Aspen Wd HYDE SK14 ....102 C1
Aspenwood Dr SALE M33 ....95 M8
Aspin La ANC M4 ....7 H1
Aspinall Cl HOR/BR BL6 ....33 J1
Aspinall Crs WALK M28 ....68 C2
Aspinall Rd WGNNW/ST WN6 ...30 E3
Aspinall St HEY OL10 ....41 H2
HOR/BR BL6 ....34 A3
MDTN M24 ....57 M5
RUSH/FAL M14 ....98 F1
WGNE/HIN WN2 ....64 D2
Aspin Wy HOR/BR BL6 ....33 M4
Aspland Rd HYDE SK14 ....102 C5
Aspull Cl WGN WN1 ....80 F3
Aspull Ct OLDE OL4 ....59 M7
Aspull Av DUK SK16 ....90 F6
Aspull St RDSH SK5 ....100 C3
Asquith Av DTN/ASHW M34 .....89 M3
Asquith Rd NEWH/MOS M40 ....74 A4
ROY/SHW OL2 ....43 J5
Assheton Av AUL OL6 ....90 E1
NEWLW WA12 ....78 D8
Assheton Crs NEWH/MOS M40 ..74 A4
Assheton Rd NEWH/MOS M40 ...74 A4
ROY/SHW OL2 ....43 J5
Assheton St MDTN M24 ....57 K2
Assheton Wy MDTN M24 ....57 K4
Assisi Gdns WGTN/LGST M12 ...88 B6
Assumption Rd MDTN M24 ....57 G1
Astan Av DROY M43 ....89 G1
Astbury Av DTN/ASHW M34 .....90 A3
Astbury Cl BURY BL9 ....5 J9
GOL/RIS/CUL WA3 ....80 E4
HALE/TIMP WA15 * 108 B6
OLDE OL4 ....60 C6
Astbury Crs EDGY/DAV SK3 ....112 A6
Astbury St RAD M26 ....54 B3
Aster Av FWTH BL4 ....52 D3
Aster Rd RNFD/HAY WA11 ....78 C6
Aster St OLD OL1 ....9 G1
Astley Cl ROY/SHW OL2 ....43 J5
Astley Ct IRL M44 ....94 B4
Astley Gdns DUK SK16 ....90 E4
Astley Gv STLY SK15 ....91 J1
Astley Hall Dr RAMS BL0 ....18 F8
Astley La BOL BL1 ....36 A1
Astley La BOLE BL2 ....23 H7
IRL M44 ....82 F7
STLY SK15 ....91 J2
Astley Rd BOL BL1 ....36 B2
BRO M7 ....71 M7
BURY BL9 ....5 J7
CHD/CHDH SK8 ....119 J3
ECC M30 ....85 G3
GLSP SK13 ....93 K8
HALE/TIMP WA15 ....117 H4
LEIGH WN7 ....66 C6
MPL/ROM SK6 ....113 G1
NEWLW WA12 ....78 F8
ROY/SHW OL2 ....43 K6
SALE M33 ....108 A1
URM M41 ....95 H2
WALK M28 ....69 G8
WALK M28 ....69 H5
WGN WN1 ....48 A2
WGNNW/ST WN6 ....31 H4
WGNW/BIL/OR WN5 ....50 C3
WHTN BL5 ....50 C1
WILM/AE SK9 ....130 D3
Averham Cl AIMK WN4 ....78 E3
Averhill WALK M28 ....68 A4
Averill St NEWH/MOS M40 ....74 A7
Averon Ri OLD OL1 ....44 A8
Aveson Av CCHDY M21 ....97 L6
Avian Dr RUSH/FAL M14 ....98 E4
Aviary Rd WALK M28 ....69 H6
Aviator Wy WYTH/NTH M22 .....118 F4
Aviemore Cl AIMK WN4 ....63 G8
RAMS BL0 ....24 D2
Avis St ROY/SHW OL2 ....43 K5
Avocet Cl LEIGH WN7 ....66 D4
NEWLW WA12 ....78 F8
Avocet Dr ALT WA14 ....107 L4
IRL M44 ....94 D1
Avon Av MILN OL16 ....29 K6
Avon Cl MILN OL16 ....29 K6
MPL/ROM SK6 ....114 B7
WALK M28 ....68 D2
Avoncliff Cl BOL BL1 ....36 A1
Avon Ct BRUN/LGST M13 * 87 M6
RAMS BL0 ....18 F5

Atholl Gv WGNS/IIMK WN3 ....63 K1
Athol Rd BRAM/HZG SK7 ....120 F7
OLDTF/WHR M16 ....98 B3
Athol St AUL OL6 ....90 F1
ECC M30 ....85 G2
GTN M18 ....100 D1
HTNM SK4 ....12 F1
RAMS BL0 ....18 F5
Atkinson Av BOLS/LL BL3 ....52 E1
Atkinson St SALE M33 ....96 A2
URM M41 ....96 A2
Atkinson St CHAD OL9 ....8 D5
ROCH OL11 ....41 M2
STKP SK1 ....13 M8
WGNE/HIN WN2 ....65 H4
Atkin St WALK M28 ....69 G2
Atlanta Av MANAIR M90 ....118 C4
Atlantic St ALT WA14 ....107 K6
Atlas Pk WYTH/NTH M22 * 119 H3
Atlas St AULW OL7 ....75 K6
DUK SK16 * 91 G4
OLDS OL8 ....9 H7
Atlow Dr NTHM/RTH M23 ....109 L7
Attenbury's La ALT WA14 ....108 B3
Attenburys Park Est
ALT WA14 * 108 B4
Attercliffe Rd CCHDY M21 ....97 K5
Attewell St OP/CLY M11 ....88 D3
Attingham Wk
WGNS/IIMK WN3 ....47 K7
Attleboro Rd
NEWH/MOS M40 ....73 K5
Attlee Av GOL/RIS/CUL WA3 .....79 L8
Attlee Wy WGTN/LGST M12 .....88 B3
Attock Cl CHAD OL9 ....8 A9
Attwood Cl HALE/TIMP WA15 ..108 F3
Attwood St WGTN/LGST M12 ....99 K1
Atwood Rd DID/WITH M20 ....110 F1
Atwood St CMANE M1 ....7 H6
Auberson Rd BOLS/LL BL3 ....52 A1
Aubrey Rd RUSH/FAL M14 ....99 H6
Aubrey St ROCH OL11 ....10 E8
SALQ M50 ....86 D5
Auburn Av HYDE SK14 ....102 A6
MPL/ROM SK6 ....101 J8
Auburn Dr URM M41 ....96 B3
Auburn Rd DTN/ASHW M34 ....101 G2
OLDTF/WHR M16 ....98 B3
Auburn St BOLS/LL BL3 ....36 A8
CMANE M1 ....7 J7
MDTN M24 ....57 M5
Auckland Dr SLFD M6 ....71 K7
Auckland Rd BNG/LEV M19 .....99 J4
Audax Wk NEWH/MOS M40 .....73 L8
Auden Cl OP/CLY M11 ....89 G3
Audenshaw Hall Gv
DTN/ASHW M34 ....89 L5
Audenshaw Rd
DTN/ASHW M34 ....89 M5
Audlem Cl NEWH/MOS M40 .....88 A2
Audley Av STRET M32 ....96 E5
Audley Rd BNG/LEV M19 * 99 J2
Audley St AUL OL6 ....91 H2
MOSL OL5 ....77 G4
Audlum Ct BURY BL9 ....5 J4
Audrey Av GTN M18 ....89 H7
Audrey St BKLY M9 ....73 J4
Aughton Cl
WGNW/BIL/OR WN5 ....62 B8
Aughton St WGNE/HIN WN2 .....48 F8
Augusta Cl WHIT OL12 ....28 B2
Augusta St WHIT OL12 ....28 B2
Augustine Webster Cl BKLY M9 ..73 H4
Augustus St ANC M4 ....7 J1
BOLS/LL BL3 ....36 D8
Augustus Wy HULME M15 ....87 C8
Auriga Wk BRO M7 ....86 F1
Austell Rd WYTH/NTH M22 .....118 F3
Austen Av BURY BL9 ....39 J6
Austen Rd ECC M30 ....85 J2
Austin Av AIMK WN4 ....63 H8
Austin Dr DID/WITH M20 ....98 F8
Austin Gv BNG/LEV M19 ....99 J4
Austin's La HOR/BR BL6 ....34 C3
Austin St LEIGH WN7 * 66 A7
Autumn St BRUN/LGST M13 .....87 M8
Avallon Cl TOT/BURYW BL8 .....24 D5
Avalon Dr DID/WITH M20 ....110 F4
Avebury Cl BRO M7 ....72 C6
GOL/RIS/CUL WA3 ....80 C4
HOR/BR BL6 ....34 C3
Avebury Rd NTHM/RTH M23 ...109 K7
Avens Rd PART M31 ....106 C1
Avenue St BOL BL1 ....2 C2
STKP SK1 ....13 K2
The Avenue BOLE BL2 ....37 J3
BRO M7 ....71 M7
BURY BL9 ....5 J7
CHD/CHDH SK8 ....119 J3
ECC M30 ....85 G3
GLSP SK13 ....93 K8
HALE/TIMP WA15 ....117 H4
LEIGH WN7 ....66 C6
MPL/ROM SK6 ....113 G1
NEWLW WA12 ....78 F8
ROY/SHW OL2 ....43 K6
SALE M33 ....108 A1
URM M41 ....95 H2
WALK M28 ....69 G8
WALK M28 ....69 H5
WGN WN1 ....48 A2
WGNNW/ST WN6 ....31 H4
WGNW/BIL/OR WN5 ....50 C3
WHTN BL5 ....50 C1
WILM/AE SK9 ....130 D3
Averham Cl AIMK WN4 ....78 E3
Averhill WALK M28 ....68 A4
Averill St NEWH/MOS M40 ....74 A7
Averon Ri OLD OL1 ....44 A8
Aveson Av CCHDY M21 ....97 L6
Avian Dr RUSH/FAL M14 ....98 E4
Aviary Rd WALK M28 ....69 H6
Aviator Wy WYTH/NTH M22 .....118 F4
Aviemore Cl AIMK WN4 ....63 G8
RAMS BL0 ....24 D2
Avis St ROY/SHW OL2 ....43 K5
Avocet Cl LEIGH WN7 ....66 D4
NEWLW WA12 ....78 F8
Avocet Dr ALT WA14 ....107 L4
IRL M44 ....94 D1
Avon Av MILN OL16 ....29 K6
Avon Cl MILN OL16 ....29 K6
MPL/ROM SK6 ....114 B7
WALK M28 ....68 D2
Avoncliff Cl BOL BL1 ....36 A1
Avon Ct BRUN/LGST M13 * 87 M6
RAMS BL0 ....18 F5

Avondale Dr RAMS BL0 ....24 C3
SLFD M6 ....70 E7
Avondale Ri WILM/AE SK9 ....127 H6
Avondale Rd BRAM/HZG SK7 ..122 B2
EDGY/DAV SK3 ....12 C7
FWTH BL4 ....52 C4
STRET M32 ....86 B8
WGN WN1 ....47 M2
WHTF M45 ....55 H3
Avondale St BOL BL1 ....35 M3
CHH M8 ....72 C5
OLDS OL8 ....59 H8
WGNNW/ST WN6 ....31 H2
Avon Dr BURY BL9 ....25 J4
Avon Gdns BNG/LEV M19 ....99 K6
Avonhead Cl HOR/BR BL6 ....33 K2
Avonlea Dr BNG/LEV M19 ....99 H6
Avonlea Rd DROY M43 ....89 H7
SALE M33 ....108 A3
Avonleigh Gdns OLD OL1 ....59 M3
Avon Rd AIMK WN4 ....64 B7
BNG/LEV M19 ....99 G6
CHAD OL9 ....58 C4
CHD/CHDH SK8 ....119 K5
FWTH BL4 ....53 L7
HALE/TIMP WA15 ....117 C4
HEY OL10 ....40 D2
ROY/SHW OL2 ....43 L4
TYLD M29 ....67 M5
WGNW/BIL/OR WN5 ....46 F5
Avon St BOL BL1 ....35 L3
EDGY/DAV SK3 ....12 H9
LEIGH WN7 ....66 E8
OLDS OL8 ....59 J8
Avril Cl RDSH SK5 ....100 C4
Avro Cl RUSH/FAL M14 ....98 E3
Avroe Rd ECC M30 ....84 C5
Avro Wy MANAIR M90 ....118 B5
Awburn Rd HYDE SK14 ....103 H3
Axbridge Wk NEWH/MOS M40 ...88 A2
Axeholme Ct HOR/BR BL6 ....33 J1
Axford Cl BRO M7 ....72 C6
Axon Sq OLDTF/WHR M16 ....87 J8
Aycliffe Av CCHDY M21 ....98 A7
Aycliffe Gv BRUN/LGST M13 .....99 H1
Aye Bridge Rd
WGNE/HIN WN2 ....64 F3
Aylesbury Av DTN/ASHW M34 ..101 J3
URM M41 ....85 H3
Aylesbury Cl ORD M5 ....86 D3
Aylesbury Crs WGNE/HIN WN2 ..65 M2
Aylesbury Gv MDTN M24 ....57 M2
Aylesby Av GTN M18 ....88 E3
Aylesford Rd RUSH/FAL M14 ....99 G1
Aylesford Wk BOL BL1 * 2 D1
Aylsham Cl MPL/ROM SK6 .....101 J7
Aylsham Ms SWIN M27 ....70 A7
Aylwin Dr SALE M33 ....108 E1
Ayr Av OLDS OL8 ....75 J1
Ayr Cl BRAM/HZG SK7 ....122 C2
Ayrefield Gv WGNNW/ST WN6 ..30 A6
Ayres Rd OLDTF/WHR M16 ....86 F8
Ayr Gv HEY OL10 ....40 D4
Ayrshire Rd BRO M7 ....71 K6
Ayr St BOLE BL2 ....22 E8
Ayrton Gv LHULT M38 ....52 D7
Aysgarth Av CHD/CHDH SK8 ...110 F6
GTN M18 ....89 H6
MPL/ROM SK6 ....102 A3
Aysgarth Cl SALE M33 ....108 A1
Ayshford Cl ALT WA14 ....107 H6
Ayton Gv RUSH/FAL M14 ....88 B8
Aytoun St CMANE M1 ....7 J5
Azalea Av GTN M18 ....89 G6

B

Babbacombe Gv BKLY M9 ....56 E7
Babbacombe Rd OFTN SK2 .....112 F6
Back Abingdon Rd BOLE BL2 .....3 L3
Back Acton St CMANE M1 * 7 J6
Back Adcroft St STKP SK1 ....13 K8
Back Adrian Rd BOL BL1 ....35 M2
Back Adrian Rd East BOL BL1 * ..35 M2
Back Ainscow St BOL BL1 ....2 C5
Back Ainsworth La BOLE BL2 .....3 L2
Back Ainsworth La East
BOLE BL2 ....3 L1
Back Ainsworth Rd North
TOT/BURYW BL8 ....38 F2
Back Ainsworth Rd South
TOT/BURYW BL8 ....38 F2
Back Albert St BOLS/LL BL3 ....36 A2
Back Albion Pl BURY BL9 ....25 J8
Back Alder St BOLS/LL BL3 ....52 C1
Back Alexander Rd BOLE BL2 * ..36 E1
Back Alexandra St BOLS/LL BL3 ..35 M8
Back Alfred St BOLS/LL BL3 * 36 E8
Back Alice St BOLS/LL BL3 * 35 M7
BOLS/LL BL3 ....53 L1
Back Alicia St BOLS/LL BL3 ....37 G8
Back All Saints' St BOL BL1 * 2 F3
Back Alston St BOLS/LL BL3 ....52 B1
Back Andrew St BURY BL9 ....5 H5
Back Andrew St North
BURY BL9 ....5 J5
Back Anglia Gv BOLS/LL BL3 ....35 M8
Back Annis Rd BOLS/LL BL3 ....35 L8
Back Anson St BOL BL1 * 36 C1
Back Apple Ter BOL BL1 * 36 A3
Back Argo St BOLS/LL BL3 * 36 A8
Back Argyle St BURY BL9 ....25 J3
Back Arlington St BOLS/LL BL3 ...52 C1
Back Arnold St BOL BL1 ....35 M3
Back Arnold Ter BOL BL1 * 35 J3
Back Ashbee St BOL BL1 ....36 B1
Back Ashford Wk BOL BL1 * 2 C1
Back Ashley St ANC M4 ....7 J1
Back Ash St BOLE BL2 ....5 J4
BURY BL9 ....5 J4
Back Ashton St BOLS/LL BL3 * ...35 L8
Back Ashworth La BOL BL1 ....22 C7
Back Ashworth St
TOT/BURYW BL8 ....4 A3
Back Astley St BOL BL1 ....36 B2
BOLS/LL BL3 ....36 D8
Back Augustus St
BOLS/LL BL3 ....36 C8
Back Augustus St West
BOLS/LL BL3 ....36 C8
Back Avenue St BOL BL1 ....2 C2
Back Avondale St BOL BL1 * 35 M3
Back Baldwin St BOLS/LL BL3 * ..36 C8
Back Baldwin St North
BOLS/LL BL3 ....36 C8
Back Balloon St ANC M4 * 7 G2
Back Banbury St BOLE BL2 ....36 F5
Back Bankfield St BOLS/LL BL3 ...35 M7
Back Bank St CHH M8 ....72 D7

Back Bantry St BOLS/LL BL3 .... 2 C9
Back Barbara St BOLS/LL BL3 .... 36 A8
Back Bark St BOL BL1 .... 2 D4
Back Bashall St BOL BL1 .... 35 M4
Back Battenberg Rd BOL BL1 .... 35 M4
Back Baxendale St BOL BL1 .... 22 B8
Back Bayley St BOL BL1 .... 2 A2
Back Baythorpe St BOL BL1 .... 36 C2
Back Baytorpe St North
 BOL BL1 .... 36 C1
Back Beaconsfield St
 BOLS/LL BL3 .... 52 C1
Back Beaconsfield Ter BOLE BL2 .... 3 J1
Back Bedford St BOL BL1 .... 36 C2
Back Beech St BOL BL1 .... 36 C2
Back Beechwood St
 BOLS/LL BL3 .... 52 C1
Back Belbeck St
 TOT/BURYW BL8 .... 38 F2
Back Bell La BURY BL9 .... 5 H3
Back Belmont Rd BOL BL1 .... 22 B7
Back Belmont Rd East BOL BL1 ..... 22 B7
Back Bennett's La BOL BL1 .... 35 M2
Back Bennett's La East BOLS/LL BL1 . 35 M2
Back Benson St BOL BL1 .... 35 L3
Back Bentinck St BOL BL1 .... 35 L3
Back Bentley St BOLE BL2 .... 3 L8
Back Bertrand Rd BOL BL1 .... 35 M6
Back Beverley St BOL BL1 .... 35 M4
Back Birch St BURY BL9 .... 5 C2
Back Blackbank St BOL BL1 .... 36 C3
Back Blackburn Rd BOL BL1 .... 36 C2
Back Blackburn Rd East
 EDGW/EG BL7 .... 22 A1
Back Blackburn Rd West
 BOL BL1 .... 36 B1
 EDGW/EG BL7 * 22 B4
Back Blackburn St BOL BL1 .... 36 C1
Back Blackwood St
 BOLS/LL BL3 .... 36 D8
Back Bolton Rd North
 TOT/BURYW BL8 .... 38 F3
Back Bolton Rd South
 TOT/BURYW BL8 .... 4 A5
Back Bolton St BOL BL1 .... 36 C2
Back Bolton St South BURY BL9 ..... 4 D4
Back Bond St West BURY BL9 .... 5 J4
Back Boundary St BOL BL1 .... 36 A2
Back Bowen St BOL BL1 .... 35 L3
Backbower La HYDE SK14 .... 102 C4
Back Bowness Rd BOLS/LL BL3 ...... 36 A8
Back Bradford Rd BOLS/LL BL3 ..... 52 D1
Back Bradford Rd West
 BOLS/LL BL3 .... 52 D1
Back Bradford St BOLE BL2 .... 3 K5
Back Bradford St East BOLE BL2 .... 3 J9
Back Bradford St South
 BOLE BL2 .... 3 H6
Back Bradford St West
 BOLE BL2 .... 3 J5
Back Bradshaw BOLE BL2 .... 22 F8
Back Bradshaw Brow West
 BOLE BL2 .... 22 F8
Back Bradshawgate BOL BL1 .... 2 F5
Back Bradshaw Rd South
 BOLE BL2 .... 23 G7
Back Bradshaw St MILN OL16 ...... 11 H2
Back Brandon St BOL BL1 .... 36 A8
Back Brandon St North
 BOLS/LL BL3 .... 36 A8
Back Brandwood St
 BOLS/LL BL3 .... 35 M8
Back Bridgeman St
 BOLS/LL BL3 .... 36 B8
Back Bridge St BOL BL1 .... 2 E3
 CSLFD M3 .... 6 E4
 NM/HAY SK22 .... 124 E3
 RAMS BL0 .... 18 F6
Back Brierley St BURY BL9 .... 4 E9
Back Brierley St South
 BURY BL9 .... 4 E9
Back Brigade St BOL BL1 .... 35 M5
Back Brindley St BOL BL1 .... 22 C8
Back Brink's Pl BOL BL1 * 2 C4
Back Bristol Av BOLE BL2 .... 3 L1
Back Bristol St BOLS/LL BL3 .... 2 B8
Back Broach St BOLS/LL BL3 .... 36 B8
Back Broad o' th' La BOL BL1 * ... 22 B8
Back Broad St BURY BL9 .... 4 E5
Back Bromwich St BOLE BL2 .... 3 J6
Back Brookfield St BOLE BL2 .... 3 H4
Back Brook St North BURY BL9 ..... 5 H1
Back Broom St BOLE BL2 .... 3 H4
 MILN OL16 .... 29 L8
Back Burnaby St BOLS/LL BL3 .... 2 A9
Back Burnham Av BOL BL1 .... 35 K3
Back Bury New Rd BOLE BL2 .... 3 H5
Back Bury New Rd East
 BOLE BL2 .... 3 J5
Back Bury Old Rd BOLE BL2 .... 3 H4
Back Bury Rd BOLE BL2 .... 37 C5
Back Bury Rd East BOLE BL2 .... 3 M4
Back Bury Rd South BOLE BL2 .... 3 L4
 BOLE BL2 .... 37 C5
Back Bushell St BOLS/LL BL3 ...... 35 L8
Back Byrom St
 TOT/BURYW BL8 .... 24 E8
Back Byrom St South
 TOT/BURYW BL8 .... 24 E8
Back Calder Rd BOLS/LL BL3 .... 52 B1
Back Caledonia St BOL BL1 .... 35 M7
Back Calvert Rd BOLS/LL BL3 ...... 52 C1
Back Cambridge St AULW OL7 .... 90 C3
Back Camp St BRO M7 * 72 A7
Back Canada St BOL BL1 .... 36 A2
 HOR/BR BL6 .... 33 L1
Back Canning St BURY BL9 .... 4 F1
Back Carl St BOL BL1 .... 35 A2
Back Carter St BOLS/LL BL3 .... 36 D8
Back Castle BOLE BL2 .... 3 J5
Back Cateaton St BURY BL9 .... 4 F2
Back Cecilia St BOLS/LL BL3 ...... 36 D8
Back Cecil St BOLE BL2 .... 3 J5
 MOSL OL5 .... 76 F4
Back Cedar St BURY BL9 .... 5 K3
Back Cedar St North BURY BL9 ...... 5 K3
Back Cemetery Rd East
 BOLE BL2 .... 3 K4
Back Cestrian St BOLS/LL BL3 ..... 52 C1
Back Chalfont St BOL BL1 .... 36 C2
Back Chapel St BNG/LEV M19 .... 99 K3
 BRAM/HZG SK7 * 122 A1
 HOR/BR BL6 .... 33 M1
 TOT/BURYW BL8 .... 24 C5
 WHIT OL12 .... 21 G5
Back Chapman St BOL BL1 .... 35 L3
Back Charles Holden St
 BOL BL1 .... 2 A6
Back Chaucer St BOL BL1 .... 36 A3
Back Cheapside BOL BL1 .... 2 E5
Back Chesham Rd North
 BURY BL9 .... 25 K8

Back Chesham Rd South
 BURY BL9 .... 25 K8
Back Chester St BURY BL9 .... 25 K8
Back China La CMANE M1 .... 7 J5
Back Chorley New Rd
 BOL BL1 .... 35 L5
Back Chorley New Rd North
 BOL BL1 .... 35 K3
Back Chorley Old Rd
 BOL BL1 .... 35 L3
Back Chorley Old Rd North
 BOL BL1 .... 35 K3
Back Chorley St BOL BL1 .... 2 C4
Back Chorley St East BOL BL1 * 2 C5
Back Church Av BOLS/LL BL3 .... 35 M8
Back Church Rd BOL BL1 .... 35 K2
Back Church Rd North BOL BL1 ..... 35 M2
Back Church St BOL BL1 .... 2 D3
 BOLS/LL BL3 .... 53 K1
Back Clarendon Rd BOLE BL2 .... 3 M4
Back Clarke St BOL BL1 * 35 M4
Back Clay St East
 EDGW/EG BL7 * 22 D5
Back Clay St West
 EDGW/EG BL7 * 22 D5
Back Clegg's Buildings
 BOL BL1 .... 3 M5
Back Clegg St BOLE BL2 .... 3 M5
Back Clifton St BURY BL9 .... 25 J8
Back Cloister St BOL BL1 .... 35 M2
Back Clyde St BOL BL1 .... 36 B2
Back Cobden St BOL BL1 .... 36 A1
Back Colenso Rd BOLE BL2 * 37 G5
Back Columbia Rd BOL BL1 .... 35 M4
Back Common St WHTN BL5 .... 49 L5
Back Coniston St BOL BL1 .... 36 C1
Back Coop St BOL BL1 .... 22 B8
Back Cornall St
 TOT/BURYW BL8 .... 38 F1
Back Corson St BOLS/LL BL3 .... 53 G2
Back Cottam St
 TOT/BURYW BL8 .... 4 A2
Back Cotton St BOL BL1 .... 36 A2
Back Cowm La WHIT OL12 .... 20 A1
Back Cox Green Rd North
 EDGW/EG BL7 * 22 C4
Back Crawford Av BOLE BL2 .... 3 J6
Back Crawford St BOLE BL2 * 3 J6
Back Crescent Av BOL BL1 .... 2 B3
Back Crescent Rd BOLS/LL BL3 ..... 36 D8
Back Crescent Rd West
 BOLS/LL BL3 .... 52 D1
Back Croft La BOLS/LL BL3 .... 3 J9
Back Cross La NEWLW WA12 .... 78 E8
Back Crostons Rd
 TOT/BURYW BL8 .... 4 B3
Back Crumpsall St North
 BOL BL1 .... 36 B1
Back Cundey St BOL BL1 .... 35 M3
Back Curzon St BOL BL1 .... 35 M5
Back Cyril St BOLS/LL BL3 .... 3 H9
Back Daisy St BOLS/LL BL3 .... 35 M8
Back Darley St FWTH BL4 .... 53 H4
Back Darwen Rd North
 EDGW/EG BL7 * 22 C4
Back Darwen Rd South
 EDGW/EG BL7 * 22 D5
Back Darwin St BOL BL1 * 36 A2
Back Deal St BOLS/LL BL3 * 52 C1
Back Deane Church La
 BOLS/LL BL3 .... 35 L8
Back Deane Church La West
 BOLS/LL BL3 .... 35 L8
Back Deane Rd North
 BOLS/LL BL3 .... 35 M7
Back Deane Rd South
 BOLS/LL BL3 .... 2 B7
Back Delamere St South
 BURY BL9 * 25 K7
Back Denton St BURY BL9 .... 25 J8
Back Derby St BOLS/LL BL3 .... 2 C5
 BURY BL9 .... 5 G4
Back Design St BOLS/LL BL3 .... 35 L8
Back Devonshire Rd BOL BL1 .... 35 K3
Back Devon St North BURY BL9 ..... 4 E8
Back Devon St South BURY BL9 ..... 4 F9
Back Dijon St BOLS/LL BL3 .... 35 M8
Back Dijon St North
 BOLS/LL BL3 .... 35 M8
Back Dobie St BOLS/LL BL3 * 36 D8
Back Doffcocker Brow
 BOL BL1 .... 35 J3
Back Dorset St BOLE BL2 .... 35 L3
Back Dougill St BOL BL1 .... 35 L3
Back Dougill St South BOL BL1 .... 35 L3
Back Drake St MILN OL16 .... 10 F6
Back Drummond St BOL BL1 .... 22 B8
Back Ducie Av BOL BL1 .... 35 M5
Back Duckworth St BURY BL9 .... 25 K8
 HOR/BR BL6 .... 33 M1
Back Dunstan St BOL BL1 .... 3 L4
Back Durham St ROCH OL11 .... 11 G8
Back Duxbury St BOL BL1 * 36 A2
Back Earnshaw St
 BOLS/LL BL3 .... 51 M1
Back Eastbank St BOL BL1 .... 36 C1
Back East St BURY BL9 .... 5 G6
Back Eckersley Rd BOL BL1 .... 36 B1
Back Eden St BOL BL1 .... 35 M5
Back Edgmont Av
 BOLS/LL BL3 .... 36 A8
Back Eldon St BURY BL9 .... 4 F1
Back Ellesmere Rd
 BOLS/LL BL3 .... 51 M1
Back Ellesmere St BOLS/LL BL3 ..... 2 A7
Back Elm St BOL BL1 .... 35 K5
Back Elmwood Gv BOL BL1 * 35 M4
Back Elmwood Gv West
 BOL BL1 .... 35 M4
Back Elsworth St CSLFD M3 .... 87 K1
Back Emmett St HOR/BR BL6 .... 33 L1
Back Empire Rd BOLE BL2 .... 37 G4
Back Empress St BOL BL1 .... 35 L3
Back Ena St BOLS/LL BL3 .... 52 D1
Back Ernest St BOL BL1 .... 2 A6
Back Eskrick St East BOL BL1 * ... 36 A2
Back Eskrick St South BOL BL1 .... 36 A2
Back Eskrick St West BOL BL1 ..... 36 A2
Back Essingdon St BOLS/LL BL3 .... 36 A8
Back Essingdon St South
 BOLS/LL BL3 .... 36 A8
Back Eustace St BOLS/LL BL3 ...... 52 D1

Back Euxton St BOLS/LL BL3 .... 36 A8
Back Everton St North
 BOL BL1 .... 36 C2
Back Ewart St BOL BL1 .... 36 B2
Back Fairhaven Rd BOL BL1 .... 36 C1
Back Fair St BOLS/LL BL3 .... 51 M2
Back Fenton St
 TOT/BURYW BL8 .... 38 F1
Back Fern St East
 BOLS/LL BL3 .... 35 M6
Back Fir St BURY BL9 .... 5 K4
Back Fletcher St BOL BL1 * 5 H4
 RAD M26 .... 53 L5
Back Fletcher St South
 BOLS/LL BL3 .... 2 E9
Back Flora St BOLS/LL BL3 * 36 B8
Back Florence Av BOLE BL2 .... 22 C8
Back Fortune St BOLS/LL BL3 .... 3 J9
Back Foundry St BURY BL9 .... 5 C5
Back Frances St BOL BL1 .... 36 A2
Back Frank St BOL BL1 .... 36 A3
 BURY BL9 .... 5 G6
Back Fylde St BOLS/LL BL3 .... 53 G2
Back Gainsborough Av
 BOLS/LL BL3 .... 51 M1
Back Garside Gv BOL BL1 * 35 M2
Back Garston St BURY BL9 .... 25 K8
Back Gaskell St BOL BL1 .... 2 B3
Back Gaskell St East BOL BL1 * 2 B3
Back Gaythorne St BOL BL1 * 36 C1
Back George Barton St
 BOLE BL2 .... 3 K1
Back George St BOLS/LL BL3 .... 36 D8
 CMANE M1 .... 7 G5
 HOR/BR BL6 .... 33 M1
Back Gibraltar St BOLS/LL BL3 ..... 2 B7
Back Gibraltar St South
 BOLS/LL BL3 .... 2 A7
Back Gigg La BURY BL9 .... 4 F9
Back Gilmour St MDTN M24 .... 57 K4
Back Gilnow Gv BOL BL1 .... 2 A6
Back Gilnow La West
 BOLS/LL BL3 .... 35 M6
Back Gilnow Rd BOL BL1 .... 35 M6
Back Glen Av BOLS/LL BL3 .... 35 L7
Back Glenboro Av
 TOT/BURYW BL8 .... 38 E2
Back Glen Bott St BOL BL1 * 36 A2
Back Gloster St BOLE BL2 .... 3 H5
Back Goldsmith St BOL BL1 .... 36 A8
Back Goodlad St
 TOT/BURYW BL8 .... 24 E8
Back Gordon Av BOLS/LL BL3 .... 35 M7
Back Gorses Mt BOLE BL2 .... 3 M8
Back Grafton St ALT WA14 .... 108 A8
 BOL BL1 .... 2 A3
Back Grantham Cl BOL BL1 * 36 B3
Back Grasmere St BOL BL1 .... 36 C2
Back Greaves St OLD OL1 * 9 K6
Back Greenhalgh St
 BOLS/LL BL3 .... 53 K1
Back Greenland Rd
 BOLS/LL BL3 .... 52 C1
Back Green La BOLS/LL BL3 .... 52 C1
Back Green La South
 BOLS/LL BL3 .... 52 C1
Back Green St MDTN M24 .... 57 L3
Back Gregory Av BOLE BL2 .... 37 H4
Back Grendon St BOLS/LL BL3 ...... 51 M1
Back Gresham St BOL BL1 .... 36 C1
Back Grosvenor St STLY SK15 ...... 91 K3
Back Grove St BOL BL1 .... 36 A2
Back Hadwin St BOL BL1 .... 2 E1
Back Halliwell La CHH M8 * 72 C5
Back Halliwell Rd BOL BL1 .... 36 B2
Back Halliwell Rd South
 BOL BL1 .... 35 L8
Back Halstead St BOLE BL2 .... 3 H5
Back Hamilton St BRO M7 * 72 A6
 BURY BL9 .... 25 J8
Back Hampson St
 NEWH/MOS M40 .... 73 C8
Back Hanson St BURY BL9 .... 25 J8
Back Hargreaves St BOL BL1 .... 36 B2
Back Harper's La South
 BOL BL1 .... 35 L2
Back Hartington St BOL BL1 * 35 M4
Back Hart St WHTN BL5 .... 49 L5
Back Harvey St
 TOT/BURYW BL8 .... 38 F1
Back Haslam St BURY BL9 * 25 K8
Back Haslam Ter BOLE BL2 * 3 L4
Back Hatfield Rd BOL BL1 .... 35 M3
Back Hawthorne Rd
 BOLS/LL BL3 .... 35 L8
Back Hawthorne Rd East
 BOLS/LL BL3 .... 35 L7
Back Hawthorn Rd West
 BOLS/LL BL3 .... 35 L7
Back Haydn St BOL BL1 .... 36 A2
Back Haydock St BOL BL1 .... 2 E2
Back Hayward St
 TOT/BURYW BL8 .... 4 A2
Back Hengist St BOLE BL2 * 3 M4
Back Hennon St BOL BL1 .... 36 A3
Back Henrietta St
 BOLS/LL BL3 .... 35 L8
Back Henry Lee St BOLS/LL BL3 .... 51 M1
Back Heywood St East
 BURY BL9 .... 5 H5
Back Heywood St West
 BURY BL9 .... 5 H6
Back High Bank St BOLE BL2 .... 3 M5
Back Higher Darcy St BOLE BL2 .... 3 L9
Back Higher Shady La West
 EDGW/EG BL7 * 22 E5
Back Higher Swan La
 BOLS/LL BL3 .... 52 A1
Back Higher Swan La West
 BOLS/LL BL3 .... 52 A1
Back High St BOLS/LL BL3 .... 36 B8
 EDGW/EG BL7 .... 16 F8
Back High St South
 BOLS/LL BL3 .... 36 B8
Back High St West
 BOLS/LL BL3 .... 36 B8
Back Hilden St BOLE BL2 .... 3 H6
Back Hilden St West BOLE BL2 ...... 3 H6
Back Hilton St BOLE BL2 .... 3 M4
 BRO M7 .... 72 A5
 BURY BL9 .... 5 G1
Back Hind St BOLE BL2 .... 3 H6
Back Holland St BOL BL1 .... 22 C8
Back Holland St East BOL BL1 * ... 22 C8
Back Holly Pl BOL BL1 * 22 C8
Back Holly St BOL BL1 .... 22 C8
Back Holly St South BURY BL9 ..... 5 J4
Back Hopefield St BOLS/LL BL3 .... 36 A8
Back Hope St BRO M7 * 72 A5
 OLD OL1 .... 59 L5

Back Horbury St
 TOT/BURYW BL8 .... 38 F2
Back Horeb St East
 BOLS/LL BL3 .... 2 A9
Back Hornby St BOL BL9 .... 25 J7
Back Hornby St East
 BURY BL9 .... 4 F2
Back Hornby St West
 BURY BL9 * 4 F2
Back Horne St North BURY BL9 ..... 4 E9
Back Horne St South BURY BL9 ..... 4 E9
Back Horsa St BOLE BL2 .... 3 J1
Back Horsa St North BOLE BL2 * 3 J1
Back Hotel St BOL BL1 * 2 E4
Back Hough La East
 EDGW/EG BL7 .... 22 D5
Back Howarden St BOL BL1 .... 22 B7
Back Howcroft St
 BOLS/LL BL3 .... 36 A8
Back Howe St BRO M7 .... 71 M5
Back Hughes St BOL BL1 .... 36 A2
Back Hulbert St
 TOT/BURYW BL8 .... 38 F3
Back Hulme St ORD M5 .... 86 F3
 TOT/BURYW BL8 .... 4 B2
Back Hulton La BOLS/LL BL3 .... 51 K2
Back Hulton La South
 BOLS/LL BL3 .... 51 K2
Back Hulton La West
 BOLS/LL BL3 .... 35 K8
Back Huntley Mount Rd
 BURY BL9 .... 5 K2
Back Hurst St BOLS/LL BL3 .... 51 M1
Back Huxley St BOL BL1 .... 35 M2
Back Ingham St BURY BL9 .... 5 H6
Back Ingham St East
 BURY BL9 .... 5 H6
Back Irlam St BOL BL1 .... 36 B1
Back Irlam St North BOL BL1 ...... 36 B1
Back Ivy Bank Rd BOL BL1 .... 22 B7
Back Ivy Rd BOL BL1 .... 35 M3
Back Ivy Rd West BOL BL1 * 35 M2
Back James St BOLS/LL BL3 .... 53 L1
Back Jauncey St BOLS/LL BL3 ...... 35 M7
Back John Brown St BOL BL1 * 2 B3
Back John Cross St
 BOLS/LL BL3 .... 36 B8
Back Johnson St BOL BL1 * 2 F6
Back Junction St CMANE M1 .... 7 K4
Back Keighley St BOL BL1 .... 35 M2
Back Kendal Rd BOL BL1 .... 35 M4
Back Kershaw St BURY BL9 .... 5 J5
Back Kingholm Gdns BOL BL1 * 36 A3
Back Kingsley St BOL BL1 .... 36 A2
Back King St BOL BL1 .... 2 D4
 OLDS OL8 .... 9 H6
Back King St North
 EDGW/EG BL7 * 22 C4
Back King St South BOLE BL2 ...... 23 G7
Back Knight St
 TOT/BURYW BL8 .... 38 F2
Back Knowl St STLY SK15 .... 91 L2
Back Knowsley Rd BOL BL1 * 35 L2
Back Knowsley St BOLE BL2 .... 2 E4
 BURY BL9 .... 4 E5
Back Kylemore Av
 BOLS/LL BL3 .... 35 L7
Back La ALT WA14 .... 106 E7
 AULW OL7 .... 75 H8
 BOL BL1 .... 2 C3
 GLSP SK13 .... 104 B6
 HALE/TIMP WA15 .... 117 H7
 HYDE SK14 .... 92 D8
 MOSL OL5 .... 76 D2
 OLDE OL4 .... 60 F3
 WGNNW/ST WN6 .... 30 C3
 WHIT OL12 .... 20 A2
 WHTN BL5 .... 51 L6
Back Lark St BOL BL1 .... 36 C2
Back Latham St BOL BL1 * 36 C2
Back Lathom St BURY BL9 .... 25 K8
Back Laurel St BURY BL9 .... 5 K4
Back Lawn St BOL BL1 .... 35 M3
Back Leachfield St BOL BL1 .... 36 A1
Back Leach St BOLS/LL BL3 .... 2 C9
Back Lee Av BOLS/LL BL3 .... 52 B1
Back Lee St UPML OL3 .... 61 L4
Back Lena St BOL BL1 .... 36 C2
Back Lenora St BOLS/LL BL3 * 35 L7
Back Lever Edge La
 BOLS/LL BL3 .... 51 M2
 BOLS/LL BL3 .... 52 C1
Back Lever Edge La South
 BOLS/LL BL3 .... 52 B1
Back Lever St BOLS/LL BL3 * 2 E9
Back Lever St North
 BOLS/LL BL3 .... 37 K8
Back Lever St South
 BOLS/LL BL3 .... 36 B8
Back Lightburne Av BOL BL1 .... 35 L5
Back Lilly St BOL BL1 .... 2 A2
Back Lincoln Rd BOL BL1 * 35 M4
Back Lindley St BOLS/LL BL3 ...... 53 L1
Back Linton Av BURY BL9 .... 25 J7
Back Longden St BOL BL1 .... 35 M4
Back Longfield Rd
 BOLS/LL BL3 .... 51 L1
Back Longsight North
 BOLE BL2 .... 23 H7
Back Longsight South
 BOLE BL2 .... 23 G7
Back Longworth Rd
 EDGW/EG BL7 .... 22 A1
Back Lonsdale St
 TOT/BURYW BL8 .... 4 A4
Back Lord St BOLS/LL BL3 .... 53 L1
 BURY BL9 .... 5 G6
Back Loxham St BOLS/LL BL3 .... 53 G2
Back Lumsden St BOLS/LL BL3 ...... 2 C9
Back Luton St BOLS/LL BL3 .... 36 D8
Back Lytton St BOL BL1 .... 36 A3
Back Mackenzie St BOL BL1 .... 22 A8
Back Malvern Av BOL BL1 .... 35 K3
 BURY BL9 .... 25 J7
Back Manchester Old Rd
 BURY BL9 .... 4 D7
Back Manchester Rd BOLE BL2 ...... 52 D1
 BOLS/LL BL3 .... 52 D1
Back Manchester Rd East
 BOLE BL2 .... 3 G8
Back Manchester Rd South
 BOLS/LL BL3 .... 3 H9
Back Manchester Rd West
 BOLS/LL BL3 .... 52 D1
Back Manchester St HEY OL10 * ... 41 H3
Back Manor St BURY BL9 .... 5 H4
Back Maple St BOLS/LL BL3 * 2 B8
Back Marion St South
 BOLS/LL BL3 .... 52 F2

Back Market St BOLS/LL BL3 .... 53 L1
 BURY BL9 .... 4 E5
 LEIGH WN7 .... 66 C7
 NEWLW WA12 .... 78 D8
 RAD M26 .... 53 L5
 WGNE/HIN WN2 * 49 G7
Back Market St West BURY BL9 ..... 4 E4
Back Markland Hill La BOL BL1 .... 35 J3
Back Markland Hill La East
 BOL BL1 .... 35 J3
Back Markland Hill La West
 BOL BL1 .... 35 J3
Back Marlborough St BOL BL1 ...... 2 A3
Back Marsh Fold La BOL BL1 * 35 M4
Back Mary St BOLS/LL BL3 * 2 B8
Back Mason St BURY BL9 .... 5 H5
Back Massie St
 CHD/CHDH SK8 .... 111 G6
Back Mawdsley St BOL BL1 .... 2 E5
Back Maxwell St BOL BL1 .... 22 B8
Back Maybank St BOLS/LL BL3 ...... 2 B9
Back Mayfield Av BOLS/LL BL3 ..... 52 E1
Back Mayor St BOL BL1 .... 2 A6
 TOT/BURYW BL8 .... 4 A2
Back Maze St BOLS/LL BL3 .... 3 M9
Back McDonna St BOL BL1 .... 35 M1
Back McKean St BOLS/LL BL3 .... 36 D8
Back McKean St North
 BOLS/LL BL3 .... 36 D8
Back Melbourne Rd
 BOLS/LL BL3 .... 35 M7
Back Melbourne St STLY SK15 ...... 91 K2
Back Mellor Gv BOL BL1 * 35 L3
Back Mellor Gv West BOL BL1 * 35 L3
Back Mellor Rd NM/HAY SK22 ..... 124 E3
Back Melrose Av BOL BL1 .... 35 L3
Back Melville St BOLS/LL BL3 ..... 52 D1
Back Mercia St BOLS/LL BL3 .... 35 M7
Back Mere Gdns BOL BL1 * 2 D3
Back Meredith St BOLS/LL BL3 ..... 52 C1
Back Merlin Gv BOL BL1 * 35 L3
Back Merton St
 TOT/BURYW BL8 .... 4 B2
Back Mesnes St WGN WN1 .... 15 G2
Back Methwold St
 BOLS/LL BL3 .... 35 M8
Back Milford Rd BOLS/LL BL3 ...... 52 B8
Back Miller St BOL BL1 .... 22 B8
Back Millet St BURY BL9 .... 4 C5
Back Mill St North
 EDGW/EG BL7 * 22 C4
Back Mill St South
 EDGW/EG BL7 * 22 C4
Back Milner Av BURY BL9 .... 25 J7
Back Minorca St BOLS/LL BL3 ...... 36 B8
Back Monmouth Av BURY BL9 ...... 25 J7
Back Moor HYDE SK14 .... 92 D8
Back Moorfield Gv BOLE BL2 .... 36 E3
Back Moorgate West BURY BL9 ..... 5 H3
Back Mornington Rd East
 BOL BL1 .... 35 M4
Back Morris Green La
 BOLS/LL BL3 .... 51 M2
Back Morris Green La East
 BOLS/LL BL3 .... 51 M2
Back Moss Ter BOL BL1 .... 2 E3
Back Mostyn Av BURY BL9 .... 25 J7
Back Mowbray St BOL BL1 .... 35 L3
Back Murton Ter BOL BL1 .... 22 C8
Back Musgrave Rd BOL BL1 .... 35 M4
Back Musgrave Rd North
 BOL BL1 .... 35 M4
Back Myrtle St BURY BL9 .... 5 K4
Back Myrtle St South BURY BL9 .... 5 K5
Back Nebo St BOLS/LL BL3 .... 36 A8
Back Nelson St HOR/BR BL6 .... 34 A1
Back Nelson St North BURY BL9 .... 4 F8
Back Nelson St South BURY BL9 .... 4 F9
Back Nevada St BOL BL1 .... 36 B3
Back Newbold St
 TOT/BURYW BL8 .... 38 F2
Back New George St
 TOT/BURYW BL8 .... 4 A3
Back Newhall La BOL BL1 .... 35 K3
Back Newport St
 BOLS/LL BL3 * 36 D8
Back Newport St South
 BOLS/LL BL3 .... 2 E6
Back Newton St BOL BL1 .... 36 B2
Back Nixon Rd BOLS/LL BL3 .... 51 M1
Back Normanby St
 BOLS/LL BL3 .... 51 M2
Back Norris St BOLS/LL BL3 .... 53 K1
Back Northern Gv BOL BL1 .... 35 M3
Back Nunnery Rd
 BOLS/LL BL3 .... 35 L8
Back Nut St BOL BL1 .... 36 A2
Back Oak St RAD M26 .... 54 F3
Back Olaf St BOLE BL2 .... 3 J1
Back Oldham St MILN OL16 .... 11 G6
Back Olga St BOL BL1 .... 36 A2
Back Olga St North BOL BL1 .... 36 A2
Back Olive Bank
 TOT/BURYW BL8 .... 24 E8
Back Oram St BURY BL9 .... 25 K8
Back Oriel St BOLS/LL BL3 .... 35 M7
Back Ormrod St BURY BL9 .... 5 G5
Back Osborne Gv BOL BL1 .... 35 M3
Back o' th' Low Rd OLDE OL4 ..... 60 C4
Back Owen's Rw HOR/BR BL6 .... 35 M3
Back Oxford Gv North BOL BL1 .... 35 M3
Back Oxford St BOL BL1 .... 5 H6
Back Packer St BOL BL1 .... 35 M2
Back Palace St BOLE BL2 .... 2 E3
Back Parkdale Rd BOLE BL2 .... 3 L1
Back Parkfield Rd BOLS/LL BL3 .... 52 D1
Back Parkhills Rd North
 BURY BL9 .... 4 E8
Back Parkhills Rd South
 BURY BL9 .... 4 F9
Back Parkinson St
 BOLS/LL BL3 * 35 M7
Back Park Rd BOL BL1 .... 2 A3
Back Park Vw BOL BL1 .... 22 C6
Back Park View Rd
 BOLS/LL BL3 .... 35 M8
Back Parsonage St BURY BL9 .... 5 J3
Backparsons La BURY BL9 .... 4 F4
Back Partington St
 BOLS/LL BL3 .... 51 M2
Back Patience St WHIT OL12 * 27 M3
Back Patterson St
 BOLS/LL BL3 * 35 K8
Back Peabody St BOLS/LL BL3 ...... 36 B8
Back Peace St BOLS/LL BL3 * 2 A9
Back Pedder St BOL BL1 .... 35 M4
Back Penarth Rd BOLS/LL BL3 ...... 35 L8
Back Pennington Rd
 BOLS/LL BL3 .... 52 C1
Back Percy St BURY BL9 .... 5 K2

Back Peter St BURY BL9 .....5 H3
Back Peveril St BOLS/LL BL3 .....51 L1
Back Phoenix St BOL BL1 .....4 D5
Back Piccadilly CMANE M1 .....7 J5
Back Pikes La West
   BOLS/LL BL3 .....35 M7
Back Pine St BOL BL1 .....36 C2
   BURY BL9 .....5 K4
Back Pleasant St BOL BL1 .....5 K2
Back Pool Fold CMANW M2 * 6 F4
Back Poplar Av BOL BL1 .....22 C8
Back Porter St BURY BL9 .....25 J8
Back Portland St AUL OL6 .....90 D2
Back Portugal St BOL BL2 .....3 J5
Back Primrose St BOL BL1 .....22 C8
Back Primula St BOL BL1 .....22 C8
Back Proctor St
   TOT/BURYW BL8 * 38 F3
Back Progress St BOL BL1 * 36 F5
Back Quay St CSLFD M3 .....6 C5
Back Quebec St BOLS/LL BL3 .....2 A9
Back Queengate BOL BL1 .....35 M4
Back Queen St BOL BL1 .....2 D5
Back Radcliffe Rd East
   BOLE BL2 * 3 J4
Back Raimond St BOL BL1 .....35 M1
Back Rainshaw St BOL BL1 .....22 C8
Back Rake St BURY BL9 .....25 J8
Back Randal St BOLS/LL BL3 .....35 M8
Back Range St BOLS/LL BL3 * 36 A8
Back Raphael St BOL BL1 .....36 A3
Back Raven St BURY BL9 .....5 G1
Back Rawson Rd BOL BL1 .....35 M3
Back Rawson Rd North
   .....35 M3
Back Raymond St BURY BL9 .....25 J7
Back Red Bank ANC M4 .....87 K1
Back Redhill Gv BOL BL1 * 2 C2
Back Regent St BURY BL9 .....4 F1
Back Ribblesdale Rd
   BOLS/LL BL3 .....36 A8
Back Richard Burch St
   BURY BL9 .....5 G2
Back Richelieu St BOLS/LL BL3 .....36 D8
Back Rigby La North
   BOLE BL2 * 22 F6
Back Rigby La South BOLE BL2 .....22 F6
Back Rishton La BOLS/LL BL3 .....52 C1
Back Rishton La East
   BOLS/LL BL3 .....52 C1
Back Rochdale Old Rd North
   BURY 5 M2
Back Rochdale Old Rd South
   BURY 5 M2
Back Rochdale Old South Rd
   BURY 39 M1
Back Rochdale Rd BURY BL9 .....5 H4
Back Rochdale Rd South
   BURY 5 H5
Back Rock Av BOL BL1 .....35 M1
Back Roland Rd BOLS/LL BL3 * 35 M7
Back Romer St BOLE BL2 .....3 M4
Back Rosamond St
   BOLS/LL BL3 .....35 M8
Back Roscow Av BOLE BL2 .....37 H4
Back Roseberry St BOLS/LL BL3 .....35 M8
Back Rossini St BOL BL1 * 36 A1
Back Rowena St BOLS/LL BL3 * 52 F2
Back Rowland St BOLS/LL BL3 * 51 L1
Back Roxalina St BOL BL1 .....36 B8
Back Royal Av BURY BL9 .....25 J7
Back Royds St MILN OL16 .....11 H9
Back Rudolph St BOLS/LL BL3 .....52 C1
Back Rumworth St
   BOLS/LL BL3 .....36 A8
Back Rushton Rd BOL BL1 * 35 L3
Back Russell Cl BOL BL1 * 35 M4
Back Russell St BOL BL1 .....35 M4
Back Rutland Gv BOL BL1 * 35 M3
Back Ryefield St BOL BL1 * 3 G1
Back St Anne's St BURY BL9 .....25 J8
Back St Ann St BOL BL1 .....36 B3
Back St Augustine St BOL BL1 .....36 A2
Back St George's Rd ANC M4 * 7 J1
   BOL BL1 .....2 D3
Back St George's Rd North
   .....2 B3
Back St Helens Rd
   BOLS/LL BL3 .....36 A8
Back St Helens Rd South
   BOLS/LL BL3 .....51 L2
Back St James's St OLD OL1 * 59 L5
Back St Mark's La CHH M8 * 72 C4
Back St Mary's Pl BURY BL9 .....4 D5
Back St Philip's Av BOLS/LL BL3 * 36 A8
Back St Thomas St East
   BOL BL1 * 36 A2
Back Salford LEIGH WN7 * 66 C7
Back Salford St BURY BL9 .....25 K8
Back Salisbury St BOLS/LL BL3 .....2 B6
Back Salisbury Ter BOLE BL2 .....37 C5
Back Sandon St West
   BOLS/LL BL3 .....36 A8
Back Sandy Bank Rd
   EDGW/EG BL7 .....17 G7
Back Sankey St BURY BL9 .....4 C4
Back Sapling Rd BOLS/LL BL3 * 51 L2
Back Sapling Rd South
   BOLS/LL BL3 .....51 L2
Back Scholes St TOT/BURYW BL8..4 A3
Back Scott St OLDS OL8 * 9 H9
Back Scowcroft St BOLE BL2 .....3 J1
Back Settle St BOLS/LL BL3 .....52 A1
Back Settle St North
   BOLS/LL BL3 .....52 B1
Back Seymour Rd BOL BL1 .....36 C1
Back Shakerley Rd TYLD M29 * 67 J3
Back Sharman St BOLS/LL BL3 .....3 J9
Back Shaw-street BURY BL9 .....5 K3
Back Shepherd St BURY BL9 .....5 G5
Back Sherwood St BOL BL1 .....36 C1
Back Shipton St BOL BL1 .....35 L3
Back Short St ATH M46 .....67 H3
Back Silverdale Rd BOLS/LL BL3 .....35 M5
Back Silver St BURY BL9 .....4 E5
Back Skipton St BOLE BL2 .....3 L3
Back Smethurst La
   BOLS/LL BL3 .....51 L2
Back Smethurst La West
   BOLS/LL BL3 .....51 L2
Back Sofa St BOL BL1 .....35 L3
Back Soho St BOL BL1 .....2 E6
Back Somerset Rd BOL BL1 .....35 L5
Back Somerville St BOL BL1 .....35 M1
Back South Cross St East
   BURY BL9 .....5 G5
Back South Pde CSLFD M3 .....6 E4
Back South St BOLS/LL BL3 .....52 B1
Back South View St BOLE BL2 .....3 M5
Back Spa Rd BOL BL1 .....2 A6
Back Spa Rd North BOL BL1 .....2 A6

Back Spa Rd West BOL BL1 * 2 A6
Back Spear St ANC M4 * 7 J3
Back Springfield St
   BOLS/LL BL3 .....36 E8
Back Spring Gdns BOL BL1 .....2 E6
   MDTN M24 .....57 K2
Back Spring St East BURY BL9 .....5 G6
Back Spring St West BURY BL9 .....5 G6
Back Square St RAMS BL0 .....18 F6
Back Stainsbury St
   BOLS/LL BL3 .....35 M8
Back Stanley St RAMS BL0 .....18 E7
Back Stephen St
   TOT/BURYW BL8 .....38 F2
Back Stewart St BOL BL1 .....36 B3
Backstone St BOLE BL2 .....3 J1
Back Sunlight Rd BOL BL1 .....35 M5
Back Sunning Hill St
   BOLS/LL BL3 * 36 A8
Back Sunnyside Rd BOL BL1 .....35 M2
Back Swan La BOLS/LL BL3 .....36 A8
Back Tavistock Rd ROCH OL11 .....2 A6
Back Teak St BURY BL9 .....5 K4
Back Tenterden St BURY BL9.....4 D5
Back Thicketford Rd
   BOLE BL2 * 36 F3
Back Thicketford Rd West
   BOLE BL2 .....36 E3
Back Thomasson Cl BOL BL1 .....36 B3
Back Thomas St ANC M4 * 7 H3
Back Thorns Rd BOL BL1 .....36 B1
Back Thorn St BOL BL1 .....36 C2
Back Thorpe St BOL BL1 .....36 A2
Back Thurnham St
   BOLS/LL BL3 * 51 M1
Back Tinline St BURY BL9 .....5 J5
Back Tonge Moor Rd
   BOLE BL2 .....36 E2
Back Tonge Moor Rd East
   BOLE BL2 .....3 J1
Back Tonge Old Rd BOLE BL2.....3 M4
Back Tong Rd BOLS/LL BL3 .....37 K8
Back Tottington Rd
   TOT/BURYW BL8 * 24 E8
Back Tottington Rd East
   BOLE BL2 .....23 H7
Back Tottington Rd North
   TOT/BURYW BL8 .....4 A2
Back Tottington Rd South
   TOT/BURYW BL8 .....4 A2
Back Tudor St BOLS/LL BL3 * 35 M8
Back Turner St ANC M4 .....7 H3
Back Turton Rd East BOLE BL2 .....22 F7
Back Turton Rd West BOLE BL2 .....22 F8
Back Uganda St BOLS/LL BL3 .....51 M1
Back Ulleswater St BOL BL1 .....36 C2
Back Union Rd BOLE BL2 .....3 H1
   NM/HAY SK22 .....124 E5
Back Unsworth St South
   BOLS/LL BL3 .....2 B9
Back Uttley St BOL BL1 .....36 B3
Back Venice St BOLS/LL BL3 .....35 M8
Back Vernon St BOL BL1 .....2 C3
   BURY BL9 .....4 F1
Back Vernon St South BOL BL1 * 2 C3
Back Vickerman St BOL BL1 .....36 A2
Back Victoria Gv BOL BL1 .....35 M3
Back Victoria Gv North
   BOL BL1 .....35 M3
Back Victory St East BOL BL1 .....35 M4
Back View St BOLS/LL BL3 .....2 A9
Back Vincent St BOL BL1 .....35 M4
Back Vine St BOLS/LL BL3 .....35 M6
Back Viola St BOL BL1 .....36 B1
Back Waldeck St BOL BL1 .....35 M5
Back Walmersley Rd East
   BURY 5 G2
Back Walmersley Rd West
   BURY BL9 .....5 G1
Back Walnut St BOL BL1 .....36 C1
Back Walshaw Rd North
   TOT/BURYW BL8 .....4 A2
Back Walshaw Rd South
   TOT/BURYW BL8 .....38 F1
Back Wapping St BOL BL1 * 36 A2
Back Wardle St BOLE BL2 .....3 K8
Back Wash La BURY BL9 .....5 J4
Back Wash La South BURY BL9 .....5 J4
Back Water St EDGW/EG BL7 .....22 A2
   STKP SK1 * 13 K2
Back Waverley Rd BOL BL1 .....36 B1
Back Webster St BOLS/LL BL3 .....36 E8
Back Wellington Rd South
   BURY BL9 .....4 E8
Back Wells St BURY BL9 .....5 G6
Back Westbank St BOL BL1 .....2 B3
Back Westbourne Av
   BOLS/LL BL3 .....52 D1
Back Weston St North
   BOLS/LL BL3 .....36 D8
Back Weston St South
   BOLS/LL BL3 .....36 C8
Back Westwood Rd BOL BL1 * 35 M4
Back Wheatfield St BOLE BL2 .....3 L8
Back Whittle Gv BOL BL1 * 35 L3
Back Whittle St
   TOT/BURYW BL8 .....4 A2
Back Wigan Rd BOLS/LL BL3 .....35 L1
Back Wigan Rd North
   BOLS/LL BL3 .....35 K8
Back Wigan Rd South
   BOLS/LL BL3 .....35 L7
Back Willows BOLS/LL BL3 .....35 L8
Back Willows La BOLS/LL BL3 .....36 A8
Back Willows La North
   BOLS/LL BL3 .....35 L8
Back Willows La South
   BOLS/LL BL3 .....35 M8
Back Wilmot St BOL BL1 .....35 M1
Back Wilton St BOL BL1 .....36 C1
Back Windermere St BOL BL1 .....35 M3
Back Windsor Gv BOL BL1 * 35 M3
Back Wolfenden St BOL BL1 * 36 B2
Back Woodbine Rd
   BOLS/LL BL3 .....51 M1
Back Woodfield St
   BOLS/LL BL3 .....52 D1
Back Woodgate St
   BOLS/LL BL3 .....52 D1
Back Wood St HOR/BR BL6 .....33 M1
   TOT/BURYW BL8 .....4 A3
Back Worcester St BOL BL1 .....36 B3
Back Wordsworth St BOL BL1 * 36 A1
Back Worsel St BOLS/LL BL3 .....35 M8
Back Worsel St North
   .....35 M8
Back Wynne St BOL BL1 .....36 B2
Back Yates St BOLE BL2 .....3 H1
Baclaw Cl WGN WN1 .....48 C3
Bacon Av DTN/ASHW M34 .....101 K5
Bacup Rd NEWH/MOS M40 .....73 K4
Badbury Cl RNFD/HAY WA11 .....78 A5
Badby Cl ANC M4 .....88 A3

Baddeley Cl EDGY/DAV SK3 .....112 A7
Badder St BOL BL1 .....2 E5
Bader Dr HEY OL10 .....41 G5
Badger Cl HYDE SK14 .....91 H8
   UPML OL3 .....42 F1
   MPL/ROM SK6. .....123 H1
Badger Edge La OLDE OL4 .....60 F1
   UPML OL3 .....44 F8
Badger La MILN OL16 .....42 F1
Badger Rd ALT WA14 .....107 M4
Badger St BURY BL9 .....5 G2
Badgers Wk
   WYTH/NTH M22 .....119 G3
Badgers Wy GLSP SK13 .....104 E5
Bag La ATH M46 .....50 E8
Bagnall Cl UPML OL3 .....61 M3
   WHIT OL12 .....27 J2
Bagot St OP/CLY M11 .....88 F2
   SWIN M27 .....69 M3
Bagshaw La WGNW/BIL/OR WN2 .....49 H2
Bagshaw St HYDE SK14. .....91 H8
Bagslate Moor La ROCH OL11 .....27 J5
Bagslate Moor Rd ROCH OL11 .....27 J5
Bagstock Av POY/DIS SK12 .....129 J2
Baguley Crs EDGY/DAV SK3 .....112 A6
   MDTN M24 .....56 D6
Baguley Dr BURY BL9 .....55 K2
Baguley La SALE M33 .....109 H2
Baguley Rd SALE M33 .....97 H8
Baguley St DROY M43 .....89 L3
Bahama Cl RNFD/HAY WA11 .....78 A4
Bahama Rd RNFD/HAY WA11 .....78 A4
Baildon Rd ROCH OL11 .....27 L3
Baildon St NEWH/MOS M40 .....73 K3
Bailey Fold WHTN M45 .....50 E4
Bailey La BOLE BL2 .....37 H3
   MANAIR M90 .....118 D3
   PART M31 .....94 C8
Bailey Rd TRPK M17 .....85 K5
Bailey St OLD OL1 * 9 L5
   OP/CLY M11 .....89 G3
   PWCH M25 .....55 M7
Bailey Wk ALT WA14 .....116 E4
Baillie St MILN OL16 .....10 F3
   RAD M26 .....39 H7
Baillie St East MILN OL16 .....11 G3
The Bails BRO M7 .....71 M6
Bainbridge Av
   GOL/RIS/CUL WA3 .....80 C4
Bainbridge Cl
   WGTN/LGST M12 * 88 A6
Bainburgh Clough OLDS OL8 .....59 M8
Baines Av IRL M44 .....94 C3
Baines St BOL BL1 .....35 L4
Bain St SWIN M27 .....70 C5
Baird St CMANE M1 .....7 K6
Baitings Cl WHIT OL12 .....26 F2
Bakehurst Cl NM/HAY SK22 .....124 E5
Baker St FWTH BL4 .....53 L6
   HEY OL10 .....41 H4
   HTNM SK4 .....13 G1
   MDTN M24 .....57 L4
   RAMS BL0 .....18 E7
   STLY SK15 .....91 L3
   WGNS/IIMK WN3 .....14 D8
Bakewell Av AUL OL6 .....76 C6
   DTN/ASHW M34 .....101 K4
Bakewell Dr
   WGNNW/ST WN6 .....31 K8
Bakewell Ms GLSP SK13 .....104 A3
Bakewell St BRAM/HZG SK7 .....122 A4
   DROY M43 .....89 H2
   ECC M30. .....84 E4
   STRET M32 .....96 D1
Bakewell St EDGY/DAV SK3 .....12 F7
   GTN M18 .....88 F8
Bala Cl ORD M5 .....86 B5
Balcarres Rd WGN WN1 .....48 B2
Balcarres Rd WGNE/HIN WN2 .....32 E8
Balcary Gv BOL BL1 .....35 L4
Balcombe Cl TOT/BURYW BL8 .....24 E5
Balderstone Rd ROCH OL11 .....42 D7
Baldock Rd DID/WITH M20 .....111 G1
Baldoine Dr WGNE/HIN WN2 .....49 L7
Baldwin Rd BNG/LEV M19 .....99 J6
Baldwin St BOLS/LL BL3 .....2 C8
   WGN WN1 .....15 J3
   WGNE/HIN WN2 .....65 L1
   WGNS/IIMK WN3 .....15 J7
   WGNW/BIL/OR WN5 .....46 E7
Bale St CMANW M2 .....6 F6
Balfern Cl WHTN BL5 .....50 B3
Balfern Fold WHTN BL5 .....50 B3
Balfour Gv RDSH SK5 .....100 C4
Balfour Rd ALT WA14 .....108 A5
   URM M41 .....95 L2
   WHIT OL12 .....27 M3
Balfour St BOLS/LL BL3 .....2 A7
   CHH M8 .....72 D4
   OLDE OL4 .....59 M5
   ROY/SHW OL2 .....43 L4
   SLFD M6 .....71 J6
Balham Wk WGTN/LGST M12 .....7 J8
Balharry Av RNFD/HAY WA11 .....78 C5
Balinge WHIT OL12 .....10 D2
Ballantine Wy NEWH/MOS M40 .....73 M8
Ballantyne Wy
   GOL/RIS/CUL WA3 .....80 B4
Ballard Cl LIT OL15 .....21 M5
Ballard Wy ROY/SHW OL2 .....45 M3
Ballater Av URM M41 .....95 K3
Ballbrook Av DID/WITH M20 .....98 D7
Balleratt St BNG/LEV M19 .....99 K3
Ball Gn STRET M32 .....96 C1
Balliol Cl MPL/ROM SK6 .....101 M8
Balliol St CHH M8 .....72 D4
   SWIN M27 .....70 B4
Balliol Wy AIMK WN4 .....63 J8
Balloon St ANC M4 .....7 G3
Ball St MILN OL16 .....11 G3
   WGNNW/ST WN6 .....47 H2
Ball Wk HYDE SK14 .....103 J3
Balmain Av GTN M18 .....99 M1
Balmain Rd URM M41 .....95 L1
Balmer Rd NTHM/RTH M23 .....109 K7
Balmfield St CHH M8 .....72 D7
Balmoral Av BOLS/LL BL3 .....53 K1

Balmoral Dr ALT WA14 .....108 C4
   DTN/ASHW M34 .....89 K8
   HEY OL10 .....40 D3
   LEIGH WN7 .....67 G6
   MPL/ROM SK6. .....123 G5
   POY/DIS SK12 .....129 H1
   STLY SK15 .....91 K1
   WGNE/HIN WN2 .....48 F8
Balmoral Gra PWCH M25 .....72 B1
Balmoral Gv
   BRAM/HZG SK7 .....122 B1
Balmoral Rd AIMK WN4 .....63 G8
   FWTH BL4 .....52 F5
   HALE/TIMP WA15 .....108 B8
   HTNM SK4 .....111 K1
   RUSH/FAL M14 .....99 C4
   SWIN M27 .....70 D2
   URM M41 .....95 M5
   WGNW/BIL/OR WN5 .....47 H6
Balmoral St GTN M18 .....88 F8
Balmore Cl BOLS/LL BL3 .....51 K1
Balm St RAMS BL0 .....18 D8
Balsam Cl BRUN/LGST M13 .....7 K9
Balshaw Av IRL M44 .....94 C2
Balshaw Cl BOLS/LL BL3 .....35 M7
Balshaw St IRL M44 .....94 D2
Baltic Rd ALT WA14 .....107 K6
Baltic St ORD M5 .....86 B2
Baltimore St
   NEWH/MOS M40 .....73 J7
   GLSP SK13 .....93 J7
   GLSP SK13 .....105 G4
Bamber Av SALE M33 .....109 J7
Bamber Cft WHTN BL5 .....50 B1
Bamber St BKLY M9 .....57 G7
Bamber Wk BOLS/LL BL3 * 35 M7
Bamburgh Cl RAD M26 .....37 M7
Bamburgh Dr AULW OL7 .....75 H7
Bamburgh Pl AIMK WN4 .....63 K7
Bamford Av DTN/ASHW M34 .....101 J4
   MDTN M24 .....57 K2
Bamford Cl BURY BL9 .....26 B8
   CHD/CHDH SK8 .....119 M4
Bamford Ct ROCH OL11 .....27 L6
Bamford Dr ROCH OL11 .....27 L6
Bamford Gdns
   HALE/TIMP WA15 .....109 G7
Bamford Gn GLSP SK13 .....104 B3
Bamford Ms GLSP SK13 .....104 B3
Bamford Prec ROCH OL11 * 27 H5
   ROCH OL11 .....27 H5
   HEY OL10 .....26 F8
   RAMS BL0 .....19 H4
   RAMS BL0 .....19 L6
Bamford St CHAD OL9 .....8 C2
   LIT OL15 .....21 K7
   OP/CLY M11 .....88 D2
   ROY/SHW OL2 .....43 H8
   STKP SK1 .....13 J6
Bamford Wy ROCH OL11 .....27 J6
Bampton Av OFTN SK2 .....112 E5
   WHTN BL5 .....50 B3
Bampton Rd WYTH/NTH M22 .....118 D3
Banbury Cl OFTN SK2 .....112 E5
Banbury Dr ALT WA14 .....108 B4
Banbury Ms SWIN M27 .....70 A3
Banbury Rd FAIL M35 .....74 B8
   MDTN M24 .....57 J7
   NTHM/RTH M23 .....109 J7
   WGNW/BIL/OR WN5 .....62 K2
Bancroft Av CHD/CHDH SK8 .....120 C5
Bancroft Cl MPL/ROM SK6 .....113 H1
Bancroft Fold HYDE SK14 .....91 L7
Bancroft Rd HALE/TIMP WA15 .....117 J1
   SWIN M27 .....70 B3
Banff Gv HEY OL10 .....40 D1
Banff Rd RUSH/FAL M14 .....87 M8
Bangor Fold LEIGH WN7 .....66 F8
Bangor Rd CHD/CHDH SK8 .....111 K6
Bangor St AUL OL6 .....91 H2
   BOL BL1 .....2 D2
   HULME M15 .....87 G7
   MILN OL16 .....11 K5
   RDSH SK5 .....100 C8
Banham Av WGNS/IIMK WN3 .....62 F1
Bank Av WGNW/BIL/OR WN5 .....46 A7
Bank Barn La WHIT OL12 .....21 H6
Bankbottom GLSP SK13 .....93 K7
Bank Bridge Rd OP/CLY M11 .....88 D1
Bankbrook WGNNW/ST WN6 .....31 K8
Bank Buildings
   WGNE/HIN WN2 * 64 D2
Bank Cl LIT OL15 .....29 K1
Banker St BOLS/LL BL3 .....3 M9
Bankes Av WGNW/BIL/OR WN5 .....46 D6
Bankfield HYDE SK14 .....91 G7
Bank Fld WHTN BL5 .....50 D5
Bankfield Av BRUN/LGST M13 .....99 H1
   DROY M43 .....89 K2
   HTNM SK4 .....12 D3
   IRL M44 .....94 A7
Bankfield Cl BOLE BL2 .....37 M3
Bankfield Dr OLDS OL8 .....75 L2
   WALK M28 .....68 D6
Bankfield La ROCH OL11 .....27 M3
Bankfield Rd CHD/CHDH SK8 .....120 B3
   FWTH BL4 .....52 C6
   MPL/ROM SK6. .....101 K7
   SALE M33 .....96 B6
   TYLD M29 .....68 B4
Bankfield St BKLY M9 .....73 C2
   BOLS/LL BL3 .....35 M8
   HTNM SK4 .....112 B1
Bank Field St RAD M26 .....54 E1
Bank Hall TOT/BURYW BL8 .....38 D2
Bankhall La HALE/TIMP WA15 .....117 G4
Bankhall Rd HTNM SK4 .....111 K2
Bank Hey WHTN BL5 * 50 C4
Bank Hill St OLDE OL4 .....59 L5
Bankhirst Cl CHH M8 .....72 D3
Bank House Cl TYLD M29 .....68 B3
Bank House Rd BKLY M9 .....72 F1
Bankhouse Rd
   TOT/BURYW BL8 .....24 F8
Banklands Cl IRL M44 .....94 A7
Bank La GLSP SK13 .....93 K5
   LHULT M38 .....51 C6
   SLFD M6 .....71 C6
   WHIT OL12 .....21 H5
Bankley St BNG/LEV M19 .....99 K3
Bank Mellor Rd NM/HAY SK22 .....124 E3
Bankmill Cl BRUN/LGST M13 .....7 K9
Bank Pas GOL/RIS/CUL WA3 * 79 K3
Bank Pl CSLFD M3 .....6 A3

Bank Rd CHH M8 .....72 D2
   MPL/ROM SK6. .....113 K1
   SKEL WN8 .....30 A7
   STLY SK15 .....77 H7
Banks Ct LEIGH WN7 .....66 A7
Banks Cft HEY OL10 .....41 G5
Bankside HALE/TIMP WA15 .....117 M8
   HYDE SK14 .....105 G5
Bank Side WHTN BL5 .....50 C4
Bankside Av AIMK WN4 .....63 K4
   RAD M26 .....39 G8
   UPML OL3 .....61 M5
Bankside Cl CHAD OL9 .....8 E5
   MPL/ROM SK6. .....114 C3
   UPML OL3 .....61 M4
   WILM/AE SK9 .....127 H3
Bankside Ct HTNM SK4 * 111 K1
Bankside Rd DID/WITH M20 .....110 E5
Banks La STKP SK1 .....112 E4
Bank Stanway Av BOLS/LL BL3 .....2 B7
Bank St BOL BL1 .....2 E4
   BRO M7 .....72 C4
   BURY BL9 .....4 D5
   CHD/CHDH SK8 .....111 H6
   CSLFD M3 .....6 A3
   DROY M43 .....89 H3
   DTN/ASHW M34 .....90 C6
   DTN/ASHW M34 .....101 L4
   EDGW/EG BL7 .....16 F8
   FWTH BL4 .....53 G4
   GLSP SK13 .....93 J7
   GOL/RIS/CUL WA3 .....79 K3
   HEY OL10 .....40 E2
   HYDE SK14 .....102 A1
   MPL/ROM SK6. .....101 L7
   NEWH/MOS M40 .....88 F1
   NM/HAY SK22 .....125 M2
   OLDE OL4 .....60 A6
   OP/CLY M11 .....88 D2
   RAD M26 .....54 E2
   RAMS BL0 .....19 H4
   ROCH OL11 .....28 D3
   ROY/SHW OL2 .....43 K5
   SALE M33 .....96 F7
   TOT/BURYW BL8 .....24 C8
   WGNE/HIN WN2 .....64 D1
   WGNW/BIL/OR WN5 .....47 H6
   WHTF M45 .....55 H3
Bankswood Cl GLSP SK13 .....93 K8
The Bank GLSP SK13 .....105 G4
Bank Top AUL OL6 .....90 F2
   HEY OL10 .....40 E1
Bank Top Gv BOL BL1 .....22 D7
Bank Top Pk OLDE OL4 .....60 A6
Bank Top St HEY OL10 .....40 E1
Bank Vale Rd NM/HAY SK22 .....125 L1
Bankwell St HULME M15 .....87 H7
Bank Wd BOL BL1 .....35 J5
Bankwood WGNNW/ST WN6 .....30 B6
Banky La SALE M33 .....95 M6
Bannach Dr CHAD OL9 .....58 D4
Bannatyne Cl NEWH/MOS M40 .....74 B3
Banner Dale Cl
   BRUN/LGST M13 .....88 C8
Bannerman Av PWCH M25 .....71 L1
Bannerman Rd DROY M43 .....89 L3
Banner St WGNE/HIN WN2 .....49 H7
   WGNS/IIMK WN3 .....15 K9
Banner Wk OP/CLY M11 * 88 C3
Bannister Dr CHD/CHDH SK8..120 B2
Bannister St BOLE BL2 .....37 H4
   OFTN SK2 .....13 K8
Bannister Wy WGNS/IIMK WN3 .....63 H2
Bann St EDGY/DAV SK3 .....13 G6
Banstead Av WYTH/NTH M22 .....110 A5
Bantry Av BKLY M9 .....72 F1
Bantry St BOLS/LL BL3 .....2 C9
Baptist St ANC M4 .....7 H3
Barathea Cl ROCH OL11 .....41 L1
Barbara Rd BOLS/LL BL3 .....51 K2
Barbeck Cl NEWH/MOS M40 .....88 B1
Barberry Cl ALT WA14 .....107 L5
Barberry Bank EDGW/EG BL7 .....22 A1
Barber Cl GLSP SK13 .....93 J7
   OP/CLY M11 * 89 H5
Barbican St DID/WITH M20 .....98 C1
Barbirolli Sq CMANW M2 .....6 D6
Barbon Wk ANC M4 .....7 L3
Barbrook Cl WGNNW/ST WN6 .....30 C2
Barbury Cl LEIGH WN7 .....66 C5
Barchester Av BOLE BL2 .....37 H3
Barcheston Rd
   CHD/CHDH SK8 .....110 F8
Barcicroft Rd
   CHD/CHDH SK8 .....110 F8
Barclay Rd POY/DIS SK12 .....129 J2
Barclays Av SLFD M6 .....71 G2
Barcliffe Av NEWH/MOS M40 .....73 M2
Barclyde St ROCH OL11 .....10 A4
Barcombe Cl OLDE OL4 .....60 A2
   STRET M52 .....96 C1
Barcroft Rd BOL BL1 .....35 L2
Barcroft St BURY BL9 .....4 F2
Bardale Gv AIMK WN4 .....78 D1
Bardell Cl POY/DIS SK12 * 129 H1
Bardney Av GOL/RIS/CUL WA3 .....79 J2
Bardon Cl BOL BL1 * 36 A3
Bardon Rd NTHM/RTH M23 .....109 J6
Bardsea Av WYTH/NTH M22 .....118 F3
Bardsley Av FAIL M35 .....74 C5
Bardsley Cl BOLE BL2 .....23 C7
   HYDE SK14 .....103 H2
Bardsley Gate Av STLY SK15 .....92 B6
Bardsley St CHAD OL9 .....74 C1
   HTNM SK4 .....112 A1
   MDTN M24 .....57 K3
   NEWH/MOS M40 .....74 A7
   OLDE OL4 .....60 B4
   OLDE OL4 .....60 B7
Bardsley Vale Av OLDS OL8 .....75 J4
Bardwell Av WHTN BL5 .....50 A4
Barehill St LIT OL15 .....21 L4
Bare St BOL BL1 .....3 H3
Barff Rd ORD M5 .....85 M2
Barfold Cl OFTN SK2 .....113 K7
Barford Dr GOL/RIS/CUL WA3 .....80 D4
   WILM/AE SK9 .....127 G3
Barford Gv HOR/BR BL6. .....34 C3
Bar Gap Rd OLD OL1 .....9 J3
Baring St CMANE M1 .....7 J7
Barkan Wy SWIN M27 .....70 C4
Barker Rd MPL/ROM SK6. .....113 J1
Barker's La SALE M33 .....96 C7
Barker St BURY BL9 .....4 D3
   CSLFD M3 .....6 C2
   HEY OL10 .....40 E3
   LEIGH WN7 .....65 M7
Barke St LIT OL15 .....29 J1
Barking St NEWH/MOS M40 .....88 B1

Bark St BOL BL1............................2 D4
  FWTH BL4...............................53 L7
Bark St East BOL BL1.....................2 E3
Barkway Rd STRET M32............96 D3
Barkwell La MOSL OL5...............76 E3
Bar La BOL BL1..............................22 B7
Barlborough Rd
  WGNW/BIL/OR WN5..............47 C7
Barlea Av NEWH/MOS M40.....120 C4
Barley Brook Meadow BOL BL1...22 C6
Barley Brook St
  WGNNW/ST WN6.....................14 D1
Barleycorn Cl SALE M33............109 K1
Barley Cft CHD/CHDH SK8.......120 B4
Barleycroft GLSP SK13................93 J8
Barley Croft Rd HYDE SK14.......91 H7
Barleycroft St
  OLDTF/WHR M16.....................87 J8
Barley Dr BRAM/HZG SK7........121 G5
Barleyfield Wk MDTN M24.........57 H3
Barley Hall St HEY OL10.............41 H1
Barlow Cl BURY BL9....................25 J7
Barlow Ct WALK M28....................69 H1
Barlow Crs MPL/ROM SK6.......114 C8
Barlow Fold BURY BL9.................39 J7
Barlow Fold Cl BURY BL9............39 H7
Barlow Fold Rd MPL/ROM SK6...114 A1
  RDSH SK5.................................100 C4
Barlow Hall Rd CCHDY M21......97 M7
Barlow La ECC M30.......................84 C7
Barlow La North RDSH SK5......100 C4
Barlow Moor Cl WHIT OL12........27 H2
Barlow Moor Ct DID/WITH M20...98 C8
Barlow Moor Rd CCHDY M21.....97 L5
  DID/WITH M20........................98 B8
Barlow Park Av BOL BL1............22 A7
Barlow Pl BRUN/LGST M13...........7 J9
Barlow Rd ALT WA14.................107 L4
  BNG/LEV M19.............................99 M3
  DUK SK16...................................91 C4
  ORD M5.......................................86 F3
  STRET M32...................................86 C8
  WILM/AE SK9...........................126 F3
Barlow's Cft CSLFD M3.................6 D3
Barlow's La South
  BRAM/HZG SK7........................121 L1
Barlow St BURY BL9........................5 G3
  ECC M30.....................................85 G3
  HEY OL10...................................41 H4
  HOR/BR BL6...............................33 M2
  MILN OL16...................................11 G4
  OLDE OL4......................................9 M7
  RAD M26.....................................54 F1
  WALK M28...................................53 G8
Barlow Wood Dr
  MPL/ROM SK6.........................123 K1
Barmeadow UPML OL3................61 J2
Barmhouse Cl HYDE SK14........102 E1
Barmhouse La HYDE SK14.......102 E1
Barmhouse Ms HYDE SK14......102 D1
Barmouth St OP/CLY M11..........88 C4
Barmouth Wk OLDS OL8.............74 E2
Barnaby Rd POY/DIS SK12.......129 H2
Barnabys Rd WHTN BL5..............50 A1
Barn Acre HOR/BR BL6................33 H3
Barnacre Rd BOLE BL2................37 J5
  NTHM/RTH M23.....................118 B1
Barnard Av HTNM SK4.................12 A2
  WHTF M45.................................55 L5
Barnard Cl AULW OL7..................75 J2
Barnard St BOLE BL2.....................3 J3
Barnbrook St BURY BL9.................5 H3
Barnby St WGN/LGST M12.........99 K1
  URM M41.....................................94 F2
Barnclose Rd WYTH/NTH M22...118 F3
Barn Ct BOLE BL2............................3 K7
Barncroft Dr HOR/BR BL6...........34 C1
Barncroft Gdns
  WYTH/NTH M22 *...................109 M7
Barncroft Rd FWTH BL4...............53 L4
Barnes Av HTNM SK4.................111 K2
Barnes Cl FWTH BL4....................53 C4
  RAMS BL0...................................24 D1
Barnes Dr FWTH BL4....................52 L3
Barnes St FWTH BL4.....................52 E3
Barnes Ter FWTH BL4...................53 K5
Barneswell St NEWH/MOS M40...73 M7
Barnet Rd BOL BL1.......................35 L2
Barnett Av DID/WITH M20...........98 E6
Barnett Dr CSLFD M3....................6 B2
Barnfield URM M41.......................95 L4
Barnfield Av MPL/ROM SK6.....114 A1
Barnfield Cl EDGW/EG BL7.........22 B2
  ORD M5.......................................86 C3
  RAD M26.....................................54 B1
  TYLD M29...................................67 J3
Barnfield Crs SALE M33..............96 C2
Barnfield Dr WALK M28...............68 E6
  WHTN BL5.................................50 D5
Barn Field La WHIT OL12............20 E5
Barnfield Ri ROY/SHW OL2.........43 K3
Barnfield Rd BNG/LEV M19........99 H8
  HYDE SK14.................................91 L7
  SWIN M27...................................70 A2
Barnfield Rd East
  EDGY/DAV SK3.......................112 C8
Barnfield Rd West
  EDGY/DAV SK3.......................112 A8
Barnfield St DTN/ASHW M34......90 A8
  HEY OL10...................................41 H2
  WHIT OL12................................28 C2
Barn Fold OLDE OL4....................60 B7
Barngate Rd MOSL OL5..............76 H4
Barngate Rd CHD/CHDH SK8...110 D6
Barngill Gv WGNS/IIMK WN3.....63 H1
Barn Gv DTN/ASHW M34............90 A5
Barnham Cl GOL/RIS/CUL WA3...79 K4
Barn Hl WHTN BL5........................50 E3
Barnhill Av PWCH M25.................71 L2
Barnhill Dr PWCH M25.................71 L2
Barnhill Rd PWCH M25................71 K1
Barnhill St RUSH/FAL M14...........87 J8
Barn Hill Ter WHTN BL5..............50 E3
Barn La GOL/RIS/CUL WA3.........79 J5
Barnley Cl IRL M44.......................94 E1
Barn Meadow EDGW/EG BL7......17 C7
Barnsdale Cl BOLE BL2................37 M3
Barnsdale Dr CHH M8..................72 D7
Barnsfold Av RUSH/FAL M14......98 F4
Barnsfold Rd MPL/ROM SK6.....123 H1
Barnside Av WALK M28................69 J4
Barnside Cl BURY BL9.................25 H4
Barnside Wy FAIL M35.................74 F5
Barns La ALT WA14....................106 D7
Barnsley St STKP SK1.................13 M6
  WGNNW/ST WN6....................47 K1
Barns Pl HALE/TIMP WA15.......117 L4
Barnstead Av DID/WITH M20......99 G7

Barnston Av RUSH/FAL M14.......98 E2
Barnston Cl BOL BL1....................22 C8
Barn St BOL BL1...............................2 D5
  OLDS OL8.....................................9 H6
  WHTF M45.................................55 J5
Barnton Cl GOL/RIS/CUL WA3...80 A5
Barnview Dr ALT WA14................94 D3
Barnwell Av GOL/RIS/CUL WA3...81 G8
Barnwell Cl DTN/ASHW M34.......90 D7
Barnwood Cl BOL BL1 *...............36 B3
Barnwood Dr BOL BL1.................36 B3
Barnwood Rd HTNM M23..........118 C1
Barnwood Ter BOL BL1................36 B3
Baroness Gv BRO M7....................71 M8
Baron Fold Crs LHULT M38.........52 C7
Baron Fold Gv LHULT M38..........52 C7
Baron Fold Rd LHULT M38 *........52 C7
Baron Gn CHD/CHDH SK8.........109 M5
Barons Ct FAIL M35......................74 A6
Baron St BURY BL9.........................4 C6
  MILN OL16...................................11 J5
Baron Wk BOLS/LL BL3...............53 M1
Barrack Hl MPL/ROM SK6.........113 K2
Barrack Hill Cl MPL/ROM SK6...113 K1
Barrack Sq WGN WN1 *..............15 C4
Barracks Rd WGNE/HIN WN2.....65 G3
Barrack St HULME M15..................6 A9
Barracks Yd WGN M41 *..............14 F4
Barra Dr URM M41........................85 C7
Barrass St OP/CLY M11................89 G5
Barratt Av MDTN M24...................57 G1
Barratt Ct BURY BL9......................5 K8
Barrfield Rd SLFD M6...................71 H8
Barr Hill Av SLFD M6....................71 H7
Barrhill Cl HULME M15................87 C6
Barrie St LEIGH WN7...................66 A4
Barrie Wy BOL BL1........................22 E8
Barrington Av CHD/CHDH SK8...120 A8
  DROY M43..................................89 J3
Barrington Cl ALT WA14............108 A6
  WGNS/IIMK WN3.....................63 C2
Barrington Rd ALT WA14..........108 A6
Barrington St OP/CLY M11..........88 F2
Barrisdale Cl BOLS/LL BL3..........35 J7
Barron Meadow LEIGH WN7......66 A5
Barrow Bridge Rd BOL BL1.........35 K1
Barrowcroft Cl WGN WN1............31 L3
Barrowdale Rd
  GOL/RIS/CUL WA3...................79 L4
Barrowfield Rd
  WYTH/NTH M22......................118 C2
Barrowfields MDTN M24..............57 K2
Barrow Hill Rd CHH M8................72 C7
Barrow La HALE/TIMP WA15.....117 K5
Barrow Meadow
  CHD/CHDH SK8.......................120 B4
Barrows Ct BOL BL1 *....................2 E6
Barrowshaw Cl WALK M28..........68 F2
Barrow St AIMK WN4...................64 A8
  ORD M5...6 A4
Barrs Fold Cl WHTN BL5..............50 A1
Barrs Fold Rd WHTN BL5.............50 A1
Barrule Av BRAM/HZG SK7.......122 A3
Barry Crs WALK M28....................68 D1
Barry Lawson Cl CHH M8 *..........72 C5
Barry Ri ALT WA14....................116 C2
Barry Rd NTHM/RTH M23..........109 L2
  RDSH SK5.................................100 C7
Barry St OLD OL1...........................59 L4
Barsham Dr BOLS/LL BL3..............2 B8
Bar St WGNE/HIN WN2................64 D3
Bar Ter WGNE/HIN WN2..............20 A5
Bartlam Pl OLD OL1........................9 M1
Bartlemore St OLD OL1.................9 M1
Bartlett Rd ROY/SHW OL2..........43 L6
Bartlett St OP/CLY M11................88 E5
Bartley Rd WYTH/NTH M22......109 M4
Barton Av URM M41.....................95 L2
Barton Cl WILM/AE SK9.............127 H2
Barton Clough
  WGNW/BIL/OR WN5...............62 B7
Barton Dock Rd STRET M32........85 K8
  URM M41.....................................85 H6
Barton Fold HYDE SK14............102 A3
Barton Hall Av ECC M30..............84 D3
Barton Highlevel Br TRPK M17...84 D5
Barton La ECC M30.......................85 C4
Barton Moss Rd ECC M30............83 M5
Barton Rd ECC M30......................84 F4
  FWTH BL4...................................52 E5
  HTNM SK4.................................111 H3
  HYDE SK14.................................90 F7
  MDTN M24.................................57 J4
  STRET M32..................................96 D1
  SWIN M27...................................70 D5
  URM M41.....................................84 F8
  WALK M28...................................69 J7
Barton St CHAD OL9........................8 E2
  CSLFD M3.....................................6 D7
  FWTH BL4...................................53 H5
  GOL/RIS/CUL WA3...................79 K4
  WGNE/HIN WN2........................64 E1
  WGNW/BIL/OR WN5...............64 E1
Barway Rd CCHDY M21...............97 J3
Barwell Cl GOL/RIS/CUL WA3....79 M3
Barwell Rd SALE M33..................96 B7
Barwell Sq FWTH BL4..................52 E2
Barwick Pl SALE M33...................96 D8
Basechurch Wk
  WGTN/LGST M12 *...................88 C6
Basford Rd OLDTF/WHR M16......97 L1
Bashall St BOL BL1.......................35 M4
Basil Ct MILN OL16.......................11 K6
Basildon Cl BRUN/LGST M13......88 A7
Basil St BOLS/LL BL3......................2 C8
  HTNM SK4....................................12 F1
  MILN OL16...................................11 K6
  RUSH/FAL M14 *.......................98 F1
Basle Cl BRAM/HZG SK7...........121 G1
Baslow Av BNG/LEV M19.............99 L2
  WGNE/HIN WN2........................65 J1
Baslow Dr BRAM/HZG SK7.......122 B4
  CHD/CHDH SK8.......................119 C4
Baslow Gv RDSH SK5.................100 C7
Baslow Ms GLSP SK13...............104 C5
Baslow Rd DROY M43...................89 J1
  DTN/ASHW M34......................101 J4
Baslow St OP/CLY M11.................88 B3
Bassenthwaite Cl MDTN M24......57 G1
Basset Av SLFD M6.......................71 M7
Bassett Gv WGNE/HIN WN3........62 E3
Bassett Wy WHIT OL12................28 B2
Bass La BURY BL9.........................25 H1
Bass St BOLE BL2............................3 L4
  DUK SK16...................................90 H6
Basswood Gn WGNE/HIN WN2...65 K1
Bastien Dr BRO M7.......................72 A6
Batchelor Cl CCHDY M21............98 B5

Bateman St HOR/BR BL6.............34 A2
Batemill Rd NM/HAY SK22........124 F2
Bates Cl ROCH OL11.....................42 A3
Bateson Dr OLDE OL4..................60 C6
Bateson St STKP SK1...................13 L3
Bateson Wy OLDS OL8 *................9 J8
Bates St BRUN/LGST M13...........88 C8
  DUK SK16...................................90 F4
Bath Cl BRAM/HZG SK7.............122 C2
Bath Crs CHD/CHDH SK8..........120 D6
  OLDTF/WHR M16.....................86 F7
Batheaston Gv LEIGH WN7.........28 A3
Bath St ALT WA14.......................116 F2
  ATH M46.....................................66 D1
  BOL BL1..2 E3
  CHAD OL9.....................................8 D8
  WGNE/HIN WN2........................48 C2
  WHIT OL12..................................11 H1
Batley St BKLY M9.........................73 H4
  MOSL OL5...................................76 E3
Batridge Rd EDGW/EG BL7.........16 D5
Batsmans Dr SWIN M27...............54 B8
Battenberg Rd BOL BL1...............35 M4
Battersbay Gv
  BRAM/HZG SK7......................122 A2
Battersby Ct OFTN SK2 *...........113 H6
Battersby St BURY BL9................26 A8
  LEIGH WN7.................................66 E8
  OP/CLY M11 *............................89 H1
  ROCH OL11.................................27 L6
  WGNE/HIN WN2........................48 E4
Battersea Rd HTNM SK4.............111 H3
Battery La WILM/AE SK9............126 B8
Batty St CHH M8...........................72 F7
Baucher Rd WGNS/IIMK WN3....47 H1
The Baum MILN OL16..................10 E3
Baverstock Cl WGNS/IIMK WN3...15 J1
Baxendale St BOL BL1..................22 B8
Baxter Gdns NTHM/RTH M23....109 K5
Baxter Rd SALE M33.....................96 E8
Baxter's Rw WGNE/HIN WN2......65 C3
Baxter St OLDS OL8.....................74 E2
  WGNNW/ST WN6.....................31 J8
Baycliffe St RAD M26 *................54 F1
Baycliff Cl WGNE/HIN WN2.........65 J1
Baycroft Gv NTHM/RTH M23....109 K3
Baydon Av BRO M7.......................72 C6
Bayfield Gv NEWH/MOS M40.....73 K3
Bayle Cl HYDE SK14.....................91 H7
Bayley Ct BOL BL1..........................2 A7
Bayley St STLY SK15....................91 H2
Baysdale Cl BOLS/LL BL3............35 J8
Bayston Wk WGTN/LGST M12...88 C6
Bay St CHAD OL9............................8 E5
  HEY OL10...................................40 E1
  WHIT OL12..................................11 H1
Bayswater Av NEWH/MOS M40...73 M8
Bayswater St BOLS/LL BL3..........51 M2
Baythorpe St BOL BL1..................36 C1
Baytree Av CHAD OL9..................58 B4
  DTN/ASHW M34......................90 D8
Baytree Dr MPL/ROM SK6.........101 J8
Baytree Gv RAMS BL0..................24 C2
Baytree La MDTN M24..................58 A4
Baytree Rd WGNNW/ST WN6......47 J2
Baytree Wk WHIT OL12................20 A3
Baywood St BKLY M9....................73 C4
Bazaar St SLFD M6........................71 K8
Bazley Rd WYTH/NTH M22........110 A3
Bazley St BOL BL1..........................35 J1
Beacomfold MPL/ROM SK6.......114 E1
Beacon Cl ATH M46.......................66 D2
Beacon Dr NTHM/RTH M23.......118 C2
Beacon Gv OLDS OL8 *.................59 M8
Beacon Hl
  WGNW/BIL/OR WN5 *............62 B5
Beacon Rd MPL/ROM SK6.........113 K4
  TRPK M17...................................85 H5
  WGNE/HIN WN2........................65 K4
  WGNNW/ST WN6.....................62 A5
  WGNW/BIL/OR WN5...............62 A6
Beaconsfield RUSH/FAL M14 *...98 F5
Beaconsfield Rd ALT WA14.......108 A5
Beaconsfield St BOLS/LL BL3.......2 A7
Beaconsfield Ter STLY SK15........77 J5
The Beacons WGNNW/ST WN6...30 A4
Beacon Vw MPL/ROM SK6.........114 C4
Beadham Dr BKLY M9...................56 F7
Beadle Av WHIT OL12..................21 H7
Beaford Dr WGNW/BIL/OR WN5...46 E7
Bealbank Cl MILN OL16...............43 K1
Beal Crs MILN OL16......................11 M1
Beal Cl HTNM SK4........................111 C1
Bealcroft Cl MILN OL16................29 K5
Beal Dr WGNE/HIN WN2.............64 D2
Beale Gv CCHDY M21...................97 L5
Bealey Av RAD M26......................39 H7
Bealey Cl GTN M18.......................88 C2
  RAD M26.....................................39 G8
Bealey Dr BURY BL9.....................39 G5
Beal La ROY/SHW OL2.................43 H6
Beaminster Rd HTNM SK4..........111 J1
Beaminster Wk
  BRUN/LGST M13 *...................87 M7
Beamish Cl BRUN/LGST M13......87 M6
Beamsley Dr WYTH/NTH M22...118 D2
Beanfields WALK M28...................69 J7
Bean Leach Av OFTN SK2..........113 J6
Bean Leach Dr OFTN SK2..........113 J6
Bean Leach Rd BRAM/HZG SK7...113 H6
Beard Crs NM/HAY SK22...........124 F4
Beard Rd GTN M18.......................88 F8
Beardsmore Dr
  GOL/RIS/CUL WA3...................80 B4
Beard St DROY M43.......................89 J3
  ROY/SHW OL2..........................59 H1
Beardwood Rd BKLY M9...............57 C8
Bearswood Cl HYDE SK14.........102 C3
Beathwaite Dr
  BRAM/HZG SK7......................120 D3
Beatrice Av CHD/CHDH SK8.....120 B2
  GTN M18.....................................89 J8
Beatrice St BOL BL1.....................35 M4
  WALK M28...................................69 L5
Beatrice St DTN/ASHW M34......101 H1
  FWTH BL4...................................52 E4
  ROCH OL11.................................10 A1
  SWIN M27...................................70 B3
Beatrice Wignall St
  DROY M43..................................89 K4
Beatrix Dr GLSP SK13................104 F3
Beatson Wk ANC M4.......................7 L4
Beattock St HULME M15 *.............6 D9
Beattock St HULME M15................6 D9
Beatty Dr WHTN BL5....................50 B3
Beauchamp St AUL OL6...............90 F1
Beaufont Dr OLDE OL4.................59 M7
Beaufort Av DID/WITH M20.........98 D7
  SALE M33.................................108 F2
  SWIN M27...................................70 A3
Beaufort Cha WILM/AE SK9......127 K3

Beaufort Cl HYDE SK14.............103 H3
  WILM/AE SK9...........................130 E2
Beaufort Ms HYDE SK14 *.........102 D1
  HYDE SK14...............................103 H1
  OFTN SK2.................................113 C8
  SALE M33.................................108 F1
Beaufort St CSLFD M3...................6 C7
  ECC M30.....................................84 E1
  PWCH M25.................................55 M8
  WGNE/HIN WN2 *....................49 G7
  WGNW/BIL/OR WN5...............47 H6
  WILM/AE SK9...........................130 D4
Beaufield St CHH M8....................72 C6
Beech Gv AULW OL7....................90 C3
  LEIGH WN7.................................81 H2
  LHULT M38................................52 B7
  RUSH/FAL M14.........................99 G4
  SALE M33...................................96 C3
  SLFD M6.....................................71 H8
  STLY SK15..................................76 F2
  TOT/BURYW BL8......................24 D3
  WGNE/HIN WN2........................47 H1
  WGNNW/ST WN6......................47 H1
  WILM/AE SK9...........................126 E6
Beech Grove Cl BURY BL9.........25 L8
Beech Hall St WGNNW/ST WN6...47 K2
Beech Hill Av WGNNW/ST WN6...47 H1
Beech Hill La WGNNW/ST WN6...47 H1
Beech Hill Rd OLDE OL4..............60 D4
Beech Holme Gv STKP SK1......112 F4
Beech Hurst Cl
  OLDTF/WHR M16 *...................98 A2
Beech La MPL/ROM SK6.............113 M2
  OLDE OL4...................................60 C4
  WILM/AE SK9...........................126 E6
Beech Ms CCHDY M21..................97 K4
  OFTN SK2.................................112 D7
Beech Mt AULW OL7.....................75 G4
  BKLY M9.....................................73 G4
Beechpark Av WYTH/NTH M22...109 M3
Beech Rd CCHDY M21..................97 L4
  CHD/CHDH SK8.......................120 D3
  EDGY/DAV SK3.......................112 B6
  GOL/RIS/CUL WA3...................79 K3
  HALE/TIMP WA15....................117 G1
  MPL/ROM SK6.........................123 H5
  SALE M33...................................97 C8
  SWIN M27...................................69 L8
Beech St AIMK WN4......................63 K6
  ATH M46.....................................67 H1
  BOL BL1..36 C2
  BURY BL9.....................................5 K4
  BURY BL9...................................24 F1
  ECC M30.....................................84 E3
  EDGW/EG BL7...........................17 C7
  FAIL M35....................................74 B4
  MDTN M24 *..............................57 J2
  MILN OL16...................................29 K8
  OLD OL1.......................................9 L5
  RAD M26.....................................54 F3
  ROCH OL11.................................27 L6
  SWIN M27...................................70 C5
Beech Tree Av
  WGNNW/ST WN6.....................30 A4
Beech Tree Houses
  WGNE/HIN WN2........................64 B6
Beechurst Rd CHD/CHDH SK8...110 F3
Beech Vw HYDE SK14.................102 D2
Beech Wk LEIGH WN7..................81 H2
  MDTN M24.................................57 J6
  STRET M32.................................96 F4
  WGNNW/ST WN6......................31 G4
  WGNS/IIMK WN3......................30 C7
Beechway MPL/ROM SK6...........123 H5
  WILM/AE SK9...........................126 D7
Beechwood ALT WA14................116 D3
  GLSP SK13...............................104 C5
  ROY/SHW OL2..........................44 A4
Beechwood Av AIMK WN4...........78 C2
  CCHDY M21...............................97 M5
  LIT OL15....................................29 K1
  MPL/ROM SK6.........................113 M2
  NEWH WA12..............................79 C8
  RAMS BL0...................................19 G5
  STLY SK15..................................76 F8
  URM M41.....................................95 H1
  WGNNW/ST WN6......................30 C7
Beechwood Ct
  TOT/BURYW BL8......................24 E7
Beechwood Crs TYLD M29..........67 K6
  WGNW/BIL/OR WN5...............46 B6
Beechwood Dr HYDE SK14........102 C3
  MOSL OL5...................................76 F2
  MPL/ROM SK6.........................114 D6
  ROY/SHW OL2..........................42 F6
  SALE M33...................................95 M8
  WALK M28...................................69 L6
  WILM/AE SK9 *.......................127 J4
Beechwood Gv
  CHD/CHDH SK8.......................120 C4
Beechwood La
  GOL/RIS/CUL WA3...................81 C8
Beechwood Rd OLDS OL8............75 J2
  PWCH M25.................................72 A1
Beechwood St BOLS/LL BL3........52 C1
Beede St OP/CLY M11...................88 E4
Beedon Av BOLS/LL BL3..............37 K8
Bee Fold La ATH M46....................66 C2
Beeford Dr WGNW/
  BIL/OR WN5...............................46 B7
Beehive Gn WHTN BL5.................50 E3
Beehive St OLDS OL8...................75 J1
Beeley St HYDE SK14.................102 B2
  SLFD M6.....................................71 L7
Beenham Cl SALE M33...............107 K4
Beeston Av BRO M7......................71 L6
  HALE/TIMP WA15....................108 C6
Beeston Gv EDGY/DAV SK3......112 B7
  LEIGH WN7.................................67 G5
  WHTF M45.................................55 K1
Beeston Rd SALE M33..................96 B8
  WILM/AE SK9...........................119 M7
Beeston St BKLY M9.....................73 H5
Beeth St OP/CLY M11...................89 H6
Beeton Gv BRUN/LGST M13.......88 B8
Beever St OLD OL1.........................9 M4
  OLDTF/WHR M16.....................86 F7
Begley Cl MPL/ROM SK6...........113 J3
Begonia Av FWTH BL4.................52 D3
Beilby Rd RNFD/HAY WA11.........78 E3
Belayse Cl BOL BL1......................35 L2
Belbeck St TOT/BURYW BL8.......38 F2
Belbeck St South
  TOT/BURYW BL8........................4 A5
Belcroft Cl WYTH/NTH M22.......110 B4
Belcroft Dr LHULT M38................52 B7
Belcroft Gv LHULT M38...............52 B7
Belding Av NEWH/MOS M40......74 C8
Beldon Rd BKLY M9......................56 F8
Belfairs Cl AULW OL7..................90 C3
Belfield Cl MILN OL16..................11 M2
Belfield Dr WHTN BL5..................49 M4
Belfield La MILN OL16..................11 M2
Belfield Mill La MILN OL16..........11 M2

Belfield Old Rd *MILN* OL16 ....11 L2
Belfield Rd *DID/WITH* M20 ......110 E1
  MILN OL16 ....11 K2
  PWCH M25 ....72 B1
Belford Av *DTN/ASHW* M34 ....100 D1
Belford Dr *BOLS/LL* BL3 ....52 E1
Belford Rd *STRET* M32 ....97 G1
Belfort Dr *ORD* M5 ....86 E4
Belfry Cl *WILM/AE* SK9 ....127 H4
Belfry Crs *WGNNW/ST* WN6 ....31 J2
Belgate Cl *WGTN/LGST* M12 ....88 D8
Belgium St *ROCH* OL11 ....27 H5
Belgrave Av *HALE* M35 ....74 E4
  MPL/ROM SK6 ....114 C6
  OLDS OL8 ....59 K8
  URM M41 ....95 H1
Belgrave Cl *LEIGH* WN7 ....80 F4
  WGNS/IIMK WN3 ....63 G1
Belgrave Ct *OLDS* OL8 ....59 J8
Belgrave Crs *ECC* M30 ....85 J1
  HOR/BR BL6 ....34 A1
  OFTN SK2 ....112 E8
Belgrave Dr *RAD* M26 ....38 D8
Belgrave Gdns *BOL* BL1 ....36 B2
Belgrave Rd *ALT* WA14 ....116 E1
  IRL M44 ....94 A7
  NEWH/MOS M40 ....74 B3
  OLDS OL8 ....59 J8
  SALE M33 ....96 D8
Belgrave St *ATH* M46 ....66 D1
  BOL BL1 ....36 B2
  HEY OL10 ....40 F3
  RAD M26 ....38 D8
  WHIT OL12 ....10 A1
Belgrave St South *BOL* BL1 ......2 C1
Belgravia Gdns *CCHDY* M21 ....97 K4
  HALE/TIMP WA15 ....117 G4
Belgravia Ms *ROY/SHW* OL2 ....43 H5
Belhaven Rd *CHH* M8 ....72 C2
Bellairs St *BOLS/LL* BL3 ....51 M1
Bella St *BOLS/LL* BL3 ....35 M8
Bell Clough Rd *DROY* M43 ......89 L1
Bell Crs *OP/CLY* M11 ....88 C4
Belldale Cl *HTNM* SK4 ....111 K2
Belldean *WGNE/HIN* WN2 ......48 D4
Belle Green La *WGNE/HIN* WN2 ....48 D4
Belle Isle Av *WHIT* OL12 ....20 B6
Bellerby Cl *WHTF* M45 ....55 H4
Belle Vue Av *WGTN/LGST* M12 ....88 C7
Belle Vue St
  WGNW/BIL/OR WN5 ....47 J5
  WGTN/LGST M12 ....88 D6
Belle Vue Ter *BOL* BL9 ....4 D6
Bellfield Av *CHD/CHDH* SK8 ..120 D3
  OLDS OL8 ....75 J2
Bellfield Cl *BKLY* M9 ....72 F2
Bellfield Vw *BOL* BL1 ....36 D1
Bellhill Gdns *SLFD* M6 ....86 C1
Bellingham Av *WGN* WN1 ......47 M2
Bellingham Cl *ROY/SHW* OL2 ....43 L4
  TOT/BURYW BL8 ....38 C2
Bellingham Dr *WGN* WN1 ......47 M2
Bellingham Mt *WGN* WN1 ......48 A1
Bellis Cl *WGTN/LGST* M12 ......88 B3
Bell La *BURY* BL9 ....5 H3
  MILN OL16 ....29 L5
  WGNW/BIL/OR WN5 ....46 E4
Bellott St *CHH* M8 ....72 D6
Bellott Wk *OLD* OL1 * 9 H2
Bellpit Cl *WALK* M28 ....68 F5
Bells Croft Av
  NEWH/MOS M40 * 73 L5
Bellshill Crs *MILN* OL16 ....11 M1
Bell St *DROY* M43 ....89 L2
  LEIGH WN7 ....66 A3
  MILN OL16 ....10 E3
  OLD OL1 ....9 M4
  WGNE/HIN WN2 ....49 H6
Bell Ter *ECC* M30 ....84 F4
Bellwood *WHTN* BL5 ....39 M1
Belmont Av *ATH* M46 ....51 J8
  DTN/ASHW M34 ....90 D6
  GOL/RIS/CUL WA3 ....79 M3
  OLDE OL4 ....60 D5
  SLFD M6 ....85 K1
  SWIN M27 ....54 A7
  WGNE/HIN WN2 ....65 J3
  WGNW/BIL/OR WN5 ....62 A1
Belmont Cl *HTNM* SK4 ....13 L1
Belmont Dr *MPL/ROM* SK6 ....114 E3
  TOT/BURYW BL8 ....38 D3
  WGNE/HIN WN2 ....32 F7
Belmont Rd *BOL* BL1 ....22 A6
  BRAM/HZG SK7 ....121 H7
  CHD/CHDH SK8 ....110 E6
  HALE/TIMP WA15 ....117 G2
  RAD M26 ....54 D3
  SALE M33 ....96 E3
  WGNE/HIN WN2 ....49 J7
Belmont St *ECC* M30 ....85 G1
  HTNM SK4 ....12 F1
  OLD OL1 ....9 G4
  OLDE OL4 ....60 B7
  SALQ M50 ....86 A3
Belmont Ter *PART* M31 * 95 G6
Belmont Vw *BOLE* BL2 ....23 J8
Belmont Wk *BRUN/LGST* M13 * ..87 M6
Belmont Wy *CHAD* OL9 ....8 D2
  HTNM SK4 ....13 L1
  WHIT OL12 ....28 B2
Belmore Rd *SALE* M33 ....108 E3
Belper Rd *ECC* M30 ....84 E4
  HTNM SK4 ....111 J3
Belroy Ct *PWCH* M25 * 71 L1
Belsay Cl *AULW* OL7 ....75 H7
Belsay Dr *NTHM/RTH* M23 ....109 K8
Belsfield Ter *AUL* OL6 * 75 M4
Belstone Av *NTHM/RTH* M23 ..118 C1
Belstone Cl *BRAM/HZG* SK7 ..121 H2
Belthorne Av *BKLY* M9 ....73 K2
Belton Av *MILN* OL16 ....11 M1
Belton Cl *GOL/RIS/CUL* WA3 ....79 K5
Beltone Cl *STRET* M32 ....96 E3
Belton Wk *CHAD* OL9 ....8 E6
Belvedere Av *ATH* M46 ....51 J8
  RDSH SK5 ....100 C2
  TOT/BURYW BL8 ....37 G3
Belvedere Cl *LEIGH* WN7 ....67 G5
Belvedere Ct *PWCH* M25 * 71 K1
Belvedere Dr *DUK* SK16 ....91 H4
  MPL/ROM SK6 ....112 F1
Belvedere Pl *WGNS/IIMK* WN3 ..47 J3
Belvedere Ri *OLDE* OL4 ....60 A1
Belvedere Rd *AIMK* WN4 ....70 F1
  NEWLW WA12 ....78 E8
  RUSH/FAL M14 ....99 H4
  SLFD M6 ....86 D1
Belvedere St *SLFD* M6 * 86 E1
Belvoir Av *BNG/LEV* M19 * 99 K2
  BRAM/HZG SK7 ....122 A4

Belvoir Mdw *MILN* OL16 ....21 J8
Belvoir St *BOLE* BL2 ....3 L4
  WGN WN1 ....15 J4
Belvor Av *DTN/ASHW* M34 ......90 B5
Belwood Rd *CCHDY* M21 ....97 K5
Bembridge Cl *RUSH/FAL* M14 ..98 F1
Bembridge Ct *EDGY/DAV* SK3 ..63 H2
Bembridge Dr *BOLS/LL* BL3 ......37 C7
Bembridge Rd
  DTN/ASHW M34 ....101 L4
Bempton Cl *OFTN* SK2 ....113 K7
Bemrose Av *ALT* WA14 ....107 H6
Bemsley Pl *ORD* M5 * 86 D4
Benbecula Wy *URM* M41 ....84 F7
Benbow Av *WGTN/LGST* M12 ..88 C7
Benbow St *SALE* M33 ....96 E1
Benbrook Wy *WYTH/NTH* M22 ..110 B8
Benchill Court Rd
  WYTH/NTH M22 ....110 B8
Benchill Dr *WYTH/NTH* M22 ..110 A7
Benchill Rd *WYTH/NTH* M22 ..109 M6
Bendall St *OP/CLY* M11 ....89 H4
Ben Davies Ct *MPL/ROM* SK6 * ..113 M2
Bendemeer *URM* M41 ....95 M1
Bendix St *ANC* M4 ....7 J2
Benedict Cl *BRO* M7 ....71 M7
Benedict Dr *DUK* SK16 ....90 F6
  OP/CLY M11 ....88 E5
  ROY/SHW OL2 ....43 L7
Benfield Av *NEWH/MOS* M40 ..73 M2
Benfield St *HEY* OL10 ....41 G2
Benfleet Cl *WGTN/LGST* M12 * ..88 D6
Bengairn Cl *WGN* WN1 ....15 M2
Bengal La *AUL* OL6 ....75 M8
Bengal St *ANC* M4 ....7 K2
  EDGY/DAV SK3 ....13 G7
  LEIGH WN7 ....66 C7
Benhale Wk *CHH* M8 * 72 C6
Benin Wk *NEWH/MOS* M40 * ..73 J4
Benjamin Fold *AIMK* WN4 ......63 L7
Benjamin St *AULW* OL7 ....90 D3
Benmore Cl *HEY* OL10 ....40 D2
Benmore Rd *BKLY* M9 ....73 J1
Bennet St *RAD* M26 ....38 A8
Bennett Cl *EDGY/DAV* SK3 ......12 C6
Bennett Dr *BRO* M7 ....72 C4
  WGNW/BIL/OR WN5 ....46 A4
Bennett Rd *CHH* M8 ....72 C5
Bennett's La *BOL* BL1 ....35 M2
Bennett St *AULW* OL7 ....90 C3
  EDGY/DAV SK3 ....12 C6
  HYDE SK14 ....90 F7
  HYDE SK14 ....93 C7
  STLY SK15 ....91 K3
  STRET M32 ....96 F3
  WGTN/LGST M12 ....88 B6
Benny La *DROY* M43 ....90 A1
Benson Cl *BRO* M7 ....72 B7
Benson St *BURY* BL9 ....5 H6
  EDGW/EG BL7 ....17 G7
Ben St *OP/CLY* M11 ....88 E2
Bentcliffe Wy *ECC* M30 ....85 K3
Bentfield Crs *MILN* OL16 ....29 K8
Bent Fold Dr *BURY* BL9 * 55 K3
Bentgate Cl *MILN* OL16 ....29 K8
Bentgate St *MILN* OL16 ....43 K1
Bentham Cl *TOT/BURYW* BL8 ..38 C7
Bentham Pl *WGNNW/ST* WN6 ..31 J2
Bentham Rd *WGNNW/ST* WN6 ..31 H3
Bent Hill St *BOLS/LL* BL3 * 35 K8
Bentinck Cl *ALT* WA14 * 107 M8
Bentinck Rd *ALT* WA14 ....107 M8
Bentinck St *AUL* OL6 ....90 D2
  BOL BL1 ....35 L3
  FWTH BL4 ....52 F3
  HULME M15 ....6 A4
  WGNS/IIMK WN3 ....47 J3
  WHIT OL12 ....27 M3
Bent La *CHH* M8 ....72 C5
  PWCH M25 ....55 M8
Bent Lanes *URM* M41 ....84 D7
Bentley Av *MDTN* M24 ....42 A7
Bentley Cl *RAD* M26 ....39 G8
Bentley Ct *FWTH* BL4 ....53 G3
Bentley Fold *TOT/BURYW* BL8 ..24 C8
Bentley Hall Cottages
  TOT/BURYW BL8 * 24 C8
Bentley Hall Rd
  TOT/BURYW BL8 ....23 M8
Bentley La *BURY* BL9 ....25 K3
Bentley Ms *WHIT* OL12 * 28 B2
Bentley Rd *BRO* M7 ....72 B4
  CCHDY M21 ....97 K3
  DTN/ASHW M34 ....101 J1
Bentley St *BOLE* BL2 ....3 L8
  CHAD OL9 ....8 B4
  FWTH BL4 ....53 G3
  OLD OL1 ....59 L4
  WHIT OL12 ....28 B2
Bentmeadows *WHIT* OL12 ......28 B3
Benton Dr *MPL/ROM* SK6 ....114 F4
Benton St *BKLY* M9 ....73 J5
Bents Av *MPL/ROM* SK6 ......113 K1
  URM M41 ....95 H3
Bents Farm Cl *LIT* OL15 * 21 K7
Bentside Rd *POY/DIS* SK12 ....123 M7
Bent Spur Rd *FWTH* BL4 ....53 K7
Bent St *CHH* M8 ....72 D7
  FWTH BL4 ....53 H5
Bentworth Cl *WHTN* BL5 ....50 C6
Bentworth Wk *BKLY* M9 ....73 H5
Beresford Av *BOLS/LL* BL3 ......35 M1
Beresford Crs *OLDE* OL4 ....60 A4
  RDSH SK5 ....100 B1
Beresford Rd *BRUN/LGST* M13 ..99 J1
  STRET M32 ....86 B8
Beresford St *FAIL* M35 ....74 B5
  MILN OL16 ....29 L8
  RUSH/FAL M14 ....98 C1
  WGNNW/ST WN6 ....14 B2
Berigan Cl *WGTN/LGST* M12 ..88 B7
Berisford Cl *HALE/TIMP* WA15 ..108 B5
Berkeley Av *CHAD* OL9 ....74 C1
  RUSH/FAL M14 ....98 B8
  STRET M32 ....85 K8
  WGNS/IIMK WN3 ....63 G2
Berkeley Cl *HYDE* SK14 ....102 A3
  LEIGH WN7 ....80 F4
  OFTN SK2 ....112 F4
Berkeley Ct *NEWLW* WA12 ......78 E2
Berkeley Crs *HYDE* SK14 ......102 A3
  RAD M26 ....37 M7
Berkeley Dr *MILN* OL16 ....28 E8
Berkeley Rd *BOL* BL1 ....22 B8
  BRAM/HZG SK7 ....122 D1
Berkeley St *AUL* OL6 ....90 D1
Berkley Av *BNG/LEV* M19 ......99 K2
Berkley Dr *ROY/SHW* OL2 ......59 G2
Berkley Wk *LIT* OL15 * 21 K7
Berkshire Cl *CHAD* OL9 ....8 D9
Berkshire Ct *BURY* BL9 ....39 J5
Berkshire Pl *CHAD* OL9 ....8 C8
Berkshire Rd *NEWH/MOS* M40 ..88 B1

Berlin Rd *EDGY/DAV* SK3 ......112 A6
Berlin St *BOLS/LL* BL3 ....35 M6
Bermondsay St *ORD* M5 ....86 E4
Bernard Gv *BOL* BL1 ....35 M2
Bernard St *BKLY* M9 ....73 G4
  GLSP SK13 ....104 F3
  WHIT OL12 ....28 B1
Berne Av *HOR/BR* BL6 ....33 K1
Berne Cl *BRAM/HZG* SK7 ......112 B8
  CHAD OL9 ....8 C7
Bernice Av *CHAD* OL9 ....8 A7
Bernice St *BOL* BL1 ....35 M2
Berriedale Cl
  OLDTF/WHR M16 * 98 A2
Berrie Gv *BNG/LEV* M19 ....99 K4
Berrington Gv *AIMK* WN4 ......78 D1
Berry Brow *NEWH/MOS* M40 ..74 B8
  UPML OL3 ....61 L7
Berry Cl *WILM/AE* SK9 ....126 E1
Berrycroft La *MPL/ROM* SK6 ..113 K1
Berryfold Wy *TYLD* M29 ....67 K4
Berry St *CMANE* M1 ....7 K7
  ECC M30 ....84 E4
  STLY SK15 ....91 M4
  SWIN M27 ....70 C2
  UPML OL3 ....61 L7
Bertha Rd *MILN* OL16 ....11 L5
Bertha St *BOL* BL1 ....36 A2
  OP/CLY M11 ....88 E5
  ROY/SHW OL2 ....43 L7
Bertie St *ROCH* OL11 ....28 A3
Bertram St *SALE* M33 ....97 H8
  WGTN/LGST M12 * 88 B6
Bertrand Rd *BOL* BL1 ....35 M5
Berwick Av *HTNM* SK4 ....111 G2
  URM M41 ....96 D2
  WHTF M45 ....55 K5
Berwick Cl *HEY* OL10 ....40 D3
  WALK M28 ....68 C5
Berwick Pl *WGN* WN1 ....15 L1
Berwick St *MILN* OL16 ....11 J6
Berwyn Av *BKLY* M9 ....72 D6
  CHD/CHDH SK8 ....111 L7
  MDTN M24 ....57 M4
Berwyn Cl *OLDS* OL8 ....75 H1
Beryl Av *TOT/BURYW* BL8 ......24 C5
Beryl St *BOL* BL1 ....36 C1
Besom La *STLY* SK15 ....92 B1
Bessemer Rd *IRL* M44 ....94 D3
Bessemer St *OP/CLY* M11 ......88 F5
Bessemer Wy *OLD* OL1 * 9 H4
Bessie's Well Pl
  WGNNW/ST WN6 * 31 J4
Bessybrook Cl *HOR/BR* BL6 ....34 F6
Beswick Dr *FAIL* M35 ....74 D6
Beswicke Royds St *MILN* OL16 ..11 L1
Beswicke St *WHIT* OL12 ....10 C2
Beswick Rw *ANC* M4 ....7 G2
Beswick St *ANC* M4 ....88 A2
  DROY M43 ....89 L3
Beta Av *STRET* M32 ....96 F3
Beta St *BOL* BL1 ....2 D2
Bethany La *MILN* OL16 ....29 M8
Bethany Ms *WGNE/HIN* WN2 ..49 L8
Bethel Av *FAIL* M35 ....74 B5
Bethel St *HEY* OL10 ....40 F2
Bethersden Rd *WGN* WN1 ......31 L8
Bethesda St *OLDS* OL8 ....59 J8
Bethnal Dr *RUSH/FAL* M14 ......98 D1
Betjeman Pl *ROY/SHW* OL2 ......44 A5
Betleymere Rd
  CHD/CHDH SK8 ....111 J8
Betley Rd *RDSH* SK5 ....100 C3
Betley St *CMANE* M1 ....7 L6
  HEY OL10 * 40 F3
Bettison Av *LEIGH* WN7 ....81 M1
Betony Cl *WHIT* OL12 ....28 A1
Betsham St *HULME* M15 ....87 J7
Bettison Av *LEIGH* WN7 ....81 M1
Bettwood Dr *CHH* M8 ....72 C7
Betula Gv *BRO* M7 ....72 A5
Betula Ms *ROCH* OL11 ....27 G4
Beulah Av *WGNW/BIL/OR* WN5 ..62 B3
Bevan Cl *WGTN/LGST* M12 ......88 B3
Bevendon Sq *BRO* M7 ....72 B6
Beveridge St *RUSH/FAL* M14 ....98 D1
Beverley Av *DTN/ASHW* M34 ..101 K2
  LEIGH WN7 ....66 D7
  URM M41 ....85 H8
  WGNW/BIL/OR WN5 ....62 B3
Beverley Cl *WHTF* M45 ....55 L3
Beverley Pl *MILN* OL16 * 11 G3
Beverley Rd *BOL* BL1 ....35 M4
  BOLS/LL BL3 ....53 J1
  OFTN SK2 ....112 F4
  SWIN M27 ....70 F5
  WGNW/BIL/OR WN5 ....46 E4
Beverley St *BKLY* M9 ....73 H3
Beverley Wk *OLDS* OL8 * 9 H9
Beverly Rd *RUSH/FAL* M14 ......99 G5
Beverston *ROCH* OL11 ....10 D7
Beverston Dr *BRO* M7 ....72 B6
Bevill Sq *CSLFD* M3 ....6 C2
Bevin Av *GOL/RIS/CUL* WA3 ....81 L8
Bevington Wk *AIMK* WN4 ......63 J7
Bevis Gn *BURY* BL9 ....25 J4
Bewick St *AIMK* WN4 ....14 D8
Bewley St *OLDS* OL8 ....75 G2
Bexhill Av *HALE/TIMP* WA15 ..108 C6
Bexhill Cl *BOLS/LL* BL3 ....53 M1
Bexhill Dr *BRUN/LGST* M13 ......99 H1
  LEIGH WN7 ....65 M2
Bexhill Rd *EDGY/DAV* SK3 ....112 B8
Bexhill Wk *CHAD* OL9 * 8 A6
Bexington Rd *OLDTF/WHR* M16 ..98 A1
Bexley Cl *GLSP* SK13 ....104 F1
  URM M41 ....84 E8
Bexley Dr *LHULT* M38 ....68 F1
  TOT/BURYW BL8 ....38 E3
Bexley Sq *CSLFD* M3 ....6 D3
Bexley St *CHAD* OL9 ....8 D8
  WGNE/HIN WN2 ....65 L1
Beyer Cl *GTN* M18 ....88 D2
Bibby La *BNG/LEV* M19 ....99 J3
Bibby St *BURY* BL9 ....39 J7
  HYDE SK14 * 91 G7
Bibury Av *WYTH/NTH* M22 ....118 D1
Bickerdike Av *WGTN/LGST* M12 ..99 L1
Bickershaw Dr *WALK* M28 ......68 C2
Bickershaw La *WGNE/HIN* WN2 ..64 F3
Bickerstaffe Cl *ROY/SHW* OL2 ..43 K7
Bickerton Rd *ALT* WA14 ......107 L7
Bickley Gv *TYLD* M29 ....67 M6
Biddall Dr *NTHM/RTH* M23 ..109 L6
Biddisham Wk
  NEWH/MOS M40 * 73 G8

Biddulph Av *OFTN* SK2 ....112 F7
Bideford Dr *BOLE* BL2 ....37 K6
  NTHM/RTH M23 ....109 J5
Bideford Rd *OFTN* SK2 ....112 F7
  ROCH OL11 ....41 L1
Bidford Cl *TYLD* M29 ....67 M3
Bidston Av *RUSH/FAL* M14 ......98 E2
Bidston Cl *ROY/SHW* OL2 ......44 A6
  TOT/BURYW BL8 ....38 C2
Bidston Dr *WILM/AE* SK9 ......127 J2
Big Fold *HOR/BR* BL6 * 33 G2
Biggin Gdns *HEY* OL10 ....41 H5
Bignor St *CHH* M8 ....72 D6
Bilbao St *BOL* BL1 ....35 M4
Bilberry St *MILN* OL16 ....11 J6
Bilbrook St *ANC* M4 ....87 L1
Billberry Cl *WHTF* M45 ....55 L4
Billing Av *WGTN/LGST* M12 ......7 L8
Billinge Ar *WGN* WN1 * 14 F3
Billinge Cl *BOL* BL1 ....35 M8
Billinge Rd *AIMK* WN4 ....62 E7
  WGNS/IIMK WN3 ....46 F8
  WGNW/BIL/OR WN5 ....47 H6
Billington Av *NEWLW* WA12 ....78 F7
Billington Rd *SWIN* M27 ....71 H4
Bill Williams Cl *OP/CLY* M11 ....88 F4
Billy La *SWIN* M27 ....70 C2
Billy's La *CHD/CHDH* SK8 ......120 C3
Bilson Dr *EDGY/DAV* SK3 ......12 B9
Binbrook Wk *BOLS/LL* BL3 ......36 B8
Bindloss Av *ECC* M30 ....85 K1
Bingham Dr
  NTHM/RTH M23 ....109 J6
Bingham St *SWIN* M27 ....70 C4
Bingley Cl *OP/CLY* M11 ....88 C4
Bingley Dr *URM* M41 ....84 C8
Bingley Rd *MILN* OL16 ....11 M5
Bingley Sq *MILN* OL16 ....11 M5
Bingley Ter *MILN* OL16 ....11 M5
Binns Nook Rd *WHIT* OL12 ......28 D2
Binns Pl *ANC* M4 ....7 K4
Binns St *STLY* SK15 ....91 H3
Binsley Cl *IRL* M44 ....94 D3
Binstead Rd *RUSH/FAL* M14 ....99 H1
Birbeck St *BOLS/LL* BL3 ....5 M1
Birchacre Gv *RUSH/FAL* M14 ..99 G5
Birchall Av
  GOL/RIS/CUL WA3 ....81 C8
Birchall Cl *DUK* SK16 ....91 G5
Birchall Gn *MPL/ROM* SK6 ....101 K7
Birchall Wy *HULME* M15 ....87 J7
Birch Av *FAIL* M35 ....74 C7
  HTNM SK4 ....99 L8
  IRL M44 ....94 A7
  MDTN M24 ....57 K5
  MPL/ROM SK6 ....114 C6
  OLD OL1 ....58 D2
  OLDS OL8 ....75 G2
  OLDTF/WHR M16 ....86 D8
  SALE M33 ....108 E1
  SLFD M6 ....71 H8
  TOT/BURYW BL8 ....24 D7
  WGNNW/ST WN6 ....21 H8
  WHIT OL12 ....21 H8
Birch Cl *WHIT* OL12 ....20 A7
Birch Crs *MILN* OL16 ....43 K1
  NEWLW WA12 ....78 D3
Birch Dr *BRAM/HZG* SK7 ......121 C2
  OLDE OL4 ....60 B7
  SWIN M27 ....70 E4
Birchenall St
  NEWH/MOS M40 ....73 J4
Birchenlea St *CHAD* OL9 ....74 D1
Birches Rd *EDGW/EG* BL7 ......17 G8
The Birches *MOSL* OL5 ....76 E3
  NM/HAY SK22 ....125 J2
  SALE M33 ....96 B7
Birchfield *BOLE* BL2 ....23 H6
Birchfield Av *ATH* M46 ....50 E8
  BURY BL9 ....40 B3
Birchfield Dr *ROCH* OL11 ....27 M7
  WALK M28 ....68 D5
Birchfield Gv *BOLS/LL* BL3 ......35 H8
Birchfield Ms *HYDE* SK14 * 102 A2
Birchfield Rd *EDGY/DAV* SK3 ..111 K5
Birchfields *HALE/TIMP* WA15 ..117 H3
  OLDE OL4 ....60 A4
Birchfields Av *BRUN/LGST* M13 ..99 H2
Birchfields Rd *BRUN/LGST* M13 ..99 H1
Birchfold Cl *LHULT* M38 ....52 E8
Birchgate Wk *BOLS/LL* BL3 ......2 D9
Birch Gn *GLSP* SK13 ....105 H3
Birch Gv *AIMK* WN4 ....62 F7
  DTN/ASHW M34 ....90 C6
  DTN/ASHW M34 ....101 H1
  HALE/TIMP WA15 ....109 H7
  PWCH M25 ....55 K6
  RAMS BL0 ....24 D1
  RUSH/FAL M14 ....99 G1
Birch Hall Cl *NM/HAY* SK22 ..125 J2
  OLDE OL4 ....60 B8
Birch Hall La
  BRUN/LGST M13 ....99 H2
Birch Hey Cl *WHIT* OL12 ....21 G8
Birch Hill Crs *WHIT* OL12 ....21 G8
Birch Hill La *WHIT* OL12 ....21 H6
Birchington Rd
  DID/WITH M20 ....98 D4
Birchinlee Av *ROY/SHW* OL2 ....58 E1
Birchin Pl *ANC* M4 * 7 H4
Birch La *BRUN/LGST* M13 ......88 B8
  DUK SK16 ....91 G5
Birchlea *HALE/TIMP* WA15 ....108 C3
Birch-lea Cl *BURY* BL9 ....39 J5
Birchleaf Gv *ORD* M5 ....85 M2
Birch Mt *WHIT* OL12 ....21 J8
Birch Polygon
  RUSH/FAL M14 ....99 G1
Birch Rd *ALT* WA14 ....107 J3
  ATH M46 ....66 B5
  CHD/CHDH SK8 ....110 D7
  CHH M8 ....56 A8
  FWTH BL4 ....53 J6
  LEIGH WN7 ....81 M1
  MDTN M24 ....57 M2
  PART M31 ....95 J3
  PART M31 ....106 A1
  POY/DIS SK12 ....129 K2
  RNFD/HAY WA11 ....78 B5
  SWIN M27 ....70 A7
  UPML OL3 ....61 M5
  WALK M28 ....68 D1
  WGNE/HIN WN2 ....64 D3
  WHIT OL12 ....21 H8
Birchside Av *GLSP* SK13 ......104 E2

Birch St *AULW* OL7 ....90 C3
  BOLE BL2 ....3 J7
  BURY BL9 ....5 G2
  DROY M43 ....89 L4
  HEY OL10 ....41 G3
  RAD M26 ....39 H7
  STLY SK15 ....76 F7
  TYLD M29 * 67 K3
  WGNE/HIN WN2 ....49 G7
  WGNNW/ST WN6 ....14 C1
  WGTN/LGST M12 ....88 B6
  WHIT OL12 ....11 L5
Birch Ter *HYDE* SK14 * 101 M2
Birch Tree Av *BRAM/HZG* SK7 ..122 C3
Birch Tree Cl *ALT* WA14 ......116 E3
Birch Tree Dr *WYTH/NTH* M22 ..118 F1
Birch Tree Rd
  GOL/RIS/CUL WA3 ....80 C4
Birch Tree Wy *HOR/BR* BL6 ....34 B3
Birchvale Av *MPL/ROM* SK6 ..114 A1
Birchvale Cl *HULME* M15 ....6 C7
Birchway *BRAM/HZG* SK7 ....120 F5
  MPL/ROM SK6 ....123 H6
Birchwood *CHAD* OL9 ....58 B5
  DROY M43 ....89 L1
Birchwood Cl *LEIGH* WN7 ......81 J1
  WGNS/IIMK WN3 ....62 F3
Birchwood Crs *HYDE* SK14 ....91 K6
Birchwood Dr *NEWH/MOS* M40 ..73 G6
  WILM/AE SK9 ....127 H5
Birchwood Rd *MDTN* M24 ......57 M4
Birchwood Wy *DUK* SK16 * 91 G6
Bird Hall Av *CHD/CHDH* SK8 ..111 H4
Birdhall Gv *BNG/LEV* M19 ......99 K4
Bird Hall Rd *CHD/CHDH* SK8 ..111 L7
Birdlip Dr *NTHM/RTH* M23 ....118 C1
Birley St *WGNE/HIN* WN2 ......48 C5
Birkby Dr *MDTN* M24 ....57 H2
Birkdale Av *ATH* M46 ....50 F7
  ROY/SHW OL2 ....59 H2
  WHTF M45 ....55 L5
Birkdale Cl *BRAM/HZG* SK7 ..121 H6
  HEY OL10 ....41 G4
  HYDE SK14 ....91 J7
Birkdale Dr *SALE* M33 ....108 B2
  TOT/BURYW BL8 ....38 C2
Birkdale Gdns *BOLS/LL* BL3 ......2 B9
Birkdale Gv *ECC* M30 ....85 J2
  RDSH SK5 ....100 C7
Birkdale Pl *SALE* M33 * 96 C6
Birkdale Rd *MILN* OL16 ....28 E8
  RDSH SK5 ....100 C2
Birkdale St *CHH* M8 ....72 D5
Birkenhills Dr *BOLS/LL* BL3 ......35 H7
Birkett Bank *WGN* WN1 ....15 L4
Birkett Cl *BOL* BL1 ....22 A6
Birkett Dr *BOL* BL1 ....22 A6
Birkett St *WGN* WN1 ....15 L4
Birkinbrook Cl *WHTF* M45 ......55 K3
Birkinheath La *ALT* WA14 ....116 D8
Birks Av *OLDE* OL4 ....60 C4
Birks Dr *TOT/BURYW* BL8 ......24 E6
Birkside Cl *WGNS/IIMK* WN3 ..63 K3
Birkworth Ct *OFTN* SK2 ....113 G6
Birley Cl *HALE/TIMP* WA15 ..108 C5
  WGNNW/ST WN6 ....30 C1
Birley Pk *DID/WITH* M20 ......110 C1
Birley St *BOL* BL1 ....22 B8
  BURY BL9 ....25 J7
  LEIGH WN7 ....66 B6
  NEWLW WA12 ....79 G8
  WHIT OL12 ....28 B3
Birling Dr *NTHM/RTH* M23 ....109 L8
Birnam Gv *HEY* OL10 ....40 D3
Birshaw Cl *ROY/SHW* OL2 ......43 L7
Birtenshaw Crs *EDGW/EG* BL7 ..22 E1
Birtle Dr *TYLD* M29 ....67 M5
Birtle Rd *BURY* BL9 ....26 B5
Birtles Av *RDSH* SK5 ....100 C1
Birtles Cl *CHD/CHDH* SK8 ....111 K8
  DUK SK16 ....91 G6
Birtles La *MCFLDN* SK10 ......131 K8
Birtlespool Rd *CHD/CHDH* SK8 ..111 J8
Birtley Wk *NEWH/MOS* M40 * ..7 M1
Birt St *NEWH/MOS* M40 ....73 G8
Birwood Rd *CHH* M8 ....72 E2
Biscay Cl *OP/CLY* M11 ....88 C3
Bishopbridge Cl *BOLS/LL* BL3 ..36 C8
Bishop Cl *OLDTF/WHR* M16 ....87 H8
Bishopdale Cl *ROY/SHW* OL2 ..43 C7
Bishopgate *CHAD* OL9 ....58 D7
Bishop Marshall Cl
  NEWH/MOS M40 * 73 G7
Bishop Marshall Wy *MDTN* M24 ..41 G8
Bishop Reeves Rd
  RNFD/HAY WA11 ....78 B5
Bishop Rd *SLFD* M6 ....70 B8
  URM M41 ....95 H2
Bishops Cl *ALT* WA14 ....116 D3
  AULW OL7 ....75 K7
  BOLS/LL BL3 ....52 D2
  CHD/CHDH SK8 ....111 K7
Bishopsgate *CMANW* M2 ....6 F7
Bishopsgate Wk *MILN* OL16 ....28 F8
Bishops Meadow *MDTN* M24 ..57 G1
Bishops Ms *SALE* M33 ....96 B6
Bishop's Rd *BOLS/LL* BL3 ......52 D2
  PWCH M25 ....71 M1
Bishop St *MDTN* M24 ....58 A5
  MILN OL16 ....28 E3
  STKP SK1 ....13 L5
Bishopton Cl *BNG/LEV* M19 ....99 M3
Bisley Av *NTHM/RTH* M23 ....109 J6
Bisley St *OLDS* OL8 ....8 F7
Bismarck St *OLDE* OL4 ....9 M8
Bispham Av *BOLE* BL2 ....37 G3
Bispham Cl *TOT/BURYW* BL8 ..38 C3
Bispham Ct
  WGNW/BIL/OR WN5 ....62 A2
Bispham Dr *AIMK* WN4 ....63 J7
Bispham Gv *BRO* M7 ....72 B5
Bispham St *BOLE* BL2 * 3 L2
Bittern Cl *POY/DIS* SK12 ......128 C1
  ROCH OL11 ....27 J5
Bittern Dr *DROY* M43 ....89 M1
Blackbank St *BOL* BL1 ....36 C2
Blackberry Cl *ALT* WA14 ......107 L4
Blackberry Dr *WGNE/HIN* WN2 ..48 F3
Blackberry La *RDSH* SK5 ......100 D5
Black Brook Rd *HTNM* SK4 ....100 A5
Blackburn Cl *GOL/RIS/CUL* WA3 ..80 C4
Blackburn Gdns *DID/WITH* M20 ..98 D3
Blackburn Pl *ORD* M5 ....86 F3
Blackburn Rd *EDGW/EG* BL7 ..16 F3
  EDGW/EG BL7 ....22 A4
Blackburn St *CSLFD* M3 ....6 A1
  OLDTF/WHR M16 ....86 F7
  PWCH M25 ....55 M8
  RAD M26 ....54 E2
Blackcap Cl *WALK* M28 ....68 C3
Blackcarr Rd *NTHM/RTH* M23 ..109 L2

Blackchapel Dr MILN OL16 ......42 E1
Blackcroft Cl SWIN M27 ......70 B4
Blackdown Gv OLDS OL8 ......75 H1
Blackfield La ALT M41 ......71 M4
Blackford Av BURY BL9 ......39 J8
Blackford Rd BNG/LEV M19 ......99 L5
Blackford Wk
  NEWH/MOS M40 ......88 A1
Blackfriars St CSLFD M3 ......6 C1
Blackfriars St CSLFD M3 ......6 E3
Blackhill Cl BRUN/LGST M13 ......7 K9
Blackhorse Av HOR/BR BL6 * 32 F1
Blackhorse Cl HOR/BR BL6 ......32 F1
Black Horse St BOL BL1 ......2 E6
  FWTH BL4 ......53 H5
  HOR/BR BL6 ......32 F1
Blackhurst Brow
  MCFLDN SK10 ......131 L1
Black La RAMS BL0 ......19 L5
Blackleach Dr WALK M28 ......53 C8
Blackledge Cl
  WGNW/BIL/OR WN5 ......46 B7
Blackledge St BOLS/LL BL3 ......35 M8
Blackley Cl BURY BL9 ......55 K2
Blackleyhurst Av
  WGNW/BIL/OR WN5 ......62 B7
Blackley New Rd BKLY M9 ......72 C1
Blackley Park Rd BKLY M9 ......73 G3
Blackley St MDTN M24 ......56 E5
  OLDTF/WHR M16 ......86 F7
Blacklock St CSLFD M3 ......72 C8
Blackmoor Av TYLD M29 ......67 L7
Blackmore Rd STRET M32 ......85 L7
Black Moss Rd ALT WA14 ......107 H5
Black Moss Rd ALT WA14 ......107 H5
Blackpool St OP/CLY M11 ......88 F2
Blackrock MOSL OL5 ......76 F6
Blackrock St OP/CLY M11 ......88 C3
Blackrod By-Pass Rd
  HOR/BR BL6 ......33 J4
Blackrod Dr TOT/BURYW BL8 ......38 D5
Black Sail Wk OL1 ......9 K1
Blackshaw Clough
  GLSP SK13 ......105 H1
Blackshaw La BOLS/LL BL3 ......35 M6
  ROY/SHW OL2 ......43 J8
  WILM/AE SK9 ......130 C3
Blackshaw Rd GLSP SK13 ......105 H1
Blackshaw St EDGY/DAV SK3 ......13 H6
Blacksmith La ROCH OL11 ......27 L8
Blacksmiths Fold ATH M46 ......67 H1
Blackstock St BRUN/LGST M13 ......87 M8
Blackstone Av MILN OL16 ......11 M2
Blackstone Rd OFTN SK2 ......113 G7
Blackthorn Av BNG/LEV M19 ......99 K5
  WGNNW/ST WN6 ......47 J1
Blackthorn Cl OLD OL12 ......28 B2
Blackthorne Cl BOL BL1 ......35 K3
Blackthorne Dr SALE M33 ......108 A2
Blackthorne Rd HYDE SK14 ......102 B6
Blackthorn Ms WHIT OL12 ......28 B2
Blackthorn Rd OLDS OL8 ......74 F4
Blackwin St WGTN/LGST M12 ......88 D0
Blackwood Dr
  NTHM/RTH M23 ......109 G4
Blackwood Cl BOLS/LL BL3 ......36 D8
Bladen Cl CHD/CHDH SK8 ......111 K8
Bladon St CMANE M1 * 7 G8
Blair Av LHULT M38 ......52 E8
  URM M41 ......95 H2
  WGNE/HIN WN2 ......65 L1
Blair Cl BRAM/HZG SK7 ......121 L4
  ROY/SHW OL2 ......43 L5
  SALE M33 ......107 M3
Blairhall Av NEWH/MOS M40 ......73 K5
Blair La BOLE BL2 ......37 G3
Blairmore Dr BOLS/LL BL3 ......35 H8
Blair Rd OLDTF/WHR M16 ......98 B3
Blair St EDGW/EG BL7 ......22 C4
  FWTH BL4 ......53 K6
  OLDTF/WHR M16 ......87 G7
  WHIT OL12 ......10 A1
Blake Cl WGNS/IIMK WN3 ......47 K7
Blakedown Wk
  WGTN/LGST M12 ......88 B7
Blake Dr OFTN SK2 ......113 H5
Blakefield Dr WALK M28 ......69 H3
Blake Gdns BOL BL1 ......36 A2
Blakelock St ROY/SHW OL2 ......43 K5
Blakemere Av SALE M33 ......109 H1
Blakemore Pk ATH M46 ......50 E8
Blakemore Wk
  WGTN/LGST M12 * 88 B3
Blake St BOL BL1 ......36 A2
  EDGW/EG BL7 ......22 D5
  MILN OL16 ......11 H3
Blakeswell Cl URM M41 ......95 C1
Blakey Cl BOLS/LL BL3 ......35 J8
Blakey St WGTN/LGST M12 ......88 D8
Blanchard St HULME M15 ......87 H7
Blanche St WHIT OL12 ......28 D2
Blanche Wk OLD OL1 ......9 L3
Bland Cl FAIL M35 ......74 B5
Blandford Av WALK M28 ......69 K4
Blandford Cl TOT/BURYW BL8 ......25 C7
  TYLD M29 ......67 K3
Blandford Ct STLY SK15 ......91 K2
Blandford Dr NEWH/MOS M40 ......73 M2
Blandford Ri HOR/BR BL6 ......34 D3
Blandford Rd ECC M30 ......84 E2
  HTNM SK4 ......12 C2
  SLFD M6 ......71 L7
Blandford St AUL OL6 ......90 D1
  STLY SK15 * 91 K2
Bland St PWCH M25 ......71 L2
Blanefield Cl CCHDY M21 ......98 B5
Blantyre Av WALK M28 ......69 H1
Blantyre Rd SWIN M27 ......70 E6
Blantyre St ECC M30 ......84 D1
  HULME M15 ......6 B8
  SWIN M27 ......70 A4
  WGNE/HIN WN2 ......49 H6
Blanwood Dr CHH M8 ......72 E5
Blaven Cl EDGY/DAV SK3 ......112 C1
Blaydon Cl WGNE/HIN WN2 ......33 G1
Blazemoss Bank OFTN SK2 ......113 G7
Bleach St WGNE/HIN WN2 ......48 F1
Bleackley St TOT/BURYW BL8 ......24 F8
Bleadale Cl WILM/AE SK9 ......127 K6
Bleak Hey Nook La UPML OL3 ......45 M5
Bleak Hey Rd WYTH/NTH M22 ......119 H2
Bleakholt Rd RAMS BL0 ......19 J3
Bleakledge Gn WGNE/HIN WN2 ......49 J5
Bleakley St WGNE/HIN WN2 ......49 J4
Bleaklow Cl WGNS/IIMK WN3 ......63 L2
Bleak St BOLE BL2 ......36 E2
Bleasby St OLDE OL4 ......59 M5
Bleasdale Cl HOR/BR BL6 ......34 C4

Bleasdale Rd BOL BL1 ......35 J2
  NEWLW WA12 ......78 E8
  WYTH/NTH M22 ......118 C2
Bleasdale St ROY/SHW OL2 ......43 G7
Bleasefell Cha WALK M28 ......68 D7
Bleatarn Rd STKP SK1 ......112 E5
Bledlow Cl ECC M30 ......85 H1
Blenheim Av OLDTF/WHR M16 ......98 A2
Blenheim Cl ALT WA14 ......116 F3
  BURY BL9 ......39 J7
  GLSP SK13 ......93 K7
  HEY OL10 ......41 G2
  POY/DIS SK12 ......122 B8
  WILM/AE SK9 ......127 H5
Blenheim Dr LEIGH WN7 ......67 H5
Blenheim Rd AIMK WN4 ......79 G2
  BOLE BL2 ......37 H5
  CHD/CHDH SK8 ......120 D2
  OLDTF/WHR M16 ......97 K1
  WGNW/BIL/OR WN5 ......46 F4
Blenheim St OLDE OL4 ......60 A3
  WHIT OL12 * 27 M3
Blenheim Wy AUL OL6 ......76 B8
Blenhall Av OLD OL1 ......60 A1
Blenmar Cl RAD M26 ......38 F7
Bleriot St BOLS/LL BL3 ......52 A1
Blessford Cl WGNE/HIN WN2 ......49 G8
Blisworth Av ECC M30 ......85 H4
Blisworth Cl ANC M4 ......88 A3
Block La CHAD OL9 ......8 B9
Blodwell St SLFD M6 ......86 C2
Blomley St ROCH OL11 ......41 M2
Bloomfield Cl CHD/CHDH SK8 ......120 A3
Bloomfield Dr BURY BL9 ......55 L1
  WALK M28 ......68 D5
Bloomfield Rd FWTH BL4 ......53 G6
Bloomfield St BOL BL1 ......36 B1
Bloomsbury Gv
  HALE/TIMP WA15 ......108 D6
Bloomsbury La
  HALE/TIMP WA15 ......108 D6
Bloom St CMANE M1 ......7 H6
  CSLFD M3 ......6 C3
  EDGY/DAV SK3 ......12 D7
  RAMS BL0 ......18 D8
Blossom Pl MILN OL16 * 10 E3
Blossom Rd PART M31 ......106 D2
Blossoms Hey CHD/CHDH SK8 ......120 A5
Blossoms La BRAM/HZG SK7 ......127 L2
Blossom St OFTN SK2 * 13 K9
Blossom St ANC M4 ......7 K3
  CSLFD M3 ......6 D2
  TYLD M29 ......67 M8
Blucher St AULW OL7 ......75 K6
  ORD M5 ......86 F3
  WGTN/LGST M12 ......88 B6
Blueball Av PWCH M25 ......56 D3
Bluebell Av NEWH/MOS M40 ......73 M4
  WGNNW/ST WN6 ......31 J8
Bluebell Cl HYDE SK14 ......91 J7
  NM/HAY SK22 ......125 L1
Bluebell Dr ROCH OL11 ......41 L1
Bluebell Gv CHD/CHDH SK8 ......111 G8
Bluebell Wy WILM/AE SK9 ......127 G3
Blueberry Dr ROY/SHW OL2 ......44 A5
Blueberry Rd ALT WA14 ......116 C4
Bluefields ROY/SHW OL2 ......44 A5
Blue Ribbon Wk SWIN M27 ......70 D3
Bluestone Dr HTNM SK4 ......111 H1
Bluestone Rd NEWH/MOS M40 ......73 K4
  RDSH SK5 ......100 D2
Blundell Cl BURY BL9 ......55 L1
Blundell La HOR/BR BL6 ......32 D2
Blundell Ms WGNS/IIMK WN3 ......47 G8
Blundells Ct WGNS/IIMK WN3 ......47 G7
Blundell St BOL BL1 ......2 D4
Blundering La STLY SK15 ......92 A6
Blunn St OLDS OL8 ......59 J8
Blyborough Cl SLFD M6 ......71 H8
Blyth Av LIT OL15 * 29 J1
Blyth Cl HALE/TIMP WA15 ......109 G6
Blythe Av BRAM/HZG SK7 ......120 E6
Blyton St HULME M15 ......87 L7
Boad St CMANE M1 ......7 K6
Boardale Dr MDTN M24 ......57 H3
Boardman Cl BOL BL1 ......36 B2
  RDSH SK5 ......100 A6
Boardman Fold Cl MDTN M24 ......57 K7
Boardman Fold Rd MDTN M24 ......57 K7
Boardman La MDTN M24 ......56 E4
Boardman Rd CHH M8 ......72 C2
Boardman St BOL BL1 ......36 B2
  ECC M30 ......85 H3
  HOR/BR BL6 ......33 G2
  HYDE SK14 ......102 A2
Board St AUL OL6 ......75 L8
  BOL BL1 ......2 A6
Boarfold La GLSP SK13 ......103 J7
Boar Green Cl NEWH/MOS M40 ......73 M5
Boarshaw Clough MDTN M24 ......57 L2
Boarshaw Clough Wy
  MDTN M24 ......57 L2
Boarshaw Crs MDTN M24 ......57 M2
Boarshaw La MDTN M24 ......58 A1
Boarshaw Rd MDTN M24 ......57 K3
Boars Head Av
  WGNNW/ST WN6 ......31 K5
Boarshurst La UPML OL3 ......61 M7
Boat La IRL M44 ......94 A7
Boatmans Rw TYLD M29 ......67 M8
Bobbin Wk ANC M4 * 7 K6
  OLDE OL4 ......9 M7
Bob Brook Cl NEWH/MOS M40 ......73 M6
Bob Massey Cl OP/CLY M11 ......88 F4
Bob's La IRL M44 ......94 A8
Boddens Hill Rd HTNM SK4 ......111 H3
Bodden St COL/RIS/CUL WA3 ......80 C8
Boddington Rd ECC M30 ......84 C3
Bodiam Rd TOT/BURYW BL8 ......24 C8
Bodley St OP/CLY M11 ......88 F2
Bodmin Cl ROY/SHW OL2 ......59 K1
Bodmin Crs RDSH SK5 ......100 E7
Bodmin Dr BRAM/HZG SK7 ......121 H5
  WGNE/HIN WN2 ......64 D3
Bodmin Rd SALE M33 ......96 A7
  TYLD M29 ......67 L4
Boggard La GLSP SK13 ......104 A7
Bogguard Rd MPL/ROM SK6 ......115 K8
Bolam Cl NTHM/RTH M23 ......109 H3
Boland Dr RUSH/FAL M14 ......99 G4

Bolbury Crs SWIN M27 ......71 G4
Bolderod Pl OLD OL1 * 9 L3
Bolderstone Pl OFTN SK2 ......113 H8
Bolderwood Dr
  WGNE/HIN WN2 ......49 G8
Bold St ALT WA14 ......116 F1
  BOL BL1 ......2 E6
  BURY BL9 ......5 H2
  HULME M15 ......87 H7
  LEIGH WN7 ......66 C7
  SWIN M27 ......70 D2
  WGNW/BIL/OR WN5 ......47 H7
Bolesworth Cl CCHDY M21 ......97 J4
Boleyn Ct HEY OL10 ......40 F3
Bolholt Ter TOT/BURYW BL8 ......24 E8
Bolivia St ORD M5 ......85 M2
Bollin Av ALT WA14 ......116 C4
Bollin Cl FWTH BL4 ......53 K6
Bollin Ct HULME M15 ......87 G6
Bollin Dr ALT WA14 ......108 B4
  SALE M33 ......108 C2
Bollings Yd BOL BL1 * 2 F6
Bollington Rd HTNM SK4 ......100 A3
  NEWH/MOS M40 ......88 A2
Bollington St AULW OL7 ......90 D3
Bollin Hl WILM/AE SK9 ......126 E4
Bollin Sq ALT WA14 ......116 D3
Bollin Wk WHTF M45 ......55 M2
  WILM/AE SK9 ......126 F5
Bollinway
  HALE/TIMP WA15 ......117 J4
Bollinwood Cha
  WILM/AE SK9 ......127 H5
Bolney St WGNE/HIN WN2 ......48 D2
Bolshaw Farm La
  CHD/CHDH SK8 ......119 L6
Bolshaw Rd
  CHD/CHDH SK8 ......119 K6
Bolton Av BNG/LEV M19 ......111 G2
  CHD/CHDH SK8 ......120 D6
Bolton Cl GOL/RIS/CUL WA3 ......80 E4
  POY/DIS SK12 ......121 M8
  PWCH M25 ......71 J2
Bolton House Rd
  WGNE/HIN WN2 ......65 J5
Bolton Old Rd ATH M46 ......67 C1
Bolton Rd AIMK WN4 ......64 B7
  AIMK WN4 ......78 A1
  ATH M46 ......51 H8
  BOLE BL2 ......22 F7
  EDGW/EG BL7 ......17 G8
  FWTH BL4 ......53 G2
  FWTH BL4 ......53 H5
  RAD M26 ......38 A8
  ROCH OL11 ......27 K8
  SLFD M6 ......70 F6
  SWIN M27 ......70 F4
  TOT/BURYW BL8 ......4 B4
  TOT/BURYW BL8 ......23 M2
  TOT/BURYW BL8 ......38 D2
  WALK M28 ......53 C8
  WGNE/HIN WN2 ......32 F7
  WHTN BL5 ......50 C4
Bolton Rd North RAMS BL0 ......18 F3
Bolton Rd West RAMS BL0 ......18 B8
Bolton Sq WGN WN1 ......15 K2
Bolton St AIMK WN4 ......63 C7
  CSLFD M3 ......6 C5
  OLDE OL4 ......9 M6
  RAD M26 ......54 C1
  RAMS BL0 ......18 D8
  RDSH SK5 ......100 B5
  TOT/BURYW BL8 ......4 B4
Bombay Rd EDGY/DAV SK3 ......12 D9
  WGNW/BIL/OR WN5 ......46 F4
Bombay St AUL OL6 ......76 A8
  CMANE M1 ......7 H7
Bonar Cl EDGY/DAV SK3 * 12 C6
Bonar Rd EDGY/DAV SK3 ......12 C7
Boncarn Dr NTHM/RTH M23 ......109 K8
Bonchurch Wk
  WGTN/LGST M12 ......88 C3
Bond Cl HOR/BR BL6 ......33 M1
Bondmark Rd OP/CLY M11 ......88 F6
Bond Sq BRO M7 * 72 B6
Bond St ATH M46 ......67 J3
  BURY BL9 ......5 J4
  DTN/ASHW M34 ......101 J1
  LEIGH WN7 ......66 C7
  RAMS BL0 ......19 H2
  STLY SK15 ......91 K1
  WGTN/LGST M12 ......7 L7
  WHIT OL12 ......28 D2
Bongs Rd OFTN SK2 ......113 J6
Bonhill Wk OP/CLY M11 ......88 C2
Bonington Ri
  MPL/ROM SK6 ......114 E4
Bonis Crs OFTN SK2 ......112 F8
Bonny Brow St MDTN M24 ......56 E5
Bonnywell Rd LEIGH WN7 ......81 J1
Bonsall St HULME M15 ......87 K6
Bonscale Crs MDTN M24 ......57 H1
Bonville Cha ALT WA14 ......117 G2
Bonville Rd ALT WA14 ......107 L7
Boodle St AUL OL6 ......75 L8
Boond St ANC M4 ......88 A3
  CSLFD M3 ......6 D2
Boonfields EDGW/EG BL7 ......22 D4
Booth Av RUSH/FAL M14 ......99 G5
Booth Bridge Cl
  MDTN M24 * 56 F5
Boothby Rd SWIN M27 ......70 B3
Boothby St OFTN SK2 ......112 F8
Booth Cl STLY SK15 ......91 J3
  TOT/BURYW BL8 ......24 D7
Boothcote
  DTN/ASHW M34 ......90 A6
Booth Dr URM M41 ......84 C7
Boothfield ECC M30 ......84 D1
Boothfield Rd
  WYTH/NTH M22 ......109 M6
Boothfields
  TOT/BURYW BL8 ......4 A3
Booth Hall Dr
  TOT/BURYW BL8 ......24 C7
Booth Hall Rd BKLY M9 ......73 K1
Booth Hill La OLD OL1 ......59 H3
Booth Rd ALT WA14 ......107 M8
  BOLS/LL BL3 ......53 L2
  DTN/ASHW M34 ......89 K5
  OLDTF/WHR M16 ......97 M1
  SALE M33 ......96 A6
  WIL M/AE SK9 ......126 E3
Boothroyden Rd BKLY M9 ......56 F6
Boothroyden Ter BKLY M9 ......56 F6
Boothsbank Av WALK M28 ......68 G6
Booth's Brow Rd AIMK WN4 ......63 G6
Booth's Hall WALK M28 ......68 G6
Booth's Hall Gv WALK M28 ......68 G6
Booth's Hall Rd WALK M28 ......68 G6
Booth's Hall Wy WALK M28 ......68 G6
Boothstown Dr WALK M28 ......68 D7

Booth St AUL OL6 * 90 E2
  BOL BL1 ......35 M1
  CHAD OL9 ......9 G6
  CMANW M2 ......6 E3
  CSLFD M3 ......6 E3
  DTN/ASHW M34 ......90 C7
  EDGY/DAV SK3 ......13 H8
  HYDE SK14 ......92 F8
  MDTN M24 ......58 A6
  OLDE OL4 ......60 B6
  STLY SK15 ......91 J4
  TOT/BURYW BL8 ......24 C7
Booth St East BRUN/LGST M13 ......87 L6
Booth St West HULME M15 ......87 K6
Booth Wy TOT/BURYW BL8 ......24 C7
Boot La BOL BL1 ......35 G3
Bootle St CMANW M2 ......6 C5
Bor Av WGNS/IIMK WN3 ......47 L8
Bordale Av BKLY M9 ......73 J5
Bordan St OP/CLY M11 ......88 C4
Borden Cl WGNE/HIN WN2 ......48 C2
Border Brook La WALK M28 ......68 D5
Border Wy BURY BL9 ......39 K6
Bordley Wk NTHM/RTH M23 ......109 H1
Bordon Rd EDGY/DAV SK3 ......12 B9
Boringdon Cl
  NEWH/MOS M40 * 73 L6
Borland Av NEWH/MOS M40 ......74 A3
Borough Av RAD M26 ......39 G7
  SWIN M27 ......70 G7
Borough Rd HALE/TIMP WA15 ......108 B8
  SALQ M50 ......86 A3
Borough St STLY SK15 ......91 K3
The Borrans WALK M28 * 68 C7
Borron Rd NEWLW WA12 ......78 E7
Borron St STKP SK1 ......13 M2
Borrowdale Av BOL BL1 ......35 K4
  CHD/CHDH SK8 ......110 E8
Borrowdale Cl ROY/SHW OL2 ......43 G6
Borrowdale Crs AULW OL7 ......75 J8
  DID/WITH M20 ......98 B8
Borrowdale Dr BURY BL9 ......55 K1
  ROCH OL11 ......27 C8
Borrowdale Rd MDTN M24 ......57 H2
  OFTN SK2 ......112 E6
  WGNW/BIL/OR WN5 * 46 E5
Borsdane Av WGNE/HIN WN2 ......49 H8
Borsden St SWIN M27 ......70 A3
Borth Av OFTN SK2 ......112 F5
Borwell St GTN M18 ......89 C7
Boscobel Rd BOLS/LL BL3 ......52 C7
Boscombe Av ECC M30 ......84 F4
Boscombe Dr BRAM/HZG SK7 ......121 J2
Boscombe Pl WGNE/HIN WN2 ......49 H8
Boscombe St RDSH SK5 ......100 C2
  RUSH/FAL M14 ......98 E2
Boscow Rd BOLS/LL BL3 ......53 K2
Bosden Av BRAM/HZG SK7 ......122 A1
Bosden Cl WILM/AE SK9 ......119 M7
Bosden Fold STKP SK1 ......13 K6
Bosdenfold Rd BRAM/HZG SK7 ......122 A1
Bosden Hall Rd
  BRAM/HZG SK7 ......122 A1
Bosdin Rd East URM M41 ......95 H3
Bosdin Rd West URM M41 ......95 H3
Bosley Av DID/WITH M20 ......98 D4
Bosley Cl WILM/AE SK9 ......127 H2
Bosley Dr POY/DIS SK12 ......129 L1
Bosley Rd EDGY/DAV SK3 ......111 K4
Bossall Av BKLY M9 ......57 H8
Bossington Cl OFTN SK2 ......112 F4
Bostock Rd HYDE SK14 ......103 K4
Bostock Wk BRUN/LGST M13 ......7 K9
Boston Cl BRAM/HZG SK7 ......120 F5
  FAIL M35 ......81 J8
  GOL/RIS/CUL WA3 ......81 J8
Boston Ct SALQ M50 ......86 B4
Boston Gv LEIGH WN7 ......66 B3
Boston St BOL BL1 * 36 B2
  HULME M15 ......87 J7
  HYDE SK14 ......102 B2
  OLDS OL8 ......59 J8
Boswell Av DTN/ASHW M34 ......90 A3
Boswell Pl WGNS/IIMK WN3 ......47 J8
Boswell Wy MDTN M24 ......42 A8
Bosworth Cl WHTF M45 ......55 M4
Bosworth Sq ROCH OL11 * 28 A8
Bosworth St OP/CLY M11 ......88 D4
  ROCH OL11 ......10 B9
Botanical Av OLDTF/WHR M16 ......86 D7
Botany Cl HEY OL10 ......40 E1
  WGNE/HIN WN2 ......48 D2
Botany La AUL OL6 ......75 M8
Botany Rd ECC M30 ......69 K8
  MPL/ROM SK6 ......101 K6
Botesworth Cl WGNE/HIN WN2 ......49 L7
Botesworth Gn MILN OL16 ......29 K7
Botham Cl HULME M15 ......87 K7
Bothwell Rd NEWH/MOS M40 ......7 M1
Bottesford Av DID/WITH M20 ......98 C3
Bottomfield Cl OLD OL1 ......9 M1
Bottomley Side BKLY M9 ......72 B1
Bottom o' th' Knotts Brow
  EDGW/EG BL7 ......23 J1
Bottom o' th' Moor BOLE BL2 ......37 G2
  HOR/BR BL6 ......34 C1
  OLD OL1 ......9 M5
Bottom St HYDE SK14 ......102 C1
Boughey St LEIGH WN7 ......66 B7
Boulden Dr TOT/BURYW BL8 ......24 F7
Boulder Dr NTHM/RTH M23 ......118 C2
Boulderstone Rd STLY SK15 ......76 D8
The Boulevard
  BRAM/HZG SK7 ......122 A2
  DID/WITH M20 ......98 B6
  HYDE SK14 ......93 C7
Boundary Cl MOSL OL5 ......76 D6
  MPL/ROM SK6 ......101 M7
Boundary Dr BOLE BL2 ......37 H3
Boundary Edge RAMS BL0 ......19 H1
Boundary Gdns BOL BL1 ......36 A2
  OLD OL1 ......9 G2
Boundary Gv DID/WITH M20 ......98 B6
Boundary La HULME M15 ......87 K6
  WGNNW/ST WN6 ......30 C1
Boundary Park Rd OLD OL1 ......58 F3
Boundary Rd CHD/CHDH SK8 ......111 C6
  IRL M44 ......94 F1
  SWIN M27 ......70 C4
Boundary St BOL BL1 ......36 A2
  BOLE BL2 ......37 L7
  LEIGH WN7 ......66 E8
  LIT OL15 ......21 M6
  ROCH OL11 ......10 D7
  TYLD M29 ......67 K3
  WGNE/HIN WN2 ......15 J6
  WGTN/LGST M12 ......88 D7
Boundary St East CMANE M1 * 7 M9
Boundary St West HULME M15 ......87 K6
Boundary Ter
  WYTH/NTH M22 * 119 H6

The Boundary SWIN M27 ......54 A8
Boundary Wk ROCH OL11 ......10 D8
Boundry Gn DTN/ASHW M34 ......90 B7
Bourdon St NEWH/MOS M40 ......88 A1
Bourget St BRO M7 * 72 C4
Bournbrook Av LHULT M38 ......52 D6
Bourne Av GOL/RIS/CUL WA3 ......80 A4
  SWIN M27 ......70 C5
Bourne Dr NEWH/MOS M40 ......73 M3
Bournelea Av BNG/LEV M19 ......99 H6
Bourne Rd ROY/SHW OL2 ......43 K4
Bourne St CHAD OL9 ......74 E2
  HTNM SK4 ......100 B8
  WILM/AE SK9 ......126 D6
Bourneville Dr
  TOT/BURYW BL8 ......38 D2
Bournville Av HTNM SK4 ......100 B8
Bournville Gv BNG/LEV M19 ......99 M8
Bourton Cl TOT/BURYW BL8 ......38 E1
Bourton Ct TYLD M29 ......68 A3
Bourton Dr GTN M18 ......88 B8
Bowden Cl GOL/RIS/CUL WA3 ......81 J8
  HYDE SK14 ......103 H3
  LEIGH WN7 ......81 M2
  NM/HAY SK22 ......125 L1
  ROCH OL11 ......42 A4
Bowden Crs NM/HAY SK22 ......124 F4
Bowden House La
  WILM/AE SK9 ......127 K4
Bowden La MPL/ROM SK6 ......114 D5
  SWIN M27 ......70 D5
Bowden Rd GLSP SK13 ......104 F1
  SWIN M27 ......70 D5
Bowden St BRAM/HZG SK7 ......122 A1
  DTN/ASHW M34 ......101 H1
Bowdon Av RUSH/FAL M14 ......98 C3
Bowdon Ri ALT WA14 ......116 F2
Bowdon Rd ALT WA14 ......116 E1
Bowdon St EDGY/DAV SK3 ......13 G7
Bowen Cl BRAM/HZG SK7 ......121 M3
Bowen St BOL BL1 ......35 L3
Bower Av BRAM/HZG SK7 ......121 M5
  HTNM SK4 ......12 D1
  WHIT OL12 ......21 H8
Bower Ct HYDE SK14 ......91 K7
Bower Cup Fold STLY SK15 ......77 H8
Bowerfield Av BRAM/HZG SK7 ......121 M4
Bowerfield Crs BRAM/HZG SK7 ......121 M4
Bowerfold La HTNM SK4 ......12 E2
Bower Gdns STLY SK15 ......92 A4
Bower Gv STLY SK15 ......91 M2
Bower Rd HALE/TIMP WA15 ......117 G3
Bowers Av URM M41 ......84 E8
Bowers St RUSH/FAL M14 ......99 G5
Bower St BRO M7 * 72 B5
  BURY BL9 * 5 G5
  NEWH/MOS M40 ......73 J7
  OLD OL1 ......9 M4
  RDSH SK5 ......100 C2
Bower Ter DROY M43 ......89 M1
Bowery Av CHD/CHDH SK8 ......120 B6
Bowes Cl TOT/BURYW BL8 ......24 E7
Bowes St RUSH/FAL M14 ......98 C1
Bowfell Dr MPL/ROM SK6 ......123 G4
Bowfell Gv BKLY M9 ......72 E1
Bowfell Rd URM M41 ......95 L2
Bowgreave Av BOLE BL2 ......37 J5
Bow Green Rd ALT WA14 ......116 C3
Bowgreen Wk HULME M15 ......87 G6
Bowker Av DTN/ASHW M34 ......101 L4
Bowker Bank Av CHH M8 ......72 C2
Bowker Cl ROCH OL11 ......27 H3
Bowkers Rw BOL BL1 ......2 E4
Bowker St BRO M7 * 72 A6
  HYDE SK14 ......102 D1
  RAD M26 ......54 D1
  WALK M28 ......68 E1
Bowlacre Rd HYDE SK14 ......102 A6
Bowland Av AIMK WN4 ......63 L8
  GOL/RIS/CUL WA3 ......79 M3
  GTN M18 ......89 K8
Bowland Cl AUL OL6 ......75 M5
  OFTN SK2 ......113 H7
  ROY/SHW OL2 ......43 H5
  TOT/BURYW BL8 ......38 B1
Bowland Dr BOL BL1 ......35 B1
Bowland Gv MILN OL16 ......29 K8
Bowland Rd DTN/ASHW M34 ......100 E1
  GLSP SK13 ......104 D4
  MPL/ROM SK6 ......101 L7
  NTHM/RTH M23 ......109 J6
Bow La ALT WA14 ......116 C4
  CMANW M2 ......6 F5
  HEY OL10 ......40 F2
Bowlee Cl WHTF M45 ......55 K3
Bowler St BNG/LEV M19 ......99 L4
  ROY/SHW OL2 ......43 L5
Bowlers Wk WHIT OL12 ......28 C2
Bowley Av WYTH/NTH M22 ......118 C2
Bowling Green St HEY OL10 ......41 G2
  HYDE SK14 ......101 M2
The Bowling Gn RAMS BL0 ......19 G1
Bowling Green Wy ROCH OL11 ......27 J6
Bowling Rd GTN M18 ......100 B1
The Bowlings WGNNW/ST WN6 ......47 K2
Bowman Crs AUL OL6 ......91 G1
Bow Meadow Gra
  WGTN/LGST M12 ......88 C8
Bowmont Cl CHD/CHDH SK8 ......111 K8
Bowness Av CHD/CHDH SK8 ......120 D3
  HTNM SK4 ......100 B6
  IRL M44 ......94 A8
  WHIT OL12 ......27 M3
Bowness Dr SALE M33 ......96 C7
Bowness Pl WGNE/HIN WN2 ......48 E4
Bowness Rd AULW OL7 ......75 J8
  BOLS/LL BL3 ......36 A8
  BOLS/LL BL3 ......37 J8
  MDTN M24 ......57 G3
Bowness St OP/CLY M11 ......89 G3
  STRET M32 ......97 G1
Bowring St BRO M7 * 71 M7
Bow St BOL BL1 ......2 E5
  CMANW M2 ......6 E4
  DUK SK16 ......90 F2
  EDGY/DAV SK3 ......12 C6
  OLD OL1 ......9 K5
  ROCH OL11 ......42 A1
Bowyer Gdns BOLS/LL BL3 ......51 J1
Boxgrove Rd SALE M33 ......96 B7
Boxhill Dr NTHM/RTH M23 * 109 K3
Box St LIT OL15 ......21 L7
  RAMS BL0 ......19 G6
Boxtree Av GTN M18 ......100 A1
Boyd St WGNNW/ST WN6 ......31 J4
Boyd's Wk DUK SK16 ......90 F5

Boyer St OLDTF/WHR M16 86 E7
Boyle St BOL BL1 35 K3
CHH M8 72 E6
Boysnope Whf ECC M30 84 A8
Brabant Rd CHD/CHDH SK8 120 D2
Brabazon Pl
WGNW/BIL/OR WN5 46 F4
Brabham Cl CCHDY M21 97 L4
Brabham Ms SWIN M27 69 M5
Brabyns Av MPL/ROM SK6 114 A1
Brabyns Brow MPL/ROM SK6 114 D5
Brabyns Rd HYDE SK14 102 B5
Bracadale Dr EDGY/DAV SK3 112 B8
Bracewell Cl WGTN/LGST M12 88 D7
Bracken Av WALK M28 69 H1
Bracken Cl BOL BL1 22 A6
DROY M43 89 M2
HEY OL10 41 G4
HYDE SK14 93 G6
MPL/ROM SK6 114 F5
OLDE OL4 60 C6
SALE M33 95 M7
Bracken Dr NTHM/RTH M23 109 L7
Brackenhurst Av MOSL OL5 77 H3
Bracken Lea WHTN BL5 50 C7
Brackenlea Dr BKLY M9 72 F2
Bracken Lea Fold WHIT OL12 27 L2
Brackenlea Pl EDGY/DAV SK3 112 A7
Bracken Rd ATH M46 67 G2
LEIGH WN7 65 L7
Brackenside RDSH SK5 100 D4
Bracken Wy GLSP SK13 105 J5
Brackenwood Cl ROY/SHW OL2 58 F2
Brackenwood Dr
CHD/CHDH SK8 111 G8
Brackenwood Ms
WILM/AE SK9 127 J3
Brackley Av HULME M15 6 A9
IRL M44 94 A6
TYLD M29 67 L3
Brackley Dr MDTN M24 57 K7
Brackley Ldg ECC M30 * 85 J1
Brackley Rd ECC M30 70 A8
HTNM SK4 100 A7
WHTN BL5 51 K4
Brackley Sq OLD OL1 * 9 M3
Brackleys St FWTH BL4 53 G4
Brackley St FWTH BL4 53 G4
OLD OL1 * 9 L3
WALK M28 52 F8
Bracondale Av BOL BL1 35 L2
Bradbourne Cl BOLS/LL BL3 2 D9
Bradburn Cl ECC M30 85 G3
Bradburn Rd IRL M44 94 B5
Bradburn St ECC M30 85 G3
Bradburn Wk CHH M8 72 E6
Bradbury Av ALT WA14 107 K7
Bradbury St AULW OL7 * 75 K8
HYDE SK14 102 B3
RAD M26 54 D2
Bradda Mt BRAM/HZG SK7 121 H2
Braddan Av SALE M33 108 F1
Bradden Cl ORD M5 86 D3
Braddocks Cl WHIT OL12 21 H8
Braddon Av URM M41 96 A1
Braddon Rd MPL/ROM SK6 101 K7
Braddon St OP/CLY M11 88 F3
Braddyll Rd WHTN BL5 51 J4
Brade Cl OP/CLY M11 88 F4
Bradfield Av SLFD M6 85 M2
Bradfield Cl RDSH SK5 100 B2
Bradfield Rd STRET M32 96 E2
URM M41 96 C2
Bradford Av BOLS/LL BL3 52 E1
Bradford Crs BOLS/LL BL3 * 36 D8
Bradford La MCFLDN SK10 130 D6
Bradford Park Dr BOLE BL2 3 K6
Bradford Rd BOLS/LL BL3 52 D2
ECC M30 70 B8
NEWH/MOS M40 88 A2
Bradford St BOLE BL2 3 H5
FWTH BL4 53 G5
OLD OL1 9 G2
WGNS/IIMK WN3 14 F6
Bradford Ter BURY BL9 4 C7
Bradgate Av CHD/CHDH SK8 119 M3
Bradgate Cl WYTH/NTH M22 110 B4
Bradgate Rd ALT WA14 107 K7
SALE M33 108 E2
Bradgate St AULW OL7 90 D3
Bradgreen Rd ECC M30 84 F1
Bradley Av BRO M7 71 L5
Bradley Cl HALE/TIMP WA15 108 B5
Bradley Dr BURY BL9 55 L2
Bradley Fold Rd BOLE BL2 37 L6
Bradley Green Rd HYDE SK14 91 J6
Bradley La MILN OL16 29 L8
RAD M26 37 L7
STRET M32 96 D5
WGNNW/ST WN6 31 J2
Bradleys Count CMANE M1 * 7 J4
Bradley Smithy Cl WHIT OL12 28 B2
Bradley St CMANE M1 7 J3
MILN OL16 29 L8
Bradney Cl BKLY M9 56 E8
Bradnor Rd WYTH/NTH M22 110 A5
Bradshaw Av DID/WITH M20 98 E5
FAIL M35 74 B7
WHTF M45 55 H2
Bradshaw Brow BOLE BL2 22 F8
Bradshaw Cl WGNNW/ST WN6 31 G3
Bradshaw Crs MPL/ROM SK6 114 D5
Bradshaw Fold Av
NEWH/MOS M40 74 A1
Bradshawgate BOL BL1 2 F5
LEIGH WN7 66 C7
WGN WN1 15 J4
Bradshaw Hall Dr BOLE BL2 22 F6
Bradshaw Hall Fold BOLE BL2 * 23 G6
Bradshaw Hall La
CHD/CHDH SK8 119 M4
Bradshaw La STRET M32 97 G4
Bradshaw Mdw BOLE BL2 23 G6
Bradshaw Rd BOLE BL2 23 G5
MPL/ROM SK6 114 C5
TOT/BURYW BL8 23 M6
Bradshaw St ANC M4 * 7 G2
ATH M46 67 G1
BRO M7 72 B6
FWTH BL4 53 G5
HEY OL10 41 H2
OLD OL1 9 K5
RAD M26 54 C1
WGN WN1 48 A2
WGNW/BIL/OR WN5 46 D6
Bradshaw St North BRO M7 72 A5
Bradstock Rd OLDTF/WHR M16 98 B1
Bradstone Rd CHH M8 72 C7
Bradwell Av DID/WITH M20 98 C6
STRET M32 96 D1
Bradwell Dr CHD/CHDH SK8 119 L5
Bradwell Pl BOLE BL2 36 E3
Bradwell Rd BRAM/HZG SK7 122 A4
GOL/RIS/CUL WA3 80 B5
Bradwen Av CHH M8 72 D3
Bradwen Cl DTN/ASHW M34 101 K3
Brady St STKP SK1 13 L2
Braeburn Ct LEIGH WN7 66 A7
Braemar Av STRET M32 96 D2
URM M41 95 K3
Braemar Dr BURY BL9 40 A2
Braemar Gv HEY OL10 40 D3
Braemar La WALK M28 68 E6
Braemar Rd BRAM/HZG SK7 122 B1
RUSH/FAL M14 99 H4
SALE M33 107 M2
Braemore Cl ROY/SHW OL2 43 H4
WGNS/IIMK WN3 62 F2
Braemore Dr HYDE SK14 103 J3
Brae Side OLDS OL8 75 H2
Braeside STRET M32 * 96 D3
Braeside Cl OFTN SK2 113 J7
Braeside Crs
WGNW/BIL/OR WN5 62 A7
Braeside Gv BOLS/LL BL3 35 H7
Braewood Cl BURY BL9 39 M1
Bragenham St GTN M18 88 F7
Braidhaven WGNNW/ST WN6 30 B5
Brailsford Rd BOLE BL2 36 F1
RUSH/FAL M14 99 H4
Braintree Rd WYTH/NTH M22 119 G4
Braithwaite WGNNW/ST WN6 30 D6
Braithwaite Rd
GOL/RIS/CUL WA3 80 A3
MDTN M24 41 G8
Brakehouse Cl MILN OL16 29 H6
Brakenhurst Dr BRO M7 * 72 C6
Brakesmere Gv WALK M28 52 C8
Braley St WGTN/LGST M12 * 7 K8
Bramah Edge Ct GLSP SK13 93 J6
Bramall Cl BURY BL9 55 L2
Bramall St HYDE SK14 91 G8
Bramble Av OLDE OL4 60 A3
ORD M5 86 F5
Bramble Bank GLSP SK13 105 H4
Bramble Cl LIT OL15 21 K7
Bramble Cft HOR/BR BL6 50 D1
Bramble Gv
WGNW/BIL/OR WN5 47 H5
The Brambles AIMK WN4 63 G7
Bramblewood WGNE/HIN WN2 49 J5
Brambling Cl DTN/ASHW M34 89 M2
OFTN SK2 113 K8
Brambling Dr WHTN BL5 50 A6
Brambling Wy
GOL/RIS/CUL WA3 80 B5
Bramcote Av BOLE BL2 3 J8
NTHM/RTH M23 109 L6
Bramdean Av BOLE BL2 23 H7
Bramfield Wk HULME M15 * 6 B9
Bramford Cl WHTN BL5 50 B6
Bramhall Av BOLE BL2 23 K8
Bramhall Cl DUK SK16 91 G6
HALE/TIMP WA15 109 G6
MILN OL16 29 H7
SALE M33 109 H1
Bramhall La EDGY/DAV SK3 112 C8
Bramhall La South
BRAM/HZG SK7 121 G6
Bramhall Moor La
BRAM/HZG SK7 121 K3
Bramhall Park Rd
BRAM/HZG SK7 120 F3
Bramhall St BOLS/LL BL3 52 E1
GTN M18 * 89 H7
Bramham Rd MPL/ROM SK6 114 D8
Bramley Av BNG/LEV M19 99 K4
STRET M32 96 E2
Bramley Cl BRAM/HZG SK7 121 G6
SWIN M27 69 M6
WILM/AE SK9 126 B8
Bramley Crs HTNM SK4 12 A4
Bramley Dr BRAM/HZG SK7 121 G6
TOT/BURYW BL8 24 F5
Bramley Meade BRO M7 72 B5
Bramley Rd BOL BL1 22 C6
BRAM/HZG SK7 121 G6
ROCH OL11 27 H4
Bramley St BRO M7 72 B7
Brammay Dr TOT/BURYW BL8 24 B7
Brampton Cl WGNE/HIN WN2 64 C3
Brampton Rd BOLS/LL BL3 51 K1
BRAM/HZG SK7 121 H2
Brampton St ATH M46 * 67 G1
Bramway BRAM/HZG SK7 120 E5
MPL/ROM SK6 123 H5
Bramwell Dr BRUN/LGST M13 87 M6
Bramwell St STKP SK1 112 E4
Bramworth Av RAMS BL0 18 E6
Brancaster Dr
GOL/RIS/CUL WA3 80 D5
Brancaster Rd CMANE M1 7 H8
Branch Cl TOT/BURYW BL8 4 C2
Branch Rd LIT OL15 29 H3
Branch St WGNE/HIN WN2 48 D5
Branch Wy RNFD/HAY WA11 78 A6
Brancker St WHTN BL5 50 F4
Brandish Cl BRUN/LGST M13 88 A8
Brandle Av TOT/BURYW BL8 24 F8
Brandlehow Dr MDTN M24 56 F2
Brandlesholme Rd
TOT/BURYW BL8 24 F6
Brandon Av CHD/CHDH SK8 119 K3
DTN/ASHW M34 100 C1
ECC M30 70 D8
WYTH/NTH M22 109 M4
Brandon Brow OLD OL1 * 9 H2
Brandon Cl TOT/BURYW BL8 25 G7
WILM/AE SK9 127 H2
Brandon Crs ROY/SHW OL2 43 K4
Brandon Rd SLFD M6 70 E7
Brandon St BOLS/LL BL3 36 A8
MILN OL16 29 H6
Brandram Rd PWCH M25 * 55 L8
Brandreth Pl WGNNW/ST WN6 31 J3
Brandsby Gdns ORD M5 * 86 D4
Brandwood OLD OL1 58 B3
Brandwood Av CCHDY M21 98 A8
Brandwood Cl WALK M28 68 D4
Brandwood St BOLS/LL BL3 35 M8
Branfield Av CHD/CHDH SK8 119 M3
Branksome Av PWCH M25 55 K8
Branksome Dr BKLY M9 56 E6
CHD/CHDH SK8 119 M3
SLFD M6 70 D7
Branksome Rd HTNM SK4 12 A4
Brannach Dr CHAD OL9 58 D4
Bransby Av BKLY M9 57 H8
Branscombe Dr SALE M33 95 M7
Branscombe Gdns
BOLS/LL BL3 * 37 G7
Bransdale Av ROY/SHW OL2 42 F8
Bransdale Cl BOLS/LL BL3 35 J8
Bransdale Dr AIMK WN4 79 G1
Bransfield Cl WGNS/IIMK WN3 63 K1
Bransford Cl AIMK WN4 78 F2
Bransford Rd OP/CLY M11 89 G4
URM M41 95 M1
Branson Cl GOL/RIS/CUL WA3 79 K2
Branson St ANC M4 88 A2
Branson Wk HALE/TIMP WA15 108 F6
Branston Rd NEWH/MOS M40 74 A2
Brantfell Gv BOLE BL2 37 J4
Branthwaite WGNE/HIN WN2 48 E3
Brantingham Rd CCHDY M21 97 L3
Brantwood Cl ROY/SHW OL2 42 F8
Brantwood Dr BOLE BL2 37 J4
Brantwood Rd BRO M7 72 A4
CHD/CHDH SK8 120 B3
HTNM SK4 99 M8
Brantwood Ter BKLY M9 * 73 J5
Brassey St AUL OL6 75 L8
MDTN M24 57 K3
Brassica Cl ECC M30 69 K8
Brassington Av CCHDY M21 97 L5
ORD M5 86 E4
Brassington Crs GLSP SK13 104 A3
Brassington Rd HTNM SK4 99 H8
Brathay Cl BOLE BL2 37 J3
WHTF M45 55 M4
Brattice Dr SWIN M27 70 F4
Bratton Cl WGNS/IIMK WN3 62 F3
Bratton Wk BRUN/LGST M13 * 88 A6
Brattray Dr MDTN M24 57 H1
Braunston Cl ECC M30 85 H4
Bray Av ECC M30 84 E1
Braybrook Dr BOL BL1 35 G5
Bray Cl CHD/CHDH SK8 120 A2
Brayford Dr WGNE/HIN WN2 32 F7
Brayford Rd WYTH/NTH M22 118 F3
Brayshaw Cl HEY OL10 40 E3
Brayside Rd DID/WITH M20 99 G8
Braystan Gdns CHD/CHDH SK8 110 E6
Braystones Cl
HALE/TIMP WA15 109 G6
Brayston Fold MDTN M24 56 F4
Brayton Av DID/WITH M20 110 F2
SALE M33 96 A7
Brayton Ct WGNE/HIN WN2 49 G6
Brazennose St CMANW M2 6 E5
Brazil Pl CMANE M1 7 H7
Brazil St CMANE M1 7 H7
Brazley Av BOLS/LL BL3 52 D1
HOR/BR BL6 34 B3
Bread St GTN M18 89 H6
Breaktemper WHTN BL5 50 B3
Breaston Av LEIGH WN7 81 M1
Brechvale Cl POY/DIS SK12 129 J1
Breckland Cl STLY SK15 92 A2
Breckland Dr BOL BL1 35 G5
Breckles Pl BOLS/LL BL3 * 2 B8
Breck Rd ECC M30 84 E2
Brecon Av BNG/LEV M19 99 J5
CHD/CHDH SK8 120 A3
DTN/ASHW M34 101 J3
URM M41 95 G1
Brecon Cl POY/DIS SK12 122 B8
ROY/SHW OL2 42 F6
WGNE/HIN WN2 64 E2
Brecon Crs AUL OL6 75 L6
Brecon Dr BURY BL9 39 H5
WGNE/HIN WN2 65 K1
Brecon Wk OLDS OL8 * 74 E2
Bredbury Dr FWTH BL4 53 H4
Bredbury Gn MPL/ROM SK6 113 K3
Bredbury Park Wy
MPL/ROM SK6 101 H7
Bredbury Rd RUSH/FAL M14 98 E2
Bredbury St CHAD OL9 8 B7
HYDE SK14 * 91 G7
Bredon Wy OLDS OL8 75 H1
Breeze Hl ATH M46 51 J7
WGNNW/ST WN6 31 L5
Breeze Hill Rd ATH M46 51 K7
OLDE OL4 60 A7
Breeze Mt PWCH M25 71 L2
Breightmet Dr BOLE BL2 37 H5
Breightmet Fold La BOLE BL2 37 J5
Breightmet St BOLE BL2 2 F6
Brellafield Dr ROY/SHW OL2 43 J3
Brenbar Crs WHIT OL12 20 B3
Brenchley Dr NTHM/RTH M23 109 K2
Brencon Av NTHM/RTH M23 108 F3
Brendall Cl OFTN SK2 113 K7
Brendon Av NEWH/MOS M40 73 K5
RDSH SK5 100 C6
Brendon Cl GLSP SK13 104 D4
Brendon Dr DTN/ASHW M34 90 A3
Brendon Hills ROY/SHW OL2 58 F1
Brennan Cl HULME M15 87 K7
Brennan Ct OLDS OL8 74 F2
Brennock Cl OP/CLY M11 88 C4
Brentbridge Rd DID/WITH M20 98 E5
Brent Cl BOLE BL2 37 L7
POY/DIS SK12 121 K8
Brentfield Av CHH M8 72 C6
Brentford Av BOL BL1 35 L2
Brentford Rd RDSH SK5 100 C6
Brentford St BKLY M9 73 H5
Brent Moor Rd BRAM/HZG SK7 121 J2
Brentnall St STKP SK1 13 J8
Brentnor Rd NEWH/MOS M40 73 M2
Brenton Av SALE M33 96 D8
Brent Rd HTNM SK4 12 D4
NTHM/RTH M23 109 K2
Brentwood SALE M33 96 D8
SLFD M6 86 B1
WGNW/BIL/OR WN5 47 G7
Brentwood Av ALT WA14 108 B5
IRL M44 94 A6
URM M41 96 A2
WALK M28 69 L6
Brentwood Cl LIT OL15 29 J1
OLDTF/WHR M16 98 C1
RDSH SK5 101 G7
STLY SK15 91 M2
Brentwood Ct PWCH M25 71 J1
Brentwood Crs ALT WA14 108 B6
Brentwood Dr CHD/CHDH SK8 110 E7
ECC M30 70 A8
FWTH BL4 52 E2
Brentwood Gv LEIGH WN7 66 C5
Brentwood Rd SWIN M27 70 A6
Brereton Cl ALT WA14 116 E3
Brereton Dr WALK M28 69 J5
Brereton Gv IRL M44 94 B6
Brereton Rd ECC M30 84 C3
WILM/AE SK9 127 J1
Breslyn St CSLFD M3 6 F1
Bretherton Rw WGN WN1 14 F4
Bretherton St WGNE/HIN WN2 48 F6
Brethren's Ct DROY M43 89 K4
Bretland Gdns HYDE SK14 103 H3
Brettargh St SLFD M6 71 K8
Brett Rd WALK M28 68 C6
Brett St WYTH/NTH M22 110 B3
Brewer's Gn BRAM/HZG SK7 121 M1
Brewer St CMANE M1 7 J4
Brewerton Rd OLDE OL4 59 M7
Brewery La LEIGH WN7 66 D7
Brewery St ALT WA14 108 A8
STKP SK1 13 K2
Brewster St BKLY M9 * 73 G4
MDTN M24 57 K2
Brian Av DROY M43 * 89 M1
Brian Redhead Ct
HULME M15 6 C9
Brian Rd FWTH BL4 52 D2
Brian St ROCH OL11 41 L2
Briaracre Ter AUL OL6 * 75 M4
Briar Av BRAM/HZG SK7 122 B2
OLDE OL4 60 A3
Briar Cl AIMK WN4 63 K8
SALE M33 95 M8
URM M41 95 K1
WGNE/HIN WN2 49 L8
WHIT OL12 27 K3
Briar Crs WYTH/NTH M22 110 B7
Briarcroft Dr ATH M46 66 D3
Briardene
DTN/ASHW M34 * 90 D8
Briardene Gdns
WYTH/NTH M22 110 B8
Briarfield EDGW/EG BL7 22 A2
Briarfield Rd
CHD/CHDH SK8 120 D1
DID/WITH M20 99 G6
FWTH BL4 52 D3
HALE/TIMP WA15 108 F6
HTNM SK4 100 B6
UPML OL3 61 K2
WALK M28 69 J5
Briar Gv CHAD OL9 58 E3
LEIGH WN7 66 B4
MPL/ROM SK6 101 K7
Briar Hill Av LHULT M38 52 B8
Briar Hill Cl LHULT M38 52 B8
Briar Hill Gv LHULT M38 52 B8
Briar Hill Wy SLFD M6 * 86 D1
Briar Hollow HTNM SK4 12 A4
Briarlands Av SALE M33 108 C2
Briarlands Cl
BRAM/HZG SK7 120 F6
Briarlea Gdns BNG/LEV M19 99 H7
Briarley Gdns MPL/ROM SK6 101 M6
Briarly WGNNW/ST WN6 31 K5
Briarmere Wk CHAD OL9 8 C4
Briar Rd GOL/RIS/CUL WA3 79 L4
WGNW/BIL/OR WN5 47 G5
Briars Mt HTNM SK4 12 A4
Briars Pk BRAM/HZG SK7 120 E3
Briarstead Cl BRAM/HZG SK7 120 F5
Briar St BOLE BL2 * 37 G5
ROCH OL11 10 B6
Briarwood WILM/AE SK9 127 G5
Briarwood Av DROY M43 89 H1
NTHM/RTH M23 109 G4
Briarwood Cha
CHD/CHDH SK8 120 D3
Briarwood Crs MPL/ROM SK6 114 C8
Briary Dr TYLD M29 67 L4
Brice St DUK SK16 90 E4
Brickbridge Rd MPL/ROM SK6 114 D7
Brickfield St GLSP SK13 93 L7
MILN OL16 28 E2
Brickhill La HALE/TIMP WA15 117 K8
Brick Houses GLSP SK13 * 103 J7
Brickkiln La ALT WA14 106 F8
Brick Kiln La WGN WN1 15 G2
Brickkiln Rw ALT WA14 116 E3
Brickley St CSLFD M3 87 K1
Brick St ANC M4 * 7 H3
BURY BL9 5 J3
Bridcam St CHH M8 72 D7
Briddon St CSLFD M3 87 J1
Brideoake St LEIGH WN7 66 E8
Brideoak St CHH M8 72 D6
OLDE OL4 60 B4
Bridestowe Av HYDE SK14 102 F1
Bride St BOL BL1 36 B2
Bridge Av MPL/ROM SK6 101 K7
Bridge Bank Rd LIT OL15 29 K1
Bridge Cl PART M31 106 D1
RAD M26 54 E2
Bridgecrest Ct
CHD/CHDH SK8 * 120 C2
Bridge Dr CHD/CHDH SK8 111 G8
WILM/AE SK9 127 H1
Bridge End WGNS/IIMK WN3 14 D4
Bridgefield Av WILM/AE SK9 127 G3
Bridgefield Crs OLDE OL4 60 C6
Bridgefield Dr BURY BL9 39 M2
Bridgefield St RAD M26 54 E1
ROCH OL11 10 B5
STKP SK1 13 H4
Bridgefold Rd ROCH OL11 27 M5
Bridgefoot Cl WALK M28 68 D7
Bridge Gv HALE/TIMP WA15 108 C5
Bridge Hall Dr BURY BL9 39 M2
Bridge Hall Fold BURY BL9 39 M2
Bridge Hall La BURY BL9 40 A2
Bridge La BRAM/HZG SK7 121 J3
Bridgelea Ms DID/WITH M20 98 E6
Bridgelea Rd DID/WITH M20 98 E6
Bridgeman Pl BOLE BL2 3 G6
Bridgeman St BOLS/LL BL3 2 E8
FWTH BL4 53 G3
Bridgeman Ter WGN WN1 14 F1
Bridgemere Cl RAD M26 38 C7
Bridgend Cl CHD/CHDH SK8 111 M8
WGTN/LGST M12 88 D6
Bridgenorth Av URM M41 96 C2
Bridgenorth Dr LIT OL15 29 J1
Bridge Rd BURY BL9 4 C6
HALE/TIMP WA15 108 F5
Bridges Av BURY BL9 39 J6
Bridges Ct BOL BL1 * 2 E6
Bridge's St ATH M46 66 E2
Bridge St BOL BL1 2 E4
BURY BL9 5 H1
CSLFD M3 6 D4
DROY M43 89 H4
DTN/ASHW M34 90 C5
FWTH BL4 53 H3
GOL/RIS/CUL WA3 79 K5
HEY OL10 40 E2
MDTN M24 * 57 K4
MILN OL16 29 J6
NM/HAY SK22 124 E3
OLD OL1 9 L6
OLD OL1 59 G3
OLDE OL4 60 C6
RAD M26 53 L4
RAMS BL0 18 F6
ROCH OL11 41 M3
ROY/SHW OL2 * 43 M4
STKP SK1 13 J3
STLY SK15 91 J3
SWIN M27 70 D4
UPML OL3 61 L5
WGNE/HIN WN2 49 G6
WGNS/IIMK WN3 14 F6
WHIT OL12 * 20 A3
WHIT OL12 28 F1
Bridge St Brow STKP SK1 13 J3
Bridgewater Cir TRPK M17 84 F6
Bridgewater Pl CMANE M1 7 G4
Bridgewater Rd ALT WA14 108 A5
SWIN M27 70 E5
WALK M28 68 D5
WALK M28 68 F2
Bridgewater St BOL BL1 2 A6
CSLFD M3 6 C7
ECC M30 84 E2
FWTH BL4 53 G4
LHULT M38 52 E8
OLD OL1 9 L3
SALE M33 96 E7
STRET M32 * 97 H2
WGNE/HIN WN2 49 H6
WGNS/IIMK WN3 14 E5
WGNW/BIL/OR WN5 14 A7
Bridgewater Viad CSLFD M3 6 D8
Bridgewater Wy
OLDTF/WHR M16 86 F6
Bridgfield Cl MPL/ROM SK6 123 G5
Bridgnorth Rd BKLY M9 72 D1
Bridle Cl DROY M43 89 M1
URM M41 95 H2
Bridle Fold RAD M26 38 D8
Bridle Rd BRAM/HZG SK7 128 D1
PWCH M25 56 B5
Bridle Wy BRAM/HZG SK7 128 D2
Bridleway NM/HAY SK22 124 F3
Bridlington Av SLFD M6 * 85 M1
Bridlington Cl
NEWH/MOS M40 73 M6
Bridport Av NEWH/MOS M40 74 A4
Bridson La BOLE BL2 37 G3
Bridson St OLDE OL4 59 M5
ORD M5 86 B3
Brief St BOLE BL2 36 F3
Brien Av ALT WA14 108 A6
Briercliffe Cl GTN M18 88 F6
Briercliffe Rd BOLS/LL BL3 35 M7
Brierfield Av ATH M46 50 F8
Brierfield Dr BURY BL9 25 H4
Brierholme Av EDGW/EG BL7 22 B3
Brierley Av FAIL M35 74 D5
WHTF M45 55 H2
Brierley Cl AUL OL6 76 D6
DTN/ASHW M34 101 H2
Brierley Dr MDTN M24 57 K5
Brierley Rd East SWIN M27 70 B3
Brierley Rd West SWIN M27 70 B3
Brierley St BURY BL9 4 E8
CHAD OL9 8 D2
DUK SK16 * 91 G3
HEY OL10 41 G2
OLDS OL8 75 J1
Brierley Wk CHAD OL9 8 D2
Brierton Dr WYTH/NTH M22 118 D3
Brierwood BOLE BL2 3 K1
Brierwood Cl ROY/SHW OL2 59 H3
Briery Av BOLE BL2 23 G6
Brigade Dr STRET M32 96 F1
Brigade St BOL BL1 35 M5
Brigadier Cl DID/WITH M20 98 E6
Brigantine Cl ORD M5 86 D4
Briggs Cl SALE M33 107 M3
Briggs Fold Cl EDGW/EG BL7 22 B2
Briggs Fold Rd EDGW/EG BL7 22 B2
Briggs Rd STRET M32 * 86 C8
Briggs St CSLFD M3 6 B1
LEIGH WN7 66 B5
Brigham St OP/CLY M11 88 F4
Bright Cir URM M41 85 H6
Brightgate Wy STRET M32 85 K7
Brightman St GTN M18 89 G6
Brighton Av BNG/LEV M19 99 J5
BOL BL1 35 K3
BRO M7 72 B6
RDSH SK5 100 C2
URM M41 95 H2
Brighton Gv HYDE SK14 102 B3
RUSH/FAL M14 99 G2
SALE M33 96 D7
URM M41 95 H2
Brighton Pl BRUN/LGST M13 87 L6
Brighton Range GTN M18 * 89 J8
Brighton Rd HTNM SK4 12 C4
OLDE OL4 60 D3
Brighton St ANC M4 87 K1
BURY BL9 5 K2
Bright Rd ECC M30 85 H2
Brightstone Wk
RUSH/FAL M14 88 B8
Bright St AUL OL6 91 G2
BURY BL9 5 J2
CHAD OL9 74 D1
DROY M43 89 L3
LEIGH WN7 66 B5
MILN OL16 11 H8
OLDS OL8 8 E8
RAD M26 38 F8
Brightwater Cl WHTF M45 55 K4
Brightwell Wk ANC M4 7 H3
Brignall Gv GOL/RIS/CUL WA3 80 A3
Brigstock Av GTN M18 88 F7
Briksdal Wy HOR/BR BL6 34 F5
Brimelow St MPL/ROM SK6 112 F1
Brimfield Av TYLD M29 67 M3
Brimmy Croft La UPML OL3 44 F1
Brimrod La ROCH OL11 10 A9
Brimscombe Av
WYTH/NTH M22 118 E2
Brindale Rd RDSH SK5 100 F8
Brindle Cl SLFD M6 71 J8
Brindle Heath Rd SLFD M6 71 J8
Brindlehurst Dr TYLD M29 68 A5
Brindle St TYLD M29 67 K3
WGNE/HIN WN2 49 J5
Brindley Av BKLY M9 56 E7
MPL/ROM SK6 114 C7
SALE M33 96 F6
WALK M28 68 D6
Brindley Cl ATH M46 66 D2
FWTH BL4 52 E4
Brindley Rd OLDTF/WHR M16 86 E7
Brindley St ECC M30 84 E1
HOR/BR BL6 * 33 M2
SWIN M27 70 C2
WALK M28 68 C6
WALK M28 69 G2
WGNW/BIL/OR WN5 46 F7
Brinell Dr IRL M44 94 C7
Brinkburn Rd BRAM/HZG SK7 122 C1
Brinklow Cl OP/CLY M11 89 H5
Brinkshaw Av WYTH/NTH M22 119 G2
Brinks La BOLE BL2 37 K5

Brinksway BOL BL1....34 F5
EDGY/DAV SK3....12 C6
Brinksworth Cl BOLE BL2....37 K4
Brinnington Crs RDSH SK5....100 E8
Brinnington Rd RDSH SK5....100 F8
STKP SK1....13 M1
Brinsop Hall La WHTN BL5....33 K7
Brinsop Sq WGTN/LGST M12....88 E6
Brinsworth Dr CHH M8....72 D6
Briony Av HALE/TIMP WA15....117 L2
Briony Cl ROY/SHW OL2....59 H2
Brisbane Cl BRAM/HZG SK7....121 H7
Brisbane St BRUN/LGST M13....87 L7
Briscoe La NEWH/MOS M40....73 K8
Briscoe Ms BOLS/LL BL3....36 D8
Briscoe St OLD OL1....9 J3
Bristle Hall Wy WHTN BL5....50 C2
Bristle St HULME M15....87 K6
Bristol Av AUL OL6....75 L5
BNG/LEV M19....99 L4
BOLE BL2....3 L1
Bristol St BRO M7....72 B5
Bristowe St OP/CLY M11....89 G1
Britain St BURY BL9....39 H6
Britannia Av ROY/SHW OL2....43 M6
Britannia Cl RAD M26....54 D1
Britannia Rd SALE M33....96 E7
WGNW/BIL/OR WN5....46 F4
Britannia St AULW OL7....90 C4
HEY OL10....40 E2
OLD OL1....9 M4
SLFD M6....71 K6
Britannia Wy BOLE BL2....36 D2
Britnall Av WGTN/LGST M12....88 D7
ROY/SHW OL2....59 H2
Briton St MILN OL16....11 J2
Brixham Av CHD/CHDH SK8....120 B5
Brixham Dr SALE M33....96 A6
Brixham Rd OLDTF/WHR M16....86 E8
Brixham Wk BRAM/HZG SK7....121 G5
BRUN/LGST M13....87 M7
Brixton Av DID/WITH M20....98 D6
Broach St BOLS/LL BL3....36 B8
Broadacre STLY SK15....92 B6
WGNNW/ST WN6....30 D2
Broad Acre WHIT OL12....27 H2
Broadbent Av AUL OL6....75 M6
DUK SK16....91 G4
STLY SK15....77 H6
Broadbent Cl ROY/SHW OL2....43 J7
Broadbent Dr BURY BL9....26 B8
Broadbent Gv HYDE SK14....103 H3
Broadbent Rd OLD OL1....59 M2
Broadbent St HYDE SK14....91 G8
SWIN M27....70 A4
Broadbottom Rd HYDE SK14....103 J2
Broadcarr La MOSL OL5....76 B5
Broadfield Cl DTN/ASHW M34....101 K2
Dr LIT OL15....29 J1
Broadfield Gv RDSH SK5....100 B1
Broadfield Rd RDSH SK5....100 B1
RUSH/FAL M14....98 D1
Broadfield Stile MILN OL16....10 D6
Broadfield St HEY OL10....40 E3
MILN OL16....10 D6
Broadford Rd BOLS/LL BL3....35 J7
Broadgate CHAD OL9....58 B8
MDTN M24....58 A6
UPML OL3....61 H3
Broadgate Meadow
SWIN M27....70 C5
Broadgreen Gdns FWTH BL4 *....53 G2
Broadhalgh Av ROCH OL11....27 K5
Broadhalgh Rd ROCH OL11....27 H5
Broadhead Rd EDGW/EG BL7....17 H5
Broadheath Cl WHTN BL5....50 D3
Broad Hey MPL/ROM SK6....114 A1
Broadhey Vw NM/HAY SK22....124 D3
Broad Hill Cl BRAM/HZG SK7....121 J3
Broadhill Rd BNG/LEV M19....99 M6
STLY SK15....76 D8
Broadhurst DTN/ASHW M34....90 D7
SWIN M27....70 C3
Broadhurst Av OLD OL1....8 C1
Broadhurst Ct BOLS/LL BL3....36 A8
Broadhurst Gv AUL OL6....75 M6
Broadhurst Rd BOLS/LL BL3 *....36 A8
EDGY/DAV SK3....13 H9
Broad Ing ROCH OL11 *....27 L3
Broadlands WGNNW/ST WN6....30 E6
Broadlands Rd WALK M28....69 M6
Broad La HALE/TIMP WA15....117 K4
MILN OL16....42 F1
UPML OL3....45 H5
Broad Lea URM M41....95 M1
Broadlea Gv WHIT OL12....27 M2
Broadlea Rd BNG/LEV M19....99 H7
Broadley Av GOL/RIS/CUL WA3....80 A5
WYTH/NTH M22....110 A8
Broadmeadow EDGW/EG BL7....22 E4
Broadmeadow Av
OLDTF/WHR M16....98 C3
Broadmoss Dr BKLY M9....73 K1
Broadmoss Rd BKLY M9....73 K1
Broadmount Ter CHAD OL9 *....58 E8
Broadoak Av WALK M28....68 C5
WYTH/NTH M22....109 M7
Broadoak Crs AUL OL6....75 L7
Broadoak Dr WYTH/NTH M22....110 A7
Broad Oak La BURY BL9....39 M1
DID/WITH M20....110 F4
WALK M28....69 L6
Broadoak Pk ECC M30....70 A8
Broadoak Rd AUL OL6....75 M6
BRAM/HZG SK7....121 H2
ROCH OL11....27 H6
WYTH/NTH M22....109 M8
Broadoaks BURY BL9....40 A1
Broadoaks Rd SALE M33....96 D8
URM M41....95 L3
Broad Oak Ter BURY BL9....40 B1
Broad o' th' La BOL BL1....22 B8
Broadriding Rd
WGNNW/ST WN6....30 B6
Broad Rd SALE M33....96 F7
Broad Shaw La MILN OL16....43 G3
Broadstone Av OLDE OL4....44 C8
Broadstone Cl PWCH M25....71 K2
WHIT OL12....27 K3
Broadstone Hall Rd North
HTNM SK4....100 A6
Broadstone Hall Rd South
HTNM SK4....100 A6
Broadstone Rd BOLE BL2....23 G7
HTNM SK4....100 A6
Broad St BURY BL9....4 E5
MDTN M24....57 K2
SLFD M6....71 H7

Broad Wk WHTN BL5....50 B5
WILM/AE SK9....126 D4
Broadway ATH M46....51 J7
BRAM/HZG SK7....121 H2
CHAD OL9....8 A1
CHD/CHDH SK8....110 F8
DROY M43....89 K4
FAIL M35....74 A4
FWTH BL4....52 D2
HALE/TIMP WA15....117 J3
HOR/BR BL6....34 A1
HYDE SK14....90 E7
IRL M44....94 D3
OFTN SK2....112 F5
PART M31....94 D8
ROY/SHW OL2....59 H1
SALE M33....96 D7
SALQ M50....86 B4
URM M41....84 E8
WALK M28....69 G3
WGNE/HIN WN2....4 K7
WILM/AE SK9....126 F6
Broadway Av CHD/CHDH SK8....111 G7
Broadway Cl URM M41....84 F8
Broadway North DROY M43....89 K4
Broadway St OLDS OL8....59 J8
The Broadway MPL/ROM SK6....101 H8
LEIGH WN7....81 H3
Broadwood HOR/BR BL6....34 F5
Broadwood Cl POY/DIS SK12....123 H5
Brocade Cl CSLFD M3....6 A1
Broche Cl ROCH OL11....41 L1
Brock Av BOLE BL2....37 J5
Brock Cl OP/CLY M11....89 G5
Brock Dr CHD/CHDH SK8....120 C4
Brockenhurst Dr BOLE BL2....37 J1
Brockford Dr BKLY M9....57 H7
Brockholes GLSP SK13....104 C4
Brockhurst Wk
WGNS/IIMK WN3....47 K7
Brocklebank Rd MILN OL16....29 G5
RUSH/FAL M14....98 F4
Brocklehurst Av BURY BL9....5 G7
Brocklehurst St BKLY M9....73 K4
Brockley Av RUSH/FAL M14....98 E2
Brock Mill La WGN WN1....31 M8
Brock Pl NEWH/MOS M40....64 C2
Brockstedes Av AIMK WN4....63 G5
Brock St CMANE M1 *....7 K4
WGN WN1....15 L4
The Brock ROY/SHW OL2....43 J4
Brockway MILN OL16....42 F1
Brocstedes Av AIMK WN4....63 G5
Brodick Dr BOLE BL2....37 J6
Brodick St NEWH/MOS M40....73 J4
Brodie Cl ECC M30....84 D2
Brogan St GTN M18....89 G7
Brogden Av GOL/RIS/CUL WA3....81 H8
Brogden Cl CHD/CHDH SK8....110 E7
Brogden Gv SALE M33....108 A3
Brogden Ter SALE M33....96 D8
Bromborough Av
DID/WITH M20....98 D4
Bromfield WHIT OL12....10 B5
Bromfield Av BKLY M9....73 G3
Bromleigh Av CHD/CHDH SK8....110 E6
Bromley Av GOL/RIS/CUL WA3....80 A5
ROY/SHW OL2....42 F5
URM M41....95 H3
Bromley Cl WGNE/HIN WN2....48 D2
Bromley Crs AUL OL6....75 L6
Bromley Cross Rd
EDGW/EG BL7....22 E5
Bromley Dr LEIGH WN7....66 A4
Bromley Rd SALE M33....108 F2
Bromley St ANC M4....87 L1
CHAD OL9....74 D2
DTN/ASHW M34....101 J1
Bromlow St OP/CLY M11....88 F7
Brompton Av FAIL M35....74 E4
RUSH/FAL M14....98 E2
STRET M32....96 C1
Brompton St OLDE OL4....9 M8
Brompton Wy WILM/AE SK9....119 J3
Bromsgrove Av ECC M30....84 C2
Bromshill Dr BRO M7....72 B6
Bromwich St BOLE BL2....3 J7
Bronington Cl WYTH/NTH M22....110 B5
Bronte Av BURY BL9....39 J6
Bronte Cl BOL BL1....36 A3
OLD OL1....44 A8
WGNS/IIMK WN3....47 K7
WHIT OL12....27 K3
Bronte St HULME M15....87 K7
Bronville Cl OLD OL1....58 F3
Brookash Rd WYTH/NTH M22....119 J4
Brook Av BNG/LEV M19....99 L2
DROY M43 *....89 H3
HALE/TIMP WA15....108 B6
HTNM SK4....100 A7
ROY/SHW OL2....43 L4
SWIN M27....70 C5
UPML OL3....61 L4
WILM/AE SK9....127 H1
Brook Bank BOLE BL2 *....37 G1
Brookbank Cl MDTN M24....57 L5
Brook Bottom Rd
NM/HAY SK22....124 B3
Brookbottom Rd RAD M26....38 C6
Brookburn Rd CCHDY M21....97 K5
Brook Cl HALE/TIMP WA15....108 B6
TYLD M29....67 K2
WHTF M45....55 L8
Brookcot Rd NTHM/RTH M23....109 J5
Brookcroft Av
WYTH/NTH M22....110 A7
Brookcroft Rd
WYTH/NTH M22....110 A7
Brookdale ATH M46....51 J6
WHIT OL12....28 B1
Brookdale Av DTN/ASHW M34....90 B5
MPL/ROM SK6....114 D8
NEWH/MOS M40....74 A8
Brookdale Cl BOL BL1....36 C2
MPL/ROM SK6....113 L7
Brookdale Pk LHULT M38 *....52 E6
Brookdale Ri BRAM/HZG SK7....121 H3
Brookdale Rd BRAM/HZG SK7....121 H3
CHD/CHDH SK8....110 C3
WGNE/HIN WN2....49 J7
Brookdale St FAIL M35....74 B5
Brookdean Cl BOL BL1....35 M1
Brookdene Rd BNG/LEV M19....99 H6
BURY BL9....55 K3
Brook Dr MPL/ROM SK6....114 D8
TYLD M29....67 M6
WHTF M45....55 L4
Brooke Dr WILM/AE SK9....119 M8
Brookes St MDTN M24....57 L2

Brooke Wy WILM/AE SK9 *....119 M8
Brook Farm Cl PART M31....106 B3
Brookfield PWCH M25....55 L8
ROY/SHW OL2....43 K3
Brookfield Av BOLE BL2....37 M3
CCHDY M21....97 M5
HALE/TIMP WA15....108 C4
MPL/ROM SK6....101 K8
POY/DIS SK12....129 G1
ROY/SHW OL2....59 H1
SLFD M6....85 M1
STKP SK1....13 M8
URM M41....95 K2
Brookfield Cl STKP SK1....13 M8
Brookfield Crs CHD/CHDH SK8....111 C8
Brookfield Dr
HALE/TIMP WA15....108 D5
LIT OL15....21 K6
SWIN M27....70 B3
WALK M28....68 C5
Brookfield Gdns
WYTH/NTH M22....109 M6
Brookfield Gv AUL OL6....91 G2
Brookfield Rd BURY BL9....25 H4
CHD/CHDH SK8....111 H7
CHH M8....72 D3
ECC M30....69 L8
GOL/RIS/CUL WA3....80 F8
WGNNW/ST WN6....30 E2
Brookfields
WGNW/BIL/OR WN5 *....46 E7
Brookfield St BOLE BL2....3 J8
LEIGH WN7....66 D6
OLDS OL8....9 J8
Brookfold FAIL M35....74 B4
Brookfold La BOLE BL2....23 J8
HYDE SK14....102 D2
Brook Fold La HYDE SK14....102 E3
Brookfold Rd HTNM SK4....100 A7
Brook Gdns BOLE BL2....23 H8
HEY OL10....40 F2
Brook Green La GTN M18....100 C1
Brook Gv IRL M44....94 C4
Brookhead Dr DID/WITH M20 *....98 C5
Brookhead Dr CHD/CHDH SK8....111 K7
Brookhey HYDE SK14....101 L1
Brookheys Rd ALT WA14....107 H2
PART M31....95 H8
Brookhill Cl UPML OL3....45 M7
Brookhouse Av ECC M30....84 D3
FWTH BL4....52 F6
Brook House Cl BOLE BL2....37 H1
TOT/BURYW BL8....24 B4
Brookhouse Mill La
TOT/BURYW BL8....38 D1
Brookhouse St WGN WN1....15 H5
Brookhurst La LHULT M38....52 B6
Brookhurst Rd GTN M18....89 G8
Brookland Av DTN/ASHW M34....101 G2
FWTH BL4....52 F5
WGNE/HIN WN2....49 G7
Brookland Gv BOL BL1....35 K2
Brookland Rd WGN WN1....47 L1
Brooklands HOR/BR BL6....33 M1
Brooklands Av AIMK WN4....79 G2
ATH M46....51 G8
CHAD OL9....8 A8
DID/WITH M20 *....98 D6
LEIGH WN7....81 H1
Brooklands Cl DTN/ASHW M34....90 A8
HTNM SK4....100 A7
IRL M44....94 C2
MOSL OL5....76 C7
Brooklands Crs SALE M33....108 A3
Brooklands Dr DROY M43....89 M1
GLSP SK13....104 E5
OLDE OL4....60 E6
WGNW/BIL/OR WN5....46 A7
Brooklands Pde OLDE OL4 *....60 E6
Brooklands Rd BRAM/HZG SK7....122 A3
NTHM/RTH M23....108 F4
PWCH M25....72 B2
RAMS BL0....24 C2
RDSH SK5....100 B2
SALE M33....108 L1
SWIN M27....70 A6
Brooklands Station Ap
SALE M33....108 D1
Brooklands St ROY/SHW OL2....43 G7
The Brooklands HEY OL10....40 F7
Brookland Ter MILN OL16 *....42 E1
Brook La BURY BL9....39 K7
HALE/TIMP WA15....108 B6
MILN OL16....42 E1
OLDE OL4....60 B6
OLDS OL8....59 K8
UPML OL3....61 J3
WGNW/BIL/OR WN5....46 E7
WILM/AE SK9....130 C1
Brooklawn Dr DID/WITH M20....98 D5
PWCH M25....55 M6
Brookleigh Rd DID/WITH M20....99 C6
Brooklet Cl OLDE OL4....60 D7
Brooklyn Av LIT OL15....21 L5
MILN OL16....21 J8
OLDTF/WHR M16....97 L2
URM M41....95 H2
Brooklyn Crs CHD/CHDH SK8....111 G7
Brook Lynn Av
GOL/RIS/CUL WA3....80 C3
Brooklyn Rd CHD/CHDH SK8....111 G7
OFTN SK2....112 F6
Brooklyn St BOL BL1....36 B3
OLD OL1....59 M3
Brook Meadow GLSP SK13....105 H3
WHTN BL5 *....50 B4
Brook Rd CHD/CHDH SK8....111 G6
HTNM SK4....99 M7
RUSH/FAL M14....98 F5
URM M41....95 M1
Brooks Av BRAM/HZG SK7....121 M1
HYDE SK14....102 B3
RAD M26....38 C6
Brooksbottom Cl RAMS BL0....18 D4
Brooks Dr CHD/CHDH SK8....119 L2
FAIL M35....74 D4
HALE/TIMP WA15....108 B6
HALE/TIMP WA15....109 H8
HALE/TIMP WA15....117 M4
Brooks End ROCH OL11....27 H1
Brookshaw St BURY BL9....5 H1
OP/CLY M11....88 D3
Brookside GLSP SK13....104 E4
OLDE OL4....60 A6
WGNS/IIMK WN3 *....47 K7

Brookside Av AIMK WN4....63 J5
DROY M43....89 M1
FWTH BL4....52 F5
OFTN SK2....113 H6
OLDE OL4....60 E6
POY/DIS SK12....129 G1
Brookside Cl ATH M46....51 H8
BOLE BL2....23 G7
CHD/CHDH SK8....111 G8
GLSP SK13....14 A3
HYDE SK14....102 D1
RAMS BL0....24 D1
Brookside Crs MDTN M24....57 M6
TOT/BURYW BL8....24 C4
WALK M28....69 H1
Brookside Dr HYDE SK14....102 D1
PWCH M25....72 A3
Brookside La MPL/ROM SK6....123 G5
Brookside Rd BOLE BL2....37 G4
CHD/CHDH SK8....110 D6
NEWH/MOS M40....73 K3
SALE M33....108 D2
Brooksmouth TOT/BURYW BL8....4 B5
Brook's Pl WHIT OL12....10 C2
Brook's Rd OLDTF/WHR M16....97 H5
Brooks St STKP SK1....13 K8
Brookstone Cl CCHDY M21....98 A6
Brook St AIMK WN4....78 F2
ATH M46....66 E1
BOL BL1....2 E4
BRAM/HZG SK7....122 A1
BURY BL9....5 H1
CHAD OL9....8 B3
CHD/CHDH SK8....111 J6
CMANE M1....7 H8
FAIL M35....74 A6
FWTH BL4....53 H4
GOL/RIS/CUL WA3....79 K5
GOL/RIS/CUL WA3....80 C3
HYDE SK14....102 B1
OLD OL1....9 M3
RAD M26....53 K5
RAD M26....54 F1
ROY/SHW OL2....59 G1
SALE M33....96 F7
SLFD M6....71 L8
SWIN M27....70 A4
WGNE/HIN WN2....48 D5
WHIT OL12....21 G6
WHTN BL5....50 C3
Brook St East AUL OL6....90 D2
Brook St West AUL OL6....90 D2
Brookthorn Cl OFTN SK2....113 J7
Brookthorpe Av BNG/LEV M19....99 H6
Brookthorpe Rd
TOT/BURYW BL8....38 D1
Brookvale WGNNW/ST WN6....14 A1
Brookview WGNE/HIN WN2....49 G8
Brookwater Cl TOT/BURYW BL8....24 C6
Brookway HALE/TIMP WA15....108 C6
LIT OL15....21 L8
OLDE OL4....60 B7
OLDE OL4....61 H6
Brookway Cl BNG/LEV M19....99 H8
Brookwood Av CHH M8....72 F4
SALE M33....108 B1
Brookwood Cl
DTN/ASHW M34....101 K5
Brooky Moor EDGW/EG BL7 *....17 H6
Broom Av BNG/LEV M19....99 L4
BRO M7....72 B4
LEIGH WN7....66 B5
RDSH SK5....100 C6
Broome Gv FAIL M35....74 C6
Broomehouse Av IRL M44....94 B4
Broome St CHAD OL9....8 E6
Broomfield SWIN M27....71 G6
Broomfield Cl BOLE BL2....37 M4
RDSH SK5....100 C6
WILM/AE SK9 *....119 H8
Broomfield Crs MDTN M24....57 G3
OFTN SK2....112 D8
Broomfield Dr CHH M8....72 D5
RDSH SK5....100 C6
Broomfield La
HALE/TIMP WA15....117 G2
Broomfield Pl
WGNNW/ST WN6....31 H3
Broomfield Rd BOLS/LL BL3....35 M7
HTNM SK4....99 M8
WGNNW/ST WN6....31 H3
Broomfields DTN/ASHW M34....90 D7
Broomfield Sq ROCH OL11 *....10 C8
Broomfield Ter MILN OL16....29 L8
WGN WN1....15 L5
Broomflat Cl WGNNW/ST WN6....31 H3
Broomgrove La
DTN/ASHW M34....90 D8
Broomhall Rd BKLY M9....56 D7
SWIN M27....71 G6
Broomhey Av WCN WN1....31 M7
Broomhey Ter WGN WN1....15 L5
Broomhill Dr BRAM/HZG SK7....120 F3
Broomholme SWIN M27....30 A5
Broomhurst Av OLDS OL8....59 G8
Broom La BNG/LEV M19....99 L4
BRO M7....72 A4
Broom Rd HALE/TIMP WA15....117 G1
PART M31....106 C2
WGNW/BIL/OR WN5....47 G5
Broomstair Rd DTN/ASHW M34....90 C6
Broom St MILN OL16....29 L8
SWIN M27....70 C5
TOT/BURYW BL8....4 B4
Broomville Av SALE M33....96 E8
Broom Wy WHTN BL5....50 D2
Broomwood Rd
HALE/TIMP WA15....108 D5
Broomwood Wk HULME M15 *....87 J6
Broseley Av DID/WITH M20....111 G3
GOL/RIS/CUL WA3....81 G8
Broseley La GOL/RIS/CUL WA3....81 G7
Broseley Rd OLDTF/WHR M16....97 K2
Brosscroft GLSP SK13....93 K6
Brosscroft St GLSP SK13....93 K6
Brosscroft Village GLSP SK13....93 K6
Brotherdale Cl ROY/SHW OL2....43 G7
Brotherod Hall Rd WHIT OL12....27 M2
Brotherton Cl HULME M15....6 A9
Brotherton Dr CSLFD M3....6 B3
Brougham St WALK M28....68 F2
Brough St WGNE/HIN WN2....65 H1
Broughton Av
GOL/RIS/CUL WA3....80 A5
LHULT M38....52 D8
Broughton Cl MDTN M24....57 G3
Broughton La BRO M7....72 A7

Broughton Rd MCFLDN SK10....129 G7
RDSH SK5....100 C8
SLFD M6....86 D1
Broughton Rd East SLFD M6....71 L8
Broughton St BOL BL1....36 A2
CHH M8....72 C7
Broughville Dr DID/WITH M20....110 F4
Brow Av MDTN M24....57 L6
Brow East BOLE BL2....22 F8
Browfield Av ORD M5....86 E5
Browfield Wy OLD OL1....59 H3
Browmere Dr DID/WITH M20....98 C8
Brown Bank Rd LIT OL15....29 J1
Browncross St CSLFD M3....6 C4
Brown Edge Rd OLDE OL4....60 B8
Brownhill Dr OLDE OL4....60 D5
Brownhill La UPML OL3....61 L3
Brownhills Cl TOT/BURYW BL8....24 D7
Brownhills Ct CCHDY M21....97 L4
Brownhill St OP/CLY M11....88 D4
Browning Av ATH M46....51 G7
DROY M43....89 K3
WGNS/IIMK WN3....47 J8
Browning Cl BOL BL1....36 A3
Browning Gv WGNNW/ST WN6....47 H1
Browning Rd MDTN M24....57 G2
OLD OL1....59 L3
RDSH SK5....100 B3
SWIN M27....70 B4
Browning St CSLFD M3....6 B8
HULME M15....87 G6
LEIGH WN7....66 A6
Brown La CHD/CHDH SK8....119 J3
Brownlea Av DUK SK16....90 F5
Brownley Court Rd
WYTH/NTH M22....110 B7
Brownley Rd WYTH/NTH M22....110 B7
Brown Lodge St LIT OL15....29 J1
Brown Lodge Dr ROY/SHW OL2....59 J2
WGNE/HIN WN2....48 E5
Brownlow Av ROY/SHW OL2....59 J2
Brownlow Cl POY/DIS SK12....129 G2
Brownlow Wy BOL BL1....2 C1
Brownmere WGNNW/ST WN6....47 J2
Brownrigg Cl MDTN M24....56 F3
Brownside Cl MILN OL16....28 F1
Brown's La WILM/AE SK9....127 J4
Brownslow Wk
BRUN/LGST M13 *....7 K9
Browns Rd BOLE BL2....37 L6
Brown St ALT WA14....116 F1
BOL BL1....2 F4
CHAD OL9....58 D5
CSLFD M3....6 D4
FAIL M35....74 B5
HEY OL10....40 F1
HOR/BR BL6....33 G2
LIT OL15....21 L7
MDTN M24....57 K2
OLD OL1....9 M4
RAD M26....38 C6
RAMS BL0....18 E2
SLFD M6....86 D3
STKP SK1....13 H3
TYLD M29 *....67 J5
WGNE/HIN WN2....48 D5
WGNE/HIN WN2....65 H3
WGNS/IIMK WN3....14 E5
WILM/AE SK9....130 D3
Brown St North LEIGH WN7....66 B7
Brown St South LEIGH WN7....66 B7
Brownsville Rd HTNM SK4....99 L7
Brownville Gv DUK SK16....91 H5
Brownwood Av SALE M33....108 B1
Brownwood Cl SALE M33....108 B1
Brows Av NTHM/RTH M23....109 K2
Brow St ROCH OL11....28 D8
Broxton Av BOLS/LL BL3....51 L1
WGNW/BIL/OR WN5....46 C5
Broxton St NEWH/MOS M40....88 C1
Broxwood Cl GTN M18....89 G7
Bruce St ROCH OL11....27 M8
Brundage Rd WYTH/NTH M22....118 F2
Brundretts Rd CCHDY M21....97 L4
Brundrett St STKP SK1....13 M1
Brunel Av ORD M5....86 E3
Brunel Cl STRET M32....97 H2
Brunel St BOL BL1....36 A1
HOR/BR BL6....33 M2
Brunet Wy WGTN/LGST M12 *....88 C2
Brunstead Cl NTHM/RTH M23....109 G6
Brunswick Av HOR/BR BL6....34 A2
Brunswick Cl BOL BL1....2 C1
Brunswick Rd ALT WA14....108 A5
DID/WITH M20....98 F6
NEWLW WA12....78 C8
Brunswick Sq OLD OL1 *....9 J7
Brunswick St BRUN/LGST M13....87 M6
BURY BL9....4 F3
DUK SK16....90 F4
HEY OL10....40 F2
LEIGH WN7....66 D8
MILN OL16....11 H2
MOSL OL5....77 G4
OLD OL1....9 J6
ROY/SHW OL2....43 L5
STRET M32....96 F4
Brunt St RUSH/FAL M14....98 E1
Brunton Rd RDSH SK5....100 C5
Bruntwood Av CHD/CHDH SK8....119 J3
Bruntwood La CHD/CHDH SK8....119 J3
Brushes Av STLY SK15....92 A1
Brushes Rd STLY SK15....92 A1
Brussels Rd EDGY/DAV SK3....112 A6
Bruton Av STRET M32....96 B3
Bryan Rd CCHDY M21....97 L2
Bryan St OLDE OL4....59 M3
Bryant Cl BRUN/LGST M13....87 M3
Bryantsfield BOL BL1....35 G6
Bryce St HYDE SK14....91 G8
Brydges Rd MPL/ROM SK6....114 B7
Brydon Av WGTN/LGST M12....7 M8
Brydon Cl SLFD M6....86 D2
Bryham St WGN WN1....15 J4
Bryndale Gv SALE M33....108 C3
Brynden Av DID/WITH M20....98 F7
Bryn Dr RDSH SK5....100 C7
Brynford Av BKLY M9....56 D7
Bryn Gates La
WGNE/HIN WN2....63 M4
Bryngs Dr BOLE BL2....23 J8
Brynhall Cl RAD M26....38 B7
Brynheys Cl LHULT M38....52 D7
Bryn St WGNE/HIN WN2....64 C5
Brynorme Rd CHH M8....72 D2
Bryn Rd AIMK WN4....63 K6
Bryn Rd South AIMK WN4....63 M8
Bryn St AIMK WN4....78 E1
WGNS/IIMK WN3....15 K8
Brynton Rd BRUN/LGST M13....99 H2
Bryn Wk BOL BL1....2 E2
Bryone Dr OFTN SK2....112 C7

Bryony Cl WGNW/BIL/OR WN5....46 A7
  WYTH/NTH M22....118 E3
Buchanan Dr WGNE/HIN WN2....65 L1
Buchanan Rd
  WGNW/BIL/OR WN5....47 H5
Buchanan St LEIGH WN7....66 B7
  RAMS BL0....18 E6
  SWIN M27....70 C3
Buchan St OP/CLY M11....88 E2
Buckden Rd HTNM SK4....100 A5
Buckfast Av OLDS OL8....59 M8
  RNFD/HAY WA11....78 C5
Buckfast Cl MDTN M24....97 L3
  CHD/CHDH SK8....120 D5
  HALE/TIMP WA15....117 K2
  POY/DIS SK12....121 M7
Buckfast Rd MDTN M24....41 J8
  SALE M33....96 A6
Buckfield Av ORD M5....86 E5
Buckhurst Rd BNG/LEV M19....99 K3
  BURY BL9....25 L1
Buckingham Av HOR/BR BL6....34 B2
  SLFD M6....86 A2
  WHTF M45....55 K5
Buckingham Cl
  WGNW/BIL/OR WN5....47 H7
Buckingham Dr DUK SK16....91 J6
  TOT/BURYW BL8....38 E4
Buckingham Park Cl
  ROY/SHW OL2....43 L4
Buckingham Rd ALT WA14....108 C3
  CCHDY M21....97 L3
  CHD/CHDH SK8....120 B2
  DROY M43....89 H3
  HTNM SK4....99 M7
  POY/DIS SK12....129 H1
  PWCH M25 *....71 L2
  STLY SK15....85 C7
  STRET M32....86 C7
  SWIN M27....70 D2
  WILM/AE SK9....126 D6
Buckingham Rd West
  HTNM SK4....99 K8
Buckingham St MILN OL16....11 H2
  OFTN SK2 *....112 D6
  ORD M5....86 C3
Buckingham Wy
  HALE/TIMP WA15....108 D6
Buckland Av BKLY M9....72 D1
Buckland Dr
  WGNW/BIL/OR WN5....46 E3
Buckland Gv HYDE SK14....102 D4
Buckland Rd SLFD M6....71 G8
Buck La SALE M33....96 B6
Buckley Av GTN M18....88 F8
Buckley Brook St WHIT OL12....28 E2
Buckley Cha MILN OL16....29 H7
Buckley Cl HYDE SK14....102 B5
Buckley Dr MPL/ROM SK6....113 K3
  UPML OL3....44 F8
Buckley Farm La WHIT OL12....28 E1
Buckley Flds WHIT OL12....28 D2
Buckley Hill La MILN OL16....29 H7
Buckley La FWTH BL4....52 F5
  WHIT OL12....28 E1
  WHTF M45....71 H1
Buckley Rd GTN M18....88 E8
  WHIT OL12....28 E8
Buckley Sq FWTH BL4....52 F5
Buckley St BURY BL9....5 G2
  CHAD OL9....58 D5
  DROY M43....89 K4
  DTN/ASHW M34....90 A5
  HEY OL10....41 C1
  MILN OL16....11 G2
  OLDE OL4....60 B7
  OP/CLY M11....89 H5
  RDSH SK5....100 B2
  ROY/SHW OL2....43 M5
  STLY SK15....91 J4
  UPML OL3....61 L4
  WGNNW/ST WN6....47 L2
Buckley St West
  WGNNW/ST WN6....47 K2
Buckley Vw WHIT OL12....28 E1
Bucklow Av PART M31....94 D8
  RUSH/FAL M14....98 E3
Bucklow Cl HYDE SK14....103 J3
  OLDE OL4....60 B1
Bucklow Vw ALT WA14....116 C4
Buckstones Rd OLD OL1....44 B6
  ROY/SHW OL2....43 M3
Buck St LEIGH WN7....66 A6
Buckthorn Cl CCHDY M21....98 A6
  HALE/TIMP WA15....109 H7
  WHTN BL5....50 D7
Buckthorn La ECC M30....84 C3
Buckton Dr STLY SK15....77 H7
Buckton Dr STLY SK15....77 J5
Buckton Vale Ms STLY SK15....77 H6
Buckwood Cl BRAM/HZG SK7....122 C1
Buddleia Gv BRO M7 *....72 A6
Bude Av RDSH SK5....100 E7
  TYLD M29....67 M4
  URM M41....95 L4
Bude Cl BRAM/HZG SK7....121 M5
Budworth Av SALE M33....109 H1
Buer Av WGNS/IIMK WN3....47 J8
Buersil Av MILN OL16....42 E1
Buersil St MILN OL16....42 E1
Buerton Av BKLY M9....56 D7
Bugle St CMANE M1 *....6 D7
Buile Dr BKLY M9....57 J8
Buile Hill Av LHULT M38....52 E8
Buile Hill Dr ORD M6....86 A1
Buile Hill Gv LHULT M38....52 E7
Buile St BRO M7....72 B5
Buiford Av WYTH/NTH M22....118 D2
Bulkeley Rd CHD/CHDH SK8....111 H6
  POY/DIS SK12....129 L1
  WILM/AE SK9....12 F6
Bulkeley St EDGY/DAV SK3....12 F6
Bullcote Gn ROY/SHW OL2....43 L8
Bullcote La ROY/SHW OL2....43 L8
Bullcroft Dr TYLD M29....67 M6
Buller Ms TOT/BURYW BL8....38 E3
Buller Rd BRUN/LGST M13....99 J2
Buller St BOLS/LL BL3....52 F2
  DROY M43....89 L4
  TOT/BURYW BL8....38 F3
Bullfinch Dr BURY BL9....25 L7
Bull Hill Crs RAD M26....54 E4
Bullock St STKP SK1....13 K9
Bullough St ATH M46....66 F2
Bullows Rd LHULT M38....52 C6
Bulteel St BOLS/LL BL3....51 M2
  ECC M30....84 E1
  WALK M28....68 B6
  WGNW/BIL/OR WN5....47 G6

Bulwer St MILN OL16....11 H2
The Bungalows
  BRAM/HZG SK7 *....113 J8
  NM/HAY SK22....124 F3
Bunkers HI MPL/ROM SK6....113 L3
  WHTF M45....71 H1
Bunkershill Rd HYDE SK14....103 H3
Bunkershill Rd
  MPL/ROM SK6....113 L4
Bunsen St CMANE M1 *....7 J4
Bunting G GOL/RIS/CUL WA3....80 E4
Bunting Ms WALK M28....68 E4
Bunyan Cl OLD OL1....44 A8
Bunyan St WHIT OL12....10 F1
Bunyard St CHH M8....72 E6
Burbage Rd NTHM/RTH M23....118 C2
Burchall Fld MILN OL16....11 K4
Burdale Dr SLFD M6....70 E8
Burder St OLDS OL8....74 F2
Burdett Av WHIT OL12....27 J3
Burdett Wy WYTH/NTH M22 *....88 B7
Burdith Av RUSH/FAL M14....98 D3
Burdon Av WYTH/NTH M22....110 B8
Burford Av BRAM/HZG SK7....120 E7
  OLDTF/WHR M16....98 A2
  URM M41....96 B1
Burford Crs WILM/AE SK9....126 C7
Burford Dr BOLS/LL BL3....2 C8
  OLDTF/WHR M16....98 A2
  SWIN M27....70 B2
Burford Gv SALE M33....108 B3
Burford Rd OLDTF/WHR M16....98 A2
Burgess Av OL6....75 M7
Burgess Dr FAIL M35....74 C5
Burgess St WGNS/IIMK WN3....15 K9
Burghley Av OLDE OL4....60 A6
Burghley Cl RAD M26....37 L7
  STLY SK15....91 K2
Burghley Dr RAD M26....37 L7
Burghley Wy WGNS/IIMK WN3....48 C7
Burgin Wk NEWH/MOS M40....72 F8
Burgundy Dr TOT/BURYW BL8....24 C5
Burke St BOL BL1....36 A2
Burkitt St HYDE SK14....102 B2
Burland Cl BRO M7....72 A7
Burland St WGNW/BIL/OR WN5....41 J5
Burleigh Cl BRAM/HZG SK7....121 J3
Burleigh Ms CCHDY M21....97 L6
Burleigh Rd STRET M32....86 B8
Burleigh St HULME M15....87 L7
Burlescombe Cl ALT WA14....107 L6
Burley Av GOL/RIS/CUL WA3....80 A3
Burley Ct HTNM SK4 *....12 C2
Burley Crs WGNS/IIMK WN3....62 F2
Burlington Av OLDS OL8....59 H6
Burlington Cl HTNM SK4....111 H2
Burlington Dr EDGY/DAV SK3....112 C8
Burlington Gdns
  EDGY/DAV SK3....112 C8
Burlington Ms EDGY/DAV SK3....112 C8
Burlington Rd ALT WA14....108 C3
  DID/WITH M20....98 F5
  ECC M30....70 B8
Burlington St AULW OL7....90 C2
  BRUN/LGST M13....87 L7
  ROCH OL11....28 D8
  WGNE/HIN WN2....49 H7
Burlton Gv WGNE/HIN WN2....48 D2
Burman St OP/CLY M11....89 J3
Burnaby St BOLS/LL BL3....2 A9
  OLDS OL8....8 D9
Burnage Av BNG/LEV M19....99 J4
Burnage Hall Rd BNG/LEV M19....99 H5
Burnage La BNG/LEV M19....111 G2
Burnage Range BNG/LEV M19....99 K3
Burnaston Gv
  WGNW/BIL/OR WN5....47 G7
Burn Bank UPML OL3....61 H7
Burnbray Av BNG/LEV M19....99 H6
Burndale Dr BURY BL9....55 K1
Burnden Rd BOLS/LL BL3....3 K9
Burnedge Wy HOR/BR BL6....33 M4
Burnedge Cl WHIT OL12....28 G6
Burnedge Fold Rd OLDE OL4....61 G6
Burnedge La OLDE OL4....60 F6
Burnell Cl NEWH/MOS M40....7 M1
Burnet Cl MILN OL16....28 F8
  TYLD M29....67 L5
Burnett Av ORD M5....86 E4
Burnett Cl NEWH/MOS M40....73 C7
Burnfell GOL/RIS/CUL WA3....80 B5
Burnfield Rd GTN M18....100 A1
Burnham Av BOL BL1....35 K3
  RDSH SK5....100 C3
Burnham Cl CHD/CHDH SK8....120 B2
  GOL/RIS/CUL WA3....81 M8
  URM M41....95 M1
Burnham Dr BNG/LEV M19....99 J5
Burnhill Ct WGNNW/ST WN6....31 H4
Burnley La CHAD OL9....8 C1
Burnley Rd BURY BL9....25 H4
Burnley St CHAD OL9....8 A3
  FAIL M35....74 D5
Burnmoor Rd BOLE BL2....37 J4
Burnsall Av GOL/RIS/CUL WA3....80 C4
  WHTF M45....55 H5
Burnsall Gv ROY/SHW OL2....43 G5
Burns Av ATH M46....51 G7
  BURY BL9....39 J6
  CHD/CHDH SK8....111 J6
  LEIGH WN7....65 M4
  SWIN M27....70 A3
Burns Cl AIMK WN4....63 J6
  OLD OL1....44 B7
  OP/CLY M11....88 C3
  WGNS/IIMK WN3....47 K8
  WGNW/BIL/OR WN5....62 A3
Burns Crs OFTN SK2....113 H5
Burns Fold DUK SK16....91 K5
Burns Gdns PWCH M25 *....71 J1
Burns Gv DROY M43....89 K2
Burnside GLSP SK13....93 J8
  HALE/TIMP WA15....117 M5
  RAMS BL0....19 C2
  ROY/SHW OL2....44 B4
  STLY SK15....92 A5
Burnside Av HTNM SK4....100 B6
  SLFD M6....70 D7
Burnside Cl HEY OL10....41 C3
  MPL/ROM SK6....113 J1
  RAD M26....38 C2
  STLY SK15....92 A5
  TYLD M29....67 L5
  WILM/AE SK9....127 C7
Burnside Crs MDTN M24....57 H1
Burnside Dr BNG/LEV M19....99 H5
Burnside Rd BOL BL1....35 L2
  CHD/CHDH SK8....110 D7
  MILN OL16....11 M7

Burns Rd DTN/ASHW M34....101 K5
  LHULT M38....52 E7
  WGNE/HIN WN2....64 E3
Burns St BOLS/LL BL3....2 E7
  HEY OL10....41 C3
Burnthorp Av BKLY M9....72 E1
Burnt Oak Rd ROCH OL11....27 H6
Burnvale WGNS/IIMK WN3....63 G2
Burrows Av CCHDY M21....97 L6
Burrs Cl TOT/BURYW BL8....24 F1
Burrswood Av BURY BL9....25 H6
Burrswood Dr BURY BL9....25 H6
Bursar Cl NEWLW WA12....79 C8
Burslem Av DID/WITH M20....98 D4
Burstead St GTN M18....89 H6
Burstock St ANC M4....87 L1
Burton Av DID/WITH M20....98 E6
  HALE/TIMP WA15....108 D3
  TOT/BURYW BL8....24 D3
Burton Gv WALK M28....69 M4
Burton Rd DID/WITH M20....98 C8
  HTNM SK4....112 B1
  MDTN M24....57 J4
  OLDE OL4....60 B6
Burton Wk CSLFD M3....6 B2
  HTNM SK4....100 B8
Burtonwood Ct MDTN M24....57 J3
Burtree St WGTN/LGST M12 *....88 D4
Burwell Cl BOLS/LL BL3....36 A8
  GLSP SK13....104 C4
  LEIGH WN7....66 D8
  WHIT OL12....28 A1
Burwell Gv NTHM/RTH M23....109 H5
Bury & Bolton Rd RAD M26....38 A5
Bury & Rochdale Old Rd
  HEY OL10....26 F7
  BURY BL9....27 G1
Bury Av OLDTF/WHR M16....97 M2
Bury New Rd BOL BL1....3 C3
  BOLE BL2....37 L5
  BRO M7....72 A5
  BURY BL9....40 A2
  PWCH M25....55 K7
  RAMS BL0....19 C6
  WHTF M45....55 J3
Bury Old Rd BOLE BL2....3 J4
  BRO M7....72 B3
  BURY BL9....19 J3
  RAMS BL0....19 J3
  WHTF M45....55 K6
Bury Pl OP/CLY M11....88 F2
Bury Rd BOLE BL2....3 L4
  EDGW/EG BL7....17 H6
  EDGW/EG BL7....23 J1
  RAD M26....38 B8
  RAMS BL0....19 C2
  ROCH OL11....27 J6
  TOT/BURYW BL8....24 C6
Bury St CSLFD M3....6 D2
  HEY OL10....40 E2
  MOSL OL5....76 F4
  RAD M26....38 F8
  RDSH SK5....112 C1
Bushell St BOLS/LL BL3....35 L8
Bushey Dr NTHM/RTH M23....109 K7
Busheyfield Cl HYDE SK14....91 C7
Bush St NEWH/MOS M40....73 H7
Busk Rd CHAD OL9....8 E2
Busk Wk CHAD OL9 *....8 D2
Butcher La BURY BL9....4 F4
  NTHM/RTH M23....109 C5
  ROY/SHW OL2....42 F7
Butcher St AIMK WN4....78 E2
Bute Av OLDS OL8....75 J1
Bute St BOL BL1....35 L3
  NEWH/MOS M40....73 J5
  SALQ M50....86 A3
Butler Gn CHAD OL9....58 D8
Butler La ANC M4....7 M1
Butler St ANC M4....7 M2
  RAMS BL0....18 D8
  WGN WN1....15 H4
Butley St BRAM/HZG SK7....113 H8
Butman St OP/CLY M11....89 J3
Buttercup Av WALK M28 *....68 C1
Buttercup Cl ATH M46....51 C7
Buttercup Dr EDGY/DAV SK3....112 A8
  OLDE OL4....60 A2
  ROCH OL11....41 L1
Butterfield Cl CHD/CHDH SK8....120 D3
Butterfield Rd WHTN BL5....51 J4
Butterhouse La UPML OL3....61 L2
Butter La CSLFD M3 *....6 E4
Butterley Cl DUK SK16....91 J5
Buttermere Av AIMK WN4....63 L7
  HEY OL10....41 C4
  SWIN M27....70 C6
  WYTH/NTH M22....118 D2
Buttermere Cl BOLS/LL BL3....37 J8
  STRET M32....96 F1
Buttermere Dr
  HALE/TIMP WA15....117 L6
  MDTN M24....57 H2
  RAMS BL0....18 E5
Buttermere Rd AULW OL7....75 J8
  CHD/CHDH SK8....119 K1
  FWTH BL4....52 B4
  OLDE OL4....60 A4
  PART M31....106 B1
Butterstile Av PWCH M25....71 J3
Butterstile Cl PWCH M25....71 J3
Butterstile La PWCH M25....71 J3
Butterwick Cl WGTN/LGST M12 *....88 D4
Butterwick Fld HOR/BR BL6....33 J1
Butterworth Hall MILN OL16....29 M7
Butterworth La CHAD OL9....74 B1
Butterworth St CHAD OL9....8 A4
  LIT OL15....21 L7
  MDTN M24....57 M5
  OLDE OL4....59 M7
  OP/CLY M11....88 D4
Butterworth Wy UPML OL3....61 L7
Butteryhouse La
  HALE/TIMP WA15....118 A2
Butt Hill Av PWCH M25....71 L1
Butt Hill Ct PWCH M25....71 L1
Butt Hill Dr PWCH M25....71 L2
Butt Hill Rd PWCH M25....71 L2
Butt La OLDE OL4....60 E8
Button Hole ROY/SHW OL2....44 A5
Button La NTHM/RTH M23....109 J2
Buttress St GTN M18....88 F6
Butts Av LEIGH WN7....81 J5
The Butts Av MILN OL16....10 E4
Butts Ct LEIGH WN7....81 K1

Butts St LEIGH WN7....81 K1
  LHULT M38....52 E7
  WGNE/HIN WN2....64 E3
Buxted Rd OLD OL1....59 L3
Buxton Av ALT OL6....76 C6
  DID/WITH M20....98 C6
Buxton Cl ATH M46....51 H8
  MILN OL16....28 E8
Buxton Crs MILN OL16....28 E8
  SALE M33....109 C5
Buxton La DROY M43....89 H4
  MPL/ROM SK6....114 B7
Buxton Ms GLSP SK13....104 B3
Buxton Old Rd POY/DIS SK12....123 M6
Buxton Pl OLDS OL8 *....9 H9
Buxton Rd BRAM/HZG SK7....122 C4
  OFTN SK2....112 D6
  POY/DIS SK12....124 C6
  STRET M32....96 D1
Buxton Ter HYDE SK14....93 C6
Bye Rd RAMS BL0....19 H5
Byfield Rd WYTH/NTH M22....109 M8
Byfleet Cl WGNS/IIMK WN3....62 F3
Byland Cl CHD/CHDH SK8....120 D6
  OLDE OL4....60 A8
Byland Cl BOL BL1....36 B2
Bylands Cl POY/DIS SK12....121 M8
Bylands Fold DUK SK16....91 C6
Byley Ri WGNNW/ST WN6....31 H4
Byng St FWTH BL4....53 C4
  HEY OL10....41 H4
Byrcland Cl WGTN/LGST M12....88 B4
Byron Av BNG/LEV M19....99 M3
  BRAM/HZG SK7....121 L3
  DROY M43....89 K2
  PWCH M25....71 J1
  RAD M26....38 A8
  SWIN M27....70 B4
  WGNE/HIN WN2....49 G7
Byron Cl WGNE/HIN WN2....64 E4
  WGNNW/ST WN6....47 H1
  WGNW/BIL/OR WN5....46 C5
Byron Dr CHD/CHDH SK8....111 J6
Byron Gv LEIGH WN7....66 B5
  RDSH SK5....100 B3
Byron Rd DTN/ASHW M34....101 J4
  MDTN M24....57 L2
  STRET M32....97 H1
  TOT/BURYW BL8....24 C2
Byron's Dr HALE/TIMP WA15....108 D6
Byron St ECC M30....85 C2
  LEIGH WN7....66 C6
  OLDS OL8....74 E2
  ROY/SHW OL2....43 H8
Byron Wk FWTH BL4....52 E6
Byrth Rd OLDS OL8....75 J4

C

Cabin La OLDE OL4....60 D1
Cablestead Wk OP/CLY M11....88 C4
Cable St ANC M4....7 H2
  BOL BL1....2 F2
  CSLFD M3....6 D2
Cabot Pl RDSH SK5....100 C8
Cabot St BRUN/LGST M13 *....87 L6
Caddington Rd CCHDY M21....97 M4
Cadishead Wy IRL M44....94 D5
Cadman Ov WGNE/HIN WN2....49 G8
Cadman's Yd
  WGNW/BIL/OR WN5....47 G7
Cadnam Dr WYTH/NTH M22....119 H1
Cadogan Pl BRO M7 *....72 B3
Cadogan St RUSH/FAL M14....87 K8
Cadum Wk BRUN/LGST M13....87 M6
Caen Av NEWH/MOS M40....73 M1
Caernarvon Cl TOT/BURYW BL8....24 C3
Caernarvon Dr BRAM/HZG SK7....121 L3
Caernarvon Rd WGNE/HIN WN2....65 K1
Caesar St ROCH OL11....42 D2
Cairn Brae NEWLW WA12....78 F3
Cairn Dr ROCH OL11....42 D2
  SLFD M6....71 M8
Cairngorm Dr BOLS/LL BL3....35 H7
Cairns Pl AUL OL6....76 A7
Cairn Wk OP/CLY M11....88 C3
Cairnwell Rd CHAD OL9....58 D4
Caister Av WHTF M45....55 K5
Caister Cl OLDTF/WHR M16....98 A4
Caistor Cl STKP SK1....112 E1
Caistor St STKP SK1....13 J9
Caithness Cl NTHM/RTH M23....109 K8
Caithness Dr BOLS/LL BL3....35 H7
Caithness Rd HEY OL10....27 H7
Cakebread St WGTN/LGST M12 *....7 L8
Calbourne Crs WGTN/LGST M12....99 L1
Calcutta St EDGY/DAV SK3....12 D9
Caldbeck Av BOL BL1....35 J3
  SALE M33....97 H7
Caldbeck Cl AIMK WN4....63 L8
Caldbeck Dr FWTH BL4....52 B5
  MDTN M24....57 H3
Calcecott Rd BKLY M9....56 D7
Calder Av IRL M44....94 C3
  LIT OL15....21 L5
  WGNE/HIN WN2....65 M1
  WYTH/NTH M22....110 A4
Calderbank Av URM M41....84 B8
Calderbank St
  WGNW/BIL/OR WN5....47 H7
Calderbeck Wy
  WYTH/NTH M22....110 B8
Calderbrook Dr
  CHD/CHDH SK8....111 K8
Calderbrook Rd LIT OL15....21 M4
Calderbrook Wy OLDE OL4....59 L7
Calderburn Cl HOR/BR BL6....34 A4
Calder Cl BURY BL9....25 K4
  POY/DIS SK12....129 H2
  RDSH SK5....100 D7
Calder Ct URM M41....84 B8
Calder Dr FWTH BL4....53 L7
  SWIN M27....70 B8
  WALK M28....68 D2
  WGNE/HIN WN2....65 M1
Calder Gv ROY/SHW OL2....43 K4
Calder Pl WGNW/BIL/OR WN5....46 B4
Calder Rd BOLS/LL BL3....52 B1

Caldershaw La WHIT OL12....27 K2
Caldershaw Rd WHIT OL12....27 K3
Calder St MILN OL16....28 E2
  ORD M5....6 A7
Caldervale Av CCHDY M21....97 M8
Calderwood Cl
  TOT/BURYW BL8....24 C8
Caldew Cl WGNE/HIN WN2....49 H8
Caldey Rd NTHM/RTH M23....109 H1
Caldford Cl WGNE/HIN WN2....32 F6
Caldon Cl ECC M30....85 G4
Caldwell Av TYLD M29....67 L8
Caldwell Cl TYLD M29....67 L7
Caldwell St RDSH SK5....100 C3
  WHTN BL5....50 C7
Caldy Dr RAMS BL0....24 D1
Caldy Rd SLFD M6....71 C8
  WILM/AE SK9....127 H1
Caleb Cl TYLD M29....67 J3
Caledon Av NEWH/MOS M40....73 K4
Caledonian Dr ECC M30....85 H4
Caledonia St BOLS/LL BL3....35 M7
  RAD M26....38 F3
Caledonia Wy STRET M32....85 K7
Cale Gn OFTN SK2....112 C6
Cale La WGNE/HIN WN2....48 C2
Cale Rd NM/HAY SK22....124 F4
Cale St OFTN SK2....13 J9
Caley St BOL BL1....35 J2
  CMANE M1....7 G8
Calf Hey LIT OL15....21 K6
Calf Hey Cl RAD M26....54 B1
Calf Hey North ROCH OL11....28 D8
Calf Hey Rd ROY/SHW OL2....44 A4
Calf Hey South ROCH OL11....28 D8
Calf La MOSL OL5....61 H8
Calgarth Dr MDTN M24....57 G1
Calgary St GTN M18....88 F7
Calico Cl CSLFD M3....6 A1
Calico Crs STLY SK15....77 K6
Calico La CHF/WBR SK23....124 E8
Calico Wood Av
  WGNNW/ST WN6....30 C5
Callaghan Wk HEY OL10....40 F3
Calland Av HYDE SK14....102 C1
Callander Ct
  WGNW/BIL/OR WN5....47 H5
Callender St RAMS BL0....18 E6
Calliards Rd MILN OL16....21 J8
Callingdon Rd CCHDY M21....98 A7
Callington Cl HYDE SK14....103 H2
Callington Dr HYDE SK14....103 H2
Callis Rd BOLS/LL BL3....35 M6
Callum Wk BRUN/LGST M13 *....87 M6
Calluna Ms DID/WITH M20 *....98 D3
Calow Dr LEIGH WN7....81 M1
Caltha St RAMS BL0....18 E6
Calthorpe Av BKLY M9....72 F5
Calton Av BRO M7....71 K5
Calton Cl WGNS/IIMK WN3....47 G8
Calve Croft Rd
  WYTH/NTH M22....119 H3
Calveley Wy WGNNW/ST WN6....31 H4
Calver Av ECC M30....84 F4
Calver Cl URM M41....95 G1
Calver Hey Cl WHTN BL5....50 F2
Calverleigh Cl BOLS/LL BL3....51 K2
Calverley Av BNG/LEV M19....99 J5
Calverley Cl WILM/AE SK9....127 G4
Calverley Wy WHIT OL12....20 C8
Calver Ms GLSP SK13....104 A2
Calverton Dr NEWH/MOS M40....73 M5
Calvert Rd BOLS/LL BL3....52 C1
Calvert St ORD M5....86 A2
Calvine Wk NEWH/MOS M40 *....87 M1
Calvin St BOL BL1....2 F1
Cambeck Cl WHTF M45....55 L3
Cambell Rd ECC M30....84 E2
Camberley Cl BRAM/HZG SK7....121 J5
  TOT/BURYW BL8....24 D7
Camberly Dr ROCH OL11....27 J6
Cambert La GTN M18....88 F7
Camberwell Crs
  WGNE/HIN WN2....48 C2
Camberwell Dr AULW OL7....75 K5
Camberwell St CHH M8 *....72 D8
  OLDS OL8....59 H8
Camberwell Wy ROY/SHW OL2....42 F8
Camborne Rd HYDE SK14....103 H1
Camborne St RUSH/FAL M14....98 C3
Cambourne Dr BOLS/LL BL3....35 K7
  WGNE/HIN WN2....65 M2
Cambo Wk HTNM SK4....111 J1
Cambrai Crs ECC M30....69 G8
Cambrian Crs WGNS/IIMK WN3....62 C2
  ROY/SHW OL2....58 F2
Cambrian Dr MILN OL16....29 K6
Cambrian Rd EDGY/DAV SK3....12 D7
Cambrian St NEWH/MOS M40....88 D2
Cambria Sq BOLS/LL BL3....35 M7
Cambria St BOLS/LL BL3....35 M7
  OLDE OL4....59 M5
Cambridge Av
  OLDTF/WHR M16....97 M2
  ROCH OL11....27 K6
  WILM/AE SK9....126 D5
Cambridge Cl FWTH BL4....52 C3
  SALE M33....108 A1
Cambridge Dr BOLS/LL BL3....37 L8
  DTN/ASHW M34....100 D1
  MPL/ROM SK6....113 H2
Cambridge Gv ECC M30....85 J2
  WHTF M45....55 K4
Cambridge Rd BKLY M9....73 G3
  CHD/CHDH SK8....110 E6
  DROY M43....89 J1
  FAIL M35....74 C7
  HALE/TIMP WA15....117 G2
  HOR/BR BL6....34 C4
  HTNM SK4....99 M7
  URM M41....95 J3
  WGNW/BIL/OR WN5....46 B4
Cambridge St ATH M46....66 F2
  AULW OL7....90 C3
  BRO M7....72 B3
  CHAD OL9....8 B9
  CMANE M1....6 F7
  DUK SK16....90 F3
  OFTN SK2....112 D6
  STLY SK15....91 K2
  WGN WN1....15 J5
Cambridge Wy WGN WN1....15 J5
Camden Av NEWH/MOS M40....73 M8
Camden Cl BOLE BL2....37 M3
Camden St MOSL OL5....77 G1
Camelford Cl HULME M15 *....87 K6
Camelia Rd BKLY M9....72 F5
Camellia Cl BOL BL1....35 L5
Camelot Cl NEWLW WA12....78 C8

Cameron Ct ROY/SHW OL2 ....43 G6
Cameron Pl
  WCGNW/BIL/OR WN5......47 H4
Cameron St BOL BL1...........22 A7
  CMANE M1 *..................6 E7
  LEIGH WN7...................66 A5
  TOT/BURYW BL8................4 A4
Camm St WGNE/HIN WN2..........6 E7
Campania St ROY/SHW OL2......59 H2
Campbell Ci TOT/BURYW BL8....24 D8
Campbell Ct FWTH BL4.........52 F2
Campbell Dr BOLS/LL BL3......51 K2
  BRUN/LGST M13...............99 J2
  SALE M33...................108 D1
  SWIN M27....................70 B6
Campbell St FWTH BL4.........52 E3
  RDSH M....................100 C3
  WCGNW/BIL/OR WN5...........47 G7
  WHIT OL12 *.................28 B2
Campbell Wy WALK M28.........68 F1
Campden Wy WILM/AE SK9......119 M8
Campion Gv WALK WN4..........63 J8
Campion Wy WHIT OL12.........27 M1
Camp Rd AIMK WN4.............78 B1
Camp St AUL OL6..............90 E1
  BRO M7......................71 M8
  CSLFD M3.....................6 D6
  TOT/BURYW BL8...............38 F1
Camrose Gdns BOL BL1.........36 B3
Camrose Wk BRUN/LGST M13 *...88 A7
Cams Acre Cl RAD M26.........54 B1
Cams La RAD M26..............54 B1
Canaan GOL/RIS/CUL WA3.......80 F4
Canada St BOL BL1............35 M2
  HOR/BR BL6..................33 L1
  NEWH/MOS M40................73 H8
  OFTN SK2...................112 D6
Canal Bank ECC M30...........84 F1
Canal Bridge La DROY M43.....89 G3
Canal Cottages Yd ANC M4 *....7 M5
Canal Rd ALT WA14...........108 B5
Canal Side ECC M30...........84 F1
Canal St CHAD OL9............74 E1
  CMANE M1.....................7 H6
  DROY M43....................89 K4
  HEY OL10....................41 H4
  HYDE SK14..................101 M1
  LIT OL15....................21 M7
  MPL/ROM SK6................114 C6
  ORD M5 *....................86 F3
  ROCH OL11...................11 H9
  STKP SK1....................13 K6
  STLY SK15...................91 K3
  WGNE/HIN WN2................15 M7
  WGNNW/ST WN6................47 J3
Canal Ter WGN WN1............15 L5
Canary Wy SWIN M27...........70 E5
Canberra Rd BRAM/HZG SK7....121 H7
  WGNW/BIL/OR WN5.............46 F3
Canberra St OP/CLY M11.......88 F2
Canberra Wy ROCH OL11........42 D1
Candahar St BOLS/LL BL3......52 D1
Candleford Pl OFTN SK2.......52
Candleford Rd DID/WITH M20 *..98 E6
Candlestick Ct BURY BL9......26 A8
Candy La MCFLDN SK10........129 G4
Canisp Cl CHAD OL9...........58 D4
Canley Cl STKP SK1...........13 K7
Canmore Cl BOLS/LL BL3.......51 K1
Cannel Fold WALK M28.........68 E5
Canning Cl WGNE/HIN WN2......48 F3
Canning Dr BOL BL1...........36 B2
Canning St BOL BL1...........36 B2
  BURY BL9.....................4 F1
  HTNM M.....................13 H2
  WCGNW/BIL/OR WN5...........47 G6
  WCGNW/BIL/OR WN5...........47 G6
  WHIT OL12...................28 B1
  WILM/AE SK9................130 C4
Cannon Rd WYTH/NTH M23......109 L3
Cannon St CSLFD M3............6 F5
Cannon Gv BOLS/LL BL3.........8
Cannon St ATH M46............67 G1
  BOLS/LL BL3..................2 B8
  CHAD OL9.....................9 G5
  CSLFD M3.....................6 A2
  ECC M30.....................85 H3
  HYDE SK14...................92 F7
  RAD M26.....................38 C7
  RAMS BL0....................18 D8
Cannon St North BOLS/LL BL3 *..2 B7
Cann St TOT/BURYW BL8........24 A5
Canon Cl WGNNW/ST WN6........31 J2
Canon Dr ALT WA14...........116 D3
Canon Flynn Ct MILN OL16.....11 M4
Canon Green Dr CSLFD M3.......6 C2
Canons Cl BOL BL1............35 L2
Canons Gv NEWH/MOS M40.......73 H7
Canonsleigh Cl CHH M8........72 D7
Canon St BURY BL9.............5 H1
  MILN OL16...................28 E2
Canonsway SWIN M27...........70 B5
Canon Tighe Ct CHAD OL9......58 D5
Canon Wilson Cl
  RNFD/HAY WA11...............78 A6
Cansfield Ct FWTH BL4........53 K6
Cansfield Gv AIMK WN4........63 K8
Canterbury Av
  GOL/RIS/CUL WA3.............80 A3
Canterbury Cl ATH M46........51 H8
  DUK SK16....................91 G6
  ROCH OL11...................27 K5
Canterbury Crs MDTN M24......58 A2
Canterbury Dr PWCH M25.......71 M2
  TOT/BURYW BL8...............25 G8
Canterbury Gdns ORD M5.......85 K8
Canterbury Gv BOLS/LL BL3....52 A1
Canterbury Pk DID/WITH M20...110 C1
Canterbury Rd
  HALE/TIMP WA15.............117 L1
  STKP SK1...................112 E3
  URM M41.....................95 M1
Canterbury St AUL OL6........75 M8
Canterfield Cl DROY M43......90 A2
Cantrell St OP/CLY M11.......88 E3
Canute Rd STRET M32..........97 H1
Canute St BOLE BL2...........36 F3
  ORD M5 *....................86 F2
  RAD M26.....................54 B1
Cape Gdns ROY/SHW OL2........43 L6
Capella Wk BRO M7............71 M8
Capenhurst Cl
  NTHM/RTH M23...............109 J8
  POY/DIS SK12...............122 B8
Capesthorne Cl
  BRAM/HZG SK7...............122 B4
Capesthorne Dr ROY/SHW OL2...43 J5
Capesthorne Rd
  BRAM/HZG SK7...............122 B4
  DUK SK16....................91 G6
  HALE/TIMP WA15.............109 G6
  MPL/ROM SK6................123 G5
  WILM/AE SK9................126 C7
Cape St DID/WITH M20.........98 F5
Capital Rd OP/CLY M11........89 G3
Capitol Cl OP/CLY M11 *......35 K1

Cappadocia Wy WHTN BL5.......50 A5
Capps St WGNE/HIN WN2........64 E1
Capricorn Rd BKLY M9.........73 L1
Capricorn Wy SLFD M6 *.......71 M8
Capstan St BKLY M9...........73 H4
Captain Clarke Rd HYDE SK14..90 E7
Captain Fold HEY OL10 *......41 H2
Captain Fold Rd LHULT M38....52 C7
Captain Lees Gdns WHTN BL5...50 D4
Captain Lees Rd WHTN BL5.....50 D4
Captain's Clough Rd BOL BL1..35 L2
Captain's La AIMK WN4........78 F1
Capton Cl BRAM/HZG SK7......121 J2
Carawood Cl
  WCGNNW/ST WN6...............30 A5
Car Bank Av ATH M46..........51 C8
Car Bank Sq ATH M46..........51 C8
Car Bank St ATH M46..........50 E8
Carberry Rd GTN M18..........89 H3
Carden Av SWIN M27...........70 A5
  URM M41.....................95 H2
Carder Cl SWIN M27...........70 C5
Carders Cl LEIGH WN7.........66 E8
Cardew Av WGNE/HIN WN2......110 B8
Cardiff Cl OLDS OL8..........74 E3
Cardiff St BRO M7............72 B5
Cardigan Dr BURY BL9.........39 H5
Cardigan Rd OLDS OL8.........74 E2
Cardigan St ROY/SHW OL2......43 H8
  SLFD M6.....................86 B3
  WHIT OL12...................28 B1
Cardinal Ms MDTN M24.........57 G2
Cardinal St CHH M8...........72 E6
  OLD OL1......................9 L5
Carding Gv CSLFD M3...........6 C1
Cardroom Rd ANC M4...........7 L4
Cardus St BNG/LEV M19........99 K3
Cardwell Gdns BOL BL1 *......36 B2
Cardwell Rd ECC M30..........84 D5
Cardwell St OLDS OL8.........75 J1
Careless La WGNE/HIN WN2.....48 C5
Caremine Av BNG/LEV M19......99 G2
Carey St BRO M7 *............72 A8
  WGNS/IIMK WN3...............63 G2
Carey Wk HULME M15...........87 J7
Carfax Fold WHIT OL12........27 L2
Carfax St GTN M18............89 G7
Carill Av NEWH/MOS M40.......73 H3
Carill Dr RUSH/FAL M14.......99 C4
Carina Pl BRO M7.............71 M8
Carisbrook Av URM M41........95 M3
Carisbrook Dr SWIN M27.......70 D6
Carisbrooke Av
  BRAM/HZG SK7...............121 M3
Carisbrooke Dr BOL BL1.......36 B1
Carisbrooke Rd LEIGH WN7.....67 G6
Carisbrook St BKLY M9........73 G5
Carlburn St OP/CLY M11.......89 G2
Carleton Rd POY/DIS SK12....122 E8
Carley Gv BKLY M9............56 F8
Carlford Gv PWCH M25.........71 J1
Carlile St EDGY/DAV SK3......13 G7
Carlin Ga HALE/TIMP WA15....108 C6
Carling Dr WYTH/NTH M22.....119 C2
Carlingford Cl EDGY/DAV SK3...112 B7
Carlisle Cl BOLS/LL BL3......53 K2
  MPL/ROM SK6................113 G3
  WHTF M45....................55 L5
Carlisle Crs AUL OL6.........75 M8
Carlisle Dr ALT WA14........108 B4
  IRL M44.....................94 D2
Carlisle St BRO M7............8 D7
  EDGW/EG BL7.................22 D4
  SWIN M27....................70 C2
  WGNE/HIN WN2 *..............49 H6
  WGNW/BIL/OR WN5.............47 G6
  WHIT OL12...................28 B1
  WILM/AE SK9................130 C4
Carloon Rd WYTH/NTH M23.....109 L3
Carlow Dr WYTH/NTH M22......119 C2
Carl St BOL BL1 *............36 A2
  BRAM/HZG SK7...............120 F7
  CHD/CHDH SK8...............120 B1
  MPL/ROM SK6................114 A1
  OLDE OL4....................60 A3
  PWCH M25....................72 B2
  WHTF M45....................55 C3
  WILM/AE SK9................127 G2
Carlton Cl BOLE BL2..........37 H1
  HOR/BR BL6..................33 G2
  WALK M28....................68 F3
Carlton Ct HALE/TIMP WA15...117 K3
Carlton Crs STKP SK1.........13 M5
  URM M41.....................96 A3
Carlton Dr CHD/CHDH SK8.....110 D6
  PWCH M25....................72 B2
Carlton Gv HOR/BR BL6........34 A3
  WGNE/HIN WN2................65 J1
Carlton Pl BRAM/HZG SK7.....122 C3
  FWTH BL4....................53 C3
Carlton Range GTN M18 *......89 J3
Carlton Rd AUL OL6...........75 M7
  BOL BL1.....................35 K4
  GOL/RIS/CUL WA3.............80 A3
  HALE/TIMP WA15.............117 G2
  HTNM SK4...................111 K2
  HYDE SK14..................102 D1
  OLDTF/WHR M16...............98 A1
  SALE M33....................96 A1
  SLFD M6.....................71 H8
  URM M41.....................95 M3
  WALK M28....................68 F3
Carlton St BOLE BL2...........3 G6
  BURY BL9.....................4 F9
  ECC M30.....................85 C1
  FWTH BL4....................53 C4
  OLDTF/WHR M16...............86 F8
  WGNS/IIMK WN3...............14 E8
Carlton Wy ROY/SHW OL2.......59 C2
Carlyle Cl CHH M8............72 D6
Carlyle Gv LEIGH WN7.........65 M4
Carlyle St BURY BL9...........4 C4
Carlyn Av SALE M33...........97 G8
Carmel Av ORD M5.............86 F5
Carmel Cl ORD M5.............86 F4
Carmel Ct BKLY M9............73 G3
Carmenna Dr BRAM/HZG SK7....121 H5
Carmichael Cl PART M31......106 D3
Carmichael St EDGY/DAV SK3...12 E8
Car Mill Ms WILM/AE SK9.....126 F3
Carmine Fold MDTN M24........57 J2
Carmona Dr PWCH M25..........55 H7
Carmona Gdns BRO M7..........71 M3
Carmoor Rd BRUN/LGST M13 *...87 M7
Carnaby St BKLY M9...........73 J3
Carna Rd RDSH SK5...........100 B3
Carnarvon St BRO M7 *........72 B5
  CSLFD M3 *..................87 J1
  OLDS OL8....................74 E2
  STKP SK1....................13 M6

Carnation Rd FWTH BL4........52 D3
  OLDE OL4....................60 B8
Carnegie Av BNG/LEV M19......99 J3
Carnegie Cl SALE M33........108 A1
Carnegie Dr WGNW/NTH WN4.....63 K7
Carnforth Av CHAD OL9........58 D6
  ROCH OL11...................42 A5
Carnforth Dr SALE M33.......108 D1
  TOT/BURYW BL8...............24 D2
Carnforth Rd CHD/CHDH SK8...111 M8
  HTNM SK4....................99 M6
Carnforth Sq MDTN M24........42 A5
Carnforth St RUSH/FAL M14....98 E1
Carnoustie BOLS/LL BL3.......51 K1
Carnoustie Cl
  NEWH/MOS M40................73 M5
  WILM/AE SK9................127 H4
Carnoustie Dr
  CHD/CHDH SK8...............119 J3
  RAMS BL0....................18 E6
Carnwood Cl
  NEWH/MOS M40................74 A8
Carolina Wy SALE M50.........86 B3
Caroline St AUL OL6..........90 F1
  BOLS/LL BL3.................36 A8
  BRO M7......................72 B8
  EDGY/DAV SK3................12 F8
  IRL M44.....................94 B4
  STLY SK15...................91 K3
  WGN WN1.....................15 M4
  WGNS/IIMK WN3...............14 E5
Carpenters La ANC M4..........7 J3
Carpenters Wk DROY M43.......89 J3
Carpenters Wy MILN OL16......28 B8
Carradale Dr SALE M33........95 M7
Carradon Dr
  WGNNW/ST WN6................31 H3
Carr Av PWCH M25.............71 J2
Carr Bank GLSP SK13.........105 H4
Carr Bank Av BKLY M9.........72 C1
Carr Bank Dr RAMS BL0........18 E5
Carr Bank Rd RAMS BL0........18 E5
Carrbrook Cl STLY SK15.......77 J6
Carrbrook Crs STLY SK15......77 J6
Carr Brook Dr ATH M46........51 H8
Carrbrook Dr ROY/SHW OL2.....59 H3
Carrbrook Rd STLY SK15.......77 J5
Carrbrook Ter RAD M26........38 E5
Carr Brow MPL/ROM SK6.......123 J5
Carr Cl STKP SK1............112 E4
Carr Common Rd
  WGNE/HIN WN2................66 A1
Carr Dr FWTH BL4 *...........52 C3
Carrfield Av EDGY/DAV SK3...112 B6
  HALE/TIMP WA15.............109 C7
  LHULT M38...................52 B8
Carrfield Gv LHULT M38.......52 B8
Carr Fold RAMS BL0...........18 E5
Carrgate Rd DTN/ASHW M34....101 L3
Carrgreen Cl BNG/LEV M19.....99 L3
Carrgreen La LYMM WA13......106 C6
Carrhill Quarry Cl MOSL OL5..76 F2
Carrhill Rd MOSL OL5.........76 F2
Carrhill Ter MOSL OL5 *......76 F2
Carrhouse La HYDE SK14.......92 F8
Carriage Dr LIT OL15.........21 M5
The Carriage Dr GLSP SK13....93 H8
The Carriages ALT WA14 *....107 M8
Carriage St OLDTF/WHR M16....87 G7
Carrick Gdns MDTN M24........41 J8
Carrie St BOL BL1............35 L4
Carrigart PWCH M25...........71 K1
Carrill Gv East BNG/LEV M19...99 G1
Carrington Dr BOLS/LL BL3....36 C8
Carrington Field St STKP SK1..112 E3
Carrington Gv LEIGH WN7 *....66 C5
Carrington La PART M31.......95 K5
  SALE M33....................96 B7
Carrington Rd RUSH/FAL M14...98 F4
  STKP SK1...................112 E2
  URM M41.....................95 H4
Carrington St CHAD OL9.......74 E1
  LEIGH WN7...................66 C5
  SWIN M27....................70 E3
Carrington Ter SWIN M27 *....70 D3
Carr La GOL/RIS/CUL WA3......80 D5
  LEIGH WN7...................81 H4
  STLY SK15...................77 J5
  UPML OL3....................45 M7
  UPML OL3....................61 L5
  WGNS/IIMK WN3...............63 K1
  WILM/AE SK9................130 A2
Carr Lea OLDE OL4............60 F6
Carr Mill Crs
  WGNW/BIL/OR WN5.............62 B8
Carr Mill Ms WILM/AE SK9 *...126 F3
Carr Mill Rd
  WGNW/BIL/OR WN5.............62 B8
Carron Av BKLY M9............73 H3
Carron Gv BOLE BL2...........37 J5
Carr Ri STLY SK15............77 J5
Carr Rd HALE/TIMP WA15......117 K2
  IRL M44.....................94 E2
Carrs Av CHD/CHDH SK8.......111 K6
Carrsdale Dr BKLY M9.........72 F2
Carrsfield Rd
  WYTH/NTH M22...............110 B6
Carrslea Cl RAD M26..........38 B7
Carrs Rd CHD/CHDH SK8.......111 J6
Carr St AUL OL6..............76 A7
  LEIGH WN7...................65 M7
  RAMS BL0....................18 E5
  SWIN M27....................70 A5
  WGNE/HIN WN2................49 G6
Carrswood Rd
  NTHM/RTH M23...............108 F4
Carruthers Cl HEY OL10.......41 J1
Carruthers St ANC M4.........88 A5
Carr Vw RNFD/HAY SK22 *.....124 F7
Carwood HALE/TIMP WA15......117 K6
Carwood Av BRAM/HZG SK7.....121 G4
Carwood Hey RAMS BL0.........18 D8
Carwood Rd
  BRAM/HZG SK7...............120 F3
  WILM/AE SK9................126 D4
Carsdale Rd WYTH/NTH M22....119 C5
Carslake Av BOL BL1..........35 M4
Carslake Rd
  NEWH/MOS M40................73 C7
  SLFD M6.....................71 G8
  WGNE/HIN WN2................49 J7
Carson Rd BNG/LEV M19........99 K4
Carstairs Av HTNM SK4.......112 D8
Carstairs Cl CHH M8..........72 C5
Car St WGNE/HIN WN2..........64 D3
Carswell Cl TYLD M29........67 M3
Carter Cl DTN/ASHW M34 *....101 J2
Carter Pl HYDE SK14 *........91 G7

Carter St BOLS/LL BL3........36 D8
  BRO M7......................72 A7
  FWTH BL4 *..................53 H7
  HYDE SK14...................91 G7
  MOSL OL5....................76 F4
  SALO M50....................85 M3
  STLY SK15...................91 L2
  WGNS/IIMK WN3...............15 K7
Carthage St OLDS OL8.........59 J8
Cartleach Gv WALK M28........68 C2
Cartleach La WALK M28........68 C2
Cartmel WHIT OL12............10 E2
Cartmel Av HTNM SK4.........100 A6
  MILN OL16...................29 J8
  WGN WN1.....................47 L1
Cartmel Cl BOLS/LL BL3.......51 C2
  BRAM/HZG SK7...............121 L1
  BURY BL9....................55 K1
  CHD/CHDH SK8...............119 J3
  OLDS OL8....................75 G1
Cartmel Crs BOLE BL2.........36 F2
  CHAD OL9....................74 C2
Cartmel Dr HALE/TIMP WA15...109 G6
Cartmel Gv WALK M28..........69 L5
Cartridge Cl WYTH/NTH M22...119 H1
Cartridge St HEY OL10........40 F2
Cartwright Gv LEIGH WN7......66 A3
Cartwright Rd CCHDY M21......97 K4
Cartwright St
  DTN/ASHW M34................90 C6
  HYDE SK14...................91 K7
Carver Av PWCH M25...........55 M7
Carver Cl OLDTF/WHR M16......86 E7
Carver Dr MPL/ROM SK6.......114 B7
Carver Rd HALE/TIMP WA15....117 C7
  MPL/ROM SK6................114 B7
Carver St OLDTF/WHR M16......86 E7
Carver Wk HULME M15 *........87 J7
Carville Gv WGNE/HIN WN2.....49 L8
Carwood Gv HOR/BR BL6........34 A3
Cascade Dr BRO M7............72 B7
Case Rd RNFD/HAY WA11........78 A6
Cashgate Ct OLDS OL8.........74 F1
Cashmere Rd EDGY/DAV SK3.....12 C9
Cashmoor Wk WGTN/LGST M12....88 B6
Cashmore Dr WGNE/HIN WN2.....48 D8
Caspian Rd ALT WA14.........107 K6
  BKLY M9.....................73 L1
Cass Av ORD M5..............86 D4
Cassidy Cl ANC M4............7 K2
Cassidy Gdns MDTN M24........41 J8
Casson Ga WHIT OL12..........28 B3
Casson St FAIL M35...........74 C5
Casterton Wy WALK M28........68 D7
Castle Av DTN/ASHW M34......101 H2
  ROCH OL11...................10 C7
Castlebrook Cl BURY BL9......39 L8
Castle Cl DROY M43...........89 L2
Castle Ct AUL OL6............75 L5
Castle Cft BOLE BL2..........37 G1
Castlecroft Av HOR/BR BL6....33 C2
Castlecroft Rd BURY BL9.......4 F6
Castledene Av SLFD M6........86 B1
Castle Edge Rd NM/HAY SK22..124 D2
Castle Farm Dr OFTN SK2.....112 E6
Castle Farm La OFTN SK2.....112 F7
  WGNE/HIN WN2................49 J3
Castlefield Av BRO M7........72 B4
Castlefield Br ORD M5........6 A6
Castleford Cl BOL BL1........2 B6
Castleford St OLD OL1........8 D1
Castle Gv LEIGH WN7..........67 G6
  RAMS BL0....................24 D2
Castle Hall Cl STLY SK15.....91 K3
Castle Hall Ct STLY SK15 *...91 K3
Castle Hall Vw STLY SK15.....91 K3
Castle Hey Cl BURY BL9.......55 M1
Castle Hi GLSP SK13.........105 H1
  NEWLW WA12..................79 H8
Castle Hill Crs ROCH OL11....10 C6
Castle Hill Dr BKLY M9.......72 F3
Castle Hill Pk MPL/ROM SK6 *..101 J6
  WGNE/HIN WN2................49 J5
Castle Hill Rd BURY BL9......25 M6
  PWCH M25....................72 A2
  WGNE/HIN WN2................49 H6
Castle Hill St BOLE BL2......36 E2
Castle La STLY SK15..........77 J4
Castlemere Cl WGNS/IIMK WN3...63 C3
Castlemere Dr ROY/SHW OL2....44 A1
Castlemere St ROCH OL11......10 C6
Castlemere Ter ROCH OL11 *...10 D7
Castle Mill La
  HALE/TIMP WA15.............117 J7
Castlemoor Av BRO M7.........71 L4
Castle Quay HULME M15........6 C8
Castlerea Cl ECC M30.........85 C4
Castlerigg Cl HTNM SK4......100 A5
Castlerigg Dr MDTN M24.......56 F2
  ROY/SHW OL2.................42 F6
Castle Ri WGNE/HIN WN2.......49 H7
Castle Rd BURY BL9...........39 M8
Castle Shaw Rd OFTN SK2.....113 H7
Castle St ATH M46............67 J3
  BOLE BL2.....................3 J6
  BURY BL9.....................4 E4
  BURY BL9.....................4 F3
  CSLFD M3.....................6 C7
  ECC M30.....................85 J2
  EDGY/DAV SK3................12 E8
  FWTH BL4 *..................53 G5
  GLSP SK13...................93 H5
  HYDE SK14..................102 C1
  MDTN M24....................58 A5
  STLY SK15...................91 K3
  WGNE/HIN WN2................49 H6
Castle St South ROCH OL11 *..42 D7
Castleton Av ALT WA14.......107 M5
  BOLE BL2....................36 E2
  CHAD OL9.....................8 C7
Castleton Dr MPL/ROM SK6....123 H6
Castleton Gv AUL OL6.........76 C6
Castleton Rd BRAM/HZG SK7...122 B3
  BRO M7......................72 B4
  ROY/SHW OL2.................42 F4
  STRET M32...................85 K8
Castleton Rd South ROCH OL11..42 D7
Castleton St ALT WA14.......107 M5
  BOLE BL2....................36 E2
  CHAD OL9.....................8 C7
Castleton Wk OP/CLY M11 *....88 C3
Castleton Wy WGNS/IIMK WN3...62 C2
Castle Wy SWIN M27...........70 D2
Castleway HALE/TIMP WA15....117 L1
  ROCH OL11...................41 L1
  SLFD M6.....................71 H8
  WGNE/HIN WN2................49 J7
Castlewood Gdns OFTN SK2....113 H7
Castlewood Rd BRO M7.........71 J4
Castle Yd STKP SK1 *.........13 G4
Catchdale Cl BKLY M9.........56 F7
Catches Cl ROCH OL11.........27 L3
Catches La ROCH OL11.........27 L3

Cateaton St BURY BL9..........4 F2
  CSLFD M3.....................6 F3
Caterham Av BOLS/LL BL3......51 J2
Caterham St ANC M4...........88 A3
Catfield Wk HULME M15 *.......6 B9
Catford Rd NTHM/RTH M23.....109 J7
Cathedral Ap CSLFD M3 *.......6 E3
Cathedral Cl DUK SK16........91 G6
Cathedral Gdns ANC M4 *......6 F3
Cathedral Gates CSLFD M3 *....6 F3
Cathedral Rd CHAD OL9........58 D3
Cathedral St CSLFD M3 *.......6 F3
Catherine Houses HTNM SK4 *...111 J3
Catherine Rd ALT WA14.......116 E1
  CHH M8......................72 B3
  MPL/ROM SK6................113 J3
  SWIN M27....................69 M5
Catherine St BOLS/LL BL3.....52 C1
  BRAM/HZG SK7...............113 H8
  BURY BL9....................39 H6
  ECC M30.....................84 D3
  HYDE SK14..................102 A1
  LEIGH WN7...................66 C5
  OLDE OL4....................60 B6
  OP/CLY M11..................89 H5
Catherine Ter WGN WN1........15 K4
Catherston Cl OLDTF/WHR M16...98 B1
Cathrine St East
  DTN/ASHW M34...............101 G1
Cathrine St West
  DTN/ASHW M34...............101 G1
Catlow La ANC M4.............7 H3
Catlow St BRO M7.............72 B8
Caton Cl BURY BL9............4 D9
Caton Dr ATH M46............46 D4
Caton St MILN OL16...........10 F6
Cato St RAMS BL0.............18 D8
Catterall Crs BOLE BL2.......23 G6
Catterick Av DID/WITH M20...110 F1
  SALE M33...................107 M2
Catterick Dr BOLS/LL BL3.....51 K3
Catterick Rd DID/WITH M20...110 F1
Catterwood Dr MPL/ROM SK6...114 C2
Cattlin Wy OLDS OL8..........74 F2
Caunce Av GOL/RIS/CUL WA3....79 K5
Caunce Rd WGN WN1............15 K3
Caunce St WGN WN1............15 K4
The Causeway ALT WA14.......108 A8
  CHAD OL9....................58 A7
Causewood Cl OLDE OL4........44 B8
Causey Dr MDTN M24...........57 G1
Cavanagh Cl BRUN/LGST M13....88 A6
Cavan Cl EDGY/DAV SK3.......111 J5
Cavan Dr RNFD/HAY WA11.......78 A3
Cavell St CMANE M1 *..........7 J4
Cavell Wy ORD M5............86 D3
Cavendish Av DID/WITH M20....98 C6
  SWIN M27....................70 F1
Cavendish Dr WGNS/IIMK WN3...63 C2
Cavendish Gdns BOLS/LL BL3...51 M1
Cavendish Gv ECC M30.........85 H1
Cavendish Ms WILM/AE SK9....126 E7
Cavendish Pl AUL OL6 *.......90 D1
Cavendish Rd ALT WA14.......116 E1
  BRAM/HZG SK7...............121 M3
  BRO M7......................72 A3
  DID/WITH M20................85 H1
  HTNM M.....................111 J2
  ROCH OL11...................42 B1
  STRET M32...................86 B8
  URM M41.....................96 B2
  WALK M28....................69 L6
Cavendish St AUL OL6.........90 E2
  HULME M15....................6 E9
  OLDS OL8.....................9 H7
Cavendish Wy ROY/SHW OL2.....58 F2
Cavenham Gv BOL BL1..........35 M4
Caversham Dr BKLY M9.........73 H4
Cawdor Av FWTH BL4...........52 F2
Cawdor Pl HALE/TIMP WA15....108 F6
Cawdor Rd RUSH/FAL M14.......98 F3
Cawdor St ECC M30............84 F3
  FWTH BL4....................52 E2
  HULME M15....................6 C9
  LEIGH WN7...................66 C8
  SWIN M27....................70 A4
  WALK M28....................69 H2
  WGNE/HIN WN2................49 L7
  WGNW/BIL/OR WN5.............47 G7
Cawley Av GOL/RIS/CUL WA3....81 K8
  PWCH M25....................71 J2
Cawley La MCFLDN SK10.......129 J5
Cawley Ter BKLY M9...........56 F7
Cawood Sq RDSH SK5..........100 F6
Cawston Wk CHH M8............72 D6
Caxton Cl WGNS/IIMK WN3......63 J2
Caxton Rd RUSH/FAL M14.......98 E3
Caxton St CSLFD M3 *..........6 D3
  HEY OL10....................41 H2
  ROCH OL11...................41 M2
Caxton Wy ORD M5.............86 E3
Caygill St CSLFD M3...........6 D2
Cayley St MILN OL16..........11 J3
Caythorpe St RUSH/FAL M14....98 D1
Cayton St WGTN/LGST M12......99 K1
C' Ct AIMK WN4...............78 E2
The Ceal MPL/ROM SK6........114 C2
  WGNNW/ST WN6................47 K2
Cecil Dr URM M41.............95 H2
Cecil Gv GTN M18.............89 G8
Cecilia St BOLS/LL BL3.......36 B8
Cecil Rd BKLY M9.............57 G8
  ECC M30.....................85 H3
  HALE/TIMP WA15.............117 G2
  STRET M32...................96 F3
Cecil St BOLE BL2............3 J5
  BURY BL9....................4 F6
  DUK SK16....................90 E4
  EDGY/DAV SK3................13 C8
  HULME M15...................87 L7
  LEIGH WN7...................66 D8
  LIT OL15....................21 K7
  MOSL OL5....................76 F4
  OLDS OL8.....................9 C9
  ROCH OL11...................10 F7
  ROY/SHW OL2.................42 F8
  STLY SK15...................91 L3
  WALK M28....................69 C5
  WGN WN1.....................15 L4
  WHIT OL12...................48 B8
Cedar Av ALT WA14...........107 M8
  ATH M46.....................50 E8
  AUL OL6.....................76 A7
  BOLS/LL BL3.................53 L2
  BRAM/HZG SK7...............122 A2
  GOL/RIS/CUL WA3.............80 C5
  HEY OL10....................40 F1
  HOR/BR BL6..................34 B3
  STLY SK15...................91 M1

WGNE/HIN WN2................65 J1
WGNNW/ST WN6.............31 J4
WHTF M45.......................55 J6
Cedar Bank CI MILN OL16....29 G5
Cedar CI GLSP OL13..........104 E2
POY/DIS SK12..................129 J1
Cedar Crs CHAD OL9.............8
RAMS BL0.........................18 F5
Cedar Dr DROY M43............89 L2
SWIN M27.........................54 A8
URM M41...........................95 M3
WGN WN1..........................48 A2
Cedar Gv AIMK WN4............63 G7
DTN/ASHW M34................101 H1
DUK SK16..........................91 J4
FWTH BL4..........................52 E4
HTNM SK4..........................99 M1
PWCH M25.........................55 K6
RNFD/HAY WA11.................78 B5
ROY/SHW OL2....................43 G6
ROY/SHW OL2....................43 L6
RUSH/FAL M14...................99 G4
WGNW/BIL/OR WN5.............46 C6
WHTN BL5..........................50 B5
Cedar La MILN OL16............43 L1
OLDE OL4...........................61 G6
Cedar Lawn
CHD/CHDH SK8 *.............120 C2
Cedar Ms AULW OL7...........75 K7
Cedar PI BRO M7.................71 M8
Cedar Rd CHD/CHDH SK8...110 D7
FAIL M35...........................74 C6
HALE/TIMP WA15..............117 G1
LEIGH WN7........................66 B4
MDTN M24..........................57 M4
MPL/ROM SK6...................114 B8
OFTN SK2.........................112 E8
PART M31.........................106 D1
SALE M33..........................96 A6
Cedars Rd WYTH/NTH M22..118 F1
Cedar St AUL OL6................76 A3
BURY BL9............................5 J3
HYDE SK14.........................91 G7
OLDE OL4...........................59 M5
WHIT OL12.........................28 C3
Cedar Vw AUL OL6..............76 B7
Cedarwood Av HTNM SK4....111 K3
Cedarwood CI WYTH/NTH M22..110 B4
Cedar Wood BOL BL1 *.........35 J4
Cedric Rd CHH M8................72 B2
OLDE OL4...........................59 M5
Cedric St ORD M5................86 A2
Celandine CI LIT OL15...........21 K7
Celandine Wk WGNS/IIMK WN3..46 E8
Celia St CHH M8..................72 E4
Cellini Sq BOL BL1...............36 A3
Celtic St STKP SK1...............13 M6
Cemetery Rd BOLE BL2...........3 K4
DROY M43..........................89 L2
DTN/ASHW M34..................90 C6
DTN/ASHW M34................101 J3
FAIL M35...........................74 C6
FWTH BL4...........................53 J3
GLSP SK13.........................93 M8
MOSL OL5..........................77 G5
ORD M5.............................86 B3
RAD M26............................38 D7
RAMS BL0...........................18 D8
ROY/SHW OL2....................42 F7
SWIN M27...........................70 B5
WGNS/IIMK WN3.................38 B2
Cemetery Rd North SWIN M27..70 B2
Cemetery St MDTN M24........57 K3
WHTN BL5..........................50 B3
Cennick CI OLDE OL4............59 M6
Ceno St OLD OL1...................9 L1
Centaur CI SWIN M27............70 C2
Centenary Ct BOLS/LL BL3....36 C8
Centenary Wy SALQ M50.......85 K3
Central Av ATH M46..............51 H8
BNG/LEV M19......................99 K2
BURY BL9............................39 C5
FWTH BL4...........................52 D4
LEIGH WN7 *.......................81 M1
LIT OL15............................21 M6
RAMS BL0...........................19 G2
SALE M33..........................108 A3
SLFD M6.............................71 H7
SWIN M27...........................54 D7
UPML OL3...........................61 M7
URM M41............................85 H6
WALK M28...........................52 F7
Central Dr BRAM/HZG SK7...120 F2
BURY BL9............................25 J4
CHD/CHDH SK8.................119 M4
CHH M8.............................72 E3
MPL/ROM SK6...................113 M1
RDSH SK5.........................100 D7
SWIN M27...........................70 E5
URM M41............................96 A2
WGNNW/ST WN6................30 E6
WHTN BL5..........................50 B3
Central Flats WGNE/HIN WN2 *..48 C3
Central Park Est TRPK M17 *..85 M6
Central Park Wy WGN WN1....15 H1
Central Rd DID/WITH M20....98 D7
MANAIR M90.....................118 E6
PART M31...........................106 C1
Central Wy ALT WA14..........108 A8
CMANW M2..........................6 F7
RAMS BL0...........................18 E6
Centre Ct LEIGH WN7...........80 E3
Centre Gdns BOL BL1............36 A3
Centre Park Rd BOL BL1..........2 A1
Centurion Gv BRO M7...........72 B7
Century Gdns WHIT OL12......10 E2
Century Ldg FWTH BL4..........52 F4
Cestrian St BOLS/LL BL3.......52 C1
Ceylon St NEWH/MOS M40....73 K6
OLDE OL4...........................60 A7
Chadbury CI HOR/BR BL6......34 E8
Chadderton Dr BURY BL9......55 K2
Chadderton Fold OLD OL1.....58 C3
Chadderton Hall Rd CHAD OL9..58 C3
Chadderton Park Rd CHAD OL9..58 C3
Chadderton Prec CHAD OL9 *...8 B4
Chadderton St ANC M4............7 J2
Chadderton Wy CHAD OL9.....58 F3
OLD OL1.............................58 F3
Chaddesley Wk OP/CLY M11 *..88 D4
Chaddock La TYLD M29..........68 A6
The Chaddock Level WALK M28..68 D7
Chadkirk Rd MPL/ROM SK6...113 M3
Chadvil Rd CHD/CHDH SK8...110 F7
Chadwell Rd OFTN SK2........113 H5
RUSH/FAL M14....................98 E1
WILM/AE SK9.....................127 G3
Chadwick Fold BURY BL9......55 K2
Chadwick Hall Rd ROCH OL11..27 L6

Chadwick La MILN OL16........42 F2
ROCH OL11.........................41 K2
Chadwick Rd ECC M30..........85 H2
URM M41............................96 C2
Chadwick St AUL OL6...........91 H1
BOLE BL2.............................3 J4
BOLS/LL BL3.......................53 L1
BURY BL9...........................26 B8
GLSP SK13........................104 E4
LEIGH WN7........................66 C6
MILN OL16..........................29 H5
MPL/ROM SK6...................114 C7
ROCH OL11.........................10 A5
STKP SK1...........................13 J7
SWIN M27...........................70 C4
WGNE/HIN WN2..................49 H6
WGNS/IIMK WN3.................14 D7
Chaffinch CI DROY M43........89 M1
OLDE OL4...........................60 B8
WYTH/NTH M22.................110 C7
Chaffinch Dr BURY BL9..........5 M1
Chaffinch Gv STLY SK15 *.....77 H5
Chain Bar La HYDE SK14.....103 J2
Chain Rd BKLY M9.................57 G7
Chain St CMANE M1................7 G5
Chalbury CI WGNE/HIN WN2 *..49 G8
Chalcombe Gra
WGTN/LGST M12 *..............88 C8
Chale CI NEWH/MOS M40......88 A1
Chale Gn BOLE BL2...............37 H1
Chalfont Av URM M41 *..........96 B2
Chalfont CI OLDS OL8...........59 L8
Chalfont Dr CHH M8..............72 D5
TYLD M29............................67 K5
WALK M28............................69 H4
Chalfont St BOL BL1.............36 C2
Chalford Rd NTHM/RTH M23..118 C1
Challenge Wy
WGNW/BIL/OR WN5.............46 F3
Challenor Sq WGTN/LGST M12 *..88 D6
Challum Dr CHAD OL9...........58 D4
Chamber Hall CI OLDS OL8....59 G8
Chamberhall St BURY BL9.......4 E2
Chamber House Dr ROCH OL11..41 L1
Chamberlain Dr WILM/AE SK9..127 H3
Chamberlain Rd STLY SK15....76 F7
Chamberlain St BOLS/LL BL3....2 F7
Chamber Rd OLDS OL8..........74 F1
ROY/SHW OL2.....................43 K5
Chambers Ct HYDE SK14.....103 K1
Chambers Field Ct ORD M5....86 D3
Champness Rd MILN OL16 *....10 F5
Chancel Av ORD M5..............86 A4
Chancel CI DUK SK16............90 F6
Chancel La WILM/AE SK9.....126 F4
Chancellor La WGTN/LGST M12..88 A4
Chancel Ms STKP SK1...........13 L4
Chancel PI CMANE M1 *...........7 L5
MILN OL16..........................10 E5
Chancery CI TYLD M29..........67 L4
Chancery La BOL BL1..............2 F5
CMANW M2............................6 F5
ROY/SHW OL2 *..................43 M5
UPML OL3...........................61 K2
Chancery St CHAD OL9...........8 D2
OLDE OL4...........................59 M6
Chancery Wk CHAD OL9 *.......8 D2
Chandler Wy GOL/RIS/CUL WA3..80 B4
Chandley St CHD/CHDH SK8 *..111 C6
Chandos Gv ORD M5.............86 A2
Chandos Rd CCHDY M21........97 M3
HTNM SK4...........................99 J6
MPL/ROM SK6....................71 L2
Chandos Rd South CCHDY M21..97 M3
Chandos St ROY/SHW OL2....43 M5
Change Wy CSLFD M3..............6 C1
Channing CI MILN OL16.........11 K7
Channing Sq MILN OL16.........11 J7
Channing St MILN OL16.........11 J7
Chanters Av ATH M46...........67 H1
The Chanters WALK M28........68 F5
Chantlers Av TOT/BURYW BL8..38 D3
Chantry CI POY/DIS SK12.....124 A7
RDSH SK5.........................100 B5
WHTN BL5............................68 F5
Chantry Fold POY/DIS SK12..124 A6
Chantry Rd POY/DIS SK12....123 M6
Chantry Wk AIMK WN4..........63 J7
Chapel Aly BOL BL1 *..............2 E4
Chapel Brow GLSP SK13........93 K5
GLSP SK13........................104 B6
Chapel CI BURY BL9..............39 L8
DUK SK16...........................90 F4
WGNS/IIMK WN3.................15 J8
Chapel Ct ALT WA14............108 A8
Chapel Dr AUL OL6..............117 L5
HALE/TIMP WA15..............117 L5
Chapelfield DI WALK M28.......68 E1
Chapel Field Rd
DTN/ASHW M34.................101 J1
Chapelfield Rd WGTN/LGST M12..7 M7
Chapel Fields La
WGNE/HIN WN2...................49 H7
Chapelfield St BOL BL1..........36 B1
Chapel Gdns TOT/BURYW BL8..24 B3
Chapel Ga MILN OL16............29 J6
Chapel Gra EDGW/EG BL7.....16 F8
Chapel Gn DTN/ASHW M34...101 J1
Chapel Green Rd
WGNE/HIN WN2...................49 H6
Chapel Gv URM M41.............96 B2
Chapel HI LIT OL15...............21 M6
Chapelhill Dr BKLY M9...........72 F1
Chapel La BKLY M9...............72 F1
GLSP SK13..........................93 J7
HALE/TIMP WA15..............117 L5
PART M31.........................106 C1
ROCH OL11.........................26 E4
ROY/SHW OL2.....................43 G8
SALE M33..........................121 K1
TOT/BURYW BL8.................18 D6
WGNS/IIMK WN3.................14 F7
WILM/AE SK9....................126 D6
Chapel Meadow WALK M28....68 E5
Chapel PI AIMK WN4 *...........78 E1
BOLS/LL BL3........................2 D1
URM M41............................85 G4
Chapel Rd IRL M44................94 D2
OLDS OL8...........................74 F1
PWCH M25..........................71 J3
SALE M33............................96 E7
SWIN M27...........................53 G8
UPML OL3...........................61 K6
WILM/AE SK9....................127 L4
WILM/AE SK9....................130 D3
WYTH/NTH M22.................110 A4
Chapelstead WHTN BL5.........50 C7

Chapel St AIMK WN4.............78 E1
ATH M46.............................67 G1
AUL OL6.............................90 F1
BNC/LEV M19......................99 K3
BOL BL1...............................3 G3
BOLS/LL BL3 *.....................53 K1
BRAM/HZG SK7.................122 A1
BURY BL9............................5 J3
CHD/CHDH SK8..................111 G7
CMANW M2............................7 G5
DROY M43...........................89 L3
DTN/ASHW M34...................90 C6
DUK SK16...........................90 F4
ECC M30............................84 F3
EDGW/EG BL7.....................22 A1
FWTH BL4...........................53 H4
GLSP SK13........................104 F3
HEY OL10 *.........................41 G2
HOR/BR BL6........................33 C2
HOR/BR BL6........................33 H1
HTNM SK4.........................111 G3
HYDE SK14........................102 A3
LEIGH WN7........................66 C6
MDTN M24..........................56 F5
MDTN M24..........................57 J4
MOSL OL5...........................76 E3
MPL/ROM SK6...................101 L7
NM/HAY SK22....................124 D6
OLDE OL4...........................60 B6
PWCH M25..........................55 K8
RNFD/HAY WA11.................78 B5
ROCH OL11.........................28 D8
ROY/SHW OL2....................43 G8
ROY/SHW OL2 *..................43 L5
STLY SK15..........................91 K2
SWIN M27...........................70 D3
TOT/BURYW BL8.................24 C5
TYLD M29............................67 K3
UPML OL3...........................61 L4
WALK M28...........................68 C6
WGNE/HIN WN2..................48 D1
WGNE/HIN WN2..................49 G7
WGNE/HIN WN2..................64 D2
WGNE/HIN WN2..................65 H3
WGNS/IIMK WN3.................14 F6
WGNW/BIL/OR WN5.............46 F7
WHIT OL12..........................20 A4
WHIT OL12..........................21 G5
WILM/AE SK9....................130 D3
Chapeltown Rd EDGW/EG BL7..22 E4
RAD M26............................54 D3
Chapeltown St CMANE M1.......7 L6
Chapel Vw DUK SK16............90 F4
Chapel View CI HYDE SK14..102 B5
Chapel Wk OLD OL1..............59 L3
Chapel Wks CHD/CHDH SK8..120 D6
CMANE M1............................6 F7
Chapelway Gdns ROY/SHW OL2..43 G6
Chaple Wy GLSP SK13...........93 J7
Chaplin CI SLFD M6...............71 H8
Chapman Ms GTN M18 *........89 G7
Chapman Rd HYDE SK14......103 H3
Chapman St BOL BL1.............35 L4
GTN M18.............................89 G6
Chappell Rd DROY M43.........89 K2
Chappeltown Rd RAD M26.....54 C3
Chapter St NEWH/MOS M40...73 H8
Charcoal Rd ALT WA14.........116 B1
Charcoal Woods ALT WA14...116 C1
Chard Dr WYTH/NTH M22....118 F3
Chardin Av MPL/ROM SK6...114 F4
Charges St AULW OL7...........90 C3
Charlcot St OP/CLY M11.........90 A3
Charity St LEIGH WN7 *..........65 M7
Charlbury Av PWCH M25.......72 A1
Charlbury Wy ROY/SHW OL2..43 K7
Charlecote Rd POY/DIS SK12..122 B8
Charles Av DTN/ASHW M34...89 K5
MPL/ROM SK6...................113 M6
Charles CI BOL BL1 *...............2 E1
RUSH/FAL M14....................87 K7
Charles Holden St BOL BL1 *....2 A6
Charles La GLSP SK13..........105 J2
MILN OL16..........................29 K7
Charles Ms MILN OL16 *.......29 K7
Charles Morris CI FAIL M35....74 E4
Charles Shaw CI OLDE OL4....60 B3
Charles St AULW OL7...........90 C2
BOL BL1...............................3 G3
BRAM/HZG SK7.................121 M1
BURY BL9............................5 G2
CHAD OL9.............................8 D7
CMANE M1............................7 H7
DROY M43 *.........................89 H3
DTN/ASHW M34...................90 C3
DUK SK16...........................90 E3
EDGW/EG BL7.....................22 A2
FWTH BL4...........................53 H3
GLSP SK13........................104 F3
GOL/RIS/CUL WA3...............79 K3
HEY OL10............................41 H4
IRL M44..............................94 B6
LEIGH WN7........................66 C5
LIT OL15.............................21 L7
ROY/SHW OL2....................43 G8
SLFD M6.............................71 H8
STKP SK1...........................13 L8
SWIN M27...........................70 A3
TYLD M29............................67 J3
WGN WN1...........................15 G1
WGNE/HIN WN2..................49 H5
WHTN BL5...........................55 J5
Charleston CI SALE M33.......108 A2
Charleston Sq URM M41.......95 L1
Charleston St OLDS OL8........59 J8
Charlestown Rd BKLY M9.......73 G2
GLSP SK13........................104 F4
Charlestown Rd East
OFTN SK2.........................121 J1
Charlestown Rd West
EDGY/DAV SK3..................121 H1
Charlestown Wy AUL OL6......90 D1
Charles Whittaker St
WHIT OL12..........................27 J3
Charlesworth Av
BOLS/LL BL3.......................52 E2
DTN/ASHW M34.................101 J4
WGNE/HIN WN2..................49 J8
Charlesworth St
OP/CLY M11........................88 C4
STKP SK1...........................13 J8
Charlock Av WHTN BL5.........50 A6
Charlock CI LEIGH WN7........81 J1
Charlock Sq ALT WA14.........107 L4
Charlotte Dr
WGNS/IIMK WN3.................47 G8
Charlotte La OLDE OL4..........61 H7
Charlotte PI HALE/TIMP WA15..117 H1

Charlotte St BOL BL1.............36 B2
CHD/CHDH SK8..................111 G7
CMANW M2............................7 G5
EDGW/EG BL7.....................16 F8
MDTN M24..........................28 D8
RAMS BL0...........................18 D8
STKP SK1...........................112 E1
Charlton Av ECC M30............85 G3
HYDE SK14.........................91 K8
RAMS BL0...........................71 L1
Charlton CI AIMK WN4...........63 K8
Charlton Dr NTHM/RTH M23..96 F8
SWIN M27...........................70 A2
Charlton Fold WALK M28.......52 F7
Charlton PI CMANE M1............7 K8
Charlton Rd BNG/LEV M19....99 J2
Charminster Dr CHH M8.........72 E4
Charmouth CI NEWLW WA12..78 E8
Charmouth Wk
WYTH/NTH M22.................119 H1
Charnley CI NEWH/MOS M40..88 B1
Charnley St WHTF M45..........55 J4
Charnock Dr BOL BL1..............2 D1
Charnock St SWIN M27..........70 D5
Charnville Rd CHD/CHDH SK8..110 C8
Charnwood Av
DTN/ASHW M34.................100 E1
Charnwood CI AUL OL6.........75 M5
ROY/SHW OL2.....................43 H4
TYLD M29............................67 L4
WALK M28...........................68 F2
Charnwood Crs
BRAM/HZG SK7.................121 M4
Charnwood Rd BKLY M9........57 G7
MPL/ROM SK6...................101 M7
Charter Av RAD M26.............54 F3
Charter CI SALE M33...........108 A1
Charterhouse Rd
WGNS/IIMK WN3.................15 J8
Charter Rd HALE/TIMP WA15..108 C8
Chartist St SLFD M6..............87 J1
MILN OL16..........................28 D8
OLD OL1...............................9 L2
Chartwell CI SLFD M6...........86 C2
Chartwell Dr NTHM/RTH M23..109 G5
Chase Briar Wd
CHD/CHDH SK8 *..............120 D3
Chasefield ALT WA14...........116 C2
Chaseley CI SLFD M6............71 H8
WHIT OL12..........................10 C2
The Chase WALK M28............69 K7
Chasewood BNG/LEV M19 *...99 K3
Chassen Av URM M41 *.........95 K3
Chassen Ct URM M41 *..........95 L3
Chassen Rd BOL BL1.............35 L5
URM M41............................95 L3
Chataway Rd CHH M8...........72 E4
Chatburn Av GOL/RIS/CUL WA3..79 H8
ROCH OL11.........................42 A5
Chatburn Gdns HEY OL10......40 C2
Chatburn Rd BOL BL1............35 J1
CCHDY M21.........................97 M4
Chatburn Sq ROCH OL11......42 A4
Chatcombe Rd
WYTH/NTH M22.................118 C2
Chatfield Rd CCHDY M21.......97 L4
Chatford CI BRO M7..............72 B8
Chatham CI BRAM/HZG SK7...120 D6
Chatham Gdns BOLS/LL BL3 *...2 B8
Chatham PI BOLS/LL BL3 *......2 B8
Chatham Rd GTN M18 *........100 B1
OLDTF/WHR M16..................97 M1
Chatham St CMANE M1............7 J5
EDGY/DAV SK3....................12 E7
HYDE SK14.........................102 A3
LEIGH WN7........................66 C5
WGN WN1............................15 K5
WGNE/HIN WN2..................48 D4
Chatsworth Av
WGNS/IIMK WN3.................15 J8
Chatsworth CI AIMK WN4......63 J8
BURY BL9............................39 K7
DROY M43...........................89 G1
HALE/TIMP WA15..............108 F7
ROY/SHW OL2.....................43 M4
URM M41............................96 B2
Chatsworth Dr LEIGH WN7....67 G5
Chatsworth Gv
OLDTF/WHR M16..................98 A2
Chatsworth Ms
BRAM/HZG SK7.................120 F2
Chatsworth Rd
BRAM/HZG SK7.................122 B3
DROY M43...........................89 H2
ECC M30.............................70 C8
GTN M18.............................88 F7
MPL/ROM SK6...................123 H6
RAD M26............................38 C7
STRET M32.........................96 C1
WALK M28............................69 L7
WILM/AE SK9....................126 C8
Chatsworth St OLDE OL4.......59 M7
WGNW/BIL/OR WN5.............46 F7
WHIT OL12..........................28 B1
Chatteris CI WGNE/HIN WN2..49 H8
Chatterton CI DID/WITH M20..98 F6
Chatterton La MPL/ROM SK6..115 K4
Chatterton Old La RAMS BL0..18 F2
Chatterton Rd RAMS BL0.......18 F2
Chatton CI TOT/BURYW BL8...38 C7
Chatwood Rd NEWH/MOS M40..74 A2
Chaucer Av DROY M43...........89 K3
DTN/ASHW M34.................101 K5
RDSH SK5.........................100 A4
Chaucer Gv LEIGH WN7........65 M4
Chaucer Ms STKP SK1.........112 E1
Chaucer PI WGN WN1...........47 M1
WGNE/HIN WN2..................64 E3
Chaucer Ri DUK SK16...........91 K5
Chaucer Rd MDTN M24.........57 L2
Chaucer St BOL BL1..............36 A3
OLDS OL8.............................9 H6
ROCH OL11.........................27 M4
ROY/SHW OL2....................43 H7
Chaucer Wk BRUN/LGST M13..87 M6
Chauncy Rd NEWH/MOS M40..74 B4
Chaytor Av NEWH/MOS M40...73 L5
Cheadle Av BRO M7..............71 K4
Cheadle Old Rd EDGY/DAV SK3..12 C9
Cheadle PI CHD/CHDH SK8 *..111 C7
Cheadle Point CHD/CHDH SK8..111 H6
Cheadle Sq BOL BL1 *.............2 D5
Cheadle St OP/CLY M11.........89 G4

Cheadle Wd CHD/CHDH SK8..120 A4
Cheam Rd HALE/TIMP WA15..108 C4
Cheapside CMANW M2.............6 F4
HYDE SK14.........................102 B1
Cheap Side MDTN M24..........57 K2
Cheapside OLD OL1.................9 H5
Cheapside Sq BOL BL1 *..........2 C5
Cheddar St GTN M18.............89 G7
Cheddington CI
CHD/CHDH SK8..................120 C5
Chedlee Dr CHD/CHDH SK8..120 A3
Chedlin Dr NTHM/RTH M23..109 G3
Chedworth Crs LHULT M38.....52 D6
Chedworth Dr
NTHM/RTH M23.................109 L6
Chedworth Gv BOLS/LL BL3 *...2 C8
Cheeryble St DROY M43.........89 J4
Cheetham Fold Rd HYDE SK14..102 A4
Cheetham HI ROY/SHW OL2...43 L6
Cheetham Hill Rd ANC M4........7 G1
CHH M8..............................72 C5
DUK SK16...........................91 G6
Cheetham PI MPL/ROM SK6..101 M8
Cheetham Rd SWIN M27........70 D5
The Cheethams HOR/BR BL6..33 H5
Cheetham St FAIL M35...........74 D4
MDTN M24..........................57 J4
MILN OL16..........................10 E3
NEWH/MOS M40..................73 H7
OLD OL1 *...........................59 L5
RAD M26............................38 F2
ROY/SHW OL2....................43 M6
Cheetwood Rd CHH M8.........72 C7
Cheetwood St BRO M7..........72 B8
Chelbourne Dr OLDS OL8......74 E2
Chelburn CI OFTN SK2.........113 C7
WGNE/HIN WN2..................65 H3
Chelford Av BOL BL1..............22 B7
GOL/RIS/CUL WA3...............80 A5
Chelford CI HALE/TIMP WA15..108 B6
MDTN M24..........................63 J2
WGNS/IIMK WN3.................63 J2
Chelford Dr SWIN M27..........70 B2
TYLD M29............................67 M6
Chelford Gv EDGY/DAV SK3..111 M7
Chelford Rd MCFLDN SK10...131 K7
OLDTF/WHR M16..................97 M1
SALE M33..........................109 H2
WILM/AE SK9....................119 M7
WILM/AE SK9....................130 A3
Chellow Dene MOSL OL5.......76 C3
Chell St BRUN/LGST M13......88 C8
Chelmarsh Av AIMK WN4.......78 F1
Chelmer CI WHTN BL5...........50 C3
Chelmer Gv HEY OL10...........40 D1
Chelmorton Gv
WGNS/IIMK WN3.................62 F2
Chelmsford Av
NEWH/MOS M40..................73 J3
Chelmsford Dr
WGNS/IIMK WN3.................47 K8
Chelmsford Ms WGN WN1.....47 M2
Chelmsford Rd EDGY/DAV SK3..12 D7
Chelmsford St OLDS OL8........9 G8
Chelsea Av RAD M26.............38 A8
Chelsea CI ROY/SHW OL2.....43 L5
WHTN BL5...........................50 B5
Chelsea Ct WHTN BL5 *.........50 A7
Chelsea Rd BOLS/LL BL3.......51 M1
NEWH/MOS M40..................73 M7
URM M41............................94 F3
Chelsea St BURY BL9.............39 J7
ROCH OL11.........................10 A9
Chelsfield Gv CCHDY M21......98 A4
Chelston Av NEWH/MOS M40..74 C2
Chelston Dr CHD/CHDH SK8..119 L6
Cheltenham Av
WGNS/IIMK WN3.................15 J8
Cheltenham Crs BRO M7.......72 B5
Cheltenham Dr NEWLW WA12..78 F7
SALE M33............................96 F8
WGNW/BIL/OR WN5.............62 A2
Cheltenham Gn MDTN M24....57 K6
Cheltenham Rd CCHDY M21...97 L2
EDGY/DAV SK3..................111 K5
MDTN M24..........................57 K6
Cheltenham St OLD OL1.........59 L3
ROCH OL11.........................28 A8
SLFD M6.............................71 K8
WGNE/HIN WN2..................48 D2
Chelwood CI BOL BL1............22 A5
Chelwood Dr DROY M43........89 J2
Chelwood Ms HOR/BR BL6......34 E5
Chelwood Pk AIMK WN4........78 E3
Chendre CI NM/HAY SK22....125 L1
Chendre Rd BKLY M9............73 L1
Cheney CI OP/CLY M11 *.......89 G5
Chepstow Av SALE M33........107 M1
Chepstow CI ROCH OL11.......27 J4
Chepstow Dr BRAM/HZG SK7..122 C2
OLD OL1.............................59 L3
Chepstow Gv LEIGH WN7......67 H5
Chepstow Rd CCHDY M21.....97 K3
SWIN M27...........................70 D2
Chepstow St CMANE M1..........6 F7
Chepstow St South
CMANE M1............................6 F7
Chequers Rd CCHDY M21......97 L4
Chequers St WGN WN1.........14 E4
Cherington CI NTHM/RTH M23..109 J1
WILM/AE SK9....................127 K1
Cherington Rd CHD/CHDH SK8..110 F8
Cheriton Av SALE M33............96 F7
Cheriton CI HYDE SK14........103 G2
Cheriton Dr BOLE BL2............37 H6
Cheriton Ri OFTN SK2..........113 K6
Cheriton Rd URM M41...........95 G2
Cherrington Dr ROCH OL11....42 A4
Cherry Av AUL OL6................75 L6
BURY BL9.............................5 M1
OLDS OL8...........................59 M1
Cherrybrook Dr
WGNS/IIMK WN3.................63 G3
Cherry CI BURY BL9..............39 K5
NEWLW WA12.....................78 C8
OFTN SK2..........................113 H5
Cherrycroft MPL/ROM SK6...114 B3
Cherry Dr SWIN M27.............69 M2
Cherry Gv LEIGH WN7...........66 C4
ROCH OL11.........................42 F6
ROY/SHW OL2....................43 M5
STLY SK15...........................91 K4
WGNNW/ST WN6.................47 J1
Cherry Hall Dr ROY/SHW OL2..43 H5
Cherry Hinton OLD OL1 *........8 E2
Cherry Holt Av HTNM SK4......99 J8
Cherry La MILN OL16.............44 C1
SALE M33..........................107 M2
Cherry Orchard CI
BRAM/HZG SK7.................120 C7
Cherry St PWCH M25 *...........55 M7

Cherryton Wk BRUN/LGST M13 .....87 M6
Cherry Tree Av FWTH BL4 .....52 A4
　POY/DIS SK12 .....129 K1
Cherry Tree Cl
　HALE/TIMP WA15 .....108 E7
　MPL/ROM SK6 .....114 B2
　WILM/AE SK9 .....127 J4
Cherry Tree Ct OFTN SK2 .....112 F8
Cherry Tree Dr BRAM/HZG SK7 .....122 C4
Cherry Tree Gv LEIGH WN7 .....66 A6
　ATH M46 .....50 E8
Cherry Tree La ALT WA14 .....116 C7
　MPL/ROM SK6 .....114 B2
　OFTN SK2 .....112 F7
　TOT/BURYW BL8 .....4 A6
Cherry Tree Rd
　CHD/CHDH SK8 .....120 B3
　GOL/RIS/CUL WA3 .....80 C4
　NTHM/RTH M23 .....109 J4
Cherry Tree Wk STRET M32 .....96 E3
Cherry Tree Wy BOLE BL2 .....22 F7
　HOR/BR BL6 .....34 B3
Cherry Wk CHD/CHDH SK8 .....120 E4
Cherrywood CHAD OL9 .....58 A5
Cherrywood Av WHTN BL5 .....51 K5
Cherrywood Cl WALK M28 .....68 E4
Chertsey Cl GTN M18 .....89 H7
　ROY/SHW OL2 .....43 L4
Chervil Cl RUSH/FAL M14 .....98 E3
Chervil Wk WGNS/IIMK WN3 .....46 F8
Chervill Wk RUSH/FAL M14 .....98 F4
Cherwell Av HEY OL10 .....40 D1
Cherwell Cl CHD/CHDH SK8 .....120 C5
　OLDS OL8 .....74 F3
　WGNE/HIN WN2 .....32 F6
　WHTF M45 .....55 K4
Cherwell Rd WHTN BL5 .....50 C2
Chesham Av BOL BL1 .....36 B2
　ROCH OL11 .....42 A5
　URM M41 .....95 H1
　WYTH/NTH M22 .....109 M8
Chesham Cl GLSP SK13 .....93 L7
　WILM/AE SK9 .....126 D8
Chesham Crs BURY BL9 .....5 J2
Chesham Fold Rd BURY BL9 .....5 L2
Chesham Pl ALT WA14 .....116 E2
Chesham Rd BURY BL9 .....25 L7
　ECC M30 * 84 F4
　OLDE OL4 .....59 M6
　WILM/AE SK9 .....126 D8
Cheshire Cl STRET M32 .....96 E3
Cheshire Ct RAMS BL0 .....19 G6
Cheshire Ring Canal Wk
　ALT WA14 .....107 H7
　MCFLDN SK10 .....129 L6
　MPL/ROM SK6 .....101 L6
　MPL/ROM SK6 .....123 G6
　POY/DIS SK12 .....122 F8
Cheshire Rd PART M31 .....106 A2
　STLY SK15 .....77 G7
Cheshire Sq STLY SK15 .....77 H7
The Cheshires MOSL OL5 .....77 G3
Cheshire St MOSL OL5 .....77 G4
Chesney Av CHAD OL9 .....74 B2
Chesshyre Av ANC M4 * 88 A3
Chessington Ri SWIN M27 .....70 D1
Chester Av BOLS/LL BL3 .....37 L8
　DUK SK16 .....91 H5
　GOL/RIS/CUL WA3 .....80 A4
　HALE/TIMP WA15 .....117 H2
　ROCH OL11 .....27 K6
　SALE M33 .....107 L3
　STLY SK15 .....92 A1
　URM M41 .....90 B1
　WHTF M45 .....55 K5
Chester Cl BOLS/LL BL3 .....37 L8
　IRL M44 .....94 A7
　WILM/AE SK9 .....127 J3
Chester Dr WHtN WN4 .....79 G2
　RAMS BL0 .....18 D8
Chesterfield Gv AUL OL6 .....91 G1
Chesterfield Cl OLDE OL4 .....59 L6
Chestergate EDGY/DAV SK3 .....12 F5
Chester Rd BRAM/HZG SK7 .....121 M4
　BRAM/HZG SK7 .....128 B2
　HULME M15 .....6 A9
　OLDTF/WHR M16 .....86 F7
　POY/DIS SK12 .....121 K8
　POY/DIS SK12 .....121 M5
　STRET M32 .....87 G8
　TYLD M29 .....68 A4
Chester St ATH M46 .....67 H2
　BURY BL9 .....25 K8
　CHAD OL9 .....8 C9
　DTN/ASHW M34 .....101 J2
　EDGY/DAV SK3 .....12 E6
　HULME M15 .....6 F9
　LEIGH WN7 .....66 C6
　PWCH M25 .....55 K7
　SWIN M27 .....70 B5
Chesterton Cl WGNS/IIMK WN3 .....14 C9
Chesterton Dr BOLS/LL BL3 .....35 L8
Chesterton Gv DROY M43 .....89 K2
Chesterton Rd
　NTHM/RTH M23 .....109 G4
Chester Wk BOL BL1 * 36 B2
Chester Wks MPL/ROM SK6 .....113 K3
Chestnut Av ATH M46 * 50 F8
　BURY BL9 .....5 A4
　CCHDY M21 .....97 L4
　CHD/CHDH SK8 .....120 E5
　DROY M43 .....89 H1
　IRL M44 .....94 B7
　LFIGH WN7 .....81 H1
　TOT/BURYW BL8 .....24 D7
　WALK M28 .....69 G2
　WHTF M45 .....55 J5
Chestnut Cl BOLS/LL BL3 .....35 L8
　NM/HAY SK22 .....125 G3
　OLDE OL4 .....60 A4
　STLY SK15 .....91 K4
　WILM/AE SK9 .....127 J4
Chestnut Crs OLDS OL8 .....75 K2
Chestnut Dr BURY BL9 .....25 J5
　LEIGH WN7 .....81 J1
　POY/DIS SK12 .....129 K1
　SALE M33 .....108 A3
　WHTN BL5 .....50 C5
Chestnut Dr South LEIGH WN7 .....81 J3
Chestnut Fold RAD M26 .....38 D8
Chestnut Gdns
　DTN/ASHW M34 .....101 H2
　HEY OL10 .....40 F3
Chestnut Gv AIMK WN4 .....64 A8
　FAIL M35 .....74 C6
　GOL/RIS/CUL WA3 .....80 C4
　RAD M26 .....54 C4
　WGNE/HIN WN2 .....49 K8
Chestnut La LEIGH WN7 .....81 J2
Chestnut Rd ECC M30 .....69 K8
Chestnut St CHAD OL9 .....74 D1

Chestnut Wy LIT OL15 .....21 K7
Chesworth Cl STKP SK1 .....13 J6
Chesworth Fold STKP SK1 .....13 J7
Chetham Cl ORD M5 * 86 E5
Chetvode Av RAMS/IIMK WN4 .....78 E3
Chetwyn Av EDGW/EG BL7 .....22 D5
　ROY/SHW OL2 .....42 F8
Chetwynd Av URM M41 .....95 M3
Chetwynd Cl SALE M33 .....96 B6
Chevassut St HULME M15 .....87 H6
Chevington Dr BKLY M9 .....73 C6
　HTNM SK4 .....111 G1
Cheviot Av CHD/CHDH SK8 .....120 B2
　OLDS OL8 .....75 H1
　ROY/SHW OL2 .....58 F1
Cheviot Cl BOL BL1 .....22 A7
　CHAD OL9 .....58 D7
　HTNM SK4 .....12 F1
　MDTN M24 .....58 A4
　MILN OL16 .....29 K6
　RAMS BL0 .....18 F8
　SLFD M6 .....86 B1
　TOT/BURYW BL8 .....38 D1
　WGNS/IIMK WN3 .....62 F2
Cheviot Rd BRAM/HZG SK7 .....121 K3
Cheviots Rd ROY/SHW OL2 .....43 K4
Cheviot St CSLFD M3 .....87 J1
Chevithorne Cl ALT WA14 .....107 L7
Chevril Cl ROCH OL11 .....41 L1
　SLFD M6 .....86 B2
Chevron Cl ALT WA14 .....108 A5
　SLFD M6 .....86 B2
Chew Brook Dr UPML OL3 .....61 L7
Chew Moor La WHTN BL5 .....50 D2
Chew V DUK SK16 .....91 J5
　UPML OL3 .....61 L8
Chew Valley Rd UPML OL3 .....61 J7
Chicago Av MANAIR M90 .....119 D5
Chichester Av ATH M46 .....66 D2
Chichester Cl LIT OL15 .....29 J1
　SALE M33 .....108 A1
Chichester Crs CHAD OL9 .....58 D3
Chichester Rd HULME M15 .....87 H1
　MPL/ROM SK6 .....113 M2
Chichester Rd South
　HULME M15 * 87 H1
Chichester St MILN OL16 .....11 J5
Chidlow Av DID/WITH M20 .....98 D5
Chidwall Rd WYTH/NTH M22 .....118 D2
Chief St OLDE OL4 .....9 M7
Chiffon Wy CSLFD M3 .....6 A1
Chigwell Cl WYTH/NTH M22 .....110 B7
Chilcote Av SALE M33 .....96 B8
Childwall Cl BOLS/LL BL3 .....52 B2
Chilgrove Av HOR/BR BL6 .....33 G3
Chilham Rd ECC M30 .....70 C8
　WALK M28 .....69 H2
Chilham St BOLS/LL BL3 .....51 L2
　SWIN M27 .....70 B6
　WGNW/BIL/OR WN5 .....46 D6
Chillingham Dr LEIGH WN7 .....66 E8
Chilmark Dr NTHM/RTH M23 .....109 K6
Chiltern Av ATH M46 .....51 J7
　URM M41 .....95 J1
Chiltern Cl AIMK WN4 .....78 F2
　BRAM/HZG SK7 .....121 K3
　RAMS BL0 .....18 F8
　ROY/SHW OL2 .....43 J4
　WALK M28 .....69 H4
Chiltern Dr BOLE BL2 .....3 J4
　HALE/TIMP WA15 .....117 H2
　OFTN SK2 .....112 D8
　ROY/SHW OL2 .....42 F8
　SWIN M27 .....70 C6
　TOT/BURYW BL8 .....24 E8
　WGNS/IIMK WN3 .....62 F1
Chiltern Gdns SALE M33 .....108 A4
Chiltern Rd GOL/RIS/CUL WA3 .....81 H8
　RAMS BL0 .....18 F8
Chiltern Wy TYLD M29 .....67 L4
Chilton Av CHAD OL9 .....58 D6
Chilton Cl LEIGH WN7 .....66 C5
Chilton Dr MDTN M24 .....57 M5
Chilworth St RUSH/FAL M14 .....98 E2
Chime Bank CHH M8 .....72 F5
Chimes Ct OLDE OL4 .....60 E7
Chimes Rd AIMK WN4 .....63 C9
China La BOL BL1 .....2 E2
　CMANE M1 .....7 J5
Chingford Wk
　BRUN/LGST M13 * 88 C3
Chinley Av NEWH/MOS M40 .....73 K4
　STRET M32 .....85 K8
Chinley Cl BRAM/HZG SK7 .....121 G1
　HTNM SK4 .....12 A1
　SALE M33 .....109 G1
Chinley St SLFD M6 .....71 L7
Chinnor Cl LEIGH WN7 .....66 C5
Chinwell Vw BNG/LEV M19 * 99 K3
Chip Hill Rd BOLS/LL BL3 .....35 K8
Chippendale Pl AUL OL6 .....76 B7
Chippenham Av OFTN SK2 .....112 F5
Chippenham Ct ANC M4 .....88 A2
Chippenham Rd ANC M4 .....7 M3
Chipping Fold MILN OL16 .....29 J7
Chipping Rd BOL BL1 .....35 J2
Chipstead Av WGTN/LGST M12 .....88 D7
Chirmside St TOT/BURYW BL8 .....38 E3
Chirton Cl RNFD/HAY WA11 .....78 A5
Chisacre Dr WGNNW/ST WN6 .....30 A5
Chiseldon Av WYTH/NTH M22 .....119 G2
Chiselhurst St CHH M8 .....72 F5
Chisholm Cl WGNNW/ST WN6 .....30 E2
Chisholme St TOT/BURYW BL8 .....24 C2
Chisholm St OP/CLY M11 .....89 G5
Chisledon Av BRO M7 * 72 C6
Chisledon Cl RNFD/HAY WA11 .....78 A5
Chislehurst Av URM M41 .....95 M1
Chislehurst Cl TOT/BURYW BL8 .....38 E3
Chiswell St WGNW/BIL/OR WN5 .....46 F7
Chiswick Dr RAD M26 .....37 L7
Chiswick Rd DID/WITH M20 .....110 F3
Chisworth Cl BRAM/HZG SK7 .....121 G1
　LEIGH WN7 .....66 B5
Chisworth St BOLE BL2 .....36 E1
Choir St BRO M7 .....72 B6
Chokeberry Cl ALT WA14 .....107 L4
Cholmondeley Av ALT WA14 * 108 A4
Cholmondeley Rd SLFD M6 .....70 E8
Chomlea Mnr SLFD M6 * 70 F7
Choral Gv BRO M7 .....72 A7
Chorley Cl TOT/BURYW BL8 .....38 C3
Chorley Hall Cl WILM/AE SK9 .....130 C3
Chorley Hall La WILM/AE SK9 .....130 B5
Chorley New Rd BOL BL1 .....35 H5
　HOR/BR BL6 .....33 L1
Chorley Old Rd BOL BL1 * 2 A2
　HOR/BR BL6 .....34 B1
Chorley Rd SALE M33 .....109 H2
　SWIN M27 .....70 A3
　WGNNW/ST WN6 .....31 L6
　WHTN BL5 .....33 M8

Chorley St BOL BL1 .....2 C3
　STRET M32 .....86 C7
　WGNS/IIMK WN3 .....15 K8
Chorley Wood Av
　BNG/LEV M19 * 99 J6
Chorlton Dr CHD/CHDH SK8 .....111 H6
Chorlton Fold ECC M30 .....70 A7
Chorlton Gv STKP SK1 .....112 E5
Chorlton Pl CCHDY M21 .....97 L3
Chorlton Rd HULME M15 .....6 B9
Chorlton St CMANE M1 .....7 H5
　OLDTF/WHR M16 .....86 F7
Chorlton Ter
　BRUN/LGST M13 * 87 L6
Chowbent Cl ATH M46 .....67 H1
Chretien Rd WYTH/NTH M22 .....110 B2
Christchurch Av ORD M5 .....86 E2
Christ Church St BOLE BL2 * 37 J2
Christ Church La BOLE BL2 * 37 J1
Christchurch Rd SALE M33 .....95 M1
Christie Rd STRET M32 .....97 H2
Christie St STKP SK1 .....13 M8
Christine St ROY/SHW OL2 .....43 L5
Christleton
　WGNNW/ST WN6 .....30 E6
Christleton Av HTNM SK4 .....100 A7
Christopher Acre
　ROCH OL11 .....27 H3
Christopher St
　NEWH/MOS M40 .....74 A8
　ORD M5 .....86 D3
　WGNS/IIMK WN3 .....15 M8
Chronnell Dr BOLE BL2 .....37 H4
Chudleigh Cl ALT WA14 .....107 L6
　BRAM/HZG SK7 .....121 J1
Chudleigh Rd CHH M8 .....72 D2
Chulsey Gate La HOR/BR BL6 .....34 D8
Chulsey St BOLS/LL BL3 .....51 L1
Chunal La GLSP SK13 .....104 F6
Church Av BOLS/LL BL3 .....35 M8
　DTN/ASHW M34 .....101 K4
　HYDE SK14 .....102 A3
　MDTN M24 .....42 A6
　NEWH/MOS M40 .....73 M7
　SLFD M6 .....86 A2
　WGNE/HIN WN2 .....65 J4
Church Bank BOL BL1 .....2 F4
Churchbank STLY SK15 .....92 A2
Church Brow ALT WA14 .....116 C2
　HYDE SK14 .....102 A3
　HYDE SK14 .....103 K1
Church Cl GLSP SK13 .....105 L7
　RAD M26 .....53 L4
　RAMS BL0 .....18 E7
　WILM/AE SK9 .....127 H1
Church Ct BURY BL9 * 5 H3
　DUK SK16 .....90 E3
Church Cft BURY BL9 .....39 L8
Churchdale Rd BKLY M9 .....56 E8
Church Dr PWCH M25 .....55 J8
　RNFD/HAY WA11 .....78 A5
Churchfield CCHDY M21 .....97 J2
Churchfield Cl RAD M26 .....54 C3
Churchfield Rd SLFD M6 .....71 G7
Churchfields ALT WA14 .....116 D3
　DTN/ASHW M34 .....90 B5
　SALE M33 .....96 A6
Churchfield Wk OP/CLY M11 * 88 D4
Church Fold GLSP SK13 .....103 M6
Churchgate BOL BL1 .....2 F4
　STKP SK1 .....13 J4
　WGNE/HIN WN2 .....96 B3
Churchgate Buildings
　CMANE M1 * 7 L6
Church Gates WGN WN1 .....14 F4
Church Gn RAD M26 .....39 G8
　SLFD M6 .....86 C1
Church Green Gdns
　GOL/RIS/CUL WA3 .....79 K3
Church Gv BRAM/HZG SK7 .....122 A4
　WGN WN1 * 15 K4
Churchill Av BOLE BL2 .....38 A3
　GOL/RIS/CUL WA3 .....81 L8
Churchill Cl HEY OL10 .....41 H4
Churchill Crs MPL/ROM SK6 .....114 A5
　RDSH SK5 .....100 B3
Churchill Dr BOLS/LL BL3 .....53 M1
　FWTH BL4 .....52 C2
Churchill Rd ALT WA14 .....108 A5
Churchill St BOLE BL2 * 3 M4
　HTNM SK4 .....112 A1
　OLDE OL4 .....9 L7
　WHIT OL12 .....27 M3
Churchill St East OLDE OL4 .....9 M7
Churchill Wy SLFD M6 .....86 D2
　TRPK M17 .....85 M5

URM M41 .....95 K4
　URM M41 .....96 A3
　WALK M28 .....69 G1
　WGNE/HIN WN2 .....64 C1
　WILM/AE SK9 .....126 C8
　WILM/AE SK9 .....127 H1
　WYTH/NTH M22 .....110 B3
Church Rd East SALE M33 .....97 G8
Church Rd West SALE M33 .....96 F8
Churchside FWTH BL4 .....52 E5
Churchside Cl BKLY M9 .....73 G5
Church Stile ALT WA14 * 108 A7
Church St WT SALE M33 * 108 A7
　ANC M4 .....7 H3
　AUL OL6 .....90 F2
　BOLE BL2 .....23 G7
　BOLE BL2 .....38 A3
　BOLS/LL BL3 .....53 J1
　BURY BL9 .....5 H3
　CHD/CHDH SK8 .....111 G6
　DROY M43 .....89 L3
　DUK SK16 .....90 E4
　ECC M30 .....85 H2
　FAIL M35 .....74 C4
　FWTH BL4 .....53 H5
　GLSP SK13 .....93 L5
　GLSP SK13 .....93 K8
　GLSP SK13 .....105 G2
　GOL/RIS/CUL WA3 .....79 L3
　HEY OL10 .....41 G2
　HOR/BR BL6 .....32 F2
　HOR/BR BL6 .....33 M1
　HTNM SK4 .....11 J8
　HYDE SK14 .....102 A3
　LEIGH WN7 .....66 C7
　LIT OL15 .....21 M7
　MDTN M24 * 57 K2
　MILN OL16 .....11 H7
　MILN OL16 .....29 K6
　MPL/ROM SK6 .....101 K7
　MPL/ROM SK6 .....114 C7
　NEWLW WA12 .....79 H8
　NM/HAY SK22 .....125 M2
　OLDE OL4 .....60 B7
　RAD M26 .....54 C2
　RAMS BL0 .....18 F6
　ROY/SHW OL2 .....43 G8
　STLY SK15 .....91 K2
　STRET M32 .....96 F3
　SWIN M27 .....70 B4
　SWIN M27 .....70 B4
　TOT/BURYW BL8 .....24 C7
　UPML OL3 .....61 J5
　WGN WN1 .....15 G3
　WGNE/HIN WN2 .....32 E6
　WGNE/HIN WN2 .....49 G7
　WGNNW/ST WN6 .....31 H3
　WGNNW/ST WN6 .....15 M7
　WGNW/BIL/OR WN5 .....46 E6
　WHIT OL12 .....14 A1
　WHIT OL12 .....20 A4
　WHTN BL5 .....50 B5
　WILM/AE SK9 .....126 F5
Church St East OLDE OL4 .....60 B4
　RAD M26 .....38 F8
Church St South GLSP SK13 .....105 H2
Church St West RAD M26 .....54 C3
Church Ter MILN OL16 .....29 K7
　OLD OL1 .....9 L1
　SALE M33 * 96 D6
　WILM/AE SK9 .....119 M8
Churchtown Av BOLE BL2 .....37 J5
Church Vw HYDE SK14 .....103 K1
　IRL M44 .....94 D2
　WHIT OL12 .....27 H2
Church Wk ALT WA14 .....108 A7
　FWTH BL4 .....52 F4
　STLY SK15 .....91 K1
　SWIN M27 .....54 C8
　TOT/BURYW BL8 * 24 C7
Churchward Sq HOR/BR BL6 .....33 M2
Churchwood Rd
　DID/WITH M20 .....110 E1
Churnet St NEWH/MOS M40 .....73 G7
Churnett Cl WHTN BL5 .....50 C2
Churning Ter IRL M44 .....94 E1
Churston Av BKLY M9 .....57 H8
Churton Av SALE M33 .....108 B1
Churton Gv WGNNW/ST WN6 .....30 C2
Churwell Av HTNM SK4 .....99 J8
Cicero St BKLY M9 .....73 H4
　OLD OL1 .....9 L1
Cinamon St WHIT OL12 .....10 A2
Cinder HI BURY BL9 * 25 L6
Cinder Hill La OLD OL1 .....58 D1
Cinder St ANC M4 * 7 L2
Cinnabar Dr MDTN M24 .....57 J2
Cinnamon Av WGNE/HIN WN2 .....49 K8
Cinnamon Cl WGNE/HIN WN2 .....49 K8
Cipher St ANC M4 .....7 L1
Circle South TRPK M17 .....86 B6
The Circuit CHD/CHDH SK8 .....120 C6
　DID/WITH M20 .....98 E7
　EDGY/DAV SK3 .....111 M6
　WILM/AE SK9 .....126 B7
Circular Rd DID/WITH M20 .....98 E7
　DTN/ASHW M34 .....101 H3
　PWCH M25 .....71 L3
Circus St CMANE M1 * 7 J5
Cirencester Cl LHULT M38 .....52 D6
Ciss La URM M41 .....96 B2
Citrus Wy SLFD M6 .....86 D2
City Av DTN/ASHW M34 * 101 H2
City Gdns DTN/ASHW M34 * 101 H2
City Rd HULME M15 .....87 G6
　WALK M28 .....68 D4
　WGNW/BIL/OR WN5 .....46 E5
City Rd East HULME M15 .....6 E9
City Wk SWIN M27 .....70 E4
Clacton Wk BRUN/LGST M13 * 87 M6
Clague St OP/CLY M11 .....88 D2
Claife Av NEWH/MOS M40 .....73 L2
Clammerclough Rd FWTH BL4 .....53 J4
Clandon Av ECC M30 .....84 D2
Clanwood Cl WGNS/IIMK WN3 .....63 H2
Clapgate MPL/ROM SK6 .....113 K3
Clap Gate La WGNS/IIMK WN3 .....61 M3
Clapgate Rd ROCH OL11 .....27 H3
Clara Gorton Ct MILN OL16 .....11 K6
Clara St CHAD OL9 .....58 F8
　OLDE OL4 .....10 E9
　WHIT OL12 .....10 E9
Clare Av WILM/AE SK9 .....127 G1
Clarebank BOL BL1 .....35 J5
Clare Cl TOT/BURYW BL8 .....25 G7

Claremont Av ALT WA14 .....108 A4
　DID/WITH M20 .....98 D7
　HTNM SK4 .....99 M7
　MPL/ROM SK6 .....113 M6
　WGNE/HIN WN2 .....49 J7
Claremont Ct BOL BL1 * 36 B3
Claremont Dr ALT WA14 .....108 A4
　LHULT M38 .....52 F7
Claremont Gdns AUL OL6 .....76 B8
Claremont Gv DID/WITH M20 .....110 D1
　HALE/TIMP WA15 .....117 C1
Claremont Range GTN M18 * 89 J7
Claremont Rd CHD/CHDH SK8 .....120 C4
　GOL/RIS/CUL WA3 .....81 G8
　MILN OL16 .....29 J7
　OFTN SK2 .....112 E8
　OLDTF/WHR M16 .....98 C1
　ROCH OL11 .....27 M5
　SALE M33 .....96 F3
　SLFD M6 .....70 F8
　WGNW/BIL/OR WN5 .....62 B7
Claremont St AUL OL6 .....76 A8
　CHAD OL9 .....8 C1
　FAIL M35 .....74 C4
　OLDS OL8 .....75 J2
　SLFD M6 .....70 F6
Clarence Ar AUL OL6 * 90 E2
Clarence Av OLDS OL8 .....59 M7
　TRPK M17 .....85 J6
　WHTF M45 .....55 K5
Clarence Ct BOL BL1 * 2 C5
Clarence Rd AUL OL6 .....75 M8
　BRUN/LGST M13 .....99 H1
　HALE/TIMP WA15 .....117 H1
　HTNM SK4 .....99 J7
　SWIN M27 .....69 M5
Clarence St AIMK WN4 .....63 J8
　ATH M46 .....67 H3
　BOL BL1 .....2 E3
　BRO M7 .....72 A8
　CMANW M2 * 6 F5
　FWTH BL4 .....53 H3
　GOL/RIS/CUL WA3 .....79 K3
　HYDE SK14 .....91 H8
　LEIGH WN7 .....66 E8
　NEWLW WA12 .....78 C8
　ROY/SHW OL2 .....59 L1
　STLY SK15 .....91 H3
　WGNE/HIN WN2 .....48 D5
　WHIT OL12 .....28 A2
Clarence Yd WGN WN1 * 14 F4
Clarendon Av
　HALE/TIMP WA15 .....108 B7
　HTNM SK4 .....111 H1
Clarendon Cottages
　WILM/AE SK9 * 126 E1
Clarendon Crs ECC M30 .....85 J1
　SALE M33 .....97 G7
Clarendon Gv BOLE BL2 .....3 J7
Clarendon Pl HYDE SK14 .....102 B2
Clarendon Rd BOLE BL2 .....3 M5
　BRAM/HZG SK7 .....122 B1
　DTN/ASHW M34 .....89 L5
　DTN/ASHW M34 .....101 J2
　ECC M30 .....85 J1
　HYDE SK14 .....102 A1
　IRL M44 .....94 B5
　MILN OL16 .....97 M2
　SALE M33 .....97 G8
　SWIN M27 .....70 C4
　URM M41 .....95 H1
Clarendon Rd West CCHDY M21 .....97 L2
Clarendon St BOLS/LL BL3 .....2 C5
　BURY BL9 .....5 H1
　DUK SK16 .....90 E4
　HULME M15 .....87 H6
　HYDE SK14 .....102 A1
　MILN OL16 .....28 E8
　MOSL OL5 .....77 G4
　RDSH SK5 .....112 C1
　WHTF M45 .....55 H4
Clare Rd BNG/LEV M19 .....99 K4
　RDSH SK5 .....100 C8
Clare St CMANE M1 .....7 K8
　DTN/ASHW M34 .....90 B8
　ORD M5 * 86 F7
Claribel St OP/CLY M11 .....88 B4
Claridge Rd CCHDY M21 .....97 K3
Clarington Gv WGN WN1 .....15 K5
Clarion St ANC M4 .....7 L1
Clark Av GTN M18 .....89 H7
Clarke Av GOL/RIS/CUL WA3 .....81 G8
　ORD M5 .....86 C5
Clarke Brow MDTN M24 .....57 K3
Clarke Crs HALE/TIMP WA15 .....117 H1
　LHULT M38 .....52 A6
Clarkes Cft BURY BL9 .....39 M1
Clarke's La WHIT OL12 .....10 B2
Clarke St AULW OL7 * 90 A1
　BOL BL1 .....35 M4
　HEY OL10 .....41 G2
　LEIGH WN7 .....66 B8
　MILN OL16 .....28 E2
Clarksfield Rd OLDE OL4 .....59 M6
Clarksfield St OLDE OL4 .....59 M6
Clark's HI PWCH M25 .....55 K8
Clarkson Cl DTN/ASHW M34 .....101 G2
Clark Wy HYDE SK14 .....102 A1
Clarkwell Cl OLD OL1 .....9 G3
Claude Av SWIN M27 .....70 A4
Claude Rd CCHDY M21 .....97 K5
Claude St CHH M8 .....72 D3
　ECC M30 .....69 J4
　SWIN M27 .....70 A4
　WGNW/BIL/OR WN5 .....47 G6
Claudia Sq STLY SK15 .....77 H7
Claughton Av BOLE BL2 .....37 J5
　WALK M28 .....68 F4
Claughton Rd
　TOT/BURYW BL8 .....24 C7
Claverton Rd
　NTHM/RTH M23 .....109 H3
Claxton Av BKLY M9 .....73 G1
Clay Bank DROY M43 .....89 H3
Claybank Dr
　TOT/BURYW BL8 .....24 C7
Clay Bank St HEY OL10 .....40 F1
Claybar Dr ECC M30 .....85 H1
Claybridge Cl
　WGNW/BIL/OR WN5 .....46 E3
Claybrook Cl ATH M46 .....66 D2
Claybrook Wk OP/CLY M11 * 88 D3
Clayburn Rd HULME M15 .....87 H6
Claycourt Av ECC M30 .....69 J2
Clayton Dr RAD M26 .....37 L7
　WGNS/IIMK WN3 .....48 C8
Clayfield Dr ROCH OL11 .....27 J4
Claygate Dr BKLY M9 .....57 G7
Clayhill Gv
　GOL/RIS/CUL WA3 .....80 E4
Claylands Cl HYDE SK14 .....93 G8

Clay La HALE/TIMP WA15 108 F8
NTHM/RTH M23 109 J8
ROCH OL11 27 H4
WILM/AE SK9 119 L7
WILM/AE SK9 126 A8
Claymere Av ROCH OL11 27 H4
Claymore St BOLS/LL BL3 52 C1
GTN M18 89 H6
Claypool Rd HOR/BR BL6 34 B3
Clay St EDGW/EG BL7 22 D5
LIT OL15 21 K7
OLDS OL8 59 H8
Claythorpe Wk PWCH M25 72 B2
Clayton Av BOLE BL2 3 L9
DID/WITH M20 110 E1
GOL/RIS/CUL WA3 80 B4
Claytonbrook Rd
OP/CLY M11 88 F3
Clayton Cl HULME M15 87 H7
TOT/BURYW BL8 38 C3
Clayton Hall Rd OP/CLY M11 88 F2
Clayton House LEIGH WN7 65 M7
Clayton La OP/CLY M11 88 E4
Clayton La South
WGTN/LGST M12 88 D5
Claytons Cl OLDE OL4 60 C5
Clayton St BOLE BL2 3 K9
CHAD OL9 74 D1
DTN/ASHW M34 101 J2
DUK SK16 91 G4
FAIL M35 * 74 B5
OP/CLY M11 88 E1
WGNS/IIMK WN3 14 D4
WHIT OL12 28 E2
Cleabarrow Dr
WALK M28 68 D7
Cleadon Av GTN M18 88 F8
Cleadon Dr South
TOT/BURYW BL8 24 F7
Clearwater Dr
DID/WITH M20 98 C7
Cleavley St ECC M30 84 E2
Clee Av BRUN/LGST M13 99 J2
Cleethorpes Av BKLY M9 72 E1
Cleeve Rd NTHM/RTH M23 109 K2
OLDE OL4 59 M6
Cleeve Wy CHD/CHDH SK8 120 D6
Clegg Hall Rd MILN OL16 29 G2
Clegg Pl AUL OL6 76 A8
Clegg's Buildings BOL BL1 * 2 C3
Clegg's La LHULT M38 52 D7
Clegg St BOLE BL2 3 M5
DROY M43 * 89 J3
LIT OL15 21 K5
MILN OL16 29 K7
MPL/ROM SK6 113 J1
OLD OL1 9 K6
OLDE OL4 60 D6
TYLD M29 67 K6
WHIT OL12 20 A2
WHTF M45 55 J5
Cleggswood Av LIT OL15 29 K1
Clelland St FWTH BL4 53 H5
Clement Av ATH M46 66 D2
Clement Ct MILN OL16 11 K6
Clementina St WHIT OL12 10 E1
Clementine Cl SLFD M6 86 E2
Clement Rd MPL/ROM SK6 114 E5
Clement Royds St WHIT OL12 10 C3
Clement Stott Cl BKLY M9 57 J8
Clement St HTNM SK4 12 F1
Cleminson St CSLFD M3 6 B3
Clemshaw Cl HEY OL10 40 F3
Clerewood Av CHD/CHDH SK8 119 K5
Clerke St BURY BL9 4 F4
Clevedon Av URM M41 96 D2
Clevedon Dr WGNS/IIMK WN3 46 F8
Clevedon Rd CHAD OL9 58 D3
Clevedon St BKLY M9 73 H5
Cleveland Av BNG/LEV M19 99 L2
HYDE SK14 * 101 M2
SLFD M6 85 M1
WGNS/IIMK WN3 62 F2
Cleveland Cl RAMS BL0 24 F1
Cleveland Dr AIMK WN4 63 M8
GOL/RIS/CUL WA3 80 A4
MILN OL16 29 K6
Cleveland Gdns BOLS/LL BL3 35 L8
Cleveland Gv ROY/SHW OL2 58 F2
Cleveland Rd CHH M8 72 E2
HALE/TIMP WA15 117 H1
HTNM SK4 99 K8
Cleveland St BOLS/LL BL3 * 35 L8
Cleveleys Av BOLE BL2 3 M3
BURY BL9 4 D9
CCHDY M21 97 M5
CHD/CHDH SK8 119 K3
MILN OL16 42 E1
Cleveleys Gv BRO M7 72 B5
Cleves Ct HEY OL10 40 F3
Clevlands Cl ROY/SHW OL2 43 K4
Cleworth Cl TYLD M29 67 M8
Cleworth Rd MDTN M24 57 J2
Cleworth St HULME M15 * 6 A9
Cleworth Wk HULME M15 6 A9
Clibran St CHH M8 72 E6
Clifden Dr WYTH/NTH M22 119 G2
Cliff Av BRO M7 71 M6
BURY BL9 25 G2
TOT/BURYW BL8 24 B5
Cliff Crs BRO M7 72 A5
Cliff Dl STLY SK15 91 J4
Cliffdale Dr CHH M8 72 D3
Cliffe Rd GLSP SK13 105 G5
Cliff Gv HTNM SK4 99 L8
Cliff Hill Rd ROY/SHW OL2 43 M3
Cliffmere Cl CHD/CHDH SK8 120 B1
Clifford Av DTN/ASHW M34 90 B7
HALE/TIMP WA15 108 D6
Clifford Rd BOLS/LL BL3 * 51 K2
POY/DIS SK12 121 L8
WILM/AE SK9 126 D6
Clifford St ECC M30 84 E4
LEIGH WN7 66 E8
ROCH OL11 10 F9
SWIN M27 70 E4
Cliff Rd WILM/AE SK9 126 F4
Cliff Side WILM/AE SK9 126 F4
Clifton Av CHD/CHDH SK8 119 J2
ECC M30 85 G1
HALE/TIMP WA15 108 B7
OLDE OL4 * 59 L7
RUSH/FAL M14 99 G4
TYLD M29 67 M6
Clifton Cl HEY OL10 40 F3
OLDE OL4 59 L7
OLDTF/WHR M16 87 G7
Clifton Ct FWTH BL4 52 E2
Clifton Crs ROY/SHW OL2 59 K1
WGN WN1 47 M2
Clifton Dr CHD/CHDH SK8 110 C7
CHD/CHDH SK8 119 J2
HOR/BR BL6 32 E1
MPL/ROM SK6 114 C5
SWIN M27 70 A2
WILM/AE SK9 126 C8
Clifton Gv
OLDTF/WHR M16 87 G7
SWIN M27 70 A2
Clifton Holmes UPML OL3 45 H7
Clifton House Rd SWIN M27 54 B8
Cliftonmill Mdw
GOL/RIS/CUL WA3 79 J4
Clifton Park Rd OFTN SK2 112 D7
Clifton Pl PWCH M25 * 55 K7
Clifton Rd AIMK WN4 63 J6
CCHDY M21 97 M4
ECC M30 85 G1
HTNM SK4 99 K8
LEIGH WN7 81 H3
MDTN M24 42 A6
PWCH M25 55 H8
SALE M33 108 E1
URM M41 95 K2
WGNW/BIL/OR WN5 62 A8
Clifton St AUL OL6 90 D1
BOL BL1 2 C3
BURY BL9 25 J8
FAIL M35 74 D3
FWTH BL4 52 E2
FWTH BL4 53 J5
LEIGH WN7 66 A7
MILN OL16 29 J6
NEWH/MOS M40 73 J8
OLDTF/WHR M16 87 G7
ROCH OL11 * 11 G9
TYLD M29 68 B4
UPML OL3 61 L7
WGN WN1 15 G1
WGNS/IIMK WN3 47 K8
WILM/AE SK9 130 D3
Clifton Vw SWIN M27 54 B8
Cliftonville Dr SWIN M27 70 E6
Cliftonville Rd MILN OL16 42 F4
Clinton Av RUSH/FAL M14 98 D2
Clinton Gdns RUSH/FAL M14 98 D2
Clinton St AUL OL6 * 76 A8
Clinton Wk OLDE OL4 * 9 L7
Clippers Quay SALQ M50 86 D6
Clipsley Crs OLDE OL4 60 A5
Cliston Wk BRAM/HZG SK7 121 J2
Clitheroe Cl HEY OL10 41 G1
Clitheroe Dr TOT/BURYW BL8 38 C2
Clitheroe Rd BRUN/LGST M13 99 J1
Clito St BKLY M9 73 J4
Clive Av WHTF M45 55 H3
Clivedale Pl BOL BL1 2 F5
Clively Av SWIN M27 70 E3
Clive Rd FAIL M35 74 B5
WHTN BL5 50 B6
Clive St ANC M4 7 J1
AULW OL7 75 K7
BOL BL1 2 F5
OLDS OL8 75 G2
Clivia Gv BRO M7 * 72 A6
Cloak St CMANE M1 7 H8
Clock House Av DROY M43 89 H1
Clockhouse Ms DROY M43 * 89 H1
Clock St CHAD OL9 74 E2
Clock Tower Cl HYDE SK14 102 B3
WALK M28 68 C1
Cloister Av LEIGH WN7 66 A3
Cloister Cl DUK SK16 90 F6
Cloister Rd HTNM SK4 111 G2
The Cloisters CHD/CHDH SK8 111 K7
MILN OL16 28 E3
SALE M33 97 G8
WHTN BL5 50 B7
Cloister St BKLY M9 73 J4
BOL BL1 35 M2
Clondberry Cl TYLD M29 68 B3
Clopton Wk HULME M15 87 H6
Closebrook Rd
WGNW/BIL/OR WN5 47 G6
Close La WGNE/HIN WN2 65 J1
WGNE/HIN WN2 65 L3
Closes Farm BOLS/LL BL3 51 L2
Close St WGNE/HIN WN2 49 J6
The Close ALT WA14 107 M7
ATH M46 51 J7
BOLE BL2 36 E1
DTN/ASHW M34 90 A8
MDTN M24 57 L1
MPL/ROM SK6 114 E3
STLY SK15 76 C8
TOT/BURYW BL8 24 F6
Clothorn Rd DID/WITH M20 98 E8
Cloudstock Gv LHULT M38 52 B7
Clough Av MPL/ROM SK6 114 F6
SALE M33 108 A3
WHTN BL5 50 C4
WILM/AE SK9 126 F2
Clough Bank BKLY M9 * 73 G2
Cloughbank RAD M26 53 M5
Clough Dr PWCH M25 55 J8
Clough End Rd HYDE SK14 103 J3
Cloughfield Av ORD M5 86 E4
Cloughfold RAD M26 53 L5
Clough Fold Rd HYDE SK14 101 M3
Clough Ga HYDE SK14 * 102 C4
OLDS OL8 75 G2
Clough Gv AIMK WN4 63 J7
WHTF M45 55 G2
Clough House Dr LEIGH WN7 66 E7
Clough House La WHIT OL12 20 F6
Clough La HEY OL10 26 F8
OLDE OL4 61 H6
PWCH M25 55 J8
Clough Meadow BOL BL1 35 G6
MPL/ROM SK6 101 M7
Clough Meadow Rd RAD M26 54 B1
Clough Park Av OLDE OL4 61 H6
Clough Rd BKLY M9 73 J4
DROY M43 89 L2
FAIL M35 74 D5
LIT OL15 21 L4
MDTN M24 57 K2
ROY/SHW OL2 44 A6
Cloughs Av CHAD OL9 58 A4
Clough Side MPL/ROM SK6 114 F5
Cloughside POY/DIS SK12 124 A6
Clough St FWTH BL4 53 J5
MDTN M24 57 L2
NEWH/MOS M40 73 M8
RAD M26 54 F3
WHIT OL12 21 G6
Clough Ter LIT OL15 * 21 L5
The Clough AIMK WN4 63 G8
AULW OL7 75 K6
BOL BL1 * 35 H4
RDSH SK5 100 E6
Clough Top Rd BKLY M9 73 K2
Cloughwood Crs
WGNNW/ST WN6 30 A5
Clovelly Av LEIGH WN7 66 C4
OLDS OL8 74 F2
Clovelly Rd CCHDY M21 97 M4
OFTN SK2 112 F4
SWIN M27 69 M5
Clovelly St NEWH/MOS M40 * 74 A7
ROCH OL11 41 L1
Clover Av EDGY/DAV SK3 112 A8
Cloverbank Av BNG/LEV M19 99 G8
Clover Crs OLDS OL8 75 M1
Clover Cft SALE M33 109 G3
Cloverdale Dr AIMK WN4 78 F2
Cloverdale Sq BOL BL1 35 K3
Clover Hall Crs MILN OL16 11 M1
Cloverley Dr HALE/TIMP WA15 108 D8
Clover Rd HALE/TIMP WA15 108 D7
MPL/ROM SK6 114 B1
Clover St WGNNW/ST WN6 47 K2
WHIT OL12 10 D3
Clover Vw MILN OL16 * 11 K3
Clowes St CHAD OL9 74 D2
CSLFD M3 6 D3
WGTN/LGST M12 88 D6
Club St OP/CLY M11 89 J5
Clumber Cl POY/DIS SK12 129 J1
Clumber Rd GTN M18 89 J8
POY/DIS SK12 129 J1
Clunton Av BOLS/LL BL3 35 L8
Clutha Rd EDGY/DAV SK3 112 C8
Clwyd Av EDGY/DAV SK3 12 F9
Clyde Av WHTF M45 55 J6
Clyde Ct MILN OL16 11 J6
Clyde Rd DID/WITH M20 98 C8
EDGY/DAV SK3 12 D8
RAD M26 38 C7
TYLD M29 67 M5
Clydesdale St OLDS OL8 59 H8
Clyde St AULW OL7 90 C3
BOL BL1 * 36 B2
LEIGH WN7 * 66 E8
OLD OL1 59 M3
Clyde Ter RAD M26 * 38 C7
Clyne St STRET M32 86 C7
Coach House Dr
WGNNW/ST WN6 30 E6
Coach La ROCH OL11 27 H7
Coach Rd HYDE SK14 92 F7
TYLD M29 67 M6
Coach St ATH M46 67 G1
Coalbrook Wk WGTN/LGST M12 88 A4
Coalburn St WGTN/LGST M12 88 C2
Coal Pit La ATH M46 66 E1
LEIGH WN7 66 B4
OLDS OL8 75 G5
WGNE/HIN WN2 65 L3
Coal Rd RAMS BL0 19 K4
Coalshaw Green Rd CHAD OL9 74 D1
Coatbridge St OP/CLY M11 88 F3
Cobalt Av URM M41 85 J6
Cobb Cl CHH M8 72 B1
Cobbett's Wy WILM/AE SK9 126 D8
Cobble Bank BKLY M9 72 F1
Cobden St AUL OL6 * 91 G2
BKLY M9 73 H3
BOL BL1 36 A1
BURY BL9 5 H2
CHAD OL9 8 B5
EDGW/EG BL7 * 22 A2
HEY OL10 41 G3
NEWLW WA12 79 G8
OLDE OL4 60 A3
RAD M26 38 C6
SLFD M6 71 J8
TYLD M29 67 K3
Coberley Av URM M41 84 C8
Cob Hall Rd STRET M32 96 F3
Cobham Av BOLS/LL BL3 52 A1
NEWH/MOS M40 73 M2
Coblers Hl UPML OL3 45 J7
Cob Moor Av
WGNW/BIL/OR WN5 62 A3
Cob Moor Rd
WGNW/BIL/OR WN5 62 A3
Cobourg St CMANE M1 7 J6
Coburg Av BRO M7 72 A8
Cochrane Av WGTN/LGST M12 88 B7
Cochrane St BOLS/LL BL3 2 F9
Cock Brow HYDE SK14 102 F5
Cock Clod St RAD M26 54 F1
Cockcroft Rd ORD M5 86 F2
Cockcroft St BKLY M9 73 G3
Cockerell Springs BOLE BL2 * 3 G6
Cocker Hl STLY SK15 91 L2
Cocker Mill La ROY/SHW OL2 43 J7
Cockers La STLY SK15 92 B4
Cocker St LHULT M38 52 D8
Cockey Moor Rd BOLE BL2 38 A3
Cockhall La WHIT OL12 20 A3
Coconut Gv SLFD M6 86 D2
Codale Dr BOLE BL2 37 J4
Coddington Av OP/CLY M11 89 H4
Code La WHTN BL5 33 L8
Coe St BOLS/LL BL3 2 E8
Coghlan Cl OP/CLY M11 * 88 E2
Coin St ROY/SHW OL2 43 H8
Colborne Av ECC M30 84 E2
MPL/ROM SK6 113 L2
RDSH SK5 * 100 C1
Colbourne Av CHH M8 72 C3
Colbourne Gv HYDE SK14 103 H2
Colburn Cl WGNS/IIMK WN3 63 K2
Colby Rd WGNS/IIMK WN3 63 L1
Colchester Av BOLE BL2 37 H4
Colchester Cl NTHM/RTH M23 109 H3
Colchester Dr FWTH BL4 52 C3
Colchester Pl HTNM SK4 12 B1
Colchester Wk OLD OL1 9 J4
Colclough Cl NEWH/MOS M40 73 L6
Coldalhurst La TYLD M29 67 L7
Coldfield Dr NTHM/RTH M23 109 J6
Cold Greave Cl MILN OL16 29 M8
Coldhurst St OLD OL1 9 G2
Coldstone Dr AIMK WN4 63 G8
Coldstream Av BKLY M9 57 G8
Cole Av NEWLW WA12 78 F8
Colebrook Dr NEWH/MOS M40 73 K6
Colebrook Rd
HALE/TIMP WA15 108 D6
Coleby Av OLDTF/WHR M16 86 F8
WYTH/NTH M22 119 H3
Coleclough Pl
GOL/RIS/CUL WA3 81 J8
Coledale Dr MDTN M24 56 F2
Coleford Gv BOL BL1 2 C6
Colemore Av DID/WITH M20 111 G1
Colenso Ct BOLE BL2 3 M4
Colenso Gv HTNM SK4 12 A1
Colenso St OLDS OL8 75 G1
Coleport Cl CHD/CHDH SK8 120 C3
Coleridge Av MDTN M24 57 M1
RAD M26 54 B1
WGNW/BIL/OR WN5 46 D6
Coleridge Cl RDSH SK5 100 B3
Coleridge Rd LIT OL15 29 J2
OLD OL1 44 B8
OLDTF/WHR M16 97 M1
RDSH SK5 100 B3
TOT/BURYW BL8 24 C2
WGNW/BIL/OR WN5 62 A3
Colerne Wy
WGNS/IIMK WN3 63 G2
Colesbourne Cl LHULT M38 52 D6
Coleshill Ri WGNS/IIMK WN3 62 F2
Coleshill St NEWH/MOS M40 88 B1
Cole St NEWH/MOS M40 73 J4
Colgate Crs RUSH/FAL M14 98 E4
Colgate La ORD M5 86 D6
Colgrove Av NEWH/MOS M40 73 M2
Colina Dr BRO M7 72 B7
Colindale Av BKLY M9 57 H8
Colindale Cl BOLS/LL BL3 * 35 M7
Colin Rd HTNM SK4 100 B8
Colin St WGN WN1 15 H1
Colinton Cl BOL BL1 36 A3
Colinwood Cl BURY BL9 55 J1
Collard St ATH M46 50 E8
Coll Dr URM M41 85 G7
College Av OLDS OL8 75 G1
WGN WN1 15 G5
College Cl BOLS/LL BL3 2 D7
OFTN SK2 112 E6
WILM/AE SK9 126 C4
College Dr OLDTF/WHR M16 97 M2
College Rd ECC M30 85 K2
OLDS OL8 59 G8
OLDTF/WHR M16 98 A2
WHIT OL12 10 B4
College St LEIGH WN7 66 D7
College Wy BOLS/LL BL3 2 C7
Collegiate Wy SWIN M27 70 C1
Collen Crs TOT/BURYW BL8 24 E6
Collett Cl WGN WN1 15 K4
Collett St OLD OL1 59 M4
Colley St MILN OL16 11 H1
STRET M32 86 C7
Collie Av SLFD M6 71 M7
Collier Av MILN OL16 29 J5
Collier Cl HYDE SK14 103 H3
Collier Hl OLDS OL8 75 G1
Collier Hill Av OLDS OL8 74 F1
Colliers Cl LEIGH WN7 81 H1
Collier's Ct ROCH OL11 42 E3
Collier St CSLFD M3 6 D2
CSLFD M3 6 D7
GLSP SK13 104 F4
SWIN M27 70 B5
WGNE/HIN WN2 49 G6
Colliery La ATH M46 50 D8
Colliery St OP/CLY M11 88 D3
Collin Av GTN M18 88 F8
Collingburn Av ORD M5 86 E5
Colling Cl IRL M44 94 D3
Collinge Av MDTN M24 57 M4
Collinge St HEY OL10 40 F2
MDTN M24 58 A5
ROY/SHW OL2 * 43 L5
TOT/BURYW BL8 24 E8
WGNE/HIN WN2 64 D2
Collingham St CHH M8 72 D8
Colling St RAMS BL0 * 18 E7
Collington Cl WGTN/LGST M12 88 D7
Collingwood Av DROY M43 89 H1
Collingwood Cl POY/DIS SK12 129 L1
Collingwood Dr SWIN M27 70 D5
Collingwood Rd BNG/LEV M19 99 J3
Collingwood St ROCH OL11 41 M4
WGNNW/ST WN6 31 H3
Collingwood Wy OLD OL1 9 J2
WHTN BL5 50 B3
Collins La WHTN BL5 50 C6
Collins St TOT/BURYW BL8 24 C8
Collins Wy CHAD OL9 74 F1
Collisdene Rd
WGNW/BIL/OR WN5 46 A6
Collop Dr HEY OL10 41 H5
Coll's La UPML OL3 45 G8
Collyhurst Av WALK M28 69 H2
Collyhurst Rd
NEWH/MOS M40 72 E8
Collyhurst St NEWH/MOS M40 72 F8
Colman Gdns ORD M5 86 E5
Colmore Dr BKLY M9 57 K8
Colmore Gv BOLE BL2 22 E8
Colmore St BOLE BL2 36 E1
Colnbrook WGNNW/ST WN6 30 E3
Colne St ROCH OL11 42 A3
Colonial Rd OFTN SK2 112 D6
Colshaw Dr WILM/AE SK9 127 H3
Colshaw Rd NTHM/RTH M23 109 K7
Colson Dr MDTN M24 57 J5
Colt Hill La UPML OL3 61 J4
Coltsfoot Cl LEIGH WN7 66 E7
Coltsfoot Dr ALT WA14 107 L4
Columbia Av GTN M18 89 J8
Columbia Rd BOL BL1 35 M4
Columbia St OLDS OL8 * 59 J8
Columbine Cl WHIT OL12 27 M1
Columbine St OP/CLY M11 89 G5
Colville Dr TOT/BURYW BL8 38 E3
Colville Gv HALE/TIMP WA15 108 D6
SALE M33 108 B3
Colville Rd OLD OL1 59 G3
Colwell Av STRET M32 96 E3
Colwick Av ALT WA14 108 B6
Colwith Av BOLE BL2 37 H3
Colwyn Av MDTN M24 57 K6
RUSH/FAL M14 99 H4
Colwyn Crs RDSH SK5 100 C7
Colwyn Dr WGNE/HIN WN2 65 M2
Colwyn Gv ATH M46 50 F7
Colwyn Rd BRAM/HZG SK7 121 H4
CHD/CHDH SK8 120 A3
SWIN M27 69 M6
Colwyn St CHAD OL9 8 E5
ROCH OL11 41 L2
SLFD M6 86 C1
Combe Cl OP/CLY M11 88 E1
Combermere Av
DID/WITH M20 98 D5
Combermere Cl
CHD/CHDH SK8 111 J8
TYLD M29 67 L3
Combermere St DUK SK16 90 F3
Combs Cl NM/HAY SK22 124 C4
Combs Ms GLSP SK13 104 A3
Comer Ter SALE M33 96 D8
Comet Rd
WGNW/BIL/OR WN5 46 F4
Comet St CMANE M1 7 K5
Commercial Av
CHD/CHDH SK8 120 A7
Commercial Brow HYDE SK14 91 H8
Commercial Rd
BRAM/HZG SK7 121 M1
Commercial St CHAD OL9 8 D7
CSLFD M3 6 D8
HYDE SK14 102 B1
Commodore Pl
WGNW/BIL/OR WN5 47 H3
Common La GOL/RIS/CUL WA3 81 G8
LEIGH WN7 65 L8
PART M31 94 F8
TYLD M29 67 K3
Common Nook WGNE/HIN WN2 48 D6
Common Side Rd WALK M28 68 C5
Common St WHTN BL5 49 L5
Commonwealth Cl LEIGH WN7 81 K1
Community St AULW OL7 90 C3
Como St BOLS/LL BL3 * 35 M8
Como Wk GTN M18 88 E6
Compass St OP/CLY M11 88 F5
Compstall Av RUSH/FAL M14 98 E3
Compstall Gv GTN M18 * 89 H6
Compstall Mills Est
MPL/ROM SK6 * 114 E2
Compstall Rd MPL/ROM SK6 114 A2
Compton Cl URM M41 94 F3
Compton Dr NTHM/RTH M23 * 118 C2
Compton Fold ROY/SHW OL2 43 M3
Compton Wy MDTN M24 57 M5
Comus St ORD M5 86 F4
Concert La CMANW M2 7 G5
Concord Av WGNS/IIMK WN3 63 L1
Concord Pl SLFD M6 71 K7
Condor Cl DROY M43 * 89 M1
Condor Pl SLFD M6 71 K7
Condor Wk BRUN/LGST M13 * 87 L6
Conduit St AUL OL6 90 F2
GLSP SK13 93 J5
OLD OL1 60 A1
Conewood Wk
BRUN/LGST M13 87 M6
Coney Gv NTHM/RTH M23 109 K5
Coneymead STLY SK15 76 D8
Congham Rd EDGY/DAV SK3 12 C7
Congleton Av RUSH/FAL M14 98 D2
Congleton Cl WILM/AE SK9 130 D4
Congleton Rd MCFLDN SK10 130 D6
Congou St CMANE M1 7 L6
Congreave St OLD OL1 9 G3
Congresbury Rd LEIGH WN7 66 A5
Coningsby Dr BKLY M9 73 G4
Coningsby Gdns
GOL/RIS/CUL WA3 80 B4
Conisber Cl EDGW/EG BL7 22 B3
Conisborough ROCH OL11 10 C7
Conisborough Pl WHTF M45 55 L5
Coniston BOL BL1 * 36 C1
Coniston Av AIMK WN4 63 L8
ATH M46 51 G7
BKLY M9 73 G4
FWTH BL4 52 B5
HYDE SK14 90 F8
LHULT M38 52 D8
OLDS OL8 75 G1
SALE M33 108 F2
WGN WN1 47 L1
WGNE/HIN WN2 48 E5
WGNW/BIL/OR WN5 46 C5
WHTF M45 55 J4
Coniston Cl BOLS/LL BL3 37 K8
CHAD OL9 58 D5
DTN/ASHW M34 100 E2
RAMS BL0 18 F5
Coniston Dr BURY BL9 39 H5
MDTN M24 57 H2
STLY SK15 91 K1
WGNE/HIN WN2 64 E4
WILM/AE SK9 119 L8
Coniston Gv AULW OL7 75 K8
HEY OL10 41 G4
LHULT M38 52 D8
ROY/SHW OL2 43 G6
Coniston Park Dr
WGNNW/ST WN6 31 K5
Coniston Rd CHD/CHDH SK8 110 E6
HOR/BR BL6 33 G1
MPL/ROM SK6 122 F4
PART M31 94 B8
RDSH SK5 100 C6
STRET M32 96 F1
SWIN M27 70 C6
TYLD M29 67 K5
URM M41 95 H4
WGNE/HIN WN2 49 H8
Coniston St LEIGH WN7 66 B7
NEWH/MOS M40 73 M7
SLFD M6 71 L8
Coniston Wk
HALE/TIMP WA15 109 G7
Conival Wy CHAD OL9 58 D3
Conmere Sq HULME M15 6 F9
Connaught Av BNG/LEV M19 99 J5
MILN OL16 42 E1
WHTF M45 55 K5
Connaught Cl WILM/AE SK9 127 G4
Connaught Sq BOLE BL2 36 E3
Connaught St OLDS OL8 9 H7
TOT/BURYW BL8 38 E3
Connel Cl BOLE BL2 37 J6
Connell Rd NTHM/RTH M23 109 K6
Connell Wy HEY OL10 * 41 J1
Connery Crs AUL OL6 76 A6
Connie St OP/CLY M11 88 F4
Conningsby Cl EDGW/EG BL7 22 C4
Connington Av BKLY M9 73 G3
Connington Cl ROY/SHW OL2 42 F8
Connor Wy CHD/CHDH SK8 110 C8
Conrad Cl OLD OL1 44 B8
WGNS/IIMK WN3 14 C9
Conran St BKLY M9 73 G5
Consett Av NTHM/RTH M23 109 K6
Consort Av
ROY/SHW OL2 42 F6
Consort Cl DUK SK16 90 F6
Consort Pl ALT WA14 116 D1
Constable Cl BOL BL1 36 A3
Constable Dr MPL/ROM SK6 114 E4
WILM/AE SK9 127 J4
Constable St GTN M18 89 H6
Constance Gdns ORD M5 86 C3
Constance Rd BOLS/LL BL3 35 M7
PART M31 106 C1
Constance St HULME M15 * 6 D8
Constantia St WGNS/IIMK WN3 64 C1
Constantine Rd MILN OL16 10 F4
Constantine St OLDE OL4 60 A6
Consul St WYTH/NTH M22 110 B3
Convamore Rd
BRAM/HZG SK7 120 F6
Convent Gv ROCH OL11 10 B8
Convent St OLDE OL4 59 M8
Conway Av BOL BL1 35 K3
IRL M44 94 C4
SWIN M27 70 E2
WHTF M45 55 J5

Conway Cl HEY OL10 ...... 40 D1
  LEIGH WN7 ...... 67 H5
  MDTN M24 ...... 57 K5
  OLDTF/WHR M16 * 97 L1
  RAMS BL0 ...... 18 E6
Conway Crs
  TOT/BURYW BL8 ...... 24 C2
  WGNW/BIL/OR WN5 ...... 62 B6
Conway Dr
  BRAM/HZG SK7 ...... 121 L3
  BURY BL9 ...... 40 A2
  HALE/TIMP WA15 ...... 108 F6
  STLY SK15 ...... 91 K1
  WGNE/HIN WN2 ...... 33 G8
  WGNW/BIL/OR WN2 ...... 62 C7
Conway Gv CHAD OL9 ...... 58 C4
Conway Rd AIMK WN4 ...... 64 B7
  CHD/CHDH SK8 ...... 120 A2
  SALE M33 ...... 109 G1
  URM M41 ...... 85 G8
  WGNE/HIN WN2 ...... 49 J8
Conway St FWTH BL4 ...... 53 C5
  RDSH SK5 ...... 100 B8
  WGNW/BIL/OR WN5 ...... 46 F7
Conyngham Rd
  RUSH/FAL M14 ...... 88 A8
Cook Av RNFD/HAY WA11 ...... 78 B5
Cooke St AIMK WN4 ...... 63 J6
  BRAM/HZG SK7 ...... 121 M1
  DTN/ASHW M34 ...... 101 J1
  FAIL M35 ...... 74 C4
  FWTH BL4 ...... 53 H5
  HYDE SK14 ...... 91 J7
Cook St BURY BL9 ...... 5 C5
  CSLFD M3 ...... 6 C3
  DTN/ASHW M34 ...... 90 C6
  ECC M30 ...... 84 F2
  EDGY/DAV SK3 ...... 12 F5
  LEIGH WN7 ...... 66 C7
  MILN OL16 ...... 28 E3
  OLDE OL4 ...... 9 G5
  WGNE/HIN WN2 ...... 64 D5
Cook Ter MILN OL16 ...... 28 E3
Cooling La TYLD M29 ...... 67 G4
Coomassie St HEY OL10 ...... 40 F2
  RAD M26 ...... 54 D1
  SLFD M6 ...... 86 C1
Coombe Cl TYLD M29 ...... 67 L4
Coombes Av HYDE SK14 ...... 102 C3
  MPL/ROM SK6 ...... 114 C7
Coombes Gv GLSP SK13 ...... 103 M7
Coombes St OFTN SK2 ...... 112 E4
Coombes Vw HYDE SK14 ...... 103 J4
Co-operation St FAIL M35 ...... 74 C3
Co-operative St
  BRAM/HZG SK7 ...... 122 A1
  LEIGH WN7 ...... 66 A7
  LHULT M38 * 52 B7
  OLDE OL4 ...... 60 C6
  ROY/SHW OL2 * 43 L5
  SLFD M6 ...... 86 C2
  UPML OL3 * 61 L4
Cooper Fold MDTN M24 ...... 41 K8
Cooper La BKLY M9 ...... 57 J1
  MDTN M24 ...... 57 J1
Coopers Gln WGNE/HIN WN2 ...... 48 D4
Cooper St BRAM/HZG SK7 ...... 122 B1
  BURY BL9 ...... 4 E4
  CMANW M2 ...... 6 F5
  DROY M43 ...... 89 H3
  DUK SK16 ...... 90 E3
  GLSP SK13 ...... 104 E4
  OFTN SK2 ...... 13 K8
  OLDE OL4 ...... 60 D5
  STRET M32 ...... 97 G3
  WHIT OL12 ...... 21 H8
Copers Wk MILN OL16 ...... 28 F2
Cooper Ter MILN OL16 ...... 11 J2
Coop St ANC M4 * 7 J2
  BOL BL1 ...... 22 B8
  WGN WN1 ...... 15 J3
Copage Dr MPL/ROM SK6 ...... 101 K8
Cope Bank BOL BL1 ...... 35 M3
Cope Bank West BOL BL1 * 35 L2
Cope Cl OP/CLY M11 * 89 H5
Copeland Av SWIN M27 ...... 70 F3
Copeland Cl MDTN M24 ...... 56 F3
Copeland Dr
  WGNNW/ST WN6 ...... 31 J2
Copeland Ms BOL BL1 ...... 35 K5
Copeland St HYDE SK14 ...... 91 K7
Copeman Cl
  BRUN/LGST M13 ...... 87 M6
Copenhagen Sq
  MILN OL16 ...... 11 H3
Copenhagen St MILN OL16 ...... 11 H3
  NEWH/MOS M40 ...... 73 K6
Copesthorne Cl
  WGNE/HIN WN2 ...... 32 F6
Cope St BOL BL1 ...... 35 M3
Copgrove Rd CCHDY SK21 ...... 97 L5
Copley Av SWIN M27 ...... 91 M2
Copley Park Ms STLY SK15 ...... 91 M2
Copley Rd CCHDY M21 ...... 97 K2
Copley St ROY/SHW OL2 * 43 L4
Coplow Dl WGNE/HIN WN2 ...... 65 H1
Copperas Cl
  WGNNW/ST WN6 ...... 30 D5
Copperas La DROY M43 ...... 89 H4
  WGNE/HIN WN2 ...... 32 D6
Copperas St ANC M4 ...... 7 H3
Copperbeech Cl
  WYTH/NTH M22 ...... 110 B3
Copper Beech Dr
  GLSP SK13 ...... 104 B3
  STLY SK15 ...... 92 A1
Copperbeech Dr
  WGNNW/ST WN6 ...... 31 L5
Copper Beech Mnr
  GLSP SK13 * 104 B3
Copperfield Cl WGN WN1 * 47 M2
Copperfield Ct ALT WA14 ...... 116 E1
Copperfield Rd
  CHD/CHDH SK8 ...... 120 D7
  POY/DIS SK12 ...... 129 H2
Copperfields HOR/BR BL6 ...... 50 A5
  WILM/AE SK9 ...... 127 G4
Copper La POY/DIS SK12 ...... 123 J6
  SALE M33 ...... 108 A3
Coppice Cl HOR/BR BL6 ...... 50 D1
  MPL/ROM SK6 ...... 101 L8
Coppice Ct CHD/CHDH SK8 ...... 119 K4
Coppice Dr
  WGN WN3 ...... 63 J1
  WGNW/BIL/OR WN5 ...... 62 A2
  WHIT OL12 ...... 20 A5
  WYTH/NTH M22 ...... 110 A3
Coppice La POY/DIS SK12 ...... 123 J6
Coppice Rd POY/DIS SK12 ...... 129 M1
Coppice St BURY BL9 ...... 5 M1
  OLDS OL8 ...... 8 E8

The Coppice BKLY M9 ...... 73 K2
  BOLE BL2 ...... 23 G7
  HALE/TIMP WA15 ...... 117 K4
  PWCH M25 ...... 55 K8
  RAD M26 ...... 38 D8
  WALK M28 ...... 69 J4
  WALK M28 ...... 69 M7
Coppice Wk DTN/ASHW M34 ...... 101 G2
Coppingford Cl WHIT OL12 ...... 27 K2
Copping St WGTN/LGST M12 ...... 88 C6
The Coppins WILM/AE SK9 ...... 126 C8
Coppleridge Dr CHH M8 ...... 72 D2
Copplestone Dr SALE M33 ...... 95 M7
Coppull La WGN WN1 ...... 48 A2
Coppull Bridge Dr MILN OL16 ...... 29 C4
Cop Rd OLD OL1 ...... 43 M8
Copse Av WYTH/NTH M22 ...... 119 C1
Copse Dr BURY BL9 ...... 25 J6
The Copse EDGW/EG BL7 ...... 22 F2
  HALE/TIMP WA15 ...... 117 M5
  MPL/ROM SK6 ...... 114 F4
  NEWLW WA12 ...... 78 D8
  WGNW/BIL/OR WN5 ...... 45 J8
Copson St DID/WITH M20 ...... 98 E5
Copster Av OLDS OL8 ...... 75 H1
Copster Hill Rd OLDS OL8 ...... 75 H1
Copster Pl OLDS OL8 ...... 75 H1
Copthall La CHH M8 ...... 72 C4
Copthorne Cl HEY OL10 ...... 41 G4
Copthorne Crs BRUN/LGST M13 ...... 99 F2
Copthorne Dr BOLE BL2 ...... 37 H6
Copthorn Wk TOT/BURYW BL8 ...... 24 C7
Coptrod Head Cl WHIT OL12 ...... 20 C8
Coral Av CHD/CHDH SK8 ...... 120 C5
Coral Gv LEIGH WN7 ...... 66 B8
Coralin Wy AIMK WN4 ...... 63 J6
Coral Rd CHD/CHDH SK8 ...... 120 C5
Coral St BRUN/LGST M13 ...... 7 J3
  WGNNW/ST WN6 ...... 47 K1
Coram St GTN M18 ...... 89 J6
Corbar Rd OFTN SK2 ...... 112 E7
Corbel Wy ECC M30 ...... 85 C1
Corbett St MILN OL16 ...... 11 H2
  OP/CLY M11 ...... 88 D3
Corbrook Rd CHAD OL9 ...... 58 B3
Corby St WGTN/LGST M12 ...... 88 D6
Corcoran Dr MPL/ROM SK6 ...... 114 C2
Corda Av WYTH/NTH M22 ...... 110 A4
Cordingley Av DROY M43 ...... 89 J4
Cordova Av DTN/ASHW M34 ...... 100 C1
Corelli St NEWH/MOS M40 ...... 73 J8
Corfe Cl URM M41 ...... 94 F3
  WGNE/HIN WN2 ...... 33 G7
Corfe Crs BRAM/HZG SK7 ...... 121 M3
Corhampton Crs ATH M46 ...... 51 H7
Corinthian Av BRO M7 ...... 71 M7
Corkland Cl AUL OL6 ...... 91 G2
Corkland Rd CCHDY M21 ...... 97 L4
Corks La POY/DIS SK12 ...... 124 A7
Cork St AUL OL6 ...... 91 G2
  BURY BL9 ...... 5 J4
  WGTN/LGST M12 ...... 88 A4
Corley Av EDGY/DAV SK3 ...... 111 J5
Corley Wk OP/CLY M11 * 88 C3
Cormallen Gv FAIL M35 ...... 74 D5
Cormorant Cl LHULT M38 ...... 68 F1
Cornall St TOT/BURYW BL8 ...... 38 F1
Cornbrook Arches
  HULME M15 ...... 86 F5
Cornbrook Cl WHIT OL12 ...... 21 G6
  WHTN BL5 ...... 50 A6
Cornbrook Gv OLDTF/WHR M16 * 87 G7
Cornbrook Park Rd
  HULME M15 ...... 86 F6
Cornbrook St OLDTF/WHR M16 * 87 G7
Cornbrook Wy
  OLDTF/WHR M16 ...... 87 G7
Corn Cl BRUN/LGST M13 ...... 87 M7
Cornelian Gv AIMK WN4 ...... 63 J7
Cornell St ANC M4 ...... 7 K2
Corner Brook HOR/BR BL6 ...... 50 D1
Corner Cft WILM/AE SK9 ...... 126 E8
Cornergate WHTN BL5 ...... 50 B7
Corner La LEIGH WN7 ...... 66 A2
Corner St AUL OL6 ...... 90 F2
Cornet St BRO M7 ...... 72 A7
Cornfield STLY SK15 ...... 92 B5
Cornfield Cl BURY BL9 ...... 25 J3
  SALE M33 ...... 109 J1
Cornfield Dr WYTH/NTH M22 ...... 118 E1
Cornfield Rd MPL/ROM SK6 ...... 114 B1
Cornfield St MILN OL16 ...... 29 K7
Corn Hey Rd SALE M33 ...... 107 M2
Cornhill Av URM M41 ...... 95 L1
Corn Hill La DTN/ASHW M34 ...... 89 K7
Cornhill Rd URM M41 ...... 95 L1
Cornhill St OLD OL1 ...... 59 M2
Cornish Wy ROY/SHW OL2 ...... 59 J1
Cornishway WYTH/NTH M22 ...... 118 F4
Cornlea Dr WALK M28 ...... 68 F5
Corn Mill Cl WHIT OL12 ...... 21 H8
Corn Mill La STLY SK15 ...... 91 L3
Corn St FAIL M35 ...... 73 M6
  GLSP SK13 ...... 105 G3
  LEIGH WN7 ...... 66 A7
  OLDE OL4 ...... 9 M3
Cornwall Av BNG/LEV M19 ...... 99 L4
  TYLD M29 ...... 67 K1
  WHTN BL5 ...... 51 J4
Cornwall Cl MPL/ROM SK6 ...... 123 G5
Cornwall Crs RDSH SK5 ...... 100 F6
  UPML OL3 ...... 45 L3
  WGN WN1 ...... 31 L3
Cornwall Dr BURY BL9 ...... 5 H9
  WGNE/HIN WN2 ...... 49 J6
Cornwallis Rd WGNS/IIMK WN3 ...... 14 A9
Cornwall Pl
  WGNW/BIL/OR WN5 ...... 46 F3
Cornwall Rd CHD/CHDH SK8 ...... 119 K4
  DROY M43 ...... 89 K1
  IRL M44 ...... 94 A7
Cornwall St CHAD OL9 ...... 8 B7
  ECC M30 ...... 84 F3
  OP/CLY M11 ...... 89 G5
Cornwell Cl WILM/AE SK9 ...... 127 H4
Corona Av HYDE SK14 ...... 102 B1
  OLDS OL8 ...... 75 C1
Coronation Av ATH M46 ...... 50 F7
  DUK SK16 ...... 91 J5
  GOL/RIS/CUL WA3 ...... 81 M5
  HEY OL10 ...... 41 H4
  HYDE SK14 ...... 102 B3
Coronation Dr LEIGH WN7 ...... 82 C1
  RNFD/HAY WA11 ...... 78 D5
Coronation Gdns RAD M26 ...... 38 B8
Coronation Rd AUL OL6 ...... 75 M6
  DROY M43 ...... 89 J1
  FAIL M35 ...... 74 B6
  RAD M26 ...... 38 C6
  WGNNW/ST WN6 ...... 47 G1

Coronation Sq CMANE M1 ...... 7 M7
Coronation St AIMK WN4 ...... 63 H6
  BOL BL1 ...... 2 E5
  DTN/ASHW M34 ...... 100 F1
  OP/CLY M11 * 88 E4
  ORD M5 ...... 86 F4
  RDSH SK5 ...... 100 B8
  SWIN M27 ...... 70 D3
  WGNS/IIMK WN3 ...... 14 E7
Coronation Wk
  WGNW/BIL/OR WN5 ...... 62 A8
Corporation Rd
  DTN/ASHW M34 ...... 90 A7
  ROCH OL11 ...... 10 D5
Corporation St ANC M4 ...... 7 G3
  BOL BL1 ...... 2 E4
  HYDE SK14 * 102 A3
  MDTN M24 ...... 57 K4
  STKP SK1 ...... 13 K3
  STLY SK15 ...... 91 L3
  WGNS/IIMK WN3 ...... 14 E7
Corran Cl ECC M30 ...... 84 C2
Corranstone Cl HOR/BR BL6 ...... 33 L1
Correction Brow
  POY/DIS SK12 ...... 122 E6
Corrie Cl DTN/ASHW M34 ...... 101 J3
Corrie Crs FWTH BL4 ...... 54 A8
Corrie Dr FWTH BL4 ...... 54 A8
Corrie Rd SWIN M27 ...... 70 C8
Corrie St LHULT M38 ...... 52 D8
Corrie Wy MPL/ROM SK6 ...... 101 H7
Corrigan St GTN M18 ...... 89 H6
Corringham Rd BNG/LEV M19 ...... 99 M5
Corring Wy BOL BL1 ...... 22 E8
Corrin Rd BOLE BL2 ...... 3 H5
Corriss Av BKLY M9 ...... 56 D7
Corry St HEY OL10 ...... 41 H7
Corsey Rd WGNE/HIN WN2 ...... 49 H8
Corsock Dr WGN WN1 ...... 15 L1
Corson St BOLS/LL BL3 ...... 53 G2
Corston Gv HOR/BR BL6 ...... 33 G3
Corwen Av BKLY M9 ...... 73 H4
Corwen Cl OLDS OL8 ...... 74 E2
Cosgate Cl WGNW/BIL/OR WN5 ...... 46 B7
Cosgrove Crs FAIL M35 ...... 74 B7
Cosgrove Rd FAIL M35 ...... 74 B7
Cosham Rd WYTH/NTH M22 ...... 119 H1
Costessey Wy WGNS/IIMK WN3 ...... 62 F1
Costobadie Cl SK14 ...... 103 J1
Cosworth Cl LEIGH WN7 ...... 66 E8
Cotaline Cl ROCH OL11 ...... 41 L1
Cotefield Av BOLS/LL BL3 ...... 52 C1
Cotefield Cl MPL/ROM SK6 * 114 C7
Cotefield Rd WYTH/NTH M22 ...... 118 D2
Cote Green La MPL/ROM SK6 ...... 114 E3
Cote Green Rd MPL/ROM SK6 ...... 114 C3
Cote La BOLS/LL BL3 ...... 21 K6
  MOSL OL5 ...... 77 H1
  NM/HAY SK22 ...... 125 M1
  UPML OL3 ...... 45 L5
Cotford Rd BOL BL1 ...... 22 C7
Cotham St CSLFD M3 ...... 87 J1
Cotman Dr MPL/ROM SK6 ...... 114 F4
Cotswold Av BRAM/HZG SK7 ...... 121 K3
  CHAD OL9 ...... 58 D7
  GOL/RIS/CUL WA3 ...... 80 A6
  ROY/SHW OL2 ...... 43 J4
  URM M41 ...... 95 J1
  WGNW/BIL/OR WN5 ...... 46 F7
Cotswold Cl GLSP SK13 ...... 104 D4
  PWCH M25 ...... 55 M7
  RAMS BL0 ...... 18 F8
Cotswold Crs MILN OL16 ...... 29 K5
  TOT/BURYW BL8 ...... 38 E1
Cotswold Dr ROY/SHW OL2 ...... 58 E1
  SLFD M6 ...... 71 C8
Cotswold Rd HTNM SK4 ...... 12 F1
Cottage Cft BOLE BL2 ...... 23 G7
Cottage Gdns MPL/ROM SK6 ...... 113 G5
Cottage Gv WILM/AE SK9 ...... 126 C7
Cottage La GLSP SK13 ...... 104 B2
The Cottages OLDE OL4 * 60 C5
Cottam Crs MPL/ROM SK6 ...... 114 C6
Cottam Gv SWIN M27 ...... 70 D5
Cottam St OLD OL1 ...... 8 A2
  TOT/BURYW BL8 ...... 4 A2
Cottenham La BRO M7 ...... 72 B4
Cottenham St BRUN/LGST M13 * 87 L6
Cotterdale Cl OLDTF/WHR M16 * 98 A2
Cotteril Cl SALE M33 ...... 108 F3
Cotterill St SLFD M6 ...... 86 D2
Cotter St WGTN/LGST M12 ...... 7 L8
Cottesmore Cl WHIT OL12 ...... 20 A1
Cottesmore Dr CHH M8 ...... 72 F4
Cottesmore Gdns
  HALE/TIMP WA15 ...... 117 L4
Cottesmore Wy
  GOL/RIS/CUL WA3 ...... 79 L3
Cottingham Dr AUL OL6 ...... 75 M8
Cottingham Rd
  WGTN/LGST M12 ...... 88 B6
Cottingley Cl BOL BL1 ...... 22 A7
Cotton Cl HYDE SK14 ...... 102 A3
Cottonfield Rd DID/WITH M20 ...... 98 F6
Cottonfields EDGW/EG BL7 ...... 22 C5
Cotton Fold MILN OL16 ...... 11 L7
Cotton Hl DID/WITH M20 ...... 98 F6
Cotton La DID/WITH M20 ...... 98 F6
Cotton Mill Crs CHAD OL9 ...... 7 K3
Cotton St ANC M4 ...... 7 K3
  BOL BL1 ...... 36 A2
  LEIGH WN7 ...... 66 A7
Cotton St East AUL OL6 ...... 90 E1
Cotton St West AUL OL6 ...... 90 D1
Cotton Tree Cl OLDE OL4 ...... 60 A4
Cotton Tree St HTNM SK4 ...... 13 G4
Cottonwood Dr SALE M33 ...... 95 M7
Cottrell Rd HALE/TIMP WA15 ...... 117 M5
Coucill Sq FWTH BL4 ...... 53 H4
Coulsden Dr BKLY M9 ...... 73 G1
Coulthart St AUL OL6 ...... 90 E1
Coulthurst St RAMS BL0 ...... 18 A6
Coulton Cl OLD OL1 ...... 9 M3
Coultshead Av
  WGNW/BIL/OR WN5 ...... 62 B6
Council Av AIMK WN4 ...... 78 E1
Councillor La CHD/CHDH SK8 ...... 111 J7
Councillor St WGTN/LGST M12 ...... 88 B7
Countess Av CHD/CHDH SK8 ...... 120 A7
Countess Gv BRO M7 ...... 72 B4
Countess La RAD M26 ...... 38 A7
Countess Pl PWCH M25 ...... 55 M7
Countess Rd DID/WITH M20 ...... 110 E1
Countess St AUL OL6 ...... 91 G2
  OFTN SK2 ...... 112 D7
Counthill Dr CHH M8 ...... 72 B2
Counthill Rd OLDE OL4 ...... 60 A3
Counting House Rd
  POY/DIS SK12 ...... 124 A7
Count St MILN OL16 ...... 11 H9
County Av AUL OL6 ...... 76 B4
County Rd LHULT M38 ...... 52 D7

County St CMANW M2 ...... 6 F5
  OLDS OL8 ...... 74 F2
Coupes Gn WHTN BL5 ...... 50 B6
Coupland Cl OLDE OL4 ...... 44 C8
  WHIT OL12 ...... 20 A4
Coupland Rd WGNE/HIN WN2 ...... 66 A1
Coupland St HULME M15 ...... 87 K7
  WHIT OL12 ...... 20 B4
Courier St GTN M18 ...... 89 H6
Courier St GTN M18 ...... 89 L8
Course Vw OLDE OL4 ...... 76 B1
Court Dr NEWH/MOS M40 ...... 74 B8
Courtfield Av BKLY M9 * 57 C8
Courthill St STKP SK1 ...... 13 M6
Courtney Gn WILM/AE SK9 ...... 127 H2
Courtney Pl ALT WA14 ...... 116 C3
Court St BOLE BL2 ...... 3 H5
  UPML OL3 ...... 61 L4
Courts Vw SALE M33 ...... 96 F7
Courtyard Dr WALK M28 ...... 68 C1
The Courtyard BOL BL1 * 36 C3
  HEY OL10 * 41 J3
  HYDE SK14 * 93 J3
Cousin Flds EDGW/EG BL7 ...... 22 F5
Covell Rd POY/DIS SK12 ...... 121 J7
Covent Gdn STKP SK1 ...... 13 J5
Coventry Av EDGY/DAV SK3 ...... 111 J5
Coventry Gv CHAD OL9 ...... 58 D3
Coventry Rd RAD M26 ...... 38 C7
Coventry St ROCH OL11 * 10 F7
Coverdale Av BOL BL1 ...... 35 K4
  ROY/SHW OL2 ...... 42 F7
Coverdale Cl HEY OL10 ...... 40 F3
Coverdale Crs WGTN/LGST M12 ...... 88 A6
Coverdale Rd WHTN BL5 ...... 50 A4
Coverham Av OLDE OL4 ...... 60 A4
Coverhill Rd OLDE OL4 ...... 60 E7
Covert Rd OLDE OL4 ...... 76 B1
  WYTH/NTH M22 ...... 110 B7
The Coverts WGNNW/ST WN6 ...... 47 J2
The Cove HALE/TIMP WA15 ...... 117 M5
Covington Pl WILM/AE SK9 ...... 126 F6
Cowan St NEWH/MOS M40 ...... 88 C1
Cowbrook Av GLSP SK13 ...... 105 H3
Cowburn Dr NM/HAY SK22 ...... 124 E3
Cowburn St CSLFD M3 ...... 87 K1
  HEY OL10 ...... 41 H4
  LEIGH WN7 ...... 66 A7
  WGNE/HIN WN2 ...... 49 J5
Cowdals Rd HOR/BR BL6 ...... 34 E8
Cowesby St RUSH/FAL M14 ...... 98 D1
Cowhill La ATH M46 ...... 51 H6
Cowie St ROY/SHW OL2 ...... 43 L4
Cow La BOLS/LL BL3 ...... 51 L2
  BRAM/HZG SK7 ...... 113 C8
  FAIL M35 ...... 74 B5
  HALE/TIMP WA15 ...... 117 H4
  HYDE SK14 ...... 93 C6
  OLDE OL4 ...... 59 M5
  ORD M5 ...... 86 F3
  SALE M33 ...... 97 H6
  WILM/AE SK9 ...... 127 C5
Cow Lees WHTN BL5 ...... 50 D3
Cowley Rd BOL BL1 ...... 22 C7
Cowley St NEWH/MOS M40 ...... 73 M6
Cowling St WGNS/IIMK WN3 ...... 14 E7
Cowlishaw ROY/SHW OL2 ...... 43 K7
Cowlishaw La ROY/SHW OL2 ...... 43 L7
Cowlishaw Rd HYDE SK14 ...... 102 C7
Cowm Park Wy North
  WHIT OL12 ...... 20 A2
Cowm Park Wy South
  WHIT OL12 ...... 20 A4
Cowper St AUL OL6 ...... 90 F1
  LEIGH WN7 ...... 66 A7
  MDTN M24 ...... 58 A5
Coxfield WGNNW/ST WN6 ...... 30 A5
Cox Green Cl EDGW/EG BL7 ...... 22 A1
Cox Green Rd EDGW/EG BL7 ...... 16 A8
Coxton Rd WYTH/NTH M22 ...... 119 C3
Cox Wy ATH M46 ...... 67 C1
Crabbe St ANC M4 ...... 87 K1
Crab La BKLY M9 ...... 56 D7
Crabtree Av HALE/TIMP WA15 ...... 117 M5
  POY/DIS SK12 ...... 124 A7
Crab Tree La ATH M46 ...... 67 G2
Crabtree La OP/CLY M11 ...... 89 C4
Crabtree Rd OLD OL1 ...... 59 L4
Craddock Rd SALE M33 ...... 108 F3
Craddock St MOSL OL5 ...... 76 F3
Cradley Av OP/CLY M11 ...... 89 G4
Crag Av BURY BL9 ...... 25 G2
Cragg Fold BURY BL9 * 25 G2
Cragg Rd OLD OL1 ...... 58 D2
Cragie St CHH M8 ...... 72 C7
Crag La BURY BL9 ...... 25 G2
Cragside Wy WILM/AE SK9 ...... 127 G6
Craig Av TOT/BURYW BL8 ...... 38 E3
  URM M41 ...... 95 K1
Craig Cl HTNM SK4 ...... 12 A4
Craighall Av BNG/LEV M19 ...... 99 K4
Craighall Rd BOL BL1 ...... 22 B6
Craiglands MILN OL16 ...... 42 E2
Craigmore Av DID/WITH M20 ...... 98 A8
Craignair Ct SWIN M27 * 70 F4
Craig Rd GTN M18 ...... 88 F2
  HTNM SK4 ...... 12 A4
Craigslands Av
  NEWH/MOS M40 ...... 73 K6
Craig Wk OLDS OL8 ...... 9 H9
Craigwell Av DID/WITH M20 ...... 110 F1
Craigwell Rd PWCH M25 ...... 72 A2
Cramer St NEWH/MOS M40 * 73 J7
Crammond Cl NEWH/MOS M40 * 73 L8
Cramond Cl BOL BL1 ...... 36 A3
  WGNS/IIMK WN3 ...... 47 G8
Cramond Wk BOL BL1 ...... 36 A3
Crampton Dr
  HALE/TIMP WA15 ...... 117 L4
Crampton La PART M31 ...... 95 G6
Cranage Rd BNG/LEV M19 ...... 99 L4
Cranark Cl BOL BL1 ...... 35 K5
Cranberry Av WGNNW/ST WN6 ...... 47 L4
Cranberry Cl ALT WA14 ...... 107 L4
Cranberry Dr BOLS/LL BL3 ...... 35 J8
  DTN/ASHW M34 ...... 100 F3
Cranberry Rd PART M31 ...... 106 C1
Cranberry St OLDE OL4 ...... 59 L7
Cranborne Cl HOR/BR BL6 ...... 34 C3
Cranbourne
  WGNNW/ST WN6 ...... 31 C3

Cranbourne Cl
  HALE/TIMP WA15 ...... 108 D6
Cranbourne Rd AULW OL7 ...... 75 L7
  CCHDY M21 ...... 97 L4
  HTNM SK4 ...... 99 L8
  OLDTF/WHR M16 ...... 86 F8
  ROCH OL11 ...... 27 H6
Cranbourne St SLFD M6 * 86 F3
Cranbourne Ter AUL OL6 ...... 75 L7
Cranbrook Av AIMK WN4 ...... 63 K8
Cranbrook Dr PWCH M25 ...... 71 M2
Cranbrook Gdns AULW OL7 * 75 L8
  GTN M18 ...... 100 B1
Cranbrook Rd ECC M30 ...... 69 K8
  GTN M18 ...... 100 B1
Cranbrook St AULW OL7 ...... 75 L8
  OLDE OL4 ...... 59 M6
  RAD M26 ...... 38 F7
Cranbrook Wk CHAD OL9 ...... 8 A7
Cranbrook Wy WGN WN1 ...... 31 L8
Cranby St WGNE/HIN WN2 ...... 49 G7
Crandon Dr DID/WITH M20 ...... 110 F4
Cranesbill Cl WYTH/NTH M22 ...... 118 E3
Crane St BOLS/LL BL3 ...... 51 L1
  WGTN/LGST M12 ...... 7 M7
Cranfield Cl NEWH/MOS M40 ...... 88 A2
Cranfield Rd HOR/BR BL6 ...... 33 L5
  WGNS/IIMK WN3 ...... 63 K1
Cranford Av DID/WITH M20 ...... 99 G8
  SALE M33 ...... 96 F6
  STRET M32 ...... 97 L3
  WHTF M45 ...... 55 H2
Cranford Cl SWIN M27 ...... 70 E6
  WHTF M45 ...... 55 H2
Cranford Dr IRL M44 ...... 94 C1
Cranford Gdns MPL/ROM SK6 ...... 114 C5
  URM M41 * 95 H1
Cranford Rd URM M41 ...... 95 H1
  WILM/AE SK9 ...... 127 H2
Cranford St BOLS/LL BL3 ...... 51 M2
Cranham Av GOL/RIS/CUL WA3 ...... 80 B5
Cranham Cl TOT/BURYW BL8 ...... 38 E1
Cranham Rd WYTH/NTH M22 ...... 118 C2
Crank Rd WGNW/BIL/OR WN5 ...... 62 A3
Crankwood Rd LEIGH WN7 ...... 65 H8
  WGNE/HIN WN2 ...... 64 E6
Cranleigh WGNNW/ST WN6 ...... 31 J4
Cranleigh Av HTNM SK4 ...... 99 J8
Cranleigh Cl HOR/BR BL6 ...... 33 G3
  OLDE OL4 ...... 60 B3
Cranleigh Dr BRAM/HZG SK7 ...... 122 C4
  CHD/CHDH SK8 ...... 111 J6
  SALE M33 ...... 96 D7
  SALE M33 ...... 108 F3
  TYLD M29 ...... 67 L4
  WALK M28 ...... 69 J4
Cranlington Dr CHH M8 ...... 72 C6
Cranmer Ct HEY OL10 ...... 40 C8
Cranmere Av BNG/LEV M19 ...... 99 M2
Cranmere Dr SALE M33 ...... 108 A8
Cranmer Rd DID/WITH M20 ...... 98 E8
Cranshaw St TYLD M29 ...... 67 L4
Cranstal Dr WGNE/HIN WN2 ...... 49 K7
Cranston Dr DID/WITH M20 ...... 110 E1
  SALE M33 ...... 109 H1
Cranston Gv CHD/CHDH SK8 ...... 110 C7
Cranswick St RUSH/FAL M14 ...... 98 D1
Crantock Dr CHD/CHDH SK8 ...... 111 L4
  STLY SK15 ...... 92 A1
Crantock St WGTN/LGST M12 ...... 99 L1
Cranwell Av GOL/RIS/CUL WA3 ...... 81 J3
Cranwell Dr BNG/LEV M19 ...... 99 H8
Cranworth Av TYLD M29 ...... 67 K6
Cranworth St STLY SK15 ...... 91 L3
Craston Rd BRUN/LGST M13 ...... 99 H1
Crathie Ct BOL BL1 ...... 35 L3
Craven Av GOL/RIS/CUL WA3 ...... 80 B5
  ORD M5 ...... 86 E4
Craven Ct ALT WA14 * 107 H5
Craven Dr ALT WA14 ...... 107 H4
  ORD M5 ...... 86 E4
Craven Gdns ROCH OL11 * 10 D8
Cravenhurst Av
  NEWH/MOS M40 ...... 73 L8
Craven Pl BOL BL1 ...... 35 J2
  OP/CLY M11 ...... 88 F2
Craven Rd ALT WA14 ...... 107 H5
  RDSH SK5 ...... 100 C6
Craven St AUL OL6 ...... 76 A7
  BURY BL9 ...... 5 L2
  OLD OL1 ...... 9 H2
  ORD M5 ...... 86 E4
Craven St East HOR/BR BL6 ...... 34 A2
Craven Ter SALE M33 ...... 96 F6
Cravenwood AUL OL6 ...... 76 C4
Cravenwood Rd CHH M8 ...... 72 D4
Crawford Av BOLE BL2 ...... 3 J6
  TYLD M29 ...... 67 J2
  WALK M28 ...... 69 J4
  WGNE/HIN WN2 ...... 32 F7
Crawford Pl WGN WN1 * 48 A1
Crawford St BOLE BL2 ...... 64 G1
  BOLE BL2 ...... 3 H5
  ECC M30 ...... 85 G1
  MILN OL16 ...... 11 H6
  NEWH/MOS M40 * 73 M7
  WGN WN1 ...... 14 F4
  WGNE/HIN WN2 ...... 32 F8
Crawley Av ECC M30 ...... 85 K1
  WYTH/NTH M22 ...... 118 F1
Crawley Cl TYLD M29 ...... 67 M3
Crawley Gv OFTN SK2 ...... 112 E6
Craydon St OP/CLY M11 ...... 88 F4
Crayfield Rd BNG/LEV M19 ...... 99 L4
Crayford Rd
  NEWH/MOS M40 ...... 73 L8
The Cray MILN OL16 ...... 29 H6
Cray Wk BRUN/LGST M13 ...... 7 J7
Creaton Wy MDTN M24 ...... 41 C8
Creden Av WYTH/NTH M22 ...... 119 H1
Creden Av WYTH/NTH M22 ...... 119 H1
Crediton Cl ALT WA14 ...... 107 L6
  HULME M15 ...... 87 H8
Crediton Dr BOLE BL2 ...... 37 K5
  WGNE/HIN WN2 ...... 49 H8
Cresbury St WGTN/LGST M12 * 88 A3
Crescent Av AIMK WN4 ...... 63 K8
  BOL BL1 ...... 2 B1
  CHH M8 * 72 D4
  FWTH BL4 ...... 53 J6
  PWCH M25 ...... 71 L2
  SWIN M27 ...... 70 C4
  WHTN BL5 ...... 51 K4
Crescent Cl DUK SK16 ...... 90 F3
  EDGY/DAV SK3 ...... 112 D7
Crescent Ct CHH M8 ...... 72 D4
  LHULT M38 ...... 52 E7
Crescent Fold HYDE SK14 * 103 L4
Crescent Gv BNG/LEV M19 ...... 99 K3
  PWCH M25 ...... 71 L2
Crescent Pk HTNM SK4 ...... 12 C4

Crescent Range
RUSH/FAL M14 ....98 F1
Crescent Rd ALT WA14 ....107 K6
BOLS/LL BL3 ....52 E1
CHAD OL9 ....74 B2
CHD/CHDH SK8 ....110 F6
CHH M8 ....72 D4
DUK SK16 ....72 D4
FWTH BL4 ....53 J6
HALE/TIMP WA15 ....117 G2
HOR/BR BL6 ....34 B4
ROCH OL11 ....27 L8
STKP SK1 ....112 E1
WILM/AE SK9 ....130 G2
Crescent St CHH M8 ....72 F4
The Crescent ALT WA14 ....107 K7
BNG/LEV M19 ....99 K3
BOLE BL2 ....23 J8
BOLS/LL BL3 ....53 L2
BURY BL9 ....5 H3
CHD/CHDH SK8 ....110 F6
DROY M43 ....89 J3
EDGW/EG BL7 ....22 D4
EDGY/DAV SK3 ....112 D8
HALE/TIMP WA15 ....108 C5
HOR/BR BL6 ....34 A3
IRL M44 ....94 E1
MCFLDN SK10 ....131 K2
MDTN M24 ....57 H4
MOSL OL5 ....76 E3
MPL/ROM SK6 ....101 G8
NM/HAY SK22 ....124 D4
PWCH M25 ....55 L8
RAD M26 ....38 A7
ROY/SHW OL2 ....43 K6
STLY SK15 ....92 A6
URM M41 ....95 J1
WGNE/HIN WN2 * 48 E5
WGNW/BIL/OR WN5 ....46 F2
WHIT OL12 * 20 A4
WHTN BL5 ....50 B5
Crescent Wy EDGY/DAV SK3 ....112 D7
Cressell Pk WGNNW/ST WN6 ....30 D2
Cressfield Wy CCHDY M21 ....98 A5
Cressingham Rd BOLS/LL BL3 ....51 L1
STRET M32 ....96 E3
Cressington Cl ORD M5 * 86 E3
Cresswell Av NM/HAY SK22 ....124 E4
Cresswell Gv DID/WITH M20 ....98 D7
Cresswell St NM/HAY SK22 ....124 E4
Crestfield Gv
WGNNW/ST WN6 ....47 J2
Crestfold LHULT M38 ....52 D8
The Crest DROY M43 ....89 J3
Crestwood Av WGNS/IIMK WN3 ....63 H1
Creswick Cl WGNE/HIN WN2 ....48 B8
Crete St OLDS OL8 ....59 J8
Crewe Rd NTHM/RTH M23 ....109 H4
Crib Fold UPML OL3 ....61 G2
Crib La UPML OL3 ....61 K2
Criccieth Rd EDGY/DAV SK3 ....111 K5
Criccieth St OLDTF/WHR M16 * 87 J8
Cricketers Wy WHTN BL5 ....50 B4
Cricketfield La WALK M28 ....68 F1
Cricket's La AUL OL6 ....90 F1
Cricket's La North AUL OL6 ....90 F1
Cricket St BOLS/LL BL3 ....2 B9
DTN/ASHW M34 * 90 D8
WGNNW/ST WN6 ....14 B3
Cricket Vw MILN OL16 ....29 J7
Cricklewood Rd
WYTH/NTH M22 ....118 C2
Crimble La ROCH OL11 ....27 H7
Crimble St WHIT OL12 ....10 B3
Crime La OLDS OL8 ....75 G5
Crimsworth Av
OLDTF/WHR M16 ....97 L2
Crinan Wk NEWH/MOS M40 * 88 A1
Cringlebarrow Cl WALK M28 ....68 C7
Cringle Cl BOLS/LL BL3 ....35 H8
Cringle Dr CHD/CHDH SK8 ....110 D6
Cringleford Wk
WGTN/LGST M12 * 88 C7
Cringle Hall Rd BNG/LEV M19 ....99 J3
Cringle Rd BNG/LEV M19 ....99 L5
Crippen St ATH M46 ....66 D3
Cripple Ga WGNNW/ST WN6 ....30 D2
Cripple Gate La ROCH OL11 ....42 B3
Crispin Rd WYTH/NTH M22 ....119 G4
Critchley Cl HYDE SK14 ....102 C3
Criterion St RDSH SK5 ....100 C2
Croal Av WGNE/HIN WN2 ....64 D2
Croal St BOL BL1 ....2 A6
Croasdale Av RUSH/FAL M14 ....98 E3
Croasdale Cl ROY/SHW OL2 ....43 H7
Croasdale St BOL BL1 * 2 F1
Crocus Dr ROY/SHW OL2 ....43 K7
Crocus St BOL BL1 ....22 C8
Croft Acres RAMS BL0 ....19 G2
Croft Av ATH M46 ....67 G2
GOL/RIS/CUL WA3 ....79 K7
PWCH M25 ....56 C4
WGNW/BIL/OR WN5 * 46 A7
Croft Bank BRO M7 * 71 M7
M18 ....89 H7
Croft Brow OLDS OL8 ....75 H2
Croft Cl HALE/TIMP WA15 ....117 L6
Croft Ct LEIGH WN7 ....80 F3
Croft Dr TOT/BURYW BL8 ....24 B6
Croft Edge UPML OL3 ....61 K7
Crofters Brook RAD M26 ....38 F8
Crofters Gn WILM/AE SK9 ....126 D6
The Crofters SALE M33 ....109 J1
Crofters Wk BOLE BL2 ....22 C2
Croft Ga BOLE BL2 ....23 H8
Croft Gates Rd MDTN M24 ....57 G5
Croft Gv LHULT M38 ....52 C7
Croft Head Dr ROY/SHW OL2 ....43 G8
Croft Hill Rd NEWH/MOS M40 ....73 H3
Croftlands RAMS BL0 ....24 D1
WGNW/BIL/OR WN5 ....46 A7
Croftlands Rd WYTH/NTH M22 ....110 B8
Croft La BOLS/LL BL3 ....51 J5
BURY BL9 ....39 K7
RAD M26 ....38 F8
Croftleigh Cl WHTF M45 ....55 H2
Croft Mnr GLSP SK13 ....93 K6
Crofton Av HALE/TIMP WA15 ....108 D4
Crofton St OLDS OL8 ....75 H1
OLDTF/WHR M16 ....87 H3
RUSH/FAL M14 ....98 C3
Croft Pl TYLD M29 ....67 J4
Croft Rd CHD/CHDH SK8 ....120 D1
SALE M33 ....109 H2
WILM/AE SK9 ....126 C8
Croftside Av WALK M28 ....69 H1
Croftside Cl WALK M28 ....69 H1
Croftside Gv WALK M28 ....69 H1
Croftside Wy WILM/AE SK9 ....127 G6

Croft St BOLS/LL BL3 ....36 E8
BRO M7 ....71 M7
BURY BL9 ....5 H4
FAIL M35 ....74 D3
GOL/RIS/CUL WA3 * 79 K4
HYDE SK14 ....102 A2
LHULT M38 ....52 C7
OP/CLY M11 ....88 E3
STLY SK15 ....91 J2
WHIT OL12 ....28 F1
WHTN BL5 ....50 B1
The Croft BURY BL9 ....39 K6
GLSP SK13 ....93 K6
HYDE SK14 ....92 D8
OLDS OL8 ....75 H2
PART M31 ....95 G6
WGNW/BIL/OR WN5 ....46 B3
Croftwood Sq
WGNW/BIL/OR WN5 ....46 F2
Croichbank TOT/BURYW BL8 ....23 L2
Cromar Rd BRAM/HZG SK7 ....122 B1
Cromarty Av CHAD OL9 ....74 C1
Cromarty Wk OP/CLY M11 ....88 C3
Crombie Av WYTH/NTH M22 ....110 A4
Crombouke Dr LEIGH WN7 ....66 B3
Crombouke Fold WALK M28 ....68 C5
Cromdale Av BOL BL1 ....35 L4
BRAM/HZG SK7 ....122 B1
Cromedale Crs
WGNNW/ST WN6 ....31 K5
Cromer Av BOLE BL2 ....3 L1
DID/WITH M20 ....98 E6
DTN/ASHW M34 ....100 D1
Cromer Dr ATH M46 ....66 D2
Cromer Rd CHD/CHDH SK8 ....111 H6
SALE M33 ....108 B3
TOT/BURYW BL8 ....25 G7
WGNS/IIMK WN3 ....63 H1
Cromer St MDTN M24 ....57 K3
OP/CLY M11 * 89 G3
ROY/SHW OL2 * 43 L5
STKP SK1 ....13 M3
WHIT OL12 ....10 D1
Cromford Av STRET M32 ....96 E1
Cromford Cl BOL BL1 ....2 C1
Cromford Dr
WGNW/BIL/OR WN5 ....46 E7
Cromford Gdns BOL BL1 ....36 C2
Cromford St OLD OL1 ....9 M2
Cromhurst St CHH M8 ....72 E4
Cromley Rd MPL/ROM SK6 ....123 G5
OFTN SK2 ....121 J1
Crompton Av BOLE BL2 ....37 H4
MILN OL16 ....42 E1
Crompton Circuit
ROY/SHW OL2 ....44 B3
UPML OL3 ....44 E2
Crompton Cl BOL BL1 ....22 D8
MPL/ROM SK6 ....114 C5
RAD M26 ....54 E4
Crompton Pl BOL BL1 * 2 F5
RAD M26 ....54 E1
Crompton St AUL OL6 ....76 B8
BOL BL1 ....3 G3
BURY BL9 ....4 E4
CHAD OL9 ....8 C5
FWTH BL4 ....53 H5
OLD OL1 ....9 L5
ROY/SHW OL2 ....43 L5
ROY/SHW OL2 * 59 H1
SWIN M27 ....70 B4
WALK M28 ....69 J2
WGN WN1 ....15 G3
WGNE/HIN WN2 ....48 E8
WGNS/IIMK WN3 ....64 C1
Crompton V BOLE BL2 ....37 G4
Crompton Wy BOLE BL2 ....3 M2
GOL/RIS/CUL WA3 ....80 A4
ROY/SHW OL2 ....43 L6
Cromwell Av CHD/CHDH SK8 ....110 D6
MPL/ROM SK6 ....113 M5
OLDTF/WHR M16 ....97 M2
RDSH SK5 ....100 D2
Cromwell Cl NEWLW WA12 ....78 D8
Cromwell Gv BNG/LEV M19 ....99 K3
BRO M7 ....71 M7
Cromwell Range
RUSH/FAL M14 ....99 G2
Cromwell Rd BRAM/HZG SK7 ....120 F6
ECC M30 ....84 F2
IRL M44 ....94 B5
MPL/ROM SK6 ....101 G6
PWCH M25 ....55 M8
ROY/SHW OL2 ....42 F6
SLFD M6 ....71 K8
STRET M32 ....97 H3
SWIN M27 ....70 B3
WHTF M45 ....55 G2
Cromwell St BOL BL1 ....2 C6
HEY OL10 ....41 G3
HTNM SK4 ....12 F1
OLD OL1 ....9 J7

Crossby Cl MDTN M24 ....57 J7
Cross Cliffe GLSP SK13 ....105 H4
Crosscliffe St OLDTF/WHR M16 ....87 J8
Crossdale Rd BKLY M9 ....56 E8
BOLE BL2 ....37 J4
Crossefield Rd CHD/CHDH SK8 ....120 C1
Crossen St BOLS/LL BL3 ....3 M9
Crossfell Av BKLY M9 ....56 F7
Cross Field Cl ROY/SHW OL2 ....43 M3
Crossfield Cl DTN/ASHW M34 ....101 K2
STLY SK15 ....91 K3
WHIT OL12 ....21 G5
Crossfield Dr RAD M26 ....54 B1
SWIN M27 ....70 B3
WALK M28 ....69 J5
WGNE/HIN WN2 ....65 M1
Crossfield Gv MPL/ROM SK6 ....114 C3
OFTN SK2 ....112 E8
Crossfield Pl ROCH OL11 ....11 G9
Crossfield Rd ECC M30 ....83 M8
HALE/TIMP WA15 ....117 K2
WHIT OL12 ....21 G5
WILM/AE SK9 ....119 M8
Crossfields EDGW/EG BL7 ....22 E4
Crossford Br SALE M33 ....96 F5
Crossford Cl BURY BL9 ....39 J8
Crossford Ct SALE M33 * 96 E6
Crossford Dr BOLS/LL BL3 ....35 H7
Crossford Dr STRET M32 ....97 G3
Crossgate Av WYTH/NTH M22 ....110 A6
Crossgate La GLSP SK13 ....93 J5
Crossgates Rd MILN OL16 ....29 J5
Crossgill TYLD M29 ....67 L7
Cross Glebe St AUL OL6 * 90 F1
Cross Gv HALE/TIMP WA15 ....108 C4
Crosshill St OLDTF/WHR M16 ....87 J8
Cross Keys St ANC M4 ....7 J2
Cross Knowle Vw URM M41 ....84 D8
Crossland Rd CCHDY M21 ....97 K4
DROY M43 ....89 K2
Crosslands PWCH M25 ....71 K1
Crosslands Rd WALK M28 ....68 C6
Cross La DROY M43 ....75 C8
GTN M18 ....89 C7
MPL/ROM SK6 ....114 B7
ORD M5 ....86 D3
RAD M26 ....38 F8
TOT/BURYW BL8 ....18 D7
WGNW/BIL/OR WN5 ....62 A1
WILM/AE SK9 ....127 K4
Cross La East PART M31 ....106 C1
Cross La West PART M31 ....106 B2
Crosslee Rd BKLY M9 ....57 H7
Cross Lees WHIT OL12 ....28 D1
Crossley Ct ANC M4 ....88 A3
Crossley Crs AUL OL6 ....76 B6
Crossley Rd BNG/LEV M19 ....99 K5
SALE M33 ....96 D6
Crossley St BOLS/LL BL3 ....37 K8
GTN M18 ....88 E6
MILN OL16 ....29 H6
ROY/SHW OL2 ....43 M5
ROY/SHW OL2 ....59 H2
STLY SK15 ....91 J2
Crossmead Dr BKLY M9 ....57 H7
Crossmeadow Cl ROCH OL11 ....27 K4
Crossmoor Crs MPL/ROM SK6 ....113 M2
Crossmoor Dr BOLE BL2 ....3 K2
Crossmoor Gv MPL/ROM SK6 ....113 M2
Cross Ormrod St BOLS/LL BL3 ....2 B7
Cross Ri GLSP SK13 ....105 H4
Cross Rd CCHDY M21 ....97 L5
CHD/CHDH SK8 ....119 K5
Cross St ALT WA14 ....108 A8
ATH M46 ....50 E8
AUL OL6 ....76 A7
AUL OL6 ....90 D2
BOL BL1 ....2 D2
BOLS/LL BL3 ....53 L1
BURY BL9 ....4 F4
CMANW M2 ....6 D3
CSLFD M3 ....6 D3
DTN/ASHW M34 ....90 B7
EDGW/EG BL7 ....22 C5
FWTH BL4 ....53 G3
FWTH BL4 ....53 L7
GLSP SK13 ....93 K7
GOL/RIS/CUL WA3 ....79 K5
HEY OL10 ....41 H3
HYDE SK14 ....93 G8
HYDE SK14 ....102 A2
LEIGH WN7 ....66 D8
MDTN M24 ....57 J4
MILN OL16 ....29 G5
MOSL OL5 * 76 F2
NM/HAY SK22 * 124 E4
OLDE OL4 ....59 L5
OLDE OL4 ....60 D6
OLDTF/WHR M16 ....87 G7
RAMS BL0 ....18 F6
ROCH OL11 ....41 M2
SALE M33 ....96 F7
STLY SK15 ....77 G8
STRET M32 ....97 G2
SWIN M27 ....70 B3
TYLD M29 ....67 J4
URM M41 ....95 M3
WALK M28 ....69 J2
WGNE/HIN WN2 ....49 G7
WGNNW/ST WN6 ....31 M3
WGNS/IIMK WN3 ....14 F6
WGNS/IIMK WN3 ....48 B3
WGNW/BIL/OR WN5 * 46 E6
WHTF M45 ....55 H2
The Cross GLSP SK13 ....93 K7
TOT/BURYW BL8 * 24 C6
Crosswaite Rd OFTN SK2 ....113 G6
Crossway BRAM/HZG SK7 ....121 G7
DID/WITH M20 ....110 E1
DROY M43 ....89 K3
OFTN SK2 ....112 D8
Crossway Cl AIMK WN4 ....64 E3
Crossways OLDS OL8 ....75 K3
Croston Cl WILM/AE SK9 ....130 E5
Croston Close Rd BURY BL9 ....25 L2
Crostons Rd TOT/BURYW BL8 ....4 B3
Croston St BOLS/LL BL3 ....35 M8
WGNE/HIN WN2 ....48 B1
Croston Wk OP/CLY M11 ....88 B3
Croton St HTNM SK4 ....111 H2
Croughton Cl OP/CLY M11 * 89 G5
Crowborough Cl HOR/BR BL6 ....34 C3
Crowborough Wk HULME M15 ....6 C9
Crowcroft Rd BRUN/LGST M13 ....99 K2
Crowden Dr GLSP SK13 ....93 K7
Crowden Rd NEWH/MOS M40 ....73 L2
Crow Hl STLY SK15 ....77 H7
Crow Hl North MDTN M24 ....57 J6

Crowhill Rd AULW OL7 ....75 J8
Crow Hl South MDTN M24 ....57 J6
Crow Hill Vw OLDE OL4 ....60 C8
Crowhurst Dr WGN WN1 ....47 L1
Crowland Gdns
CHD/CHDH SK8 ....120 D6
Crowland Rd BOLE BL2 ....36 F2
NTHM/RTH M23 ....118 D1
Crow La RAMS BL0 ....18 F6
Crow La East NEWLW WA12 ....78 E8
Crow La West NEWLW WA12 ....78 D8
Crowley La OLDE OL4 ....60 A3
Crowley Rd BKLY M9 ....73 J4
HALE/TIMP WA15 ....108 E6
Crown Ct BRAM/HZG SK7 ....121 M1
Crowndale EDGW/EG BL7 ....17 G5
Crowneast St ROCH OL11 ....27 M5
Crown Fields Cl NEWLW WA12 ....78 E7
Crown Gdns EDGW/EG BL7 ....17 G6
MILN OL16 ....11 H9
NEWLW WA12 ....78 E8
Crowngreen Rd ECC M30 ....85 H3
Crown Gv LEIGH WN7 ....67 G6
Crown Hl MOSL OL5 ....77 G4
Crownhill Dr DROY M43 ....89 K2
Crown La ANC M4 ....7 H1
HOR/BR BL6 ....33 J1
Crown Park Dr
NEWLW WA12 ....78 E8
Crown Passages
HALE/TIMP WA15 ....117 G2
Crown Point Av
NEWH/MOS M40 * 73 M7
Crown Rd HEY OL10 ....40 E2
Crown Sq CSLFD M3 ....6 D5
Crown St ATH M46 ....66 F1
AUL OL6 ....90 E2
BOL BL1 ....2 C1
CSLFD M3 ....6 D5
DTN/ASHW M34 ....90 B8
FAIL M35 ....74 C4
HULME M15 ....6 C8
MILN OL16 ....11 J9
MPL/ROM SK6 ....101 G8
NEWH/MOS M40 ....73 M7
ROY/SHW OL2 ....43 L5
WGNE/HIN WN2 ....48 F6
WGNS/IIMK WN3 ....14 E7
Crowther Av ORD M5 ....86 D4
Crowther Dr GTN M18 ....89 G3
LIT OL15 ....21 J8
MILN OL16 ....28 E8
Crowthorn Dr NTHM/RTH M23 ....118 D2
Crowthorn Rd AULW OL7 ....90 C3
EDGW/EG BL7 ....17 J3
HTNM SK4 ....100 A5
Crowton Av SALE M33 ....108 A3
Crow Trees La EDGW/EG BL7 ....16 F5
Crow Wood Rd
GOL/RIS/CUL WA3 ....80 A3
Croxdale Cl AULW OL7 ....75 J7
Croxton Av MILN OL16 ....11 L3
Croxton Cl MPL/ROM SK6 ....114 D7
SALE M33 ....108 A2
Croyde Cl BOLE BL2 ....37 J2
WYTH/NTH M22 ....119 H5
Croydon Av LEIGH WN7 ....66 C4
ROCH OL11 ....42 A5
ROY/SHW OL2 ....42 F6
Croydon Dr NEWH/MOS M40 ....73 M8
Croydon Sq ROCH OL11 ....42 A4
Crummock Cl BOLS/LL BL3 ....53 J1
Crummock Dr MDTN M24 ....57 H1
WGNS/IIMK WN3 ....63 J1
Crummock Rd
CHD/CHDH SK8 ....119 K1
FWTH BL4 ....52 B5
Crumpsall La CHH M8 ....72 C2
Crumpsall St BOL BL1 ....36 B2
Crumpsall V CHH M8 ....72 E2
Crumpsall Wy CHH M8 ....72 E3
Crundale Rd BOL BL1 ....35 L4
Cruttenden Rd OFTN SK2 ....112 F8
Cryer St DROY M43 ....89 K1
Crystal Cl WGNE/HIN WN2 ....64 D1
Cubley Rd BRO M7 ....72 B4
Cuckoo Gv PWCH M25 ....55 L6
Cuckoo La BURY BL9 ....39 M2
PWCH M25 ....55 L6
Cuddington Av
DID/WITH M20 ....98 D4
Cuddington Crs
EDGY/DAV SK3 ....112 A6
Cudworth Rd BKLY M9 ....56 D7
Culand St WGTN/LGST M12 ....88 B6
Culbert Av DID/WITH M20 ....110 F1
Culcheth Av MPL/ROM SK6 ....114 C6
Culcheth Av WGNE/HIN WN2 ....64 B8
Culcheth Hall Dr
GOL/RIS/CUL WA3 ....81 J8
Culcheth La
NEWH/MOS M40 ....73 M8
Culcheth Rd ALT WA14 ....116 F1
Culcross Av WGNS/IIMK WN3 ....46 F8
Culford Cl WGTN/LGST M12 ....88 B7
Culham Cl BOL BL1 * 36 A2
Cullen Cl WGNE/HIN WN2 ....48 D4
Cullen Gv BKLY M9 ....73 H1
Cullercoats Wk
WGTN/LGST M12 * 99 L1
Culmere Rd WYTH/NTH M22 ....118 F5
Culraven WGNE/HIN WN2 * 32 E5
Culross Av BOLS/LL BL3 ....35 H6
NEWH/MOS M40 ....74 B3
Culvercliff Wk CSLFD M3 ....6 C6
Culver Rd EDGY/DAV SK3 ....112 A7
Culvert St MILN OL16 ....29 G6
OLDE OL4 ....60 B3
WGNNW/ST WN6 ....31 K2
Culverwell Dr ORD M5 ....86 E2
Cumber Cl WILM/AE SK9 ....126 B8
Cumber Dr WILM/AE SK9 ....126 B8
Cumberland Av DUK SK16 ....91 H4
HEY OL10 ....40 D2
RDSH SK5 ....100 D3
SWIN M27 ....70 C2
TYLD M29 ....67 G2
Cumberland Cl BURY BL9 ....39 H6
OLD OL1 ....59 G3
Cumberland Dr ALT WA14 ....116 C4
Cumberland Gv AULW OL7 ....75 L8

Cumberland Rd ATH M46 ....51 H8
BKLY M9 * 73 G3
PART M31 ....106 A2
ROCH OL11 ....42 C2
SALE M33 ....108 F2
URM M41 ....95 M3
Cumberland St BRO M7 ....72 A8
STLY SK15 ....91 J2
WGN WN1 ....15 K1
Cumber La WILM/AE SK9 ....126 B8
Cumbrae Gdns ORD M5 ....86 B3
Cumbrae Rd BNG/LEV M19 ....99 M3
Cumbrian Cl BRUN/LGST M13 * 87 M6
ROY/SHW OL2 ....43 J4
WGNE/HIN WN2 ....64 E2
Cumbria Wk SLFD M6 ....71 L8
Cummings St OLDS OL8 ....74 F2
Cunard Cl BRUN/LGST M13 ....87 M6
Cuncliffe Dr ROY/SHW OL2 ....44 A5
Cundey St BOL BL1 * 35 M3
Cundiff Rd CCHDY M21 ....97 L6
Cundy St HYDE SK14 ....91 H8
Cunliffe Av NEWLW WA12 ....78 E7
RAMS BL0 ....18 D8
Cunliffe Brow BOL BL1 ....35 L3
Cunliffe Ct LEIGH WN7 ....65 K8
Cunliffe Dr SALE M33 ....108 F1
Cunliffe St EDGY/DAV SK3 ....12 D6
HYDE SK14 ....90 F8
LEIGH WN7 ....65 M7
RAMS BL0 ....18 F5
Cunningham Dr BURY BL9 ....55 L3
WYTH/NTH M22 ....119 J4
Cunningham Rd WHTN BL5 ....49 M5
Cunningham Wy OLD OL1 ....9 J2
Curate St STKP SK1 ....13 M5
Curlew Cl GOL/RIS/CUL WA3 ....80 A4
ROCH OL11 ....27 J5
Curlew Dr IRL M44 ....94 B2
Curlew Rd OLDE OL4 ....60 B8
Curlew Wy GLSP SK13 ....104 C3
Currier La AUL OL6 ....90 F2
Curtels Cl WALK M28 ....69 M5
Curtis Gv GLSP SK13 ....93 K7
Curtis Rd BNG/LEV M19 ....99 M3
HTNM SK4 ....111 K2
Curtis St BOLS/LL BL3 ....51 M2
WGNW/BIL/OR WN5 ....47 G6
Curzon Av RUSH/FAL M14 ....88 B3
Curzon Cl ROCH OL11 ....42 C2
Curzon Dr HALE/TIMP WA15 ....108 E6
Curzon Gn OFTN SK2 ....113 G4
Curzon Ms WILM/AE SK9 ....126 E6
Curzon Rd AUL OL6 ....75 M8
BOL BL1 ....35 M5
BRO M7 ....72 A5
CHD/CHDH SK8 ....119 K5
OFTN SK2 ....113 G5
POY/DIS SK12 ....129 J2
ROCH OL11 ....42 C2
SALE M33 ....96 E7
STRET M32 ....96 D1
Curzon St MOSL OL5 ....76 F3
OLD OL1 ....9 J5
Cutacre Cl TYLD M29 ....67 L3
Cutacre La WHTN BL5 ....52 A6
Cutgate Cl NTHM/RTH M23 ....109 H3
Cutgate Rd WHIT OL12 ....27 L3
Cuthbert Av BNG/LEV M19 ....99 L2
Cuthbert Mayne Ct MILN OL16 ....10 D7
Cuthbert Rd CHD/CHDH SK8 ....111 H6
Cuthbert St BOLS/LL BL3 ....51 K2
WGNS/IIMK WN3 ....47 G6
Cutland St NEWH/MOS M40 ....73 K6
Cutland Wy LIT OL15 ....21 J3
Cut La WHIT OL12 ....27 J3
Cutler Hill Rd FAIL M35 ....74 F5
Cutnook La IRL M44 ....83 J7
Cutter Cl ORD M5 ....86 D4
Cycle St OP/CLY M11 ....88 E4
Cyclone St OP/CLY M11 ....88 C4
Cygnet St WGNS/IIMK WN3 ....14 E7
Cygnus Av BRO M7 ....86 F1
Cymbal Ct RDSH SK5 ....112 B1
Cynthia Dr MPL/ROM SK6 ....114 C7
Cypress Av CHAD OL9 ....8 A3
Cypress Cl EDGY/DAV SK3 ....12 C6
Cypress Gdns MILN OL16 ....29 G5
Cypress Gv DTN/ASHW M34 ....101 K1
FWTH BL4 * 53 J5
Cypress Oaks STLY SK15 ....92 A1
Cypress Rd DROY M43 ....89 K1
ECC M30 ....69 K8
OLDE OL4 ....60 A4
WGNW/BIL/OR WN5 ....47 H6
Cypress St MDTN M24 ....57 M4
Cypress Wy MPL/ROM SK6 ....123 J1
Cyprus Cl OLDE OL4 ....60 A7
ORD M5 ....86 C3
Cyprus St STRET M32 ....97 G2
Cyril St ROY/SHW OL2 ....43 M5
RUSH/FAL M14 ....98 E1
Cyrus St NEWH/MOS M40 ....88 B2

D

Daccamill Dr SWIN M27 ....70 C6
Dacre Av OLDTF/WHR M16 ....97 L2
Dacre Cl MDTN M24 ....56 E3
Dacre Rd ROCH OL11 ....42 D8
Dacres Av UPML OL3 ....61 J8
Dacres Dr UPML OL3 ....61 J8
Dacres Rd UPML OL3 ....61 J8
Daffodil Cl WHIT OL12 ....28 B1
Daffodil Rd FWTH BL4 ....52 D3
Daffodil St BOL BL1 ....22 C7
Dagenham Rd RUSH/FAL M14 * 98 F1
Dagmar St WALK M28 ....52 F8
Dagnall Av CCHDY M21 ....97 L6
Dahlia Cl BNG/LEV M19 ....99 J6
WHIT OL12 ....28 A1
Daimler St CHH M8 ....72 D6
Dain Cl DUK SK16 ....91 L3
Daine Av NTHM/RTH M23 ....109 L3
Dainton St WGTN/LGST M12 ....88 A5
Daintry Cl HULME M15 ....87 J6
Daintry Rd CHAD OL9 ....8 A5
Dairydale Cl IRL M44 ....94 E1
Dairyground Rd
BRAM/HZG SK7 ....121 C5
Dairyhouse La ALT WA14 ....107 L3
Dairy House La
BRAM/HZG SK7 ....127 M1
Dairy House Rd
BRAM/HZG SK7 ....120 D7
Dairy St CHAD OL9 ....8 A5
Daisy Av BRUN/LGST M13 ....88 B3
FWTH BL4 ....52 D3
Daisy Bank NEWH/MOS M40 ....73 M7
Daisy Bank Av SWIN M27 ....70 F6

Daisybank Cl WGNE/HIN WN2.....49 G7
Daisy Bank La CHD/CHDH SK8...119 J3
Daisy Bank Rd RUSH/FAL M14....88 B8
Daisyfield HOR/BR BL6 *.........34 A3
Daisyfield Cl WYTH/NTH M22....118 E3
Daisyfield Ct TOT/BURYW BL8....38 F3
Daisy Hall Dr WHTN BL5..........50 B7
Daisyhill Cl WHTN BL5...........50 C7
Daisyhill Ct WHTN BL5...........50 C7
Daisy Ms EDGY/DAV SK3..........112 A8
Daisy Rd WGNW/BIL/OR WN5.......47 H6
Daisy St BOLS/LL BL3............35 M8
  CHAD OL9......................8 E4
  CHAD OL9.....................58 D4
  OFTN SK2.....................13 K9
  TOT/BURYW BL8.................4 A5
  WHIT OL12....................10 C3
Daisy Wy MPL/ROM SK6..........123 H5
Dakerwood Cl
  NEWH/MOS M40.................73 M7
Dakins Rd LEIGH WN7............81 L2
Dakley St OP/CLY M11...........88 F5
Dakota Av SALQ M50.............86 B4
Dakota South SALQ M50..........86 C4
Dalbeatie Ri WGN WN1...........15 M1
Dalbeattie St BKLY M9..........73 H4
Dalberg St WGTN/LGST M12.......88 B8
Dalbury Dr NEWH/MOS M40........72 F7
Dalby Av SWIN M27..............70 B5
Dalby Gv STKP SK1..............13 M4
Dalby Rd WGNE/HIN WN2..........49 L7
Dale Av BRAM/HZG SK7..........121 H4
  ECC M30......................84 F1
  MOSL OL5.....................77 H1
Dalebank ATH M46...............50 F7
Dalebank Ms SWIN M27...........54 A7
Dalebeck Cl WHTF M45...........55 L4
Dale Brook Av DUK SK16.........91 G6
Dalebrook Ct HTNM SK4..........12 D4
Dalebrook Rd SALE M33.........108 F3
Dalecrest WGNW/BIL/OR WN5......62 A3
Daleford Sq BRUN/LGST M13 *.....7 K9
Dalegarth Av BOL BL1...........34 F5
Dale Gv AULW OL7...............75 K7
  HALE/TIMP WA15..............108 C5
  IRL M44......................94 B6
  LEIGH WN7....................81 M1
Dalehead Dr ROY/SHW OL2........44 A5
Dalehead Gv LEIGH WN7..........65 M8
Dale La UPML OL3...............45 J7
Dale Lee WHTN BL5..............50 D4
Dale Rd GOL/RIS/CUL WA3........79 K5
  MDTN M24.....................57 L2
  MPL/ROM SK6.................114 B5
  NM/HAY SK22.................124 E5
Dales Av CHH M8................72 C2
  WHTF M45.....................55 G3
Dalesbrook Cl BOLS/LL BL3......37 K8
Dales Brow BOL BL1.............22 C6
  SWIN M27 *...................70 A6
Dales Brow Av AULW OL7.........75 L7
Dalesfield Crs MOSL OL5........77 H3
Dalesford Cl LEIGH WN7.........80 F4
Dales Gv WALK M28..............69 J3
Daleside Av AIMK WN4...........63 K4
Dales La WHTF M45..............55 H3
Dalesman Cl BKLY M9............73 J1
Dalesman Dr OLD OL1............60 A1
Dalesman Wk HULME M15 *........87 J6
Dales Park Dr SWIN M27 *.......70 A6
Dale St AUL OL6................76 D6
  CMANE M1......................7 J4
  EDGY/DAV SK3.................12 E9
  FWTH BL4.....................53 H3
  LEIGH WN7....................65 M7
  MDTN M24.....................57 L5
  MILN OL16....................11 L4
  MILN OL16....................29 J6
  RAD M26......................18 F4
  RAMS BL0.....................18 D8
  ROY/SHW OL2..................43 L6
  STLY SK15....................91 J3
  SWIN M27.....................70 B6
  TOT/BURYW BL8................24 F8
  WGNS/IIMK WN3................64 C1
  WHTF M45.....................55 H3
  WHTN BL5.....................50 C7
Dale St East AUL OL6...........90 D2
  HOR/BR BL6...................34 A3
Dale St West AUL OL6...........90 D2
  HOR/BR BL6...................34 A3
Daleswood Av WHTF M45..........55 G3
Dale Vw DTN/ASHW M34..........101 K5
  HYDE SK14...................102 A4
  LIT OL15.....................29 J2
  NEWLW WA12...................79 H8
Dalham Av BKLY M9..............73 K2
Dalkeith Gv BOLS/LL BL3........35 J7
Dalkeith Rd RDSH SK5..........100 C5
  WGNE/HIN WN2.................49 K7
Dalkeith St GTN M18............88 E6
Dallas Ct SALQ M50.............86 B4
Dalley Av BRO M7...............72 A8
Dallimore Rd NTHM/RTH M23....109 H6
Dalmahoy Cl NEWH/MOS M40.......73 M4
Dalmain Cl CHH M8..............72 C6
Dalmeny Ter ROCH OL11..........28 C8
Dalmorton Rd CCHDY M21.........98 A4
Dalny St BNG/LEV M19...........99 L3
Dalston Av FAIL M35............74 E4
Dalston Dr BRAM/HZG SK7.......120 E7
  DID/WITH M20................110 F2
Dalston Gv WGNS/IIMK WN3.......63 G1
Dalton Av MILN OL16............29 G5
  RUSH/FAL M14.................98 D2
  STRET M32....................85 J3
  WHTF M45.....................55 J2
Dalton Cl MILN OL16............29 K5
  RAMS BL0.....................18 D8
  WGNW/BIL/OR WN5..............46 E5
Dalton Fold WHTN BL5...........50 C7
Dalton Gdns URM M41............95 L1
Dalton Gv AIMK WN4.............63 K3
  HTNM SK4.....................99 M8
Dalton St ANC M4...............7 J2
  CHAD OL9......................8 A4
  ECC M30......................85 G1
  FAIL M35.....................74 B4
  OLD OL1.......................9 M2
  SALE M33.....................96 F6
  TOT/BURYW BL8................38 E2
Daltry St OLD OL1..............9 M2
Dalveen Av URM M41.............84 C5
Dalveen Dr HALE/TIMP WA15....108 C5
Dalwood Cl WGNE/HIN WN2........49 J7
Dalymount Cl BOLE BL2..........36 E2

Damask Av CSLFD M3..............6 A2
Dame Hollow CHD/CHDH SK8.....119 M5
Dameral Cl CHH M8..............72 D6
Damery Ct BRAM/HZG SK7.......121 G4
Damery Rd BRAM/HZG SK7.......121 G4
Dam St OL9......................8 E2
Dam Head Dr BKLY M9............73 H1
Damian Dr NEWLW WA12...........78 D7
Damien St BNG/LEV M19..........99 L2
Dam La AIMK WN4................79 J1
Dams Head Fold WHTN BL5........50 C3
Damson Gn MDTN M24.............57 M4
Dam Bank MPL/ROM SK6.........113 M6
Danby Cl HYDE SK14.............91 J8
Danby St OLD OL1...............9 G2
Danby Pl HYDE SK14.............91 J8
Danby Rd BOLS/LL BL3...........52 B1
  HYDE SK14....................91 J8
Dane Av EDGY/DAV SK3..........111 K4
  PART M31.....................94 C8
Dane Bank Dr POY/DIS SK12....123 M6
Danebank Ms DTN/ASHW M34.....100 E3
Danebank Wk BRUN/LGST M13 *.....7 K9
Dane Cl BRAM/HZG SK7.........120 F2
Danebury Cl WGNE/HIN WN2.......49 G8
Dane Cl BRAM/HZG SK7.........120 F2
Danecroft Cl BRUN/LGST M13....88 A7
Dane Dr WILM/AE SK9...........127 H6
Danefield Cl CHD/CHDH SK8....119 M4
Danefield Rd SALE M33..........96 F6
Dane Hill Cl POY/DIS SK12....123 M7
Daneholme Rd BNG/LEV M19.......99 H1
Dane Ms SALE M33 *.............96 E6
Dane Rd DTN/ASHW M34.........100 D3
  SALE M33.....................96 F6
Danes Av WGNE/HIN WN2..........49 H6
Danes Brook Cl
  WGNE/HIN WN2.................49 H6
Danesbury Cl
  WGNW/BIL/OR WN5..............62 B8
Danesbury Ri BOLE BL2..........22 E8
Danes Gv WGNE/HIN WN2..........49 H5
Daneshill PWCH M25.............55 L6
Danesmoor Dr BURY BL9..........25 K8
Danesmoor Rd DID/WITH M20....110 A3
Danes Rd RUSH/FAL M14..........99 G2
Dane St BOLS/LL BL3 *..........35 M8
  OLDE OL4.....................59 M5
  OP/CLY M11...................89 H5
  WHIT OL12....................10 C5
Danesway PWCH M25..............72 A2
  SWIN M27.....................70 F6
  WGN WN1......................47 L1
Danesway Ct BOL BL1............36 A2
Daneswood Av BKLY M9 *.........57 J8
  WHIT OL12....................20 A5
Danett Cl WGTN/LGST M12........88 D6
Danforth Gv BNG/LEV M19........99 L4
Daniel Adamson Av PART M31...106 A1
Daniel Adamson Rd SALQ M50....86 A4
Daniel Fold WHIT OL12..........27 L2
Daniel's La STKP SK1...........13 J7
Daniel St BRAM/HZG SK7.......122 A2
  HEY OL10.....................40 E2
  OLD OL1......................59 M4
  ROY/SHW OL2..................59 K1
  WHIT OL12....................20 B3
Danisher La OLDS OL8...........75 J4
Dannywood Cl HYDE SK14.......101 M4
Danson St NEWH/MOS M40.........88 B1
Dantall Av BKLY M9.............73 K2
Dante Cl ECC M30...............70 D8
Danty St DUK SK16..............90 E3
Dantzic St ANC M4..............7 G3
  ANC M4......................87 L1
Danwood Cl DTN/ASHW M34......101 L3
Darbishire St BOL BL1...........3 G4
Darby La WGNE/HIN WN2..........49 M4
Darby Rd IRL M44...............94 D6
Darbyshire Cl BOL BL1..........35 M4
Darbyshire St RAD M26..........54 D7
Darcy St BOLE BL2...............3 L8
Darden Cl HTNM SK4............111 H1
Darell Wk CHH M8...............72 E6
Daresbury Av URM M41...........84 A8
Daresbury Cl EDGY/DAV SK3....112 A7
  SALE M33....................109 J1
Daresbury Rd CCHDY M21.........97 J3
Daresbury St CHH M8............72 D5
Dargai St OP/CLY M11...........89 G3
Dargle Rd SALE M33.............96 E6
Darian Av WYTH/NTH M22.......118 F4
Daric Cl LEIGH WN7.............80 F3
Dark La HOR/BR BL6.............32 E1
  MOSL OL5.....................77 G3
  MPL/ROM SK6.................113 G1
  UPML OL3.....................45 H6
  UPML OL3.....................61 K4
  WGTN/LGST M12................88 A4
Darley Av CCHDY M21...........110 E7
  CHD/CHDH SK8................110 B8
  DID/WITH M20.................98 B8
  ECC M30......................84 F4
  FWTH BL4.....................53 H3
Darley Gv FWTH BL4.............53 H3
Darley Rd BRAM/HZG SK7.......122 B5
  OLDTF/WHR M16................97 M1
  ROCH OL11....................28 C8
  WGNS/IIMK WN3................63 L1
Darley St BOL BL1..............36 A3
  FWTH BL4.....................53 H4
  OP/CLY M11...................88 B3
  SALE M33.....................96 E6
  STRET M32....................86 B8
Darley Ter BOL BL1 *...........36 A3
Darlington Rd DID/WITH M20....98 D6
  ROCH OL11....................42 C1
Darlington St TYLD M29.........67 K3
Darlington St East TYLD M29...67 L3
  WGN WN1......................15 J5
Darliston Av BKLY M9...........56 D7
Darnall Av DID/WITH M20........98 D4
Darnborough Dr WYTH/NTH M22..118 D3
Darnhall St WGNS/IIMK WN3 *....48 C5
Darnley Av WALK M28............68 F3
Darnley St OLDTF/WHR M16.......87 G3
Darnton Rd AUL OL6.............91 H1
Darran Av WGNS/IIMK WN3........63 J1
Darras Rd GTN M18..............99 M1
Dart Cl CHAD OL9...............58 C4
Dartford Av ECC M30............84 E4
  RDSH SK5....................100 E6
Dartford Cl WGTN/LGST M12......88 A6
Dartford Rd URM M41............95 M3
Dartington Cl BRAM/HZG SK7...121 G1
  NTHM/RTH M23................109 G6

Dartington Rd WGNE/HIN WN2.....64 C2
Dartmouth Cl OLDS OL8..........59 J8
Dartmouth Crs RDSH SK5........100 F7
Dartmouth Rd CCHDY M21.........97 M4
  WHTF M45.....................55 K5
Dartnall Cl POY/DIS SK12.....123 J8
Darton Av NEWH/MOS M40.........88 B1
Darvel Av AIMK WN4.............62 F8
Darvel Cl BOLE BL2.............37 J6
Darwell Av ECC M30.............84 F4
Darwen Rd EDGW/EG BL7..........22 C4
Darwen St OLDTF/WHR M16........86 F2
Darwin Gv BRAM/HZG SK7.......121 G6
Darwin St AULW OL7.............90 D2
  BOL BL1......................36 A2
  HYDE SK14....................91 K6
  OLDE OL4.....................59 M7
Dashwood Rd PWCH M25...........55 J7
Datchett Ter ROCH OL11.........28 C8
Dauntesy Av SWIN M27...........71 C5
Davehall Av WILM/AE SK9.......126 E5
Davenfield Gv DID/WITH M20....110 E1
Davenfield Rd DID/WITH M20....110 E1
Davenham Rd RDSH SK5..........100 C2
  SALE M33.....................96 B6
  WILM/AE SK9.................119 M8
Davenhill Rd BNG/LEV M19.......99 K4
Davenport Av DID/WITH M20......98 E5
  WILM/AE SK9.................126 C8
Davenport Dr MPL/ROM SK6.....101 L6
Davenport Fold Rd BOLE BL2 *...23 K8
Davenport Gdns BOL BL1 *.......2 D3
Davenport Park Rd OFTN SK2...112 D7
Davenport St BOL BL1............2 C3
  DROY M43.....................89 H3
  DTN/ASHW M34.................90 B4
  ROCH OL11....................42 C1
Daventry Rd CCHDY M21..........98 A4
Daveylands URM M41.............84 C7
  WILM/AE SK9.................127 H6
Davey La WILM/AE SK9..........130 D2
David Brow BOLS/LL BL3.........51 K2
David Cl DTN/ASHW M34.........101 K3
David Lewis Cl MILN OL16.......11 L6
David's Crs OLDE OL4...........60 C5
David's Farm Cl MDTN M24.......57 M5
Davids La OLDE OL4.............60 C5
Davidson Dr MDTN M24...........57 M6
David's Rd DROY M43............89 H2
David St DTN/ASHW M34.........101 K3
  RDSH SK5....................100 B4
  TOT/BURYW BL8................38 F1
  WHIT OL12....................28 C3
David St North WHIT OL12 *....28 C3
Davies Rd MPL/ROM SK6........113 G1
  NEWLW WA12...................78 F8
  PART M31....................106 D1
Davies Sq HULME M15 *..........87 K8
Davies St AULW OL7.............90 C3
  FWTH BL4.....................53 K5
  OLD OL1.......................8 D7
  WGNE/HIN WN2.................64 D2
Davy Av SWIN M27...............71 G2
Davy St NEWH/MOS M40...........72 E8
Davyhulme Rd STRET M32.........96 F1
  URM M41......................84 F1
Davyhulme Rd East STRET M32...97 G1
Davyhulme St WHIT OL12.........28 D3
Davy St NEWH/MOS M40...........72 E8
Dawber Delph
  WGNNW/ST WN6.................30 A4
Dawber St AIMK WN4.............64 A8
Dawley Cl AIMK WN4.............78 D1
Dawlish Av CHAD OL9............58 C3
  CHD/CHDH SK8................120 B4
  DROY M43.....................89 H2
  RDSH SK5....................100 F7
Dawlish Cl BRAM/HZG SK7.......121 G5
  HYDE SK14...................103 H1
Dawlish Rd CCHDY M21...........96 B7
  SALE M33.....................96 B5
Dawlish Wy GOL/RIS/CUL WA3....79 J3
Dawnay St OP/CLY M11 *.........88 E5
Dawn St ROY/SHW OL2............43 L6
Dawood Sq
  WGNW/BIL/OR WN5..............46 E7
Dawson Av WGNNW/ST WN6.........47 K1
Dawson La BOL BL1...............2 C4
  CHD/CHDH SK8................119 M4
Dawson St ATH M46 *............66 F1
  BURY BL9.....................25 K8
  CSLFD M3......................6 B7
  CSLFD M3 *....................6 A7
  HEY OL10.....................40 F2
  HYDE SK14...................102 B3
  OLDE OL4.....................60 B7
  STKP SK1....................112 E1
  SWIN M27.....................70 D4
Day Dr FAIL M35................74 C2
Day Gv HYDE SK14..............103 K1
Daylesford Cl CHD/CHDH SK8...110 B3
Daylesford Crs CHD/CHDH SK8..110 B3
Daylesford Rd CHD/CHDH SK8...111 G3
Deacon Cl ALT WA14............116 D3
Deacons Cl STKP SK1............13 L4
Deacons Dr SLFD M6.............71 G6
Deacon St MILN OL16............28 E3
Deakin St WGNS/IIMK WN3........15 K9
Deal Av RDSH SK5..............100 E6
Deal Cl NEWH/MOS M40...........74 A7
Dealey Rd BOLS/LL BL3..........35 K8
Deal St BOLS/LL BL3............52 C1
  BURY BL9......................5 K3
  CSLFD M3 *....................6 D3
  HYDE SK14...................102 B2
Deal Wk CHAD OL9...............58 D6
Dean Av NEWH/MOS M40...........73 L6
  OLDTF/WHR M16................97 L1
Deanbank Av BNG/LEV M19........99 J4
Dean Bank Dr MILN OL16.........29 J1
Dean Brook Cl NEWH/MOS M40....73 M5
Dean Cl FWTH BL4...............52 C4
  PART M31.....................94 C8
  RAMS BL0.....................19 G1
  WHTF M45.....................55 G5
  WILM/AE SK9.................127 G3
Dean Ct BOL BL1.................2 F5
  GOL/RIS/CUL WA3..............79 K5
  HULME M15 *..................87 K6
Deancourt ROCH OL11............28 B6
Dean Crs WGNW/BIL/OR WN5.......46 E7
Dean Dr ALT WA14..............116 D3
  WILM/AE SK9.................127 G3
Deane Av BOLS/LL BL3...........35 L7
  CHD/CHDH SK8................111 J4
  HALE/TIMP WA15..............115 M3
Deane Church La BOLS/LL BL3...35 L7
Deane Rd BOLS/LL BL3...........35 M7
Deanery Wy STKP SK1 *..........13 J3

Dean La BRAM/HZG SK7..........122 A4
Dean Meadow NEWLW WA12.........78 F8
Dean Moor Rd BRAM/HZG SK7....121 J2
Dean Rd CSLFD M3................6 D1
  GOL/RIS/CUL WA3.............79 K5
  GTN M18......................88 E6
  IRL M44......................94 B6
Dean Row Rd WILM/AE SK9......127 J1
Deanscourt Av SWIN M27.........70 B5
Deansgate BOL BL1...............2 E4
  HULME M15....................6 D9
  WGNE/HIN WN2.................49 H6
Deanshut Rd OLDS OL8...........75 K2
Dean's Rd SWIN M27.............70 B5
Dean St AUL OL6................90 D1
  CMANE M1......................7 K4
  FAIL M35.....................74 B4
  MILN OL16....................28 E3
  MOSL OL5.....................76 E3
  RAD M26......................54 C1
  STLY SK15....................91 K3
Deansway SWIN M27..............70 D2
Deanswood Dr BKLY M9...........56 D7
Dean Ter AUL OL6...............75 L3
Deanwater Ct
  CHD/CHDH SK8 *..............119 M5
  STRET M32....................96 F1
Deanway NEWH/MOS M40...........73 K4
  URM M41......................95 G2
  WILM/AE SK9.................127 G4
Dean Wood Av
  WGNW/BIL/OR WN5..............46 B3
Dearden Av LHULT M38...........52 D7
Dearden Clough RAMS BL0........19 H2
Dearden Fold RAMS BL0..........19 H2
  TOT/BURYW BL8................38 F3
Deardens St TOT/BURYW BL8.....38 F3
Dearden St BOLS/LL BL3.........87 K6
  HULME M15....................6 D9
  LIT OL15.....................21 M6
  STLY SK15....................91 K2
Dearmans Pl CSLFD M3............6 D3
Dearne Dr STRET M32............97 H2
Dearnley Cl LIT OL15...........21 K8
Debdale Av GTN M18.............89 J8
Debdale La GTN M18.............89 J8
  TYLD M29.....................67 G2
Deben Cl WGNNW/ST WN6..........31 G3
Debenham Av NEWH/MOS M40.......73 M4
Debenham Ct FWTH BL4...........53 C5
Debenham Rd STRET M32..........96 D3
De Brook Cl URM M41............95 H3
Dee Av HALE/TIMP WA15.........109 C7
Deepcar St BNG/LEV M19.........99 K2
Deepdale LEIGH WN7.............81 M1
  OLDE OL4.....................60 A6
Deepdale Av DID/WITH M20.......98 D4
  MILN OL16....................11 M7
  ROY/SHW OL2..................42 F4
Deepdale Dr SWIN M27...........71 G5
Deepdale Rd BRUN/LGST M13 *....7 K9
Deeping Av OLDTF/WHR M16.......98 A2
Deeplish La BURY BL9...........25 H3
Deeplish Rd ROCH OL11..........10 F8
Deeplish St ROCH OL11..........10 F8
Deeracre Av OFTN SK2..........112 F6
Deerfold Cl GTN M18............89 G7
Deerhurst Dr CHH M8............72 C6
Dee Rd TYLD M29................67 G2
Deeroak Cl GTN M18.............88 E6
Deerpark Rd OLDTF/WHR M16 *....98 A1
Deerwood V HYDE SK14..........103 H3
Defence St BOLS/LL BL3..........2 B7
Defiance St ATH M46............66 F1
Degas Cl BRO M7................71 L4
Delacourt Rd RUSH/FAL M14.....98 D4
Delafield Av WCTN/LGST M12.....99 K2
Delaford Av WALK M28...........69 G2
Delaford Cl EDGY/DAV SK3.....112 B8
Delahays Dr HALE/TIMP WA15...117 J2
Delahays Range GTN M18.........89 J7
Delahays Rd HALE/TIMP WA15...117 H2
Delaine Rd DID/WITH M20........98 F6
Delamere Av GOL/RIS/CUL WA3...80 C6
  ROY/SHW OL2..................44 A7
  SALE M33....................109 H1
  SLFD M6......................70 F6
  STRET M32....................70 E2
  SWIN M27.....................70 E2
  WHTF M45.....................55 H4
Delamere Cl BRAM/HZG SK7.....122 C1
  MPL/ROM SK6................101 M7
  STLY SK15....................77 H6
Delamere Rd BNG/LEV M19........99 K4
  BRAM/HZG SK7...............122 C1
  CHD/CHDH SK8................110 E7
  DTN/ASHW M34................100 E2
  MILN OL16....................29 J3
  OFTN SK2....................112 E8
  URM M41......................95 J2
  WILM/AE SK9.................119 M8
Delamere St AUL OL6............90 E2
  BURY BL9.....................25 K7
  OLDS OL8.....................59 J8
  OP/CLY M11...................89 J5
Delamer Rd ALT WA14...........116 C1
Delaunays Rd CHH M8............72 C2
  SALE M33.....................96 C8
Delbooth Av URM M41............84 A8
Delegarte St WGNS/IIMK WN3.....15 M3
Delfhaven Ct WGNNW/ST WN6......31 K5
Delfur Rd BRAM/HZG SK7.......121 H5
Dell Rd IRL M44................94 A4 (?)
  WHIT OL12....................27 M3
Dellar St WHIT OL12............27 M3
Dell Av SWIN M27...............47 H1
Dell Cl OLDE OL4...............60 C5
Dellcot Cl PWCH M25............72 A2
  SLFD M6......................70 E7
Dellcot La WALK M28............69 J7
Dellhide Cl OLDE OL4...........60 D6
Dell Meadow WHIT OL12..........27 M1
Dell Side WHIT OL12............27 M2
Dell Side Wy WHIT OL12.........27 M2
The Dell BOLE BL2..............22 A5
Dellside MPL/ROM SK6..........123 G2 (?)
Dellside Av AIMK WN4...........63 G6
Dell St BOL BL1................3 H3
Delph Brook Wy EDGW/EG BL7....22 A2

Delph Gv LEIGH WN7.............66 A3
Delph Hi BOL BL1...............35 H2
Delph Hill Cl BOL BL1..........35 H2
Delphi Av WALK M28.............69 G2
Delph La BOLE BL2..............37 M3
  UPML OL3.....................45 J7
Delph New Rd UPML OL3..........45 J3
Delph Rd UPML OL3..............44 F5
Delphside Cl
  WGNW/BIL/OR WN5..............46 A7
Delph St BOLS/LL BL3............2 B9
  MILN OL16....................29 J6
  WGNNW/ST WN6.................14 D1
The Delph WALK M28.............69 J6
Delside Av NEWH/MOS M40........73 K4
Delta Cl ROY/SHW OL2...........59 G2
Delta Rd DTN/ASHW M34..........90 B3
Delves Rd ALT WA14............108 A4
Delvino Wk RUSH/FAL M14........87 K3
Delwood Gdns
  WYTH/NTH M22...............110 A8
De-massey Cl MPL/ROM SK6 *...101 L6
Demesne Crs STLY SK15..........91 M3
Demesne Dr STLY SK15...........91 M3
Demesne Rd OLDTF/WHR M16.......98 B2
Demmings Rd CHD/CHDH SK8.....111 J7
Dempsey Dr BURY BL9............55 L2
Denbigh Cl BRAM/HZG SK7......121 G4
Denbigh Dr ROY/SHW OL2.........43 J6
Denbigh Gv ATH M46.............50 F7
Denbigh Pl ORD M5..............86 D3
Denbigh Rd BOLE BL2.............3 J8
  DTN/ASHW M34.................90 J3
  SWIN M27.....................70 D2
Denbigh St HTNM SK4............12 F1
  OLDS OL8.....................75 J1
Denbury Wk HULME M15...........87 H7
Denbury Gn BRAM/HZG SK7......121 J3
Denbydale Wy ROY/SHW OL2.......42 F8
Denby La HTNM SK4.............100 A8
Denby Rd DUK SK16..............90 F5
Dene Av WILM/AE SK9...........127 ..
Dene Bank BOLE BL2.............22 F7
Dene Brow DTN/ASHW M34........101 L4
Dene Ct HTNM SK4...............12 C2
Dene Dr MDTN M24...............57 J5
Denefield Cl MPL/ROM SK6.....114 C3
Deneford Rd DID/WITH M20......110 D2
Dene Gv LEIGH WN7..............65 L8
Dene Hollow RDSH SK5..........100 D3
Denehurst St
  WGTN/LGST M12 *.............88 C6
Dene Pk DID/WITH M20..........110 D2
Dene Rd DID/WITH M20..........110 D2
Dene Rd West DID/WITH M20....110 D2
Deneside BRAM/HZG SK7.........122 B1
Denes St BOLE BL2..............22 F7
  LEIGH WN7....................65 L8
Denesway SALE M33.............120 E5
Deneway BRAM/HZG SK7..........120 E5
  HTNM SK4.....................12 C2
  MPL/ROM SK6................123 H5
Deneway Cl HTNM SK4............12 C3
Deneway Ms HTNM SK4............12 C3
Denewell Cl BRUN/LGST M13......88 A7
Denford Cl WGNS/IIMK WN3.......63 J1
Denham Cl BOL BL1..............22 D7
Denham Dr BRAM/HZG SK7.......120 F5
  IRL M44......................94 D3
  WGNS/IIMK WN3................63 K1
Denham St BRUN/LGST M13........88 A8
Denhill Rd HULME M15...........87 J8
Denholme Rd ROCH OL11.........28 C8
Denhurst Rd LIT OL15...........21 L6
Denis Av OLDTF/WHR M16.........98 B2
Denison Rd BRAM/HZG SK7......122 A4
  RUSH/FAL M14.................98 F1
Denison St RUSH/FAL M14........98 F1
Deniston Rd HTNM SK4...........99 J3
Den La OLDE OL4................60 C5
  UPML OL3.....................61 L4
Denmark Rd HULME M15...........87 K9
  SALE M33.....................96 E6
Denmark St ALT WA14...........108 A2
  CHAD OL9......................8 D2
  MILN OL16....................11 J7
  OLDE OL4.....................59 L5
Denmark Wy CHAD OL9.............8 D3
Denmore Rd NEWH/MOS M40........73 M2
Dennington Dr URM M41..........84 D8
Dennison Av DID/WITH M20.......98 D6
Dennison Rd CHD/CHDH SK8.....120 C4
Denshaw Cl BNG/LEV M19........111 H1
Denshaw Rd UPML OL3............44 F1
Densmead Wk NEWH/MOS M40 *.....7 M1
Denson Rd HALE/TIMP WA15.....108 E4
Denstone Av ECC M30............85 H1
  SALE M33....................108 B1
  URM M41......................95 M1
Denstone Crs BOLE BL2..........37 G2
Denstone Rd RDSH SK5..........100 C5
  SLFD M6......................70 F6
  URM M41......................95 M1
Dentdale Cl BOL BL1............35 G6
Denton Av WGNW/BIL/OR WN5.....46 E4
Denton Hall Farm Rd
  DTN/ASHW M34...............100 F2
Denton La CHAD OL9..............8 A7
Denton Rd BOLE BL2.............37 L6
  DTN/ASHW M34.................90 B7
Denton St BURY BL9..............4 F1
  HEY OL10.....................40 F3
  WHIT OL12....................10 E1
Denver Av NEWH/MOS M40.........88 A1
Denver Dr HALE/TIMP WA15.....108 C6
Denver Rd ROCH OL11............28 C8
Denville Crs WYTH/NTH M22....119 G1
Denzell Gdns ALT WA14 *.......116 C1
Depleach Rd CHD/CHDH SK8.....111 G7
Deptford Av NTHM/RTH M23.....108 A3
De Quincey Cl ALT WA14........108 A3
Deramore Cl AUL OL6............91 H1
Deramore St RUSH/FAL M14.......98 F1
Derby Av SLFD M6...............86 B2
Derby Ct CHAD OL9..............58 B3
  SALE M33....................108 F1
Derby Gv BNG/LEV M19...........99 L3
Derby Range HTNM SK4...........99 L8
Derby Rd AUL OL6...............90 E1
  GOL/RIS/CUL WA3.............79 M3
  HTNM SK4.....................99 M8
  NM/HAY SK22.................124 F3
  ORD M5.......................86 B2
  RAD M26......................53 K4

RUSH/FAL M14 ... 98 F5
SALE M33 ... 96 C1
URM M41 ... 96 A1
WHTF M45 ... 55 K6
Derbyshire Av STRET M32 ... 96 E1
Derbyshire Crs STRET M32 ... 96 D1
Derbyshire Gv STRET M32 ... 96 D1
Derbyshire La STRET M32 ... 96 E2
Derbyshire La West STRET M32 ... 96 D1
Derbyshire Level GLSP SK13 ... 105 J6
Derbyshire Rd NEWH/MOS M40 ... 74 A8
  PART M31 ... 122 F2
  POY/DIS SK12 ... 126 F7
  SALE M33 ... 96 F8
  WGNS/IIMK WN3 ... 63 G3
Derbyshire Rd South
  SALE M33 ... 109 G2
Derbyshire Rw BOL BL1 * ... 36 B1
Derbyshire St OP/CLY M11 ... 88 F5
Derby St ALT WA14 ... 108 B7
  ATH M46 ... 50 F8
  AULW OL7 ... 75 K7
  BOLS/LL BL3 ... 2 C8
  BURY BL9 ... 5 G4
  CHAD OL9 ... 8 C9
  CHH M8 ... 72 B7
  DTN/ASHW M34 ... 90 A8
  EDGY/DAV SK3 ... 12 F7
  FAIL M35 ... 74 D3
  GLSP SK13 ... 104 F4
  HEY OL10 ... 40 E2
  HOR/BR BL6 ... 34 A3
  LEIGH WN7 ... 66 D8
  MOSL OL5 ... 77 G4
  MPL/ROM SK6 ... 114 C7
  PWCH M25 ... 55 K8
  RAMS BL0 ... 19 G6
  ROCH OL11 ... 11 G8
  WGNS/IIMK WN3 ... 4 C8
  WHTN BL5 ... 50 C3
Dereham Av TOT/BURYW BL8 ... 25 C7
Dereham Wy WGNS/IIMK WN3 ... 63 G3
Derg St SLFD M6 ... 86 C2
Derker St OLD OL1 ... 9 M3
Dermot Murphy Cl
  DID/WITH M20 ... 98 C6
Dernford Av BNG/LEV M19 ... 99 J7
Derngate Dr WGNNW/ST WN6 ... 31 K5
Derry Av WYTH/NTH M22 ... 110 B8
Derwent Av AULW OL7 ... 75 K8
  CCHDY M21 ... 98 A7
  DROY M43 ... 89 H3
  GOL/RIS/CUL WA3 ... 79 M3
  HALE/TIMP WA15 * ... 109 G7
  HEY OL10 ... 41 G4
  MILN OL16 ... 29 L6
  WGNE/HIN WN2 ... 48 E5
  WHTF M45 ... 55 L4
Derwent Cl BOLS/LL BL3 ... 53 J1
  DTN/ASHW M34 ... 100 E2
  GLSP SK13 ... 105 J4
  LEIGH WN7 ... 81 H1
  PART M31 ... 94 C8
  WALK M28 ... 69 M5
  WHTF M45 ... 55 L5
Derwent Dr BRAM/HZG SK7 ... 120 E7
  BURY BL9 ... 39 G5
  CHAD OL9 ... 58 D5
  FWTH BL4 ... 53 L7
  LIT OL15 ... 29 J2
  ROY/SHW OL2 ... 43 K4
  SALE M33 ... 108 D2
  WILM/AE SK9 ... 119 L7
Derwent Pl WGNW/BIL/OR WN5 ... 46 F5
Derwent Rd AIMK WN4 ... 64 B7
  FWTH BL4 ... 52 C5
  MDTN M24 ... 57 H1
  MPL/ROM SK6 ... 123 G4
  STRET M32 ... 97 G1
  URM M41 ... 95 H2
  WGNE/HIN WN2 ... 49 H7
  WGNW/BIL/OR WN5 ... 46 C4
Derwent St CHH M8 ... 72 F6
  DROY M43 * ... 89 G3
  LEIGH WN7 ... 81 H1
  ORD M5 ... 86 F4
  TYLD M29 ... 67 K5
  WHIT OL12 ... 28 C3
Derwent Ter STLY SK15 ... 76 D3
Derwent Wy LEIGH WN7 ... 80 E3
Design St BOLS/LL BL3 ... 51 L1
Desmond Rd WYTH/NTH M22 ... 110 B8
Desmond St ATH M46 ... 66 D2
De Trafford Dr WGNE/HIN WN2 ... 48 E4
The De Traffords IRL M44 ... 94 B2
Dettingen St SLFD M6 ... 71 H6
Deva St BRAM/HZG SK7 ... 121 M3
  POY/DIS SK12 ... 121 K8
Deva Sq CHAD OL9 ... 8 C9
Deverill Av GTN M18 ... 89 J8
Devine Cl CSLFD M3 ... 6 A2
  ROY/SHW OL2 ... 43 G6
Devisdale Gra ALT WA14 * ... 116 D1
Devisdale Rd ALT WA14 ... 107 L8
Devoke Av WALK M28 ... 69 H2
Devoke Gv FWTH BL4 ... 52 B4
Devon Av BNG/LEV M19 ... 99 J4
  WHTF M45 ... 55 H3
Devon Cl BOLS/LL BL3 ... 37 L8
  RDSH SK5 ... 85 M8
  ROY/SHW OL2 ... 43 J5
  SLFD M6 ... 85 K1
  WGNE/HIN WN2 ... 33 G7
  WGNW/BIL/OR WN5 ... 46 A2
Devon Dr BOLE BL2 ... 37 M3
  UPML OL3 ... 45 M8
  WGN WN1 ... 31 L3
Devonport Crs ROY/SHW OL2 ... 43 J8
Devon Rd DROY M43 ... 89 K1
  FAIL M35 ... 74 B6
  IRL M44 ... 94 A7
  PART M31 ... 106 B2
  TYLD M29 ... 67 J2
  URM M41 ... 95 H3
Devonshire Cl HEY OL10 ... 40 D3
  URM M41 ... 96 B2
Devonshire Dr WALK M28 ... 68 B6
  WILM/AE SK9 ... 127 J4
Devonshire Park Rd OFTN SK2 ... 112 D7
Devonshire Pl PWCH M25 ... 55 K7
Devonshire Rd ALT WA14 ... 107 M6
  ATH M46 ... 50 F7
  BOL BL1 ... 35 L4
  BRAM/HZG SK7 ... 122 B4
  CCHDY M21 ... 97 M4
  ECC M30 ... 85 H2
  HTNM SK4 ... 12 A2
  ROCH OL11 ... 28 A8
  SLFD M6 ... 85 K1
  WHTN BL5 ... 50 B1

WALK M28 ... 52 F6
Devonshire St BRO M7 ... 72 B6
  BRUN/LGST M13 ... 88 A4
Devonshire St East FAIL M35 * ... 74 A7
Devonshire St North
  WGTN/LGST M12 ... 88 A5
Devonshire St South
  BRUN/LGST M13 ... 88 A7
Devon St BOLE BL2 ... 3 H5
  BURY BL9 ... 4 E8
  CHAD OL9 ... 58 E8
  FWTH BL4 ... 53 G2
  LEIGH WN7 ... 67 G8
  ROCH OL11 ... 10 E7
  SWIN M27 ... 70 D2
  WGNE/HIN WN2 ... 49 H7
Devon Wy OLDS OL8 ... 74 F2
Dewar Cl OP/CLY M11 ... 88 D3
Dewberry Cl TYLD M29 ... 68 B3
Dewes Av SWIN M27 ... 70 E2
Dewham Cl WHTN BL5 ... 50 C3
Dewhirst Rd WHIT OL12 ... 20 D7
Dewhirst St WHIT OL12 ... 20 D8
Dew Meadow Cl WHIT OL12 ... 28 C2
Dewsnap Cl DUK SK16 * ... 90 F6
Dewsnap La DUK SK16 ... 90 F6
  HYDE SK14 ... 92 D6
Dew Wy CHAD OL9 ... 8 E4
Dexter Rd BKLY M9 ... 56 D7
Deyne Av PWCH M25 ... 55 L8
  RUSH/FAL M14 ... 87 M8
Deyne St ORD M5 ... 86 B2
Dial Ct FWTH BL4 * ... 53 G4
Dial Park Rd OFTN SK2 ... 113 G8
Dial Rd HALE/TIMP WA15 ... 117 L4
  OFTN SK2 ... 112 F7
Dialstone La OFTN SK2 ... 112 F5
Diamond St LEIGH WN7 ... 66 B8
  OFTN SK2 ... 112 D6
  WGNNW/ST WN6 ... 47 K1
Diamond Ter MPL/ROM SK6 ... 123 H1
Diane Av AIMK WN4 ... 64 B8
Dicconson Crs WGN WN1 ... 15 G2
Dicconson La WHTN BL5 ... 33 K8
Dicconson St WGN WN1 ... 14 F1
Dicconson Ter WGN WN1 ... 14 F1
Dicken Gn La ROCH OL11 ... 28 C8
Dicken Green La ROCH OL11 ... 28 C8
Dickens Cl CHD/CHDH SK8 ... 120 D7
Dickens Dr WGNE/HIN WN2 ... 64 E4
Dickens La POY/DIS SK12 ... 129 J1
Dickenson Rd RUSH/FAL M14 ... 99 G1
Dickenson St WGNE/HIN WN2 ... 49 H8
Dickens Pl WGNS/IIMK WN3 ... 47 J3
Dickens Rd ECC M30 ... 85 C3
Dickens St HEY OL10 * ... 40 E2
  OLD OL1 ... 44 B8
Dickinson Cl BOL BL1 * ... 36 B3
Dickinson St BOL BL1 ... 36 B3
  CMANE M1 ... 7 G6
Didcot Rd WYTH/NTH M22 ... 118 E3
Didley Sq WGTN/LGST M12 ... 88 D6
Didsbury Gv WGNE/HIN WN2 ... 49 G7
Didsbury Pk DID/WITH M20 ... 110 F3
Didsbury Rd HTNM SK4 ... 12 B4
Digby Rd ROCH OL11 ... 28 C8
Dig Gate La MILN OL16 ... 43 H1
Diggles La ROCH OL11 ... 27 H6
Diggle St ROY/SHW OL2 ... 43 L6
  WGNNW/ST WN6 ... 14 C2
Diglands Av NM/HAY SK22 ... 124 F3
Dijon St BOLS/LL BL3 ... 35 M8
Dilham Ct BOL BL1 ... 35 M4
Dillmoss Wk HULME M15 * ... 87 G6
Dillon Dr WGTN/LGST M12 ... 88 B7
Dilworth Cl HEY OL10 ... 40 C2
Dilworth Ct OFTN SK2 ... 113 H7
Dilworth St HULME M15 ... 87 L7
Dimple Pk EDGW/EG BL7 ... 22 A1
Dingle Av ROY/SHW OL2 ... 43 M3
  WILM/AE SK9 ... 130 A1
Dingle Bank Rd
  BRAM/HZG SK7 ... 120 F3
Dingle Cl GLSP SK13 ... 104 D3
  MPL/ROM SK6 ... 114 A2
Dingle Dr DROY M43 ... 89 J4
Dingle Gv CHD/CHDH SK8 ... 110 C6
Dingle Rd MDTN M24 ... 57 H6
Dingle Ter AUL OL6 ... 75 L2
The Dingle BRAM/HZG SK7 ... 120 E3
  HYDE SK14 ... 102 B6
Dingle Wk BOL BL1 ... 2 E1
  WGNNW/ST WN6 ... 31 G8
Dinmor Rd WYTH/NTH M22 ... 118 F4
Dinnington Dr CHH M8 ... 72 C6
Dinorwic Cl CHH M8 ... 72 D2
Dinsdale Dr BOLS/LL BL3 ... 2 A8
Dinting Av DID/WITH M20 ... 98 D5
Dinting La GLSP SK13 ... 104 D3
Dinting Rd GLSP SK13 ... 104 E2
Dinton St HULME M15 ... 86 F5
Dirty La OLDE OL4 ... 60 L3
  UPML OL3 ... 45 L4
Dirty Leech WHIT OL12 ... 20 D6
Discovery Pk HTNM SK4 * ... 99 M7
Disley Av DID/WITH M20 ... 98 C6
Disley St ROCH OL11 ... 28 A8
Distaff Rd POY/DIS SK12 ... 121 K8
Ditton Brook WHTN BL5 ... 50 C3
Ditton Mead Cl WHIT OL12 ... 28 E2
Division St BOLS/LL BL3 ... 52 C1
  WHIT OL12 ... 28 E2
Dixey St HOR/BR BL6 ... 33 L5
Dixon Av BRO M7 ... 72 A6
  NEWLW WA12 ... 78 F7
  WGNNW/ST WN6 ... 30 D7
Dixon Cl RNFD/HAY WA11 ... 78 D4
  SALE M33 ... 109 G2
Dixon Closes ROCH OL11 ... 27 H5
Dixon Dr SWIN M27 ... 54 B8
  WGNNW/ST WN6 ... 30 D7
Dixon Green Dr FWTH BL4 ... 52 F3
Dixon St AUL OL6 ... 76 A3
  HOR/BR BL6 ... 33 L1
  IRL M44 ... 94 B4
  MDTN M24 ... 57 K2
  NEWH/MOS M40 ... 73 J6
  OLD OL1 ... 9 H3
  OLDE OL4 ... 60 B4
  ROCH OL11 ... 28 A8
  SLFD M6 ... 71 J6
  WHTN BL5 ... 50 B1

Dobb Brow Rd WHTN BL5 ... 50 A5
Dobb Hedge Cl
  HALE/TIMP WA15 ... 117 L6
Dobbin Dr ROCH OL11 ... 42 C1
Dobbinets La
  HALE/TIMP WA15 ... 117 M1
Dobbinetts La
  HALE/TIMP WA15 ... 109 H8
Dobcross Cl BRUN/LGST M13 ... 99 J3
Dobcross New Rd UPML OL3 ... 61 K3
Dobhill St FWTH BL4 ... 53 H4
Dobroyd St CHH M8 ... 72 D4
Dobson Cl BRUN/LGST M13 ... 88 A6
Dobson Rd BOL BL1 ... 35 M5
  WGNNW/ST WN6 ... 30 B2
Dobson Pkwy
  WGNNW/HIN WN2 ... 48 D6
Dobson St BOL BL1 ... 36 A2
Doctor Fold La HEY OL10 ... 40 F7
Doctor La OLDE OL4 ... 60 F3
Doctors La OLDE OL4 ... 60 F3
Doctor's Nook LEIGH WN7 ... 66 C7
Dodd La ORD M5 ... 86 D4
Doddington Wk
  DTN/ASHW M34 * ... 101 H3
Dodd La WHTN BL5 ... 49 L1
Dodd's Farm La
  WGNE/HIN WN2 ... 49 H1
Dodd St ORD M5 ... 86 A2
Dodge Fold OFTN SK2 ... 113 H6
Dodge Hl HTNM SK4 ... 13 H2
Dodgson St MILN OL16 ... 11 H7
Dodhurst Rd
  WGNE/HIN WN2 ... 49 J6
Dodworth Cl
  NEWH/MOS M40 ... 87 J6
Doe Brow SWIN M27 ... 54 B8
Doefield Av WALK M28 ... 69 G4
Doeford Cl
  GOL/RIS/CUL WA3 ... 81 H7
Doe Hey Gv FWTH BL4 ... 52 E3
Doe Hey Rd BOLS/LL BL3 ... 52 E2
Doffcocker Brow BOL BL1 ... 35 J3
Doffcocker La
  BOL BL1 ... 35 J3
Dogford Rd ROY/SHW OL2 ... 43 C7
Dog Hill Lne ROY/SHW OL2 ... 44 C5
Dolbey St ORD M5 ... 86 B3
Dolefield CSLFD M3 ... 6 D5
D'Olivera Ct MDTN M24 ... 57 H2
Dollond St BKLY M9 ... 73 H3
Dolphin Pl
  WGTN/LGST M12 ... 7 M9
Dolphin St WGTN/LGST M12 ... 7 M9
Doman St BOLS/LL BL3 ... 2 E9
Dombey Rd POY/DIS SK12 ... 129 K2
Domestic Ap MANAIR M90 ... 118 E6
The Dome WA14 * ... 108 A8
Domett St BKLY M9 ... 72 F2
Dominic Cl NTHM/RTH M23 ... 109 H3
Donald Av HYDE SK14 ... 102 C3
Donald St CMANE M1 * ... 7 H7
Dona St STKP SK1 ... 13 M6
Don Av SLFD M6 ... 85 M2
Doncaster Av DID/WITH M20 ... 98 D5
Doncaster Cl BOLS/LL BL3 ... 53 J1
  OLD OL1 ... 44 A8
Doncaster Wk OLD OL1 ... 9 J4
Donhead Wk BRUN/LGST M13 * ... 87 M6
Donkey La WILM/AE SK9 ... 126 E7
Donleigh St NEWH/MOS M40 ... 74 A7
Donnington Rd OCH OL11 ... 10 C7
Donnington Av
  CHD/CHDH SK8 ... 111 J7
Donnington Cl LEIGH WN7 ... 81 G3
Donnington Gdns WALK M28 * ... 69 G1
Donnington Rd GTN M18 ... 89 M7
  RAD M26 ... 37 M7
Donnison St WGTN/LGST M12 ... 88 C6
Donovan Av NEWH/MOS M40 ... 72 F8
Don St BOLS/LL BL3 ... 52 A1
  MDTN M24 ... 57 M3
Doodson Av IRL M44 ... 94 C2
Doodson Sq FWTH BL4 ... 53 G4
Dooley La MPL/ROM SK6 ... 113 L5
Dootson St WGNE/HIN WN2 ... 49 K6
  WGNE/HIN WN2 ... 64 D3
Dorac Av CHD/CHDH SK8 ... 119 L6
Dora St RAMS BL0 ... 18 D8
Dorchester Av BOLE BL2 ... 37 H3
  DTN/ASHW M34 ... 101 J3
  PWCH M25 ... 71 M2
  URM M41 ... 96 C1
Dorchester Cl
  CHD/CHDH SK8 ... 120 B3
  SALE M33 ... 108 C2
Dorchester Dr
  NTHM/RTH M23 ... 109 H3
  ROY/SHW OL2 ... 59 G2
Dorchester Gv HEY OL10 ... 40 F4
Dorchester Rd
  BRAM/HZG SK7 ... 121 K3
  SWIN M27 ... 70 C6
Dorclyn Av URM M41 ... 96 A2
Dorfield Cl MPL/ROM SK6 ... 113 H1
Doric Av MPL/ROM SK6 ... 113 G2
Doric Cl OP/CLY M11 ... 88 C5
Doric Gn WGNW/BIL/OR WN5 ... 62 A1
Doris Av BOLE BL2 ... 37 G5
Doris Rd EDGY/DAV SK3 ... 12 C7
Doris St MDTN M24 ... 57 K2
Dorket Gv WHTN BL5 ... 50 A4
Dorking Av NEWH/MOS M40 ... 73 K8
Dorking Cl BOL BL1 ... 36 C2
  STKP SK1 ... 13 K4
Dorlan Av GTN M18 ... 89 J8
Dorland Gv OFTN SK2 ... 112 E5
Dorman St OP/CLY M11 ... 89 G5
Dormer St BOL BL1 ... 36 C1
Dorney St GTN M18 ... 89 G7
Dorning Rd SWIN M27 ... 70 D5
Dorning St ATH M46 ... 67 J3
  ECC M30 ... 85 G3
  FWTH BL4 ... 53 H4
  HOR/BR BL6 ... 33 H5
  LEIGH WN7 ... 66 D7
  TOT/BURYW BL8 * ... 24 D8
  WGN WN1 ... 14 E3
Dorothy Gv LEIGH WN7 ... 66 B8
Dorothy Rd BRAM/HZG SK7 ... 122 B3
Dorothy St BRO M7 ... 72 C5
  RAMS BL0 ... 18 E7
Dorrington Rd
  EDGY/DAV SK3 ... 111 K5
  SALE M33 ... 96 A8
Dorris St BNG/LEV M19 ... 99 J4
Dorrit Cl POY/DIS SK12 ... 129 K2

Dorset Av BRAM/HZG SK7 ... 120 F3
  CHD/CHDH SK8 ... 111 M8
  DTN/ASHW M34 ... 89 M4
  FWTH BL4 ... 52 F2
  RDSH SK5 ... 100 F7
  ROY/SHW OL2 ... 43 J5
  RUSH/FAL M14 ... 98 D2
  TYLD M29 ... 67 J3
  UPML OL3 ... 45 M8
Dorset Cl FWTH BL4 ... 52 F4
  HEY OL10 ... 40 D3
  WGNW/BIL/OR WN5 ... 46 F5
Dorset Dr BURY BL9 ... 5 H8
Dorset Rd ALT WA14 ... 107 L8
  ATH M46 ... 50 F8
  BNG/LEV M19 ... 99 M3
  DROY M43 ... 89 J1
  FAIL M35 ... 74 C7
  IRL M44 ... 94 A7
  WGN WN1 ... 31 L3
Dorset St AUL OL6 ... 91 G2
  BOLE BL2 ... 3 H5
  CHAD OL9 ... 8 C9
  LEIGH WN7 ... 67 G8
  STRET M32 ... 97 G3
  SWIN M27 ... 70 C2
  WGNE/HIN WN2 ... 49 H6
Dorsey St ANC M4 * ... 7 J3
Dorstone Cl
  NEWH/MOS M40 ... 73 M8
  WGNE/HIN WN2 ... 49 L7
Dorwood Av BKLY M9 ... 56 F7
Dotterel Cl LEIGH WN7 ... 66 B8
Doughty Av ECC M30 ... 85 J1
Douglas Av STRET M32 ... 97 G1
  TOT/BURYW BL8 ... 38 E2
Douglas Cl WHTF M45 ... 55 H4
Douglas Dr WGNNW/ST WN6 ... 30 C7
  WGNW/BIL/OR WN5 ... 14 B6
Douglas Gn SLFD M6 ... 71 K7
Douglas Pk ATH M46 ... 67 H2
Douglas Rd ATH M46 ... 67 H2
  BRAM/HZG SK7 ... 122 A1
  EDGY/DAV SK3 ... 112 B8
  LEIGH WN7 ... 65 M5
  WALK M28 ... 69 M5
  WGN WN1 ... 15 J1
  WGNNW/ST WN6 ... 30 E2
Douglas St ATH M46 ... 67 H2
  AUL OL6 ... 91 G1
  BOL BL1 * ... 22 B7
  BRO M7 ... 72 A6
  FAIL M35 ... 74 D5
  HYDE SK14 ... 102 B2
  NEWH/MOS M40 ... 7 G1
  OLD OL1 ... 9 L3
  RAMS BL0 ... 18 E6
  SWIN M27 ... 70 D5
  WGNE/HIN WN2 ... 48 F8
  WGNW/BIL/OR WN5 ... 14 B6
Douglas Vw WGN WN1 ... 31 L6
Doulton St NEWH/MOS M40 ... 73 M4
Dounby Av ECC M30 ... 84 E1
Douro St NEWH/MOS M40 ... 73 J7
Dove Bank Rd BOLS/LL BL3 ... 37 J8
Dovebrook Cl GLSP SK15 ... 77 H5
Dovecote CI LEIGH WN7 ... 66 A8
Dovecote Cl EDGW/EG BL7 ... 22 E4
Dovecote La LHULT M38 ... 68 B1
  OLDE OL4 ... 60 C5
Dovecote Ms CCHDY M21 ... 97 K5
Dovedale Av DID/WITH M20 ... 98 D5
  DROY M43 ... 89 H2
  ECC M30 ... 72 A1
  PWCH M25 ... 71 K1
  URM M41 ... 96 A1
Dovedale Cl MPL/ROM SK6 ... 123 G5
  GLSP SK13 ... 105 J3
Dovedale Crs AIMK WN4 ... 63 K4
Dovedale Dr WGNNW/ST WN6 ... 31 K5
  WHIT OL12 ... 14 D4
Dovedale Rd AIMK WN4 ... 63 K4
  BOLE BL2 ... 37 J2
  OFTN SK2 ... 113 G5
Dovedale St FAIL M35 ... 74 B5
Dove Dr BURY BL9 ... 5 L1
  IRL M44 ... 94 D1
Dovehouse Cl WHTF M45 ... 55 G4
Doveleys Rd SLFD M6 ... 71 G8
Dovenby Fold WGNE/HIN WN2 ... 48 D5
Dover Cl TOT/BURYW BL8 ... 24 D3
Dovercourt Av HTNM SK4 ... 99 J8
Dovercourt Av HTNM SK4 * ... 111 J1
Dover Gv BOLS/LL BL3 ... 2 B8
Dover Rd SWIN M27 ... 70 D2
Dover St BRUN/LGST M13 ... 87 L6
  CHAD OL9 ... 8 D8
  ECC M30 ... 84 E2
  FWTH BL4 ... 52 F2
  MILN OL16 ... 28 E2
  RDSH SK5 * ... 100 B5
Dovestone Crs DUK SK16 ... 91 J5
Dovestone Wk
  NEWH/MOS M40 * ... 74 B3
Doveston Rd SALE M33 ... 96 E8
Dove St BOL BL1 ... 22 B8
  GOL/RIS/CUL WA3 ... 81 G4
  OLDE OL4 ... 59 M6
  ROCH OL11 ... 10 E7
Dovey Cl TYLD M29 ... 67 M5
Dower St WGNE/HIN WN2 ... 49 M6
Dow Fold TOT/BURYW BL8 ... 38 D1
Dowland Cl NTHM/RTH M23 * ... 109 J2
Dow La TOT/BURYW BL8 ... 38 D1
Dowling Cl WGNNW/ST WN6 ... 47 G1
Dowling St ROCH OL11 ... 10 F7
Downall Green Rd AIMK WN4 ... 63 K6
Downesway WILM/AE SK9 ... 130 C3
Downes Wy WYTH/NTH M22 ... 110 B6
Downfield Cl RAMS BL0 ... 18 D6
Downfields RDSH SK5 ... 100 D3
Downgreen Rd BOLE BL2 ... 37 H1
Downhall Gn BOL BL1 ... 3 G1
Downham Av BOLE BL2 * ... 3 M3
Downham Cha
  HALE/TIMP WA15 ... 108 E6
Downham Cl ROY/SHW OL2 ... 58 F2
Downham Crs PWCH M25 ... 72 B1
Downham Gdns PWCH M25 ... 72 B1
Downham Rd HEY OL10 ... 40 D2
Downham Wk
  NTHM/RTH M23 ... 109 G4
Downhill Cl OLD OL1 ... 9 J1
Downing Cl AULW OL7 ... 75 J6
Downing St WGNE/HIN WN2 ... 64 D3

Downing St AULW OL7 ... 75 J6
  CMANE M1 ... 7 J8
  LEIGH WN7 * ... 66 C7
Downley Cl OLD OL12 ... 27 K2
Downley Dr ANC M4 ... 7 M3
Downs Dr ALT WA14 ... 108 B4
Downshaw Rd AULW OL7 ... 75 K6
The Downs ALT WA14 ... 116 F1
  CHD/CHDH SK8 ... 119 M1
  MDTN M24 ... 57 L6
  PWCH M25 ... 71 K1
  WGNS/IIMK WN3 ... 46 F8
Downton Av RNFD/HAY WA11 ... 78 D3
Dowry Rd OLDE OL4 ... 60 B5
Dowry St OLDS OL8 ... 75 J1
Dowson Rd HYDE SK14 ... 102 B3
Dowson St BOLE BL2 ... 3 H5
Dow St HYDE SK14 ... 91 G7
Doyle Av MPL/ROM SK6 ... 113 G5
Doyle Cl OLD OL1 ... 44 B8
Doyle Rd BOLS/LL BL3 ... 51 H5
Drake Av FWTH BL4 ... 53 G6
  IRL M44 ... 94 B6
  WYTH/NTH M22 ... 118 C2
Drake Cl OLD OL1 ... 9 J2
Drake Ct RDSH SK5 ... 100 B8
Drake Hall WHTN BL5 ... 50 A1
Drake Rd ALT WA14 ... 107 L4
Drake St ATH M46 ... 66 F7
  ROCH OL11 ... 10 E6
Drapers Ct GOL/RIS/CUL WA3 ... 80 C5
Draycott Cl WGNE/HIN WN2 ... 65 J1
Draycott St BOL BL1 ... 36 C3
Draycott St East BOL BL1 ... 36 C2
Drayfields DROY M43 ... 90 A2
Drayford Cl NTHM/RTH M23 ... 109 J2
Drayton Cl BOL BL1 ... 36 A2
  SALE M33 ... 108 B3
  WILM/AE SK9 ... 127 H3
Drayton Dr CHD/CHDH SK8 ... 119 K6
Drayton Gv HALE/TIMP WA15 ... 108 D3
Drayton Wk HULME M15 ... 87 H4
Drayton Wk OLDTF/WHR M16 ... 86 F7
Dresden St NEWH/MOS M40 ... 73 M8
Drewett St NEWH/MOS M40 ... 73 H8
Dreyfus Av OP/CLY M11 ... 88 F2
Driffield St ECC M30 ... 84 F4
  RUSH/FAL M14 ... 98 D3
Drill Wk ANC M4 ... 7 M4
Drinkwater Rd PWCH M25 ... 71 J3
Driscoll St BRUN/LGST M13 ... 99 J1
The Drive ATH M46 ... 50 F8
  BRO M7 ... 71 M4
  BURY BL9 ... 25 J7
  CHD/CHDH SK8 ... 111 M8
  DID/WITH M20 ... 110 F1
  HALE/TIMP WA15 ... 117 M4
  LEIGH WN7 ... 81 J1
  MPL/ROM SK6 ... 113 G1
  PWCH M25 ... 55 L8
  RAMS BL0 ... 19 G2
  RDSH SK5 ... 100 F8
  SALE M33 ... 108 B3
Droitwich Rd NEWH/MOS M40 ... 73 G8
Dronfield Rd SLFD M6 ... 71 G8
  WYTH/NTH M22 ... 110 A4
Droughts La PWCH M25 ... 56 A4
Droxford Gv ATH M46 ... 51 H7
  NEWH/MOS M40 ... 74 A7
Droylsden Rd DTN/ASHW M34 ... 89 L3
Druid St EDGW/EG BL7 ... 22 A1
Druids Cl EDGW/EG BL7 ... 22 A1
Druid St AIMK WN4 ... 78 F2
Drummer's La AIMK WN4 ... 63 H5
Drummond Sq
  WGNW/BIL/OR WN5 ... 47 H5
Drummond St BOL BL1 * ... 22 B8
Drummond Wy LEIGH WN7 ... 66 E7
Drury La CHAD OL9 ... 74 D1
Drury St BNG/LEV M19 ... 99 K3
Dryad Cl SWIN M27 ... 70 C2
Drybrook Cl BRUN/LGST M13 ... 88 D7
Dryburgh Av BOL BL1 ... 36 A1
Dryden Av AIMK WN4 ... 63 J5
  CHD/CHDH SK8 ... 111 H6
  SWIN M27 ... 70 A5
Dryden Cl DUK SK16 ... 91 L5
  MPL/ROM SK6 ... 114 C8
  WGNS/IIMK WN3 ... 47 K7
Dryden Rd OLDTF/WHR M16 ... 97 H1
Dryden St BRUN/LGST M13 ... 87 M6
Dryhurst Dr POY/DIS SK12 ... 123 M6
Dryhurst La POY/DIS SK12 ... 123 M6
Dryhurst Wk HULME M15 ... 87 K6
Drymoss OLDS OL8 ... 75 J3
Drysdale Vw BOL BL1 ... 22 B8
Dryton Wk WGNE/HIN WN2 ... 48 D5
Drywood Av WALK M28 ... 69 K7
Ducal St ANC M4 ... 7 G2
Duchess Park CI ROY/SHW OL2 ... 43 L4
Duchess Rd CHH M8 ... 72 C4
Duchess St OLDS OL8 ... 43 K4
Duchess Wk BOLS/LL BL3 ... 35 L8
Duchy Av WALK M28 ... 69 G4
  WHTN BL5 ... 51 K4
Duchy Bank SLFD M6 ... 71 G6
Duchy Rd SLFD M6 ... 71 H7
Duchy St EDGY/DAV SK3 ... 12 C2
  SLFD M6 ... 86 C2
Ducie Av BOL BL1 ... 35 M5
  OLDS OL8 ... 75 J2
  RAD M26 ... 38 C7
  WHTF M45 ... 55 J4
Duckshaw La FWTH BL4 ... 52 F4
Duckworth Rd PWCH M25 ... 71 J1
Duckworth St BURY BL9 ... 25 K8
  ROY/SHW OL2 ... 43 K5
Duddon Av BOLE BL2 ... 37 J3
Duddon Cl WHTF M45 ... 55 L4
Duddon Cl WGNNW/ST WN6 ... 31 J5
Dudley Av BOLE BL2 ... 3 M1
  WHTF M45 ... 55 J4
Dudley Cl HULME M15 ... 87 H7
Dudley Rd HALE/TIMP WA15 ... 108 G5
  IRL M44 ... 94 A8
  OLDTF/WHR M16 ... 98 A1
  SALE M33 ... 96 F6
  SWIN M27 ... 70 C2
Dudley St AIMK WN4 ... 63 K7
  BRO M7 ... 72 A6
  ECC M30 ... 84 F3
  OLDE OL4 ... 60 A6
Dudlow Wk HULME M15 * ... 87 G6
Dudwell Cl BOL BL1 ... 35 M3
Duerden St BOLS/LL BL3 * ... 51 K2
Duffield Ct MDTN M24 ... 57 J7
Duffield Gdns MDTN M24 ... 57 J7
Duffield Rd MDTN M24 ... 57 J7
  SLFD M6 ... 71 G7
Duffins Cl WHIT OL12 ... 28 A1
Dugdale Av BKLY M9 ... 56 H8

Dugie St RAMS BL0 ....18 E5
Duke Av CHD/CHDH SK8 .....120 D6
　GOL/RIS/CUL WA3...............81 M5
Duke Ct OLDTF/WHR M16.......87 C7
Dukefield St WYTH/NTH M22...110 B4
Duke Pl CSLFD M3 * 6 C7
Duke Rd BOLE BL2 ....37 M3
　HYDE SK14...........................91 J7
Dukes Fold GLSP SK15.........104 C5
Dukes Platting AUL OL6.........76 C7
Dukes St GLSP SK15.............104 F4
Duke St AIMK WN4..................78 F1
　AUL OL6 * 90 E2
　BOL BL1.................................2 D3
　BRO M7................................72 A7
　CSLFD M3...............................6 C7
　CSLFD M3...............................6 C7
　DTN/ASHW M34...................101 H1
　ECC M30...............................69 M8
　FAIL M35...............................74 D4
　GOL/RIS/CUL WA3..............79 K3
　HEY OL10............................40 E2
　LEIGH WN7..........................66 D8
　LHULT M38...........................52 D7
　LIT OL15..............................21 L7
　MOSL OL5............................77 H3
　RAD M26..............................54 F2
　RAMS BL0.............................18 D8
　ROY/SHW OL2......................43 M6
　STKP SK1.............................13 J5
　STLY SK15...........................91 J3
　TYLD M29.............................67 M6
　WALK M28............................69 L2
　WGN WN1............................47 M2
　WGNE/HIN WN2....................64 D1
　WGNS/IIMK WN3..................47 J8
　WHIT OL12...........................28 C3
　WILM/AE SK9......................130 E2
Duke St North BOL BL1.............2 D2
Dukes Wk HALE/TIMP WA15...117 H1
Dukinfield Rd HYDE SK14.......90 F7
Dukinfield St LEIGH WN7 *.......66 D7
Dulford Wk BRUN/LGST M13 *..87 M7
Dulgar St OP/CLY M11 *...........88 E2
Dulverton Gdns BOLS/LL BL3 *..53 L2
Dulverton St NEWH/MOS M40...73 L6
Dulwich Cl SALE M33.............108 A1
Dulwich St ANC M4..................87 L1
Dumbarton Cl RDSH SK5.......100 C6
Dumbarton Dr HEY OL10.........40 D3
Dumbarton Gn
　WGNNW/ST WN6..................47 H2
Dumbarton Rd RDSH SK5......100 C5
Dumbell St SWIN M27..............70 C2
Dumber La SALE M33..............96 C6
Dumers Cl RAD M26.................39 C8
Dumers La RAD M26................39 H7
Dumfries Av UPML OL3.............44 F2
Dumfries Dr UPML OL3.............44 F2
Dumfries Hollow HEY OL10......41 J1
Dunbar Av NTHM/RTH M23....118 C1
Dunbar Dr BOLS/LL BL3...........36 B8
Dunbar Gv HEY OL10..............40 C4
Dunbar St OLD OL1....................9 C3
Dunblane Av BOLS/LL BL3........35 H7
　HTNM SK4............................12 A1
Dunblane Gv HEY OL10...........40 D4
Duncan Av NEWLW WA12.........78 F7
Duncan Pl WGNW/BIL/OR WN5..47 H5
Duncan Rd BRUN/LGST M13....99 J1
Duncan St BRO M7...................71 M6
　DUK SK16.............................90 E6
　HOR/BR BL6.........................35 C6
　ORD M5.................................86 F4
Dunchurch Cl HOR/BR BL6.......35 C6
Dunchurch Rd SALE M33.........96 B8
Dun Cl CSLFD M3.......................6 B3
Duncombe Cl BRAM/HZG SK7..121 J1
Duncombe Dr NEWH/MOS M40..73 L5
Duncombe Rd BOLS/LL BL3......52 B2
Duncombe St BRO M7...............72 B6
Duncote Gv ROY/SHW OL2.......43 J7
Dundee Cl HEY OL10...............40 C3
Dundee La RAMS BL0...............18 E6
Dundonald Rd CHD/CHDH SK8..120 D5
　DID/WITH M20.....................110 F1
Dundonald St OFTN SK2.........112 C6
Dundraw Cl MDTN M24.............56 E3
Dundrennan Cl POY/DIS SK12..121 M7
Dunecroft DTN/ASHW M34 *.....90 D2
Dunedin Dr RUSH/FAL M14.......98 B2
Dunedin Dr SALE M33.............71 J7
Dunelm Dr SALE M33..............108 A1
Dunham Av GOL/RIS/CUL WA3..79 J3
Dunham Cl WHTN BL5..............50 A7
Dunham Gv LEIGH WN7............81 M7
Dunham Lawn ALT WA14.........107 L7
Dunham Ms ALT WA14...........116 A3
Dunham Ri ALT WA14.............107 M8
Dunham Rd ALT WA14.............107 L8
　ALT WA14............................116 B2
　DUK SK16.............................91 G6
　LYMM WA13.........................106 B5
　PART M31.............................95 C8
　WILM/AE SK9......................119 M7
Dunham St HULME M15............87 H6
　OLDE OL4.............................60 B4
Dunkeld Rd NTHM/RTH M23...109 J6
Dunkerley Av FAIL M35............74 C5
Dunkerley St AULW OL7...........75 K7
　OLDE OL4..............................59 M5
　ROY/SHW OL2......................43 C8
Dunkery Rd WYTH/NTH M22...118 F3
Dunkirk La HYDE SK14.............90 F8
Dunkirk Ri WHIT OL12..............10 C4
Dunkirk Rd WHTF M45..............55 J3
Dunkirk St DROY M43...............89 L3
Dunley Cl WGTN/LGST M12 *....88 D7
Dunlin Av NEWLW WA12...........78 F8
Dunlin Cl BOLE BL2....................3 H8
　OFTN SK2............................113 K7
　POY/DIS SK12.....................128 E1
　ROCH OL11...........................27 J5
Dunlin Dr IRL M44....................94 D1
Dunlin Gv LEIGH WN7..............66 E7
Dunlop Av ROCH OL11.............42 B1
Dunlop St CSLFD M3 * 6 B1
Dunmail Cl TYLD M29...............67 M6
Dunmail Dr MDTN M24.............57 H1
Dunmaston Av
　HALE/TIMP WA15................109 C5
Dunmore Cl CHD/CHDH SK8...110 D6
Dunmow Ct OFTN SK2............113 H7
Dunne La GLSP SK13..............105 H2
Dunnisher Rd NTHM/RTH M23..109 L8
Dunnock Cl OFTN SK2............113 J7
Dunollie Rd SALE M33............109 H1
Dunoon Cl HEY OL10...............40 D3
Dunoon Dr BOL BL1..................22 A7
Dunoon Rd RDSH SK5............100 C5
　WGNE/HIN WN2....................33 C7

Dunrobin Cl HEY OL10.............40 D4
Dunscar Cl WHTF M45..............55 C5
Dunscore Rd
　WGNS/IIMK WN3...................63 H1
Dunsdale Dr AIMK WN4............78 F1
Dunsfold Dr
　NTHM/RTH M23...................109 G4
Dunsley Av
　NEWH/MOS M40...................74 A2
Dunsmore Cl
　OLDTF/WHR M16..................87 C8
Dunsop Dr BOL BL1..................35 J1
Dunstable WHIT OL12..............10 D2
Dunstable St BNG/LEV M19......99 L3
Dunstall Rd
　WYTH/NTH M22..................110 B7
Dunstan St BOLE BL2................3 L4
Dunstar Av
　DTN/ASHW M34...................90 B5
Dunster Av BKLY M9.................57 H8
　RDSH SK5............................100 F7
　ROCH OL11...........................10 C9
　SWIN M27.............................70 E2
　WGNE/HIN WN2....................64 D3
Dunster Dr URM M41................94 F3
Dunster Pl WALK M28..............68 C5
Dunster Rd WALK M28.............68 C5
Dunsters Av
　TOT/BURYW BL8...................24 F7
Dunsterville Ter ROCH OL11 *...10 C9
Dunston St OP/CLY M11............88 F4
Dunton Gn RDSH SK5.............100 E6
Dunvegan Rd
　BRAM/HZG SK7...................122 B3
Dunwood Av ROY/SHW OL2.....43 M4
Dunwoods Park Cts
　ROY/SHW OL2......................43 M3
Durban St LEIGH WN7.............98 E1
Durant St ANC M4 *...................7 J1
Durban Cl ROY/SHW OL2.........43 K6
Durban Rd BOL BL1..................22 B7
Durban St ATH M46..................66 D2
　AULW OL7.............................90 B3
　OLDS OL8.............................74 F1
　ROCH OL11...........................41 M2
Durden Ms
　ROY/SHW OL2......................43 L6
Durham Av URM M41................96 B1
Durham Cl BOLS/LL BL3...........37 L8
　DUK SK16.............................91 G6
　MPL/ROM SK6.....................113 K3
　TYLD M29.............................67 K1
Durham Crs FAIL M35...............74 D6
Durham Dr AUL OL6.................76 A4
　BURY BL9..............................5 H3
　RAMS BL0.............................24 D1
Durham Rd SLFD M6................71 M8
　WGNE/HIN WN2....................49 H7
Durham St BKLY M9..................73 H5
　BOL BL1................................36 C2
　CHAD OL9.............................89 K4
　DROY M43.............................89 K4
　RAD M26...............................37 M3
　RDSH SK5............................100 B2
　ROCH OL11...........................10 F8
　WGN WN1............................15 L1
Durley Av CHH M8....................72 E5
　HALE/TIMP WA15................108 C5
Durling St WGTN/LGST M12 *...7 M9
Durnford Av URM M41..............96 D2
Durnford Cl WHIT OL12............27 C2
Durnford St MDTN M24............57 J3
Durrell Wy GOL/RIS/CUL WA3..80 B4
Durrington Pl WHTN BL5...........50 B3
Dursley Dr AIMK WN4...............64 A8
Dutton Cv LEIGH WN7..............81 M2
Dutton St CSLFD M3.................87 J1
Duty St BOL BL1.......................36 B1
Duxbury Av BOLE BL2...............23 H7
　BOLS/LL BL3.........................37 K7
Duxbury Dr BURY BL9................5 M4
Duxbury St BOL BL1..................36 A2
Dyche St ANC M4 *....................7 J2
Dye House La MILN OL16...........28 F1
　NM/HAY SK22......................124 E4
Dye La MPL/ROM SK6.............113 L2
Dyers Ct LIT OL15....................21 L6
Dyer St GOL/RIS/CUL WA3........88 D4
　OP/CLY M11...........................88 D4
　ORD M5.................................86 F5
Dyserth Gv RDSH SK5............100 C7
Dyson Cl FWTH BL4..................53 C4
Dyson Gv OLDE OL4 *...............60 C4
Dyson St FWTH BL4..................53 C5
　MOSL OL5............................77 H1
Dystelegh Rd POY/DIS SK12...123 M7

E

Eades St SLFD M6....................86 D1
Eadington St CHH M8...............72 D3
Eafield Av MILN OL16...............29 J3
Eafield Cl MILN OL16...............29 J5
Eafield Rd LIT OL15.................29 H1
　MILN OL16............................28 F3
Eagar St NEWH/MOS M40.......73 M6
Eagle Ct UPML OL3..................45 J7
Eagle Dr SLFD M6....................71 K7
Eagle Mill Ct UPML OL3 *.........45 J7
Eagle St ANC M4 *.....................7 H2
　BOLE BL2...............................3 H4
　CHAD OL9.............................58 D5
　ROCH OL11 *.........................11 G5
Eagley Brook Wy BOL BL1........36 C1
Eagley Brow BOL BL1...............22 C5
Eagley Dr TOT/BURYW BL8......38 D3
Eagley Vw TOT/BURYW BL8.....38 D3
Eagley Wy BOL BL1..................22 C6
Ealand Cha HOR/BR BL6..........33 J1
Ealing Av RUSH/FAL M14.........98 E2
Ealing Pl BNG/LEV M19 *..........99 K6
Ealing Rd EDGY/DAV SK3.........12 C9
Eames Av RAD M26..................55 K4
Earby Gv BKLY M9....................73 J1
Earlesdon Crs LHULT M38........52 D7
Earle Rd BRAM/HZG SK7........121 C2
Earlesfield Cl SALE M33..........108 A2
Earle St AULW OL7...................90 C3
Earl Rd CHD/CHDH SK8..........120 A7
　HTNM SK4.............................99 M8
　RAMS BL0.............................18 E6
Earlston Av DTN/ASHW M34....100 D1

Earl St ATH M46.......................66 E2
　BRO M7.................................72 A8
　BURY BL9...............................5 G4
　DTN/ASHW M34.....................89 K8
　EDGY/DAV SK3.....................12 F7
　HEY OL10.............................40 F2
　MOSL OL5............................55 M8
　PWCH M25............................19 G6
　ROCH OL11...........................41 M4
　SALE M33..............................96 F7
　WGN WN1............................47 M2
　WGNE/HIN WN2....................48 D5
Earls Wy FAIL M35...................74 A6
Earl Sway GLSP SK13.............104 E4
Earlswood Wk BOLS/LL BL3.....36 C8
Earl Wk WGTN/LGST M12 *......88 C8
Early Bank STLY SK15..............91 M5
Early Bank Rd HYDE SK14........91 L6
Earnshaw Av STKP SK1...........112 E3
　WHIT OL12............................28 B1
Earnshaw Cl AULW OL7 *.........75 J7
Earnshaw St BOLS/LL BL3 *.....51 M1
　HYDE SK14...........................93 C8
Easby Cl CHD/CHDH SK8........120 D6
　POY/DIS SK12.....................121 M7
Easby Rd MDTN M24................57 J1
Easdale Cl URM M41................95 J1
Easedale Rd BOL BL1...............35 K4
　NEWH/MOS M40...................73 M4
East Aisle Rd TRPK M17...........85 M6
East Av BNG/LEV M19...............99 J5
　CHD/CHDH SK8...................119 M4
　GOL/RIS/CUL WA3................79 M5
　LEIGH WN7...........................81 K1
　STLY SK15............................55 K1
　WHTF M45............................55 H2
Eastbank St BOL BL1................36 C2
East Bond St LEIGH WN7..........66 D7
East Bourne Gv BOL BL1...........35 K4
Eastbourne St OLDS OL8..........59 L8
　ROCH OL11...........................10 C9
East Bridgewater St
　LEIGH WN7...........................66 D8
Eastbrook Av NEWH/MOS M40...87 H1
Eastburn Av NEWH/MOS M40....87 H1
East Central Dr SWIN M27........70 E5
Eastchurch Cl FWTH BL4..........53 C5
Eastcombe Av BRO M7.............71 L5
Eastcote Rd RDSH SK5...........100 C5
East Crs MDTN M24..................57 J5
Eastdale Pl ALT WA14 *...........108 A5
East Downs Rd ALT WA14......116 C2
East Dr BURY BL9.....................39 L8
　MPL/ROM SK6.....................123 H1
　SLFD M6................................71 H7
　SWIN M27.............................70 E5
Easterdale OLDE OL4................59 M6
Eastern Av SWIN M27...............71 C2
Eastern By-Pass OP/CLY M11...88 F2
　OP/CLY M11...........................89 C4
Eastern Cir BNG/LEV M19.........99 K6
Eastfield SLFD M6....................71 H8
Eastfield Av MDTN M24............57 K5
　NEWH/MOS M40...................88 B1
Eastfields RAD M26..................38 B7
Eastford Sq NEWH/MOS M40...72 B8
Eastgarth WGNE/HIN WN2.......64 E2
Eastgate WHIT OL12................10 D3
Eastgate St AULW OL7.............90 D3
East Gate St MILN OL16............10 F3
East Gra OP/CLY M11...............88 F1
East Gv BRUN/LGST M13..........87 M7
Eastgrove Av BOL BL1...............22 B5
Eastham Av BURY BL9..............25 H6
　RUSH/FAL M14.....................98 E3
Eastham St BRUN/LGST M13 *..52 E7
Easthaven Av OP/CLY M11 *......88 F2
East Hill St OLDE OL4 *..............9 M7
Eastholme Dr BNG/LEV M19.....99 L3
Easthope Cl DID/WITH M20......98 E5
East Lancashire Rd
　GOL/RIS/CUL WA3................80 C5
　GOL/RIS/CUL WA3................82 A2
　NEWLW WA12......................79 G5
　RNFD/HAY WA11..................78 C5
　SWIN M27.............................70 B6
　TYLD M29.............................67 M7
　WALK M28.............................68 F5
Eastlands Rd BKLY M9..............57 C7
East Lea DTN/ASHW M34........101 K1
Eastleigh Av SLFD M6...............72 B4
Eastleigh Crs LEIGH WN7.........81 L1
Eastleigh Dr NEWH/MOS M40...88 A1
Eastleigh Rd CHD/CHDH SK8...119 K3
　PWCH M25............................72 B1
East Lynn Dr WALK M28............69 K2
East Meade BOLS/LL BL3.........52 B2
　CCHDY M21...........................97 L5
　PWCH M25............................72 A2
　SWIN M27.............................70 B6
East Moor WALK M28................68 D5
Eastmoor Dr NEWH/MOS M40..74 A8
Eastmoor Gv BOLS/LL BL3.......51 L2
East Mt WGNW/BIL/OR WN5....46 C6
East Newton St ANC M4............7 L8
Easton Cl MDTN M24................57 M5
　WGNS/IIMK WN3...................63 K2
Easton Dr CHD/CHDH SK8......111 K7
Easton Rd DROY M43...............89 H2
East Ordsall La CSLFD M3..........6 C7
Eastover MPL/ROM SK6.........113 K4
Eastpark Cl BRUN/LGST M13...87 M6
East Park Cl BRUN/LGST M13...87 M6
East Philip St CSLFD M3...........87 H1
East Rd BOL BL1.......................22 B8
　GTN M18...............................99 L1
　MANAIR M90.......................118 E6
　STLY SK15............................77 H6
　STRET M32...........................85 L8
　URM M41..............................85 J2
　WGTN/LGST M12..................99 K1
East St AIMK WN4....................64 A8
　ATH M46...............................67 J3
　AUL OL6...............................76 A8
　BURY BL9...............................5 J4
　DTN/ASHW M34.....................90 C6
　MILN OL16............................11 G2
　MILN OL16............................29 G5
　RAD M26...............................54 C1
　WGNE/HIN WN2....................65 L1
　WHIT OL12............................21 M6
East Union St OLDTF/WHR M16..86 F6
East Vw BURY BL9....................24 F1
　MDTN M24............................57 J4
East Wk EDGW/EG BL7............22 F2
Eastville Gdns BNG/LEV M19....99 H7
East Wk EDGW/EG BL7............22 A2
Eastward Av WILM/AE SK9.....126 D6

Edge Fold FWTH BL4 *..............51 M3
Edge Fold Crs WALK M28.........69 G4
Edge Fold Rd WALK M28...........69 G3
Edge Gn WALK M28 *................68 F4
Edge Green La
　GOL/RIS/CUL WA3................79 J2
Edge Green Rd AIMK WN4........64 C8
Edge Green St AIMK WN4.........64 A8
Edge Hall Rd
　WGNW/BIL/OR WN5..............46 B8
Edge Hill Av ROY/SHW OL2......59 H2
Edgehill Cha WILM/AE SK9......127 J5
Edgehill Cl ORD M5..................86 C2
Edge Hill Rd BOLS/LL BL3.........51 L1
　ROY/SHW OL2......................59 H1
Edgehill Rd SLFD M6................85 M1
Edgehill St ANC M4 *..................7 H3
Edge La DROY M43...................89 H3
　EDGW/EG BL7.......................16 D4
　HYDE SK14...........................92 B8
　STRET M32...........................97 H3
Edge Lane Rd OLD OL1.............9 K2
Edge Lane St ROY/SHW OL2.....43 H8
Edgeley Fold EDGY/DAV SK3....12 E9
Edgeley Rd EDGY/DAV SK3......12 C9
　URM M41..............................95 K4
Edgemoor ALT WA14..............116 C2
Edgemoor Cl OLDE OL4............60 A3
　RAD M26...............................38 B7
Edgemoor Dr ROCH OL11.........27 J7
Edgerley Pl AIMK WN4..............78 D1
Edgerton Rd GOL/RIS/CUL WA3..80 B4
　LIT OL15...............................21 H3
Edge Vw OLD OL1....................58 B3
Edgeware Av PWCH M25..........56 C8
Edge Ware Rd WGNS/IIMK WN3..63 C1
Edgeware Rd CHAD OL9...........74 B1
　ECC M30...............................69 K8
Edgewater ORD M5..................86 A4
Edgeway WILM/AE SK9...........126 F7
Edgeway Rd WGNS/IIMK WN3...63 K3
Edgewood WGNNW/ST WN6....30 D7
Edgeworth Av BOLE BL2............38 A3
Edgeworth Dr RUSH/FAL M14...99 H5
Edgeworth Rd
　GOL/RIS/CUL WA3................79 J3
　WGNE/HIN WN2....................65 K1
Edgeworth V EDGW/EG BL7.....17 H6
Edgmont Av BOLS/LL BL3.........36 A8
Edgware Rd NEWH/MOS M40...73 L8
Edgworth Cl HEY OL10.............40 D2
Edgworth Dr TOT/BURYW BL8..38 D3
Edilom Rd CHH M8....................72 B2
Edinburgh Cl CHD/CHDH SK8...111 J6
　WGNE/HIN WN2....................48 D4
Edinburgh Dr MPL/ROM SK6...101 M8
　WGNE/HIN WN2....................65 L1
　WGNW/BIL/OR WN5..............47 G7
Edinburgh Sq NEWH/MOS M40..73 G8
Edinburgh Wy ROCH OL11.......28 A8
Edington WHIT OL12................10 D2
Edison Rd ECC M30..................84 F4
Edison St OP/CLY M11..............89 H5
Edith Av RUSH/FAL M14...........98 D2
Edith Cavell Cl OP/CLY M11 *....88 F3
Edith St BOL BL1......................35 M6
　FWTH BL4.............................52 E2
　OLDS OL8.............................75 J1
　WGNS/IIMK WN3...................14 D5
Edlin Cl WGTN/LGST M12.........88 B7
Edlingham ROCH OL11.............10 C9
Edlinburgh Cl SALE M33.........108 A1
Edmonds St MDTN M24............57 L3
Edmonton Rd EDGY/DAV SK3..112 D8
　NEWH/MOS M40...................73 L5
Edmund Cl HTNM SK4............112 B1
Edmund Dr LEIGH WN7.............65 M7
Edmunds Ct BOLS/LL BL3..........2 B7
Edmunds Fold LIT OL15............21 K6
Edmund St CSLFD M3 *..............6 C3
　DROY M43.............................89 K4
　FAIL M35...............................74 C4
　RAD M26...............................54 E2
　ROY/SHW OL2......................43 M5
　SLFD M6................................71 K8
　WHIT OL12............................10 A2
Edna Rd LEIGH WN7.................66 D8
Edna St HYDE SK14................102 A2
Edridge Wy WGNE/HIN WN2....48 F8
Edson Rd CHH M8....................72 C1
Edward Av CCHDY M21...........97 J5
　LIT OL15...............................29 J1
　MPL/ROM SK6.....................113 H1
　SLFD M6................................85 M1
Edward Charlton Rd
　OLDTF/WHR M16..................97 K2
Edward Ct ALT WA14..............107 L5
Edward Dr AIMK WN4...............63 L8
Edward Ms CHAD OL9................8 D8
Edward Rd BRO M7..................57 G7
　ROY/SHW OL2......................43 K6
Edwards Cl MPL/ROM SK6......114 D7
Edwards Dr WHTF M45.............55 L4
Edward St AUL OL6...................91 H2
　BKLY M9................................73 H4
　BOLS/LL BL3...........................2 A8
　BRO M7..................................72 B8
　BURY BL9...............................4 F6
　CHAD OL9...............................8 D5
　CHAD OL9.............................58 D5
　DROY M43.............................90 A5
　DTN/ASHW M34.....................90 C6
　DUK SK16.............................90 F6
　FWTH BL4.............................52 E2
　GLSP SK13..........................104 F3
　HOR/BR BL6.........................35 C6
　HYDE SK14.........................101 M1
　LEIGH WN7...........................66 D8
　MDTN M24............................57 J2
　MILN OL16............................11 H2
　MPL/ROM SK6.....................114 D3
　PWCH M25............................55 L4
　RAD M26...............................38 B7
　RAD M26...............................54 E2
　SALE M33..............................97 H8
　STKP SK1..............................13 H6
　WGN WN1............................15 M4
　WGN WN1............................15 K5
　WHIT OL12............................20 B2
　WHIT OL12............................21 H8
　WHTN BL5............................50 B4
Edwin Rd OP/CLY M11..............88 E3
Edwin St BURY BL9....................5 J4
　STKP SK1..............................112 E4
　WGN WN1............................15 K5
Eeasbrook URM M41................96 A3
Egbert St NEWH/MOS M40.......73 L5
Egerton Ct WALK M28 *............69 K4

Egerton Crs DID/WITH M20 * 98 E5
Egerton Dr SALE M33 * 96 E7
Egerton Gv WALK M28 .....69 G1
Egerton Ldg EDGW/EG BL7 .....22 B3
Egerton Pk WALK M28 .....69 L5
RUSH M14 .....99 G4
Egerton Moss
HALE/TIMP WA15 .....117 G7
Egerton Pk WALK M28 .....69 L5
Egerton Rd ROY/SHW OL2 .....43 K6
Egerton Rd ECC M30 .....70 A8
EDGY/DAV SK3 .....112 D8
HALE/TIMP WA15 .....117 J2
RUSH/FAL M14 .....99 G4
WALK M28 .....69 G1
WHTF M45 .....55 J3
WILM/AE SK9 .....126 F4
Egerton Rd North CCHDY M21 .....97 M3
HTNM SK4 .....99 M7
Egerton Rd South CCHDY M21 .....97 M4
HTNM SK4 .....99 M8
Egerton St AUL OL6 .....90 F1
CSLFD M3 6
DROY M43 .....89 L3
DTN/ASHW M34 .....90 A7
ECC M30 .....84 E2
FWTH BL4 .....52 F5
HEY OL10 .....40 F3
HULME M15 .....6 B8
MDTN M24 * 56 F5
MOSL OL5 .....76 F2
OLD OL1 .....9 K4
PWCH M25 .....55 M8
WGNE/HIN WN2 .....64 E5
Egerton Ter RUSH/FAL M14 .....99 G4
Egerton V EDGW/EG BL7 .....22 A2
Eggar Cl TYLD M29 .....67 L5
Eggington St
NEWH/MOS M40 .....72 F7
Egham Ct BOLE BL2 * 3 J1
Egmont St CHH M8 .....72 D4
MOSL OL5 .....76 F2
SLFD M6 .....71 H6
Egremont Av DID/WITH M20 .....98 D5
Egremont Cl WHTF M45 .....55 G3
Egremont Ct BRO M7 .....71 M4
Egremont Gv EDGY/DAV SK3 .....12 A5
Egremont Rd MILN OL16 .....29 H8
Egret Dr IRL M44 .....94 D1
Egyptian St BOL BL1 .....2 E1
Egypt La PWCH M25 .....56 B2
Ehlinger Av GLSP SK13 .....93 K7
Eida Wy TRPK M17 .....85 M4
Eight Acre WHTF M45 .....54 F5
Eighth Av OLDS OL8 .....75 G3
Eighth St TRPK M17 .....85 M6
Eileen Gv RUSH/FAL M14 .....98 F2
Eileen Gv West RUSH/FAL M14 .....98 F2
Elaine Av BKLY M9 .....73 L2
Elaine Cl AIMK WN4 .....64 A7
Elbe St WGTN/LGST M12 * 7 M7
Elbow La ROCH OL11 .....11 G6
Elbow St BNG/LEV M19 .....99 K3
Elbut La BURY BL9 .....26 C7
Elcho Ct ALT WA14 * 116 D2
Elcho Rd ALT WA14 .....116 D1
Elcombe Av GOL/RIS/CUL WA3 .....80 B5
Elcot Cl NEWH/MOS M40 * 72 F7
Elderberry Cl UPML OL3 .....45 M7
WGN WN1 .....31 L3
Elderberry Wy WILM/AE SK9 .....127 J4
Elder Cl OFTN SK2 .....113 G4
TOT/BURYW BL8 .....24 C7
Eldercot Gv BOLS/LL BL3 .....35 K8
Eldercot Rd BOLS/LL BL3 .....35 K8
Eldercroft Rd
HALE/TIMP WA15 .....108 F7
Elder Dr BOLS/LL BL3 .....37 H7
Elderfield Dr MPL/ROM SK6 .....101 J8
Elder Gv NEWH/MOS M40 .....74 C2
Eldermount Rd BKLY M9 .....73 G2
Elder Rd OLDE OL4 .....60 D6
Elder St MILN OL16 .....11 J8
Elderwood CHAD OL9 .....58 B5
Eldon Cl DTN/ASHW M34 .....90 M6
Eldon Gdns AIMK WN4 .....63 K6
Eldon Pl ECC M30 .....84 F3
Eldon Prec OLDS OL8 * 9 H8
Eldon Rd EDGY/DAV SK3 .....12 D8
IRL M44 .....94 D2
Eldon St BOLE BL2 .....36 E3
BURY BL9 .....4 F1
LEIGH WN7 .....66 A6
OLDS OL8 .....9 J8
Eldon Street Est OLDS OL8 * 9 J8
Eldridge Dr NEWH/MOS M40 .....73 K7
Eldroth Av WYTH/NTH M22 .....118 F1
Eleanor Rd CCHDY M21 .....97 J4
ROY/SHW OL2 .....59 H2
Eleanor St BOL BL1 .....22 D7
OLD OL1 .....8 F2
WGNS/IIMK WN3 .....14 C6
Electo St OP/CLY M11 .....89 H5
Elevator Rd TRPK M17 .....86 B6
Eleventh St TRPK M17 .....86 A6
Elf Mill Cl EDGY/DAV SK3 .....112 B6
Elford Gv GTN M18 .....89 K8
Elgar St WGTN/LGST M12 .....99 K1
DID/WITH M20 * 111 G1
Elgin Cl WGNE/HIN WN2 .....48 D4
Elgin Dr SALE M33 .....109 H1
Elgin Rd DUK SK16 .....90 F6
OLDE OL4 .....60 B6
Elgin St AULW OL7 .....75 K8
BOL BL1 .....35 M2
STLY SK15 .....91 L3
Elgol Cl EDGY/DAV SK3 .....112 A5
Elgol Dr BOLS/LL BL3 .....35 H7
Elham Cl RAD M26 .....53 M5
Eliot Cl WGNS/IIMK WN3 .....47 K7
Eliot Rd ECC M30 .....85 C3
Eli St CHAD OL9 .....74 D1
Eliza Ann St ECC M30 .....84 F3
NEWH/MOS M40 .....72 F8
Elizabethan Dr
WGNS/IIMK WN3 .....48 B8
Elizabethan Wy MILN OL16 .....29 H6
Elizabeth Av CHAD OL9 .....74 D1
DTN/ASHW M34 .....90 B7
POY/DIS SK12 .....123 M7
ROY/SHW OL2 .....43 J5
STKP SK1 .....13 K7
WGNE/HIN WN2 .....65 H3
Elizabeth Ct HTNM SK4 .....12 C7
Elizabeth Gv ROY/SHW OL2 .....43 L6
Elizabeth Rd PART M31 .....94 C8
RNFD/HAY WA11 .....78 B5
Elizabeth Slinger Rd
DID/WITH M20 .....98 B8

Elizabeth St ATH M46 .....67 G1
AUL OL6 .....75 L8
CHH M8 .....72 D7
DTN/ASHW M34 .....101 G1
HEY OL10 .....40 F2
HYDE SK14 .....102 A1
LEIGH WN7 .....81 L1
RAD M26 .....54 D1
RAMS BL0 .....19 G1
ROCH OL11 .....41 M1
SWIN M27 .....70 D3
WGNE/HIN WN2 .....48 D4
WHTF M45 .....55 J5
Eliza St HULME M15 .....87 H6
RAMS BL0 .....19 G6
Elkanagh Gdns SLFD M6 .....86 C1
Elkstone Av LHULT M38 .....52 D6
Elkstone Cl WGNS/IIMK WN3 .....62 F2
Elkwood Cl WGN WN1 .....31 L8
Elladene Pk CCHDY M21 .....97 M4
Ellanby Cl RUSH/FAL M14 .....98 F1
Elland Cl BURY BL9 .....55 L2
WHTN BL5 .....50 A1
Ellaston Dr URM M41 * 96 A2
Ellastone Gv SLFD M6 .....70 F8
Ellbourne Rd BKLY M9 .....72 D1
Ellenbrook Cl
WGTN/LGST M12 .....88 E6
Ellenbrook Rd WALK M28 .....68 E4
Ellen Brook Rd
WYTH/NTH M22 .....118 F4
Ellendale Gra WALK M28 .....68 E4
Ellen Gv FWTH BL4 .....54 A7
Ellenhall Cl BKLY M9 .....73 C4
Ellenor Dr TYLD M29 .....67 M5
Ellenroad Ap MILN OL16 .....29 K8
Ellenrod Dr WHIT OL12 .....27 K2
Ellenrod La WHIT OL12 .....27 K2
Ellenshaw Cl WHIT OL12 .....27 K2
Ellen St BOL BL1 .....35 M1
CHAD OL9 .....8 C3
DROY M43 .....89 L4
HTNM SK4 .....112 A1
WGN WN1 .....15 H5
Ellen Wilkinson Crs
WGTN/LGST M12 .....88 D7
Elleray Cl BOLS/LL BL3 .....53 M1
Elleray Rd MDTN M24 .....57 J7
SLFD M6 .....71 G7
Ellerbeck Cl BOLE BL2 .....22 F7
Ellerbeck Crs WALK M28 .....68 F5
Ellerby Av SWIN M27 .....70 D1
Ellerscroft NM/HAY SK22 * 125 G3
Ellesmere Av AUL OL6 .....75 M5
ECC M30 .....85 H2
MPL/ROM SK6 .....114 C6
WALK M28 .....68 F1
Ellesmere Cir URM M41 .....85 G5
Ellesmere Cl DUK SK16 .....91 H5
Ellesmere Dr CHD/CHDH SK8 .....111 K7
Ellesmere Gdns BOLS/LL BL3 .....52 A1
Ellesmere Rd AIMK WN4 .....63 J7
ALT WA14 .....108 A6
BOLS/LL BL3 .....51 M1
CCHDY M21 .....97 M3
ECC M30 .....70 B8
EDGY/DAV SK3 .....12 E5
GOL/RIS/CUL WA3 .....81 H8
WGNW/BIL/OR WN5 .....47 G6
Ellesmere Rd North HTNM SK4 .....99 M7
Ellesmere Rd South
CCHDY M21 .....97 M4
ECC M30 .....85 G3
FAIL M35 .....74 C4
FWTH BL4 .....53 G4
LEIGH WN7 .....66 C3
LHULT M38 .....68 F1
ROCH OL11 .....10 E8
SWIN M27 .....70 A5
SWIN M27 .....70 D3
TYLD M29 .....67 K3
TYLD M29 .....67 M7
Ellesmere Ter RUSH/FAL M14 .....99 G5
Ellingham Cl OP/CLY M11 .....88 C3
Elliot Sq OLD OL1 * 9 H3
Elliot St BOL BL1 .....35 M1
OLDE OL4 .....60 B6
Elliott Av GOL/RIS/CUL WA3 .....79 L3
HYDE SK14 .....91 C7
WGNE/HIN WN2 .....49 G5
Elliott Dr SALE M33 .....96 B3
TYLD M29 .....67 H4
WHIT OL12 .....11 C2
Ellis Crs WALK M28 .....68 L1
Ellis Dr CHH M8 .....72 E3
Ellis Fold WHIT OL12 .....27 H2
Ellis La MDTN M24 .....56 E4
Ellison St HYDE SK14 .....93 C7
Ellison St GLSP SK13 .....105 C3
Ellis Rd WGNW/BIL/OR WN5 .....62 A3
Ellis St BOLS/LL BL3 .....2 B8
CHH M8 .....72 B8
HULME M15 .....87 H6
HYDE SK14 .....102 C2
TOT/BURYW BL8 * 38 E2
WGN WN1 .....15 K1
Elliston Sq WGTN/LGST M12 .....88 D6
Ellonby Ri HOR/BR BL6 .....34 F7
Ellor St SLFD M6 .....86 C1
Ellwood Dr STKP SK1 .....112 E3
Elly Clough ROY/SHW OL2 * 58 F1
Elm Av AIMK WN4 .....63 C7
GOL/RIS/CUL WA3 .....79 K3
HOR/BR BL6 .....34 B3
RAD M26 .....54 C4
WGNNW/ST WN6 .....31 J4
WGNW/BIL/OR WN5 .....47 H6
Elmbank Av DID/WITH M20 .....98 B8
Elmbank Rd MDTN M24 .....57 M4
Elmbridge Wk BOLS/LL BL3 * 2 A8
Elm Cl HYDE SK14 .....92 D8
POY/DIS SK12 .....129 K1
Elm Crs WALK M28 .....68 E2
WILM/AE SK9 .....130 E2
Elm Cft WGN WN1 .....31 L8
Elmdale CHD/CHDH SK8 .....119 K2
Elmdale Wk HULME M15 * 87 K6
Elm Dr STRET M32 .....96 F4
WGNNW/BIL/OR WN5 .....62 A7
Elmfield WGNNW/ST WN6 .....30 E6
Elmfield Av AIMK WN4 .....74 F6
WYTH/NTH M22 .....110 B4
Elmfield Dr MPL/ROM SK6 .....114 D6
Elmfield Rd DTN/ASHW M34 .....89 M4
EDGY/DAV SK3 .....111 G1
WGN WN1 .....31 L7
WILM/AE SK9 .....130 E2
Elmfield St BOL BL1 .....36 C2
CHH M8 .....72 D6
Elmgate Gv BNG/LEV M19 .....99 K3

Elm Gv AUL OL6 .....75 M7
DID/WITH M20 .....110 G1
DROY M43 .....89 G2
DTN/ASHW M34 .....90 A8
EDGW/EG BL7 .....22 B3
FAIL M35 .....74 E4
GLSP SK13 .....104 C3
HYDE SK14 .....102 C2
MILN OL16 .....43 K1
OLDE OL4 .....60 E6
PWCH M25 .....55 K6
ROCH OL11 .....10 D9
SALE M33 .....96 E6
SWIN M27 .....69 L3
URM M41 .....96 B2
WHIT OL12 .....21 G7
WILM/AE SK9 .....130 E2
Elmham Wk
NEWH/MOS M40 .....72 F8
Elmhow Gv WGNS/IIMK WN3 .....63 G2
Elmhurst Dr BNG/LEV M19 .....99 J7
Elmira Wy ORD M5 .....86 D6
Elmley Cl OFTN SK2 .....113 K7
Elmore Wd LIT OL15 .....21 K6
Elmpark Ga WHIT OL12 .....27 L1
Elmpark Gv WHIT OL12 .....27 L1
Elmpark V WHIT OL12 .....27 L1
Elmpark Vw WHIT OL12 .....27 L1
Elmpark Wy WHIT OL12 .....27 L1
Elmridge LEIGH WN7 .....66 E6
Elmridge Dr
HALE/TIMP WA15 .....117 L4
Elm Rd BOLS/LL BL3 .....53 L2
CHD/CHDH SK8 .....110 D7
DID/WITH M20 .....98 D8
FWTH BL4 .....53 J7
HALE/TIMP WA15 .....117 G1
MPL/ROM SK6 .....123 H1
OLDE OL4 .....75 G3
RNFD/HAY WA11 * 78 B5
WGNE/HIN WN2 .....64 F5
WHTN BL5 .....50 B5
Elm Rd South EDGY/DAV SK3 .....111 K5
Elmsbury St AIMK WN4 .....63 J5
Elms Cl WHTF M45 .....55 J4
Elmscott Wk BRUN/LGST M13 * 88 A7
Elmsdale Av BKLY M9 .....56 F7
Elmsfield Av ROCH OL11 .....27 H5
Elmsleigh Rd CHD/CHDH SK8 .....119 J3
Elmsmere Rd DID/WITH M20 .....111 J3
Elms Rd HTNM SK4 .....99 L7
STLY SK15 .....92 A1
WHTF M45 .....55 J3
Elms St WHTF M45 .....55 J3
Elmstead Av DID/WITH M20 .....98 D6
Elmsted Cl CHD/CHDH SK8 .....120 D1
Elmstone Cl BKLY M9 .....72 F2
Elmstone Dr ROY/SHW OL2 .....43 G7
Elmstone Gv BOL BL1 * 2 E1
Elm St BURY BL9 .....5 K5
ECC M30 .....85 G3
FAIL M35 .....74 C4
FWTH BL4 .....53 G6
HEY OL10 .....41 G2
LEIGH WN7 .....81 J1
MDTN M24 .....57 M4
MPL/ROM SK6 .....101 J8
RAMS BL0 .....19 C6
RAMS BL0 .....19 H1
SWIN M27 .....70 B3
TYLD M29 .....67 K3
WGNE/HIN WN2 .....64 D7
WHIT OL12 .....20 B2
WHIT OL12 .....28 C3
Elmsway BRAM/HZG SK7 .....120 E5
HALE/TIMP WA15 .....117 K4
MPL/ROM SK6 .....123 G6
Elmswood Av RUSH/FAL M14 .....98 C3
Elmswood Dr HYDE SK14 * 102 D1
Elmsworth Av BNG/LEV M19 .....99 J8
Elmton Rd BKLY M9 .....73 H1
Elm Tree Cl FAIL M35 .....74 E5
Elm Tree Dr DUK SK16 .....91 J5
WYTH/NTH M22 .....118 F1
Elmtree Dr HTNM SK4 .....12 B3
Elm Tree La GOL/RIS/CUL WA3 .....80 C5
Elmwood SALE M33 .....95 M8
Elmwood Av AIMK WN4 .....78 D2
Elmwood Cl WHTN BL5 .....51 K6
Elmwood Dr ROY/SHW OL2 .....42 F7
Elmwood Gv BKLY M9 .....73 J5
BOL BL1 * 35 M4
FWTH BL4 .....52 F6
Elmwood Pk STLY SK15 .....92 A1
Elnup Av WGNNW/ST WN6 .....30 C6
Elsa Rd BNG/LEV M19 .....99 M3
Elsdon Dr ATH M46 .....51 H8
GTN M18 .....89 G6
Elsdon Gdns BOLE BL2 .....36 E3
Elsdon Rd BRUN/LGST M13 .....99 H2
Elsfield Cl BOL BL1 * 36 A2
Elsham Dr WALK M28 .....68 D8
Elsham Gdns GTN M18 .....88 D8
Elsie St BKLY M9 .....73 H4
FWTH BL4 .....52 F5
RAMS BL0 .....18 D8
Elsinore Av IRL M44 .....94 D3
Elsinore Cl FAIL M35 .....74 E5
Elsinore Rd OLDTF/WHR M16 .....86 D6
Elsinore St BOLE BL2 .....36 E1
Elsma Rd NEWH/MOS M40 .....74 B8
Elsmore Rd RUSH/FAL M14 .....98 D3
Elson Dr HYDE SK14 .....102 B5
Elstead Gv AIMK WN4 .....63 G8
Elsted Rd UPML OL3 .....61 J7
Elston Av NEWLW WA12 .....78 F7
Elstree Av NEWH/MOS M40 .....73 L8
Elswick Av BOLS/LL BL3 .....35 L7
BRAM/HZG SK7 .....121 L4
CCHDY M21 .....98 A8
Elsworth Cl RAD M26 .....54 E3
Elsworth Dr BOL BL1 .....22 C8
Elsworth St CSLFD M3 .....87 K1
Elterwater Cl TOT/BURYW BL8 * 24 D7
Eltham Av OFTN SK2 * 112 F7
Eltham Cl AIMK WN4 .....79 L1
Eltham Dr URM M41 .....84 F8
Eltham St BNG/LEV M19 .....99 K2
Elton Av BNG/LEV M19 .....99 K4
FWTH BL4 .....52 E5
Elton Brook Cl TOT/BURYW BL8 .....38 E1
Elton Cl COL/RIS/CUL WA3 .....80 B5
WHTF M45 .....55 K4
WILM/AE SK9 .....127 J3
Elton Dr BRAM/HZG SK7 .....121 H4
Elton Rd SALE M33 .....108 G4

Elton St BOLE BL2 .....3 H4
BRO M7 .....87 C1
ROCH OL11 .....41 M3
STRET M32 .....86 C7
Elton Vale Rd TOT/BURYW BL8 .....38 E2
Elvate Crs CHH M8 .....72 B7
Elverdon Cl HULME M15 .....87 H7
Elverston Cl WYTH/NTH M22 .....110 B3
Elverston Wy CHAD OL9 .....8 C3
Elvey St NEWH/MOS M40 .....73 J7
Elvington Cl
WGNW/BIL/OR WN5 .....46 E3
Elvington Crs WALK M28 .....68 F4
Elway Rd AIMK WN4 .....78 F1
Elwick Cl OLDTF/WHR M16 .....98 C1
Elworthy Gv WGN WN1 .....48 B2
Elwyn Av BNG/LEV M19 .....99 K6
Elwyn Av WYTH/NTH M22 .....110 A5
Ely Av STRET M32 .....96 C1
Ely Cl WALK M28 .....68 C4
Ely Crs FAIL M35 .....74 C7
Ely Dr TOT/BURYW BL8 .....4 C1
TYLD M29 .....67 M5
Ely Gv BOL BL1 * 2 D1
Elysian St OP/CLY M11 .....88 F4
Ely St CHAD OL9 .....8 B9
Emaline Gra SLFD M6 .....86 B2
Embankment Rd EDGW/EG BL7 .....16 F7
Ember St OP/CLY M11 * 89 C2
Embla Wk BOLS/LL BL3 .....36 D8
Embleton Cl BOLE BL2 .....23 H8
Embleton Cl BOLE BL2 .....23 H8
Embsay Cl BOL BL1 .....22 A7
Emerald Av LEIGH WN7 .....66 B8
Emerald Dr OLDE OL4 .....60 B1
Emerald Rd WYTH/NTH M22 .....119 H5
Emerald St BOL BL1 .....36 C1
DTN/ASHW M34 .....101 H1
WGNNW/ST WN6 .....47 K1
Emerson Av ECC M30 .....85 K1
Emerson Dr MDTN M24 .....57 J3
Emerson St ORD M5 .....86 A2
Emery Av CCHDY M21 .....97 M6
Emery Cl ALT WA14 .....108 A5
HTNM SK4 .....99 M8
Emily Beavan Cl OP/CLY M11 .....88 F4
Emily Cl FAIL M35 .....74 D3
Emily Pl DROY M43 .....89 J3
Emley St BNG/LEV M19 .....99 L3
Emlyn Gv CHD/CHDH SK8 .....111 K6
Emlyn St FWTH BL4 .....52 F3
SWIN M27 .....70 A4
WALK M28 .....69 G1
Emlyn St BOL BL1 * 48 F7
Emmanuel Cl BOLS/LL BL3 * 2 B8
Emmanuel Pl BOLS/LL BL3 * 2 B8
Emma St OLDS OL8 .....75 J1
WHIT OL12 .....10 C2
Emmerson St SWIN M27 .....70 C3
Emmett St HOR/BR BL6 .....33 L1
Emmett St East
NEWH/MOS M40 .....73 H7
Emmott Cl HEY OL10 .....40 F2
Emmott Wy OLD OL1 .....9 K6
Empire Rd BOLE BL2 .....37 G4
DUK SK16 .....90 F6
Empire St CHH M8 .....72 C8
HEY OL10 .....41 G2
LEIGH WN7 .....81 J1
MDTN M24 .....57 M4
MPL/ROM SK6 .....101 J8
RAMS BL0 .....19 C6
SWIN M27 .....70 B3
TYLD M29 .....67 K3
WGNE/HIN WN2 .....64 D7
Empress Av MPL/ROM SK6 .....114 C7
Empress Dr HTNM SK4 .....100 A8
LEIGH WN7 .....67 H6
Empress St BOL BL1 * 35 L3
CHH M8 .....72 C4
OLDTF/WHR M16 .....86 F5
Emsworth Dr SALE M33 .....108 F3
Ena Crs LEIGH WN7 .....65 H5
Ena St BOLS/LL BL3 .....52 D1
OLDE OL4 .....59 M3
Enbridge St ORD M5 * 86 M3
Encombe Pl CSLFD M3 6
Endcott Cl GTN M18 .....88 E6
Enderby Rd NEWH/MOS M40 .....73 L8
Ending Rake WHIT OL12 .....20 A8
Endon Dr CCHDY M21 .....98 B6
Endon St BOL BL1 .....35 L3
Endsleigh Rd DID/WITH M20 .....98 F6
Endsley Av WALK M28 .....68 D4
Energy St NEWH/MOS M40 * 88 E1
Enfield Av BNG/LEV M19 .....99 K6
OLDS OL8 .....75 H1
Enfield Cl BOL BL1 .....36 B3
BURY BL9 .....39 J7
ECC M30 .....85 G4
Enfield Dr OP/CLY M11 .....88 F2
Enfield Gv LEIGH WN7 .....66 D6
Enfield Rd ECC M30 .....70 A8
SWIN M27 .....70 C6
Enfield St HYDE SK14 * 102 B5
WALK M28 .....53 G7
WGNW/BIL/OR WN5 .....46 E3
Enford Av WYTH/NTH M22 .....118 C2
Engell Cl GTN M18 .....88 F7
Engine St WGNE/HIN WN2 .....48 D5
Engine Fold Rd WALK M28 .....68 A5
Engine La ATH M46 .....51 K8
Engine St CHAD OL9 .....58 E8
Engledene BOL BL1 .....22 A6
English St LEIGH WN7 .....66 D6
Enid Cl BRO M7 .....72 B7
Enid Pl WGNE/HIN WN2 .....64 C4
Ennerdale Av AIMK WN4 .....63 L8
BOLE BL2 .....37 J2
CCHDY M21 .....98 A8
ROY/SHW OL2 .....43 J5
SWIN M27 .....70 C6
Ennerdale Cl BOLS/LL BL3 .....53 J1
CHD/CHDH SK8 .....119 K1
HALE/TIMP WA15 .....108 D5
SALE M33 .....96 E8
Ennerdale Dr BURY BL9 .....55 K2
CHD/CHDH SK8 .....119 K1
HALE/TIMP WA15 .....108 F5
MDTN M24 .....57 J7
Ennerdale Gv FWTH BL4 .....52 C4
Ennerdale Pl WGNE/HIN WN2 .....48 E4
Ennerdale Rd LEIGH WN7 .....66 F6
MDTN M24 .....57 H2
MPL/ROM SK6 .....101 L8
PART M31 .....106 B1
ROCH OL11 .....27 L8
STKP SK1 .....112 E5
STRET M32 .....96 C1
TYLD M29 .....67 L5
Ennerdale Ter STLY SK15 .....91 K1
Ennis Cl WYTH/NTH M22 .....118 D3
Ennismore Av ECC M30 .....85 K4
Ensor Wy NM/HAY SK22 .....124 E5
Enstone Dr NEWH/MOS M40 .....74 A3
Enstone Wy TYLD M29 .....67 M3
Enterprise Pk HOR/BR BL6 .....33 M4
Enterprise Wy
GOL/RIS/CUL WA3 .....80 D5

Entwisle Av URM M41 .....84 E6
Entwisle Rd MILN OL16 .....11 G3
Entwisle Rw FWTH BL4 .....53 G4
Entwisle St FWTH BL4 * 53 G3
MILN OL16 .....29 H6
SWIN M27 .....70 A3
Entwistle Gv LEIGH WN7 .....81 M1
Entwistle Hall La EDGW/EG BL7 .....16 E1
Entwistle St BOLE BL2 .....3 K2
Enver Rd CHH M8 .....72 E4
Enville Rd ALT WA14 .....116 A3
NEWH/MOS M40 .....73 L3
SLFD M6 .....71 H6
Enville St AUL OL6 .....90 F1
BKLY M9 .....73 G1
DTN/ASHW M34 .....90 B5
Envoy Cl WGNW/BIL/OR WN5 .....47 H3
Ephraim's Fold WGNE/HIN WN2 .....33 G6
Epping Cl AUL OL6 .....75 M5
CHAD OL9 .....58 B4
Epping Dr SALE M33 .....95 M7
Epping Rd DTN/ASHW M34 .....100 E2
Epping St HULME M15 .....87 H8
Eppleworth Ri SWIN M27 .....70 D1
Epsom Av BNG/LEV M19 .....99 J8
SALE M33 .....107 M2
WILM/AE SK9 .....120 A8
Epsom Cl BRAM/HZG SK7 .....122 B2
ROCH OL11 .....27 H4
Epsom Dr WGNE/HIN WN2 .....64 C5
Epworth St ANC M4 .....7 M5
Equitable St MILN OL16 .....29 J7
OLDE OL4 .....60 A4
Era St BOLE BL2 .....37 H1
SALE M33 .....96 E5
Ercall Av WGTN/LGST M12 .....88 C5
Erica Av OLDE OL4 .....44 C8
Erica Cl RDSH SK5 .....100 C4
Erica Dr BNG/LEV M19 .....99 H8
Eric Brook Cl RUSH/FAL M14 .....98 F1
Eric Bullows Cl
WYTH/NTH M22 .....118 E3
Eric St LIT OL15 .....21 L6
OLDE OL4 .....59 M6
Erin Cl CHAD OL9 .....8 A8
Erin St OP/CLY M11 * 89 H5
Erith Cl RDSH SK5 .....100 E6
Erith Rd OLDE OL4 .....59 L6
Erlesmere Av DTN/ASHW M34 .....90 D8
Erlesmere Cl OLDE OL4 .....44 D8
Erlington Av OLDTF/WHR M16 .....97 L1
Ermen Rd ECC M30 .....84 F4
Ermington Dr CHH M8 .....72 A8
Erneley Cl WGTN/LGST M12 .....99 L1
Ernest St BOL BL1 .....2 A5
CHD/CHDH SK8 .....110 F6
OFTN SK2 .....112 D6
PWCH M25 .....55 J8
Ernest Ter WHIT OL12 .....28 C3
Ernlouen Av BOL BL1 .....35 K4
Ernocroft Gv GTN M18 * 89 H6
Ernocroft La MPL/ROM SK6 .....115 H1
Ernocroft Rd MPL/ROM SK6 .....114 E3
Erradale Crs WGNS/IIMK WN3 .....63 G2
Errington Cl OFTN SK2 .....113 H6
Errington Cl BOLS/LL BL3 .....35 J7
Errington Dr BRO M7 .....72 A8
Errol Av BKLY M9 .....56 D7
WYTH/NTH M22 .....109 M8
Erwood Crs BNG/LEV M19 .....99 K5
Erwood Rd BNG/LEV M19 .....99 K5
Erskine Cl BOLS/LL BL3 .....35 H7
Erskine Pl WGNE/HIN WN2 .....64 E3
Erskine Rd BKLY M9 .....57 H7
PART M31 .....106 C1
Erskine St HULME M15 .....87 G6
MPL/ROM SK6 .....114 C2
Erwin St NEWH/MOS M40 .....73 L6
Erwood Rd BNG/LEV M19 .....99 K5
Eryngo St STKP SK1 .....13 M5
Escott St OLDTF/WHR M16 .....98 C1
Escow Dr SALE M33 .....108 E4
Esk Cl URM M41 .....84 D8
Eskdale CHD/CHDH SK8 .....110 F8
Eskdale Av BOLE BL2 .....37 J2
BRAM/HZG SK7 .....120 E7
DID/WITH M20 .....98 D5
HOR/BR BL6 .....34 B3
MPL/ROM SK6 .....101 L7
OLDS OL8 .....59 G8
ROCH OL11 .....27 L8
ROY/SHW OL2 .....43 G5
WGN WN1 .....47 L1
Eskdale Cl BURY BL9 .....55 L1
Eskdale Dr HALE/TIMP WA15 .....108 F5
MDTN M24 .....57 J7
Eskdale Gv FWTH BL4 .....52 C4
Eskdale Ms UPML OL3 * 61 L7
WGNE/HIN WN2 .....49 H1
Eskrick St BOL BL1 .....36 A2
Eskrigge Cl BRO M7 .....72 C4
Esmond Rd CHH M8 .....72 D5
Esmont Dr MDTN M24 .....57 H1
The Esplanade MILN OL16 .....10 D5
Essex Av BURY BL9 .....40 B3
DID/WITH M20 .....98 B8
DROY M43 .....89 K1
EDGY/DAV SK3 .....12 B7
Essex Cl FAIL M35 .....74 C7
ROY/SHW OL2 .....43 J5
Essex Dr BURY BL9 .....5 G9
Essex Pl TYLD M29 .....67 J1
Essex Rd GTN M18 .....100 C1
RDSH SK5 .....100 F7
WGN WN1 .....31 L1
Essex St CMANW M2 .....6 F5
HOR/BR BL6 .....34 A3
ROCH OL11 .....10 E7
WGN WN1 .....15 K2
Essex Wy OLDTF/WHR M16 .....87 C7
Essingden St BOLS/LL BL3 .....36 A8
Essington Dr NEWH/MOS M40 .....73 H7
Estate St OLDS OL8 .....59 J8
Estate St South OLDS OL8 .....59 J8
Est Bank Rd RAMS BL0 .....24 D1
Esther St OLDE OL4 .....59 M5
Esthwaite Dr TYLD M29 .....67 G3
Estonfield Dr URM M41 .....96 C2
Eston St BRUN/LGST M13 .....88 A8
Eswick St OP/CLY M11 .....88 F3
Etchells St STKP SK1 .....13 J4
Etchell St NEWH/MOS M40 * 72 F7
Ethel Av BKLY M9 .....57 G8
SWIN M27 .....70 E4
Ethel Ct MILN OL16 .....11 G6
Ethel St BOLS/LL BL3 .....2 C8
OLDS OL8 .....75 J1
WHIT OL12 .....10 C2
Ethel Ter BNG/LEV M19 .....99 M3

Etherley Cl IRL M44 .... 94 D2
Etherow Av MPL/ROM SK6 .... 114 D2
Etherow Brow HYDE SK14 .... 103 L4
NEWH/MOS M40 * 74 C2
Etherow Wy CLSP SK13 .... 93 K3
Etherstone St CHH M8 .... 72 F4
LEIGH WN7 .... 66 B8
Eton Av OLDS OL8 .... 75 H1
Eton Cl OLDTF/WHR M16 .... 87 H7
ROCH OL11 .... 27 L6
Eton Ct OLDTF/WHR M16 * 87 H7
Eton Dr CHD/CHDH SK8 .... 119 L2
Eton Hill Rd RAD M26 .... 38 F7
Eton St LEIGH WN7 .... 81 J1
Eton Wy WGNW/BIL/OR WN5 .... 46 C4
Eton Wy North RAD M26 .... 38 F7
Eton Wy South RAD M26 .... 38 F7
Etruria Cl BRUN/LGST M13 .... 88 B7
Ettington Cl TOT/BURYW BL8 .... 38 C1
Ettrick Cl OP/CLY M11 .... 89 G5
Euclid Cl IRL M44 .... 88 B3
Europa Ga TRPK M17 .... 86 A7
Europa Wy EDGY/DAV SK3 .... 111 M6
RAD M26 .... 53 L5
TRPK M17 .... 86 A7
Eustace St BOLS/LL BL3 .... 52 D1
CHAD OL9 .... 8 B1
Euston Av BKLY M9 .... 73 K1
Euxton Cl TOT/BURYW BL8 .... 38 D4
Evan Cl DID/WITH M20 .... 110 D1
Evans Cl DID/WITH M20 .... 110 D1
RNFD/HAY WA11 .... 78 C5
Evans Rd ECC M30 .... 84 D3
Evans St AUL OL6 .... 6 D1
CSLFD M5 .... 6 D1
LEIGH WN7 .... 66 C7
MDTN M24 .... 57 L4
OLD OL1 .... 9 J3
Evanstone Cl HOR/BR BL6 .... 33 L1
Evan St NEWH/MOS M40 .... 73 H7
Eva Rd EDGY/DAV SK3 .... 111 K5
Eva St LEIGH WN7 .... 65 M5
RUSH/FAL M14 .... 98 F1
WHIT OL12 .... 28 D2
Evelyn St OLD OL1 .... 59 L3
RUSH/FAL M14 .... 99 G4
Evening St FAIL M35 .... 74 C4
Evenley Cl OP/CLY M11 * 89 H6
Everard Cl WALK M28 .... 68 E4
Everard St ORD M5 .... 86 F5
Everbrom Rd BOLS/LL BL3 .... 51 K2
Everest Av AULW OL7 .... 75 L7
Everest Cl HYDE SK14 .... 91 K8
Everest Pl WGN WN1 .... 47 M2
Everest Rd ATH M46 .... 50 F7
HYDE SK14 .... 91 K8
Everest St ROCH OL11 .... 42 D2
Everett Rd DID/WITH M20 .... 98 E6
Everglade OLDS OL8 .... 75 H5
The Evergreens HOR/BR BL6 .... 34 B3
Everleigh Cl BOLE BL2 .... 23 H7
Everleigh Dr BRO M7 .... 72 C6
Eversden Ct BRO M7 * 72 B8
Everside Dr CHH M8 .... 72 B6
Eversley Rd DID/WITH M20 .... 110 D1
Everton Rd OLDS OL8 .... 75 C1
RDSH SK5 .... 100 A4
Everton St AIMK WN4 .... 63 C7
SWIN M27 .... 70 B4
Every St ANC M4 .... 88 A3
BURY BL9 .... 4 F1
RAMS BL0 * 19 G6
Evesham Av GLSP SK13 .... 93 K7
HTNM SK4 .... 12 A1
NTHM/RTH M23 .... 109 G5
Evesham Cl BOLS/LL BL3 .... 2 B7
LEIGH WN7 .... 81 G3
MDTN M24 .... 57 L7
Evesham Dr FWTH BL4 .... 52 E2
Evesham Drive WILM/AE SK9 * 127 G2
Evesham Gdns MDTN M24 * 57 L7
Evesham Gv AUL OL6 .... 75 M5
SALE M33 .... 97 H8
Evesham Rd BKLY M9 .... 73 K2
CHD/CHDH SK8 .... 111 K8
MDTN M24 .... 57 K7
Evesham Wk BOLS/LL BL3 .... 2 B7
MDTN M24 .... 57 L7
OLDS OL8 .... 9 H9
Eveside Cl CHD/CHDH SK8 .... 111 L8
Eve St OLDS OL8 .... 75 J2
Ewan St GTN M18 .... 89 G6
Ewart Av ORD M5 .... 86 D3
Ewart St BOL BL1 .... 36 B2
Ewhurst Av SWIN M27 .... 70 A6
Ewing St CHH M8 .... 72 D3
Ewood OLDS OL8 .... 75 K4
Ewood Dr TOT/BURYW BL8 .... 38 D4
Exbourne Rd WYTH/NTH M22 .... 118 E3
Exbury WHIT OL12 .... 10 D2
Exbury St RUSH/FAL M14 .... 99 G5
Excelsior Gdns HEY OL10 .... 41 J4
Excelsior Ter LIT OL15 .... 29 J1
Exchange Quay ORD M5 .... 86 D6
Exchange Sq CSLFD M5 .... 6 F3
Exchange St BOL BL1 * 2 E5
CSLFD M3 * 6 F4
EDGY/DAV SK3 .... 13 G5
RAMS BL0 .... 19 G1
Exeter Av BOLE BL2 .... 36 E2
DTN/ASHW M34 .... 101 J4
ECC M30 .... 70 D8
FWTH BL4 .... 52 C3
RAD M26 .... 38 D2
Exeter Cl CHD/CHDH SK8 .... 120 B4
DUK SK16 .... 90 F6
Exeter Dr AUL OL6 .... 76 A5
IRL M44 .... 94 C3
WGNE/HIN WN2 .... 33 G7
Exeter Gv ROCH OL11 .... 10 F8
Exeter Rd RDSH SK5 .... 100 F7
URM M41 .... 85 G8
WGNE/HIN WN2 .... 49 H7
Exeter St ROCH OL11 .... 10 F8
SLFD M6 .... 86 B2
Exford Av WGNS/IIMK WN3 .... 47 L8
Exford Cl NEWH/MOS M40 .... 88 A1
RDSH SK5 .... 100 C6
Exford Dr BOLE BL2 .... 37 K6
Exit Rd West MANAIR M90 .... 118 C6
Exmoor Cl AUL OL6 .... 75 M5
Exmouth Av RDSH SK5 .... 100 F7
Exmouth Pl MILN OL16 .... 42 D1
Exmouth Sq MILN OL16 * 42 D1
Exmouth Rd SALE M33 .... 96 A7
Exmouth Wk OLDTF/WHR M16 .... 98 B1
Eyam Gv OFTN SK2 .... 113 C8
Eyam Ms GLSP SK13 .... 104 A3
Eyam Rd BRAM/HZG SK7 .... 122 A4

Eycott Dr MDTN M24 .... 57 G3
Eyebrook Rd ALT WA14 .... 116 C3
Eyet Cl LEIGH WN7 .... 66 B7
Eyet St LEIGH WN7 .... 66 B7
Eynford Av RDSH SK5 .... 100 F1
Eyre St HULME M15 .... 87 K7

F

Faber St ANC M4 .... 87 K1
Factory Brow HOR/BR BL6 .... 33 G1
MDTN M24 .... 56 F5
Factory Fold WGNE/HIN WN2 * 48 D5
Factory La BKLY M9 .... 73 G3
CSLFD M3 * 6 A4
Factory St MDTN M24 .... 54 E1
RAD M26 .... 54 E1
RAMS BL0 .... 18 F5
TYLD M29 .... 67 J3
Factory St East ATH M46 .... 66 F1
Factory St West ATH M46 .... 66 F1
Faggy St WGNS/IIMK WN3 .... 15 G6
Failsworth Rd FAIL M35 .... 74 E5
Fair Acres BOLE BL2 .... 37 H1
Fairacres WGNNW/ST WN6 .... 30 E3
Fairacres Rd MPL/ROM SK6 .... 123 G4
Fairbairn St HOR/BR BL6 .... 33 L2
Fairbank Dr MDTN M24 .... 57 G2
Fairbottom St OLD OL1 .... 9 K5
Fairbourne Av WGNS/IIMK WN3 .... 47 K8
WILM/AE SK9 .... 126 D8
WILM/AE SK9 .... 130 E1
Fairbourne Cl WILM/AE SK9 .... 126 D8
Fairbourne Dr
HALE/TIMP WA15 .... 108 E3
WILM/AE SK9 .... 126 D8
Fairbourne Rd BNG/LEV M19 .... 99 J3
DTN/ASHW M34 .... 101 J2
Fairbrook Dr SLFD M6 .... 86 B2
Fairbrother St ORD M5 .... 86 D5
Fairburn Cl URM M41 .... 84 D8
Fairclough St BOLS/LL BL3 .... 36 C8
OP/CLY M11 .... 88 D2
WGN WN1 .... 15 H5
WGNE/HIN WN2 .... 49 G6
Fairfax Av DID/WITH M20 .... 98 D3
HALE/TIMP WA15 .... 108 D6
Fairfax Cl MPL/ROM SK6 .... 114 A5
WILM/AE SK9 .... 126 D8
Fairfax Dr LIT OL15 .... 29 J1
WILM/AE SK9 .... 126 D8
Fairfax Rd PWCH M25 .... 55 K7
Fairfield Av CHD/CHDH SK8 .... 120 E2
DROY M43 .... 89 K5
MPL/ROM SK6 .... 101 K8
WGNE/HIN WN2 .... 64 D3
WGNW/BIL/OR WN5 .... 47 C7
Fairfield Dr BURY BL9 .... 40 A1
Fairfield Rd DROY M43 .... 89 K4
FWTH BL4 .... 52 F3
HALE/TIMP WA15 .... 108 F7
MDTN M24 .... 57 H3
OP/CLY M11 .... 89 H5
Fairfields EDGW/EG BL7 .... 22 C4
OLDS OL8 .... 75 J2
Fairfield Sq DROY M43 .... 89 K4
Fairfield St CMANE M1 .... 7 K7
SLFD M6 .... 71 G7
WGNW/BIL/OR WN5 .... 46 F7
Fairford Cl RDSH SK5 .... 100 C7
Fairford Dr BOLS/LL BL3 .... 2 C9
RDSH SK5 .... 100 C7
WILM/AE SK9 .... 127 H5
Fairhaven Av CCHDY M21 .... 97 L5
WHTF M45 .... 55 C5
WHTN BL5 .... 50 E4
Fairhaven Cl BRAM/HZG SK7 .... 121 H5
TOT/BURYW/LGST M12 .... 88 C6
Fairhills Rd IRL M44 .... 94 D4
Fairholme Av AIMK WN4 .... 63 J8
URM M41 .... 95 M2
Fairholme Rd DID/WITH M20 .... 98 F6
HTNM SK4 .... 12 D1
Fairhope Av SLFD M6 .... 70 F8
Fairhurst Av WGNNW/ST WN6 .... 31 G1
Fairhurst Dr WALK M28 .... 68 C2
Fairhurst St LEIGH WN7 .... 66 B7
WGNS/IIMK WN3 .... 14 D4
Fairisle Cl OP/CLY M11 .... 88 C3
Fairlands Rd BURY BL9 .... 25 J5
SALE M33 .... 108 C2
Fairlands St ROCH OL11 .... 42 E2
Fairlawn HTNM SK4 .... 12 E1
Fairlawn Cl RUSH/FAL M14 .... 87 K8
Fairlea Av DID/WITH M20 .... 110 F2
Fairlee Av DTN/ASHW M34 .... 89 M3
Fairleigh Av SLFD M6 .... 85 M1
Fairless Rd ECC M30 .... 85 C3
Fairlie Av BOLS/LL BL3 .... 35 J7
Fairlie Dr HALE/TIMP WA15 .... 108 E4
Fairlyn Cl WHTN BL5 .... 51 K5
Fairlyn Dr WHTN BL5 .... 51 K5
Fairman Dr WGNE/HIN WN2 .... 49 H5
Fairman St OLDTF/WHR M16 .... 98 C1
Fairmead Rd NTHM/RTH M23 .... 109 M3
Fairmile Dr DID/WITH M20 .... 110 F4
Fairmount Av BOLE BL2 .... 37 H4
Fairmount Rd SWIN M27 .... 69 L6
Fairoak Ct BOLS/LL BL3 .... 2 A8
Fair Oak Rd BNG/LEV M19 .... 99 J7
Fairstead Cl WHTN BL5 .... 50 A4
Fairstead Wk OP/CLY M11 .... 89 F6
Fair St BOLS/LL BL3 * 51 M2
CMANE M1 .... 7 K6
SWIN M27 .... 70 D3
Fair Vw WGNW/BIL/OR WN5 .... 62 A7
Fairview Av BNG/LEV M19 .... 99 J2
DTN/ASHW M34 .... 100 D3
Fairview Dr MPL/ROM SK6 .... 114 C5
Fairview Rd DTN/ASHW M34 .... 100 D3
HALE/TIMP WA15 .... 108 F2
Fairway BRAM/HZG SK7 .... 120 F6
CHD/CHDH SK8 .... 110 E8
DROY M43 .... 89 K4
PWCH M25 .... 72 A2
ROCH OL11 .... 27 M5
SWIN M27 .... 70 F5
WHIT OL12 .... 20 A5
Fairway Av BOLE BL2 .... 23 K8
NTHM/RTH M23 .... 109 G5
Fairway Crs ROY/SHW OL2 .... 43 C6
Fairway Dr SALE M33 .... 108 B2
Fairway Rd BURY BL9 .... 25 L7
OLDE OL4 .... 60 B8
Fairways HOR/BR BL6 .... 33 M1

Fairways Cl GLSP SK13 .... 105 J3
The Fairways AIMK WN4 .... 78 A2
WHTF M45 .... 55 J6
WHTN BL5 .... 50 B4
The Fairway NEWH/MOS M40 .... 74 A4
OFTN SK2 .... 113 G5
Fairwood Rd NTHM/RTH M23 .... 109 G5
Fairy Bank Crs NM/HAY SK22 .... 125 M1
Fairy Bank Rd NM/HAY SK22 .... 125 M1
Fairy La CHH M8 .... 72 B7
SALE M33 .... 97 J8
SALE M33 .... 109 L1
Fairy St TOT/BURYW BL8 .... 4 A5
Fairywell Cl WILM/AE SK9 .... 127 H3
Fairywell Dr SALE M33 .... 108 D3
Fairywell Rd
HALE/TIMP WA15 .... 108 E5
Faith St BOL BL1 .... 35 K3
LEIGH WN7 .... 65 M7
Falcon Av URM M41 .... 96 B2
Falcon Cl BURY BL9 .... 5 J1
LEIGH WN7 .... 66 F7
NM/HAY SK22 .... 124 F4
WHIT OL12 .... 27 G2
Falcon Crs SWIN M27 .... 70 E2
Falcon Dr CHAD OL9 .... 8 C3
IRL M44 .... 83 L8
LHULT M38 .... 52 D7
MDTN M24 .... 57 H1
Falconers Gn WGNS/IIMK WN3 .... 47 L7
Falcon St OLDS OL8 .... 9 H4
Falconwood Cha WALK M28 .... 68 E6
Falconwood Cl
WGNNW/ST WN6 .... 14 C2
Falfield Dr CHH M8 .... 72 E7
Falinge Fold WHIT OL12 .... 28 A3
Falinge Ms WHIT OL12 .... 10 C3
Falinge Rd WHIT OL12 .... 10 D7
Falkirk Dr BOLE BL2 .... 37 J6
WGNE/HIN WN2 .... 48 D4
Falkirk Gv WGNW/BIL/OR WN5 .... 46 F4
Falkirk St OLDE OL4 .... 59 M5
ROCH OL11 .... 27 M4
Falkland Av NEWH/MOS M40 .... 73 G8
ROCH OL11 .... 27 M4
Falkland Cl OLDS OL8 .... 44 B8
Falkland Dr AIMK WN4 .... 62 F8
Falkland Rd BOLE BL2 .... 37 K5
Fall Birch Rd HOR/BR BL6 .... 34 C4
Fallons Rd WALK M28 .... 69 M3
Fallow Av GTN M18 .... 100 A5
Fallow Cl WHTN BL5 .... 50 B2
Fallowfield Av ORD M5 .... 86 D4
Fallowfield Dr WHIT OL12 .... 28 A2
Fallow Fields Dr RDSH SK5 .... 100 D3
Fallowfield Wy ATH M46 .... 67 H3
The Fallows CHAD OL9 .... 58 D7
Falls Gv WYTH/NTH M22 .... 118 C5
Falmer Cl GTN M18 .... 89 J6
TOT/BURYW BL8 .... 24 F6
Falmer Dr WYTH/NTH M22 .... 118 F3
Falmouth Av SALE M33 .... 96 A7
URM M41 .... 95 H1
Falmouth Crs RDSH SK5 .... 100 F7
Falmouth Rd IRL M44 .... 94 E2
Falmouth St NEWH/MOS M40 .... 73 J8
OLDS OL8 .... 9 J9
ROCH OL11 .... 11 G7
Falsgrave Cl NEWH/MOS M40 .... 73 K7
Falshaw Dr BURY BL9 .... 25 H4
Falstaff Ms MPL/ROM SK6 .... 113 K1
Falston Av NEWH/MOS M40 .... 74 A2
Falstone Av RAMS BL0 .... 18 F8
Falstone Cl WGNS/IIMK WN3 .... 63 G8
Falterley Rd NTHM/RTH M23 .... 109 H4
Fancroft Rd WYTH/NTH M22 .... 109 M7
Faraday Av CHH M8 .... 72 D6
SWIN M27 .... 71 G2
Faraday Dr BOL BL1 .... 36 B3
Faraday Ri WHIT OL12 .... 27 L3
Faraday St CMANE M1 .... 7 J4
Farcroft Av RAD M26 .... 38 F7
Farcroft Cl NTHM/RTH M23 .... 109 J4
OFTN SK2 .... 113 H5
Far Cromwell Rd
MPL/ROM SK6 .... 101 G6
Fardale ROY/SHW OL2 .... 43 L6
Farden Dr NTHM/RTH M23 .... 109 G4
Fardon Cl WGNE/HIN WN2 .... 49 J8
Farewell Cl ROCH OL11 .... 41 M2
Far Hey Cl RAD M26 .... 54 B1
Farholme ROY/SHW OL2 .... 58 F2
Faringdon ROCH OL11 .... 10 C7
Faringdon Wk BOLS/LL BL3 .... 2 B7
Farland Pl BOLS/LL BL3 .... 35 J7
Farlands Dr DID/WITH M20 .... 110 E3
Farlands Ri MILN OL16 .... 42 F1
Far La GTN M18 .... 89 G8
Farley Av GTN M18 .... 89 K8
Farley Ct CHD/CHDH SK8 .... 118 D8
Farley Rd SALE M33 .... 108 F2
Farley Wy RDSH SK5 .... 100 B3
Farliegh Cl WHTN BL5 .... 50 D2
Farman St BOLS/LL BL3 * 52 A1
Farm Av STRET M32 .... 85 K8
Farm Cl HTNM SK4 .... 99 M6
TOT/BURYW BL8 .... 24 C6
Farmers Cl SALE M33 .... 109 K2
Farmer St HTNM SK4 .... 112 A1
Farmfield SALE M33 .... 96 B6
Farm Hl PWCH M25 .... 55 K7
Farmlands Wk OLD OL1 .... 43 M8
Farm La HYDE SK14 .... 102 A4
POY/DIS SK12 .... 123 J6
PWCH M25 .... 56 B4
WALK M28 .... 69 J7
WGNE/HIN WN2 .... 48 D2
Farm Meadow Rd
WGNW/BIL/OR WN5 .... 46 B7
Farm Rd OLDS OL8 .... 74 F4
Farmside Av IRL M44 .... 94 D1
Farmstead Cl FAIL M35 .... 74 F6
Farm St FAIL M35 .... 74 A6
HEY OL10 .... 41 H4
OLD OL1 .... 58 E3
Farm Wy ALT WA14 .... 116 A2
Farm Yd BNG/LEV M19 .... 99 K3
Farn Av RDSH SK5 .... 100 B2
Farnborough Av OLDE OL4 .... 60 A6
Farnborough Rd BOL BL1 .... 22 B6
NEWH/MOS M40 .... 88 A1
Farndale Av AIMK WN4 .... 63 J8
Farndale Sq LHULT M38 .... 68 F1
Farndon Av BRAM/HZG SK7 .... 113 J8
Farndon Cl SALE M33 .... 109 H1
Farndon Dr HALE/TIMP WA15 .... 108 D6
Farndon Rd RDSH SK5 .... 100 D4
Farnham Av BKLY M9 .... 57 G7

Farnham Cl BOL BL1 * 2 C1
CHD/CHDH SK8 .... 120 C5
LEIGH WN7 .... 66 C6
Farnham Dr IRL M44 .... 94 D3
Farnley Cl WHIT OL12 .... 27 J2
Farnley St WGTN/LGST M12 * 88 D6
Farnsworth Cl AULW OL7 .... 75 L7
Farnworth Dr RUSH/FAL M14 .... 98 F2
Farnworth St BOLS/LL BL3 * 35 M8
HEY OL10 .... 40 F7
LEIGH WN7 .... 66 E8
Farrand Rd OLDS OL8 .... 74 E2
Farrant Rd WGTN/LGST M12 .... 99 K1
Farrar Rd DROY M43 .... 89 J4
Farr Cl WGNS/IIMK WN3 .... 47 J7
Farrell St BRO M7 .... 87 H1
WGNW/BIL/OR WN5 .... 46 F7
Farrer Rd BRUN/LGST M13 .... 99 J2
Far Ridings MPL/ROM SK6 .... 114 A1
Farrier Cl SALE M33 .... 109 J1
Farrier's Cft WGNNW/ST WN6 .... 47 H1
Farriers La ROCH OL11 .... 27 L8
Farringdon St SLFD M6 .... 86 B1
Farrowdale Av ROY/SHW OL2 .... 43 L6
Farrow St ROY/SHW OL2 .... 43 L6
Farrow St East ROY/SHW OL2 .... 43 L6
Farr St EDGY/DAV SK3 .... 12 C6
Farwood Cl OLDTF/WHR M16 .... 86 F7
Far Woodseats La GLSP SK13 .... 105 J7
Fastnet St OP/CLY M11 .... 88 D4
Faulkenhurst Ms OLD OL1 .... 8 C1
Faulkenhurst St OLD OL1 .... 8 C1
Faulkner Dr HALE/TIMP WA15 .... 108 E8
Faulkner Rd STRET M32 .... 97 H3
Faulkner St BOLS/LL BL3 .... 2 D9
CMANE M1 .... 7 G6
MILN OL16 .... 10 F4
Fauvel Rd GLSP SK13 .... 104 F3
Faversham Brow OLD OL1 * 9 H2
Faversham St NEWH/MOS M40 .... 73 L5
Fawborough Rd
NTHM/RTH M23 .... 109 J3
Fawcetts Fold WHTN BL5 .... 34 B8
Fawcett St BOLE BL2 .... 3 K4
Fawley Av HYDE SK14 .... 102 A3
Fawley Gv WYTH/NTH M22 .... 110 A8
Fawns Keep STLY SK15 .... 92 B6
WILM/AE SK9 .... 127 H5
Fay Av BKLY M9 .... 73 L2
Fay Gdns GLSP SK13 .... 93 H8
Faywood Dr MPL/ROM SK6 .... 114 D6
Fearney Side BOLS/LL BL3 .... 53 J1
Fearnham Cl LEIGH WN7 .... 81 G3
Fearnhead Cl FWTH BL4 .... 53 H4
Fearnhead St BOLS/LL BL3 .... 35 M8
Featherstall Brook Vie LIT OL15 .... 21 L7
Featherstall Rd LIT OL15 .... 21 K7
Featherstall Rd North OLD OL1 .... 8 A5
Featherstall Rd South CHAD OL9 .... 8 A7
Fecit La RAMS BL0 .... 19 L4
Federation St ANC M4 .... 7 G2
PWCH M25 .... 55 J7
Feldom Rd NTHM/RTH M23 .... 109 J2
Fellbridge Cl WHTN BL5 .... 50 D3
Fellbrigg Cl GTN M18 .... 99 H1
Fellfoot Cl WALK M28 .... 68 E5
Fellpark Rd NTHM/RTH M23 .... 109 K2
Fells Gv WALK M28 .... 69 J3
Fellside BOLE BL2 .... 37 K6
Fellside Cl TOT/BURYW BL8 .... 24 C3
Fellside Gdns LIT OL15 .... 21 K5
Fellside Gn STLY SK15 .... 91 K4
Fell St LEIGH WN7 .... 65 M7
TOT/BURYW BL8 .... 38 F7
Felltop Dr RDSH SK5 .... 100 D4
Felskirk Rd WYTH/NTH M22 .... 118 D1
Felsted BOL BL1 .... 35 H4
Felt Ct DTN/ASHW M34 .... 100 F3
Felthorpe Dr CHH M8 .... 72 C6
Felton Av WYTH/NTH M22 .... 118 E1
Felton Cl BURY BL9 .... 39 K7
Felton Wk BOL BL1 .... 36 B2
Fencegate Av HTNM SK4 .... 100 A7
Fence St OFTN SK2 .... 113 H5
Fenchurch Av NEWH/MOS M40 .... 73 M8
Fencot Dr WGTN/LGST M12 .... 88 C7
Fenella St BRUN/LGST M13 .... 88 B8
Fenham Cl NEWH/MOS M40 .... 72 F7
Fenmore Av GTN M18 .... 99 L1
Fennel St ANC M4 .... 6 F2
Fenners Cl BOLS/LL BL3 .... 52 A1
Fenney St BRO M7 .... 72 B7
Fenney St East BRO M7 .... 72 B6
Fenside Rd WYTH/NTH M22 .... 110 B7
Fenton Av BRAM/HZG SK7 .... 122 A3
Fenton Ms ROCH OL11 .... 10 D8
Fenton St OLDE OL4 .... 59 L6
ROCH OL11 .... 10 D8
ROY/SHW OL2 .... 43 J2
TOT/BURYW BL8 .... 38 F1
WGTN/LGST M12 .... 87 M4
Fenton Wy WGNE/HIN WN2 .... 49 J8
Fenwick Cl WHTN BL5 .... 50 B2
Fenwick Dr HTNM SK4 .... 111 H1
MDTN M24 .... 57 K4
Fenwick St HULME M15 .... 87 K6
ROCH OL11 .... 11 G8
Ferdinand St NEWH/MOS M40 * 73 C8
Fereday St WALK M28 .... 52 F8
Ferguson Gdns WHIT OL12 .... 28 C1
Ferguson Ri
WGNW/BIL/OR WN5 .... 47 H4
Ferguson Wy OLDE OL4 .... 60 A3
Fernacre SALE M33 .... 96 A7
Fernally St HYDE SK14 .... 102 B3
Fern Av URM M41 .... 95 K2
Fern Bank NEWH/MOS M40 * 73 M5
Fernbank RAD M26 .... 54 D4
Fern Bank STLY SK15 .... 91 M4
Fern Bank Cl STLY SK15 .... 91 M4
Fern Bank Dr NTHM/RTH M23 .... 109 H4
Fernbray Av BNG/LEV M19 .... 99 G8
Fernbray Rd WGNE/HIN WN2 .... 49 J7
Fernbrook Cl BRUN/LGST M13 .... 88 B7
Fern Cl ATH M46 .... 67 G2
MDTN M24 .... 58 A4
MPL/ROM SK6 .... 114 C6
OLDE OL4 .... 60 C6
WGNNW/ST WN6 .... 30 C5
Fern Clough BOL BL1 .... 35 J5
Fernclough Rd BKLY M9 .... 73 G6
Fern Crs STLY SK15 .... 91 M4
Ferndale HYDE SK14 .... 91 K7
Ferndale Av MILN OL16 .... 42 F3
OFTN SK2 .... 112 D8
WHTF M45 .... 54 F1
Ferndale Cl OLDE OL4 .... 60 A8

Ferndale Gdns BNG/LEV M19 .... 99 H6
Ferndale Rd SALE M33 .... 108 E2
Fern Dene WHIT OL12 .... 27 L2
Ferndene Rd DID/WITH M20 .... 98 E7
WHTF M45 .... 55 M5
Ferndown Av CHD/CHDH SK8 .... 119 K3
CHAD OL9 .... 58 A5
Ferndown Dr IRL M44 .... 94 D1
Ferndown Rd BOLE BL2 .... 37 H1
NTHM/RTH M23 .... 109 G4
Ferney Field Rd MDTN M24 .... 58 B6
Ferngate Dr DID/WITH M20 .... 98 E6
Ferngrove BURY BL9 .... 5 M1
Fernhill MPL/ROM SK6 .... 114 E6
Fernhill Av BOLS/LL BL3 .... 35 K8
Fernhill Cl GLSP SK13 .... 105 G1
Fernhill Dr GTN M18 .... 88 E8
Fern Hill La WHIT OL12 .... 27 K1
Fernhills EDGW/EG BL7 .... 22 B2
Fernhill St BURY BL9 .... 4 F2
Fernholme Ct OLDS OL8 .... 58 F8
Fernhurst Cl WGNS/IIMK WN3 .... 15 M8
Fernhurst Rd DID/WITH M20 .... 98 F7
Fernie St ANC M4 * 87 K1
Fernilee Cl NM/HAY SK22 .... 124 E3
Fern Lea CHD/CHDH SK8 .... 119 K3
Fernlea HALE/TIMP WA15 .... 117 H3
Fern Lea OLD OL1 .... 8 C1
Fernlea Cl GLSP SK13 .... 93 H8
WHIT OL12 .... 27 L2
Fernlea Crs SWIN M27 .... 70 B5
Fernlea Gv AIMK WN4 .... 63 C7
Fern Lea Gv LHULT M38 .... 52 C8
Fernleigh HOR/BR BL6 * 34 A3
Fernleigh Av BNG/LEV M19 .... 99 M3
Fernleigh Dr OLDTF/WHR M16 * 86 F7
Fernley Av DTN/ASHW M34 .... 101 K2
Fernley Rd OFTN SK2 .... 112 E6
Fern Lodge AUL OL6 .... 76 A7
Ferns Gv BOL BL1 .... 35 L5
Fernside Av DID/WITH M20 .... 99 G7
Fernside Gv WALK M28 * 53 G8
WGNS/IIMK WN3 .... 63 G3
Fernside Wy WHIT OL12 .... 27 K3
Fernstead BOLS/LL BL3 .... 35 M6
Fernstone Cl HOR/BR BL6 .... 33 K1
Fern St BOLS/LL BL3 .... 35 M6
BURY BL9 .... 4 E2
CHAD OL9 .... 58 D4
CHH M8 .... 53 H3
FWTH BL4 .... 53 H3
OLDS OL8 .... 9 G6
RAMS BL0 .... 19 G6
ROCH OL11 .... 21 G6
WHIT OL12 .... 21 G6
Fernthorpe Av UPML OL3 .... 61 M3
Fern Vw HALE/TIMP WA15 .... 109 H7
Fernview Dr RAMS BL0 .... 24 E3
Fernwood MPL/ROM SK6 .... 114 F5
Fernwood Av GTN M18 .... 100 A1
Fernwood Gv WILM/AE SK9 .... 127 G4
Ferrand Rd LIT OL15 .... 21 M6
Ferrer St AIMK WN4 .... 63 J6
Ferring Wk CHAD OL9 * 8 A7
Ferris St OP/CLY M11 .... 89 G4
Ferrous Wy IRL M44 .... 94 C6
Ferryhill Rd IRL M44 .... 94 D2
Ferrymasters Wy IRL M44 .... 94 D3
Ferry Rd IRL M44 .... 94 C2
Ferry St OP/CLY M11 .... 88 B4
Festival Dr MCFLDN SK10 .... 131 J6
Fettler Cl SWIN M27 .... 70 B6
Feversham Ct ECC M30 .... 70 D6
Fewston Cl BOL BL1 .... 22 B7
Fiddlers La IRL M44 .... 94 E1
Field Bank Gv BNG/LEV M19 .... 99 L3
Field Cl BRAM/HZG SK7 .... 120 F8
MPL/ROM SK6 .... 114 A7
Fieldcroft ROCH OL11 .... 27 L5
Fielden Cl CCHDY M21 .... 97 L3
Fielden Ct CCHDY M21 .... 97 L3
Fielden Rd DID/WITH M20 .... 98 C7
Fielders Wy SWIN M27 .... 54 D8
Fieldfare Av NEWH/MOS M40 .... 73 L8
Fieldfare Cl GOL/RIS/CUL WA3 .... 80 A7
Fieldfare Wy AULW OL7 .... 75 K5
Fieldhead Av ROCH OL11 .... 27 L5
TOT/BURYW BL8 .... 38 D3
TYLD M29 .... 67 G1
Fieldhead Ms WILM/AE SK9 .... 127 J4
Fieldhead Rd WILM/AE SK9 .... 127 J4
Field House La MPL/ROM SK6 .... 114 D7
Fieldhouse Rd WHIT OL12 .... 28 C2
Fielding Av POY/DIS SK12 .... 129 J2
Fielding St ECC M30 .... 84 F3
MDTN M24 .... 57 K2
OLDE OL4 .... 76 A7
Field Pl DID/WITH M20 .... 110 E1
Field Rd MILN OL16 .... 29 G5
SALE M33 .... 96 B6
Fields Crs HYDE SK14 .... 93 G6
Fieldsend Cl STLY SK15 .... 92 A4
Fieldsend Dr LEIGH WN7 .... 80 F4
Fields End Fold ECC M30 .... 83 H4
Fields Farm Cl HYDE SK14 .... 103 G3
Fields Farm Rd HYDE SK14 .... 103 H2
Fields Gv HYDE SK14 .... 103 G3
Fields New Rd CHAD OL9 .... 58 D7
The Fields WGNNW/ST WN6 .... 31 J4
Field St DROY M43 .... 89 L4
FAIL M35 .... 74 B5
GTN M18 .... 89 H6
HYDE SK14 .... 91 K6
MPL/ROM SK6 .... 113 J1
ROCH OL11 .... 28 D1
SLFD M6 .... 49 H8
WGNE/HIN WN2 .... 14 C3
WGNNW/ST WN6 .... 48 C8
WGNS/IIMK WN3 .... 48 C8
Fieldsway OLDS OL8 .... 75 H2
Field Vale Dr RDSH SK5 .... 100 D3
Fieldvale Rd SALE M33 .... 108 B3
Field View Wk
OLDTF/WHR M16 .... 98 C2
Field Wk HALE/TIMP WA15 * 117 K1
Fieldway MILN OL16 .... 44 A1
WGNE/HIN WN2 .... 64 E2
Fife Av CHAD OL9 .... 58 C8
Fifield Cl OLDS OL8 .... 75 K1
Fifth Av BOL BL1 .... 35 L5
BOLS/LL BL3 .... 36 A8
BURY BL9 .... 26 A8
DUK SK16 .... 90 E5
OLDS OL8 .... 74 F2
OP/CLY M11 .... 88 F2
TRPK M17 .... 85 M7
Fifth St TRPK M17 .... 85 M7

Filbert St OLD OL1 59 M3
Filby Wk NEWH/MOS M40 73 H8
Fildes St MDTN M24 58 A5
Filey Av OLDTF/WHR M16 98 A2
URM M41 84 D8
Filey Dr SLFD M6 71 G6
Filey Rd OFTN SK2 112 F5
RUSH/FAL M14 99 G4
Filey St MILN OL16 28 F2
Filton Av BOLS/LL BL3 * 2 B8
Finance St LIT OL15 21 J7
Finborough Cl
OLDTF/WHR M16 87 H8
Finchale Dr HALE/TIMP WA15 117 K3
Finchdale Gdns
GOL/RIS/CUL WA3 80 E4
Finchley Av NEWH/MOS M40 73 M8
Finchley Cl TOT/BURYW BL8 38 E4
Finchley Crs WGNE/HIN WN2 48 D3
Finchley Gv NEWH/MOS M40 73 K3
Finchley Rd HALE/TIMP WA15 117 G1
RUSH/FAL M14 98 E4
Finch Mill Av WGNNW/ST WN6 30 A5
Finchwood Rd
WYTH/NTH M22 110 B7
Findon Rd NTHM/RTH M23 109 K6
Finger Post BOLS/LL BL3 37 K8
Finghall Rd URM M41 95 L2
Finishing Wk ANC M4 7 M4
Finland Rd EDGY/DAV SK3 12 F9
Finlan Rd MDTN M24 42 B7
Finlay Ct WGNW/BIL/OR WN5 47 H4
Finlay St FWTH BL4 * 53 G4
Finlow Hill La MCFLDN SK10 131 H6
Finney Cl WILM/AE SK9 127 G2
Finney Dr CCHDY M21 97 K5
WILM/AE SK9 127 G2
Finney Gv RNFD/HAY WA11 78 B6
Finney La CHD/CHDH SK8 119 J4
Finney St BOLS/LL BL3 * 36 C8
Finningley Rd BKLY M9 56 E6
Finny Bank Rd SALE M33 96 D6
Finsbury Av NEWH/MOS M40 73 M8
Finsbury Cl OLDS OL8 59 L8
Finsbury Rd RDSH SK5 100 B4
Finsbury St ROCH OL11 10 A9
Finsbury Wy WILM/AE SK9 127 J2
Finstock Cl ECC M30 84 E3
Fintry Gv ECC M30 85 G3
Fir Av BRAM/HZG SK7 121 G4
Firbank Cl AULW OL7 90 C2
Fir Bank Rd ROY/SHW OL2 43 G6
Firbank Rd NTHM/RTH M23 109 K7
WGNS/IIMK WN3 63 L1
Firbarn Cl MILN OL16 29 G5
Firbeck Dr ANC M4 88 A2
Fir Cl POY/DIS SK12 129 J1
Fircroft WGNNW/ST WN6 30 D2
Fircroft Rd OLDS OL8 75 K2
Firdale Av NEWH/MOS M40 74 B3
Firdale Wk CHAD OL9 8 C4
Firecrest Cl WALK M28 68 E4
Firefly Cl CSLFD M3 6 A4
Fire Station Sq ORD M5 * 86 F2
Fire Station Yd ROCH OL11 10 F6
Firethorn Av BNG/LEV M19 99 J6
Firethorn Cl WHTN BL5 50 C2
Firethorn Dr HYDE SK14 102 D2
Firfield Gv WALK M28 69 J1
Fir Gv BNG/LEV M19 99 K3
CHAD OL9 8 B2
WGNNW/ST WN6 47 K1
Firgrove Av MILN OL16 29 G4
Firgrove Gdns MILN OL16 29 G4
Fir La ROY/SHW OL2 43 G6
Fir Rd BRAM/HZG SK7 121 G4
DTN/ASHW M34 101 K1
FWTH BL4 52 E4
MPL/ROM SK6 114 B8
SWIN M27 70 B6
Firs Av AUL OL6 75 L8
FAIL M35 74 B5
OLDTF/WHR M16 97 L2
Firsby Av MPL/ROM SK6 101 J8
Firsby St BNG/LEV M19 99 K3
Firs Cottages WGNE/HIN WN2 * 49 G3
Firs Gv CHD/CHDH SK8 110 D8
Firs La LEIGH WN7 65 M7
Firs Park Crs WGNE/HIN WN2 49 G3
Firs Rd CHD/CHDH SK8 119 J1
SALE M33 96 B7
WHTN BL5 51 J6
First Av ATH M46 51 G8
BOLS/LL BL3 37 J8
OLDS OL8 75 G2
OP/CLY M11 89 G2
POY/DIS SK12 129 H3
STLY SK15 77 H7
SWIN M27 70 A7
TOT/BURYW BL8 24 C6
TRPK M17 86 A7
TYLD M29 67 M8
WGNE/HIN WN2 49 G7
WGNNW/ST WN6 47 K2
The Firs ALT WA14 116 D2
Fir St BOL BL1 36 C2
BURY BL9 5 J4
ECC M30 85 G3
FAIL M35 74 B5
HEY OL10 41 H3
HTNM SK4 13 G3
IRL M44 94 A7
NEWH/MOS M40 73 G8
OLDTF/WHR M16 * 86 F8
RAD M26 54 E2
RAMS BL0 19 G5
ROY/SHW OL2 43 G7
SLFD M6 86 C2
Firs Wy SALE M33 107 M1
Firswood Dr HYDE SK14 102 D1
ROY/SHW OL2 42 F7
SWIN M27 70 B6
Firswood Mt CHD/CHDH SK8 110 D8
Firth St OLD OL1 9 K6
Fir Tree Av GOL/RIS/CUL WA3 80 C4
OLDS OL8 75 K2
SALE M33 95 M8
WALK M28 68 E6
Fir Tree Cl DUK SK16 91 J5
Fir Tree Crs DUK SK16 91 J4
WGNS/IIMK WN3 64 C1
Fir Tree Dr HYDE SK14 91 H7
WGNS/IIMK WN3 64 C1
Fir Tree La DUK SK16 91 J5
Fir Tree St WGNS/IIMK WN3 * 48 C8
Fir Tree Wy HOR/BR BL6 34 B3
Firvale Av CHD/CHDH SK8 119 K3
Firvale Cl LEIGH WN7 65 M7
Firwood Av FWTH BL4 52 F6
URM M41 96 D3
Firwood Cl OFTN SK2 112 F4
Firwood Crs RAD M26 54 E3
Firwood Gv AIMK WN4 78 C2
BOLE BL2 36 E2
Firwood La BOLE BL2 36 F1
Firwood Pk CHAD OL9 58 B5
Fishbourne Sq
RUSH/FAL M14 * 98 F1
Fisher Av WGNE/HIN WN2 64 F5
Fisher Cl WGNS/IIMK WN3 14 A9
Fisher Dr WGNW/BIL/OR WN5 46 B6
Fisherfield WHIT OL12 27 J3
Fishermore Rd URM M41 95 H2
Fishers Br NM/HAY SK22 125 M2
Fisher St OLD OL1 9 K3
Fishwick St MILN OL16 11 H7
Fistral Av CHD/CHDH SK8 119 L4
Fistral Crs STLY SK15 92 A1
Fitton Av CCHDY M21 97 L6
Fitton Crs SWIN M27 70 C1
Fitton Hill Rd OLDS OL8 75 K1
Fitton St MILN OL16 11 H2
ROY/SHW OL2 43 J5
ROY/SHW OL2 43 J8
Fitzadam St WGN WN1 14 E3
Fitzalan St GLSP SK13 104 F3
Fitzgeorge St
NEWH/MOS M40 72 F7
Fitzgerald Cl PWCH M25 71 J2
Fitzgerald Wy SLFD M6 * 86 C1
Fitzhugh St BOL BL1 * 22 D7
Fitzroy St AULW OL7 90 C3
DROY M43 89 L4
STLY SK15 77 G8
Fitzwarren St SLFD M6 86 C2
Fitzwilliam St BRO M7 72 A8
Five Quarters RAD M26 38 B7
Flagcroft Dr NTHM/RTH M23 109 L7
Flagg Wood Av MPL/ROM SK6 114 A5
Flag Rw ANC M4 * 87 L1
Flagship Av ORD M5 * 86 E4
Flake La ROY/SHW OL2 43 G8
Flamborough Wk
RUSH/FAL M14 * 98 E1
Flamingo Cl WGTN/LGST M12 88 D6
Flamstead Av NTHM/RTH M23 109 H6
Flannel St WHIT OL12 11 G2
Flapper Fold La ATH M46 50 F8
Flashfields PWCH M25 71 J3
Flash St NEWH/MOS M40 73 M6
Flatley Cl HULME M15 87 K6
Flavian Wk OP/CLY M11 * 88 E4
Flaxcroft Rd WYTH/NTH M22 118 D2
Flaxfield Av STLY SK15 92 A2
Flaxman Ri OLD OL1 43 M8
Flaxpool Cl OLDTF/WHR M16 87 H8
Flax St CSLFD M3 6 B1
RAMS BL0 18 D8
Fleece St MILN OL16 10 E4
OLDE OL4 * 59 L5
Fleeson St RUSH/FAL M14 98 F1
Fleet St AUL OL6 90 D2
GTN M18 89 J6
HOR/BR BL6 34 A1
HYDE SK14 91 H8
OLDE OL4 59 M5
WGNW/BIL/OR WN5 46 E6
Fleetwood Dr NEWLW WA12 78 E8
Fleetwood Rd WALK M28 68 D1
Fleming Cl WHIT OL12 21 H7
Fleming Dr AIMK WN4 64 A8
Fleming Pl CHAD OL9 8 F6
Fleming Rd WYTH/NTH M22 118 F2
Flemish Rd DTN/ASHW M34 101 L2
Fletcher Av ATH M46 51 G7
SWIN M27 70 D1
Fletcher Cl CHAD OL9 8 E6
HEY OL10 41 G2
Fletcher Dr ALT WA14 116 E3
POY/DIS SK12 123 H6
Fletcher Fold Rd BURY BL9 39 J6
Fletcher Sq CMANE M1 * 7 L5
Fletcher's Rd LIT OL15 29 H1
Fletcher St ATH M46 * 66 F1
AUL OL6 90 F1
BOLS/LL BL3 2 D8
BOLS/LL BL3 53 L1
BURY BL9 5 H4
FWTH BL4 53 G4
NEWH/MOS M40 73 J7
RAD M26 38 F8
ROCH OL11 11 H9
STKP SK1 13 J4
Fletsand Rd WILM/AE SK9 127 G6
Fletton Cl WHIT OL12 28 B2
Fletton Ms WHIT OL12 27 M2
Flint Cl BRAM/HZG SK7 121 L3
OP/CLY M11 * 88 E2
Flint St DROY M43 89 L2
EDGY/DAV SK3 13 H8
OLD OL1 59 M4
Flitcroft Ct BOLS/LL BL3 * 36 C8
Flitcroft St OLDE OL4 59 M8
Flixton Rd URM M41 95 J3
Floatshall Rd NTHM/RTH M23 109 J8
Floats Rd NTHM/RTH M23 109 H7
Flockton Av WGNNW/ST WN6 31 G8
Flora St AIMK WN4 78 E2
BKLY M9 72 F1
OLD OL1 9 H4
Florence Av BOL BL1 22 C8
Florence Ct EDGY/DAV SK3 * 12 B9
Florence Park Ct
DID/WITH M20 98 F8
Florence St BOLS/LL BL3 * 36 A8
DROY M43 89 L4
ECC M30 84 E3
FAIL M35 74 C4
HTNM SK4 13 H2
MILN OL16 11 K7
SALE M33 96 E6
WGN WN1 15 L4
Florence Wy HYDE SK14 93 G7
Florida St OLDS OL8 9 G8
Florin Gdns SLFD M6 86 C1
Florist St EDGY/DAV SK3 13 H9
Flowery Bank OLDS OL8 59 H8
Flowery Fld OFTN SK2 121 J1
Flowery Field Gn HYDE SK14 90 F8
Floyd Av CCHDY M21 97 M6
Floyer Rd BKLY M9 57 H8
Foden La BRAM/HZG SK7 128 B1
Foggbrook Cl OFTN SK2 113 H6
Fogg La BOLS/LL BL3 53 H1
Fog La BNG/LEV M19 99 G8
DID/WITH M20 98 E8
Fold Av DROY M43 89 L2
Fold Crs STLY SK15 77 J6
Fold Gdns WHIT OL12 27 L1
Fold Gn CHAD OL9 58 D6
Fold Ms BRAM/HZG SK7 122 A1
Fold Rd RAD M26 53 M5
Folds HOR/BR BL6 32 F1
Folds Rd BOL BL1 3 G3
Fold St BOL BL1 * 2 F5
BURY BL9 4 C4
GOL/RIS/CUL WA3 79 K3
HEY OL10 41 H2
NEWH/MOS M40 73 K4
The Fold BKLY M9 73 G1
ROY/SHW OL2 43 K8
URM M41 95 K1
Fold Vw EDGW/EG BL7 22 B3
OLDS OL8 75 K2
Foleshill Av BKLY M9 73 G5
Foley Gdns HEY OL10 41 H5
Foley St WGNE/HIN WN2 49 G7
Foliage Crs RDSH SK5 100 E7
Foliage Gdns RDSH SK5 100 F7
Foliage Rd RDSH SK5 100 E8
Folkestone Rd
OP/CLY M11 89 G2
Folkestone Rd East
OP/CLY M11 89 G2
Folkestone Rd West
OP/CLY M11 88 F2
Follows St GTN M18 89 G6
Folly La SWIN M27 70 A7
Folly Wk WHIT OL12 10 F1
Fonthill Gv SALE M33 108 C3
Fontwell Cl
OLDTF/WHR M16 97 M1
WGNNW/ST WN6 31 J3
Fontwell La OLD OL1 59 K3
Fontwell Rd BOLS/LL BL3 53 K2
Fooley Cl DROY M43 89 H4
Footman Cl TYLD M29 67 L5
Foot Mill Crs WHIT OL12 28 A2
Foot Wood Crs WHIT OL12 28 A2
Forber Crs GTN M18 99 M1
Forbes Cl SALE M33 109 G2
STKP SK1 112 E4
WGNE/HIN WN2 49 H5
Forbes Pk BRAM/HZG SK7 120 F5
Forbes Rd STKP SK1 112 E3
Forbes St MPL/ROM SK6 101 J8
Fordbank Rd DID/WITH M20 110 D2
Ford Gdns ROCH OL11 27 L6
Ford Gv HYDE SK14 92 D8
Fordham Gv BOL BL1 35 M4
Fordland Cl
GOL/RIS/CUL WA3 80 B3
Ford La DID/WITH M20 110 D2
SLFD M6 71 K8
WYTH/NTH M22 110 B3
Ford Ldg DID/WITH M20 110 E2
Ford's La BRAM/HZG SK7 120 F6
Ford St CSLFD M3 6 B3
DUK SK16 90 F6
EDGY/DAV SK3 12 E5
RAD M26 53 K4
WGTN/LGST M12 88 A6
Fordyce Wy WGNE/HIN WN2 48 D4
Foreland Cl NEWH/MOS M40 73 G7
Forest Av WGNNW/ST WN6 47 H1
Forest Cl DUK SK16 90 F6
Forest Ct URM M41 95 G1
Forest Dr HALE/TIMP WA15 108 C6
SALE M33 108 B2
WGNNW/ST WN6 30 D2
WHTN BL5 50 D4
Forester Hill Av BOLS/LL BL3 52 C1
Forester Hill Cl BOLS/LL BL3 52 C1
Forest Gdns PART M31 106 A1
Forest Range BNG/LEV M19 99 K3
Forest Rd BOL BL1 35 L1
Forest St AUL OL6 75 M8
ECC M30 69 K8
OLDS OL8 75 J2
Forest Vw WHIT OL12 28 A2
Forest Wy EDGW/EG BL7 22 F6
Forfar St BOL BL1 22 B7
Forge St OLDE OL4 59 L5
WGN WN1 15 L5
Formby Av ATH M46 51 G8
CCHDY M21 98 A5
Formby Dr CHD/CHDH SK8 119 K4
Formby Rd SLFD M6 71 H7
Forres Gv AIMK WN4 62 F8
Forrester Dr ROY/SHW OL2 44 A4
STLY SK15 91 K3
Forresters Cl WGNE/HIN WN2 65 H4
Forresters Gn TRPK M17 86 B6
Forrester St WALK M28 69 K4
Forrest Rd DTN/ASHW M34 101 L3
Forshaw Av GTN M18 89 J7
Forster St GOL/RIS/CUL WA3 79 K3
Forsyth St WHIT OL12 27 H2
Fortescue Rd OFTN SK2 113 G5
Forth Pl RAD M26 38 C7
Forth Rd RAD M26 38 C7
Forth St LEIGH WN7 66 F8
Forton Av BOLE BL2 37 H5
Forton Rd WGNS/IIMK WN3 63 J2
Fortran Cl ORD M5 86 D3
Fort Rd PWCH M25 72 A2
Fortrose Av BKLY M9 73 J4
Fortuna Gv BNG/LEV M19 99 J4
Fortune St BOLS/LL BL3 3 J9
Fortyacre Dr MPL/ROM SK6 113 H1
Forum Gv BRO M7 72 B7
Fosbrook Av DID/WITH M20 98 F8
Foscarn Dr NTHM/RTH M23 109 L7
Fossgill Av BOLE BL2 22 F7
Foster Av WGNS/IIMK WN3 15 L8
Foster Ct BURY BL9 26 A8
Foster La BOLE BL2 37 J3
Fosters Buildings
WGNNW/ST WN6 14 D3
Foster St DTN/ASHW M34 101 J1
OLDE OL4 59 M6
RAD M26 54 C1
WGNNW/ST WN6 14 B2
Fotherby Dr BKLY M9 73 G1
Fotherby Pl WGNS/IIMK WN3 63 K1
Foulds Av TOT/BURYW BL8 38 D2
Foundry La ANC M4 7 J3
WGNS/IIMK WN3 47 G8
Foundry St BOLS/LL BL3 2 F8
BOLS/LL BL3 53 K1
BURY BL9 5 G5
DUK SK16 90 F4
HEY OL10 40 F2
LEIGH WN7 66 E8
OLDS OL8 9 G7
RAD M26 54 D1
WGNE/HIN WN2 49 G7
Fountain Av HALE/TIMP WA15 117 K2
Fountain Gdns OLD OL1 8 F1
Fountain Pk WHTN BL5 49 M7
Fountain Pl WHTF M45 55 J5
Fountains Av BOLE BL2 36 F3
RNFD/HAY WA11 78 C5
Fountains Cl TYLD M29 67 M5
Fountains Rd CHD/CHDH SK8 120 E6
STRET M32 96 C1
Fountain St AUL OL6 76 B8
BURY BL9 5 J5
CMANW M2 7 G5
ECC M30 85 G4
HYDE SK14 102 C1
MDTN M24 57 J4
OLD OL1 9 H5
TOT/BURYW BL8 4 A5
Fountain St North BURY BL9 5 H4
Fountains Wk CHAD OL9 * 58 D7
DUK SK16 90 F6
GOL/RIS/CUL WA3 80 E4
Fouracres Rd NTHM/RTH M23 109 J7
Four Lane Ends URM M41 95 H4
Four Lanes HYDE SK14 92 D8
Four Lanes Wy ROCH OL11 26 F2
Fourmarts Rd
WGNW/BIL/OR WN5 46 F2
Four Stalls End LIT OL15 21 L8
Fourteen Meadows Rd
WGNS/IIMK WN3 14 D7
Fourth Av BOL BL1 35 L5
BOLS/LL BL3 37 J8
BURY BL9 25 M8
CHAD OL9 58 D7
OLDS OL8 74 F2
OP/CLY M11 88 F1
STLY SK15 77 H6
SWIN M27 70 A7
Fourth St TRPK M17 85 M7
Fourways TRPK M17 85 K6
Four Yards CMANW M2 6 F5
Fovant Crs RDSH SK5 100 B3
Fowler Av GTN M18 89 J5
Fowler Cl WGN WN1 15 K4
Fowler St OLDS OL8 74 F1
Fowley Common La
GOL/RIS/CUL WA3 81 L7
Fownhope Av SALE M33 108 C1
Fownhope Rd SALE M33 108 C1
Foxall Cl MDTN M24 56 F5
Foxall St MDTN M24 56 F5
Foxbank St BRUN/LGST M13 88 B8
Fox Bench Cl BRAM/HZG SK7 120 E6
Foxbench Wk CCHDY M21 98 A6
Fox Cl HALE/TIMP WA15 108 C6
Foxcroft St LIT OL15 21 K7
Foxdale Cl EDGW/EG BL7 17 H6
Foxdale St OP/CLY M11 88 F3
Foxdene Gv WGNS/IIMK WN3 63 H2
Foxdenton Dr STRET M32 96 C1
Foxdenton La MDTN M24 58 B6
Foxendale Wk BOLS/LL BL3 * 2 E9
Foxfield Cl TOT/BURYW BL8 24 E7
Foxfield Dr OLDS OL8 74 F3
Foxfield Gv WGNNW/ST WN6 30 E6
Foxfield Rd NTHM/RTH M23 118 C1
Foxfold Cl WALK M28 68 C5
Foxglove Cl GOL/RIS/CUL WA3 80 A4
WGNNW/ST WN6 31 G2
Foxglove Ct WHIT OL12 28 A1
Foxglove Dr ALT WA14 107 M4
BURY BL9 40 A1
Foxglove La STLY SK15 91 J1
Foxhall Rd DTN/ASHW M34 90 A8
HALE/TIMP WA15 108 B6
Foxham Dr BRO M7 72 B6
Foxhill ALT WA14 107 K7
Fox Hl ROY/SHW OL2 43 H4
Foxhill Cha OFTN SK2 113 K7
Foxhill Dr STLY SK15 91 M4
Foxhill Rd ECC M30 84 C3
Fox Hill Rd ROCH OL11 42 A4
Foxholes Cl WHIT OL12 28 D3
Foxholes La WHIT OL12 28 E2
Foxholes Rd HYDE SK14 102 A4
WHIT OL12 28 D2
Foxlair Rd WYTH/NTH M22 118 D1
Foxland Rd CHD/CHDH SK8 110 E8
Foxlea GLSP SK13 104 C4
Foxley Gv BOLS/LL BL3 2 B6
Fox Park Rd OLDS OL8 74 F3
Fox Platt Rd MOSL OL5 * 76 E3
Fox Platt Ter MOSL OL5 76 F4
Fox St BURY BL9 5 G2
ECC M30 85 J2
EDGY/DAV SK3 12 E7
HEY OL10 40 F2
HOR/BR BL6 33 M2
MILN OL16 11 J2
MILN OL16 29 H6
OLDS OL8 74 F2
Foxton St MDTN M24 56 F5
Foxwood Cl
WGNW/BIL/OR WN5 46 B7
Foxwood Dr HYDE SK14 91 H8
MOSL OL5 77 G2
Foxwood Gdns BNG/LEV M19 99 H7
Foynes Cl NEWH/MOS M40 * 73 G7
Foy St AIMK WN4 * 78 E1
Framingham Rd SALE M33 108 E2
Frampton Cl MDTN M24 57 L5
Fram St BKLY M9 73 J4
SLFD M6 * 86 B2
Frances Av CHD/CHDH SK8 110 D6
Frances Pl ATH M46 66 D3
Frances St BOL BL1 36 A2
BRUN/LGST M13 87 L6
CHD/CHDH SK8 111 H6
EDGY/DAV SK3 13 H6
HYDE SK14 101 M1
IRL M44 94 B7
MILN OL16 29 G1
OLD OL1 59 K3
Frances St West HYDE SK14 101 M1
France St WGNE/HIN WN2 49 G6
WGNW/BIL/OR WN5 14 A6
WHTN BL5 50 B6
Francis Av ECC M30 85 H2
WALK M28 69 J2
Francis Rd DID/WITH M20 98 F7
IRL M44 94 C4
Francis St CSLFD M3 87 J1
DTN/ASHW M34 101 L4
ECC M30 85 G1
FAIL M35 74 C5
FWTH BL4 52 F3
LEIGH WN7 66 B5
TYLD M29 68 A4
WGNE/HIN WN2 49 G7
Frankby Cl SWIN M27 * 70 F5
Frank Fold HEY OL10 40 D2
Frankford Av BOL BL1 35 M2
Frankford Sq BOL BL1 * 35 M2
Frankland Cl OP/CLY M11 88 E2
Franklin Cl OLD OL1 9 H3
Franklin Rd DROY M43 89 K3
Franklin St ECC M30 85 G2
MILN OL16 11 J9
OLD OL1 9 H3
Franklyn Av URM M41 95 H2
Franklyn Rd GTN M18 89 H6
Frank Perkins Wy IRL M44 94 C5
Frank St BOL BL1 36 A3
BURY BL9 5 G6
FAIL M35 74 B5
HYDE SK14 102 B2
SLFD M6 71 K8
Frankton Rd WHTF M45 55 J5
Franton Rd OP/CLY M11 88 E2
Fraser Av SALE M33 109 H1
Fraser Pl TRPK M17 86 A7
Fraser Rd CHH M8 72 C3
WGNW/BIL/OR WN5 47 H5
Fraser St AUL OL6 90 F1
MILN OL16 28 E8
ROY/SHW OL2 43 K4
SWIN M27 70 D3
Frawley Av NEWLW WA12 78 E7
Frecheville Ct BURY BL9 4 D7
Freckleton Av CCHDY M21 97 M8
Freckleton Dr TOT/BURYW BL8 38 C4
Freckleton St WGN WN1 47 M2
Frederica Gdns WGNE/HIN WN2 64 D1
Frederick Av ROY/SHW OL2 * 43 K7
Frederick Rd SLFD M6 86 E1
Frederick St AIMK WN4 63 K7
AUL OL6 91 H2
CHAD OL9 8 B3
CSLFD M3 6 C3
DTN/ASHW M34 90 C7
FWTH BL4 53 G4
LIT OL15 21 L6
OLDS OL8 8 E9
RAMS BL0 18 E7
WGNE/HIN WN2 49 G7
WGNS/IIMK WN3 15 J8
Frederick Ter BKLY M9 * 73 G3
Frederic St WGN WN1 15 L4
Fred Tilson Cl RUSH/FAL M14 98 D1
Freehold St ROCH OL11 10 D8
Freelands TYLD M29 67 M3
Freeman Av AUL OL6 91 G1
Freeman Rd DUK SK16 90 F6
Freeman Sq HULME M15 * 87 K6
Freemantle St EDGY/DAV SK3 12 D6
Freesia Av WALK M28 68 C1
Freestone Cl TOT/BURYW BL8 4 C2
Freetown GLSP SK13 104 F5
Freetown Cl RUSH/FAL M14 87 K8
Freetrade St ROCH OL11 10 D8
Fremantle Av GTN M18 100 A1
French Av OLD OL1 59 M3
STLY SK15 91 M3
French Barn La BKLY M9 72 F1
French Gv BOLS/LL BL3 37 G7
French St AUL OL6 76 A8
STLY SK15 91 M3
Frenchwood Ct
WGNE/HIN WN2 32 F8
Fresca Rd OLD OL1 44 A8
Fresh Ct GLSP SK13 104 C5
Freshfield CHD/CHDH SK8 119 K3
Freshfield Av ATH M46 50 F8
BOLS/LL BL3 52 A2
HYDE SK14 102 A3
PWCH M25 55 M6
Freshfield Cl FAIL M35 74 D6
MPL/ROM SK6 114 E3
Freshfield Gv BOLS/LL BL3 52 C2
Freshfield Rd HTNM SK4 111 J2
WGNE/HIN WN2 49 J7
WGNS/IIMK WN3 63 H1
Freshfields RAD M26 38 A7
Freshpool Wy WYTH/NTH M22 110 B6
Freshville St CMANE M1 * 7 K6
Freshwater Dr AUL OL6 76 B8
DTN/ASHW M34 101 L4
Freshwater St GTN M18 89 H6
Freshwinds Ct OLDE OL4 60 A8
Fresnel Cl HYDE SK14 91 L6
Frewland Av EDGY/DAV SK3 112 C8
Freya Gv ORD M5 86 F4
Friarmere Rd UPML OL3 45 H7
Friars Cl ALT WA14 116 D3
TYLD M29 68 A3
WILM/AE SK9 126 C4
Friars Crs ROCH OL11 42 C2
Friar's Rd SALE M33 96 E8
Friendship Av GTN M18 * 89 H8
Frieston WHIT OL12 20 B8
Frieston Rd ALT WA14 108 B4
Friezland Cl STLY SK15 77 H7
Friezland La UPML OL3 61 K8
Frimley Gdns WYTH/NTH M22 118 F1
Frinton Av NEWH/MOS M40 * 74 A1
Frinton Cl SALE M33 108 C3
Frinton Rd BOLS/LL BL3 51 L1
Frith Rd DID/WITH M20 98 F7
Frith St WGNW/BIL/OR WN5 14 B5
Frobisher Cl BRUN/LGST M13 88 A7
Frobisher Pl RDSH SK5 100 B8
Frodesley Wk
WGTN/LGST M12 * 88 C6
Frodsham Av HTNM SK4 12 C1
Frodsham Cl WGNNW/ST WN6 47 G1
Frodsham Rd SALE M33 109 H2
Frodsham St RUSH/FAL M14 * 98 E1
Frog La WGNNW/ST WN6 14 C3
Frogley St BOLE BL2 * 36 E1
Frogmore Av HYDE SK14 102 B5
Frome Av OFTN SK2 112 F7
URM M41 95 L4
Frome Cl TYLD M29 67 L6
Frome Dr CHH M8 72 E5
Frome St OLDE OL4 59 M6
Frostlands St OLDTF/WHR M16 98 B1
Frost St ANC M4 * 88 A3
OLDS OL8 59 H8
Froxmer St GTN M18 88 F6
Fryent Cl HOR/BR BL6 33 G2
Fulbeck Av WGNS/IIMK WN3 63 K2
Fulbrook Dr CHD/CHDH SK8 120 C6
Fulbrook Wy TYLD M29 67 M3
Fulford St OLDTF/WHR M16 86 F8
Fulham Av NEWH/MOS M40 73 L7
Fulham St OLDE OL4 59 M6
Fullerton Rd HTNM SK4 12 A2
Full Pot La ROCH OL11 27 H4
Fulmar Cl POY/DIS SK12 121 J8
WHTN BL5 50 A6
Fulmar Dr OFTN SK2 113 J7
SALE M33 107 M3
Fulmards Cl WILM/AE SK9 127 G5
Fulmar Gdns ROCH OL11 27 J5
Fulmer Dr ANC M4 7 M2
Fulmere Ct SWIN M27 70 A6
Fulneck Sq DROY M43 89 K4
Fulshaw Av WILM/AE SK9 126 E6
Fulshaw Ct WILM/AE SK9 126 E7
Fulshaw Pk WILM/AE SK9 126 E7
Fulshaw Pk South
WILM/AE SK9 126 D8
Fulstone Ms OFTN SK2 112 E6

Fulwell Av *TYLD* M29.....67 H4
Fulwood Av *BKLY* M9.....57 J8
Fulwood Cl *TOT/BURYW* BL8.....38 C3
Fulwood Rd
  GOL/RIS/CUL WA3.....80 B6
Furbarn La *ROCH* OL11.....27 G4
Furbarn Rd *ROCH* OL11.....27 G4
Furlong Cl *WGNE/HIN* WN2.....64 C5
Furlong Rd *WYTH/NTH* M22.....118 D2
Furnace St *DUK* SK16.....90 B3
  HYDE SK14.....90 F8
Furness Av *AULW* OL7.....75 J7
  BOLE BL2.....36 E2
  HEY OL10.....26 F8
  LIT OL15.....21 L6
  OLDS OL8.....59 M8
  WHTF M45.....55 K4
Furness Cl *GLSP* SK13.....105 L4
  MILN OL16.....29 H6
  POY/DIS SK12.....121 L8
Furness Crs *LEIGH* WN7.....66 A3
Furness Gv *STKP* SK4.....111 K3
Furness Lodge Cl
  CHF/WBR SK23.....124 F8
Furness Rd *BOL* BL1.....35 L5
  CHD/CHDH SK8.....120 E6
  MDTN M24.....57 J1
  RUSH/FAL M14.....98 F3
  URM M41.....96 A1
Furness Sq *BOLE* BL2.....36 E2
Furnival Rd *GTN* M18.....88 F6
Furnival St *LEIGH* WN7.....66 C5
  RDSH SK5.....100 B2
Furrow Dr *ECC* M30.....69 L8
Further Fld *ROCH* OL11.....27 G3
Further Heights Rd *WHIT* OL12.....28 B2
Further Hey Cl *OLDE* OL4.....60 B5
Further La *HYDE* SK14.....103 H1
Further Pits *ROCH* OL11.....27 M5
Furze Av *WHTN* BL5.....50 C5
Furzegate *MILN* OL16.....42 F1
Furze La *OLDE* OL4.....60 A3
Fushia Gv *BRO* M7 *.....72 A6
Futura Pk *HOR/BR* BL6.....33 M3
Fylde Av *BOLE* BL2.....37 H5
  CHD/CHDH SK8.....119 L4
Fylde Rd *HTNM* SK4.....111 K2
Fylde St *BOLS/LL* BL3.....53 L2
Fylde St East *BOLS/LL* BL3.....53 G2

G

Gable Av *WILM/AE* SK9.....126 E5
Gable Dr *MDTN* M24.....57 H5
The Gables *SALE* M33 *.....108 E1
Gable St *BOLE* BL2 -.....23 G7
  OP/CLY M11.....88 C4
Gabriel's Ter *MDTN* M24.....57 M5
The Gabriels *ROY/SHW* OL2.....43 J5
Gadbury Av *ATH* M46.....66 E1
Gadbury Fold *ATH* M46.....66 D2
Gaddum St *ALT* WA14.....116 C3
  DID/WITH M20.....110 F1
Gadfield Gv *ATH* M46.....66 D1
Gadwall Cl *WALK* M28.....69 G4
Gail Av *HTNM* SK4.....12 E2
Gail Cl *FAIL* M35.....74 B7
Gainford Av *CHD/CHDH* SK8.....110 E8
Gainford Gdns *NEWH/MOS* M40.....73 L3
Gainford Rd *RDSH* SK5.....100 C3
Gainford Wk *BOLS/LL* BL3 *.....36 B8
Gainsborough Av *BOLS/LL* BL3.....51 M1
  DID/WITH M20 *.....98 F7
  MPL/ROM SK6.....114 E4
  OLDS OL8.....59 H8
  STRET M32.....97 J1
Gainsborough Cl
  WGNS/IIMK WN3.....63 G1
  WILM/AE SK9.....127 H4
Gainsborough Dr
  CHD/CHDH SK8.....111 J6
  ROCH OL11.....42 C1
Gainsborough Rd *CHAD* OL9.....58 B4
  DTN/ASHW M34.....90 A3
  RAMS BL0.....24 D3
Gainsborough St *BRO* M7.....72 B5
Gairloch Av *STRET* M32.....96 E2
Gair Rd *RDSH* SK5.....100 C8
Gair St *HYDE* SK14.....91 C8
Gaitskell Cl *WGTN/LGST* M12.....88 B3
Galbraith Rd *DID/WITH* M20.....110 F1
Galbraith St *CMANE* M1 *.....7 H7
Galbraith Wy *ROCH* OL11.....27 H4
Gale Dr *MDTN* M24.....57 G2
Gale Rd *PWCH* M25.....71 J1
Gales Ter *ROCH* OL11.....10 C9
Gale St *HEY* OL10.....40 E2
  WHIT OL12.....28 C1
Galgate Cl *HULME* M15.....6 C9
  TOT/BURYW BL8.....38 C3
Galindo St *BOLE* BL2.....36 E2
Galland St *OLDE* OL4.....60 A5
Galloway Cl *BOLS/LL* BL3.....35 H7
  HEY OL10.....40 C3
Galloway Dr *SWIN* M27.....54 C8
Galloway Rd *SWIN* M27 *.....70 A6
Gallowsclough Rd *STLY* SK15.....92 B3
Galston St *OP/CLY* M11.....88 D4
Galsworthy Av *CHH* M8.....72 D4
Galvin Rd *BKLY* M9.....72 E1
Galway St *OLD* OL1 *.....9 J6
Galwey Gv *WGN* WN1.....31 M8
Gambleside Cl *WALK* M28.....68 C4
Gamble St *LEIGH* WN7.....66 D7
Gambrel Bank Rd *AUL* OL6.....75 L6
Gambrel Gv *AUL* OL6.....75 L6
Game St *OLDE* OL4.....59 M7
Gamma Wk *OP/CLY* M11.....88 E2
Gandy La *WHIT* OL12.....20 A8
Gantley Av *WGNW/BIL/OR* WN5.....46 A8
Gantley Crs
  WGNW/BIL/OR WN5.....62 A1
Gantley Rd *WGNW/BIL/OR* WN5.....46 A8
Gantock Wk *RUSH/FAL* M14.....98 F1
Ganton Av *WHTF* M45.....55 G5
Garbrook Av *BKLY* M9.....56 F7
Garden Av *DROY* M43.....89 L2
  STRET M32.....97 G2
  SWIN M27.....70 A5
Garden City *RAMS* BL0.....24 D4
Garden Cl *LIT* OL15.....29 J2
Gardenfold Wy *DROY* M43.....89 L2
Garden La *ALT* WA14.....108 A7
  CSLFD M3.....6 D2
  MILN OL16.....11 G3
  WALK M28.....68 D6
Garden Ms *AUL* OL6 *.....91 G2

Garden Rw *HEY* OL10.....26 E8
The Gardens *BOL* BL1.....22 C6
  EDGW/EG BL7.....17 H8
Garden St *DTN/ASHW* M34.....90 C6
  ECC M30.....85 H3
  FWTH BL4.....52 A1
  HEY OL10.....40 F1
  HYDE SK14.....91 H8
  MILN OL16.....29 L8
  OFTN SK2 *.....112 F7
  OLD OL1.....9 M4
  RAMS BL0.....18 F8
  TOT/BURYW BL8.....24 C5
  TYLD M29.....67 M1
Garden Ter *ROY/SHW* OL2.....42 F5
Garden Wk *AUL* OL6.....75 M8
Garden Wall Cl *ORD* M5.....86 F4
Garden Wy *LIT* OL15.....29 J2
Gardinar Cl *WGN* WN1.....31 L3
Gardner Rd *PWCH* M25.....55 J8
Gardner St *SLFD* M6.....86 D1
  WGTN/LGST M12.....88 E6
Garfield Av *BNG/LEV* M19.....99 L3
Garfield Cl *ROCH* OL11.....27 H4
Garfield Gv *BOLS/LL* BL3.....2 B7
Garfield St *BOLS/LL* BL3.....51 M1
  STKP SK1 *.....13 L2
Garforth Av *ANC* M4 *.....7 M2
Garforth Crs *DROY* M43.....89 M1
Garforth Ri *BOL* BL1.....35 K5
Garforth St *CHAD* OL9.....8 C4
Gargrave Av *BOL* BL1.....35 J2
Gargrave St *BRO* M7.....71 J4
Garland Rd *WYTH/NTH* M22.....119 G1
Garlick St *OLD* OL9.....9 C6
  GTN M18.....89 G7
  HYDE SK14 *.....102 C1
Garnant Cl *BKLY* M9.....73 J4
Garner Av
  HALE/TIMP WA15.....108 D3
Garner Cl *ALT* WA14.....116 F2
Garner Dr *ECC* M30 *.....84 F1
  ORD M5.....86 A1
  TYLD M29.....67 M1
Garner's La *EDGY/DAV* SK3.....112 A8
  EDGY/DAV SK3.....112 C7
Garnet St *OLD* OL1.....59 L4
Garnett Cl *HYDE* SK14.....103 H1
Garnett Rd *HYDE* SK14.....103 H1
Garnett St *BOL* BL1.....36 B1
  RAMS BL0.....18 E7
  STKP SK1 *.....13 J5
Garratt Wy *GTN* M18.....88 F7
Garret Gv *ROY/SHW* OL2.....43 M5
Garrett Hall Rd *WALK* M28.....68 B5
Garretts La *TYLD* M29.....68 A5
Garrett Wk *EDGY/DAV* SK3.....12 C6
Garrick Gdns *WYTH/NTH* M22.....110 A8
Garsdale Cl *BURY* BL9.....39 K5
Garsdale La *BOL* BL1.....35 G5
Garside Av *COL/RIS/CUL* WA3.....80 A5
Garside Gv *BOL* BL1.....35 H2
  WGNS/IIMK WN3.....63 H2
Garside Hey Rd
  TOT/BURYW BL8.....24 F6
Garside St *BOL* BL1.....2 C5
  DTN/ASHW M34 *.....101 J2
  HYDE SK14.....102 B3
Garstang Av *BOLE* BL2.....37 H6
Garstang Dr *TOT/BURYW* BL8.....38 C3
Garston Av *ATH* M46.....50 E7
Garston Cl *HTNM* SK4.....12 D1
  LEIGH WN7.....66 B3
Garston St *BURY* BL9.....25 K8
Garswood Crs
  WGNW/BIL/OR WN5.....62 B3
Garswood Dr *TOT/BURYW* BL8.....24 E6
Garswood Rd *AIMK* WN4.....62 E8
  BOLS/LL BL3.....52 B2
  RUSH/FAL M14.....98 D2
  WGNW/BIL/OR WN5.....62 B8
Garswood St *AIMK* WN4.....78 E1
Garth Av *HALE/TIMP* WA15.....108 B6
Garthland Rd *BRAM/HZG* SK7.....122 B1
Garthmere Rd *ATH* M46.....51 J7
Garthorne Cl *OLDTF/WHR* M16 *.....87 H8
Garthorp Rd *NTHM/RTH* M23.....109 H3
Garth Rd *MPL/ROM* SK6.....114 D6
  OFTN SK2.....112 F6
  WYTH/NTH M22.....110 A3
The Garth *ORD* M5.....86 A2
Garthwaite Av *OLDS* OL8.....75 H1
Garton Dr *COL/RIS/CUL* WA3.....80 B3
Gartside Av *AULW* OL7 *.....90 B3
  CSLFD M3.....6 D5
  OLDE OL4.....59 L7
  UPML OL3 *.....45 H8
Garwick Rd *BOL* BL1.....35 L1
Garwood St *HULME* M15.....6 D9
Gascoyne St *RUSH/FAL* M14.....98 E1
Gaskell Cl *LIT* OL15 *.....21 L6
Gaskell Ri *OLD* OL1.....44 B7
Gaskell Rd *ALT* WA14.....108 A6
  ECC M30.....85 H3
Gaskell St *BOL* BL1.....2 C2
  DUK SK16 *.....90 E3
  NEWH/MOS M40.....73 M7
  SWIN M27.....70 C2
  WGNE/HIN WN2.....49 H5
Gaskill St *HEY* OL10.....40 D2
Gas St *AUL* OL6.....90 E1
  BOL BL1.....2 C5
  FWTH BL4.....53 G3
  HEY OL10.....41 G2
  HTNM SK4.....13 G4
  HYDE SK14.....93 H7
  ROCH OL11.....10 C5
  WGNE/HIN WN2.....64 E2
Gatcombe Sq *RUSH/FAL* M14.....98 F1
Gateacre Wk *NTHM/RTH* M23.....109 H5
Gate Field Cl *RAD* M26.....54 B1
Gategill Gv *WGNW/BIL/OR* WN5.....62 A2
Gatehead Cft *UPML* OL3.....61 J1
Gatehead Ms *UPML* OL3.....61 J1
Gatehead Rd *UPML* OL3.....61 J1
Gatehouse Rd *WALK* M28.....52 D8
Gate Keeper Fold *AULW* OL7.....75 K5
Gatemere Cl *WALK* M28.....68 E4
Gatesgarth Rd *MDTN* M24.....56 F7
Gateshead Cl *RUSH/FAL* M14.....87 L3
Gate St *DUK* SK16.....90 D6
  OP/CLY M11.....88 D2
  ROCH OL11.....10 F9
Gateway Crs *CHAD* OL9.....58 B8
Gateway Rd *GTN* M18.....88 F6
The Gateways *SWIN* M27.....70 C3
The Gateway *NEWH/MOS* M40.....73 H6
Gathill Cl *CHD/CHDH* SK8.....120 B3
Gathurst Hall
  WGNNW/ST WN6 *.....46 A1
Gathurst La *WGNNW/ST* WN6.....30 D7

Gathurst Rd
  WGNW/BIL/OR WN5.....46 B4
Gathurst St *GTN* M18.....89 H6
Gatley Av *RUSH/FAL* M14.....98 D3
Gatley Brow *OLD* OL1 *.....9 H2
Gatley Cl *TYLD* M29.....67 L3
Gatley Gn *CHD/CHDH* SK8.....110 D7
Gatley Rd *CHD/CHDH* SK8.....110 F7
  SALE M33.....109 H1
Gatling Av *WGTN/LGST* M12.....99 K2
Gatwick Av *NTHM/RTH* M23.....109 L6
Gavin Av *ORD* M5.....86 D3
Gawsworth Av *DID/WITH* M20.....110 F3
Gawsworth Cl *BRAM/HZG* SK7.....121 C7
  EDGY/DAV SK3.....112 A7
  GLSP SK13.....93 K7
  HALE/TIMP WA15.....109 G6
  POY/DIS SK12.....129 K2
  ROY/SHW OL2.....43 J5
Gawsworth Ms
  CHD/CHDH SK8.....110 E7
Gawsworth Rd
  GOL/RIS/CUL WA3.....79 J3
  SALE M33.....109 H2
Gawthorne Cl *BRAM/HZG* SK7.....121 L2
Gawthorpe Cl *BURY* BL9.....39 K7
Gaydon Rd *SALE* M33.....96 A8
Gaynor Rd *RNFD/HAY* WA11.....78 C5
Gaythorne St *BOL* BL1.....36 C1
Gaythorn St *ORD* M5.....86 F5
Gayton Cl *WGNS/IIMK* WN3.....63 C1
Geddington Rd *ALT* WA14.....107 M5
Gee Cross Fold *HYDE* SK14.....102 B5
Gee La *ECC* M30.....84 E1
Gee St *EDGY/DAV* SK3.....12 F8
Gellert Pl *WHTN* BL5.....50 B6
Gellert Rd *WHTN* BL5.....50 B6
Gemini Gv *SLFD* M6.....71 M8
Gencoyne Dr *BOL* BL1.....22 A6
Gendre Rd *EDGW/EG* BL7.....22 D4
Geneva Rd *BRAM/HZG* SK7.....120 F1
Geneva Ter *ROCH* OL11.....27 M4
Geneva Wk *CHH* M8.....8 C6
Genista Gv *BRO* M7 *.....72 A6
Geoffrey St *BURY* BL9.....5 H1
  RAMS BL0.....18 D4
  WHTN BL5.....51 J4
George Barton St *BOLE* BL2.....3 J1
George La *MPL/ROM* SK6.....101 K8
George Leigh St *ANC* M4.....7 J3
George Mann Cl
  WYTH/NTH M22.....118 D3
George Richards Wy
  ALT WA14.....107 L5
George Rd *RAMS* BL0.....18 E7
George's Cl *POY/DIS* SK12.....129 J1
Georges La *WGN* WN1.....15 M4
George Sq *OLD* OL1.....9 H6
George's Rd *HTNM* SK4.....12 F5
  SALE M33.....108 E1
George's Rd West
  POY/DIS SK12.....129 J1
George's Ter
  WGNW/BIL/OR WN5.....46 A7
George St *AIMK* WN4.....63 M8
  ATH M46.....67 G1
  AUL OL6.....90 F1
  BURY BL9.....5 G3
  CHAD OL9.....58 D5
  CMANE M1.....7 G6
  DTN/ASHW M34 *.....101 K1
  ECC M30.....84 F3
  FAIL M35.....74 C4
  FWTH BL4.....52 E5
  GLSP SK13.....104 F4
  HEY OL10.....40 E1
  HOR/BR BL6.....33 H1
  IRL M44.....94 C1
  LIT OL15.....21 M7
  MILN OL16.....11 G2
  MILN OL16.....29 G1
  MILN OL16.....29 H5
  MOSL OL5.....76 F3
  MPL/ROM SK6.....114 E2
  NEWLW WA12 *.....78 D8
  OLD OL1.....9 H6
  PWCH M25.....71 L3
  RAD M26.....54 C1
  ROY/SHW OL2.....43 M4
  STKP SK1.....13 L4
  STLY SK15.....91 K2
  URM M41.....96 B2
  WGNE/HIN WN2.....48 C5
  WGNE/HIN WN2.....49 H8
  WHIT OL12.....20 A4
  WHTF M45.....55 H1
  WHTN BL5.....50 C4
  WILM/AE SK9.....130 D3
George St East *STKP* SK1.....112 E4
George St North *BRO* M7.....72 C4
George St South *BRO* M7.....72 B4
George St West *STKP* SK1.....112 E4
Georgette Dr *CSLFD* M3.....6 D1
Georgia Av *DID/WITH* M20.....98 C6
Georgiana St *FWTH* BL4.....52 E5
Georgina Ct *BOLS/LL* BL3.....51 L2
Georgina St *BOLS/LL* BL3.....51 L2
Gerald Av *CHH* M8.....72 D4
Gerald Rd *SLFD* M6.....71 K7
Gerard Av *AIMK* WN4.....78 E1
Germain Cl *BKLY* M9.....56 F7
Gerrard Av *HALE/TIMP* WA15.....108 D4
Gerrard Cl *WGNE/HIN* WN2.....49 G2
Gerrard Rd *WGNW/BIL/OR* WN5.....62 B7
Gerrards Cl *IRL* M44.....94 D2
Gerrards Gdns *HYDE* SK14.....102 B5
Gerrards Hollow *HYDE* SK14.....102 A5
The Gerrards *HYDE* SK14.....102 A5
Gerrard St *FWTH* BL4.....53 H4
  LEIGH WN7.....66 C7
  ROCH OL11.....42 D3
  SLFD M6.....86 D1
  STLY SK15.....91 L3
  WHTN BL5.....50 B5
Gerrards Wd *HYDE* SK14.....102 A5
Gertrude St *ORD* M5.....86 D4
Gervis Cl *NEWH/MOS* M40 *.....73 C7
Ghyll Gv *WALK* M28.....69 H2
Giants Hall Rd *WGNNW/ST* WN6.....47 H1
Giants Seat Gv *SWIN* M27.....71 H4
Gibb Av *GTN* M18.....88 D2
Gibbon's Rd *AIMK* WN4.....78 A2
Gibbon St *BOLS/LL* BL3.....2 E5
  OP/CLY M11.....88 D2
Gibb Rd *WALK* M28.....69 C6
Gibfield Dr *ATH* M46.....66 D2
Gib La *NTHM/RTH* M23.....109 M4
Gibraltar La *DTN/ASHW* M34.....101 L4
Gibraltar St *BOLS/LL* BL3.....2 C8
  OLDE OL4.....60 A7

Gibsmere Cl *HALE/TIMP* WA15.....109 C6
Gibson Av *GTN* M18.....89 J5
Gibson Dr *WALK* M28.....68 D1
Gibson La *WALK* M28.....68 D1
Gibson Pl *ANC* M4.....87 K1
Gibsons Rd *HTNM* SK4.....99 L8
Gibson St *BOLE* BL2.....36 F3
  MILN OL16.....11 M2
  OLDE OL4 *.....59 M6
  WGNE/HIN WN2.....65 C2
Gibson Wy *ALT* WA14.....107 M4
Gibwood Rd *WYTH/NTH* M22.....109 M4
Gidlow Av *GOL/RIS/CUL* WA3.....47 K4
Gidlow La *WGNNW/ST* WN6.....14 C2
  WGNNW/ST WN6.....31 K8
Gidlow St *GTN* M18.....89 H6
  WGNE/HIN WN2.....48 D4
  WGNE/HIN WN2.....49 C6
Gifford Av *BKLY* M9.....57 J8
Gifford Pl *WGNE/HIN* WN2.....49 J8
Gigg La *BURY* BL9.....5 H9
Gilbertbank *MPL/ROM* SK6.....101 K8
Gilbert Rd *HALE/TIMP* WA15.....117 K8
Gilbert St *ECC* M30.....84 C4
  HULME M15.....6 D8
  RAMS BL0.....18 F3
  SLFD M6 *.....86 C3
  WALK M28.....68 F3
  WGNE/HIN WN2.....48 F7
Gilbrook Wy *MILN* OL16.....42 E2
Gilchrist Rd *IRL* M44.....94 B6
Gilda Brook Rd *ECC* M30.....85 K3
Gilda Crs *ECC* M30.....85 K3
Gilda Rd *WALK* M28.....68 B5
Gildenhall *FAIL* M35.....74 D5
Gilderdale Cl *ROY/SHW* OL2.....43 L4
Gilderdale St *BKLY* M9.....56 E6
Gildridge Rd
  OLDTF/WHR M16.....98 B3
Gilesgate *RUSH/FAL* M14.....98 E1
Giles St *WGTN/LGST* M12.....88 D8
Gillan Rd *WGNNW/ST* WN6.....47 L2
Gill Av *WGNNW/ST* WN6.....30 E6
Gillbent Rd *CHD/CHDH* SK8.....120 C6
Gillbrook Rd *DID/WITH* M20.....110 E2
Gillbrow Crs *WGN* WN1.....48 C3
Gillemere Gv *ROY/SHW* OL2.....43 M5
Gillers Gn *WALK* M28.....68 C5
Gillford Av *BKLY* M9.....73 J4
Gillingham Rd *ECC* M30.....84 C2
Gillingham Sq *OP/CLY* M11.....88 C4
Gill St *BKLY* M9.....73 J3
  STKP SK1.....112 E1
Gillwood Dr *MPL/ROM* SK6.....113 J5
Gilman Cl *BKLY* M9 *.....72 F2
Gilman St *BKLY* M9 *.....72 F2
Gilmerton Dr
  NEWH/MOS M40 *.....73 M7
Gilmore Dr *PWCH* M25.....55 L7
Gilmore St *EDGY/DAV* SK3.....13 K4
Gilmour St *MDTN* M24.....57 K4
Gilmour Ter *BKLY* M9.....73 J3
Gilnow Gdns *BOL* BL1.....35 M6
Gilnow Gv *BOL* BL1 *.....2 A6
Gilnow La *BOLS/LL* BL3.....35 M6
Gilnow Rd *BOL* BL1.....35 M6
Gilpin Pl *WGNE/HIN* WN2.....64 C2
Gilpin Rd *URM* M41.....96 C3
Gilroy St *WGN* WN1.....15 J4
Giltbrook Av *NEWH/MOS* M40.....73 H8
Gilwell Dr *NTHM/RTH* M23.....109 J3
Gilwood Gv *MDTN* M24.....41 J8
Gin Croft La *RAMS* BL0.....19 H1
Gingham Pk *RAD* M26.....38 D7
Gipsy La *OFTN* SK2.....112 F6
  ROCH OL11.....41 M1
Gird La *MPL/ROM* SK6.....115 H3
Girton Av *WGNW/BIL/OR* WN5.....63 J8
Girton Cl *BRO* M7.....72 B8
Girton St *BOLS/LL* BL3.....51 M1
  BRO M7.....72 B8
Girvan Av *NEWH/MOS* M40.....74 A2
Girvan Cl *BOLS/LL* BL3.....51 M1
Girvan Crs *AIMK* WN4.....62 F8
Gisborn Dr *SLFD* M6.....71 J7
Gisburn Av *BOL* BL1.....35 H2
  GOL/RIS/CUL WA3.....79 J2
Gisburne Av *WGNW/BIL/OR* WN5.....46 B4
Gisburn Dr *TOT/BURYW* BL8.....38 B1
Gisburn Rd *NEWH/MOS* M40.....74 A2
Givendale Dr *CHH* M8.....72 D2
Givvons Fold *OLDE* OL4.....60 A3
Glabyn Av *HOR/BR* BL6.....34 C4
Gladden Hey Dr
  WGNS/IIMK WN3.....63 G3
Glade Brow *OLDE* OL4 *.....60 D6
Gladeside Rd *WYTH/NTH* M22.....109 M6
Glade St *BOL* BL1.....35 M5
The Glade *BOL* BL1.....2 A1
  HTNM SK4.....111 K3
  WGNNW/ST WN6.....30 E6
Gladewood Cl *WILM/AE* SK9.....127 G4
Gladstone Cl *BOL* BL1 *.....36 B2
  GLSP SK13.....105 C4
Gladstone Crs *ROCH* OL11.....42 D1
Gladstone Gv *HTNM* SK4.....111 K1
Gladstone Pl *FWTH* BL4.....52 E5
Gladstone Rd *ALT* WA14.....108 A6
  ECC M30.....85 H2
  FWTH BL4.....52 F3
  URM M41.....96 B2
Gladstone St *BOL* BL1.....36 B2
  BURY BL9.....5 K3
  GLSP SK13.....93 J5
  GLSP SK13.....104 F4
  OFTN SK2.....112 F8
  OLDE OL4.....59 L4
  SWIN M27.....70 D4
Gladstone Terrace Rd
  UPML OL3.....61 K8
Gladstone Wy *NEWLW* WA12.....78 B8
Gladwyn Av *DID/WITH* M20.....98 B8
Gladys St *BOLS/LL* BL3.....53 L2
Glaisdale *OLDE* OL4.....60 A6
Glaisdale Cl *AIMK* WN4.....78 F1
  BOLE BL2.....36 E2
Glaisdale St *BOLE* BL2.....36 E2
Glamis Av *HEY* OL10.....41 H5
  OP/CLY M11.....88 F1
  STRET M32.....96 F3
Glamis Cl *LEIGH* WN7.....66 C6
Glamorgan Pl *CHAD* OL9.....58 C8
Glandon Dr *CHD/CHDH* SK8.....120 C5
Glanford Av *BKLY* M9.....72 D1
Glanvor Rd *EDGY/DAV* SK3.....12 C7
Glassbrook St *WGNNW/ST* WN6.....14 C1
Glasshouse St *ANC* M4.....7 L1
Glaswen Gv *RDSH* SK5.....100 C8
Glazebrook Cl *HEY* OL10.....40 F1
Glazebury Dr *NTHM/RTH* M23.....109 L1
  WHTN BL5.....50 C2
Glazedale Av *ROY/SHW* OL2.....42 F8
Glaze Wk *WHTF* M45.....55 M2
Gleaves Av *BOLE* BL2.....23 K8
Gleaves Rd *ECC* M30.....85 H3
Gleave St *BOL* BL1 *.....2 C1
  SALE M33.....96 E6
Glebe Av *AIMK* WN4.....78 E2
Glebe Cl *WGNNW/ST* WN6.....31 H3
Glebe End St *WGNNW/ST* WN6.....14 D3
Glebeland Cl *BOLS/LL* BL3.....35 K7
Glebelands Rd
  NTHM/RTH M23.....109 J6
  PWCH M25.....55 M8
  SALE M33.....96 D6
Glebe La *OLD* OL1.....60 B1
Glebe Rd *URM* M41.....96 A2
  WGNNW/ST WN6.....31 J4
Glebe St *BOLE* BL2.....3 G6
  CHAD OL9.....74 D1
  LEIGH WN7.....66 C6
  RAD M26.....54 E1
  ROY/SHW OL2.....43 J5
  STKP SK1.....13 M5
  WGNE/HIN WN2.....48 F7
  WHTN BL5.....50 B3
Gleden St *NEWH/MOS* M40.....88 B2
Gledhall St *STLY* SK15.....91 K2
Gledhill Av *ORD* M5.....86 B6
Gledhill Cl *ROY/SHW* OL2.....43 K3
Gledhill St *DID/WITH* M20.....98 E5
Gledhill Wy *EDGW/EG* BL7.....22 D4
Glegg St *WGNE/HIN* WN2.....49 J8
Glemsford Cl *NEWH/MOS* M40 *.....73 L6
  WGNS/IIMK WN3.....63 L1
Glenacre Gdns *GTN* M18.....100 B1
Glenart *ECC* M30.....85 H1
Glen Av *BKLY* M9.....73 H3
  BOLS/LL BL3.....53 L7
  FWTH BL4.....53 L6
  SALE M33.....96 D6
  SWIN M27.....70 A4
  WALK M28.....69 K4
Glenavon Dr *ROY/SHW* OL2.....43 J4
  WHIT OL12.....28 B2
Glenbarry Cl *BRUN/LGST* M13.....87 L6
Glenbarry St *WGTN/LGST* M12.....88 A4
Glenbeck Cl *HOR/BR* BL6.....34 A3
Glenbeck Rd *WHTF* M45.....55 H5
Glenboro Av *TOT/BURYW* BL8.....38 E2
Glen Bott St *BOL* BL1.....36 A2
Glenbourne Pk
  BRAM/HZG SK7.....120 F7
Glenbranter Av
  WGNE/HIN WN2.....48 D4
Glenbrook Gdns *FWTH* BL4.....53 C2
Glenbrook Hi *GLSP* SK13.....104 F2
Glenbrook Rd *BKLY* M9.....56 D7
Glenburn St *BOLS/LL* BL3.....52 A1
Glenby Av *WYTH/NTH* M22.....119 H1
Glencar *WHTN* BL5.....50 A5
Glencastle Rd *GTN* M18.....88 F7
Glencoe Cl *HEY* OL10.....40 B3
Glencoe Dr *BOLE* BL2.....37 J6
  SALE M33.....107 M2
Glencoe St *OLDS* OL8 *.....74 F2
Glen Cottages *BOL* BL1 *.....35 H2
Glencross Av *OLDTF/WHR* M16.....97 K2
Glendale *SWIN* M27.....69 M6
Glendale Av *AIMK* WN4.....63 M8
  BNG/LEV M19.....99 J6
  BURY BL9.....55 J1
Glendale Ct *OLDS* OL8.....59 J8
Glendale Dr *BOLS/LL* BL3.....35 J8
Glendale Rd *ECC* M30.....85 K1
  GTN M18.....88 F8
  WALK M28.....68 C5
Glendene Av *BRAM/HZG* SK7.....120 F7
  DROY M43.....89 M1
Glenden Foot *WHIT* OL12.....28 A1
Glendevon Cl *BOLS/LL* BL3.....35 J8
  WGNE/HIN WN2.....48 D4
Glendevon Pl *WHTF* M45.....55 L5
Glendinning St *SLFD* M6.....86 B2
Glendon Ct *OLD* OL1.....44 B8
Glendon Crs *AUL* OL6.....75 L5
Glendore *ORD* M5.....85 M2
Glendower Dr *NEWH/MOS* M40.....72 F7
Glen Dr *WGNNW/ST* WN6.....30 B4
Gleneagles *BOLS/LL* BL3.....51 J1
Gleneagles Av *HEY* OL10.....41 G4
Gleneagles Cl *BRAM/HZG* SK7.....121 J5
  WILM/AE SK9.....127 H4
Gleneagles Rd *CHD/CHDH* SK8.....119 L3
  URM M41.....84 B8
Gleneagles Wy *RAMS* BL0.....18 E7
Glenfield *ALT* WA14.....107 L8
Glenfield Cl *OLDE* OL4.....60 A6
Glenfield Dr *POY/DIS* SK12.....129 H1
Glenfield Rd *HTNM* SK4.....100 A8
Glenfield Sq *FWTH* BL4.....52 F4
Glenfyne Rd *SLFD* M6.....71 C7
Glen Gdns *WHIT* OL12.....28 C1
Glengarth *UPML* OL3.....61 L5
Glengarth Dr *HOR/BR* BL6.....34 A4
Glen Gv *MDTN* M24.....57 M6
  ROY/SHW OL2.....43 M5
Glenhaven Av *URM* M41.....95 M2
Glenholme Rd *BRAM/HZG* SK7.....120 F5
Glenhurst Rd *BNG/LEV* M19 *.....99 H7
Glenilla Av *WALK* M28.....69 H5
Glenlea Dr *DID/WITH* M20.....110 E4
Glenmaye Gv *WGNE/HIN* WN2.....49 K7
Glenmere Cl *PWCH* M25.....55 J6
Glenmere Rd *DID/WITH* M20.....110 F4
Glenmoor Rd *STKP* SK1.....13 L5
Glenmore Av *DID/WITH* M20.....98 B8
  FWTH BL4.....52 D2
Glenmore Cl *BOLS/LL* BL3.....35 H7
  ROCH OL11.....27 H7
Glenmore Dr *CHH* M8.....72 E5
  FAIL M35.....74 E4
Glenmore Gv *DUK* SK16.....91 G2
Glenmore Rd *TOT/BURYW* BL8.....24 C2
Glenmuir Cl *IRL* M44.....94 D2
Glenolden St *OP/CLY* M11.....89 C2
Glenpark *LEIGH* WN7.....66 D6
Glenridding Cl *OLD* OL1.....59 K3
Glenridge Cl *BOL* BL1.....36 C2

Glen Ri HALE/TIMP WA15 108 D7
Glen Rd OLDE OL4 59 M6
Glen Royd WHIT OL12 27 M3
Glensdale Dr NEWH/MOS M40 74 B3
Glenshee Dr BOLS/LL BL3 35 J7
Glenside Av GTN M18 100 A1
Glenside Dr BOLS/LL BL3 52 C2
MPL/ROM SK6 101 L7
WILM/AE SK9 127 G6
Glenside Gdns FAIL M35 74 D5
Glenside Gv WALK M28 69 H1
Glen St RAMS BL0 18 E5
SALQ M50 86 D5
The Glen BOL BL1 35 H5
MDTN M24 57 L6
Glenthorn Av BKLY M9 57 G6
Glenthorne St BOL BL1 36 B3
Glenthorn Gv SALE M33 108 E1
Glentrool Ms BOL BL1 35 K5
Glent Vw STLY SK15 76 D8
Glentwood ALT WA14 116 F3
Glenvale Cl RAD M26 54 E1
Glen Vw ROY/SHW OL2 43 G7
Glenview Rd TYLD M29 67 J2
Glenville Rd CHH M8 72 C7
Glenville Wy DTN/ASHW M34 101 K2
Glenwood Av HYDE SK14 91 G7
Glenwood Cl RAD M26 54 E2
Glenwood Dr BKLY M9 73 H5
MDTN M24 57 M2
Glenwood Gv OFTN SK2 121 K1
Glenwyn Av BKLY M9 57 H8
Globe Cl OLDTF/WHR M16 87 G7
Globe La DUK SK16 90 E5
EDGW/EG BL7 22 A1
Globe Sq DUK SK16 90 D5
Globe St OLDE OL4 59 L5
Glodwick Rd OLDE OL4 59 L7
Glossop Brook Rd GLSP SK13 104 E3
Glossop Rd GLSP SK13 104 A4
MPL/ROM SK6 103 H8
Glossop Wy WGNE/HIN WN2 49 H8
Gloster St BOLE BL2 3 H5
Gloucester Av BNG/LEV M19 99 L4
GOL/RIS/CUL WA3 79 L4
HEY OL10 40 F5
HOR/BR BL6 34 A2
MPL/ROM SK6 114 C6
WHIT OL12 21 H8
WHTF M45 55 J4
Gloucester Cl AUL OL6 76 A4
Gloucester Crs WGNE/HIN WN2 49 H6
Gloucester Dr SALE M33 96 A8
UPML OL3 45 M8
Gloucester Pl ATH M46 51 G8
SLFD M6 86 D1
Gloucester Ri DUK SK16 91 K5
Gloucester Rd CHD/CHDH SK8 119 L5
DROY M43 89 K1
DTN/ASHW M34 100 D2
HYDE SK14 102 B4
MDTN M24 57 K6
POY/DIS SK12 129 H1
SLFD M6 70 F8
URM M41 96 A3
WGNW/BIL/OR WN5 46 F6
Gloucester St ATH M46 66 F1
CMANE M1 6 F8
ORD M5 86 F4
SLFD M6 71 K8
Gloucester St North CHAD OL9 8 C9
Gloucester Wy GLSP SK13 105 J4
Glover Dr HYDE SK14 102 B2
Glover St LEIGH WN7 65 M4
Glyn Av HALE/TIMP WA15 117 J2
Glynne St FWTH BL4 52 F4
Glynrene Dr SWIN M27 69 M2
Glynwood Pk FWTH BL4 52 F3
Goadsby St ANC M4 7 H2
Goats Gate Ter WHTF M45 * 55 G2
Godbert Av CCHDY M21 97 M7
Goddard La GLSP SK13 93 K6
Goddard St OLDS OL8 59 J8
Godfrey Av DROY M43 89 G1
Godfrey Range GTN M18 89 J8
Godfrey Rd SLFD M6 70 F7
Godlee Dr SWIN M27 70 B5
Godley Cl OP/CLY M11 88 F5
Godley Hill Rd HYDE SK14 102 E1
Godley St HYDE SK14 91 J8
Godmond Hall Dr WALK M28 68 C7
Godolphin Cl ECC M30 70 B8
Godson St OLD OL1 9 G1
Godward Rd NM/HAY SK22 124 D4
Godwin St GTN M18 89 H6
Golborne Av DID/WITH M20 98 C5
Golborne Dale Rd
NEWLW WA12 79 K8
Golborne Gallery WGN WN1 * 14 F3
Golborne Pl WGN WN1 * 15 K3
Golborne Rd AIMK WN4 64 A8
GOL/RIS/CUL WA3 79 M4
Golborne St NEWLW WA12 79 H8
Goldbourne Dr ROY/SHW OL2 43 L4
Goldbrook Cl HEY OL10 41 H3
Goldcrest Cl WALK M28 68 E5
WYTH/NTH M22 110 C7
Goldenhill Av OP/CLY M11 88 F1
Golden St ECC M30 85 G3
ROY/SHW OL2 44 B4
Goldenways WGN WN1 47 M2
Goldfinch Dr BURY BL9 25 M7
Goldfinch Wy DROY M43 89 M1
Goldie Av WYTH/NTH M22 119 H3
Goldrill Av BOLE BL2 37 J4
Goldrill Gdns BOLE BL2 37 J4
Goldsmith Av OLD OL1 44 B8
ORD M5 86 A2
Goldsmith Pl WGNS/IIMK WN3 47 K8
Goldsmith Rd RDSH SK5 100 A3
Goldsmith St BOLS/LL BL3 36 A8
Gold St CMANE M1 * 7 H5
Goldswcrthy Rd URM M41 95 H2
Goldsworth Rd OLD OL1 60 A1
Goldsworthy Rd URM M41 95 H1
Golf Rd HALE/TIMP WA15 117 H1
SALE M33 97 J8
Golfview Dr ECC M30 70 A8
Gooch St HOR/BR BL6 33 L2
Goodacre HYDE SK14 91 L6
Gooden St HEY OL10 41 H3
Goodiers Dr ORD M5 86 D4
Goodier St NEWH/MOS M40 73 H7
SALE M33 96 D8
Goodier Vw HYDE SK14 91 J7
Goodison Cl BURY BL9 55 L1
Goodlad St TOT/BURYW BL8 24 E8
Goodman St BKLY M9 73 H3
Goodrich ROCH OL11 10 C7
Goodridge Av WYTH/NTH M22 118 E2
Goodrington Rd WILM/AE SK9 127 J2
Goodshaw Rd WALK M28 68 F4
Good Shepherd Cl MILN OL16 11 H3
Goodwill Cl SWIN M27 70 C5
Goodwin Sq BKLY M9 * 73 G5
Goodwin St BOL BL1 3 G3
Goodwood Av
NTHM/RTH M23 109 G4
SALE M33 95 M8
Goodwood Cl BOLS/LL BL3 53 J1
Goodwood Crs
HALE/TIMP WA15 108 F6
Goodwood Dr EDGY/DAV SK3 112 B8
OLD OL1 59 L3
SWIN M27 70 E5
Goodwood Rd MPL/ROM SK6 114 B7
Goole St OP/CLY M11 88 D4
Goose Cote Hl EDGW/EG BL7 22 B3
Goose Gn ALT WA14 108 A8
Goose La WHIT OL12 10 E2
Goosetrey Cl WILM/AE SK9 127 J3
Goostrey Av DID/WITH M20 98 C4
Gordon Av AIMK WN4 63 H8
BNG/LEV M19 99 L3
BOLS/LL BL3 35 M7
BRAM/HZG SK7 121 M1
CHAD OL9 74 D1
OLDE OL4 59 M6
RNFD/HAY WA11 78 C5
Gordon Cl WGNW/BIL/OR WN5 47 H4
Gordon Ct LIT OL15 21 M6
Gordon Pl DID/WITH M20 98 E7
Gordon Rd ECC M30 85 G1
SALE M33 96 E6
SWIN M27 69 M6
Gordonstoun Crs
WGNW/BIL/OR WN5 46 C5
Gordon St AUL OL6 * 76 A8
BRO M7 72 A8
BURY BL9 4 D1
CHAD OL9 58 C8
GTN M18 89 H6
HTNM SK4 13 H2
HYDE SK14 102 B2
LEIGH WN7 66 C6
MILN OL16 43 L1
OLDE OL4 60 D6
OLDTF/WHR M16 87 G8
ROCH OL11 * 11 H9
ROY/SHW OL2 43 M5
STLY SK15 91 L3
WGN WN1 15 L5
Gordon Ter BKLY M9 * 73 H4
Gordon Wy HEY OL10 40 C3
Gore Av FAIL M35 74 E5
ORD M5 86 A2
Gorebrook Ct WGTN/LGST M12 88 D8
Gore Cl BURY BL9 39 M3
Gore Crs ORD M5 86 A1
Goredale Av GTN M18 100 B1
Gore Dr ORD M5 86 A1
Gorelan Rd GTN M18 * 89 G7
Gore St CMANE M1 7 J5
CSLFD M3 6 C4
SLFD M6 86 D1
WGNW/BIL/OR WN5 46 E6
Goring Av GTN M18 89 G6
Gorman St WGNNW/ST WN6 14 B3
Gorman Wk WGNS/IIMK WN3 14 A9
Gorrells Wy ROCH OL11 42 A1
Gorrels Cl ROCH OL11 42 A1
Gorrel St ROCH OL11 11 H9
Gorse Av DROY M43 89 M2
MOSL OL5 77 H3
MPL/ROM SK6 114 B6
OLDS OL8 75 M1
STRET M32 97 J1
Gorse Bank BURY BL9 39 M1
Gorse Bank Rd
HALE/TIMP WA15 117 L5
Gorse Crs STRET M32 97 J1
Gorse Dr LHULT M38 52 C6
STRET M32 97 J1
Gorsefield Cl RAD M26 38 D8
Gorsefield Dr SWIN M27 70 C5
Gorsefield Hey WILM/AE SK9 127 J4
Gorse Hall Cl DUK SK16 * 91 J5
Gorse Hall Dr STLY SK15 91 K4
Gorse Hall Rd DUK SK16 91 J5
Gorselands CHD/CHDH SK8 120 D7
Gorse La STRET M32 97 J1
Gorse Rd MILN OL16 29 J6
SWIN M27 70 B6
WALK M28 69 H2
Gorses Dr WGNE/HIN WN2 32 F6
Gorses Mt BOLE BL2 3 M8
Gorse Sq PART M31 106 A1
Gorses Rd BOLE BL2 3 M8
BOLS/LL BL3 37 G7
Gorse St CHAD OL9 58 C8
STRET M32 97 H1
The Gorse ALT WA14 116 D4
Gorse Wy GLSP SK13 105 H5
Gorseway RDSH SK5 100 E8
Gorsey Av WYTH/NTH M22 109 M8
Gorsey Bank Rd EDGY/DAV SK3 12 B6
Gorsey Brow HYDE SK14 103 K3
MPL/ROM SK6 113 K2
WGNW/BIL/OR WN5 62 A7
Gorsey Brow Cl
WGNW/BIL/OR WN5 62 A7
Gorsey Clough Wk
TOT/BURYW BL8 24 C7
Gorsey Dr WYTH/NTH M22 109 M8
Gorseyfields DROY M43 89 K4
Gorsey Gv WHTN BL5 50 A5
Gorsey Hey WHTN BL5 50 B5
Gorsey Hill St HEY OL10 41 G3
Gorsey Intakes HYDE SK14 103 K4
Gorsey La ALT WA14 107 L7
AUL OL6 76 C6
LYMM WA13 106 D6
Gorsey Mount St STKP SK1 13 K5
Gorsey Rd WILM/AE SK9 126 D5
WYTH/NTH M22 109 M8
Gorsey Wy AUL OL6 76 B6
Gorston Wk WYTH/NTH M22 118 E4
Gort Cl BURY BL9 55 L3
Gorton Crs DTN/ASHW M34 100 F2
Gorton Gv WALK M28 52 F7
Gorton La WGTN/LGST M12 88 D6
Gorton Rd OP/CLY M11 88 C5
RDSH SK5 100 C4
Gorton St AULW OL7 90 C3
BOLE BL2 3 G6
CHAD OL9 8 B7
CSLFD M3 * 6 E2
ECC M30 84 D3
FWTH BL4 52 E5
HEY OL10 41 H2
Gortonvilla Wk
WGTN/LGST M12 88 C6
Gosforth Cl OLD OL1 59 K3
TOT/BURYW BL8 24 F7
Goshen La BURY BL9 39 J6
Gosport Sq BRO M7 72 A7
Goss Hall St OLDE OL4 * 59 M6
Gotha Wk BRUN/LGST M13 * 87 M6
Gotherage Cl
MPL/ROM SK6 114 B2
Gotherage La MPL/ROM SK6 114 B2
Gothic Cl MPL/ROM SK6 114 C2
Gough St EDGY/DAV SK3 12 F5
HEY OL10 * 41 H2
Goulden Rd DID/WITH M20 98 D7
Goulden St ANC M4 7 J2
SLFD M6 86 B2
Goulder Rd GTN M18 100 B1
Gould St
DTN/ASHW M34 101 H1
OLD OL1 59 L4
Gourham Dr
CHD/CHDH SK8 120 B2
Govan St
WYTH/NTH M22 110 B3
Gowan Dr MDTN M24 57 G3
Gowanlock's St BOL BL1 36 B2
Gowan Rd OLDTF/WHR M16 98 B3
Gower Av BRAM/HZG SK7 121 L1
Gowerdale Rd RDSH SK5 100 F7
Gower Hey
Gdns HYDE SK14 102 B3
Gower Rd HTNM SK4 100 A8
HYDE SK14 102 A3
Gowers St MILN OL16 11 J2
Gower St AUL OL6 * 90 F1
BOL BL1 2 A3
FWTH BL4 52 F3
LEIGH WN7 66 B8
OLD OL1 9 L4
SWIN M27 70 D3
WGNW/BIL/OR WN5 14 A7
Gowran Pk OLDE OL4 60 A6
Gowy Cl WILM/AE SK9 127 J3
Goyt Av MPL/ROM SK6 114 C8
Goyt Crs MPL/ROM SK6 113 J1
STKP SK1 112 E1
Goyt Hey Av
WGNW/BIL/OR WN5 62 B8
Goyt Rd MPL/ROM SK6 114 C8
NM/HAY SK22 124 E6
POY/DIS SK12 123 M7
STKP SK1 112 E1
Goyt Valley Rd
MPL/ROM SK6 113 J2
Goyt Vw NM/HAY SK22 124 D6
Goyt Wy MPL/ROM SK6 114 C3
MPL/ROM SK6 114 E7
NM/HAY SK22 124 B3
NM/HAY SK22 124 E6
POY/DIS SK12 124 C5
Grace St LEIGH WN7 65 M7
WHIT OL12 28 D2
Grace Wk ANC M4 88 A3
Gracie Av OLD OL1 59 L3
Gradwell St EDGY/DAV SK3 12 F6
Grafton Av ECC M30 70 D8
Grafton Ct MILN OL16 11 K7
The Graftons ALT WA14 * 108 A8
Grafton St ALT WA14 108 A8
ATH M46 66 D3
AUL OL6 91 G2
BOL BL1 2 A3
BRUN/LGST M13 87 L7
BURY BL9 4 F9
FAIL M35 74 C4
HTNM SK4 112 B1
MILN OL16 11 K7
OLD OL1 44 B8
STLY SK15 92 A1
Graham Dr POY/DIS SK12 123 L6
Graham Rd SLFD M6 70 F8
STKP SK1 112 E4
Graham St AULW OL7 90 C3
BOL BL1 * 2 E2
OP/CLY M11 88 D4
WGNE/HIN WN2 64 D3
Grainger Av WGTN/LGST M12 99 K1
Grains Rd ROY/SHW OL2 43 M5
UPML OL3 44 E7
Grain Vw ORD M5 * 86 D4
Gralam Cl SALE M33 109 H3
Grammar School Rd OLDS OL8 74 E2
Grampian Cl CHAD OL9 58 D7
Grampian Wy
GOL/RIS/CUL WA3 80 A3
ROY/SHW OL2 43 K4
Granada Ms OLDTF/WHR M16 * 98 B3
Granada Rd DTN/ASHW M34 100 D1
Granary La WALK M28 69 J8
Granary Wy SALE M33 108 C2
Granby Rd CHD/CHDH SK8 120 D4
HALE/TIMP WA15 108 D3
OFTN SK2 112 E7
STRET M32 97 H3
SWIN M27 69 M5
Granby Rw CMANE M1 7 J7
Granby St CHAD OL9 74 D2
TOT/BURYW BL8 24 C8
Grandale St RUSH/FAL M14 * 98 F1
Grand Central Sq STKP SK1 * 13 H6
Grandidge St ROCH OL11 10 D8
Grand Union Wy ECC M30 85 G4
Granford Cl ALT WA14 * 108 A5
Grange Av BNG/LEV M19 99 J4
BOLS/LL BL3 53 M1
CHD/CHDH SK8 120 B1
ECC M30 70 A8
HALE/TIMP WA15 108 E5
HALE/TIMP WA15 117 J2
HTNM SK4 99 M7
MILN OL16 29 J8
OLDS OL8 58 F8
STRET M32 97 G2
SWIN M27 70 A2
URM M41 95 H2
WGNS/IIMK WN3 14 D9
WGNW/BIL/OR WN5 46 E5
Grange Cl GOL/RIS/CUL WA3 79 M6
HYDE SK14 102 C3
Grange Ct OLDS OL8 * 58 F8
Grange Crs URM M41 95 M3
Grange Dr BKLY M9 73 J1
ECC M30 70 A8
Grangeforth Rd CHH M8 72 C4
Grange Gv WHTF M45 55 J4
Grange La DID/WITH M20 110 E2
UPML OL3 45 J6
Grange Park Av AUL OL6 76 C6
CHD/CHDH SK8 111 G7
WILM/AE SK9 126 E4
Grangepark Rd BKLY M9 73 J1
Grange Park Rd
CHD/CHDH SK8 111 G7
EDGW/EG BL7 22 F6
Grange Pl IRL M44 94 A7
Grange Rd AIMK WN4 63 J6
ALT WA14 116 E3
BOLS/LL BL3 35 L7
BRAM/HZG SK7 121 J2
CCHDY M21 97 K2
ECC M30 69 J8
EDGW/EG BL7 22 F5
FWTH BL4 52 D3
HALE/TIMP WA15 108 E5
MDTN M24 42 A6
RNFD/HAY WA11 78 A7
SALE M33 96 C8
TOT/BURYW BL8 38 E2
URM M41 95 M3
WALK M28 68 B5
WGNE/HIN WN2 65 H3
WHIT OL12 20 B2
Grange Rd North HYDE SK14 102 C2
Grange Rd South HYDE SK14 102 C3
Grange St CHAD OL9 9 G4
FAIL M35 74 A6
LEIGH WN7 81 H1
SLFD M6 86 B2
WGNE/HIN WN2 49 G8
The Grange HYDE SK14 102 C3
OLD OL1 * 59 L4
RUSH/FAL M14 98 F1
WHTN BL5 49 M4
Grangethorpe Dr
BNG/LEV M19 99 H5
Grangethorpe Rd
RUSH/FAL M14 98 F2
URM M41 95 M3
Grange Va RNFD/HAY WA11 78 A6
Grangeway WILM/AE SK9 119 M8
Grangewood EDGW/EG BL7 22 F5
Grangewood Dr BKLY M9 73 G5
Granite St OLD OL1 59 L4
Gransden Dr CHH M8 72 F6
Granshaw St NEWH/MOS M40 88 B1
Gransmoor Av OP/CLY M11 89 J5
Gransmoor Rd OP/CLY M11 89 J5
Grantchester Pl FWTH BL4 52 C3
Grantchester Wy BOLE BL2 37 H3
Grant Cl BKLY M9 73 G2
Grantham Cl BOL BL1 * 36 B3
Grantham Dr TOT/BURYW BL8 25 G7
Grantham Gv WGNE/HIN WN2 48 C2
Grantham Rd HTNM SK4 12 D3
Grantham St OLDE OL4 9 M8
Grantley St AIMK WN4 63 K7
Grant Rd WGNS/IIMK WN3 63 K1
Grants La RAMS BL0 18 F6
Grant St FWTH BL4 52 E2
ROCH OL11 42 A2
Grantwood AIMK WN4 63 K7
Granville Av BRO M7 72 B4
Granville Cl CHAD OL9 8 C4
Granville Ct MILN OL16 43 L1
Granville Gdns DID/WITH M20 110 D2
Granville Rd BOLS/LL BL3 51 M1
CHD/CHDH SK8 111 M7
DTN/ASHW M34 89 L3
HALE/TIMP WA15 108 F6
RUSH/FAL M14 98 F4
URM M41 96 B1
WILM/AE SK9 126 D7
Granville St AUL OL6 91 G2
CHAD OL9 8 C3
ECC M30 85 G1
FWTH BL4 53 G3
LEIGH WN7 66 C5
OLD OL1 9 G1
WALK M28 68 F1
WGNE/HIN WN2 * 49 H7
Granville Wk CHAD OL9 8 C3
Graphite Wy GLSP SK13 93 H7
Grasmere Av BOLS/LL BL3 37 K8
FWTH BL4 52 C5
HEY OL10 41 G4
HTNM SK4 100 B6
SWIN M27 69 M2
URM M41 95 H3
WGNE/HIN WN2 48 D5
WGNE/HIN WN2 49 H8
WGNW/BIL/OR WN5 46 C4
WHTF M45 54 F5
Grasmere Cl STLY SK15 76 D8
Grasmere Crs BRAM/HZG SK7 121 G4
ECC M30 69 L8
MPL/ROM SK6 123 G3
Grasmere Dr AIMK WN4 63 L7
BURY BL9 39 K5
Grasmere Gv AULW OL7 75 J8
Grasmere Rd CHD/CHDH SK8 119 K1
HALE/TIMP WA15 108 F6
OLDE OL4 59 M6
PART M31 106 B1
ROY/SHW OL2 43 G6
SALE M33 108 F2
STRET M32 97 G1
SWIN M27 70 C6
WGNW/BIL/OR WN5 46 F5
WILM/AE SK9 130 D3
Grasmere St BOL BL1 36 C2
LEIGH WN7 66 B7
WGTN/LGST M12 99 L1
WHIT OL12 28 C3
Grasmere Ter WGNE/HIN WN2 64 E4
Grasmere Wk MDTN M24 57 J2
Grason Av WILM/AE SK9 127 G3
Grasscroft RDSH SK5 100 F6
Grasscroft Cl RUSH/FAL M14 98 C2
Grasscroft Rd STLY SK15 91 K3
WGNE/HIN WN2 49 K8
Grassfield Av BRO M7 71 M6
Grassholme Dr OFTN SK2 113 L7
Grassingham Gdns SLFD M6 86 C1
Grassington Av
NEWH/MOS M40 73 K3
Grassington Ct
TOT/BURYW BL8 24 B8
Grassington Dr BURY BL9 40 B3
Grassington Pl BOLE BL2 36 D3
Grass Md DTN/ASHW M34 101 K4
Grassmoor Crs GLSP SK13 104 A2
Gratrix Av ORD M5 86 E5
Gratrix La SALE M33 109 J1
Gratrix St GTN M18 89 H8
Gratten Ct WALK M28 52 F8
Gravel Bank Rd MPL/ROM SK6 101 L6
Gravel La CSLFD M3 6 E2
WILM/AE SK9 126 D7
Gravel Wks OLDE OL4 59 L5
Gravenmoor Dr BRO M7 72 B6
Grave Oak La LEIGH WN7 81 L3
Graver La NEWH/MOS M40 74 A7
Gray Av RNFD/HAY WA11 78 A6
Gray Cl HYDE SK14 103 J1
WGNE/HIN WN2 48 D2
Graymar Rd LHULT M38 52 D8
Graymarsh Dr POY/DIS SK12 129 J2
Graysands Rd
HALE/TIMP WA15 117 H1
Grayson Av WHTF M45 55 K5
Grayson Rd LHULT M38 52 E8
Grayson's Cl WGN WN1 15 G1
Grayson Wy UPML OL3 61 L6
Gray St BOL BL1 2 D2
Gray St North BOL BL1 2 E2
Graythorpe Wk ORD M5 * 86 D3
Graythorp Wk RUSH/FAL M14 98 E1
Graythwaite Rd BOL BL1 35 J2
Grazing Dr IRL M44 94 F1
Greame St OLDTF/WHR M16 98 C1
Great Acre WGN WN1 15 J1
Great Ancoats St ANC M4 7 J3
CMANE M1 88 A4
Great Bank Rd WHTN BL5 50 A2
Great Bent Cl WHIT OL12 21 H8
Great Boys Cl TYLD M29 68 B3
Great Bridgewater St
CMANE M1 6 E7
Great Cheetham St East
BRO M7 72 B6
Great Cheetham St West
BRO M7 71 M7
Great Clowes St BRO M7 72 A5
Great Delph RNFD/HAY WA11 78 A5
Great Ducie St CHH M8 72 C8
CSLFD M3 6 F1
Great Eaves Rd RAMS BL0 18 F5
Great Egerton St STKP SK1 13 H3
Greatfield Rd WYTH/NTH M22 109 L8
Great Flatt WHIT OL12 27 L3
Great Fold LEIGH WN7 67 H8
Great Gable Cl OLD OL1 9 L2
Great Gates Cl ROCH OL11 28 D8
Great Gates Rd ROCH OL11 42 D2
Great George St CSLFD M3 6 A3
MILN OL16 10 F5
WGNS/IIMK WN3 14 E4
Great Hall Cl RAD M26 38 D8
Great Heaton Cl MDTN M24 * 56 F5
Great Holme BOLS/LL BL3 52 C1
Great Howarth WHIT OL12 20 F8
Great Jackson St HULME M15 6 C8
Great John St CSLFD M3 6 C6
Great Jones St WGTN/LGST M12 88 D6
Great Lee WHIT OL12 28 A1
Great Lee Wk WHIT OL12 28 A2
Great Marlborough St
CMANE M1 6 F7
Great Marld Cl BOL BL1 35 J2
Great Meadow ROY/SHW OL2 43 J3
Great Moor St BOL BL1 2 E6
OFTN SK2 112 E7
Great Moss Rd TYLD M29 82 F2
Great Newton St
NEWH/MOS M40 73 M7
Great Norbury St HYDE SK14 102 A2
Great Portwood St STKP SK1 13 K2
Great Southern St
RUSH/FAL M14 98 E1
Great Stone Cl RAD M26 * 54 A1
Great Stone Rd STRET M32 86 C8
Great Stones Cl EDGW/EG BL7 22 B2
Great St CMANE M1 7 M6
Great Underbank STKP SK1 13 J4
Great Western St
OLDTF/WHR M16 87 H8
Greave MPL/ROM SK6 102 A8
Greave Av ROCH OL11 27 L4
Greave Fold MPL/ROM SK6 101 M8
Greave Rd STKP SK1 112 F4
Greaves Av FAIL M35 74 B6
Greaves Cl WGNNW/ST WN6 30 C4
Greaves Rd WILM/AE SK9 126 C4
Greaves St MOSL OL5 76 F2
OLD OL1 9 K6
OLDE OL4 60 C6
ROY/SHW OL2 * 43 M5
Greave St ROY/SHW OL2 43 M5
Grebe Cl POY/DIS SK12 121 K8
WGNS/IIMK WN3 46 E8
Grecian Crs BOLS/LL BL3 36 C8
Grecian St BRO M7 71 M7
Grecian St North BRO M7 71 M7
Grecian Ter BRO M7 * 71 M7
Gredle Cl URM M41 96 C2
Greeba Rd NTHM/RTH M23 109 H6
Greek St CMANE M1 7 J9
EDGY/DAV SK3 13 H7
Greenacre WGN WN1 15 J1
Green Acre WHTN BL5 50 C5
Greenacre Cl RAMS BL0 19 H5
Greenacre La WALK M28 69 J8
Green Acre Pk BOL BL1 * 36 C3
Greenacres EDGW/EG BL7 17 H6
Greenacres Cl LEIGH WN7 80 E4
Greenacres Dr BNG/LEV M19 99 H8
Greenacres Rd OLDE OL4 59 M5
Greenall St AIMK WN4 63 L7
Green Av BOLS/LL BL3 52 E1
LHULT M38 52 B7
SWIN M27 70 C5
TYLD M29 67 K8
Green Bank BOLE BL2 37 H1
GLSP SK13 104 C5
Greenbank FWTH BL4 52 F3
WGNE/HIN WN2 64 E5
WGNE/HIN WN2 65 K1
Greenbank Av CHD/CHDH SK8 110 D7
HTNM SK4 111 H2
SWIN M27 * 70 A6
UPML OL3 61 M3
WGNW/BIL/OR WN5 62 A1
Greenbank Crs MPL/ROM SK6 114 C8
Greenbank Dr LIT OL15 29 J1
Greenbank Rd BOLS/LL BL3 * 35 L8
CHD/CHDH SK8 110 D6
MPL/ROM SK6 114 E3
RAD M26 38 C7
SALE M33 96 B7
SLFD M6 86 B1
WHIT OL12 28 D2
Green Bank Ter HTNM SK4 13 H2
Greenbank Ter MDTN M24 57 M3
Greenbarn Wy HOR/BR BL6 33 G3
Greenbeech Cl MPL/ROM SK6 114 B5
Green Booth Cl DUK SK16 91 J5
Greenbooth Rd WHIT OL12 27 G1
Green Bridge Cl ROCH OL11 * 28 C8
Greenbridge La UPML OL3 61 K7
Green Brook Cl BURY BL9 25 K8
Greenbrook St BURY BL9 25 K8
Greenbrow Rd
NTHM/RTH M23 118 B1
Greenburn Dr BOLE BL2 37 H2
Green Cl ATH M46 67 H3
CHD/CHDH SK8 110 D6
Green Common La ATH M46 50 E6
Green Ct GOL/RIS/CUL WA3 80 E3
Greencourt Dr LHULT M38 52 C8

Green Cts ALT WA14 116 D1
Green Cft MPL/ROM SK6 114 A1
Greencroft Meadow
ROY/SHW OL2 43 J7
Greencroft Rd ECC M30 69 L8
Greencroft Wy MILN OL16 29 G1
Greendale ATH M46 51 H8
Greendale Crs LEIGH WN7 66 F8
Greendale Dr BKLY M9 73 H1
RAD M26 54 E3
Greendale Gv DTN/ASHW M34 101 L4
Green Dr BNG/LEV M19 99 J3
HALE/TIMP WA15 108 D5
HOR/BR BL6 34 F5
WILM/AE SK9 127 H2
Green End BNG/LEV M19 99 H7
DTN/ASHW M34 101 L4
Green End Rd BNG/LEV M19 99 H8
Greenfield Av ECC M30 84 D5
URM M41 96 A2
WGNE/HIN WN2 15 M6
Greenfield Cl EDGY/DAV SK3 112 B6
HALE/TIMP WA15 108 F6
NM/HAY SK22 124 C4
TOT/BURYW BL8 38 D3
WHTN BL5 50 D3
Greenfield Ct HEY OL10 41 G3
Greenfield La MILN OL16 29 G1
ROCH OL11 28 D8
ROY/SHW OL2 43 L6
Greenfield Rd ATH M46 51 H7
Greenfields WGNNW/ST WN6 31 K8
Greenfields Cl NEWLW WA12 78 F8
WGNE/HIN WN2 49 J6
Greenfields Crs AIMK WN4 63 L8
Greenfield St DTN/ASHW M34 90 A5
GLSP SK13 93 K6
HYDE SK14 102 A2
ROCH OL11 28 D8
Greenfield Vw
WGNW/BIL/OR WN5 62 A8
Green Fold GTN M18 89 J6
Greenfold Av FWTH BL4 52 E5
Green Fold La WHTN BL5 50 B5
Greenfold Wy LEIGH WN7 81 L2
Greenford Cl CHD/CHDH SK8 111 L8
WGNW/BIL/OR WN5 46 A6
Greenford Rd CHH M8 72 D5
Green Gables Cl
CHD/CHDH SK8 119 K3
Greengate CSLFD M3 6 E2
HALE/TIMP WA15 117 M5
HYDE SK14 102 A4
MDTN M24 57 M7
NEWH/MOS M40 73 M1
Greengate Cl WHIT OL12 21 H8
Greengate East
NEWH/MOS M40 73 M1
Greengate La BOLE BL2 37 J4
PWCH M25 55 K8
Greengate Rd DTN/ASHW M34 90 D8
Greengate St OLDE OL4 9 L8
Greengate West CSLFD M3 6 C1
Greengrove Bank MILN OL16 28 F1
Greenhalgh Moss La
TOT/BURYW BL8 24 E7
Greenhalgh St FAIL M35 73 M6
HTNM SK4 13 H2
Greenhalgh Wk ANC M4 7 L3
Green Hall Cl ATH M46 51 J7
Green Hall Ms WILM/AE SK9 126 F6
Greenham Rd NTHM/RTH M23 109 J3
Greenhaven Cl WALK M28 69 J1
Green Hayes Av WGN WN1 47 M1
Greenhey WGNW/BIL/OR WN5 46 D5
Greenheys BOLE BL2 37 H1
DROY M43 89 K2
Greenheys Crs TOT/BURYW BL8 24 B3
Greenheys La HULME M15 87 J7
Greenheys La West
HULME M15 87 J7
Greenheys Rd LHULT M38 52 B6
Greenhill OLD OL1 9 L6
PWCH M25 55 K8
Greenhill Av BOLS/LL BL3 35 L7
FWTH BL4 52 F6
ROY/SHW OL2 43 H3
SALE M33 96 D6
WHIT OL12 10 C2
Greenhill Crs
WGNW/BIL/OR WN5 62 C7
Greenhill La BOLS/LL BL3 35 J8
Greenhill Pas OLD OL1 9 L6
Green Hill Rd HYDE SK14 102 D1
Greenhill Rd CHH M8 72 D5
HALE/TIMP WA15 108 F6
MDTN M24 57 M5
TOT/BURYW BL8 38 D3
WGNW/BIL/OR WN5 62 C7
Green Hill St EDGY/DAV SK3 12 E8
Green Hill Ter EDGY/DAV SK3 12 E8
Greenhill Ter OLDE OL4 9 L7
Greenhill Wk POY/DIS SK12 123 M6
Green Hollow Fold STLY SK15 77 G8
Greenholm Cl NEWH/MOS M40 74 A3
Greenhow St DROY M43 89 J4
Greenhurst Crs OLDS OL8 75 K2
Greenhurst La AUL OL6 76 B6
Greenhurst Rd AUL OL6 76 A5
Greenhythe Rd
CHD/CHDH SK8 119 L6
Greening Rd BNG/LEV M19 99 L2
Greenland Av WGNNW/ST WN6 31 H4
Greenland Cl TYLD M29 67 L6
Greenland Rd BOLS/LL BL3 52 C2
TYLD M29 67 L6
Greenlands Cl CHD/CHDH SK8 120 A4
Greenland St CHH M8 72 C5
SLFD M6 * 86 B2
Green La AUL OL6 75 L7
BOLS/LL BL3 52 C1
BRAM/HZG SK7 121 M1
ECC M30 84 F2
FAIL M35 74 B8
FWTH BL4 53 K5
GLSP SK13 93 J8
GLSP SK13 104 C4
GOL/RIS/CUL WA3 80 D2
GTN M18 89 G6
HALE/TIMP WA15 108 E8
HEY OL10 41 H2
HEY OL10 * 41 H4
HTNM SK4 12 A1
HTNM SK4 12 C1
HTNM SK4 12 E3
HYDE SK14 92 F6
HYDE SK14 102 D3
IRL M44 94 A7
LEIGH WN7 66 F7
MDTN M24 57 L3
MDTN M24 58 A5
MPL/ROM SK6 113 L3
OLDE OL4 60 D2
OLDS OL8 75 H2
POY/DIS SK12 122 E8
POY/DIS SK12 123 M7
SALE M33 96 B6
WGNE/HIN WN2 49 L7
WGNNW/ST WN6 31 H4
WGNW/BIL/OR WN5 62 A1
WHIT OL12 * 10 D2
WHTF M45 55 J3
WILM/AE SK9 126 F5
WILM/AE SK9 130 C4
Green La North
HALE/TIMP WA15 108 E8
Greenlea Av GTN M18 100 A1
Greenleach La WALK M28 69 J4
Greenlea Cl
WGNW/BIL/OR WN5 46 A7
Greenleaf Cl WALK M28 68 C6
Greenleas HOR/BR BL6 34 F6
Greenlees St WHIT OL12 10 E2
Greenleigh Cl BOL BL1 22 A7
Greenmans La UPML OL3 77 K1
Green Meadow WHIT OL12 21 H8
Green Mdw
GOL/RIS/CUL WA3 80 B7
MPL/ROM SK6 114 C5
WHTN BL5 50 A5
Green Meadows Dr
MPL/ROM SK6 114 C5
Green Meadows Wk
WYTH/NTH M22 119 G3
Greenmount Cl
TOT/BURYW BL8 24 C2
Greenmount Ct BOL BL1 35 K4
Greenmount Dr HEY OL10 41 J5
TOT/BURYW BL8 24 C1
Greenmount La BOL BL1 35 J4
Greenmount Pk FWTH BL4 53 K6
Greenoak RAD M26 53 M5
Greenoak Dr SALE M33 108 F3
WALK M28 52 F7
Greenock Cl BOLS/LL BL3 35 H7
Greenough St ATH M46 66 D3
WGN WN1 15 J3
Greenpark Cl
TOT/BURYW BL8 24 B3
Greenpark Rd
WYTH/NTH M22 110 A3
Green Park Vw OLD OL1 60 A2
Green Pastures HTNM SK4 111 H3
Green Pine Rd HOR/BR BL6 34 A5
Greenrigg Cl
WGNNW/ST WN6 31 J5
Green Rd PART M31 106 B1
Greenroyd Av BOLE BL2 37 H2
Greenroyde ROCH OL11 * 10 C9
Greens Arms Rd
EDGW/EG BL7 16 B5
Greensbridge Gdns WHTN BL5 50 C3
Greenshall La POY/DIS SK12 124 B6
Greenshank Cl LEIGH WN7 66 E7
NEWLW WA12 78 D8
ROCH OL11 * 27 J5
Greenside BOLE BL2 37 M3
HTNM SK4 111 K3
WALK M28 69 K7
Greenside Av FWTH BL4 53 J6
OLDE OL4 60 A2
Greenside Cl DUK SK16 91 K4
TOT/BURYW BL8 23 L1
Greenside Crs DROY M43 89 J1
Greenside Dr ALT WA14 117 G3
IRL M44 94 C3
TOT/BURYW BL8 24 C4
Greenside La DROY M43 89 H1
Greenside Pl DTN/ASHW M34 101 K4
Greenside St OP/CLY M11 88 E3
Greenside Vw HYDE SK14 91 J7
Greenside Wy MDTN M24 57 M7
Greenslate Ct
WGNW/BIL/OR WN5 62 B1
Green & Slater Homes
HTNM SK4 * 111 K1
Greenslate Rd
WGNW/BIL/OR WN5 62 B1
Greensmith Wy WHTN BL5 50 B2
Greenson Dr MDTN M24 57 H5
Greenstead Av CHH M8 72 D4
The Greens WHIT OL12 20 A3
Greenstone Av HOR/BR BL6 33 K1
Greenstone Dr SLFD M6 71 J7
Green St ATH M46 67 H3
BOL BL1 2 F4
ECC M30 84 E4
EDGY/DAV SK3 112 C6
FWTH BL4 52 F3
HYDE SK14 102 B3
MDTN M24 57 M3
OLDS OL8 8 F7
RAD M26 54 D1
RAMS BL0 * 19 H1
RUSH/FAL M14 99 J4
STRET M32 96 F4
TOT/BURYW BL8 24 C8
TYLD M29 67 K3
WGNE/HIN WN2 64 E2
WGNS/IIMK WN3 14 F7
WILM/AE SK9 130 D3
Greensward Cl
WGNNW/ST WN6 30 E3
The Green CHD/CHDH SK8 120 B4
GLSP SK13 104 D5
HTNM SK4 12 C2
MPL/ROM SK6 123 J1
OLDS OL8 75 K1
ROCH OL11 41 M1
SWIN M27 70 E2
TOT/BURYW BL8 24 C3
WALK M28 69 J7
WGNW/BIL/OR WN5 46 E6
WILM/AE SK9 127 J1
Greenthorne Av HTNM SK4 100 A5
Greenthorne Cl EDGW/EG BL7 17 H5
Green Tree Gdns
MPL/ROM SK6 113 L2
Greenvale ROCH OL11 27 G4
WGNNW/ST WN6 30 C8
Greenvale Dr CHD/CHDH SK8 110 F6
Greenview Cha OLDE OL4 60 E7
Greenview Dr DID/WITH M20 110 F4
ROCH OL11 27 J4
Green Villa Pk WILM/AE SK9 126 C8
Green Wk ALT WA14 116 C1
CHD/CHDH SK8 110 D6
HALE/TIMP WA15 108 C5
OLDTF/WHR M16 97 M2
STRET M32 96 E2
Green Wks PWCH M25 71 M1
Greenwatch Cl ECC M30 84 F3
Green Wy BOL BL1 36 E1
ROCH OL11 41 L3
Greenway AIMK WN4 63 K8
ALT WA14 107 K7
BRAM/HZG SK7 120 F6
HOR/BR BL6 34 C1
HYDE SK14 102 A3
MDTN M24 57 H7
MPL/ROM SK6 114 B3
ROY/SHW OL2 43 J5
WILM/AE SK9 126 E6
WYTH/NTH M22 110 B4
Greenway Av BNG/LEV M19 99 L4
Green Way Cl BOL BL1 22 E8
Greenway Cl SALE M33 108 A1
TOT/BURYW BL8 38 E1
Greenway Dr MOSL OL5 76 F2
Greenway Rd CHD/CHDH SK8 119 L6
HALE/TIMP WA15 108 D3
Greenways AULW OL7 75 J6
LEIGH WN7 66 D6
NEWH/MOS M40 74 A3
WGNNW/ST WN6 31 K6
WGNW/BIL/OR WN5 62 A1
Greenwich Cl NEWH/MOS M40 74 A8
ROCH OL11 27 J6
Greenwood Av AUL OL6 75 M7
HOR/BR BL6 34 A3
OFTN SK2 112 F6
SWIN M27 70 E3
WALK M28 68 F1
WGNW/BIL/OR WN5 47 H5
Greenwood Cl
HALE/TIMP WA15 109 G7
WALK M28 68 B5
Greenwood Dr WILM/AE SK9 127 H4
Greenwood La HOR/BR BL6 34 B3
Greenwood Rd
WGNNW/ST WN6 31 H2
WYTH/NTH M22 109 M7
Greenwoods La BOLE BL2 23 J8
Greenwood St ALT WA14 108 A8
FWTH BL4 53 G4
LIT OL15 21 M7
MILN OL16 10 F5
OLDE OL4 59 M4
OLDS OL8 * 75 J3
SLFD M6 71 J8
Greenwood V BOL BL1 36 C1
Greenwood V South BOL BL1 * 36 C1
Greer St OP/CLY M11 88 F4
Greetland Dr BKLY M9 57 J8
Gregge St HEY OL10 41 H4
Greg Ms WILM/AE SK9 126 F2
Gregory Av ATH M46 50 F7
BOLE BL2 37 H4
MPL/ROM SK6 113 L3
Gregory St HYDE SK14 91 H7
OLDS OL8 74 F1
WGNE/HIN WN2 * 48 F6
WGTN/LGST M12 88 C6
WHTN BL5 49 K5
Gregory Wy RDSH SK5 100 C6
Gregson Fld BOLS/LL BL3 36 B8
Gregson Rd RDSH SK5 100 B6
Gregson St OLD OL1 9 K6
Greg St RDSH SK5 100 B6
Grelley Wk RUSH/FAL M14 98 E1
Grenaby Av WGNE/HIN WN2 49 K7
Grendale Av BRAM/HZG SK7 122 A3
STKP SK1 112 E3
Grendon Av OLDS OL8 75 H1
Grendon St BOLS/LL BL3 51 M1
Grendon Wk WGTN/LGST M12 88 D6
Grenfel Cl WGNS/IIMK WN3 14 B9
Grenfell Rd DID/WITH M20 110 D1
Grenham Av HULME M15 87 G6
Grenville Rd BRAM/HZG SK7 121 L1
Grenville St DUK SK16 90 F4
EDGY/DAV SK3 12 E6
STLY SK15 77 G8
Gresford Cl CCHDY M21 97 K4
Gresham Cl WHTF M45 55 G5
Gresham Dr CHAD OL9 8 D5
Gresham St BOL BL1 36 C1
DTN/ASHW M34 90 C8
Gresham Wk HTNM SK4 112 B1
Gresham Wy SALE M33 108 D3
Gresley Av HOR/BR BL6 33 L1
Gresley Cl WGN WN1 15 K4
Gresty Av WYTH/NTH M22 119 H3
Greswell St DTN/ASHW M34 90 B8
Greta Av CHD/CHDH SK8 119 L6
Gretna Rd ATH M46 66 D3
Greton Cl BRUN/LGST M13 88 B8
Gretton Cl ROY/SHW OL2 43 J8
Greville St BRUN/LGST M13 99 H1
Grey Cl MPL/ROM SK6 101 K8
Greyfriars AIMK WN4 78 C1
Greyfriars Rd WYTH/NTH M22 118 D2
Greyhound Dr SLFD M6 71 L7
Greyhound Rd MCFLDN SK10 131 L7
Grey Knotts WALK M28 68 D7
Greylag Crs WALK M28 69 G4
Greylands Cl SALE M33 96 B8
Greylands Rd DID/WITH M20 110 F4
Grey Mare La OP/CLY M11 88 D4
Greymont Rd BURY BL9 25 J6
Grey Rd AIMK WN4 63 K8
ALT WA14 107 M7
Greystoke Av BNG/LEV M19 99 M3
HALE/TIMP WA15 109 G6
SALE M33 108 E1
Greystoke Crs WHTF M45 55 H2
Greystoke Dr BOL BL1 22 A6
MDTN M24 57 G2
WILM/AE SK9 130 D2
Greystoke La FAIL M35 74 A6
Greystoke St STKP SK1 13 M5
Greystone Av CCHDY M21 98 C4
WGNE/HIN WN2 32 F7
Grey St AUL OL6 90 F1
DTN/ASHW M34 101 G1
MDTN M24 57 J3
PWCH M25 55 M8
STLY SK15 91 M3
WGTN/LGST M12 88 B6
Greyswood Av CHH M8 72 C6
Greytown Cl SLFD M6 71 J7
Greywood Av BURY BL9 5 L4
Grierson St BOL BL1 36 B1
OLDTF/WHR M16 87 H8
Griffe La BURY BL9 55 M1
Griffin Cl BURY BL9 5 K1
NM/HAY SK22 124 E6
Griffin Ct CSLFD M3 * 6 C3
Griffin Gv BNG/LEV M19 99 K4
Griffin La CHD/CHDH SK8 119 M5
Griffin Rd FAIL M35 74 A5
Griffin St BRO M7 71 M6
Griffiths Cl BRO M7 * 72 A8
Griffiths St NEWH/MOS M40 73 M7
Grimes St WHIT OL12 27 J3
Grime St RAMS BL0 18 D8
Grimscott Cl BKLY M9 * 73 J3
Grimshaw Av FAIL M35 74 D4
Grimshaw Cl MPL/ROM SK6 101 K8
Grimshaw Ct GOL/RIS/CUL WA3 79 K3
Grimshaw La MDTN M24 57 L5
NEWH/MOS M40 73 J7
Grimshaw St FAIL M35 * 74 B4
GOL/RIS/CUL WA3 79 K3
STKP SK1 13 M4
Grimstead Cl NTHM/RTH M23 109 H6
Grindall Av NEWH/MOS M40 73 L2
Grindley Av CCHDY M21 98 A7
Grindlow St BRUN/LGST M13 88 B7
Grindon Av BRO M7 71 K5
Grindrod St RAD M26 38 D8
Grindsbrook Rd RAD M26 38 C5
Grinton Av BRUN/LGST M13 99 H2
Grisdale Dr MDTN M24 57 H2
Grisdale Rd BOLS/LL BL3 35 M7
Grisebeck Wy OLD OL1 9 H4
Grisedale Av ROY/SHW OL2 42 F4
Grisedale Cl GTN M18 88 F8
MDTN M24 57 G1
Grisedale Rd ROCH OL11 27 L8
Gristlehurst La BURY BL9 26 C7
Grizebeck Cl GTN M18 88 F6
Grizedale Cl BOL BL1 35 J2
STLY SK15 77 H5
Grizedale Dr WGNE/HIN WN2 48 D5
Grizedale Rd MPL/ROM SK6 101 L8
Groby Pl ALT WA14 107 M7
Groby Rd ALT WA14 107 M8
CCHDY M21 97 L4
DTN/ASHW M34 90 B5
Groby Rd North
DTN/ASHW M34 90 A4
Groby St OLDS OL8 75 K1
STLY SK15 91 M3
Groom St CMANE M1 * 7 J9
Grosvenor Av
GOL/RIS/CUL WA3 80 A4
WHTF M45 55 H4
Grosvenor Cl WALK M28 52 F7
WILM/AE SK9 126 E8
Grosvenor Ct AULW OL7 90 D3
CHD/CHDH SK8 111 G6
Grosvenor Crs HYDE SK14 101 M3
Grosvenor Dr POY/DIS SK12 129 G1
WALK M28 52 F7
Grosvenor Gdns BRO M7 72 A8
STLY SK15 * 91 K3
WYTH/NTH M22 110 B6
Grosvenor House Sq STLY SK15 91 K3
Grosvenor Pl AULW OL7 * 90 D3
Grosvenor Rd ALT WA14 108 B6
CHD/CHDH SK8 111 M8
ECC M30 84 D1
HTNM SK4 12 A1
HYDE SK14 102 A3
LEIGH WN7 66 A6
MPL/ROM SK6 114 C5
OLDTF/WHR M16 98 A2
SALE M33 96 C7
SWIN M27 70 E5
URM M41 95 M2
WALK M28 52 F7
WHTF M45 55 H3
Grosvenor Sq SALE M33 96 D8
Grosvenor St AULW OL7 90 D3
BOLE BL2 3 G7
BOLS/LL BL3 37 K8
BRAM/HZG SK7 121 M1
BRUN/LGST M13 7 J9
BURY BL9 4 F8
DTN/ASHW M34 90 A8
EDGY/DAV SK3 13 J7
FWTH BL4 53 J4
HEY OL10 40 F3
PWCH M25 55 M8
RAD M26 54 C1
ROCH OL11 41 M3
STLY SK15 91 K3
STRET M32 97 G2
SWIN M27 70 C2
WGNE/HIN WN2 49 G7
WGNW/BIL/OR WN5 47 J6
Grosvenor Wy ROY/SHW OL2 59 G2
Grotton Hollow OLDE OL4 60 E6
Grotton Mdw OLDE OL4 60 E7
Grouse St WHIT OL12 28 C3
Grove Av FAIL M35 74 B7
WILM/AE SK9 126 E5
Grove Bank OLDE OL4 61 H7
Grove Cl RUSH/FAL M14 98 F1
Grove Ct BRAM/HZG SK7 * 122 A1
SALE M33 97 G8
Grove Hl WALK M28 68 C6
Grovehurst SWIN M27 69 L6
Grove La CHD/CHDH SK8 120 D7
DID/WITH M20 110 E2
HALE/TIMP WA15 108 D6
HALE/TIMP WA15 117 J1
WGNNW/ST WN6 31 J4
Grove Ms WALK M28 * 69 G1
Grove Pl WGNNW/ST WN6 31 J4
Grove Rd HALE/TIMP WA15 117 G1
MDTN M24 57 L2
STLY SK15 77 G8
UPML OL3 61 L5
Grove St AIMK WN4 63 K8
AULW OL7 75 H7
BOL BL1 36 A2
BRAM/HZG SK7 * 122 A1
BRO M7 72 B7
DROY M43 89 J4
DUK SK16 91 G3
FWTH BL4 53 H4
HEY OL10 41 H2
LEIGH WN7 66 E8
NM/HAY SK22 124 D5
OLD OL1 9 M4
ROCH OL11 10 D8
UPML OL3 61 L7
WILM/AE SK9 * 126 F5
The Grove ALT WA14 * 108 A7
BOLE BL2 3 K8
BOLS/LL BL3 53 L1
CHD/CHDH SK8 120 C6
DID/WITH M20 110 E3
ECC M30 85 J3
GLSP SK13 93 J8
GOL/RIS/CUL WA3 80 A3
OFTN SK2 13 H9
ROY/SHW OL2 43 K6
SALE M33 108 E1
UPML OL3 61 J3
URM M41 95 J3
WGNE/HIN WN2 15 L6
Grove Wy WILM/AE SK9 126 F5
Grovewood Cl AULW OL7 75 H7
Grovewood Dr
WGNNW/ST WN6 30 B5
Grundey St BRAM/HZG SK7 122 A2
Grundy Av PWCH M25 71 H2
Grundy Cl BURY BL9 5 H7
Grundy La BURY BL9 4 E9
Grundy Rd FWTH BL4 53 H5
Grundy's Cl TYLD M29 67 M7
Grundy St BOLS/LL BL3 36 A8
GOL/RIS/CUL WA3 79 K5
HEY OL10 41 H4
HTNM SK4 111 H2
WALK M28 69 J1
WHTN BL5 50 B3
Guardian Cl WHIT OL12 21 H7
Guardian Ms NTHM/RTH M23 * 108 F3
Guernsey Cl BNG/LEV M19 * 99 K6
Guest Rd PWCH M25 55 K6
Guest St LEIGH WN7 66 D7
Guide La AULW OL7 90 B4
Guide Post Sq
BRUN/LGST M13 * 88 A6
Guide Post St BRUN/LGST M13 88 A6
Guide St SALQ M50 85 M3
Guido St BOL BL1 36 A2
FAIL M35 74 B5
Guild Av WALK M28 69 G2
Guildford Av CHD/CHDH SK8 120 C6
Guildford Cl STKP SK1 112 E5
Guildford Crs WGNNW/ST WN6 47 J1
Guildford Dr AUL OL6 75 M5
Guildford Gv MDTN M24 57 M1
Guildford Rd BNG/LEV M19 99 L2
BOL BL1 35 L2
DUK SK16 91 K5
SLFD M6 70 E8
URM M41 85 H8
Guildford St MILN OL16 * 11 G5
Guildhall Cl HULME M15 87 K7
Guild St EDGW/EG BL7 22 E6
Guilford Rd ECC M30 84 E3
Guinness Rd TRPK M17 85 K4
Guiseley Cl BURY BL9 25 H4
Gullane Cl NEWH/MOS M40 73 M5
Gull Cl POY/DIS SK12 128 F1
Gulvain Pl CHAD OL9 58 C4
Gun Rd GLSP SK13 115 L1
MPL/ROM SK6 115 M5
Gunson St NEWH/MOS M40 7 M1
Gun St ANC M4 7 K3
Gunters Av WHTN BL5 50 B6
Gurner Av ORD M5 86 E5
Gurney St ANC M4 88 A3
Gutter La RAMS BL0 18 E5
Guy Fawkes St ORD M5 86 E5
Guywood La MPL/ROM SK6 113 M1
Gwelo St OP/CLY M11 88 D2
Gwenbury Av STKP SK1 112 E3
Gwendor Av CHH M8 72 C1
Gwladys St STLY SK15 77 H6
Gylden Cl HYDE SK14 91 L7
Gypsy La ROCH OL11 41 M1

H

Habergham Cl WALK M28 68 F5
Hackberry Cl ALT WA14 107 L4
Hacken Bridge Rd BOLS/LL BL3 37 G8
Hacken La BOLS/LL BL3 36 F8
Hackford Cl BOL BL1 35 M4
TOT/BURYW BL8 25 G7
Hacking St BRO M7 72 B6
BURY BL9 5 H5
PWCH M25 55 K8
Hackle St OP/CLY M11 88 F2
Hackleton Cl ANC M4 88 A3
Hackness Rd CCHDY M21 97 K4
Hackney Av NEWH/MOS M40 73 M8
Hackney Cl RAD M26 38 D7
Hackworth Cl WGN WN1 15 K4
Hadbutt La TYLD M29 67 J8
Haddington Dr BKLY M9 73 H1
Haddon Av NEWH/MOS M40 74 B3
Haddon Cl BURY BL9 39 K7
MPL/ROM SK6 123 G6
WILM/AE SK9 130 C2
Haddon Gv HALE/TIMP WA15 108 C5
RDSH SK5 100 B5
SALE M33 108 D1
Haddon Hall Rd DROY M43 89 H2
Haddon Ms GLSP SK13 104 A2
Haddon Rd BRAM/HZG SK7 122 A3
CCHDY M21 98 A7
CHD/CHDH SK8 119 L5
ECC M30 84 F4
GOL/RIS/CUL WA3 80 A3
WALK M28 69 M7
WGNS/IIMK WN3 63 H1
Haddon St SLFD M6 71 L7
STRET M32 86 A8
Haddon Wy ROY/SHW OL2 43 M4
Hadfield Cl RUSH/FAL M14 99 G1
Hadfield Crs AUL OL6 76 B7
Hadfield Pl GLSP SK13 104 F4
Hadfield Rd GLSP SK13 93 J8
Hadfields Av HYDE SK14 93 G7
Hadfield Sq GLSP SK13 104 F4
Hadfield St BRO M7 72 B6
DUK SK16 90 D5
GLSP SK13 104 F4
OLDS OL8 75 H1
OLDTF/WHR M16 86 F6
Hadleigh Cl BOL BL1 22 D6
Hadley Av BRUN/LGST M13 99 H2
Hadley Cl CHD/CHDH SK8 120 B3
Hadley St SLFD M6 71 L7
Hadlow Gn RDSH SK5 100 E6
Hadlow Wk
NEWH/MOS M40 * 88 A1
Hadwin St BOL BL1 2 E1
Hafton Rd BRO M7 71 L6
Hag Bank La POY/DIS SK12 123 M5
Haggate ROY/SHW OL2 58 F1
Haggate Crs ROY/SHW OL2 58 F1
Hagley Rd ORD M5 86 D6
The Haggs BURY BL9 39 K7
Haguebar Rd NM/HAY SK22 124 B4
Hague Bush Cl
GOL/RIS/CUL WA3 * 80 B3
Hague Fold Rd NM/HAY SK22 124 B4
Hague Rd DID/WITH M20 98 D7
HYDE SK14 103 M2
Hague St AUL OL6 75 M8
GLSP SK13 105 G5
NEWH/MOS M40 73 J7
OLDE OL4 60 B4
Haig Ct TOT/BURYW BL8 38 E3
Haigh Av HTNM SK4 100 B7
Haigh Hall Cl RAMS BL0 18 E8
Haigh La CHAD OL9 58 B3
Haigh Pk HTNM SK4 100 B7
Haigh Rd WGNE/HIN WN2 32 F7

Haigh St BOL BL1 ....2 E2
ROCH OL11 ....11 G7
Haigh Vw WGN WN1 ....48 A2
WGNS/IIMK WN3
Haig Rd STRET M32 ....97 C1
TOT/BURYW BL8 ....38 E2
Haig St WGNS/IIMK WN3 ....14 D5
Haile Dr WALK M28 ....68 C6
Hailsham Cl TOT/BURYW BL8 ....24 F5
Hail St RAMS BL0 ....18 D8
Halbury Wk BOL BL1 * 36 C2
Halcyon Cl WHIT OL12 ....27 L2
Haldon Rd DID/WITH M20 ....99 G7
Hale Av POY/DIS SK12 ....129 H2
Hale Bank WHTN BL5 ....50 C3
Hale Cl LEIGH WN7 ....81 L2
Hale Gv AIMK WN4 ....63 J7
Hale La FAIL M35 ....74 B4
Hale Low Rd HALE/TIMP WA15 ....117 H1
Hale Rd HALE/TIMP WA15 ....117 G1
HALE/TIMP WA15 ....117 J2
HTNM SK4 ....12 C1
Hales Cl DROY M43 ....89 J1
Halesden Rd HTNM SK4 ....100 A7
Halesfield WGNE/HIN WN2 ....65 J3
Halesworth Wk
NEWH/MOS M40 * 72 F8
Hale Vw ALT WA14 * 116 F2
Halewood Av GOL/RIS/CUL WA3 ....79 J3
Hale Wd Cl RDSH SK5 ....100 C4
Haley St CHH M8 ....6 B3
Half Acre RAD M26 ....38 C6
Half Acre Dr ROY/SHW OL2 ....27 M6
Half Acre La HOR/BR BL6 ....32 F3
ROCH OL11 ....27 L6
Half Acre Ms ROCH OL11 ....27 L6
Half Acre Rd ROCH OL11 ....27 L6
Halfacre Rd WYTH/NTH M22 ....109 M8
Half Edge La ECC M30 ....85 J1
Half Moon La OFTN SK2 ....113 H6
Halford Dr NEWH/MOS M40 ....73 M1
Half St CSLFD M3 ....6 D1
Halifax Rd MILN OL16 ....28 E2
Halifax St AUL OL6 ....75 L8
Hallacres La CHD/CHDH SK8 ....120 A4
Hallam Rd NEWH/MOS M40 ....73 L7
Hallam St OFTN SK2 ....112 D6
RAD M26 ....39 C8
Hallas Gv NTHM/RTH M23 ....109 L3
RUSH/FAL M14 ....99 G1
SALE M33 ....96 B6
STLY SK15 ....76 F7
Hall Bank ECC M30 ....84 F2
Hallbottom St HYDE SK14 ....91 J7
Hallbridge Gdns BOL BL1 ....36 D1
Hall Cl HYDE SK14 ....92 D7
WGNNW/ST WN6 ....30 E6
The Hall Coppice EDGW/EG BL7 ....22 A3
Hallcroft PART M31 ....94 C8
Hallcroft Gdns MILN OL16 ....29 H6
Hall Dr HYDE SK14 ....92 D7
MDTN M24 ....57 J6
Hall Farm Av URM M41 ....95 L1
Hall Farm Cl BRAM/HZG SK7 ....122 C1
Hall Fold WHIT OL12 ....20 D8
Hall Gdns WHIT OL12 ....27 M2
Hallgate WGN WN1 ....14 F4
WHTN BL5 ....50 B7
Hallgate Dr CHD/CHDH SK8 ....119 J2
Hall Gn Cl DUK SK16 ....90 F3
Hall Green Rd DUK SK16 ....90 F3
Hall Gv RUSH/FAL M14 ....99 G1
Hall House La LEIGH WN7 ....66 F7
Halliday Rd NEWH/MOS M40 ....73 L8
Halliford Rd NEWH/MOS M40 ....73 K6
Hallington Cl BOLS/LL BL3 ....36 C6
Hall i' th' Wood La BOL BL1 ....22 D8
Halliwell Av OLDS OL8 ....75 H1
Halliwell La CHH M8 ....72 C5
Halliwell Rd BOL BL1 ....36 A2
PWCH M25 ....71 J3
Halliwell St BOL BL1 * 36 A2
CHAD OL9 * 74 D3
MILN OL16 ....29 H5
WHIT OL12 ....10 C3
Halliwell St West CHH M8 * 72 C5
Hall La FWTH BL4 ....53 H1
HOR/BR BL6 ....34 B5
MPL/ROM SK6 ....101 L6
NTHM/RTH M23 ....109 L6
PART M31 ....94 C8
WGN WN1 ....32 A8
WGNE/HIN WN2 ....49 J8
WGNNW/ST WN6 ....30 A2
WGNW/BIL/OR WN5 ....46 C8
Hall Lane Gv WGNE/HIN WN2 ....49 G4
Hall Lee Dr WHTN BL5 ....50 D5
Hall Meadow CHD/CHDH SK8 ....120 A3
Hall Meadow Rd GLSP SK13 ....105 G2
Hall Moss La BRAM/HZG SK7 ....120 E8
Hall Moss Rd BKLY M9 ....73 K1
Hallows Av CCHDY M21 ....97 M7
Hallows Farm Av WHIT OL12 ....28 A2
Hall Pool Dr OFTN SK2 ....113 H5
Hall Rd ALT WA14 ....116 E3
AUL OL6 ....75 M7
BRAM/HZG SK7 ....120 F3
RNFD/HAY WA11 ....78 B5
RUSH/FAL M14 ....99 G1
WILM/AE SK9 ....126 E5
WILM/AE SK9 ....127 J1
Hallroyd Brow OLD OL1 ....9 H2
Hallstead Av LHULT M38 ....52 B8
Hallstead Gv LHULT M38 ....52 B8
Hall St AUL OL6 ....91 H2
BOLS/LL BL3 ....53 C6
BURY BL9 ....24 F3
CHD/CHDH SK8 ....111 G6
CMANW M2 ....6 F6
FAIL M35 ....74 A6
HEY OL10 ....41 G3
HYDE SK14 ....101 L1
MDTN M24 ....57 M4
NM/HAY SK22 ....124 D4
OLDE OL4 ....59 L5
RAD M26 ....38 C6
ROY/SHW OL2 ....43 G8
STKP SK1 ....112 E4
SWIN M27 ....70 C2
TOT/BURYW BL8 ....4 D1
TOT/BURYW BL8 ....24 B7
WGN WN1 ....15 H5
WGNE/HIN WN2 ....68 C5
WGNE/HIN WN2 ....49 G4
WHIT OL12 ....20 A4
Hallsville Rd BNG/LEV M19 ....99 H3
Halls Wy UPML OL3 ....61 K6
Hallsworth Rd ECC M30 ....85 H5
Hallview Wy WALK M28 ....68 C1
Hall Wood Av RNFD/HAY WA11 ....78 C4

Hallwood Av SLFD M6 ....70 F8
Hallwood Rd NTHM/RTH M23 ....109 K6
WILM/AE SK9 ....127 L1
Hall Wood Rd WILM/AE SK9 ....127 L2
Hallworth Av DTN/ASHW M34 ....89 C8
Hallworth Rd CHH M8 ....72 E4
Hallworthy Cl LEIGH WN7 ....80 E3
Halmore Rd NEWH/MOS M40 ....88 C2
Halsall Cl BURY BL9 ....25 J6
Halsall Dr BOLS/LL BL3 ....52 B2
Halsbury Cl WGTN/LGST M12 ....88 B6
Halsey Cl CHAD OL9 ....74 B1
Halshaw La FWTH BL4 ....53 J5
Halsmere Dr BKLY M9 ....73 H1
Halstead Av CCHDY M21 ....97 K5
SLFD M6 ....71 H7
Halstead Dr IRL M44 ....94 E2
Halstead Gv CHD/CHDH SK8 ....110 C7
LEIGH WN7 ....66 E7
Halstead St BOLE BL2 ....3 H5
BURY BL9 ....25 K7
Halstead Wk BURY BL9 * 25 K7
Halstock Wk NEWH/MOS M40 ....73 C7
Halstone Av WILM/AE SK9 ....126 C8
Halston St HULME M15 ....87 H6
Halter Cl RAD M26 ....38 D7
Halton Bank SLFD M6 ....71 J8
Halton Dr HALE/TIMP WA15 ....108 E3
Halton Rd OP/CLY M11 ....88 F2
Halton St BOLE BL2 ....2 K5
HYDE SK14 ....102 C1
RNFD/HAY WA11 * 78 B6
Halvard Av BURY BL9 ....25 J6
Halvard Ct BURY BL9 ....25 J6
Halvis Gv OLDTF/WHR M16 ....97 L2
Hambleden Cl BOLS/LL BL3 ....35 J7
Hambledon Cl ATH M46 ....51 H7
Hambleton Av TOT/BURYW BL8 ....38 C3
Hambleton Dr SALE M33 ....96 A7
Hambleton Rd CHD/CHDH SK8 ....119 L4
Hamblett St LEIGH WN7 ....65 L7
Hambridge Cl CHH M8 ....72 D5
Hamel St BOLS/LL BL3 ....52 A1
HYDE SK14 ....91 J7
Hamer Dr OLDTF/WHR M16 ....87 C7
Hamer Hall Crs WHIT OL12 ....28 E3
Hamer Hl BKLY M9 ....72 F1
Hamer La MILN OL16 ....11 J1
Hamer St BOLE BL2 ....36 E5
HEY OL10 ....40 E2
RAD M26 ....38 F8
RAMS BL0 ....24 E2
Hamerton Rd NEWH/MOS M40 ....72 F8
Hamilcar Av ECC M30 ....85 H2
Hamilton Av ECC M30 ....85 H3
IRL M44 ....94 A8
ROY/SHW OL2 ....58 E1
Hamilton Cl PWCH M25 ....71 K1
TOT/BURYW BL8 ....38 E1
Hamilton Ct
WCNW/BIL/OR WN5 ....47 H4
Hamilton Crs HTNM SK4 ....12 H4
Hamilton Gv OLDTF/WHR M16 ....87 C7
Hamilton Rd ECC M30 * 84 E1
PWCH M25 ....71 K1
Hamilton Rd AIMK WN4 ....62 F8
BRUN/LGST M13 ....99 J1
PWCH M25 ....71 K1
TYLD M29 ....68 A6
WGNE/HIN WN2 ....49 J8
WHTF M45 ....55 H4
Hamilton Sq HTNM SK4 ....13 C1
WCNW/BIL/OR WN5 ....47 H4
Hamilton St ATH M46 ....66 F2
AULW OL7 ....90 C3
BOL BL1 ....22 B8
BRO M7 * 72 A5
BURY BL9 ....25 J8
CHAD OL9 ....58 D5
ECC M30 ....84 E1
LEIGH WN7 ....66 A6
OLDE OL4 ....9 M6
OLDTF/WHR M16 ....87 C7
STLY SK15 ....91 J2
SWIN M27 ....70 A3
Hamilton Wy HEY OL10 ....40 B3
Hamlet Dr SALE M33 ....96 B6
The Hamlet HOR/BR BL6 ....34 E4
Hammersmith Rd GTN M18 ....88 F6
Hammett Rd CCHDY M21 ....97 K4
Hammond Av HTNM SK4 ....100 D1
Hamnet Cl BOL BL1 ....22 D7
Hamnett St HYDE SK14 * 102 A2
OP/CLY M11 ....88 D4
Hamon Rd HALE/TIMP WA15 ....108 B8
Hampden Crs GTN M18 ....88 F7
Hampden Gv ECC M30 ....85 C2
Hampden Pl
WGNNW/ST WN6 ....47 G3
Hampden Rd PWCH M25 ....55 L8
ROY/SHW OL2 ....44 A6
SALE M33 ....108 D1
Hampden St HEY OL10 ....41 G3
ROCH OL11 ....10 F6
Hampshire Cl BURY BL9 ....5 J9
GLSP SK13 ....105 J4
Hampshire Rd CHAD OL9 ....8 B8
DROY M43 ....89 K1
PART M31 ....106 F2
RDSH SK5 ....100 F7
Hampshire St BRO M7 ....72 A7
Hampson Av AIMK WN4 ....78 E2
ECC M30 ....84 E3
Hampson Crs WILM/AE SK9 ....119 L8
Hampson Fold RAD M26 ....38 C8
Hampson Mill La BURY BL9 ....39 J7
Hampson Rd AUL OL6 ....76 B6
STRET M32 ....96 F2
Hampson St ATH M46 ....66 F1
CSLFD M3 ....6 B6
DROY M43 ....89 K2
ECC M30 ....73 C8
NEWH/MOS M40 * 73 C8
RAD M26 ....38 C6
SALE M33 ....97 C8
STKP SK1 ....112 E4
SWIN M27 ....70 D3
Hampstead Av URM M41 ....95 H3
Hampstead Dr OFTN SK2 ....112 F7
WHTF M45 ....55 H4
Hampstead La OFTN SK2 ....112 F7
Hampstead Rd
WGNNW/ST WN6 ....31 G3
Hampton Gv ALT WA14 ....108 B5
BURY BL9 ....5 J6
CHD/CHDH SK8 ....120 A2
FAIL M35 ....74 D4
IRL M44 ....94 A4
URM M41 ....96 A3
Hampton Rd BOLS/LL BL3 ....52 D1
CCHDY M21 ....97 J3
FAIL M35 ....74 D4
IRL M44 ....94 A4
URM M41 ....96 A3
Hampton St OLDS OL8 ....59 G8

Hamsell Rd BRUN/LGST M13 ....7 L9
Hanborough Ct TYLD M29 ....67 H4
Hancock St RUSH/FAL M14 ....98 E3
Hancock St STRET M32 ....97 G4
Handel Av URM M41 ....95 K2
Handel Ms SALE M33 ....96 F8
Handel St BOL BL1 ....36 A1
Handforth Gv BRUN/LGST M13 ....99 H2
Handforth Rd RDSH SK5 ....100 C7
WILM/AE SK9 ....127 J3
Hand La LEIGH WN7 ....81 H3
Handley Av RUSH/FAL M14 ....98 E3
Handley Cl EDGY/DAV SK3 ....111 M7
Handley Gdns BOL BL1 ....35 L5
Handley Rd BRAM/HZG SK7 ....121 G1
Handley St BURY BL9 ....4 F9
WHIT OL12 * 10 B2
Hands La ROCH OL11 ....27 K5
Handsworth St
WGTN/LGST M12 ....88 A5
Hanging Chadder La
ROY/SHW OL2 ....42 F5
Hankinson Cl PART M31 ....106 C2
Hankinson Wy SLFD M6 ....86 D1
Hanley Cl MDTN M24 ....57 J3
POY/DIS SK12 ....123 M7
Hanlith Ms BNG/LEV M19 ....99 J4
Hanlon St CHH M8 ....72 C3
Hanmer St WGNE/HIN WN2 ....49 C7
Hannah Baldwin Cl
OP/CLY M11 ....88 C4
Hannah St WGTN/LGST M12 ....99 K2
Hannerton Rd ROY/SHW OL2 ....44 A4
Hannesburg Gdns
NTHM/RTH M23 ....109 J8
Hannet Ct BRO M7 ....72 A5
Hanover Ct BRO M7 ....72 B4
WALK M28 ....69 L6
Hanover Crs RUSH/FAL M14 ....88 A4
Hanover Gdns BRO M7 ....72 B4
Hanover Rd ALT WA14 ....107 L5
WGNE/HIN WN2 ....48 F6
Hanover St ANC M4 ....7 G2
BOL BL1 ....2 E4
LEIGH WN7 ....66 D6
LIT OL15 ....21 L7
MOSL OL5 ....76 F2
ROCH OL11 ....41 M2
STLY SK15 ....91 J2
Hanover St North
DTN/ASHW M34 ....90 B4
Hanover St South
DTN/ASHW M34 * 90 B4
Hansby Cl OLD OL1 ....59 H3
Hansdon Cl CHH M8 ....72 D6
Hansom Dr ATH M46 ....66 D4
Hanson Cl MDTN M24 ....57 L3
Hanson Ms STKP SK1 ....112 E2
Hanson Pk NEWH/MOS M40 ....57 M4
Hanson Rd NEWH/MOS M40 ....73 K5
Hanson St BURY BL9 ....25 J8
MDTN M24 ....57 K4
OLDE OL4 ....59 M5
Hanstock WGNW/BIL/OR WN5 ....46 A7
Hanwell Cl LEIGH WN7 ....81 H3
Hanworth Cl BRUN/LGST M13 ....7 K9
Hapton Av STRET M32 ....97 G3
Hapton Pl HTNM SK4 ....13 C1
Hapton St BNG/LEV M19 ....99 K3
Harbern Cl ECC M30 ....84 F2
Harbern Dr LEIGH WN7 ....66 A2
Harbord St MDTN M24 ....57 K4
Harboro Gv SALE M33 ....96 C8
Harboro Rd SALE M33 ....96 C8
Harboro Wy SALE M33 ....96 C8
Harbour Farm Rd HYDE SK14 ....91 H7
Harbour La EDGW/EG BL7 ....17 G7
MILN OL16 ....29 J7
Harbour La North MILN OL16 ....29 J6
Harbourne Av WALK M28 ....68 F4
Harbourne Cl WALK M28 ....68 F4
Harbury Cl BOLS/LL BL3 ....51 K1
WGNNW/ST WN6 ....47 J2
Harbury Crs WYTH/NTH M22 ....109 M7
Harcles Dr RAMS BL0 ....24 E2
Harcombe Rd DID/WITH M20 ....98 F6
Harcourt Av URM M41 ....96 C5
Harcourt Cl URM M41 ....96 C5
Harcourt Rd ALT WA14 ....108 A6
SALE M33 ....96 D6
Harcourt St OLD OL1 ....59 L4
RDSH SK5 ....100 C4
STRET M32 ....97 H1
WALK M28 ....53 C7
Hardacre St WGNS/IIMK WN3 ....15 J3
Hardberry Pl OFTN SK2 ....113 H6
Hardcastle Av CCHDY M21 ....97 M6
Hardcastle Cl BOLE BL2 ....22 F6
Hardcastle Gdns BOLE BL2 ....22 F6
Hardcastle Rd EDGY/DAV SK3 ....12 F9
Hardcastle St BOL BL1 ....36 C2
Harden Dr BOLE BL2 ....37 G2
Harden Hills ROY/SHW OL2 ....44 A4
Hardfield Rd MDTN M24 ....57 K7
Hardfield St HEY OL10 ....41 G2
Hardicker St HTNM SK4 ....99 L5
Hardie Av FWTH BL4 ....52 E5
Harding Av ANC M4 ....88 A3
CSLFD M3 ....6 E2
HYDE SK14 ....91 G7
SLFD M6 ....71 K8
STKP SK15 ....112 E3
Hard La WHIT OL12 ....20 E4
Hardman Av MPL/ROM SK6 ....113 K1
PWCH M25 ....72 A2
Hardman Cl RAD M26 ....38 C6
Hardman La FAIL M35 ....74 A4
Hardman Rd RDSH SK5 ....100 C4
Hardmans EDGW/EG BL7 ....22 C5
Hardmans La EDGW/EG BL7 ....22 C4
Hardman's Ms WHTF M45 ....55 J6
Hardman's Rd WHTF M45 ....55 K6
Hardman St BURY BL9 ....4 F1
CHAD OL9 ....74 E1
CSLFD M3 ....6 D5
EDGY/DAV SK3 ....12 F6
FAIL M35 ....74 A4
FWTH BL4 ....53 H5
HEY OL10 ....41 G2
RAD M26 ....38 C6
WGNS/IIMK WN3 ....14 D2
Hardon Gv BRUN/LGST M13 ....99 J2
Hardrow Cl WGNS/IIMK WN3 ....63 L2
Hardrush Fold FAIL M35 ....74 D6
Hardshaw Cl BRUN/LGST M13 * 87 L6
Hardwicke Rd POY/DIS SK12 ....122 B8
Hardwicke St ROCH OL11 ....10 F4
Hardwick Rd AIMK WN4 ....63 K7
PART M31 ....106 D1

Hardwick St AULW OL7 ....90 C2
Hardwood Cl CHH M8 ....72 C5
Hardy Av CCHDY M21 ....97 K4
Hardybutts WGN WN1 ....15 H4
WGN WN1 ....15 K5
Hardy Cl ROCH OL11 ....42 C1
WHTN BL5 ....50 B1
Hardy Dr BRAM/HZG SK7 ....120 F5
HALE/TIMP WA15 ....108 C5
Hardy Gv SWIN M27 ....70 A7
WALK M28 ....69 J4
Hardy La CCHDY M21 ....97 M6
Hardy Mill Rd BOLE BL2 ....37 J1
Hardy St AUL OL6 ....76 B6
ECC M30 ....84 E3
OLDE OL4 ....9 M8
WGNNW/ST WN6 ....14 C1
Hardywood Rd
DTN/ASHW M34 ....101 K5
Harebell Cl WALK M28 * 68 C1
Harebell Cl WHIT OL12 ....28 A1
Harecastle Av ECC M30 ....85 H4
Haredale Dr CHH M8 ....72 E6
Hare Dr BURY BL9 ....39 L8
Harefield Av ROCH OL11 ....10 F8
WILM/AE SK9 ....126 E7
Harefield Dr DID/WITH M20 ....110 D2
HEY OL10 ....41 J3
WILM/AE SK9 ....126 E7
Harefield Rd WILM/AE SK9 ....120 A3
Harehill Cl BRUN/LGST M13 ....7 K8
Hare Hill Rd HYDE SK14 ....102 F2
LIT OL15 ....21 L6
Hareshill Rd HEY OL10 ....40 F5
Hare St ANC M4 ....7 H3
ROCH OL11 ....10 F8
Harewood HYDE SK14 ....103 K4
Harewood Av ROCH OL11 ....27 G2
SALE M33 ....96 A8
Harewood Dr ROCH OL11 ....26 F3
ROY/SHW OL2 ....42 F7
Harewood Gv RDSH SK5 ....100 B4
Harewood Rd IRL M44 ....94 E2
ROCH OL11 ....26 F2
ROY/SHW OL2 ....43 M4
WGNE/HIN WN2 ....48 F6
Harewood St ANC M4 ....7 G2
BOL BL1 ....2 E1
LEIGH WN7 ....66 D6
LIT OL15 ....21 L7
MOSL OL5 ....76 F2
ROCH OL11 ....41 M2
STLY SK15 ....91 J2
Harford Cl BRAM/HZG SK7 ....121 J3
Hargate Av WHIT OL12 ....27 K2
Hargate Cl BURY BL9 ....25 J5
Hargate Dr HALE/TIMP WA15 ....117 J3
IRL M44 ....94 D1
Hargate Hill La GLSP SK13 ....104 B5
Hargrave Cl BKLY M9 ....56 F6
Hargreaves Rd
HALE/TIMP WA15 ....108 F6
Hargreave's St ANC M4 ....87 K1
BOL BL1 * 36 B2
CHAD OL9 ....8 D6
OLD OL1 ....9 H4
ROCH OL11 ....27 M8
Harkerside Cl CCHDY M21 ....97 M4
Harkness St WGTN/LGST M12 ....7 M9
Harland Dr AIMK WN4 ....78 F1
CHH M8 ....72 E5
Harland Wy WHIT OL12 ....27 K2
Harlea Av WGNE/HIN WN2 ....49 K8
Harlech Av WGNE/HIN WN2 ....49 K8
WHTF M45 ....55 L6
Harlech Dr BRAM/HZG SK7 ....121 L3
Harlech St AIMK WN4 ....63 J7
Harleen Gv OFTN SK2 ....113 G5
Harlesden Crs BOLS/LL BL3 * 35 L7
Harley Av BOLE BL2 ....37 H1
BOLE BL2 ....38 A3
RUSH/FAL M14 ....99 H1
Harley Ct MDTN M24 ....57 J3
SALE M33 ....95 F7
Harley Rd MDTN M24 ....57 J3
SALE M33 ....95 F7
Harley St AUL OL6 * 90 E1
OP/CLY M11 ....89 G4
Harling Rd WYTH/NTH M22 ....110 A5
Harlow Dr GTN M18 ....100 A1
Harlyn Av BRAM/HZG SK7 ....121 H5
Harmer Cl NEWH/MOS M40 ....73 K7
Harmol Gv AULW OL7 ....75 J6
Harmony St OLDE OL4 ....9 L8
Harmsworth Dr HTNM SK4 ....99 L7
Harmuir Cl WGNNW/ST WN6 ....31 H8
Harold Av AIMK WN4 ....63 K7
DUK SK16 ....91 G3
GTN M18 ....88 J8
Haroldene St BOLE BL2 ....36 E2
Harold Lees Rd HEY OL10 ....41 J1
Harold Priestnall Cl
NEWH/MOS M40 ....73 L7
Harold Rd BOL BL1 ....36 A2
CHAD OL9 ....8 E5
FAIL M35 ....74 B5
MDTN M24 ....57 H4
OLDTF/WHR M16 ....86 F6
PWCH M25 ....55 J8
STKP SK1 ....112 F4
WGNE/HIN WN2 ....33 G7
Harper Ct EDGY/DAV SK3 ....13 H8
Harper Fold Rd RAD M26 ....54 B1
Harper Green Rd FWTH BL4 ....52 E3
Harper Pl AUL OL6 ....90 F1
Harper Rd WYTH/NTH M22 ....110 B5
Harper Sq ROY/SHW OL2 ....43 M5
Harper St EDGY/DAV SK3 ....13 G8
FWTH BL4 ....52 F3
OLDS OL8 ....59 H8
ROCH OL11 ....10 C9
WGN WN1 ....15 K5
Harpford Dr BOLE BL2 ....37 K7
Harp Rd TRPK M17 ....85 K4
Harptree Gv LEIGH WN7 ....66 A5
Harpurhey Rd CHH M8 ....72 E4
Harridge Av STLY SK15 ....92 A2
WALK M28 ....69 G7
The Harridge WHIT OL12 ....27 M1
Harridge St WHIT OL12 ....27 M1
Harrier Cl LEIGH WN7 ....66 E7
WALK M28 ....69 G7
WYTH/NTH M22 ....110 B3
Harriet St ANC M4 ....7 M2
MILN OL16 ....11 G5
Harringay Rd NEWH/MOS M40 ....73 J4
Harrington Cl BURY BL9 ....39 K5
Harrington Rd ALT WA14 ....107 L7
Harrington St GTN M18 ....89 H7

Harris Av DTN/ASHW M34 ....100 E1
URM M41 ....85 G7
Harris Cl DTN/ASHW M34 ....100 E1
HEY OL10 ....40 B3
Harris Dr BURY BL9 ....55 L2
HYDE SK14 ....91 K8
Harrison Av BNG/LEV M19 ....99 L2
Harrison Cl WHIT OL12 ....27 J3
Harrison Crs HOR/BR BL6 ....32 F1
Harrisons Dr MPL/ROM SK6 ....101 M7
Harrison St ANC M4 ....88 A3
BRO M7 ....72 A8
ECC M30 ....84 D4
HYDE SK14 ....102 C4
LHULT M38 ....52 D8
OFTN SK2 ....13 K9
OLD OL1 ....9 J6
RAMS BL0 ....18 F5
STLY SK15 ....91 K2
WGNE/HIN WN2 ....65 L1
WGNW/BIL/OR WN5 ....14 A7
Harrison Wy NEWLW WA12 ....78 F8
Harris Rd WGNNW/ST WN6 ....30 E2
Harris St BOLS/LL BL3 ....2 C7
BRO M7 ....72 B8
Harrogate Av PWCH M25 ....72 A2
Harrogate Cl OP/CLY M11 ....89 H5
Harrogate Dr RDSH SK5 ....100 B4
Harrogate Rd RDSH SK5 ....100 B3
Harrogate St WGN WN1 ....15 C5
Harrop Edge La UPML OL3 ....45 L7
Harrop Edge Rd HYDE SK14 ....92 B8
Harrop Fold OLDS OL8 ....75 K3
Harrop Green La UPML OL3 ....45 M7
Harrop Fold La MCFLDN SK10 ....129 J7
Harrop La UPML OL3 ....45 K7
Harrop Rd HALE/TIMP WA15 ....117 H2
Harrop St BOLS/LL BL3 ....35 K8
GTN M18 ....89 G3
STKP SK1 ....13 J8
STLY SK15 ....91 J2
WALK M28 ....68 C1
Harrow Av BNG/LEV M19 ....99 K6
OLDS OL8 ....75 G1
ROCH OL11 ....27 K6
Harrowby Dr NEWH/MOS M40 ....73 C7
Harrowby Fold FWTH BL4 ....52 F4
Harrowby La FWTH BL4 ....52 F4
Harrowby Rd BOL BL1 ....35 J2
BOLS/LL BL3 ....51 K1
SWIN M27 ....70 B5
Harrowby St FWTH BL4 ....52 E4
WGNW/BIL/OR WN5 ....47 H6
Harrow Cl BURY BL9 ....39 J7
WGNW/BIL/OR WN5 ....46 C4
WILM/AE SK9 ....127 H4
Harrow Crs LEIGH WN7 ....81 J1
Harrow Dr SALE M33 ....108 D2
Harrow Ms ROY/SHW OL2 ....43 L5
Harrow Pl WGNS/IIMK WN3 ....48 C8
Harrow Rd BOL BL1 ....35 L5
SALE M33 ....108 D2
WGNW/BIL/OR WN5 ....47 G3
Harrow St CHH M8 ....72 E3
ROCH OL11 ....42 E2
Harrycroft Rd MPL/ROM SK6 ....101 L7
Harry Hall Gdns BRO M7 * 71 M8
Harry Rd RDSH SK5 ....100 C4
Harry Rowley Cl
WYTH/NTH M22 ....118 C2
Harry's Ct LEIGH WN7 ....66 A7
Harry St CHAD OL9 ....8 D7
ROCH OL11 ....41 L1
ROY/SHW OL2 ....59 K2
Harry Thorneycroft Wk
OP/CLY M11 ....88 B2
Harrytown MPL/ROM SK6 ....113 K2
Harswell Cl WGNW/BIL/OR WN5 ....46 B7
Hart Av DROY M43 ....89 L3
SALE M33 ....109 J1
Hart Ct MOSL OL5 ....76 E2
Hart Dr BURY BL9 ....39 L8
Harter St CMANE M1 ....7 C6
Hartfield Cl BRUN/LGST M13 ....87 M6
Hartfield Wk BOLE BL2 ....3 J3
Hartford Av HEY OL10 ....40 E2
HTNM SK4 ....100 A6
WILM/AE SK9 ....126 D7
Hartford Cl HEY OL10 ....40 E1
Hartford Gdns
HALE/TIMP WA15 ....109 G7
Hartford Rd SALE M33 ....95 H8
URM M41 ....85 H8
WHTN BL5 ....50 C7
Hartford Sq CHAD OL9 * 8 D7
Hartford St DTN/ASHW M34 * 90 B7
Hart Hill Dr ORD M5 ....86 A1
Harthill St CHH M8 ....72 C7
Hartington Ct URM M41 ....96 B2
Hartington Dr BRAM/HZG SK7 ....122 A4
OP/CLY M11 ....88 E1
WGNNW/ST WN6 ....31 J5
Hartington Rd ALT WA14 ....108 A5
BOL BL1 ....35 M4
BRAM/HZG SK7 ....121 G6
CCHDY M21 ....97 K3
CHD/CHDH SK8 ....119 M4
ECC M30 ....84 D1
MPL/ROM SK6 ....123 G6
OFTN SK2 ....113 G8
Hartis Av BRO M7 ....72 B6
Hartland Cl OFTN SK2 ....112 F4
POY/DIS SK12 ....121 M7
TYLD M29 ....67 L4
Hartland St HEY OL10 ....41 G2
Hartlebury ROCH OL11 ....10 D7
Hartlepool Cl RUSH/FAL M14 ....98 E1
Hartley Av PWCH M25 ....71 M1
WGN WN1 ....15 K5
Hartley Gv IRL M44 ....94 E5
WGNW/BIL/OR WN5 ....46 E5
Hartley Hall Gdns
OLDTF/WHR M16 ....98 B3
Hartley La ROCH OL11 ....27 M1
Hartley Rd ALT WA14 ....107 M7
CCHDY M21 ....97 K3
Hartley St EDGY/DAV SK3 ....12 E7
HEY OL10 ....41 G2
HOR/BR BL6 ....33 L2
LIT OL15 ....29 C5
MILN OL16 ....11 J1
NEWH/MOS M40 ....73 J4
STLY SK15 ....91 J2
WGNW/BIL/OR WN5 ....21 G6
WHIT OL12 ....21 G6
Hartley Ter WGNS/IIMK WN3 ....14 F6
Hart Mill Cl MOSL OL5 ....76 E2
Harton Av GTN M18 ....99 M1
Harton Cl ROY/SHW OL2 ....43 C6
Hart Rd RUSH/FAL M14 ....98 E3

Harts Farm Ms *LEIGH* WN7 ......66 C5
Hartshead Av *AUL* OL6 ......75 M6
  STLY SK15 ......91 K1
Hartshead Cl *AUL* OL6. ......76 B8
  OP/CLY M11 ......89 K5
Hartshead Crs *FAIL* M35 ......74 F6
Hartshead Rd *AUL* OL6 ......75 M6
Hartshead St *OLDE* OL4 ......60 C7
Hartshead Vw *HYDE* SK14 ......102 C3
Hartsop Dr *MDTN* M24 ......56 F2
Hartspring Av *SWIN* M27 ......70 D5
Hart St *ALT* WA14 ......108 B7
  CMANE M1 ......7 H6
  DROY M43 ......89 K2
  TYLD M29 ......67 M4
  WHTN BL5 ......45 L3
Hartswell Cl *GOL/RIS/CUL* WA3 ......79 K5
Hartswood Cl *DTN/ASHW* M34 ......90 D8
Hartswood Rd *DID/WITH* M20 ......99 G6
Hartwell Cl *BOLE* BL2 ......36 F2
  OP/CLY M11 ......88 C4
Harvard Cl *MPL/ROM* SK6 ......101 M1
Harvard Rd *SLFD* M6. ......85 M1
Harvard Rd *GTN* M18 ......88 C7
Harvest Cl *ROCH* OL11 ......28 D8
Harvest Cl *SALE* M33 ......109 K1
  SLFD M6. ......71 H7
Harvest Pk *BOL* BL1 ......35 M4
Harvey Ct *LEIGH* WN7 ......80 E3
Harvey La *GOL/RIS/CUL* WA3 ......79 J3
Harvey St *BOL* BL1. ......36 A1
  STKP SK1 ......13 J4
  TOT/BURYW BL8 ......38 F1
  WGNS/IIMK WN3 ......15 J7
  WHIT OL12 ......28 E3
Harvin Gv *DTN/ASHW* M34 ......101 K2
Harwich Cl *BNG/LEV* M19 * 99 K3
  RDSH SK5 ......100 F6
Harwin Cl *WHIT* OL12. ......28 A1
Harwood Ct *SLFD* M6. ......71 L8
Harwood Crs *TOT/BURYW* BL8 ......24 E5
Harwood Dr *TOT/BURYW* BL8 ......38 D3
Harwood Gv *BOLE* BL2 *. 36 E3
Harwood Meadow *BOLE* BL2 ......37 J1
Harwood Rd *BNG/LEV* M19 ......99 H6
  BOLE BL2. ......23 L8
  HTNM SK4 ......111 H2
Harwood St *HTNM* SK4 ......13 G1
  LIT OL15 ......21 K7
Harwood V *BOLE* BL2. ......37 H7
Haseldine Cl *AIMK* WN4 ......63 J6
Haseley Cl *POY/DIS* SK12 ......122 A7
  RAD M26 ......37 L7
  TYLD M29 ......67 K4
Haselhurst Wk
  NTHM/RTH M23. ......109 J2
Hasguard Cl *BOL* BL1. ......35 J5
Haskoll St *HOR/BR* BL6. ......34 A3
Haslam Brow *BURY* BL9 * 4 D8
Haslam Cl *WGNW/BIL/OR* WN5 ......31 J5
Haslam Hall Ms *BOL* BL1 ......35 H5
Haslam Hey Cl *BOLE* BL2 * 37 M3
  TOT/BURYW BL8 ......38 C2
Haslam Rd *EDGY/DAV* SK3 ......112 B6
Haslam St *BOLS/LL* BL3 ......2 B9
  BURY BL9 ......25 K8
  MDTN M24 * 57 M5
  WHIT OL12 ......10 B2
Haslemere Av
  HALE/TIMP WA15 ......117 L6
Haslemere Dr *CHD/CHDH* SK8 ......120 C3
Haslemere Rd *DID/WITH* M20 ......99 G6
  URM M41 ......95 L3
Haslington Rd *WYTH/NTH* M22. ......119 G2
Hasper Av *DID/WITH* M20 ......98 D5
Hassall Av *DID/WITH* M20 ......98 C4
Hassall St *RAD* M26 ......39 H7
  STLY SK15 * 91 L3
Hassnes Cl *WGNS/IIMK* WN3. ......15 H7
Hassop Av *BRO* M7 ......71 K5
Hassop Ct *OP/CLY* M11 ......88 B3
Hassop Rd *RDSH* SK5. ......100 D3
Hastings Av *CCHDY* M21 ......97 K4
  WHTF M45 ......55 L5
Hastings Cl *CHD/CHDH* SK8 ......120 E2
  STKP SK1 ......112 E5
  WHTF M45 ......55 L5
Hastings Dr *URM* M41 ......95 H1
Hastings Rd *BOL* BL1 ......35 L4
  ECC M30. ......69 K8
  PWCH M25 ......55 M7
Hastings St *ROCH* OL11 ......10 F8
Haston Cl *RDSH* SK5. ......100 C8
Hasty La *HALE/TIMP* WA15 ......118 B5
Hatchett Rd *WYTH/NTH* M22 ......119 G2
Hatchmere Cl *CHD/CHDH* SK8. ......111 J8
  HALE/TIMP WA15 ......109 C6
Hatfield Av *BNG/LEV* M19 ......99 J6
Hatfield Rd *BOL* BL1 ......35 M3
Hatford Cl *TYLD* M29 ......67 M3
Hathaway Ct *LEIGH* WN7 ......66 E5
Hathaway Dr *BOL* BL1 ......22 D7
Hathaway Gdns
  MPL/ROM SK6 ......113 J1
Hathaway Rd *BURY* BL9 ......55 K1
Hatherley Rd *DID/WITH* M20. ......99 G2
Hatherlow *MPL/ROM* SK6 ......113 G2
Hatherlow La *BRAM/HZG* SK7 ......121 M2
Hatherop Cl *ECC* M30. ......84 E3
Hathersage Av *SLFD* M6. ......71 J7
Hathersage Dr *GLSP* SK13 ......105 J4
Hathersage Rd
  BRUN/LGST M13 ......87 M3
Hathersage St *CHAD* OL9 ......8 C7
Hathershaw La *OLDS* OL8 ......75 J1
Hatro Ct *URM* M41 ......96 D3
Hatters Ct *STKP* SK1 ......13 K7
Hattersley Rd East *HYDE* SK14 ......103 H2
Hattersley Rd West
  HYDE SK14 ......102 F3
Hatter St *ANC* M4 ......7 J2
Hatton Av *ATH* M46 ......51 G7
Hatton Fold *ATH* M46 ......66 E2
Hatton Gv *BOL* BL1 ......22 D7
Hattons Ct *STRET* M32 ......96 F1
Hattons Rd *TRPK* M17 ......85 L6
Hatton St *STKP* SK1 ......13 H1
  WGTN/LGST M12 ......99 K1
Haugh Hill Rd *OLDE* OL4 ......60 D1
Haugh La *MILN* OL16 ......29 M8
Haughton Cl *MPL/ROM* SK6 ......112 C2
Haughton Dr *WYTH/NTH* M22. ......110 A3
Haughton Green Rd
  DTN/ASHW M34 ......101 L4
Haughton Hall Rd
  DTN/ASHW M34 ......101 K1
Haughton St *DTN/ASHW* M34 ......90 C7
  HYDE SK14 ......102 B3
Havana Cl *OP/CLY* M11 ......88 C3
Haveley Rd *WYTH/NTH* M22 ......109 M7
Havelock Dr *BRO* M7. ......72 A4
Havelock St *OLDS* OL8 ......9 J9

Havenbrook Gv *RAMS* BL0 * 24 D1
Haven Cl *BRAM/HZG* SK7. ......121 L3
  OLDE OL4. ......61 G6
  RAD M26. ......38 A7
Haven Dr *DROY* M43. ......89 H2
Haven La *OLDE* OL4. ......60 B1
Havenscroft Av *ECC* M30. ......85 G4
Havenside Cl *OLDE* OL4. ......60 B1
Haven St *SLFD* M6. ......86 B3
The Haven *HALE/TIMP* WA15 ......117 H1
Havenwood Rd *WGN* WN1. ......31 L8
Havercroft Cl
  WGNS/IIMK WN3. ......63 H1
Haverfield Rd *BKLY* M9. ......73 H1
Haverford St *WGTN/LGST* M12. ......88 C5
Haverhill Gv *BOLE* BL2. ......36 E2
Haversham Rd *CHH* M8. ......72 B2
Havers Rd *GTN* M18 ......88 H7
Havisham Cl *HOR/BR* BL6. ......34 E8
Hawarde Cl *NEWLW* WA12. ......78 D3
Hawarden Av
  OLDTF/WHR M16. ......97 M2
Hawarden Rd *ALT* WA14. ......108 A6
Haw Clough La *UPML* OL3. ......61 M6
Hawdraw Gn *OFTN* SK2. ......112 F4
Hawes Av *FWTH* BL4. ......52 B5
  RUSH/FAL M14. ......99 H5
  SWIN M27 * 70 C6
Hawes Cl *OFTN* SK2. ......112 D6
Hawes Crs *AIMK* WN4 ......63 L7
Haweswater Av *TYLD* M29. ......67 L5
  WGNE/HIN WN2. ......48 E5
Haweswater Cl
  DTN/ASHW M34 ......100 D2
Haweswater Crs
  BURY BL9 ......39 L7
Haweswater Dr
  MDTN M24 ......57 H2
Hawfinch Gv
  WALK M28. ......69 G4
Hawk Cl *BURY* BL9 * 5 K1
Hawker Av *BOLS/LL* BL3. ......52 A1
Hawkeshead Rd *CHH* M8. ......72 E6
Hawke St *STLY* SK15 ......91 M3
Hawk Green Rd
  MPL/ROM SK6. ......123 H1
Hawkhurst Rd
  BRUN/LGST M13 ......99 J1
Hawkhurst St *LEIGH* WN7. ......66 F8
Hawkins St *RDSH* SK5 ......100 B8
Hawkley Av
  WGNS/IIMK WN3. ......63 J2
Hawkridge Cl *WHTN* BL5. ......50 C6
Hawkridge Dr
  NTHM/RTH M23 ......109 J2
Hawkrigg Cl
  WGNW/BIL/OR WN6 ......31 J5
Hawk Rd *IRL* M44 ......94 D1
  NM/HAY SK22 ......124 F4
Hawkshaw Cl *TOT/BURYW* BL8. ......23 L1
  WGNE/HIN WN2 ......48 D1
Hawkshaw Ct *ORD* M5. ......86 D3
Hawkshaw La *TOT/BURYW* BL8. ......17 L6
Hawkshead Dr *BOLS/LL* BL3. ......51 K1
  MDTN M24 ......57 H3
  ROY/SHW OL2 ......43 G6
Hawkshead Fold *GLSP* SK13. ......105 H1
Hawkshead Rd *GLSP* SK13. ......105 H1
  ROY/SHW OL2 ......43 K4
Hawksheath Cl *EDGW/EG* BL7. ......22 C3
Hawksley St *HOR/BR* BL6. ......34 A2
  OLDS OL8 ......74 F1
Hawksmoor Dr *ROY/SHW* OL2. ......43 L4
Hawkstone Av *DROY* M43 ......89 H1
  WHTF M45 ......55 G5
Hawkstone Cl *BOLE* BL2 ......37 H1
Hawkswick Dr
  NTHM/RTH M23. ......109 K2
Hawkworth *TYLD* M29 ......67 L7
Hawley Dr *HALE/TIMP* WA15 ......117 H7
Hawley Gn *WHIT* OL12. ......28 A2
Hawley La *HALE/TIMP* WA15 ......117 K4
Hawley St *BNG/LEV* M19 * 99 L4
Haworth Av *RAMS* BL0. ......24 E2
Haworth Cl *BURY* BL9 ......39 J6
Haworth Dr *STRET* M32 ......96 D1
Haworth Rd *GTN* M18 ......88 F8
Haworth St *EDGW/EG* BL7. ......17 G7
  OLD OL1 * 9 H2
  RAD M26 ......54 E1
  TOT/BURYW BL8 ......24 C8
  WGNE/HIN WN2 * 49 G6
Hawthorn Av *AIMK* WN4 ......62 F7
  ECC M30. ......85 G1
  HALE/TIMP WA15 ......108 C5
  MPL/ROM SK6. ......114 A6
  RAD M26 ......54 C3
  RAMS BL0 ......19 H2
  RAMS BL0 ......24 D2
  TOT/BURYW BL8 ......24 F8
  URM M41 ......96 C3
  WGN WN1 ......31 L6
  WGNE/HIN WN2 ......65 K1
  WGNW/BIL/OR WN5. ......46 C6
  WGNW/BIL/OR WN5. ......47 G6
  WILM/AE SK9. ......126 E5
Hawthorn Bank *GLSP* SK13. ......93 J8
Hawthorn Crs *OLDS* OL8. ......75 J2
  ROY/SHW OL2 * 43 L6
  TOT/BURYW BL8 ......24 C5
Hawthorn Dr *BNG/LEV* M19. ......99 J5
  IRL M44 ......94 A7
  SLFD M6 ......70 D8
  STLY SK15 ......91 J4
  SWIN M27 ......70 F5
Hawthorne Av *FWTH* BL4. ......52 E4
  GOL/RIS/CUL WA3. ......81 M7
  HOR/BR BL6. ......34 B3
Hawthorne Dr *WALK* M28. ......69 L5
Hawthorne Gv *AULW* OL7. ......90 C3
  CHAD OL9. ......8 B2
  LEIGH WN7 * 66 B5
  MPL/ROM SK6. ......101 M4
  POY/DIS SK12. ......122 E8

Hawthorn Rd *CHD/CHDH* SK8 ......110 D7
  DROY M43 ......89 M2
  DTN/ASHW M34 ......89 L8
  FWTH BL4 ......53 L7
  HALE/TIMP WA15. ......117 G1
  HTNM SK4. ......111 K2
  NEWH/MOS M40 ......74 B3
  OLDS OL8 ......74 E3
  ROCH OL11 ......27 H6
  STRET M32. ......97 H4
  WHTN BL5. ......50 C5
Hawthorn Rd South
  DROY M43. ......89 M2
The Hawthorns
  DTN/ASHW M34 ......90 A6
Hawthorn St *DTN/ASHW* M34. ......90 B6
  GTN M18. ......89 G6
  WILM/AE SK9. ......126 E6
Hawthorn Ter *HTNM* SK4. ......12 A1
Hawthorn Vw *WILM/AE* SK9 ......126 E5
Hawthorn Wk *LIT* OL15 ......21 K7
  WILM/AE SK9 * 126 E5
Hawthorpe Gv *UPML* OL3. ......61 L4
Haxby Rd *GTN* M18. ......100 A1
Haxey Wk *HOR/BR* BL6. ......33 J1
Hayburn Rd *DTN/ASHW* M23. ......109 L5
Hayburn Rd *OFTN* SK2. ......112 F4
Haycock Cl *STLY* SK15. ......92 B5
Hay Cft *CHD/CHDH* SK8. ......120 A4
Haydn Av *RUSH/FAL* M14. ......87 L8
Haydn Fold *GLSP* SK13 ......104 A6
Haydock Av *SALE* M33. ......107 M2
Haydock Cl *STRET* M32 ......86 C8
Haydock Dr *BRAM/HZG* SK7 ......122 B2
  HALE/TIMP WA15. ......68 E6
Haydock La *EDGW/EG* BL7. ......22 C4
  RNFD/HAY WA11. ......78 A4
Haydock Park Gdns
  NEWLW WA12. ......78 E3
Haydock St *AIMK* WN4 ......78 E2
  BOL BL1. ......2 E2
  NEWLW WA12 ......78 D8
Haye's Rd *IRL* M44 ......94 B7
Hayes St *LEIGH* WN7. ......65 K8
  LEIGH WN7 ......66 B5
Hayeswater Rd *URM* M41 ......84 F8
Hayfell Rd *WGNS/IIMK* WN3. ......63 J3
Hayfield Av *MPL/ROM* SK6. ......101 K8
  TYLD M29. ......67 M6
Hayfield Cl *MDTN* M24 ......57 M1
  OLDE OL4. ......44 C8
  TOT/BURYW BL8 ......24 C3
  WGTN/LGST M12 ......88 B6
Hayfield Rd *MPL/ROM* SK6. ......101 K8
  NM/HAY SK22. ......125 G3
  SLFD M6 ......70 E8
Hayfield St *SALE* M33. ......96 D8
Hayfield Wk *HALE/TIMP* WA15. ......108 F6
Hayle Rd *OLD* OL1 * 44 A8
Hayley St *WGTN/LGST* M12 * 88 B3
Hayling Cl *TOT/BURYW* BL8. ......24 F7
Hayling Rd *SALE* M33. ......96 B7
Haymaker Ri *WHIT* OL12. ......21 G6
Hayman Av *LEIGH* WN7. ......81 G2
Haymarket *BURY* BL9. ......4 F5
The Haymarket *BURY* BL9 *. 4 F4
Haymill Av *LHULT* M38. ......52 D6
Haymond Cl *SLFD* M6. ......71 K6
Haynes St *BOLS/LL* BL3. ......51 L1
  WHIT OL12 ......10 F2
Haysbrook Av *LHULT* M38. ......52 C8
Haysbrook Cl *AULW* OL7. ......75 K5
Haythorp Av *WYTH/NTH* M22. ......119 C5
Hayward Av *BOLS/LL* BL3. ......53 M1
Hayward Gv *WGNW/BIL/OR* WN6. ......31 G2
Haywards Cl *GLSP* SK13. ......104 F1
Hayward St *TOT/BURYW* BL8 ......24 A2
Haywood Cl *GOL/RIS/CUL* WA3. ......80 B3
Hazel Av *OL6. ......76 B6
  BURY BL9. ......5 L4
  CHD/CHDH SK8 ......111 H7
  LHULT M38. ......52 B7
  MILN OL16. ......43 K1
  MPL/ROM SK6. ......114 A2
  OLDTF/WHR M16. ......98 A2
  RAD M26 ......53 K4
  RAMS BL0 ......24 E3
  SALE M33. ......108 E1
  SWIN M27 ......70 D5
  TOT/BURYW BL8. ......24 C7
  WGNNW/ST WN6 ......31 K8
  WHTN BL5. ......50 C5
Hazelbadge Cl *POY/DIS* SK12 ......121 L8
Hazelbadge Rd *POY/DIS* SK12. ......121 L8
Hazelbank Av *DID/WITH* M20. ......98 E5
Hazelbottom Rd *CHH* M8. ......72 E5
Hazel Cl *DROY* M43. ......89 M2
  MPL/ROM SK6. ......114 B8
Hazelcroft *WILM/AE* SK9. ......130 C4
Hazeldene *CHAD* OL9. ......58 A6
Hazel-dene Cl *BURY* BL9. ......39 J5
Hazeldene Rd *NEWH/MOS* M40. ......74 B3
Hazel Dr *OFTN* SK2 ......113 G6
  POY/DIS SK12 ......129 K1
  WYTH/NTH M22. ......119 G3
Hazel Gv *CHAD* OL9. ......8 B2
  FWTH BL4 ......52 E4
  GOL/RIS/CUL WA3. ......79 L4
  LEIGH WN7 ......66 B5
  ORD M5. ......85 M2
  RAD M26 ......54 C4
  URM M41 ......96 E2
Hazel Hall La *TOT/BURYW* BL8 ......24 A3
Hazelhurst Cl *BOL* BL1. ......36 B2
  RAMS BL0 ......18 B8
Hazelhurst Dr *MDTN* M24 ......41 J8
Hazelhurst Fold *WALK* M28 ......69 M5
Hazelhurst Rd *AUL* OL6. ......76 D8
  WALK M28. ......69 L5
Hazel La *GOL/RIS/CUL* WA3. ......80 C2
Hazelmere Av *ECC* M30. ......69 L8
Hazelmere Gdns
  WGNE/HIN WN2. ......49 H8
Hazel Mt *EDGW/EG* BL7 ......22 B2
Hazel Rd *ALT* WA14 ......108 A7
  ALT WA14. ......116 F2
  GLSP SK13 ......104 F1
  HALE/TIMP WA15 ......108 G4
  OFTN SK2 ......112 C6
  WHTF M45 ......55 L4
Hazel St *BRAM/HZG* SK7 * 122 A1
  DTN/ASHW M34 ......90 B6
  RAMS BL0 ......18 D8
Hazel Ter *BKLY* M9 * 57 C8
Hazelton Cl *LEIGH* WN7 * 81 H5
Hazelwell *SALE* M33. ......108 E1
Hazelwood *CHAD* OL9 ......58 A6
Hazelwood Av *BOLE* BL2. ......37 H1
Hazelwood Cl *HYDE* SK14 ......102 D2

Hazelwood Dr *BURY* BL9 ......25 J5
  BURY BL9. ......90 B6
Hazelwood Rd *BOL* BL1. ......35 L2
  BRAM/HZG SK7 ......122 A2
  HALE/TIMP WA15 ......117 G2
  OFTN SK2. ......112 D8
  WGN WN1. ......31 L8
  WILM/AE SK9. ......127 H4
  WYTH/NTH M22 ......118 F4
Hazelhurst Gv *AIMK* WN4 ......78 F1
Hazlemere *FWTH* BL4 ......53 K5
Headen Av
  WGNW/BIL/OR WN5. ......46 E7
Headingley Dr
  OLDTF/WHR M16 ......97 K1
Headingley Rd *RUSH/FAL* M14. ......99 C5
Headingley Wy *BOLS/LL* BL3. ......52 A1
Headlands Dr *PWCH* M25 ......71 K2
Headlands Rd *BRAM/HZG* SK7 ......121 K8
Headlands St *WHIT* OL12. ......28 B3
Heady Hill Cl *HEY* OL10. ......40 D3
Heady Hill Rd *HEY* OL10 ......40 D2
Heald Av *RUSH/FAL* M14. ......98 E1
Heald Cl *ALT* WA14. ......116 E2
  LIT OL15. ......29 K1
  WHIT OL12 ......27 M1
Heald Dr *ALT* WA14. ......116 E2
  WHIT OL12 ......27 M1
Heald Gv *CHD/CHDH* SK8. ......119 J3
  RUSH/FAL M14. ......98 E1
Heald La *LIT* OL15 ......29 K1
Heald Pl *RUSH/FAL* M14. ......98 E1
Heald Rd *ALT* WA14. ......116 E2
Healds Gn *OLD* OL1 ......58 C1
Heald St *STKP* SK1 ......13 L2
Healdwood Rd *MPL/ROM* SK6 ......101 M8
Healey Av *HEY* OL10. ......41 H1
Healey Cl *BRO* M7 ......71 M4
  NTHM/RTH M23 ......109 J2
Healey Gv *WHIT* OL12 ......20 A7
Healey La *WHIT* OL12. ......20 B8
Healey St *MILN* OL16. ......10 D6
Healing St *ROCH* OL11 ......11 H9
Heanor Av *DTN/ASHW* M34 ......101 K4
Heap Br *BURY* BL9 ......39 M2
Heap Brow *BURY* BL9. ......40 A2
Heap St *ROCH* OL11 ......41 M3
Heaplands *TOT/BURYW* BL8 ......24 C3
Heap Rd *WHIT* OL12 ......27 G2
Heaps Farm Ct *STLY* SK15 ......92 A4
Heap St *BOLS/LL* BL3. ......36 B8
  BURY BL9 ......40 A3
  OLDE OL4 ......59 M5
  RAD M26 ......54 E1
  WHTF M45 * 55 J5
Heapworth Av *RAMS* BL0 ......18 E6
Heapy Cl *TOT/BURYW* BL8 ......24 C3
Heardman Av *WGNNW/ST* WN6. ......14 B1
Heath Av *BRO* M7 ......71 M8
  RAMS BL0 ......24 E5
Heathbank Rd *BKLY* M9. ......56 F7
  CHD/CHDH SK8 ......120 B4
  EDGY/DAV SK3 ......12 B9
Heathcliffe Wk
  BRUN/LGST M13 ......87 M7
Heath Cl *BOLS/LL* BL3 ......51 L2
Heathcote Av *HTNM* SK4. ......111 M1
Heathcote Rd *GTN* M18 ......88 F8
Heath Crs *OFTN* SK2. ......112 C7
Heather Av *DROY* M43 ......89 M2
  IRL M44 ......94 A6
  ROY/SHW OL2 ......44 A4
Heather Bank
  TOT/BURYW BL8 * 24 B5
Heather Bank Cl *GLSP* SK13 ......104 D5
Heather Brae *NEWLW* WA12 ......78 D8
Heather Brow *STLY* SK15 ......92 B5
Heather Cl *OLDE* OL4 ......60 A1
Heatherdale Dr *CHH* M8. ......72 D6
Heather Falls *NM/HAY* SK22 ......124 D4
Heatherfield *BOL* BL1. ......22 A7
  EDGW/EG BL7 ......17 H6
Heatherfield Ct *WILM/AE* SK9 ......127 J4
Heather Gv *AIMK* WN4 ......64 B8
  DROY M43 ......89 L4
  HYDE SK14 ......93 G6
  LEIGH WN7 ......66 B5
  WGNW/BIL/OR WN5. ......47 G4
Heather Lea *DTN/ASHW* M34. ......101 K2
Heather Rd *ALT* WA14. ......117 G3
Heatherside *RDSH* SK5. ......100 D3
  STLY SK15. ......92 A2
Heatherside Av *MOSL* OL5. ......77 H5
Heatherside Rd *RAMS* BL0. ......18 E5
The Heathers *OFTN* SK2. ......112 E8
Heather St *OP/CLY* M11 ......88 E2
Heather Wy *MPL/ROM* SK6 ......114 B7
Heath Farm La *PART* M31. ......106 E1
Heathfield *BOLE* BL2 ......23 J8
  WALK M28. ......69 J7
  WILM/AE SK9. ......127 J4
Heathfield Av *CHD/CHDH* SK8. ......110 E7
  DTN/ASHW M34 ......90 E7
  HTNM SK4. ......99 M7
Heathfield Cl *SALE* M33. ......109 J1
  OFTN SK2. ......112 C6
Heathfields *UPML* OL3. ......61 M4
Heathfield St *NEWH/MOS* M40. ......73 M7
Heath Gdns *WGNE/HIN* WN2. ......49 J3
Heathland Av *BRO* M7. ......71 L3
Heathlands Dr *PWCH* M25. ......71 H2
Heathland Ter *EDGY/DAV* SK3. ......13 H9
Heath La *GOL/RIS/CUL* WA3. ......80 A6
  LEIGH WN7 ......65 L2
Heathlea *WGNE/HIN* WN2. ......65 M2
Heathlea Cl *BOL* BL1. ......22 B6
Heathmoor Av
  GOL/RIS/CUL WA3. ......80 A6
Heath Pl *BRO* M7 ......71 M8
Heath Rd *AIMK* WN4 ......78 E2
  CHH M8. ......72 C5
  GOL/RIS/CUL WA3. ......79 K4
  ROCH OL11 ......10 B6

The Heath *AULW* OL7 ......75 K5
  GLSP SK13. ......104 F1
  MDTN M24. ......57 L6
Heathwood *UPML* OL3. ......77 M1
Heathwood Rd *BNG/LEV* M19. ......99 H8
Heatley Rd *MILN* OL16. ......29 G8
Heaton Av *BOL* BL1. ......35 J3
  BOLE BL2. ......37 K8
  BOLS/LL BL3. ......37 K8
  BRAM/HZG SK7. ......52 F4
  FWTH BL4. ......52 F4
Heaton Cl *BURY* BL9. ......39 K7
  HTNM SK4. ......111 K1
Heaton Ct *BURY* BL9. ......39 H5
Heaton Dr *BURY* BL9. ......39 H5
Heaton Fold *BURY* BL9. ......4 E9
Heaton Grange Dr *BOL* BL1. ......35 K5
Heaton Gv *BURY* BL9. ......39 H5
Heaton La *HTNM* SK4. ......12 F4
Heaton Moor Rd *HTNM* SK4. ......111 K1
Heaton Mt *BOL* BL1. ......35 J3
Heaton Park Rd *BKLY* M9. ......56 D7
Heaton Park Rd West
  BKLY M9. ......56 D7
Heaton Rd *BOLE* BL2. ......37 L7
  DID/WITH M20. ......98 F5
  HOR/BR BL6. ......33 G6
  HTNM SK4. ......112 A1
Heatons Gv *WHTN* BL5. ......50 D2
Heaton St *BRO* M7. ......72 B5
  DTN/ASHW M34 ......101 L1
  MDTN M24. ......56 E5
  MILN OL16. ......29 K7
  PWCH M25. ......55 M8
  WGN WN1. ......47 M2
  WGNE/HIN WN2. ......31 H3
  WGNS/IIMK WN3. ......15 K7
Heaviley Gv *OFTN* SK2. ......112 C6
Hebble Butt Cl *MILN* OL16 * 29 H6
Hebble Cl *BOLE* BL2. ......37 H1
Hebden Av *WHIT* OL12. ......20 A7
Hebden Cl *GOL/RIS/CUL* WA3. ......81 M8
  MPL/ROM SK6. ......101 M1
  SLFD M6 ......85 M1
Hebden Dr *GLSP* SK13. ......105 J4
Hebden Wk *HULME* M15. ......87 J7
Hebdon Cl *AIMK* WN4. ......63 J6
Heber St *LIT* OL15. ......21 M7
Heber St *RAD* M26. ......54 D1
  WGNE/HIN WN2. ......48 C5
Hebron St *ROY/SHW* OL2. ......59 K1
Hector Av *MILN* OL16. ......11 J2
Hector Rd *BRUN/LGST* M13. ......99 J1
  WGNW/BIL/OR WN5. ......47 G3
Heddles Ct *LEIGH* WN7 * 66 B8
Heddon Cl *HTNM* SK4. ......111 H1
Hedgemead *WGNNW/ST* WN6. ......30 A2
Hedge Rows *WHIT* OL12. ......20 B2
The Hedgerows *HYDE* SK14. ......102 D1
  RNFD/HAY WA11. ......78 C5
Hedges St *FAIL* M35. ......74 D4
Hedley St *BOL* BL1. ......35 M2
Heeley St *WGN* WN1. ......47 L2
Heginbottom Crs *AUL* OL6. ......75 M7
Heights Av *WHIT* OL12. ......28 B3
Heights Cl *WHIT* OL12. ......28 B2
Heights La *OLD* OL1. ......58 C2
  UPML OL3. ......45 G5
  WHIT OL12. ......28 B3
The Heights *HOR/BR* BL6. ......34 A3
Helena St *SLFD* M6. ......70 F7
Helen St *AIMK* WN4. ......63 H8
  BRO M7. ......71 M7
  ECC M30. ......84 E4
  FWTH BL4. ......53 G4
  GOL/RIS/CUL WA3. ......79 J3
Helensville Av *SLFD* M6. ......71 J7
Helga St *NEWH/MOS* M40. ......73 G8
Helias Cl *WALK* M28. ......68 C1
Hell Nook *GOL/RIS/CUL* WA3. ......79 J3
Helmclough Wy *WALK* M28. ......68 F4
Helmet St *CMANE* M1. ......7 M7
Helmsdale *WALK* M28. ......68 F2
Helmsdale Av *BOLS/LL* BL3. ......35 J6
Helmsdale Cl *RAMS* BL0. ......24 D1
Helmshore Av *OLDE* OL4. ......60 A1
Helmshore Rd *TOT/BURYW* BL8. ......18 D4
Helmshore Wk *BRUN/LGST* M13. ......7 H1
Helmshore Wy *ROY/SHW* OL2. ......43 L4
Helmsman Wy
  WGNS/IIMK WN3. ......14 D3
Helsby Cl *OLDE* OL4. ......60 D6
Helsby Gdns *BOL* BL1. ......22 C8
Helsby Rd *SALE* M33. ......109 H2
Helsby Wk *WGTN/LGST* M12. ......88 B3
Helsby Wy *WGNS/IIMK* WN3. ......62 F2
Helston Cl *BRAM/HZG* SK7. ......121 K5
  IRL M44 ......94 E2
Helston Dr *ROY/SHW* OL2. ......43 G7
Helston Gv *CHD/CHDH* SK8. ......119 L4
Helston Wy *TYLD* M29. ......67 M4
Helvellyn Dr *MDTN* M24. ......57 G2
Helvellyn Rd
  WGNW/BIL/OR WN5. ......46 E5
Helvellyn Wk *OLD* OL1. ......9 L1
Hembury Av *BNG/LEV* M19. ......99 H8
Hembury Cl *MDTN* M24. ......57 L2
Hemfield Ct *WGNE/HIN* WN2. ......48 E4
Hemfield Rd *WGNE/HIN* WN2. ......48 E4
Hemley Cl *WHTN* BL5. ......50 A6
Hemlock Av *OLDS* OL8. ......75 H1
Hemming Dr *ECC* M30. ......85 G4
Hemmington Dr *BKLY* M9. ......73 G5
Hemmons Rd *WGTN/LGST* M12. ......99 C3
Hempcroft Rd
  HALE/TIMP WA15. ......108 F7
Hempshaw La *STKP* SK1. ......13 K8
Hemsley St *BKLY* M9. ......73 H4
Hemsley St South *BKLY* M9. ......73 H4
Hemswell Cl *SLFD* M6. ......71 H8
Hemsworth Rd *BOL* BL1. ......100 A1
  GTN M18. ......88 E6
Henbury Rd *MPL/ROM* SK6. ......101 L6
Henbury La *CHD/CHDH* SK8. ......120 B6
Henbury Rd *WILM/AE* SK9 * 119 M8
Henbury St *OFTN* SK2. ......112 F8
  RUSH/FAL M14. ......98 D1
Henderson Av *SWIN* M27. ......70 C1
Henderson St *BNG/LEV* M19. ......99 L4
  LIT OL15. ......21 L7
  WHIT OL12. ......28 E1
Henderville St *LIT* OL15. ......21 L6
Hendham Cl *BRAM/HZG* SK7. ......121 L3
Hendham Dr *ALT* WA14. ......107 L2
Hendham V *BKLY* M9. ......72 F1
  EDGY/DAV SK3 ......111 K5
Hendon Dr *BURY* BL9 ......39 J7
  EDGY/DAV SK3 ......111 K5
Hendon Gv *LEIGH* WN7 ......66 C4
Hendon Rd *BKLY* M9. ......56 F8
  WGNW/BIL/OR WN5. ......47 G4

Hendon St *LEIGH* WN7 .... 66 C4
Hendriff Pl *WHIT* OL12 * 28 C3
Hen Fold Rd *TYLD* M29 .... 67 M5
Hengist St *BOLE* BL2 .... 3 M4
 GTN M18 .... 89 C8
Henley Av *CHD/CHDH* SK8 .... 120 B2
 IRL M44 .... 94 B6
 OLDTF/WHR M16 .... 97 L1
Henley Cl *TOT/BURYW* BL8 .... 38 E4
Henley Dr *AUL* OL7 .... 75 J8
 HALE/TIMP WA15 .... 108 C5
Henley Gv *BOLS/LL* BL3 .... 51 M1
Henley Pl *BNG/LEV* M19 .... 99 K6
Henley St *CHAD* OL9 .... 74 D1
 OLD OL1 .... 8 F2
 WGNE/HIN WN2 .... 32 E6
 WHIT OL12 .... 10 D1
Henley Ter *ROCH* OL11 .... 10 C9
Henniker Rd *BOLS/LL* BL3 .... 51 K1
Henniker St *SWIN* M27 .... 70 B6
 WALK M28 .... 69 G3
Hennon St *BOL* BL1 .... 36 A3
Henrietta St *AUL* OL6 .... 75 L8
 BOLS/LL BL3 .... 35 L8
 LEIGH WN7 .... 66 C7
 OLDTF/WHR M16 .... 86 F8
Henry Herman St *BOLS/LL* BL3 * 51 K1
Henry Lee St *BOLS/LL* BL3 * 51 M1
Henry Park St *WGN* WN1 .... 15 L5
Henry St *ANC* M4 .... 7 J3
 BOLE BL2 .... 3 G7
 DROY M43 .... 89 K3
 DTN/ASHW M34 * 101 L4
 ECC M30 .... 84 F3
 FAIL M35 .... 74 C5
 GLSP SK13 .... 104 F3
 HYDE SK14 .... 102 A2
 LEIGH WN7 .... 81 K1
 LIT OL15 .... 29 J1
 MDTN M24 .... 57 J4
 OLDTF/WHR M16 .... 55 M7
 PWCH M25 .... 55 M7
 RAMS BL0 .... 19 G5
 ROCH OL11 .... 10 E6
 STKP SK1 .... 112 E4
 TYLD M29 .... 67 K3
 WGNS/IIMK WN3 .... 48 B8
 WHIT OL12 .... 21 G5
Henshall La *ALT* WA14 .... 108 A1
Henshaw Ct *OLDTF/WHR* M16 .... 86 E8
Henshaw La *CHAD* OL9 .... 74 C2
Henshaw St *OLD* OL1 .... 9 H5
 STRET M32 .... 97 G2
Henshaw Wk *BOL* BL1 .... 36 B2
Henson Gv *HALE/TIMP* WA15 .... 108 D8
Henthorn St *ROY/SHW* OL2 .... 43 L6
Henton Wk *NEWH/MOS* M40 .... 72 F8
Henty Cl *ECC* M30 .... 84 E3
Henwick Hall Av *RAMS* BL0 .... 18 E8
Henwood Rd *DID/WITH* M20 .... 98 F7
Hepley Rd *POY/DIS* SK12 .... 129 L1
Hepple Cl *HTNM* SK4 .... 111 J1
Heppleton Rd *NEWH/MOS* M40 .... 74 A2
Hepple Wk *AULW* OL7 * 75 H7
Hepton St *OLD* OL1 .... 9 G3
Hepworth Cl *GOL/RIS/CUL* WA3 .... 79 J2
Hepworth St *HYDE* SK14 .... 102 B5
Herbert St *BOLS/LL* BL3 .... 51 L8
 CHAD OL9 .... 8 B5
 CHH M8 * 72 C7
 DROY M43 .... 89 J3
 DTN/ASHW M34 .... 90 D8
 EDGY/DAV SK3 .... 12 F4
 OLDE OL4 .... 60 A3
 PWCH M25 .... 55 J8
 RAD M26 .... 38 C7
 STRET M32 .... 97 G2
 WGNS/IIMK WN3 .... 14 D5
 WHTN BL5 .... 50 B2
Hereford Av
 GOL/RIS/CUL WA3 * 79 L4
Hereford Cl *AIMK* WN4 .... 78 F2
 AUL OL6 .... 76 A5
 ROY/SHW OL2 .... 43 J5
Hereford Crs *BOLS/LL* BL3 .... 37 L8
Hereford Dr *BURY* BL9 .... 5 G3
 PWCH M25 .... 71 M2
 SWIN M27 .... 70 C6
 WILM/AE SK9 .... 127 J1
Hereford Gv *URM* M41 .... 95 M2
Hereford Rd *BOL* BL1 .... 35 L4
 CHD/CHDH SK8 .... 111 K8
 ECC M30 .... 70 D7
 RDSH SK5 .... 100 F7
 WGNE/HIN WN2 .... 49 J6
Hereford St *BOL* BL1 .... 36 C2
 OLDE OL4 .... 8 C8
 ROCH OL11 .... 11 G8
 SALE M33 .... 96 E8
Hereford Wy *MDTN* M24 .... 57 M3
 STLY SK15 .... 77 M5
Herevale Gra *WALK* M28 .... 68 E5
Herevale Hall Dr *RAMS* BL0 .... 18 E8
Heristone Av *DTN/ASHW* M34 .... 101 H1
Heritage Gdns *DID/WITH* M20 .... 110 E2
Herle Dr *WYTH/NTH* M22 .... 118 E3
Hermitage Av *MPL/ROM* SK6 .... 114 C2
Hermitage Cl *WGNNW/ST* WN6 .... 30 B5
Hermitage Gdns
 MPL/ROM SK6 .... 114 C2
Hermitage Rd *CHH* M8 .... 72 D4
 HALE/TIMP WA15 .... 117 J1
Hermon Av *OLDS* OL8 .... 75 H1
Herne St *OP/CLY* M11 .... 88 D4
Heron Av *DUK* SK16 .... 91 K5
Heron Cl *GLSP* SK13 .... 105 H4
Heron Ct *SLFD* M6 .... 85 L1
Herondale Cl *NEWH/MOS* M40 .... 73 L7
Heron Dr *DTN/ASHW* M34 .... 89 M3
 IRL M44 .... 94 D1
 POY/DIS SK12 .... 128 E1
 WGNS/IIMK WN3 .... 63 H2
Heron MI *OLDS* OL8 * 75 G1
Heron Pl *WGNW/BIL/OR* WN5 .... 46 F4
Heron St *EDGY/DAV* SK3 .... 12 F7
 HULME M15 .... 87 H7
 OLDS OL8 .... 74 F1
 SWIN M27 .... 70 D3
Heron's Wy *BOLE* BL2 .... 3 G8
Herons Whf *WGNNW/ST* WN6 .... 30 A5
Heron Vw *GLSP* SK13 .... 104 C4
Heron Wk *ORD* M5 .... 6 A8
Herristone Rd *CHH* M8 .... 72 B3
Herrod Av *HTNM* SK4 .... 100 D7
Herschel St *NEWH/MOS* M40 .... 73 H4
Hersey St *SLFD* M6 * 86 B2
Hertford Dr *TYLD* M29 .... 67 K1
Hertford Rd *BKLY* M9 .... 73 C3
Hertfordshire Park Cl
 ROY/SHW OL2 * 43 L4
Hertford St *AULW* OL7 .... 90 D3
Hesford Av *BKLY* M9 .... 73 J5

Hesketh Av *BOL* BL1 .... 22 C7
 DID/WITH M20 .... 110 D1
 ROY/SHW OL2 .... 43 K7
Hesketh Ct *ATH* M46 .... 66 F1
Hesketh Dr *WGNNW/ST* WN6 .... 30 D2
Hesketh Meadow La
 GOL/RIS/CUL WA3 .... 80 L4
Hesketh Rd *MILN* OL16 .... 11 L4
 SALE M33 .... 108 C1
Hesketh St *ATH* M46 .... 51 J8
 HTNM SK4 .... 13 C1
 LEIGH WN7 .... 66 A7
 WGNW/BIL/OR WN5 .... 47 H5
Hesnall Cl *GOL/RIS/CUL* WA3 .... 81 M4
Hessel St *SALQ* M50 .... 86 A3
Hester Wk *HULME* M15 * 87 J6
Heston Av *BRUN/LGST* M13 .... 99 H2
Heston Dr *URM* M41 .... 95 M1
Heswall Av *DID/WITH* M20 .... 98 E5
Heswall Dr *TOT/BURYW* BL8 .... 24 F7
Heswall Rd *RDSH* SK5 .... 100 C3
Hetherington Wk
 DID/WITH M20 * 110 D4
Hethorn St *NEWH/MOS* M40 .... 73 M7
Hetton Av *BRUN/LGST* M13 .... 99 H2
Heversham Av *ROY/SHW* OL2 .... 44 A5
Hewart Cl *NEWH/MOS* M40 .... 72 F8
Hewart Dr *BURY* BL9 .... 39 M2
Hewitt Av *DTN/ASHW* M34 .... 100 C1
Hewitt St *HULME* M15 .... 6 C8
Hewlett Rd *CCHDY* M21 .... 97 K3
Hewlett St *BOLE* BL2 .... 3 G5
 WGN WN1 .... 15 C4
 WHTN BL5 .... 49 L5
Hexham Av *BOL* BL1 .... 35 J3
 WGNS/IIMK WN3 .... 63 J1
Hexham Cl *ATH* M46 .... 51 H8
 CHAD OL9 .... 8 C4
 OFTN SK2 .... 113 H7
Hexham Rd *GTN* M18 .... 88 E8
Hexon Cl *SLFD* M6 .... 86 B1
Hey Bottom La *WHIT* OL12 .... 20 E6
Heybrook Rd *WHTF* M45 .... 55 H6
 NTHM/RTH M23 .... 109 L7
Heybrook St *MILN* OL16 * 11 J1
Heybury Cl *OP/CLY* M11 .... 88 C4
Hey Crs *OLDE* OL4 .... 60 C5
Heycrofts Vw *RAMS* BL0 .... 19 H1
Heyes Av *HALE/TIMP* WA15 .... 108 A5
 RNFD/HAY WA11 .... 78 A7
Heyes Dr *HALE/TIMP* WA15 .... 108 A5
Heyes La *HALE/TIMP* WA15 .... 108 A5
 WILM/AE SK9 .... 130 E2
Heyes Leigh
 HALE/TIMP WA15 * 108 E5
Heyes Rd *WGNW/BIL/OR* WN5 .... 46 B6
Heyes Ter *HALE/TIMP* WA15 * 108 E4
Hey Flake La *UPML* OL3 .... 45 M5
Heyford Av *NEWH/MOS* M40 .... 74 A2
Heyford Rd
 WGNW/BIL/OR WN5 .... 47 G4
Hey Head La *LIT* OL15 .... 21 M4
Heyheads New Rd *STLY* SK15 .... 77 H5
Heyland Rd *ROY/SHW* OL2 .... 43 K7
Heyland Rt *NTHM/RTH* M23 .... 109 K6
Heyridge Dr *WYTH/NTH* M22 .... 119 H4
Heyrod St *CMANE* M1 .... 7 L6
 STLY SK15 .... 77 G7
Heyrose Wk *HULME* M15 * 87 G6
Heys Av *MPL/ROM* SK6 .... 114 B1
 NTHM/RTH M23 .... 109 K3
 SWIN M27 .... 70 A4
Heysbank Rd *POY/DIS* SK12 .... 123 M7
Heys Cl North *SWIN* M27 .... 69 M2
Heyscroft Rd *DID/WITH* M20 .... 98 F6
 HTNM SK4 .... 111 K2
Heysham Av *DID/WITH* M20 .... 98 C5
Heysham Rd
 WGNW/BIL/OR WN5 .... 46 E5
Hey Shoot La
 GOL/RIS/CUL WA3 .... 81 M7
Heyside *ROY/SHW* OL2 .... 43 K8
Heyside Av *ROY/SHW* OL2 .... 59 K1
Heyside Cl *STLY* SK15 .... 77 H6
Heyside Wy *BURY* BL9 .... 5 H6
Heys La *HEY* OL10 .... 40 D2
 MPL/ROM SK6 .... 114 B1
Heys Rd *AUL* OL6 .... 91 G1
 PWCH M25 .... 55 L7
Heys St *TOT/BURYW* BL8 .... 4 B4
The Heys *AUL* OL6 .... 91 G1
 PWCH M25 .... 55 L7
 RDSH SK5 .... 100 D3
Hey St *MILN* OL16 .... 11 J3
 WGNNW/ST WN6 .... 14 D3
 WGNS/IIMK WN3 .... 64 C1
Heys Vw *PWCH* M25 .... 55 L7
The Hey *ROY/SHW* OL2 * 44 B3
Heythrop Cl *WHTF* M45 .... 55 J6
Heywood Av *GOL/RIS/CUL* WA3 .... 79 L3
 OLDE OL4 .... 60 D4
 SWIN M27 .... 70 E2
Heywood Cl *WILM/AE* SK9 .... 130 E2
Heywood Fold Rd *OLDE* OL4 .... 60 C5
Heywood Gdns *BOLS/LL* BL3 .... 36 B8
 PWCH M25 .... 55 L8
Heywood Gv *SALE* M33 .... 96 D6
Heywood Hall Rd *HEY* OL10 .... 41 G1
Heywood La *OLDE* OL4 .... 60 D5
Heywood Old Rd *HEY* OL10 .... 40 F3
 MDTN M24 .... 56 D4
Heywood Pk *PWCH* M25 .... 71 L1
 ROCH OL11 .... 41 L2
 SALE M33 .... 108 E1
 WILM/AE SK9 .... 130 E1
Heywoods Hollow *BOL* BL1 .... 36 C1
Heywood St *BOL* BL1 .... 2 E2
 BOLS/LL BL3 .... 53 L1
 BURY BL9 .... 5 H6
 CHH M8 .... 72 D6
 FAIL M35 .... 74 A5
 OLDE OL4 .... 60 B4
 SWIN M27 .... 70 B4
Heywood Wy *SLFD* M6 .... 86 C1
Heyworth Av *DTN/ASHW* M34 .... 90 A7
Heyworth St *MPL/ROM* SK6 .... 114 A1
Hibbert Av *DTN/ASHW* M34 .... 90 A7
 HYDE SK14 .... 102 B3
Hibbert Crs *FAIL* M35 .... 74 D5
Hibbert La *MPL/ROM* SK6 .... 114 C7
Hibbert St *BOL* BL1 .... 36 C2
 HTNM SK4 .... 100 B7
 NM/HAY SK22 * 124 D6
 OLDE OL4 .... 60 C5
 RUSH/FAL M14 .... 98 F1
Hibernia St *BOLS/LL* BL3 .... 35 M7
Hibernia Wy *STRET* M32 .... 85 K7
Hibson Av *WHIT* OL12 .... 27 H2
Hibson Cl *WHIT* OL12 .... 21 G6
Hickenfield Rd *HYDE* SK14 .... 91 L7
Hicken Pl *HYDE* SK14 .... 91 J7

Hickton Dr *ALT* WA14 .... 107 L7
Hieland Rd *WGN* WN1 .... 48 B2
Higginshaw La *OLD* OL1 .... 59 K2
Higginshaw Rd *OLD* OL1 .... 9 L1
Higginson Rd *RDSH* SK5 .... 100 B5
Higgs Cl *OLDE* OL4 .... 60 C5
Higham Cl *ROY/SHW* OL2 .... 43 K7
Higham La *HYDE* SK14 .... 102 C4
Higham St *CHD/CHDH* SK8 .... 120 C4
Higham Vw *SLFD* M6 .... 86 D7
High Ash Gv
 DTN/ASHW M34 .... 90 A5
High Av *BOLE* BL2 .... 37 H5
High Bank *ALT* WA14 .... 108 A7
 ATH M46 .... 51 K6
 EDGW/EG BL7 .... 22 C5
 GTN M18 .... 89 H7
Highbank *GLSP* SK13 .... 93 J5
High Bank Av *STLY* SK15 .... 92 A5
High Bank Cl *IRL* M44 .... 94 A6
Highbank Crs *PWCH* M25 .... 71 M1
Highbank Dr
 DID/WITH M20 .... 110 C4
High Bank Gv *PWCH* M25 .... 71 M1
High Bank La *HOR/BR* BL6 .... 34 E5
High Bank Rd *DROY* M43 .... 89 J4
 HYDE SK14 .... 102 C5
 SWIN M27 .... 70 E4
Highbank Rd *BURY* BL9 .... 55 J1
 GLSP SK13 .... 105 J5
 MILN OL16 .... 43 M1
High Bank Side *STKP* SK1 .... 13 J4
High Bank St *BOLE* BL2 .... 3 M5
High Barn Cl *ROCH* OL11 .... 10 C9
High Barn La *WHIT* OL12 .... 20 A1
High Barn Rd *MDTN* M24 .... 57 K5
 ROY/SHW OL2 .... 43 J8
High Barn St *ROY/SHW* OL2 .... 43 H8
High Beeches *BOLE* BL2 .... 37 L7
High Beeches Crs *AIMK* WN4 .... 63 K6
High Bent Av
 CHD/CHDH SK8 .... 120 C6
Highbridge Cl *BOLE* BL2 .... 37 K6
Highbury Av *IRL* M44 .... 94 D3
 URM M41 .... 95 H2
Highbury Cl *WHTN* BL5 .... 50 A6
Highbury Rd *HTNM* SK4 .... 99 M6
 OLDTF/WHR M16 .... 98 B3
Highbury Wy *ROY/SHW* OL2 .... 43 G6
Highclere Av *CHH* M8 .... 72 C6
Highclere Rd *CHH* M8 .... 72 C6
Highcliffe Ct *WGNNW/ST* WN6 .... 31 J5
Highcliffe Rd *BKLY* M9 .... 72 D1
Highclove La *WALK* M28 .... 68 C7
High Crest Av *CHD/CHDH* SK8 .... 110 C7
Highcrest Gv *TYLD* M29 .... 68 A3
Highcroft *BOL* BL1 .... 36 D1
 HYDE SK14 .... 102 B5
Highcroft Av *DID/WITH* M20 .... 98 B8
High Croft Cl *DUK* SK16 .... 91 K4
Highcroft Rd *MPL/ROM* SK6 .... 113 M1
Highcroft Wy *WHIT* OL12 .... 20 D8
Highdales Rd *NTHM/RTH* M23 .... 109 L7
High Elm Dr *HALE/TIMP* WA15 .... 117 L4
High Elm Rd *HALE/TIMP* WA15 .... 117 M5
High Elms *CHD/CHDH* SK8 .... 120 D7
Higher Ainsworth Rd *RAD* M26 .... 38 B5
Higher Ardwick
 WGTN/LGST M12 .... 7 M9
Higher Arthurs *UPML* OL3 .... 61 L6
Higher Bank Rd *LIT* OL15 .... 29 K1
Higher Barlow Rw *STKP* SK1 .... 13 K6
Higher Barn *HOR/BR* BL6 .... 34 C1
Higher Bank Rd *GLSP* SK13 .... 93 H8
Higher Bents La
 MPL/ROM SK6 .... 113 J1
Higher Bridge St *BOL* BL1 .... 2 E2
Higherbrook Cl *HOR/BR* BL6 .... 34 A3
Higher Bury St *HTNM* SK4 .... 12 E3
Higher Cambridge St
 HULME M15 .... 87 K7
Higher Carr La *UPML* OL3 .... 61 L5
Higher Chatham St
 HULME M15 * 87 K6
Higher Cleggswood Av
 LIT OL15 .... 29 K1
Higher Cft *ECC* M30 .... 84 D4
 WHTF M45 .... 54 F6
Higher Crossbank *OLDE* OL4 .... 60 C5
Higher Cross La *UPML* OL3 .... 61 M5
Higher Damshead *WHTN* BL5 .... 50 C4
Higher Darcy St *BOLE* BL2 .... 3 L8
Higher Dean St *RAD* M26 .... 54 B1
Higher Downs *ALT* WA14 .... 116 C1
Higher Drake Meadow
 WHTN BL5 .... 50 A7
Higher Dunscar *EDGW/EG* BL7 .... 22 B3
Higher Fold Farm
 MPL/ROM SK6 * 123 G3
Higher Fold La *RAMS* BL0 .... 19 H5
Higher Fullwood *OLD* OL1 .... 44 A8
Higher Gn *AUL* OL6 .... 75 M8
Higher Green La *TYLD* M29 .... 67 M6
Higher Henry St *HYDE* SK14 .... 102 A3
Higher Highfield Ct
 WGNE/HIN WN2 * 32 E6
Higher Hillgate *STKP* SK1 .... 13 K6
Higher House Cl *CHAD* OL9 .... 58 D8
Higher Knowles *HOR/BR* BL6 .... 34 B2
Higher La *WGNE/HIN* WN2 .... 32 D8
 WHTF M45 .... 55 H4
Higher Lime Rd *OLDS* OL8 .... 74 F4
Higher Ldg *WHIT* OL12 .... 26 F2
Higher Lomax La *HEY* OL10 .... 40 E1
Higher Lydgate Pk *OLDE* OL4 .... 60 F6
Higher Market St *FWTH* BL4 .... 53 H4
Higher Mdw *BNG/LEV* M19 .... 99 M3
Higher Ormond St
 HULME M15 * 87 K6
Higher Oswald St *ANC* M4 * 7 H2
Higher Pk *ROY/SHW* OL2 .... 43 M3
Higher Pit La *BOLE* BL2 .... 38 B4
Higher Ridings *EDGW/EG* BL7 .... 22 C5
Higher Ri *ROY/SHW* OL2 .... 43 K3
Higher Rd *URM* M41 .... 96 B2
Higher Rw *BURY* BL9 .... 5 K2
Higher Shady La *EDGW/EG* BL7 .... 22 F5
Higher Shore Rd *LIT* OL15 .... 21 J5
Higher Southfield *WHTN* BL5 .... 50 B5
Higher Summerseat *RAMS* BL0 .... 24 E3
Higher Swan La *BOLS/LL* BL3 .... 36 A8
Higher Tame St *STLY* SK15 .... 91 L2
Higher Turf La *OLDE* OL4 .... 60 E4
Higher Wharf St *AULW* OL7 .... 90 E2
Higher Wheat La *MILN* OL16 .... 11 L3
Higher Wood St *MDTN* M24 .... 57 J2
Highfield *CHD/CHDH* SK8 .... 119 L1
 SALE M33 .... 108 A1
 WGNS/IIMK WN3 .... 47 G8

Highfield Av *ATH* M46 .... 51 H7
 BOLE BL2 .... 37 K1
 GOL/RIS/CUL WA3 .... 79 J4
 HEY OL10 .... 40 D2
 LEIGH WN7 .... 81 H1
 MPL/ROM SK6 .... 113 J2
 RAD M26 .... 54 F3
 WALK M28 .... 69 J1
 WGN WN1 .... 15 L1
 WGNNW/ST WN6 .... 30 D7
Highfield Cl *EDGY/DAV* SK3 .... 112 C8
 HYDE SK14 .... 91 G7
 STRET M32 .... 96 F4
Highfield Crs *WILM/AE* SK9 .... 127 G3
Highfield Dr *ECC* M30 .... 85 G1
 FWTH BL4 .... 52 D5
 MDTN M24 .... 57 J3
 MOSL OL5 .... 76 C2
 ROY/SHW OL2 .... 59 H2
 SWIN M27 .... 70 A4
 URM M41 .... 95 M1
 WGNNW/ST WN6 .... 31 J5
Highfield Est
 WILM/AE SK9 .... 127 G3
Highfield Gdns *HYDE* SK14 .... 93 G7
 HYDE SK14 .... 102 C1
Highfield Gln *AUL* OL6 .... 76 C7
Highfield Grange Av
 WGNS/IIMK WN3 .... 63 G2
Highfield Gv
 WGNE/HIN WN2 .... 32 F7
Highfield La *BURY* BL9 .... 55 J1
 GOL/RIS/CUL WA3 .... 79 M7
Highfield Pk *HTNM* SK4 .... 111 J2
Highfield Park Rd
 BNG/LEV M19 .... 101 H8
Highfield Pkwy
 BRAM/HZG SK7 .... 120 F8
Highfield Pl *GTN* M18 * 89 J8
 PWCH M25 .... 55 K7
Highfield Range *GTN* M18 * 89 J8
Highfield Rd
 BNG/LEV M19 .... 99 M3
 BOL BL1 .... 35 J2
 BRAM/HZG SK7 .... 121 H1
 BRAM/HZG SK7 .... 122 C2
 CHD/CHDH SK8 .... 120 B3
 ECC M30 .... 70 A8
 FWTH BL4 .... 52 B4
 GLSP SK13 .... 105 G4
 HALE/TIMP WA15 .... 108 E1
 HALE/TIMP WA15 .... 117 J2
 HOR/BR BL6 .... 33 H3
 LHULT M38 .... 52 C7
 MILN OL16 .... 29 K6
 MPL/ROM SK6 .... 114 C2
 POY/DIS SK12 * 121 J8
 PWCH M25 .... 55 K6
 RAMS BL0 .... 19 G1
 ROCH OL11 .... 27 H3
 SLFD M6 .... 86 C1
 STRET M32 .... 96 F4
Highfield St *BRO* M7 .... 72 C5
 CHAD OL9 .... 8 C8
 DTN/ASHW M34 .... 90 C6
 DUK SK16 .... 90 E3
 EDGY/DAV SK3 .... 12 C6
 MDTN M24 .... 57 L4
Highfield Ter *BKLY* M9 .... 73 C4
 NM/HAY SK22 * 124 F4
 OLDE OL4 .... 60 A2
Highgate *BOLS/LL* BL3 .... 50 F2
 URM M41 .... 84 D8
Highgate Crs *GTN* M18 .... 89 C8
 WGNNW/ST WN6 .... 30 B5
Highgate Dr *LHULT* M38 .... 52 B7
 ROY/SHW OL2 .... 42 F5
 WHIT OL12 .... 20 A6
Highgate La *LHULT* M38 .... 52 B7
Highgate Rd *ALT* WA14 .... 107 L8
 NM/HAY SK22 .... 125 M2
High Gates *SALE* M33 .... 97 H7
Highgrove *HALE/TIMP* WA15 .... 108 D3
Highgrove Cl *BOL* BL1 .... 36 C1
High Grove Rd *CHD/CHDH* SK8 .... 110 F7
 OLDE OL4 .... 61 H7
The Highgrove *BOL* BL1 .... 35 J5
High Hill Rd *NM/HAY* SK22 .... 124 F3
High Houses *BOL* BL1 * 22 A6
High Hurst Cl *MDTN* M24 * 56 F5
Highland Rd *EDGW/EG* BL7 .... 22 F4
 HOR/BR BL6 .... 34 B3
Highlands *LIT* OL15 .... 29 K1
 ROY/SHW OL2 .... 58 F1
Highlands Dr *OFTN* SK2 .... 113 J6
Highlands Rd *OFTN* SK2 .... 113 J6
 ROCH OL11 .... 27 G7
 ROY/SHW OL2 .... 43 J4
 ROY/SHW OL2 .... 58 F1
The Highlands *MOSL* OL5 * 76 E3
High La *CCHDY* M21 .... 97 L4
 GLSP SK13 .... 104 B5
 MPL/ROM SK6 .... 101 C8
High Lea *CHD/CHDH* SK8 .... 110 F7
High Lea Rd *NM/HAY* SK22 .... 124 C4
High Lee La *OLDE* OL4 .... 44 E8
High Legh Rd *OP/CLY* M11 .... 89 G4
High Level Rd *ROCH* OL11 .... 10 F7
Highmarsh Crs *NEWLW* WA12 .... 78 E9
High Meadow
 CHD/CHDH SK8 * 120 A4
Highmeadow *RAD* M26 .... 54 C3
High Mdw *EDGW/EG* BL7 .... 22 E4
 GLSP SK13 .... 104 E5
 MPL/ROM SK6 .... 113 M1
Highmead St *GTN* M18 .... 89 G7
Highmead Wk *OLDTF/WHR* M16 * 87 G7
High Moor Crs *OLDE* OL4 .... 60 B3
Highmore Dr *BKLY* M9 .... 73 H1
High Mt *BOLE* BL2 .... 37 H1
High Pk *WGNNW/ST* WN6 .... 30 F6
High Peak Rd *AUL* OL6 .... 76 D6
 WHIT OL12 .... 20 A6
High Peak St *NEWH/MOS* M40 .... 73 L6
High Rid La *HOR/BR* BL6 .... 34 E3
Highshore Dr *CHH* M8 .... 72 C5
High Stile St *FWTH* BL4 .... 53 H5
Highstone Dr *CHH* M8 .... 72 C6
Highstones Gdns *GLSP* SK13 * 105 J2
High St *ALT* WA14 .... 108 A5
 ANC M4 .... 7 G2
 ATH M46 .... 67 G4
 BOLS/LL BL3 .... 36 B8
 BRAM/HZG SK7 .... 122 B2
 CHD/CHDH SK8 .... 111 H4
 DROY M43 .... 89 K3
 EDGW/EG BL7 .... 16 F7
 GOL/RIS/CUL WA3 .... 79 K4
 HEY OL10 .... 40 C7

HYDE SK14 .... 102 C2
 LEIGH WN7 .... 66 D3
 LIT OL15 .... 21 K7
 MDTN M24 .... 57 K3
 MOSL OL5 .... 77 G2
 NEWLW WA12 .... 79 G8
 NM/HAY SK22 .... 124 E4
 OLD OL1 .... 9 G6
 OLDE OL4 .... 60 B6
 ROY/SHW OL2 * 43 G8
 STKP SK1 .... 13 J4
 STLY SK15 .... 91 K5
 TOT/BURYW BL8 .... 38 C1
 TYLD M29 .... 67 J3
 TYLD M29 .... 67 L7
 UPML OL3 .... 45 J8
 UPML OL3 .... 61 L4
 WALK M28 .... 68 F1
 WGN WN1 .... 48 A2
 WGNE/HIN WN2 .... 48 E1
 WGNNW/ST WN3 .... 31 J1
 WHIT OL12 .... 10 E3
High St East *GLSP* SK13 .... 105 G3
High St West *GLSP* SK13 .... 104 E3
Highthorne Gn *ROY/SHW* OL2 .... 42 F4
Highview *GLSP* SK13 .... 104 D5
High View St *BOL* BL1 .... 22 B7
 BOLS/LL BL3 * 35 M8
Highwood *ROCH* OL11 .... 27 H5
Highwood Cl *BOLE* BL2 * 37 J3
 GLSP SK13 .... 104 C5
High Wood Fold
 MPL/ROM SK6 .... 114 F4
Highwoods Cl *AIMK* WN4 .... 63 L7
Highworth Cl *BOLS/LL* BL3 * 2 C9
Highworth Dr *NEWH/MOS* M40 .... 74 A2
Higifield Av *SALE* M33 .... 108 C1
Higson Av *CCHDY* M21 .... 97 L5
 ECC M30 .... 84 F4
 MPL/ROM SK6 .... 113 J2
Hilary Av *ATH* M46 .... 50 F7
 CHD/CHDH SK8 .... 119 M4
 GOL/RIS/CUL WA3 .... 80 A3
 OLDS OL8 .... 75 J3
Hilary Gv *FWTH* BL4 .... 52 F5
Hilary Rd *WYTH/NTH* M22 .... 118 D3
Hilary St *ROCH* OL11 * 42 A3
Hilbre Av *ROY/SHW* OL2 .... 59 C2
Hilbury Av *BKLY* M9 .... 73 C3
Hilda Av *CHD/CHDH* SK8 .... 111 H7
 TOT/BURYW BL8 .... 24 C6
Hilda Gv *RDSH* SK5 .... 100 C8
Hilda Rd *HYDE* SK14 .... 102 A5
Hilda St *BOLS/LL* BL3 .... 36 D8
 CHAD OL9 .... 8 F4
 HEY OL10 .... 40 D1
 LEIGH WN7 .... 65 M6
Hilden Ct *OLDTF/WHR* M16 * 87 G8
Hilden St *BOLE* BL2 .... 3 H6
Hildbrook Cl *NTHM/RTH* M23 .... 109 L6
Hildyard St
 WGNW/BIL/OR WN5 .... 14 A8
Hiley Rd *ECC* M30 .... 84 C4
Hilgay Cl *WGNS/IIMK* WN3 .... 63 G1
Hillam Cl *URM* M41 .... 96 C3
Hillary Av *AULW* OL7 .... 75 L7
Hillary Rd *HYDE* SK14 .... 91 K7
Hillbank *WGNNW/ST* WN6 .... 31 K1
Hillbank Cl *BOL* BL1 .... 35 M1
Hill Bank Cl *STLY* SK15 .... 77 G7
Hillbank St *MDTN* M24 .... 42 A6
Hillbeck Crs *AIMK* WN4 .... 63 G8
Hillbre Wy *WILM/AE* SK9 .... 119 M8
Hillbrook Av *NEWH/MOS* M40 .... 73 L2
Hillbrook Rd *BRAM/HZG* SK7 .... 120 F6
 STKP SK1 .... 112 F4
Hillbury Rd *BRAM/HZG* SK7 .... 121 H3
Hill Cl *OLDE* OL4 .... 59 M7
 OLDE OL4 .... 30 B5
Hillcote Wk *GTN* M18 * 88 E6
Hill Cot Rd *BOL* BL1 .... 22 C7
Hill Court Ms *MPL/ROM* SK6 .... 113 L2
Hillcourt Rd *MPL/ROM* SK6 .... 113 L2
 MPL/ROM SK6 .... 123 C5
Hillcourt St *CMANE* M1 * 7 H9
Hill Crs *BKLY* M9 .... 72 D1
 LEIGH WN7 .... 81 G2
Hill Crest *ATH* M46 .... 51 J7
Hillcrest *HYDE* SK14 .... 102 C5
 MDTN M24 .... 57 J1
 SLFD M6 * 85 K1
 WGNE/HIN WN2 .... 64 D7
Hillcrest Av *HEY* OL10 .... 40 D4
 LEIGH WN7 .... 81 G2
Hillcrest Crs *HEY* OL10 .... 40 D4
Hillcrest Dr *BNG/LEV* M19 .... 99 M5
 DTN/ASHW M34 .... 101 L3
Hillcrest Rd *BRAM/HZG* SK7 .... 121 H3
 OFTN SK2 .... 112 F6
 PWCH M25 .... 55 M7
 ROCH OL11 .... 41 M2
 TYLD M29 .... 67 G3
Hillcroft *OFTN* SK2 .... 113 H6
 OLDS OL8 .... 75 K4
Hillcroft Cl *CHH* M8 .... 72 D4
Hilldale Av *BKLY* M9 .... 57 G8
Hill Dr *WILM/AE* SK9 .... 127 H5
Hill End *MPL/ROM* SK6 * 102 A8
Hillend *MPL/ROM* SK6 .... 102 A8
Hillend La *HYDE* SK14 .... 103 J3
Hillend Pl *NTHM/RTH* M23 .... 109 K2
Hillend Rd *NTHM/RTH* M23 .... 109 K2
Hill End Rd *UPML* OL3 .... 45 J8
Hill Farm Cl *OLDS* OL8 .... 75 L1
Hillfield *ORD* M5 .... 6 B9
Hillfield Cl *BRUN/LGST* M13 .... 88 A7
Hillfield Dr *BOLE* BL2 .... 38 D5
 WALK M28 .... 68 D5
Hillfoot Wk *HULME* M15 * 87 G6
Hillgate Av *ORD* M5 .... 86 B8
Hillgate St *AUL* OL6 .... 75 M8
Hillgate St *BKLY* M9 .... 73 H4
Hillier St North *BKLY* M9 .... 73 H4
Hillier St *BKLY* M9 .... 73 H4
Hillingdon Dr *NEWH/MOS* M40 .... 73 L2
Hillingdon Rd *STRET* M32 .... 97 H2
 WHTF M45 .... 54 F5
Hillington Rd *EDGY/DAV* SK3 .... 111 M6
 SALE M33 .... 96 B8
Hillkirk Dr *WHIT* OL12 .... 10 D1
Hillkirk St *OP/CLY* M11 .... 88 B1
Hill La *BKLY* M9 .... 57 G8
 BOLE BL2 .... 3 H1
 HOR/BR BL6 .... 32 E1
Hillman Cl *NEWH/MOS* M40 .... 73 H7

Hill Mt DUK SK16 91 K4
Hillreed WGNNW/ST WN6 14 A1
Hill Ri ALT WA14 107 K7
MPL/ROM SK6 113 L2
RAMS BL0 18 D8
Hillsborough Dr BURY BL9 55 L2
Hill's Ct TOT/BURYW BL8 24 E8
Hillsdale Gv BOLE BL2 37 H1
Hill Side BOL BL1 35 J5
Hillside Av AIMK WN4 63 J4
ATH M46 51 H8
BRO M7 71 K4
EDGW/EG BL7 22 E5
FWTH BL4 52 F5
HOR/BR BL6 33 H3
HYDE SK14 102 C6
OLDE OL4 59 M5
OLDE OL4 60 E7
ROY/SHW OL2 43 H7
ROY/SHW OL2 44 A5
STLY SK15 77 J6
UPML OL3 61 M1
WALK M28 52 F8
WHTF M45 55 H2
Hillside Cl BOLE BL2 23 H7
BOLS/LL BL3 51 G2
BRAM/HZG SK7 121 J5
GLSP SK13 104 B1
NEWH/MOS M40 73 K3
POY/DIS SK12 123 M6
WGNS/IIMK WN3 63 G1
WGNW/BIL/OR WN5 62 A8
Hillside Crs AUL OL6 76 C7
BURY BL9 25 J6
Hillside Dr MDTN M24 57 L3
SWIN M27 71 G6
Hillside Gv MPL/ROM SK6 114 E3
Hillside Rd HALE/TIMP WA15 117 J1
MPL/ROM SK6 101 M7
OFTN SK2 113 G5
RAMS BL0 18 D7
Hillside St BOLS/LL BL3 2 A9
Hillside Vw DTN/ASHW M34 101 K5
NM/HAY SK22 124 C4
Hillside Wk WHIT OL12 20 B8
Hillside Wy WHIT OL12 20 A3
Hills La BURY BL9 55 M2
Hillspring Rd OLDE OL4 60 D6
Hillstone Av WHIT OL12 20 A8
Hillstone Cl TOT/BURYW BL8 24 C2
Hill St AULW OL7 90 D2
BRO M7 72 A6
BURY BL9 24 F1
DID/WITH M20 98 E5
HEY OL10 40 F2
LEIGH WN7 66 B7
MDTN M24 57 K1
MILN OL16 11 H4
MPL/ROM SK6 113 L2
OLDE OL4 59 L5
RAD M26 38 C8
ROY/SHW OL2 43 M6
TOT/BURYW BL8 24 C8
WGNE/HIN WN2 49 G6
WGNNW/ST WN6 14 D1
Hill Top ATH M46 51 J7
BOLS/LL BL3 37 K8
HALE/TIMP WA15 117 J3
MPL/ROM SK6 113 L1
Hill Top Av CHD/CHDH SK8 120 D4
PWCH M25 55 L8
WILM/AE SK9 126 F4
Hilltop Av BKLY M9 73 G1
WHTF M45 55 L4
Hill Top Ct CHD/CHDH SK8 120 D3
Hill Top Dr HALE/TIMP WA15 117 J2
ROCH OL11 42 D2
Hilltop Dr MPL/ROM SK6 113 M5
ROY/SHW OL2 59 H2
TOT/BURYW BL8 24 B6
Hilltop Gv WHTF M45 55 L4
Hill Top La UPML OL3 45 G8
Hilltop Rd GLSP SK13 104 E1
Hill Top Rd WALK M28 53 G8
Hill Vw STLY SK15 92 A6
Hill View Cl OLD OL1 59 M2
Hillview Rd BOL BL1 * 22 B8
DTN/ASHW M34 100 D3
Hillwood Av CHH M8 72 C1
Hillwood Dr GLSP SK13 105 J4
Hillyard St TOT/BURYW BL8 38 F1
Hilly Cft EDGW/EG BL7 22 C4
Hilmarton Cl BOLE BL2 23 H7
Hilrose Av URM M41 96 C2
Hilton Av HOR/BR BL6 33 K1
URM M41 96 A2
Hilton Cl LEIGH WN7 66 D7
Hilton Ct EDGY/DAV SK3 * 13 G6
Hilton Crs AUL OL6 75 M7
PWCH M25 71 L2
WALK M28 68 E6
Hilton Dr AULW OL7 75 J7
PWCH M25 71 L2
Hilton Fold La MDTN M24 57 L3
Hilton Gv POY/DIS SK12 121 M8
WALK M28 68 E1
Hilton La PWCH M25 71 K2
WALK M28 68 E2
Hilton Pl WGNE/HIN WN2 32 F6
Hilton Rd BRAM/HZG SK7 121 H2
BURY BL9 4 F5
POY/DIS SK12 122 E7
POY/DIS SK12 123 K5
WYTH/NTH M22 110 B7
Hiltons Cl OLDS OL8 9 G9
Hiltons Farm Cl
DTN/ASHW M34 90 B7
Hilton Sq SWIN M27 70 D3
Hilton St AIMK WN4 78 E1
ANC M4 7 H3
BOLE BL2 3 M4
BRO M7 72 B7
BURY BL9 5 G1
EDGY/DAV SK3 12 F6
HYDE SK14 * 91 J7
LHULT M38 52 D8
WGN WN1 15 H2
WGNS/IIMK WN3 15 K8
Hilton St North BRO M7 72 A6
Hilton Wk MDTN M24 56 F4
Himley Rd OP/CLY M11 88 F1
Hinchcombe Cl LHULT M38 * 52 D6
Hinchley Rd BKLY M9 73 L1
Hinchley Wy SWIN M27 70 C2
Hinckley St OP/CLY M11 88 C4
Hindburn Cl WHTF M45 55 L4
Hindburn Dr WALK M28 68 D4
Hinde St NEWH/MOS M40 73 K4
Hind Hill St HEY OL10 41 G3
Hindle Dr ROY/SHW OL2 58 F1
Hindles Cl ATH M46 66 D2
Hindle St RAD M26 54 D1
Hindley Av WYTH/NTH M22 118 D2
Hindley Mill La WGNE/HIN WN2 49 H5
Hindley Rd WHTN BL5 50 A7
Hindley St AULW OL7 90 C3
STKP SK1 13 K7
Hindley Wk WGN WN1 * 14 F3
Hind Rd WGNW/BIL/OR WN5 47 G4
Hindsford Cl NTHM/RTH M23 109 G3
Hindsford St ATH M46 67 J3
Hinds La BURY BL9 38 F5
TOT/BURYW BL8 4 A8
Hind St BOLE BL2 3 M4
Hinkler Av BOLS/LL BL3 52 D1
Hinton WHIT OL12 10 B1
Hinton Cl ROCH OL11 27 H6
Hinton Gv HYDE SK14 102 D4
Hinton St ANC M4 * 7 K1
OLDS OL8 9 K8
Hipley Cl MPL/ROM SK6 101 K7
Hirons La OLDE OL4 60 D7
Hirst Av WALK M28 53 G7
Hitchen Cl DUK SK16 91 J5
Hitchen Dr DUK SK16 91 J5
Hitchin Wk BRUN/LGST M13 87 M7
Hive St OLDS OL8 74 E2
Hoade St WGNE/HIN WN2 49 H5
Hobart Cl BRAM/HZG SK7 121 H8
Hobart St BOL BL1 36 A2
GTN M18 89 G7
Hobby Gv LEIGH WN7 66 E7
Hob Hey La GOL/RIS/CUL WA3 81 G8
Hob Hl STLY SK15 91 J3
Hobhill Mdw GLSP SK13 105 G5
Hob La EDGW/EG BL7 16 F5
Hob Mill Ri MOSL OL5 61 H8
Hobson Ct DTN/ASHW M34 90 B6
Hobson Crs DTN/ASHW M34 90 B6
Hobson Moor Rd HYDE SK14 92 C6
Hobson St FAIL M35 74 A6
OLD OL1 9 J7
OP/CLY M11 89 K5
RDSH SK5 100 C2
Hockenhull Cl WYTH/NTH M22 119 G2
Hocker La MCFLDN SK10 130 E7
Hockerley Cl SALE M33 96 A7
Hockery Vw WGNE/HIN WN2 48 F8
Hockley Cl POY/DIS SK12 129 K1
Hockley Paddock
POY/DIS SK12 129 K1
Hockley Rd NTHM/RTH M23 109 J7
POY/DIS SK12 129 K1
Hodder Av LIT OL15 21 K6
WGNE/HIN WN2 64 C2
Hodder Bank OFTN SK2 113 H7
Hodder Cl WGNW/BIL/OR WN5 47 G5
Hodder Wy WHTF M45 55 M4
Hoddesdon St CHH M8 72 E5
Hodge Clough Rd OLD OL1 43 M8
Hodge La HYDE SK14 103 J4
SLFD M6 86 C3
Hodge Rd OLD OL1 60 A1
WALK M28 69 G2
Hodges St WGNNW/ST WN6 47 K2
Hodge St BKLY M9 73 J3
Hodgson Dr HALE/TIMP WA15 108 D4
Hodgson St AUL OL6 90 D2
CHH M8 72 C7
Hodnet Dr AIMK WN4 78 F1
Hodnett Av URM M41 95 H3
Hodson Fold OLDS OL8 75 H2
Hodson Rd SWIN M27 70 B2
Hodson St WGNS/IIMK WN3 14 F6
Hogarth Ri OLD OL1 44 A8
Hogarth Rd MPL/ROM SK6 114 E4
ROCH OL11 42 C2
Holbeach Cl TOT/BURYW BL8 25 G7
WGNE/HIN WN2 49 H8
Holbeck TYLD M29 67 L7
Holbeck Av WHIT OL12 20 B8
Holbeck Cl HOR/BR BL6 34 A4
Holbeck Gv RUSH/FAL M14 88 B8
Holbeton Cl CHH M8 72 B7
Holborn Av FAIL M35 74 E5
LEIGH WN7 66 C4
RAD M26 38 B8
WGNS/IIMK WN3 14 D9
Holborn Dr CHH M8 72 E7
Holborn Gdns ROCH OL11 10 A8
Holborn Sq ROCH OL11 10 A8
Holborn St ROCH OL11 10 A8
STKP SK1 13 J5
Holbrook Av LHULT M38 52 D6
Holbrook St CMANE M1 * 7 H7
Holcombe Av GOL/RIS/CUL WA3 79 M4
TOT/BURYW BL8 38 E2
Holcombe Cl ALT WA14 107 L6
FWTH BL4 53 K7
OLDE OL4 60 D5
SLFD M6 86 D2
Holcombe Ct RAMS BL0 24 C2
Holcombe Crs FWTH BL4 53 K6
Holcombe Lee RAMS BL0 24 D1
Holcombe Old Rd
TOT/BURYW BL8 18 D7
TOT/BURYW BL8 24 C1
Holcombe Rd BOLS/LL BL3 53 J1
RUSH/FAL M14 99 H5
TOT/BURYW BL8 24 C2
Holcombe View Cl OLDE OL4 60 A2
Holden Av BOL BL1 22 B6
BURY BL9 26 B8
OLDTF/WHR M16 98 B3
RAMS BL0 18 D7
Holden Brook Cl LEIGH WN7 66 E7
Holden Clough Dr AULW OL7 75 L5
Holden Fold La ROY/SHW OL2 58 F2
Holden Lea WHTN BL5 50 B1
Holden Rd BRO M7 72 A3
LEIGH WN7 66 D7
Holden St AUL OL6 75 M8
OLDS OL8 75 J1
WHIT OL12 * 28 D2
Holden Wk WGNW/BIL/OR WN5 47 H7
Holder Av BOLS/LL BL3 37 L7
Holderness Dr ROY/SHW OL2 58 F2
Holdgate Cl HULME M15 87 H7
Holding St WGNE/HIN WN2 49 G6
Holdsworth St SWIN M27 70 A5
Holebottom AUL OL6 75 M6
Hole House Fold
MPL/ROM SK6 113 L2
Holford Av RUSH/FAL M14 98 E2
Holford Wk MILN OL16 29 G5
Holgate Dr WGNW/BIL/OR WN5 46 B7
Holgate St OLDE OL4 60 B3
Holhouse La TOT/BURYW BL8 24 C2
Holiday La OFTN SK2 113 J6
Holkar Mdw EDGW/EG BL7 22 E4
Holker Cl BRUN/LGST M13 88 A8
POY/DIS SK12 122 B8
Holkham Cl ANC M4 * 7 M3
Holland Av STLY SK15 91 K2
Holland Cl UPML OL3 45 H8
Holland Ct POY/DIS SK12 129 J1
RAD M26 38 F8
Holland Gv AUL OL6 75 L6
Holland Ri WHIT OL12 10 D3
Holland Rd BRAM/HZG SK7 121 G5
CHH M8 72 C2
HYDE SK14 91 J7
Holland St BOL BL1 22 C8
DTN/ASHW M34 90 A8
HEY OL10 41 G2
MILN OL16 21 H8
NEWH/MOS M40 88 A2
RAD M26 38 F8
SLFD M6 71 J7
WHIT OL12 10 C4
Holland St East
DTN/ASHW M34 90 A8
Holland St West
DTN/ASHW M34 89 M8
Hollies Dr MPL/ROM SK6 114 D7
Hollies La WILM/AE SK9 127 K5
The Hollies ATH M46 * 67 G1
CHD/CHDH SK8 * 110 E7
DID/WITH M20 110 C1
WGN WN1 48 A1
WGNE/HIN WN2 * 32 F7
Hollin Acre WHTN BL5 50 C4
Hollin Bank HTNM SK4 100 A5
Hollinbrook WGNNW/ST WN6 47 J2
Hollin Crs UPML OL3 61 H8
Hollin Cross La GLSP SK13 104 F4
Hollin Dr MDTN M24 41 H8
Holliney Av WYTH/NTH M22 119 H3
Holliney Rd WYTH/NTH M22 119 H3
Holling Gn MDTN M24 57 K1
Hollingwood Cl AIMK WN4 78 D1
Hollingworth Av
NEWH/MOS M40 74 C2
Hollingworth Cl STKP SK1 * 13 J6
Hollingworth Dr
MPL/ROM SK6 123 H1
Hollingworth Fold LIT OL15 * 29 M2
Hollingworth Rd LIT OL15 21 M8
MPL/ROM SK6 101 H8
Hollingworth St CHAD OL9 74 E1
Hollinhall St OLDE OL4 59 M5
Hollin Hey Rd BOL BL1 35 H1
Hollinhey Ter HYDE SK14 92 F8
Hollinhurst Dr HOR/BR BL6 34 F5
Hollinhurst Rd RAD M26 54 F2
Hollin La MDTN M24 41 J8
ROCH OL11 27 H6
WILM/AE SK9 119 H7
Hollins FWTH BL4 * 52 A4
Hollins Av HYDE SK14 102 B5
OLDE OL4 60 C4
Hollins Brook Cl BURY BL9 * 39 L7
Hollins Brook Wy BURY BL9 39 L6
Hollins Brow BURY BL9 39 J8
Hollins Cl AIMK WN4 63 G8
BURY BL9 39 L8
TYLD M29 67 K4
Hollinsclough Cl
WYTH/NTH M22 110 B7
Hollinscroft Av
HALE/TIMP WA15 109 G7
Hollins Green Rd
MPL/ROM SK6 114 C6
Hollins Gv SALE M33 96 D8
WGTN/LGST M12 99 K1
Hollins La BURY BL9 39 K7
MOSL OL5 77 G3
MPL/ROM SK6 114 C6
MPL/ROM SK6 114 F4
RAMS BL0 19 H3
Hollins Ms BURY BL9 39 M8
GLSP SK13 104 A2
Hollinsmoor Rd NM/HAY SK22 115 M5
Hollins Mt MPL/ROM SK6 114 E4
Hollins Rd OLDE OL4 60 C4
OLDS OL8 74 F2
OLDS OL8 75 J1
WGNE/HIN WN2 49 K7
WGNS/IIMK WN3 63 K1
Hollins St BOLE BL2 3 J7
OLDE OL4 60 C6
STLY SK15 91 J4
Hollinswood Rd BOLE BL2 3 K6
WALK M28 68 E6
Hollinwell Cl MDTN M24 41 J8
Hollinwood Av CHAD OL9 74 D2
NEWH/MOS M40 74 A2
Hollinwood La MPL/ROM SK6 123 K2
Hollinwood Rd POY/DIS SK12 123 M6
Holloway Dr WALK M28 69 M3
Hollowbrook Wy WHIT OL12 28 A2
Hollowell La HOR/BR BL6 34 A3
Hollow End RDSH SK5 100 E5
Hollowfield ROCH OL11 27 G3
Hollow Mdw RAD M26 53 M6
Hollowspell WHIT OL12 28 F1
The Hollows CHD/CHDH SK8 * 119 L3
Hollow Vale Dr RDSH SK5 100 D4
Holly Av CHD/CHDH SK8 111 G7
URM M41 95 L2
WALK M28 69 H2
Holly Bank DROY M43 89 M1
GLSP SK13 105 H4
HYDE SK14 93 G7
NEWH/MOS M40 * 73 M5
ROY/SHW OL2 43 G7
SALE M33 108 F1
Hollybank Ri DUK SK16 91 J4
Holly Bank Rd WILM/AE SK9 126 F3
Hollybank St RAD M26 54 C1
Hollybrook Dene
MPL/ROM SK6 114 B2
Hollybush Sq GOL/RIS/CUL WA3 80 B3
Hollybush St GTN M18 89 H6
Holly Cl HALE/TIMP WA15 108 D6
Holly Ct HYDE SK14 102 D2
Hollycroft Av BOLE BL2 37 H7
WYTH/NTH M22 110 A6
Hollydene WGNE/HIN WN2 * 32 E7
Holly Dene Dr HOR/BR BL6 34 E5
Holly Dr SALE M33 96 D8
Hollyedge Dr PWCH M25 71 K2
Holly Fold WHTF M45 55 J3
Holly Gra ALT WA14 116 F2
BRAM/HZG SK7 121 H1
Holly Gv BOL BL1 35 M3
CHAD OL9 8 B3
DTN/ASHW M34 101 K1
FWTH BL4 52 D4
HOR/BR BL6 34 E5
LEIGH WN7 66 B5
OLDE OL4 60 B4
SALE M33 97 G8
STLY SK15 91 H4
Holly Heath Dr WGN WN1 31 L8
Hollyhedge Av
WYTH/NTH M22 110 A7
Hollyhedge Court Rd
WYTH/NTH M22 110 B7
Hollyhedge Rd
NTHM/RTH M23 109 L7
Hollyhey Dr NTHM/RTH M23 109 L3
Hollyhouse Dr MPL/ROM SK6 101 K7
Holly House Dr URM M41 95 J2
Hollyhurst WALK M28 69 L6
Holly La OLDS OL8 74 F2
WILM/AE SK9 119 G7
Holly Mill Crs BOL BL1 22 C8
Hollymount Av OFTN SK2 112 F7
Hollymount Dr OFTN SK2 112 F7
OLDE OL4 60 B1
Hollymount Gdns OFTN SK2 113 G7
Hollymount Rd OFTN SK2 112 F7
Holly Oak Gdns HEY OL10 40 F3
Holly Rd BRAM/HZG SK7 121 G7
GOL/RIS/CUL WA3 79 M4
HTNM SK4 99 M7
MPL/ROM SK6 123 H5
POY/DIS SK12 129 J1
SWIN M27 70 A6
WGNE/HIN WN2 32 E7
WGNW/BIL/OR WN5 47 H6
Holly Rd North WILM/AE SK9 126 E6
Holly Rd South WILM/AE SK9 126 E7
Holly Royde Cl DID/WITH M20 98 D6
Holly St BOL BL1 22 C8
BURY BL9 5 J4
BURY BL9 24 F1
DROY M43 89 G2
MILN OL16 42 E2
STKP SK1 13 M5
TOT/BURYW BL8 24 C6
WGTN/LGST M12 88 B4
WHIT OL12 21 G6
Hollythorn Av CHD/CHDH SK8 120 E5
Hollyway WYTH/NTH M22 110 B4
Hollywood Rd BOL BL1 35 L2
MPL/ROM SK6 115 H4
Hollywood Wy HTNM SK4 12 E5
Holmbrook TYLD M29 67 M3
Holmbrook Wk CHH M8 72 D6
Holm Ct SLFD M6 * 86 D1
Holmcroft Rd GTN M18 100 A2
Holmdale Av BNG/LEV M19 99 H7
Holme Av TOT/BURYW BL8 24 F7
WGN WN1 47 M2
Holme Beech Gv OFTN SK2 * 112 F4
Holmebrook Dr HOR/BR BL6 34 A4
Holme Ct WGN WN1 * 47 M2
Holme Crs ROY/SHW OL2 58 F2
Holmefield SALE M33 96 E8
Holme Park Gdns WALK M28 68 D7
Holme Park Wy FAIL M35 74 E5
Holme Rd DID/WITH M20 110 C1
Holmes Cottages BOL BL1 * 35 M1
Holmes House Av
WGNS/IIMK WN3 62 F1
Holmes Rd WHIT OL12 10 B4
Holmes St BOLS/LL BL3 36 C8
CHD/CHDH SK8 111 H6
OFTN SK2 13 H8
WHIT OL12 10 B3
WHIT OL12 28 F1
Holme St HYDE SK14 102 A2
Holmeswood Cl WILM/AE SK9 127 G4
Holmeswood Rd BOLS/LL BL3 52 A2
Holme Ter WGN WN1 47 L1
Holmfield Av BKLY M9 73 J5
PWCH M25 71 M1
Holmfield Av West BKLY M9 73 J6
Holmfield Cl HTNM SK4 112 A1
Holmfield Dr CHD/CHDH SK8 120 D4
Holmfield Gn BOLS/LL BL3 51 J1
Holmfirth St BRUN/LGST M13 88 C8
Holmlea Rd DROY M43 89 H2
Holmleigh Av BKLY M9 73 H3
Holmpark Rd OP/CLY M11 89 J5
Holmsfield Cl WGNE/HIN WN2 48 D2
Holmside Gdns BNG/LEV M19 99 G8
Holmwood ALT WA14 116 C1
Holmwood Cl AIMK WN4 63 K7
Holmwood Rd DID/WITH M20 98 E7
Holroyd St MILN OL16 11 G5
OP/CLY M11 * 88 D4
Holset Dr ALT WA14 107 L7
Holst Av CHH M8 72 D6
Holstein Av WHIT OL12 20 B8
Holt Av WGNW/BIL/OR WN5 62 A8
Holtby St BKLY M9 73 H3
Holt Crs WGNW/BIL/OR WN5 62 A8
Holthouse Rd TOT/BURYW BL8 24 B7
Holt La FAIL M35 74 E5
Holt Lane Ms FAIL M35 74 D5
Holton Wy WGNS/IIMK WN3 63 H3
Holts La OLDE OL4 60 A8
WILM/AE SK9 126 D1
Holts Ter WHIT OL12 28 B2
Holt St ALT WA14 107 M5
BOLS/LL BL3 2 A8
DTN/ASHW M34 90 B4
ECC M30 84 F4
LEIGH WN7 66 B5
MILN OL16 * 29 K7
NEWH/MOS M40 73 J7
OLDE OL4 59 M4
RAMS BL0 19 G6
STKP SK1 13 K7
SWIN M27 70 C2
TYLD M29 67 K3
WGN WN1 15 M4
WGNE/HIN WN2 48 F7
WGNNW/ST WN6 47 J3
WGNS/IIMK WN3 47 K8
WGNW/BIL/OR WN5 46 A7
WHIT OL12 20 A3
Holt St West RAMS BL0 18 E7
Holtswell Cl GOL/RIS/CUL WA3 80 B3
Holt Town NEWH/MOS M40 88 B2
Holwick Rd NTHM/RTH M23 109 J3
Holwood Dr OLDTF/WHR M16 98 B4
Holy Harbour St BOL BL1 * 35 M2
Holyhurst Wk BOL BL1 * 36 B2
Holyoake Rd WALK M28 69 G2
Holyoake St DROY M43 89 M2
Holyoak St NEWH/MOS M40 73 M6
Holyrood Cl PWCH M25 55 M6
Holyrood Dr PWCH M25 55 M6
SWIN M27 69 M5
Holyrood Gv PWCH M25 55 M6
Holyrood Rd PWCH M25 55 M7
Holyrood St NEWH/MOS M40 74 A8
OLD OL1 59 K3
Holywood St RUSH/FAL M14 98 E1
Homebury Dr OP/CLY M11 * 88 E2
Home Dr MDTN M24 57 J6
Home Farm Av HYDE SK14 103 J3
Homelands Cl SALE M33 108 C2
Homelands Rd SALE M33 108 C2
Homer Dr MPL/ROM SK6 114 E4
Homerton Rd NEWH/MOS M40 73 L8
Homestead Av
RNFD/HAY WA11 * 78 B5
Homestead Cl PART M31 94 D8
Homestead Crs BNG/LEV M19 111 G1
Homestead Gdns WHIT OL12 21 H7
Homestead Rd POY/DIS SK12 123 L6
Hometel RUSH/FAL M14 98 F3
Homewood Av
WYTH/NTH M22 110 A3
Homewood Rd
WYTH/NTH M22 109 M3
Honduras St OLDE OL4 9 M5
Hondwith Cl BOLE BL2 22 E7
Honeybourne Cl TYLD M29 67 M3
Honeycombe Cottages
CHD/CHDH SK8 * 111 H7
Honey St CHH M8 72 D8
Honeysuckle Av
WGNNW/ST WN6 47 J1
Honeysuckle Cl MPL/ROM SK6 101 K7
NTHM/RTH M23 109 G3
Honeysuckle Dr STLY SK15 91 L2
Honeysuckle Wy WHIT OL12 28 A1
Honeywell La OLDS OL8 75 J1
Honeywood Cl RAMS BL0 24 D1
Honford Rd WYTH/NTH M22 109 L8
Hong Kong Av
HALE/TIMP WA15 118 C4
Honister Dr MDTN M24 57 J2
Honister Rd BKLY M9 73 J5
WGNW/BIL/OR WN5 46 E6
Honister Wy ROCH OL11 27 L8
Honiton Av HYDE SK14 102 F2
Honiton Cl CHAD OL9 58 B3
HEY OL10 40 F4
LEIGH WN7 66 A2
Honiton Dr BOLE BL2 37 K6
Honiton Gv RAD M26 38 A7
Honiton Wy ALT WA14 107 L6
Honor St BRUN/LGST M13 99 H1
Hood Cl TYLD M29 68 A3
Hood Gv LEIGH WN7 81 L1
Hood Sq OLDE OL4 60 D7
Hood St ANC M4 7 K3
Hook St WGNE/HIN WN2 48 C5
Hoole Cl CHD/CHDH SK8 111 K7
Hooley Range HTNM SK4 111 L1
Hooper St EDGY/DAV SK3 13 H5
OLDE OL4 9 M7
WGTN/LGST M12 88 A4
Hooten La LEIGH WN7 81 M1
Hooton St BOLS/LL BL3 51 M1
NEWH/MOS M40 88 B1
Hopcroft Cl BKLY M9 56 E6
Hope Av BOLE BL2 3 K7
BOLE BL2 23 H7
LHULT M38 52 E8
STRET M32 96 E1
WILM/AE SK9 127 H1
Hope Carr La LEIGH WN7 81 L2
Hope Carr Rd LEIGH WN7 81 L1
Hope Carr Wy LEIGH WN7 81 K1
Hopecourt Cl SLFD M6 70 E8
Hope Crs WGNNW/ST WN6 30 E6
Hopedale Rd RDSH SK5 100 C6
Hopefield St BOLS/LL BL3 36 A8
Hope Fold Av ATH M46 66 E2
Hopefold Dr WALK M28 69 H2
Hope Green Wy POY/DIS SK12 129 H2
Hope Hey La LHULT M38 52 C7
Hope La GOL/RIS/CUL WA3 82 B2
MCFLDN SK10 129 J3
Hopelea St DID/WITH M20 98 E5
Hope Park Cl PWCH M25 71 L1
Hope Park Rd PWCH M25 71 L1
Hope Pl ROCH OL11 * 41 M3
Hope Rd PWCH M25 71 K2
RUSH/FAL M14 88 A8
SALE M33 108 E1
Hopes Carr STKP SK1 13 K5
Hope St AIMK WN4 64 A7
AUL OL6 76 A8
BRAM/HZG SK7 121 M2
BRO M7 72 A5
CMANE M1 7 J5
DTN/ASHW M34 90 B7
DUK SK16 90 F4
GLSP SK13 105 H2
HEY OL10 41 J4
HOR/BR BL6 33 H4
HTNM SK4 12 F4
LEIGH WN7 66 C7
LHULT M38 52 D8
OLD OL1 59 L5
ORD M5 86 F3
RAMS BL0 18 E7
ROY/SHW OL2 43 L5
SWIN M27 70 D4
TYLD M29 67 L7
WGN WN1 * 14 F3
WGNE/HIN WN2 49 J1
WGNE/HIN WN2 49 J6
WGNS/IIMK WN3 48 B8
WHIT OL12 10 E2
Hope Ter DUK SK16 * 90 E4
EDGY/DAV SK3 * 13 H7
Hopkin Av OLD OL1 59 L4
Hopkins Fld ALT WA14 116 D3
Hopkinson Av DTN/ASHW M34 90 B7
Hopkinson Cl UPML OL3 61 L4
Hopkinson Rd BKLY M9 57 G7
Hopkins St HYDE SK14 91 H8
Hopkin St OLD OL1 9 K5
WGTN/LGST M12 99 K1
Hoppet La DROY M43 89 M2
Hopton Av WYTH/NTH M22 119 G1
Hopwood Av ECC M30 85 G1
HEY OL10 41 G4
Hopwood Cl BURY BL9 55 J1
GOL/RIS/CUL WA3 80 C4
Hopwood Rd MDTN M24 41 K8
Hopwood St CSLFD M3 * 6 D2
NEWH/MOS M40 73 L6
SWIN M27 70 D4
Horace Barnes Cl
RUSH/FAL M14 98 D1
Horace Gv HTNM SK4 100 B8
Horace St BOL BL1 36 A2
Horatio St GTN M18 * 89 J6
Horbury Av GTN M18 100 A1
Horbury Dr TOT/BURYW BL8 38 F2
Horeb St BOLS/LL BL3 2 A9
Horest La UPML OL3 44 E4
Horkers Nook WHTN BL5 50 A5
Horley Cl TOT/BURYW BL8 24 F5
Hornbeam Cl
HALE/TIMP WA15 109 H7
SALE M33 95 M7
Hornbeam Ct SLFD M6 86 D1
Hornbeam Crs AIMK WN4 78 E1
Hornbeam Rd BNG/LEV M19 99 L2

Hornby Av *BKLY* M9..........57 H7
Hornby Dr *BOLS/LL* BL3..........51 G2
Hornby Gv *LEIGH* WN7..........67 G5
Hornby Rd *STRET* M32..........86 C8
Hornby St *WGN* WN1..........47 M2
Hornby St *BURY* BL9..........4 E1
CHH M8..........72 C8
HEY OL10..........41 G3
MDTN M24..........57 K4
OLDS OL8..........8 F8
Horncastle Cl *GOL/RIS/CUL* WA3..........80 C4
TOT/BURYW BL8..........25 G7
Horncastle Rd *NEWH/MOS* M40..........73 L3
Hornchurch Ct *HEY* OL10..........41 H5
Hornchurch St *HULME* M15..........87 H6
Horne Dr *ANC* M4..........7 M3
Horne Gv *WGNS/IIMK* WN3..........14 A9
Horne St *BURY* BL9..........4 E9
Hornsea Cl *CHAD* OL9..........58 C5
TOT/BURYW BL8..........38 C2
Hornsea Rd *OFTN* SK2..........113 K7
Hornsea Wk *OP/CLY* M11 *..........88 D3
Hornsey Gv *WGNS/IIMK* WN3..........63 C1
Horridge Av *NEWLW* WA12..........78 F7
Horridge Fold *EDGW/EG* BL7 *..........22 B1
Horridge Fold Av *WHTN* BL5..........51 J2
Horridge St *TOT/BURYW* BL8..........24 E8
Horrobin Fold *EDGW/EG* BL7 *..........22 F2
Horrobin La *EDGW/EG* BL7..........22 F2
Horrocks Fold Av *BOL* BL1..........22 A6
Horrocks Rd *EDGW/BL* BL7..........17 G5
Horsa St *BOLE* BL2..........3 J1
Horsedge St *OLD* OL1..........9 K3
Horsefield Av *WHIT* OL12..........20 A6
Horsefield Cl *CCHDY* M21..........98 B5
Horseforth La *UPML* OL3..........61 K8
Horseshoe La *EDGW/EG* BL7..........22 D4
MDTN M24..........58 C6
WILM/AE SK9..........130 D2
Horsfield St *BOLS/LL* BL3..........35 K8
Horsham Av *BRAM/HZG* SK7..........121 L3
Horsham Cl *TOT/BURYW* BL8..........24 F5
WHTN BL5..........50 C6
Horsham Gv *WGNE/HIN* WN2..........48 C2
Horsham St *SLFD* M6..........86 B2
Horstead Wk *BNG/LEV* M19..........99 K2
Horton Av *BOL* BL1..........22 B6
Horton Rd *RUSH/FAL* M14..........98 D2
Horton St *STKP* SK1..........13 L9
WGNW/BIL/OR WN5..........47 H2
Hortree Rd *STRET* M32..........97 H2
Horwood Crs *DID/WITH* M20..........99 H2
Hoscar Dr *BNG/LEV* M19..........99 H5
The Hoskers *WHTN* BL5..........50 A5
Hoskins Cl *WGTN/LGST* M12..........88 D7
Hospital Rd *EDGW/EG* BL7..........22 D4
SWIN M27..........70 E5
Hotel Rd *MANAIR* M90..........118 C5
Hotel St *BOL* BL1..........2 E5
Hothersall Rd *RDSH* SK5..........100 C5
Hotspur Cl *RUSH/FAL* M14..........98 D4
Hough Cl *OLDS* OL8..........75 K2
Hough End Av *CCHDY* M21..........97 M6
Houghend Crs *DID/WITH* M20..........98 B5
Hough Fold Wy *BOLE* BL2..........23 G8
Hough Gn *HALE/TIMP* WA15..........117 G7
Hough Hall Rd
NEWH/MOS M40..........73 J4
Hough Hill Rd *STLY* SK15..........91 L4
Hough La *EDGW/EG* BL7..........22 C5
HYDE SK14..........91 J7
MDTN M24..........42 C7
TYLD M29..........67 M4
WILM/AE SK9..........127 H6
Hough St *BOLS/LL* BL3..........35 K8
TYLD M29..........68 A4
Houghton Av *OLDS* OL8..........75 G2
WGNW/BIL/OR WN5..........47 H2
Houghton Cl *MILN* OL16..........11 L6
NM/HAY SK22..........125 L2
Houghton La *SWIN* M27..........70 A7
WGNNW/ST WN6..........30 C6
Houghton Rd *CHH* M8..........72 C3
Houghton St *BOLS/LL* BL3..........2 C8
BURY BL9..........4 D7
LEIGH WN7..........66 C6
ROY/SHW OL2..........59 H2
SWIN M27..........71 G6
Hough Wk *BRO* M7..........86 F1
Houghwood Gra *AIMK* WN4..........78 C1
Houldsworth Av *ALT* WA14..........108 B5
Houldsworth Ml *RDSH* SK5..........100 B5
Houldsworth St *CMANE* M1..........7 J3
RAD M26..........38 C7
RDSH SK5..........100 B5
Houseley Av *CHAD* OL9..........74 D1
Houseman Gv *WGNS/IIMK* WN6..........47 K2
Housley Cl *WGNS/IIMK* WN3..........47 K2
Houson St *OLDS* OL8..........9 J8
Houston Pk *SALQ* M50..........86 C3
Hove Cl *TOT/BURYW* BL8..........24 C3
Hoveden St *CHH* M8..........72 C8
Hove Dr *RUSH/FAL* M14..........99 H5
Hove St *BOLS/LL* BL3..........35 M7
Hove St North *BOLS/LL* BL3 *..........35 M7
Hovey Cl *CHH* M8 *..........72 C5
Hovingham St *MILN* OL16..........11 J3
Hovis St *OP/CLY* M11..........88 F4
Howard Av *BOLS/LL* BL3..........35 K8
CHD/CHDH SK8..........120 C3
ECC M30..........85 C1
FWTH BL4..........53 J5
HTNM SK4..........99 H6
Howard Cl *GLSP* SK13..........104 E2
MPL/ROM SK6..........113 K2
Howard Ct *AUL* OL6..........90 E1
HALE/TIMP WA15..........108 E4
Howard Dr *HALE/TIMP* WA15..........117 J3
Howard Hl *BURY* BL9..........39 K8
Howardian Cl *OLDS* OL8..........75 H2
Howard La *DTN/ASHW* M34..........90 C8
Howard Pl *MILN* OL16..........10 C3
Howard Rd *WYTH/NTH* M22..........110 A3
Howards La *MOSL* OL5..........77 H3
WGNW/BIL/OR WN5..........46 C3
Howards Meadow *GLSP* SK13..........104 E3
Howard St *AULW* OL7..........75 K8
BOL BL1..........36 C3
CHH M8..........72 B8
DTN/ASHW M34..........90 C6
GLSP SK13..........104 F3
OLDE OL4..........60 B4
ORD M5..........86 D4
RAD M26..........54 E1
ROY/SHW OL2..........43 K5
STKP SK1..........13 J2

STLY SK15..........77 G8
STRET M32..........97 G2
WGNW/BIL/OR WN5..........46 F7
WHIT OL12..........10 D2
Howarth Av *WALK* M28..........69 H5
Howarth Cross St *MILN* OL16..........28 E2
Howarth Dr *IRL* M44..........94 C3
Howarth Farm Wy *WHIT* OL12..........28 F1
Howarth Fold *EDGW/EG* BL7 *..........22 A1
Howarth Sq *MILN* OL16..........11 H3
Howarth St *FWTH* BL4..........53 C5
LEIGH WN7..........66 B8
LIT OL15..........21 M6
OLDTF/WHR M16..........86 F8
WHTN BL5..........50 C4
Howbridge Cl *WALK* M28..........68 F4
Howbro Dr *AULW* OL7..........75 H7
How Clough Cl *WALK* M28..........69 J2
How Clough Dr *WALK* M28..........69 J2
Howcroft Cl *BOL* BL1..........2 C3
Howden Cl *RDSH* SK5..........100 B3
Howden Dr *WGNS/IIMK* WN3..........47 K8
Howden Rd *BKLY* M9..........56 F7
NM/HAY SK22..........124 E3
Howe Bridge Cl *ATH* M46..........66 D3
Howe Dr *RAMS* BL0..........24 A2
Howell Cft North *BOL* BL1 *..........2 E5
Howell Cft South *BOL* BL1 *..........2 E5
Howells Av *SALE* M33..........96 D7
Howe St *AULW* OL7..........90 B4
BRO M7..........71 M5
Howgill Crs *OLDS* OL8..........75 H1
Howgill St *OP/CLY* M11..........89 G3
How Lea Dr *BURY* BL9..........25 J6
Howsin Av *BOLE* BL2..........22 E8
Howton Cl *WGTN/LGST* M12..........88 D3
Howty Cl *WILM/AE* SK9..........127 H3
Hoxton Cl *MPL/ROM* SK6..........101 K8
Hoy Dr *URM* M41..........85 G7
Hoylake Cl *LEIGH* WN7..........81 C2
NEWH/MOS M40..........74 A4
Hoylake Rd *EDGY/DAV* SK3..........111 K4
SALE M33..........109 J2
Hoyland Cl *WGTN/LGST* M12..........88 C6
Hoyle Av *OLDS* OL8..........9 K8
Hoyle Cl *WALK* M28..........68 E1
Hoyles Ct *RAD* M26..........38 F8
Hoyle's Ter *MILN* OL16 *..........29 H6
Hoyle St *RAD* M26..........54 E3
WGTN/LGST M12..........7 M7
WHIT OL12..........20 B1
Hoyle Wk *BRUN/LGST* M13 *..........87 L6
Hucclecote Av
WYTH/NTH M22..........118 C2
Hucklow Cl *NTHM/RTH* M23..........118 C2
Hudcar La *BURY* BL9..........5 H1
Huddart Cl *ORD* M5..........86 E4
Huddersfield Rd *MILN* OL16..........29 M8
MOSL OL5..........77 H2
OLDE OL4..........59 L5
STLY SK15..........91 M2
UPML OL3..........61 K8
UPML OL3..........61 M1
Hudson Gv *GOL/RIS/CUL* WA3..........80 B4
Hudson Rd *BOLS/LL* BL3..........51 L1
HYDE SK14..........102 B5
Hudson St *OLDTF/WHR* M16..........74 D2
Hudsons Wk *ROCH* OL11..........27 L5
Hudswell Cl *WHTF* M45..........55 H4
Hughenden Ct
TOT/BURYW BL8 *..........24 C5
Hughes Cl *BURY* BL9..........5 H3
FAIL M35..........74 B4
Hughes St *BOL* BL1..........36 A2
OP/CLY M11..........88 B4
Hughley Cl *ROY/SHW* OL2..........43 J8
Hugh Lupus St *BOL* BL1..........22 D7
Hugh Oldham Dr *BRO* M7..........71 M6
Hugh St *MILN* OL16..........11 H6
Hughtrede St *MILN* OL16 *..........42 E1
Hugo St *FWTH* BL4..........52 E2
NEWH/MOS M40..........73 K5
ROCH OL11..........42 A2
Hulbert St *MDTN* M24..........57 L3
TOT/BURYW BL8..........38 F3
Hullet Cl *WGNNW/ST* WN6..........30 B4
Hull Mill La *UPML* OL3..........45 J7
Hull Sq *CSLFD* M3..........6 A2
Hully St *STLY* SK15..........91 J2
Hulme Av *WALK* M28..........68 B4
Hulme Gv *LEIGH* WN7..........65 M6
Hulme Hall Av *CHD/CHDH* SK8..........120 C4
Hulme Hall Cl *CHD/CHDH* SK8..........120 C4
Hulme Hall Crs *CHD/CHDH* SK8..........120 C4
Hulme Hall La *NEWH/MOS* M40..........73 H8
Hulme Hall Rd *HULME* M15..........6 A9
Hulme Pl *ORD* M5 *..........86 F3
Hulme Rd *BOLE* BL2..........23 H6
DTN/ASHW M34..........100 A1
HTNM SK4..........100 A7
LEIGH WN7..........65 M6
RAD M26..........53 M6
SALE M33..........109 C1
Hulmes Rd *NEWH/MOS* M40..........74 B7
Hulme St *AUL* OL6..........76 A8
BOL BL1..........2 F3
HULME M15..........6 D9
OLDS OL8..........59 H8
ORD M5..........86 D5
STKP SK1..........112 E5
TOT/BURYW BL8..........8 B2
Hulton Av *WALK* M28..........68 A4
Hulton Cl *BOLS/LL* BL3..........35 K8
Hulton Dr *BOLS/LL* BL3..........51 K1
OLDTF/WHR M16..........87 H8
Hulton La *BOLS/LL* BL3..........51 K1
Hulton St *DTN/ASHW* M34..........90 B8
FAIL M35..........74 A5
ORD M5..........86 D5
Humber Dr *BURY* BL9..........25 J4
Humber Pl *WGNW/BIL/OR* WN5..........46 F5
Humber Rd *MILN* OL16..........29 K6
TYLD M29..........67 M5
Humber St *CHH* M8..........72 D5
SLFD M6..........86 A3
Hume St *BNG/LEV* M19 *..........99 L4
MILN OL16..........11 H7
Humphrey Crs *URM* M41..........96 D2
Humphrey La *URM* M41..........96 D2
Humphrey Pk *URM* M41..........96 D3
Humphrey Rd *OLDTF/WHR* M16..........86 E7
Humphrey St *BOLS/LL* BL3..........51 M1
DROY M43..........74 F8
Hyde Sq *MDTN* M24..........57 H4
Hyde St *BOLS/LL* BL3..........51 M1
DROY M43..........74 B4
FWTH BL4..........53 J5
Hydon Brook Wk *ROCH* OL11..........27 M8
Hydra Cl *BRO* M7..........86 F1
Hydrangea Cl *SALE* M33..........95 M7
Hylydale Av
CHD/CHDH SK8..........110 E6
Hylton Dr *CHD/CHDH* SK8..........120 E4
Hypatia St *BOLE* BL2..........3 K4
Hythe Cl *RUSH/FAL* M14..........98 F1
Hythe Rd *EDGY/DAV* SK3..........12 A7
Hythe St *BOLS/LL* BL3 *..........35 K8
Hythe Wk *CHAD* OL9..........8 A7

Hunters Cha
WGNW/BIL/OR WN5..........62 B3
Hunters Cl *MPL/ROM* SK6..........113 J1
WILM/AE SK9 *..........127 K3
Hunters Ct *STLY* SK15..........92 A4
Hunters Gn *RAMS* BL0..........24 C1
Hunters Hl *BURY* BL9..........39 L8
Hunters Hill La *UPML* OL3..........45 M6
Hunters La *GLSP* SK13..........104 C4
MILN OL16..........10 E3
OLD OL1..........9 K5
Hunters Ms *SALE* M33..........96 D8
WILM/AE SK9..........127 C5
Hunters Pool La *MCFLDN* SK10..........131 M4
Hunterston Av *ECC* M30..........85 K2
Hunt Fold Dr *TOT/BURYW* BL8..........24 C3
Huntingdon Av *CHAD* OL9..........8 B8
Huntingdon Crs *RDSH* SK5..........100 F7
Huntingdon Wk *BOL* BL1..........36 B2
Huntington Av *DID/WITH* M20..........98 D5
Hunt La *CHAD* OL9..........58 D5
Huntley Mount Rd *BURY* BL9..........5 L1
Huntley Rd *CHH* M8..........72 B2
EDGY/DAV SK3..........12 A9
Huntley St *BURY* BL9..........5 L1
Huntly Cha *WILM/AE* SK9..........127 H6
Hunt Rd *HYDE* SK14..........91 K7
RNFD/HAY WA11..........78 B6
Huntroyde Av *BOLE* BL2..........3 K1
Hunts Bank *CSLFD* M3..........6 F2
Huntsham Cl *ALT* WA14..........107 L6
Huntsman Dr *IRL* M44..........94 C5
Huntspill Rd *ALT* WA14..........108 A4
Hunts Rd *SLFD* M6..........71 G7
Hunt St *ATH* M46..........67 G1
BKLY M9..........73 G3
WGN WN1..........15 K5
Hurdlow Av *BRO* M7..........71 K5
Hurdlow Ms *GLSP* SK13..........104 A3
Hurdsfield Rd *OFTN* SK2..........112 F8
Hurford Av *GTN* M18..........89 G6
Hurlbote Cl *WILM/AE* SK9..........119 M7
Hurley Dr *CHD/CHDH* SK8..........120 A2
Hurlston Rd *BOLS/LL* BL3..........52 A2
Hurst Av *CHD/CHDH* SK8..........120 E6
SALE M33..........107 M1
Hurstbank Av *BNG/LEV* M19..........99 C8
Hurst Bank Rd *AUL* OL6..........76 F3
Hurstbourne Av *OP/CLY* M11..........88 E1
Hurst Brook Cl *AUL* OL6..........75 M8
Hurstbrook Cl *GLSP* SK13..........105 J3
Hurstbrook Dr *STRET* M32..........96 C2
Hurst Cl *GLSP* SK13..........105 J3
WHTN BL5..........51 H1
Hurst Crs *GLSP* SK13..........105 H4
Hurstead Gn *WHIT* OL12 *..........21 H8
Hurstead Rd *MILN* OL16..........29 J6
Hurst Green Cl *RAD* M26..........38 C4
RDSH SK5..........100 D1
Hurst Gv *AUL* OL6..........76 B7
Hurst Hall Dr *AUL* OL6..........76 D7
Hursthead Rd *CHD/CHDH* SK8..........120 D5
Hursthead Wk *BRUN/LGST* M13 *..........7 K9
Hurst Hill Crs *AUL* OL6..........76 A8
Hurst La *GOL/RIS/CUL* WA3..........81 L6
Hurst Lea Ct *WILM/AE* SK9..........130 D1
Hurst Lea Rd *NM/HAY* SK22..........124 E5
Hurst Meadow *MILN* OL16..........42 C7
Hurst Mill La *GOL/RIS/CUL* WA3..........81 M4
Hurst Rd *GLSP* SK13..........105 J3
Hurst St *BOLS/LL* BL3..........51 M1
BURY BL9..........5 J6
CHAD OL9..........8 E5
DUK SK16..........90 D6
LEIGH WN7..........80 B1
RDSH SK5..........100 D1
ROCH OL11..........11 H9
WALK M28..........52 F6
WGNE/HIN WN2..........48 F6
Hurstvale Av *CHD/CHDH* SK8..........119 K3
Hurstville Rd *CCHDY* M21..........97 L6
Hurstway Dr *BKLY* M9..........73 H1
Hurstwood *AUL* OL6..........76 C6
BOL BL1..........22 A7
Hurstwood Cl *OLDS* OL8..........59 M8
Hurstwood Ct *BOLS/LL* BL3..........36 F8
Hurstwood Gv *OFTN* SK2..........113 K6
Huskisson Wy *NEWLW* WA12..........78 E8
Hus St *DROY* M43..........89 J4
Husteads La *UPML* OL3..........61 H3
Hutchins La *OLDE* OL4..........60 A3
Hutchinson Rd *ROCH* OL11..........27 C3
Hutchinson St *ROCH* OL11..........27 L6
Hutchinson Wy *RAD* M26..........54 D2
Hutton Av *AUL* OL6..........91 H2
WALK M28..........68 C6
Hutton Cl *GOL/RIS/CUL* WA3..........81 H7
Hutton St *WCN* WN1..........15 J3
Huxley Av *CHH* M8..........72 D6
Huxley Cl *BRAM/HZG* SK7..........121 C5
Huxley Dr *BRAM/HZG* SK7..........121 C5
Huxley Pl *WGNS/IIMK* WN3..........47 K7
Huxley St *ALT* WA14..........108 A5
BOL BL1..........35 M2
OLDE OL4..........59 M7
Huxton Gn *BRAM/HZG* SK7..........121 J2
Hyacinth Cl *EDGY/DAV* SK3..........112 A7
RNFD/HAY WA11..........78 C6
Hyacinth Wk *PART* M31..........106 B2
Hyatt Crs *WGNNW/ST* WN6..........30 F1
Hyde Bank Rd *NM/HAY* SK22..........124 E5
Hyde Dr *WALK* M28..........68 F2
Hyde Fold Cl *BNG/LEV* M19..........99 J3
Hyde Pl *BRUN/LGST* M13 *..........87 M7
Hyde Rd *DTN/ASHW* M34..........101 J1
GTN M18..........89 J3
HYDE SK14..........103 J1
MDTN M24..........58 B6
MPL/ROM SK6..........101 L7
WALK M28..........68 F2
WGTN/LGST M12..........7 M9

I

Ibsley *WHIT* OL12..........10 D2
Ice House Cl *WALK* M28..........68 C1
Iceland St *SLFD* M6..........86 B2
Idonia St *BOL* BL1..........36 A1
Ilex Gv *BRO* M7..........72 A6
Ilford St *OP/CLY* M11..........88 E2
Ilfracombe Rd *OFTN* SK2..........113 C4
Ilfracombe St *NEWH/MOS* M40..........74 A6
Ilkeston Dr *WGNE/HIN* WN2..........49 J1
Ilkley Cl *BOLE* BL2..........3 L4
CHAD OL9..........8 B7
Ilkley Crs *RDSH* SK5..........100 F4
Ilkley Dr *URM* M41..........84 D8
Ilkley St *NEWH/MOS* M40..........73 K3
Ilk St *OP/CLY* M11..........88 E2
Illingworth Av *STLY* SK15..........91 M3
Illiona Dr *BRO* M7..........72 A6
Ilminster *OLDS* OL11..........10 C7
Ilminster Av *NEWH/MOS* M40..........74 A8
Ilthorpe Wk *NEWH/MOS* M40 *..........73 L3
Imex Business Pk *BRUN/LGST* M13 *..........87 M6
Imogen Ct *SLFD* M6..........86 D3
Imperial Dr *LEIGH* WN7..........67 G6
Imperial Ter *SALE* M33..........96 D6
Ina Av *BOL* BL1..........35 J3
Ince Cl *DID/WITH* M20..........98 E5
HTNM SK4..........112 B1
Ince Green La *WGNS/IIMK* WN3..........15 L7
Ince Hall Av *WGNE/HIN* WN2..........14 F4
Ince St *HTNM* SK4..........112 B1
Incham Dr *WILM/AE* SK9..........119 C7
Inchfield *ROCH* OL11..........27 H4
Inchfield Rd *NEWH/MOS* M40..........73 J3
Inchley Rd *BRUN/LGST* M13..........7 J9
Inchwood Ms *OLDE* OL4..........44 B8
Incline Rd *OLDS* OL8..........9 L8
Independent St *BOLS/LL* BL3..........53 K1
Indigo St *SLFD* M6..........71 L7
Indus Pl *BRO* M7..........71 M8
Industrial St *RAMS* BL0..........18 F3
WHTN BL5..........50 C5
Industry Rd *WHIT* OL12..........10 E1
Industry St *CHAD* OL9..........58 D8
LIT OL15..........21 M7
ROCH OL11..........27 H3
WHIT OL12..........20 B1
Infant St *PWCH* M25 *..........55 M8
Infirmary St *BOL* BL1..........2 F5
Ingersol Rd *HOR/BR* BL6..........34 B4
Ingham Rd *ALT* WA14..........108 A3
Inghams La *LIT* OL15..........21 M7
Ingham St *BURY* BL9..........5 H6
LEIGH WN7..........66 B4
NEWH/MOS M40 *..........74 B8
OLD OL1..........9 L5
Inghamwood Cl *BRO* M7..........72 C5
Ingleby Av *BKLY* M9..........57 J8
Ingleby Cl *ROY/SHW* OL2..........43 K4
WGNNW/ST WN6..........31 G2
WHTN BL5..........50 C2
Ingleby Ct *STRET* M32..........97 H3
Ingleby Wy *ROY/SHW* OL2..........43 K4
Ingledene Av *BRO* M7..........72 B3
Ingledene Gv *BOL* BL1 *..........35 K2
Ingle Dr *OFTN* SK2..........112 F5
Inglefield *ROCH* OL11..........27 H3
Inglehead Cl *DTN/ASHW* M34..........101 K2
Inglenook Cl *PART* M31..........95 J5
Ingle Rd *CHD/CHDH* SK8..........111 K6
Ingles Fold *WALK* M28..........68 E4
Inglesham Cl *LEIGH* WN7..........83 H3
Ingleton Av *CHH* M8..........72 E5
Ingleton Cl *BOLE* BL2..........23 G8
CHD/CHDH SK8..........110 F6
NEWLW WA12 *..........78 E8
ROY/SHW OL2..........43 G7
Ingleton Ms *TOT/BURYW* BL8..........24 E8
Ingleton Rd *EDGY/DAV* SK3..........12 C7
Inglewhite *BOL* BL1 *..........35 G3
Inglewhite Av *WGN* WN1..........47 M2
Inglewhite Crs *WGN* WN1 *..........47 M2
Inglewood *AULW* OL7..........75 J7
Inglewood Av *WGN* WN1..........15 K5
Inglewood Cl *AULW* OL7..........75 J7
BURY BL9..........5 M1
PART M31..........94 B8
Inglewood Hollow *STLY* SK15..........91 M4
Inglewood Rd *CHAD* OL9..........58 D3
Inglewood Wk *BRUN/LGST* M13 *..........87 M6
Inglis St *LIT* OL15..........21 M6
Ingoe Cl *HEY* OL10..........41 J9
Ingoldsby Av *BRUN/LGST* M13..........88 A3
Ingram Dr *HTNM* SK4..........111 H1
Ingram St *WGNE/HIN* WN2..........64 D1
WGNNW/ST WN6..........14 A1
Ings Av *WHIT* OL12..........27 L2
Ings La *WHIT* OL12..........27 M3
Inkerman St *HYDE* SK14..........90 F8
NEWH/MOS M40..........73 C7
WHIT OL12 *..........10 E1
Ink St *MILN* OL16..........10 C4
Inman St *BURY* BL9..........4 D8
DTN/ASHW M34..........101 J1
Innes St *WGTN/LGST* M12..........99 L1
Innis Av *NEWH/MOS* M40..........73 M7
Institute St *BOL* BL1..........3 C5
Instow Cl *BRUN/LGST* M13 *..........88 A7
CHAD OL9..........58 C3
Intake La *UPML* OL3..........77 L1
International Ap *MANAIR* M90..........118 D5
Invar Rd *WALK* M28..........70 A3
Inverbeg Dr *BOLE* BL2..........37 K5
Inverlael Av *BOL* BL1..........35 L4
Inverness Av *BKLY* M9..........57 K8
Inverness Rd *DUK* SK16..........90 F5
Inward Dr *WGNNW/ST* WN6..........30 D7
Inwood Wk *CHH* M8..........72 F6
Inworth Cl *WHTN* BL5..........50 C6
Iona Pl *BOLE* BL2..........36 F2
Iona Wy *URM* M41..........85 G7
Ionian Gdns *BRO* M7..........71 M7
Ipswich St *ROCH* OL11..........10 C1
Iqbal Cl *WGTN/LGST* M12..........88 D7
Ireby Cl *MDTN* M24..........56 F2
Iredale Cr
WGNNW/ST WN6..........31 J5
Iredine St *OP/CLY* M11..........88 F3
Irene Av *HYDE* SK14..........91 K6
Iris Av *FWTH* BL4..........52 D3
FWTH BL4..........53 J5
OP/CLY M11..........88 C3
Iris St *OLDS* OL8..........75 J2
RAMS BL0..........18 E3
Irkdale St *CHH* M8..........72 F6
Irk Vale Dr *OLD* OL1..........58 B3
Irlam Av *ECC* M30..........85 C3
Irlam Rd *IRL* M44..........94 A3
SALE M33..........96 F7
Irlam Sq *SLFD* M6..........86 C1
Irlam St *BOL* BL1..........36 D1
NEWH/MOS M40..........73 H7
Irlam Wharf Rd *IRL* M44..........94 D6
Irma St *BOL* BL1..........36 C1

Ironmonger La *WGNS/IIMK* WN3..........14 F7
Iron St *DTN/ASHW* M34..........101 J1
HOR/BR BL6..........33 M2
NEWH/MOS M40..........88 B1
Irvin Dr *WYTH/NTH* M22..........119 J4
Irvine Av *WALK* M28..........68 D6
Irvine St *LEIGH* WN7..........66 C6
Irving Cl *OFTN* SK2..........121 J1
Irving St *BOL* BL1..........36 B2
OLDS OL8..........74 E2
Irvin St *NEWH/MOS* M40..........73 M6
Irwell Av *ECC* M30..........85 J3
LHULT M38..........52 E8
Irwell Gv *ECC* M30..........85 J3
Irwell Pl *ECC* M30..........85 J3
ORD M5..........86 F3
RAD M26..........53 L4
WGNW/BIL/OR WN5..........46 F6
Irwell Rd *WGNW/BIL/OR* WN5..........46 C5
Irwell Sculpture Trail *BRO* M7..........71 M6
Irwell St *BURY* BL9..........4 D5
CSLFD M3..........6 C4
CSLFD M3..........72 B8
RAD M26..........53 K5
RAD M26..........54 E2
RAMS BL0..........18 F6
Irwell Valley Wy *CMANW* BL9..........25 G3
RAMS BL0..........18 F8
Irwin Dr *WILM/AE* SK9..........119 C7
Irwin Rd *ALT* WA14..........107 M4
Irwin St *DTN/ASHW* M34..........101 H1
Isaac Cl *ORD* M5..........86 D4
Isaac St *BOL* BL1..........35 M4
Isabella Cl *OLDTF/WHR* M16..........86 F8
Isabella Sq *WHIT* OL12..........28 C2
Isabella St *WHIT* OL12..........28 C2
Isabel Wk *BOLS/LL* BL3..........2 A9
Isaiah St *OLDS* OL8 *..........59 J8
Isa St *RAMS* BL0..........18 D8
Isca St *OP/CLY* M11..........88 C3
Isel Wk *BOLE* BL2..........3 L2
Isherwood Dr *MPL/ROM* SK6..........114 A6
Isherwood Fold *EDGW/EG* BL7..........17 C5
Isherwood Rd *PART* M31..........95 J6
Isherwood St *HEY* OL10..........41 H3
LEIGH WN7..........66 B4
ROCH OL11..........11 G8
Isis Cl *BRO* M7..........71 K4
Islington Rd *OFTN* SK2..........112 F8
Islington St *CSLFD* M3..........6 B3
Islington Wy *CSLFD* M3..........6 A4
Isobel Cl *ECC* M30..........84 C3
OLDTF/WHR M16..........86 F8
Ivanhoe Av *GOL/RIS/CUL* WA3..........80 A3
Ivanhoe Ct *BOLS/LL* BL3..........52 F2
Ivanhoe St *BOLS/LL* BL3..........52 F2
OLD OL1..........59 M3
Iveagh Ct *MILN* OL16..........11 J7
Ivor St *ROCH* OL11..........41 L1
Ivy Bank Cl *BOL* BL1..........22 B7
Ivy Bank Rd *BOL* BL1..........22 B7
Ivybridge Cl *BRUN/LGST* M13..........88 A7
Ivy Cl *DROY* M43..........89 J2
ROY/SHW OL2..........43 L5
Ivy Cottages *WHIT* OL12..........10 A1
Ivycroft *GLSP* SK13..........93 H8
Ivydale Dr *LEIGH* WN7..........66 A7
Ivy Dr *MDTN* M24..........57 J6
Ivy Farm Gdns
GOL/RIS/CUL WA3..........81 C8
Ivygreen Dr *OLDE* OL4..........60 C6
Ivygreen Rd *CCHDY* M21..........97 J4
Ivy Gv *FWTH* BL4..........52 E4
FWTH BL4..........53 J5
LHULT M38..........52 C8
Ivy House Rd *GOL/RIS/CUL* WA3..........80 A3
Ivyleaf Sq *BRO* M7..........72 B6
Ivylea Rd *BNG/LEV* M19..........99 H8
Ivy Rd *BOL* BL1..........35 M3
GOL/RIS/CUL WA3..........79 L4
POY/DIS SK12..........129 J1
TOT/BURYW BL8..........38 G2
WHTN BL5..........50 C5
Ivy St *AIMK* WN4..........78 E1
BOLS/LL BL3..........35 M8
ECC M30..........85 K4
NEWH/MOS M40..........73 K4
WGN WN1..........14 E3

J

Jack Brady Cl *NTHM/RTH* M23..........109 H8
Jackdaw Rd *TOT/BURYW* BL8..........24 C2
Jack La *DROY* M43..........89 M2
URM M41..........96 B2
Jackman Av *HEY* OL10..........41 C5
Jackroom Dr *ANC* M4 *..........7 L4
Jack's La *WHTN* BL5..........49 K5
Jackson Av *DUK* SK16..........91 G4
Jackson Cl *HALE/TIMP* WA15..........108 F5
OLDS OL8..........9 G8
Jackson Ct *URM* M41..........95 K1
Jackson Crs *HULME* M15..........6 D9
Jackson Gdns *DTN/ASHW* M34..........101 G2
Jackson Ms *OLDE* OL4..........60 A3
Jacksons Edge Rd
POY/DIS SK12..........128 D5
Jacksons La *BRAM/HZG* SK7..........121 K4
Jacksons Rw *CMANW* M2..........6 E6
Jackson St *AUL* OL6..........75 L8
CHD/CHDH SK8..........111 H6
FAIL M35..........74 A6
FWTH BL4..........53 J5
FWTH BL4..........53 J5
GLSP SK13..........93 M7
HYDE SK14..........102 A2
HYDE SK14..........103 K1
MDTN M24..........57 L3
MILN OL16..........11 K7
OLDE OL4..........59 L2
RAD M26..........54 E2
SALE M33..........97 G2
STRET M32..........96 F3
WALK M28..........68 D1
WGNE/HIN WN2..........48 D5
WHIT OL12..........20 B1
WHTF M45..........55 J3
Jack St *BOLE* BL2..........3 L1
Jack Taylor Ct *WHIT* OL12 *..........11 J1
Jacob Bright Ms *WHIT* OL12..........28 B1
Jacobite Cl *BRO* M7..........71 M3
Jacobsen Av *HYDE* SK14..........91 J8
Jacob St *WGNE/HIN* WN2..........49 G6
Jaffrey St *LEIGH* WN7..........66 B4
James Andrew St *MDTN* M24 *..........57 L3
James Brindley Basin
CMANE M1..........7 L5
James Butterworth Ct
MILN OL16..........11 J4

James Butterworth St
  MILN OL16 .....11 K6
James Cl DUK SK16 .....91 H4
  WGNS/IIMK WN3 .....14 F6
James Corbett Rd SALQ M50 .....85 M3
James Dr HYDE SK14 .....102 B2
James Henry Av ORD M5 .....86 E4
James Hill St LIT OL15 .....21 M7
James Leech St STKP SK1 .....13 H6
James Leigh St CMANE M1 .....7 G7
James Pl WGNNW/ST WN6 .....31 G2
James Rd RNFD/HAY WA11 .....78 C5
  ROY/SHW OL2 .....43 L4
James Sq WGNNW/ST WN6 .....31 G2
James's St OLDE OL4 .....60 A3
James St ATH M46 .....67 H3
  BOLS/LL BL3 .....53 L1
  BURY BL9 .....5 J6
  DROY M43 .....89 L2
  DTN/ASHW M34 .....90 B4
  DTN/ASHW M34 * 101 K1
  DUK SK16 * 91 H4
  EDGW/EG BL7 .....22 A1
  EDGY/DAV SK3 .....13 G8
  FAIL M35 .....74 D4
  FWTH BL4 .....53 J4
  GLSP SK13 .....104 F4
  HEY OL10 .....41 G2
  HOR/BR BL6 .....33 J1
  LIT OL15 .....21 K7
  MPL/ROM SK6 .....101 K7
  NEWH/MOS M40 .....88 A1
  ORD M5 .....6 A4
  PWCH M25 .....55 K7
  RAD M26 .....54 E2
  ROY/SHW OL2 .....43 K7
  SALE M33 .....97 G8
  TYLD M29 .....67 J4
  WGNE/HIN WN2 .....64 B5
  WGNS/IIMK WN3 .....15 J7
  WHIT OL12 * 11 G1
  WHIT OL12 .....20 B2
  WHTN BL5 .....50 B2
James St North RAD M26 .....54 E2
James St South CHAD OL9 * 58 D5
Jamieson Cl CHH M8 .....72 B7
Jammy St CHAD OL9 .....8 C7
Jane St CHAD OL9 .....8 E7
  WHIT OL12 .....10 C2
Janus Dr OLD OL1 .....8 F1
Japan St BRO M7 .....72 C5
Jardine Wy CHAD OL9 .....58 C8
Jarvis St OLDE OL4 .....9 M7
  WHIT OL12 .....28 C3
Jasmine Av DROY M43 .....89 M2
Jasmine Cl NTHM/RTH M23 .....109 H3
Jasmine Gv BOLS/LL BL3 .....52 B1
Jasmine Rd
  WGNW/BIL/OR WN5 * 47 C5
Jason St ANC M4 .....87 L1
Jauncey St BOLS/LL BL3 .....35 M7
Jayton Av DID/WITH M20 .....110 E5
Jean Av LEIGH WN7 .....81 K7
Jean Cl BNG/LEV M19 .....99 K2
Jedburgh Av BOL BL1 .....35 L4
Jefferson Wy WHIT OL12 .....28 C1
Jeffrey Dr DUK SK16 .....91 H4
Jeffrey St WGNE/HIN WN2 .....48 D4
Jehlum Cl CHH M8 .....72 E5
Jellicoe Av IRL M44 .....94 B6
Jenkinson St HULME M15 .....7 H9
  WGNE/HIN WN2 .....49 C6
Jennaby Wk BOL BL1 .....36 B2
Jennet Hey AIMK WN4 .....63 J6
Jennet's La COL/RIS/CUL WA3 .....81 M3
Jennings Av ORD M5 .....86 D4
Jennings Cl HYDE SK14 .....91 L7
  ORD M5 .....86 D4
Jennings St EDGY/DAV SK3 .....12 F9
Jennison Cl WGTN/LGST M12 .....88 E2
Jenny La BRAM/HZG SK7 .....128 C1
Jenny Lind Cl BOLS/LL BL3 .....52 F2
Jenny St OLDS OL8 .....74 F2
Jepheys Pl WHIT OL12 .....28 C3
Jepheys St WHIT OL12 .....28 C3
Jepson St OFTN SK2 .....112 D6
Jericho Rd BURY BL9 .....26 B8
Jermyn St WHIT OL12 .....11 G2
Jerrold St LIT OL15 .....21 M7
Jersey Rd RDSH SK5 .....100 C8
Jersey St ANC M4 .....7 K3
  AUL OL6 .....75 J1
Jerusalem Pl CMANW M2 * 6 E2
Jesmond Av PWCH M25 .....71 J1
Jesmond Dr TOT/BURYW BL8 .....24 F7
Jesmond Gv CHD/CHDH SK8 .....120 D4
Jespersen St OLD OL1 .....9 J4
Jessamine Av BRO M7 .....72 A8
Jessel Cl BRUN/LGST M13 .....87 M6
Jessica Wy LEIGH WN7 .....65 L8
Jessie St BOLS/LL BL3 .....35 M7
  NEWH/MOS M40 .....73 K4
Jessop Dr MPL/ROM SK6 .....114 C4
Jessop Forge BOLS/LL BL3 .....53 K1
Jessop St GTN M18 .....89 C7
Jethro St BOLE BL2 .....3 L3
  BOLE BL2 .....22 F8
Jetson St GTN M18 .....89 M1
Jimmy McMullen Wk
  RUSH/FAL M14 * 98 D1
Jinnah Cl OLDE OL4 .....59 M7
  OP/CLY M11 .....88 F4
J J Thomson Ms
  RUSH/FAL M14 * 98 F3
Joan St NEWH/MOS M40 .....73 K5
Jobling St OP/CLY M11 .....88 C4
Jocelyn St NEWH/MOS M40 .....73 H6
Joddrell St CSLFD M3 .....6 D5
Jodrell St NM/HAY SK22 .....124 D3
Joel La HYDE SK14 .....102 C5
Johannesburg Gdns
  NTHM/RTH M23 .....109 J3
John Ashworth St WHIT OL12 .....28 E3
John Atkinson Ct ORD M5 * 86 A2
John Av CHD/CHDH SK8 .....111 H7
John Beeley Av OP/CLY M11 .....89 C4
John Booth St OLDE OL4 .....60 C7
John Brown St BOL BL1 * 2 C3
John Clynes Av
  NEWH/MOS M40 * 87 M1
John Cross St BOLS/LL BL3 .....36 B8
John Dalton St CMANW M2 .....6 E5
  GLSP SK13 .....93 H7
John Foran Cl OP/CLY M11 .....88 F4
John Gilbert Wy TRPK M17 .....86 B7
John Heywood St OP/CLY M11 .....88 F4
John Kennedy Gdn HYDE SK14 .....103 K1
John Kennedy Rd NM/HAY SK22 .....103 J1
John Knott St OLDE OL4 .....60 C6
John Lee Fold MDTN M24 .....57 K3
John Nash Crs HULME M15 .....87 H4

Johnny King Cl
  NEWH/MOS M40 .....73 C7
John Roberts Cl ROCH OL11 .....10 D8
Johns Cl CCHDY M21 .....97 L1
John Shepley St HYDE SK14 .....102 B2
John Smeaton Ct CMANE M1 .....7 L5
Johnson Av NEWLW WA12 .....78 E7
  WGNE/HIN WN2 .....65 H3
Johnsonbrook Rd HYDE SK14 .....91 C7
Johnson Cl LEIGH WN7 .....65 L8
Johnson Fold Av BOL BL1 .....35 H7
Johnson Gv MDTN M24 .....57 H4
Johnson's Sq NEWH/MOS M40 .....73 G8
Johnson St ATH M46 .....66 D3
  BOL BL1 .....2 F6
  CSLFD M3 .....6 C2
  HULME M15 .....87 G6
  RAD M26 .....54 E2
  SWIN M27 .....71 C6
  TYLD M29 .....67 K3
  WGNW/BIL/OR WN5 .....46 E6
Johns Pl MPL/ROM SK6 .....113 M2
Johnston WHIT OL12 .....10 D2
Johnston Av LIT OL15 * 29 J1
John St AIMK WN4 .....64 A7
  ALT WA14 .....108 A8
  ANC M4 .....7 H3
  BOLS/LL BL3 * 53 L1
  BRAM/HZG SK7 .....121 M1
  BRO M7 .....72 A8
  BURY BL9 .....4 F3
  CSLFD M3 .....6 D2
  DROY M43 .....89 J4
  DTN/ASHW M34 * 90 C8
  ECC M30 .....84 E3
  EDGW/EG BL7 .....22 D5
  FAIL M35 .....74 C1
  FWTH BL4 .....53 H4
  GLSP SK13 .....104 F4
  GOL/RIS/CUL WA3 .....79 K4
  HEY OL10 .....41 G2
  HYDE SK14 .....102 A2
  IRL M44 .....94 B7
  LEIGH WN7 .....66 C7
  LIT OL15 .....21 L7
  MILN OL16 .....11 C3
  MILN OL16 .....28 F1
  MPL/ROM SK6 .....101 K7
  MPL/ROM SK6 .....113 M2
  MPL/ROM SK6 .....114 D7
  MPL/ROM SK6 .....114 E2
  OLDS OL8 .....9 G6
  PWCH M25 .....56 B4
  ROY/SHW OL2 .....43 C8
  ROY/SHW OL2 .....43 K7
  SALE M33 .....96 F2
  STKP SK1 .....13 J6
  STLY SK15 .....76 F7
  SWIN M27 .....70 D4
  TYLD M29 .....67 K3
  WALK M28 .....53 C8
  WGN WN1 .....15 J4
  WGNE/HIN WN2 .....48 D4
  WGNW/BIL/OR WN5 .....47 G7
  WHIT OL12 .....20 A3
Joiner St ANC M4 .....7 H4
Join Rd SALE M33 .....97 C8
Jolly Brows BOLE BL2 .....37 C1
Jonas St BKLY M9 .....73 H4
  CSLFD M3 .....87 H1
Jonathan Fold LEIGH WN7 .....67 G7
Jones Sq STKP SK1 .....13 K8
Jones St BOL BL1 .....2 E2
  GLSP SK13 .....104 E5
  MILN OL16 .....11 H7
  OLD OL1 .....9 J3
  RAD M26 .....38 E8
  ROY/SHW OL2 .....59 H2
  SLFD M6 .....86 C1
Jonquil Dr WALK M28 .....68 C2
Jopson St MDTN M24 .....57 L3
Jordan Av ROY/SHW OL2 * 43 M3
Jordan St GLSP SK13 .....105 H3
  HULME M15 .....6 D8
Josephine Dr SWIN M27 .....70 D5
Joseph Johnson Ms
  WYTH/NTH M22 * 110 B3
Joseph St ECC M30 .....84 E3
  FAIL M35 .....74 D4
  FWTH BL4 .....53 G4
  LIT OL15 .....21 M6
  MDTN M24 .....57 J3
  MPL/ROM SK6 * 114 D6
  RAD M26 .....54 E2
Joshua La MDTN M24 .....58 A5
Josslyn Rd ORD M5 .....86 A1
Jo St ORD M5 .....86 D3
Joule Cl ORD M5 .....86 C4
Joules Ct STKP SK1 .....13 K5
Joule St BKLY M9 .....73 H3
Jowett St OLD OL1 .....59 M3
  RDSH SK5 .....100 C8
Jowett's Wk AULW OL7 .....90 D2
Jowkin La ROCH OL11 .....27 C5
Joyce St NEWH/MOS M40 .....73 L5
Joynson Av BRO M7 .....72 A8
Joynson St SALE M33 .....96 E7
Joy St RAMS BL0 .....18 E6
  WHIT OL12 .....28 C2
Jubilee Av DUK SK16 .....91 H3
  RAD M26 .....54 F4
  WGNW/BIL/OR WN5 .....46 A8
Jubilee Crs RNFD/HAY WA11 .....78 C5
Jubilee Gdns NM/HAY SK22 .....124 E5
Jubilee Houses WALK M28 * 68 F1
Jubilee Rd MDTN M24 .....57 L3
Jubilee St AULW OL7 .....90 C3
  NM/HAY SK22 .....124 E5
  ROY/SHW OL2 .....43 M5
  SLFD M6 .....86 C2
Jubilee Ter MDTN M24 .....57 L2
Jubilee Wy BURY BL9 .....4 C5
Judith St WHIT OL12 .....10 D3
Judson Av CCHDY M21 .....97 M7
Julia St CSLFD M3 .....6 E1
  WHIT OL12 .....10 D3
Julius St BNG/LEV M19 .....99 L4
Junction Aly MILN OL16 .....10 F5
Junction Rd BOLS/LL BL3 .....35 J7
  OFTN SK2 .....13 J8
Junction Rd West
  HOR/BR BL6 .....35 C7
Junction St HYDE SK14 .....90 F7
  MDTN M24 .....58 A6
  OLDS OL8 .....9 G8
Junction Ter WGNS/IIMK WN3 .....15 L8

June Av HTNM SK4 .....12 B3
  LEIGH WN7 .....65 M6
Juniper Bank RDSH SK5 .....100 D4
Juniper Cl BOL BL1 .....36 B3
  OLDE OL4 .....44 C8
  SALE M33 .....96 B8
Juniper Dr MILN OL16 .....29 G6
  WGNE/HIN WN2 .....65 J1
Juno St OLD OL1 .....9 L1
Jupiter Gv WGNS/IIMK WN3 .....63 H2
Jura Cl DUK SK16 .....91 G4
Jura Dr URM M41 .....85 H7
Jura Gv HEY OL10 .....40 E3
Jurby Av BKLY M9 .....56 F8
Jury St CHH M8 .....72 C8
  LEIGH WN7 .....66 B5
Justene Cl COL/RIS/CUL WA3 .....79 K2
Justin Cl BRUN/LGST M13 .....7 J9
Jutland Av ROCH OL11 .....27 M4
Jutland Gv WHTN BL5 .....50 B3
Jutland St CMANE M1 .....7 K5

K

Kale St BRUN/LGST M13 .....7 K9
Kalima Gv BRO M7 .....72 A6
Kane Ct GOL/RIS/CUL WA3 .....80 D3
Kansas Av SALQ M50 .....86 B4
Kara St SLFD M6 .....86 B2
Karen Rd WGN WN1 .....15 L4
Kate St RAMS BL0 .....18 E6
Kathan Cl MILN OL16 .....11 K5
Katherine Rd OFTN SK2 .....112 F7
Katherine St AULW OL7 * 90 C2
Kathleen Gv RUSH/FAL M14 .....98 F2
Kathleen St WHIT OL12 .....10 B4
Kay Av MPL/ROM SK6 .....113 M3
Kay Brow HEY OL10 .....40 F2
  RAMS BL0 .....18 F6
Kay Cl WGN WN1 .....15 J4
Kayfields BOLE BL2 .....23 H8
Kay's Av STKP SK1 .....112 E3
Kays Gdns CSLFD M3 .....6 B2
Kay St ATH M46 .....67 G2
  BOL BL1 .....2 E1
  BOL BL1 .....2 F3
  BOLS/LL BL3 .....53 L1
  BURY BL9 .....5 J2
  BURY BL9 .....24 F1
  EDGW/EG BL7 .....16 F8
  HEY OL10 .....40 F2
  OP/CLY M11 .....88 C5
  ROCH OL11 .....10 D8
  SLFD M6 .....71 J6
  STLY SK15 .....91 K3
Kay St Wood Rd MPL/ROM SK6 .....114 A6
Keadby Cl ECC M30 .....85 G4
Keal Dr IRL M44 .....83 L8
Kearsley Dr BOLS/LL BL3 .....52 E1
Kearsley Hall Rd RAD M26 .....53 M5
Kearsley Rd CHH M8 .....72 D2
  RAD M26 .....53 M4
Kearsley St ECC M30 .....84 E2
  LEIGH WN7 .....66 A7
  WGNNW/ST WN6 .....14 D2
Kearsley V RAD M26 .....53 L4
Kearton Dr ECC M30 .....85 K3
Keary Cl GTN M18 .....89 G6
Keaton Cl SLFD M6 .....71 H8
Keats Av DROY M43 .....89 K2
  DTN/ASHW M34 .....101 K4
  WGNNW/ST WN6 .....47 M1
  WGNS/IIMK WN3 .....14 C9
  WGNW/BIL/OR WN5 .....62 A3
  WHIT OL12 .....27 K3
Keats Crs RAD M26 .....38 C8
Keats Fold DUK SK16 .....91 L5
Keats Ms NTHM/RTH M23 .....108 F4
Keats Rd ECC M30 .....85 G3
  OLD OL1 .....59 L3
  TOT/BURYW BL8 .....24 C2
Keats St LEIGH WN7 .....66 A5
Keats Wy WGNE/HIN WN2 .....64 E3
Keb La OLDS OL8 .....75 K4
Keble Av OLDS OL8 .....75 H1
Keble Gv LEIGH WN7 .....65 K4
Keble St WGNE/HIN WN2 .....48 C5
Kedleston Av RUSH/FAL M14 .....98 F1
Kedleston Gn OFTN SK2 .....113 G5
Keele Cl NEWH/MOS M40 .....87 M1
Keele Wk NEWH/MOS M40 .....87 M1
Keepers Dr WHIT OL12 .....27 H2
The Keep BOL BL1 .....35 H5
Keighley Av DROY M43 .....89 K1
Keighley Cl TOT/BURYW BL8 .....38 C2
Keighley St BOL BL1 .....35 M2
Keilder Ms BOL BL1 .....35 K4
Keith Dr EDGY/DAV SK3 .....12 A9
Keith Wk NEWH/MOS M40 .....88 A1
Kelboro Av DTN/ASHW M34 .....90 A5
Kelbrook Rd OP/CLY M11 .....88 E4
Kelby Av NTHM/RTH M23 .....109 H5
Keld Cl TOT/BURYW BL8 .....24 E7
Kelfield Av NTHM/RTH M23 .....108 F6
Kellaton Cl WGNS/IIMK WN3 .....15 K7
Kellbank Rd WGNS/IIMK WN3 .....63 H1
Kellbrook Crs BRO M7 .....71 K4
Kellet Cl WGNW/BIL/OR WN5 .....47 C5
Kellets Rw WALK M28 * 53 C7
Kellett St BOL BL1 .....22 C6
  MILN OL16 .....11 J3
Kelling Wk HULME M15 .....6 B9
Kells Gv WGNNW/ST WN6 .....47 J2
Kelmarsh Cl OP/CLY M11 .....89 C5
Kelmscott Av EDGY/DAV SK3 .....112 A6
Kelsall Crs EDGY/DAV SK3 .....112 A6
Kelsall Dr DROY M43 .....89 J1
  HALE/TIMP WA15 .....108 F6
Kelsall Rd CHD/CHDH SK8 .....111 K7
Kelsall St CHAD OL9 .....8 E6
  MILN OL16 .....10 F3
  SALE M33 .....96 D8
  WGTN/LGST M12 .....88 C6
Kelso Cl OLDS OL8 .....75 J3
Kelso Gv WGNE/HIN WN2 .....49 C8
Kelson Av AULW OL7 .....75 K7
Kelstern Av BRUN/LGST M13 .....99 H1
Kelstern Sq BRUN/LGST M13 .....99 H1
Kelton Cl RDSH SK5 .....100 C7
Kelverlow St OLDE OL4 .....59 M6
Kelvin Av MDTN M24 .....56 F5
  SALE M33 .....96 E7
Kelvindale Dr
  HALE/TIMP WA15 .....108 F5
  STLY SK15 .....91 K3
Kelvin Gv CHH M8 .....72 D6
  WGNS/IIMK WN3 .....63 J2
Kelvington Dr BKLY M9 .....73 G6
Kelvin St ANC M4 .....7 H3
  AULW OL7 .....90 C4

Kensington St BOL BL1 .....2 C4
  HYDE SK14 .....102 B3
  ROCH OL11 .....28 B8
  RUSH/FAL M14 .....98 D1
Kenslow Av CHH M8 .....72 C2
Kensworth Cl BOL BL1 * 36 A3
Kensworth Dr BOL BL1 .....36 A3
Kent Av CHAD OL9 .....58 D6
  CHD/CHDH SK8 .....111 M8
  DROY M43 .....89 H3
Kent Cl UPML OL3 .....45 M8
  WALK M28 .....68 D2
Kent Ct BOL BL1 * 2 D3
Kent Dr BURY BL9 .....5 G8
  FWTH BL4 .....53 L6
Kentford Dr NEWH/MOS M40 .....72 F8
Kentford Rd BOL BL1 .....2 D1
Kentmere Av WHIT OL12 .....28 E1
Kentmere Cl CHD/CHDH SK8 .....119 K1
Kentmere Dr MDTN M24 .....57 H1
  TYLD M29 .....67 L1
Kentmere Gv FWTH BL4 .....52 C5
Kentmere Rd BOLE BL2 .....37 J3
  HALE/TIMP WA15 .....109 G6
Kentmore Cl HTNM SK4 .....111 H2
  WGTN/LGST M12 .....88 D5
Kenton Av GTN M18 .....99 M1
Kenton Cl BOL BL1 .....36 A3
  DTN/ASHW M34 .....90 E6
Kenton Rd ROY/SHW OL2 .....43 K5
Kenton St OLDS OL8 .....59 L7
Kent Rd ATH M46 .....50 F8
  DTN/ASHW M34 .....100 D2
  EDGY/DAV SK3 .....12 A7
  FAIL M35 .....74 B6
  GLSP SK13 .....105 G3
  PART M31 .....106 B2
  TYLD M29 .....67 J2
Kent Rd East RUSH/FAL M14 .....99 G1
Kent Rd West RUSH/FAL M14 .....98 F1
Kentsford Dr RAD M26 .....37 K7
Kentstone Av BNG/LEV M19 .....111 G1
Kent St BOL BL1 .....72 A8
  BRO M7 .....72 A8
  CMANW M2 * 6 F4
  LEIGH WN7 .....67 G8
  OLDS OL8 .....59 J8
  ROCH OL11 .....10 E7
  SWIN M27 .....70 E5
  WGN WN1 .....15 J5
Kentucky St OLDE OL4 .....59 M6
Kentwell Cl DUK SK16 .....90 F5
Kenwick Dr NEWH/MOS M40 .....56 B2
Kenwood Av BNG/LEV M19 .....99 J6
  BRAM/HZG SK7 .....120 F7
  CHD/CHDH SK8 .....110 D6
  HALE/TIMP WA15 .....117 J2
  LEIGH WN7 .....66 F7
Kenwood Cl LEIGH WN7 .....66 F8
  STRET M32 .....97 H2
Kenwood La WALK M28 .....69 J7
Kenwood Rd BOL BL1 .....35 L1
  RDSH SK5 .....100 D2
  STRET M32 .....97 H3
Kenworthy Av AUL OL6 .....76 A7
Kenworthy Cl HYDE SK14 .....103 H3
Kenworthy Gdns UPML OL3 .....61 L4
Kenworthy La WYTH/NTH M22 .....110 A2
Kenworthy St MILN OL16 .....91 K3
  STLY SK15 .....91 K3
Kenwright St ANC M4 .....7 H2
Kenwyn St NEWH/MOS M40 .....88 B1
Kenyon Av DUK SK16 .....91 H6
  OLDS OL8 .....75 J1
  SALE M33 .....109 H2
Kenyon Cl HYDE SK14 .....91 H7
Kenyon Fold ROCH OL11 .....27 H7
Kenyon Gv WALK M28 .....68 B1
Kenyon La GOL/RIS/CUL WA3 .....80 C6
  MDTN M24 .....57 H4
  NEWH/MOS M40 .....73 K4
  PWCH M25 .....55 M8
Kenyon Rd BOLE BL2 .....37 L7
  WGN WN1 .....47 M2
  WGNNW/ST WN6 .....31 G2
Kenyons La North
  RNFD/HAY WA11 .....78 C4
Kenyon's La South
  RNFD/HAY WA11 .....78 C4
Kenyon St AUL OL6 .....90 C1
  BURY BL9 .....5 H2
  DUK SK16 .....91 H6
  GTN M18 .....89 H6
  HEY OL10 .....40 F2
  LEIGH WN7 .....66 B7
  RAMS BL0 .....18 F5
Kenyon Ter LHULT M38 .....68 C1
Kenyon Wy LHULT M38 .....68 C1
  TOT/BURYW BL8 .....38 C1
Keppel Rd CCHDY M21 .....97 L3
Keppel St AUL OL6 .....90 F1
Kepplecove Meadow
  WALK M28 .....68 C7
Kepwick Dr WYTH/NTH M22 .....119 G3
Kerans Dr WHTN BL5 .....50 B3
Kerenhappuch St RAMS BL0 .....18 E7
Kerfoot Cl
  WYTH/NTH M22 .....110 B4
Kerfoot St LEIGH WN7 .....66 F6
Kermoor Av BOL BL1 .....22 B6
Kerne Gv NTHM/RTH M23 .....109 K3
Kerrera Dr ORD M5 * 86 A3
Kerridge Dr
  MPL/ROM SK6 .....101 J8
Kerris Cl WYTH/NTH M22 .....119 G3
Kerr St BKLY M9 .....73 G1
Kerry Gv BOLE BL2 .....3 K2
Kersal Av LHULT M38 .....52 E8
  SWIN M27 .....70 F4
Kersal Bank BRO M7 .....71 M4
Kersal Cl PWCH M25 .....71 K3
Kersal Crag BRO M7 .....71 M3
Kersal Dr HALE/TIMP WA15 .....108 F5
Kersal Hall Av BRO M7 .....71 L4
Kersal Rd PWCH M25 .....71 J3
Kersal Vale Rd PWCH M25 .....71 L3
Kerscott Rd
  NTHM/RTH M23 .....109 H2
Kersh Av BNG/LEV M19 .....99 L3
Kershaw Av BOLS/LL BL3 .....37 K8
  PWCH M25 .....71 J2
  SALE M33 .....109 G2
Kershaw Dr CHAD OL9 .....58 A8
Kershaw Gv
  DTN/ASHW M34 .....89 L4
Kershaw La DTN/ASHW M34 .....89 M4
Kershaw Rd FAIL M35 .....74 C4

Kershaw St AULW OL7...90 C4
BOLE BL2...22 F7
BOLS/LL BL3...2 B8
BURY BL9...5 H5
DROY M43...89 J3
GLSP SK13...104 F4
HEY OL10...40 E2
ROY/SHW OL2...43 G7
ROY/SHW OL2...43 L5
TYLD M29...67 K3
WGNW/BIL/OR WN5...46 E6
WHIT OL12 *...10 E1
Kershaw St East ROY/SHW OL2...43 L5
Kershaw Wk WGTN/LGST M12...88 A6
Kershaw Wy NEWLW WA12...78 F7
Kershope Gv ORD M5...86 D4
Kersley St OLDE OL4...59 L6
Kerwin Wk OP/CLY M11 *...88 D4
Kerwood Dr ROY/SHW OL2...59 H1
Kesteven Rd BKLY M9...73 C5
Keston Av BKLY M9...73 K1
DROY M43...89 H3
Keston Crs RDSH SK5...100 E6
Keston Rd OLD OL1...59 M3
Kestor St BOLE BL2...3 J4
Kestrel Av GLSP SK13...104 C4
Kestrel Av DTN/ASHW M34...89 M3
FWTH BL4...52 C5
LHULT M38...52 D7
OLDE OL4...59 M7
SWIN M27...70 E2
Kestrel Cl HYDE SK14...91 H8
MPL/ROM SK6...123 J1
PWCH M25...55 K6
Kestrel Dr AIMK WN4...63 M6
BURY BL9...5 K1
IRL M44...94 D1
Kestrel Rd TRPK M17...85 J4
Kestrel St BOL BL1 *...3 G3
Kestrel Wk WGTN/LGST M12...88 D4
Keswick Av AULW OL7...75 J7
CHAD OL9...58 D5
CHD/CHDH SK8...119 K1
DTN/ASHW M34...90 A8
HYDE SK14...90 F8
OLDS OL8...59 K8
URM M41...95 H3
Keswick Cl BRUN/LGST M13...88 A4
IRL M44...94 A8
MDTN M24...57 G2
STLY SK15...76 D8
Keswick Dr BRAM/HZG SK7...120 E7
BURY BL9...39 G5
Keswick Pl WGNE/HIN WN2...48 D5
Keswick Rd HALE/TIMP WA15...109 G6
HTNM SK4...123 G4
MPL/ROM SK6...128 B5
STRET M32...96 F1
WALK M28...69 J2
Keswick St BOL BL1...36 C2
ROCH OL11...41 L2
Kettering Rd BNG/LEV M19...99 L2
Kettleshulme Wy
POY/DIS SK12...129 L2
Ketton Cl OP/CLY M11...89 H1
Kevin Av ROY/SHW OL2...59 H2
Kevin St BNG/LEV M19...99 L4
Kew Av HYDE SK14...102 B3
Kew Dr CHD/CHDH SK8...120 A2
URM M41...84 D8
Kew Gdns NEWH/MOS M40...73 K3
Kew Rd FAIL M35...74 D4
OLDE OL4...59 L6
ROCH OL11...42 D1
Key Ct DTN/ASHW M34...101 K4
Keymer St OP/CLY M11...88 B2
Keynsham Rd OP/CLY M11...88 E1
Keystone Cl SLFD M6...71 H8
Key West Cl OP/CLY M11...88 C3
Keyworth Wk NEWH/MOS M40...73 H8
Khartoum St OLDTF/WHR M16...87 G7
OP/CLY M11...89 G2
Kibbles Brow EDGW/EG BL7...22 E4
Kibboth Crew RAMS BL0...18 E5
Kibworth Av WHTF M45...55 H4
Kidderminster Wy CHAD OL9...58 C3
Kidd Rd GLSP SK13...105 H6
Kid Glove Rd WGNS/IIMK WN3...79 L3
Kid St MDTN M24 *...57 J3
Kiel Cl ECC M30...85 H4
Kielder Cl AIMK WN4...63 J5
Kielder Hl MDTN M24...41 J8
Kilbride Av BOLE BL2...37 J6
Kilbuck La RNFD/HAY WA11...78 D4
Kilburn Av AIMK WN4...64 A8
BKLY M9...57 G7
Kilburn Cl CHD/CHDH SK8...119 L5
LEIGH WN7...66 A3
Kilburn Dr WGNNW/ST WN6...30 E5
Kilburn Gv WGNS/IIMK WN3...63 C1
Kilburn Rd EDGY/DAV SK3...12 D8
RAD M26...38 A3
Kilburn St OLD OL1...59 M3
Kilcoby Av SWIN M27...71 H4
Kildale Cl BOLS/LL BL3...35 H8
Kildare Crs ROCH OL11...42 D2
Kildare Rd CCHDY M21...98 A4
SWIN M27...70 B3
Kildare St FWTH BL4...52 F5
WGNE/HIN WN2...48 F7
WGNS/IIMK WN3...47 J8
Kildonan Dr BOLS/LL BL3...35 K4
Killer St RAMS BL0 *...18 F6
Killington Cl WGNS/IIMK WN3...63 G1
Killingworth Ms HOR/BR BL6 *...34 A3
Killon St BURY BL9...5 H7
Kilmaine Av BKLY M9...73 L1
Kilmaine Dr BOLS/LL BL3...35 H1
Kilmington Dr CHH M8...72 C6
Kilmory Dr BOLE BL2...37 J6
Kilmory Fold GLSP SK13...105 H1
Kiln Bank La WHIT OL12...20 A2
Kilnbrook Cl AUL OL6...60 E8
Kiln Brow EDGW/EG BL7...22 F4
Kiln Cft MPL/ROM SK6...113 J3
Kiln Croft La WILM/AE SK9...120 A8
Kilner Cl BURY BL9...39 L8
Kilnerdeyne Ter MILN OL16...10 D6
Kilner Wk NEWH/MOS M40...72 F8
Kiln Fld EDGW/EG BL7...22 C4
Kiln Hill Cl OLD OL1...58 C2
Kiln Hill La OLD OL1...58 C2
Kilnhurst Wk BOL BL1 *...2 B3
Kiln La GLSP SK13...93 K7
MILN OL16...29 K5
Kilnside Dr BKLY M9...73 G5
Kiln St RAMS BL0...18 E5
Kiln Wk WHIT OL12...28 B2
Kilnwick Cl GTN M18...99 L1
The Kilphin HOR/BR BL6...34 E4
Kilrush Av ECC M30...85 G4

Kilsby Cl FWTH BL4...52 E2
HOR/BR BL6...34 F6
Kilsby Wk NEWH/MOS M40...73 G8
Kilshaw St WGNW/BIL/OR WN5...46 F7
Kilton Wk NEWH/MOS M40 *...72 F8
Kilvert Dr SALE M33...96 C2
Kilvert St TRPK M17...86 D7
Kilworth Av SALE M33...108 C1
Kilworth Dr HOR/BR BL6...35 G6
Kilworth St ROCH OL11...10 B9
Kimberley Av AIMK WN4...78 E1
Kimberley Pl AIMK WN4...78 E1
Kimberley Rd BOL BL1...22 B7
Kimberley St BRO M7 *...72 B5
EDGY/DAV SK3...13 H9
OLDS OL8...74 F1
Kimberley Wk HULME M15...6 B9
Kimberly St WGNNW/ST WN6...14 E1
Kimble Cl TOT/BURYW BL8...24 C2
Kimbolton Cl WGTN/LGST M12...88 D5
Kinburn Rd BNG/LEV M19...111 G2
Kincardine Rd BRUN/LGST M13...7 J9
Kincraig Cl BOLS/LL BL3...35 H8
OP/CLY M11...88 F3
Kinder Av AUL OL6...76 D6
OLDE OL4...60 A7
Kinder Cl GLSP SK13...104 D4
Kinder Dr MPL/ROM SK6...114 D6
Kinder Fold STLY SK15...92 A6
Kinder Gv AIMK WN4...63 J6
MPL/ROM SK6...114 B2
Kinders Cl OLDE OL4...61 L7
Kinders Fold LIT OL15...21 K5
Kinders La UPML OL3...61 M6
Kinders Ms UPML OL3 *...61 L7
Kinder St EDGY/DAV SK3...13 G8
STLY SK15...91 K2
Kinderton Av DID/WITH M20...98 E5
Kinder Wy MDTN M24...57 J2
Kineton Wk BRUN/LGST M13...87 M6
Kingham Dr ANC M4...7 M2
King Albert St ROY/SHW OL2...43 L5
King Charles Ct GLSP SK13...105 G5
King Cup Cl GLSP SK13...105 H4
King Edward Av GLSP SK13...105 G3
King Edward Rd HYDE SK14...102 B5
King Edward St BNG/LEV M19...99 L3
ECC M30...84 F2
ORD M5...86 E4
Kingfisher Av DTN/ASHW M34...89 M4
Kingfisher Cl WGTN/LGST M12...88 B7
Kingfisher Ct AIMK WN4...63 L6
Kingfisher Dr BURY BL9...25 L8
FWTH BL4...52 C5
Kingfisher Ms OFTN SK2...13 C8
Kingfisher Wy GLSP SK13...104 C4
King George Cl AIMK WN4...78 E1
King George Rd HYDE SK14...102 B3
RNFD/HAY WA11...78 D5
Kingham Dr ANC M4...7 M2
Kingholm Gdns BOL BL1 *...36 A3
King La OLD OL1...44 B8
Kingmoor Av RAD M26...38 B3
King's Acre ALT WA14...116 C3
Kings CHD/CHDH SK8...110 D8
CHH M8...72 D4
GOL/RIS/CUL WA3...80 C5
WHTF M45...55 H2
Kingsbridge Av BOLE BL2...38 A3
HYDE SK14...102 F2
Kingsbridge Cl MPL/ROM SK6...114 B5
Kingsbridge Dr DUK SK16...90 E5
Kingsbridge Rd BKLY M9...72 F5
OLDS OL8 *...59 L7
Kingsbrook Rd
OLDTF/WHR M16...98 B4
Kingsbury Av BOL BL1...35 K3
Kingsbury Ct TOT/BURYW BL8...24 D6
Kingsbury Dr WILM/AE SK9...127 H4
Kingsbury Rd OP/CLY M11...88 F2
Kingscliffe St BKLY M9...73 H5
King's Cl BRAM/HZG SK7...121 H2
GTN M18...89 J6
PWCH M25...55 M7
WILM/AE SK9...126 E6
Kings Ct RDSH SK5...13 J1
Kingscourt Ct WGN WN1...15 K5
Kings Crs OLDTF/WHR M16...97 L1
TYLD M29...67 H4
Kingsdale Rd BNG/LEV M19...99 K8
Kingsdale Rd GTN M18...89 K8
Kingsdown Crs WGN WN1...31 M8
Kingsdown Dr BOL BL1 *...2 E1
Kingsdown Gdns BOL BL1 *...2 E1
Kingsdown Rd WGNE/HIN WN2...64 E5
WYTH/NTH M22...118 E3
Kingsdown Rd CHH M8...72 D4
HTNM SK4...111 K1
MDTN M24...57 G4
MPL/ROM SK6...114 B5
Kingsfield Dr DID/WITH M20...110 F2
Kingsfield Wy TYLD M29...67 L4
Kings Fold ATH M46...67 H1
Kingsfold Av NEWH/MOS M40 *...72 F8
Kingsford St ORD M5...86 A2
King's Gdns LEIGH WN7...66 F7
Kingsgate BOL BL1 *...2 D1
Kingsgate Rd WYTH/NTH M22...118 E3
Kings Gv STRET M32...97 J1
WHIT OL12...21 G8
Kingsheath Av OP/CLY M11...88 E1
Kingshill Ct WGNNW/ST WN6...31 J5
Kingshill Rd CCHDY M21...97 K4
Kingsholme Rd
WYTH/NTH M22...118 C2
Kingsland Cl NEWH/MOS M40...88 A1
Kingsland Rd EDGY/DAV SK3...111 K5
FWTH BL4...52 C5
ROCH OL11...41 L1
Kings La STRET M32...97 J1
Kingslea Rd DID/WITH M20...98 F7
Kingsleigh Rd HTNM SK4...99 J8
Kingsley Av BKLY M9...73 J5
BRO M7...71 K5
HTNM SK4...100 B8
STRET M32...97 J1
URM M41...95 L2
WGNNW/ST WN6...63 J1
WHTF M45...55 K5
WILM/AE SK9...127 G6
Kingsley Cl AUL OL6...76 D7
DTN/ASHW M34...101 G3
OLDE OL4...60 B7
Kingsley Dr CHD/CHDH SK8...120 C1
OLDE OL4...60 B7
Kingsley Gv DTN/ASHW M34...89 M4
Kingsley Rd HALE/TIMP WA15...108 E3
MDTN M24...57 L2
OLDE OL4...59 M6
SWIN M27...70 A3
WALK M28...68 F1
WGNE/HIN WN2 *...49 J7
WYTH/NTH M22...110 A4

Kingsley St BOL BL1...36 A2
LEIGH WN7...65 M5
TOT/BURYW BL8...38 E2
King's Lynn Cl DID/WITH M20...110 E1
Kingsmead Ms BKLY M9...56 F7
Kingsmede WGN WN1...48 A1
Kingsmere Av BNG/LEV M19...99 J3
Kingsmill Av BNG/LEV M19...99 L4
Kingsmoor Flds GLSP SK13...105 G1
Kingsmoor Rd GLSP SK13...105 G2
Kingsnorth Rd URM M41...95 C1
Kingsoak Cl WGN WN1...15 H3
Kings Pk ATH M46...66 D4
King's Rd AIMK WN4...63 K7
AUL OL6...75 M8
BRAM/HZG SK7...122 A1
CHAD OL9...58 D8
CHD/CHDH SK8...120 C1
DTN/ASHW M34...89 K7
GOL/RIS/CUL WA3...79 K5
IRL M44...94 B6
MILN OL16...11 J9
MPL/ROM SK6...113 K1
OLDS OL8...9 K9
OLDTF/WHR M16...97 K1
PWCH M25...71 M2
ROY/SHW OL2...43 K6
SALE M33...96 C8
STRET M32...97 H2
WILM/AE SK9...126 C4
Kings Ter STRET M32...97 J1
Kingston Av BOLE BL2...3 L1
CHAD OL9...58 D8
DID/WITH M20...110 E3
OLD OL1 *...59 L3
Kingston Cl BRO M7...72 A4
HYDE SK14...103 H2
ROY/SHW OL2...43 L5
SALE M33...108 A2
TOT/BURYW BL8...38 E4
WGNS/IIMK WN3...63 L1
Kingston Dr ROY/SHW OL2...42 F6
SALE M33...97 G7
URM M41...95 L4
Kingston Gdns HYDE SK14...101 L1
Kingston Gv BKLY M9...57 J8
Kingston Hl CHD/CHDH SK8...119 G8
Kingston Ml CHD/CHDH SK8...119 G8
Kingston Pl CHD/CHDH SK8...120 A2
Kingston Rd DID/WITH M20...110 E3
FAIL M35...74 E5
RAD M26...38 F6
WILM/AE SK9...119 L8
Kingston St EDGY/DAV SK3...12 F5
King St BOL BL1...2 D4
BOLE BL2...23 G7
BRO M7...72 B5
CMANW M2...6 F4
CSLFD M3...6 D2
DROY M43...89 K4
DTN/ASHW M34...90 C6
DUK SK16...90 E4
ECC M30...85 J3
EDGW/EG BL7...22 C4
FAIL M35...74 A6
FWTH BL4...53 G4
GLSP SK13...104 F4
HEY OL10...41 G3
HYDE SK14...93 G7
HYDE SK14...102 A1
HYDE SK14...103 K4
LEIGH WN7...66 C8
MDTN M24...57 K3
MILN OL16...10 E4
MOSL OL5...77 G3
OLDS OL8...9 H6
OLDE OL4...60 A5
RAD M26...54 E2
RAMS BL0...18 F6
SLFD M6...71 G7
STLY SK15...91 K2
UPML OL3...45 J8
WGN WN1...14 F4
WGNE/HIN WN2...48 D5
WGNE/HIN WN2 *...48 D1
WHIT OL12...20 E1
King St East ROCH OL11...10 E8
STKP SK1...13 J2
King St South ROCH OL11...10 D8
King St West CSLFD M3...6 E4
EDGY/DAV SK3...13 G6
HTNM SK4...12 F4
WGN WN1...14 F4
Kings Vw HTNM SK4 *...12 D4
Kingsway ALT WA14...108 A7
BNG/LEV M19...99 H3
BRAM/HZG SK7...121 H2
DID/WITH M20...110 F5
DID/WITH M20...111 G2
DUK SK16...91 H5
FWTH BL4...53 J6
MDTN M24...57 J6
MPL/ROM SK6...113 H1
STRET M32...96 F3
SWIN M27...70 F6
WALK M28...69 G4
WGN WN1...48 A2
WHTF M45...15 M6
Kingsway Av BNG/LEV M19...99 J3
Kingsway Cl OLDS OL8...9 G9
Kingsway Crs BNG/LEV M19...99 J3
Kingsway Pk URM M41...85 G8
Kingswear Dr BOL BL1...35 M3
Kingswood Gv RDSH SK5...100 C3
Kingswood Rd ECC M30...69 G8
MDTN M24...57 J6
PWCH M25...55 J7
RUSH/FAL M14...99 H5
Kingthorpe Gdns
BOLS/LL BL3 *...36 B8
King William St ECC M30...84 D1
SALQ M50...86 D4
King Wk TYLD M29...67 J3
Kingwood Av BOL BL1...35 J4
Kingwood Crs
WGNW/BIL/OR WN5...47 G6
Kinlay Rd FWTH BL4...52 E3
Kinlet Rd WGNS/IIMK WN3...46 F8
Kinley Cl WGTN/LGST M12...88 E8
Kinloch Dr BOL BL1...35 L5
Kinloch Gdns OLDS OL8...59 K8
Kinloch St OLDS OL8...59 K8
OP/CLY M11...88 D2
Kinmel Av RDSH SK5...100 F8
Kinnaird Crs STKP SK1...112 E4
Kinnaird Rd DID/WITH M20...98 F7
Kinnerly Gv WALK M28...68 F1
Kinniside Cl WGNS/IIMK WN3...63 K2

Kinross Av AIMK WN4...62 F8
OFTN SK2...121 J1
Kinross Cl RAMS BL0...24 D2
Kinross Dr BOLS/LL BL3...35 J7
Kinross Rd RUSH/FAL M14...99 H1
Kinsey Av NTHM/RTH M23...109 J5
Kinsley Dr WALK M28...68 F2
Kintbury St WGNE/HIN WN2...64 C5
Kintore Av BRAM/HZG SK7...122 B2
Kintyre Av ORD M5...86 B5
Kintyre Cl OP/CLY M11 *...88 F3
Kintyre Dr BOLS/LL BL3...35 H7
Kinver Rd NEWH/MOS M40...73 M2
Kipling Av DROY M43...89 K5
DTN/ASHW M34...101 K5
WGNS/IIMK WN3...47 K8
Kipling Cl OFTN SK2...113 H5
Kipling Gv LEIGH WN7...66 A5
Kipling St BRO M7...72 A6
Kippax Av WGNW/BIL/OR WN5...46 E3
Kippax St RUSH/FAL M14...98 E1
Kirby Av ATH M46...50 F7
CHAD OL9...74 A1
SALE M33...108 A3
SWIN M27...70 A7
Kirby Rd LEIGH WN7...66 B6
Kirkbank St CHAD OL9...8 F3
Kirkbeck LEIGH WN7...81 M1
Kirkby Av NEWH/MOS M40...74 A2
Kirkby Cl BURY BL9...39 H5
Kirkby Dr SALE M33...109 G2
Kirkdale Av NEWH/MOS M40...74 A2
Kirkdale Dr ROY/SHW OL2...42 F7
Kirkebrok Rd BOLS/LL BL3...35 K8
Kirkfell Dr MPL/ROM SK6...123 C4
TYLD M29...67 L5
Kirkfenton Cl WHTN BL5...50 C3
Kirkhall Wk NEWH/MOS M40 *...7 M1
Kirkhall La BOL BL1...35 M4
LEIGH WN7...66 B6
Kirkham Av GOL/RIS/CUL WA3 *...80 B6
GTN M18...89 G6
Kirkham Cl DTN/ASHW M34...101 J1
Kirkham Rd CHD/CHDH SK8...119 L4
TYLD M29...67 L5
Kirkham St BOLE BL2 *...8 L1
LHULT M38...52 D7
SALQ M50...86 B3
WGNE/HIN WN2...64 E4
Kirkhaven Sq NEWH/MOS M40...73 M8
Kirkhill Gra WHTN BL5...50 D2
Kirkhope Dr BOL BL1...36 A3
Kirkhope Wk BOL BL1...2 B1
Kirklands BOLE BL2...37 G2
SALE M33...108 D2
Kirklee Av CHAD OL9...58 D3
Kirklee Rd ROCH OL11...42 A2
Kirklees St TOT/BURYW BL8...24 D5
WGN WN1...15 L4
Kirkless La WGNE/HIN WN2...48 E3
Kirkless St WGNE/HIN WN2...48 D1
Kirkless Vls WGNE/HIN WN2 *...48 D2
Kirkley St HYDE SK14...102 A3
Kirklinton Dr BKLY M9...73 C6
Kirkman Av ECC M30...84 F4
Kirkman Cl GTN M18...89 G8
Kirkmanshulme La GTN M18...88 E7
Kirkman St BURY BL9...55 J1
Kirkpatrick St WGNE/HIN WN2...65 L1
Kirk Rd BNG/LEV M19...99 L5
Kirkstall WHIT OL10...40 F1
LIT OL15...21 L6
Kirkstall Av HEY OL10...40 F1
Kirkstall Cl POY/DIS SK12...121 M8
Kirkstall Rd MDTN M24...57 J1
URM M41...96 B1
Kirkstall Sq BRUN/LGST M13...87 M6
Kirkstead Cl OP/CLY M11...88 D4
Kirkstead Rd CHD/CHDH SK8...119 G8
Kirkstead Wy GOL/RIS/CUL WA3...79 K4
Kirkstile Crs WGNS/IIMK WN3...63 H2
Kirkstile Pl SWIN M27...54 B8
Kirkstone WGNW/BIL/OR WN5...46 E5
Kirkstone Av WALK M28...69 J3
Kirkstone Cl OLD OL1...9 K1
Kirkstone Dr MDTN M24...57 H2
ROY/SHW OL2...42 F6
Kirkstone Rd HYDE SK14...90 F7
NEWH/MOS M40...73 M2
Kirk St GTN M18...89 G7
Kirkwall Dr BOLE BL2...3 K8
Kirkway BKLY M9...57 K8
MDTN M24...57 K6
ROCH OL11...42 C2
Kirkwood Cl WGNE/HIN WN2...48 C2
Kirkwood Dr NEWH/MOS M40...72 F8
Kirtley Av ECC M30...85 G1
Kirtlington Cl ROY/SHW OL2...43 K7
Kitchener Av BOLS/LL BL3...52 E1
TOT/BURYW BL8...38 F2
Kitchener St BURY BL9...55 J1
Kitchener Wy FWTH BL4...52 C3
Kite Gv LEIGH WN7...66 E7
Kitepool St ECC M30 *...84 D1
Kitter St WHIT OL12...28 F1
Kitt Green Rd
WGNW/BIL/OR WN5...46 F4
Kittiwake Cl TYLD M29...67 K5
Kitt's Moss La BRAM/HZG SK7...120 F6
Kitty Wheeldon Gdns
SALE M33 *...96 D7
Kiveton Cl WALK M28...68 F2
Kiveton Dr AIMK WN4...78 E2
Kiwi St SLFD M6...86 E2
Knaresborough Cl RDSH SK5...100 B3
Knaresborough Rd
WGNE/HIN WN2...49 H8
Knarr Barn La UPML OL3...61 G1
Knarr La UPML OL3...61 H2
Knight Crs MDTN M24...57 G1
Knightley Wk NEWH/MOS M40...73 G7
Knightsbridge STKP SK1...13 J1
Knightsbridge Cl BRO M7...72 A4
WILM/AE SK9...127 H1
Knightscliffe Crs
WGNNW/ST WN6...30 B6
Knight's Cv PWCH M25...55 L7
Knightshill Crs
WGNNW/ST WN6...14 A1
Knight St AULW OL7...90 C2
BOL BL1...2 E2
DID/WITH M20...110 E2
HYDE SK14...102 C3
TOT/BURYW BL8 *...38 F2
Knightswood BOLS/LL BL3...51 G2
Knightswood Rd CHH M8...72 D5
Knightwake Rd NM/HAY SK22...124 C4
Kniveton Rd WGTN/LGST M12...88 C6

Kniveton Rd WGTN/LGST M12...88 C1
Knivton St HYDE SK14...102 C1
Knole Av POY/DIS SK12...122 B8
Knoll St BRO M7...72 A5
NM/HAY SK22...124 D4
ROCH OL11...41 L1
The Knoll MOSL OL5...76 E3
ROY/SHW OL2...43 M6
Knott Fold HYDE SK14...102 A4
Knott Hill La UPML OL3...45 H8
Knott La BOL BL1...35 L4
HYDE SK14...102 A4
Knott Lanes OLDS OL8...75 H4
Knotts Brow EDGW/EG BL7...17 J8
Knott St ORD M5...86 A3
Knowe Av WYTH/NTH M22...118 F3
Knowl Cl DTN/ASHW M34...100 D2
RAMS BL0...19 K5
Knowldale Wy WGTN/LGST M12...88 B8
Knowle Av AULW OL7...75 K8
Knowle Dr PWCH M25...71 K2
Knowle Pk WILM/AE SK9...127 G1
Knowle Rd MPL/ROM SK6...114 C6
Knowles Av WGNS/IIMK WN3...47 J8
Knowles Edge St BOL BL1...35 M4
WGN WN1...15 L3
Knowles Pl HULME M15...6 F9
WGN WN1...15 L3
Knowles St RAD M26...38 D8
WGNS/IIMK WN3...15 K8
The Knowles OLDS OL8...74 E3
Knowl Hill Dr WHIT OL12...27 H4
Knowl Rd MILN OL16...29 G6
ROY/SHW OL2...43 M6
Knowls La OLDE OL4...60 C7
Knowl St OLDS OL8...74 F2
STLY SK15...91 L2
Knowl Syke St WHIT OL12...21 G5
Knowl Vw LIT OL15...29 J2
TOT/BURYW BL8...24 D6
Knowsley Av AIMK WN4...50 F8
GOL/RIS/CUL WA3...79 L3
OLDE OL4...60 D5
ORD M5...86 E4
URM M41...95 G5
Knowsley Crs STKP SK1...112 E4
Knowsley Dr LEIGH WN7...81 H2
SWIN M27...70 A6
Knowsley Gra BOL BL1...35 G5
Knowsley Gn OLDE OL4...60 D5
ORD M5 *...86 E4
Knowsley Gv HOR/BR BL6...34 A3
Knowsley Rd BOL BL1...35 L2
BOLE BL2...37 M3
BRAM/HZG SK7...122 B4
STKP SK1...112 E4
WGNNW/ST WN6...47 K1
WHTF M45...55 J4
Knowsley St BOL BL1...2 D5
BURY BL9...4 D7
CHH M8...72 D8
LEIGH WN7...66 A7
WHIT OL12...10 D2
Knowsley Ter OLDE OL4...60 D5
STKP SK1...112 E4
Knutsford Av HTNM SK4...100 A3
SALE M33...97 H8
Knutsford Rd GTN M18...88 F8
WILM/AE SK9...126 D7
Knutsford St SLFD M6...86 B2
Knutshaw Crs BOLS/LL BL3...51 G2
Knypersley Av OFTN SK2...112 F5
Krokus Sq CHAD OL9...58 D5
Kylemore Av BOLS/LL BL3...35 G3
Kyle Rd BRAM/HZG SK7...122 B3
Kynder St DTN/ASHW M34...101 J1

L

Labrador Quay SALQ M50...86 C5
Labtec St SWIN M27...70 D4
Laburnum Av ATH M46...67 H1
AUL OL6...75 M8
CHAD OL9...8 B1
DTN/ASHW M34...89 M3
ECC M30...84 D4
FAIL M35...74 C6
HYDE SK14...102 A4
LEIGH WN7...66 B4
ROY/SHW OL2...43 L6
STLY SK15...91 J4
SWIN M27...70 B6
TOT/BURYW BL8...24 C5
WGNS/IIMK WN3...15 M7
WHTF M45...55 K3
Laburnum Cl HALE/TIMP WA15...108 E7
WHTF M45...55 K3
Laburnum Dr WGNNW/ST WN6...31 K8
Laburnum Gv HOR/BR BL6...34 A3
PWCH M25...55 K7
TYLD M29...68 A3
Laburnum La
HALE/TIMP WA15...117 L4
MILN OL16...43 K1
Laburnum Pk BOLE BL2...22 F7
Laburnum Rd DTN/ASHW M34...100 C1
FWTH BL4...52 E4
GOL/RIS/CUL WA3...80 C4
GTN M18...89 G8
IRL M44...94 A7
MDTN M24...57 M4
OLDS OL8...74 F4
URM M41...84 E8
WALK M28...69 H2
Laburnum St AIMK WN4...78 E2
ATH M46...67 H1
BOL BL1...2 E2
SLFD M6...86 C2
Laburnum Ter ROCH OL11...28 B8
Laburnum Wy EDGY/DAV SK3...12 B6
LIT OL15...21 K5
Lacerta Ms BRO M7...86 F1
Lacey Av WILM/AE SK9...126 F4
Lacey Ct WILM/AE SK9...126 F4
Lacey Gn WILM/AE SK9...127 G3
Lackford Dr NEWH/MOS M40...72 F8
Lacrosse Av OLDS OL8...58 F8
Lacy Gv STRET M32...97 J1
Lacy St STKP SK1...13 J4
STRET M32...97 J1
Lacy Wk WGTN/LGST M12...88 A4
Ladbrooke Cl AUL OL6...75 M8
Ladbrooke Rd AUL OL6...75 M8
Ladcastle Rd UPML OL3...61 K3
UPML OL3...61 K6
Ladhill La UPML OL3...61 L7
Ladies La WGNE/HIN WN2...49 J5
Ladybarn Av GOL/RIS/CUL WA3...79 J5
Ladybarn Crs BRAM/HZG SK7...121 H6
RUSH/FAL M14...99 J3

Ladybarn La RUSH/FAL M14 ....99 G4
Ladybarn Rd RUSH/FAL M14 ....99 G4
Ladybower CHD/CHDH SK8 ....120 E1
Ladybridge Av WALK M28 ....68 F4
Lady Bridge La BOL BL1 ....35 J5
Ladybridge Ri CHD/CHDH SK8 .....120 E1
Ladybridge Rd CHD/CHDH SK8 ....120 E1
Ladybrook Av
    HALE/TIMP WA15 ....108 E5
Ladybrook Rd
    BRAM/HZG SK7 ....120 E3
Ladyfield St WILM/AE SK9 ....126 F5
Ladyfield Ter WILM/AE SK9 ....127 G5
Ladyhill Vw WALK M28 ....68 F4
Ladyhouse Cl MILN OL16 ....29 K8
Ladyhouse La MILN OL16 ....29 K7
Lady Kelvin Rd ALT WA14 ....107 M6
Lady La WGNS/IIMK WN3 ....47 H8
Ladymere Dr WALK M28 ....68 E4
Ladypit Rd CHF/WBR SK23 ....125 H8
Lady Rd OLDE OL4 ....60 B6
Ladys Cl POY/DIS SK12 ....122 A8
Ladyshore Rd BOLS/LL BL3 ....53 M2
Ladyshore Rd BOLS/LL BL3 ....53 M2
Ladysmith Av AIMK WN4 ....78 F1
    BURY BL9 ....25 K7
Ladysmith Dr AUL OL6 ....76 C7
Ladysmith Rd AUL OL6 ....76 C7
    DID/WITH M20 ....110 F2
Ladysmith St EDGY/DAV SK3 ....13 H9
    OLDS OL8 ....74 H1
The Ladysmith AUL OL6 ....76 C7
Ladythorn Av MPL/ROM SK6 ....114 D7
Ladythorn Ct PWCH M25 ....71 K2
Ladythorn Crs BRAM/HZG SK7 ....121 H6
Ladythorne Av PWCH M25 ....71 K2
Ladythorne Dr PWCH M25 ....71 K2
Ladythorn Gv BRAM/HZG SK7 .....121 G6
Ladythorn Rd BRAM/HZG SK7 .....121 G6
Ladywell Av LHULT M38 ....52 D8
Ladywell Cl BRAM/HZG SK7 ....121 J2
Ladywell Gv LHULT M38 ....52 D7
Lagos Cl RUSH/FAL M14 ....87 K8
Laindon Rd RUSH/FAL M14 ....99 H1
Laithwaite Rd
    WGNW/BIL/OR WN5 ....47 G6
Lake Bank LIT OL15 ....29 K1
Lake Dr MDTN M24 ....57 J5
Lakeland Av AIMK WN4 ....63 M8
Lakeland Crs BURY BL9 ....39 H6
Lakeland Dr ROY/SHW OL2 * 42 F4
Lakelands Dr BOLS/LL BL3 ....35 J7
Lakenheath Cl BOL BL1 ....22 C6
Lakenheath Dr BOL BL1 ....22 C6
Lake Rd DTN/ASHW M34 ....90 C8
    STLY SK15 ....76 C8
    TRPK M17 ....85 M5
Lakes Dr WGNW/BIL/OR WN5 ....46 B6
Lake Side BURY BL9 ....39 J8
    LEIGH WN7 ....66 A6
    LIT OL15 ....29 K2
Lakeside CHD/CHDH SK8 ....119 L2
    GLSP SK13 ....93 K6
Lakeside Av AULW OL7 ....75 J8
    BOLS/LL BL3 ....52 D2
    WALK M28 ....53 G7
    WGNW/BIL/OR WN5 ....62 B1
Lakeside Cl GTN M18 ....89 J6
Lakeside Dr POY/DIS SK12 ....122 A4
Lakeside Gn OFTN SK2 ....112 F6
Lakeside Ri BKLY M9 ....72 D1
Lakeside Wy BURY BL9 ....4 E7
Lakes Rd DUK SK16 ....90 F4
    MPL/ROM SK6 ....114 E7
Lakes Ter WGNE/HIN WN2 ....48 D5
Lake St BOLS/LL BL3 * 2 E9
    LEIGH WN7 ....66 D6
    OFTN SK2 ....112 E7
Lakeswood DUK SK16 * 90 E4
Lake Vw BKLY M9 ....73 H1
Lakin St NEWH/MOS M40 ....73 K5
Laleham Gn BRAM/HZG SK7 ....120 F1
Lamb Cl WGTN/LGST M12 * 88 C7
Lamb Ct CSLFD M3 * 6 C3
Lamberhead Rd
    WGNW/BIL/OR WN5 ....46 E6
Lambert Dr SALE M33 ....96 A6
Lamberton Dr NTHM/RTH M23 ......109 H6
Lambert Av MDTN M24 ....57 G5
Lambeth Av FAIL M35 ....74 C4
Lambeth Cl HOR/BR BL6 ....34 A1
Lambeth Cl MPL/ROM SK6 ....101 K7
    RDSH SK5 ....100 C5
Lambeth Rd NEWH/MOS M40 ....73 M8
    RDSH SK5 ....100 C5
Lambeth Ter ROCH OL11 ....10 A9
Lambgates GLSP SK13 ....93 K5
Lamb La ALT WA14 ....116 F7
    CSLFD M3 ....6 C3
Lambley Cl LEIGH WN7 ....66 A4
Lambourn Cl BOLS/LL BL3 * 2 C8
    POY/DIS SK12 ....121 M8
Lambourne Cl WYTH/NTH M22 ......118 F4
Lambourne Gv MILN OL16 ....29 J7
Lambourn Rd URM M41 ....84 A8
Lamb St WGN WN1 ....15 K1
Lambton Cl CCHDY M21 ....98 A4
    WALK M28 ....69 M6
Lambton St BOLS/LL BL3 ....51 J2
    ECC M30 ....69 L8
    WGNW/BIL/OR WN5 ....46 E7
Lamburn Av
    NEWH/MOS M40 * 74 A2
Lamerton Wy WILM/AE SK9 ....127 J2
Lamorna Cl BRO M7 ....71 L4
Lamphey Cl BOL BL1 ....35 G4
Lamplight Wy SWIN M27 ....71 H5
Lamport Cl CMANE M1 * 7 J8
Lamport Ct CMANE M1 * 7 J8
Lampson St CHH M8 ....72 B8
Lamport St ALT WA14 ....108 A5
Lamsholme Cl BNG/LEV M19 ....99 K2
Lanark Av WYTH/NTH M22 ....110 A4
Lanark Cl BRAM/HZG SK7 ....122 C2
    HEY OL10 ....40 C3
Lanbury Dr CHH M8 ....72 C5
Lancashire Cl CHAD OL9 ....8 C8
Lancashire Hl HTNM SK4 ....13 H1
Lancashire St
    NEWH/MOS M40 ....73 J7
Lancaster Av ATH M46 ....67 G4
    FAIL M35 ....74 B5
    FWTH BL4 ....52 C4
    GOL/RIS/CUL WA3 ....79 M4
    HOR/BR BL6 ....34 A2
    MDTN M24 ....57 M5
    RAMS BL0 ....18 D8
    TYLD M29 ....67 K1
    URM M41 ....96 B1
    WHTF M45 ....55 K5

Lancaster Cl BOL BL1 ....3 C5
    BRAM/HZG SK7 ....121 M4
    MPL/ROM SK6 ....113 K3
    NEWLW WA12 ....78 C8
Lancaster Dr BOLS/LL BL3 ....37 L8
    BURY BL9 ....25 J4
    PWCH M25 ....71 M2
Lancaster Rd DID/WITH M20 ....110 D1
    DROY M43 ....89 J1
    DTN/ASHW M34 ....101 J3
    SLFD M6 ....70 E8
    WGNE/HIN WN2 ....49 J7
    WGNW/BIL/OR WN5 ....46 F3
    WILM/AE SK9 ....127 J3
Lancaster St CHAD OL9 ....74 D1
    MOSL OL5 ....76 E5
    RAD M26 ....54 B1
    STKP SK1 ....13 L2
    WGNS/IIMK WN3 ....15 K7
Lancaster Wk BOL BL1 * 36 B2
Lancelot Rd WYTH/NTH M22 ....119 H2
Lancelyn Dr WILM/AE SK9 ....127 H4
Lance Wood Pl
    WGNW/BIL/OR WN5 ....47 G6
Lanchester Dr BOLS/LL BL3 ....2 A8
Lanchester St
    NEWH/MOS M40 ....88 B1
Lancing Av DID/WITH M20 ....111 G1
Lancing Wk CHAD OL9 * 58 D6
Landau Dr WALK M28 ....68 C1
Landcross Rd
    RUSH/FAL M14 ....98 F3
Landedmans MILN BL5 ....50 C5
Lander Gv BKLY M9 ....73 H7
Land Gate La AIMK WN4 ....63 K5
Landkey Cl NTHM/RTH M23 ....109 J2
Land La WILM/AE SK9 ....127 G6
Landmark Ct BOL BL1 ....35 J3
Landor Cl GOL/RIS/CUL WA3 ....80 B4
Landos Rd
    NEWH/MOS M40 ....7 M1
Landrace Dr WALK M28 ....68 E6
Landsberg Rd FAIL M35 ....74 E4
Landseer Dr MPL/ROM SK6 ....114 E5
Landseer St OLDS OL8 ....9 L8
Lands End Rd MDTN M24 ....56 E5
Landside LEIGH WN7 ....81 J2
Land St WGNNW/ST WN6 ....14 D3
Laneside Av ROY/SHW OL2 ....44 A5
Laneside Cl LIT OL15 ....21 L6
Laneside Dr BRAM/HZG SK7 ....121 J3
Laneside Rd DID/WITH M20 ....110 F4
    NM/HAY SK22 ....125 H6
The Lane BOL BL1 ....35 C5
Lanfield Dr CHH M8 ....72 C5
Langcroft Dr NEWH/MOS M40 ....73 H7
Langdale Av BNG/LEV M19 ....99 L4
    GOL/RIS/CUL WA3 ....79 M3
    MILN OL16 ....42 F4
    OLDS OL8 ....59 C8
    WGN WN1 ....47 L2
    WGNE/HIN WN2 ....48 E4
Langdale Cl CHD/CHDH SK8 ....119 L1
    DTN/ASHW M34 ....101 H3
    HALE/TIMP WA15 ....108 B7
    MPL/ROM SK6 ....123 G4
Langdale Crs WGNE/HIN WN2 ....64 C4
    WGNW/BIL/OR WN5 ....46 E4
Langdale Dr BURY BL9 ....55 K1
    MDTN M24 ....57 J1
    WALK M28 ....53 L7
Langdale Gv WGNE/HIN WN2 ....64 E1
Langdale Rd BRAM/HZG SK7 ....120 E7
    HTNM SK4 ....99 M6
    MPL/ROM SK6 ....101 L7
    PART M31 ....106 B1
    RUSH/FAL M14 ....88 A3
    SALE M33 ....108 B3
    STRET M32 * 96 F1
    WGNE/HIN WN2 ....49 H7
    WGNW/BIL/OR WN5 ....46 E5
Langdale St BOLS/LL BL3 ....52 B1
    FWTH BL4 ....52 F5
    LEIGH WN7 ....66 B7
Langden Cl GOL/RIS/CUL WA3 ....81 C3
    ROY/SHW OL2 ....43 K4
Langdon Cl BOL BL1 ....2 B2
Langfield GOL/RIS/CUL WA3 ....80 B5
Langfield Av OLDTF/WHR M16 ....98 A1
Langfield Crs DROY M43 * 89 M2
Langford Dr IRL M44 ....94 D3
Langford Gdns BOLS/LL BL3 ....36 B8
Langford Rd DID/WITH M20 ....99 M8
    HTNM SK4 ....99 M8
Langford St DTN/ASHW M34 * 101 J1
Langham Cl BOL BL1 ....22 D6
Langham Ct STRET M32 ....85 K8
Langham Gv HALE/TIMP WA15 ......108 E4
Langham Rd ALT WA14 ....116 E2
    HTNM SK4 ....12 B4
    OLDS OL8 ....59 H8
    SLFD M6 ....86 C2
    WGNNW/ST WN6 ....31 G3
Langham St AULW OL7 ....75 K7
Langholm Cl WGNS/IIMK WN3 ....63 H1
Langholm Dr BOLE BL2 ....37 J6
Langholme Cl HULME M15 * 6 D9
Langholme Pl ECC M30 ....85 G2
Langholme Wy HEY OL10 ....40 C3
Langholm Rd AIMK WN4 ....62 F8
Langland Cl BNG/LEV M19 ....100 A2
Langland Dr ECC M30 ....84 F5
Langley Av BRAM/HZG SK7 ....121 K3
    MDTN M24 ....71 H8
    OLDE OL4 ....60 E7
    PWCH M25 ....55 L6
Langley Cl GOL/RIS/CUL WA3 ....79 M3
    URM M41 ....84 A8
    WGNNW/ST WN6 ....31 H2
Langley Ct GLSP SK13 ....93 K5
Langley Dr BRAM/HZG SK7 ....121 K3
    WALK M28 ....68 B6
    WILM/AE SK9 ....127 J3
Langley Gdns PWCH M25 ....55 L6
Langley Hall Rd PWCH M25 ....55 L6
Langley La HEY OL10 ....40 F8
Langley Platt La TYLD M29 ....67 G4

Langley Rd PWCH M25 ....55 K7
    RUSH/FAL M14 ....98 F3
    SALE M33 ....96 B8
    SWIN M27 ....71 J4
Langley Rd South SLFD M6 ....71 J8
Langley St WGNW/BIL/OR WN5 ....47 G6
Langness St OP/CLY M11 ....88 F3
Lango St OLDTF/WHR M16 * 86 F8
Langport Av WGTN/LGST M12 ....88 B7
Langset Av WGTN/HIN WN2 ....49 G6
Langsett Av SLFD M6 ....85 M1
Langshaw Rd BOLS/LL BL3 ....35 M7
Langshaw St OLDTF/WHR M16 ....86 B7
    SLFD M6 ....86 B2
Langshaw Wk BOLS/LL BL3 * 35 M7
Langside Av BKLY M9 ....57 H8
Langside Dr BOLS/LL BL3 ....35 H8
Langstone Cl HOR/BR BL6 ....33 L1
Langston Gn BRAM/HZG SK7 ....121 J5
Langston St CSLFD M3 * 87 J1
Langthorne St BNG/LEV M19 ....99 L4
Langthorne Wk BOLS/LL BL3 ....2 A7
Langton Av WGNNW/ST WN6 ....31 H4
Langton Cl FAIL M35 ....74 E4
    NEWLW WA12 ....78 D8
Langton Pl WGNNW/ST WN6 ....31 H3
Langton St HEY OL10 ....40 F1
    MDTN M24 ....57 K4
    SLFD M6 ....86 B2
Langton Ter ROCH OL11 ....28 B2
Langtree Cl WALK M28 ....68 C4
Langtree La WGNNW/ST WN6 ....31 C1
Langworthy Av LHULT M38 ....52 E8
Langworthy Rd
    NEWH/MOS M40 ....73 K5
    SLFD M6 ....86 C1
Lanhill Dr CHH M8 ....72 F6
Lankro Wy TRPK M17 ....85 J3
Lansbury St
    WGNW/BIL/OR WN5 ....46 D6
Lansdale Gdns BNG/LEV M19 ....99 H7
Lansdale St ECC M30 ....84 D4
Lansdown Cl CHD/CHDH SK8 ....120 E5
Lansdowne Av DTN/ASHW M34 ....89 M3
    MPL/ROM SK6 ....114 A2
Lansdowne Ct CHAD OL9 ....8 A6
    RAMS BL0 ....18 E7
Lansdowne Dr WALK M28 ....68 F4
Lansdowne Rd ALT WA14 ....108 A6
    ATH M46 ....51 J7
    BOLE BL2 ....36 E3
    CHAD OL9 ....8 C6
    CHH M8 ....72 D4
    ECC M30 ....85 G1
    SALE M33 ....96 D6
    URM M41 ....95 H4
Lansdowne Rd North
    URM M41 ....95 H3
Lansdowne St ROCH OL11 ....27 M5
Lanstead Dr NEWH/MOS M40 ....88 B2
Lantern Pike Vw
    NM/HAY SK22 ....125 J2
Lantern Vw NM/HAY SK22 ....124 D3
Lapwing Cl GOL/RIS/CUL WA3 ....80 A4
    ROCH OL11 ....27 H5
    STLY SK15 ....76 D8
Lapwing La DID/WITH M20 ....98 D7
    RDSH SK5 ....100 F6
Larch Av CHD/CHDH SK8 ....120 C5
    RAD M26 ....54 E3
    STRET M32 ....97 G3
    SWIN M27 ....69 M6
    WGNW/BIL/OR WN5 ....47 G6
Larch Cl FAIL M35 ....74 C6
    GOL/RIS/CUL WA3 ....80 C5
    MPL/ROM SK6 ....114 B7
    NTHM/RTH M23 ....108 A7
    POY/DIS SK12 ....129 K1
    WGNW/BIL/OR WN5 ....62 A7
The Larches MOSL OL5 ....77 G3
Larch Gv ATH M46 ....50 F4
    CHAD OL9 ....8 B2
    SWIN M27 ....69 L2
Larch Rd DTN/ASHW M34 ....101 K1
    ECC M30 ....69 M8
    LEIGH WN7 ....66 B4
    PART M31 ....106 B1
    RNFD/HAY WA11 * 78 K5
Larch St BURY BL9 ....5 L4
    OLDS OL8 ....8 F5
Larchview Rd MDTN M24 ....57 M4
Larch Wy GLSP SK13 ....105 K4
Larchway BRAM/HZG SK7 ....120 E5
    MILN OL16 ....29 G5
    MPL/ROM SK6 ....123 H6
Larchwood CHAD OL9 ....58 B5
Larchwood Av BKLY M9 ....73 J5
Larchwood Cl SALE M33 ....95 M8
Larchwood Dr WGN WN1 ....31 L8
    WILM/AE SK9 ....127 J4
Larchwood St BOL BL1 ....36 C2
Larke Ri DID/WITH M20 ....110 C1
Larkfield Av LHULT M38 ....52 C7
    WGN WN1 ....31 L8
Larkfield Cl AULW OL7 ....75 L5
    TOT/BURYW BL8 ....24 B2
Larkfield Gv BOLE BL2 * 3 K2
Larkfield Ms LHULT M38 ....52 C7
Larkhall Ri WYTH/NTH M22 ....110 B7
Lark Hl FWTH BL4 ....53 G5
    STLY SK15 ....76 D8
Larkhill Av WGNNW/ST WN6 ....31 J4
Larkhill Cl HALE/TIMP WA15 ....108 E6
Lark Hill La UPML OL3 ....45 K8
Larkhill Pl WHIT OL12 ....28 B3
Larkhill Rd CHD/CHDH SK8 ....111 M7
Lark Hill Rd EDGY/DAV SK3 ....12 D6
    UPML OL3 ....61 J2
Larkhill Vw CHD/CHDH SK8 ....111 M7
Larkhill Wk CHH M8 ....72 F6
Larkside Av WALK M28 ....69 H1
Larkspur Cl BOL BL1 ....36 D1
    LEIGH WN7 ....81 J1
Larks Ri DROY M43 ....90 A2
Lark St BOL BL1 ....2 F5
    FWTH BL4 ....53 G5
    OLD OL1 * 60 A1
Larkswood Dr STLY SK15 ....77 H5
Larmuth Av CCHDY M21 ....97 M6
Larne Av EDGY/DAV SK3 ....12 D4
    STRET M32 ....96 F2
Larne St OP/CLY M11 ....88 D4
Larwood Av HTNM SK4 ....12 A4
Lascar Av ORD M5 ....86 D4
Lashbrook Cl NEWH/MOS M40 ....73 G8
Lassell Fold HYDE SK14 ....91 L6
Lassell St OP/CLY M11 * 89 H1
Lastingham St NEWH/MOS M40 ....73 M6
Latchford St AULW OL7 ....75 K8
Latchmere Rd RUSH/FAL M14 ....98 F4

Latham Av NEWLW WA12 ....78 F8
Latham Cl MPL/ROM SK6 ....101 J7
Latham La WGNW/BIL/OR WN5 ....46 D4
Latham Rd HOR/BR BL6 ....32 F7
Latham St BOL BL1 ....36 C2
    OP/CLY M11 ....89 J5
Lathbury Rd BKLY M9 ....73 G6
Lathom Gv SALE M33 ....109 H1
Lathom Hall Av OLDE OL4 * 60 D5
Lathom Rd DID/WITH M20 ....99 G5
    IRL M44 ....94 C4
Latimer Cl
    WGNW/BIL/OR WN5 * 46 C5
Latimer St OLDE OL4 ....9 M7
Latin St MILN OL16 ....10 D6
Latrigg Crs MDTN M24 ....56 F2
Latrobe St DROY M43 ....89 K4
Lauderdale Crs
    BRUN/LGST M13 ....87 M9
Launceston Cl BRAM/HZG SK7 ......121 H5
    OLDS OL8 ....59 M8
Launceston Rd RAD M26 ....38 A7
Laundry St SLFD M6 ....71 J8
Laura St BURY BL9 ....24 E3
Laureate Wy DTN/ASHW M34 ....101 K5
Laurel Av BOLS/LL BL3 ....37 H7
    CHAD OL9 ....58 A4
    CHD/CHDH SK8 ....111 G7
    RUSH/FAL M14 ....98 D2
    STLY SK15 ....91 L4
Laurel Bank Gdns BKLY M9 ....57 L8
Laurel Cl BOL BL1 ....2 E2
    MILN OL16 ....11 J6
Laurel Crs WGNE/HIN WN2 ....65 K1
Laurel Dr HALE/TIMP WA15 ....108 E3
    LHULT M38 ....52 D8
Laurel End La HTNM SK4 ....111 K1
Laurel Gn DTN/ASHW M34 ....101 K2
Laurel Gv AIMK WN4 ....63 L8
    GOL/RIS/CUL WA3 ....80 A4
    LEIGH WN7 ....66 B4
    SLFD M6 ....85 M2
Laurel Wk PART M31 ....106 B2
Laurel Wy BRAM/HZG SK7 ....120 F4
Laurence Cl WGTN/LGST M12 ....88 D6
Laurence Cl OLDE OL4 ....60 C6
Lauria Ter BOLE BL2 ....38 A3
Laurie Pl WHIT OL12 * 28 C3
Lausanne Rd BRAM/HZG SK7 ....121 C5
    DID/WITH M20 ....98 C8
Lavender Cl NTHM/RTH M23 ....109 H3
    SALE M33 ....95 M7
Lavender Rd FWTH BL4 ....52 D3
    OLDE OL4 ....60 B4
    WGNNW/ST WN6 ....47 J1
Lavenders Brow STKP SK1 ....13 K4
Lavender St RAD M26 ....54 A1
Lavenham Av OP/CLY M11 ....89 C3
Lavenham Cl BRAM/HZG SK7 ....122 A4
    BURY BL9 ....55 J1
Laverton Cl BURY BL9 ....40 B3
Lavington Av CHD/CHDH SK8 ....111 K7
Lavington Gv GTN M18 ....89 D7
Lavinia St ECC M30 ....84 E2
Lavister Av BNG/LEV M19 ....111 G1
Lawefield Crs SWIN M27 ....54 A7
Lawers Av CHAD OL9 ....58 D4
Lawflat WHIT OL12 ....21 G7
Lawler Av ORD M5 ....86 E6
Lawnbank Cl MDTN M24 ....57 H3
Lawn Cl OLDS OL8 ....75 M1
Lawndale Cl RAD M26 ....54 E2
Lawn Dr HALE/TIMP WA15 ....108 B6
    SWIN M27 ....70 B5
Lawnfold GLSP SK13 ....93 H8
Lawngreen Av CCHDY M21 ....97 K5
Lawnside Ms DID/WITH M20 ....98 D7
The Lawns ALT WA14 ....116 E1
Lawn St BOL BL1 ....2 A1
Lawnswood ROCH OL11 ....27 K3
Lawnswood Dr SWIN M27 ....70 D6
    TYLD M29 ....68 A3
Lawnswood Park Rd SWIN M27 ....70 D6
Lawrence Cl WHIT OL12 ....30 D3
Lawrence Ct WGNE/HIN WN2 ....64 E3
Lawrence Pl POY/DIS SK12 ....129 K1
Lawrence Rd ALT WA14 ....107 M6
    BRAM/HZG SK7 ....122 A1
    URM M41 ....95 H1
Lawrence St BURY BL9 ....39 J8
    EDGY/DAV SK3 ....13 H5
Lawrie Av RAMS BL0 ....18 E7
Lawson Av CHD/CHDH SK8 ....110 E7
    LEIGH WN7 ....66 B3
Lawson Cl MDTN M24 ....41 K8
    WALK M28 ....69 M5
Lawson Gv SALE M33 ....96 B6
Lawson Rd BOL BL1 ....35 M2
Lawson St BKLY M9 ....72 F2
    BOL BL1 ....22 B8
Law St ROCH OL11 ....27 M7
Lawton Av BRAM/HZG SK7 ....121 C4
Lawton Cl MPL/ROM SK6 ....113 J3
Lawton Moor Rd
    NTHM/RTH M23 ....109 L3
Lawton Rd HTNM SK4 ....99 M8
Lawton Sq UPML OL3 * 45 J8
Lawton St DROY M43 ....89 L2
    OP/CLY M11 ....89 G5
    STLY SK15 ....91 L3
    UPML OL3 ....45 H8
    WHIT OL12 ....11 G1
Laxey Av ATH M46 ....67 H2
Laxey Crs LEIGH WN7 ....81 K2
Laxey St NEWH/MOS M40 * 73 L5
Laxfield Dr BOLS/LL BL3 ....35 H6
Layard St AUL OL6 ....90 D1
Laycock Av BOLE BL2 ....36 C1
    STLY SK15 ....77 H8
Laycock Crs FAIL M35 ....74 C4
Laycock Dr DUK SK16 ....91 K5
Laycock Gv FAIL M35 ....74 C5
Laycock St MILN OL16 ....29 G1
Layfield Cl TOT/BURYW BL8 ....24 C4
Layland Av GOL/RIS/CUL WA3 ....81 H8
Laystall St CMANE M1 ....7 K4
Laythe Barn Cl MILN OL16 ....29 G8
Layton Av HYDE SK14 ....91 L1

Layton Cl STKP SK1 ....13 L6
    WGNW/BIL/OR WN5 ....47 G7
Layton Dr FWTH BL4 ....53 J6
    MPL/ROM SK6 ....113 J6
Layton St NEWH/MOS M40 ....88 A2
Lazenby Crs AIMK WN4 ....78 C1
Lazonby Av WGNNW/ST WN6 ....49 J1
Leabank St BNG/LEV M19 ....99 K3
Leabrook Dr NEWH/MOS M40 ....74 B4
Leaburn Dr BNG/LEV M19 ....99 H8
Leach Cl MILN OL16 ....18 E2
Leaches Rd RAMS BL0 ....19 G4
Leach St BOLS/LL BL3 ....2 C9
    FWTH BL4 ....53 H3
    GTN M18 ....88 E7
    MILN OL16 ....11 J6
    MILN OL16 ....29 J7
    PWCH M25 ....55 J8
    ROY/SHW OL2 ....43 M6
Leach Wk OLDE OL4 ....60 B4
Leaconfield Dr WALK M28 ....69 J5
Lea Ct FAIL M35 ....74 B5
Leacroft Av BOLE BL2 ....37 C7
Leacroft Rd CCHDY M21 ....98 A7
Leadale Cl BNG/LEV M19 ....99 K2
Leadale Ri OLDE OL4 * 61 G5
Leader St WGN WN1 ....15 L4
    WGNW/BIL/OR WN5 ....46 F6
Leader Williams Rd IRL M44 ....94 C3
Lea Dr BKLY M9 ....73 J1
Leafield TYLD M29 ....67 M3
Leafield Av DID/WITH M20 ....99 K3
Leafield Cl RAD M26 ....54 B1
Leafield Dr CHD/CHDH SK8 ....120 E6
    WALK M28 ....68 D6
Leafield Rd POY/DIS SK12 ....123 G4
Leaford Av DTN/ASHW M34 ....90 A8
Leaford Cl DTN/ASHW M34 ....90 A8
Leaf St BOLE BL2 ....3 L8
    HULME M15 ....87 G6
    RDSH SK5 ....100 B5
Leagate URM M41 ....96 C3
Lea Gate Cl BOLE BL2 ....23 G7
    WGNS/IIMK WN3 * 63 H1
League St MILN OL16 ....11 H8
Leaholme Cl NEWH/MOS M40 ....74 A7
Leak St LIT OL15 * 21 M7
Leal Holme Av NEWH/MOS WN2 ......48 D2
Leamington Av BURY BL9 ....25 H4
    DID/WITH M20 ....98 C3
Leamington Rd ECC M30 ....84 E1
    RDSH SK5 ....100 B3
    URM M41 ....95 L1
Leamington St OLDE OL4 ....59 M4
    OP/CLY M11 ....89 C5
    WHIT OL12 ....10 D2
Lea Mount Dr BURY BL9 ....26 A8
Leander Cl BKLY M9 ....73 H2
Leander Dr ROCH OL11 ....42 A3
Lea Rd CHD/CHDH SK8 ....119 K3
    HTNM SK4 ....99 L8
    NM/HAY SK22 ....125 L1
Leaside Av OLD OL1 ....58 D2
Leaside Cl WHIT OL12 ....28 A2
Leaside Dr DID/WITH M20 ....99 G7
Leaside Gv WALK M28 ....69 H1
Leaside Wy WILM/AE SK9 ....117 K1
The Leas HALE/TIMP WA15 ....117 L7
Lea St NM/HAY SK22 ....124 C4
    WGNS/IIMK WN3 ....14 C5
Leaton Av NTHM/RTH M23 ....109 K6
Leavale Cl LHULT M38 ....52 C7
Lea Vw ROY/SHW OL2 ....58 F1
    WGN WN1 ....15 M3
Leaway WGNE/HIN WN2 ....15 M5
    WHIT OL12 ....21 G5
Lecester Rd CHH M8 ....72 E6
Leckenby Cl WALK M28 ....68 F4
Leconfield Dr BKLY M9 ....73 H1
Leconfield Rd ECC M30 ....69 J8
Lecturers Cl BOLS/LL BL3 ....2 E8
Ledbrooke Cl ORD M5 ....86 C5
Ledburn Cl HULME M15 ....87 G6
Ledbury Av URM M41 ....95 M1
Ledbury Cl MDTN M24 ....57 K6
Ledbury Rd FAIL M35 ....74 B8
Ledbury St LEIGH WN7 * 66 C6
Ledge Ley CHD/CHDH SK8 ....120 B4
Ledmore Gv AIMK WN4 ....78 A1
Ledsham Av BKLY M9 ....56 D7
Ledson Rd NTHM/RTH M23 ....109 J7
Ledward La ALT WA14 ....116 D2
Lee Av ALT WA14 ....107 M5
    BOLS/LL BL3 ....52 A1
Lee Bank WHTN BL5 ....50 D4
Lee Av AUL OL6 ....76 B7
Leech Brook Av
    DTN/ASHW M34 ....90 B7
Leech Brook Cl
    DTN/ASHW M34 ....90 B6
Leech St HYDE SK14 ....102 C2
    STLY SK15 ....91 K3
Lee Cl IRL M44 ....94 C3
Lee Ct WYTH/NTH M22 * 110 B4
Lee Crs STRET M32 ....97 H2
Lee Dale Cl
    DTN/ASHW M34 ....101 K2
Leeds Cl BURY BL9 ....55 L2
Leeds St WGNS/IIMK WN3 ....14 D5
Leefields Cl UPML OL3 ....61 L4
Lee Ga BOLE BL2 ....23 G7
Leegate Cl HTNM SK4 ....99 K8
Leegate Dr BKLY M9 ....57 J8
Leegate Gdns HTNM SK4 ....99 K8
Leegrange Rd BKLY M9 ....57 J6
Lee Gv FWTH BL4 ....52 C4
Lee Head GLSP SK13 ....103 M7
Leek St RAD M26 ....54 B1
Lee La EDGW/EG BL7 ....16 E2
    WGNE/HIN WN2 ....64 E4
Leemans Hill St
    TOT/BURYW BL8 ....24 D7
Lee Mt GLSP SK13 ....104 F3
Lees Av DTN/ASHW M34 ....101 H2
Leeside HTNM SK4 ....111 K3
Lees La MCFLDN SK10 ....127 M5
Lees New Rd AUL OL6 ....76 A3
    OLDE OL4 ....60 C8
Lees Park Av DROY M43 ....89 M4
Lees Rd AUL OL6 ....76 B1
    BRAM/HZG SK7 ....120 F7
    MOSL OL5 ....76 B1
    OLDE OL4 ....60 C8

Lees St AUL OL6 ....75 L8
DROY M43 ....89 L2
GTN M18 ....89 H6
MDTN M24 ....58 A5
MOSL OL5 * 76 F2
OLDS OL8 ....75 J4
STLY SK15 ....91 K2
SWIN M27 ....70 C3
Lees St East ROY/SHW OL2 ....43 L3
Leestone Rd WYTH/NTH M22 ....110 B6
Lee Av ATH M46 ....67 C2
BURY BL9 ....25 J4
LIT OL15 ....11 M6
MDTN M24 ....57 J1
OLDS OL8 ....8 F7
STKP SK1 ....13 J5
UPML OL3 ....61 L4
Leesway OLDE OL4 ....60 B7
Leesway Dr DTN/ASHW M34 ....101 K2
Leeswood Av CCHDY M21 ....97 M6
Lee Vale Dr GLSP SK13 ....104 A5
Leewood SWIN M27 ....54 A8
Left Bank CSLFD M3 ....6 D4
Le Gendre St BOLE BL2 ....36 F3
Legh Cl POY/DIS SK12 ....129 J1
Legh Dr DTN/ASHW M34 ....89 L3
MPL/ROM SK6 ....101 L6
Legh Rd BRO M7 ....72 A4
MCFLDN SK10 ....129 C7
POY/DIS SK12 ....123 J6
SALE M33 ....109 H1
Legh St AIMK WN4 ....78 E2
BRO M7 ....72 A4
ECC M30 ....84 F3
GOL/RIS/CUL WA3 ....79 K4
Legion Gv BRO M7 ....72 B6
Legwood Ct URM M41 ....95 M2
Leicester Av BRO M7 * 72 C4
DROY M43 ....89 J1
DTN/ASHW M34 ....101 J3
HALE/TIMP WA15 ....108 D4
HOR/BR BL6 ....33 K1
NEWH/MOS M40 ....49 J7
Leicester Dr GLSP SK13 ....105 J5
Leicester Rd BRO M7 ....72 B5
FAIL M35 ....74 D7
HALE/TIMP WA15 ....117 G2
SALE M33 ....96 F2
TYLD M29 ....67 K2
WHTF M45 ....55 C3
Leicester St AULW OL7 ....75 L8
OLDE OL4 ....59 L6
RDSH SK5 ....100 E6
ROCH OL11 ....11 G8
Leigh Ar WGN WN1 ....14 F1
Leigh Av MPL/ROM SK6 ....114 B6
SWIN M27 ....70 A7
Leighbrook Rd RUSH/FAL M14 ....98 E4
Leigh Cl TOT/BURYW BL8 ....24 B5
Leigh Fold HYDE SK14 ....91 H7
Leigh La TOT/BURYW BL8 ....38 D1
Leigh Rd ATH M46 ....66 F7
HALE/TIMP WA15 ....117 G2
WALK M28 ....68 C6
WGNE/HIN WN2 ....65 L3
WHTN BL5 ....50 C5
WILM/AE SK9 ....126 E4
Leigh St FWTH BL4 ....53 G4
HEY OL10 ....40 F2
HYDE SK14 ....102 B2
LEIGH WN7 ....65 M7
MILN OL16 ....29 J1
TOT/BURYW BL8 ....24 C8
WGN WN1 ....15 J5
WGNE/HIN WN2 ....49 J1
WGNE/HIN WN2 ....65 L3
WHTN BL5 ....50 B3
Leighton Av ATH M46 ....66 F7
BOL BL1 ....35 L4
LIT OL15 ....29 J2
Leighton Dr LEIGH WN7 ....80 E3
MPL/ROM SK6 ....114 F4
Leighton Rd OLDTF/WHR M16 ....86 F8
Leighton St ATH M46 ....66 E1
NEWH/MOS M40 ....73 K4
Leinster Rd SWIN M27 ....70 B5
Leinster St FWTH BL4 ....52 F4
Leith Av SALE M33 ....97 H8
Leith Pl OLDS OL8 ....75 J2
Leith Rd SALE M33 ....97 H8
Le Mans Crs BOL BL1 ....2 E5
Lemnos St OLD OL1 ....9 L4
Lemon St TYLD M29 ....67 J4
Lena St BOL BL1 ....36 C2
CMANE M1 ....7 J5
Len Cox Wk ANC M4 * 7 J3
Lenfield La OLD OL1 ....59 H3
Leng Rd NEWH/MOS M40 ....74 A7
Lenham Cl RDSH SK5 ....100 E6
Lenham Gdns BOLE BL2 ....37 H6
Lennox Gdns BOLS/LL BL3 ....51 J3
Lennox St AUL OL6 ....90 F1
Lenora St BOLS/LL BL3 ....51 J4
Lenten Gv HEY OL10 ....41 H5
Lentmead Dr BKLY M9 ....73 K3
Lenton Gdns WYTH/NTH M22 ....110 B7
Lentworth Dr WALK M28 ....52 F7
Leominster Dr WYTH/NTH M22 ....119 C1
Leominster Rd MDTN M24 * 57 L6
Leonardin Cl ROY/SHW OL2 ....43 J4
Leonard St BOLS/LL BL3 ....52 B1
ROCH OL11 ....41 M3
Leopold Av DID/WITH M20 ....98 D7
Leopold St ROCH OL11 ....10 A5
WGNW/BIL/OR WN5 ....46 E7
Lepp Crs TOT/BURYW BL8 ....24 C7
Lepton Dr BKLY M9 ....73 J2
Lerryn Dr BRAM/HZG SK7 ....120 F3
Lesley Rd URM M41 ....96 D3
CHAD OL9 ....74 E1
Leslie Av BURY BL9 ....55 J1
Leslie Gv HALE/TIMP WA15 ....108 D4
Leslie Hough Wy SLFD M6 ....86 L1
Leslie St BOL BL1 ....3 J1
RUSH/FAL M14 ....98 C1
Lessingham Av WGN WN1 ....47 L1
Lester Rd LHULT M38 ....52 E7
Lester St STRET M32 ....97 G2
Letchworth Av ROCH OL11 ....11 G9
Letchworth St RUSH/FAL M14 ....98 E1
Letham St OLDS OL8 ....75 J2
Letitia St HOR/BR BL6 ....33 K1
Levedale Rd BKLY M9 ....73 J1
Leven Cl FWTH BL4 ....53 L7
Levengreave Cl WGNE/HIN WN2 ....65 M1
Levenhurst Rd CHH M8 ....72 C4
Levens Cl CHD/CHDH SK8 ....110 E8
Levens Dr BOLE BL2 ....37 H3
Levenshulme Rd GTN M18 ....89 G8

Levenshulme Ter BNG/LEV M19 * 99 K3
Levens Pl WGNE/HIN WN2 ....48 D4
WGNW/BIL/OR WN5 ....46 B9
Levens Rd BRAM/HZG SK7 ....121 G3
Levens St NEWH/MOS M40 ....73 K5
SLFD M6 ....71 L7
Lever Av SWIN M27 ....70 E2
Lever Edge La BOLS/LL BL3 ....51 M2
Leverett Cl ALT WA14 ....107 K7
Lever Gv BOLE BL2 ....3 H8
Lever Hall Rd BOLE BL2 ....37 G5
Leverhulme Av BOLS/LL BL3 ....52 D1
Lever St BOLE BL2 ....3 G8
BOLS/LL BL3 ....2 F9
BOLS/LL BL3 ....121 M4
BRAM/HZG SK7 ....121 M4
CMANE M1 ....7 J4
HEY OL10 ....41 G1
MDTN M24 ....57 K3
RAD M26 ....38 C7
RAMS BL0 ....18 F6
TYLD M29 ....67 J3
WHTN BL5 ....50 B1
Lever Wk MDTN M24 ....57 J5
Levington Dr OLDS OL8 ....75 K4
Levi St BOL BL1 ....35 J3
Lewes Av DTN/ASHW M34 ....101 J3
Lewis Av BKLY M9 ....73 H3
URM M41 ....85 G7
Lewis Cl WGNS/IIMK WN3 ....14 B9
Lewis Dr HEY OL10 ....40 C3
Lewisham Av NEWH/MOS M40 ....73 L8
Lewisham Cl ROY/SHW OL2 * 42 F6
Lewis Rd DROY M43 ....89 H2
RDSH SK5 ....100 C3
Lewis St ECC M30 ....85 G3
HEY OL10 * 41 H1
NEWH/MOS M40 ....88 A1
ROY/SHW OL2 ....43 L7
Lewtas St ECC M30 ....85 H3
Lexton Av CHH M8 ....72 E2
Leybourne Av BNG/LEV M19 ....99 L3
Leybourne St BOL BL1 ....36 B2
Leybrook Rd WYTH/NTH M22 ....118 E1
Leyburn Av ROY/SHW OL2 ....43 G8
STRET M32 ....96 F2
URM M41 ....95 K3
Leyburn Cl WGN WN1 ....15 M2
WHTF M45 ....55 H4
Leyburne Rd OFTN SK2 ....112 F6
Leyburn Gv MPL/ROM SK6 ....113 M2
Leyburn Rd NEWH/MOS M40 ....73 M2
Leycett Dr NTHM/RTH M23 ....109 K3
Ley Crs TYLD M29 ....67 K3
Leycroft St CMANE M1 ....7 K6
Ley Dr HEY OL10 ....41 H5
Leyfield Av MPL/ROM SK6 ....113 M2
Leyfield Rd MILN OL16 ....29 G6
Leygate Vw NM/HAY SK22 ....124 D4
Ley Hey Av MPL/ROM SK6 ....114 C5
Ley Hey Rd MPL/ROM SK6 ....114 C5
Leyland Av CHD/CHDH SK8 ....110 E6
DID/WITH M20 ....111 G1
IRL M44 ....83 L8
WGNE/HIN WN2 ....65 G1
Leyland Green Rd AIMK WN4 ....62 F7
Leyland Mill La WGN WN1 ....32 A8
Leylands La HYDE SK14 ....103 H6
Leyland St BURY BL9 ....39 J8
HTNM SK4 ....13 G4
MILN OL16 ....48 F8
WGNE/HIN WN2 ....64 E3
Ley La MPL/ROM SK6 ....114 F4
Ley Rd TYLD M29 ....67 L6
Leyton Av RUSH/FAL M14 ....108 B4
Leyton Cl FWTH BL4 ....52 C3
Leyton Dr BURY BL9 ....39 J7
Leyton St WHIT OL12 ....28 C2
Leywell Dr OLD OL1 ....60 A1
Leywell Rd BKLY M9 ....73 J4
Library La CHAD OL9 ....8 F3
Library St WGN WN1 ....15 G4
WHTN BL5 ....50 C4
Libra St BOL BL1 ....36 A2
Lichens Crs OLDS OL8 ....75 K1
Lichfield Av AUL OL6 ....76 A5
BOLE BL2 ....36 E2
GOL/RIS/CUL WA3 ....80 A4
HALE/TIMP WA15 ....117 G2
RDSH SK5 ....100 B5
TYLD M29 ....67 M5
Lichfield Cl FWTH BL4 ....52 D4
CHH M8 ....72 E5
PWCH M25 ....71 M2
SWIN M27 ....70 C6
TOT/BURYW BL8 ....4 C1
Lichfield Dr CHAD OL9 ....58 D3
CHH M8 ....72 E5
PWCH M25 ....71 M2
SWIN M27 ....70 C6
TOT/BURYW BL8 ....4 C1
Lichfield Gv AIMK WN4 ....78 F2
Lichfield Rd ECC M30 ....70 C8
RAD M26 ....38 A7
URM M41 ....85 G8
Lichfield St SLFD M6 ....71 K7
WGNW/BIL/OR WN5 ....46 F7
Lichfield Ter MILN OL16 ....28 F8
Lichfield Wk MPL/ROM SK6 ....113 K3
Lidbrook Wk WGTN/LGST M12 ....88 B6
Liddington Hall Dr RAMS BL0 ....18 E8
Lidgate Cl WGNS/IIMK WN3 ....63 G1
Lidgett Cl LHULT M38 ....52 F1
Lidiard St CHH M8 ....72 D3
Liffey Av WYTH/NTH M22 ....119 G1
Lifton Av NEWH/MOS M40 ....73 H8
Light Alders La POY/DIS SK12 ....123 J5
Lightborne Rd SALE M33 ....96 A8
Lightbounds Rd BOL BL1 ....35 J1
Lightbourne Av SWIN M27 ....70 C5
Lightbowne Rd NEWH/MOS M40 ....73 J4
Lightburn Av LIT OL15 ....21 K8
Lightburne Av BOL BL1 ....35 L8
LEIGH WN7 ....81 H1
Lighthorne Av EDGY/DAV SK3 ....111 J5
Lighthorne Gv EDGY/DAV SK3 ....111 J5
Lighthorne Rd EDGY/DAV SK3 ....111 J5
Light Oaks Rd GOL/RIS/CUL WA3 ....81 M6
SLFD M6 ....70 E8
Lightshaw La GOL/RIS/CUL WA3 ....64 D8
Lightwood WALK M28 ....68 C6
Lightwood Cl FWTH BL4 ....53 H3
Lignum Av CHAD OL9 ....8 A7

Lilac Av AIMK WN4 ....63 G7
BURY BL9 ....39 G5
HYDE SK14 ....102 A4
LEIGH WN7 ....66 B5
ROCH OL11 ....11 G7
SWIN M27 ....70 D4
WGNW/ST WN6 ....47 K1
Lilac Ct SLFD M6 ....86 D2
Lilac Gv CHAD OL9 ....8 B2
NEWH/MOS M40 ....73 K3
PWCH M25 ....55 K6
WGNW/BIL/OR WN5 ....62 A8
Lilac La OLDS OL8 ....75 G2
Lilac Rd GOL/RIS/CUL WA3 ....79 K3
HALE/TIMP WA15 ....117 J1
ROCH OL11 ....42 C2
Lilac St OFTN SK2 ....112 C6
Lilac View Cl ROY/SHW OL2 ....43 M6
Lila St BKLY M9 ....73 J5
Lilburn Cl RAMS BL0 ....18 F8
Liley St MILN OL16 ....11 H5
Lilford Cl WGTN/LGST M12 ....88 D6
LEIGH WN7 ....66 B8
Lilian Dr WGNNW/ST WN6 ....47 L1
Lilian Gv RDSH SK5 ....100 C3
Lillian St OLDTF/WHR M16 ....86 F8
Lilly St BOL BL1 ....2 A1
HYDE SK14 ....102 C4
Lilmore Av CHH M8 ....72 F6
NEWH/MOS M40 ....73 M6
ROY/SHW OL2 ....42 F5
URM M41 ....95 J1
Lily Av FWTH BL4 ....52 E3
Lily Cl EDGY/DAV SK3 ....112 A7
Lily Hill St WHTF M45 ....55 H2
Lily La BKLY M9 ....73 J5
WGNE/HIN WN2 ....64 D4
Lily Lanes AUL OL6 ....76 B4
Lily Pl AIMK WN4 ....78 F2
Lily St AIMK WN4 ....64 B7
ECC M30 ....84 E3
MDTN M24 ....57 M4
MILN OL16 ....29 J6
OLD OL1 ....9 G1
ROY/SHW OL2 ....43 G1
Lima St BURY BL9 ....5 L2
Limbert Cir CHH M8 ....72 F3
Lime Av LEIGH WN7 ....66 B4
NM/HAY SK22 ....124 F3
SWIN M27 ....69 M6
URM M41 ....95 L2
WHTF M45 ....55 J4
Lime Bank St WGTN/LGST M12 ....88 A4
Limebrook Cl OP/CLY M11 ....89 H5
Lime Cl DUK SK16 ....91 C6
SLFD M6 ....86 D1
WGNE/HIN WN2 ....64 D5
Lime Ct SLFD M6 * 86 D1
Lime Crs OLDTF/WHR M16 ....86 E8
Limeditch Rd FAIL M35 ....74 E4
Lime Fld MILN OL16 ....29 H5
Limefield MDTN M24 ....57 C5
MOSL OL5 ....76 E2
WGN WN1 ....15 H3
Limefield Av FWTH BL4 ....53 G3
Limefield Brow BURY BL9 ....25 J3
Limefield Cl BRO M7 ....72 A3
BURY BL9 ....25 J5
RAD M26 ....54 A1
Limefield Ter BNG/LEV M19 ....99 K3
Lime Gdns DUK SK16 ....90 F4
MDTN M24 ....57 H4
Lime Ga OLDS OL8 ....74 F2
Lime Gn OLDS OL8 ....75 G3
Lime Green Rd OLDS OL8 ....74 F4
Lime Gv AUL OL6 ....75 M7
BURY BL9 ....25 J5
CHD/CHDH SK8 ....111 G6
DTN/ASHW M34 ....90 C8
GOL/RIS/CUL WA3 ....80 A6
HALE/TIMP WA15 ....108 F6
HEY OL10 ....40 F1
LIT OL15 ....21 K7
OLDTF/WHR M16 ....86 E8
PWCH M25 ....55 K6
ROY/SHW OL2 ....43 G6
STLY SK15 ....91 H4
WALK M28 ....68 C6
WGNE/HIN WN2 ....65 J1
Lime La FAIL M35 ....74 C4
Limehurst Av AULW OL7 ....75 K6
RUSH/FAL M14 ....98 C4
Limehurst Ct AULW OL7 ....75 K6
Lime Kiln La MPL/ROM SK6 ....114 D7
Limekiln La WGTN/LGST M12 ....88 A4
Lime La FAIL M35 ....74 F3
Limers Ga WHIT OL12 ....20 D7
Limerston Dr NEWH/MOS M40 ....73 J7
Limes Av WGNNW/ST WN6 ....31 L6
Limesdale Cl BOLE BL2 ....37 L7
Limeside Rd OLDS OL8 ....74 F2
Limestead Av CHH M8 ....72 D4
The Limes GOL/RIS/CUL WA3 ....80 A6
GOL/RIS/CUL WA3 ....81 G8
Lime St ATH M46 ....66 C1
BURY BL9 ....25 J6
DUK SK16 ....90 E4
ECC M30 ....85 H4
FWTH BL4 ....53 G3
MPL/ROM SK6 ....101 H8
NEWH/MOS M40 ....73 H7
OLD OL1 ....8 D2
ROCH OL11 ....27 M8
TYLD M29 ....67 J3
WGN WN1 ....15 H3
Lime Tree Cl URM M41 ....96 B2
Lime Tree Gv FAIL M35 ....74 E5
Limetrees Rd MDTN M24 ....57 J8
Lime Wk WGNS/IIMK WN3 ....48 C8
Limewood Meadow
TYLD M29 ....67 J3

Lincoln Cl AUL OL6 ....76 A4
LEIGH WN7 ....80 F4
ROCH OL11 ....11 G7
TYLD M29 ....67 K2
Lincoln Ct AIMK WN4 ....78 F2
Lincoln Dr AIMK WN4 ....5 G8
HALE/TIMP WA15 ....108 E2
LIT OL15 ....29 K1
WGNE/HIN WN2 ....33 G7
Lincoln Gv BOLE BL2 ....23 J8
BRUN/LGST M13 ....87 M7
SALE M33 ....96 F4
Lincoln Leach Ct ROCH OL11 ....10 E8
Lincoln Pl WGNW/BIL/OR WN5 ....46 F4
Lincoln Ri MPL/ROM SK6 ....113 K3
Lincoln Rd BOL BL1 ....35 L4
FAIL M35 ....74 D6
MDTN M24 ....57 M7
WGNE/HIN WN2 ....49 H7
WILM/AE SK9 ....127 J3
Lincoln St BRUN/LGST M13 ....88 C8
CHAD OL9 ....8 B8
ECC M30 ....84 F3
ROCH OL11 ....11 G7
Lincoln Wy GLSP SK13 ....105 J4
Lincombe Rd WYTH/NTH M22 ....118 E4
Lincroft Rd WGNE/HIN WN2 ....65 K1
Linda Dr BRAM/HZG SK7 ....121 M3
Lindale Av BOL BL1 ....35 J4
BURY BL9 ....55 K1
CHAD OL9 ....58 D6
NEWH/MOS M40 ....74 A2
ROY/SHW OL2 ....42 F5
URM M41 ....95 J1
Lindale Cl WALK M28 ....68 B5
Lindale Dr MDTN M24 ....57 H1
Lindale Ri ROY/SHW OL2 ....44 A5
Lindbury Av OFTN SK2 ....112 F5
Linden Av AIMK WN4 ....63 J7
ATH M46 ....66 E2
BOLS/LL BL3 ....37 K7
DTN/ASHW M34 ....90 A5
HALE/TIMP WA15 ....108 B7
OLDE OL4 ....60 A4
RAMS BL0 ....19 G6
SALE M33 ....71 H6
SWIN M27 ....70 A5
WGNW/BIL/OR WN5 ....46 B6
Linden Cl DTN/ASHW M34 ....101 K1
RAMS BL0 ....19 G5
Linden Crs TOT/BURYW BL8 ....24 C7
Linden Dr ORD M5 ....86 C3
Linden Gv BRAM/HZG SK7 ....120 F8
LEIGH WN7 ....66 B5
OFTN SK2 ....112 E8
RUSH/FAL M14 ....98 C3
WGNW/BIL/OR WN5 ....46 B6
Linden Pk BNG/LEV M19 ....99 K4
Linden Rd CHD/CHDH SK8 ....120 C1
DID/WITH M20 ....98 D8
DTN/ASHW M34 ....101 K1
STLY SK15 ....92 A5
WALK M28 ....68 C6
WGNE/HIN WN2 ....49 H5
Linden St BNG/LEV M19 ....99 L3
RAD M26 ....54 A1
Linden Wk BOLE BL2 ....22 E7
Lindenwood CHAD OL9 ....58 B4
Lindeth Av GTN M18 ....89 G8
Lindfield Dr BOL BL1 ....36 B3
Lindfield Est North WILM/AE SK9 ....126 E6
Lindfield Est South WILM/AE SK9 ....126 E6
Lindfield Rd RDSH SK5 ....100 A3
Lindinis Av ORD M5 ....86 D2
Lindisfarne WHIT OL12 ....10 D3
Lindisfarne Av GOL/RIS/CUL WA3 ....80 A7
Lindisfarne Cl SALE M33 ....108 C3
Lindisfarne Dr POY/DIS SK12 ....121 M8
Lindisfarne Pl BOLE BL2 ....36 F2
Lindisfarne Rd AULW OL7 ....75 H7
Lindley Gv EDGY/DAV SK3 ....112 A7
Lindley St BOLS/LL BL3 * 53 L1
FWTH BL4 ....53 L1
LEIGH WN7 ....66 D7
Lindleywood Rd RUSH/FAL M14 ....99 H4
Lindon Wy DROY M43 ....89 H4
Lindop Rd HALE/TIMP WA15 ....117 H3
Lindow Cl TOT/BURYW BL8 ....24 F6
Lindow Ct MPL/ROM SK6 ....113 L5
Lindow Fold Dr WILM/AE SK9 ....126 B8
Lindow La WILM/AE SK9 ....126 C6
Lindow Rd OLDTF/WHR M16 ....97 C2
Lindow St SALE M33 ....109 H1
LEIGH WN7 ....66 A7
Lindrick Av WHTF M45 ....55 C6
Lindrick Cl NEWH/MOS M40 ....73 M5
Lindrick Ter BOLS/LL BL3 * 2 A9
Lindsay Av BNG/LEV M19 ....99 J3
CHD/CHDH SK8 ....120 D3
SWIN M27 ....70 B5
Lindsay Cl OLDE OL4 * 60 A2
Lindsay Rd BNG/LEV M19 ....99 J3
Lindsay St HOR/BR BL6 ....34 A3
STLY SK15 ....91 L2
WGNE/HIN WN2 ....32 E7
Lindsell Rd ALT WA14 ....107 M4
Lindsgate Dr HALE/TIMP WA15 ....108 E5
Lindside Wk NEWH/MOS M40 ....88 A2
Lindum Av OLDTF/WHR M16 ....98 A1
Lindum St RUSH/FAL M14 ....98 E1
Lindwall Cl NTHM/RTH M23 ....109 L2
Linehan Cl HTNM SK4 ....111 G2
Lineholme ROY/SHW OL2 ....58 F2
Linen Ct CSLFD M3 ....6 A1
Lines Rd DROY M43 ....89 L3
IRL M44 ....94 D1
Linfield Cl BOLE BL2 ....23 G8
Linfield St OP/CLY M11 ....88 D3
Linford Av NEWH/MOS M40 ....73 M2
Lingard La MPL/ROM SK6 ....101 G7
Lingard Rd WYTH/NTH M22 ....110 A3
Lingards La TYLD M29 ....67 K8
Lingard St LEIGH WN7 ....66 B8
RDSH SK5 ....100 C4
Lingcrest Rd HTNM SK4 ....99 M6
Lingdale Rd CHD/CHDH SK8 ....120 B2
Lingfield Av SALE M33 ....108 B3
Lingfield Cl FWTH BL4 ....52 F5
TOT/BURYW BL8 ....24 F6
Lingfield Crs WGNNW/ST WN6 ....47 H1
Lingholme Dr MDTN M24 ....56 F2

Lingmell Cl BOL BL1 ....35 J2
MDTN M24 ....57 G2
URM M41 ....84 C8
Lingmoor Cl MDTN M24 ....56 F2
WGNS/IIMK WN3 ....63 K3
Lingmoor Dr TYLD M29 ....67 L5
Lingmoor Rd BOL BL1 ....35 J3
Lingmoor Wk HULME M15 * 87 G8
Linhope Cl HTNM SK4 ....111 L1
Link Av URM M41 ....96 D3
Linkfield Dr WALK M28 ....68 C6
Link La OLDS OL8 ....75 H2
Link Rd OLDE OL4 ....60 C5
SALE M33 ....108 A2
Links Av FAIL M35 ....74 C7
Links Crs PWCH M25 ....72 B2
Links Dr HOR/BR BL6 ....34 E5
Linksfield DTN/ASHW M34 ....90 C7
Linkside Av ROY/SHW OL2 ....43 G7
Links Pl AUL OL6 ....76 B5
Links Ri URM M41 ....84 D8
Links Rd BOLE BL2 ....37 K1
HEY OL10 ....41 G4
HOR/BR BL6 ....34 E5
MPL/ROM SK6 ....114 A1
MPL/ROM SK6 ....114 C8
WILM/AE SK9 ....130 B1
The Links NEWH/MOS M40 ....73 M5
Links Vw PWCH M25 ....71 K3
ROCH OL11 ....27 L6
Links Wy CHAD OL9 ....8 C3
Linksway CHD/CHDH SK8 ....110 D8
PWCH M25 ....72 A2
SWIN M27 ....70 D6
Linksway Cl HTNM SK4 ....99 K7
Linksway Dr BURY BL9 ....55 K1
The Link RDSH SK5 ....100 F6
ROY/SHW OL2 ....43 J3
WILM/AE SK9 ....127 H1
Linkway Av AIMK WN4 ....64 B7
The Linkway HOR/BR BL6 ....33 K4
Linley Av RAD M26 ....39 H7
Linley Cl WGNNW/ST WN6 ....30 E8
Linley Dr OLDE OL4 ....60 A8
Linley Gv RAMS BL0 ....24 D2
Linley Rd CHD/CHDH SK8 ....120 D4
SALE M33 ....96 F3
WGNW/BIL/OR WN5 ....47 G7
Linnell Dr ROCH OL11 ....27 H4
Linnet Cl DTN/ASHW M34 ....89 M2
OFTN SK2 ....113 J7
WGTN/LGST M12 ....88 C8
Linnet Dr BURY BL9 ....5 L1
IRL M44 ....94 D1
LEIGH WN7 ....66 E7
Linnet Hl ROCH OL11 ....27 H6
Linnet's Wood Ms WALK M28 ....69 H3
Linney La ROY/SHW OL2 ....43 M5
Linney Rd BRAM/HZG SK7 ....120 F2
Linney Sq WGN WN1 ....15 K3
Linn St CHH M8 ....72 D3
Linslade Gdns BOLS/LL BL3 * 2 C7
Linsley St CSLFD M3 ....6 D2
Linstead Dr CHH M8 ....72 C6
Linstock Wy ATH M46 ....66 D1
Linthorpe Wk BOLS/LL BL3 ....35 L8
Linton Av BURY BL9 ....25 J3
DTN/ASHW M34 ....100 D1
GOL/RIS/CUL WA3 ....79 J2
Linton Cl ANC M4 ....88 A4
Linton Rd SALE M33 ....96 F6
Linton Wk BRO M7 ....71 J4
Linwood Cl WGNE/HIN WN2 ....49 G8
Linwood Gv WGTN/LGST M12 ....99 K2
Linwood St NEWH/MOS M40 ....73 M6
Lion Brow BKLY M9 ....73 G2
Lion Fold La BKLY M9 ....73 G2
Lion La HOR/BR BL6 ....32 F7
Lions Dr SWIN M27 ....70 F5
Lion St BKLY M9 ....73 G2
Liptrot St WGNW/BIL/OR WN5 ....14 A6
Lisbon St ROCH OL11 ....27 L4
Lisburn Av OLDTF/WHR M16 ....97 M3
SALE M33 ....108 C1
Lisburne Av OFTN SK2 ....113 G6
Lisburne Cl OFTN SK2 * 113 G6
Lisburne La OFTN SK2 ....112 F7
Lisburn Rd NEWH/MOS M40 ....73 K4
Liscard Av RUSH/FAL M14 ....98 E3
Liscard St ATH M46 ....66 E1
Lisetta Av OLDE OL4 * 59 L7
Liskeard Av ROY/SHW OL2 ....43 G8
Liskeard Cl MILN OL16 ....11 L1
Liskeard Dr BRAM/HZG SK7 ....121 G5
Lisle St WHIT OL12 ....11 G2
Lismore Av BOLS/LL BL3 ....35 J5
EDGY/DAV SK3 ....12 A7
Lismore Rd DUK SK16 ....91 G5
Lismore Wy URM M41 ....85 G7
Lissadel St SLFD M6 ....71 K8
Lisson Gv HALE/TIMP WA15 ....117 G2
Lister Rd MDTN M24 ....56 F6
Lister St BOLS/LL BL3 ....51 L1
Liston St DUK SK16 ....91 J4
Litcham Cl CMANE M1 * 7 J8
Litchfield Gv WALK M28 ....69 L5
Litherland Av WYTH/NTH M22 ....119 G2
Litherland Rd BOLS/LL BL3 ....52 B2
SALE M33 ....109 H1
Little 66 BURY BL9 ....39 G6
Little Ancoats St CMANE M1 ....7 J3
Little Bank St OLDE OL4 ....59 L6
Littlebourne Wk BOL BL1 ....2 F1
Littlebrook Cl CHD/CHDH SK8 ....111 M8
GLSP SK13 ....93 K8
Little Brook Rd SALE M33 ....107 M3
Little Brow EDGW/EG BL7 ....22 D5
Little Clegg Rd LIT OL15 ....21 K5
Littledale St WHIT OL12 ....10 C3
Little David St CMANE M1 ....7 H6
Little Ees La SALE M33 ....96 C5
Little Egerton St STKP SK1 ....13 H3
Little Factory St TYLD M29 ....67 J3
Littlefields HYDE SK14 ....92 D8
Little Flatt WHIT OL12 ....27 L3
Littlegate WHTN BL5 ....50 B7
Little Gn MDTN M24 ....58 B1
Littlegreen Gdns SLFD M6 ....86 C2
Little Harwood Lee BOLE BL2 ....37 C1
Littlehaven Cl WGTN/LGST M12 ....88 B7
Little Heath La ALT WA14 ....107 C7
Little Hey St ROY/SHW OL2 ....43 L8
Littlehills Cl MDTN M24 ....57 H3
Little Holme Wk BOLS/LL BL3 * 36 C6
Little Howarth Wy WHIT OL12 * 21 G8
Little John St CSLFD M3 ....6 C5
Little La WGNS/IIMK WN3 ....47 H6
Little Lever St CMANE M1 ....7 J4
Little London WGN WN1 ....15 H5
Little Meadow Rd ALT WA14 ....116 D3

Little Mdw EDGW/EG BL7 * 22 C5
Little Moor Clough
  EDGW/EG BL7 ...... 22 B2
Little Moor Cottages STKP SK1 .. 112 E4
Littlemoor La OLDE OL4 ...... 59 M4
Littlemoor Rd UPML OL3 ...... 45 L8
Littlemoor Rd HYDE SK14 ...... 103 K2
Little Moss La SWIN M27 ...... 70 C2
Littlemoss Rd DROY M43 ...... 89 M1
Little Nelson St ANC M4 * 7 J4
Little Oak Cl OLDE OL4 ...... 60 B6
Little Pasture LEIGH WN7 ...... 66 A5
Little Peter St HULME M15 ...... 6 D8
Little Pitt St CMANE M1 * 7 J4
Little Quay St CSLFD M3 ...... 6 E5
Little Scotland HOR/BR BL6 ...... 32 E2
Little Stones Rd EDGW/EG BL7 .. 22 B2
Littleton Gv WGNS/IIMK WN3 .... 31 H2
Littleton Rd BRO M7 ...... 71 K4
Little Underbank STKP SK1 ...... 13 J4
Littlewood Av BURY BL9 ...... 25 J7
Littlewood Rd WYTH/NTH M22 .. 109 M8
Littlewood St SLFD M6 ...... 86 B2
Littondale Cl ROY/SHW OL2 ...... 43 H7
Litton Ms GLSP SK13 ...... 104 B3
Liverpool Cl STKP SK1 ...... 100 B5
Liverpool Rd AIMK WN4 ...... 78 A2
  CSLFD M3 ...... 6 B6
  ECC M30 ...... 84 A6
  IRL M44 ...... 94 A7
  IRL M44 ...... 94 E1
  WGNW/HIN WN2 ...... 64 E1
Liverpool Rd RDSH SK5 ...... 100 B5
  SLFD M6 ...... 86 B2
Liverstudd Av RDSH SK5 ...... 100 C4
Livesey St ANC M4 ...... 87 M1
  BNG/LEV M19 ...... 99 K4
  OLD OL1 ...... 59 M4
Livingston Av WYTH/NTH M22 .. 118 D2
Livingstone Av MOSL OL5 ...... 76 E3
Livingstone St OLDE OL4 ...... 60 B7
Livsey Ct BOL BL1 ...... 2 A1
Livsey La HEY OL10 ...... 40 D2
Livsey St MILN OL16 ...... 11 G5
  WHTF M45 ...... 55 H4
Liza St LEIGH WN7 ...... 66 B4
Lizmar Ter BKLY M9 ...... 73 J4
Llanberis Rd CHD/CHDH SK8 .. 120 A3
Llanfair Rd EDGY/DAV SK3 ...... 12 D7
Lloyd Av CHD/CHDH SK8 ...... 110 D6
Lloyd Ct LEIGH WN7 * 66 B5
Lloyd Gdns ALT WA14 ...... 116 F1
Lloyd Rd BNG/LEV M19 ...... 99 L5
Lloyd Sq WA14 ...... 108 A8
Lloyd St WA14 ...... 108 A8
  CMANW M2 ...... 6 F5
  HEY OL10 ...... 41 G3
  HTNM SK4 ...... 12 F2
  ROCH OL11 ...... 10 D9
  WHIT OL12 ...... 20 A3
Lloyd St South RUSH/FAL M14 .. 98 D3
Lobden Crs WHIT OL12 ...... 20 B5
Lobelia Av FWTH BL4 ...... 52 D3
Lobley Cl WHIT OL12 ...... 28 E2
Local Board St
  WGNE/HIN WN2 * 48 C5
Lochawe Cl HEY OL10 ...... 40 D3
Lochinver Gv HEY OL10 ...... 40 D3
Lochmaddy Cl BRAM/HZG SK7 .. 122 E8
Loch Cl HEY OL10 ...... 41 H4
Lockerbie Pl WGNS/IIMK WN3 .... 63 H2
Locker La AIMK WN4 ...... 64 C8
Lockett Gdns CSLFD M3 ...... 6 C2
Lockett Rd AIMK WN4 ...... 63 L6
Lockett St CHH M8 ...... 86 E4
  SLFD M6 ...... 71 K7
Lockhart Cl WGTN/LGST M12 .... 88 D7
Lockhart St MILN OL16 ...... 11 K8
Lockingate St AUL OL6 ...... 75 M6
Locking Gate Ri OLDE OL4 ...... 60 B3
Lock Keepers Ms SWIN M27 ...... 71 C4
Locklands La IRL M44 ...... 94 D2
Lock La HOR/BR BL6 ...... 34 F8
  PART M31 ...... 106 B1
Lock Rd ALT WA14 ...... 107 M6
Lockside MPL/ROM SK6 ...... 114 C6
Lockside Vw MOSL OL5 ...... 77 H1
Locksley Cl HTNM SK4 ...... 12 D1
Locks Vw WGN WN1 ...... 15 M4
Lockton Cl CMANE M1 ...... 7 K8
  RDSH SK5 ...... 100 B6
Lockton Ct CMANE M1 ...... 7 J8
Lockwood St WGTN/LGST M12 .. 99 L1
Lodge Av URM M41 ...... 96 B2
Lodge Bank GLSP SK13 ...... 93 K6
  HOR/BR BL6 ...... 33 J1
Lodge Bank Rd LIT OL15 ...... 29 J1
Lodge Brow RAD M26 ...... 54 E2
Lodge Cl DUK SK16 ...... 91 H5
Lodge Ct HTNM SK4 ...... 111 J2
  HYDE SK14 ...... 92 D8
Lodge Dr TYLD M29 ...... 67 L6
Lodge Farm Cl BRAM/HZG SK7 .. 121 G2
Lodge Fold DROY M43 ...... 89 L2
Lodge Gn DUK SK16 ...... 91 H5
Lodge Gv ATH M46 ...... 67 H3
Lodge La ATH M46 ...... 67 G3
  DUK SK16 ...... 91 G4
  HYDE SK14 ...... 91 G8
  LEIGH WN7 ...... 67 H8
  NEWLW WA12 ...... 78 E5
  UPML OL3 ...... 45 H7
Lodge Mill La RAMS BL0 ...... 19 K3
Lodgepole Cl ECC M30 ...... 84 C4
Lodge Rd ATH M46 ...... 67 H3
  RAD M26 ...... 54 E2
  WGNW/BIL/OR WN5 ...... 46 B8
Lodgeside Cl DROY M43 ...... 89 L2
Lodge St AULW OL7 ...... 90 C3
  HYDE SK14 ...... 91 H7
  LIT OL15 ...... 21 M7
  MDTN M24 ...... 57 K3
  NEWH/MOS M40 ...... 73 H7
  RAMS BL0 ...... 18 F6
  RAMS BL0 ...... 19 H4
  WHIT OL12 ...... 21 G6
The Lodge GLSP SK13 ...... 93 K6
Lodge Vw DROY M43 ...... 89 L2
  RAMS BL0 ...... 19 K4
Loeminster Pl WGNE/HIN WN2 .. 15 M6
Loen Crs BOL BL1 ...... 35 M1
Loganberry Av SLFD M6 ...... 86 D1
Logan St BOL BL1 ...... 22 B7
Logwood Av TOT/BURYW BL8 ...... 4 C2
  WGNW/BIL/OR WN5 ...... 47 H5
Logwood Pl
  WGNW/BIL/OR WN5 ...... 47 H4
Loire Dr WGNW/BIL/OR WN5 .... 14 A3
Loisíné Cl ROCH OL11 ...... 41 L1
Lolla Gdns CHH M8 ...... 72 B7
Lomas St BNG/LEV M19 ...... 111 G1

Lomas St EDGY/DAV SK3 ...... 12 F8
  FAIL M35 ...... 74 D3
  STRET M32 ...... 97 L2
Lomax St BOL BL1 ...... 36 B2
  BURY BL9 ...... 5 H3
  CMANE M1 ...... 7 J4
  RAD M26 ...... 54 D2
  WGNE/HIN WN2 ...... 64 D2
  WHIT OL12 ...... 10 F2
  WHTF M45 * 55 H2
Lomax's Buildings BOLE BL2 ...... 2 F6
Lombard Ct MPL/ROM SK6 ...... 101 J8
Lombard Gv RUSH/FAL M14 ...... 98 F4
Lombard St ATH M46 ...... 66 E1
  OLD OL1 ...... 9 H4
  WHIT OL12 ...... 10 B3
Lombardy Ct SLFD M6 * 86 D1
Lomond Av HALE/TIMP WA15 .. 117 J4
  STRET M32 ...... 97 G1
Lomond Cl OFTN SK2 ...... 121 J1
Lomond Dr TOT/BURYW BL8 ...... 24 F8
Lomond Pl BOLS/LL BL3 ...... 35 H6
Lomond Rd WYTH/NTH M22 .. 119 H2
Lomond Ter MILN OL16 ...... 28 F3
London Flds
  WGNW/BIL/OR WN5 ...... 62 B7
London Pl STKP SK1 ...... 13 J5
London Rd BRAM/HZG SK7 ...... 113 C8
  CMANE M1 ...... 7 K7
  OLD OL1 ...... 59 L3
  WILM/AE SK9 ...... 130 D3
London Rd North
  POY/DIS SK12 ...... 121 M8
London Rd South
  POY/DIS SK12 ...... 129 H2
London Sq STKP SK1 ...... 13 J5
London St BOLS/LL BL3 ...... 36 B8
  SLFD M6 ...... 71 L8
  WHTF M45 ...... 55 J5
Long Acres Dr WHIT OL12 ...... 20 B3
Longacres La WHIT OL12 ...... 20 B3
Longacres Rd
  HALE/TIMP WA15 ...... 117 L5
Longbow Ct BRO M7 * 72 A8
Longbridge Rd TRPK M17 ...... 85 K6
Longbrook WGNNW/ST WN6 .... 30 E6
Long Cswy ATH M46 ...... 66 E5
  FWTH BL4 ...... 53 C5
Longcliffe Wk BOL BL1 * 36 C2
Long Clough ROY/SHW OL2 ...... 58 F2
Longclough Dr GLSP SK13 ...... 104 D4
Longcrag Wk HULME M15 * 87 J7
Longcroft TYLD M29 ...... 67 H8
Longcroft Dr ALT WA14 ...... 107 H8
Longcroft Gv DTN/ASHW M34 .. 89 J1
  NTHM/RTH M23 ...... 109 K5
Long Croft La CHD/CHDH SK8 .. 120 E7
Longdale Cl ROY/SHW OL2 ...... 42 F8
Longdale Dr HYDE SK14 ...... 103 K1
Longden Av OLDE OL4 ...... 60 M7
Longden Rd WGTN/LGST M12 .... 99 J1
Longden St BOL BL1 ...... 35 M4
Longdendale Ct BRAM/HZG SK7 * .. 128 A3

Longdendale Rd
  WGNNW/ST WN6 ...... 31 G4
Longfellow Av BOLS/LL BL3 ...... 51 L1
Longfellow Cl WGNS/IIMK WN3 .. 47 K7
Longfellow Crs OLD OL1 ...... 44 A8
Longfield BURY BL9 * 25 K8
Longfield Av CHD/CHDH SK8 .. 119 L5
  HALE/TIMP WA15 ...... 108 F6
  URM M41 ...... 95 L2
Longfield Cl HYDE SK14 ...... 91 H6
Longfield Crs OLDE OL4 ...... 59 M5
Longfield Dr URM M41 ...... 95 L2
Longfield La OLDE OL4 ...... 60 A3
Longfield Pk ROY/SHW OL2 ...... 43 K7
Longfield Rd BOLS/LL BL3 ...... 51 L2
  NTHM/RTH M23 ...... 109 J4
  ROCH OL11 ...... 27 M4
  ROY/SHW OL2 ...... 43 K6
Longford Av BOL BL1 ...... 35 M2
  STRET M32 ...... 97 H2
Longford Cl STRET M32 ...... 97 H1
Longford Pk STRET M32 ...... 97 H1
Longford Pl RUSH/FAL M14 ...... 88 B8
Longford Rd RDSH SK5 ...... 100 C3
  STRET M32 ...... 97 H1
Longford Rd West
  BNG/LEV M19 ...... 100 A3
Longford St GTN M18 ...... 89 G6
  HEY OL10 ...... 40 F2
Long Grain Pl OFTN SK2 ...... 113 G7
Longham Cl BRAM/HZG SK7 ...... 120 E8
  OP/CLY M11 ...... 88 B3
Long Hey HALE/TIMP WA15 ...... 117 L6
Longhey Rd WYTH/NTH M22 .. 110 A7
Long Hl ROCH OL11 ...... 28 A8
Longhirst Cl BOL BL1 ...... 35 L1
Longhope Rd WYTH/NTH M22 .. 118 E1
Longhurst La MPL/ROM SK6 .. 114 E5
Longhurst Rd BKLY M9 ...... 56 E8
  WGNE/HIN WN2 ...... 49 J8
Longlands Av HYDE SK14 ...... 102 E1
Longlands Dr HYDE SK14 ...... 102 E1
  NM/HAY SK22 ...... 124 D4
Longlands Rd NM/HAY SK22 .. 124 D4
Long La BOLE BL2 ...... 37 G7
  BURY BL9 ...... 25 J5
  CHAD OL9 ...... 74 C1
  GLSP SK13 ...... 103 M5
  UPML OL3 ...... 61 K2
  WGNE/HIN WN2 ...... 49 K8
  WHTN BL5 ...... 50 B3
Longlevens Rd
  WYTH/NTH M22 ...... 118 E2
Longley Av WALK M28 ...... 69 L6
Longley La WYTH/NTH M22 .. 110 B5
Longley St OLD OL1 ...... 9 L7
  ROY/SHW OL2 ...... 43 L7
  WALK M28 ...... 69 G2
Long Marl Dr WILM/AE SK9 .. 120 B8
Longmead Av AIMK WN4 ...... 63 J3
  BRAM/HZG SK7 ...... 121 M3
Longmeade Gdns
  WILM/AE SK9 ...... 127 G6
Longmeadow CHD/CHDH SK8 .. 120 C5
Long Meadow EDGW/EG BL7 .. 22 F5
  HYDE SK14 ...... 91 J6
Longmeadow Gv
  DTN/ASHW M34 ...... 101 H2
Longmeadow Pas HYDE SK14 .. 102 A1
Long Meadow Pas
  HYDE SK14 * 102 A1
Longmead Rd SLFD M6 ...... 71 G7
Longmead Wy MDTN M24 ...... 57 K3
Longmere Av WYTH/NTH M22 .. 118 F1
Longnor Ms GLSP SK13 ...... 104 A2

Longnor Rd BRAM/HZG SK7 .. 122 A5
  CHD/CHDH SK8 ...... 119 M5
Longport Av DID/WITH M20 ...... 98 D5
Longridge EDGW/EG BL7 ...... 22 F4
Longridge Av STLY SK15 ...... 76 D8
  WGNNW/ST WN6 ...... 31 J4
Longridge Crs BOL BL1 ...... 35 J2
Longridge Dr HEY OL10 ...... 40 C2
  TOT/BURYW BL8 ...... 38 D4
Long Rw STLY SK15 ...... 77 J5
Long Rushes ROY/SHW OL2 ...... 43 J4
Longshaw Av SWIN M27 ...... 70 C3
  WGNW/BIL/OR WN5 ...... 62 B3
Longshaw Cl
  WGNW/BIL/OR WN5 ...... 62 B3
Longshaw Common
  WGNW/BIL/OR WN5 ...... 62 B3
Longshaw Dr LHULT M38 ...... 52 D8
Longshaw Old Rd
  WGNW/BIL/OR WN5 ...... 62 B3
Longshoot Cl WGN WN1 ...... 15 J4
Longshut La OFTN SK2 ...... 13 J8
Longshut La West OFTN SK2 .. 13 H8
Longsides Rd
  HALE/TIMP WA15 ...... 117 L5
Longsight BOLE BL2 ...... 23 G7
  CHD/CHDH SK8 ...... 120 B7
Longsight La BOLE BL2 ...... 23 G8
  CHD/CHDH SK8 ...... 120 B7
Longsight Rd BOLE BL2 ...... 37 G5
  GTN M18 ...... 99 L1
  RAMS BL0 ...... 24 D2
Longsight St HTNM SK4 ...... 12 E3
Longson St BOL BL1 ...... 3 J1
Long St GTN M18 ...... 89 H6
  MDTN M24 ...... 57 K3
  SWIN M27 ...... 70 C5
Longton Av DID/WITH M20 ...... 98 D5
  GOL/RIS/CUL WA3 ...... 79 M4
Longton Rd BKLY M9 ...... 56 F8
  SLFD M6 ...... 70 F7
Longton St BURY BL9 ...... 39 J8
  WGNE/HIN WN2 ...... 49 G7
Longtown Gdns BOL BL1 * 36 B2
Longview Dr SWIN M27 ...... 69 M3
Longwall Av WALK M28 ...... 68 F4
Longwood Av OFTN SK2 ...... 112 E6
Longwood Cl MPL/ROM SK6 .. 114 E1
Longwood Rd TRPK M17 ...... 85 L6
  WYTH/NTH M22 ...... 119 C1
Longworth Av HOR/BR BL6 ...... 32 F1
Longworth Cl URM M41 ...... 95 C3
Longworth Clough
  EDGW/EG BL7 ...... 22 A2
Longworth La EDGW/EG BL7 .. 22 A4
Longworth St BOLE BL2 ...... 3 L4
  CSLFD M3 ...... 6 D6
Lonsdale Av LEIGH WN7 ...... 81 G2
  MILN OL16 ...... 11 K9
  RDSH SK5 ...... 100 C1
  SWIN M27 ...... 70 A7
  URM M41 ...... 84 E8
Lonsdale Rd BNG/LEV M19 ...... 99 L2
  BOL BL1 ...... 35 L4
  OLDS OL8 ...... 74 E2
Lonsdale St NEWH/MOS M40 .. 73 M6
  TOT/BURYW BL8 ...... 38 D7
Lonsdale Wk
  WGNW/BIL/OR WN5 ...... 46 E4
Loom St ANC M4 ...... 7 K3
Loonies Ct STKP SK1 * 13 J6
Lord Av ATH M46 * 67 H3
Lord Byron Sq SALQ M50 ...... 86 A4
Lord Derby Rd HYDE SK14 .. 102 B6
Lord Gv ATH M46 ...... 67 J3
Lord La FAIL M35 ...... 74 B8
Lord Napier Dr ORD M5 ...... 86 D5
Lord North St NEWH/MOS M40 .. 73 H8
Lord's Av ORD M5 ...... 86 A2
Lordsfields Av AULW OL7 ...... 75 L8
Lords Fold BOL BL1 * 35 J3
Lord Sheldon Wy AULW OL7 ...... 90 C1
Lordship Cl BKLY M9 ...... 73 J3
Lord Sq AIMK WN4 ...... 64 A8
Lord's Stile La EDGW/EG BL7 .. 22 E5
Lord St AIMK WN4 ...... 64 A8
  ANC M4 ...... 87 K1
  ATH M46 ...... 67 H3
  AUL OL6 ...... 75 L8
  BURY BL9 ...... 5 G5
  BURY BL9 ...... 39 M3
  DTN/ASHW M34 ...... 89 K8
  DUK SK16 ...... 91 J4
  FWTH BL4 ...... 53 H4
  GLSP SK13 ...... 104 F3
  HYDE SK14 ...... 93 G8
  LEIGH WN7 ...... 66 C7
  MDTN M24 ...... 57 K3
  OLD OL1 ...... 9 J4
  RAD M26 ...... 54 D1
  STKP SK1 ...... 13 J5
  TYLD M29 ...... 67 J6
  WGN WN1 ...... 15 G1
  WGNE/HIN WN2 ...... 48 D5
  WGNE/HIN WN2 ...... 49 G7
  WHTN BL5 ...... 50 B3
Lordy Cl WGNNW/ST WN6 ...... 31 L5
Loretto Rd URM M41 ...... 96 C3
Lorgill Cl EDGY/DAV SK3 ...... 112 C8
Loring St NEWH/MOS M40 ...... 73 M7
Lorland Rd EDGY/DAV SK3 ...... 12 A9
Lorna Gv CHD/CHDH SK8 ...... 110 C6
Lorna Rd CHD/CHDH SK8 ...... 120 D2
Lorna Wy IRL M44 ...... 94 E1
Lorne Av ROY/SHW OL2 ...... 58 E1
Lorne Gv EDGY/DAV SK3 ...... 112 B6
  URM M41 ...... 96 B2
Lorne Rd RUSH/FAL M14 ...... 98 F4
Lorne St BOL BL1 ...... 2 E4
  BRUN/LGST M13 ...... 87 M7
  ECC M30 ...... 84 E4
  FWTH BL4 ...... 52 F2
  HEY OL10 ...... 41 G3
  MOSL OL5 ...... 76 F3
  OLDS OL8 ...... 59 H8
  WGN WN1 ...... 15 K4
  WHIT OL12 ...... 28 E1
Lorne Wy HEY OL10 ...... 40 C3
Lorraine Cl HEY OL10 ...... 41 H4
Lorraine Rd HALE/TIMP WA15 .. 108 D7
Lorton Cl MDTN M24 ...... 56 F2
  WALK M28 ...... 68 C6
Lorton Gv BOLE BL2 ...... 37 J4
Lostock Av BNG/LEV M19 ...... 99 L3
  BRAM/HZG SK7 ...... 121 K3
  POY/DIS SK12 ...... 121 K8
  SALE M33 ...... 97 H4
  URM M41 ...... 95 L1
Lostock Cl HEY OL10 ...... 40 E1
  WGNW/BIL/OR WN5 ...... 62 B7
Lostock Dr BURY BL9 ...... 25 J4
Lostock Gv STRET M32 ...... 96 F1
Lostock Hall Rd POY/DIS SK12 .. 128 F1

Lostock Junction La
  HOR/BR BL6 ...... 34 F6
Lostock La HOR/BR BL6 ...... 34 B6
Lostock Park Dr HOR/BR BL6 .. 34 D5
Lostock Rd ORD M5 ...... 86 B2
  POY/DIS SK12 ...... 129 G2
  URM M41 ...... 84 F8
  WILM/AE SK9 ...... 119 K8
Lostock St NEWH/MOS M40 ...... 88 A1
Lostock Wy WILM/AE SK9 .. 119 K8
Lothian Av ECC M30 ...... 84 E1
Lottery Rw BOL BL1 * 2 F5
Lottery St EDGY/DAV SK3 ...... 12 F5
Lottie St SWIN M27 ...... 70 D4
Loughborough Cl SALE M33 .. 108 A1
Loughfield URM M41 ...... 95 K2
Loughrigg Av ROY/SHW OL2 ...... 42 F4
Loughrigg Cl OFTN SK2 ...... 67 L5
Louisa St BOL BL1 ...... 36 A2
  OP/CLY M11 ...... 89 G4
  WALK M28 ...... 53 C8
Louis Av BURY BL9 ...... 25 J8
Louise Cl WHIT OL12 ...... 28 F1
Louise Gdns WHIT OL12 ...... 28 E1
  WHTN BL5 ...... 50 B6
Louise St WHIT OL12 ...... 28 E1
Louvain St FAIL M35 ...... 74 B5
Lovalle St BOL BL1 ...... 35 M3
Lovat Rd BOLE BL2 ...... 37 J5
Love La HTNM SK4 ...... 13 G2
  RAMS BL0 ...... 19 H3
Lovell Dr BKLY M9 ...... 91 J8
Lovers' La ATH M46 ...... 66 C2
  OLDE OL4 ...... 60 F6
Low Bank Rd AIMK WN4 ...... 63 J8
Lowbrook Av BKLY M9 ...... 73 L1
Lowcroft Crs CHAD OL9 ...... 58 C4
Low Crompton Rd
  ROY/SHW OL2 ...... 43 H6
Lowcross Rd NEWH/MOS M40 .. 73 K6
Lowe Av ATH M46 ...... 50 F7
Lowe Gn ROY/SHW OL2 ...... 43 H7
Lower Mill La WGNE/HIN WN2 .. 49 G7
Lower Albion St CMANE M1 ...... 7 J7
Lower Alma St DUK SK16 ...... 90 E3
Lowerbank DTN/ASHW M34 ...... 90 F1
Lower Bank GLSP SK13 ...... 105 G4
Lower Bank Cl GLSP SK13 ...... 104 C1
Lower Bank St BURY BL9 ...... 4 F5
Lower Barn Rd GLSP SK13 ...... 93 H8
Lower Beechwood ROCH OL11 .. 10 B8
Lower Bennett St HYDE SK14 .. 90 F8
Lower Bents La MPL/ROM SK6 .. 101 J8
Lower Birches OLDE OL4 ...... 60 C8
Lower Bridgeman St BOLE BL2 .. 3 G7
Lower Broadacre STLY SK15 .. 92 B6
Lowerbrook Cl HOR/BR BL6 ...... 34 A3
Lower Brook La WALK M28 * .. 69 K7
Lower Brook St CMANE M1 ...... 7 J6
Lower Broughton Rd BRO M7 .. 71 M7
Lower Bury St HTNM SK4 ...... 12 E4
Lower Byrom St CSLFD M3 ...... 6 C6
Lower Carr La UPML OL3 ...... 61 L6
Lower Carrs AUL OL6 ...... 76 A7
Lower Chatham St CMANE M1 .. 7 G8
Lower Cliffe NM/HAY SK22 * .. 124 A2
Lower Crft WHTF M45 ...... 54 F6
Lowercroft Rd TOT/BURYW BL8 .. 38 C2
Lower Crossbank OLDE OL4 ...... 60 C4
Lower Darcy St BOLE BL2 ...... 3 L9
Lower Dingle OLD OL1 ...... 43 M8
Lower Drake Fold WHTN BL5 .. 50 B7
Lower Edge Av OLD OL1 ...... 9 G7
Lower Falinge WHIT OL12 ...... 10 E2
Lower Fold OFTN SK2 ...... 113 J7
Lowerfields OLDS OL8 ...... 59 L8
Lower Flds UPML OL3 ...... 61 K3
Lowerfields Ri ROY/SHW OL2 .. 43 J4
Lower Fold DTN/ASHW M34 .. 101 K2
  MPL/ROM SK6 ...... 114 C4
Lower Fold Av ROY/SHW OL2 .. 43 K8
Lower Fold Cl WHIT OL12 ...... 20 A8
Lowerfold Crs WHIT OL12 ...... 20 A8
Lowerfold Dr WHIT OL12 ...... 20 A8
Lowerfold Wy WHIT OL12 ...... 20 A8
Lower Frenches Dr UPML OL3 .. 61 K6
Lower Goodwin Cl BOLE BL2 .. 37 H1
Lower Gn AUL OL6 ...... 75 M8
  MDTN M24 ...... 57 J7
  WHIT OL12 ...... 27 M3
Lower Green La TYLD M29 ...... 82 F2
Lower Greenshall La
  POY/DIS SK12 ...... 124 D6
Lower Hague NM/HAY SK22 .. 124 A4
Lower Hardman St CSLFD M3 .. 6 C5
Lower Hey La MOSL OL5 ...... 77 H1
Lower Hillgate STKP SK1 ...... 13 K5
Lower House Dr HOR/BR BL6 .. 34 F5
Lower House La WHIT OL12 ...... 20 F5
Lower House St OLD OL1 ...... 59 L4
Lower House Wk EDGW/EG BL7 .. 22 D4
Lower Jowkin La ROCH OL11 .. 27 C5
Lower Knoll Rd UPML OL3 ...... 45 M7
Lower Landedmans WHTN BL5 .. 50 C5
Lower Leigh Rd WHTN BL5 ...... 50 C7
Lower Lime Rd OLDS OL8 ...... 74 F5
Lower Longshoot WGN WN1 .. 15 J3
Lower Lyndon Av
  WGNNW/ST WN6 ...... 30 D6
Lower Makinson Fold
  HOR/BR BL6 * 34 A3
Lower Marlands EDGW/EG BL7 .. 22 C3
Lower Md EDGW/EG BL7 ...... 22 C3
Lower Meadow EDGW/EG BL7 .. 17 C3
Lower Meadow Rd
  WILM/AE SK9 ...... 120 A8
Lower Moat Cl HTNM SK4 ...... 112 B1
Lower Monton Rd ECC M30 ...... 85 H2
Lower Mosley St CMANE M1 ...... 6 E7
Lower Moss La HULME M15 ...... 6 A9
  WHTF M45 ...... 55 H4
Lower New Rw WALK M28 ...... 68 B5
Lower Ormond St CMANE M1 .. 7 G8
Lower Park Crs POY/DIS SK12 .. 121 H6
Lower Park Rd POY/DIS SK12 .. 121 H7
  RUSH/FAL M14 ...... 87 M8
Lower Rawson St FWTH BL4 ...... 53 H4
Lower Rd RAMS BL0 ...... 19 G4
Lower Rock St NM/HAY SK22 .. 124 A4
Lower St Stephen St
  WGNNW/ST WN6 ...... 14 C3
Lower Seedley Rd SLFD M6 ...... 86 B1
Lower Sheriff St WHIT OL12 .. 10 C3
Lower Southfield WHTN BL5 .. 50 B5
Lower St FWTH BL4 ...... 52 F5
  MILN OL16 ...... 29 G8
Lower Strines Rd
  MPL/ROM SK6 ...... 114 D7
Lower Sutherland St SWIN M27 .. 70 B4

Lower Tenterfield ROCH OL11 .. 27 G2
Lower Tong EDGW/EG BL7 ...... 22 C5
Lower Turf La OLDE OL4 ...... 61 G6
Lower Tweedale St ROCH OL11 .. 10 F7
Lower Victoria St CHAD OL9 .. 8 E8
Lower Wharf St AUL OL6 ...... 90 E2
Lower Wheat End MILN OL16 .. 11 K6
Lower Woodhill Rd
  TOT/BURYW BL8 ...... 4 C3
Lowerwood La BOLE BL2 ...... 36 E3
Lowes Rd BURY BL9 ...... 25 J6
Lowestead Rd OP/CLY M11 ...... 88 F2
The Lowes ALT WA14 ...... 116 F1
Lowestoft St RUSH/FAL M14 .. 98 E2
Lowe St DTN/ASHW M34 ...... 101 L1
  GOL/RIS/CUL WA3 ...... 79 K4
  RAD M26 ...... 38 C8
  STKP SK1 ...... 13 J5
Loweswater Av TYLD M29 ...... 67 K5
Loweswater Rd
  CHD/CHDH SK8 ...... 119 K1
  FWTH BL4 ...... 52 B8
Lowfield Av AUL OL6 ...... 76 C7
  DROY M43 ...... 89 J1
Lowfield Gdns
  GOL/RIS/CUL WA3 ...... 80 B5
Lowfield Gv OFTN SK2 ...... 13 J9
Lowfield Rd EDGY/DAV SK3 ...... 13 H9
Low Gate La UPML OL3 ...... 45 K3
Low Hall Cl WHIT OL12 ...... 28 F1
Low Hill WHIT OL12 ...... 28 F1
Lowhouse Cl MILN OL16 ...... 29 K5
Lowick Av BOLS/LL BL3 ...... 52 D1
Lowick Cl BRAM/HZG SK7 ...... 121 M2
Lowick Gn MPL/ROM SK6 ...... 101 J7
Lowland Gv AULW OL7 ...... 75 K6
Lowland Rd OFTN SK2 ...... 112 E8
Lowlands Cl MDTN M24 ...... 57 M8
Low Lea Rd MPL/ROM SK6 .. 114 C6
Low Leighton Rd
  NM/HAY SK22 ...... 124 F5
Low Mdw ROY/SHW OL2 ...... 43 G6
Lowndes Cl OFTN SK2 ...... 112 E5
Lowndes La OFTN SK2 ...... 112 E5
Lowndes St BOL BL1 ...... 35 L4
Lowndes Wk
  BRUN/LGST M13 * 87 M6
Lownorth Rd WYTH/NTH M22 .. 119 G4
Lowood Av URM M41 ...... 84 C3
Lowood St LEIGH WN7 ...... 66 C7
Lowry Ct DTN/ASHW M34 ...... 89 K8
Lowry Dr MPL/ROM SK6 ...... 114 E4
  SWIN M27 ...... 70 C3
Lowry Gv HYDE SK14 ...... 103 J1
Lowry Houses ECC M30 * 85 H2
Lowry Wk BOL BL1 ...... 35 L4
Lowside Av BOL BL1 ...... 34 F6
  MPL/ROM SK6 ...... 101 M7
Lowside Dr OLDE OL4 ...... 59 L7
Low's Pl WHIT OL12 ...... 22 C3
Lowstern Cl EDGW/EG BL7 ...... 22 C3
The Lows OLDE OL4 ...... 59 L7
Lowther Av GOL/RIS/CUL WA3 .. 81 J8
  GTN M18 ...... 99 L1
  HALE/TIMP WA15 ...... 108 D6
  ROY/SHW OL2 ...... 42 F4
Lowther Cl PWCH M25 ...... 71 K1
Lowther Crs MDTN M24 ...... 57 H3
Lowther Dr LEIGH WN7 ...... 67 G5
Lowther Gdns URM M41 ...... 95 J2
Lowther Rd CHH M8 ...... 72 D3
  PWCH M25 ...... 71 J1
  ROCH OL11 ...... 28 B8
Lowther St BOLS/LL BL3 ...... 52 C3
Lowthorpe St RUSH/FAL M14 .. 98 D2
Lowton Av BKLY M9 ...... 73 J5
Lowton Gdns GOL/RIS/CUL WA3 .. 79 L3
Lowton Rd GOL/RIS/CUL WA3 .. 79 L3
  SALE M33 ...... 108 A2
Lowton St RAD M26 ...... 38 D8
Low Wood Cl BRAM/HZG SK7 .. 120 E3
Low Wood Rd DTN/ASHW M34 .. 89 K8
Loxford Cl HULME M15 ...... 6 F9
Loxham St BOLS/LL BL3 ...... 53 G2
Loxton Crs WGNS/IIMK WN3 .. 63 H1
Lubeck St BKLY M9 ...... 73 H4
Lucas Rd FWTH BL4 ...... 52 D4
Lucas St BURY BL9 ...... 5 J2
  OLDE OL4 ...... 60 C6
Lucas Wk OP/CLY M11 * 88 C4
Lucerne Cl CHAD OL9 ...... 8 C1
Lucerne Rd BRAM/HZG SK7 .. 121 G1
Lucien Cl WGTN/LGST M12 ...... 88 B7
Luciol Cl TYLD M29 ...... 67 M3
Lucknow St ROCH OL11 ...... 10 E9
Lucy St BOL BL1 ...... 35 K3
  BRO M7 ...... 72 A7
  EDGY/DAV SK3 ...... 13 G7
  HULME M15 ...... 6 C9
Ludford Gv SALE M33 ...... 108 C2
Ludgate Hl ANC M4 * 7 J1
Ludgate Rd NEWH/MOS M40 .. 73 M8
  ROCH OL11 ...... 42 D2
Ludgate St ANC M4 ...... 7 H1
Ludlow Av WGNE/HIN WN2 ...... 49 K8
  WHTF M45 ...... 55 L6
Ludlow Dr LEIGH WN7 ...... 67 G5
Ludlow Pk OLDE OL4 ...... 60 A6
Ludlow Rd OFTN SK2 ...... 112 F4
Ludlow St WGNNW/ST WN6 ...... 30 F1
Ludovic Ter WGN WN1 ...... 15 M8
Lugano Rd BRAM/HZG SK7 .. 121 G1
Luke Rd DROY M43 ...... 89 L3
Luke St AIMK WN4 ...... 64 A7
Lullington Cl WYTH/NTH M22 .. 118 E3
Lullington Rd SLFD M6 ...... 71 G8
Lulworth Av URM M41 ...... 84 C8
Lulworth Cl TOT/BURYW BL8 .. 24 F6
Lulworth Crs FAIL M35 ...... 74 D4
Lulworth Dr WGNE/HIN WN2 .. 49 K8
Lulworth Gdns
  NTHM/RTH M23 ...... 109 J4
Lulworth Rd BOLS/LL BL3 ...... 51 K4
  ECC M30 ...... 84 F2
  MDTN M24 ...... 57 L2
Lumb Carr Av RAMS BL0 ...... 18 D8
Lumb Carr Rd RAMS BL0 ...... 18 D8
Lumb Cl BRAM/HZG SK7 ...... 121 G6
Lumber La WALK M28 ...... 69 H4
Lumb La BRAM/HZG SK7 ...... 121 G6
  DROY M43 ...... 89 M3
  DTN/ASHW M34 ...... 89 M3
Lumley Cl RUSH/FAL M14 ...... 87 L8
Lumn Hollow HYDE SK14 ...... 102 B2
Lumn Rd HYDE SK14 ...... 102 B2
Lumn's La SWIN M27 ...... 70 F2
Lumsden St BOL BL1 ...... 3 G3

Lumwood BOL BL1 35 L1
Luna St ANC M4 7 J3
Lund Av RAD M26 54 E4
Lund St OLDTF/WHR M16 86 F6
Lundy Av CCHDY M21 97 M7
Lune Cl WHTF M45 55 K4
Lunedale Gn OFTN SK2 113 H6
Lune Dr WHTF M45 55 K4
Lune Gv HEY OL10 40 D1
LEIGH WN7 65 M7
Lunehurst GOL/RIS/CUL WA3 80 B4
Lune Rd WGNE/HIN WN2 64 D2
Lune St OLDS OL8 59 H8
Lune Wy RDSH SK5 100 C7
Lunn Av GTN M18 89 J6
Luntswood Gv NEWLW WA12 78 D8
Lupin Av FWTH BL4 52 D3
Lupin Cl OLD OL1 60 B1
Lupin Dr RNFD/HAY WA11 78 C6
Lupton St CSLFD M3 * 6 B3
DTN/ASHW M34 90 C8
Lurden Wk CHAD OL9 * 58 D8
Lurdin La WGNNW/ST WN6 31 L5
Lurgan Av SALE M33 108 F1
Lutener Av ALT WA14 107 M4
Luton Dr NTHM/RTH M23 109 K8
Luton Gv ATH M46 66 E1
Luton Rd RDSH SK5 100 C4
Luton St BOLS/LL BL3 36 D8
TOT/BURYW BL8 38 E3
Luxhall Wk NEWH/MOS M40 73 L7
Luxor Gv DTN/ASHW M34 100 C1
Luzley Brook Rd ROY/SHW OL2 43 K7
Luzley Rd AUL OL6 76 E7
Lyceum Pas MILN OL16 10 E4
Lyceum Pl HULME M15 * 7 G9
Lychgate WGNW/BIL/OR WN5 47 H7
Lychgate Ct OLDE OL4 76 B1
Lychgate Ms HTNM SK4 * 111 H2
Lydbrook Cl BOL BL1 2 C6
Lydden Av OP/CLY M11 * 89 G1
Lydford ROCH OL11 10 D7
Lydford Gdns BOLE BL2 37 J7
Lydford Gn WGNNW/ST WN6 31 J4
Lydford St SLFD M6 71 L8
Lydford Wk BRUN/LGST M13 * 87 M6
Lydgate Av BOLE BL2 37 H4
Lydgate Cl DTN/ASHW M34 101 L3
STLY SK15 77 H6
WHTF M45 55 K4
Lydgate Dr OLDE OL4 59 M7
Lydgate Rd DROY M43 89 H1
SALE M33 108 F2
Lydiate Cl BOLS/LL BL3 52 C2
Lydiat La WILM/AE SK9 130 D4
Lydney Av CHD/CHDH SK8 119 L5
Lydney Rd URM M41 95 G1
Lyefield Av WGN WN1 15 M2
Lyefield Wk MILN OL16 11 J6
Lymbridge Dr HOR/BR BL6 33 G2
Lyme Av WILM/AE SK9 126 F3
Lyme Clough Wy MDTN M24 41 J8
Lymefield Dr WALK M28 68 D5
Lymefield Gv OFTN SK2 112 E6
Lyme Gv ALT WA14 107 M8
DROY M43 89 J4
MPL/ROM SK6 114 A2
MPL/ROM SK6 114 C7
OFTN SK2 13 J8
Lyme Rd BRAM/HZG SK7 122 A3
POY/DIS SK12 123 J5
Lymes ALT WA14 116 E3
Lyme St BRAM/HZG SK7 * 121 M1
HTNM SK4 111 H2
RNFD/HAY WA11 78 B6
Lymewood Dr POY/DIS SK12 123 K6
WILM/AE SK9 * 127 J4
Lymington Cl MDTN M24 57 L7
Lymington Dr NTHM/RTH M23 109 G4
Lymm Cl EDGY/DAV SK3 112 A6
WALK M28 68 D1
Lymn St WGNE/HIN WN2 64 E1
Lynbridge Cl
WGNW/BIL/OR WN5 46 B7
Lyncombe Cl CHD/CHDH SK8 120 D6
Lyndale Av RDSH SK5 100 C1
SWIN M27 70 A6
Lyndale Dr LIT OL15 21 L6
Lyndene Av WALK M28 69 K4
Lyndene Gdns CHD/CHDH SK8 110 E6
Lyndene Rd WYTH/NTH M22 110 A7
Lyndhurst Av AUL OL6 75 L7
BRAM/HZG SK7 121 L3
CHAD OL9 58 C7
DTN/ASHW M34 * 101 H1
IRL M44 94 E1
MPL/ROM SK6 101 J8
PWCH M25 72 B1
ROCH OL11 42 A4
SALE M33 108 C1
URM M41 84 F8
Lyndhurst Cl WILM/AE SK9 126 B7
Lyndhurst Dr
HALE/TIMP WA15 117 J2
Lyndhurst Rd DID/WITH M20 98 D8
OLDS OL8 75 G1
RDSH SK5 * 100 B2
STRET M32 96 E2
Lyndhurst St SLFD M6 86 B2
Lyndhurst Vw DUK SK16 * 90 F3
Lyndon Av WGNNW/ST WN6 30 E5
Lyndon Cl OLDE OL4 60 E4
TOT/BURYW BL8 24 C6
Lyndon Rd IRL M44 94 C3
Lyne Av GLSP SK13 104 D4
Lyne Edge Crs DUK SK16 91 J5
Lyne Edge Rd DUK SK16 91 K5
Lyne Vw HYDE SK14 91 K6
Lyngard Cl WILM/AE SK9 127 H3
Lyngate Cl STKP SK1 13 L6
Lyn Gv HEY OL10 40 D1
Lynham Dr HEY OL10 41 G4
Lynmouth Av DID/WITH M20 98 D6
OLDS OL8 75 J1
RDSH SK5 100 B5
ROY/SHW OL2 58 F1
URM M41 95 L4
Lynmouth Cl CHAD OL9 58 B3
RAD M26 38 F8
WGNNW/ST WN6 47 K2
Lynmouth Gv PWCH M25 71 J1
Lynn Av SALE M33 96 F6
Lynndene Ct HEY OL10 * 40 F1
Lynn Dr DROY M43 89 H2
Lynne Cl GLSP SK13 105 J4
Lynn St CHAD OL9 58 F8
Lynnwood Dr ROCH OL11 27 L4
Lynnwood Rd BNG/LEV M19 111 G2
Lynroyle Wy ROCH OL11 42 A1
Lynsted Av BOLS/LL BL3 52 D1
Lynstock Wy HOR/BR BL6 34 B6
Lynthorpe Av IRL M44 94 A6
Lynthorpe Rd NEWH/MOS M40 74 A2
Lynton Av HYDE SK14 102 F2
IRL M44 94 B6
OLDS OL8 74 F2
ROCH OL11 41 L1
SWIN M27 70 C3
URM M41 94 F2
WGNNW/ST WN6 47 K1
Lynton Cl CHAD OL9 58 C3
Lynton Crs WALK M28 69 G4
Lynton Dr BNG/LEV M19 99 J5
MPL/ROM SK6 123 G4
PWCH M25 55 M6
Lynton Gv HALE/TIMP WA15 108 D7
Lynton La WILM/AE SK9 130 D2
Lynton Lea RAD M26 38 F8
Lynton Ms WILM/AE SK9 130 D2
Lynton Park Rd
CHD/CHDH SK8 120 B4
Lynton Rd BOLS/LL BL3 51 M2
CCHDY M21 97 K3
CHD/CHDH SK8 110 F7
HTNM SK4 99 L7
SWIN M27 70 C3
TYLD M29 68 A4
WGNE/HIN WN2 49 J6
Lynton St LEIGH WN7 66 A7
RUSH/FAL M14 * 98 E2
Lyntonvale Av CHD/CHDH SK8 110 D6
Lynway Dr DID/WITH M20 98 E7
Lynway Gv MDTN M24 57 L2
Lynwell Rd ECC M30 85 G2
Lynwood HALE/TIMP WA15 117 J4
Lynwood Av BOLS/LL BL3 52 E2
ECC M30 85 G2
GOL/RIS/CUL WA3 80 B6
OLDTF/WHR M16 97 M2
Lynwood Cl AULW OL7 75 K5
Lynwood Dr OLDE OL4 60 B5
Lynwood Gv ATH M46 66 E1
BOLE BL2 23 G8
DTN/ASHW M34 89 M3
HTNM SK4 99 M6
SALE M33 96 F7
Lyon Gv WALK M28 69 K4
Lyon Rd ALT WA14 107 M5
FWTH BL4 53 H7
WGNNW/ST WN6 47 K2
Lyons Dr TOT/BURYW BL8 38 D3
Lyons Fold SALE M33 96 E6
Lyons Rd TRPK M17 85 K5
Lyon St AIMK WN4 63 J5
ROY/SHW OL2 43 L5
SWIN M27 70 B5
WGNS/IIMK WN3 14 E5
Lyra Pl BRO M7 86 F1
Lysander Cl RUSH/FAL M14 98 D4
Lytham Av CCHDY M21 97 M5
Lytham Cl AUL OL6 76 B6
Lytham Dr BRAM/HZG SK7 121 J5
HEY OL10 40 F3
Lytham Rd AIMK WN4 63 J7
CHD/CHDH SK8 119 K3
RUSH/FAL M14 99 J3
URM M41 94 F2
Lytham St EDGY/DAV SK3 112 C6
WHIT OL12 28 B1
Lytherton Av IRL M44 94 A8
Lyth St RUSH/FAL M14 99 G5
Lytton Av CHH M8 72 D6
Lytton Rd DROY M43 89 K2
Lytton St BOL BL1 36 A2

M

Mabel Av BOLS/LL BL3 52 D1
WALK M28 69 K5
Mabel Rd FAIL M35 74 D3
Mabel's Brow FWTH BL4 53 H5
Mabel St BOL BL1 35 M4
NEWH/MOS M40 74 A7
WGNW/BIL/OR WN5 47 H6
WHIT OL12 28 A2
WHTN BL5 50 C6
Maberry Cl WGNNW/ST WN6 30 A5
Mabfield Rd RUSH/FAL M14 98 F3
Mableden Cl CHD/CHDH SK8 119 M4
Mabs Ct AUL OL6 91 G2
Macaulay St ROCH OL11 41 M3
ROY/SHW OL2 43 H8
Macauley Cl DUK SK16 91 K5
Macauley Pl WGNS/IIMK WN3 47 J8
Macauley Rd OLDTF/WHR M16 97 L2
RDSH SK5 100 A3
Macclesfield Cl WGNE/HIN WN2 48 F7
Macclesfield Rd
BRAM/HZG SK7 122 B4
MCFLDN SK10 131 H5
WILM/AE SK9 127 G6
WILM/AE SK9 130 F4
Macdonald Av FWTH BL4 52 D5
WGNS/IIMK WN3 63 K1
Macdonald Rd IRL M44 94 B5
Macdonald St OLDS OL8 59 J8
WGNW/BIL/OR WN5 46 E6
Macefin Av CCHDY M21 98 A8
Macfarren St WGTN/LGST M12 99 K1
Mackenzie Av WGNS/IIMK WN3 63 K1
Mackenzie Gv BOL BL1 22 A8
Mackenzie Rd BRO M7 71 L6
Mackenzie St BOL BL1 22 A8
WGTN/LGST M12 99 K1
Mackenzie Wk OLD OL1 44 B7
Mackeson Dr AUL OL6 76 B8
Mackeson Rd AUL OL6 76 B8
Mackintosh Wy OLD OL1 9 J4
Mackworth St HULME M15 87 G7
Maclaren Dr CHH M8 72 B3
Maclure Rd ROCH OL11 10 F6
Macnair Ct MPL/ROM SK6 114 D7
Macnair Ms MPL/ROM SK6 114 D8
Madams Wood Rd WALK M28 68 C1
Maddison Rd DROY M43 89 J4
Madeley Cl ALT WA14 117 G4
WGNS/IIMK WN3 63 H1
Madeley Dr CHAD OL9 8 B7
Madeley Gdns BOL BL1 36 B2
WHIT OL12 10 A1
Maden's Sq LIT OL15 21 M7
Maden St TYLD M29 67 J6
Maden Wk CHAD OL9 * 8 B3
Madison Av CHD/CHDH SK8 120 C2
DTN/ASHW M34 89 M4
Madison Gdns WHTN BL5 50 D2
Madison Pk WHTN BL5 50 C2
Madison St GTN M18 89 H6
Madras Rd EDGY/DAV SK3 12 D9
Maesbrook Dr TYLD M29 67 K4
Mafeking Av BURY BL9 25 K7
Mafeking Pl AIMK WN4 78 F1
Mafeking Rd BOLE BL2 * 37 H5
Mafeking St OLDS OL8 74 F1
Magdala St HEY OL10 * 41 H4
OLD OL1 9 G2
Magdalen Dr AIMK WN4 63 J8
Magda Rd OFTN SK2 112 F7
Magenta Av IRL M44 94 B6
Magnolia Cl SALE M33 95 M7
Magnolia Dr CHH M8 * 72 D6
Magpie Cl DROY M43 89 M1
Magpie La OLDE OL4 60 B8
Magpie Wk OP/CLY M11 * 88 C3
Maguire Av GLSP SK13 93 K6
Maher Gdns HULME M15 87 H8
Mahood St EDGY/DAV SK3 12 F8
Maida St BNG/LEV M19 99 L2
Maiden Cl AULW OL7 75 K6
Maidford Cl ANC M4 * 88 A3
STRET M32 97 H2
Maidstone Av CCHDY M21 97 K3
Maidstone Cl LEIGH WN7 65 M2
Maidstone Ms CCHDY M21 97 K3
Maidstone Rd BNG/LEV M19 111 G2
Main Av BNG/LEV M19 99 J5
TRPK M17 85 M8
Main Dr ALT WA14 116 A1
OLD OL1 59 G3
Maine Rd RUSH/FAL M14 98 D2
Mainprice Cl SLFD M6 71 J8
Main Rd CHAD OL9 8 D4
SWIN M27 71 G1
Mains Av WGNE/HIN WN2 64 C5
Main St FAIL M35 74 C4
HYDE SK14 91 G8
WGNW/BIL/OR WN5 62 B7
Mainwaring Dr WILM/AE SK9 127 H4
Mainwaring Ter
NTHM/RTH M23 109 K2
Mainway MDTN M24 57 J6
Mainway East MDTN M24 57 M6
Mainwood Rd
HALE/TIMP WA15 108 F7
Maismore Rd WYTH/NTH M22 118 C3
Maitland Av CCHDY M21 97 M8
Maitland Cl WHIT OL12 28 F1
Maitland St STKP SK1 112 E5
Maitland Wk CHAD OL9 * 8 B3
Major St CMANE M1 7 H6
MILN OL16 29 J6
RAMS BL0 18 E6
WGNW/BIL/OR WN5 46 F6
Makants Cl ATH M46 51 J6
TYLD M29 68 B4
Makerfield Dr NEWLW WA12 78 D8
Makerfield Wy WGNE/HIN WN2 48 E5
Makinson Ar WGN WN1 14 F3
Makinson Av HOR/BR BL6 34 B3
WGNE/HIN WN2 49 G5
Makin St CMANE M1 * 7 H7
Makkah Cl NEWH/MOS M40 73 K7
Malaga Av MANAIR M90 118 D5
Malakoff St STLY SK15 91 H4
Malbrook Wk
BRUN/LGST M13 * 87 M6
Malby St OLD OL1 9 J3
Malcolm Av SWIN M27 70 D2
Malcolm Dr SWIN M27 70 D2
Malcolm St ROCH OL11 42 A1
Malden Gv NTHM/RTH M23 109 K5
Maldon Cl BOLS/LL BL3 53 K1
OFTN SK2 113 L7
WGNE/HIN WN2 48 C2
Maldon Crs SWIN M27 70 C6
Maldon Dr ECC M30 70 B8
Maldon Rd WGNNW/ST WN6 31 J4
Maldon St ROCH OL11 10 F8
Maldwyn Av BOLS/LL BL3 51 L2
CHH M8 72 D2
Maleham St BRO M7 * 72 B6
Malgam Dr DID/WITH M20 110 E4
Malham Av WGNS/IIMK WN3 63 K2
Malham Cl LEIGH WN7 65 M7
ROY/SHW OL2 43 G8
Malham Ct OFTN SK2 113 G6
Malham Dr WHTF M45 55 K4
Malika Pl AIMK WN4 * 63 H6
Mallard Cl DUK SK16 91 H5
OFTN SK2 113 K7
OLDS OL8 75 G2
Mallard Crs POY/DIS SK12 121 J8
Mallard Dr HOR/BR BL6 33 K1
Mallard Gn ALT WA14 107 L4
Mallards Reach MPL/ROM SK6 113 L2
Mallard St CMANE M1 * 7 G8
Mallet Crs BOL BL1 35 J2
Malling Rd NTHM/RTH M23 109 K8
Mallison St BOL BL1 36 C1
Mallory Av AULW OL7 75 L7
Mallory Dr LEIGH WN7 66 E7
Mallory Rd HYDE SK14 91 K8
Mallow Cft MILN OL16 28 F8
Mallowdale WALK M28 68 E4
Mallowdale Av RUSH/FAL M14 98 E4
Mallowdale Cl BOL BL1 35 G6
Mallowdale Rd OFTN SK2 113 H7
Mallow St HULME M15 87 H6
The Mall BURY BL9 4 F5
STLY SK15 92 B6
Mally Gdns MOSL OL5 77 G4
Malmesbury Cl POY/DIS SK12 121 M8
Malmesbury Rd
CHD/CHDH SK8 120 D6
Malpas Av WGN WN1 15 J1
Malpas Cl CHD/CHDH SK8 111 K7
WILM/AE SK9 127 J3
Malpas Dr ALT WA14 108 B4
Malpas St OLD OL1 9 K4
WGTN/LGST M12 88 D6
Malpas Wk OLDTF/WHR M16 * 87 G7
Malrae HALE/TIMP WA15 * 117 G3
Malsham Rd NTHM/RTH M23 109 J2
Malta Cl MDTN M24 58 A5
Malta St ANC M4 88 A3
OLDE OL4 60 A6
Maltby Ct OLDE OL4 60 C7
Maltby Dr BOLS/LL BL3 51 M2
Maltby Rd NTHM/RTH M23 109 J6
Maltings La ROCH OL11 41 M3
Malton Av BOLS/LL BL3 35 K8
CCHDY M21 97 L5
GOL/RIS/CUL WA3 80 B5
WHTF M45 55 J2
Malton Cl CHAD OL9 58 C3
LEIGH WN7 65 M6
Malton Dr ALT WA14 107 L6
BRAM/HZG SK7 121 M5
Malton Rd HTNM SK4 99 K8
WALK M28 68 B5
Malton St OLDS OL8 8 F8
Malt St HULME M15 6 A9
Malus Ct SLFD M6 86 D1
Malverley Dr LEIGH WN7 66 F7
Malvern Av ATH M46 51 J7
AUL OL6 75 M5
BOL BL1 35 K3
BURY BL9 25 J7
CHD/CHDH SK8 110 C7
DROY M43 89 M2
URM M41 95 L2
WGNE/HIN WN2 49 K8
Malvern Cl AIMK WN4 63 L8
FWTH BL4 52 C3
HTNM SK4 12 F1
MILN OL16 29 K5
PWCH M25 55 M7
ROY/SHW OL2 43 J4
ROY/SHW OL2 58 F1
SWIN M27 71 G6
WGNS/IIMK WN3 62 F1
Malvern Crs
WGNS/IIMK WN3 48 C8
Malvern Dr ALT WA14 107 L7
SWIN M27 71 G6
Malvern Gv DID/WITH M20 98 D6
SLFD M6 85 M1
WALK M28 69 G1
Malvern Ri GLSP SK13 93 K7
Malvern Rd MDTN M24 57 K7
Malvern Rw HULME M15 * 86 F6
Malvern St OLDS OL8 8 F8
WGNNW/ST WN6 30 F1
Malvern St East ROCH OL11 27 M5
Malvern St West ROCH OL11 27 M5
Malvern Ter LEIGH WN7 81 J1
Manby Rd GTN M18 88 E8
Manby Sq GTN M18 88 E8
Manchester Chambers
OLD OL1 9 H5
Manchester New Rd
MDTN M24 57 J6
PART M31 106 C1
Manchester Old Rd
BURY BL9 4 D7
MDTN M24 56 F5
Manchester Rd ALT WA14 108 A6
AULW OL7 90 B3
BOLE BL2 3 G8
BOLS/LL BL3 52 F1
BURY BL9 4 E5
BURY BL9 39 H6
CCHDY M21 97 L3
DID/WITH M20 111 G4
DROY M43 89 H3
DTN/ASHW M34 89 K8
DTN/ASHW M34 89 L5
DTN/ASHW M34 101 H1
FWTH BL4 53 L6
GLSP SK13 93 J5
HEY OL10 41 G6
HOR/BR BL6 33 G2
HTNM SK4 100 A7
HYDE SK14 101 L1
LEIGH WN7 66 F8
MDTN M24 42 A5
MOSL OL5 76 F5
OLDS OL8 58 F8
PART M31 94 D8
RAMS BL0 19 H6
RAMS BL0 19 H7
ROCH OL11 10 A9
ROCH OL11 41 M1
ROY/SHW OL2 43 K7
SWIN M27 54 A8
SWIN M27 70 A3
TYLD M29 67 K8
TYLD M29 67 L3
UPML OL3 61 J8
WALK M28 69 G1
WGN WN1 15 M4
WGNE/HIN WN2 48 D5
WHTN BL5 50 C2
WILM/AE SK9 127 G4
Manchester Rd East
LHULT M38 52 D8
Manchester Rd North
DTN/ASHW M34 89 M8
Manchester Rd South
DTN/ASHW M34 100 F1
Manchester Rd West
LHULT M38 52 B7
Manchester St CHAD OL9 8 E8
HEY OL10 41 G2
OLDTF/WHR M16 86 F7
Manchet St ROCH OL11 41 L3
Mancroft Av BOLS/LL BL3 36 A8
Mancroft Ter BOLS/LL BL3 * 36 A8
Mancroft Wk CMANE M1 7 J8
Mancunian Rd
DTN/ASHW M34 101 K4
Mancunian Wy WGTN/LGST M12 7 M8
Mandalay Gdns
MPL/ROM SK6 114 A5
Mandarin Gn ALT WA14 107 L4
Mandarin Wk SLFD M6 * 86 D1
Manderville Cl WGNS/IIMK WN3 63 G2
Mandeville St BNG/LEV M19 99 L4
Mandley Av NEWH/MOS M40 * 74 A2
Mandley Cl BOLS/LL BL3 37 L7
Mandley Park Av BRO M7 72 B5
Mandon Cl RAD M26 38 B7
Manesty Cl MDTN M24 56 F2
Manet Cl BRO M7 71 L4
Mangle St CMANE M1 7 J4
Mango Pl SLFD M6 86 D2
Manifold Dr MPL/ROM SK6 123 H6
Manifold St SLFD M6 71 L7
Manilla Wk OP/CLY M11 88 C3
Manipur St OP/CLY M11 88 B4
Manley Av GOL/RIS/CUL WA3 79 J2
SWIN M27 54 C8
Manley Cl BURY BL9 24 F2
LEIGH WN7 66 A4
Manley Crs WHTN BL5 50 E3
Manley Gv BRAM/HZG SK7 121 G6
HYDE SK14 103 J1
Manley Rd CCHDY M21 97 M3
OLDS OL8 59 H8
OLDTF/WHR M16 98 B2
ROCH OL11 27 M8
SALE M33 108 C3
Manley St BRO M7 72 A6
WGNS/IIMK WN3 15 K8
Manley Ter BOL BL1 * 22 B8
Manning Av WGNNW/ST WN6 47 K2
Manningham Rd BOLS/LL BL3 35 L7
Mannington Dr BKLY M9 72 F6
Mannock St OLDS OL8 8 F8
The Manns UPML OL3 61 J7
Manor Av BOLS/LL BL3 53 M1
GOL/RIS/CUL WA3 79 M4
NEWLW WA12 78 C8
OLDTF/WHR M16 98 A2
SALE M33 96 A8
URM M41 96 A3
Manor Cl CHAD OL9 8 C3
CHD/CHDH SK8 120 E4
DTN/ASHW M34 101 L2
OLDE OL4 61 H7
WILM/AE SK9 126 C4
Manor Ct GOL/RIS/CUL WA3 79 M4
STRET M32 96 E3
Manor Dr CCHDY M21 98 A8
ROY/SHW OL2 59 H1
Manor Farm Cl AULW OL7 75 J7
Manor Farm Ri OLDE OL4 60 A5
Manorfield Cl BOL BL1 35 K3
Manor Gdns WILM/AE SK9 127 H5
Manor Gate Rd BOLE BL2 37 K4
Manor Gv LEIGH WN7 81 M1
WGNE/HIN WN2 32 E7
WGNW/BIL/OR WN5 46 E4
Manor Hill Rd MPL/ROM SK6 114 C6
Manorial Dr LHULT M38 52 B7
Manor Ml CHAD OL9 * 8 C2
Manor Mill Cl MILN OL16 29 G1
Manor Pk URM M41 * 96 A3
Manor Park Rd GLSP SK13 105 H3
Manor Pl WGNS/IIMK WN3 15 M8
Manor Rd BNG/LEV M19 99 L2
CHD/CHDH SK8 120 E3
DROY M43 89 H3
DTN/ASHW M34 89 L5
DTN/ASHW M34 101 L3
HALE/TIMP WA15 108 B8
HYDE SK14 91 J7
MDTN M24 57 J6
MPL/ROM SK6 101 L7
MPL/ROM SK6 114 C5
OLDE OL4 59 M8
RDSH SK5 100 E7
RNFD/HAY WA11 78 D5
ROY/SHW OL2 43 K5
SALE M33 96 E7
SLFD M6 71 G8
STRET M32 96 E3
SWIN M27 70 C6
TYLD M29 67 M6
WGNE/HIN WN2 49 J7
WGNNW/ST WN6 30 D6
WILM/AE SK9 126 C4
Manor St BOL BL1 2 F4
BURY BL9 5 H4
DTN/ASHW M34 90 C5
FWTH BL4 52 F5
FWTH BL4 53 L7
GLSP SK13 105 G3
GOL/RIS/CUL WA3 79 L3
MDTN M24 57 K2
MOSL OL5 76 F2
RAMS BL0 18 E5
ROY/SHW OL2 59 K2
WGN WN1 14 F4
WGNW/BIL/OR WN5 47 J6
WGTN/LGST M12 7 L8
Manor Vw MPL/ROM SK6 101 L7
Mansart Cl AIMK WN4 79 G1
Manse Gdns NEWLW WA12 79 G8
Mansell Wy HOR/BR BL6 34 A4
The Manse MOSL OL5 76 F4
Mansfield Av BKLY M9 57 G8
DTN/ASHW M34 90 A7
RAMS BL0 24 E3
Mansfield Cl AULW OL7 90 C3
DTN/ASHW M34 90 A7
Mansfield Crs DTN/ASHW M34 90 A8
Mansfield Dr BKLY M9 57 H8
Mansfield Gra ROCH OL11 27 M6
Mansfield Gv BOL BL1 35 L3
Mansfield Rd BKLY M9 57 H8
HYDE SK14 102 B3
MOSL OL5 77 H3
OLDS OL8 59 L7
ROCH OL11 27 H5
URM M41 95 K3
Mansfield St AULW OL7 90 B4
GOL/RIS/CUL WA3 79 H3
Mansford Dr NEWH/MOS M40 73 J7
Manshaw Crs DTN/ASHW M34 89 K5
Manshaw Rd OP/CLY M11 89 K5
Mansion Av WHTF M45 55 H1
Manson Av HULME M15 6 A9
Manstead Wk
NEWH/MOS M40 * 88 B2
Manston Dr CHD/CHDH SK8 120 C2
Manswood Dr CHH M8 72 D5
Manthorpe Av WALK M28 69 K5
Mantley La UPML OL3 44 D5
Manton Av BKLY M9 73 L1
DTN/ASHW M34 100 D1
Manton Cl BRO M7 72 C6
Manvers St RDSH SK5 112 B1
Manwaring St FAIL M35 74 B4
Maple Av ATH M46 50 E8
BOL BL1 * 35 L3
BURY BL9 5 L4
CCHDY M21 97 L4
CHD/CHDH SK8 120 B2
DTN/ASHW M34 89 L3
DTN/ASHW M34 101 H1
ECC M30 69 K8
GOL/RIS/CUL WA3 80 C5
HALE/TIMP WA15 109 H7
HOR/BR BL6 34 B3
MPL/ROM SK6 114 C8
POY/DIS SK12 124 C6
POY/DIS SK12 129 K1
STLY SK15 91 J4
STRET M32 97 G3
WGNE/HIN WN2 65 J1
WHTF M45 55 J5
Maple Cl FWTH BL4 53 J7
MDTN M24 58 A4
OFTN SK2 112 E6
ROY/SHW OL2 * 43 J4
SLFD M6 86 C1
WGNW/BIL/OR WN5 62 A7
Maple Crs LEIGH WN7 66 B5
Maplecroft STKP SK1 112 E4
Mapledon Rd BKLY M9 73 J4
Maple Dr
WGNE/HIN WN2 64 E5
Maplefield Dr WALK M28 68 E5
Maple Gv FAIL M35 74 B7
NEWH/MOS M40 74 B2
PWCH M25 55 K6
RAMS BL0 19 G7
TOT/BURYW BL8 24 D7
WALK M28 69 G4
WGNNW/ST WN6 47 K1
Maple Rd BRAM/HZG SK7 121 G7
CHAD OL9 8 B1
FWTH BL4 52 D4
NTHM/RTH M23 108 F4
PART M31 106 B1
SWIN M27 70 B6
WILM/AE SK9 130 E2

Maple Rd West
  NTHM/RTH M23..........108 F4
Maple St *AIMK* WN4..........63 K6
  BOLE BL2..........22 F7
  BOLS/LL BL3..........2 B8
  OLDS OL8..........74 F1
  ROCH OL11..........10 B6
Maple Wk *NTHM/RTH* M23..........108 F4
Maplewood Cl *BKLY* M9..........72 Y4
  ROY/SHW OL2..........58 F2
Maplewood Ct *BRO* M7..........72 A5
Maplewood Gdns *BOL* BL1 *..........36 B2
Maplewood House *BOL* BL1..........36 B3
Maplewood Rd *WILM/AE* SK9..........127 J4
Mapley Av *WYTH/NTH* M22..........110 A4
Maplin Cl *BRUN/LGST* M13..........7 L9
Maplin Dr *OFTN* SK2..........113 K7
Marble St *CMANW* M2..........7 G4
  OLD OL1 *..........59 L4
Marbury Av *RUSH/FAL* M14..........98 E3
Marbury Cl *EDGY/DAV* SK3..........111 K5
  URM M41..........95 G1
Marbury Gv *WGNNW/ST* WN6..........31 H4
Marbury Rd *HTNM* SK4..........100 A3
  WILM/AE SK9 *..........126 E3
Marcer Rd *NEWH/MOS* M40..........88 A2
March Av *HTNM* SK4..........12 B3
Marchbank *WGNE/HIN* WN2..........48 D2
Marchbank St *CHAD* SK8..........110 F6
March Dr *TOT/BURYW* BL8..........25 G7
Marchers Ms *ECC* M30..........84 E3
Marchioness St *GTN* M18 *..........89 J6
March St *MILN* OL16..........11 H4
Marchwood Av *CCHDY* M21..........98 A3
Marcliffe Dr *BNG/LEV* M19..........99 M3
  ROCH OL11..........27 L6
Marcliff Gv *WHIT* OL12..........12 A3
Marcroft Pl *ROCH* OL11..........28 D8
Marcus Gv *RUSH/FAL* M14..........98 F2
Marcus St *BOL* BL1..........35 L3
Mardale Av *DID/WITH* M20..........98 F7
  ROY/SHW OL2..........42 F4
  SWIN M27..........69 M2
  URM M41..........95 J1
Mardale Cl *ATH* M46..........50 F7
  BOLE BL2..........37 J3
  OLDE OL4..........60 A5
  PWCH M25..........55 M5
  STLY SK15..........91 K1
Mardale Dr *BOLE* BL2..........37 J3
  CHD/CHDH SK8..........110 E6
  MDTN M24..........57 H3
Mardale Rd *SWIN* M27..........70 A6
Mardyke *WHIT* OL12..........10 D3
Marfield Av *CHAD* OL9..........58 D7
Marford Cl *WYTH/NTH* M22..........110 A6
Marford Crs *SALE* M33..........108 C2
Margaret Ashton Cl *BKLY* M9 *..........73 J5
Margaret Av *BURY* BL9..........5 G6
  WGNNW/ST WN6..........30 F8
Margaret Rd *DROY* M43 *..........89 J2
  DTN/ASHW M34..........90 D8
Margaret Sands St *HULME* M15 *..........87 G6
Margaret St *AUL* OL6..........90 D2
  BURY BL9..........5 G6
  HEY OL10..........41 H2
  OLDS OL8..........74 E2
  RDSH SK5..........100 B5
  ROY/SHW OL2 *..........43 L6
  WGNE/HIN WN2..........49 C6
  WGNNW/ST WN6..........14 C2
Margate Av *NEWH/MOS* M40..........73 L7
Margate Rd *RDSH* SK5..........100 C5
Margrove Cha *CMANW* M2 *..........34 F7
Margrove Cl *FAIL* M35..........74 F5
Margrove Rd *SLFD* M6..........70 F8
Margrov Cl *WHIT* OL12..........28 D7
Marguerita Rd *NEWH/MOS* M40..........74 A8
Marham Cl *CCHDY* M21 *..........98 B6
  HYDE SK14..........91 G6
Marian Rd *RNFD/HAY* WA11..........78 B5
Maria St *BOL* BL1..........36 B2
Marie Cl *DTN/ASHW* M34..........101 J2
Marie St *BRO* M7..........72 B5
Marigold St *ROCH* OL11..........10 E9
  WGNNW/BIL/OR WN5..........47 C5
Mariman Dr *CHH* M8..........72 D2
Marina Av *DTN/ASHW* M34..........101 K3
Marina Cl *WILM/AE* SK9..........119 M7
  WGNNW/BIL/OR WN5..........47 C7
Marina Crs *OP/CLY* M11..........88 C1
Marina Dr *MPL/ROM* SK6..........113 M5
  WGNNW/BIL/OR WN5..........47 C7
Marina Rd *DROY* M43..........89 L2
  MPL/ROM SK6..........101 H8
Marine Av *PART* M31..........106 A1
Marion Pl *WGNE/HIN* WN2..........64 C4
Marion St *BOLS/LL* BL3..........52 F2
  OLDS OL8..........75 J1
Maritime Cl *NEWLW* WA12..........78 F7
Marjorie Cl *GTN* M18..........88 E6
Mark Av *SLFD* M6..........71 L8
Markenfield Dr *ROY/SHW* OL2..........43 J5
Market Ap *AIMK* WN4 *..........78 E1
Market Pde *BURY* BL9..........5 J4
Market Pl *AUL* OL6..........90 E1
  BURY BL9 *..........4 E4
  HYDE SK14 *..........103 K1
  LEIGH WN7..........66 C7
  MDTN M24..........57 K3
  OLD OL1 *..........9 H5
  RAMS BL0..........18 F5
  STKP SK1..........13 J3
  WGN WN1..........14 F4
  WGNNW/ST WN6..........31 H3
Market St *ALT* WA14..........108 A8
  ATH M46..........66 F1
  BOL BL1..........2 E4
  BOLS/LL BL3..........53 K1
  BURY BL9..........5 H3
  CMANE M1..........7 G4
  DROY M43..........89 K4
  DTN/ASHW M34..........101 J1
  FWTH BL4..........53 G3
  GLSP SK13..........104 F4
  HEY OL10..........40 F2
  HYDE SK14..........92 D8
  HYDE SK14..........93 G7
  HYDE SK14..........102 A1
  MDTN M24..........57 J3
  MOSL OL5..........76 F3
  NEWLW WA12..........78 D8
  NM/HAY SK22..........124 D5
  POY/DIS SK12..........123 M6
  RAD M26..........53 L4
  ROY/SHW OL2..........43 L6
  STLY SK15..........91 K2
  SWIN M27..........70 D3

  TOT/BURYW BL8..........24 C6
  TYLD M29..........67 J3
  WGN WN1..........14 F3
  WGNE/HIN WN2..........49 G7
  WGNNW/ST WN6..........31 H3
  WHIT OL12..........20 A6
  WHTN BL5..........50 B4
Market Wk *SALE* M33 *..........96 E8
Market Wy *SLFD* M6..........86 C1
Markfield Av *BRUN/LGST* M13..........88 A7
Markham Cl *WGTN/LGST* M12..........88 B4
Markham St *HYDE* SK14..........91 G2
Markington St *RUSH/FAL* M14..........98 D1
Markland Hl *BOL* BL1..........35 H4
Markland Hill Cl *BOL* BL1..........35 J3
Markland Hill La *BOL* BL1..........35 J3
Marklands Rd *TYLD* M29..........67 K8
Markland St *BOL* BL1..........102 B3
  HYDE SK14..........18 F6
  RAMS BL0 *..........15 L5
  WGN WN1..........44 A6
Mark La *ROY/SHW* OL2..........54 D1
Marks St *RAD* M26..........8 F4
Mark St *CHAD* OL9..........68 C5
  WALK M28..........11 H1
  WHIT OL12..........45 J8
Markwood *UPML* OL3..........75 K3
Marland Av *CHD/CHDH* SK8..........120 B2
  OLDS OL8..........27 L8
  ROCH OL11..........100 C4
Marland Cl *ROCH* OL11..........27 L8
Marland Crs *RDSH* SK5..........27 L8
Marland Fold *ROCH* OL11..........27 L8
Marland Fold La *OLDS* OL8..........75 J5
Marland Gn *ROCH* OL11..........27 M7
Marland Hill Rd *ROCH* OL11..........27 L8
Marland Old Rd *ROCH* OL11..........74 D1
Marland St *CHAD* OL9..........97 G1
Marland Wy *STRET* M32
Marlborough Av
  CHD/CHDH SK8..........120 C3
  OLDTF/WHR M16..........97 M3
  WGNS/IIMK WN3..........48 C8
  WILM/AE SK9..........130 C3
Marlborough Cl *AULW* OL7..........90 B4
  DTN/ASHW M34..........101 J1
  MPL/ROM SK6..........114 A5
  RAMS BL0..........24 F1
Marlborough Dr *FAIL* M35..........74 B6
  HTNM SK4 *..........100 A8
Marlborough Gdns *FWTH* BL4..........52 C4
Marlborough Rd *ALT* WA14..........116 F2
  ATH M46..........51 H8
  BRO M7..........72 C6
  ECC M30..........70 D8
  HYDE SK14..........102 B4
  IRL M44..........94 E1
  ROY/SHW OL2..........59 H2
  SALE M33..........96 E8
  STRET M32..........96 F1
  URM M41..........95 J2
Marlborough St *AULW* OL7..........90 C3
  BOL BL1..........2 A3
  HEY OL10..........41 H4
  OLDE OL4..........9 L7
  WHIT OL12..........27 M3
Marlborough Wy
  RNFD/HAY WA11..........78 B4
Marlbrook Dr *WHTN* BL5..........50 B7
Marlbrook Ms *WHTN* BL5 *..........50 C7
Marlbrook Wk *BOLS/LL* BL3..........36 C8
Marlcroft Av *HTNM* SK4..........12 B3
Marlcroft Ct *NTHM/RTH* M23..........109 K5
Marld Crs *BOL* BL1..........35 J2
Marle Av *MOSL* OL5..........77 H3
Marle Cft *WHTF* M45..........54 F6
Marled Hey *EDGW/EG* BL7..........17 G7
Marle Ri *MOSL* OL5..........77 H3
Marler Rd *HYDE* SK14..........91 H8
Marley Cl *HALE/TIMP* WA15..........108 C5
Marley Dr *SALE* M33..........96 D6
Marleyer Cl *NEWH/MOS* M40..........73 M5
Marleyer Ri *MPL/ROM* SK6..........113 K4
Marley Rd *BNG/LEV* M19..........99 L4
  POY/DIS SK12..........129 J2
Marlfield Rd
  HALE/TIMP WA15..........117 M6
  ROY/SHW OL2..........43 H4
Marlfield St *BKLY* M9..........73 H3
Marl Gv *WGNW/BIL/OR* WN5..........46 A8
Marlhill Cl *OFTN* SK2..........113 H7
Marlinford Dr
  NEWH/MOS M40..........73 M7
Marlor St *DTN/ASHW* M34..........90 B8
Marlow Brow *GLSP* SK13..........93 K8
Marlow Cl *BOLE* BL2..........37 J3
  CHD/CHDH SK8..........120 B2
  URM M41..........84 E8
Marlow Dr *ALT* WA14..........116 B2
  IRL M44..........94 D1
  SWIN M27..........70 B6
  WILM/AE SK9..........119 L7
Marlowe Cl
  WGNS/IIMK WN3..........47 K7
Marlowe Dr
  DID/WITH M20..........98 E8
Marlowe Wks *MPL/ROM* SK6..........113 H2
Marlow Rd *BKLY* M9..........73 H3
Marlow St *GLSP* SK13..........93 K8
Marlwood Rd *BOL* BL1..........35 J2
Marmion Cl *GOL/RIS/CUL* WA3..........80 B8
Marmion Dr *CCHDY* M21..........97 K4
Marne Av *AUL* OL6..........76 C7
  WYTH/NTH M22..........110 B7
Marne Crs *ROCH* OL11..........27 M5
Marnland Gv *BOLS/LL* BL3..........35 H8
Marnock Cl *WGNE/HIN* WN2..........65 J4
Maroon Rd *WYTH/NTH* M22..........119 H5
Marple Av *BOL* BL1..........22 D8
Marple Cl *OLDS* OL8..........75 G2
  WGNNW/ST WN6..........30 D2
Marple Gv *STRET* M32..........96 F1
Marple Hall Dr *MPL/ROM* SK6..........114 A3
Marple Old Rd *OFTN* SK2..........113 K6
Marple Rd *GLSP* SK13..........103 K7
  OFTN SK2..........113 G5
Marple St *HULME* M15..........87 G7
Marquis Av *BURY* BL9..........25 H8
Marquis Dr *CHD/CHDH* SK8..........119 M5
Marquis St *BNG/LEV* M19..........100 A3
Marrick Cl *WGNS/IIMK* WN3..........63 K5
Marriotts Ct *CMANW* M2..........7 G5
Marriott St *DID/WITH* M20..........98 E6
  MILN OL16..........13 K7
Mars Av *BOLS/LL* BL3..........51 M1
Marsden Cl *AULW* OL7..........75 H7
  MILN OL16..........42 F2
Marsden Dr *HALE/TIMP* WA15..........108 F6
Marsden Rd *BOL* BL1..........2 D4
  MPL/ROM SK6..........113 M1

Marsden St *BURY* BL9..........4 F2
  CMANW M2..........6 F4
  ECC M30..........84 F1
  GLSP SK13..........93 K8
  MDTN M24..........57 M5
  WALK M28..........68 C6
  WGN WN1..........15 G3
  WGNS/IIMK WN3..........48 B8
  WGNW/BIL/OR WN5..........47 J5
  WHTN BL5..........50 B4
Marsett Cl *WHIT* OL12..........27 J3
Marshall Cl *AUL* OL6..........91 G2
  OLD OL1 *..........9 G2
Marshall Rd *BNG/LEV* M19..........99 K3
Marshall Stevens Wy
  TRPK M17..........85 L7
Marshall St *ANC* M4..........7 J2
  LEIGH WN7..........66 B8
  MILN OL16..........11 K5
  WGTN/LGST M12..........87 M6
Marsham Cl *BRUN/LGST* M13..........88 B8
  OLDE OL4..........60 E7
Marsham Dr *BRAM/HZG* SK7..........121 K3
  WHTN BL5..........50 B3
Marshbank *WHTN* BL5..........50 B3
Marshbrook Cl *WGNE/HIN* WN2..........49 K6
Marshbrook Dr *BKLY* M9..........72 F3
Marsh Brook Fold *WHTN* BL5..........49 K5
Marshbrook Rd *URM* M41..........95 M1
Marsh Cl *EDGY/DAV* SK3..........112 A6
Marshdale Rd *BOL* BL1..........35 J4
Marshfield Rd
  HALE/TIMP WA15..........108 F7
Marshfield Wk
  BRUN/LGST M13 *..........87 M6
Marsh Fold La *BOL* BL1..........35 M4
Marsh Gn *WGNW/BIL/OR* WN5..........47 G3
Marsh Hey Cl *LHULT* M38..........52 D4
Marsh La *FWTH* BL4..........52 D4
  KNUT WA16..........116 C8
  NM/HAY SK22..........124 F6
  WGN WN1..........15 G3
Marsh Rd *BOLS/LL* BL3..........37 K8
  LHULT M38..........52 E8
Marsh Rw *WGNE/HIN* WN2..........49 K8
  WHTN BL5..........50 B3
Marshway Dr *NEWLW* WA12..........78 E8
Marsland Av
  HALE/TIMP WA15..........108 E4
Marsland Cl
  DTN/ASHW M34..........100 E1
Marsland Green La *TYLD* M29..........67 H8
Marsland Rd
  HALE/TIMP WA15..........108 E4
  MPL/ROM SK6..........114 D5
  SALE M33..........108 D1
Marslands *UPML* OL3..........61 L1
Marsland St
  BRAM/HZG SK7 *..........121 M2
  STKP SK1..........13 K1
Marsland St North *BRO* M7..........72 B5
Marsland St South *BRO* M7..........72 C5
Marsland Ter *STKP* SK1..........112 E4
Mars St *CHAD* OL9..........8 D4
  EDGW/EG BL7..........17 H6
Marston Cl *FAIL* M35..........74 B6
  HOR/BR BL6..........34 C4
  WHTF M45..........55 M4
Marston Gn *IRL* M44..........94 D2
Marston Rd *BRO* M7..........72 B4
  STRET M32..........97 H2
Marston Wy South *CMANE* M1 *..........6 F4
Marsworth Dr *ANC* M4 *..........7 M3
Martens Rd *IRL* M44..........94 C7
Marthall Dr *SALE* M33..........109 H2
Martham Dr *OFTN* SK2..........113 K7
Martha's Ter *MILN* OL16..........28 E1
Martha St *BOLS/LL* BL3 *..........36 A8
  OLD OL1..........8 F3
Martin Av *BOLS/LL* BL3..........53 M1
  NEWLW WA12..........78 E7
  OLDE OL4..........59 M7
Martin Cl *DTN/ASHW* M34..........90 C7
  OFTN SK2..........113 J7
Martindale Cl *ROY/SHW* OL2..........43 H7
Martindale Crs *MDTN* M24..........57 C1
  WGNW/BIL/OR WN5..........47 M6
  WGTN/LGST M12..........88 B6
Martindale Gdns *BOL* BL1..........36 B2
Martin Dr *IRL* M44..........83 K8
Martingale Cl *RAD* M26..........38 D7
Martingale Wy *DROY* M43..........90 A1
Martin Gv *FWTH* BL4..........53 J5
Martin La *WHIT* OL12..........27 L3
Martin Rd *SWIN* M27..........70 E2
Martinsclough *HOR/BR* BL6..........34 F6
Martins Ct *WGNE/HIN* WN2..........49 K6
Martinscroft Rd
  NTHM/RTH M23..........109 K7
Martins Fld *WHIT* OL12..........27 J3
Martin St *ATH* M46 *..........67 G1
  BURY BL9..........40 A1
  DTN/ASHW M34..........90 C5
  EDGW/EG BL7..........17 G8
  HYDE SK14..........102 B2
  ORD M5..........6 C7
Martland Av *GOL/RIS/CUL* WA3..........80 A5
  WGNNW/ST WN6..........30 C7
Martland Crs *WGNNW/ST* WN6..........47 H1
Martland Mill La
  WGNW/BIL/OR WN5..........47 G2
Martlesham Wk *ANC* M4 *..........7 H3
Martlet Av *POY/DIS* SK12..........123 L6
  ROCH OL11..........27 H5
Martlet Cl *RUSH/FAL* M14..........98 D3
Martlew Dr *ATH* M46..........51 H8
Martock Av *WYTH/NTH* M22..........119 G1
Marton Av *BOLE* BL2..........3 L2
  DID/WITH M20..........110 F2
Marton Cl *GOL/RIS/CUL* WA3..........81 M3
Marton Dr *IRL* M44..........94 D1
Marton Gra *PWCH* M25..........72 B2
Marton Gn *EDGY/DAV* SK3..........112 A6
Marton Gv *HTNM* SK4..........100 B6
Marton Pl *SALE* M33..........96 B8
Marus Av *WGNS/IIMK* WN3..........63 J1
Marwick Cl *WGNNW/ST* WN6..........31 G5
Marwood Cl *ALT* WA14..........107 L6
  RAD M26..........53 K4
Marwood Dr *NTHM/RTH* M23..........118 B1
Maryfield Cl *GOL/RIS/CUL* WA3..........79 K5
Maryfield Ct *OLDTF/WHR* M16 *..........98 B4
Mary France St *HULME* M15..........87 H5
Mary Hulton Ct *WHTN* BL5..........50 D4
Maryland Av *BOLE* BL2..........37 C5
Marylebone Cl *WGN* WN1..........48 A1
Marylebone Pl *WGN* WN1..........47 M1
Marylon Dr *WYTH/NTH* M22..........110 D4
Maryport Dr *HALE/TIMP* WA15..........108 F6

Mary St *CHD/CHDH* SK8..........111 G6
  CSLFD M3..........87 J1
  DROY M43..........89 J3
  DTN/ASHW M34 *..........90 C4
  DUK SK16..........53 C5
  FWTH BL4..........40 F2
  HEY OL10..........101 N1
  HYDE SK14..........18 E7
  RAMS BL0..........13 L3
  STKP SK1..........67 K3
  TYLD M29..........72 C5
Masboro St *CHH* M8..........22 B5
Masbury Cl *BOL* BL1..........38 B8
Masefield Av *LEIGH* WN7..........66 A5
  PWCH M25..........71 J1
  RAD M26..........46 D6
Masefield Cl *DUK* SK16..........91 L5
Masefield Crs *DROY* M43..........89 K3
Masefield Dr *FWTH* BL4..........52 E5
  HTNM SK4..........111 K7
  WGNS/IIMK WN3..........47 K7
Masefield Gv *RDSH* SK5..........100 B3
Masefield Rd *BOLS/LL* BL3..........37 L8
  DROY M43..........89 K3
  OLD OL1..........59 L2
Mason Cl *AIMK* WN4..........64 A8
Mason Gdns *BOLS/LL* BL3..........2 C7
Mason La *ATH* M46..........67 H2
Masons Gv *GLSP* SK13..........93 K6
Mason St *ANC* M4..........7 J2
  AULW OL7..........90 C3
  BURY BL9..........5 H5
  EDCW/EG BL7 *..........22 B5
  HOR/BR BL6..........33 K1
  MILN OL16..........10 F5
  WGNE/HIN WN2..........64 E4
  WGNS/IIMK WN3..........14 D5
Massey Av *AUL* OL6..........75 M6
  FAIL M35..........74 E4
Massey Cft *WHIT* OL12..........20 A5
Massey Rd *HALE/TIMP* WA15..........108 B8
  SALE M33..........97 H8
Massey St *BURY* BL9..........5 K2
  STKP SK1..........13 J5
  WILM/AE SK9..........130 D3
Massey Wk *WYTH/NTH* M22..........119 H3
Massie St *CHD/CHDH* SK8..........111 G6
Matham Wk *HULME* M15..........7 G9
Mather Av *ECC* M30..........85 K7
  GOL/RIS/CUL WA3..........80 B6
  PWCH M25..........71 M3
  WHTF M45..........55 J2
Mather Cl *WHTF* M45..........55 J3
Mather Fold Rd *WALK* M28..........68 C3
Mather La *LEIGH* WN7..........66 D8
Mather Rd *BURY* BL9..........25 J5
  ECC M30..........85 K2
Mather St *ATH* M46..........67 C1
  BOLS/LL BL3 *..........2 C7
  FAIL M35..........74 A5
  FWTH BL4..........53 H4
  RAD M26..........54 D1
Mather Wy *SLFD* M6 *..........86 D1
Matheson Dr
  WGNW/BIL/OR WN5..........47 G4
Matissee Wy *BRO* M7..........71 L4
Matley Cl *HYDE* SK14..........91 L7
Matley Gn *RDSH* SK5..........100 F6
Matley La *STLY* SK15..........91 M6
Matlock Av *AUL* OL6..........76 C6
  DID/WITH M20..........98 E8
  DTN/ASHW M34..........101 K4
  URM M41..........95 L4
Matlock Cl *ATH* M46..........67 C2
  FAIL M35..........74 B8
  SALE M33..........96 F8
Matlock Dr *BRAM/HZG* SK7..........122 A4
Matlock Rd *CHD/CHDH* SK8..........119 L5
  RDSH SK5..........100 D3
  STRET M32..........96 D1
Matlock St *ECC* M30..........84 F4
Matt Busby Cl *SWIN* M27..........70 E5
Matthew Cl *GLSP* SK13..........93 K5
  OLDS OL8..........59 M8
Matthew Moss La *ROCH* OL11..........27 L8
Matthews Av *FWTH* BL4..........53 C5
Matthews La *BRUN/LGST* M13..........88 C3
Matthew's St *WGTN/LGST* M12..........88 C1
Matthew St *MPL/ROM* SK6..........114 D6
Mattison St *OP/CLY* M11..........89 H5
Maud St *BOLE* BL2..........22 F7
  WHIT OL12..........28 D2
Maudsley Dr *CHH* M8..........72 F4
Maudsley St *BOL* BL1..........2 E4
Maxwell Av *OFTN* SK2..........112 F7
Maxwell St *BOL* BL1..........22 B8
  BURY BL9..........5 K3
Max Woosnam Wk
  RUSH/FAL M14..........98 D1
Mayall St *MOSL* OL5..........76 F3
Mayall St East *OLDE* OL4 *..........59 M5
Mayan Av *CSLFD* M3..........6 A2
May Av *CHD/CHDH* SK8..........120 D6
  HTNM SK4..........12 C3
  LEIGH WN7..........66 A6
  WGNE/HIN WN2..........64 C5
Maybank St *BOLS/LL* BL3..........2 A8
Mayberth Av *CHH* M8..........72 D2
Maybreck Cl *BOLS/LL* BL3..........35 M7
Mayburn Cl *MDTN* M24..........57 M7
Maybury St *OP/CLY* M11..........89 H6
Maycroft *OLD* OL1 *..........59 J7
May Dr *BNG/LEV* M19..........99 C2
Mayer St *OFTN* SK2..........112 F5
Mayes Gdns *ANC* M4..........88 C1
Mayes St *ANC* M4..........7 H2
Mayfair *HOR/BR* BL6..........34 A1
Mayfair Av *RAD* M26..........38 A8
  SLFD M6..........85 L1
  URM M41..........95 L3
  WHTF M45 *..........55 J5

Mayfair Cl *DUK* SK16..........91 J4
  POY/DIS SK12..........122 A7
Mayfair Ct *HALE/TIMP* WA15 *..........108 E5
Mayfair Crs *FAIL* M35..........74 E4
Mayfair Dr *ATH* M46..........51 J8
  IRL M44..........94 D2
  ROY/SHW OL2..........59 G2
  SALE M33..........108 B2
  WGNE/HIN WN2..........49 G2
  WGNS/IIMK WN3
Mayfair Gdns *ROCH* OL11..........10 A9
Mayfair Ms *DID/WITH* M20 *..........98 C8
Mayfair Pk *DID/WITH* M20..........98 C8
Mayfair Rd *WYTH/NTH* M22..........110 B8
Mayfield *BOLE* BL2..........23 C7
Mayfield Av *BOLS/LL* BL3..........52 E1
  DTN/ASHW M34..........101 K5
  FWTH BL4..........52 F5
  OLDE OL4..........60 D5
  RDSH SK5..........100 C7
  SALE M33..........97 H8
  STRET M32..........96 E3
  WALK M28..........69 G1
  WALK M28..........69 C8
Mayfield Cl *HALE/TIMP* WA15..........108 E6
  RAMS BL0..........24 D2
Mayfield Dr *LEIGH* WN7..........80 F4
Mayfield Gv *GTN* M18..........100 C1
  RDSH SK5..........100 C7
  WILM/AE SK9..........130 E7
Mayfield Houses *RAD* M26 *..........54 B2
Mayfield Rd *BRAM/HZG* SK7..........71 L3
  BRO M7..........108 E6
  HALE/TIMP WA15..........114 E3
  MPL/ROM SK6..........59 L3
  OLD OL1..........98 B3
  OLDTF/WHR M16..........24 D2
  RAMS BL0..........47 C3
  WGNW/BIL/OR WN5
Mayfield St *AIMK* WN4 *..........78 D1
  ATH M46..........66 F1
  DTN/ASHW M34..........90 B7
  MILN OL16..........11 K1
Mayfield Ter *MILN* OL16..........28 E3
Mayflower Av *ORD* M5..........86 B7
Mayflower Cl *GLSP* SK13..........105 H4
Mayford Rd *BNG/LEV* M19..........99 K2
Maygate *CHAD* OL9..........8 E2
May Gv *BNG/LEV* M19..........99 L4
Mayhill Dr *SLFD* M6..........70 D8
  WALK M28..........69 K4
Mayhurst Av *CCHDY* M21..........110 A1
Mayorlowe Av *RDSH* SK5..........100 F8
Mayor's Rd *HALE/TIMP* WA15..........108 B8
Mayor St *BOL* BL1..........2 D2
  TOT/BURYW BL8..........4 A2
Mayo St *CMANE* M1 *..........7 H8
Maypool Dr *RDSH* SK5..........100 C6
May Rd *CHD/CHDH* SK8..........120 C6
  OLDTF/WHR M16..........98 A1
  SWIN M27..........70 E6
May St *BOLE* BL2..........3 H5
  ECC M30..........69 M8
  EDGW/EG BL7..........17 H6
  GOL/RIS/CUL WA3..........79 L2
  HEY OL10 *..........41 H4
  LEIGH WN7..........65 M7
  NEWH/MOS M40..........73 M7
  OLDS OL8..........58 F8
  RAD M26..........54 D1
Mayton St *OP/CLY* M11..........88 D4
May Tree Dr *WGN* WN1..........31 L8
Mayville Dr *DID/WITH* M20..........98 E7
Maywood Av *DID/WITH* M20..........110 E4
Maze St *BOLS/LL* BL3..........37 C7
Mcconnell Rd *NEWH/MOS* M40..........73 K5
McCormack Dr *WGN* WN1..........15 J4
McCready Dr *ORD* M5 *..........86 E4
McDonna St *BOL* BL1..........35 M1
McDonough Cl *OLDS* OL8..........75 K1
McKean St *BOLS/LL* BL3..........36 C2
McKie Cl *OLDS* OL8..........75 K1
McLaren Cl *CCHDY* M21..........97 K3
McLean Dr *IRL* M44..........83 K8
Mc Naught St *MILN* OL16..........11 J7
Menachin Av *CCHDY* M21..........97 J7
Meade Cl *URM* M41..........95 J1
Meade Gv *BRUN/LGST* M13..........99 M2
Meade Hill Rd *CHH* M8..........71 L3
The Meade *BOLS/LL* BL3..........52 B2
  WILM/AE SK9..........126 F4
Meadfoot Av *PWCH* M25..........71 M1
Meadfoot Rd *GTN* M18..........89 C6
Meadland Gv *BOL* BL1..........22 C8
Meadow Av *HALE/TIMP* WA15..........117 K1
  SWIN M27..........70 E3
Meadowbank *AULW* OL7..........75 K6
Meadow Bank *CCHDY* M21..........97 K5
  GLSP SK13..........104 C5
  HALE/TIMP WA15..........108 D5
  HTNM SK4..........12 B3
  HYDE SK14..........93 C6
  MPL/ROM SK6..........113 J1
Meadowbank Av *ATH* M46..........51 H8
Meadowbank Cl *FAIL* M35..........74 D6
Meadow Bank Ct *OLDE* OL4..........60 B8
Meadow Bank Ct *STRET* M32..........96 C6
Meadowbank Gdns
  GOL/RIS/CUL WA3..........81 M5
Meadowbank Rd *BOLS/LL* BL3..........51 L2
Meadowbrook Cl *BURY* BL9..........5 M1
  HOR/BR BL6..........50 F1
Meadow Brook Wy
  CHD/CHDH SK8..........111 L8
Meadow Brow *WILM/AE* SK9..........130 U2
Meadow Cl *BOLS/LL* BL3..........53 L2
  DTN/ASHW M34..........101 K5
  HALE/TIMP WA15..........117 K1
  HEY OL10..........40 F2
  LEIGH WN7..........81 H2
  MOSL OL5..........77 H1
  MPL/ROM SK6..........101 K7
  MPL/ROM SK6..........123 H4
  STRET M32..........96 C3
  WILM/AE SK9..........126 C8
Meadow Cl *CCHDY* M21..........97 J4
Meadow Cft *BRAM/HZG* SK7..........122 A1
  WHTF M45..........54 F6
Meadowcroft *AIMK* WN4..........63 J6
  HYDE SK14..........92 C8
  RAD M26..........38 C7
  RAMS BL0..........50 C5
Meadowcroft La *OLD* OL1..........9 M1
Meadowcroft Wy *LEIGH* WN7..........81 L2
Meadowfield *HOR/BR* BL6..........34 D6
  MILN OL16..........42 E1
Meadowfield Cl *GLSP* SK13..........104 C1
Meadowfield Ct *HYDE* SK14..........91 C6
Meadowfield Dr *WALK* M28..........68 E6
Meadow Fold *UPML* OL3..........61 M4

Meadowgate URM M41 96 A3
  WALK M28 69 J4
Meadowgate Rd SLFD M6 85 M2
Meadow Head Av WHIT OL12 20 B8
Meadow La ALT WA14 106 D8
  BOLE BL2 37 K5
  DTN/ASHW M34 101 K5
  DUK SK16 91 G4
  OLDS OL8 75 H2
  POY/DIS SK12 123 M6
  WALK M28 69 J7
Meadow Pit La WGNE/HIN WN2 32 E4
Meadow Ri GLSP SK13 104 C5
  ROY/SHW OL2 43 K3
Meadow Rd BRO M7 86 F2
  MDTN M24 57 H6
  URM M41 96 A3
Meadows Cl BRAM/HZG SK7 122 A1
  WGNE/HIN WN2 49 G7
Meadowside BRAM/HZG SK7 120 E2
  MCFLDN SK10 129 M4
  MILN OL16 29 M8
  POY/DIS SK12 124 C6
Meadowside Av AIMK WN4 63 K4
  BOLE BL2 3 M4
  IRL M44 94 D2
  WALK M28 53 H8
  WYTH/NTH M22 110 A8
Meadowside Cl RAD M26 38 D7
Meadowside Gv WALK M28 69 H1
Meadowside Rd
  WGNE/HIN WN2 49 K8
Meadows La BOLE BL2 37 J1
Meadows Rd CHD/CHDH SK8 119 K3
  CHD/CHDH SK8 120 B4
  HTNM SK4 99 M6
  NM/HAY SK22 125 M2
  SALE M33 96 F6
The Meadows IRL M44 94 A6
  MDTN M24 57 K3
  MPL/ROM SK6 101 L8
  OLDE OL4 60 D6
  PWCH M25 55 L8
  RAD M26 38 B7
  UPML OL3 61 L5
  WHIT OL12 20 A3
Meadow St HYDE SK14 102 B3
  NM/HAY SK22 124 D4
  OFTN SK2 112 F7
The Meadow BOL BL1 35 G5
Meadowvale Dr
  WGNW/BIL/OR WN5 46 F6
Meadow Vw WHIT OL12 27 K3
Meadow Wk FWTH BL4 52 D5
  LIT OL15 21 K7
Meadow Wy EDGW/EG BL7 17 G6
  HALE/TIMP WA15 117 K1
  HOR/BR BL6 33 H4
  NEWH/MOS M40 73 K3
  TOT/BURYW BL8 24 B6
  WILM/AE SK9 126 C8
Meadscroft Dr WILM/AE SK9 130 C3
Meads Gv FWTH BL4 52 A4
  TYLD M29 67 M6
The Meads CHAD OL9 58 D6
The Mead CCHDY M21 97 L5
  ORD M5 86 B2
Meadway BRAM/HZG SK7 121 C7
  BURY BL9 39 J6
  CHAD OL9 74 B2
  DUK SK16 91 H5
  GOL/RIS/CUL WA3 80 A4
  MPL/ROM SK6 123 H4
  POY/DIS SK12 121 K7
  RAMS BL0 18 F3
  ROCH OL11 27 L8
  SALE M33 108 D2
  STLY SK15 92 B6
  TYLD M29 68 A3
  WGNE/HIN WN2 15 M6
Meadway Cl HOR/BR BL6 34 A1
  SALE M33 108 D1
Meadway Rd CHD/CHDH SK8 120 D1
Mealhouse Brow STKP SK1 13 J4
Mealhouse Ct ATH M46 66 F1
Mealhouse La ATH M46 66 F1
  BOL BL1 2 E4
Meal St HTNM SK4 112 B1
  NM/HAY SK22 124 E4
Meanley Rd LEIGH WN7 67 J5
Meanley St TYLD M29 67 M6
Meanwood Fold ROCH OL11 27 M4
  WHIT OL12 10 A2
Measham Ms CMANE M1 7 G3
Meddings Cl WILM/AE SK9 130 D4
Medina Cl CHD/CHDH SK8 111 J8
Medlar Wy AIMK WN4 63 J7
Medley St WHIT OL12 28 C3
Medlock Dr OLDS OL8 75 K3
Medlock St DROY M43 89 K2
  HULME M15 6 B8
  OLD OL1 9 M4
Medlock Valley Wy OLDE OL4 44 D7
  WGNE/HIN WN2 64 D2
  WHTF M45 55 M4
Medway Cl AIMK WN4 63 J6
  LEIGH WN7 80 F4
  OLDS OL8 74 F1
  ORD M5 86 A1
  WILM/AE SK9 127 H2
Medway Crs ALT WA14 107 M6
Medway Dr FWTH BL4 53 L7
  HOR/BR BL6 34 A1
Medway Pl WGNW/BIL/OR WN5 47 G5
Medway Rd OLDS OL8 74 F1
  ROY/SHW OL2 43 K4
  WALK M28 68 E1
The Medway HEY OL10 40 E1
Medway Wk NEWH/MOS M40 88 A1
Meech St OP/CLY M11 88 F4
Meek St ROY/SHW OL2 59 K2
Meerbrook Rd EDGY/DAV SK3 111 K4
Mee's Sq ECC M30 85 G6
Megfield WHTN BL5 50 B6
Megna Cl CHAD OL9 8 D3
Melandra Castle Rd GLSP SK13 104 B2
Melandra Crs HYDE SK14 103 H1
Melandra Rd GLSP SK13 104 A1
Melanie Cl GLSP SK13 104 C4
Melanie Dr RDSH SK5 100 C4
Melba St OP/CLY M11 89 G1
Melbecks Wk NTHM/RTH M23 109 J2
Melbourne Av CHAD OL9 58 D5
  MANAIR M90 118 C4
  STRET M32 97 C2
Melbourne Cl HOR/BR BL6 33 M1
  ROCH OL11 42 D2
Melbourne Gv HOR/BR BL6 33 M1

Melbourne Rd BOLS/LL BL3 35 L7
  BRAM/HZG SK7 121 C6
  ROCH OL11 42 D2
Melbourne St BKLY M9 73 H4
  BRO M7 72 A7
  CHAD OL9 8 A4
  DTN/ASHW M34 101 H2
  HULME M15 6 D9
  RDSH SK5 100 C3
  STLY SK15 91 K3
  SWIN M27 70 E4
Melbourne St North AUL OL6 75 M8
Melbourne St South AUL OL6 90 F1
Melbury Av DID/WITH M20 99 G8
Melbury Dr HOR/BR BL6 34 C4
Melbury Rd CHD/CHDH SK8 120 D6
Meldon Rd BRUN/LGST M13 99 H2
Meldrum St OLDS OL8 59 J8
Melford Av NEWH/MOS M40 74 B3
  WGNW/BIL/OR WN5 62 A1
Melford Dr AIMK WN4 63 K8
  WGNW/BIL/OR WN5 62 A1
Melford Gv OLDE OL4 60 A6
Melford Rd BRAM/HZG SK7 122 B3
Melfort Av STRET M32 97 H3
Meliden Crs BOL BL1 35 L3
  WYTH/NTH M22 119 C2
Melksham Cl ORD M5 86 C2
Mellalieu St MDTN M24 57 H3
  ROY/SHW OL2 59 H2
Melland Av CCHDY M21 97 M1
Melland Rd GTN M18 99 H1
Meller Rd BRUN/LGST M13 99 J2
Melling Av CHAD OL9 58 B3
  HTNM SK4 100 B6
Melling Cl LEIGH WN7 81 J3
Melling Rd OLDE OL4 59 M6
Mellings Av
  WGNW/BIL/OR WN5 62 B3
Melling St WGNW/BIL/OR WN5 47 H7
  WGTN/LGST M12 88 D3
Mellodew Dr OL1 60 A1
Mellor Brook Dr
  WGNE/HIN WN2 64 D2
Mellor Brow HEY OL10 40 E2
Mellor Cl AUL OL6 91 H2
  WGNNW/ST WN6 31 H7
Mellor Ct OLDS OL8 113 H5
Mellor Dr BURY BL9 39 C5
  WALK M28 68 F3
Mellor Gv BOL BL1 35 L3
Mellor Rd AUL OL6 76 C8
  CHD/CHDH SK8 120 D3
  NM/HAY SK22 124 E1
Mellors Rd TRPK M17 85 C5
Mellor St DROY M43 89 J3
  ECC M30 85 C3
  FAIL M35 74 A5
  NEWH/MOS M40 88 A1
  OLDE OL4 60 B6
  OLDS OL8 74 F2
  PWCH M25 55 J8
  RAD M26 54 E2
  ROCH OL11 10 A3
  ROY/SHW OL2 43 G7
  STRET M32 86 A8
Mellor Wy CHAD OL9 58 D8
Mellowstone Dr CCHDY M21 98 C4
Melloy Pl CHH M8 72 D8
Melmerby Cl AIMK WN4 78 C1
Melon Pl SLFD M6 86 E2
Melrose WHIT OL12 10 D3
Melrose Av BOL BL1 35 K3
  DID/WITH M20 110 F1
  ECC M30 69 K8
  EDGY/DAV SK3 111 J5
  HEY OL10 40 F1
  LEIGH WN7 66 A7
  LIT OL15 21 L5
  SALE M33 108 C1
  TOT/BURYW BL8 38 F1
Melrose Cl WHTF M45 55 J2
Melrose Crs EDGY/DAV SK3 112 A8
  HALE/TIMP WA15 117 K3
  POY/DIS SK12 122 F7
Melrose Dr WGNS/IIMK WN3 63 C1
Melrose Gdns RAD M26 38 B7
Melrose Rd BOLS/LL BL3 53 J1
  RAD M26 38 B7
Melrose St NEWH/MOS M40 73 M7
  OLD OL1 59 L3
  RAMS BL0 24 E2
  ROCH OL11 10 A5
Melsomby Rd NTHM/RTH M23 109 K2
Meltham Av DID/WITH M20 98 D8
Meltham Cl HTNM SK4 111 H3
Meltham Pl BOLS/LL BL3 35 M8
Meltham Rd HTNM SK4 111 H3
Melton Av DTN/ASHW M34 100 D1
  URM M41 94 F1
Melton Cl HEY OL10 40 E3
  TYLD M29 67 L4
  WALK M28 68 F2
Melton Dr BURY BL9 39 K7
Melton Rd CHH M8 72 B3
Melton St BKLY M9 73 J3
  HEY OL10 40 E3
  RAD M26 38 C8
  RDSH SK5 100 C8
Melverley Rd BKLY M9 56 D7
Melverley St WGNS/IIMK WN3 14 C6
Melville Cl OP/CLY M11 89 H5
Melville Rd FWTH BL4 53 J6
  STRET M32 96 E1
Melville St AUL OL6 75 L8
  BOLS/LL BL3 36 D3
  CSLFD M3 6 D3
  OLDE OL4 60 B7
  ROCH OL11 42 A3
Melvin Av WYTH/NTH M22 110 B8
Melyncourt Rd HYDE SK14 103 H1
Memorial Cottages SWIN M27 70 C1
Memorial Rd WALK M28 69 C1
Menai Gv CHD/CHDH SK8 111 J8
Menai Rd EDGY/DAV SK3 112 B6
Menai St BOLS/LL BL3 35 M8
Mendip Av WGNS/IIMK WN3 62 F1
  WYTH/NTH M22 110 D3
Mendip Cl BOLE BL2 37 K5
  CHAD OL9 58 D7
  CHD/CHDH SK8 119 K5
  HTNM SK4 13 C1
  ROY/SHW OL2 58 F1
Mendip Crs TOT/BURYW BL8 38 D1
Mendip Dr BOLE BL2 37 K6
  MILN OL16 29 K6
Mendip Rd OLDS OL8 75 C1
Mendips Cl ROY/SHW OL2 43 J4
Menston Av NEWH/MOS M40 74 B3
Mentmore Rd MILN OL16 29 C5

Mentone Crs WYTH/NTH M22 110 B8
Mentone Rd HTNM SK4 111 L1
Mentor St BRUN/LGST M13 99 J1
Mercer La ROCH OL11 27 H4
Mercer Rd GTN M18 89 C7
  HEY OL10 41 C5
Mercer St BNG/LEV M19 99 L3
  DROY M43 89 L2
  NEWLW WA12 79 C8
Merchants Crs
  GOL/RIS/CUL WA3 80 B3
Merchants Quay SALO M50 86 D6
Mercian Ml AUL OL6 * 90 E1
Mercian Wy EDGY/DAV SK3 12 F8
Mercia St BOLS/LL BL3 35 M7
Mercury Pk URM M41 * 85 J6
Mercury Wy URM M41 85 J7
Mere Av DROY M43 89 H4
  LEIGH WN7 66 A7
  MDTN M24 57 K6
  SLFD M6 86 B2
Merebank Cl ROCH OL11 27 H4
Mere Bank Cl WALK M28 68 F1
Mere Cl BURY BL9 39 L7
  DTN/ASHW M34 100 E2
  SALE M33 109 J1
Mereclough Av WALK M28 69 J3
Meredew Av SWIN M27 70 B6
Meredith St BOLS/LL BL3 52 C1
  RUSH/FAL M14 99 C5
Mere Dr DID/WITH M20 98 E8
  SWIN M27 70 D2
Merefield Av ROCH OL11 10 C9
Merefield St WGNE/HIN WN2 49 H8
Merefield Rd
  HALE/TIMP WA15 108 C7
  ROCH OL11 10 C9
Merefield Ter ROCH OL11 * 10 C9
Mere Fold WALK M28 68 C1
Mere Gdns BOL BL1 2 C2
Merehall Cl BOL BL1 2 C2
Merehall Dr BOL BL1 2 C2
Merehall St BOL BL1 2 C2
Mereland Av DID/WITH M20 98 F8
Mereland Cl
  WGNW/BIL/OR WN5 46 B6
Mere La ROCH OL11 10 E8
Meremanor WALK M28 69 J3
Merepool Cl MPL/ROM SK6 113 M5
Mere Rd AIMK WN4 63 H8
  NEWLW WA12 79 J8
Mere Side STLY SK15 76 C8
Mereside Cl CHD/CHDH SK8 111 J8
Mereside Gv WALK M28 69 H1
Mere St LEIGH WN7 66 A7
  ROCH OL11 10 E7
  WGNW/BIL/OR WN5 14 A8
The Mere AUL OL6 76 B6
  CHD/CHDH SK8 111 J8
Mere Wk BOL BL1 2 C2
Merewood Av WYTH/NTH M22 110 A6
Meriden Cl RAD M26 38 C6
Meriden Gv HOR/BR BL6 35 C6
Meridian Pl DID/WITH M20 98 D3
Merinall Cl MILN OL16 11 M5
Meriton Rd WILM/AE SK9 119 L3
Merlewood Av BNG/LEV M19 99 M5
  DTN/ASHW M34 * 89 L3
  UPML OL3 61 L4
Merlewood Dr SWIN M27 69 M6
  TYLD M29 67 L4
Merlin Cl LIT OL15 29 K2
  OFTN SK2 113 K6
  OLDS OL8 75 K4
Merlin Dr SWIN M27 70 E2
Merlin Gv BOL BL1 35 L3
Merlin Rd IRL M44 83 K8
  MILN OL16 29 J6
Merlyn Av DID/WITH M20 98 F3
  DTN/ASHW M34 101 K2
  SALE M33 96 F7
Merrick Av WYTH/NTH M22 110 B8
Merrick St HEY OL10 41 H1
Merridale Rd NEWH/MOS M40 73 M3
The Merridale
  HALE/TIMP WA15 117 J4
Merrill St ANC M4 88 B4
Merriman St OLDTF/WHR M16 87 H8
Merrion St FWTH BL4 52 F2
Merrow Wk CMANE M1 7 J8
Merrybent Cl OFTN SK2 113 C8
Merrybower Rd BRO M7 72 B4
Merrydale Av ECC M30 70 B4
Merryman Hall WHIT OL12 * 28 E2
Merseybank Av CCHDY M21 98 A8
Mersey Bank Rd GLSP SK13 93 J8
Mersey Cl WGNE/HIN WN2 65 M1
Mersey Crs DID/WITH M20 110 A1
Mersey Dr PART M31 94 D8
  WHTF M45 55 L3
Mersey Mdw DID/WITH M20 110 C1
  HTNM SK4 111 J2
  SALE M33 96 E6
  WGNE/HIN WN2 44 C5
  WGNW/BIL/OR WN5 46 C6
Mersey Rd North M35 74 D3
Mersey Sq STKP SK1 13 H4
Mersey St DROY M43 89 H4
  LEIGH WN7 65 M8
  STKP SK1 13 L2

Mesnes Park Ter WGN WN1 14 F2
Mesnes Rd WGN WN1 47 M2
Mesnes St WGN WN1 14 F2
Mesnes Ter WGN WN1 14 F2
Metcalfe Ct LHULT M38 * 52 C8
Metcalfe Dr MPL/ROM SK6 113 L2
Metcalf Gdns UPML OL3 61 L4
Metfield Pl BOL BL1 35 L4
Methuen St WGTN/LGST M12 99 L1
Methwold St BOLS/LL BL3 * 35 M8
The Mews BOL BL1 35 L4
  CHD/CHDH SK8 110 E7
  NEWH/MOS M40 88 B1
  PWCH M25 71 L1
  SALE M33 * 108 F7
  WGNE/HIN WN2 49 G7
  WHTF M45 * 55 G4
Mexborough St OLDE OL4 60 A4
Meyer St EDGY/DAV SK3 * 112 C6
Meynell Dr LEIGH WN7 81 J2
Meyrick Rd WGNW/BIL/OR WN5 14 A7
Miall St ROCH OL11 10 F8
Micawber Rd POY/DIS SK12 129 J2
Michael Ct MDTN M24 57 J4
Michael Wife La RAMS BL0 19 J2
Michigan Av SALQ M50 86 C4
Mickleby St NEWH/MOS M40 * 7 M1
Mickleham Av OFTN SK2 113 H7
Micklehurst Gn OFTN SK2 113 H7
Micklehurst Rd MOSL OL5 77 H3
Mickleton ATH M46 51 H8
Middlebourne St SLFD M6 86 B2
Middle Ga OLDS OL8 75 H2
Middle Gn AUL OL6 75 M8
Middleham St RUSH/FAL M14 98 D2
Middle Hillgate STKP SK1 13 K5
Middle Hl WHIT OL12 20 D8
Middlesex Dr BURY BL9 5 G8
Middlesex Rd BKLY M9 73 G2
  RDSH SK5 100 F6
Middlesex Wk CHAD OL9 8 F6
Middlestone Dr BKLY M9 73 G5
Middle St WHIT OL12 20 A3
Middleton Av FAIL M35 74 C5
Middleton Dr BURY BL9 55 J1
Middleton Old Rd BKLY M9 56 C7
  CHAD OL9 8 B4
  CHH M8 72 C2
  HEY OL10 41 H4
  RDSH SK5 100 C2
  ROY/SHW OL2 58 E1
Middleton Wy MDTN M24 57 J4
Middle Turn EDGW/EG BL7 17 G5
Middleway OLDE OL4 60 E7
Middlewood GOL/RIS/CUL WA3 80 B4
Middlewood Dr HTNM SK4 111 K3
Middlewood Gv CHAD OL9 58 D5
Middle Wood La LIT OL15 21 J6
Middlewood Rd
  MPL/ROM SK6 122 F5
  POY/DIS SK12 122 C8
Middlewood St ORD M5 86 F3
Middlewood Wy
  BRAM/HZG SK7 122 E4
  MCFLDN SK10 129 M3
Midford Av ECC M30 84 E2
Midford Dr BOL BL1 22 B5
Midge Hall Dr ROCH OL11 27 K6
Midge Hl MOSL OL5 61 G8
Midgley Av GTN M18 89 H6
Midgley Crs AUL OL6 76 B8
Midgley Dr MILN OL16 42 E2
Midgley St SWIN M27 70 A6
Midgrove La UPML OL3 45 M1
Midhurst Av NEWH/MOS M40 * 73 L8
Midhurst Cl CHD/CHDH SK8 120 E4
Midhurst St ROCH OL11 10 F9
Midland Rd BRAM/HZG SK7 121 G1
  RDSH SK5 100 C2
Midland St WGTN/LGST M12 88 A5
Midland Ter ALT WA14 116 F2
  NM/HAY SK22 124 E5
Midland Wk BRAM/HZG SK7 121 G1
Midlothian St OP/CLY M11 88 E2
Midville Rd OP/CLY M11 88 F1
Midway CHD/CHDH SK8 120 D7
Midway Dr POY/DIS SK12 129 H2
Midway St WGTN/LGST M12 99 K2
Milan St BRO M7 72 B6
Milbourne Rd BURY BL9 25 J6
Milburn Av NTHM/RTH M23 109 L2
Milburn Dr BOLE BL2 37 J4
Milbury Dr LIT OL15 29 K2
Milden Cl DID/WITH M20 * 98 E7
Mildred Av OLDE OL4 60 E7
  PWCH M25 71 M2
  ROY/SHW OL2 59 H2
Mildred St BRO M7 71 M7
Mile End La OFTN SK2 112 F6
  TOT/BURYW BL8 38 D4
Miles La WGNNW/ST WN6 30 B5
Miles St BOL BL1 36 A2
  HYDE SK14 102 C2
  OLD OL1 9 M1
  WGTN/LGST M12 88 D5
Milford Av OLDS OL8 74 F2
Milford Brow OLDE OL4 60 B5
Milford Crs LIT OL15 21 M6
Milford Dr BNG/LEV M19 99 M5
Milford Gv OFTN SK2 112 F5
Milford Rd BOLE BL2 23 J8
  BOLS/LL BL3 52 B1
  WGNE/HIN WN2 48 C2
Milford St BKLY M9 73 G2
  SLFD M6 86 B3
  WGNS/IIMK WN3 15 K8
  WHIT OL12 28 C3

Millbank St CMANE M1 7 L5
  HEY OL10 40 E2
Millbeck Farm
  WGNW/BIL/OR WN5 47 G5
Millbeck Gv BOLS/LL BL3 * 36 B5
Millbeck Rd MDTN M24 57 G2
Millbeck St HULME M15 87 K6
Millbrae Gdns ROY/SHW OL2 43 J5
Millbrook Av NEWH/MOS M40 51 H7
  DTN/ASHW M34 101 G3
Millbrook Bank ROCH OL11 27 G3
Millbrook Cl GOL/RIS/CUL WA3 81 M7
  ROY/SHW OL2 44 A5
Millbrook Fold BRAM/HZG SK7 122 C5
Millbrook Rd NTHM/RTH M23 109 K8
Millbrook St STKP SK1 13 J6
Mill Brow AUL OL6 75 M8
  CHH M8 72 F2
  HYDE SK14 103 H4
  MPL/ROM SK6 115 G4
  OLD OL1 58 D2
  WALK M28 69 J6
Mill Brow Rd MPL/ROM SK6 115 G4
Mill Court Dr RAD M26 53 L4
Millcrest Cl WALK M28 68 C7
Mill Cft BOL BL1 2 B2
  ROY/SHW OL2 43 M6
Millcroft
  WGNW/BIL/OR WN5 46 A7
Mill Croft Cl WHIT OL12 26 F2
Mill Croft La UPML OL3 45 J4
Milldale Cl ATH M46 66 F1
  HOR/BR BL6 34 F5
Miller Rd OLDS OL8 75 J1
Millers Brook Cl HEY OL10 * 41 G1
Millers Cl SALE M33 109 K1
Millers Ct ORD M5 85 K2
Millersdale Ct GLSP SK13 105 J3
Miller's La ATH M46 67 G3
  WGNE/HIN WN2 64 D3
Millers St ECC M30 84 F3
Miller St ANC M4 7 H2
  AUL OL6 75 L8
  BOL BL1 22 B8
  BURY BL9 24 F2
  HEY OL10 41 G2
  RAD M26 38 C5
Millett St BURY BL9 4 C5
  RAMS BL0 19 C5
Millfield Ct HALE/TIMP WA15 117 C2
Millfield Dr WALK M28 68 C6
Millfield Gv MILN OL16 11 J7
Millfield La AIMK WN4 78 B3
Millfield Rd BOLE BL2 37 K5
Millfold WHIT OL12 20 B2
Mill Fold Gdns LIT OL15 21 L8
Mill Fold Rd MDTN M24 57 J3
Millford Av URM M41 95 H3
Mill Ga MILN OL16 28 E2
  OLDS OL8 75 G1
Millgate ANC M4 * 7 G3
  EDGW/EG BL7 22 A2
  STKP SK1 13 K3
  UPML OL3 45 J8
  WGN WN1 15 H4
Millgate La DID/WITH M20 110 E3
Mill Green St WGTN/LGST M12 * 88 A4
Millhall Cl HULME M15 87 H7
Millhead Av NEWH/MOS M40 88 B2
Mill HI BOLE BL2 52 B6
  LHULT M38 52 B6
Mill Hill Av POY/DIS SK12 121 M5
Mill Hill Caravan Pk BOLE BL2 3 H3
Mill Hill Gv HYDE SK14 103 J3
Mill Hill Hollow POY/DIS SK12 121 M5
Mill Hill St BOLE BL2 3 H3
Millhouse Av NTHM/RTH M23 109 K8
Mill House Cl WHIT OL12 21 H8
Millhouse St RAMS BL0 19 H4
Milliner Ct OFTN SK2 * 113 G5
Millingford Av
  GOL/RIS/CUL WA3 79 G3
Millingford Gv AIMK WN4 78 E1
Millington Wk HULME M15 87 G6
Mill La AUL OL6 90 E2
  BRAM/HZG SK7 122 B4
  CHAD OL9 58 F8
  CHD/CHDH SK8 111 G6
  CHD/CHDH SK8 120 D1
  DTN/ASHW M34 101 L3
  FAIL M35 73 M5
  HALE/TIMP WA15 118 A3
  LEIGH WN7 66 E8
  MCFLDN SK10 128 C6
  MCFLDN SK10 128 C6
  MOSL OL5 76 F2
  MPL/ROM SK6 101 K7
  MPL/ROM SK6 113 K5
  RDSH SK5 100 D5
  ROY/SHW OL2 42 F8
  TOT/BURYW BL8 24 E8
  UPML OL3 61 G3
  WGNE/HIN WN2 49 J1
  WHTN BL5 50 B8
Mill Nook WHIT OL12 28 C1
Millom Av NTHM/RTH M23 109 L3
Millom Cl MILN OL16 11 L1
Millom Ct HALE/TIMP WA15 * 109 G6
Millom Dr BURY BL9 55 K2
Millom Pl CHD/CHDH SK8 119 K1
Millow St ANC M4 * 7 G1
Millpond Av BOLS/LL BL3 52 D1
Mill Pond Av NM/HAY SK22 124 F3
Mill Pond Cl ROY/SHW OL2 43 L6
Mill Rd BURY BL9 25 J4
  WGNW/BIL/OR WN5 46 A7
  WILM/AE SK9 126 F5
Mills Farm Cl OLDS OL8 75 K3
Mills Hill Rd MDTN M24 58 A3
Mills St HEY OL10 40 E2
  WHIT OL12 20 B3
Millstone Cl MPL/ROM SK6 113 K1
  POY/DIS SK12 122 B7
Millstone Rd BOL BL1 35 J3
Millstream La NEWH/MOS M40 89 H1
Mill St AIMK WN4 78 F2
  ALT WA14 108 B7
  ATH M46 67 H3
  BOL BL1 36 A4
  BRAM/HZG SK7 121 H1
  EDGW/EG BL7 22 C4
  FAIL M35 73 M5
  FWTH BL4 52 F4
  GLSP SK13 105 G3
  GOL/RIS/CUL WA3 79 K4
  HYDE SK14 91 H7
  LEIGH WN7 66 D8
  MOSL OL5 76 F2
  OP/CLY M11 88 D4
  RAD M26 54 C2

RAMS BL0 .... 18 D8
ROY/SHW OL2 .... 43 G8
SLFD M41 .... 71 K8
STLY SK15 .... 91 M3
TOT/BURYW BL8 .... 24 C4
UPML OL3 .... 61 L4
WALK M28 .... 68 D5
WGNE/HIN WN2 .... 49 G7
WGNS/IIMK WN3 .... 14 E5
WHTN BL5 .... 50 C4
WILM/AE SK9 .... 126 F5
Milltown GLSP SK13 .... 105 G3
Milltown St RAD M26 .... 54 C1
Mill View La HOR/BR BL6 .... 34 B1
Millway HALE/TIMP WA15 .... 117 L5
Millwell La BOL BL1 .... 2 E4
Millwood Cl AIMK WN4 .... 63 K7
　CHD/CHDH SK8 .... 120 A4
Millwood Ct BURY BL9 .... 39 J6
Millwood Ter HYDE SK14 .... 101 M2
Millwright St NEWH/MOS M40 .... 73 L7
Mill Yd BURY 5 H3
Milne Cl WGTN/LGST M12 .... 88 D6
　BURY BL9 .... 25 J7
Milner Av ALT WA14 .... 107 L5
　RAD M26 .... 54 B1
　SWIN M27 .... 70 D4
　WHIT OL12 .... 20 A4
Milnes Av LEIGH WN7 .... 81 J2
Milne St CHAD OL9 .... 8 B4
　CHAD OL9 .... 8 C1
　CHAD OL9 .... 8 C1
　OLD OL1 .... 59 K2
　ROCH OL11 .... 41 M2
　ROY/SHW OL2 .... 43 L6
Milngate Cl MILN OL16 .... 42 F1
Milnholme BOL BL1 .... 35 L1
Milnrow Cl BRUN/LGST M13 .... 7 K8
Milnrow Rd LIT OL15 .... 29 J2
　MILN OL16 .... 11 L5
　ROY/SHW OL2 .... 43 L5
Milnthorpe Rd BOLE BL2 .... 37 H4
Milnthorpe St SLFD M6 .... 71 K7
Milnthorpe Wy
　WGTN/LGST M12 .... 88 B6
Milo St BKLY M9 .... 73 C1
Milsom Av BOLS/LL BL3 .... 51 M1
Milton Av BOLS/LL BL3 .... 37 L8
　BOLS/LL BL3 .... 51 L1
　DROY M43 .... 89 K3
　IRL M44 .... 94 B6
　ORD M5 .... 86 A2
　STLY SK15 .... 77 H8
Milton Cl DUK SK16 .... 91 L5
　MPL/ROM SK6 .... 114 C4
　STRET M32 .... 97 H1
Milton Ct BNG/LEV M19 .... 99 H8
Milton Crs CHD/CHDH SK8 .... 110 F7
　FWTH BL4 .... 52 E6
Milton Dr CHAD OL9 .... 58 D6
　HALE/TIMP WA15 .... 108 D3
　POY/DIS SK12 .... 121 M8
　SALE M33 .... 96 D6
Milton Gv OLDTF/WHR M16 .... 97 M2
　SALE M33 .... 96 D6
　WGN WN1 .... 47 M1
　WGNW/BIL/OR WN5 .... 46 D6
　WGNW/BIL/OR WN5 .... 62 A3
Milton Pl SLFD M6 .... 86 D1
Milton Rd BRAM/HZG SK7 .... 121 G5
　DTN/ASHW M34 .... 90 A3
　GOL/RIS/CUL WA3 .... 80 A5
　PWCH M25 .... 55 M7
　RAD M26 .... 38 B2
　STRET M32 .... 97 H1
　SWIN M27 .... 70 A3
Milton St BRO M7 .... 72 B8
　ECC M30 .... 85 G2
　HYDE SK14 .... 91 G8
　LEIGH WN7 .... 66 B7
　MDTN M24 .... 57 J3
　MILN OL16 .... 10 F4
　MOSL OL5 .... 76 F2
　RAMS BL0 .... 18 G6
　ROY/SHW OL2 .... 43 H7
Milton Vw MOSL OL5 .... 77 G2
Milverton Av HYDE SK14 .... 102 F5
Milverton Cl HOR/BR BL6 .... 35 C7
Milverton Dr BRAM/HZG SK7 .... 120 D7
Milverton Rd RUSH/FAL M14 .... 99 G1
Milverton Wk HYDE SK14 .... 102 F2
Milwain Dr HTNM SK4 .... 99 M6
Milwain Rd BNG/LEV M19 .... 99 J3
　STRET M32 .... 96 F3
Mimosa Dr SWIN M27 .... 70 C2
Mincing St ANC M4 *.................. 7 H1
Minden Cl DID/WITH M20 .... 98 F8
　TOT/BURYW BL8 .... 38 E2
Minden Pde BURY BL9 .... 4 F5
Minden St SLFD M6 .... 71 H6
Minehead Av DID/WITH M20 .... 98 C5
　LEIGH WN7 .... 66 A2
　URM M41 .... 95 L4
Minerva Rd DUK SK16 .... 90 F2
　FWTH BL4 .... 52 C3
Mine St HEY OL10 .... 27 G8
Mine Wy RNFD/HAY WA11 *.................. 78 C5
Minnie St BOLS/LL BL3 *.................. 35 L8
　WHIT OL12 *.................. 10 B2
Minoan Gdns BRO M7 .... 71 M7
Minorca Cl ROCH OL11 .... 27 M4
Minorca St BOLS/LL BL3 .... 36 B3
Minor St FAIL M35 .... 74 D4
　OLDS OL8 .... 9 H8
　ROCH OL11 .... 41 M3
Minshull St CMANE M1 *.................. 7 H5
Minshull St South CMANE M1 *.................. 7 J6
Minstead Cl HYDE SK14 .... 102 F3
Minster Cl BOLE BL2 .... 36 F2
　DUK SK16 .... 91 G6
Minster Dr ALT WA14 .... 116 C3
　CHD/CHDH SK8 .... 111 K7
　URM M41 .... 95 K1
Minster Gv TYLD M29 .... 67 L5
Minsterley Pde
　WYTH/NTH M22 .... 118 E3
Minster Rd BKLY M9 .... 73 J4
　BOLE BL2 .... 36 F2
Minster Wy CHAD OL9 .... 58 D3
Minstrel Cl SWIN M27 .... 70 A5
　WGNE/HIN WN2 .... 64 C5
Minton St NEWH/MOS M40 .... 73 M4
　OLDE OL4 .... 9 L8
Minto St AULW OL7 .... 75 K8
Mint St RAMS BL0 .... 18 F2
Mirabel St CSLFD M3 .... 6 E1
Mirfield Av BKLY M9 .... 57 G8
　HTNM SK4 .... 12 A3
　OLDS OL8 .... 59 H8
Mirfield Cl GOL/RIS/CUL WA3 .... 80 A5

Mirfield Dr ECC M30 .... 70 A8
　MDTN M24 .... 57 J3
　URM M41 .... 84 F8
Mirfield Rd BKLY M9 .... 57 G8
Miriam Gv LEIGH WN7 .... 66 D8
Miriam St BOLS/LL BL3 *.................. 35 L8
　FAIL M35 .... 74 B7
Miry La WGNNW/ST WN6 .... 14 A2
　WHTN BL5 .... 50 B7
Mission St HEY OL10 .... 40 F2
Missouri Av SALQ M50 .... 86 B3
Mistletoe Gv CSLFD M3 *.................. 6 B1
Mitcham Av BKLY M9 .... 73 K1
Mitchell Cl CHD/CHDH SK8 *.................. 110 C6
Mitchell Hey WHIT OL12 .... 10 C4
Mitchell Rd WGNW/BIL/OR WN5 .... 62 B7
Mitchells Quay FAIL M35 .... 74 B5
Mitchell St AIMK WN4 .... 78 F2
　ECC M30 .... 84 F1
　GOL/RIS/CUL WA3 .... 80 D5
　LEIGH WN7 .... 65 L7
　MILN OL16 .... 28 F1
　NEWH/MOS M40 .... 73 L7
　OLD OL1 .... 8 F2
　OP/CLY M11 *.................. 88 C3
　TOT/BURYW BL8 .... 24 C6
　WGNE/HIN WN2 .... 48 D5
　WGNW/BIL/OR WN5 .... 47 J6
　WHIT OL12 .... 10 B3
Mitchell Wk BNG/LEV M19 .... 99 H4
Mitford Rd RUSH/FAL M14 .... 98 F5
Mitford St STRET M32 .... 96 F3
Mitre Rd BRUN/LGST M13 .... 88 C8
Mitre St BOL BL1 .... 22 B8
　FAIL M35 .... 74 C4
Mitton Cl GOL/RIS/CUL WA3 .... 81 H7
　HEY OL10 .... 40 C2
　TOT/BURYW BL8 .... 38 C2
Mizzy Rd WHIT OL12 .... 10 B1
Moadlock MPL/ROM SK6 .... 101 M8
Moat Av WYTH/NTH M22 .... 109 M6
Moatfield Gdns BOL BL1 .... 2 A2
Moat Gdns WYTH/NTH M22 .... 109 M8
Moat Hall Av ECC M30 .... 84 D4
Moat House St WGNE/HIN WN2 .... 48 D5
Moat Rd WYTH/NTH M22 .... 109 M8
Mobberley Cl BNG/LEV M19 .... 99 H8
Mobberley Rd BOLE BL2 .... 37 G4
　WILM/AE SK9 .... 126 A3
Mocha Pde BRO M7 .... 87 G1
Modbury Cl BRAM/HZG SK7 .... 121 G3
Mode Hill La WHTF M45 .... 55 M4
Model Cottages
　HALE/TIMP WA15 *.................. 109 G8
Mode Wheel Rd South
　SALQ M50 .... 86 A3
Modwen Rd ORD M5 *.................. 86 E6
Moelfre Dr CHD/CHDH SK8 .... 120 E5
Moffat Cl BOLE BL2 .... 37 J6
Moggle La MCFLDN SK10 .... 129 K3
Moisant St BOLS/LL BL3 .... 52 A1
Mold St BOL BL1 .... 36 B1
　OLD OL1 .... 9 H2
Molesworth St MILN OL16 .... 11 G5
Mollets Wd DTN/ASHW M34 .... 90 D7
Mollington Rd WYTH/NTH M22 .... 119 G4
Mollis Gv OLD OL1 .... 60 B1
Molyneux Rd BNG/LEV M19 .... 99 H8
　WHTN BL5 .... 50 E3
Molyneux St WGN WN1 .... 15 J3
　WHIT OL12 .... 10 A2
Mona Av CHD/CHDH SK8 .... 119 M3
　STRET M32 .... 96 F3
Monaco Dr WYTH/NTH M22 .... 110 A2
Monarch Cl IRL M44 .... 94 B6
　ROY/SHW OL2 .... 59 H2
Mona Rd CHAD OL9 .... 8 A9
Monart Rd BKLY M9 .... 73 H1
Mona St HYDE SK14 .... 102 B2
　SLFD M6 .... 71 K8
　WGN WN1 .... 14 E3
Mona Wy IRL M44 .... 94 E4
Moncrieffe St BOLS/LL BL3 *.................. 3 G8
Mond Rd IRL M44 .... 83 L8
Money Ash Rd
　HALE/TIMP WA15 .... 116 F1
Monfa Av OFTN SK2 .... 112 D8
Monica Av CHH M8 .... 72 C2
Monica Gv BNG/LEV M19 .... 99 J4
Monica Ter AIMK WN4 .... 78 E2
Monks Cl MILN OL16 .... 29 H6
Monksdale Av URM M41 .... 95 L2
Monks Hall Gv ECC M30 .... 85 J2
Monks La BOLE BL2 .... 37 G2
Monks' Rd GLSP SK13 .... 104 B6
Monkton Av GTN M18 .... 99 M1
Monkwood Dr BKLY M9 .... 73 H4
Monmouth Av BURY BL9 .... 25 J7
　SALE M33 .... 96 C7
Monmouth Crs AIMK WN4 .... 78 F2
Monmouth Rd
　CHD/CHDH SK8 .... 120 D3
Monmouth St CHAD OL9 .... 8 C9
　GTN M18 .... 89 H6
　MDTN M24 .... 57 M4
　ROCH OL11 .... 10 E8
Monroe Cl SLFD M6 .... 71 H8
　WGNS/IIMK WN3 .... 63 K1
Monsal Av BRO M7 .... 71 K5
　OFTN SK2 .... 113 G5
Monsall Cl BURY BL9 .... 55 K2
Monsall Rd NEWH/MOS M40 .... 73 H6
Monsall St NEWH/MOS M40 .... 73 G7
　OLDS OL8 .... 75 H1
Mons Av ROCH OL11 .... 27 M4
Montague Av AUL OL6 .... 91 G1
　OLDTF/WHR M16 .... 86 D7
　SALE M33 .... 96 C7
Montague St BOLS/LL BL3 *.................. 51 L1
Montague Wy STLY SK15 .... 91 K2
Montagu Rd OFTN SK2 .... 113 G6
Montagu St MPL/ROM SK6 .... 114 C2
Montana Sq OP/CLY M11 .... 89 H5
Montcliffe Crs OLDTF/WHR M16 .... 98 C2
Monteagle St BKLY M9 .... 56 E8
Montford Ri WGNE/HIN WN2 .... 48 D2
Montford St SALQ M50 .... 86 D4
Montfort Cl WHTN BL5 .... 50 A6
Montgomery ROCH OL11 .... 10 D7
Montgomery Dr BURY BL9 .... 55 L2
Montgomery Rd
　BRUN/LGST M13 .... 99 J2
Montgomery St OLDS OL8 .... 74 F7
　ROCH OL11 .... 27 M8
Montgomery Wy RAD M26 .... 37 M7
Monton Av ECC M30 .... 85 H1
Montondale ECC M30 .... 84 H1
Montonfields Rd ECC M30 .... 84 F1
Monton Gn ECC M30 .... 70 A8
Monton La ECC M30 .... 85 H2
Monton Mill Gdns ECC M30 .... 84 F1

Monton Rd ECC M30 .... 85 G1
　RDSH SK5 .... 100 F8
Monton St BOLS/LL BL3 .... 52 B1
　RAD M26 .... 54 C1
　RUSH/FAL M14 .... 87 K8
Montpellior Rd
　WYTH/NTH M22 .... 118 E2
Montreal St BNG/LEV M19 .... 99 L3
　OLDS OL8 .... 59 J8
Montrose Av BOLE BL2 .... 3 L1
　DID/WITH M20 .... 110 C3
　DUK SK16 .... 90 F5
　OFTN SK2 .... 121 J1
　RAMS BL0 .... 24 D2
　STRET M32 .... 96 F3
　WGNW/BIL/OR WN5 .... 46 F5
Montrose Crs BNG/LEV M19 .... 99 K3
Montrose Dr EDGW/EG BL7 .... 22 F5
Montrose St ROCH OL11 .... 41 M4
Montserrat Brow BOL BL1 .... 34 F1
Montserrat Rd BOL BL1 .... 35 G2
Monument Man WGN WN1 *.................. 47 M2
Monument Rd WGN WN3 .... 48 A2
Monyash Ms GLSP SK13 .... 104 A3
Monyash Vw WGNE/HIN WN2 .... 65 J1
Moody St WGNNW/ST WN6 .... 31 H3
Moon Gv RUSH/FAL M14 .... 99 G2
Moon St CHAD OL9 .... 8 D4
Moor Av WGNNW/ST WN6 .... 30 D4
Moor Bank La MILN OL16 .... 29 G8
Moorbank La BLO 19 L5
Moorbottom Rd
　TOT/BURYW BL8 .... 18 D6
Moorby Av BNG/LEV M19 .... 99 H8
Moorby St OLD OL1 .... 9 L3
Moorby Wk BOLS/LL BL3 *.................. 2 E9
Moorclose St MDTN M24 .... 57 M4
Moorcock Av SWIN M27 .... 70 E4
Moor Crs UPML OL3 .... 61 L1
　ROCH OL11 .... 42 C1
Moorcroft Dr BNG/LEV M19 .... 99 J5
Moorcroft Rd NTHM/RTH M23 .... 109 J3
Moorcroft St DROY M43 .... 89 K3
　OLDS OL8 .... 9 J7
Moordale Av OLDE OL4 .... 60 B3
Moordale St DID/WITH M20 .... 98 D7
Moordown Cl CHH M8 .... 72 C6
Moor Edge Rd MOSL OL5 .... 77 J3
Mooredge Ter ROY/SHW OL2 .... 59 H2
Moore Dr RNFD/HAY WA11 .... 78 C6
Moore End WYTH/NTH M22 .... 110 A4
Moor End Av BRO M7 .... 71 M4
Moore's Ct BOL BL1 .... 35 M4
Moores La WGNNW/ST WN6 .... 31 G2
Moore St MILN OL16 .... 10 F5
　WGN WN1 .... 48 A2
Moore St East WGN WN1 .... 15 K1
Moorfield EDGW/EG BL7 .... 17 G6
　WALK M28 .... 68 C5
　WALK M28 .... 69 J4
Moorfield Av DID/WITH M20 .... 98 F5
　DTN/ASHW M34 .... 101 K3
　LIT OL15 .... 21 L5
　STLY SK15 .... 92 A5
Moorfield Cha FWTH BL4 .... 53 G5
Moorfield Cl IRL M44 *.................. 94 E1
　SWIN M27 .... 70 A6
Moorfield Crs
　GOL/RIS/CUL WA3 .... 80 D5
Moorfield Dr HYDE SK14 *.................. 91 H7
　WILM/AE SK9 .... 126 C5
Moorfield Gv BOLE BL2 .... 36 E3
　HTNM SK4 .... 99 J8
Moorfield Hts STLY SK15 .... 77 H5
Moorfield Ms ROY/SHW OL2 *.................. 58 K6
Moorfield Pl WHIT OL12 *.................. 28 E3
Moorfield Rd DID/WITH M20 .... 98 C8
　IRL M44 .... 94 E1
　OLDS OL8 .... 74 E2
　SLFD M6 .... 71 G7
　SWIN M27 .... 69 M6
Moorfield St
　DID/WITH M20 .... 98 E5
　HYDE SK14 .... 93 G6
　WGNE/HIN WN1 .... 64 E1
Moorfield Ter HYDE SK14 .... 93 G7
Moor Ga BOLE BL2 .... 23 G7
Moorgate BURY 5 G3
Moorgate Av DID/WITH M20 .... 98 C6
　ROCH OL11 .... 27 K5
Moorgate Ct BOLE BL2 .... 3 K1
Moorgate Dr STLY SK15 .... 77 H6
　TYLD M29 .... 67 M6
Moorgate La LIT OL15 .... 21 J5
Moorgate Ms STLY SK15 *.................. 77 H5
Moorgate Rd RAD M26 .... 38 B4
　STLY SK15 .... 77 H5
Moorgate St UPML OL3 .... 61 L4
Moorhead St ANC M4 *.................. 7 K1
Moorhey Rd LHULT M38 .... 52 C6
Moorhey St OLDE OL4 .... 59 L6
Moor Hl ROCH OL11 .... 27 J3
Moorhouse Farm
　MILN OL16 .... 29 H6
Moor House Fold
　MILN OL16 .... 29 H6
Moorings Cl WGN WN1 .... 15 M4
Moorings Rd TRPK M17 .... 85 L4
The Moorings MOSL OL5 .... 77 H1
　POY/DIS SK12 .... 124 A6
　WALK M28 .... 69 K7
Moorland Av CHH M8 .... 72 C2
　DROY M43 .... 89 H3
　MILN OL16 .... 29 K6
　ROCH OL11 .... 27 J5
　SALE M33 .... 108 F1
　UPML OL3 .... 61 J1
　WHIT OL12 .... 20 A6
Moorland Crs WHIT OL12 .... 20 B5
Moorland Dr CHD/CHDH SK8 .... 120 B4
　HOR/BR BL6 .... 34 C1
　LHULT M38 .... 52 C6
Moorland Gv BOL BL1 .... 35 K2
Moorland Rd AIMK WN4 .... 64 B7
　DID/WITH M20 .... 110 D1
　OFTN SK2 .... 112 D3
　STLY SK15 .... 77 M7
　WGNE/HIN WN2 .... 48 F7
Moorlands Av LEIGH WN7 .... 81 J7
　URM M41 *.................. 95 L1
Moorlands Crs MOSL OL5 .... 77 G3
Moorlands Dr MOSL OL5 .... 77 H1
Moorlands St ROY/SHW OL2 .... 43 H8
Moorland St WHIT OL12 .... 28 B3
Moorlands Vw
　BOLS/LL BL3 .... 51 K2
Moorland Ter WHIT OL12 .... 10 F4

Moor La BOL BL1 .... 2 D5
　BRAM/HZG SK7 .... 128 B1
　BRO M7 .... 71 K4
　LEIGH WN7 .... 66 B3
　NTHM/RTH M23 .... 109 K2
　UPML OL3 .... 61 M2
　WILM/AE SK9 .... 126 A7
Moor Nook SALE M33 .... 109 G1
Moor Park Av ROCH OL11 .... 41 L2
Moor Park Rd DID/WITH M20 .... 110 F4
Moor Platt Cl HOR/BR BL6 .... 34 C1
Moor Rd NTHM/RTH M23 .... 109 H4
　TOT/BURYW BL8 .... 18 D6
　WGNW/BIL/OR WN5 .... 46 B6
Moorsholme Av
　NEWH/MOS M40 .... 73 K5
Moorside HALE/TIMP WA15 *.................. 108 C5
　ROCH OL11 .... 42 C1
　SWIN M27 .... 70 A5
Moorside Av BOL BL1 .... 35 K2
　BOLE BL2 .... 38 A3
　DROY M43 .... 89 M1
　FWTH BL4 .... 52 E5
　OLDE OL4 .... 44 C8
Moorside Cl GLSP SK13 .... 104 E4
Moorside Ct DTN/ASHW M34 .... 90 F8
Moorside Crs DROY M43 .... 89 M2
Moorside La DTN/ASHW M34 .... 90 D8
Moor Side La BLO RAMS 19 L5
Moorside Rd BRO M7 .... 71 M3
　EDGW/EG BL7 .... 17 G3
　HTNM SK4 .... 111 K2
　MOSL OL5 .... 77 H3
　SWIN M27 .... 69 M5
　TOT/BURYW BL8 .... 24 C6
　URM M41 .... 95 H1
Moorside St DROY M43 .... 89 L2
Moorside Vw TOT/BURYW BL8 .... 24 C6
Moorside Wk
　WGNW/BIL/OR WN5 .... 46 B4
Moorsley Dr BKLY M9 .... 57 J8
Moor St BURY BL9 .... 5 G3
　ECC M30 .... 84 E3
　HEY OL10 .... 40 F2
　OLD OL1 .... 59 L5
　ROY/SHW OL2 .... 43 K6
Moorswood Dr OLDS OL8 .... 59 M8
Moorton Av BNG/LEV M19 .... 99 J5
Moorton Pk BNG/LEV M19 .... 99 J5
Moortop Cl BKLY M9 .... 56 F7
Moor View OL12 .... 27 J3
Moor Wy TOT/BURYW BL8 .... 23 L1
Moorway BKLY M9 .... 57 M8
Moorwood Dr OLDS OL8 .... 59 M8
　SALE M33 .... 108 C3
Mora Av CHAD OL9 .... 8 B1
Moran Cl WILM/AE SK9 .... 127 K1
Morano Dr WGNE/HIN WN2 .... 64 D1
Moran Wk HULME M15 .... 87 H4
Morar Dr BOLE BL2 .... 37 K5
Morar Rd DUK SK16 .... 91 G5
Mora St BKLY M9 .... 73 J1
Moravian Cl DUK SK16 .... 90 F3
Moravian Fld DROY M43 *.................. 89 K4
Moray Cl RAMS BL0 .... 18 D8
Moray Rd CHAD OL9 .... 8 B8
Morbourne Cl WGTN/LGST M12 .... 88 B6
Morden Av AIMK WN4 .... 64 A8
Morecambe Cl NEWH/MOS M40 .... 73 L6
Morely St LEIGH WN7 .... 66 A7
Moresby Dr DID/WITH M20 .... 110 E4
Moreton Av BRAM/HZG SK7 .... 121 G4
　SALE M33 .... 108 B1
　STRET M32 .... 97 G3
　WHTF M45 .... 55 J3
Moreton La OFTN SK2 .... 112 F5
Moreton St CHAD OL9 .... 58 C4
Morgan Pl RDSH SK5 .... 100 C8
Morgan St LIT OL15 .... 21 M7
Morgans Wy GOL/RIS/CUL WA3 .... 80 B2
Morillon Rd IRL M44 .... 83 K3
Morland Rd NM/HAY SK22 .... 125 J2
　OLDTF/WHR M16 .... 86 F8
Morley Av RUSH/FAL M14 .... 98 D3
　SWIN M27 .... 70 B2
Morley Green Rd
　WILM/AE SK9 .... 126 A3
Morley Rd RAD M26 .... 38 A4
Morley's La TYLD M29 .... 82 D1
Morley St ATH M46 .... 66 F1
　BOLS/LL BL3 .... 2 B6
　BURY BL9 .... 4 F5
　GLSP SK13 .... 105 G4
　MILN OL16 .... 11 J1
　WHTF M45 .... 55 J4
Morley Wy UPML OL3 .... 61 L7
Morna Wk WGTN/LGST M12 .... 88 A4
Morningside Cl MILN OL16 *.................. 11 J8
　OP/CLY M11 .... 89 J5
Morningside Dr
　DID/WITH M20 .... 110 F4
Mornington Av
　CHD/CHDH SK8 .... 111 G8
Mornington Crs RUSH/FAL M14 .... 98 D4
Mornington Rd ATH M46 .... 51 J6
　BOL BL1 .... 35 L4
　CHD/CHDH SK8 .... 111 G8
　ROCH OL11 .... 27 K7
　SALE M33 .... 97 G7
　WGNE/HIN WN2 .... 49 J7
Morpeth Cl AULW OL7 .... 75 H8
　WGTN/LGST M12 .... 88 B7
Morpeth St SWIN M27 .... 70 B6
Morrell Rd WYTH/NTH M22 .... 110 B4
Morris Fold Dr HOR/BR BL6 .... 34 F6
Morris Gn BOLS/LL BL3 .... 51 K2
Morris Green La BOLS/LL BL3 .... 51 M2
Morris Green St BOLS/LL BL3 *.................. 51 M2
Morris Gv URM M41 .... 95 H4
Morrison St BOLS/LL BL3 .... 52 A1
Morris St BOL BL1 .... 3 G4
　DID/WITH M20 .... 98 E5
　OLDE OL4 .... 9 M8
　RAD M26 .... 39 H7
　TYLD M29 .... 67 J3
　WGN WN1 .... 15 H4
　WGNE/HIN WN2 .... 49 G7
　WGNS/IIMK WN3 .... 48 B1
Morrowfield Av CHH M8 .... 72 C5
Morse Rd NEWH/MOS M40 .... 73 L7

Mortar St OLDE OL4 .... 59 M5
Mortfield Gdns BOL BL1 .... 2 A2
Mortfield La BOL BL1 *.................. 2 A2
Mortimer Av BKLY M9 .... 57 H8
Mortimer St OLD OL1 .... 9 L2
Mortlake Cl WALK M28 .... 68 C1
Mortlake Dr NEWH/MOS M40 .... 73 L7
Mort La TYLD M29 .... 68 B2
Morton Av WGNS/IIMK WN3 .... 14 D9
Morton Cl WGNS/IIMK WN3 .... 62 F2
Morton St FAIL M35 .... 74 B5
　HTNM SK4 .... 100 B8
　MDTN M24 .... 57 K3
　RAD M26 .... 54 E2
Mort St FWTH BL4 .... 52 E5
　LEIGH WN7 .... 65 L7
　WGNE/HIN WN2 .... 49 K7
　WGNNW/ST WN6 .... 14 B1
Morven Av BRAM/HZG SK7 .... 122 B1
Morven Dr NTHM/RTH M23 .... 109 K2
Morven Gv BOLE BL2 .... 37 J5
Morville Dr WGNS/IIMK WN3 .... 47 L8
Morville Rd CCHDY M21 .... 98 A3
Morville St CMANE M1 *.................. 7 L6
Moscow Rd EDGW/EG BL7 .... 13 G7
Moscow Rd East EDGW/EG BL7 .... 13 G7
Mosedale Cl NTHM/RTH M23 .... 109 H6
　TYLD M29 .... 67 M6
Mosedale Rd MDTN M24 .... 57 G2
Moseldene Rd OFTN SK2 .... 113 G7
Moseley Rd BNG/LEV M19 .... 99 J3
　CHD/CHDH SK8 .... 120 B1
　RUSH/FAL M14 .... 99 H4
Moseley St EDGY/DAV SK3 .... 13 G7
Mosley Av BURY BL9 .... 25 J7
　RAMS BL0 .... 24 E2
Mosley Cl HALE/TIMP WA15 .... 108 C5
Mosley Common Rd WALK M28 .... 68 B5
Mosley Rd HALE/TIMP WA15 .... 108 E6
　TRPK M17 .... 85 M4
Mosley Rd North TRPK M17 .... 85 M4
Mosley St CMANE M1 .... 6 F5
　CMANW M27 .... 26 C8
Mossack Av WYTH/NTH M22 .... 118 F3
Moss Av LEIGH WN7 .... 11 M6
　MILN OL16 .... 11 M6
　WGNW/BIL/OR WN5 .... 62 A1
Moss Bank BRAM/HZG SK7 .... 120 E7
　CHH M8 .... 72 D4
Moss Bank Av DROY M43 .... 89 M2
Moss Bank Cl BOL BL1 .... 22 A8
Mossbank Cl GLSP SK13 .... 93 H8
Moss Bank Ct DROY M43 *.................. 89 M2
Mossbank Gv HEY OL10 .... 69 M2
Moss Bank Gv SWIN M27 .... 69 M2
Moss Bank Pk BOL BL1 *.................. 35 J1
Moss Bank Rd SWIN M27 .... 70 A2
Moss Bank Wy BOL BL1 .... 35 H3
Mossbray Av BNG/LEV M19 .... 99 G5
Moss Bridge Rd MILN OL16 .... 11 K8
Moss Brook Rd BKLY M9 .... 73 H1
Moss Cl RAD M26 .... 38 A7
Mossclough Ct BKLY M9 .... 57 H5
Moss Colliery Rd SWIN M27 .... 70 B1
Mosscot Wk BRUN/LGST M13 .... 7 K8
Moss Croft Cl URM M41 .... 95 H1
Mossdale Av BOL BL1 .... 35 G3
Mossdale Rd AIMK WN4 .... 63 K4
　NTHM/RTH M23 .... 109 G2
　SALE M33 .... 108 C3
Mossdown Rd ROY/SHW OL2 .... 59 L1
Moss Dr HOR/BR BL6 .... 34 C1
Moss Farm Cl MILN OL16 .... 11 L2
Mossfield Cl BURY BL9 .... 5 L2
　HTNM SK4 .... 12 A2
Mossfield Ct BOL BL1 .... 2 C2
Mossfield Gv BKLY M9 .... 57 K8
Mossfield Rd FWTH BL4 .... 52 E4
　FWTH BL4 .... 53 J7
　HALE/TIMP WA15 .... 109 G6
　SWIN M27 .... 70 B2
Moss Fold TYLD M29 .... 67 M5
Moss Gate Rd ROY/SHW OL2 .... 43 J4
Moss Grange Av
　OLDTF/WHR M16 .... 98 A1
Moss Gv PART M31 .... 95 H8
Moss Gv ROY/SHW OL2 .... 43 H3
　WGNNW/ST WN6 .... 31 H4
Mossgrove Rd
　HALE/TIMP WA15 .... 108 C5
Mosshall Cl HULME M15 .... 87 G6
Moss Hall Rd BURY BL9 .... 40 A8
Moss Hey Dr NTHM/RTH M23 .... 109 M3
Moss Hey St ROY/SHW OL2 .... 43 M6
Moss House La WALK M28 .... 68 D8
Moss House Ter BKLY M9 *.................. 56 F7
Mossland Cl HEY OL10 .... 41 G4
Mossland Gv BOLS/LL BL3 .... 51 G2
Moss La AULW OL6 .... 90 B2
　BOL BL1 .... 35 K1
　BRAM/HZG SK7 .... 120 E7
　FWTH BL4 .... 53 L7
　GOL/RIS/CUL WA3 .... 79 L7
　HALE/TIMP WA15 .... 108 B8
　HALE/TIMP WA15 .... 108 C5
　HOR/BR BL6 .... 33 J2
　HYDE SK14 .... 103 J4
　IRL M44 .... 94 A7
　LYMM WA13 .... 106 B3
　MCFLDN SK10 .... 131 K2
　MDTN M24 .... 57 J7
　MILN OL16 .... 11 G6
　PART M31 .... 106 D1
　ROY/SHW OL2 .... 59 K1
　SALE M33 .... 96 B3
　SALE M33 .... 107 L1
　SWIN M27 .... 70 A3
　TYLD M29 .... 82 D3
　URM M41 .... 85 H7
　WALK M28 .... 68 H1
　WGNE/HIN WN2 .... 49 J4
　WGNNW/ST WN6 .... 30 D1
　WHTF M45 .... 55 J4
　WILM/AE SK9 .... 119 G6
　WILM/AE SK9 .... 130 E3
Moss La East
　OLDTF/WHR M16 .... 87 H8
Moss La West HULME M15 .... 87 H8
　RUSH/FAL M14 .... 87 K8
Moss Lea BOL BL1 .... 22 A8
Moss Lee Gv CHH M8 .... 72 C1
Mossley Rd AUL OL6 .... 90 F1
　OLDS OL8 .... 61 G8
Moss Meadow WHTN BL5 .... 50 B2
Moss Meadow Rd SLFD M6 *.................. 70 F8
Mossmere Rd
　CHD/CHDH SK8 .... 111 K8
Moss Mill St MILN OL16 .... 11 J8
Moss Park Rd STRET M32 .... 96 D2
Moss Pl BURY BL9 .... 4 E9

Moss Rd SALE M33 95 L8
STRET M32 96 F1
WGNW/BIL/OR WN5 62 A1
WILM/AE SK9 130 F2
Moss Rose WILM/AE SK9 130 E2
Moss Rw BURY BL9 4 F6
Moss Shaw Wy RAD M26 38 B7
Moss Side La MILN OL16 11 M9
Moss Side Rd IRL M44 94 A6
Moss St BRO M7 72 A7
BURY BL9 4 E5
BURY BL9 25 G2
DROY M43 89 L2
FWTH BL4 53 H3
HEY OL10 40 F2
HYDE SK14 93 G7
MILN OL16 11 J6
OLDE OL4 60 B4
WGNNW/ST WN6 14 B1
WGNS/IIMK WN3 64 C1
WGNW/BIL/OR WN5 * 46 E6
Moss St West AULW OL7 90 C2
Moss Ter MILN OL16 11 J6
WGNW/BIL/OR WN5 46 E7
The Moss MDTN M24 57 L6
Moss Vale Crs STRET M32 85 J8
Moss Vale Rd STRET M32 96 C1
Moss View Rd BOLE BL2 37 H4
PART M31 106 D1
Mossway MDTN M24 57 J7
Moss Wy SALE M33 96 B8
Mosswood Pk DID/WITH M20 110 E4
Mosswood Rd WILM/AE SK9 127 J3
Mossylea Cl MDTN M24 57 L7
Mossy Lea Fold
WGNNW/ST WN6 30 C1
Moston Bank Av BKLY M9 73 H5
Moston La BKLY M9 73 H4
NEWH/MOS M40 73 K4
Moston La East
NEWH/MOS M40 74 B3
Moston Rd MDTN M24 58 A6
RDSH SK5 100 C5
Moston St BRO M7 72 C5
Mostyn Av BURY BL9 25 J7
CHD/CHDH SK8 120 A3
RUSH/FAL M14 99 H4
Mostyn Rd BRAM/HZG SK7 121 L3
Mostyn St DUK SK16 91 J4
Motcombe Farm Rd
CHD/CHDH SK8 119 K3
Motcombe Gv CHD/CHDH SK8 119 J1
Motcombe Rd CHD/CHDH SK8 119 J2
Motherwell Av BNG/LEV M19 99 K3
Mottershead Av BOLS/LL BL3 37 K8
Mottershead Rd
WYTH/NTH M22 109 L8
Mottram Av CCHDY M21 97 M7
Mottram Cl CHD/CHDH SK8 111 K7
Mottram Dr HALE/TIMP WA15 108 D7
WGNS/IIMK WN3 47 L7
Mottram Fold STKP SK1 13 J6
Mottram Moor HYDE SK14 92 F8
Mottram Old Rd HYDE SK14 102 D4
STLY SK15 91 M3
Mottram Rd HYDE SK14 102 C2
HYDE SK14 103 K4
SALE M33 109 H1
STLY SK15 91 M3
WILM/AE SK9 130 E3
Mottram St STKP SK1 13 J6
Mough La CHAD OL9 74 A1
Mouldsworth Av
DID/WITH M20 98 D5
HTNM SK4 100 A6
Moulton St CHH M8 72 B8
Mouncey St CMANE M1 * 7 G8
Mountain Ash WHIT OL12 27 L1
Mountain Ash Cl SALE M33 95 M7
WHIT OL12 27 L1
Mountain Gv WALK M28 52 F8
Mountain St MOSL OL5 76 F3
NEWH/MOS M40 74 A8
STKP SK1 13 M3
WALK M28 52 F8
Mount Av LIT OL15 21 L5
WHIT OL12 21 J8
Mountbatten Av DUK SK16 91 J6
Mountbatten Cl BURY BL9 55 L2
Mountbatten St GTN M18 88 F7
Mount Carmel Crs ORD M5 * 86 F5
Mount Crs WGNW/BIL/OR WN5 46 C6
Mount Dr MPL/ROM SK6 114 C7
URM M41 96 C2
Mountfield PWCH M25 55 L8
Mountfield Rd BRAM/HZG SK7 121 G7
EDGY/DAV SK3 12 D9
Mountfield Wk OP/CLY M11 88 C3
Mount Fold MDTN M24 57 K5
Mountford Av CHH M8 * 72 C2
Mount Gv CHD/CHDH SK8 110 C7
Mount La UPML OL3 61 H3
Mountmorres Cl WHTN BL5 51 J5
Mount Pleasant BOLS/LL BL3 * 3 M9
BRAM/HZG SK7 121 M1
BURY BL9 25 J1
MDTN M24 56 F4
PWCH M25 56 B4
WILM/AE SK9 126 F3
Mount Pleasant Rd
DTN/ASHW M34 101 J2
FWTH BL4 52 C4
Mount Pleasant St AUL OL6 75 M8
DTN/ASHW M34 90 C6
HOR/BR BL6 34 A3
OLDE OL4 * 59 L5
Mount Pleasant Wk RAD M26 38 D8
Mount Rd GTN M18 * 88 F7
HTNM SK4 12 D2
HYDE SK14 102 D6
MDTN M24 57 K5
PWCH M25 55 M5
Mountroyal Cl HYDE SK14 91 J7
Mount St Joseph's Rd
BOLS/LL BL3 35 L7
Mountside Cl WHIT OL12 28 C2
Mountside Crs PWCH M25 55 J8
Mount Sion Houses RAD M26 * 54 A2
Mount Sion Rd RAD M26 54 B2
Mount Skip La LHULT M38 52 D8
Mount St BOL BL1 36 B3
CMANW M2 6 F6
CSLFD M3 6 B2
ECC M30 84 F4
GLSP SK13 104 F4
HEY OL10 41 G3
HOR/BR BL6 34 A3
HYDE SK14 102 B2
LEIGH WN7 65 M8
RAMS BL0 18 E5
ROCH OL11 41 M3
ROY/SHW OL2 59 H1
SWIN M27 70 C5
WHIT OL12 10 C3
The Mount ALT WA14 108 A7
HALE/TIMP WA15 117 L4
Mount Vw WGNS/IIMK WN3 15 J9
Mount View Rd ROY/SHW OL2 44 A6
Mount Zion Rd BURY BL9 39 J7
Mousell St CHH M8 72 D8
Mouselow Cl GLSP SK13 104 C1
Mowbray Av PWCH M25 71 M2
SALE M33 108 F1
Mowbray St AULW OL7 90 C2
BOL BL1 * 35 L3
OLD OL1 9 K6
ROCH OL11 41 L1
STKP SK1 13 K6
Mow Halls La UPML OL3 61 K3
Moxley Rd CHH M8 72 B3
Moxon Wy AIMK WN4 64 A8
Moyse Av TOT/BURYW BL8 24 C7
Mozart Cl ANC M4 7 M2
Muirfield Av MPL/ROM SK6 101 K8
Muirfield Cl BOLS/LL BL3 51 J1
HEY OL10 41 G3
NEWH/MOS M40 73 M5
WILM/AE SK9 127 H4
Muirfield Dr TYLD M29 67 M5
Mulberry Av GOL/RIS/CUL WA3 80 C5
Mulberry Cl CHD/CHDH SK8 119 L5
RAD M26 54 D2
ROCH OL11 42 B2
WGNW/BIL/OR WN5 47 G6
Mulberry Ct SLFD M6 * 86 D1
Mulberry Ms HTNM SK4 13 G2
Mulberry Mount St
EDGY/DAV SK3 13 H7
Mulberry Rd SLFD M6 86 D2
Mulberry St AUL OL6 * 90 F1
CMANW M2 6 E5
Mulberry Wk DROY M43 89 H4
SALE M33 96 A6
Mule St BOLE BL2 3 H3
Mulgrave Rd WALK M28 69 K4
Mulgrave St BOLS/LL BL3 51 M2
SWIN M27 70 A3
Mullacre Rd WYTH/NTH M22 110 A6
Mull Av WGTN/LGST M12 88 B7
Mullein Cl GOL/RIS/CUL WA3 80 A4
Mulliner St BOL BL1 * 36 C3
Mullins Av NEWLW WA12 78 F7
Mullion Cl BNG/LEV M19 100 A2
Mullion Dr HALE/TIMP WA15 108 B5
Mullion Wk CHH M8 72 E6
Mulmount Cl OLDS OL8 74 F1
Mumps Rbt OLD OL1 9 M5
Munday St ANC M4 88 A3
Municipal Cl HEY OL10 * 41 G2
Munn Rd BKLY M9 56 E7
Munro Av WGNW/BIL/OR WN5 46 B6
WYTH/NTH M22 119 H2
Munster St ANC M4 * 7 G1
Muriel St BRO M7 72 A7
HEY OL10 41 H2
MILN OL16 11 K8
Murieston Rd
HALE/TIMP WA15 117 G2
Murphy Cl WGNS/IIMK WN3 14 B9
Murrayfield ROCH OL11 27 H6
Murray Rd BURY BL9 4 F5
Murray St ANC M4 7 L3
ATH M46 66 E2
BRO M7 72 A6
Musabbir Sq MILN OL16 * 11 G3
Musbury Av CHD/CHDH SK8 120 D2
Museum St CMANW M2 6 F6
Musgrave Gdns BOL BL1 35 M4
Musgrave Rd BOL BL1 35 M4
WYTH/NTH M22 118 F1
Muslin St ORD M5 86 F3
Muter Av WYTH/NTH M22 119 H2
Mutual St HEY OL10 41 H1
Mycroft Cl LEIGH WN7 66 B4
Myerscroft Cl NEWH/MOS M40 74 A8
Myrrh St BOL BL1 36 B1
Myrtle Av AIMK WN4 63 J6
LEIGH WN7 66 B5
Myrtle Bank PWCH M25 71 K3
Myrtle Cl OLDS OL8 9 H9
Myrtle Gdns BURY BL9 5 K4
Myrtle Gv DROY M43 89 M2
DTN/ASHW M34 100 C1
PWCH M25 71 L2
WGNW/BIL/OR WN5 * 62 A8
WHTF M45 55 G2
Myrtleleaf Gv ORD M5 * 86 A2
Myrtle Pl BRO M7 71 M8
Myrtle Rd MDTN M24 57 M3
PART M31 106 A2
Myrtle St BOL BL1 2 B3
EDGY/DAV SK3 12 B8
OLDTF/WHR M16 * 86 F8
OP/CLY M11 88 B4
WGN WN1 14 E4
Myrtle St North BURY BL9 5 K4
Myrtle St South BURY BL9 5 K5
My St ORD M5 86 B3
Mytham Rd BOLS/LL BL3 53 L1
Mytton Rd BOL BL1 35 L1
Mytton St HULME M15 87 H7

N

Nabbs Fold TOT/BURYW BL8 24 C1
Nabbs Wy TOT/BURYW BL8 24 D3
Naburn Cl RDSH SK5 100 F6
Naburn Dr WGNW/BIL/OR WN5 46 B7
Naburn St BRUN/LGST M13 88 A8
Nada Rd CHH M8 72 C3
Nadine St SLFD M6 86 B1
Nadin St OLDS OL8 75 H1
Nairn Cl NEWH/MOS M40 * 88 B1
WGNNW/ST WN6 31 G3
Nallgate MILN OL16 42 F2
Nall St BNG/LEV M19 99 L5
MILN OL16 29 H6
Nameplate Cl ECC M30 84 E2
Nancy St HULME M15 87 G6
Nandywell BOLS/LL BL3 53 L1
Nangreave Rd OFTN SK2 112 E6
Nangreaves St LEIGH WN7 65 M7
Nan Nook Rd NTHM/RTH M23 109 J3
Nansen Av ECC M30 84 F1
Nansen Cl STRET M32 86 B8
Nansen Rd CHD/CHDH SK8 110 D8
Nansen St OP/CLY M11 88 B4
SLFD M6 86 B2
STRET M32 86 B8
Nansmoss La WILM/AE SK9 126 B3
Nantwich Av WHIT OL12 28 C1
Nantwich Rd RUSH/FAL M14 98 D3
Nantwich Wk BOLS/LL BL3 * 36 B8
Napier Ct HULME M15 * 86 F6
Napier Gn ORD M5 86 E5
Napier Rd CCHDY M21 97 L4
ECC M30 84 F1
HTNM SK4 111 L1
Napier St BRAM/HZG SK7 121 M1
HYDE SK14 102 B3
ROY/SHW OL2 43 L4
SWIN M27 70 A5
Napier St East OLDS OL8 8 F8
Napier St West OLDS OL8 8 D9
Naples Rd EDGY/DAV SK3 111 L6
Naples St ANC M4 7 J1
Narbonne Av ECC M30 70 D8
Narborough Cl WGNE/HIN WN2 49 H8
Narbuth Dr CHH M8 72 C5
Narrowgate Brow
ROY/SHW OL2 43 G5
Narrow La MCFLDN SK10 129 L3
The Narrows ALT WA14 107 M8
Naseby Av BKLY M9 57 J8
Naseby Pl PWCH M25 55 M7
Naseby Rd RDSH SK5 100 B4
Naseby Wk WHTF M45 55 M4
Nash Rd TRPK M17 85 H4
Nash St HULME M15 87 H6
Nasmyth Av DTN/ASHW M34 90 D8
Nasmyth Rd ECC M30 84 F4
Nasmyth St CHH M8 72 F7
HOR/BR BL6 33 M1
Nately Rd OLDTF/WHR M16 * 97 K2
Nathan Dr CSLFD M3 6 C2
RNFD/HAY WA11 78 B6
Nathans Rd WYTH/NTH M22 109 M8
National Dr ORD M5 86 D4
Naunton Av LEIGH WN7 65 M7
Naunton Rd MDTN M24 57 L5
Naval St ANC M4 7 L3
Nave Ct SLFD M6 71 J8
Navenby Av OLDTF/WHR M16 86 F8
Navenby Rd WGNS/IIMK WN3 63 K2
Navigation Cl LEIGH WN7 66 B8
Navigation Rd ALT WA14 108 A5
Naylor Av GOL/RIS/CUL WA3 79 L4
Naylorfarm Av
WGNNW/ST WN6 30 C7
Naylor St ATH M46 66 F1
NEWH/MOS M40 88 A1
OLD OL1 9 H4
Nazeby Wk CHAD OL9 8 D9
Naze Ct OLD OL1 * 9 G2
Neal Av AUL OL6 91 G1
CHD/CHDH SK8 119 J4
Neale Av UPML OL3 61 M7
Neale Rd CCHDY M21 97 K5
Near Birches Pde OLDE OL4 60 B8
Nearbrook Rd WYTH/NTH M22 109 M8
Nearcroft Rd NTHM/RTH M23 109 L5
Near Hey Cl RAD M26 54 B1
Nearmaker Av
WYTH/NTH M22 109 M8
Nearmaker Rd
WYTH/NTH M22 109 M8
Neary Wy URM M41 84 F7
Neasden Gv BOLS/LL BL3 * 35 M7
Neath Av WYTH/NTH M22 110 A5
Neath Cl POY/DIS SK12 121 M7
WHTF M45 55 M5
Neath Fold BOLS/LL BL3 52 A1
Neath St CHAD OL9 8 F5
Nebo St BOLS/LL BL3 36 A8
Nebraska St BOL BL1 * 36 B3
Neden Cl OP/CLY M11 88 E4
Needham Av CCHDY M21 97 L4
Needwood Cl NEWH/MOS M40 73 G7
Needwood Rd MPL/ROM SK6 101 M7
Neenton Sq WGTN/LGST M12 88 D5
Neild Gdns LEIGH WN7 66 B8
Neild St CMANE M1 7 K7
OLDS OL8 59 H8
Neill St BRO M7 72 B8
Neilson Cl MDTN M24 57 M5
Nell Carrs RAMS BL0 19 H5
Nellie St HEY OL10 40 E2
Nell La CCHDY M21 98 B6
Nell St BOL BL1 22 C8
Nel Pan La LEIGH WN7 65 M4
Nelson Av ECC M30 85 G1
POY/DIS SK12 129 L1
Nelson Cl POY/DIS SK12 129 L1
Nelson Dr DROY M43 89 G2
IRL M44 94 B6
WGNE/HIN WN2 48 D4
Nelson Fold SWIN M27 70 D3
Nelson Rd BKLY M9 57 G7
Nelson Sq BOL BL1 2 F5
Nelson St ATH M46 66 E1
BOLS/LL BL3 3 G9
BOLS/LL BL3 * 53 L1
BRAM/HZG SK7 113 J8
BRO M7 72 A7
BRUN/LGST M13 87 L7
BURY BL9 4 F9
DTN/ASHW M34 90 C6
ECC M30 85 G2
FWTH BL4 53 H4
HEY OL10 41 G3
HOR/BR BL6 34 A1
HYDE SK14 102 B2
LIT OL15 21 M7
MDTN M24 57 M5
MILN OL16 10 F5
NEWH/MOS M40 73 G8
OLDE OL4 * 60 B7
ORD M5 86 B3
STRET M32 97 G3
TYLD M29 67 L4
WGNE/HIN WN2 49 G6
Nelson Wy CHAD OL9 * 58 D8
Nelstrop Crs HTNM SK4 100 A6
Nelstrop Rd HTNM SK4 99 M6
Nelstrop Rd North
BNG/LEV M19 100 A4
Nene Gv WGNE/HIN WN2 49 H8
Nepaul Rd BKLY M9 73 H3
Neptune Gdns BRO M7 71 M8
Nesbit St BOLE BL2 * 36 E1
Nesfield Rd NTHM/RTH M23 109 J2
Neston Av BOL BL1 22 C7
DID/WITH M20 98 D6
SALE M33 109 H2
Neston Cl ROY/SHW OL2 44 A5
Neston Gv EDGY/DAV SK3 112 A7
Neston Rd MILN OL16 28 F8
TOT/BURYW BL8 24 C8
Neston St OP/CLY M11 89 J5
Neston Wy WILM/AE SK9 127 H1
Netherbury Cl GTN M18 99 M1
Netherby Rd WGNNW/ST WN6 47 K1
Nethercote Av
NTHM/RTH M23 109 L6
Nethercroft ROCH OL11 27 H4
Nethercroft Rd
HALE/TIMP WA15 108 F7
Netherfield Cl OLDS OL8 58 F8
Netherfield Rd BOLS/LL BL3 52 B2
Netherfields LEIGH WN7 66 A5
WILM/AE SK9 130 D4
Netherhey La ROY/SHW OL2 58 F2
Nether Hey St OLDS OL8 59 L8
Netherhouse Rd ROY/SHW OL2 43 K5
Netherland St SALQ M50 86 C3
Netherlees OLDE OL4 60 A7
Nether St HYDE SK14 102 C4
WGTN/LGST M12 * 7 L7
Netherton Rd RUSH/FAL M14 98 D3
Nethervale Dr BKLY M9 73 H5
Netherwood FAIL M35 74 E4
Netherwood Rd
WYTH/NTH M22 109 M5
Netherwood Wy WHTN BL5 50 D2
Netley Av WHIT OL12 28 C1
Netley Gv OLDS OL8 * 59 M8
Netley Rd NTHM/RTH M23 109 K8
Nettlebarn Rd WYTH/NTH M22 109 M7
Nettleford Rd CCHDY M21 98 B4
Nettleton Gv BKLY M9 73 J3
Nevada St BOL BL1 * 36 B3
Nevendon Dr NTHM/RTH M23 109 J8
Nevern Cl BOL BL1 35 J4
Nevile Rd BRO M7 71 L4
Neville Cardus Wk
RUSH/FAL M14 98 F2
Neville Cl BOL BL1 2 D3
Neville Dr IRL M44 83 K8
Neville St BRAM/HZG SK7 121 M1
CHAD OL9 8 D4
WGNE/HIN WN2 64 D1
Nevill Rd BRAM/HZG SK7 121 G2
Nevin Av CHD/CHDH SK8 120 A3
Nevin Cl BRAM/HZG SK7 121 J5
Nevin Rd NEWH/MOS M40 74 A3
Nevis Gv BOL BL1 22 A7
Nevis St ROCH OL11 42 D2
Nevy Fold Av HOR/BR BL6 34 C1
New Allen St NEWH/MOS M40 87 M1
Newall Gv LEIGH WN7 66 C5
Newall Rd NTHM/RTH M23 118 B1
Newall St CHAD OL9 74 E2
LIT OL15 21 M6
Newark Av RAD M26 37 M7
RUSH/FAL M14 98 E1
Newark Park Wy ROY/SHW OL2 42 F6
Newark Rd RDSH SK5 100 C7
SWIN M27 70 E2
WGNE/HIN WN2 48 F8
WHIT OL12 28 C1
Newark Sq WHIT OL12 28 C1
Newark St WGNNW/ST WN6 14 A1
New Bailey St CSLFD M3 6 C4
Newbank Cha CHAD OL9 58 D4
Newbank Cl MDTN M24 57 L5
UPML OL3 61 J3
New Bank St TYLD M29 * 67 K4
WGTN/LGST M12 88 B7
New Barn Av AIMK WN4 78 F1
New Barn Cl ROY/SHW OL2 43 K5
New Barn La LEIGH WN7 81 H2
ROCH OL11 10 B9
New Barns Av CCHDY M21 97 M6
New Barn St BOL BL1 35 L3
MILN OL16 11 H9
ROY/SHW OL2 43 K5
New Barton St SLFD M6 70 F7
Newbeck Cl HOR/BR BL6 34 A3
Newbeck St ANC M4 * 7 H2
New Beech Rd HTNM SK4 111 H2
New Beech St HYDE SK14 102 A1
Newberry Gv EDGY/DAV SK3 112 A7
Newbold Hall Dr MILN OL16 11 L4
Newbold Moss MILN OL16 11 K4
Newbold St MILN OL16 11 M4
TOT/BURYW BL8 38 F2
Newboult Rd CHD/CHDH SK8 111 H6
Newbourne Cl BRAM/HZG SK7 121 M1
Newbreak Cl OLDE OL4 60 A4
Newbridge Cl AIMK WN4 78 A1
Newbridge Gdns BOLE BL2 23 H8
New Bridge Gdns BURY BL9 39 H7
Newbridge La STKP SK1 13 L4
New Bridge St CSLFD M3 6 F1
Newbridge Vw MOSL OL5 * 77 G4
New Briggs Fold EDGW/EG BL7 22 B2
New Broad La MILN OL16 42 F1
Newbrook Av CCHDY M21 110 A1
Newbrook Rd ATH M46 51 J6
New Brunswick St HOR/BR BL6 33 L1
New Buildings Pl MILN OL16 10 E3
Newburn Av BKLY M9 57 J8
Newburn Cl WGNS/IIMK WN3 47 H8
Newbury Av SALE M33 95 M8
Newbury Cl CHD/CHDH SK8 120 C6
Newbury Ct
HALE/TIMP WA15 * 108 C6
Newbury Dr ECC M30 84 E1
URM M41 84 F7
Newbury Gv HEY OL10 40 F4
Newbury Rd BOLS/LL BL3 53 J1
CHD/CHDH SK8 119 L5
Newbury Wk BOL BL1 * 2 C2
CHAD OL9 8 C4
Newby Cl BURY BL9 39 K5
Newby Dr ALT WA14 * 108 A6
CHD/CHDH SK8 110 D7
MDTN M24 57 J1
SALE M33 109 G1
Newby Rd BOLE BL2 37 H3
BRAM/HZG SK7 121 M2
HTNM SK4 12 C3
Newby Sq
WGNW/BIL/OR WN5 * 46 E7
Newcastle St HULME M15 6 F9
New Chapel La HOR/BR BL6 34 C2
Newchurch OLDS OL8 75 K4
New Church Ct WHTF M45 * 55 J5
Newchurch Pl ROCH OL11 * 41 M3
New Church Rd BOL BL1 35 J2
New Church St RAD M26 54 E1
Newchurch St OP/CLY M11 88 C4
ROCH OL11 41 M3
New City Rd WALK M28 68 D4
Newcliffe Rd BKLY M9 57 J8
New Coin St ROY/SHW OL2 59 G1
Newcombe Cl OP/CLY M11 88 C3
Newcombe Dr LHULT M38 52 C6
Newcombe Rd RAMS BL0 24 D3
Newcombe St CSLFD M3 * 87 J1
New Copper Moss
HALE/TIMP WA15 108 C8
New Court Dr
EDGW/EG BL7 22 B1
Newcroft FAIL M35 74 E6
Newcroft Crs URM M41 96 C3
Newcroft Dr BKLY M9 72 F3
EDGY/DAV SK3 112 A6
URM M41 96 C3
Newcroft Rd URM M41 96 C3
New Cross St ORD M5 85 M2
SWIN M27 70 D5
Newdale Rd WGTN/LGST M12 99 L2
New Drake Gn WHTN BL5 50 B7
Newearth Rd WALK M28 68 E4
New Earth St MOSL OL5 77 G2
OLDE OL4 59 M7
New Ellesmere Ap WALK M28 52 F8
New Elm Rd CSLFD M3 6 B7
Newenden Rd WGN WN1 31 L8
New Field Cl MILN OL16 11 L3
RAD M26 54 B1
Newfield Head La MILN OL16 29 M6
Newfield Vw MILN OL16 29 K6
New Forest Rd
NTHM/RTH M23 108 F4
Newgate MILN OL16 10 E4
Newgate Av WGNNW/ST WN6 30 B3
Newgate Cottages WHTN BL5 * 51 K3
Newgate Dr LHULT M38 52 C6
Newgate Rd SALE M33 107 L3
WILM/AE SK9 126 B5
New George St
TOT/BURYW BL8 38 F1
New Hall Av BRO M7 72 A4
CHD/CHDH SK8 119 K5
Newhall Av BOLE BL2 37 L6
ECC M30 84 D5
New Hall Cl SALE M33 97 J8
Newhall Dr NTHM/RTH M23 109 K2
New Hall La BOL BL1 35 K4
New Hall Ms BOL BL1 35 G3
New Hall Pl BOL BL1 35 K4
New Hall Rd BRO M7 72 A5
BURY BL9 26 B8
SALE M33 * 109 J1
Newhall Rd RDSH SK5 100 D2
Newham Av OP/CLY M11 88 E2
Newham Dr TOT/BURYW BL8 38 E4
Newhart Gv WALK M28 68 F2
Newhaven Av LEIGH WN7 66 C4
OP/CLY M11 89 J5
Newhaven Cl CHD/CHDH SK8 120 E2
TOT/BURYW BL8 24 F5
New Herbert St SLFD M6 70 F7
Newhey Av WYTH/NTH M22 110 A7
New Hey Rd CHD/CHDH SK8 111 H7
Newhey Rd MILN OL16 29 K8
WYTH/NTH M22 110 A8
New Heys Wy BOLE BL2 23 G6
New Holder St BOL BL1 2 C5
Newholme Gdns WALK M28 68 F1
Newholme Rd DID/WITH M20 98 B7
Newhouse Cl WHIT OL12 21 G6
Newhouse Crs ROCH OL11 27 H4
Newhouse Dr WGNS/IIMK WN3 63 G3
Newhouse Rd HEY OL10 41 G4
New Houses OLDE OL4 60 F4
Newington Av CHH M8 72 C1
Newington Ct ALT WA14 116 D1
Newington Dr BOL BL1 * 2 E1
TOT/BURYW BL8 38 D4
Newington Wk BOL BL1 * 2 D1
New Islington ANC M4 7 M3
New Kings Head Yd CSLFD M3 * 6 E2
Newland Av
WGNW/BIL/OR WN5 47 G7
Newland Dr WHTN BL5 51 J5
Newland Ms GOL/RIS/CUL WA3 81 H7
Newlands FAIL M35 74 B8
Newlands Av BOLE BL2 37 J3
BRAM/HZG SK7 121 G4
CHD/CHDH SK8 120 C5
ECC M30 84 C4
IRL M44 94 C1
TYLD M29 67 K6
WHIT OL12 28 C1
WHTF M45 * 55 H3
Newlands Cl CHD/CHDH SK8 120 C5
WHIT OL12 28 C1
Newlands Dr DID/WITH M20 110 F4
GLSP SK13 93 J8
GOL/RIS/CUL WA3 79 M4
HOR/BR BL6 33 H5
PWCH M25 55 K7
SWIN M27 70 F6
WILM/AE SK9 126 C7
Newlands Rd CHD/CHDH SK8 111 H6
LEIGH WN7 81 J1
NTHM/RTH M23 109 J4
Newland St CHH M8 72 E3
New La BOLE BL2 37 G3
ECC M30 84 E2
MDTN M24 57 K3
ROY/SHW OL2 43 G8
New Lane Ct BOLE BL2 37 H2
New Lawns RDSH SK5 100 D3
Newlea Cl BOL BL1 35 M2
New Lees St AUL OL6 75 A7
New Lester Cl TYLD M29 67 L3
New Lester Wy LHULT M38 52 B8
New Ldg WGN WN1 47 M2
Newlyn Av STLY SK15 92 A1
Newlyn Cl BRAM/HZG SK7 121 M3
Newlyn Dr AIMK WN4 78 E2
MPL/ROM SK6 113 K1
SALE M33 108 F3
Newlyn St RUSH/FAL M14 98 E2
Newman Av WGNNW/ST WN6 47 K2
Newman Cl WGNE/HIN WN2 48 F6
Newman St AUL OL6 90 D1
HYDE SK14 102 B1
MILN OL16 28 F1
WGN WN1 48 B2
New Market CMANW M2 6 F4
Newmarket Cl SALE M33 107 L2
Newmarket Gv AULW OL7 75 H7
New Market La CMANW M2 6 F4
Newmarket Rd AULW OL7 75 H7
BOLS/LL BL3 53 K2
New Market St WGN WN1 14 F3
New Meadow HOR/BR BL6 34 F5
New Miles La
WGNNW/ST WN6 30 C6
New Mills Rd GLSP SK13 103 M8
NM/HAY SK22 125 K2
New Mill St LIT OL15 21 L7
New Moor La
BRAM/HZG SK7 121 M1
New Moss Rd IRL M44 94 A6
New Mount St ANC M4 * 7 H1
Newnham St BOL BL1 36 C1
New Park Rd ORD M5 86 E5
Newpark Wk CHH M8 72 D6
Newport Av RDSH SK5 100 B5
Newport Rd BOLS/LL BL3 52 D1
CCHDY M21 97 K3
DTN/ASHW M34 101 L4

Newport St *BOL* BL1................................2 E6
FWTH BL4.......................................53 G5
MDTN M24.......................................57 M3
OLDS OL8..8 E8
RUSH/FAL M14...............................98 E1
SLFD M6..86 B2
TOT/BURYW BL8.............................24 D7
Newquay Av *BOLE* BL2......................38 A3
RDSH SK5..100 B5
Newquay Dr *DRAM/HZG* SK7....121 H5
New Quay St *CSLFD* M3......................6 C4
New Radcliffe St *OLD* L1.......................9 H5
New Raven Ct *BOLS/LL* BL3 *.........53 L1
New Ridd Ri *HYDE* SK14.............102 A4
New Riven Ct *BOLS/LL* BL3..............53 L1
New Rd *GLSP* SK13............................93 J5
LIT OL15...21 J8
OLDS OL8..59 H8
RAD M26...54 E2
WGNE/HIN WN2................................32 D6
New Royd Av *OLDE* OL4....................60 E3
Newry Rd *ECC* M30............................85 H4
Newry St *BOL* BL1.............................36 A1
Newsham Cl *BOLS/LL* BL3...................2 E4
Newsham Rd *EDGY/DAV* SK3.......112 B6
Newsham Wk
WGNNW/ST WN6 *..........................14 A1
WGTN/LGST M12 *..........................99 L1
Newshaw La *GLSP* SK13.................104 C1
Newsholme St *CHH* M8.....................72 C5
New Springs *BOL* BL1......................35 L1
Newstead *WHIT* OL12........................10 D3
DID/WITH M20....................................99 G7
Newstead Cl *POY/DIS* SK12..........121 H7
Newstead Dr *BOLS/LL* BL3..............51 K2
Newstead Gv *MPL/ROM* SK6........113 J1
Newstead Rd *URM* M41.....................96 B1
WGNS/IIMK WN3...............................63 H1
Newstead Ter
HALE/TIMP WA15...........................108 C5
New St *ALT* WA14............................107 H8
BOLS/LL BL3.......................................2 D6
DROY M43..89 K4
ECC M30...84 F3
HYDE SK14.......................................103 K4
LIT OL15...21 K8
MILN OL16..29 K7
NEWH/MOS M40..............................73 H8
NM/HAY SK22.................................124 E5
OLDE OL4..60 B6
RAD M26...54 E2
STLY SK15..91 K4
SWIN M27..70 D3
TOT/BURYW BL8...............................24 C6
UPML OL3..61 L4
WGNE/HIN WN2................................64 D3
WGNW/BIL/OR WN5.........................46 E7
WHIT OL12..28 D2
New Tempest Rd *HOR/BR* BL6........34 F8
New Ter *HYDE* SK14........................102 B3
New Thomas St *SLFD* M6 *..............71 K8
Newton Av *DID/WITH* M20................98 D6
WGTN/LGST M12................................88 C2
Newton Cl *WGN* WN1.........................48 A2
Newton Crs *MDTN* M24.....................57 C1
Newton Dr *TOT/BURYW* BL8...........24 D4
Newton Gdns
GOL/RIS/CUL WA3.............................80 C4
New Tong Fld *EDGW/EG* BL7..........22 C5
Newton Hall Rd *HYDE* SK14............90 F7
Newton La *GOL/RIS/CUL* WA3........79 J5
Newton Rd *ALT* WA14.....................108 B5
FAIL M35...74 B7
GOL/RIS/CUL WA3.............................80 B6
MDTN M24...56 C5
URM M41...95 M2
WGNW/BIL/OR WN5.........................46 E5
WILM/AE SK9...................................126 E5
Newton St *AUL* OL6 *........................90 F1
BOL BL1..36 B2
BURY BL9...25 J6
CMANE M1..7 J4
DROY M43...89 M1
EDGY/DAV SK3..................................13 G7
FAIL M35 *...91 G8
LEIGH WN7...65 J6
MILN OL16..11 J9
STLY SK15...91 J2
STRET M32..97 G3
Newton Ter *BOL* BL1 *.......................36 B2
Newton Wk *BOL* BL1.........................36 B2
Newton Wood Rd *DUK* SK16...........90 F6
Newtown Av *DTN/ASHW* M34.......101 J2
Newtown Cl *OP/CLY* M11.................88 E4
SWIN M27..70 C2
Newtown St *PWCH* M25...................55 M8
ROY/SHW OL2....................................43 L6
New Union St *ANC* M4........................7 L3
New Vernon St *BURY* BL9.................5 G1
New Viaduct St
NEWH/MOS M40..............................88 B2
Newville Dr *DID/WITH* M20...............98 D5
New Vine St *HULME* M15 *...............87 J6
New Wakefield St *CMANE* M1............6 F8
New Wy *WHIT* OL12..........................20 A3
New York *BOLS/LL* BL3.....................35 J8
New York St *HEY* OL10.....................40 E2
New Zealand Rd *STKP* SK1...........13 M3
Neyland Cl *BOL* BL1...........................35 J5
Ney St *AULW* OL7..............................75 J6
Niagara St *OFTN* SK2.....................112 D6
Nicholas Cft *ANC* M4..........................7 G3
Nicholas Owen Cl *OP/CLY* M11 *....88 F4
Nicholas Rd *OLDS* OL8.....................59 H8
Nicholas St *BOLE* BL2.........................3 H3
CMANW M2...7 G5
Nicholls St *SLFD* M6 *.......................86 E1
Nicholson Rd *HYDE* SK14................90 F7
Nicholson Sq *DUK* SK16 *................90 H4
Nicholson St *HTNM* SK4....................13 H2
OLDE OL4..60 B6
ROCH OL11...10 B8
Nichols St *SLFD* M6..........................86 E1
Nickleby Rd *POY/DIS* SK12...........129 J7
Nicolas St *CCHDY* M21......................97 K3
Nicol Mere Dr *AIMK* WN4.................63 H4
Nicol Rd *AIMK* WN4...........................63 H4
Nield Rd *DTN/ASHW* M34..............101 J1
Nield's Brow *ALT* WA14 *...............116 E2
Nield St *MOSL* OL5.............................76 E2
Nields Wy *MPL/ROM* SK6..............115 G3
Nigel Rd *BKLY* M9..............................73 J5
Nigher Moss Av *MILN* OL16.............11 M6
Nightingale Cl *WILM/AE* SK9.........126 F3
Nightingale Dr
DTN/ASHW M34..............................89 M2
Nightingale Gdns
NTHM/RTH M23...............................109 K3
Nightingale Rd
HOR/BR BL6..32 F1

Nile St *AULW* OL7...............................90 C4
BOLS/LL BL3..2 E8
MILN OL16...11 H3
OLD OL1...9 H3
Nile Ter *BRO* M7................................72 A7
Nimble Nook *CHAD* OL9.....................58 D7
Nina Dr *NEWH/MOS* M40.................73 M1
Nine Acre Dr *ORD* M5........................86 E5
Ninehouse La *BOLS/LL* BL3.............36 B8
Ninfield Rd *NTHM/RTH* M23.........109 L8
Ninth Av *OLDS* OL8............................75 C3
Nipper La *WHTF* M45.........................55 H3
Nisbet Av *WYTH/NTH* M22............119 C1
Niven St *WGTN/LGST* M12................7 L8
Nixon Rd *BOLS/LL* BL3......................51 M1
Nixon Rd South *BOLS/LL* BL3........51 M1
Nixon St *EDGY/DAV* SK3.................13 H7
FAIL M35...74 B5
ROCH OL11...41 L1
No 11 Pas *DID/WITH* M20 *..............98 C7
Noble Meadow *WHIT* OL12 *............21 H8
Noble St *BOLS/LL* BL3........................2 C8
LEIGH WN7...66 D7
OLDS OL8...59 J8
Noel Dr *SALE* M33............................97 G8
Noel St *BOL* BL1..................................2 D4
Nolan St *BKLY* M9..............................73 H5
Nona St *SLFD* M6..............................86 B2
Nook Farm Av *WHIT* OL12...............28 C1
Nook Flds *BOLE* BL2.........................37 H2
Nook La *AUL* OL6...............................76 A6
GOL/RIS/CUL WA3.............................79 L4
TYLD M29..83 G2
The Nook *ECC* M30...........................84 D1
URM M41...96 A3
WALK M28..69 J4
WGNNW/ST WN6...............................30 B5
Noon Sun Cl *UPML* OL3....................61 K8
Noon Sun St *WHIT* OL12..................28 C3
Norbet Wk *BKLY* M9 *.......................73 H5
Norbreck Av *CCHDY* M21.................97 L5
CHD/CHDH SK8...............................111 K6
Norbreck Crs *WGNNW/ST* WN6....47 K3
Norbreck Gdns *BOLS/LL* BL3............3 L3
Norbreck St *BOLE* BL2........................3 L3
Norburn Rd *BRUN/LGST* M13........99 J2
Norbury Av *MPL/ROM* SK6............114 B6
OLDE OL4...60 F6
SALE M33...96 C8
SLFD M6..71 C7
WGNW/BIL/OR WN5.........................62 A6
Norbury Cl *NEWH/MOS* M40 *.......73 C8
Norbury Crs *BRAM/HZG* SK7........121 M2
Norbury Dr *MPL/ROM* SK6............114 C6
Norbury Gv *BOL* BL1.........................22 C8
BRAM/HZG SK7.................................121 M2
SWIN M27..70 C3
Norbury Hollow Rd
BRAM/HZG SK7.................................122 D4
Norbury La *OLDS* OL8.......................76 A1
Norbury Ms *MPL/ROM* SK6...........114 B6
Norbury St *BRO* M7...........................72 B6
LEIGH WN7...66 A7
MILN OL16 *.......................................28 E8
STKP SK1..13 J5
Norcot Wk *HULME* M15 *.................87 G6
Norcross Cl *OFTN* SK2....................113 C7
Nordale Pk *WHIT* OL12.....................27 G2
Nordek Cl *ROY/SHW* OL2.................43 G7
Nordek Dr *ROY/SHW* OL2................42 F7
Norden Av *DID/WITH* M20................98 D6
Norden Cl *ROCH* OL11.......................26 F7
Norden Ct *BOLS/LL* BL3....................36 B8
Norden Rd *ROCH* OL11.....................27 C7
Nordens Dr *CHAD* OL9......................58 C3
Nordens St *CHAD* OL9......................58 C4
Norden Wy *ROCH* OL11.....................26 F7
Norden Av *PWCH* M25.......................55 M1
Norfield Cl *DUK* SK16........................90 F4
Norfolk Av *DROY* M43........................89 J1
DTN/ASHW M34..............................100 D1
GTN M18..88 F2
HEY OL10...40 C2
HTNM SK4...99 M6
WHTF M45...55 K4
Norfolk Cl *BOLS/LL* BL3....................37 L8
ROY/SHW OL2....................................43 J5
WGNE/HIN WN2................................49 K6
Norfolk Crs *FAIL* M35........................74 B6
Norfolk Dr *FWTH* BL4........................53 C3
Norfolk Gdns *URM* M41....................95 C1
Norfolk Rd *ATH* M46...........................50 F7
GTN M18..88 F8
WGNW/BIL/OR WN5.........................62 B3
Norfolk St *CHAD* OL9.........................58 F8
CMANW M2...6 F4
GLSP SK13...105 C3
HYDE SK14...102 A2
ROCH OL11...10 D6
SLFD M6..71 K7
WALK M28..53 C6
WGNNW/ST WN6...............................47 K2
WGNW/BIL/OR WN5.........................14 A7
Norfolk Wy *ROY/SHW* OL2..............59 C2
Norford Wy *ROCH* OL11....................27 H5
Norgate Dr *DID/WITH* M20.............110 L1
Norlan Av *DTN/ASHW* M34..............90 B3
Norleigh Rd
WYTH/NTH M22...............................110 A4
Norley Av *STRET* M32........................97 J1
Norley Cl *OLD* OL1..............................58 E2
Norley Dr *BNG/LEV* M19..................99 M2
Norley Hall Av
WGNW/BIL/OR WN5.........................46 F6
Norley Rd *LEIGH* WN7......................65 L3
WGNW/BIL/OR WN5.........................46 E5
Norman Av *BRAM/HZG* SK7..........121 L1
RNFD/HAY WA11...............................78 D5
Normanby Cl *WGN* WA14................107 L8
Normanby Gv *SWIN* M27..................70 B3
Normanby Rd *WALK* M28..................68 F3
Normanby St *BOLS/LL* BL3..............51 L2
RUSH/FAL M14.................................87 K8
SWIN M27..70 B3
WGNW/BIL/OR WN5.........................46 E6
Norman Cl *MDTN* M24 *....................57 M1
Normandale Av *BOL* BL1...................35 K3
Normandy Crs *RAD* M26....................54 F1
Norman Gv *RDSH* SK5....................100 B5
WGTN/LGST M12 *...........................88 C2
Norman Rd *ALT* WA14.....................107 M6
AUL OL6...75 M6
BRO M7..72 B5
HTNM SK4...111 J1
ROCH OL11...10 D7
RUSH/FAL M14.................................99 C2
SALE M33...96 E8
STLY SK15...91 J2
Norman Rd West *BKLY* M9 *...........73 J5
Norman's Pl *ALT* WA14...................108 A8

Norman St *BURY* BL9..........................5 K1
FAIL M35...74 D3
HYDE SK14.......................................102 B2
MDTN M24...57 J3
OLD OL1...8 F3
WGTN/LGST M12...............................88 F2
Normanton Av *SLFD* M6..................85 M1
Normanton Cl
WGNNW/ST WN6..............................31 H8
Normanton Dr *BKLY* M9....................57 H8
Normanton Rd *EDGY/DAV* SK3.....111 K5
Norman Weall Ct *MDTN* M24 *.......57 K2
Normington St *OLDE* OL4.................59 L5
Norreys Av *URM* M41.........................95 H1
Norreys St *MILN* OL16.......................11 G3
Norris Av *HTNM* SK4..........................12 C3
Norris Bank Ter *HTNM* SK4.............12 C3
Norris Hill Dr *HTNM* SK4...................12 C2
Norris Rd *SALE* M33........................108 F2
Norris St *BOLS/LL* BL3........................2 C8
BOLS/LL BL3.......................................53 L1
FWTH BL4...52 F5
TYLD M29..67 K4
Northallerton Rd *BRO* M7..................71 L6
Northam Cl *WGNNW/ST* WN6........31 G3
Northampton Rd
NEWH/MOS M40..............................73 H6
North Av *BNG/LEV* M19....................99 J5
BURY BL9...39 L8
FWTH BL4...52 D4
STLY SK15...91 K1
TOT/BURYW BL8...............................24 C2
UPML OL3..61 M7
URM M41...85 H5
North Back Rock *BURY* BL9...............4 F4
Northbank Gdns *BNG/LEV* M19.....99 H6
North Blackfield La *BRO* M7............71 M4
Northbourne St *SLFD* M6.................86 B2
Northbrook Av *CHH* M8.....................56 C8
North Brook Rd *GLSP* SK13.............93 H8
North Cir *WHTF* M45..........................55 J5
North Clifden La *BRO* M7.................72 B6
Northcliffe Rd *OFTN* SK2...............112 F4
North Cl *GLSP* SK13..........................93 J5
Northcombe Rd
EDGY/DAV SK3.................................112 B7
Northcote Av *WYTH/NTH* M22......118 F1
Northcote Rd *BRAM/HZG* SK7......121 H1
North Crs *NEWH/MOS* M40.............74 A1
OP/CLY M11..89 C1
North Cft *OLDS* OL8..........................75 L1
Northdale Rd *BKLY* M9......................56 C7
North Dean St *SWIN* M27..................70 D3
Northdene Dr *ROCH* OL11................27 J6
Northdown Av *HULME* M15..............87 G6
NM/HAY SK22...................................101 M7
North Downs Rd
CHD/CHDH SK8...............................120 C6
Northdowns Rd *ROY/SHW* OL2......43 J4
North Dr *DTN/ASHW* M34.................89 M3
SWIN M27..70 E5
North Edge *LEIGH* WN7....................66 E6
Northenden Rd
CHD/CHDH SK8...............................110 D7
SALE M33...96 F8
Northend Rd *STLY* SK15...................91 M1
Northen Gv *DID/WITH* M20...............98 C3
Northern Av *SWIN* M27......................70 F1
Northern Gv *BOL* BL1........................35 M3
Northern Service Rd
NTHM/RTH M23 *............................109 J7
Northfield Av *NEWH/MOS* M40.......74 C2
Northfield Dr *WILM/AE* SK9...........127 H4
Northfield Rd *BURY* BL9....................25 J6
NEWH/MOS M40..............................74 C2
Northfield St *BOLS/LL* BL3...............35 M7
Northfleet Rd *ECC* M30.....................84 C4
North Florida Rd
RNFD/HAY WA11...............................78 A4
North Ga *OLDS* OL8...........................75 H1
Northgate *WHIT* OL12.......................20 A5
Northgate La *OLD* OL1.......................44 B8
Northgate Rd *EDGY/DAV* SK3.........12 C6
North George St *CSLFD* M3................6 A2
North Gv *BRUN/LGST* M13..............88 A7
URM M41...95 M3
WALK M28..68 F1
North Hill Rd *CSLFD* M3.....................6 B1
Northland Rd *BKLY* M9......................73 K1
BOL BL1..22 C6
Northlands *RAD* M26..........................38 B7
North La *TYLD* M29............................67 K6
WHIT OL12...10 F2
Northleach Cl *TOT/BURYW* BL8.....38 D7
Northleigh Dr *PWCH* M25 *.............72 A1
Northleigh Rd *OLDTF/WHR* M16.....97 L1
North Lonsdale St *STRET* M32 *.....97 H1
North M *CCHDY* M21.........................97 K3
North Nook *OLDE* OL4 *....................60 F6
Northolme Gdns *BNG/LEV* M19.....99 H8
Northolt Av *LEIGH* WN7....................66 C4
Northolt Ct *OP/CLY* M11 *................89 C2
Northolt Dr *BOLS/LL* BL3.................36 C8
Northolt Fold *HEY* OL10....................41 H5
North Pde *CSLFD* M3...........................6 C4
MILN OL16...29 M8
SALE M33...109 C2
North Park Rd *BRAM/HZG* SK7....121 C2
North Phoebe St *ORD* M5................86 E4
North Pl *STKP* SK1.............................13 J4
Northridge Rd *BKLY* M9....................57 C6
North Ri *UPML* OL3............................61 L7
North Rd *ATH* M46.............................50 A7
DTN/ASHW M34................................90 A3
GLSP SK13..104 F1
HALE/TIMP WA15.............................117 J4
MANAIR M90.....................................118 C6
NM/HAY SK22...................................125 H1
OP/CLY M11..88 F2
PART M31..95 J3
PWCH M25..55 J7
STRET M32..85 J3
Northside Av *URM* M41......................95 J3
North Star Dr *CSLFD* M3.....................6 A4
Northstead Av
DTN/ASHW M34..............................101 J2
North St *AIMK* WN4............................64 A7
ATH M46...67 H1
AUL OL6...90 D2
CHH M8..72 D6
HEY OL10...40 E2
LEIGH WN7...66 C1
MILN OL16...11 G2
RAD M26...38 F8
RAMS BL0..18 F2
RNFD/HAY WA11...............................78 B6
ROY/SHW OL2....................................59 C1
WHIT OL12...10 C4
Northumberland Av *AULW* OL7.....75 L8

Northumberland Cl
OLDTF/WHR M16..............................86 F7
Northumberland Crs
OLDTF/WHR M16 *...........................86 F7
Northumberland Rd
OLDTF/WHR M16..............................86 F8
PART M31..106 B2
RDSH SK5..100 E6
Northumberland St *BRO* M7.............72 A5
WGN WN1..15 L1
Northumberland Wy
WYTH/NTH M22...............................110 B6
Northurst Dr *CHH* M8........................72 C1
North Vale Rd
HALE/TIMP WA15.............................108 C6
North Veiw *WHTF* M45.......................55 H2
North View Cl *OLDE* OL4...................60 C4
Northward Rd *WILM/AE* SK9.........126 D6
North Wy *BOL* BL1.............................35 J1
North Wy *HYDE* SK14.....................102 F6
RDSH SK5..100 F6
Northway *WGN* WN1.........................14 F2
Northways *WGNNW/ST* WN6.........31 G2
Northwell St *LEIGH* WN7..................66 B4
North Western St
BNG/LEV M19....................................99 K4
CMANE M1...7 L6
Northwold Cl *WGNS/IIMK* WN3......62 F1
BOL BL1..35 H4
Northwood *BOLE* BL2........................23 C8
Northwood Av *NEWLW* WA12.........79 J8
Northwood Crs *BOLS/LL* BL3 *.......35 M7
Northwood Gv *SALE* M33................96 E8
Norton Av *DTN/ASHW* M34............100 D1
SALE M33...96 A7
URM M41...85 M2
WGTN/LGST M12...............................99 L1
Norton Gra *PWCH* M25.....................72 A1
Norton Gv *HTNM* SK4........................12 B4
Norton Rd *WALK* M28.........................68 B5
WHIT OL12...28 C1
Norton St *BOL* BL1.............................36 C1
BRO M7..72 B5
CMANE M1 *..7 M5
CSLFD M3..6 E2
NEWH/MOS M40..............................73 H8
Norview Dr *DID/WITH* M20.............110 E5
Norville Av *NEWH/MOS* M40...........74 A1
Norway Gv *RDSH* SK5.....................100 A1
Norway St *BOL* BL1 *..........................36 A2
SLFD M6..86 B2
STRET M32..97 H1
Norweb Wy *LEIGH* WN7...................81 L1
Norwell Rd *WYTH/NTH* M22..........110 B7
Norwich Av *AIMK* WN4......................79 C4
CHAD OL9..58 D3
DTN/ASHW M34................................101 J3
GOL/RIS/CUL WA3.............................80 A4
ROCH OL11...27 K5
Norwich Cl *AUL* OL6...........................76 A4
DUK SK16..91 K5
Norwich Dr *TOT/BURYW* BL8..........8 J2
Norwich Rd *STRET* M32...................96 C1
Norwick St *ROCH* OL11....................11 C8
Norwick Cl *BOLS/LL* BL3..................35 H8
Norwood *PWCH* M25.........................71 L2
Norwood Av *AIMK* WN4....................63 J6
BRAM/HZG SK7.................................120 F7
BRO M7..71 L4
CHD/CHDH SK8...............................120 C1
DID/WITH M20....................................99 G8
GOL/RIS/CUL WA3.............................80 B5
MPL/ROM SK6...................................122 F5
TYLD M29..67 K6
WGNNW/ST WN6...............................47 K6
Norwood Cl *ROY/SHW* OL2.............59 H2
WALK M28..68 F1
Norwood Crs *ROY/SHW* OL2..........59 H2
Norwood Dr *HALE/TIMP* WA15.....109 C7
SWIN M27..70 A5
Norwood Gv *BOL* BL1 *.....................70 A5
Norwood Rd *CHD/CHDH* SK8........110 E6
OFTN SK2..112 E8
STRET M32..97 H3
Nostell Rd *AIMK* WN4........................63 K7
Nottingham Av *RDSH* SK5.............100 C3
Nottingham Cl *RDSH* SK5..............100 C3
Nottingham Dr *AUL* OL6...................75 L5
BOL BL1..2 C1
FAIL M35...74 D7
RDSH SK5..100 F6
Nottingham Pl *WGN* WN1.................15 L1
Nottingham Dr *MDTN* M24 *...........57 K1
Nudger Cl *UPML* OL3........................61 J2
Nudger Gn *UPML* OL3.......................61 K2
Nuffield Cl *BOL* BL1...........................35 J4
Nuffield Rd *WYTH/NTH* M22..........110 B6
Nugent Rd *BOLS/LL* BL3..................52 B1
Nugget St *OLDE* OL4 *.......................9 L8
Nuneaton Dr
NEWH/MOS M40..............................88 A1
Nuneham Av
DID/WITH M20....................................98 F5
Nunfield Cl *NEWH/MOS* M40...........73 L2
Nunnery Rd *BOLS/LL* BL3................35 L8
Nunthorpe Dr *CHH* M8......................72 F4
Nursery Av
HALE/TIMP WA15.............................117 G4
Nursery Cl *GLSP* SK13.....................104 F4
OFTN SK2..113 C5
SALE M33...97 C8
Nursery Dr *POY/DIS* SK12.............121 M8
Nursery Gdns *MILN* OL16.................11 M3
Nursery Gv *PART* M31.....................106 A8
Nursery La *EDGY/DAV* SK3..........111 K5
MCFLDN SK10...................................130 A7
WILM/AE SK9...................................126 D6
Nursery Rd *CHD/CHDH* SK8..........120 B3
FAIL M35...74 D6
HTNM SK4...55 K6
PWCH M25..55 J7
URM M41...95 J3
Nursery St *OLDTF/WHR* M16..........98 C1
SLFD M6..86 B1
Nuthatch Av *WALK* M28...................69 C4
Nuthurst Rd
NEWH/MOS M40..............................73 M3
Nutsford V *WGTN/LGST* M12..........88 C8
Nut St *BOL* BL1 *...............................36 A2
Nuttall Av *BOLS/LL* BL3...................53 H1
HOR/BR BL6..33 K1
RAD M26...38 F8
RAMS BL0..18 F7
Nuttall Cl *RAMS* BL0.........................18 F7
Nuttall Hall Rd
RAMS BL0..19 G8
Nuttall La *RAMS* BL0.........................18 F7
Nuttall Ms *WHTF* M45 *....................55 J4
Nuttall Rd *RAMS* BL0........................18 F7
Nuttall Sq *BURY* BL9.........................39 J7

Nuttall St *ATH* M46.............................67 H1
BURY BL9...5 H6
IRL M44..94 B6
MILN OL16...11 C5
OLDS OL8...59 L8
OLDTF/WHR M16..............................86 F7
OP/CLY M11..88 D5
Nutt La *PWCH* M25...........................56 B4
Nutt St *WGN* WN1..............................15 K1

O

Oadby Cl *WGTN/LGST* M12..............88 D8
Oadby Pl *RDSH* SK5.........................100 C1
Oak Av *BOLS/LL* BL3..........................53 L1
CCHDY M21...97 J6
CHD/CHDH SK8................................120 B2
GOL/RIS/CUL WA3.............................79 L4
HTNM SK4...12 A2
IRL M44..94 A7
MDTN M24...57 K5
MPL/ROM SK6...................................113 M2
POY/DIS SK12...................................124 C6
RAMS BL0..24 D2
RNFD/HAY WA11...............................78 B5
ROY/SHW OL2....................................43 C6
WGNE/HIN WN2................................64 F5
WGNE/HIN WN2................................65 K1
WGNNW/ST WN6...............................31 J4
WHTF M45...55 J5
WILM/AE SK9...................................126 D5
Oak Bank *BKLY* M9............................73 C4
PWCH M25..71 J3
Oakbank *WGNE/HIN* WN2................64 L1
Oak Bank Av *BKLY* M9......................73 J3
Oakbank Av *CHAD* OL9.....................58 B4
Oak Bank Cl *WHTF* M45....................55 L4
Oakbank Dr *BOL* BL1..........................22 A6
Oakbarton *HOR/BR* BL6.....................34 F8
Oakcliffe Rd *NTHM/RTH* M23........109 K5
WHIT OL12...21 C8
Oak Cl *HYDE* SK14.............................92 D8
WILM/AE SK9...................................126 D6
Oak Coppice *BOL* BL1........................35 K5
Oakcroft *STLY* SK15...........................92 B5
Oakcroft Wy *WYTH/NTH* M22........110 B6
Oakdale *BOLE* BL2.............................23 C8
Oakdale Cl *WHTF* M45.......................55 G4
Oakdale Cl *UPML* OL3.......................61 H1
Oakdale Dr *CHD/CHDH* SK8...........119 G2
DID/WITH M20....................................110 F3
TYLD M29..67 M6
Oak Dene *UPML* OL3.........................61 K8
Oakdene *WALK* M28..........................69 L6
Oakdene Av *CHD/CHDH* SK8..........119 K5
HTNM SK4...100 A7
Oakdene Crs *MPL/ROM* SK6..........114 C5
Oakdene Gdns *MPL/ROM* SK6.......114 C5
Oakdene Rd *HALE/TIMP* WA15.....108 A4
MDTN M24...57 M4
MPL/ROM SK6...................................114 C5
Oakdene St *BKLY* M9.........................73 J4
Oak Dr *BRAM/HZG* SK7..................120 E5
DTN/ASHW M34..............................89 K8
MPL/ROM SK6...................................114 A6
RUSH/FAL M14.................................99 C3
Oaken Bank Rd *HEY* OL10................41 J6
Oakenbottom Rd *BOLE* BL2.............37 C6
Oaken Clough *AULW* OL7.................75 J6
Oaken Clough Cl *WILM/AE* SK9....127 H2
Oaken Clough Dr *BOL* BL1................35 J2
Oakenclough Dr *BOL* BL1..................35 J2
Oakenden Cl *AIMK* WN4....................63 K6
Oakengates *WGNNW/ST* WN6........31 J3
Oakenrod Hl *ROCH* OL11..................27 M5
Oakenshaw Av *WHIT* OL12...............20 A6
Oakenshaw Vw *WHIT* OL12.............20 A6
Oaker Av *DID/WITH* M20...................98 B3
The Oakes *GLSP* SK13....................104 D5
Oakfield *DUK* SK16.............................91 H6
PWCH M25..72 A1
SALE M33...96 D7
Oakfield Av *ATH* M46.........................50 F8
CHD/CHDH SK8...............................111 H6
DROY M43...89 J3
GOL/RIS/CUL WA3.............................79 J3
OLDTF/WHR M16..............................97 K1
OLDTF/WHR M16..............................98 A1
STLY SK15...77 H6
Oakfield Cl *BRAM/HZG* SK7..........121 C8
HOR/BR BL6..34 C2
WILM/AE SK9...................................130 C1
Oakfield Crs *WGNE/HIN* WN2.........32 F7
Oakfield Dr *LHULT* M38....................52 B7
Oakfield Gv *FWTH* BL4......................52 F6
GTN M18..89 C8
Oakfield Rd *DID/WITH* M20.............110 D1
EDGY/DAV SK3..................................112 C7
GLSP SK13...108 B1
HALE/TIMP WA15.............................108 A4
HYDE SK14...91 H7
POY/DIS SK12...................................122 B8
WILM/AE SK9...................................130 C2
Oakfield St *CHH* M8............................72 C6
HALE/TIMP WA15.............................108 A4
Oakfield Ter *ROCH* OL11..................27 M4
Oakfold Av *AUL* OL6...........................76 A6
Oakford Wk *BOLS/LL* BL3.................35 M8
Oak Gates *EDGW/EG* BL7.................22 B3
Oak Gv *AUL* OL6................................76 A6
CHD/CHDH SK8...............................111 H7
POY/DIS SK12...................................121 M8
URM M41...96 B2
Oakham Av *DID/WITH* M20...............98 D4
Oakham Cl *TOT/BURYW* BL8..........25 H7
Oakham Ms *BRO* M7.........................71 M3
Oakham Rd *DTN/ASHW* M34 *......101 K3
Oakhead *LEIGH* WN7........................81 M1
Oak Hl *LIT* OL15..................................21 K7
Oakhill Cl *BOLE* BL2...........................37 K5
Oak Hill Cl *WGN* WN1 *.....................47 L1
Oakhill Wy *CHH* M8............................72 C5
Oakhouse Dr *CCHDY* M21................97 L5
Oakhurst Cha *WILM/AE* SK9.........130 C2
Oakhurst Dr *EDGY/DAV* SK3..........111 L7
Oakhurst Gdns *PWCH* M25..............55 K8
Oakhurst V *WHTN* BL5......................49 M5

Oaklands Dr BRAM/HZG SK7 122 A3
HYDE SK14 102 D2
PWCH M25 55 L7
SALE M33 96 D7
Oaklands Pk OLDE OL4 61 H7
Oaklands Rd BRO M7 71 K5
GOL/RIS/CUL WA3 80 C5
RAMS BL0 19 G2
ROY/SHW OL2 59 H2
SWIN M27 70 A6
UPML OL3 61 J7
Oak La WHTF M45 55 L4
WILM/AE SK9 126 D6
Oaklea WGNNW/ST WN6 30 D2
Oak Lea Av WILM/AE SK9 126 E7
Oaklea Rd SALE M33 96 B6
Oakleigh Av BNG/LEV M19 99 J5
BOLS/LL BL3 52 D2
HALE/TIMP WA15 108 D5
Oakleigh Cl HEY OL10 41 H5
Oakleigh Rd CHD/CHDH SK8 120 A4
Oakley Av WGNW/BIL/OR WN5 62 A6
Oakley Cl NEWH/MOS M40 73 M7
RAD M26 54 D4
Oakley Dr OLD OL1 44 A8
WGNW/BIL/OR WN5 47 H6
Oakley Pk BOL BL1 35 J5
Oakley St ORD M5 86 A3
Oakley Vls HTNM SK4 12 B1
The Oaklings WGNE/HIN WN2 65 K1
Oak Ldg BRAM/HZG SK7 * 121 H5
Oakmere Av ECC M30 69 M8
Oakmere Cl WYTH/NTH M22 110 A8
Oakmere Rd CHD/CHDH SK8 111 J8
WILM/AE SK9 119 M7
Oak Ms WILM/AE SK9 127 G3
Oakmoor Dr BRO M7 71 K4
Oakmoor Rd NTHM/RTH M23 109 K6
Oak Mt DID/WITH M20 * 110 E2
Oak Rd BRO M7 71 M6
CHD/CHDH SK8 111 H6
DID/WITH M20 98 E7
FAIL M35 74 C6
HALE/TIMP WA15 117 G1
MCFLDN SK10 131 L3
OLDS OL8 74 F2
PART M31 106 A2
SALE M33 97 G8
Oaks Av BOLE BL2 22 F8
NM/HAY SK22 125 M2
Oak Shaw Cl BKLY M9 73 G2
Oakshaw Dr WHIT OL12 27 K3
Oaks La BOLE BL2 22 E7
The Oaks CHD/CHDH SK8 119 J2
HYDE SK14 102 D1
Oak St ANC M4 7 J3
ATH M46 66 D3
BRAM/HZG SK7 121 M1
DTN/ASHW M34 90 C6
ECC M30 85 G3
EDGY/DAV SK3 12 B7
GLSP SK13 104 F3
HEY OL10 40 E1
HYDE SK14 91 H8
LEIGH WN7 81 J1
MDTN M24 * 58 A5
MILN OL16 10 E5
MILN OL16 43 K1
RAMS BL0 * 18 E7
ROY/SHW OL2 43 M5
SWIN M27 70 D3
TYLD M29 67 K3
WGN WN1 15 K4
Oak Tree Cl ATH M46 66 D3
OFTN SK2 113 G4
Oak Tree Ct CHD/CHDH SK8 111 H7
Oak Tree Crs STLY SK15 91 L4
Oak Tree Dr DUK SK16 91 J5
Oak Vw OLD OL1 8 E1
Oak View Rd UPML OL3 61 L7
Oakville Dr SLFD M6 70 D8
Oakville Ter NEWH/MOS M40 73 J3
Oakway DID/WITH M20 110 F4
MDTN M24 41 J8
Oakwell Dr BRO M7 72 B3
BURY BL9 55 L1
Oakwell Man BRO M7 72 B3
Oakwood CHAD OL9 58 B5
GLSP SK13 104 C4
SALE M33 95 M8
Oakwood Av AIMK WN4 78 D2
CHD/CHDH SK8 110 E7
DTN/ASHW M34 90 B5
NEWH/MOS M40 74 A3
SWIN M27 54 B8
WALK M28 69 J2
WGNNW/ST WN6 30 C7
WILM/AE SK9 126 C6
Oakwood Cl TOT/BURYW BL8 38 E1
Oakwood Ct ALT WA14 116 D4
Oakwood Dr BOL BL1 35 J4
LEIGH WN7 81 H3
SLFD M6 70 E7
WALK M28 69 J2
Oakwood La ALT WA14 116 C3
Oakwood Rd MPL/ROM SK6 113 M2
POY/DIS SK12 * 123 M6
Oakworth Cft OLDE OL4 44 C8
Oakworth Dr BOL BL1 22 A7
Oakworth St BKLY M9 72 F1
Oatlands WILM/AE SK9 130 E4
Oatlands Rd WYTH/NTH M22 118 E2
Oat St STKP SK1 13 L8
Oban Av NEWH/MOS M40 73 L8
OLD OL1 59 L3
Oban Crs EDGY/DAV SK3 112 A8
Oban Dr AIMK WN4 62 F8
SALE M33 109 H1
Oban Gv BOL BL1 22 B7
Oban St BOL BL1 * 36 A1
Oban Wy WGNE/HIN WN2 * 33 G7
Oberlin St OLDE OL4 60 A5
ROCH OL11 10 B9
Occlestone Cl SALE M33 109 H3
Occupiers La BRAM/HZG SK7 * 122 D3
Ocean St ALT WA14 107 L6
Ockendon Dr BKLY M9 73 H5
Octagon Ct BOL BL1 * 2 E5
Octavia Dr NEWH/MOS M40 73 M8
Odell St OP/CLY M11 * 88 E5
Odessa Av SLFD M6 70 E8
Odette St GTN M18 88 F8
Offerton Dr OFTN SK2 113 G5
Offerton Fold OFTN SK2 112 F5
Offerton Gn OFTN SK2 113 K6
Offerton La OFTN SK2 112 F4
Offerton Rd BRAM/HZG SK7 122 C1
OFTN SK2 113 K8
Offerton St HOR/BR BL6 33 K1
STKP SK1 112 E2
Off Grove Rd STLY SK15 77 G8
Off Ridge Hill La STLY SK15 * 91 J2
Off Stamford St STLY SK15 * 77 G8
Ogbourne Wk BRUN/LGST M13 87 M6
Ogden Cl HEY OL10 40 D2
WHTF M45 55 K3
Ogden Gv CHD/CHDH SK8 * 110 C8
Ogden La OP/CLY M11 89 G5
Ogden Rd BRAM/HZG SK7 120 F7
FAIL M35 74 B6
Ogden Sq DUK SK16 90 E4
Ogden St CHAD OL9 8 B3
DID/WITH M20 110 E1
HYDE SK14 103 L4
MDTN M24 57 K4
OLDE OL4 * 60 A6
PWCH M25 55 M8
ROCH OL11 41 M2
SWIN M27 70 C5
Ogwen Dr PWCH M25 55 L7
Ohio Av SALQ M50 86 C4
Okehampton Cl RAD M26 37 M7
Okehampton Crs SALE M33 96 A7
Okell Gv LEIGH WN7 66 A7
Okeover Rd BRO M7 72 A4
Olaf St BOLE BL2 3 J1
Olanyian Dr CHH M8 72 B7
Old Bank Cl MPL/ROM SK6 113 K1
Old Bank St CMANW M2 6 F4
Old Bank Vw OLD OL1 43 M8
Old Barn Pl EDGW/EG BL7 22 D4
Old Barton Rd ECC M30 84 F5
Old Beechfield Gdns
WGNNW/ST WN6 31 G3
Old Bent La WHIT OL12 20 E5
Old Birley St HULME M15 87 J7
Old Boston RNFD/HAY WA11 78 D5
Oldbridge Dr WGNE/HIN WN2 49 G6
Old Broadway DID/WITH M20 98 F7
Old Brook Cl ROY/SHW OL2 44 A4
Oldbrook Fold
HALE/TIMP WA15 108 E8
Old Brow MOSL OL5 76 F4
Old Brow La MILN OL16 28 F1
Old Brown Ct MOSL OL5 76 F4
Oldbury Cl HEY OL10 41 G5
NEWH/MOS M40 88 A1
Oldcastle Av DID/WITH M20 98 D5
Old Chapel St EDGY/DAV SK3 12 D8
Old Church Ms DUK SK16 91 H4
Old Church St NEWH/MOS M40 73 L6
OLD OL1 9 K5
Old Clay Dr WHIT OL12 21 H8
Old Clough La WALK M28 69 J4
Oldcott Cl WALK M28 68 C7
Old Court St HYDE SK14 102 A2
The Old Ctyd
WYTH/NTH M22 * 110 C7
Old Cft OLDE OL4 60 D6
Old Croft Ms STKP SK1 112 E5
Old Crofts Bank URM M41 84 F8
Old Cross St AUL OL6 * 90 F1
Old Dairy Ms HYDE SK14 90 F7
Old Delph Rd ROCH OL11 27 J3
Old Doctors St TOT/BURYW BL8 24 C5
Old Eagley Ms BOL BL1 22 C6
Old Edge La ROY/SHW OL2 59 H2
Old Elm St BRUN/LGST M13 * 87 M6
Oldershaw Dr BKLY M9 73 G6
Old Farm Crs DROY M43 89 J4
Old Farm Dr OFTN SK2 113 J6
Oldfield Cl WHTN BL5 50 C4
Oldfield Dr HALE/TIMP WA15 108 C6
Oldfield Gv SALE M33 96 F7
Oldfield Ms ALT WA14 107 M7
Oldfield Rd ALT WA14 107 K7
ORD M5 86 F5
PWCH M25 55 M5
SALE M33 96 F7
Oldfield St OP/CLY M11 88 E3
Old Fold WGNW/BIL/OR WN5 46 E6
Old Fold Rd WGNE/HIN WN2 33 G7
WHTN BL5 49 L5
Old Gardens St STKP SK1 13 K6
The Old Gdn
HALE/TIMP WA15 108 E5
Oldgate Wk HULME M15 * 87 G6
Old Gn BOLE BL2 23 H6
Old Greenwood La
HOR/BR BL6 34 A3
Old Ground St RAMS BL0 * 18 F6
Old Hall Cl GLSP SK13 105 G2
TOT/BURYW BL8 24 E5
Old Hall Clough
HOR/BR BL6 34 F5
Old Hall Crs WILM/AE SK9 127 J1
Old Hall Dr AIMK WN4 78 D2
GTN M18 89 G8
OFTN SK2 113 H6
Old Hall La BRAM/HZG SK7 128 C4
HOR/BR BL6 34 F3
HYDE SK14 102 E5
MPL/ROM SK6 114 F7
PWCH M25 56 C5
RUSH/FAL M14 99 G3
WALK M28 69 H5
WHTF M45 54 F6
WHTN BL5 50 B7
Old Hall Mill La ATH M46 66 D4
Old Hall Rd BRO M7 72 A4
CHD/CHDH SK8 110 D6
NEWH/MOS M40 73 L5
SALE M33 97 H8
STRET M32 85 K8
WHTF M45 54 F5
Old Hall Sq GLSP SK13 93 K7
Old Hall St DUK SK16 90 D5
FWTH BL4 53 H5
MDTN M24 41 H2
OP/CLY M11 * 89 H5
WGNS/IIMK WN3 15 L8
Old Hall St North BOL BL1 2 E5
Oldham Av STKP SK1 112 E3
Oldham Dr MPL/ROM SK6 101 K8
Oldham Rd ANC M4 7 K2
AULW OL7 75 K8
FAIL M35 74 E4
MDTN M24 57 J4
MILN OL16 10 F5
NEWH/MOS M40 73 M6
OLDE OL4 60 D6
ROCH OL11 11 G7
ROCH OL11 42 E4
ROY/SHW OL2 59 H2
UPML OL3 44 D6
UPML OL3 61 G3
Oldhams La BOL BL1 22 A7
Oldham Sq NM/HAY SK22 * 124 E5
Oldham St CMANE M1 7 H4
DROY M43 89 L2
DTN/ASHW M34 100 F2
HYDE SK14 102 A2
ORD M5 6 A5
RDSH SK5 * 100 B5
Oldham Wy CHAD OL9 8 F4
MILN OL16 43 J3
MOSL OL5 76 D2
OLDE OL4 61 G7
OLDS OL8 9 G7
UPML OL3 44 D2
UPML OL3 45 K2
Old Kiln La BOL BL1 35 G2
OLDE OL4 60 D4
Oldknow Rd MPL/ROM SK6 114 D6
Old La BURY BL9 25 J4
CHAD OL9 58 E8
GLSP SK13 104 D5
HOR/BR BL6 34 C2
LHULT M38 52 C7
OLDE OL4 60 C4
OLDE OL4 61 H6
OP/CLY M11 89 G5
WGN WN1 31 L8
WGNNW/ST WN6 30 E6
WHTN BL5 50 A4
Old Lansdowne Rd
DID/WITH M20 98 C8
Old Lees St AUL OL6 76 A7
Old Malt La DID/WITH M20 98 D5
Old Manor Pk ATH M46 66 D2
Old Market Pl ALT WA14 108 A7
Old Market St BKLY M9 72 F2
Old Meadow Dr
DTN/ASHW M34 90 C7
Old Meadow La
HALE/TIMP WA15 117 L1
Old Medlock St CSLFD M3 * 6 B6
Old Mill Cl SWIN M27 70 E4
Old Mill La BRAM/HZG SK7 122 C4
OLDE OL4 60 D7
Old Mills Hl MDTN M24 58 A3
Old Mill St ANC M4 7 M4
Oldmill St WHIT OL12 10 E2
Old Moat La DID/WITH M20 98 E6
Oldmoor Rd MPL/ROM SK6 101 H7
Old Moss La GOL/RIS/CUL WA3 82 A6
Old Mount St ANC M4 7 H1
Old Nans La BOLE BL2 37 J2
Old Nursery Fold BOLE BL2 23 H8
Old Oak Cl BOLE BL2 37 L7
Old Oak Dr DTN/ASHW M34 101 K1
Old Oake Cl WALK M28 * 69 H2
Old Oak St DID/WITH M20 110 E1
Old Orch WILM/AE SK9 126 E5
The Old Orch
HALE/TIMP WA15 108 E4
Old Pack Horse Rd UPML OL3 45 L6
Old Park La TRPK M17 84 F6
Old Parrin La ECC M30 84 E1
Old Pasture Cl OFTN SK2 113 G5
Old Pepper La WGNNW/ST WN6 30 E2
Old Quarry La EDGW/EG BL7 22 C3
Old Rectory Gdns
CHD/CHDH SK8 111 G7
Old River Cl IRL M44 94 D2
Old Rd AIMK WN4 63 K7
AUL OL6 76 C7
BKLY M9 73 G2
BOL BL1 36 B1
CHD/CHDH SK8 111 J6
CHF/WBR SK23 124 F8
DUK SK16 90 F4
FAIL M35 74 B5
GLSP SK13 93 K5
HTNM SK4 112 B1
HYDE SK14 91 G8
HYDE SK14 92 C7
MILN OL16 21 J8
STLY SK15 91 M4
WILM/AE SK9 126 F4
WILM/AE SK9 127 H1
Old School Dr BKLY M9 * 72 F2
Old School La CHD/CHDH SK8 120 C4
Old School Ms DUK SK16 * 91 H4
Old School Pl AIMK WN4 78 D1
Old Shaw St ORD M5 * 86 D4
The Old Stables
DTN/ASHW M34 90 C6
Old Station St ECC M30 84 F3
Oldstead Gv BOLS/LL BL3 35 J8
Old St AUL OL6 90 E2
HYDE SK14 103 K4
OLDE OL4 60 A7
STLY SK15 91 K3
Old Swan Cl EDGW/EG BL7 * 22 B2
Old Towns Cl TOT/BURYW BL8 24 C5
Old Vicarage WHTN BL5 50 B7
Old Vicarage Gdns WALK M28 69 G1
Old Vicarage Rd HOR/BR BL6 34 C1
Old Wellington Rd ECC M30 85 H2
Old Wells Cl LHULT M38 52 D6
Oldwood Rd NTHM/RTH M23 118 C1
Old Wool La CHD/CHDH SK8 111 J8
Old York St HULME M15 87 H6
Olebrook Cl WGTN/LGST M12 88 A6
Oleo Ter IRL M44 94 F1
Olga St BOL BL1 36 A2
Olga Ter BKLY M9 * 73 G2
Olivant St BURY BL9 4 D8
Olive Bank TOT/BURYW BL8 24 E8
Olive Gv WGNNW/ST WN6 47 J1
Oliver Cl LIT OL15 21 K7
Olive Rd HALE/TIMP WA15 108 D4
Oliver St ATH M46 67 G1
EDGY/DAV SK3 13 J7
OP/CLY M11 * 88 C4
Olive Shapley Av
DID/WITH M20 110 E1
Olive St BOLS/LL BL3 36 A8
FAIL M35 74 B4
HEY OL10 41 H2
RAD M26 54 F1
ROCH OL11 * 41 M3
TOT/BURYW BL8 4 B4
Olivia Gv RUSH/FAL M14 99 G1
Ollerbarrow Rd
HALE/TIMP WA15 117 G2
Ollerbrook Ct BOL BL1 36 C2
Ollersett Av NM/HAY SK22 124 E4
Ollersett Dr NM/HAY SK22 124 F4
Ollersett La NM/HAY SK22 124 F4
Ollerton WHIT OL12 10 D3
Ollerton Av SALE M33 96 A7
Ollerton Cl WGNE/HIN WN2 48 D2
Ollerton Dr FAIL M35 74 C6
Ollerton Rd WILM/AE SK9 119 M7
Ollerton St BOL BL1 22 C6
Ollier Av WGTN/LGST M12 99 K2
Olney ROCH OL11 10 D7
Olney Av WYTH/NTH M22 110 A6
Olney St BRUN/LGST M13 88 A8
Olsberg Cl RAD M26 38 F8
Olwen Crs RDSH SK5 100 C4
Olympic Ct SALQ M50 86 C4
Omer Av BRUN/LGST M13 99 J2
Omer Dr BNG/LEV M19 99 H5
Onchan Av OLDE OL4 59 L6
One Ash Cl WHIT OL12 28 C2
One Oak La WILM/AE SK9 127 K5
Onslow Av NEWH/MOS M40 74 B3
Onslow Cl OLD OL1 9 G3
Onslow Rd EDGY/DAV SK3 12 C7
Onslow St ROCH OL11 27 M8
Onward St HYDE SK14 102 A2
Oozewood Rd MDTN M24 42 D7
Opal Ct RUSH/FAL M14 * 99 G4
Opal Gv LEIGH WN7 66 B8
Opal St BNG/LEV M19 99 L4
Openshaw Fold Rd BURY BL9 39 G5
Openshaw La IRL M44 94 B6
Openshaw Pl FWTH BL4 52 E4
Openshaw St BURY BL9 5 H6
Orama Av SLFD M6 70 D8
Orama Ml WHIT OL12 * 20 A4
Oram St BURY BL9 25 K8
Orange Hill Rd PWCH M25 55 M7
Orange St SLFD M6 86 D1
Orbital Wy DTN/ASHW M34 101 G1
Orchard Av BOL BL1 36 C1
GTN M18 89 H8
PART M31 94 C8
WALK M28 68 E5
Orchard Cl CHD/CHDH SK8 120 E5
LEIGH WN7 66 C5
POY/DIS SK12 129 J1
WGNNW/ST WN6 30 D5
WILM/AE SK9 126 D7
Orchard Ct OFTN SK2 * 113 G6
WGNW/BIL/OR WN5 62 A1
Orchard Crs MCFLDN SK10 130 C6
Orchard Dr GLSP SK13 104 B3
HALE/TIMP WA15 117 J1
WILM/AE SK9 127 J2
Orchard Gdns BOLE BL2 37 J1
Orchard Gn WILM/AE SK9 130 E3
Orchard Gv DID/WITH M20 98 C7
ROY/SHW OL2 43 K5
Orchard La LEIGH WN7 66 C5
Orchard Pl HALE/TIMP WA15 108 E5
POY/DIS SK12 * 121 M8
SALE M33 96 E7
Orchard Ri HYDE SK14 102 C4
Orchard Rd FAIL M35 74 C5
HALE/TIMP WA15 108 B7
MPL/ROM SK6 114 E2
Orchard Rd East
WYTH/NTH M22 110 A2
Orchard Rd West
WYTH/NTH M22 110 A2
The Orchards
WGNW/BIL/OR WN5 46 B7
Orchard St AIMK WN4 78 F1
DID/WITH M20 98 C7
HEY OL10 41 H1
HYDE SK14 102 B2
SLFD M6 71 K8
STKP SK1 13 K4
WGN WN1 15 H3
The Orchard WHTN BL5 50 B3
Orchard V EDGY/DAV SK3 111 M6
Orchid Av FWTH BL4 52 E3
Orchid Cl IRL M44 94 B4
OLD OL1 8 E1
Orchid Dr BURY BL9 39 K5
Orchid Gdns CHD/CHDH SK8 110 C6
Orchid St BKLY M9 73 G5
Ordsall Av LHULT M38 52 E8
Ordsall Dr ORD M5 86 E5
Ordsall La ORD M5 6 A6
Oregon Av OLD OL1 9 G1
Oregon Cl BRUN/LGST M13 87 M6
Orford Av POY/DIS SK12 123 M7
Orford Cl GOL/RIS/CUL WA3 79 K5
MPL/ROM SK6 123 G5
Orford Ct LEIGH WN7 81 L2
Orford Rd NEWH/MOS M40 73 M7
PWCH M25 55 K7
Organ St LEIGH WN7 66 B7
WGNE/HIN WN2 65 L1
Oriel Av OLDS OL8 75 H1
Oriel Cl CHAD OL9 58 D8
OFTN SK2 112 E6
Oriel Rd AIMK WN4 63 J8
DID/WITH M20 98 D8
Oriel St BOLS/LL BL3 35 M7
ROCH OL11 10 F9
Orient Rd SLFD M6 70 D8
Orient St BRO M7 72 C5
Oriole Cl WALK M28 68 E5
Oriole Dr WALK M28 68 E4
Orion Pl BRO M7 * 71 M8
Orkney Cl NTHM/RTH M23 109 K8
RAD M26 38 E8
Orkney Dr URM M41 85 G7
Orlanda Av SLFD M6 70 D8
Orlanda Dr BRO M7 72 C6
Orlando St BOLE BL2 3 G8
Orleans Wy OLD OL1 9 H4
Orley Wk OLD OL1 44 A8
Orme Av MDTN M24 57 K5
SLFD M6 70 E8
Orme Cl OP/CLY M11 88 B3
URM M41 96 C2
Ormerod Av ROY/SHW OL2 59 H1
Ormerod Cl MPL/ROM SK6 113 J3
Ormerod St HEY OL10 41 H3
Orme St OLDE OL4 9 L8
STKP SK1 * 112 E2
WILM/AE SK9 130 D3
Ormonde Av SLFD M6 70 E8
Ormonde Ct AUL OL6 75 M8
Ormond St BOLS/LL BL3 37 G7
BURY BL9 5 H3
Ormrod St BOLE BL2 22 F7
BOLS/LL BL3 2 D6
BURY BL9 5 J5
FWTH BL4 52 F4
Ormsby Av GTN M18 88 E8
Ormsby Cl EDGY/DAV SK3 112 B8
WGNNW/ST WN6 31 H3
Ormsgill Cl HULME M15 87 J6
Orms Gill Pl OFTN SK2 * 113 H6
Ormsgill St HULME M15 87 J6
Ormside Cl WGNE/HIN WN2 65 L1
Ormskirk Av DID/WITH M20 98 C6
Ormskirk Cl TOT/BURYW BL8 38 C4
Ormskirk Rd RDSH SK5 100 C6
WGNW/BIL/OR WN5 14 B6
Ormston Gv LEIGH WN7 66 C5
Ornatus St BOL BL1 * 22 C7
Orphanage St HTNM SK4 13 H1
Orpington Dr TOT/BURYW BL8 38 E3
Orpington Rd BKLY M9 73 H5
Orpington St
WGNW/BIL/OR WN5 46 F6
Orrell Ar WGN WN1 14 F3
Orrell Gdns
WGNW/BIL/OR WN5 46 C6
Orrell Hall Cl
WGNW/BIL/OR WN5 46 E5
Orrell Rd WGNW/BIL/OR WN5 46 B5
Orrell St OP/CLY M11 * 89 G4
TOT/BURYW BL8 4 B3
WGN WN1 15 J6
Orrel St SLFD M6 86 B2
Orrishmere Rd CHD/CHDH SK8 120 B1
Orron St LIT OL15 21 L7
Orsett Cl NEWH/MOS M40 87 M1
Orthes Gv HTNM SK4 100 A7
Orton Av NTHM/RTH M23 109 K3
Orton Rd NTHM/RTH M23 109 K3
Orton Wy AIMK WN4 78 C1
Orvietto Av SLFD M6 70 D8
Orville Dr BNG/LEV M19 99 J5
Orwell Av DTN/ASHW M34 100 D1
WYTH/NTH M22 110 A6
Orwell Cl TOT/BURYW BL8 4 C2
WGNNW/ST WN6 47 H1
WILM/AE SK9 127 H2
Orwell Rd BOL BL1 35 L2
Osborne Cl TOT/BURYW BL8 38 E4
Osborne Ct ATH M46 66 F1
Osborne Dr SWIN M27 70 F5
Osborne Gv BOL BL1 35 M3
CHD/CHDH SK8 119 J1
LEIGH WN7 67 G6
Osborne Pl GLSP SK13 93 K7
Osborne Rd AIMK WN4 63 K8
BKLY M9 * 73 H5
BNG/LEV M19 99 J3
DTN/ASHW M34 90 C8
GOL/RIS/CUL WA3 80 B5
HALE/TIMP WA15 108 B7
HYDE SK14 102 B3
OFTN SK2 13 J9
OLDS OL8 8 E9
SLFD M6 * 85 K1
Osborne St CHAD OL9 8 D3
HEY OL10 41 G3
MPL/ROM SK6 112 F1
NEWH/MOS M40 72 F8
ROCH OL11 10 D9
ROY/SHW OL2 43 L6
SLFD M6 86 C1
Osborne Ter SALE M33 96 E8
Osbourne Cl FWTH BL4 53 G3
WILM/AE SK9 127 H6
Osbourne Pl ALT WA14 108 A8
Osbourne St DID/WITH M20 110 D1
Oscar St BOL BL1 * 35 M2
NEWH/MOS M40 73 K5
Oscott Av LHULT M38 52 D7
Oscroft Cl CHH M8 72 C6
Osmond St OLDE OL4 59 M5
Osmund Av BOLE BL2 37 G5
Osprey Av WHTN BL5 49 M6
Osprey Cl DUK SK16 91 H5
HULME M15 87 H7
Osprey Dr DROY M43 89 M1
IRL M44 94 D1
WILM/AE SK9 127 G4
The Ospreys WGNS/IIMK WN3 62 F1
Osprey Wk BRUN/LGST M13 * 87 M6
Ossory St RUSH/FAL M14 98 E1
Osterley Rd BKLY M9 73 K1
Ostlers Ga DROY M43 90 A2
Ostrich La PWCH M25 71 M1
Oswald Cl SLFD M6 71 K7
Oswald La CCHDY M21 97 L3
Oswald Rd CCHDY M21 97 L2
Oswald St ANC M4 7 G1
ANC M4 * 88 A3
BOLS/LL BL3 35 M8
CHAD OL9 8 E2
MILN OL16 11 H2
RDSH SK5 100 C1
ROY/SHW OL2 43 M4
Oswestry Cl TOT/BURYW BL8 24 B4
Otago Rd OLDE OL4 59 M3
Otago St OLDE OL4 * 59 M3
Othello Dr ECC M30 85 G2
Otley Av SLFD M6 85 M1
Otley Cl CHAD OL9 8 B7
Otley Gv EDGY/DAV SK3 112 A8
Otmoor Wy ROY/SHW OL2 43 K8
Otranto Av SLFD M6 70 E8
Ottawa Cl NTHM/RTH M23 109 J8
Ott Cl HULME M15 87 J6
Otterburn Pl OFTN SK2 113 G6
Otterbury Cl TOT/BURYW BL8 38 C2
Otter Dr BURY BL9 39 L8
CHH M8 72 B7
Otterspool Rd MPL/ROM SK6 113 L1
Otterwood Sq
WGNW/BIL/OR WN5 46 F2
Oulder Hl ROCH OL11 27 K5
Oulder Hill Dr ROCH OL11 27 L5
Oulder Mt ROCH OL11 * 27 L5
Ouldfield Cl MILN OL16 11 J6
Oulton Av SALE M33 97 H7
Oulton Cl LEIGH WN7 66 D8
Oulton St BOL BL1 22 D7
Oulton Wk NEWH/MOS M40 88 A2
Oundle Cl RUSH/FAL M14 98 F1
Ouse St SALQ M50 85 M3
Outram Cl MPL/ROM SK6 * 114 C8
Outram Rd DUK SK16 90 E6
Outram Sq DROY M43 * 89 K4
Outrington Dr OP/CLY M11 88 D4
Outwood Av SWIN M27 54 A8
Outwood Dr CHD/CHDH SK8 119 J4
Outwood Gv BOL BL1 22 B7
Outwood La MANAIR M90 118 E4
Outwood La West
MANAIR M90 118 D4
Outwood Rd CHD/CHDH SK8 119 K4
RAD M26 54 D3
Oval Dr DUK SK16 90 E5
The Oval CHD/CHDH SK8 119 K4
WGNNW/ST WN6 30 C7
Oven Hill Rd NM/HAY SK22 125 J4
Overbeck Cl WGNNW/ST WN6 31 K8
Overbridge Rd BRO M7 72 B8
Overbrook Av NEWH/MOS M40 73 G7
Overbrook Dr PWCH M25 71 L1
Overdale SWIN M27 70 D6
Overdale Cl OLD OL1 9 H1
Overdale Crs URM M41 95 J2
Overdale Dr BOL BL1 35 K5
GLSP SK13 104 E4
Overdale Rd MPL/ROM SK6 113 K4
POY/DIS SK12 124 B6
WYTH/NTH M22 110 A7
Overdell Dr WHIT OL12 27 M1
Overdene Cl HOR/BR BL6 34 E6
Overens St OLDE OL4 59 L5
Overfield Wy WHIT OL12 28 C2
Overgreen BOLE BL2 37 H1
Overhill Dr WILM/AE SK9 127 J5
Overhill La WILM/AE SK9 127 J5

Overhill Rd CHAD OL9 ....58 C4
Over Hill Rd NM/HAY SK22 ....125 J7
Overhill Rd WILM/AE SK9 ....127 H5
Overhill Wy WGNS/IIMK WN3 ....63 G1
Overlea Dr BNG/LEV M19 ....99 H1
Overshores Rd EDGW/EG BL7 ....16 D5
Overstone Dr CHH M8 ....72 C5
Overton Av WYTH/NTH M22 ....110 A7
Overton Cl RAD M26 ....54 E3
Overton Crs BRAM/HZG SK7 ....113 H8
  SALE M33 ....108 A2
Overton Rd WYTH/NTH M22 ....110 A7
Overton St LEIGH WN7 ....66 B8
Overt St ROCH OL11 ....10 F8
Overwood Rd WYTH/NTH M22 ....110 A4
Owenington Gv LHULT M38 ....52 D7
Owens Cl CHAD OL9 ....58 B4
Owens Farm Dr OFTN SK2 ....113 H5
Owens Pk RUSH/FAL M14 * 99 G3
Owen St ECC M30 ....84 E3
  EDGY/DAV SK3 ....12 F5
  LEIGH WN7 * 66 A7
  OLD OL1 ....60 B1
  SLFD M6 ....71 K7
Owlerbarrow Rd
  TOT/BURYW BL8 ....38 D1
Owler La CHAD OL9 ....74 A1
Owlwood Cl LHULT M38 ....68 B1
Owlwood Dr LHULT M38 ....68 B1
Owsten Ct HOR/BR BL6 ....33 J1
Oxbridge Cl SALE M33 ....108 A1
Oxbrow Wy WHTF M45 ....55 K4
Oxburgh Rd WGNS/IIMK WN3 ....48 C8
Oxendale Dr MDTN M24 ....56 F3
Oxenhurst Gn OFTN SK2 ....113 H7
Oxford Av DROY M43 ....89 J1
  ROCH OL11 ....27 K6
  SALE M33 ....96 A3
  WHTF M45 ....55 K4
Oxford Cl FWTH BL4 ....52 C4
Oxford Ct CMANW M2 * 6 F7
  OLDTF/WHR M16 * 87 G7
  WGN WN1 * 15 J2
Oxford Dr MDTN M24 ....57 M2
  MPL/ROM SK6 ....101 M8
Oxford Gv BOL BL1 ....2 A2
Oxford Ml AULW OL7 * 90 C4
Oxford Pl MILN OL16 ....11 H9
  RUSH/FAL M14 ....87 M8
Oxford Rd ALT WA14 ....116 F1
  ATH M46 ....50 E7
  BOLS/LL BL3 ....53 J1
  BRUN/LGST M13 ....87 L7
  CMANE M1 ....7 G8
  DUK SK16 ....91 G4
  HOR/BR BL6 ....34 C4
  SLFD M6 ....70 D8
  WGNW/BIL/OR WN5 ....46 C5
Oxford St BOL BL1 ....2 E5
  BURY BL9 ....5 H6
  CHAD OL9 ....8 C9
  CMANE M1 ....6 F6
  ECC M30 ....85 H3
  LEIGH WN7 ....66 C5
  ROY/SHW OL2 ....43 L5
  STLY SK15 ....77 G8
  WGNE/HIN WN2 ....49 J5
Oxford St East AULW OL7 ....90 C4
Oxford St West AULW OL7 ....90 C4
Oxford Wy HTNM SK4 ....12 F1
  WHIT OL12 ....28 B2
Ox Ga BOLE BL2 ....23 G7
Ox Hey Cl HOR/BR BL6 ....34 B4
  RAMS BL0 ....18 F5
Ox Hey La HOR/BR BL6 ....34 C5
  UPML OL3 ....61 J8
Oxlea Gv WHTN BL5 ....50 B5
Oxney Rd RUSH/FAL M14 ....87 M8
Ox St RAMS BL0 ....18 E7
Oxton Av WYTH/NTH M22 ....109 M8
Oxton St OP/CLY M11 ....89 J5

P

Pacific Rd ALT WA14 ....107 K6
Pacific Wy SALQ M50 ....85 M4
Packer St BOL BL1 ....35 M2
  MILN OL16 ....10 E4
Packwood Cha CHAD OL9 ....58 C4
Padbury Cl URM M41 ....95 G3
Padbury Wy BOLE BL2 ....37 H2
Padden Brook MPL/ROM SK6 ....113 L2
Paddington Av
  NEWH/MOS M40 * 73 L7
Paddington Cl SLFD M6 ....86 D2
Paddison St SWIN M27 ....70 B5
Paddock Cl ATH M46 ....51 H7
Paddock Cha POY/DIS SK12 ....122 B6
Paddock La ALT WA14 ....106 D7
  FAIL M35 ....74 C7
  LYMM WA13 ....106 A5
Paddock Ri WGNNW/ST WN6 ....47 H1
Paddock Rd HYDE SK14 * 102 A4
The Paddocks EDGY/DAV SK3 ....112 D7
Paddock St WGTN/LGST M12 ....7 L8
The Paddock AIMK WN4 ....63 J6
  BRAM/HZG SK7 ....120 F3
  CHD/CHDH SK8 ....111 H7
  HALE/TIMP WA15 ....108 E8
  HYDE SK14 ....93 H7
  RAMS BL0 ....18 D1
  UPML OL3 ....61 J8
  WALK M28 ....69 H5
Paderborn Ct BOL BL1 ....2 C6
Padfield Cl SLFD M6 ....105 G5
Padfield Main Rd GLSP SK13 ....93 L6
Padiham Cl BURY BL9 ....39 G5
  LEIGH WN7 ....66 D7
Padstow Cl HYDE SK14 ....103 G1
Padstow Dr BRAM/HZG SK7 ....121 H5
Padstow St NEWH/MOS M40 * 88 B1
Padstow Wk HYDE SK14 ....103 G1
Pagan St MILN OL16 ....10 F3
Pagefield Cl WGNNW/ST WN6 ....14 C2
Pagefield St WGNNW/ST WN6 ....14 C1
Paget St NEWH/MOS M40 ....73 G7
Pagnall Ct CHAD OL9 ....8 A8
Paignton Av BNG/LEV M19 ....99 J4
  HYDE SK14 ....102 F3
Paignton Cl
  WGNW/BIL/OR WN5 ....62 B4
Paignton Dr SALE M33 ....96 A7
Paignton Gv RDSH SK5 ....100 B5
Pailin Dr DROY M43 ....89 M2
Painswick Rd WYTH/NTH M22 ....118 D3
Paintin Cl HOR/BR BL6 ....35 G6
Paisley Pk FWTH BL4 ....52 A4
Paiton St BOL BL1 ....35 M5

Palace Ar AIMK WN4 ....78 E1
Palace Gdns ROY/SHW OL2 ....59 G2
Palace Rd AUL OL6 ....76 B7
  SALE M33 ....96 D7
Palace St BOL BL1 ....2 E3
  BURY BL9 ....5 J5
  CHAD OL9 ....8 D5
Palatine Av DID/WITH M20 ....98 C6
Palatine Cl IRL M44 ....94 C6
  WGNS/IIMK WN3 ....47 H8
Palatine Crs DID/WITH M20 ....98 E7
Palatine Dr BURY BL9 ....25 J4
Palatine Rd DID/WITH M20 ....110 C1
  ROCH OL11 ....27 K4
  WYTH/NTH M22 ....110 B2
Palatine Sq LEIGH WN7 ....66 A7
Palatine St BOL BL1 ....2 E4
  DTN/ASHW M34 ....90 B7
  MILN OL16 ....11 L5
  RAMS BL0 ....18 F6
Palewood Cl WGN WN1 ....15 K1
Paley St BOL BL1 * 2 F4
Palfrey Pl WGTN/LGST M12 ....7 M9
Palgrave Av NEWH/MOS M40 ....73 C7
Palin St WGNE/HIN WN2 ....65 L1
Palin Wood Rd UPML OL3 ....45 J7
Pall Ml CMANW M2 ....6 F5
Palma Av HALE/TIMP WA15 ....118 C4
Palm Av AIMK WN4 ....63 C7
Palm Cl SALE M33 ....95 M7
Palmer Av CHD/CHDH SK8 ....111 J6
Palmer Cl OLDS OL8 ....59 J8
Palmer Gv LEIGH WN7 ....66 B3
Palmerston Av
  OLDTF/WHR M16 ....98 A2
Palmerston Cl DTN/ASHW M34 ....100 E1
  RAMS BL0 ....24 E1
  WGNE/HIN WN2 ....48 F1
Palmerston Rd
  DTN/ASHW M34 ....100 E1
  OFTN SK2 ....121 K1
Palmerston St WGTN/LGST M12 ....88 A4
Palmerston St BRO M7 ....71 M7
  DUK SK16 ....90 E8
  SALE M33 ....96 D8
Palm Gv CHAD OL9 ....8 B2
  WGNW/BIL/OR WN5 ....47 G6
Palm St BOL BL1 ....36 C1
  BRUN/LGST M13 ....99 J1
  DROY M43 ....89 G2
  OLDE OL4 ....59 M4
Pandora St DID/WITH M20 ....98 D7
Panfield Rd WYTH/NTH M22 ....109 M8
Pangbourne Av URM M41 ....96 D1
Pangbourne Cl EDGY/DAV SK3 ....111 M6
Pankhurst Wk RUSH/FAL M14 ....98 C1
Panmure St OLDS OL8 ....59 J8
Pansy Rd FWTH BL4 ....52 B4
Panton St HOR/BR BL6 ....34 A3
Paper Mill Rd EDGW/EG BL7 ....22 C5
Paprika Cl OP/CLY M11 ....89 C5
Parade Rd MANAIR M90 ....118 C4
Paradise St DTN/ASHW M34 ....90 C5
  GLSP SK13 ....93 K7
  RAMS BL0 ....18 F6
Paramel Av BOLS/LL BL3 ....37 L7
Parbold Av DID/WITH M20 ....98 D5
The Parchments NEWLW WA12 ....79 L3
Pargate Cha ROCH OL11 ....27 K4
Paris Av ORD M5 ....86 E5
  WGNS/IIMK WN3 ....62 F1
Paris St BOLS/LL BL3 ....35 L8
Park 66 BURY BL9 * 39 L6
Park Av ALT WA14 ....108 B4
  BNG/LEV M19 ....99 J3
  BOL BL1 * 22 B8
  BRAM/HZG SK7 ....120 F7
  BRO M7 ....72 C4
  CHAD OL9 ....58 E3
  CHD/CHDH SK8 ....120 B3
  EDGY/DAV SK3 ....111 J5
  FAIL M35 ....74 A4
  GOL/RIS/CUL WA3 ....79 J2
  HALE/TIMP WA15 ....117 H3
  HYDE SK14 ....91 G8
  MPL/ROM SK6 ....113 M2
  OLDTF/WHR M16 ....86 F7
  POY/DIS SK12 ....122 A8
  PWCH M25 ....55 L8
  RAD M26 ....39 G8
  RAMS BL0 ....19 G6
  SALE M33 ....96 D6
  URM M41 ....95 M2
  WGNNW/ST WN6 ....30 C5
  WGNW/BIL/OR WN5 ....62 B3
  WHTF M45 ....55 G6
  WILM/AE SK9 ....127 G4
Park Bank ATH M46 ....51 J6
Park Bridge Rd AULW OL7 ....75 K5
Parkbrook La
  WGNNW/ST WN6 ....30 E5
Parkbrook Rd
  NTHM/RTH M23 ....109 L5
Park Brow Cl CCHDY M21 ....97 M5
Park Cl ALT WA14 ....108 C4
  CHAD OL9 ....8 A1
  GLSP SK13 ....105 G2
  STLY SK15 ....91 J1
  WHTF M45 ....55 J6
Park Cottages BOL BL1 * 35 M1
  ROY/SHW OL2 ....43 J4
Park Court Ms
  CHD/CHDH SK8 * 111 H8
Park Crs AUL OL6 ....91 H2
  CHAD OL9 ....58 C3
  GLSP SK13 ....104 E1
  RUSH/FAL M14 ....98 F1
  WGN WN1 ....14 E1
  WILM/AE SK9 ....126 F3
Park Crs West WGN WN1 ....14 D2
Parkdale CHAD OL9 ....58 E3
  TYLD M29 ....67 L7
Parkdale Av
  DTN/ASHW M34 ....90 A5
  GTN M18 ....88 F7
Parkdale Rd BOLE BL2 ....3 L1
Parkdene Cl BOLE BL2 ....23 G8
Park Dene Dr GLSP SK13 ....104 F2
Park Dr ECC M30 ....70 A8
  HALE/TIMP WA15 ....108 D5
  HALE/TIMP WA15 ....117 H3
  HTNM SK4 ....12 B3
  HYDE SK14 ....91 G8
  OLDTF/WHR M16 ....97 M2
  WILM/AE SK9 ....126 F3
Park Edge WHTN BL5 ....50 D5
Parkedge Cl LEIGH WN7 ....81 H1
Parkend Dr LEIGH WN7 ....81 G2
Parkend Rd NTHM/RTH M23 ....109 K7
Parker St BURY BL9 ....5 H5
  CMANE M1 ....7 H5

Parkfield CHAD OL9 ....58 D3
  DROY M43 ....89 K2
  ECC M30 * 83 M8
  ORD M5 ....86 A2
  WGNE/HIN WN2 ....49 L6
Parkfield Av FWTH BL4 ....52 F5
  MPL/ROM SK6 ....114 C6
  OLDS OL8 ....74 E2
  RUSH/FAL M14 ....98 E1
  TYLD M29 ....67 L6
  URM M41 ....95 L5
Parkfield Cl LEIGH WN7 ....66 D5
  TYLD M29 ....67 L6
Parkfield Dr MDTN M24 ....57 H4
  TYLD M29 ....68 A3
Parkfield Rd ALT WA14 ....107 M8
  BOLS/LL BL3 ....52 C1
  CHD/CHDH SK8 ....120 B3
  OLDE OL4 ....61 H6
Parkfield Rd North
  NEWH/MOS M40 ....74 B2
Parkfield Rd South
  DID/WITH M20 ....98 D8
Parkfields STLY SK15 ....92 A1
  WGNE/HIN WN2 ....64 E5
Parkfield St MILN OL16 ....42 E2
  RUSH/FAL M14 ....98 E1
Parkgate CHAD OL9 ....58 E3
  TOT/BURYW BL8 ....24 B7
Park Gate Av DID/WITH M20 ....98 E6
Park Gate Cl MPL/ROM SK6 ....101 M7
Parkgate Dr BOL BL1 ....22 C7
  OFTN SK2 ....112 E8
  SWIN M27 ....70 E5
Parkgate Rd ALT WA14 ....107 M4
Park Gates Av CHD/CHDH SK8 ....120 E3
Park Gates Dr CHD/CHDH SK8 ....120 E3
Park Gv BNG/LEV M19 ....99 K2
  HTNM SK4 ....99 L8
  RAD M26 ....38 C8
  WALK M28 ....69 G4
Parkham Cl WHTN BL5 ....50 C6
Park Hey Dr WGNNW/ST WN6 ....30 B5
Park Hl PWCH M25 * 72 A2
Parkhill Av NEWH/MOS M40 ....88 E2
Park Hill Cl NM/HAY SK22 ....124 E3
Park Hill Dr WHTF M45 ....55 H4
Park Hill Rd HALE/TIMP WA15 ....117 J3
Parkhills Cl BURY BL9 ....5 G8
Parkhills Rd BURY BL9 ....4 F9
Park Hill St BOL BL1 ....2 A3
Park House Bridge Est
  SLFD M6 * 71 J5
Park House Bridge Rd SLFD M6 ....71 J6
Parkhouse St OP/CLY M11 ....88 F7
Parkhurst Av NEWH/MOS M40 ....74 B3
Parkin Cl DUK SK16 ....90 F4
Parkinson St BOLS/LL BL3 ....35 M7
  BURY BL9 ....25 J3
Parkin St WGTN/LGST M12 ....99 K1
Parklake Av BRO M7 ....72 B4
Parkland Av NM/HAY SK22 ....124 E3
Parklands ROY/SHW OL2 ....42 F6
  ROY/SHW OL2 ....44 A4
  WHTF M45 ....55 H4
Parklands Dr SALE M33 ....108 A2
  WGNE/HIN WN2 ....32 F5
Parklands Rd NTHM/RTH M23 ....109 J5
The Parklands HTNM SK4 ....100 B8
  RAMS BL0 ....53 L4
Parklands Wy POY/DIS SK12 ....122 A6
Park La BRO M7 ....72 A4
  DUK SK16 ....90 F4
  HALE/TIMP WA15 ....117 J3
  HOR/BR BL6 ....34 A1
  OLDS OL8 ....75 J8
  POY/DIS SK12 ....122 A8
  ROY/SHW OL2 ....43 H7
  SLFD M6 ....70 F7
  STKP SK1 ....112 E4
  UPML OL3 ....61 M7
  WGNE/HIN WN2 ....64 E5
  WGNE/HIN WN2 ....65 H6
  WHIT OL12 ....10 E3
  WHTF M45 ....55 H5
Park Lane Ct WHTF M45 * 55 G5
Park La West SWIN M27 ....71 G5
Parkleigh Dr NEWH/MOS M40 ....74 B2
Park Ldg BNG/LEV M19 ....99 K3
Park Lodge Cl CHD/CHDH SK8 ....111 H8
Park Meadow WHTN BL5 ....50 D4
Park Ms OLDTF/WHR M16 ....97 M2
Parkmount Rd BKLY M9 ....73 H3
Park Pde AUL OL6 ....90 D2
  ROY/SHW OL2 ....43 M3
Park Pl ANC M4 ....87 K1
  HTNM SK4 ....111 J2
  PWCH M25 ....55 M7
  SLFD M6 ....85 K1
Park Range RUSH/FAL M14 ....99 G1
Park Ri MPL/ROM SK6 ....113 M1
Park Rd ALT WA14 ....116 C2
  BOL BL1 ....2 A5
  BOLS/LL BL3 ....37 J8
  BURY BL9 ....4 E1
  CHD/CHDH SK8 ....110 C6
  CHD/CHDH SK8 ....111 H6
  CHD/CHDH SK8 ....120 E3
  DTN/ASHW M34 ....90 A4
  DTN/ASHW M34 ....101 H1
  DUK SK16 ....91 G3
  ECC M30 ....70 A8
  GLSP SK13 ....104 C4
  GOL/RIS/CUL WA3 ....79 J5
  HALE/TIMP WA15 ....108 C4
  HALE/TIMP WA15 ....117 H3
  HTNM SK4 ....12 B3
  HYDE SK14 ....91 G8
  MDTN M24 ....57 J4
  MPL/ROM SK6 ....113 M1
  NM/HAY SK22 ....124 E5
  OLDS OL8 ....9 J8
  PART M31 ....106 D1
  POY/DIS SK12 ....123 H6
  PWCH M25 ....72 A1
  RAMS BL0 ....24 C1
  SALE M33 ....96 D6
  SLFD M6 ....70 B2
  STRET M32 ....96 F2
  WALK M28 ....68 F3
  WGN WN1 ....14 E1
  WGNNW/ST WN6 ....31 H4
  WGNNW/ST WN6 ....50 A7
  WHTN BL5 ....50 A7
  WILM/AE SK9 ....126 F6
Park Rd North URM M41 ....95 M2
Park Rd South URM M41 ....95 M2
Park Rw BOL BL1 ....22 C6
  WALK M28 ....111 J3
Park Seventeen WHTF M45 ....55 J4
Parkside MDTN M24 ....57 H6
  WGNE/HIN WN2 ....49 H6
Park Side Av ROY/SHW OL2 ....43 M4
Parkside Av AIMK WN4 ....72 B4
  BRO M7 ....72 B4
  ECC M30 ....84 F3
  FAIL M35 ....74 B7
  WALK M28 ....69 G3
Parkside Cl MPL/ROM SK6 ....122 F4
  RAD M26 ....54 E1
  RAD M26 ....54 E1
Parkside Crs
  WGNW/BIL/OR WN5 ....46 C6
Parkside La MPL/ROM SK6 ....114 F6
Parkside Ms WHTF M45 ....55 J3
Parkside Rd RUSH/FAL M14 ....98 C2
  SALE M33 ....109 G1
Parkside St BOLE BL2 * 36 F3
  WGTN/LGST M12 * 7 M8
Parkside Wk BRAM/HZG SK7 ....121 G1
  BURY BL9 ....4 F7
Parks Nook FWTH BL4 ....52 F5
Park Sq AUL OL6 ....76 B8
  OLDTF/WHR M16 ....97 K2
Parkstead Dr BKLY M9 ....73 H5
The Parks NEWLW WA12 ....78 E3
Parkstone Av GTN M18 ....89 J6
  WHTF M45 ....55 J4
Parkstone Cl TOT/BURYW BL8 ....38 C2
Parkstone Dr SWIN M27 ....70 E6
Parkstone La WALK M28 ....69 J8
Parkstone Rd IRL M44 ....94 D1
Park St ATH M46 ....51 H8
  AUL OL6 ....90 C2
  BOL BL1 ....2 A3
  BRO M7 ....71 M4
  CSLFD M3 ....6 A4
  CSLFD M3 ....87 J1
  DROY M43 ....89 M2
  DTN/ASHW M34 ....101 C1
  FWTH BL4 ....53 G3
  HEY OL10 ....41 H4
  MILN OL16 ....10 E6
  MOSL OL5 ....76 F4
  MPL/ROM SK6 ....113 J1
  OLDS OL8 ....9 H7
  PWCH M25 ....55 M8
  RAD M26 ....38 F8
  ROY/SHW OL2 ....43 L6
  ROY/SHW OL2 ....43 L6
  STKP SK1 ....91 L3
  STLY SK15 ....91 L3
  SWIN M27 ....70 F6
  TYLD M29 ....67 K3
  WGNS/IIMK WN3 ....14 E1
Parksway BKLY M9 ....56 E6
  PWCH M25 ....71 M2
  SWIN M27 ....70 F6
Parks Yd BURY BL9 ....4 E4
Park Ter HEY OL10 ....41 G1
  MOSL OL5 ....76 F4
The Park OLDE OL4 ....61 G4
  UPML OL3 ....61 M7
Park Vw AIMK WN4 ....78 E2
  BKLY M9 ....72 F6
  CHAD OL9 ....58 D3
  DTN/ASHW M34 * 90 A4
  EDGY/DAV SK3 ....111 J5
  FWTH BL4 ....53 G3
  FWTH BL4 ....53 J5
  LIT OL15 ....21 M6
  RUSH/FAL M14 * 99 H5
  STKP SK1 ....112 E5
  WGNW/BIL/OR WN5 * 64 E7
Park View Ct PWCH M25 * 71 L1
Park View Ri NM/HAY SK22 ....124 E3
Park View Rd BOLS/LL BL3 * 53 J5
  PWCH M25 ....71 L1
Parkville Rd DID/WITH M20 ....98 F7
  WHTF M45 ....55 M5
Park Wy STRET M32 ....85 J8
Parkway BRAM/HZG SK7 ....121 G2
  CHAD OL9 ....58 D3
  DTN/ASHW M34 ....100 F1
  EDGY/DAV SK3 ....111 J5
  LHULT M38 ....68 B1
  NM/HAY SK22 ....124 F4
  ROCH OL11 ....27 L4
  WGNNW/ST WN6 ....30 A7
  WHTN BL5 ....50 A7
  WILM/AE SK9 ....126 F6
Parkway Gv LHULT M38 ....52 B8
Parkwood Cl
  WGNS/IIMK WN3 ....15 L8
Parkwood Dr WHTN BL5 ....51 J5
Parkwood Rd
  NTHM/RTH M23 ....109 M5
Parliament Pl BURY BL9 ....4 D7
Parliament St BURY BL9 ....4 E7
  WGNS/IIMK WN3 ....15 J7
Parndon Dr OFTN SK2 ....112 F5
Parnell Av WYTH/NTH M22 ....110 A4
Parnell Cl TYLD M29 ....67 L7
Parnham Cl RAD M26 ....37 L7
Parrbrook Cl BURY BL9 ....55 K3
Parr Cl FWTH BL4 ....52 E4
Parrenthorn Rd PWCH M25 ....55 M5
Parrfield Rd WALK M28 ....69 K5
Parr Fold BURY BL9 ....55 L2
Parr Fold Av WALK M28 ....68 F3
Parrin La ECC M30 ....84 F1
Parr La BURY BL9 ....55 K3
Parrot St BOLS/LL BL3 ....2 C9
  OP/CLY M11 * 88 F3
Parrs Mount Ms HTNM SK4 ....111 J2
Parr St ECC M30 ....85 G3
  OP/CLY M11 * 89 H1
  TYLD M29 ....67 J4
Parrs Wood Av
  DID/WITH M20 ....110 F3
Parrs Wood La DID/WITH M20 ....111 G3
Parrs Wood Rd
  DID/WITH M20 ....110 F3
Parry Md MPL/ROM SK6 ....101 K8
Parry Rd WGTN/LGST M12 ....88 C3
Parslow Av CHH M8 ....72 C2
Parsonage Cl BURY BL9 ....5 J4
  ORD M5 ....85 K1
Parsonage Dr WALK M28 ....68 F2
Parsonage Gdns CSLFD M3 * 6 C4
Parsonage La CSLFD M3 * 6 C2
Parsonage Rd DID/WITH M20 ....98 F5
  HTNM SK4 ....99 L8
  RAD M26 * 53 M6
  URM M41 ....84 E8
  WALK M28 ....68 F2

Parsonage St BURY BL9 ....5 J4
  CHH M8 ....72 C3
  HTNM SK4 ....13 C3
  HULME M15 ....87 H7
  HYDE SK14 * 102 A2
Parsonage Wk MILN OL16 * 29 J3
Parsonage Wy CHD/CHDH SK8 ....111 K7
  LEIGH WN7 ....66 B6
Parsons Dr MDTN M24 ....57 J3
Parsons Fld SLFD M6 * 71 K7
Parson's La BURY BL9 ....4 F5
Parson's Wk WGN WN1 ....14 E2
Parsons Wy BKLY M9 ....73 H5
Parth St BURY BL9 ....40 A3
Partington Ct FWTH BL4 ....52 F3
  GLSP SK13 ....105 J3
Partington La SWIN M27 ....70 B5
Partington Pk GLSP SK13 ....104 F2
  ROCH OL11 ....41 M4
Partington Pl SALE M33 ....96 C1
Partington St BOLS/LL BL3 ....51 M2
  ECC M30 ....85 C1
  FAIL M35 ....74 C5
  HEY OL10 ....40 D2
  NEWH/MOS M40 ....73 J7
  OLD OL1 ....9 L5
  ROCH OL11 ....41 L2
  WALK M28 ....69 M4
  WGNW/BIL/OR WN5 ....47 M4
Partridge Av NTHM/RTH M23 ....109 L6
Partridge Cl ROCH OL11 ....27 L5
Partridge Ct OFTN SK2 ....112 E8
Partridge Ri DROY M43 ....90 A1
Partridge Rd FAIL M35 ....74 F6
Partridge St STRET M32 ....86 C5
Partridge Wy CHAD OL9 ....58 A4
Part St WHTN BL5 ....50 B2
Parvet Av DROY M43 ....89 J1
Pascal St BNG/LEV M19 ....99 K4
Passmonds Crs ROCH OL11 ....27 L4
Passmonds Wy ROCH OL11 ....27 L4
Pass St CHAD OL9 ....8 E7
The Pass MILN OL16 ....11 H3
Paston Rd WYTH/NTH M22 ....110 A5
Pasture Cl AIMK WN4 ....63 K4
  HEY OL10 ....40 E5
Pasturefield Cl SALE M33 ....109 J1
Pasture Field Rd
  WYTH/NTH M22 ....119 H3
Pasturegreen Wy IRL M44 ....94 E3
Pastures La OLDE OL4 ....60 E4
Patch Croft Rd
  WYTH/NTH M22 ....119 H3
Patchett St WGTN/LGST M12 ....88 C3
Patch La BRAM/HZG SK7 ....121 G2
Pateley Sq WGNNW/ST WN6 ....47 L2
Patey St WGTN/LGST M12 ....99 K1
Patience St WHIT OL12 ....27 M3
Patmos St RAMS BL0 ....19 G6
Paton Av BOLS/LL BL3 ....52 D1
Paton Ct BRO M7 ....71 M8
Paton St CMANE M1 ....7 J5
  WHIT OL12 ....28 A1
Patricia Dr WALK M28 ....69 H2
Patricroft Rd WGNE/HIN WN2 ....15 M7
Patten St DID/WITH M20 ....98 E6
Patterdale Av AULW OL7 ....75 J7
  URM M41 ....84 E8
Patterdale Cl OLD OL1 ....9 L1
  ROCH OL11 ....41 M1
Patterdale Dr BURY BL9 ....39 H5
  MDTN M24 ....57 H2
Patterdale Pl WGNE/HIN WN2 ....48 D5
Patterdale Rd AIMK WN4 ....63 K4
  AULW OL7 ....75 J7
  BOLE BL2 ....23 H8
  LEIGH WN7 ....66 A3
  MPL/ROM SK6 ....101 L8
  PART M31 ....106 B1
  STKP SK1 ....112 E6
  WYTH/NTH M22 ....110 B4
Patterson Av CCHDY M21 ....97 K3
Patterson St BOLS/LL BL3 ....35 K8
  DTN/ASHW M34 ....90 C8
  NEWLW WA12 ....78 E8
  WHTN BL5 ....49 L5
Patting Cl IRL M44 ....94 F1
Pattishall Cl ANC M4 ....88 A3
Pattison Cl WHIT OL12 ....27 M1
Patton Cl BURY BL9 ....55 L2
Paulden Av NTHM/RTH M23 ....109 L6
  OLDE OL4 ....60 B3
Paulden Dr FAIL M35 ....74 D5
Paulette St BOL BL1 ....36 B2
Paulhan Rd DID/WITH M20 ....99 G8
Paulhan St BOLS/LL BL3 ....52 B1
Pauline St WGNE/HIN WN2 ....65 L3
Pavilion Cl WHIT OL12 ....28 C2
Pavilion Dr AUL OL6 ....76 A7
Pavilion Gdns WHTN BL5 ....50 B4
The Pavilions CHD/CHDH SK8 ....111 G8
Pavilion Wk RAD M26 ....38 C8
Paxford Pl WILM/AE SK9 ....126 E4
Paythorne Gn OFTN SK2 ....113 H7
Peabody St BOLS/LL BL3 ....36 B8
Peacefield MPL/ROM SK6 ....114 B7
Peace St ATH M46 ....67 H1
  BOLS/LL BL3 ....2 A9
  FAIL M35 * 74 D3
  TYLD M29 ....67 J6
Peaceville Rd BNG/LEV M19 ....99 J3
Peach Bank MDTN M24 ....57 H4
Peach Gv RNFD/HAY WA11 * 62 C4
Peach Rd OLDE OL4 ....60 A4
Peach St PWCH M25 ....55 M7
Peach Tree Cl BRO M7 * 72 C5
Peach Tree Ct SLFD M6 * 86 D2
Peacock Av SLFD M6 ....71 H7
Peacock Cl GLSP SK13 ....93 H8
  GTN M18 ....88 F6
Peacock Dr CHD/CHDH SK8 ....119 K6
Peacock Fold LEIGH WN7 ....66 A6
Peacock Gv GTN M18 ....89 G8
Peak Av ATH M46 ....50 F7
Peak Bank MPL/ROM SK6 ....113 K2
Peak Cl OLDE OL4 ....44 C8
Peakdale Av CHD/CHDH SK8 ....119 J3
Peakdale Rd DROY M43 ....89 H1
  GLSP SK13 ....104 B1
  MPL/ROM SK6 ....114 C8
Peaknaze Cl GLSP SK13 ....104 D4
  SWIN M27 ....70 E4
Peak Rd NM/HAY SK22 ....124 F4
Peak St BOL BL1 ....36 A2
  CHAD OL9 ....8 C7
  CMANE M1 ....7 K5
  STKP SK1 ....13 L4
Peak Vw GLSP SK13 ....93 J8
Pear Av BURY BL9 ....5 M1
Pear Cl MDTN M24 ....57 L6
Peardale Cl ECC M30 ....84 F4
Pearl Av BRO M7 ....72 B3

Pearl Mill Cl OLDS OL8 .....59 L8
Pearl St BRAM/HZG SK7 .....113 H8
DTN/ASHW M34 .....101 H1
ROCH OL11 .....27 M4
WGNNW/ST WN6 .....47 L1
Pearly Bank OLD OL1 .....44 A8
Pearn Rd BNG/LEV M19 .....99 J7
Pearson Cl MILN OL16 .....29 J5
PART M31 .....106 D1
Pearson Gv OLDE OL4 .....60 B6
Pearson St BURY BL9 .....5 K2
DUK SK16 .....90 F6
MILN OL16 .....11 M2
RDSH SK5 .....112 C1
Peart Av MPL/ROM SK6 .....101 M6
Pear Tree Cl GLSP SK13 .....93 H8
MPL/ROM SK6 .....114 E4
SLFD M6 .....86 D2
Pear Tree Ct SLFD M6 .....86 D2
WGNE/HIN WN2 .....32 F6
Pear Tree Dr FWTH BL4 .....52 D5
STLY SK15 .....91 L2
Pear Tree Gv TYLD M29 .....68 B3
Peart St DTN/ASHW M34 .....101 H1
Peary St ANC M4 .....87 L1
Peaslake Cl MPL/ROM SK6 .....114 A2
Peatfield Av SWIN M27 .....70 A2
Peatfield Wk HULME M15 * 87 J7
Pebble Cl STLY SK15 .....76 D8
Pebworth Cl MDTN M24 .....57 J7
Peckford Dr NEWH/MOS M40 .....73 K7
Peckforton Cl CHD/CHDH SK8 .....110 D7
Peckmill Cl WILM/AE SK9 .....127 J3
Pedder St BOL BL1 .....35 M3
Pedler Brow La WHIT OL12 .....21 J6
Pedley Hi MCFLDN SK10 .....129 K5
Pedley La BRUN/LGST M13 * 7 K8
Peebles Cl AIMK WN4 .....62 F8
Peebles Dr NEWH/MOS M40 .....74 A8
Peel Av ALT WA14 .....116 F2
Peel Brow RAMS BL0 .....19 G6
Peel Cir URM M41 .....85 H6
Peel Cl ATH M46 .....67 H1
Peel Cross Rd ORD M5 .....86 D3
Peel Dr LHULT M38 .....52 C8
SALE M33 .....97 H8
Peelgate Dr CHD/CHDH SK8 .....119 J2
Peel Green Rd ECC M30 .....84 F4
Peel Gv WALK M28 .....69 H4
WGTN/LGST M12 .....88 D8
Peel Hall Av TYLD M29 .....67 L3
Peel Hall Rd RAMS BL0 .....24 E2
WYTH/NTH M22 .....119 H1
Peel La CHH M8 .....72 D8
HEY OL10 .....40 E1
LHULT M38 .....52 C8
TYLD M29 .....67 L8
Peel Moat Rd HTNM SK4 .....99 L7
Peel Mt RAMS BL0 .....18 D8
SLFD M6 .....86 E1
Peel Park Crs LHULT M38 .....52 C8
Peel Rd HALE/TIMP WA15 .....117 G1
Peels Av OLDE OL4 .....60 D5
Peel St AUL OL6 .....90 E1
CHAD OL9 .....8 B6
DROY M43 .....89 J4
DTN/ASHW M34 .....90 B8
DUK SK16 .....90 F3
ECC M30 .....85 J2
FAIL M35 .....74 A6
FWTH BL4 .....53 H4
GLSP SK13 .....93 M7
HEY OL10 .....40 E2
HYDE SK14 .....102 C3
LEIGH WN7 .....66 B7
LIT OL15 .....11 M7
OFTN SK2 .....112 C6
RAD M26 .....54 E2
STLY SK15 .....91 J3
WGNE/HIN WN2 .....64 D2
WHIT OL12 .....10 C2
WHTN BL5 .....50 B3
Peel Vw TOT/BURYW BL8 .....24 D6
Peel Wk BURY BL9 .....4 E4
BURY BL9 .....25 H4
RAMS BL0 .....24 E1
TOT/BURYW BL8 .....4 D1
TOT/BURYW BL8 .....18 C7
TOT/BURYW BL8 .....25 G6
Peel Wy BURY BL9 .....4 E4
Peelwood Av LHULT M38 .....52 D8
Peelwood Gv ATH M46 .....67 H2
Peers Cl URM M41 .....84 A8
Peers St TOT/BURYW BL8 .....4 A5
Pegamoid St BOLE BL2 .....36 E3
Pegasus Ct ROCH OL11 * 27 M6
Pegasus Sq BRO M7 .....86 F1
Pegwell Dr BRO M7 .....72 B7
Pekin St AUL OL6 .....75 M8
Pelham Gv WGNE/HIN WN2 .....49 G8
Pelham PI CHH M8 .....72 E2
Pelham St AULW OL7 .....90 B4
BOLS/LL BL3 .....51 M1
OLDS OL8 .....75 J2
Pellowe Rd OLDS OL8 .....75 H1
Pelton Av SWIN M27 .....70 A2
Pemberlei Rd WGNE/HIN WN2 .....49 G2
Pemberton Rd WGNS/IIMK WN3 .....62 E3
Pemberton St BOL BL1 * 22 B8
LHULT M38 .....52 E8
ROCH OL11 .....41 M2
Pemberton Wy ROY/SHW OL2 .....43 L4
Pembridge Fold MDTN M24 .....57 M4
Pembridge Rd BKLY M9 .....57 J8
Pembroke Av ECC M30 .....85 G2
SALE M33 .....96 A8
Pembroke Cl BRUN/LGST M13 .....88 A6
Pembroke Ct BRAM/HZG SK7 * 122 A2
WHIT OL12 .....10 E1
Pembroke Dr BURY BL9 .....39 H5
OLDE OL4 .....44 B8
Pembroke Rd WGNE/HIN WN2 .....65 M1
WGNW/BIL/OR WN5 .....47 G3
Pembroke St BOL BL1 .....2 B1
BRO M7 .....72 B6
LIT OL15 .....21 M6
OLDS OL8 * 8 F7
SLFD M6 .....86 B3
Pembry Cl RDSH SK5 .....100 E7
Pembury Cl WYTH/NTH M22 .....118 E1
Penarth Rd BOLS/LL BL3 .....35 L8
WYTH/NTH M22 .....110 A4
Penbury Rd WGN WN1 .....31 L7
Pencarrow Cl DID/WITH M20 .....110 C1
Pencombe Cl WGTN/LGST M12 * 88 D3
Pencroft Wy HULME M15 .....87 K7
Pendale Av CHH M8 .....72 E4
Pendeen Cl TYLD M29 .....67 K5
WYTH/NTH M22 .....119 G3
Pendennis ROCH OL11 .....10 D7
Pendennis HOR/BR BL6 .....35 G7

Pendennis Cl RAD M26 .....37 M7
Pendennis Crs WGNE/HIN WN2 .....65 K1
Pendennis Rd HTNM SK4 .....12 D1
Pendle Av BOL BL1 .....22 B6
Pendlebury Cl PWCH M25 .....71 J2
Pendlebury Fold BOLS/LL BL3 .....51 G2
Pendlebury La WGN WN1 .....31 M6
WGNE/HIN WN2 .....32 B5
Pendlebury Rd CHD/CHDH SK8 .....110 D6
SWIN M27 .....70 D4
Pendlebury St BOL BL1 .....36 C1
Pendle Cl OLDE OL4 .....60 A7
TOT/BURYW BL8 .....38 E1
WGNW/BIL/OR WN5 .....47 G7
Pendle Ct BOL BL1 .....36 A3
LEIGH WN7 .....66 E8
Pendlecroft Av SWIN M27 .....70 F5
Pendlegreen Cl OP/CLY M11 .....88 C4
Pendle Gv ROY/SHW OL2 .....59 J1
GOL/RIS/CUL WA3 .....79 M3
Pendleton Gn SLFD M6 * 86 C1
Pendleton Wy SLFD M6 .....86 F1
Pendleway SWIN M27 .....70 D3
Pendragon PI FAIL M35 .....74 D5
Penelope Rd SLFD M6 .....71 G7
Penerly Dr BKLY M9 .....73 G6
Penfield Cl CMANE M1 .....7 J8
Penfold Wk WGTN/LGST M12 * 7 K7
Pengwern Av BOLS/LL BL3 .....35 L7
Penhale Ms BRAM/HZG SK7 .....121 H5
Penistone Av BKLY M9 .....73 K1
MILN OL16 .....11 M7
SLFD M6 .....85 M1
Penketh Av GTN M18 .....88 E8
TYLD M29 .....67 L6
Penketh St WCGNW/ST WN6 .....47 L1
Penleach Av LEIGH WN7 .....66 E7
Penmere Av SALE M33 .....108 B3
Penmoor Cha BRAM/HZG SK7 .....121 K3
Penmore Cl ROY/SHW OL2 .....43 M5
Pennant Dr PWCH M25 .....55 J3
Pennant St OLD OL1 .....59 L4
Pennell Dr WGNS/IIMK WN3 .....47 J7
Pennell St OP/CLY M11 .....89 C3
Penn Gn CHD/CHDH SK8 .....120 D3
Penn House Cl BRAM/HZG SK7 .....121 G5
Pennine Av CHAD OL9 .....58 D7
WGNS/IIMK WN3 .....62 F1
Pennine Bridleway WHIT OL12 .....20 B6
TOT/BURYW BL8 .....38 D1
Pennine Cl STLY SK15 .....92 A1
AUL OL6 .....76 B8
MILN OL16 .....29 K7
WHIT OL12 .....21 G6
Pennine Gv AUL OL6 .....76 B6
LEIGH WN7 .....65 M4
Pennine Rd BRAM/HZG SK7 .....121 K3
GLSP SK13 .....104 D4
MPL/ROM SK6 .....101 M6
Pennine V ROY/SHW OL2 .....43 M4
Pennine Vw DTN/ASHW M34 .....90 B7
MOSL OL5 .....77 G3
ROY/SHW OL2 .....43 H8
STLY SK15 .....77 G5
Pennington Av LEIGH WN7 .....81 H1
Pennington Cl LHULT M38 .....52 D8
WGNE/HIN WN2 .....49 H3
Pennington Gdns LEIGH WN7 .....81 H1
WGNE/HIN WN2 .....49 H2
Pennington Green La
WGNE/HIN WN2 .....48 D4
Pennington La WGNE/HIN WN2 .....32 B3
WGNE/HIN WN2 .....48 D4
Pennington Rd BOLS/LL BL3 .....52 C1
LEIGH WN7 .....81 J1
Pennington St CHAD OL9 .....74 E1
TOT/BURYW BL8 .....24 B8
WALK M28 .....69 H2
WGNE/HIN WN2 .....49 G6
WGTN/LGST M12 .....99 K2
Pennon Cl BRO M7 .....72 B6
Penn St FWTH BL4 .....52 F5
HEY OL10 .....41 G3
HOR/BR BL6 .....33 J4
MILN OL16 .....10 F3
NEWH/MOS M40 .....73 J4
OLDS OL8 .....8 E8
Penny Bridge La URM M41 .....95 K2
Pennygate Cl WGNE/HIN WN2 .....49 G6
Pennyhurst St WGNS/IIMK WN3 .....14 D5
Penny La RDSH SK5 .....13 J1
RNFD/HAY WA11 .....78 D5
Penny Meadow AUL OL6 .....90 F1
Pennymoor Dr ALT WA14 .....107 L6
Penrhos Av CHD/CHDH SK8 .....110 C8
Penrhyn Av CHD/CHDH SK8 .....120 A3
MDTN M24 .....57 K5
Penrhyn Crs BRAM/HZG SK7 .....121 L3
PWCH M25 .....55 L8
Penrhyn Dr BRAM/HZG SK7 .....121 L3
PWCH M25 .....55 L8
Penrhyn Gv ATH M46 .....50 F7
Penrhyn Rd EDGY/DAV SK3 .....12 A3
Penrice Cl RAD M26 .....38 A7
Penrice Fold WALK M28 .....68 E5
Penrith Av AULW OL7 .....75 J7
BOL BL1 .....35 K3
OLDS OL8 .....74 F1
RDSH SK5 .....100 C3
SALE M33 .....108 F2
WALK M28 .....69 J2
WHTF M45 .....55 K5
Penrith Cl PART M31 .....94 B8
Penrith Crs AIMK WN4 .....63 L1
Penrith St ROCH OL11 .....10 F9
Penrod PI SLFD M6 .....71 L8
Penrose Cl CHH M8 .....72 D6
Penrose Gdns MDTN M24 .....57 L3
Penrose St BOLE BL2 .....3 L4
Penrose Wk MDTN M24 .....57 M4
Penroy Av DID/WITH M20 .....110 A1
Penruddock Wk
BRUN/LGST M13 * 88 C8
Penry Av IRL M44 .....94 B6
Penryn Av ROY/SHW OL2 .....59 J1
SALE M33 .....108 D3
Pensarn Av RUSH/FAL M14 .....99 H4
Pensarn Gv RDSH SK5 .....100 E2
Pensby Cl SWIN M27 .....70 F5
Pensford Ct BOLE BL2 .....3 H6
Pensford Rd NTHM/RTH M23 .....118 B1
Penshaw Av WGNS/IIMK WN3 .....63 L1
Penshurst Rd RDSH SK5 .....100 E6
Penson St WGN WN1 .....48 A2
Penswick Rd WGNE/HIN WN2 .....66 A1
Penthorpe Dr ROY/SHW OL2 .....59 J1
Pentland Av NEWH/MOS M40 .....73 M2
Pentland Ct BRAM/HZG SK7 .....121 K3
Pentlands Av BRO M7 .....72 A6

The Pentlands ROY/SHW OL2 .....43 J4
Pentland Ter BOL BL1 * 36 B3
Pentland Wy HYDE SK14 .....91 L6
Pentwyn Gv NTHM/RTH M23 .....109 L5
Penwell Fold OLD OL1 * 9 H1
Penworthham St
NEWH/MOS M40 .....73 J8
Penydarren Av BOLS/LL BL3 .....52 F2
Penzance St NEWH/MOS M40 .....88 B1
Penzance St
NEWH/MOS M40 * 88 B1
Peover Av SALE M33 .....97 H8
Peover Rd WILM/AE SK9 .....120 A7
Pepler Av NTHM/RTH M23 .....109 L2
Pepperhill Rd OLDTF/WHR M16 .....87 J8
Pepper La WGNNW/ST WN6 .....30 E1
Pepper Mill La WGN WN1 .....15 H6
Peppermint Cl MILN OL16 .....29 M8
Pepper Rd BRAM/HZG SK7 .....121 K2
Pepperwood Dr
WGNS/IIMK WN3 .....63 H2
Pepys PI WGNS/IIMK WN3 .....47 K8
Perch St WGN WN1 .....15 K2
Percival Cl CHH M8 * 72 C6
Percival Rd DROY M43 .....89 L3
Percival Wy WGNW/HIN WN2 .....48 F8
Percy Dr ORD M5 .....86 E5
Percy Rd DTN/ASHW M34 .....101 H2
Percy St BOL BL1 * 36 C2
BURY BL9 .....5 J2
FWTH BL4 * 53 H5
HULME M15 .....87 G6
MILN OL16 .....11 J9
OLDE OL4 .....59 M5
RAMS BL0 .....18 C7
STKP SK1 .....13 J3
STLY SK15 .....91 L3
Peregrine Crs DROY M43 .....89 M1
Peregrine Dr IRL M44 .....94 D7
Peregrine Rd OFTN SK2 .....113 K8
Peregrine St HULME M15 .....87 H7
Perendale Ri BOL BL1 .....22 B8
Perivale Dr OLDS OL8 .....59 L8
Pernham St OLDE OL4 .....59 M5
Perrin St HYDE SK14 .....102 A2
Perry Av HYDE SK14 .....91 K8
Perrygate Av DID/WITH M20 .....98 D6
Perrymead PWCH M25 .....55 L6
Perryn PI WGNNW/ST WN6 .....31 J3
Perry Rd HALE/TIMP WA15 .....108 F1
Pershore WHIT OL12 .....10 D3
Pershore Rd MDTN M24 .....57 K1
Perth Av CHAD OL9 .....58 D8
WGNE/HIN WN2 .....48 A3
Perth Cl BRAM/HZG SK7 .....121 G2
Perth Rd ROCH OL11 .....42 E7
Perth St BOLS/LL BL3 .....51 M1
ROY/SHW OL2 .....43 K8
SWIN M27 .....70 A5
Peru St CSLFD M3 .....6 A2
Peterborough Cl AUL OL6 .....75 L6
Peterborough Dr BOL BL1 .....2 D1
Peterborough St BOL BL1 .....2 D1
Peterborough Wk BOL BL1 .....2 D1
Peterhead Cl BOL BL1 .....2 B1
Peterhead Wk ORD M5 * 86 D3
Peterhouse Gdns
MPL/ROM SK6 .....101 M8
Peterloo Ct SLFD M6 * 86 D2
Peter Moss Wy BNG/LEV M19 .....99 M3
Petersburg Rd EDGY/DAV SK3 .....111 M6
Petersfield Dr NTHM/RTH M23 .....109 G5
Petersfield Gdns
GOL/RIS/CUL WA3 .....81 H8
Petersfield Wk BOL BL1 * 2 C1
Peter St AIMK WN4 .....78 F1
ALT WA14 .....116 F1
BRAM/HZG SK7 .....121 M1
BURY BL9 .....5 G2
CMANE M1 .....7 J5
DTN/ASHW M34 .....101 K1
ECC M30 .....85 G3
GLSP SK13 .....93 K6
GOL/RIS/CUL WA3 .....79 K4
LEIGH WN7 .....66 E8
OLD OL1 .....9 J6
STKP SK1 .....13 L2
TYLD M29 .....67 J3
WGNE/HIN WN2 .....49 G7
WGNW/BIL/OR WN5 .....46 E4
WHTN BL5 .....49 K5
Peterswood Cl
WYTH/NTH M22 .....118 D3
Peterwood Gdns STRET M32 .....96 D3
Petheridge Dr
WYTH/NTH M22 .....118 D3
Petrel Av POY/DIS SK12 .....121 J8
Petrel Cl DROY M43 .....89 M1
EDGY/DAV SK3 .....112 A6
ROCH OL11 .....27 J5
TYLD M29 .....67 K4
Petrie St WHIT OL12 .....10 E1
Petticoat La WGNE/HIN WN2 .....48 E5
Petts Crs LIT OL15 .....21 L6
Petworth Av WGNS/IIMK WN3 .....63 G2
Petworth Cl WYTH/NTH M22 .....110 B7
Petworth Rd CHAD OL9 .....8 A4
Pevensey Rd SLFD M6 .....71 H7
Pevensey Wk CHAD OL9 .....8 A4
Peveril Av WNM/HAY SK22 .....124 E3
Peveril Cl WHTF M45 .....55 M5
Peveril Ct GLSP SK13 .....105 J4
Peveril Crs CCHDY M21 .....97 K2
Peveril Dr BRAM/HZG SK7 .....122 B4
Peveril Gdns CHD/CHDH SK8 .....124 C6
Peveril Ms POY/DIS SK12 .....124 C6
Peveril Rd ALT WA14 .....107 M5
OLD OL1 .....59 M3
ORD M5 .....86 A2
Peveril St BOLS/LL BL3 .....51 L1
Peveril Ter HYDE SK14 .....102 C4
Pewfist Gn WHTN BL5 .....50 B6
The Pewfist Spinney
WHTN BL5 .....50 A5
The Pewfist WHTN BL5 .....50 B5
Pewsey Rd WYTH/NTH M22 .....119 H1
Pexwood OLD OL1 .....58 B3
Pheasant Cl WALK M28 .....68 E6
Pheasant Dr CCHDY M21 .....98 A5
Pheasant Ri ALT WA14 .....116 A3
Phelan Cl NEWH/MOS M40 .....72 F7
Phethean St BOLE BL2 .....3 H1
FWTH BL4 .....52 F3
Philip Av DTN/ASHW M34 .....90 A7
Philip Cl WGNW/BIL/OR WN5 .....47 G7
Philip Dr SALE M33 .....108 E2
Philip Howard Rd GLSP SK13 .....104 F4
Philips Av FWTH BL4 .....53 G5
Philips Park Rd OP/CLY M11 .....88 B2
WHTF M45 .....54 F7

Philip St BOLS/LL BL3 .....2 B9
ECC M30 .....85 G3
OLDE OL4 .....59 M4
ROCH OL11 .....10 F8
Phillimore St OLDE OL4 .....60 B7
Philips Park Rd WHTF M45 .....55 H3
Phillips St WALK M28 .....69 H1
Phipps St WGN WN1 .....14 C5
Phoebe St BOLS/LL BL3 * 35 M8
ORD M5 .....86 D4
Phoenix Cl HEY OL10 .....41 J4
Phoenix St BOL BL1 .....3 G2
BURY BL9 .....4 C4
CMANW M2 * 7 G4
FWTH BL4 .....53 C5
LIT OL15 .....21 M6
OLD OL1 .....9 J7
WHIT OL12 .....27 M3
Phoenix Wy HULME M15 .....87 J7
RAD M26 .....54 D2
URM M41 .....85 H6
Phyllis St MDTN M24 .....57 M5
WHIT OL12 .....27 L3
Picadilly St OLDE OL4 .....60 B7
Piccadilly CMANE M1 .....7 J5
STKP SK1 .....13 J5
Piccadilly Plaza CMANE M1 * 7 H5
Piccadilly South CMANE M1 * 7 H5
Piccard Cl ANC M4 .....7 L1
Pickering Cl HALE/TIMP WA15 .....108 D5
RAD M26 .....53 K4
TOT/BURYW BL8 .....24 E7
URM M41 .....95 L2
Pickering St HULME M15 .....87 H7
Pickford Av BOLS/LL BL3 .....53 M1
Pickford Ct DUK SK16 * 90 F4
Pickford Ms DUK SK16 * 90 F4
Pickford's Brow STKP SK1 .....13 J4
Pickford St ANC M4 .....7 K3
Pickhill La UPML OL3 .....61 L4
Pickhill Ms UPML OL3 .....61 L4
Pickley Gdns LEIGH WN7 .....66 B3
Pickmere Av DID/WITH M20 .....98 E4
Pickmere Cl DROY M43 .....89 M1
SALE M33 .....109 J2
Pickmere Gdns
CHD/CHDH SK8 .....111 J7
Pickmere Ms UPML OL3 .....61 L4
Pickmere Rd WILM/AE SK9 .....119 M7
Picksley St LEIGH WN7 .....66 B7
Pickthorn Cl WGNE/HIN WN2 .....64 L1
Pickup St MILN OL16 .....11 C5
WGNE/HIN WN2 .....48 C5
Pickwick Rd POY/DIS SK12 .....129 H1
Picton Cl CSLFD M3 .....6 C2
Picton Dr WILM/AE SK9 .....127 J3
Picton Sq OLDE OL4 .....75 K6
Picton St AULW OL7 .....75 K6
BRO M7 .....87 G1
Picton Wk OLDTF/WHR M16 .....98 C1
Piele Rd RNFD/HAY WA11 .....78 B5
Pierce St OLD OL1 .....59 M3
Piercy Av ANC M4 .....88 A3
FAIL M35 * 74 B5
Piethorne Cl MILN OL16 .....29 M8
Pigeon St CMANE M1 .....7 K4
Pigginshaw WILM/AE SK9 .....126 C4
Pigott St FWTH BL4 .....52 F5
Pigot St WGNW/BIL/OR WN5 .....46 E6
Pike Av ATH M46 .....66 D2
Pike Cl NM/HAY SK22 .....125 L1
Pike Fold La BKLY M9 .....72 F1
Pike Rd BOLS/LL BL3 .....36 A8
Pike's La GLSP SK13 .....104 E4
Pike St ROCH OL11 .....10 F9
Pike View Cl OLDE OL4 .....59 L7
Pilgrim Dr OP/CLY M11 .....88 C3
Pilgrims Wy
WGNNW/ST WN6 .....31 K5
Pilgrim Wy OLD OL1 .....60 A1
Pilkington Dr WHTF M45 .....55 L2
Pilkington Rd BKLY M9 .....73 K2
FWTH BL4 .....53 J6
RAD M26 .....38 C7
Pilkington St BOLS/LL BL3 .....2 D8
MDTN M24 .....57 M7
RAMS BL0 .....18 E7
WGNE/HIN WN2 .....49 G6
Pilkington Wy RAD M26 .....54 D2
Pilling Fld EDGW/EG BL7 .....22 B3
Pilling St
DTN/ASHW M34 .....101 J1
LEIGH WN7 .....66 A7
NEWH/MOS M40 .....73 J7
TOT/BURYW BL8 .....38 F1
WHIT OL12 .....10 B2
Pilning St BOLS/LL BL3 .....36 D8
Pilot St BURY BL9 .....5 G7
Pilsley Cl
WGNW/BIL/OR WN5 .....46 D3
Pilsworth Rd BURY BL9 .....39 K6
HEY OL10 .....40 C5
Pilsworth Wy BURY BL9 .....39 K6
Pimblett Rd
RNFD/HAY WA11 .....78 B5
Pimblett St CSLFD M3 .....87 J1
GOL/RIS/CUL WA3 .....79 K5
Pimhole Fold BURY BL9 .....5 J5
Pimhole Rd BURY BL9 .....5 J5
Pimlico Cl BRO M7 * 72 A6
Pimlott Gv HYDE SK14 .....91 G7
PWCH M25 .....71 H2
Pimlott Rd BL1 .....36 E1
Pimmcroft Wy SALE M33 .....109 J1
Pine Av WHTF M45 .....55 J5
Pine Cl DTN/ASHW M34 .....90 B6
MPL/ROM SK6 .....114 B8
Pine Gv DTN/ASHW M34 .....101 K1
DUK SK16 .....91 J4
ECC M30 .....70 B8
FWTH BL4 .....52 E4
GOL/RIS/CUL WA3 .....79 M4
PWCH M25 .....55 K6
ROY/SHW OL2 .....43 G6
SALE M33 .....96 A6
SWIN M27 .....70 A4
WHTN BL5 .....50 B7

Pine St AUL OL6 .....75 L8
BOL BL1 .....36 C2
BURY BL9 .....5 K4
CHAD OL9 .....58 D4
CMANE M1 .....7 J5
HEY OL10 .....41 G2
HYDE SK14 .....91 G7
LIT OL15 .....21 M6
MDTN M24 .....57 M5
MILN OL16 .....11 J5
MILN OL16 .....43 L1
MPL/ROM SK6 .....101 L7
TYLD M29 .....67 K3
Pine St North BURY BL9 .....5 K3
Pine St South BURY BL9 .....5 K4
Pinetop Cl CCHDY M21 .....98 A5
Pine Tree Rd OLDS OL8 .....75 C3
Pinetree St GTN M18 .....88 F7
Pinevale WGNNW/ST WN6 .....31 K5
Pine Vw WGNS/IIMK WN3 .....62 E3
Pineway OLDE OL4 .....60 C6
Pinewood AIMK WN4 .....78 D2
ALT WA14 .....116 C2
CHAD OL9 .....58 B5
SALE M33 .....96 A8
Pinewood Cl BOL BL1 .....36 B2
DUK SK16 .....90 F3
HTNM SK4 .....111 K1
WGNE/HIN WN2 .....64 E5
Pinewood Crs WGNE/HIN WN2 .....15 M7
WGNW/BIL/OR WN5 .....46 B6
Pinewood Rd CCHDY M21 * 97 K5
WILM/AE SK9 .....127 G3
The Pinewoods MPL/ROM SK6 .....101 L7
Pinfold GLSP SK13 .....93 H8
Pinfold Av BKLY M9 .....73 K2
Pinfold Cl HALE/TIMP WA15 .....117 M5
WHTN BL5 .....50 A6
Pinfold Dr CHD/CHDH SK8 .....120 C5
Pinfold La HALE/TIMP WA15 .....118 B6
MPL/ROM SK6 .....102 B8
WHTF M45 .....55 H4
Pinfold Rd WALK M28 .....68 F3
Pinfold St WGNE/HIN WN2 .....48 D5
Pingate Dr CHD/CHDH SK8 .....120 C6
Pingate La CHD/CHDH SK8 .....120 C6
Pingate La South
CHD/CHDH SK8 .....120 C6
Pingle La UPML OL3 .....45 C7
Pingot Av NTHM/RTH M23 .....109 L3
Pingot La HYDE SK14 .....103 M2
Pingot Rd NM/HAY SK22 .....125 C4
WGNW/BIL/OR WN5 .....62 B7
Pingot St NM/HAY SK22 .....125 L1
The Pingot IRL M44 .....94 E1
LEIGH WN7 .....66 A7
Pingott La GLSP SK13 .....93 K7
Pink Bank La WGTN/LGST M12 .....88 E8
Pinnacle Dr EDGW/EG BL7 .....22 A2
Pinner PI BNG/LEV M19 .....99 K7
Pinners Cl RAMS BL0 .....18 F5
Pinnington La STRET M32 * 97 G3
Pinnington Rd GTN M18 .....89 C6
Pintail Av EDGY/DAV SK3 .....112 A6
Pintail Cl WHIT OL12 .....27 L2
Pioneer Rd SWIN M27 .....71 H5
Pioneer St LIT OL15 .....21 M7
OP/CLY M11 .....88 E1
ROCH OL11 .....11 G7
Piperhill Av WYTH/NTH M22 .....110 A3
Pipers Cl ROCH OL11 .....27 G4
Pipers Ct IRL M44 .....94 F1
The Pipers GOL/RIS/CUL WA3 .....80 C4
Pipewell Av GTN M18 .....88 E7
Pipit Cl DTN/ASHW M34 .....89 M2
Pitchcombe Rd
WYTH/NTH M22 .....118 D2
Pitcombe Cl BOL BL1 .....22 A5
Pitfield Gdns NTHM/RTH M23 .....109 J5
Pitfield La BOLE BL2 .....37 J1
Pitfield St BOLE BL2 .....3 J3
Pit La ROY/SHW OL2 .....42 F4
Pitman Cl OP/CLY M11 .....88 D3
Pits Farm Av ROCH OL11 .....27 M5
Pitsford Rd NEWH/MOS M40 .....73 H7
Pitshouse La WHIT OL12 * 27 H2
Pit St CHAD OL9 .....58 E8
DTN/ASHW M34 .....101 J1
HEY OL10 .....40 F2
HYDE SK14 .....102 A1
OLDE OL4 .....9 M7
RAD M26 .....54 B1
WGNS/IIMK WN3 .....14 C5
WGNS/IIMK WN3 * 15 J7
Pitt St East OLDE OL4 .....59 L7
Pixmore Av BOL BL1 .....22 E8
Place Rd ALT WA14 .....107 M6
Plain Pit St HYDE SK14 .....90 F7
Plainsfield Cl
OLDTF/WHR M16 .....87 J3
Plainsfield St
OLDTF/WHR M16 .....87 H8
Plane Av
WGNW/BIL/OR WN5 .....47 H5
Plane Ct SLFD M6 * 86 D2
Plane Rd FAIL M35 .....74 C3
Plane St OLDE OL4 .....59 L5
Plane Tree Cl
MPL/ROM SK6 .....114 A7
Plane Tree Gv
RNFD/HAY WA11 * 78 D5
Planetree Rd
HALE/TIMP WA15 .....117 J2
Plane Tree Rd PART M31 .....106 A1
Planet Wy DTN/ASHW M34 .....90 B7
Plank La LEIGH WN7 .....65 K8
Plantation Av WALK M28 .....52 F8
Plantation Gates WGN WN1 .....48 B2
Plantation Rd EDGW/EG BL7 .....17 J1
Plantation St AUL OL6 .....91 G3
GTN M18 .....88 F7
Plant Cl SALE M33 .....96 D7
Plant Hill Rd BKLY M9 .....56 F7
Plant St CMANE M1 .....7 J5
Plant Ter BKLY M9 * 9 K5
Plate St OLD OL1 .....9 K5
Platford Dr CHAD OL9 .....58 B8
Platt Av AUL OL6 .....75 M6
Plattbrook Cl
RUSH/FAL M14 .....98 E3
Platt Cl LEIGH WN7 .....66 B7
Platt Cft LEIGH WN7 .....66 E8
Platt Fold Rd LEIGH WN7 .....66 E8
Platt Fold St LEIGH WN7 .....66 D7
Platt Hill Av BOLS/LL BL3 .....35 K8
Platting Gv AULW OL7 .....75 J7
Platting La ROCH OL11 .....28 C8
Platting Rd OLDE OL4 .....60 F5

Platt La RUSH/FAL M14 ...... 98 C3
UPML OL3 ...... 61 J2
WGN WN1 ...... 15 K3
WGN WN1 ...... 31 L1
WGNE/HIN WN2 ...... 50 E6
WHTN BL5 ...... 50 D4
Platts Dr IRL M44 ...... 94 D2
Platt St CHD/CHDH SK8 ...... 111 H6
DUK SK16 ...... 90 D5
GLSP SK13 ...... 93 L7
LEIGH WN7 ...... 66 C6
OLDE OL4 ...... 9 H8
Plattwood Wk HULME M15 * 87 G6
Playfair Cl HEY OL10 ...... 41 H5
Playfair St BOL BL1 ...... 22 C6
RUSH/FAL M14 ...... 87 L8
Pleachway HTNM SK4 ...... 111 J2
Pleasance Wy NEWLW WA12 ...... 78 F8
Pleasant Gdns BOL BL1 * 2 C2
Pleasant Rd ECC M30 ...... 85 H3
Pleasant St BKLY M9 ...... 73 H5
HEY OL10 ...... 26 F8
ROCH OL11 ...... 41 M2
TOT/BURYW BL8 ...... 24 C8
Pleasant Wy CHD/CHDH SK8 ...... 120 E6
Pleasington Dr
NEWH/MOS M40 ...... 73 M2
TOT/BURYW BL8 ...... 38 B2
Plevna St BOLE BL2 ...... 3 H4
Plodder La FWTH BL4 ...... 52 A4
WHTN BL5 ...... 51 K4
Ploughbank Dr CCHDY M21 ...... 98 B5
Plough Cl URM M41 ...... 94 F3
Plough Flds WALK M28 ...... 68 C7
Ploughfields WHTN BL5 ...... 50 B1
Plough St DUK SK16 ...... 91 G4
Plover Cl GLSP SK13 ...... 105 H4
ROCH OL11 ...... 27 H5
Plover Dr ALT WA14 ...... 107 L4
BURY BL9 ...... 25 L8
IRL M44 ...... 83 K8
Plover Wy GOL/RIS/CUL WA3 ...... 80 B4
Plowden Av BOLS/LL BL3 ...... 51 M1
Plowden Rd WYTH/NTH M22 ...... 118 D2
Plowley Cl DID/WITH M20 ...... 110 E2
Plucksbridge Rd
MPL/ROM SK6 ...... 123 J1
Plumbley Dr OLDTF/WHR M16 ...... 97 J1
Plumbley St OP/CLY M11 * 89 G1
Plumley Cl EDGY/DAV SK3 ...... 112 C7
Plumley Rd WILM/AE SK9 ...... 119 M7
Plummer Av CCHDY M21 ...... 97 L6
Plumpton Cl ROY/SHW OL2 ...... 59 H3
Plumpton Dr BURY BL9 ...... 25 H6
Plumpton Rd ROCH OL11 ...... 42 E4
Plumpton Wk
BRUN/LGST M13 * 88 C8
Plum St OLDS OL8 ...... 8 E8
Plum Tree Ct SLFD M6 ...... 86 D2
Plunge Rd RAMS BL0 ...... 19 H1
Pluto Cl SLFD M6 * 6 A1
Plymouth Av BRUN/LGST M13 ...... 88 B7
Plymouth Cl AUL OL6 ...... 75 M5
Plymouth Dr BRAM/HZG SK7 ...... 121 H5
FWTH BL4 ...... 52 C4
Plymouth Gv BRUN/LGST M13 ...... 88 A7
EDGY/DAV SK3 ...... 12 A8
RAD M26 ...... 38 C7
WGNNW/ST WN6 ...... 31 K5
Plymouth Gv West
BRUN/LGST M13 ...... 88 B7
Plymouth Rd SALE M33 ...... 96 A7
Plymouth St OLDS OL8 ...... 59 J8
Plymouth Vw BRUN/LGST M13 ...... 87 M6
Plymtree Cl CHH M8 ...... 72 B2
Pochard Dr ALT WA14 ...... 107 L5
POY/DIS SK12 ...... 121 J8
Pochin St NEWH/MOS M40 ...... 88 B1
Pocket Nook La
GOL/RIS/CUL WA3 ...... 80 E5
Pocket Nook Rd HOR/BR BL6 ...... 50 E1
Pocklington Dr
NTHM/RTH M23 ...... 109 J5
Podnor La MPL/ROM SK6 ...... 115 K6
Podsmead Rd WYTH/NTH M22 ...... 118 D2
Poet's Nook LEIGH WN7 ...... 66 B8
Poise Brook Dr OFTN SK2 ...... 113 J7
Poise Brook Rd OFTN SK2 ...... 113 J7
Poise Cl BRAM/HZG SK7 ...... 122 C1
Poke St WGNW/BIL/OR WN5 ...... 46 E6
Poland St ANC M4 ...... 7 L2
DTN/ASHW M34 ...... 90 B4
Polden Cl OLDS OL8 ...... 75 H1
Polding St SLFD M6 ...... 48 B8
Poleacre La MPL/ROM SK6 ...... 101 M6
Polebrook Cl WGN/LGST M12 ...... 88 A6
Pole Ct BURY BL9 * 55 M1
Polefield Ap PWCH M25 ...... 55 L6
Polefield Cir PWCH M25 ...... 55 L6
Polefield Gdns PWCH M25 ...... 55 L6
Polefield Gra PWCH M25 ...... 55 L6
Polefield Gv PWCH M25 ...... 55 L6
Polefield Hall Rd PWCH M25 ...... 55 L6
Polefield Rd BKLY M9 ...... 73 G2
PWCH M25 ...... 55 L5
Polegate Dr LEIGH WN7 ...... 66 A2
Pole La BURY BL9 ...... 55 M4
FAIL M35 ...... 74 C4
WHIT M45 ...... 55 K4
Pole St BOLE BL2 ...... 3 J1
WGNNW/ST WN6 ...... 31 H3
Polesworth Cl WGN/LGST M12 ...... 88 D6
Police St ALT WA14 ...... 108 A7
CMANW M2 ...... 6 E4
ECC M30 ...... 85 K1
Pollard Ct OLD OL1 * 9 G2
Pollards La BURY BL9 ...... 24 F2
Pollard Sq PART M31 ...... 106 D1
Pollard St East ANC M4 ...... 7 M5
Pollard St East ANC M4 ...... 88 A5
Pollen Cl SALE M33 ...... 108 F2
Pollen Rd ALT WA14 ...... 107 M6
Polletts Av RDSH SK5 ...... 100 F6
Pollit Cft MPL/ROM SK6 ...... 113 J3
Pollitt Av AUL OL6 ...... 75 H4
Pollitt Cl WGN/LGST M12 * 88 C6
Pollitts Cl ECC M30 ...... 84 C2
Polonia Ct OLDS OL8 ...... 74 F1
Polperro Cl ROY/SHW OL2 ...... 43 K8
Polruan Rd CCHDY M21 ...... 97 L5
Polworth Rd BKLY M9 ...... 73 H3
Polygon Av BRUN/LGST M13 ...... 87 M6
Polygon Rd CHH M8 ...... 72 D4
Polygon St BRUN/LGST M13 ...... 7 L9
The Polygon BRO M7 ...... 71 M6
ECC M30 ...... 85 K2
Pomfret St SLFD M6 * 70 F7
WGTN/LGST M12 ...... 88 D6
Pomona Crs ORD M5 ...... 86 E5
Pomona Strd HULME M15 ...... 86 F6
ORD M5 ...... 86 D2
Pomona St ROCH OL11 ...... 10 F9

Ponds Cl CCHDY M21 * 97 L3
Pond St GOL/RIS/CUL WA3 ...... 80 D4
Pondwater Cl WALK M28 ...... 68 C1
Ponsford Av BKLY M9 ...... 73 K1
Ponsonby Rd STRET M32 ...... 97 G1
Pontefract Cl SWIN M27 ...... 70 E5
Pool Bank St MDTN M24 ...... 56 F5
Poolcroft SALE M33 ...... 109 J1
Poole Cl BRAM/HZG SK7 ...... 120 F3
Pooley Cl MDTN M24 ...... 56 E3
Poolfield Cl RAD M26 ...... 54 B1
Pool Fold FAIL M35 ...... 74 D6
Pool House Rd POY/DIS SK12 ...... 122 E7
Poolstock WGNS/IIMK WN3 ...... 14 F8
Poolstock La WGNS/IIMK WN3 ...... 47 K8
Pool St BOL BL1 ...... 2 D4
OLDS OL8 ...... 59 J8
WGNE/HIN WN2 ...... 49 G8
WGNS/IIMK WN3 ...... 14 E8
Pool Ter BOL BL1 ...... 35 K2
Poolton Rd BKLY M9 ...... 56 E8
Poorfield St OLDS OL8 ...... 9 H8
Poplar Av AIMK WN4 ...... 63 C7
ALT WA14 ...... 108 A6
BNG/LEV M19 ...... 99 L5
BOL BL1 ...... 22 C8
BOLE BL2 ...... 22 F6
BURY BL9 ...... 25 L8
HOR/BR BL6 ...... 34 B3
NM/HAY SK22 ...... 124 C8
OLDE OL4 ...... 60 F8
OLDS OL8 ...... 75 G2
WGNW/BIL/OR WN5 ...... 47 C6
WILM/AE SK9 ...... 126 C7
Poplar Cl CHD/CHDH SK8 ...... 110 E7
Poplar Ct DTN/ASHW M34 * 90 C6
EDGY/DAV SK3 * 112 C7
Poplar Dr PWCH M25 ...... 71 K2
Poplar Gv CTN M18 ...... 89 G8
IRL M44 ...... 94 A6
OFTN SK2 ...... 112 F8
RAMS BL0 ...... 18 D4
SALE M33 ...... 108 E1
URM M41 ...... 96 B2
WGNE/HIN WN2 ...... 65 L2
WHTN BL5 ...... 50 B4
Poplar Rd BNG/LEV M19 ...... 111 G1
DUK SK16 ...... 91 J5
ECC M30 ...... 70 B8
STRET M32 ...... 96 F4
SWIN M27 ...... 70 A5
WALK M28 ...... 69 H2
Poplars Rd STLY SK15 ...... 92 A1
The Poplars LEIGH WN7 ...... 80 F4
MOSL OL5 ...... 77 H3
Poplar St DTN/ASHW M34 ...... 90 C6
FAIL M35 ...... 74 A6
GOL/RIS/CUL WA3 ...... 79 L3
HTNM SK4 ...... 111 H2
LEIGH WN7 ...... 81 J1
TYLD M29 ...... 67 K3
Poplar Wk CHAD OL9 ...... 8 A3
Poplar Wy MPL/ROM SK6 ...... 123 J4
Poplin Dr CSLFD M3 ...... 6 D1
Poppy Cl CHAD OL9 ...... 58 A5
NTHM/RTH M23 ...... 109 H3
Poppyfield Vw ROCH OL11 ...... 27 H4
Poppythorn La PWCH M25 ...... 55 K7
Porchester Dr RAD M26 ...... 37 M7
Porchfield Sq CSLFD M3 ...... 6 D6
Porlock Av DTN/ASHW M34 ...... 89 M4
HYDE SK14 ...... 102 F2
Porlock Cl STKP SK1 ...... 112 F4
WGNE/HIN WN2 ...... 30 D3
Porlock Rd NTHM/RTH M23 ...... 109 L6
URM M41 ...... 95 L4
Porritt Cl ROCH OL11 ...... 27 H6
Porritt St BURY BL9 ...... 5 L1
Porritt Wy RAMS BL0 ...... 18 F5
Portal Gv DTN/ASHW M34 ...... 101 L3
Porter Av NEWLW WA12 ...... 78 F7
Porter Dr NEWH/MOS M40 ...... 73 G6
Porterfield Dr TYLD M29 ...... 67 K4
Porter St BURY BL9 ...... 25 J8
Porters Wood Cl
WGNW/BIL/OR WN5 ...... 46 E5
Portfield Cl BOL BL1 ...... 35 J4
Porthleven Crs TYLD M29 ...... 67 M4
Porthleven Dr
NTHM/RTH M23 ...... 109 H6
Portinscale Cl TOT/BURYW BL8 ...... 38 E1
Portland Cl BRAM/HZG SK7 ...... 121 K3
WGNE/HIN WN2 ...... 64 D3
Portland Crs BRUN/LGST M13 ...... 88 A3
Portland Gv HTNM SK4 ...... 99 L8
Portland Houses
MPL/ROM SK6 * 114 B7
Portland Pl AULW OL7 ...... 90 D3
HOR/BR BL6 ...... 34 B4
Portland Rd ALT WA14 ...... 116 F1
BRUN/LGST M13 ...... 99 J1
ECC M30 ...... 85 J1
NM/HAY SK22 ...... 124 F3
STRET M32 ...... 97 H1
SWIN M27 ...... 70 D5
WALK M28 ...... 52 F7
Portland St BOL BL1 ...... 5 H1
BURY BL9 ...... 5 H1
CMANE M1 ...... 7 G6
MILN OL16 ...... 10 F3
NEWLW WA12 ...... 78 C8
WGNW/BIL/OR WN5 ...... 47 H6
Portland St North AUL OL6 ...... 90 D2
Portland St South AUL OL6 ...... 90 D2
Portloe Rd CHD/CHDH SK8 ...... 119 K6
Portman Cl OLDTF/WHR M16 ...... 98 B1
Portrea Cl EDGY/DAV SK3 ...... 112 B7
Portree Cl ECC M30 ...... 84 C2
Portrush Rd WYTH/NTH M22 ...... 119 G2
Portside Cl WALK M28 ...... 68 C7
Portsmouth Cl BRO M7 ...... 72 A7
Portsmouth St BRUN/LGST M13 ...... 87 L1
Port Soderick Av ORD M5 ...... 86 D3
Portstone Cl OLDTF/WHR M16 ...... 87 H8
Portstone St
OLDTF/WHR M16 * 87 H8
Port St CMANE M1 ...... 7 J4
OLDS OL8 ...... 59 J8
STKP SK1 ...... 13 G3
Portugal Rd PWCH M25 ...... 71 L2
Portugal St ANC M4 ...... 7 M1
AULW OL7 ...... 90 C4
BOLE BL2 ...... 3 J5
Portugal St East CMANE M1 ...... 7 L6
Portville Rd BNG/LEV M19 ...... 99 K2
Portway WYTH/NTH M22 ...... 118 B3
Portwood Pl RDSH SK5 ...... 13 J2
Posnett St EDGY/DAV SK3 ...... 12 C6
Postal St CMANE M1 * 7 J4
Postbridge Cl BRUN/LGST M13 ...... 87 M6
Post Office St ALT WA14 ...... 108 A3

Post St GLSP SK13 ...... 93 L7
Potato Whf CSLFD M3 ...... 6 B7
Pot Hi AUL OL6 ...... 75 M8
Pot Hill Sq AUL OL6 * 75 M8
Potter Rd GLSP SK13 ...... 104 B1
Potters La BKLY M9 ...... 73 H5
Potter St BURY BL9 ...... 5 J2
RAD M26 ...... 39 C8
Pottery La OP/CLY M11 ...... 88 D4
Pottery Rd WGNS/IIMK WN3 ...... 14 C6
Pottery Ter WGNS/IIMK WN3 ...... 14 D6
Pottinger St AULW OL7 ...... 90 C4
Pott St SWIN M27 ...... 70 C2
Poulton Av BOLE BL2 ...... 37 H5
Poulton Dr AIMK WN4 ...... 63 J8
Poulton St OP/CLY M11 ...... 89 H5
Poundswick La
WYTH/NTH M22 ...... 118 F1
Powder Mill Cl IRL M44 ...... 94 D3
Powell Av HYDE SK14 ...... 102 B1
Powell Rd OLDTF/WHR M16 ...... 86 F8
OP/CLY M11 ...... 89 G2
TOT/BURYW BL8 ...... 38 E3
Powell St WGN WN1 ...... 15 G2
WGNE/HIN WN2 ...... 64 E3
Powicke Dr MPL/ROM SK6 ...... 113 J5
Powicke Wk MPL/ROM SK6 ...... 113 K3
Powis Rd URM M41 ...... 94 F3
Pownall Av BRAM/HZG SK7 ...... 121 H5
DID/WITH M20 ...... 98 D4
Pownall Rd ALT WA14 ...... 116 F2
CHD/CHDH SK8 ...... 120 C3
WILM/AE SK9 ...... 126 A4
Pownall St BRAM/HZG SK7 ...... 121 M1
LEIGH WN7 ...... 66 D7
Powys St ATH M46 ...... 67 H5
Poynings Dr WYTH/NTH M22 ...... 118 E3
Poynt Cha WALK M28 ...... 68 D7
Poynter St NEWH/MOS M40 ...... 73 M3
Poynton St BURY BL9 ...... 5 H7
HULME M15 * 87 J6
Praed Rd TRPK M17 ...... 85 M7
Praeton Cl ATH M46 ...... 66 D3
The Precinct EDGY/DAV SK3 * 13 C8
HYDE SK14 * 93 C7
OFTN SK2 * 113 C6
Preece Cl HYDE SK14 ...... 91 K8
Preesall Av CHD/CHDH SK8 ...... 119 K4
Preesall Cl TOT/BURYW BL8 ...... 38 C4
Prefect Pl WGNW/BIL/OR WN5 ...... 46 F4
Premier Rd CHH M8 ...... 72 C8
Premier St OLDTF/WHR M16 ...... 87 G8
Prenton St OP/CLY M11 ...... 89 H4
Prenton Wy TOT/BURYW BL8 ...... 24 C7
Presall St BOLE BL2 * 3 L3
Presbyterian Fold
WGNE/HIN WN2 ...... 49 C6
Prescot Av ATH M46 ...... 51 H8
TYLD M29 ...... 67 M3
Prescot Cl BURY BL9 ...... 5 H7
Prescot Rd BKLY M9 ...... 73 G5
HALE/TIMP WA15 ...... 117 H2
Prescott Av GOL/RIS/CUL WA3 ...... 79 J2
Prescott La
WGNW/BIL/OR WN5 ...... 46 E4
Prescott Rd WILM/AE SK9 ...... 126 F3
Prescott St BOLS/LL BL3 * 35 M8
GOL/RIS/CUL WA3 ...... 79 K3
LEIGH WN7 ...... 66 C6
MILN OL16 ...... 28 F2
WALK M28 ...... 68 E1
WGNE/HIN WN2 ...... 49 G7
WGNS/IIMK WN3 ...... 14 C4
Press St OP/CLY M11 ...... 89 G5
Presswood Ct SLFD M6 ...... 70 F6
Prestage St OLDTF/WHR M16 ...... 87 G8
WGTN/LGST M12 ...... 99 L2
Prestbury Av
HALE/TIMP WA15 ...... 108 B6
RUSH/FAL M14 ...... 98 C3
WGNS/IIMK WN3 ...... 63 H1
Prestbury Cl BURY BL9 ...... 5 H7
OFTN SK2 ...... 113 C8
Prestbury Dr MPL/ROM SK6 ...... 113 H1
OLD OL1 ...... 59 C3
Prestbury Rd BOL BL1 ...... 22 D7
MCFLDN SK10 ...... 131 K6
WILM/AE SK9 ...... 127 J7
Prestfield Rd WHTF M45 ...... 55 K5
Presto Gdns BOLS/LL BL3 * 35 L8
Prestolee Rd BOLS/LL BL3 ...... 53 K3
RAD M26 ...... 53 M3
Preston Av ECC M30 ...... 85 K1
IRL M44 ...... 94 C5
Preston Cl ECC M30 * 85 K1
Preston Rd BNG/LEV M19 ...... 99 K4
WGNNW/ST WN6 ...... 31 K1
Preston St BOLS/LL BL3 * 36 E8
CTN M18 ...... 88 F6
MDTN M24 ...... 57 K4
OLDE OL4 ...... 9 L7
WHIT OL12 ...... 27 M4
Presto St BOLS/LL BL3 ...... 35 L8
FWTH BL4 ...... 53 H3
Prestt Gv WGNS/IIMK WN3 ...... 14 B9
Prestwich Av OFTN SK2 ...... 66 E7
Prestwich Hills PWCH M25 ...... 71 K2
Prestwich Park Rd South
PWCH M25 ...... 71 K1
Prestwich St ATH M46 ...... 50 E8
Prestwood Cl BOL BL1 ...... 35 M3
Prestwood Dr BOL BL1 ...... 36 A3
Prestwood Rd FWTH BL4 ...... 52 D3
SLFD M6 ...... 70 F8
Pretoria Rd AIMK WN4 ...... 63 K8
BOLE BL2 ...... 37 H5
OLDS OL8 ...... 74 F1
Pretoria St WHIT OL12 * 27 M3
Prettywood BURY BL9 ...... 40 A2
Price St ANC M4 * 88 A3
BURY BL9 ...... 5 H7
DUK SK16 ...... 90 F4
FWTH BL4 ...... 53 C4
Prichard St STRET M32 ...... 97 G2
Pridmouth Rd
DID/WITH M20 ...... 98 F6
Priest Av CHD/CHDH SK8 ...... 110 D8
Priestfields LEIGH WN7 ...... 66 E7
Priest La MCFLDN SK10 ...... 131 L3
Priestley Rd WALK M28 ...... 69 M4
Priestley Wy ROY/SHW OL2 ...... 44 A5
Priestnall Rd HTNM SK4 ...... 111 J1
Priestners Wy LEIGH WN7 ...... 66 B6
Priest St STKP SK1 ...... 13 K9
Priestwood Av OLDE OL4 ...... 44 C8
Primrose Av FWTH BL4 ...... 52 D3
HYDE SK14 ...... 102 A5
MPL/ROM SK6 ...... 114 B6
UPML OL3 ...... 61 M3
URM M41 * 96 A2
WALK M28 ...... 68 C2

Primrose Bank ALT WA14 ...... 116 E3
OLDS OL8 ...... 9 G9
TOT/BURYW BL8 ...... 24 B5
WALK M28 ...... 68 E2
Primrose Cl BOLE BL2 ...... 23 K8
ORD M5 ...... 86 B2
Primrose Cottages ALT WA14 * 116 E3
Primrose Crs HYDE SK14 ...... 102 A4
Primrose Dr BURY BL9 ...... 26 A8
DROY M43 ...... 89 M1
Primrose Gv RNFD/HAY WA11 ...... 78 B5
WGNW/BIL/OR WN5 * 47 H5
Primrose Hl GLSP SK13 ...... 104 E4
Primrose La GLSP SK13 ...... 104 D3
WGNNW/ST WN6 ...... 31 G2
Primrose St ANC M4 ...... 7 K2
BOL BL1 ...... 22 C8
FWTH BL4 ...... 53 H5
LEIGH WN7 * 66 A7
OLDS OL8 ...... 9 H8
WHIT OL12 ...... 10 B3
Primrose St North TYLD M29 ...... 67 K3
Primrose Ter GLSP SK13 ...... 104 E4
Primrose Vw AIMK WN4 ...... 78 E2
Primrose Wk OLDS OL8 ...... 9 H8
Primula Dr GOL/RIS/CUL WA3 ...... 80 A4
Primula St BOL BL1 ...... 22 C8
Prince Albert Av
BNG/LEV M19 * 99 K2
Prince Charlie St OLD OL1 ...... 59 L4
Princedom St BKLY M9 ...... 73 H4
Prince Edward Av
DTN/ASHW M34 ...... 101 K2
OLDE OL4 ...... 59 M5
Prince George St OLD OL1 ...... 59 M3
Prince Mead Pl TRPK M17 ...... 85 L7
Prince Rd POY/DIS SK12 ...... 122 E7
Prince's Av BOLS/LL BL3 ...... 37 L8
DID/WITH M20 ...... 98 D8
IRL M44 ...... 94 F1
MPL/ROM SK6 ...... 113 K1
TYLD M29 ...... 67 K6
Princes Ct ECC M30 * 85 C1
Prince's Dr MPL/ROM SK6 ...... 114 B5
SALE M33 ...... 109 C1
Princes Gdns LEIGH WN7 ...... 66 F7
Princes Pk WGNNW/ST WN6 ...... 30 C8
Princes Rd ALT WA14 ...... 108 A6
HTNM SK4 ...... 99 K8
MPL/ROM SK6 ...... 113 K1
SALE M33 ...... 108 F1
Princess Av AIMK WN4 ...... 78 E1
ATH M46 ...... 50 F7
CHD/CHDH SK8 ...... 120 C1
DTN/ASHW M34 ...... 101 H1
FWTH BL4 ...... 53 J7
PWCH M25 ...... 71 M2
RNFD/HAY WA11 ...... 78 D5
WHIT OL12 ...... 21 G8
Princess Cl DUK SK16 ...... 91 G4
HEY OL10 ...... 41 G3
MOSL OL5 ...... 77 H4
Princess Dr MDTN M24 ...... 57 H4
Princess Gv FWTH BL4 ...... 53 C4
Princess Pde BURY BL9 ...... 4 F5
RUSH/FAL M14 ...... 98 C3
Princess Pkwy
WYTH/NTH M22 ...... 109 M4
Princess Rd AIMK WN4 ...... 78 E1
CHAD OL9 ...... 74 B1
DID/WITH M20 ...... 110 A1
HOR/BR BL6 ...... 34 E5
HULME M15 ...... 29 G5
MILN OL16 ...... 29 G5
PWCH M25 * 55 M8
ROY/SHW OL2 ...... 43 K6
RUSH/FAL M14 ...... 98 C3
URM M41 ...... 95 L2
WGNNW/ST WN6 ...... 30 F8
WILM/AE SK9 ...... 126 D7
Princess St ALT WA14 ...... 107 M4
AUL OL6 ...... 76 A8
BOL BL1 ...... 2 F5
CMANW M2 ...... 6 E6
ECC M30 ...... 84 F2
FAIL M35 ...... 74 B5
GLSP SK13 ...... 104 C4
HYDE SK14 ...... 102 B2
LEIGH WN7 ...... 66 D7
OLDE OL4 ...... 60 B6
RAD M26 ...... 54 B1
SLFD M6 ...... 71 K8
SWIN M27 ...... 70 D5
WGNE/HIN WN2 ...... 48 F7
WGNS/IIMK WN3 ...... 14 F6
WHIT OL12 ...... 10 F1
Prince's St STKP SK1 ...... 13 H4
Prince St AIMK WN4 ...... 63 K7
BOL BL1 ...... 2 F5
HEY OL10 ...... 41 G2
MILN OL16 ...... 11 H9
OLD OL1 ...... 9 L3
RAMS BL0 ...... 18 F6
Princes Av BRAM/HZG SK7 ...... 121 J5
Princethorpe Cl HOR/BR BL6 ...... 35 G6
Princeton Cl SLFD M6 ...... 85 M1
Prinknash Rd WYTH/NTH M22 ...... 118 F3
Printers Cl BNG/LEV M19 ...... 111 G2
Printers Dr STLY SK15 ...... 77 K5
Printers Fold HYDE SK14 ...... 93 G7
EDGW/EG BL7 ...... 93 G7
Printers Pk HYDE SK14 ...... 93 H7
Printer St OLD OL1 ...... 9 J6
OP/CLY M11 * 89 G4
Printon Av BKLY M9 ...... 56 B8
Printshop La ATH M46 ...... 67 H3
Printworks La BNG/LEV M19 ...... 99 M3
Printworks Rd STLY SK15 ...... 91 L1
Prior St OLDS OL8 ...... 59 L8
Priory Av BRO M7 ...... 71 M6
CCHDY M21 ...... 98 C1
LEIGH WN7 ...... 66 A3
Priory Cl DUK SK16 ...... 91 G4
OLDS OL8 ...... 75 G1
SALE M33 ...... 108 F1
WGNW/BIL/OR WN5 ...... 46 E7
Priory Ct RDSH SK5 ...... 100 B4
Priory Gv BRO M7 ...... 71 M6
CHAD OL9 ...... 58 D8
Priory La RDSH SK5 ...... 100 B4
Priory Pl BOLE BL2 ...... 36 F2
Priory Rd AIMK WN4 ...... 63 J7
ALT WA14 ...... 116 D4
CHD/CHDH SK8 ...... 111 K4
SALE M33 ...... 97 G3
SWIN M27 ...... 70 B4
WILM/AE SK9 ...... 126 C4
Priory St ALT WA14 ...... 116 E4
The Priory BRO M7 ...... 71 M6
Pritchard St CMANE M1 * 7 H7
Privet St OLDE OL4 ...... 60 A3
Proctor Cl WGNW/BIL/OR WN5 ...... 47 H3

Proctor St TOT/BURYW BL8 ...... 38 F3
Prodesse Ct WGNE/HIN WN2 ...... 49 G6
Progress Av AUL OL6 ...... 90 C7
Progress St AUL OL6 ...... 90 D1
BOL BL1 ...... 36 C3
ROCH OL11 ...... 41 M3
WGNE/HIN WN2 ...... 49 G7
Promenade HEY OL10 ...... 41 H2
Props Hall Dr FAIL M35 ...... 74 B6
Prospect Av FWTH BL4 ...... 53 C5
IRL M44 ...... 94 B6
Prospect Ct TOT/BURYW BL8 ...... 24 C5
Prospect Dr FAIL M35 ...... 74 C7
HALE/TIMP WA15 ...... 117 M5
Prospect Hl BOLE BL2 ...... 23 J8
Prospect Pl AUL OL6 ...... 76 A7
FWTH BL4 ...... 52 F5
HEY OL10 ...... 41 G1
Prospect Rd AUL OL6 ...... 76 B7
CHAD OL9 ...... 58 C4
DUK SK16 ...... 91 G4
IRL M44 ...... 94 B6
WGNNW/ST WN6 ...... 31 H5
Prospect St BOL BL1 ...... 36 C3
HEY OL10 ...... 41 H4
LIT OL15 ...... 21 M6
ROCH OL11 ...... 28 B3
TYLD M29 ...... 67 M3
WGNE/HIN WN2 ...... 49 G7
Prospect Ter TOT/BURYW BL8 ...... 4 B1
Prospect V CHD/CHDH SK8 ...... 119 K3
Prospect Vw SWIN M27 ...... 70 D5
Prosser Av ATH M46 ...... 66 D2
Prout St WGTN/LGST M12 ...... 99 K1
Provender Cl ALT WA14 ...... 108 A4
Providence St ANC M4 ...... 88 A3
AUL OL6 * 75 M8
BOLS/LL BL3 ...... 2 B8
DTN/ASHW M34 ...... 90 C5
Provident Av BNG/LEV M19 ...... 99 M3
Provident St ROY/SHW OL2 * 43 L5
Provident Wy
HALE/TIMP WA15 ...... 108 D5
Provis Rd CCHDY M21 ...... 97 L5
Prubella Av DTN/ASHW M34 ...... 92 B5
Pryce Av WGNE/HIN WN2 ...... 15 M5
Pryce St BOL BL1 ...... 2 B1
Pryme St HULME M15 ...... 6 C8
Pudding La HYDE SK14 ...... 102 F1
Puffin Av POY/DIS SK12 ...... 128 K1
Puffingate Cl STLY SK15 ...... 77 H5
Pulborough Cl TOT/BURYW BL8 ...... 24 C5
Pulford Av CCHDY M21 ...... 98 A8
Pulford Rd SALE M33 ...... 108 F2
Pullman Cl BNG/LEV M19 ...... 99 K3
Pullman Dr STRET M32 ...... 96 C2
Pullman St ROCH OL11 ...... 10 F9
Pump St NEWH/MOS M40 ...... 49 G7
Punch La BOLS/LL BL3 ...... 51 G2
Punch St BOLS/LL BL3 ...... 2 B7
The Pungle WHTN BL5 ...... 50 A7
Purbeck Cl WYTH/NTH M22 ...... 118 E3
Purbeck Dr HOR/BR BL6 ...... 34 C4
TOT/BURYW BL8 ...... 24 F6
Purbeck Wy TYLD M29 ...... 67 K5
Purcell Cl BOL BL1 ...... 36 C3
Purcell St WGTN/LGST M12 ...... 99 K1
Purdon St BURY BL9 ...... 5 J6
Purley Av NTHM/RTH M23 ...... 109 L3
Purple St BOL BL1 ...... 2 F4
Purslow Cl WGTN/LGST M12 ...... 88 B8
Putney Cl OLD OL1 ...... 59 H5
Pye Cl RNFD/HAY WA11 ...... 78 E4
Pyegrove GLSP SK13 ...... 105 J3
Pyegrove Rd GLSP SK13 ...... 105 H3
Pyke St WGN WN1 ...... 15 J1
Pymgate Dr CHD/CHDH SK8 ...... 119 J2
Pymgate La CHD/CHDH SK8 ...... 119 J2
Pym St ECC M30 ...... 85 C2
HEY OL10 ...... 41 G3
NEWH/MOS M40 ...... 73 J4
Pyramid Ct BRO M7 ...... 72 A6
Pyrus Cl ECC M30 ...... 84 C4
Pytha Fold Rd DID/WITH M20 ...... 99 G7

Q

The Quadrant BKLY M9 ...... 73 K1
DROY M43 ...... 89 K1
MPL/ROM SK6 ...... 113 K2
STKP SK1 ...... 112 E3
Quail Dr IRL M44 ...... 94 D1
Quail St OLDE OL4 ...... 59 M7
Quakerfields WHTN BL5 ...... 50 A5
Quakers Fld TOT/BURYW BL8 ...... 24 C4
Quakers' Pl WGNNW/ST WN6 ...... 31 H3
Quantock Cl HTNM SK4 ...... 13 C2
WGNS/IIMK WN3 ...... 62 F2
Quantock Dr OLDS OL8 ...... 75 J1
Quantock St
OLDTF/WHR M16 * 87 H8
Quarlton Dr
TOT/BURYW BL8 ...... 23 L1
Quarmby Rd GTN M18 ...... 89 J8
Quarry Bank Rd
WILM/AE SK9 ...... 126 D1
Quarry Cl GLSP SK13 ...... 105 G3
Quarry Clough STLY SK15 ...... 92 A4
Quarry Hts STLY SK15 ...... 91 J4
Quarry La UPML OL3 ...... 61 G3
Quarry Pl WGN WN1 ...... 15 J3
Quarry Pond Rd WALK M28 ...... 68 C1
Quarry Ri MPL/ROM SK6 ...... 113 L2
STLY SK15 ...... 91 J4
Quarry Rd FWTH BL4 ...... 53 K5
MPL/ROM SK6 ...... 113 L2
NM/HAY SK22 ...... 124 F5
NM/HAY SK22 ...... 125 H1
Quarry St MPL/ROM SK6 * 101 J2
RAD M26 ...... 54 E1
RAMS BL0 ...... 19 G6
STLY SK15 ...... 91 J3
WHIT OL12 ...... 10 D3
Quarry Wk OP/CLY M11 * 88 D3
Quayside LEIGH WN7 ...... 66 B8
Quayside Cl WALK M28 ...... 68 C3
The Quays SALQ M50 ...... 86 C5
Quay St CSLFD M3 ...... 6 C5
CSLFD M3 ...... 6 D3
HEY OL10 ...... 41 H3
Quay Vw ORD M5 ...... 86 D4
Quebec Pl BOLS/LL BL3 ...... 35 M7
Quebec St BOLS/LL BL3 ...... 2 A9
CHAD OL9 ...... 8 D3
DTN/ASHW M34 ...... 90 B8
Queen Alexandra Cl ORD M5 * 86 F4
Queen Ann Dr WALK M28 ...... 68 C5
Queenhill Dr HYDE SK14 ...... 91 J7
Queenhill Rd
WYTH/NTH M22 ...... 110 B3

Queen's Av AIMK WN4.............63 L8
ATH M46.................................50 F7
EDGW/EG BL7.........................22 D5
GOL/RIS/CUL WA3...................81 M5
MPL/ROM SK6.........................113 K1
WHIT OL12..............................21 G8
Queensbrook BOL BL1...............2 C4
Queensbury Cl BOL BL1..............22 A7
WILM/AE SK9...........................127 H4
Queensbury Pde
NEWH/MOS M40 *....................88 B1
Queens Cl HTNM SK4................111 K2
HYDE SK14..............................102 B5
WALK M28...............................68 C5
Queens Ct NEWH/MOS M40.......73 G7
Queens Dr CHD/CHDH SK8........120 C1
GLSP SK13..............................105 J3
GOL/RIS/CUL WA3....................79 M4
HTNM SK4...............................111 K2
HYDE SK14..............................102 C5
NEWLW WA12..........................78 F7
PWCH M25...............................71 M2
ROCH OL11..............................42 B1
Queensferry St
NEWH/MOS M40.......................73 M6
Queens Gdns LEIGH WN7...........66 F7
Queensgate BOL BL1.................35 L4
BRAM/HZG SK7........................121 G2
Queensgate Dr
ROY/SHW OL2..........................42 F6
Queen's Gv WGTN/LGST M12.....88 D8
Queens Hall Rd WGN WN1 *.......14 F4
Queensland Rd GTN M18............88 E7
Queensmere Dr SWIN M27..........70 D2
Queens Pk BOL BL1 *.................2 C5
Queen's Park Rd HEY OL10........41 G1
Queens Pl BURY BL9..................24 F2
Queen's Rd AIMK WN4...............78 E1
AUL OL6..................................76 A8
BOLS/LL BL3............................35 L8
BRAM/HZG SK7........................122 A1
CHAD OL9................................58 D5
CHD/CHDH SK8........................111 J8
CHH M8...................................72 E7
HALE/TIMP WA15.....................117 C1
LIT OL15.................................21 M7
MPL/ROM SK6..........................113 K1
NEWH/MOS M40.......................73 G7
OLDS OL8................................9 L8
RNFD/HAY WA11......................78 D5
SALE M33................................96 C8
URM M41..................................96 A3
WILM/AE SK9...........................126 F6
Queenston Rd DID/WITH M20.....98 D8
Queen St AUL OL6.....................91 C1
BOL BL1...................................2 D5
BURY BL9................................5 H4
CHD/CHDH SK8........................111 H6
CSLFD M3.................................6 E5
CSLFD M3.................................6 E5
DTN/ASHW M34........................90 B8
DTN/ASHW M34........................90 C6
DUK SK16................................90 E3
ECC M30 *...............................85 J3
FAIL M35.................................74 B5
FWTH BL4................................53 G4
GLSP SK13..............................93 K8
GLSP SK13..............................104 E4
GOL/RIS/CUL WA3 *.................79 L4
HEY OL10................................41 G2
HOR/BR BL6.............................33 K1
HYDE SK14..............................102 B3
LEIGH WN7 *...........................66 D8
LHULT M38..............................52 E8
LIT OL15.................................21 M7
MDTN M24...............................57 J3
MOSL OL5................................76 F3
MPL/ROM SK6..........................114 C6
OLD OL1..................................9 K5
RAD M26..................................54 F2
RAMS BL0...............................18 E7
ROY/SHW OL2..........................43 J3
ROY/SHW OL2..........................43 L6
SLFD M6..................................6 D1
STLY SK15 *............................91 K2
TOT/BURYW BL8.......................24 D7
WGNE/HIN WN2........................49 G6
WGNE/HIN WN2........................64 D2
WGNW/BIL/OR WN5..................47 G7
WHIT OL12...............................21 G8
WHTN BL5...............................50 B4
Queen St West DID/WITH M20....98 C5
Queens Vw LIT OL15.................29 K1
Queensway BNG/LEV M19..........111 G2
CHD/CHDH SK8........................119 L4
DUK SK16................................91 J5
FWTH BL4................................53 J6
IRL M44..................................94 C2
LEIGH WN7..............................67 G7
MOSL OL5................................77 G5
PART M31................................94 C8
POY/DIS SK12..........................129 H1
ROCH OL11..............................42 A1
SWIN M27................................70 D2
UPML OL3................................61 L6
URM M41.................................85 H8
WALK M28...............................47 L2
WGN WN1................................47 L2
WGNE/HIN WN2........................48 D4
WGNNW/ST WN6......................30 C4
Queen Victoria St ECC M30........84 F2
ROCH OL11..............................42 D1
Quenby St HULME M15..............87 H7
Quendon Av BRO M7..................72 B8
Quickedge La OLDE OL4.............44 C8
Quickedge Rd MOSL OL5............76 F2
OLDE OL4................................60 F8
Quick Rd MOSL OL5..................60 F8
Quick Vw MOSL OL5..................77 H1
Quill Ct IRL M44.......................94 B6
Quilter Gv BKLY M9...................72 F6
Quinney Crs OLDTF/WHR M16....98 C1
Quinn St OP/CLY M11................10 D3
Quinton WHIT OL12...................10 D3
Quinton Wk BRUN/LGST M13.....87 L6

R

Rabbit La HYDE SK14..................92 D6
Raby St OLDTF/WHR M16...........87 H8
RUSH/FAL M14.........................98 C3
Racecourse Pk WILM/AE SK9......126 D6
Racecourse Rd WILM/AE SK9......126 C6
Racefield Rd ALT WA14..............107 M8
The Race WCTN/LGST M12.........7 M8
Rachel St WGTN/LGST M12........7 M8
Rackhouse Rd
NTHM/RTH M23.......................109 L3

Radbourne Cl WGTN/LGST M12...88 D6
Radbourne Gv BOLS/LL BL3........35 J8
Radcliffe Gv LEIGH WN7.............66 C5
Radcliffe Moor Rd BOLE BL2.......37 L7
Radcliffe New Rd RAD M26.........54 F2
WHTF M45................................55 H3
Radcliffe Park Crs SLFD M6.........70 F7
Radcliffe Park Rd SLFD M6..........70 F7
Radcliffe Rd BOLE BL2................3 J3
BOLS/LL BL3............................37 H7
BURY BL9................................39 H5
OLDE OL4................................60 A2
Radcliffe St OLD OL1..................9 J4
OLDE OL4................................60 D6
ROY/SHW OL2..........................43 H8
Radclyffe Cl OLD OL9.................8 B3
MDTN M24...............................57 K2
Radelan Gv RAD M26.................38 A8
Radford Cl OFTN SK2.................113 C5
Radford Dr BKLY M9..................73 H4
IRL M44..................................94 D1
Radford St BRO M7....................71 M4
Radium St ANC M4....................7 K2
Radlet Dr HALE/TIMP WA15........108 D4
Radlett Wk BRUN/LGST M13 *.....87 M7
Radley Cl BOL BL1.....................35 K3
SALE M33................................108 A1
Radley St DROY M43.................89 H4
OLDTF/WHR M16......................98 C1
Radnor Av DTN/ASHW M34.........100 E1
Radnor Cl WGNE/HIN WN2.........65 K1
Radnor Dr LEIGH WN7...............66 D7
Radnormere Dr
CHD/CHDH SK8........................111 J8
Radnor St CHAD OL9.................8 C8
CTN M18.................................88 F8
HULME M15.............................87 J7
STRET M32...............................97 G3
Radstock Cl BOL BL1.................22 B5
RUSH/FAL M14........................98 E3
Radstock Rd STRET M32............96 F2
Radway TYLD M29.....................67 M3
Raeburn Dr MPL/ROM SK6.........114 E4
Rae St EDGY/DAV SK3...............12 D6
Raglan Av SWIN M27.................70 E2
WHTF M45................................55 L5
Raglan Dr ALT WA14..................108 A4
Raglan Rd SALE M33.................108 C1
STRET M32...............................96 E1
Raglan St BOL BL1.....................36 A2
HYDE SK14..............................101 M2
ROCH OL11..............................41 M3
Raglan Wk HULME M15 *...........87 J6
Ragley Cl POY/DIS SK12............122 B8
Raikes La BOLS/LL BL3..............36 E8
Raikes Rd BOLS/LL BL3.............37 C7
Raikes Wy BOLS/LL BL3.............37 C7
Railton Av OLDTF/WHR M16.......98 A1
Railton Ter BKLY M9 *...............73 J5
Railway Ap ROCH OL11..............41 M2
Railway Rd CHAD OL9................8 E7
CHAD OL9................................74 D2
GOL/RIS/CUL WA3 *.................79 L4
LEIGH WN7..............................66 B7
STKP SK1.................................13 H6
STRET M32...............................86 C7
URM M41.................................97 C3
Railway St ALT WA14.................108 A8
ATH M46.................................50 E8
BURY BL9................................24 E2
DUK SK16................................90 E4
FWTH BL4................................53 H5
GLSP SK13..............................93 K7
GLSP SK13..............................104 F3
CTN M18.................................88 F6
HEY OL10................................41 H3
HTNM SK4...............................12 F4
LIT OL15.................................21 M7
MILN OL16...............................11 G6
MILN OL16...............................29 M8
RAD M26..................................54 D2
RAMS BL0...............................18 F6
WGNE/HIN WN2........................49 H5
WGNNW/ST WN6......................14 B2
Railway Ter TOT/BURYW BL8......4 A6
Railway Vw OLDE OL4...............60 C6
ROY/SHW OL2..........................43 M4
Raimond St BOL BL1..................35 M1
Rainbow Cl CCHDY M21.............97 L5
Rainbow Dr ATH M46.................51 G8
Raincliff Av BRUN/LGST M13......99 J2
Raines Crest MILN OL16.............29 K6
Rainford Av DID/WITH M20.........98 D4
HALE/TIMP WA15.....................108 D7
Rainford Rd
WGNW/BIL/OR WN5..................62 A7
Rainford St BOLE BL2.................22 F6
Rainforth St BRUN/LGST M13.....99 J1
Rainham Dr CHH M8..................72 D5
Rainham Wy CHAD OL9 *...........8 B7
RDSH SK5................................100 B3
Rainow Av DROY M43................89 H4
Rainow Dr POY/DIS SK12............129 L2
Rainow Rd EDGY/DAV SK3 *.......111 M6
Rainshaw St BOL BL1.................22 C8
OLDE OL4 *..............................60 A4
Rainsough Av PWCH M25...........71 J3
Rainsough Brow PWCH M25.......71 J3
Rainsough Cl PWCH M25............71 K3
Rainwood CHAD OL9.................58 B4
Raithby Dr WGNS/IIMK WN3.......63 K1
Raja Cl CHH M8........................72 E5
Rake ROCH OL11.......................27 C5
Rake La SWIN M27....................70 C1
Rake St BURY BL9.....................25 J8
Rakewood Dr OLDE OL4.............44 C8
Rakewood Rd LIT OL15..............29 L1
Raleigh Cl DID/WITH M20...........98 D7
OLD OL1..................................9 J2
Raleigh St RDSH SK5.................100 B8
STRET M32...............................97 G2
Ralli Cts CSLFD M3....................6 C4
Ralph Av HYDE SK14.................102 B5
Ralph Green St CHAD OL9..........74 E2
Ralphs La DUK SK16.................90 F5
UPML OL3................................45 G2
Ralph St BOL BL1......................36 A2
OP/CLY M11.............................89 G3
Ralston Cl BRO M7....................72 C4
Ralstone Av OLDS OL8...............59 J8
Ramage Wk WGTN/LGST M12....88 B3
Ramilies Av CHD/CHDH SK8.......120 D3
Rampit Cl RNFD/HAY WA11.......78 C5
Ramp Rd East MANAIR M90........118 D5
Ramp Rd South MANAIR M90......118 D5
Ramp Rd West MANAIR M90........118 D5
Ramsay Av FWTH BL4................52 E5
Ramsay Pl MILN OL16................11 G3
Ramsay St BOL BL1...................22 B8
MILN OL16...............................11 G3
Ramsay Ter MILN OL16 *...........11 G3

Ramsbottom La RAMS BL0.........18 F5
Ramsbottom Rd HOR/BR BL6......33 L1
TOT/BURYW BL8.......................23 K2
Ramsbury Dr NEWH/MOS M40....74 A2
Ramsdale Rd BRAM/HZG SK7.....121 G4
Ramsdale St CHAD OL9..............58 D5
Ramsden Cl GLSP SK13..............104 F2
OLD OL1..................................9 G4
WGNS/IIMK WN3......................14 B9
Ramsden Crs OLD OL1...............9 G4
Ramsden Fold SWIN M27............70 C2
Ramsden Rd WHIT OL12.............21 G3
Ramsden St AUL OL6.................75 C7
BOLS/LL BL3............................37 G7
OLD OL1..................................9 G4
Ramsey Av BNG/LEV M19...........100 A3
ATH M46.................................67 H2
Ramsey Cl AIMK WN4................78 E2
ATH M46.................................67 H2
Ramsey Gv TOT/BURYW BL8......38 E2
Ramsey St CHAD OL9.................8 A9
LEIGH WN7 *...........................66 D8
NEWH/MOS M40......................73 L5
OLD OL1..................................59 L4
Ramsgate Rd NEWH/MOS M40....73 M8
RDSH SK5................................100 C5
Ramsgate St BRO M7.................72 B7
Ramsgill Cl NTHM/RTH M23.......109 L2
Ramsgreave Cl BURY BL9...........39 C5
Ram St LHULT M38....................52 C8
Ramwell Gdns BOLS/LL BL3 *.....36 C8
Ramwells Brow EDGW/EG BL7....22 A3
Ramwells Ct EDGW/EG BL7 *......22 A3
Ramwells Ms EDGW/EG BL7 *.....22 A3
Ranby Av BKLY M9....................57 J8
Randale Dr BURY BL9................55 K2
Randall Av WGNNW/ST WN6......30 D7
Randal St BOLS/LL BL3...............36 B8
Randerson St WGTN/LGST M12 *.7 L3
Randlesham St PWCH M25.........55 M8
Randolph Pl EDGY/DAV SK3........13 H8
Randolph Rd FWTH BL4..............53 J5
Randolph St BNG/LEV M19.........99 K2
BOLS/LL BL3............................2 A6
OLDS OL8................................74 F2
Rands Clough Dr WALK M28.......68 C6
Rand St OLD OL1......................60 A3
Ranelagh Rd SWIN M27..............70 F5
Ranelagh St OP/CLY M11............88 C3
Raneley Gv ROCH OL11.............42 D2
Ranford Rd BNG/LEV M19..........99 K4
Range Dr MPL/ROM SK6.............101 M6
Range La UPML OL3..................45 G3
Rangemore Av
WYTH/NTH M22 *....................110 A4
Range Rd EDGY/DAV SK3...........13 H9
OLDTF/WHR M16......................98 B1
STLY SK15...............................91 L4
Range St BOLS/LL BL3...............36 A8
OP/CLY M11.............................88 F4
Ranicar Steet WGNE/HIN WN2....65 M1
Rankine Ter BOLS/LL BL3 *.........2 B8
Ranmore Av AIMK WN4..............63 G8
Rannoch Rd BOLE BL2................37 J5
Ransfield Rd CCHDY M21...........97 K2
Ranulph Ct SLFD M6 *...............71 G7
Ranworth Av HTNM SK4.............111 J2
Ranworth Cl BOL BL1.................36 B2
Ranworth Dr GOL/RIS/CUL WA3..80 B5
Raper St OLDE OL4....................59 M4
Raphael St BOL BL1...................36 A2
Rappax Rd HALE/TIMP WA15......117 J4
Rasbottom St BOLS/LL BL3.........2 B7
Raspberry La IRL M44................83 J8
Rassbottom Brow STLY SK15 *....91 J2
Rassbottom St STLY SK15...........91 J2
Rassey Cl WGNNW/ST WN6........31 K5
Ratcliffe Av IRL M44..................94 D3
Ratcliffe Rd WGNE/HIN WN2......32 F6
Ratcliffe St BNG/LEV M19...........99 L3
LEIGH WN7..............................66 C6
STKP SK1.................................13 J7
TYLD M29................................67 L3
WGNNW/ST WN6......................14 B3
Rathan Rd URM M41..................84 F8
Rathbone St MILN OL16..............11 L5
Rathbourne Av BKLY M9............73 C1
Rathen Av WGNE/HIN WN2........48 D3
Rathen Rd DID/WITH M20...........98 E2
Rathmel Rd NTHM/RTH M23.......109 J2
Rathmore Av NEWH/MOS M40....73 H7
Rathvale Dr WYTH/NTH M22.......118 A3
Rathybank Cl BOL BL1................35 M3
Rattenbury Ct SLFD M6..............70 F7
Raveden Cl BOL BL1..................35 M1
Raveley Av RUSH/FAL M14.........99 G4
Ravelston Dr BKLY M9...............73 G6
Raven Av CHAD OL9..................58 D7
Raven Cl DROY M43..................89 M1
HALE/TIMP WA15.....................108 D7
Ravendale Cl WHIT OL12 *..........27 K3
Raven Dr IRL M44.....................94 D1
Ravenfield Gv BOL BL1 *............2 B2
Ravenhead Cl RUSH/FAL M14.....99 G4
Ravenhead Sq STLY SK15...........77 H7
Ravenhurst Dr BOL BL1..............35 G6
Ravenna Av NTHM/RTH M23.......109 C5
Ravenoak Av BNG/LEV M19........99 L4
Ravenoak Dr FAIL M35...............74 D4
Ravenoak Park Rd
CHD/CHDH SK8........................120 D4
Ravenoak Rd CHD/CHDH SK8.....120 D4
OFTN SK2................................112 D8
Raven Rd BOLS/LL BL3..............35 K8
Ravensbury St OP/CLY M11........88 C2
Ravenscar Crs
WYTH/NTH M22.......................118 A3
Ravens Cl PWCH M25................72 B2
Ravenscraig Rd LHULT M38........52 E6
Ravensdale Gdns ECC M30.........85 H1
Ravensdale Rd BOL BL1.............35 G6
Ravensdale St RUSH/FAL M14.....98 F1
Ravens Holme BOL BL1..............35 H5
Ravenside Pk CHAD OL9.............58 D7
Ravenstonedale Dr
ROY/SHW OL2..........................43 H7
Ravenstone Dr SALE M33...........97 H7
UPML OL3................................61 M1
Raven St BURY BL9...................5 G1
ROCH OL11..............................27 C3
WGTN/LGST M12......................7 M7
Ravensway PWCH M25...............72 A2
Ravens Wd BOL BL1..................35 H5
Ravenswood Av HTNM SK4.........111 K3
WGNS/IIMK WN3......................63 G1
Ravenswood Dr BKLY M9............73 H1
BOL BL1..................................35 H5
CHD/CHDH SK8........................120 D4
WGNE/HIN WN2........................49 H6

Ravenwood Dr DTN/ASHW M34....90 B6
HALE/TIMP WA15.....................117 M5
Ravine Av BKLY M9....................73 H5
Rawcliffe Av BOLE BL2...............37 J5
Rawcliffe St RUSH/FAL M14........98 F1
Rawdon Cl BNG/LEV M19...........99 L3
Rawkin Cl HULME M15...............87 H7
Rawlyn Rd BOL BL1...................35 J3
Rawpool Gdns
NTHM/RTH M23.......................109 K5
Rawson Av FWTH BL4................53 H3
Rawson Rd BOL BL1..................35 M3
Rawsons Rake TOT/BURYW BL8..18 D6
Rawson St FWTH BL4.................53 G3
Rawsthorne Av GTN M18............100 A2
RAMS BL0...............................19 G2
Rawsthorne St BOL BL1.............36 B2
TYLD M29................................68 A4
Rawstron St WHIT OL12.............20 A3
Raycroft Av BKLY M9.................73 H5
Raydale Cl GOL/RIS/CUL WA3.....80 B4
Raydon Av NEWH/MOS M40 *.....73 G7
Rayleigh Av OP/CLY M11............89 J5
Raymond Av BURY BL9..............25 J7
CHAD OL9................................74 E1
Raymond Rd NTHM/RTH M23.....109 L2
Raymond St SWIN M27..............70 C3
Rayner La AULW OL7.................90 A3
Rayners Cl STLY SK15................91 J3
Rayner St STKP SK1...................112 E4
Raynham Av DID/WITH M20........110 E1
Raynham St AUL OL6.................90 F1
Rayson Hill Dr BKLY M9.............72 F2
Reabrook Av WGTN/LGST M12....88 B4
The Reach WALK M28.................69 H2
Read Cl BURY BL9.....................39 C5
ROY/SHW OL2..........................43 L6
Reade Av URM M41...................95 H3
Reading Cl OP/CLY M11.............88 F4
Reading Dr SALE M33................96 A8
Reading St SLFD M6..................71 L7
Readitt Wk OP/CLY M11.............88 E2
Read St HYDE SK14...................101 M1
Read St West HYDE SK14...........101 M1
Reaney Wk WGTN/LGST M12 *....88 B2
Reather Wk NEWH/MOS M40......87 M1
Rebecca St CHH M8...................72 D4
Recreation Av AIMK WN4............64 A8
Recreation Dr
WGNW/BIL/OR WN5 *...............62 B7
Recreation Rd FAIL M35.............74 D3
Recreation St BOLE BL2..............23 H7
BOLS/LL BL3............................36 B8
PWCH M25...............................55 M8
Rectory Av CHH M8...................72 D3
GOL/RIS/CUL WA3....................79 M4
SWIN M27...............................55 L8
Rectory Cl DTN/ASHW M34.........101 K2
RAD M26..................................39 C8
Rectory Flds STKP SK1...............13 L4
Rectory Gdns PWCH M25............55 L8
WHTN BL5...............................50 B8
Rectory Gn PWCH M25...............55 K8
STKP SK1.................................13 L4
Rectory Gv PWCH M25...............71 L1
Rectory La BURY BL9.................26 A1
PWCH M25...............................55 K8
WGNNW/ST WN6......................31 J3
Rectory St MDTN M24................57 J3
The Rectory BURY BL9 *.............55 L1
Redacre POY/DIS SK12...............122 B6
Redbank Av GTN M18.................89 G1
Red Bank ANC M4.....................7 K1
Red Bank Rd RAD M26...............38 C7
Redbarn Cl MPL/ROM SK6.........101 J8
Redbourne Dr URM M41.............84 C8
Redbrick Ct AULW OL7...............90 D3
Redbrook Av NEWH/MOS M40....73 H7
Redbrook Cl FWTH BL4..............53 H3
Redbrook Rd
HALE/TIMP WA15.....................109 C6
PART M31................................106 B2
WGNS/IIMK WN3......................15 K7
Red Brook St ROCH OL11...........10 B5
Redbrook Wy MCFLDN SK10.......129 C7
Redbrow Hollow
MPL/ROM SK6..........................114 D2
Redburn Cl WGNS/IIMK WN3......14 D8
Redburn Rd NTHM/RTH M23.......109 L5
Redby St OP/CLY M11................88 E5
Redcar Av DID/WITH M20...........98 E6
URM M41.................................84 D8
Redcar Cl BRAM/HZG SK7..........122 C3
OLD OL1..................................59 L3
Redcar Rd BOLS/LL BL3.............53 K1
SWIN M27...............................70 F5
Redcar St WHIT OL12.................10 D1
Red Cedar Pk BOLE BL2.............37 C7
Redcliffe Av RUSH/FAL M14........98 F1
Redclyffe Rd DID/WITH M20........98 D7
ECC M30.................................85 C4
Redcot BOL BL1 *.....................35 L5
Redcote St NEWH/MOS M40.......73 K4
Redcourt Av DID/WITH M20........98 E8
Redcroft Gdns BNG/LEV M19......99 L8
Redcroft Rd SALE M33...............96 B6
Redcross St WHIT OL12..............10 E1
Redcross St North WHIT OL12.....10 E1
Reddaway Cl SLFD M6...............71 H1
Reddish Cl BOLE BL2..................23 H7
Reddish La GTN M18..................100 B1
Reddish Rd RDSH SK5...............100 C7
Reddish Vale Rd RDSH SK5.........100 D4
Redesmere Cl DROY M43...........89 L3
HALE/TIMP WA15.....................108 D6
Redesmere Dr CHD/CHDH SK8....111 J8
WILM/AE SK9...........................130 C3
Redesmere Pk URM M41............95 L4
Redfearn Wd WHIT OL12 *.........10 E1
Redfern Av SALE M33.................103 H1
Redfern Cl GLSP SK13................93 K6
Redfern St ANC M4....................7 G3
Redfern Wy ROCH OL11.............27 G3
Redfield Cft LEIGH WN7.............66 D7
Redford Cl LEIGH WN7...............66 D7
Redford Dr BRAM/HZG SK7........121 J2
Redford Rd CHH M8...................72 B4
Redford St TOT/BURYW BL8........38 F1
Redgate GLSP SK13...................93 M8
HYDE SK14..............................102 A4
Redgate La WGTN/LGST M12......88 D3
Redgate Rd AIMK WN4...............63 G7
Redgate Wk CCHDY M21............97 L3
Redgate Wy FWTH BL4...............52 C3
Redgrave Pas OLDE OL4.............60 A4
Redgrave Ri WGNS/IIMK WN3.....63 G1
Redgrave St OLDE OL4...............60 A4
Red Hall St OLDE OL4................59 M6
Redhill Dr MPL/ROM SK6...........113 G1
Redhill Gv BOL BL1....................35 J2
Redhill St ANC M4.....................7 K4
Red Hill Wy WGNE/HIN WN2 *....49 G6
Red House La ALT WA14.............106 F4
Redhouse La MPL/ROM SK6........101 J8
POY/DIS SK12..........................124 A6
Redington Dr WALK M28.............68 D7
Redisher Cl RAMS BL0...............24 C1
Redisher Cft RAMS BL0..............24 C1
Redisher La TOT/BURYW BL8......24 B1
Redland Av RDSH SK5................100 C7
Redland Cl LIT OL15...................21 M6
Redland Ct WGNE/HIN WN2........64 B5
Redland Crs CCHDY M21............97 L5
Red La BOLE BL2.......................37 G3
POY/DIS SK12..........................123 K1
LIT OL12.................................28 E2
Red Lion St ANC M4 *................7 H3
Redmain Gv GOL/RIS/CUL WA3...80 B4
Redmans Pl ECC M30.................84 E3
Redmayne Cl NEWLW WA12........78 E8
Redmere Dr BURY BL9................5 J9
Redmere Gv RUSH/FAL M14........98 F4
Redmire Ms DUK SK16...............91 J5
Redmond Cl DTN/ASHW M34......90 B5
Redmoor La POY/DIS SK12..........124 C3
Redmoor Sq BRUN/LGST M13 *...7 K8
Redmoss Rw SWIN M27.............71 C4
Rednal Wk WGNS/IIMK WN3.......14 D8
Redpol Av LEIGH WN7................66 G6
Red Rock La RAD M26................54 A6
WGN WN1...............................32 M4
Red Rose Crs BNG/LEV M19........99 M5
Redruth St RUSH/FAL M14..........98 E2
Redshank Cl NEWLW WA12........78 E8
Redshank Gv LEIGH WN7...........66 G6
Redshaw Av BOLE BL2...............22 F6
Redshaw Cl RUSH/FAL M14.........99 G3
Redstart Cl GOL/RIS/CUL WA3....80 B4
Redstart Gv WALK M28...............69 G4
Redstock Cl WHTN BL5..............50 D3
Redstone Rd BNG/LEV M19.........111 G1
Red St ATH M46........................67 H1
Redthorn Av BNG/LEV M19.........99 J5
Redthorpe Cl BOLE BL2..............36 E3
Redvale Rd BRO M7...................72 B6
Redvales Rd BURY BL9...............39 H5
Redvers St OLD OL1...................8 F5
Redwater Cl WALK M28...............68 D6
Redwing Rd TOT/BURYW BL8......24 C2
Redwood CHAD OL9...................58 A5
SALE M33................................95 M8
WGNNW/ST WN6......................30 E6
WHTN BL5...............................50 A6
Redwood Av WGNNW/ST WN6....47 J1
WGNW/BIL/OR WN5..................46 D6
Redwood Cl EDGY/DAV SK3........12 A7
WHIT OL12..............................27 L1
Redwood Dr CHH M8..................72 E7
DTN/ASHW M34.......................90 B6
MPL/ROM SK6..........................113 G1
Redwood La OLDE OL4...............60 B5
Redwood Park Gv MILN OL16......29 C5
Redwood Rd UPML OL3..............61 M5
Redwood St SLFD M6.................71 H1
Reeceton Gdns BOL BL1.............35 H5
Reedbank RAD M26...................54 D4
Reed Ct OLD OL1 *....................9 G2
Reed Crs WGNS/IIMK WN3.........47 K8
Reedham Cl BOL BL1..................35 M4
Reedham Wk CHAD OL9 *..........58 B8
NEWH/MOS M40 *....................73 G2
Reed Hl MILN OL16...................10 E3
Reedley Dr WALK M28................68 F4
Reedmace Cl WALK M28.............69 H3
Reedshaw Bank OFTN SK2..........113 C7
Reedshaw Rd BKLY M9...............72 F6
Reedsmere Cl
WGNW/BIL/OR WN5..................47 J6
Reed St GTN M18......................89 C6
OLD OL1 *...............................9 L5
Reedymoor WHTN BL5...............50 B8
Reeman Cl MPL/ROM SK6...........101 K8
Reepham Cl WGNS/IIMK WN3.....62 F1
Reeve Cl OFTN SK2...................113 J7
Reeves Rd CCHDY M21..............97 L5
Reeves St LEIGH WN7................66 C6
Reeve St GOL/RIS/CUL WA3........80 C4
Reevey Av BRAM/HZG SK7..........121 C2
Reform St WHIT OL12.................10 E2
Reform Wk OP/CLY M11.............88 E4
Regaby Gv WGNE/HIN WN2........49 K7
Regal Cl WHTF M45....................55 L4
Regal Fold WHIT OL12................20 F8
Regan Av CCHDY M21................98 A5
Regan St BOL BL1......................36 A1
RAD M26..................................54 A6
Regatta Cl CHAD OL9.................74 D1
Regatta St SLFD M6...................71 J6
Regatta Cl GLSP SK13................105 G3
NEWH/MOS M40......................73 G7
OLDS OL8................................59 G8
Regency Ct
HALE/TIMP WA15 *..................117 K3
ROCH OL11..............................15 H3
WGN WN1...............................15 H3
Regency Gdns CHD/CHDH SK8....120 A4
HYDE SK14..............................91 J8
Regency Ldg PWCH M25 *..........71 K1
Regency Pk WILM/AE SK9...........126 D7
Regent Av AIMK WN4.................63 J7
LHULT M38..............................52 F8
RUSH/FAL M14.........................98 C2
Regent Cl BRAM/HZG SK7..........121 J8
CHD/CHDH SK8........................111 M8
HEY OL10................................40 E3
WILM/AE SK9...........................126 F7
Regent Ct HTNM SK4.................99 M7
Regent Crs FAIL M35..................74 B6
ROY/SHW OL2..........................59 G2
Regent Dr DTN/ASHW M34.........101 G3
HOR/BR BL6.............................34 C6
LEIGH WN7..............................67 G5
Regent Rd ALT WA14.................108 A8
HOR/BR BL6.............................34 C6
OFTN SK2................................112 D6
ORD M5..................................86 C3
WGNE/HIN WN2........................64 D1
Regents Dr MOSL OL5................77 G5
Regents Hl HOR/BR BL6.............34 F6
Regents Pk Rd WGN WN1...........47 L4
Regent Sq ORD M5....................86 C4
The Regents
WILM/AE SK9...........................127 G4

Regent St ATH M46.....67 H2
  BURY BL9.....4 F1
  ECC M30.....85 K2
  GLSP SK13.....105 G3
  HEY OL10.....15 J1
  LIT OL15.....21 M7
  MDTN M24.....57 J2
  NEWH/MOS M40.....74 A7
  OLD OL1.....9 L5
  RAMS BL0.....18 D8
  WGNE/HIN WN2.....48 F7
  WHIT OL12.....28 C3
Regent Wk FWTH BL4 *.....53 G4
Regina Av STLY SK15.....91 K2
Regina Crs LEIGH WN7.....67 H6
Reginald St BOLS/LL BL3 *.....51 K2
  ECC M30.....84 D4
  OP/CLY M11.....89 J5
  SWIN M27.....70 A3
Reid CI DTN/ASHW M34.....101 K4
Reigate CI TOT/BURYW BL8 *.....38 E3
Reigate Rd URM M41.....95 H4
Reilly St HULME M15.....87 J6
Reins Lee Av OLDS OL8.....75 K2
Reins Lee Rd AULW OL7.....75 K6
Reliance St NEWH/MOS M40.....73 H6
Rembrandt Wk OLD OL1.....44 A7
Rena CI HTNM SK4.....12 E1
Rendel CI STRET M32.....97 G2
Renfrew Av STLY SK15.....91 K2
Renfrew Dr BOLS/LL BL3.....51 K2
Renfrew Rd WGNE/HIN WN2.....33 G7
Rennie CI STRET M32.....97 G2
Renshaw Av ECC M30.....85 G3
Renshaw Dr BURY BL9.....5 M2
Renshaw St ECC M30.....85 G3
Renton Rd BOLS/LL BL3.....51 L1
  STRET M32.....97 H2
  WYTH/NTH M22.....110 A8
Renwick Sq AIMK WN4.....78 C1
Repton Av DROY M43.....89 C1
  DTN/ASHW M34.....100 D1
  HYDE SK14.....102 B1
  NEWH/MOS M40.....74 B3
  OLDS OL8.....75 G1
  URM M41.....95 G2
  WGNS/IIMK WN3.....48 C8
Repton CI SALE M33.....108 A1
Reservoir Rd EDGY/DAV SK3.....12 F9
Reservoir St CSLFD M3.....6 D1
  MILN OL16.....11 L2
  SLFD M6.....86 C2
  WGNE/HIN WN2.....48 D4
  WGNE/HIN WN2.....49 J1
The Residences PWCH M25.....71 M1
Retford Av MILN OL16.....28 E8
Retford CI TOT/BURYW BL8.....38 E3
Retford St OLDE OL4 *.....59 L7
Retiro St OLD OL1.....9 K5
The Retreat MPL/ROM SK6.....113 L3
Reuben St HTNM SK4.....100 B8
Revers St TOT/BURYW BL8.....4 B3
Reveton Gn BRAM/HZG SK7.....121 J2
Rexcine Wy HYDE SK14.....91 K7
Reynard Rd CCHDY M21.....97 L5
Reynard St HYDE SK14.....102 A1
Reynell Rd BRUN/LGST M13.....99 J2
Reyner St AUL OL6.....91 H2
  CMANE M1.....7 G6
Reynolds CI WHTN BL5.....51 J6
Reynolds Dr GTN M18.....89 G6
  MPL/ROM SK6.....114 E4
  WHTN BL5.....51 J5
Reynolds Ms WILM/AE SK9.....127 J4
Reynolds Rd OLDTF/WHR M16.....86 F8
Reynold St HYDE SK14.....102 A2
Rhine CI TOT/BURYW BL8.....24 C5
Rhine Dr BURY BL9.....72 B7
Rhiwlas Dr BURY BL9.....5 G8
Rhodes Av OLDE OL4.....60 C7
  UPML OL3.....61 M3
Rhodes Bank OLD OL1.....9 L6
Rhodes Crs ROCH OL11.....42 C1
Rhodes Dr BURY BL9.....55 K2
Rhodes HI OLDE OL4.....60 C7
Rhodes St GLSP SK13.....93 L7
  HYDE SK14.....101 M1
  NEWH/MOS M40.....73 H8
  OLD OL1.....9 L5
  OLDE OL4.....60 C5
  WHIT OL12.....28 E1
Rhodes St North HYDE SK14.....101 M1
Rhode St TOT/BURYW BL8.....24 C6
Rhodeswood Dr GLSP SK13.....93 K6
Rhos Av CHD/CHDH SK8.....120 B3
  MDTN M24.....57 K5
  RUSH/FAL M14.....99 H4
Rhos Dr BRAM/HZG SK7.....121 M3
Rhosleigh Av BOL BL1.....22 B8
Rhyl Fold LEIGH WN7 *.....67 H7
Rialto Gdns BRO M7.....72 B6
Ribbesford Rd WGNS/IIMK WN3.....46 F8
Ribble Av BOLE BL2.....37 H5
  CHAD OL9.....58 C3
  LIT OL15.....21 K6
Ribble Dr BURY BL9.....25 J4
  FWTH BL4.....53 L7
  WALK M28.....68 C6
  WGNW/BIL/OR WN5.....46 D6
  WHTF M45.....55 K3
Ribble Gv LEIGH WN7.....65 M7
Ribble Rd OLDS OL8.....74 F1
  WGNE/HIN WN2.....48 D4
  WGNNW/ST WN6.....30 E2
Ribblesdale CI HEY OL10 *.....41 H5
Ribblesdale Dr
  NEWH/MOS M40.....72 F7
Ribblesdale Rd BOLS/LL BL3.....36 A8
Ribble St ROCH OL11.....28 B4
Ribbleton CI TOT/BURYW BL8.....38 C3
Ribchester Dr BURY BL9.....39 G5
Ribchester Gv BOLE BL2.....37 H3
Riber Bank GLSP SK13.....104 B3
Ribston St HULME M15.....87 H6
Rice St CSLFD M3.....6 C7
Richard Burch St BURY BL9.....5 G2
Richard Gwyn CI WHTF M45.....50 M2 [55 M2]
Richards CI DTN/ASHW M34.....90 B5
Richards St WHTF M45.....55 J3
Richardson Rd ECC M30.....85 G7
Richardson St OP/CLY M11.....89 H5
  STKP SK1.....13 L9
Richards St WGNNW/ST WN6.....30 E1
Richard St FAIL M35.....74 C5
  RAD M26.....54 C1
  RAMS BL0.....19 H5
  ROCH OL11.....10 F6
  STKP SK1.....13 K2
  WGN WN1.....15 J7
Richbell CI IRL M44.....94 C5
Richborough CI BRO M7.....72 B7
Richelieu St BOLS/LL BL3.....36 D8

Richmond Av CHAD OL9.....58 D8
  PWCH M25.....71 M3
  ROY/SHW OL2.....43 G8
  URM M41.....96 B0
  WALK M28.....69 M4 [119 M7]
Richmond CI DUK SK16.....91 G6
  GLSP SK13.....93 K7
  GOL/RIS/CUL WA3.....81 G8
  MILN OL16.....42 F1
  MOSL OL5.....77 H4
  ROY/SHW OL2.....43 L7
  SALE M33.....109 J1
  STLY SK15.....91 K3
  TOT/BURYW BL8.....24 C6
  WGN WN1.....31 L5
  WHTF M45.....55 C5
Richmond Crs MOSL OL5.....77 H4
Richmond Dr LEIGH WN7.....67 H5
  WALK M28.....69 M4
Richmond Gdns BOLS/LL BL3.....52 E1
Richmond Gn ALT WA14.....116 D2
  BRAM/HZG SK7 *.....121 H6
Richmond Gv BRUN/LGST M13.....88 B8
  CHD/CHDH SK8.....120 B3
  FWTH BL4 *.....52 D3
  LEIGH WN7.....67 G6
Richmond Gv East
  WGTN/LGST M12.....88 B7
Richmond Hl
  WGNW/BIL/OR WN5.....46 F6
Richmond Hill Rd
  CHD/CHDH SK8.....110 F7
Richmond Rd AIMK WN4.....63 J7
  ALT WA14.....108 A7
  ALT WA14.....116 D2
  DTN/ASHW M34 *.....100 D1
  DUK SK16.....91 G6
  FAIL M35.....74 D4
  HTNM SK4.....111 J2
  MPL/ROM SK6.....113 M1
  OLDS/FAL M14.....99 G4
  TRPK M17.....85 K5
  WALK M28.....68 B5
  WGNE/HIN WN2.....65 K1
Richmond St AULW OL7.....75 J8
  AULW OL7.....90 C1
  BURY BL9.....4 E9
  CMANE M1.....7 H6
  CSLFD M3.....6 C1
  DROY M43 *.....89 M2
  DTN/ASHW M34.....90 B6
  HYDE SK14.....102 B2
  STLY SK15.....91 L2
  WGN WN1.....14 E3
  WGNS/IIMK WN3.....47 K7
Richmond Wk CHAD OL9.....8 E6
Ricroft Rd MPL/ROM SK6.....114 E1
Ridding Av WYTH/NTH M22.....119 G1
Ridding CI OFTN SK2.....113 G6
Riddings CI HALE/TIMP WA15.....108 C4
Riddings Rd HALE/TIMP WA15.....108 D4
  HALE/TIMP WA15.....117 H3
Ridge Av HALE/TIMP WA15.....117 L6
  MPL/ROM SK6.....114 D8
  WGN WN1.....31 L5
Ridge CI GLSP SK13.....93 H8
  MPL/ROM SK6.....114 B2
  WHTF M45.....55 L4
Ridgecroft AULW OL7.....75 L6
The Ridgedales OLD OL1.....44 B8
Ridge End Fold MPL/ROM SK6.....123 J3
Ridgefield CMANW M2.....6 E5
Ridgefield St FAIL M35.....74 B6
Ridgegreen WALK M28 *.....68 D7
Ridge Gv WHTF M45.....55 L4
Ridge Hill La STLY SK15.....91 K1
Ridgemont Av HTNM SK4.....12 B2
Ridgemont CI HOR/BR BL6.....34 C1
Ridge Pk BRAM/HZG SK7.....120 F6
Ridge Rd MPL/ROM SK6.....114 D8
Ridge Top La NM/HAY SK22.....125 M2
Ridgeway BOL BL1 *.....2 E4
  GOL/RIS/CUL WA3.....80 B5
  SWIN M27.....70 E3
  WILM/AE SK9.....127 G5
Ridgeway Gates BOL BL1 *.....2 E4
Ridgeway Rd
  HALE/TIMP WA15.....108 F7
Ridgeway St NEWH/MOS M40.....88 A2
The Ridgeway POY/DIS SK12.....123 L5
Ridgewell Av GOL/RIS/CUL WA3.....80 A4
Ridgewood Av CHAD OL9.....58 B4
  NEWH/MOS M40.....73 H7
Ridgmont Dr HOR/BR BL6.....34 C1
  WALK M28.....68 C6
Ridgmont Rd BRAM/HZG SK7.....121 G8
Ridgway HOR/BR BL6.....32 F2
The Ridgway MPL/ROM SK6.....113 K3
Riding CI SALE M33.....97 J8
  TYLD M29.....68 A5
Riding Fold DROY M43.....89 M1
Riding Fold La WALK M28.....69 K7
Riding Ga BOLE BL2.....23 H6
Riding Gate Ms BOLE BL2.....23 H6
Riding Head La RAMS BL0.....19 J4
Riding La AIMK WN4.....64 B7
Ridings Gn UPML OL3.....61 K2
Ridings Rd GLSP SK13.....93 J7
Ridings St NEWH/MOS M40.....73 J7
  OP/CLY M11.....88 E4
The Ridings RNFD/HAY WA11.....78 A6
Ridley Dr ALT WA14.....108 B3
Ridley Gv SALE M33.....109 J1
Ridley St OLDE OL4.....9 M7
Ridley Wk HULME M15 *.....87 J2
Ridling La HYDE SK14.....102 B2
Ridsdale Av DID/WITH M20.....98 D6
Ridyard St LHULT M38.....52 F8
  WGNE/HIN WN2.....64 C1
  WGNW/BIL/OR WN5.....47 H5
Riefield BOL BL1.....35 L1
Rifle Rd SALE M33.....97 J7
Rifle St OLD OL1.....9 J3
Riga Rd RUSH/FAL M14.....98 F3
Riga St ANC M4.....7 H2
Rigby Av HOR/BR BL6.....32 F2
Rigby Ct BOLS/LL BL3.....36 C3
Rigby Gv LHULT M38.....53 H6
Rigby La BOLE BL2.....23 G7
Rigbys La AIMK WN4.....79 G1
Rigby St AIMK WN4.....78 D1
  ALT WA14.....116 E1
  BOLS/LL BL3.....36 C8
  BRO M7.....72 A5
  GOL/RIS/CUL WA3.....79 K4
  WGNE/HIN WN2.....49 H6
Rigel St ANC M4.....7 M1

Rigton CI WGTN/LGST M12.....88 D7
Rildene Wk ROCH OL11.....27 G4
Riley CI SALE M33.....107 L3
Riley Ct BOL BL1.....36 C3
Riley La WGNE/HIN WN2.....32 E5
Riley Sq WGN WN1.....15 J5
Riley St ATH M46.....66 D3
Riley Wood CI MPL/ROM SK6 *.....113 J5
Rimington Av
  GOL/RIS/CUL WA3.....79 M3
Rimington Fold MDTN M24.....41 G8
Rimmer CI OP/CLY M11.....88 B4
Rimmington CI BKLY M9.....73 K2
Rimsdale CI CHD/CHDH SK8.....119 J1
Rimworth Dr NEWH/MOS M40.....72 F8
Rindle Rd TYLD M29.....82 F4
Ringcroft Gdns
  NEWH/MOS M40.....73 L3
Ringley Av GOL/RIS/CUL WA3.....79 J3
Ringley Cha WHTF M45.....55 H4
Ringley CI WHTF M45.....55 G5
Ringley Dr WHTF M45.....55 G5
Ringley Gv BOL BL1.....22 B7
Ringley Hey WHTF M45.....55 G4
Ringley Mdw RAD M26.....53 M5
Ringley Old Brow RAD M26.....53 M5
Ringley Pk WHTF M45.....55 G4
Ringley Rd RAD M26.....53 L4
  RAD M26.....54 A5
  RAD M26.....54 A4
Ringley Rd West RAD M26.....54 B4
Ringley St BKLY M9 *.....73 C4
Ringlow Av SWIN M27.....69 M5
Ringlow Park Rd SWIN M27.....69 M6
Ring Lows La WHIT OL12.....20 E1
Ringmer Dr WYTH/NTH M22.....118 E3
Ringmere Ct OLD OL1 *.....9 H2
Ringmore Rd BRAM/HZG SK7.....121 J2
Ring-o-bells La POY/DIS SK12.....123 M6
Ringstead CI WILM/AE SK9.....127 H3
Ringstead Dr NEWH/MOS M40.....87 M1
  WILM/AE SK9.....127 H3
Ringstone PWCH M25.....71 K1
Ringway Av LEIGH WN7.....66 C4
Ringway Gv SALE M33.....109 H2
Ringway Rd MANAIR M90.....118 C5
  WYTH/NTH M22.....119 G5
Ringway Rd West
  WYTH/NTH M22.....118 E4
Ringwood Av BRAM/HZG SK7.....121 K3
  DTN/ASHW M34.....89 M3
  HYDE SK14.....102 D3
  RAD M26.....54 E3
  RAMS BL0.....18 D8
  WGTN/LGST M12.....99 G2
Ringwood Wy CHAD OL9.....8 C3
Rink St RUSH/FAL M14.....99 G5
Ripley Av CHD/CHDH SK8.....120 D7
  OFTN SK2.....112 E8
Ripley CI ANC M4 *.....88 A4
  BRAM/HZG SK7.....122 A4
Ripley Crs URM M41.....84 C7
  WGNS/IIMK WN3.....46 F8
Ripley Dr LEIGH WN7.....66 C6
Ripley St BOLE BL2.....22 E8
Ripon Av BOL BL1.....35 J3
  GOL/RIS/CUL WA3.....80 A4
  WHTF M45.....55 J2
Ripon CI BOLS/LL BL3.....53 J1
  CHAD OL9.....8 B7
  HALE/TIMP WA15.....117 L3
  NEWLW WA12.....78 F8
  RAD M26.....39 G7
  STKP SK1.....13 J7
  WHTF M45.....55 J2
Ripon Crs STRET M32.....96 C1
Ripon Dr BRAM/HZG SK7.....122 A4
  BOL BL1.....35 J3
Ripon Gv SALE M33.....96 C6
Ripon Hall Av RAMS BL0.....18 E8
Ripon Rd STRET M32.....96 D1
Ripon St AUL OL6 *.....90 F1
  OLD OL1.....8 F2
Rippenden Av CCHDY M21.....97 K2
Rippingham Rd
  DID/WITH M20.....98 E5
Rippleton Rd WYTH/NTH M22.....110 B8
Ripponden Rd OLDE OL4.....60 A3
  UPML OL3.....45 G2
Ripponden St OLD OL1.....59 M3
The Rises GLSP SK13.....93 J7
The Rise OLDE OL4.....60 C5
  WGNNW/ST WN6.....46 F1
Rishton Av BOLS/LL BL3.....52 C2
Rishton La BOLS/LL BL3.....52 C1
Rishworth CI OFTN SK2.....113 L1
Rishworth Dr NEWH/MOS M40.....74 B4
Rishworth Ri ROY/SHW OL2.....43 J9
Rising La OLDS OL8.....75 H2
Risley St OLD OL1.....9 J2
Rissington Av
  NTHM/RTH M23.....109 L3
Rita Av RUSH/FAL M14 *.....98 E1
Ritson CI GTN M18.....88 E6
Riva Rd BNG/LEV M19.....111 G2
River PI HULME M15.....6 D8
  MILN OL16 *.....29 J6
Riversdale Dr OLDS OL8.....75 K3
Riversdale Rd CHD/CHDH SK8.....110 F7
Riversdale Vw MPL/ROM SK6.....101 K7
The Rivers Edge WHIT OL12.....20 B4
Rivershill SALE M33.....96 D6
Rivershill Dr HEY OL10.....40 F3
Rivershill Gdns
  HALE/TIMP WA15.....117 L6
Riverside BOL BL1.....36 C2
  BRO M7.....86 F1
  DUK SK16.....90 F2
  OLD OL1.....58 B7
Riverside Av IRL M44.....94 D3
  WGN WN1.....15 L1
Riverside CI GLSP SK13.....105 G5
Riverside Ct MPL/ROM SK6 *.....114 D4

Riverside Dr BURY BL9.....24 E1
  MILN OL16.....28 F2
  RAD M26.....53 L4
  URM M41.....83 L4
Riverside Gdns SALE M33.....96 D6
Riverside Rd RAD M26.....39 G8
Rivers La URM M41.....84 F7
Riversleigh CI BOL BL1.....35 J3
Rivers St WGNE/HIN WN5.....46 B6
Riverstone Br LIT OL15.....21 M7
Riverstone Dr NTHM/RTH M23.....109 L3
River St BOLE BL2.....23 H7
  HEY OL10.....27 G8
  HULME M15.....6 E9
  MILN OL16.....10 F4
  RAD M26.....54 E1
  RAMS BL0.....18 F6
  STKP SK1.....112 E1
  WGTN/LGST M12.....7 M7
  WILM/AE SK9.....126 F4
Riverton Rd DID/WITH M20.....110 E5
River Vw RDSH SK5.....100 D5
Riverview Wk BOL BL1 *.....2 A1
River Wy WGN WN1.....15 G4
Riviera Ct WHIT OL12.....26 F2
Rivington Av GOL/RIS/CUL WA3.....79 M3
  SWIN M27.....70 F5
  WGN WN1.....47 L3
Rivington Ct WHTF M45.....55 L4
Rivington Dr ROY/SHW OL2.....44 A5
  TOT/BURYW BL8.....38 D3
  WGNE/HIN WN2.....65 J3
Rivington Gv DTN/ASHW M34.....89 M4
  IRL M44.....94 A6
Rivington Rd
  HALE/TIMP WA15.....117 H2
  OLDE OL4.....60 D5
  SLFD M6.....70 F8
Rivington St ATH M46.....66 D2
  HOR/BR BL6.....33 H1
  OLD OL1.....9 J1
  WHIT OL12.....10 F1
Rivington Wk
  WGTN/LGST M12 *.....88 B7
Rivington Wy WGNNW/ST WN6.....31 J4
Rixon St OLDE OL4 *.....60 A3
Rixson St OLDE OL4 *.....60 A3
Rix St BOL BL1.....36 B2
Rixton Dr TYLD M29.....67 L4
Rixtonleys Dr IRL M44.....94 E4
Roach Bank Rd BURY BL9.....39 M5
Roaches Ms MOSL OL5.....77 G1
Roaches Wy MOSL OL5.....77 H1
Roachill CI ALT WA14.....107 L7
Roach PI MILN OL16.....11 G3
Roach St BURY BL9.....39 J8
Roach V MILN OL16.....28 F2
Roachwood CI CHAD OL9.....58 B5
Roading Brook Rd BOLE BL2.....37 L1
Road La WHIT OL12.....20 B8
Roads Ford Av MILN OL16.....11 J3
Roadside Ct GOL/RIS/CUL WA3.....79 M4
Roan Wy WILM/AE SK9.....130 E4
Roaring Gate La
  HALE/TIMP WA15.....118 A1
Robert Hall St ORD M5.....86 E5
Robert Lawrence Ct
  URM M41 *.....95 K3
Robert Malcolm CI
  NEWH/MOS M40.....73 G7
Robert Owen Gdns
  WYTH/NTH M22 *.....110 A4
Robert Salt Ct ALT WA14.....108 B6
Robertscroft CI
  WYTH/NTH M22.....109 M8
Robertshaw Av CCHDY M21.....97 L6
Robertshaw St LEIGH WN7.....66 B5
Robertson St RAD M26.....38 D8
Roberts St ECC M30.....85 G3
Robert St ATH M46.....67 H3
  BOLE BL2 *.....23 H7
  CSLFD M3.....87 J1
  DUK SK16.....90 E4
  FAIL M35.....74 D3
  HEY OL10.....41 H4
  HYDE SK14.....101 M2
  MILN OL16.....10 F3
  NEWH/MOS M40.....73 J7
  OLDS OL8.....74 E2
  PWCH M25.....55 M8
  RAMS BL0.....18 F4
  SALE M33.....97 H8
  TOT/BURYW BL8.....38 F1
  WGNE/HIN WN2.....64 D1
Robeson Wy WYTH/NTH M22.....110 C6
Robin Cft MPL/ROM SK6.....113 C1
Robin Dr IRL M44.....94 D1
Robin Hill Dr WGNNW/ST WN6.....30 E1
Robin Hill La WGNNW/ST WN6.....30 E1
Robin Hood St CHH M8.....72 C4
Robinia CI ECC M30.....84 C4
Robin Park Rd
  WGNW/BIL/OR WN5.....14 B6
Robin Rd ALT WA14.....107 M3
Robins CI BRAM/HZG SK7.....121 G5
  DROY M43.....89 M1
Robin's La BRAM/HZG SK7.....121 G5
Robinson Pk STLY SK15.....91 H3
Robinson St CHAD OL9.....8 A7
  EDGY/DAV SK3.....12 F8
  HYDE SK14 *.....102 C1
  MILN OL16.....11 G4
  OLDS OL8.....75 J1
  STLY SK15.....91 J3
Robin St OLD OL1.....9 G2
Robinsway ALT WA14.....116 E3
Robinswood Rd
  WYTH/NTH M22.....118 F3
Rob La NEWLW WA12.....79 H3
Robson Av URM M41.....85 H5
Robson St OLD OL1.....9 K6
Robson Wy
  GOL/RIS/CUL WA3.....80 C3
Roby Rd ECC M30.....84 F4
Roby St CMANE M1.....7 J5
Roby Well Wy
  WGNW/BIL/OR WN5.....62 A7
Roch Av HEY OL10.....40 D2
Roch Bank BKLY M9.....72 C4
Rochbury CI ROCH OL11.....27 J6
Roch CI WHTF M45.....55 L3
Roch Crs WHTF M45.....55 L3
Rochdale La HEY OL10.....41 G2
  ROY/SHW OL2.....43 G7
Rochdale Old Rd BURY BL9.....39 M1

Rochdale Rd ANC M4.....7 J2
  BKLY M9.....73 G5
  BURY BL9.....5 H4
  HEY OL10.....41 G2
  MDTN M24.....29 G5
  MILN OL16.....29 G5
  NEWH/MOS M40.....72 F8
  OLD OL1.....9 G3
  RAMS BL0.....19 K3
  ROY/SHW OL2.....42 F6
  UPML OL3.....44 E1
Rochdale Rd East HEY OL10.....41 J1
Rochdale Wy MILN OL16.....43 H2
Roche Gdns CHD/CHDH SK8.....120 D6
Roche Rd UPML OL3.....45 H7
Rochester Av BOLE BL2.....37 H3
  CCHDY M21.....98 A6
  PWCH M25.....71 M2
  WALK M28.....68 F3
Rochester CI AUL OL6.....75 M5
  DUK SK16.....91 K5
  GOL/RIS/CUL WA3.....79 K4
Rochester Dr ALT WA14.....108 B3
Rochester Gv BRAM/HZG SK7.....122 A1
Rochester Rd URM M41.....85 G8
Rochester Wy CHAD OL9.....8 A7
Rochford Av WHTF M45.....55 G5
Rochford CI WHTF M45.....55 G5
Rochford Rd ECC M30.....84 C4
Roch Mills Crs ROCH OL11.....27 M7
Roch Mills Gdns ROCH OL11.....27 M7
Roch PI WGNE/HIN WN2.....64 C2
Roch St MILN OL16.....28 E3
Roch Valley Wy ROCH OL11.....27 M7
Roch Wy WHTF M45.....55 L3
Rockall Wk OP/CLY M11 *.....88 C3
Rock Av BOL BL1.....35 K2
Rock Bank BRO M7 *.....71 F5
Rockbourne CI WGNE/HIN WN2.....49 G8
Rockdove Av HULME M15.....6 E9
Rocket Wy CSLFD M3.....6 B4
Rockfield Dr BKLY M9 *.....73 H4
Rock Fold EDGW/EG BL7 *.....22 C3
Rockhampton St GTN M18.....89 H7
Rockhouse CI ECC M30.....85 C4
Rockingham CI ROY/SHW OL2.....43 H4
  WGTN/LGST M12.....88 B3
Rockingham Dr
  WGNE/HIN WN2.....48 F8
Rockley Gdns SLFD M6.....71 J8
Rocklyn Av NEWH/MOS M40.....73 M2
Rocklynes MPL/ROM SK6.....113 L2
Rockmead Dr BKLY M9.....73 H1
Rock Mill La NM/HAY SK22.....124 D5
Rock Rd URM M41.....96 C2
  WALK M28.....83 L2
Rock St AULW OL7.....75 K7
  BRO M7.....72 A6
  GOL/RIS/CUL WA3.....79 K2
  HEY OL10.....41 H3
  HOR/BR BL6.....33 L1
  HYDE SK14.....102 D5
  NM/HAY SK22.....124 D5
  OLD OL1.....9 J1
  OP/CLY M11.....89 H5
  RAD M26.....54 E2
  RAMS BL0.....19 H5
Rock Ter EDGW/EG BL7 *.....22 C3
  MOSL OL5.....77 G1
The Rock BURY BL9.....5 H5
Rocky Bank Ter
  WGNS/IIMK WN3 *.....15 K9
Rocky La ECC M30.....70 A8
Roda St BKLY M9.....73 J5
Rodborough Rd
  NTHM/RTH M23.....118 C3
Rodeheath CI WILM/AE SK9.....127 H5
Roden St NEWH/MOS M40.....73 K6
Rodepool CI WILM/AE SK9.....127 G3
Rodgers CI WHTN BL5.....50 B6
Rodgers Wy WHTN BL5.....50 B6
Rodmell Av NEWH/MOS M40 *.....73 G7
Rodmell CI EDGW/EG BL7.....22 C5
Rodmill Ct RUSH/FAL M14.....98 F1
Rodmill Dr CHD/CHDH SK8.....110 D8
Rodney Ct ANC M4.....7 L1
Rodney Dr MPL/ROM SK6.....101 K7
Rodney St ANC M4.....7 M2
  ATH M46.....66 F2
  AUL OL6.....76 A8
  CSLFD M3.....6 A4
  ROCH OL11.....15 G5
  WGN WN1.....15 G5
Roeacre St HEY OL10.....41 H3
Roebuck Gdns SALE M33 *.....96 D8
Roebuck La OLDE OL4.....96 D8
  SALE M33.....96 D8
Roebuck Ms WGNE/HIN WN2.....65 M1
Roecliffe CI WGNS/IIMK WN3.....14 E8
Roe Cross Gn HYDE SK14.....92 C7
Roe Cross Rd HYDE SK14.....92 C7
Roedean Gdns URM M41.....95 G2
Roefield Ter WHIT OL12.....27 M4
Roe Gn WALK M28.....69 K4
Roe Green Av WALK M28.....69 K4
Roe La OLDE OL4.....60 A4
Roe St ANC M4.....7 L1
  WHIT OL12.....27 M3
Rogate Dr NTHM/RTH M23.....109 K7
Roger CI MPL/ROM SK6.....113 J3
Rogerson CI HALE/TIMP WA15.....108 F3
Rogerstead BOLS/LL BL3 *.....35 M6
Roger St ANC M4.....87 K1
Rogerton CI LEIGH WN7.....66 E8
Roger Wy CHD/CHDH SK8.....120 C2
Rokeby Av GOL/RIS/CUL WA3.....80 A3
  STRET M32.....97 G1
Rokeden NEWLW WA12.....79 G8
Roker Av BRUN/LGST M13.....99 K2
Roker Park Av DTN/ASHW M34.....90 B5
Roland Rd BOLS/LL BL3.....36 C8
  RDSH SK5.....100 C5
Rolla St CSLFD M3.....6 D2
Rollesby CI TOT/BURYW BL8.....25 G7
Rolleston Av ANC M4.....7 M2
Rollins La MPL/ROM SK6.....114 D3
Rolls Crs HULME M15.....6 E9
Rollswood Dr NEWH/MOS M40.....73 K6
Romana Sq ALT WA14.....108 B4
Roman Rd AIMK WN4.....63 K7
  FAIL M35.....74 D4
  HTNM SK4.....13 H3
  PWCH M25.....55 J8
  ROY/SHW OL2.....59 G1
Roman St RAD M26.....54 B1
  NEWH/MOS M40 *.....74 D3
Rome Rd NEWH/MOS M40.....73 K7
Romer Av NEWH/MOS M40 *.....74 D3
Romer St BOLE BL2.....3 M5
Romford Av DTN/ASHW M34.....90 F4
  LEIGH WN7.....66 C6

Romford Cl OLDS OL8 ...... 9 H9
Romford Pl WGNE/HIN WN2 ...... 49 H7
Romford Rd SALE M33 ...... 96 B6
Romford St WGNE/HIN WN2 ...... 49 G7
Romiley Crs BOLE BL2 ...... 37 G4
Romiley Dr BOLE BL2 ...... 37 G4
Romiley Sq WGNNW/ST WN6 ...... 31 H4
Romiley St SLFD M6 ...... 71 G7
  STKP SK1 ...... 112 E2
Romley Rd URM M41 ...... 85 G8
Romney Av ROCH OL11 ...... 42 B2
Romney Cha BOL BL1 ...... 22 B8
Romney Rd BOL BL1 ...... 35 H2
Romney St AUL OL6 ...... 90 F1
  NEWH/MOS M40 ...... 73 K4
  SLFD M6 ...... 71 K7
Romney Wk CHAD OL9 ...... 8 A7
Romney Wy RDSH SK5 ...... 100 E6
  WGN WN1 ...... 47 L1
Romsey WHIT OL12 ...... 10 D3
Romsey Av MDTN M24 ...... 57 J1
Romsey Dr
  CHD/CHDH SK8 ...... 120 D6
Romsey Gv WGTN/LGST M12 ...... 88 D6
Romsley Dr BOLS/LL BL3 ...... 51 M1
Rona Cl WGTN/LGST M12 ...... 88 C7
Ronaldsay Gdns ORD M5 ...... 86 B3
Ronald St OLDE 59 M5
  OP/CLY M11 ...... 89 C3
  ROCH OL11 ...... 41 M3
Rondin Cl WGTN/LGST M12 ...... 88 B5
Rondin Rd WGTN/LGST M12 ...... 88 B5
Roocroft St BOLS/LL BL3 ...... 2 B1
Roocroft Sq HOR/BR BL6 ...... 32 F2
Roods La ROCH OL11 ...... 26 F3
Rookery Av AIMK WN4 ...... 78 E2
  GTN M18 ...... 89 J6
  WGNNW/ST WN6 ...... 30 B4
Rookery Cl STLY SK15 ...... 92 B5
Rookerypool Cl WILM/AE SK9 ...... 127 H2
The Rookery NEWLW WA12 ...... 79 C8
Rooke St ECC M30 ...... 84 D4
Rookfield Av SALE M33 ...... 96 F7
Rookley Wk RUSH/FAL M14 * 98 F1
Rook St HULME M15 ...... 87 H7
  OLDE OL4 ...... 59 M7
  RAMS BL0 ...... 18 F6
Rookswood Dr ROCH OL11 ...... 41 L1
Rookway MDTN M24 ...... 57 J5
Rookwood OLD OL1 ...... 58 B3
Rookwood Av
  NTHM/RTH M23 ...... 109 J5
Rooley Moor Rd WHIT OL12 ...... 27 K1
Rooley St WHIT OL12 ...... 27 M3
Roosevelt Rd FWTH BL4 ...... 53 J5
Ropefield Wy WHIT OL12 ...... 28 B1
Rope St WHIT OL12 ...... 10 E2
Rope Wk CSLFD M3 ...... 6 A4
Rosa Gv BRO M7 ...... 72 A6
Rosamond Dr CSLFD M3 ...... 6 B3
Rosamond St West
  HULME M15 ...... 87 K6
Rosary Cl OLDS OL8 ...... 75 J3
Rosary Rd OLDS OL8 ...... 75 K3
Roscoe Av WHTN BL5 ...... 50 C5
Roscoe Rd IRL M44 ...... 94 B3
Roscoe St EDGY/DAV SK3 ...... 12 F6
  OLD OL1 ...... 9 L5
  WGN WN1 ...... 15 K5
Roscow Av BOLE BL2 ...... 37 H4
Roscow Rd FWTH BL4 ...... 53 K6
Rose Acre WALK M28 ...... 68 E5
Roseacre Cl CHD/CHDH SK8 ...... 119 L3
Rose Av IRL M44 ...... 94 C3
  LIT OL15 ...... 29 J1
  RNFD/HAY WA11 ...... 78 B6
  ROCH OL11 ...... 27 G2
  WGNE/HIN WN2 ...... 64 E5
  WGNNW/ST WN6 ...... 47 J1
Rosebank HOR/BR BL6 ...... 34 F5
  RAMS BL0 ...... 19 G3
Rosebank Cl BOLE BL2 ...... 37 M3
Rose Bank Cl HYDE SK14 ...... 93 C7
  WGN WN1 ...... 31 L8
Rosebank Rd NEWH/MOS M40 ...... 73 G6
Rosebay Cl ROY/SHW OL2 ...... 43 J8
Roseberry Cl RAMS BL0 ...... 24 F1
Roseberry Rd AIMK WN4 ...... 63 K7
Roseberry St BOLS/LL BL3 ...... 35 M8
  OLDS OL8 * 8 F7
Rosebery St OFTN SK2 ...... 113 G8
  RUSH/FAL M14 ...... 98 C1
  WHTN BL5 ...... 50 C4
Rosebridge Ct WGN WN1 * 15 M5
Rosebridge Wy WGN WN1 ...... 15 M5
Rosebury Av LEIGH WN7 ...... 66 D7
  OLD OL1 ...... 59 L3
Rosebury Gv LEIGH WN7 ...... 66 E6
Rose Cottage Rd
  DID/WITH M20 ...... 98 E5
Rose Crs IRL M44 ...... 94 C3
Rosecroft Cl EDGY/DAV SK3 ...... 112 B8
Rosedale Av ATH M46 ...... 66 F1
  BOL BL1 ...... 22 B7
  GOL/RIS/CUL WA3 ...... 79 M5
Rosedale Cl OLD OL1 ...... 59 L3
Rosedale Ct DTN/ASHW M34 * 101 H1
Rosedale Dr LEIGH WN7 ...... 66 A7
Rosedale Rd HTNM SK4 ...... 100 A3
  RUSH/FAL M14 ...... 98 D2
Rosedale Wy DUK SK16 ...... 90 F6
Rosefield Cl EDGY/DAV SK3 ...... 111 B7
Rosefield Crs MILN OL16 ...... 11 K5
Rosegarth Av DID/WITH M20 ...... 98 A8
Rose Gv FWTH BL4 ...... 53 J5
  TOT/BURYW BL8 ...... 38 D2
Rosehay Av DTN/ASHW M34 ...... 101 J2
Rose Hey La FAIL M35 ...... 74 B8
Rose Hl BOLE BL2 * 3 H6
  DTN/ASHW M34 ...... 101 J4
  STLY SK15 ...... 91 J4
  UPML OL3 ...... 61 J1
Rose Hill Av NEWH/MOS M40 * 73 L8
  WGNW/BIL/OR WN5 ...... 46 F6
Rose Hill Cl EDGW/EG BL7 ...... 22 C1
Rosehill Cl SLFD M6 ...... 86 C2
Rose Hill Rd AUL OL6 ...... 76 C7
Rose Hill St HEY OL10 ...... 40 E2
Rose Hill Vw AIMK WN4 ...... 63 J5
Roseland Av DID/WITH M20 ...... 98 E4
Roseland Dr PWCH M25 ...... 55 M6
Roselands Av SALE M33 ...... 108 C2
Rose La MPL/ROM SK6 ...... 114 B2
Rose Lea BOLE BL2 ...... 23 H8
Rosemary Crs WGN WN1 ...... 48 A2

Rosemary Dr HYDE SK14 ...... 102 A5
  LIT OL15 ...... 21 K6
Rosemary Gv BRO M7 ...... 71 M7
Rosemary La STKP SK1 ...... 13 L5
  WHTN BL5 ...... 51 L6
Rosemary Rd CHAD OL9 ...... 58 B4
Rosemount HYDE SK14 ...... 91 C7
Rose Mt MDTN M24 ...... 57 J2
Rosemount Crs HYDE SK14 ...... 91 C7
Roseneath BRAM/HZG SK7 ...... 120 F3
Roseneath Av BNG/LEV M19 ...... 99 H3
Roseneath Gv BOLS/LL BL3 ...... 52 A1
Roseneath Rd BOLS/LL BL3 ...... 52 A1
  URM M41 ...... 95 M1
Rosen Sq CHAD OL9 ...... 8 A4
Rose St BOLE BL2 ...... 3 G8
  CHAD OL9 ...... 74 D1
  MDTN M24 ...... 57 M4
  RDSH SK5 ...... 112 C1
  WGN WN1 ...... 15 M5
  WGNE/HIN WN2 ...... 49 G7
Rose Ter STLY SK15 ...... 91 K3
Rosethorns Cl MDTN M24 ...... 41 J8
Rose V CHD/CHDH SK8 ...... 119 K3
Rosevale Av BNG/LEV M19 ...... 99 H4
Roseway BRAM/HZG SK6 ...... 121 H2
Rosewell Cl
  NEWH/MOS M40 ...... 73 C8
Rosewood ROCH OL11 ...... 27 H3
  WHTN BL5 ...... 49 M6
Rosewood Av DROY M43 ...... 89 M1
  HTNM SK4 ...... 111 K3
  TOT/BURYW BL8 ...... 24 D6
Rosewood Cl DUK SK16 ...... 91 G6
  WGNE/HIN WN2 ...... 64 E5
Rosewood Crs CHAD OL9 ...... 8 B1
Rosewood Gdns
  CHD/CHDH SK8 ...... 110 C6
Rosford Av RUSH/FAL M14 ...... 98 C2
Rosgill Cl HTNM SK4 ...... 111 H2
Rosgill Dr MDTN M24 ...... 57 G3
Rosina Cl AIMK WN4 ...... 63 J6
Rosina St OP/CLY M11 ...... 89 J5
Rosley Rd WGNS/IIMK WN3 ...... 63 L1
Roslin St OP/CLY M11 ...... 89 G2
Roslyn Av URM M41 ...... 95 H4
Roslyn Rd EDGY/DAV SK3 ...... 112 B7
Rossall Av RAD M26 ...... 54 F4
  STRET M32 ...... 96 F1
Rossall Cl BOLE BL2 ...... 3 L2
Rossall Crs LEIGH WN7 ...... 81 K1
Rossall Dr BRAM/HZG SK7 ...... 121 H6
Rossall Rd BOLE BL2 ...... 3 L2
  WHIT OL12 ...... 28 D2
Rossall St BOLE BL2 ...... 3 L2
Rossall Wy SLFD M6 ...... 86 D1
Ross Av CHAD OL9 ...... 74 C1
  EDGY/DAV SK3 ...... 112 B7
  WHTF M45 ...... 55 J6
Ross Cl WGNE/HIN WN2 ...... 48 C2
  WGNW/BIL/OR WN5 ...... 62 B7
Rossdale Gv WGNNW/ST WN6 ...... 31 K5
Ross Dr SWIN M27 ...... 54 B8
Rossenclough Rd
  WILM/AE SK9 ...... 127 H3
Rossendale Av BKLY M9 ...... 73 J3
Rossendale Cl ROY/SHW OL2 ...... 44 A5
Rossendale Rd CHD/CHDH SK8 ...... 119 L4
Rossendale Wy RAMS BL0 ...... 18 B2
  RAW/HAS BB4 ...... 18 B1
  WHIT OL12 ...... 20 A6
  WHIT OL12 ...... 20 L1
Rossett Av HALE/TIMP WA15 ...... 108 D4
  WYTH/NTH M22 ...... 118 F3
Rossett Cl WGNS/IIMK WN3 ...... 63 G3
Rossett Dr URM M41 ...... 84 C8
Ross Gv URM M41 ...... 95 M2
Rosshill Wk HULME M15 * 87 G6
Rossington St NEWH/MOS M40 ...... 74 A7
Rossini St BOL BL1 ...... 35 K3
Ross Lave La DTN/ASHW M34 ...... 100 F3
Rosslyn Cv HALE/TIMP WA15 ...... 108 D6
Rosslyn Rd CHD/CHDH SK8 ...... 119 M3
  NEWH/MOS M40 ...... 73 K3
  OLDTF/WHR M16 ...... 97 K2
Rossmere Av ROCH OL11 ...... 27 M6
Rossmill La HALE/TIMP WA15 ...... 117 L5
Ross St OLDS OL8 ...... 8 F8
Rostherne Av
  GOL/RIS/CUL WA3 ...... 80 A4
  MPL/ROM SK6 ...... 123 M4
  RUSH/FAL M14 ...... 98 D3
Rostherne Gdns BOLS/LL BL3 ...... 35 L8
Rostherne Rd EDGY/DAV SK3 ...... 112 B7
  SALE M33 ...... 109 J1
  WILM/AE SK9 ...... 126 C7
Rostherne St ALT WA14 ...... 116 F1
  SLFD M6 * 86 B3
Rosthernmere Rd
  CHD/CHDH SK8 ...... 111 J8
Rosthwaite Cl MDTN M24 ...... 56 F3
  WGNS/IIMK WN3 ...... 63 K2
Roston Rd BRO M7 ...... 72 B4
Rostrevor Rd EDGY/DAV SK3 ...... 112 B7
Rostron Av RAMS BL0 ...... 18 E6
Rostron Rd BNG/LEV M19 ...... 99 L3
Rothay Cl BOLE BL2 ...... 37 J3
  WHTF M45 ...... 55 M4
Rothay Dr MDTN M24 ...... 57 H1
  RDSH SK5 ...... 100 C4
Rothay St LEIGH WN7 ...... 66 B8
Rothbury Av AULW OL7 ...... 75 H7
Rothbury Cl TOT/BURYW BL8 ...... 38 C2
Rothbury Ct BOLS/LL BL3 ...... 51 L1
Rotherby Rd WYTH/NTH M22 ...... 110 B8
Rotherdale Av
  HALE/TIMP WA15 ...... 109 G7
Rotherham Cl HOR/BR BL6 ...... 33 J2
Rotherwood Av STRET M32 ...... 97 H1
Rotherwood Rd WILM/AE SK9 ...... 126 B7
Rothesay Av DUK SK16 ...... 90 F5
Rothesay Crs SALE M33 ...... 107 M2
Rothesay Rd BOLS/LL BL3 * 51 L1
  DUK SK16 ...... 90 F5
  OLD OL1 ...... 59 M3
Rothesay Ter MILN OL16 ...... 28 F8
Rothiemay Rd URM M41 ...... 95 H3
Rothley Av WYTH/NTH M22 ...... 110 A7
Rothman Cl NEWH/MOS M40 ...... 73 M6
Rothwell Crs BOLS/LL BL3 ...... 52 B6
Rothwell La LHULT M38 ...... 52 B7
Rothwell Rd GOL/RIS/CUL WA3 ...... 79 M3
Rothwell St BOLS/LL BL3 ...... 2 D9
  FAIL M35 ...... 74 B6
  NEWH/MOS M40 ...... 73 M6
  RAMS BL0 ...... 18 E6
  ROY/SHW OL2 ...... 58 F1
  WALK M28 ...... 69 J1
  WHIT OL12 ...... 28 B7

Rottingdene Dr
  WYTH/NTH M22 ...... 118 E3
Roughey Gdns
  WYTH/NTH M22 ...... 109 M8
Rough Hey Wk MILN OL16 ...... 11 J7
Rough Hill La BURY BL9 ...... 26 B8
Roughlea Av GOL/RIS/CUL WA3 ...... 81 G8
Roughlee Av SWIN M27 ...... 70 A5
Roughtown Rd MOSL OL5 ...... 77 G2
Round Barn EDGW/EG BL7 * 16 E1
Roundcroft MPL/ROM SK6 ...... 114 A1
Roundhey CHD/CHDH SK8 ...... 119 K4
Round Hey MOSL OL5 ...... 76 F4
Round Hill Gl GLSP SK13 ...... 104 C3
Roundhill Wy OLDE OL4 ...... 60 B3
Round House Av WGN WN1 ...... 15 L1
Roundmoor Rd
  WGNNW/ST WN6 ...... 31 K5
Roundthorn La WHTN BL5 ...... 50 B5
Round Thorn Rd MDTN M24 ...... 57 L5
Roundthorn Rd
  NTHM/RTH M23 ...... 109 J6
  OLDE OL4 ...... 59 M7
Roundway BRAM/HZG SK6 ...... 120 F6
Round Wy NM/HAY SK22 ...... 124 F4
Roundwood Rd
  WYTH/NTH M22 ...... 110 A5
Roundy La MCFLDN SK10 ...... 129 K7
Rousdon Cl NEWH/MOS M40 * 73 G7
Rouse St ROCH OL11 ...... 27 M8
Roving Bridge Ri SWIN M27 ...... 71 C4
Rowan Av GOL/RIS/CUL WA3 ...... 80 C5
  HOR/BR BL6 ...... 34 B3
  OLDTF/WHR M16 ...... 97 M1
  SALE M33 ...... 108 F2
  URM M41 ...... 96 A1
  WGNNW/ST WN6 ...... 47 J3
Rowan Cl FAIL M35 ...... 74 C7
  WHIT OL12 ...... 27 K1
Rowan Crs DUK SK16 ...... 91 J5
Rowan Dr BURY BL9 ...... 5 L3
  CHD/CHDH SK8 ...... 120 E4
Rowanhill Wk OP/CLY M11
Rowanlea PWCH M25 * 55 M8
Rowan Pl PWCH M25 ...... 71 L1
Rowans STLY SK15 ...... 91 M1
Rowanside Dr WILM/AE SK9 ...... 127 J4
The Rowans BOL BL1 ...... 35 H5
  MOSL OL5 ...... 77 G3
Rowan St HYDE SK14 ...... 102 C3
Rowanswood Dr HYDE SK14 ...... 102 C3
Rowan Tree Dr SALE M33 ...... 108 C3
Rowan Tree Rd OLDS OL8 ...... 75 C3
Rowan Wk GLSP SK13 ...... 93 H8
Rowanwood CHAD OL9 ...... 58 B5
Rowany Cl PWCH M25 ...... 71 K2
Rowarth Av DTN/ASHW M34 ...... 101 K4
Rowarth Rd NTHM/RTH M23 ...... 118 B2
Rowbottom Sq WGN WN1 ...... 14 F4
Rowbottom Wk OLDS OL8 * 9 H9
Rowcon Cl DTN/ASHW M34 ...... 90 B7
Rowden Rd OLDE OL4 ...... 60 B8
Rowe Gn DTN/ASHW M34 ...... 101 J2
Rowena St BOLS/LL BL3 ...... 52 F2
Rowendale St HULME M15 * 6 E7
Rowe St TYLD M29 ...... 67 L4
Rowfield Dr NTHM/RTH M23 ...... 118 B1
Rowland Av URM M41 ...... 96 B1
Rowland Ct MILN OL16 ...... 11 J7
Rowlands Rd BURY BL9 ...... 25 H3
Rowland St ATH M46 ...... 67 G2
  MILN OL16 ...... 11 K7
  ORD M5 ...... 86 D4
Rowlandsway
  WYTH/NTH M22 ...... 118 F2
Rowley Av OLDE OL4 ...... 60 B8
Rowley Rd BRAM/HZG SK7 ...... 122 A4
Rowley St AUL OL6 ...... 76 A6
Rowood Av CHH M8 ...... 72 E6
  RDSH SK5 ...... 100 C2
Rowrah Crs MDTN M24 ...... 56 E3
Rowsley Av BOL BL1 ...... 35 K3
  DID/WITH M20 ...... 98 B8
Rowsley Gv RDSH SK5 ...... 100 E6
Rowsley Ms GLSP SK13 ...... 104 B2
Rowsley Rd ECC M30 ...... 84 F4
  STRET M32 ...... 96 D1
Rowsley St OP/CLY M11 ...... 88 B2
  ORD M5 ...... 71 L7
Rowson Ct SALE M33 * 97 G8
Rowson Dr IRL M44 ...... 94 A6
Rowton St BOLE BL2 ...... 36 E1
Roxalina St BOLS/LL BL3 ...... 36 B8
Roxburgh St GTN M18 ...... 89 G7
Roxbury Av OLDE OL4 ...... 60 A7
Roxby Cl WALK M28 ...... 68 E1
Roxholme Wk WYTH/NTH M22 ...... 118 E4
Roxton St NTHM SK4 ...... 99 M6
Royal Ar WGN WN1 ...... 15 G3
Royal Av BURY BL9 ...... 25 J7
  CCHDY M21 ...... 97 K5
  DROY M43 ...... 89 L2
  HEY OL10 ...... 41 G3
  URM M41 ...... 96 A2
Royal Court Dr BOL BL1 ...... 2 B3
Royal Crs CHD/CHDH SK8 ...... 119 L2
Royal Dr LEIGH WN7 ...... 67 G6
Royal Ex CMANW M2 * 7 G5
Royal Exchange Ar
  CMANW M2 * 6 F4
Royal Gdns ALT WA14 ...... 116 B2
Royal George St
  EDGY/DAV SK3 ...... 13 H7
Royal Oak Rd NTHM/RTH M23 ...... 109 K5
Royal Pde OLD OL1 ...... 9 G1
Royal Rd POY/DIS SK12 ...... 123 M7
Royal St MILN OL16 ...... 28 F2
Royalthorn Dr
  WYTH/NTH M22 ...... 109 M6
Royalthorn Rd
  WYTH/NTH M22 ...... 110 A6
Royce Av HALE/TIMP WA15 ...... 108 C3
Royce Rd HULME M15 ...... 87 H6
Roydale St NEWH/MOS M40 ...... 88 B3
Royden Av BKLY M9 ...... 64 B8
  IRL M44 ...... 94 C4
  WGNW/BIL/OR WN5 ...... 63 J1
Royden Crs
  WGNW/BIL/OR WN5 ...... 62 B7
Royden Rd WGNW/BIL/OR WN5 ...... 62 B7
Royds Cl BRUN/LGST M13 ...... 88 C7
Royds Pl MILN OL16 ...... 11 H8
Royds St BURY BL9 ...... 26 A8
  MILN OL16 ...... 11 J8
  MILN OL16 ...... 11 K7
  TOT/BURYW BL8 ...... 24 C3

Royds St West MILN OL16 ...... 11 H9
Royd St OLDS OL8 ...... 58 F8
Royle Av GLSP SK13 ...... 105 G2
Royle Barn Rd ROCH OL11 ...... 41 M2
Royle Cl OFTN SK2 ...... 112 D7
  OLDS OL8 ...... 75 J1
Royle Green Rd
  WYTH/NTH M22 ...... 110 B4
Royle Rd ROCH OL11 ...... 42 A1
Royle St DTN/ASHW M34 ...... 90 C7
  OFTN SK2 ...... 13 K8
  RUSH/FAL M14 ...... 98 E3
  SLFD M6 ...... 86 C2
  WALK M28 ...... 69 G2
Royley ROY/SHW OL2 ...... 58 F1
Royley Crs ROY/SHW OL2 ...... 58 F1
Royley Rd OLDS OL8 ...... 59 H8
Royon Dr EDGY/DAV SK3 ...... 12 A9
Royston Av BOLE BL2 ...... 3 K2
  DTN/ASHW M34 ...... 100 C1
  OLDTF/WHR M16 ...... 97 J4
Royston Cl GOL/RIS/CUL WA3 ...... 80 B4
  TOT/BURYW BL8 ...... 24 E7
Royston Rd OLDTF/WHR M16 ...... 97 L1
  URM M41 ...... 96 B1
Royton Av SALE M33 ...... 109 H2
Rozel Sq CSLFD M3 ...... 6 D6
Ruabon Crs WGNE/HIN WN2 ...... 49 J8
Ruabon Rd DID/WITH M20 ...... 110 F2
Rubens Cl MPL/ROM SK6 ...... 114 F4
Ruby Gv LEIGH WN7 ...... 66 B8
Ruby St BOL BL1 ...... 36 C1
  BURY BL9 ...... 24 F1
  DTN/ASHW M34 ...... 101 H1
  HULME M15 ...... 87 G8
Rudcroft Cl BRUN/LGST M13 ...... 87 L6
Rudding St ROY/SHW OL2 ...... 59 K2
Ruddpark Rd
  WYTH/NTH M22 ...... 118 F3
Rudd St NEWH/MOS M40 ...... 73 K5
Rudford Gdns BOLS/LL BL3 ...... 36 C8
Rudgwick Dr TOT/BURYW BL8 ...... 24 F5
Rudheath Av DID/WITH M20 ...... 98 D5
Rudman Dr ORD M5 ...... 86 D4
Rudman St AULW OL7 ...... 90 D3
  WHIT OL12 ...... 28 A1
Rudolph St BOLS/LL BL3 ...... 52 C1
Rudston Av NEWH/MOS M40 ...... 73 L2
Rudyard Av MDTN M24 ...... 57 M1
  ROCH OL11 ...... 42 B2
  SALE M33 ...... 108 B2
Rudyard Gv HTNM SK4 ...... 100 A6
  ROCH OL11 ...... 42 B2
  SALE M33 ...... 108 B2
Rudyard Rd SLFD M6 ...... 70 F7
Rudyard St BRO M7 ...... 72 A6
Ruecroft Cl WGNNW/ST WN6 ...... 30 A4
Rufford Av HYDE SK14 ...... 102 C3
  ROCH OL11 ...... 28 A8
Rufford Cl AUL OL6 ...... 75 M5
  WHTF M45 ...... 55 K2
Rufford Dr BOLS/LL BL3 ...... 52 A2
  WHTF M45 ...... 55 J2
Rufford Pl GTN M18 * 89 J8
  TYLD M29 ...... 67 L8
Rufford Rd OLDTF/WHR M16 ...... 98 A1
Rufus St RUSH/FAL M14 ...... 99 H5
Rugby Dr SALE M33 ...... 108 D2
Rugby Rd LEIGH WN7 ...... 81 J1
  SLFD M6 ...... 85 K1
  WHIT OL12 ...... 11 G1
Rugby St CHH M8 ...... 72 B8
Rugeley St SLFD M6 ...... 71 L7
Ruins La BOLE BL2 ...... 23 H8
Ruislip Av NEWH/MOS M40 ...... 73 H7
Ruislip Cl OLDS OL8 ...... 59 L8
Rumbles La UPML OL3 ...... 45 J8
Rumworth Rd HOR/BR BL6 ...... 34 F6
Rumworth St BOLS/LL BL3 ...... 36 A8
Runcorn St HULME M15 ...... 86 F5
Runger La HALE/TIMP WA15 ...... 118 B4
Runhall Cl WGTN/LGST M12 ...... 88 D6
Runnymeade SWIN M27 ...... 70 D6
Runnymede Ct EDGY/DAV SK3 ...... 12 D9
Runnymede Ct BOLS/LL BL3 ...... 2 A8
  ROY/SHW OL2 ...... 43 J8
Runshaw Av WGNNW/ST WN6 ...... 30 B4
Rupert St BOLS/LL BL3 ...... 52 C1
  NEWH/MOS M40 ...... 74 B8
  RAD M26 ...... 54 E3
  RDSH SK5 ...... 100 B5
  WGN WN1 ...... 15 K5
  ROCH OL11 ...... 27 M3
Ruscombe Fold MDTN M24 ...... 57 G1
Rush Acre Cl RAD M26 ...... 54 E4
Rush Bank ROY/SHW OL2 ...... 43 J4
Rushbrooke Av OP/CLY M11 ...... 88 F1
Rushbury Dr ROY/SHW OL2 ...... 43 K8
Rushcroft Rd ROY/SHW OL2 ...... 43 J4
Rushdene WGNS/IIMK WN3 ...... 47 K8
Rushden Rd BNG/LEV M19 ...... 99 L2
Rushen St OP/CLY M11 ...... 88 F3
The Rushes GLSP SK13 ...... 93 J8
Rushey Cl HALE/TIMP WA15 ...... 117 M5
Rushey Fld EDGW/EG BL7 ...... 22 C4
Rushey Fold La BOL BL1 ...... 36 A2
Rusheylea Cl BOL BL1 ...... 36 A2
Rushey Rd WYTH/NTH M22 ...... 109 M7
Rushfield Dr BRUN/LGST M13 ...... 99 H1
Rushfield Rd CHD/CHDH SK8 ...... 120 C6
Rushford Av BNG/LEV M19 ...... 99 K2
Rushford Gv BOL BL1 ...... 22 C8
Rushford St WGTN/LGST M12 ...... 88 D8
Rush Gv UPML OL3 ...... 61 L5
Rush Hill Rd UPML OL3 ...... 61 L5
Rush Hill Ter UPML OL3 ...... 61 L5
Rushlake Gdns ROCH OL11 ...... 27 H4
Rushley Av BRO M7 ...... 71 L6
Rushmere AUL OL6 ...... 76 B6
Rushmere Av BNG/LEV M19 ...... 99 L3
Rushmere Dr TOT/BURYW BL8 ...... 24 F7
Rushmere Wk OLDTF/WHR M16 * 87 C7
Rushmoor Av AIMK WN4 ...... 64 B8
Rushmoor Cl IRL M44 ...... 94 D2
Rush Mt ROY/SHW OL2 ...... 43 J3
Rusholme Gv RUSH/FAL M14 ...... 98 F1
Rusholme Pl RUSH/FAL M14 * 87 M8
Rushside Rd CHD/CHDH SK8 ...... 120 B6
Rush St DUK SK16 ...... 91 H3
Rushton Av LEIGH WN7 ...... 66 A4
  NEWLW WA12 ...... 78 E8
Rushton Cl MPL/ROM SK6 * 114 D7
Rushton Dr BRAM/HZG SK7 ...... 113 M1
  MPL/ROM SK6 ...... 113 M1
Rushton Fold MCFLDN SK10 ...... 131 K2

Rushton Gv OLDE OL4 ...... 60 B1
  OP/CLY M11 ...... 89 H5
Rushton Rd BOL BL1 ...... 35 L3
  CHD/CHDH SK8 ...... 120 C6
  EDGY/DAV SK3 ...... 112 B7
Rushton St DID/WITH M20 ...... 69 G2
Rushway Av BKLY M9 ...... 73 L2
Rushwick Av NEWH/MOS M40 ...... 73 H8
Rushworth Ct HTNM SK4 ...... 99 M7
Rushyfield Crs MPL/ROM SK6 ...... 114 A1
Rushy Hill Vw WHIT OL12 * 27 L3
Rushy Vw NEWLW WA12 ...... 78 D8
Ruskin Av CHAD OL9 ...... 74 C1
  DTN/ASHW M34 ...... 89 M5
  DTN/ASHW M34 ...... 101 H3
  FWTH BL4 ...... 53 J5
  NEWLW WA12 ...... 78 E8
  RUSH/FAL M14 ...... 87 L8
  WGNS/IIMK WN3 ...... 63 J3
  WGNE/HIN WN2 ...... 64 E3
Ruskin Crs PWCH M25 ...... 71 J1
Ruskin Dr SALE M33 ...... 95 M8
Ruskin Gdns MPL/ROM SK6 ...... 113 L1
Ruskin Gv MPL/ROM SK6 ...... 113 K1
Ruskington Dr BKLY M9 ...... 73 G5
Ruskin Rd BOLS/LL BL3 ...... 37 L8
  DROY M43 ...... 89 K2
  OLDTF/WHR M16 ...... 97 H1
  PWCH M25 ...... 71 J1
  RDSH SK5 ...... 100 B3
  ROCH OL11 ...... 42 B2
Ruskin St OLD OL1 ...... 8 F3
  RAD M26 ...... 38 F8
Rusland Ct OFTN SK2 * 112 E5
Rusland Dr BOLE BL2 ...... 37 H2
Russeldene Rd
  WGNS/IIMK WN3 ...... 63 H1
Russell Av MPL/ROM SK6 ...... 123 C5
  OLDTF/WHR M16 ...... 98 A2
  SALE M33 ...... 97 G7
Russell Cl BOL BL1 ...... 35 M4
Russell Ct FWTH BL4 ...... 53 H4
  LHULT M38 ...... 68 F1
Russell Dr IRL M44 ...... 94 D2
Russell Gdns HTNM SK4 ...... 12 A4
Russell Rd OLDTF/WHR M16 ...... 98 A1
  PART M31 ...... 106 D1
  SLFD M6 ...... 70 E7
Russell St ATH M46 ...... 66 F1
  AUL OL6 ...... 76 A8
  BURY BL9 ...... 5 G1
  CHAD OL9 ...... 8 B2
  CHH M8 ...... 72 C6
  DUK SK16 ...... 90 F4
  ECC M30 ...... 85 H2
  FWTH BL4 ...... 53 C5
  HEY OL10 ...... 41 H3
  LHULT M38 ...... 68 F1
  MOSL OL5 ...... 76 F3
  OFTN SK2 ...... 112 D6
  OLDTF/WHR M16 ...... 98 C1
  PWCH M25 ...... 55 M8
  WGNE/HIN WN2 ...... 48 D4
  WGNE/HIN WN2 ...... 65 M3
Russet Rd BKLY M9 ...... 73 G3
Russet Wy WILM/AE SK9 ...... 130 E3
Ruth Av NEWH/MOS M40 ...... 74 B3
Ruthen La OLDTF/WHR M16 ...... 86 E8
Rutherford Av RUSH/FAL M14 ...... 98 E1
Rutherford Cl HYDE SK14 ...... 102 A2
Rutherford Dr WHTN BL5 ...... 51 J3
Rutherglade Cl
  NEWH/MOS M40 ...... 72 F4
Rutherglen Dr BOLS/LL BL3 ...... 35 M6
Rutherglen Wk
  NEWH/MOS M40 ...... 73 H7
Ruthin Av BKLY M9 ...... 56 F7
  CHD/CHDH SK8 ...... 120 A2
  MDTN M24 ...... 57 K6
Ruthin Cl OLDS OL8 ...... 74 E2
Ruth St BOL BL1 ...... 2 C3
  BURY BL9 ...... 5 G1
  GTN M18 ...... 100 A1
  OLD OL1 ...... 9 K3
  WHIT OL12 ...... 20 B3
Rutland ROCH OL11 ...... 10 D7
  DID/WITH M20 ...... 98 D7
  GOL/RIS/CUL WA3 ...... 80 A5
  OLDTF/WHR M16 ...... 97 K1
  SWIN M27 ...... 70 C2
  URM M41 ...... 96 B2
Rutland Cl AUL OL6 ...... 91 C2
  BOLS/LL BL3 ...... 37 L8
  CHD/CHDH SK8 ...... 110 G2
Rutland Crs RDSH SK5 ...... 101 C2
Rutland Dr AIMK WN4 ...... 63 M8
  BRO M7 ...... 71 M4
  BURY BL9 ...... 5 H9
Rutland Gv BOL BL1 ...... 35 M3
  FWTH BL4 * 52 F5
Rutland La SALE M33 ...... 97 K7
Rutland Rd ALT WA14 ...... 108 A6
  BRAM/HZG SK7 ...... 122 A4
  DROY M43 ...... 89 H2
  ECC M30 ...... 85 J1
  IRL M44 ...... 94 A7
  PART M31 ...... 106 B2
  TYLD M29 ...... 67 J2
  WALK M28 ...... 69 G3
  WGNE/HIN WN2 ...... 65 M3
Rutland St AUL OL6 ...... 91 C2
  BOLS/LL BL3 ...... 36 A8
  CHAD OL9 ...... 8 C3
  FAIL M35 * 74 C4
  GTN M18 ...... 89 H6
  HEY OL10 ...... 41 G1
  HYDE SK14 ...... 91 C7
  LEIGH WN7 ...... 67 H8
  SWIN M27 ...... 70 B3
Rutland Wy ROY/SHW OL2 ...... 43 M4
Rutter's La BRAM/HZG SK7 ...... 121 C2
Ryall Av ORD M5 ...... 86 E4
Ryall Av South ORD M5 ...... 86 E4
Ryan St OP/CLY M11 ...... 89 H5
Rydal Av BRAM/HZG SK7 ...... 121 L1
  CHAD OL9 ...... 58 B3
  DROY M43 ...... 89 H3
  ECC M30 ...... 69 L8
  HYDE SK14 ...... 90 F7
  MDTN M24 ...... 56 F4
  MPL/ROM SK6 ...... 123 C4
  ROY/SHW OL2 ...... 42 F4
  SALE M33 ...... 96 C3
  URM M41 ...... 95 K4
  WGNE/HIN WN2 ...... 49 H1
  WGNW/BIL/OR WN5 ...... 46 C5
Rydal Cl AIMK WN4 ...... 63 M8
  BURY BL9 ...... 39 H5
  CHD/CHDH SK8 ...... 119 K1

DTN/ASHW M34 ....100 E2
HOR/BR BL6 ....32 F1
WALK M28 ....67 K5
Rydal Ct BOL BL1 * 35 J3
Rydal Crs SWIN M27 ......70 C6
Rydal Gv BOL BL1 ....69 H3
Rydal Dr HALE/TIMP WA15 .117 H4
Rydal Gv AULW OL7 ....75 J8
FWTH BL4 ....52 C5
HEY OL10 ....41 G4
WHTF M45 ....55 J4
Rydal Pl WGNE/HIN WN2 ...48 E4
WGNE/HIN WN2 ....64 E4
Rydal Rd BOL BL1 ....35 K4
BOLS/LL BL3 ....53 K1
STRET M32 ....97 G1
Rydal St LEIGH WN7 ......66 B7
Ryde Av ALT WA14 ....108 B5
HTNM SK4 ....12 L4
Ryder Av ALT WA14 ......108 B5
Ryder Brow GTN M18 ......89 G8
Ryderbrow Rd GTN M18 ...89 G8
Ryder Gv LEIGH WN7 ......81 M2
Ryder St BOL BL1 ....35 M2
HEY OL10 ....41 G2
NEWH/MOS M40 ....73 C8
Ryde St BOLS/LL BL3 * 35 K8
WGNNW/BIL/OR WN5 ....47 H6
Rydings La WHIT OL12 ....20 E6
Rydings Rd WHIT OL12 ....20 F7
Rydley St BOLE BL2 ....3 J6
Ryebank Gv AUL OL6 ......76 A7
Ryebank Ms CCHDY M21 * ..97 J3
Ryebank Rd CCHDY M21 ...97 J4
Rye Bank Rd OLDTF/WHR M16 .97 K2
Ryeburn Av WYTH/NTH M22 .118 F1
Ryeburn Dr BOLE BL2 ......22 E7
Ryeburne St OLDE OL4 ....59 M5
Ryeburn Wk URM M41 .....84 C8
Rye Cft WHTF M45 ....54 F5
Rye Croft Av SLFD M6 .....85 D3
Ryecroft Av GOL/RIS/CUL WA3 .80 G3
HEY OL10 ....41 H2
TOT/BURYW BL8 ....24 C6
Ryecroft Cl OP/CLY M11 ....74 C1
Ryecroft Dr WHTN BL5 ....50 A1
Ryecroft Gv NTHM/RTH M23 .109 K5
WALK M28 ....69 J8
Ryecroft La DTN/ASHW M34 .90 B5
Ryecroft Rd STRET M32 ...96 F3
Ryecroft St AULW OL7 ....90 C3
Ryecroft Vw DTN/ASHW M34 .89 M4
Ryedale Av NEWH/MOS M40 .73 C7
Ryedale Cl HTNM SK4 ......12 B1
Ryefield Cl HALE/TIMP WA15 .108 F7
Ryefield Rd SALE M33 .....107 M2
Ryefields ROCH OL11 ......27 K6
Ryefields Dr UPML OL3 ....61 L3
Ryefield St BOL BL1 ....3 G1
Ryeford Cl WGNS/IIMK WN3 .15 M8
Rye HI WHTN BL5 * 50 C4
Ryeland Cl MILN OL16 .....28 E8
Ryelands WHTN BL5 ....50 C4
Ryelands Ct WHTN BL5 * ...50 C4
Rye St HEY OL10 ....41 H1
Rylance St OP/CLY M11 ....88 B3
Rylands St GTN M18 * 89 H6
WGNNW/ST WN6 ....47 K2
Rylane Wk NEWH/MOS M40 .73 C7
Ryley Av BOLS/LL BL3 .....35 L7
Ryleys La WILM/AE SK9 ...130 C3
Ryley St BOLS/LL BL3 * 2 L7
Rylstone Av CCHDY M21 ..110 A1
Ryther Gv BKLY M9 ....56 E7
Ryton Av GTN M18 ....99 M1
Ryton Cl WGNS/IIMK WN3 .14 D8

S

Sabden Brook Dr
WGNE/HIN WN2 ....64 C2
Sabden Cl BURY BL9 ....25 J3
HEY OL10 ....40 D2
NEWH/MOS M40 ....88 B1
Sabden Rd BOL BL1 ....35 H2
Sabrina St HTN M8 ....72 B7
Sackville St ROY/SHW OL2 .43 K3
Sackville St AUL OL6 ......90 E1
BOLE BL2 * 3 M4
CMANE M1 ....7 H7
CSLFD M3 ....6 C3
ROCH OL11 ....41 M3
Saddleback Cl WALK M28 ..68 E6
Saddleback Crs
WGNNW/BIL/OR WN5 ......46 E5
Saddleback Rd
WGNNW/BIL/OR WN5 ......46 E5
Saddlecote Cl WALK M28 ..69 K8
Saddlecote La CHH M8 .....72 E4
Saddle Gv DROY M43 ....90 A1
Saddle St BOLE BL2 ....36 C2
Saddlewood Av BNG/LEV M19 .111 C2
Sadie Av STRET M32 ....85 K8
Sadler Ct HULME M15 * 87 H7
Sadler St BOLS/LL BL3 .....36 D8
MDTN M24 ....57 J3
Saffron Cl GOL/RIS/CUL WA3 .80 B5
Saffron Dr OLDE OL4 ......60 A2
Sagars Rd WILM/AE SK9 ..119 L8
Sagar St CHH M8 ....72 C6
St Agnes Rd BRUN/LGST M13 .99 J2
St Agnes St RDSH SK5 ....100 C1
St Aidan's Cl ROCH OL11 ..10 A9
WGNNW/BIL/OR WN5 ......62 C6
St Aidan's Gv BRO M7 .....71 L6
St Albans Av AUL OL6 .....75 L6
HTNM SK4 ....99 M7
NEWH/MOS M40 ....73 L7
St Albans Cl OLDS OL8 ....59 J8
RNFD/HAY WA11 ....78 C5
St Albans Crs ALT WA14 ..107 M4
St Alban's St MILN OL16 ..10 D6
NM/HAY SK22 ....124 C4
St Alban's Ter CHH M8 ....72 C7
ROCH OL11 ....10 C7
St Aldates MPL/ROM SK6 ..113 J2
St Aldwyn's Rd DID/WITH M20 .98 E7
St Ambrose Gdns SLFD M6 * .86 C2
St Ambrose Rd OLD OL1 ...59 M3
TYLD M29 ....67 K7
St Andrew's Av DROY M43 .89 H3
ECC M30 ....85 H3
HALE/TIMP WA15 ....108 B5
St Andrews Cl HTNM SK4 ..99 L8
LIT OL15 ....21 J8
Saint Andrew's Cl
MPL/ROM SK6 ....113 L3
St Andrew's Cl RAMS BL0 ..18 F7
St Andrews Cl BOL BL1 * ...2 E5

St Andrew's Crs
WGNE/HIN WN2 ....49 G7
St Andrew's Dr HEY OL10 ..41 G3
LEIGH WN7 ....66 F7
WGNNW/ST WN6 ....30 F8
St Andrews Rd CHD/CHDH SK8 .119 L5
HOR/BR BL6 ....34 D5
HTNM SK4 ....38 D8
RAD M26 ....38 C2
STRET M32 ....96 E2
St Andrew's Sq CMANE M1 .7 M6
St Andrew's St CMANE M1 .7 L6
St Andrew's Vw RAD M26 ..38 C2
St Anne's Av ATH M46 .....67 H1
ROY/SHW OL2 ....59 H1
SLFD M6 ....86 B1
St Anne's Ct DTN/ASHW M34 .90 C6
SALE M33 ....33 J8
SLFD M6 * 71 J8
WGNNW/ST WN6 ....30 D7
St Anne's Crs OLDE OL4 ...60 C7
St Anne's Dr DTN/ASHW M34 .90 C6
WGNNW/ST WN6 ....30 D7
St Anne's Gdns HEY OL10 ..41 J2
St Annes Meadow
TOT/BURYW BL8 ....24 C5
St Annes Rd CCHDY M21 ..97 L5
DTN/ASHW M34 ....90 C6
DTN/ASHW M34 ....90 D8
St Annes Sq UPML OL3 ....45 J8
St Annes St BURY BL9 * ...25 J8
HYDE SK14 ....103 K4
St Anns Cl PWCH M25 .....71 K1
St Anns Pas CMANW M2 ....6 F4
St Ann's Rd BRAM/HZG SK7 .121 L3
MILN OL16 ....29 J8
PWCH M25 ....71 J1
St Ann's Rd North
CHD/CHDH SK8 ....119 K3
St Ann's Rd South
CHD/CHDH SK8 ....119 L3
St Ann's Sq CHD/CHDH SK8 .119 L4
CMANW M2 ....6 F4
St Ann's St CMANW M2 ....6 E4
SALE M33 ....109 J1
SWIN M27 ....70 B4
St Ann St BOL BL1 ....36 B3
St Anthonys Dr MOSL OL5 .77 G2
St Asaphs Dr AUL OL6 .....75 L6
St Aubin's Rd BOLE BL2 ....3 J7
St Aubyn's Rd WGN WN1 * .31 M8
St Augustine's Rd
EDGY/DAV SK3 ....12 B7
St Augustine St BOL BL1 ..36 A2
NEWH/MOS M40 ....73 H7
St Austell Av TYLD M29 ....67 M4
St Austell Cl CHD/CHDH SK8 .119 K4
TOT/BURYW BL8 ....24 C2
St Austell Rd OLDTF/WHR M16 .98 B4
St Austells Dr PWCH M25 ..55 L7
SWIN M27 ....70 F6
St Barnabas's Dr LIT OL15 .21 L6
St Barnabas Sq OP/CLY M11 .88 A7
St Bartholomew's Dr ORD M5 .86 F4
St Bartholomew St
BOLS/LL BL3 ....36 D8
St Bede's La BOLS/LL BL3 ..51 L2
St Bees Cl CHD/CHDH SK8 .119 K1
RUSH/FAL M14 ....87 K8
St Bees Rd BOLE BL2 ......36 F2
St Benedicts Av
WGTN/LGST M12 * 88 C6
St Benedict's Sq
WGTN/LGST M12 ....88 C6
St Bernard's Av SLFD M6 ..71 M7
St Boniface Rd BRO M7 ....71 M8
St Brannocks Rd CCHDY M21 .97 H3
CHD/CHDH SK8 ....120 D5
St Brelades Dr BRO M7 ....72 C4
St Brendans Rd DID/WITH M20 .98 E5
St Brendans Rd North
DID/WITH M20 ....98 E5
St Brides Wy OLDTF/WHR M16 .87 G7
St Catherines Dr FWTH BL4 .52 C4
St Catherine's Rd
DID/WITH M20 ....98 E5
St Chads Av MPL/ROM SK6 .113 M2
St Chad's Cl MILN OL16 ....10 F6
St Chads Ct MILN OL16 ....10 F6
St Chads Crs OLDS OL8 ...75 G3
UPML OL3 ....61 M4
St Chads Gv MPL/ROM SK6 .113 M2
St Chad's Rd DID/WITH M20 .99 C5
St Chad's St CHH M8 * 7 J2
St Charles Cl GLSP SK13 ...93 J7
St Christopher Ct
WGNNW/ST WN6 * 30 F8
St Christophers Av AUL OL6 .76 B6
St Christophers Cl
DID/WITH M20 ....98 C6
St Christophers Dr
MPL/ROM SK6 ....113 K2
St Christopher's Rd AUL OL6 .76 A6
St Clair Rd TOT/BURYW BL8 .24 C1
St Clare Ter HOR/BR BL6 * .34 C4
St Clements Ct OLDS OL8 ...9 J8
St Clement's Dr ORD M5 ...86 E5
St Clements Fold URM M41 .96 B2
St Clements Rd CCHDY M21 .97 K5
WGN WN1 ....47 M1
St Clement's St
WGNS/IIMK WN3 ....48 C8
St Cuthberts Fold OLDS OL8 .75 K3
St Davids Av MPL/ROM SK6 .113 L2
St David's Cl AUL OL6 .....76 B6
St David's Crs WGNE/HIN WN2 .32 E7
St David's Rd BRAM/HZG SK7 .121 L3
CHD/CHDH SK8 ....111 K7
St Domingo Pl OLD OL1 * ...9 H5
St Dominics Ms BOLS/LL BL3 .51 M1
St Dominics Wy MDTN M24 .57 K5
St Edmund Hall Cl RAMS BL0 .18 F4
St Edmund's Rd
NEWH/MOS M40 ....73 H6
St Edmund St BOL BL1 * 2 D4
St Elisabeth's Wy RDSH SK5 .100 B5
St Elizabeth's Rd
WGNE/HIN WN2 ....32 E7
St Elmo Av OFTN SK2 .....113 G5
St Elmo Pk POY/DIS SK12 .122 B4
St Ethelbert's Av BOLS/LL BL3 .35 L7
St Gabriel's Cl ROCH OL11 .42 A3
St George's Av
HALE/TIMP WA15 ....108 D4
WHTN BL5 ....50 B6
St George's Ct ALT WA14 ..107 L5
BOL BL1 * 2 E3
HYDE SK14 * 102 A3
STRET M32 * 96 F3
TYLD M29 * 67 J4
St George's Crs
HALE/TIMP WA15 ....108 D4

SLFD M6 * 85 K1
WALK M28 ....69 G2
St Georges Dr HYDE SK14 .102 A3
NEWH/MOS M40 ....73 L5
St Georges Gdns
DTN/ASHW M34 ....101 K3
St George's Pl ATH M46 * ..50 E4
St George's Rd BOL BL1 ...39 M8
BURY BL9 ....39 H3
DROY M43 ....89 J1
NM/HAY SK22 ....124 E4
PART M31 ....95 C6
ROCH OL11 ....27 J4
RUSH/FAL M14 ....99 H5
STRET M32 ....96 F2
St Georges Sq BOL BL1 * ...2 E3
CHAD OL9 ....74 B1
St George's St BOL BL1 * ...2 E3
STLY SK15 ....91 K1
TYLD M29 ....67 J4
St George's Wy SLFD M6 ..71 K8
St Germain St FWTH BL4 ..52 F4
St Giles Dr HYDE SK14 ....102 C2
St Gregorys Cl FWTH BL4 ..52 F5
St Gregorys Rd WGTN/LGST M12 .7 M8
St Helena Rd BOL BL1 * 2 C4
St Helens Rd BOLS/LL BL3 .35 M8
GOL/RIS/CUL WA3 ....80 E4
LEIGH WN7 ....81 G3
WHTN BL5 ....51 K3
St Helier's Dr BRO M7 .....72 C4
St Heliers St BOLS/LL BL3 .36 A8
St Hilarys Pk WILM/AE SK9 .130 D3
St Hilda's Dr OLD OL1 ....8 F2
St Hilda's Rd DTN/ASHW M34 .90 B6
OLDTF/WHR M16 ....86 F7
WYTH/NTH M22 ....110 A3
St Hilda's Vw DTN/ASHW M34 .90 B7
St Hugh's Cl ALT WA14 ...108 B4
St Ignatius Wk ORD M5 * ..86 E4
St Ives Av CHD/CHDH SK8 .111 K6
St Ives Crs SALE M33 .....108 D5
St Ives Rd RUSH/FAL M14 .98 E2
St James Av BOLE BL2 * ...37 H4
TOT/BURYW BL8 ....52 B8
St James Cl GLSP SK13 ...104 F4
MILN OL16 ....42 F4
St James Ct HALE/TIMP WA15 .108 B8
SLFD M6 * 85 L1
St James Crs WGNE/HIN WN2 .65 J4
St James Dr SALE M33 ....108 D1
WILM/AE SK9 ....126 E6
St James Gv WGNS/IIMK WN3 .14 E8
St James Rd HTNM SK4 ....99 J7
WGNW/BIL/OR WN5 ......46 A8
St James's Gv ALT WA14 ..108 C3
St James's Rd BRO M7 ....72 B6
St James's Sq CMANW M2 ..6 E5
St James's St OLD OL1 .....59 L5
HEY OL10 ....40 F7
St James St AUL OL6 * 91 G2
CMANE M1 ....7 G6
ECC M30 * 85 H2
FWTH BL4 ....52 E5
HEY OL10 ....40 F2
MILN OL16 ....29 J5
ROY/SHW OL2 ....43 L5
WHTN BL5 ....50 C7
St James' Wy CHD/CHDH SK8 .120 B6
WHTN BL5 ....50 A1
St John's Av DROY M43 ....89 J1
DUK SK16 ....91 H4
MPL/ROM SK6 ....113 L2
St Johns Ct BRO M7 * 72 A6
HYDE SK14 ....102 C1
MILN OL16 ....11 J6
OLDE OL4 ....60 C5
RAD M26 ....54 E2
WGNE/HIN WN2 ....64 E3
WHTN BL5 ....50 B1
St John's Dr HYDE SK14 ..102 C1
MILN OL16 ....11 J6
St John's Gdns MOSL OL5 ..76 F2
St John's Rd ALT WA14 ...116 E1
BRAM/HZG SK7 ....121 K3
BRUN/LGST M13 ....88 C3
DTN/ASHW M34 ....90 C7
HOR/BR BL6 ....34 E8
HTNM SK4 ....111 H2
OLDTF/WHR M16 ....86 F8
WALK M28 ....68 C5
WGNE/HIN WN2 ....32 E8
WILM/AE SK9 ....130 B1
St John's St BRO M7 ....72 A6
CHAD OL9 ....8 D7
FWTH BL4 ....53 H4
RAD M26 ....54 E2
WGNE/HIN WN2 ....64 E4
St John St ATH M46 * 67 C1
CSLFD M3 ....6 D6
DUK SK16 ....85 G3
HOR/BR BL6 ....33 L1
IRL M44 ....94 D2
NM/HAY SK22 ....125 C1
OLDE OL4 ....60 B6
SWIN M27 ....71 G6
WALK M28 ....52 F8
WGNW/BIL/OR WN5 ......46 E6
St John's Wk CHAD OL9 * ..8 D7
EDGY/DAV SK3 * 12 B6
St Johns Wd HOR/BR BL6 ..34 E8
St Josephs Av WHTF M45 ..55 M5
St Josephs Cl ROY/SHW OL2 .43 M4
St Joseph's Dr MILN OL16 .28 E8
ORD M5 ....86 E4
St Joseph St BOL BL1 .....36 A2
St Katherines Dr HOR/BR BL6 .32 F1
St Kilda Av FWTH BL4 .....53 J6
St Kildas Av DROY M43 ....89 J1
St Kilda's Dr BRO M7 ......72 C4
St Lawrence Quay SALQ M50 .86 C5
St Lawrence Rd
DTN/ASHW M34 ....101 J1
St Leonard's Av HOR/BR BL6 .34 C3
St Leonard's Ct SALE M33 .96 C8
St Leonards Dr
HALE/TIMP WA15 ....108 C6
St Leonard's Rd HTNM SK4 .100 A7
St Leonards Rd MDTN M24 .57 K3
St Lesmo Rd EDGY/DAV SK3 .12 C8
St Luke's Av GOL/RIS/CUL WA3 .80 A4
St Lukes Ct CHAD OL9 .....58 D5
St Luke's Dr
WGNNW/BIL/OR WN5 .....46 A8
St Luke's Rd SLFD M6 .....86 A2
St Luke St ROCH OL11 .....10 F9
St Malo Rd WGN WN1 .....31 M8
St Margaret's Av BNG/LEV M19 .99 J6
St Margaret's Rd ALT WA14 .107 M8

BOL BL1 * 35 L4
PWCH M25 ....55 M6
St Margarets Gdns OLDS OL8 * .74 F1
BOL BL1 ....35 L4
CHD/CHDH SK8 ....111 K6
NEWH/MOS M40 ....74 A1
PWCH M25 ....55 M7
St Mark's Av ALT WA14 ...107 K7
ROY/SHW OL2 ....43 K8
WGNW/BIL/OR WN5 ......47 J5
St Mark's Crs WALK M28 ..69 G3
St Mark's La BURY BL9 * ...5 G1
St Mark's Sq BURY BL9 ....5 G1
St Mark St BNG/LEV M19 ..99 H3
BOLS/LL BL3 ....2 E9
MPL/ROM SK6 ....101 K8
St Mark St DUK SK16 .....90 E3
St Mark's Vw BOLS/LL BL3 * .2 E9
St Marks Wk BOLS/LL BL3 ..36 B8
St Martin's Av HTNM SK4 ..12 C3
St Martins Cl DROY M43 ...89 J1
HYDE SK14 ....102 C2
St Martin's Dr BRO M7 ....72 C4
St Martin's Rd MPL/ROM SK6 .114 D6
OLDS OL8 ....75 K2
SALE M33 ....96 B6
St Martin's St ROCH OL11 .41 M3
St Mary's Av BOLS/LL BL3 .35 K7
DTN/ASHW M34 ....101 K4
St Mary's Cl ATH M46 .....67 H2
MILN OL16 ....28 E8
NEWH/MOS M40 ....55 K8
STKP SK1 ....13 L4
WGNE/HIN WN2 * 32 E7
St Mary's Ct GOL/RIS/CUL WA3 .80 E3
NEWH/MOS M40 ....73 L4
OLD OL1 * 9 H4
St Mary's Crest UPML OL3 .61 M7
St Mary's Dr CHD/CHDH SK8 * .111 J6
RDSH SK5 ....100 C7
UPML OL3 ....61 M7
St Mary's Est OLD OL1 * 9 J4
St Mary's Ga CMANE M1 ...7 H4
MILN OL16 ....10 D3
ROY/SHW OL2 * 43 L5
UPML OL3 * 61 L7
St Mary's Hall Rd CHH M8 .72 C3
MILN OL16 ....28 E8
St Mary's Parsonage CSLFD M3 .6 E4
St Mary's Pl BURY BL9 .....4 F4
St Mary's Rd ALT WA14 ...116 D2
ECC M30 ....85 J2
GLSP SK13 ....104 F4
HYDE SK14 ....91 J7
NEWH/MOS M40 ....73 L5
NM/HAY SK22 ....124 D4
POY/DIS SK12 ....123 M7
PWCH M25 ....55 K8
SALE M33 ....96 C7
WALK M28 ....52 F8
WGNE/HIN WN2 ....32 E6
St Mary's St CSLFD M3 * ...6 E4
HULME M15 ....87 H7
OLD OL1 ....9 J3
OLDTF/WHR M16 ....87 H8
St Mary's Wy LEIGH WN7 * .66 C7
OLD OL1 * 9 H4
STKP SK1 ....13 L7
St Matthew's Cl
WGNS/IIMK WN3 ....46 F8
St Matthews Ct STRET M32 * .96 F3
St Matthew's Dr OLD OL1 ..58 D2
St Matthews Gra BOL BL1 * .36 B3
St Matthew's Rd
EDGY/DAV SK3 ....12 F7
St Matthews Ter
EDGY/DAV SK3 * 12 F7
St Matthews Wk BOL BL1 * .36 B3
St Mawes Ct RAD M26 * ...37 M7
St Michael's Av ATH M46 ..66 D3
BOLS/LL BL3 ....52 E2
BRAM/HZG SK7 ....121 L3
St Michaels Cl TOT/BURYW BL8 .38 D4
St Michaels Cl SALE M33 ..96 B6
WGN WN1 ....15 C1
St Michaels Gdns WHTF M45 .55 L5
St Michael's Rd HYDE SK14 .102 C2
St Michael's Sq ANC M4 * ..7 H1
St Modwen Rd STRET M32 .85 J7
St Nicholas Rd
GOL/RIS/CUL WA3 ....80 D4
HULME M15 ....6 C9
St Osmund's Dr BOLE BL2 .37 H5
St Osmund's Gv BOLE BL2 .37 H5
St Oswalds Rd AIMK WN4 ..78 D2
BNG/LEV M19 ....99 L2
St Patrick St WGN WN1 ....15 K4
St Patricks Wy WGN WN1 ..15 L4
St Paul's Av WGNS/IIMK WN3 .47 J8
St Pauls Cl STLY SK15 ....91 M2
St Paul's Ct RAD M26 .....54 D3
WALK M28 ....69 C2
St Paul's Hill Rd HYDE SK14 .102 C2
St Paul's Rd BRO M7 ......71 M6
DID/WITH M20 ....98 F6
HTNM SK4 ....99 J3
WALK M28 * 69 H2
St Paul's St BURY BL9 * 5 J3
HYDE SK14 ....102 B1
RAMS BL0 ....18 F6
STKP SK1 ....13 M1
STLY SK15 ....91 M2
St Pauls Vis BURY BL9 .....5 J3
St Peter's Av BOL BL1 .....2 E5
St Peters Cl AULW OL7 ....90 C2
St Peters Ct STRET M32 * .97 H1
St Peter's Dr HYDE SK14 ..102 C2
St Petersgate STKP SK1 ...13 J4
St Peter's Rd BURY BL9 ....39 J6
SWIN M27 ....70 B5
St Peters Sq CMANE M1 * ..6 F6
CMANW M2 ....6 F6
STKP SK1 ....13 H4
St Peter's St AUL OL6 .....90 D2
MILN OL16 ....11 J7
St Peter's Ter FWTH BL4 ..53 C5
St Peter's Wy BOL BL1 .....2 E5
BOLE BL2 * 3 H6
BOLS/LL BL3 * 2 E6
FWTH BL4 ....53 C2
St Philip's Av BOLS/LL BL3 .36 A8
St Philip's Pl CSLFD M3 * ...6 B3
St Philip's St GTN M18 .....89 C8
St Prestwich's Rd OP/CLY M11 .59 H5
St Richards Cl ATH M46 ....50 E4
St Saviour's Rd OFTN SK2 .112 F7
Saintsbridge Rd
WYTH/NTH M22 ....118 E2
St Simons Cl OFTN SK2 ...112 F4
St Simon St CSLFD M3 .....6 C1
St Stephen's Av

DTN/ASHW M34 ....90 B4
WGN WN1 ....48 B2
St Stephen's Cl BOLE BL2 ...3 L1
BRUN/LGST M13 ....88 A7
TYLD M29 ....67 K7
St Stephens Ct BKLY M9 * ..73 G5
St Stephen's Rd
WGNNW/ST WN6 ....30 F3
St Stephens Gv BOL OL1 ...5 C3
St Stephen St CSLFD M3 ...6 C3
OLD OL1 ....9 L3
St Stephens Vw ROY/SHW OL2 .43 K8
St Teresa's Rd OLDTF/WHR M16 .97 K1
St Thomas Ct BURY BL9 ....5 J4
UPML OL3 * 45 H8
St Thomas' Pl CHH M8 ....72 D8
St Thomas's Cir OLDS OL8 ..8 F9
St Thomas's Pl STKP SK1 ..13 J7
St Thomas St BOL BL1 * ...36 A2
WGNS/IIMK WN3 ....14 F6
St Thomas St North OLDS OL8 .8 F8
St Thomas St South OLDS OL8 .8 F9
St Vincent St ANC M4 * 7 M3
St Werburghs Rd CCHDY M21 .97 M8
St Wilfred's Dr WHIT OL12 * .20 B8
St Wilfrid's Rd WGNNW/ST WN6 .31 J4
St Wilfrids St HULME M15 ..87 H6
St Williams Av BOLS/LL BL3 .52 B1
Salcombe Av BOLE BL2 ....38 A3
Salcombe Cl SALE M33 ....96 B5
WGN WN1 ....48 B2
Salcombe Gv BOLE BL2 ....37 J6
Salcombe Rd OFTN SK2 ...112 F4
OP/CLY M11 ....89 G4
Salcot Wk NEWH/MOS M40 * .87 M1
Sale Heys Rd SALE M33 ...108 C3
Sale La TYLD M29 ....68 A3
WALK M28 ....68 A3
Salem Gv OLDE OL4 ....60 A6
Sale Rd NTHM/RTH M23 ...109 K6
Salesbury Wy WGNS/IIMK WN3 .63 K2
Sales's La BURY BL9 ......25 L2
Sales St LIT OL15 ....21 M6
Salford Rd WHTN BL5 .....51 K4
Salford St BURY BL9 ....5 J4
OLDE OL4 ....59 M7
Salik Gdns ROCH OL11 ....10 E8
Salisbury Av HEY OL10 ....40 F4
WGNE/HIN WN2 ....49 H6
Salisbury Crs AUL OL6 ....76 A5
Salisbury Dr DUK SK16 ....91 K5
PWCH M25 ....71 M2
Salisbury Rd AIMK WN4 * ..63 K7
CCHDY M21 ....97 L3
ECC M30 ....85 J2
HOR/BR BL6 ....34 C3
OLDE OL4 ....60 A6
RAD M26 ....38 B7
RNFD/HAY WA11 ....78 B4
SWIN M27 ....70 B5
URM M41 ....85 C8
WHTF M45 ....55 J4
Salisbury St BOLS/LL BL3 ..53 M1
GLSP SK13 ....93 K7
GOL/RIS/CUL WA3 ....79 K4
MDTN M24 ....57 L3
RDSH SK5 ....100 C4
ROY/SHW OL2 ....43 J4
RUSH/FAL M14 ....87 K8
Salisbury Ter BOLS/LL BL3 .53 M1
Salisbury Wy TYLD M29 ...67 C1
Salkeld Av AIMK WN4 .....78 C1
Salkeld St ROCH OL11 ....10 F9
Sallowfields
WGNW/BIL/OR WN5 ......46 A7
Salmon Flds ROY/SHW OL2 .59 J1
Salmon St ANC M4 * 7 H3
WGN WN1 ....7 K1
Salmsbury Hall Cl RAMS BL0 .18 E8
Salop St BOLE BL2 ....3 G6
SLFD M6 ....71 K8
Saltash Cl WYTH/NTH M22 .118 F3
Saltdene Rd WYTH/NTH M22 .118 E3
Saltergate BOLS/LL BL3 ...35 J8
Saltergate Ms ORD M5 * ...86 D2
Salters Ct ATH M46 ....66 D1
Salterton Dr BOLS/LL BL3 .51 J2
Salteye Rd ECC M30 ......84 D3
Saltford Av ANC M4 * 7 M3
Saltford Ct ANC M4 * 7 M3
Salthill Av HEY OL10 ......41 H5
Salthouse Cl TOT/BURYW BL8 .24 F6
Saltire Gdns BRO M7 ......72 B4
Saltney Av DID/WITH M20 .98 C5
Saltram Cl RAD M26 ......37 M7
Saltram Rd WGNS/IIMK WN3 .46 F8
Saltrush Rd WYTH/NTH M22 .118 F2
Salts Dr LIT OL15 ....21 L6
Salts St ROY/SHW OL2 ....43 L5
Saltwood Gv BOL BL1 .....2 E1
Salutation St HULME M15 ..87 J6
Salvin Cl AIMK WN4 ....79 G1
Salwick Cl WGNS/IIMK WN3 .46 F8
Sam Cowan Cl RUSH/FAL M14 .98 D1
Samian Gdns BRO M7 .....71 M7
Samlesbury Cl
DID/WITH M20 ....110 C1
ROY/SHW OL2 ....43 J5
Samouth Cl NEWH/MOS M40 .88 A1
Sampson Sq RUSH/FAL M14 .87 K8
Sam Rd UPML OL3 ....45 M8
Samson St MILN OL16 ....11 M2
Sam Swire St HULME M15 .87 H7
Samuel La ROY/SHW OL2 ..43 H4
Samuel Ogden St CMANE M1 .7 H7
Samuel St ATH M46 ....66 D1
BNG/LEV M19 ....99 L4
BURY BL9 ....5 J4
FAIL M35 ....74 C2
HTNM SK4 ....112 A1
ROCH OL11 ....41 M2
Sanby Av GTN M18 ....88 F8
Sanby Rd GTN M18 ....88 F8
Sanctuary The HULME M15 .87 J7
The Sanctuary HULME M15 .87 H6
Sandacre Rd
NTHM/RTH M23 ....109 L5
Sandalwood WHTN BL5 ...50 A6
Sandalwood Dr
WGNNW/ST WN6 ....47 J1
Sandbach Av RUSH/FAL M14 .98 C4
Sandbach Rd RDSH SK5 ...100 B2
SALE M33 ....109 J1
Sandbank Gdns WHIT OL12 .20 A2
Sand Banks BOL BL1 ......22 C6
Sandbed La MOSL OL5 ....76 F2
UPML OL3 * 45 K7
Sandbrook Gdns
WGNW/BIL/OR WN5 ......46 A7
Sandbrook Pk ROCH OL11 * .28 B8
Sandbrook Rd WGNW/BIL/OR WN5 .46 A7
Sandbrook Wy

Sandbrook Wy DTN/ASHW M34 ...90 C7
ROCH OL11 ...28 B8
Sandby Dr MPL/ROM SK6 ...114 E4
Sanderling Cl WHTN BL5 ...50 A6
Sanderling Dr LEIGH WN7 ...66 D7
Sanderling Rd NEWLW WA12 ...78 F8
OFTN SK2 ...113 K7
Sanderson Cl WALK M28 ...69 L4
Sanderson's Cft LEIGH WN7 ...69 F8
Sanderson St BURY BL9 ...5 J3
LEIGH WN7 ...66 B7
NEWH/MOS M40 ...73 H7
Sanderstead Dr BKLY M9 ...73 H1
Sandfield Cl GOL/RIS/CUL WA3 ...80 B4
Sandfield Crs GOL/RIS/CUL WA3 ...81 M5
Sandfield Rd HOR/BR BL6 ...34 F6
Sandfold La BNG/LEV M19 ...99 M2
Sandford Av GTN M18 * ...89 C6
Sandford Cl BOLE BL2 ...37 H1
Sandford Rd SALE M33 ...109 J1
Sandford Station La RDSH SK5 ...100 A2
Sandford St RAD M26 ...39 G8
Sandgate Av OP/CLY M11 ...89 G2
RAD M26 ...53 L5
Sandgate Cl LEIGH WN7 ...66 C6
Sandgate Dr URM M41 ...84 F8
Sandgate Rd CHAD OL9 ...8 A7
WHTF M45 ...55 L5
Sandham St BOLS/LL BL3 ...36 C8
Sandham Wk BOLS/LL BL3 * ...36 C8
Sandheys DTN/ASHW M34 ...90 C7
Sandhill Cl BOLS/LL BL3 ...36 A4
Sandheys Gv GTN M18 ...89 H8
Sandhill La GLSP SK13 ...115 K1
MPL/ROM SK6 ...115 H3
Sandhill St HYDE SK14 ...102 C1
Sandhill Wk WYTH/NTH M22 ...118 D2
Sandhole La ROCH OL11 ...27 H7
Sand Hole La ROCH OL11 ...42 C3
Sand Hole Rd FWTH BL4 ...53 L6
Sandhurst Av DID/WITH M20 ...98 D6
Sandhurst Cl TOT/BURYW BL8 ...38 B7
Sandhurst Ct BOLE BL2 ...37 H6
Sandhurst Dr BOLE BL2 ...37 H6
WILM/AE SK9 ...127 G4
Sandhurst Rd DID/WITH M20 ...110 E2
OFTN SK2 ...112 E7
Sandhurst St OLDE OL4 ...59 M8
Sandhutton Rd BKLY M9 ...73 G3
Sandiacre WGNNW/ST WN6 ...31 H4
Sandilands Rd
NTHM/RTH M23 ...109 G4
Sandileigh Av CHD/CHDH SK8 ...111 K6
DID/WITH M20 ...98 E7
HALE/TIMP WA15 ...117 H1
RDSH SK5 ...100 E8
Sandileigh Dr BOL BL1 ...36 E1
HALE/TIMP WA15 ...117 H1
Sandiway BRAM/HZG SK7 ...121 G2
GLSP SK13 ...105 J5
HEY OL10 ...41 F2
IRL M44 ...94 D2
MPL/ROM SK6 ...113 J1
WHTN BL5 ...50 A4
Sandiway Cl MPL/ROM SK6 ...114 C4
Sandiway Dr DID/WITH M20 ...110 D1
Sandiway Pl ALT WA14 ...108 A2
Sandiway Rd ALT WA14 ...108 A6
SALE M33 ...96 C8
WILM/AE SK9 ...119 M7
Sand La MCFLDN SK10 ...130 C7
Sandling Dr GOL/RIS/CUL WA3 ...79 K2
Sandon St BOLS/LL BL3 ...36 A8
Sandown Av SLFD M6 ...86 B2
Sandown Cl GOL/RIS/CUL WA3 * ...81 J8
OLD OL1 ...59 K3
WILM/AE SK9 ...127 H4
Sandown Crs BOLS/LL BL3 ...53 K2
GTN M18 ...100 A1
Sandown Dr DTN/ASHW M34 ...101 L4
HALE/TIMP WA15 ...117 M6
SALE M33 ...108 B1
Sandown Gdns URM M41 ...95 K2
Sandown Rd BOLE BL2 ...37 J1
BRAM/HZG SK7 ...122 C3
BURY BL9 ...55 K2
EDGY/DAV SK3 ...12 A7
WGNNW/ST WN6 ...47 H1
Sandown St GTN M18 ...89 H6
Sandpiper Cl DUK SK16 ...91 H5
FWTH BL4 ...52 C5
NEWLW WA12 ...78 F8
ROCH OL11 ...27 J5
Sandpiper Dr EDGY/DAV SK3 ...112 A6
Sandpiper Rd WGNS/IIMK WN3 ...46 E8
Sandray Cl BOLS/LL BL3 ...35 J7
Sandray Gv ORD M5 ...86 B3
Sandridge Cl FWTH BL4 ...53 H4
Sandridge Wk WGTN/LGST M12 ...88 B2
Sandringham Av
DTN/ASHW M34 ...90 A6
DTN/ASHW M34 ...100 D1
STLY SK15 ...91 K1
Sandringham Cl ALT WA14 ...116 B3
WGNW/BIL/OR WN5 ...47 H7
Sandringham Dr DUK SK16 ...91 J6
HTNM SK4 ...111 K3
LEIGH WN7 ...67 H5
MILN OL16 ...29 K6
POY/DIS SK12 ...129 H1
TOT/BURYW BL8 ...24 D3
Sandringham Gra PWCH M25 ...72 B1
Sandringham Rd
BRAM/HZG SK7 ...122 B2
CHD/CHDH SK8 ...120 C1
HOR/BR BL6 ...34 A2
HYDE SK14 ...102 B5
MPL/ROM SK6 ...112 F1
WALK M28 ...68 D6
WGNE/HIN WN2 ...49 H8
Sandringham St GTN M18 ...88 D7
Sandringham Wy
ROY/SHW OL2 ...42 F6
WILM/AE SK9 ...126 E6
Sands Av CHAD OL9 ...58 B4
Sands Cl HYDE SK14 ...103 G3
Sandsend Cl CHH M8 ...72 B7
Sandsend Rd URM M41 ...95 M1
Sandstone Rd MILN OL16 ...29 J5
WGNS/IIMK WN3 ...63 J1
Sandstone Wy CCHDY M21 ...98 A6
Sand St NEWH/MOS M40 ...72 F8
STLY SK15 ...91 J4
Sandway WGNNW/ST WN6 ...47 J2
Sandwell Dr SALE M33 ...96 C8
Sandwich Rd ECC M30 ...85 J1
Sandwich St WALK M28 ...69 G2
Sandwith Cl WGNS/IIMK WN3 ...63 L2
Sandwood Av BOLS/LL BL3 ...35 H7
Sandy Acre MOSL OL5 ...76 A4

Sandyacre Cl WHTN BL5 ...51 K6
Sandy Bank ROY/SHW OL2 ...43 J4
Sandy Bank Av HYDE SK14 ...103 G3
Sandybank Cl GLSP SK13 ...93 H8
Sandy Bank Rd CHH M8 ...72 C4
Sandy Bank Wk
HYDE SK14 * ...103 G3
Sandybrook Cl
TOT/BURYW BL8 ...24 C6
Sandybrook Dr BKLY M9 ...72 F2
Sandy Brow BKLY M9 ...73 G2
Sandy Cl BURY BL9 ...39 J8
Sandy Ct GOL/RIS/CUL WA3 ...80 D3
Sandycroft Av WGN WN1 ...14 F1
WYTH/NTH M22 ...118 F1
Sandygate Cl SWIN M27 ...70 B5
Sandy Gv DUK SK16 ...91 G4
SLFD M6 ...86 B1
SWIN M27 ...70 C4
Sandy Haven Cl HYDE SK14 ...103 G3
Sandyhill Rd BKLY M9 ...72 F2
Sandyhills BOLS/LL BL3 ...36 B8
Sandylands Dr PWCH M25 ...71 J3
Sandy La CCHDY M21 ...97 L4
DROY M43 ...89 M1
DUK SK16 ...91 G4
GLSP SK13 ...103 K8
GOL/RIS/CUL WA3 ...79 J4
GOL/RIS/CUL WA3 ...80 D2
IRL M44 ...94 D1
MDTN M24 ...57 L5
MPL/ROM SK6 ...113 M1
NTHM/RTH M23 ...109 G5
OLDS OL8 * ...8 F7
PWCH M25 ...71 K2
RDSH SK5 ...112 B1
ROCH OL11 ...27 M5
ROY/SHW OL2 ...43 G8
SLFD M6 ...86 B1
STRET M32 ...96 C5
TYLD M29 ...67 K8
UPML OL3 ...61 L2
WGNE/HIN WN2 ...49 K6
WGNW/BIL/OR WN5 ...46 A8
WILM/AE SK9 ...126 D4
Sandy Meade PWCH M25 ...71 K1
Sandy Pk WGNE/HIN WN2 ...49 K6
Sandywarps IRL M44 ...94 D4
Sandyway PWCH M25 * ...71 K1
Sandy Wy WGNE/HIN WN2 ...49 J6
Sandywell Cl OP/CLY M11 ...89 G5
Sandywell St OP/CLY M11 ...89 G4
Sandy Wd SLFD M6 ...86 B1
Sangster Ct ORD M5 ...86 D4
Sankey Gv BKLY M9 ...72 F1
Sankey St BURY BL9 ...4 C4
GOL/RIS/CUL WA3 ...79 K4
Santiago St RUSH/FAL M14 ...98 E1
Santley St WGTN/LGST M12 ...99 K1
Santon Av RUSH/FAL M14 ...99 H4
Santon Dr GOL/RIS/CUL WA3 ...80 B4
Sapling Gv SALE M33 ...108 A2
Sapling Rd BOLS/LL BL3 ...51 M3
SWIN M27 ...70 A7
Sarah Butterworth Ct
MILN OL16 ...11 K5
Sarah Butterworth St
MILN OL16 ...11 K6
Sarah St ECC M30 ...84 E3
MDTN M24 ...57 J4
OP/CLY M11 ...88 C4
RAMS BL0 ...19 H1
ROCH OL11 * ...10 F7
ROY/SHW OL2 ...43 L7
WGNE/HIN WN2 ...65 L2
Sargent Dr OLDTF/WHR M16 * ...87 H8
Sargent Rd MPL/ROM SK6 ...113 G2
Sark Rd CCHDY M21 ...97 K2
Sarn Av WYTH/NTH M22 ...110 A8
Sarsfield Av GOL/RIS/CUL WA3 ...80 A4
Satinwood Cl AIMK WN4 ...78 C2
Saturn Gv SLFD M6 ...71 M8
Saunton Av BOLE BL2 ...37 J2
Saunton Rd OP/CLY M11 ...89 G4
Sautridge Cl MDTN M24 ...42 A5
Savernake Rd MPL/ROM SK6 ...101 M7
Savick Av BOLE BL2 ...37 H5
Saville Rd CHD/CHDH SK8 ...110 E6
RAD M26 ...38 C5
Saville St BOLE BL2 ...3 G5
MDTN M24 ...58 A5
Saviours Ter BOLS/LL BL3 * ...35 M7
Savio Wy MDTN M24 ...57 K5
Savoy Ct WHTF M45 ...55 H5
Savoy Dr ROY/SHW OL2 ...59 G2
Savoy St OLDE OL4 ...59 L7
ROCH OL11 ...27 M4
Sawley Av GOL/RIS/CUL WA3 ...80 A3
LIT OL15 ...21 L5
OLDE OL4 ...60 A8
WGNNW/ST WN6 ...47 J1
WHTF M45 ...55 J2
Sawley Dr CHD/CHDH SK8 ...120 D6
Sawley Rd NEWH/MOS M40 ...73 H6
Sawmill Wy LIT OL15 ...21 L8
Sawpit St LYMM WA13 ...106 D3
Saw St BOL BL1 ...36 B2
Sawyer Brow HYDE SK14 ...91 J8
Sawyer Dr AIMK WN4 ...79 G1
Sawyer St TOT/BURYW BL8 ...24 E8
WHIT OL12 ...10 E1
Saxby Av EDGW/EG BL7 ...22 C4
Saxby St SLFD M6 ...70 F7
Saxelby Dr CHH M8 ...72 E6
Saxfield Dr NTHM/RTH M23 ...109 M6
Saxon Av CHH M8 ...72 D2
DUK SK16 ...90 F4
Saxon Cl TOT/BURYW BL8 ...38 E2
Saxon Dr CHAD OL9 ...58 B4
DROY M43 ...89 K2
DTN/ASHW M34 ...90 B5
Saxonholme Rd ROCH OL11 ...41 M5
Saxon St DROY M43 ...89 J7
DTN/ASHW M34 ...101 J1
MDTN M24 ...57 J4
NEWH/MOS M40 ...88 B1
OLDE OL4 ...59 M5
RAD M26 ...54 C1
Saxthorpe Cl SALE M33 ...96 A7
WGNS/IIMK WN3 ...46 F8
Saxthorpe Wk WGTN/LGST M12 ...88 B2
Saxwood Cl WHIT OL12 ...27 L5
Saxwood Av BKLY M9 ...73 G3
Scafell Av WALK M28 * ...68 E7
Scafell Cl MPL/ROM SK6 ...123 G4
OLD OL1 ...9 K1
Scafell Dr WGNW/BIL/OR WN5 ...46 E6
Scale St ORD M5 ...86 B3
Scaliot Cl NM/HAY SK22 ...124 D4
Scant Rw HOR/BR BL6 * ...34 F1

Scarborough St
NEWH/MOS M40 ...73 K4
Scarcroft Rd WGTN/LGST M12 ...88 D7
Scardale Av BOL BL1 ...35 K3
Scarfield Dr ROCH OL11 ...27 H5
Scargill Cl RUSH/FAL M14 * ...98 F4
Scarisbrick Av DID/WITH M20 ...111 G1
Scarisbrick Rd BNG/LEV M19 ...99 J4
Scarr Av RAD M26 ...54 F3
Scarr Dr WHIT OL12 ...28 C2
Scarr La ROY/SHW OL2 ...43 M5
Scarsdale Rd RUSH/FAL M14 ...88 B8
Scarsdale St SLFD M6 ...86 E1
Scarthwood Cl BOLE BL2 ...23 H7
Scawfell Av BOLE BL2 ...36 E2
Schofield Gdns LEIGH WN7 ...81 H1
Schofield Rd DROY M43 ...89 L3
ECC M30 ...84 D3
Schofield St FAIL M35 * ...74 C4
HEY OL10 ...41 G3
LEIGH WN7 ...81 H1
MILN OL16 ...29 K7
OLDS OL8 ...75 H1
OP/CLY M11 ...88 F2
ROCH OL11 ...28 D8
ROY/SHW OL2 ...43 G7
Scholars Dr DID/WITH M20 ...98 D5
Scholars Dr DID/WITH M20 ...98 D5
Scholes Dr NEWH/MOS M40 ...74 B2
Scholes La PWCH M25 ...71 M1
Scholes St CHAD OL9 ...58 D8
FAIL M35 ...74 D3
OLD OL1 ...9 L1
ROCH OL11 ...41 M3
SWIN M27 ...70 D4
TOT/BURYW BL8 ...38 F1
Scholes Wk PWCH M25 ...71 M1
Scholey St BOLE BL2 * ...3 H9
Scholfield Av URM M41 ...96 C3
School Av AUL OL6 ...76 A6
STRET M32 * ...97 J1
WGN WN1 ...15 K1
School Brow BURY BL9 ...4 F4
MPL/ROM SK6 ...113 J2
WALK M28 ...69 J6
WGNW/BIL/OR WN5 ...62 B7
School Cl POY/DIS SK12 ...129 K1
School Ct ANC M4 ...7 L3
EDGY/DAV SK3 ...112 C6
RAMS BL0 ...19 G3
School Crs STLY SK15 ...91 K1
School Dr WGNW/BIL/OR WN5 ...62 B7
Schoolfold La MCFLDN SK10 ...129 L5
School Gv DID/WITH M20 ...98 F6
PWCH M25 ...71 K2
School Gv West
DID/WITH M20 * ...98 F6
School Hl BOL BL1 ...2 D2
School House Flats OLDS OL8 * ...74 F2
School La ALT WA14 ...107 G8
BOL BL1 ...35 L5
BOLS/LL BL3 ...37 J8
BURY BL9 ...26 A8
DID/WITH M20 ...110 F1
EDGW/EG BL7 ...17 G4
HTNM SK4 ...99 M7
HYDE SK14 ...102 B5
IRL M44 ...94 A7
IRL M44 ...94 C2
MCFLDN SK10 ...130 C6
MILN OL16 ...10 E5
MPL/ROM SK6 ...102 E8
MPL/ROM SK6 ...114 F1
PART M31 ...95 H6
POY/DIS SK12 ...129 K1
ROCH OL11 ...26 F4
STLY SK15 ...77 H5
WGN WN1 ...15 H3
WGNE/HIN WN2 ...32 B4
WGNNW/ST WN6 ...31 G3
School Ms MILN OL16 * ...29 L8
School Rd ECC M30 ...84 D4
FAIL M35 ...74 C5
HALE/TIMP WA15 ...117 H1
OLDS OL8 ...74 F2
SALE M33 ...96 D7
STRET M32 ...96 F2
WILM/AE SK9 ...119 M8
Schools Hl CHD/CHDH SK8 ...119 M1
Schoolside Cl CHH M8 ...72 E6
Schoolside La MDTN M24 ...56 F5
Schools Rd GTN M18 ...89 H7
School St AIMK WN4 ...64 A7
ANC M4 ...7 H1
BOLS/LL BL3 ...53 L1
BRAM/HZG SK7 ...122 A2
Bury BL9 ...5 K6
ECC M30 ...84 E1
EDGW/EG BL7 ...22 C5
GOL/RIS/CUL WA3 ...79 K4
HEY OL10 ...40 F7
HOR/BR BL6 ...33 M1
LEIGH WN7 ...66 B4
LIT OL15 ...21 J7
OLDE OL4 ...60 D6
RAD M26 ...54 C1
RAMS BL0 ...18 E7
TYLD M29 ...67 J6
UPML OL3 ...61 L4
WGN WN1 ...15 H3
WGNE/HIN WN2 ...48 C5
WHIT OL12 ...10 E3
School Ter GOL/RIS/CUL WA3 * ...79 K4
School Wk OLDTF/WHR M16 * ...87 G7
School Wy WGNW/BIL/OR WN5 ...46 B7
Schuter Rd RUSH/FAL M14 ...98 F1
Schwabe St MDTN M24 ...56 F4
Scobell St TOT/BURYW BL8 ...24 F7
Scoltock Wy OLD OL1 * ...9 J4
Score St OP/CLY M11 ...88 D3
Scorton Av BOLE BL2 ...37 J5
Scorton St BOL BL1 * ...35 M4
Scotland Hall Rd
NEWH/MOS M40 ...73 L8
Scotland La BURY BL9 ...25 M4
Scotland St AUL OL6 ...90 F2
NEWH/MOS M40 ...73 M7
Scot La WGNE/HIN WN2 ...33 G6
WGNW/BIL/OR WN5 ...47 H3
Scott Av CCHDY M21 ...97 L2
ECC M30 ...84 F1
WGNE/HIN WN2 ...49 H6

Scott Cl RDSH SK5 ...100 C8
Scott Dr HALE/TIMP WA15 ...108 C8
MPL/ROM SK6 ...114 C4
Scottfield OLDS OL8 ...9 H9
Scottfield Rd OLDS OL8 ...9 H9
Scott Ga DTN/ASHW M34 ...90 B5
Scottia Rd ECC M30 ...84 C4
Scott Rd DROY M43 ...89 K1
DTN/ASHW M34 ...101 H3
GOL/RIS/CUL WA3 ...80 A4
PWCH M25 ...71 J1
Scott St LEIGH WN7 ...66 A7
OLDS OL8 ...9 J9
RAD M26 ...54 A5
TYLD M29 ...67 M8
WGNNW/ST WN6 ...47 J2
WHTN BL5 ...50 B2
Scott Whf LEIGH WN7 ...66 E8
Scotty Brook Crs
GLSP SK13 ...105 H4
Scout Dr NTHM/RTH M23 ...109 J8
Scout Gn MDTN M24 ...57 K1
Scout Rd RAMS BL0 ...19 K2
Scout Vw TOT/BURYW BL8 ...24 A6
Scovell St BRO M7 ...72 A6
Scowcroft La ROY/SHW OL2 ...43 K6
Scowcroft St BOLE BL2 ...3 J1
Scroggins La PART M31 ...94 C8
Scropton St NEWH/MOS M40 ...73 G7
Seabright Wk OP/CLY M11 * ...88 C3
Seabrook Crs URM M41 ...85 G8
Seabrook Rd NEWH/MOS M40 ...73 M8
Seacombe Av RUSH/FAL M14 ...98 D3
Seacombe Gv EDGY/DAV SK3 ...12 A7
Seaford Rd BOLE BL2 ...23 H6
SLFD M6 ...71 L7
Seaforth Av ATH M46 ...66 C1
Seaforth Rd BOL BL1 ...22 B7
Seaham Dr TOT/BURYW BL8 ...24 F7
Seaham Wk RUSH/FAL M14 ...98 F1
Sealand Cl SALE M33 ...109 H2
Sealand Dr ECC M30 ...84 D4
Sealand Rd NTHM/RTH M23 ...109 G3
Seale Av DTN/ASHW M34 ...90 A5
Sealey Wk NEWH/MOS M40 * ...73 H8
Seal Rd BRAM/HZG SK7 ...121 J5
Seaman Wy WGNE/HIN WN2 ...48 E5
Seamon's Dr ALT WA14 ...107 K7
Seamon's Rd ALT WA14 ...107 K6
Searby Rd BNG/LEV M19 ...99 G3
Searness Rd MDTN M24 ...56 F2
Seascale Av WGN WN1 ...15 M1
Seascale Crs WGN WN1 ...47 M1
Seathwaite Cl MDTN M24 ...56 F3
TYLD M29 ...67 K5
Seathwaite Rd FWTH BL4 ...52 C3
Seatoller Dr MDTN M24 ...56 F3
Seatoller Pl
WGNW/BIL/OR WN5 ...46 E5
Seaton Cl BRAM/HZG SK7 ...121 M3
Seaton Ms AULW OL7 ...75 H8
Seaton Rd BOL BL1 ...35 M2
Sebastian Cl MPL/ROM SK6 ...114 C5
Sebastopol Wk ANC M4 ...7 L3
Second Av ATH M46 ...51 G8
BOL BL1 ...35 L5
BOLS/LL BL3 ...37 J8
BURY BL9 ...26 A8
OLDS OL8 ...74 F2
OP/CLY M11 ...89 G2
POY/DIS SK12 ...129 H3
STLY SK15 ...77 H7
SWIN M27 ...70 A7
TRPK M17 ...86 A7
TYLD M29 ...67 L8
WGNNW/ST WN6 ...47 K2
Section St BOL BL1 ...2 E6
Sedan Cl ORD M5 ...86 D3
Sedburgh Cl SALE M33 ...108 A1
Sedbury Cl NTHM/RTH M23 ...109 J3
Seddon Av GTN M18 ...89 G6
RAD M26 ...39 H7
Seddon Cl ATH M46 ...66 F1
RAD M26 ...39 D8
Seddon Gdns RAD M26 ...53 K4
Seddon House Dr
WGNNW/ST WN6 ...47 H1
Seddon La RAD M26 ...53 K4
Seddon Rd ALT WA14 ...116 F2
Seddon St BNG/LEV M19 ...99 L2
BOLS/LL BL3 * ...53 L1
LHULT M38 ...52 C7
RAD M26 ...54 D7
WHTN BL5 ...50 B2
Sedgeborough Rd
OLDTF/WHR M16 ...98 B1
Sedge Cl RDSH SK5 ...100 D4
Sedgefield Cl ORD M5 ...86 D2
Sedgefield Dr BOL BL1 ...35 L1
WGNNW/ST WN6 ...47 H1
Sedgefield Pk OLDE OL4 ...60 A6
Sedgefield Rd RAD M26 ...54 C4
Sedgeford Cl WILM/AE SK9 ...127 G3
Sedgeford Rd NEWH/MOS M40 ...73 G7
Sedgely WGNNW/ST WN6 ...31 K5
Sedgemoor Cl CHD/CHDH SK8 ...120 D2
Sedgemoor V BOLE BL2 ...37 J2
Sedgemoor Wy OLD OL1 * ...9 H4
Sedgley Av MILN OL16 ...28 E8
PWCH M25 ...71 M2
Sedgley Cl MDTN M24 ...57 M5
Sedgley Dr WHTN BL5 ...50 B7
Sedgley Park Rd PWCH M25 ...71 M2
Sedgley Rd CHH M8 ...72 D4
Sedgley St MDTN M24 ...57 M5
Sedgwick Cl ATH M46 ...67 H1
WHTN BL5 ...50 C6
Sedwyn St WGN WN1 ...15 K1
Seedfield Rd BURY BL9 ...25 J7
Seedley Av LHULT M38 ...52 E8
Seedley Park Rd SLFD M6 ...86 B2
Seedley Rd SLFD M6 ...86 B1
Seedley St RUSH/FAL M14 ...98 E1
Seedley Ter SLFD M6 ...86 B1
Seedley View Rd ORD M5 ...86 B1
Seed St BOL BL1 ...35 M5
Seel St MOSL OL5 ...76 E3
Sefton Av ATH M46 ...50 F7
WGNW/BIL/OR WN5 ...46 A7
Sefton Cl BRUN/LGST M13 ...87 L1
MDTN M24 ...57 H1
OLD OL1 ...43 M8
WGNE/HIN WN2 ...46 A7
Sefton Crs SALE M33 ...96 E6
Sefton Dr BURY BL9 ...25 K6
SWIN M27 ...70 A7
WALK M28 ...69 K4
WILM/AE SK9 ...127 G2
Sefton Fold Dr
WGNW/BIL/OR WN5 ...62 A7

Sefton Fold Gdns
WGNW/BIL/OR WN5 ...62 A7
Sefton La HOR/BR BL6 ...34 B3
Sefton Rd AIMK WN4 ...63 J6
BOL BL1 ...2 A1
CCHDY M21 ...97 L4
MDTN M24 ...57 H4
SALE M33 ...96 E7
SWIN M27 ...70 C3
WGNS/IIMK WN3 ...47 J8
WGNW/BIL/OR WN5 ...46 A7
Sefton St BURY BL9 ...25 J6
CHAD OL9 ...74 D2
CHH M8 ...72 D4
GLSP SK13 ...104 F4
HEY OL10 ...41 H3
LEIGH WN7 ...66 C7
RAD M26 ...54 F3
ROCH OL11 ...10 F3
WHTF M45 ...55 J5
Sefton Vw WGNW/BIL/OR WN5 ...46 A7
Segal Cl BRO M7 ...72 A5
Selborne Rd CCHDY M21 ...97 L3
Selbourne Cl WHTN BL5 ...50 D3
Selbourne St LEIGH WN7 ...66 C5
Selby Av CHD/CHDH SK8 ...58 C3
WHTF M45 ...55 J2
Selby Cl MILN OL16 ...29 H6
POY/DIS SK12 * ...121 H1
RAD M26 ...39 G7
STRET M32 ...96 C1
Selby Dr SLFD M6 ...85 L1
URM M41 ...84 C7
WGNS/IIMK WN3 ...46 F8
Selby Gdns CHD/CHDH SK8 ...120 C6
Selby Rd MDTN M24 ...57 J1
STRET M32 ...96 D1
Selby St HTNM SK4 ...100 E8
MILN OL16 ...11 J2
OP/CLY M11 ...89 G2
Selham Wk BRUN/LGST M13 * ...7 L7
Selhurst Av OP/CLY M11 ...88 F2
Selkirk Av AIMK WN4 ...63 G8
OLDS OL8 ...59 G8
Selkirk Dr BKLY M9 ...73 J1
Selkirk Gv WGNW/BIL/OR WN5 ...46 A7
Selkirk Rd BOL BL1 ...22 A7
CHAD OL9 ...58 C8
Sellars Sq DROY M43 ...89 K4
Sellers Wy CHAD OL9 ...74 D1
Selsby Av ECC M30 ...84 C2
Selsey Av EDGY/DAV SK3 ...111 J3
SALE M33 ...108 C1
Selsey Dr DID/WITH M20 ...110 F4
Selside Wk RUSH/FAL M14 ...98 F4
Selstead Rd WYTH/NTH M22 ...118 C3
Selston Rd BKLY M9 ...56 E8
Selworth Av SALE M33 ...97 H8
Selworthy Rd OLDTF/WHR M16 ...87 H8
Selwyn Av BKLY M9 ...73 G4
Selwyn Cl NEWLW WA12 ...78 E7
OLDS OL8 * ...9 G8
Selwyn Dr CHD/CHDH SK8 ...120 C5
Selwyn St BOLE BL2 ...3 H7
LEIGH WN7 ...66 C6
OLDS OL8 ...9 G8
Senecar Cl WGNE/HIN WN2 ...48 E2
Senior Av RUSH/FAL M14 ...99 H5
Senior Rd ECC M30 ...84 C4
Senior St CSLFD M3 ...6 D1
Senior Vw HYDE SK14 * ...91 H7
Sennicar La WGN WN1 ...31 M7
Sepal Cl RDSH SK5 ...100 C3
Sephton St WGNS/IIMK WN3 ...15 M7
Sepia Gv MDTN M24 ...57 J3
Sequoia St BKLY M9 ...73 H4
Sergeants La WHTF M45 ...54 F5
Serin Cl OFTN SK2 ...113 J8
Service St EDGY/DAV SK3 ...12 B6
Sesame Gdns IRL M44 ...94 F1
Set STLY SK15 ...91 J3
Sett Cl NM/HAY SK22 ...124 D5
Settle Cl TOT/BURYW BL8 ...38 C2
Settle St BOLS/LL BL3 ...52 B1
BOLS/LL BL3 ...53 M2
Sett Valley Trail NM/HAY SK22 ...125 H2
Sevenacres UPML OL3 ...45 J7
Seven Acres La WHIT OL12 ...27 H2
Seven Acres Rd WHIT OL12 ...27 H1
Seven Oaks LEIGH WN7 ...66 D6
Sevenoaks Av HTNM SK4 ...99 K3
URM M41 ...85 G8
Sevenoaks Dr BOLS/LL BL3 ...52 B1
SWIN M27 ...70 D6
Sevenoaks Rd CHD/CHDH SK8 ...110 E4
Sevenoaks Wk
BRUN/LGST M13 * ...87 M7
Seven Stars Rd
WGNS/IIMK WN3 ...14 C5
Seven Stiles Dr MPL/ROM SK6 ...114 B5
Seventh Av OLDS OL8 ...74 F3
Severn Cl ALT WA14 ...107 M6
BURY BL9 ...25 J5
WGNW/BIL/OR WN5 ...62 A8
Severn Dr BRAM/HZG SK7 ...120 E6
MILN OL16 ...29 K6
WGNE/HIN WN2 ...65 M1
Severn Rd AIMK WN4 ...64 B7
CHAD OL9 ...58 C4
HEY OL10 ...40 D1
OLDS OL8 ...74 E3
Severn St LEIGH WN7 ...66 E8
Severn Wy FWTH BL4 ...53 L7
RDSH SK5 ...100 C2
Seville St ROY/SHW OL2 ...43 K7
ROY/SHW OL2 ...59 H2
Sewell Wy LHULT M38 ...68 C1
Sewerby Cl OLDTF/WHR M16 ...87 J8
Sewerby St
OLDTF/WHR M16 ...87 H8
Sexa St OP/CLY M11 ...89 G4
Sexton St GLSP SK13 ...93 J5
HEY OL10 ...40 F2
Seymour Av OP/CLY M11 ...89 G2
Seymour Cl OLDTF/WHR M16 ...86 F7
Seymour Dr BOLE BL2 ...22 F7
Seymour Gv FWTH BL4 ...52 D3
HALE/TIMP WA15 ...108 D2
MILN OL16 ...42 E1
MPL/ROM SK6 ...114 B6
OLDTF/WHR M16 ...86 E8
SALE M33 ...96 E8
Seymour Pl OLDTF/WHR M16 * ...86 E7
Seymour Rd BOL BL1 ...36 C1
CHD/CHDH SK8 ...120 C4
CHH M8 ...72 C3
OFTN SK2 ...112 E6
Seymour Rd South
OP/CLY M11 ...89 G2

Seymour St BOLE BL2 22 F6
DTN/ASHW M34 90 A8
GTN M18 89 G6
HEY OL10 40 F3
RAD M26 54 E1
Shackleton Gv BOL BL1 35 J2
Shackleton St ECC M30 84 F1
Shackliffe Rd NEWH/MOS M40 73 L2
Shaddock Av WHIT OL12 27 J3
Shade Av OLDE OL4 60 C7
Shadowbrook Av
NTHM/RTH M23 109 K8
Shadowbrook Cl OLD OL1 9 H1
Shadowmoss Rd
WYTH/NTH M22 119 G4
Shadows La MOSL OL5 61 H8
Shadwell Gv LEIGH WN7 65 M4
Shadwell St East HEY OL10 41 H1
Shadwell St West HEY OL10 41 G1
Shadworth Cl MOSL OL5 61 H8
Shady La EDGW/EG BL7 22 E6
NTHM/RTH M23 109 G6
Shady Oak Rd OFTN SK2 113 J6
Shaftesbury Av
CHD/CHDH SK8 120 E3
ECC M30 84 F4
HALE/TIMP WA15 108 E7
HOR/BR BL6 34 C4
LIT OL15 29 K2
Shaftesbury Dr WHIT OL12 21 H6
Shaftesbury Gdns URM M41 94 F2
Shaftesbury Rd CHH M8 72 D5
EDGY/DAV SK3 111 K6
SWIN M27 70 C5
Shaftsbury Dr HEY OL10 40 F4
Shaftsbury Rd
WGNW/BIL/OR WN5 46 D4
Shaftsbury St WGNNW/ST WN6 47 J1
Shaftway Cl RNFD/HAY WA11 78 C5
Shakerley La ATH M46 51 J8
Shakerley Rd TYLD M29 67 J3
Shakespeare Av BURY BL9 39 J6
DTN/ASHW M34 101 J4
RAD M26 38 B8
STLY SK15 77 H8
Shakespeare Crs DROY M43 89 K2
ECC M30 85 G2
Shakespeare Dr
CHD/CHDH SK8 111 J6
Shakespeare Gv
WGNS/IIMK WN3 47 K8
Shakespeare Rd DROY M43 89 K2
MPL/ROM SK6 113 H1
OLD OL1 59 L2
PWCH M25 71 J1
SWIN M27 70 A4
Shakespeare Wk
BRUN/LGST M13 87 M7
Shakleton Av BKLY M9 73 K1
Shalbourne Rd WALK M28 68 F1
Shaldon Dr NEWH/MOS M40 74 B8
Shalebrook Cl ATH M46 66 D2
Shalemere Ct ATH M46 66 D2
Shalewood Ct ATH M46 66 D2
Shalfleet Cl BOLE BL2 23 H7
Shambles Sq CMANE M1 6 F3
Shandon Av WYTH/NTH M22 110 A3
Shanklin Av URM M41 95 M2
Shanklin Cl CCHDY M21 97 K3
DTN/ASHW M34 * 101 L4
Shanklin Wk BOLS/LL BL3 3 M9
Shanley Ct CHAD OL9 * 8 B3
Shannon Cl HEY OL10 40 D1
Shannon Rd WYTH/NTH M22 110 B8
Shap Av HALE/TIMP WA15 109 G7
Shap Dr WALK M28 69 J2
Shap Ga WGNW/BIL/OR WN5 46 E5
Sharcott Cl OLDTF/WHR M16 87 J8
Shardlow Cl NEWH/MOS M40 73 G8
Shared St WGN WN1 15 J6
Shargate Cl WILM/AE SK9 127 G3
Sharman St BOLS/LL BL3 3 J9
Sharnford Cl BOLE BL2 3 J7
Sharnford Sq WGTN/LGST M12 88 D6
Sharon Av OLDE OL4 61 G6
Sharon Cl AULW OL7 90 B3
Sharon Sq WGNE/HIN WN2 64 C4
Sharples Av BOL BL1 22 B6
Sharples Dr TOT/BURYW BL8 24 C8
Sharples Gn EDGW/EG BL7 17 G6
Sharples Hall Dr BOL BL1 22 C6
Sharples Hall Fold BOL BL1 22 C7
Sharples Hall Ms BOL BL1 22 C6
Sharples Hall St OLDE OL4 60 A3
Sharples Pk BOL BL1 22 A8
Sharples St HTNM SK4 112 B1
Sharp St ANC M4 7 J1
MDTN M24 57 K4
PWCH M25 * 55 K8
TOT/BURYW BL8 24 E8
WALK M28 69 H1
WGNS/IIMK WN3 15 K8
Sharrington Dr
NTHM/RTH M23 109 H6
Sharston Rd WYTH/NTH M22 110 B5
Shaving La WALK M28 69 G3
Shaw Av HYDE SK14 102 C4
Shawbrook Av WALK M28 68 E4
Shawbrook Rd BNG/LEV M19 99 K7
Shawbury Cl HOR/BR BL6 33 G3
Shawbury Gv SALE M33 108 C2
Shawbury Rd NTHM/RTH M23 109 L8
Shawbury St MDTN M24 57 M5
Shawclough Cl WHIT OL12 28 A1
Shawclough Dr WHIT OL12 27 M1
Shawclough Ri WHIT OL12 * 28 A2
Shawclough Rd WHIT OL12 27 M1
Shawclough Wy WHIT OL12 27 M1
Shawcroft Cl ROY/SHW OL2 43 K7
Shawcross Fold STKP SK1 13 J3
Shawcross La WYTH/NTH M22 110 C4
Shawcross St HYDE SK14 102 C4
SLFD M6 86 C3
STKP SK1 13 K7
Shawdene Rd WYTH/NTH M22 109 M4
Shawe Hall Av URM M41 95 K4
Shawe Hall Crs URM M41 95 K4
Shawe Rd URM M41 95 K2
Shawe Vw URM M41 95 K2
Shawfield Cl RUSH/FAL M14 98 D4
Shawfield La WHIT OL12 27 K2
Shawfield Rd GLSP SK13 104 C1
Shawfields STLY SK15 92 A1
Shawford Rd NEWH/MOS M40 73 M2
Shawgreen Cl HULME M15 87 G6
Shaw Hall Av HYDE SK14 91 L7
Shaw Hall Bank Rd UPML OL3 61 J7
Shaw Hall Cl UPML OL3 61 J7
Shaw Head Dr FAIL M35 74 C6
Shaw Heath EDGY/DAV SK3 13 H7
Shawheath Cl HULME M15 87 G6
Shawhill Wk NEWH/MOS M40 88 B2
Shaw La GLSP SK13 104 C1
MILN OL16 29 J4
Shawlea Av BNG/LEV M19 99 H6
Shaw Moor Av STLY SK15 91 M3
Shaw Rd HTNM SK4 99 L7
MILN OL16 42 F4
MILN OL16 43 L1
OLD OL1 9 L2
ROY/SHW OL2 43 J8
Shaw Rd South EDGY/DAV SK3 13 J9
EDGY/DAV SK3 112 B6
Shaws Fold OLDE OL4 60 E6
Shaws La UPML OL3 61 M5
Shaw's Rd ALT WA14 108 A8
Shaw St AIMK WN4 63 L7
AUL OL6 91 G1
BOLS/LL BL3 2 C8
BURY BL9 5 K3
CSLFD M3 6 F1
FWTH BL4 * 52 F2
GLSP SK13 104 F4
HYDE SK14 92 D8
OLD OL1 9 K4
OLDE OL4 60 D6
RNFD/HAY WA11 78 B6
ROY/SHW OL2 43 H8
UPML OL3 61 K7
WGN WN1 15 G1
WHIT OL12 28 E2
Shay Av HALE/TIMP WA15 118 A3
Shayfield Av CHAD OL9 58 B5
WYTH/NTH M22 110 A7
Shayfield Dr WYTH/NTH M22 110 A7
Shayfield Rd WYTH/NTH M22 110 A7
Shay La HALE/TIMP WA15 117 M3
Sheader Dr ORD M5 85 M2
Sheaf Field Wk RAD M26 38 D8
Sheard Av AUL OL6 76 A6
Sheardhall Av POY/DIS SK12 124 A7
Shearer Wy SWIN M27 71 G5
Shearing Av WHIT OL12 27 J3
Shearsby Cl HULME M15 87 H6
Shearwater Av TYLD M29 67 K4
Shearwater Dr WALK M28 68 F1
WHTN BL5 50 A6
Shearwater Gdns ECC M30 84 D4
Shearwater Rd OFTN SK2 113 J7
The Sheddings BOLS/LL BL3 36 D8
Shed St WHIT OL12 20 B3
Sheepfoot La OLD OL1 59 G3
PWCH M25 72 A1
Sheepfoot Wk OLD OL1 59 G3
Sheep Gap WHIT OL12 27 L3
Sheep Gate Dr TOT/BURYW BL8 24 B7
Sheep Hey RAMS BL0 * 19 G3
Sheerness St GTN M18 89 G7
Sheffield Rd GLSP SK13 105 H3
HYDE SK14 91 J8
Sheffield St CMANE M1 7 K6
HTNM SK4 13 H1
Shefford Cl OP/CLY M11 88 C4
Shefford Crs WGNS/IIMK WN3 62 F2
Sheiling Ct ALT WA14 107 M8
The Sheilings GOL/RIS/CUL WA3 80 C4
Shelbourne Av BOL BL1 35 L2
Shelburne Dr WGNE/HIN WN2 48 F8
Shelden Ms GLSP SK13 104 A3
Shelderton Cl NEWH/MOS M40 73 K5
Sheldon Av WGNNW/ST WN6 31 H2
Sheldon Cl PART M31 106 C1
Sheldon Ct AULW OL7 75 L7
Sheldon Rd BRAM/HZG SK7 122 A5
Sheldon St OP/CLY M11 88 E2
Sheldrake Cl DUK SK16 91 H5
Sheldrake Rd ALT WA14 107 L4
Sheldwich Cl LEIGH WN7 81 J1
Shelfield Cl ROCH OL11 27 J3
Shelfield La ROCH OL11 27 J3
Shelford Av GTN M18 88 E8
Shelley Av MDTN M24 57 L2
Shelley Dr WGNE/HIN WN2 64 E3
WGNW/BIL/OR WN5 46 D6
Shelley Gv DROY M43 89 K3
HYDE SK14 91 G8
STLY SK15 77 H8
Shelley Ri DUK SK16 91 L5
Shelley Rd CHAD OL9 74 C1
LHULT M38 * 52 D7
OLD OL1 59 M3
PWCH M25 71 J1
RDSH SK5 100 A3
SWIN M27 70 A4
Shelley St LEIGH WN7 65 M5
NEWH/MOS M40 73 M4
Shelley Wk BOL BL1 36 A3
Shellingford Cl
WGNNW/ST WN6 30 A5
Shelton Av SALE M33 96 A8
Shenfield Wk NEWH/MOS M40 88 A1
Shenhurst Cl WILM/AE SK9 126 C8
Shentonfield Rd
WYTH/NTH M22 110 B6
Shenton Park Av SALE M33 107 M3
Shenton St HYDE SK14 90 F8
Shepherd Cross St BOL BL1 35 M3
Shepherds Cl HOR/BR BL6 32 F1
TOT/BURYW BL8 24 C3
Shepherd's Dr HOR/BR BL6 34 D1
Shepherd St BKLY M9 * 73 G3
BURY BL9 5 G6
HEY OL10 * 40 F2
ROCH OL11 27 G3
ROY/SHW OL2 43 H8
TOT/BURYW BL8 24 C4
WHIT OL12 * 10 E2
Shepherds Wy MILN OL16 29 H7
Shepley Av BOLS/LL BL3 35 M7
Shepley Cl BRAM/HZG SK7 121 M4
DUK SK16 91 G4
Shepley Dr BRAM/HZG SK7 121 M3
Shepley La MPL/ROM SK6 114 C8
Shepley Rd DTN/ASHW M34 90 C6
Shepley St DTN/ASHW M34 90 C5
FAIL M35 74 D3
GLSP SK13 105 H2
HYDE SK14 102 B2
OLDE OL4 * 60 B6
Shepton Av WGNE/HIN WN2 64 D3
Shepton Cl BOL BL1 22 A5
Shepton Dr NTHM/RTH M23 118 C2
Sheraton Cl
WGNW/BIL/OR WN5 46 E3
Sheraton Rd OLDS OL8 59 H8
Sherborne Av WGNE/HIN WN2 49 K7
Sherborne Rd EDGY/DAV SK3 111 K5
URM M41 96 B1
WGNW/BIL/OR WN5 46 D4
Sherborne St CHH M8 72 C8
Sherborne St West CSLFD M3 87 H1
Sherbourne Cl CHD/CHDH SK8 120 D6
OLDS OL8 59 M8
RAD M26 38 A7
Sherbourne Dr HEY OL10 40 D1
Sherbourne Pl WGNS/IIMK WN3 15 K9
Sherbourne Rd BOL BL1 35 K3
MDTN M24 57 J1
Sherbourne St PWCH M25 * 55 K8
Sherbrook Cl SALE M33 108 C1
Sherbrooke Av UPML OL3 61 M3
Sherbrooke Rd POY/DIS SK12 123 M6
Sherbrook Ri WILM/AE SK9 127 G6
Sherdley Ct CHH M8 72 D3
Sherdley Rd CHH M8 72 D3
Sherford Cl BRAM/HZG SK7 121 J2
Sheridan Av GOL/RIS/CUL WA3 80 A5
Sheridan Wy CHAD OL9 * 58 B4
Sheriffs Dr TYLD M29 68 A3
Sheriff St BOLE BL2 36 E3
MILN OL16 29 K7
WHIT OL12 10 C3
Sheringham Dr HYDE SK14 102 D1
SWIN M27 70 C6
TOT/BURYW BL8 24 F7
Sheringham Pl BOLS/LL BL3 2 A9
Sheringham Rd DID/WITH M20 99 G5
Sherlock Av RNFD/HAY WA11 78 B5
Sherlock St RUSH/FAL M14 99 G5
Sherratt St ANC M4 7 K2
Sherrington St
WGTN/LGST M12 99 K1
Sherway Dr HALE/TIMP WA15 108 F6
Sherwell Rd BKLY M9 72 E1
Sherwin Wy ROCH OL11 42 A3
Sherwood Av AIMK WN4 * 63 M8
BRO M7 71 L5
DROY M43 89 M2
HTNM SK4 111 K3
RAD M26 38 C4
RUSH/FAL M14 98 F4
SALE M33 96 F7
TYLD M29 67 K6
Sherwood Cl AUL OL6 75 M5
MPL/ROM SK6 114 C8
ORD M5 86 A1
TOT/BURYW BL8 24 C5
Sherwood Crs WGNE/HIN WN2 64 D2
WGNW/BIL/OR WN5 47 G5
Sherwood Dr SWIN M27 70 E5
WGNW/BIL/OR WN5 47 G5
Sherwood Fold GLSP SK13 104 A5
Sherwood Gv LEIGH WN7 81 L2
WGNW/BIL/OR WN5 47 G5
Sherwood Rd DTN/ASHW M34 100 E1
MPL/ROM SK6 101 L7
Sherwood St BOL BL1 36 C1
OLD OL1 8 E2
ROCH OL11 42 A2
RUSH/FAL M14 98 F4
Sherwood Wy ROY/SHW OL2 43 H4
Shetland Rd NEWH/MOS M40 88 A1
Shetland Wy RAD M26 38 D7
URM M41 85 G7
Shevington Gdns
NTHM/RTH M23 109 L3
Shevington La
WGNNW/ST WN6 30 D6
Shevington Moor
WGNNW/ST WN6 30 D2
Shieldborn Dr BKLY M9 73 G5
Shield Cl OLDS OL8 9 G7
Shield Dr WALK M28 69 M4
Shield St EDGY/DAV SK3 13 G6
Shiel St WALK M28 69 G1
Shiers Dr CHD/CHDH SK8 111 H8
Shiffnall St BOLE BL2 3 G6
Shildon Cl WGNE/HIN WN2 48 C2
Shilford Dr ANC M4 7 K1
Shillingford Rd FWTH BL4 52 F4
Shillingstone Cl BOLE BL2 37 K1
Shillington Cl WALK M28 68 C1
Shiloh La OLDE OL4 60 E2
Shiloh Rd MPL/ROM SK6 115 M5
Shilton Gdns BOLS/LL BL3 2 C8
Shilton St RAMS BL0 18 E7
Shipgate BOL BL1 2 F4
Shipham Cl LEIGH WN7 66 A5
Shipla Cl CHAD OL9 9 G4
Ship La OLDE OL4 44 E7
Shipley Av SLFD M6 85 M1
Shipley Vw URM M41 84 C7
Shipper Bottom La RAMS BL0 19 H6
Shippey St RUSH/FAL M14 99 G5
Shipston Cl TOT/BURYW BL8 38 E1
Shipton St BOL BL1 35 L3
Shirburn ROCH OL11 10 D7
Shirebrook Dr GLSP SK13 105 J4
RAD M26 38 E8
Shireburn Av BOLE BL2 3 M3
Shiredale Cl CHD/CHDH SK8 111 L8
Shiredale Dr BKLY M9 73 G5
Shiregreen Av NEWH/MOS M40 72 F7
Shirehills PWCH M25 71 K1
Shireoak Rd DID/WITH M20 99 G5
Shires Cl WGNE/HIN WN2 49 H8
The Shires DROY M43 90 A1
RAD M26 38 D7
Shire Wy GLSP SK13 105 H1
Shirewell Rd
WGNW/BIL/OR WN5 46 B7
Shirley Av BRO M7 71 K5
CHAD OL9 74 B2
CHD/CHDH SK8 119 L6
DTN/ASHW M34 89 M4
DTN/ASHW M34 100 C1
ECC M30 84 F4
HYDE SK14 91 G7
MPL/ROM SK6 114 B6
STRET M32 97 J1
SWIN M27 70 F5
Shirley Cl BRAM/HZG SK7 121 L2
Shirley Gv EDGY/DAV SK3 112 B7
Shirley Rd CHH M8 72 D5
Shirley St ROCH OL11 41 M2
Shoecroft Av DTN/ASHW M34 101 H2
Sholver Hill Cl OLD OL1 44 B8
Sholver La OLD OL1 44 A8
Shone Av WYTH/NTH M22 119 H2
Shore Av ROY/SHW OL2 43 M3
Shoreditch Cl HTNM SK4 99 L7
Shorefield Cl MILN OL16 29 J5
Shorefield Mt EDGW/EG BL7 22 B4
Shore Fold LIT OL15 21 K6
Shoreham Wk CHAD OL9 * 58 D6
Shore La LIT OL15 21 K6
Shore Mt LIT OL15 21 K6
Shore Rd LIT OL15 21 K5
Shore St MILN OL16 29 J6
OLD OL1 9 M4
Shoreswood BOL BL1 22 A7
Shorland St SWIN M27 69 M5
Shorrocks St TOT/BURYW BL8 38 C1
Short Av DROY M43 89 J4
Shortcroft St HULME M15 6 E8
Shortland Crs BNG/LEV M19 111 G1
Shortland Pl
WGNE/HIN WN2 65 K4
Shortlands Av BURY BL9 5 G8
Short St BRAM/HZG SK7 121 M1
BRO M7 87 H1
CMANE M1 7 H4
GOL/RIS/CUL WA3 * 79 L3
HEY OL10 40 E3
HTNM SK4 13 G1
RNFD/HAY WA11 78 B6
WGNW/BIL/OR WN5 46 E6
Short St East HTNM SK4 13 H1
Shotton Wk
RUSH/FAL M14 * 98 E1
Shrewsbury Cl
WGNE/HIN WN2 49 J6
Shrewsbury Ct
OLDTF/WHR M16 * 87 G7
Shrewsbury Gdns
CHD/CHDH SK8 120 E6
Shrewsbury Rd BOL BL1 35 L4
DROY M43 89 K2
PWCH M25 71 K1
SALE M33 108 D2
Shrewsbury St GLSP SK13 104 F3
OLDE OL4 59 M4
OLDTF/WHR M16 87 G7
Shrigley Cl
WILM/AE SK9 127 H3
Shrigley Rd MCFLDN SK10 129 M8
Shropshire Av RDSH SK5 100 F6
Shropshire Dr GLSP SK13 105 J4
Shropshire Rd FAIL M35 74 D6
Shropshire Sq
WGTN/LGST M12 * 88 B6
Shrowbridge Wk
WGTN/LGST M12 88 D6
Shudehill ANC M4 7 H2
NM/HAY SK22 * 125 M1
Shudehill Cl NM/HAY SK22 125 M1
Shudehill Rd WALK M28 68 D3
Shurdington Rd ATH M46 51 J7
Shurmer St BOLS/LL BL3 35 M8
Shutt La UPML OL3 61 J2
Shuttle Hillock Rd
WGNE/HIN WN2 65 J5
Shuttle St ECC M30 * 85 J2
RAD M26 54 F3
TYLD M29 67 J3
WGNE/HIN WN2 49 H6
Shuttleworth Cl
OLDTF/WHR M16 98 B4
Shutts La STLY SK15 92 A4
Siam St OP/CLY M11 88 C4
Sibley Av AIMK WN4 64 A8
Sibley Rd HTNM SK4 111 L1
Sibley St GTN M18 89 G7
Sibson Rd CCHDY M21 97 K3
SALE M33 96 D8
Sickle St CMANW M2 7 G4
OLDE OL4 9 L8
Sidbrook St WGNE/HIN WN2 48 F7
Sidbury Rd CCHDY M21 97 M4
Sidcup Rd NTHM/RTH M23 109 J7
Siddall St HEY OL10 41 H4
OLD OL1 9 J3
RAD M26 38 D8
ROY/SHW OL2 43 L5
WGTN/LGST M12 88 C7
Siddeley St LEIGH WN7 66 A7
Siddington Av DID/WITH M20 98 D5
EDGY/DAV SK3 111 M6
Siddington Rd POY/DIS SK12 129 K2
WILM/AE SK9 * 119 M7
Siddow Common LEIGH WN7 81 K1
Side Av ALT WA14 116 E3
Sidebotham St MPL/ROM SK6 101 J8
Sidebottom St DROY M43 * 89 J3
OLDE OL4 60 B4
STLY SK15 91 K2
Side St OLDS OL8 74 F2
OP/CLY M11 88 E3
Sidford Cl BOLS/LL BL3 37 G7
The Sidings WALK M28 69 K7
Sidlaw Cl OLDS OL8 75 J2
Sidley Av BKLY M9 57 J8
Sidley St HYDE SK14 102 C1
Sidmouth Av URM M41 95 H1
Sidmouth Dr BKLY M9 73 G2
Sidmouth Gv CHD/CHDH SK8 120 B5
WGNS/IIMK WN3 63 H1
Sidmouth Rd SALE M33 96 A7
Sidmouth St CHAD OL9 8 B8
DTN/ASHW M34 90 A5
Sidney Rd BKLY M9 73 G3
Sidney St BOLS/LL BL3 2 F8
CMANE M1 7 H9
CSLFD M3 6 B3
CSLFD M3 * 6 E5
LEIGH WN7 66 D7
OLD OL1 59 K3
Sidwell Wk ANC M4 * 88 A3
Siebers Bank WHIT OL12 * 28 A2
Siemens Rd IRL M44 94 B7
Siemens St HOR/BR BL6 33 M2
Sienna Cl IRL M44 94 B6
Signal Cl ECC M30 84 E2
Signal Dr NEWH/MOS M40 73 G6
Signet Wk CHH M8 72 E7
Silas St AUL OL6 * 76 A7
Silburn Wy MDTN M24 56 F5
Silchester Dr NEWH/MOS M40 73 G6
Silchester Wy BOLE BL2 37 H3
Silcock St GOL/RIS/CUL WA3 79 K4
Silfield Cl OP/CLY M11 88 B3
Silkhey Gv WALK M28 69 G3
Silkin Cl BRUN/LGST M13 7 J9
Silkstone St OP/CLY M11 88 F5
Silk St ANC M4 7 M1
CSLFD M3 6 A1
GLSP SK13 105 H3
LEIGH WN7 66 C7
MDTN M24 57 J4
NEWH/MOS M40 73 M6
ROCH OL11 28 A8
WHTN BL5 * 50 B3
Sillavan Wy CSLFD M3 6 C3
Sillitoe Dr WGNNW/ST WN6 14 C2
Silsbury Gv WGNNW/ST WN6 31 K4
Silsden Av BKLY M9 56 E7
GOL/RIS/CUL WA3 80 E4
Silton St BKLY M9 73 J5
Silverbirch Cl SALE M33 108 A2
Silver Birches DTN/ASHW M34 101 L3
Silver Birch Gv AIMK WN4 63 K7
SWIN M27 70 E6
Silver Birch Ms DUK SK16 91 H5
Silverbirch Wy FAIL M35 74 C5
Silver Cl DUK SK16 90 E5
Silvercroft St HULME M15 6 C8
Silverdale SWIN M27 70 D2
WGN WN1 47 M2
Silverdale Av CHAD OL9 58 D7
DTN/ASHW M34 101 K2
IRL M44 83 L8
PWCH M25 72 B2
WGNE/HIN WN2 48 D4
Silverdale Cl BURY BL9 5 J9
MPL/ROM SK6 123 G4
Silverdale Ct WGN WN1 15 J4
Silverdale Dr OLDE OL4 60 C6
WILM/AE SK9 126 E8
Silverdale Rd BOL BL1 35 M5
CCHDY M21 97 M3
CHD/CHDH SK8 110 E8
FWTH BL4 52 D3
HTNM SK4 99 M8
NEWLW WA12 78 E8
WGNE/HIN WN2 49 J7
WGNW/BIL/OR WN5 46 E4
Silverdale St OP/CLY M11 89 J5
Silver Hl MILN OL16 29 J6
Silver Hill Rd HYDE SK14 102 B3
Silver Jubilee Wk ANC M4 7 J3
Silverlea Dr BKLY M9 72 F2
Silvermere AUL OL6 76 B6
Silver Spring HYDE SK14 102 C4
Silverstone Dr NEWH/MOS M40 74 A8
Silver St BURY BL9 4 E5
CMANE M1 7 H5
IRL M44 83 L8
OLD OL1 9 H6
RAMS BL0 18 F6
WGNE/HIN WN2 64 E2
WHIT OL12 10 B2
WHTF M45 * 55 H3
Silver Ter WGN WN1 15 H4
Silverthorne Cl STLY SK15 91 K3
Silverton Cl HYDE SK14 103 G2
Silverton Gv BOL BL1 22 C8
MDTN M24 41 G8
Silverwell La BOL BL1 2 F5
Silverwell St BOL BL1 2 F5
NEWH/MOS M40 74 A7
Silverwell Yd BOL BL1 2 F5
Silverwood CHAD OL9 58 B5
Silverwood Av CCHDY M21 97 L4
Silvester St HOR/BR BL6 * 33 G2
Silvington Wy WGNE/HIN WN2 48 D2
Simeon St ANC M4 * 7 J1
MILN OL16 29 J6
Simfield Cl WGNNW/ST WN6 31 G3
Simister Dr BURY BL9 55 K2
Simister Gn PWCH M25 56 B4
Simister La MDTN M24 56 D3
PWCH M25 56 A4
Simister Rd FAIL M35 74 C5
Simister St BKLY M9 73 H4
Simkin Wy OLDS OL8 75 K3
Simmondley Gv GLSP SK13 104 D4
Simmondley La GLSP SK13 104 D4
Simmondley New Rd
GLSP SK13 104 D5
Simms Cl CSLFD M3 6 A3
Simonbury Cl TOT/BURYW BL8 38 C2
Simon Freeman Cl
BNG/LEV M19 99 M6
Simon La MDTN M24 56 D2
Simons Cl GLSP SK13 104 D5
SALE M33 108 D1
Simonsway NTHM/RTH M23 118 C1
Simpkin St WGNE/HIN WN2 64 E3
Simpson Av SWIN M27 70 F2
Simpson Gv WALK M28 68 D6
Simpson Hill Cl HEY OL10 41 J1
Simpson Rd WALK M28 68 E6
Simpson St ANC M4 7 J1
CHAD OL9 58 E8
EDGY/DAV SK3 * 13 H7
HYDE SK14 101 M1
OP/CLY M11 88 D3
WILM/AE SK9 * 126 D6
Sinclair Pl WGNW/BIL/OR WN5 47 H4
Sinclair St ROCH OL11 42 A1
Sinderland La ALT WA14 106 F3
ALT WA14 107 H3
Sinderland Rd ALT WA14 106 F3
ALT WA14 107 L4
Sindsley Gv BOLS/LL BL3 52 B1
Sindsley Rd SWIN M27 70 A2
Singapore Av MANAIR M90 118 C4
Singleton Av BOLE BL2 37 J5
Singleton Cl BRO M7 71 M3
Singleton Gv WHTN BL5 50 E4
Singleton Rd BRO M7 71 M3
HTNM SK4 99 L8
Singleton St RAD M26 38 A8
Sion St RAD M26 54 C2
Sirdar St OP/CLY M11 * 89 J4
Sirius Pl BRO M7 87 G1
Sir Matt Busby Wy TRPK M17 86 C7
Sir Richard Fairey Rd
HTNM SK4 99 K5
Sir Robert Thomas Ct
BKLY M9 * 73 G4
Siskin Cl LEIGH WN7 66 E7
Siskin Rd OFTN SK2 113 J7
Sisley Cl BRO M7 71 L4
Sisson St FAIL M35 74 B5
Sisters' St DROY M43 89 K4
Sitch La NM/HAY SK22 125 H1
Sittingbourne Rd WGN WN1 31 M8
Sixpools Gv WALK M28 68 F4
Sixth Av BOL BL1 35 L5
BOLS/LL BL3 37 J8
BURY BL9 26 A8
OLDS OL8 74 F3
Sixth St TRPK M17 86 A7
Size House Pl LEIGH WN7 * 66 D8
Size St WHIT OL12 20 B3
Skagen Ct BOL BL1 2 D1
Skaife Rd SALE M33 97 H8
Skarratt Cl WGTN/LGST M12 88 C6
Skegness Cl TOT/BURYW BL8 25 G7
Skellorn Green La
MCFLDN SK10 129 J4
Skelton Gv BOLE BL2 37 J4
BRUN/LGST M13 99 J2
Skelton Rd ALT WA14 108 B5
STRET M32 97 G1
Skelton St AIMK WN4 63 J6
Skelwith Av BOLS/LL BL3 52 C2
Skelwith Cl URM M41 84 D8
Skerry Cl BRUN/LGST M13 7 K9
Skerton Rd OLDTF/WHR M16 86 E8
Skiddaw Cl MDTN M24 57 G1
Skiddaw Pl WGNW/BIL/OR WN5 46 F6
Skip Pl ANC M4 87 K1
Skipton Av CHAD OL9 58 C3
NEWH/MOS M40 74 A3
WGNE/HIN WN2 49 K8
Skipton Cl BRAM/HZG SK7 121 L4
RDSH SK5 100 B4
TOT/BURYW BL8 38 C2

Skipton Dr URM M41 ... 84 C7
Skipton St BOLE BL2 ... 3 L4
  OLDS OL8 ... 59 L8
Skipton Wk BOLE BL2 ... 3 L4
Skull House La
  WGNW/ST NW6 ... 30 A4
Skye Cl HEY OL10 ... 40 C3
Skye Rd MPL/ROM SK6 ... 114 A1
Skye Rd URM M41 ... 85 G7
Slackcote La UPML OL3 ... 44 F5
Slackey Brow FWTH BL4 ... 53 M7
Slackey Fold
  WGNE/HIN WN2 ... 65 L3
Slack Fold La FWTH BL4 ... 52 A3
Slack Ga WHIT OL12 ... 20 C4
Slack Gate La OL3 ... 65 C4
Slack Hall OLDE OL4 ... 60 C4
Slack La BOLE BL2 ... 23 H5
  SWIN M27 ... 70 D3
  UPML OL3 ... 45 G6
  WHTN BL5 ... 50 C2
Slack Rd BKLY M9 ... 72 F3
Slack St HYDE SK14 ... 91 J8
  MILN OL16 ... 10 F4
Slade Gv BRUN/LGST M13 ... 99 J1
Slade Hall Rd
  WGTN/LGST M12 ... 99 K2
Slade La BNG/LEV M19 ... 99 J4
  MCFLDN SK10 ... 131 H7
Slade Mt BNG/LEV M19 * ... 99 J4
Sladen St WHIT OL12 ... 10 E1
Slade St BOLS/LL BL3 ... 53 K1
Slades View Gv UPML OL3 ... 45 M7
Slag La GOL/RIS/CUL WA3 ... 80 C2
Slaidburn Av BOLE BL2 ... 37 J6
Slaidburn Cl MILN OL16 ... 29 J7
  WGNS/IIMK WN3 ... 63 K1
Slaidburn Crs
  GOL/RIS/CUL WA3 ... 79 J2
Slaidburn Dr TOT/BURYW BL8 ... 38 B1
Slaithwaite Dr OP/CLY M11 ... 88 F2
Slant Cl GLSP SK13 ... 105 G4
Slateacre Rd HYDE SK14 ... 102 C5
Slate Av ANC M4 ... 7 M4
Slatelands Av GLSP SK13 ... 104 E4
Slatelands Rd GLSP SK13 ... 104 E4
Slate La AULW OL7 ... 90 B4
  DTN/ASHW M34 ... 89 M4
Slaterfield BOLS/LL BL3 * ... 3 G2
Slater La BOL BL1 ... 2 D2
Slater's Nook WHTN BL5 ... 50 B3
Slater St BOL BL1 ... 2 D2
  CHAD OL9 ... 6 G6
  ECC M30 ... 84 C2
  FAIL M35 ... 74 C3
  FWTH BL4 ... 53 C4
Slater St North LEIGH WN7 ... 66 A7
Slate Whf HULME M15 * ... 6 B7
Slawson Wy HEY OL10 ... 41 J1
Sleaford Cl NEWH/MOS M40 ... 88 A1
  TOT/BURYW BL8 ... 25 G7
Sledbrook St
  WGNW/BIL/OR WN5 * ... 46 F7
Sleddale Cl OFTN SK2 ... 113 G2
Sledmere Cl BOL BL1 ... 36 C2
  OP/CLY M11 ... 88 D3
Sledmoor Rd NTHM/RTH M23 ... 109 J3
Slimbridge Cl BOLE BL2 ... 37 K3
Sloane Av OLDE OL6 ... 91 K4
Sloane St BOLS/LL BL3 ... 51 L1
  OP/CLY M11 ... 88 C2
Smallbridge Cl WALK M28 ... 68 F4
Smallbrook La LEIGH WN7 ... 66 E1
Smallbrook Rd ROY/SHW OL2 ... 43 M2
Smalldale Av OLDTF/WHR M16 ... 98 C1
Smalley St ROCH OL11 ... 41 M2
  WGNNW/ST WN6 ... 31 H3
Smallfield Dr BKLY M9 ... 73 C4
Smallridge Cl NEWH/MOS M40 ... 88 A1
Smallshaw Cl AIMK WN4 ... 78 D2
Smallshaw La AUL OL6 ... 75 M7
Smallwood St NEWH/MOS M40 ... 73 M6
Smart St WGTN/LGST M12 ... 99 K1
Smeaton Cl STRET M32 ... 97 H2
Smeaton St CHH M8 ... 72 F4
  HOR/BR BL6 ... 33 M2
Smedley Av BOLS/LL BL3 ... 52 D1
Smedley La CH M8 ... 72 E6
Smedley Rd CHH M8 ... 72 E6
Smethurst Hall Rd BURY BL9 ... 26 C8
Smethurst La BOLS/LL BL3 ... 51 L2
  WGNW/BIL/OR WN5 ... 46 F7
Smethurst St BKLY M9 ... 73 G3
  HEY OL10 ... 40 E2
  MDTN M24 ... 58 A5
  TOT/BURYW BL8 ... 24 E8
  WGNW/BIL/OR WN5 ... 46 F7
Smith Av WGNW/BIL/OR WN5 ... 46 E4
Smith Brow HOR/BR BL6 ... 32 F2
Smithfold La WALK M28 ... 68 D1
Smith Hl MILN OL16 ... 29 J8
Smithies Av MDTN M24 ... 57 K2
Smithies St HEY OL10 ... 41 H2
Smithills Croft Rd BOL BL1 ... 35 L1
Smithills Dr BOL BL1 ... 35 J2
Smithills Hall Cl RAMS BL0 ... 18 E8
Smith La EDGW/EG BL7 ... 22 F1
Smith's La WGNE/HIN WN2 ... 65 K4
Smiths Lawn WILM/AE SK9 ... 126 E7
Smith's Rd BOLS/LL BL3 ... 53 G1
Smith St ATH M46 * ... 67 H3
  AULW OL7 ... 90 C3
  BURY BL9 ... 5 H2
  CHD/CHDH SK8 * ... 111 J4
  DTN/ASHW M34 ... 101 J2
  HEY OL10 ... 41 G2
  HYDE SK14 ... 91 G8
  LEIGH WN7 ... 66 D7
  LIT OL15 ... 21 M7
  MILN OL16 ... 10 F4
  MOSL OL5 ... 76 E2
  OLDE OL4 ... 60 B4
  OLDTF/WHR M16 ... 86 E7
  RAMS BL0 ... 18 E7
  WALK M28 ... 69 G1
  WGNE/HIN WN2 ... 32 B7
Smithwood Av WGNE/HIN WN2 ... 49 J6
Smithybridge Rd LIT OL15 ... 29 J1
  MILN OL16 ... 21 J8
Smithy Cl GLSP SK13 ... 105 G3
Smithy Cft EDGW/EG BL7 ... 22 F1
Smithy Fold WHIT OL12 ... 27 M3
Smithy Fold Rd HYDE SK14 ... 102 B4
Smithy Glen Dr
  WGNW/BIL/OR WN5 ... 46 B8
Smithy Gn CHD/CHDH SK8 * ... 120 C4
  MPL/ROM SK6 ... 101 L7
  WGNE/HIN WN2 ... 48 C5
Smithy Gv AUL OL6 ... 75 M8
Smithy Hl BOLS/LL BL3 ... 35 K8

Smithy La ALT WA14 ... 116 A1
  CSLFD M3 * ... 6 E4
  HYDE SK14 ... 102 B3
  MCFLDN SK10 ... 131 M2
  MPL/ROM SK6 ... 115 J3
  PART M31 ... 106 C1
  UPML OL3 ... 61 L4
Smithy St HEY OL10 ... 121 M1
  LEIGH WN7 ... 66 C8
  RAMS BL0 ... 18 F6
Smock La AIMK WN4 ... 62 F8
Smyrna St HEY OL10 ... 40 F3
  OLDE OL4 * ... 59 M7
  ORD M5 ... 86 B3
  RAD M26 ... 38 C8
Snake Pass GLSP SK13 ... 105 M4
Snape St RAD M26 ... 38 C7
Snell St ANC M4 ... 88 A3
Snipe Av ROCH OL11 ... 27 J5
Snipe Cl POY/DIS SK12 ... 128 E1
Snipe Rd OLDS OL8 ... 75 L2
Snipe St BOLS/LL BL3 ... 2 F1
Snipe Wy AULW OL7 ... 90 A3
Snowden Av URM M41 ... 95 L4
  WGNS/IIMK WN3 ... 47 K8
Snowden St BOL BL1 ... 2 C3
  HEY OL10 ... 41 H4
  OLDS OL8 ... 59 J8
Snowdon Rd ECC M30 ... 85 K1
Snowdon St ROCH OL11 ... 42 D2
Snow Hill Rd BOLS/LL BL3 ... 37 G7
Snydale Cl WHTN BL5 ... 50 D2
Snydale Wy BOLS/LL BL3 ... 51 G2
  WHTN BL5 ... 50 D2
Soane Cl AIMK WN4 ... 79 G1
Soapstone Wy IRL M44 ... 94 D4
Soap St ANC M4 ... 7 H3
Society St ROY/SHW OL2 ... 43 L5
Sofa Cl BOL BL1 ... 35 L3
Soham Cl WGNE/HIN WN2 ... 49 H8
Soho St BOL BL1 ... 2 E6
  OLDE OL4 ... 59 L5
  WGNW/BIL/OR WN5 ... 14 A5
Solent Av CHH M8 ... 72 D2
Solent Dr BOLS/LL BL3 ... 3 M8
Sole St WGN WN1 ... 15 L1
Solness St BURY BL9 ... 25 J6
Soloman Rd ALT WA14 ... 107 M3
Solway Cl AIMK WN4 ... 63 K8
  BOLS/LL BL3 ... 52 A1
  OLDS OL8 ... 9 H9
  SWIN M27 ... 54 B8
Solway Rd WYTH/NTH M22 ... 110 B4
Somerby Dr WYTH/NTH M22 ... 118 C3
Somerdale Av BOL BL1 ... 35 K5
Somerfield Av BKLY M9 ... 73 C3
Somerfield Rd BKLY M9 ... 73 G3
Somerford Rd RDSH SK5 ... 100 D2
Somersby Dr EDGW/EG BL7 ... 22 C4
Somerset Av ROY/SHW OL2 ... 43 J5
  TYLD M29 ... 67 J1
Somerset Cl IRL M44 ... 94 E4
  RDSH SK5 ... 100 F8
Somerset Dr BURY BL9 ... 5 G9
Somerset Gv ROCH OL11 ... 27 K4
Somerset Pl SALE M33 ... 96 E6
Somerset Rd ALT WA14 ... 108 A6
  ATH M46 ... 66 E4
  BOL BL1 ... 35 L4
  DROY M43 ... 89 K1
  ECC M30 ... 70 D8
  FAIL M35 ... 74 B6
  WGNW/BIL/OR WN5 ... 46 F6
Somerset St OLDE OL4 ... 59 M6
Somers Rd RDSH SK5 ... 100 C3
Somerton Av SALE M33 ... 108 F1
  WYTH/NTH M22 ... 118 E1
Somerton Cl WGNNW/ST WN6 ... 31 C3
Somerton Rd BOLE BL2 ... 37 J7
Somerville Gdns
  HALE/TIMP WA15 ... 108 C5
Somerville Rd WGN WN1 ... 31 M8
Somerville Sq BOL BL1 ... 35 M1
Somerville St BOL BL1 ... 35 M1
Somerwood Wk
  WGTN/LGST M12 * ... 88 C6
Sonning Dr BOLS/LL BL3 ... 51 K2
Sopwith Dr RUSH/FAL M14 ... 98 D3
Sorby Rd IRL M44 ... 94 D5
Sorrel Bank SLFD M6 ... 71 J4
Sorrel Dr LIT OL15 ... 21 K6
Sorrell Bank RDSH SK5 ... 100 A4
Sorrel St HULME M15 ... 87 H6
Sorrel Wy OLDE OL4 ... 60 B2
Sorton St CMANE M1 * ... 7 H8
Sossmoss La MCFLDN SK10 ... 130 A6
Soudan Rd OFTN SK2 ... 112 D6
Soudan St MDTN M24 ... 57 M3
Sougher's La AIMK WN4 ... 63 J6
The Sound UPML OL3 ... 45 J8
Sourace Fold STLY SK15 ... 91 L1
South Acre Dr WILM/AE SK9 ... 127 H1
Southall St CSLFD M3 ... 87 J1
Southampton Cl BRO M7 ... 72 C7
Southam St BRO M7 ... 72 C5
South Av BNG/LEV M19 ... 99 J5
  FWTH BL4 ... 53 J7
  HEY OL10 ... 40 E2
  LEIGH WN7 ... 81 M1
  SWIN M27 ... 70 A7
  UPML OL3 ... 61 L6
  URM M41 ... 85 H6
  WHTF M45 ... 55 H3
South Back Rock BURY BL9 ... 4 F4
South Bank WILM/AE SK9 * ... 130 E2
Southbank BNG/LEV M19 ... 99 G7
South Bank Rd BURY BL9 ... 4 D7
Southbourne Av URM M41 ... 96 C2
Southbourne St SLFD M6 ... 86 B2
Southbrook Av CHH M8 ... 72 C1
Southbrook Cl GLSP SK13 ... 93 H8
Southbrook Gv BOLS/LL BL3 ... 52 C1
Southcliffe Rd RDSH SK5 ... 100 C6
South Cliffe St OP/CLY M11 ... 89 J3
South Cl BURY BL9 ... 55 K1
  GLSP SK13 ... 93 J7
  WILM/AE SK9 ... 126 D6
Southcourt LEIGH WN7 ... 66 E6
South Crs NEWH/MOS M40 ... 74 A1
  OP/CLY M11 ... 89 G2
South Cft OLDS OL8 ... 75 L1
Southcross Rd GTN M18 ... 100 A1
South Croston St
  OLDTF/WHR M16 ... 87 G4
Southdene Av DID/WITH M20 ... 98 B8
Southdown Cl HTNM SK4 ... 12 F2
  ROCH OL11 ... 27 M8
Southdown Crs BKLY M9 ... 73 K2
  CHD/CHDH SK8 ... 120 B4
Southdown Dr WALK M28 ... 68 C6

Southdowns Cl ROY/SHW OL2 ... 43 J4
South Downs Dr ALT WA14 ... 116 H4
South Downs Rd ALT WA14 ... 116 F3
South Dr BOLE BL2 ... 37 H1
  CCHDY M21 ... 97 L5
  CHD/CHDH SK8 ... 110 D8
  HALE/TIMP WA15 ... 108 D5
  WILM/AE SK9 ... 126 F6
Southend Av HULME M15 ... 87 G6
Southend St BOLS/LL BL3 ... 51 M1
Southern Ap SWIN M27 ... 70 F7
Southernby Cl
  BRUN/LGST M13 * ... 88 C8
Southern Cl BRAM/HZG SK7 ... 121 H3
  DTN/ASHW M34 ... 101 H4
Southern Crs BRAM/HZG SK7 ... 121 H3
Southern Rd SALE M33 ... 96 B6
Southern's Fold
  WGNE/HIN WN2 ... 48 D1
Southern St CSLFD M3 ... 6 D7
  SLFD M6 ... 86 B2
  WALK M28 ... 53 C7
  WGNW/BIL/OR WN5 ... 47 G7
Southey Cl LIT OL15 ... 29 J2
Southfield Av BURY BL9 ... 25 H6
Southfield Cl DUK SK16 ... 91 G6
Southfield Dr WHTN BL5 ... 50 C5
Southfields Av OP/CLY M11 ... 88 F2
Southfields Dr
  HALE/TIMP WA15 ... 108 D5
Southfield St BOLS/LL BL3 ... 36 M5
South Gdns TYLD M29 * ... 67 K7
Southgarth Rd SLFD M6 ... 86 B1
Southgate BOLE BL2 ... 23 H8
  OLDE OL4 ... 60 A7
Southgate Av
  NEWH/MOS M40 * ... 73 K8
Southgate College Land
  CSLFD M3 ... 6 E4
Southgate Rd BURY BL9 ... 55 J1
  CHAD OL9 ... 74 B1
Southgate St OLD OL1 ... 9 K6
South Gv BRUN/LGST M13 ... 88 A7
  SALE M33 ... 108 E1
  WALK M28 ... 68 F2
  WILM/AE SK9 ... 130 D3
Southgrove Av BOL BL1 ... 22 B6
South Hey LEIGH WN7 ... 65 M7
South Hi OLDE OL4 ... 60 C7
South Hill St OLDE OL4 ... 9 M7
South King St CSLFD M3 ... 6 E4
  ECC M30 ... 84 E2
Southlands Av ECC M30 ... 84 C4
  WGNNW/ST WN6 ... 31 H4
South La TYLD M29 ... 67 K7
South Langworthy Rd ORD M5 ... 86 C3
Southlea Rd DID/WITH M20 ... 99 G7
Southleigh Dr BOLE BL2 ... 37 K6
Southlink OLDE OL4 * ... 9 M6
South Lonsdale St STRET M32 ... 97 H1
South Marlow St GLSP SK13 ... 93 K8
South Mdw POY/DIS SK12 ... 121 K7
South Meade CCHDY M21 ... 97 L5
  HALE/TIMP WA15 ... 108 D5
  PWCH M25 ... 72 A2
South Meadway
  MPL/ROM SK6 ... 123 H5
Southmere Cl BKLY M9 ... 73 M2
South Mesnefield Rd BRO M7 ... 71 K5
Southmill St CMANW M2 ... 6 E6
Southmoor Rd
  NTHM/RTH M23 ... 109 H7
Southmoor Wk BOLS/LL BL3 * ... 2 C9
South Oak La WILM/AE SK9 ... 126 D6
Southover WHTN BL5 ... 50 B6
South Pde BRAM/HZG SK7 ... 121 H2
  MILN OL16 ... 10 E4
South Park Dr POY/DIS SK12 ... 122 A8
South Park Rd CHD/CHDH SK8 ... 110 E6
Southpool Cl BRAM/HZG SK7 ... 121 J2
South Pump St CMANE M1 * ... 7 J6
South Radford St BRO M7 ... 71 K5
South Rdg DTN/ASHW M34 ... 90 C7
South Rd ALT WA14 ... 116 E2
  DID/WITH M20 ... 110 E2
  STRET M32 ... 85 K8
  SWIN M27 ... 71 G2
  TRPK M17 ... 85 M8
South Rw PWCH M25 ... 71 J3
South Royd St TOT/BURYW BL8 ... 24 C5
Southsea St OP/CLY M11 ... 89 G5
Southside MPL/ROM SK6 ... 101 H6
  WILM/AE SK9 ... 118 D8
South St ATH M46 ... 67 H3
  AULW OL7 ... 90 B4
  BOLS/LL BL3 ... 52 B1
  MILN OL16 ... 11 G3
  OLDS OL8 ... 74 E2
  OP/CLY M11 ... 88 F5
  RAMS BL0 ... 19 G6
  WGTN/LGST M12 ... 88 B7
  WHIT OL12 ... 28 A1
South Ter BURY BL9 ... 39 G5
South Terrace Ct MILN OL16 ... 11 H9
South Vale Crs
  HALE/TIMP WA15 ... 108 C7
South Vw ATH M46 ... 66 F1
  MPL/ROM SK6 ... 101 M6
  RDSH SK5 ... 100 C1
  ROCH OL11 ... 27 H6
  STLY SK15 ... 77 J6
South View Gdns
  CHD/CHDH SK8 ... 119 L1
Southview Rd GLSP SK13 ... 105 J3
South View Rd MILN OL16 ... 29 H1
South View St BOLE BL2 ... 3 M5
South View Ter MILN OL16 ... 21 J8
Southview Wk OLDE OL4 * ... 60 B3
Southward Rd RNFD/HAY WA11 ... 78 D1
Southwark Dr DUK SK16 ... 91 G6
Southway ALT WA14 ... 108 B6
  AULW OL7 ... 75 K6
  DROY M43 ... 89 K4
  NEWH/MOS M40 ... 74 C2
South Wy OLDS OL8 ... 75 H2
Southwell Cl BOL BL1 ... 35 J3
  GOL/RIS/CUL WA3 ... 79 M4
  MPL/ROM SK6 ... 113 K3
Southwell Gdns AUL OL6 ... 75 L4
Southwell St NEWH/MOS M40 ... 73 H5
Southwick Rd NTHM/RTH M23 ... 109 K2
South William St CSLFD M3 * ... 6 A4
Southwood Cl BOLS/LL BL3 ... 52 C1
Southwood Dr BKLY M9 ... 72 F1
South Woodley Gdns RAD M26 ... 54 B4

Southwood Rd OFTN SK2 ... 112 E8
Southworth Rd NEWLW WA12 ... 79 J8
Southyard St BNG/LEV M19 * ... 99 J1
Sovereign Cl
  GOL/RIS/CUL WA3 ... 80 B5
Sovereign Fold Rd LEIGH WN7 ... 66 B4
Sovereign Rd WGN WN1 ... 15 H6
Sowerby Cl SLFD M6 ... 71 K8
Sowerby Cl TOT/BURYW BL8 ... 38 C2
Spa Cl RDSH SK5 ... 100 B4
Spa Crs LHULT M38 ... 52 D6
Spa Gv LHULT M38 ... 52 D6
Spa La LHULT M38 ... 52 D6
  OLDE OL4 ... 60 A7
Spalding Dr NTHM/RTH M23 ... 118 C2
Sparkford Av NTHM/RTH M23 ... 109 C3
Sparkle St CMANE M1 ... 7 K5
Sparrow Cl RDSH SK5 ... 100 B2
Sparrowfield Cl STLY SK15 ... 77 H5
Sparrow Hl MILN OL16 ... 10 D5
Sparrow St ROY/SHW OL2 ... 59 H2
Sparta Av WALK M28 ... 68 F2
Sparta Wk OP/CLY M11 ... 88 C2
Sparth Bottoms Rd ROCH OL11 ... 10 B6
Sparthfield Av ROCH OL11 ... 10 C9
Sparthfield Rd HTNM SK4 ... 12 E1
Sparth La HTNM SK4 ... 12 E1
Sparth Rd NEWH/MOS M40 ... 74 A7
Spa St HULME M15 ... 87 L7
Spath Cl WILM/AE SK9 ... 119 M4
Spath La East CHD/CHDH SK8 ... 120 D7
Spath Rd DID/WITH M20 ... 110 D1
Spath Wk CHD/CHDH SK8 ... 120 D7
Spawell Cl GOL/RIS/CUL WA3 ... 80 B3
Spaw St CSLFD M3 ... 6 C3
Speakman Av LEIGH WN7 ... 66 E7
  NEWLW WA12 ... 78 F7
Spear St CMANE M1 ... 7 J4
Spectator St ANC M4 ... 88 A3
Speedwell Cl GLSP SK13 ... 93 J5
  GOL/RIS/CUL WA3 ... 80 B4
Spelding Dr WGNNW/ST WN6 ... 31 G8
Spencer Av BOLS/LL BL3 ... 53 M1
  HYDE SK14 ... 91 G7
  OLDTF/WHR M16 ... 97 M7
  WHTF M45 ... 55 H2
Spencer La ROCH OL11 ... 27 H7
Spencer Rd West
  WGNNW/ST WN6 ... 47 K1
Spencer's La
  WGNW/BIL/OR WN5 ... 46 A5
Spencer St CHAD OL9 ... 58 E8
  DUK SK16 ... 90 F4
  ECC M30 ... 84 F3
  MOSL OL5 ... 76 E2
  OLD OL1 ... 9 M3
  RAD M26 * ... 38 F8
  RAMS BL0 ... 18 E7
  RDSH SK5 ... 100 C4
  TOT/BURYW BL8 ... 4 A3
Spender Av CHH M8 ... 72 D6
Spen Fold LIT OL15 ... 21 L8
  TOT/BURYW BL8 ... 17 M8
Spenleach La TOT/BURYW BL8 ... 17 M8
Spenlow LEIGH WN7 ... 81 M1
Spenlow Cl POY/DIS SK12 ... 129 J3
Spennithorne Rd URM M41 ... 95 L2
Spenser St DTN/ASHW M34 ... 101 K4
  RAD M26 ... 38 D8
Spenwood Rd LIT OL15 ... 21 K7
Spey Cl ALT WA14 ... 107 M6
Speyside Cl WHTF M45 * ... 55 K4
Spilsby Sq WGNS/IIMK WN3 ... 63 K2
Spindle Av STLY SK15 ... 91 M1
Spindle Cft FWTH BL4 ... 53 G8
Spindle Hillock AIMK WN4 ... 63 G8
Spindlepoint Dr WALK M28 ... 68 D4
Spindle Wk WHTN BL5 ... 50 C6
Spindlewood Cl STLY SK15 ... 92 A2
Spindlewood Rd
  WGNS/IIMK WN3 ... 15 L8
Spingfield St BOLS/LL BL3 ... 36 D8
Spingdale LHULT M38 ... 52 A6
Spinks St OLDE OL4 ... 59 L7
Spinnerbottom NM/HAY SK22 ... 125 D8
Spinnerette Cl LEIGH WN7 ... 66 D7
Spinners Gdns WHIT OL12 ... 21 G8
Spinners Gn WHIT OL12 ... 28 C2
Spinners La POY/DIS SK12 ... 121 L8
Spinners Ms BOL BL1 ... 2 A2
Spinners Wy OLDE OL4 ... 44 C8
Spinney Cl GLSP SK13 ... 104 F2
Spinney Dr BURY BL9 ... 25 J6
  SALE M33 ... 108 A1
Spinney Gv DTN/ASHW M34 ... 90 C7
Spinney Nook BOLE BL2 ... 37 K6
Spinney Rd NTHM/RTH M23 ... 109 J3
The Spinney CHD/CHDH SK8 ... 120 A1
  EDGW/EG BL7 ... 22 F2
  OLDE OL4 ... 60 D4
  URM M41 ... 95 K2
  WALK M28 ... 69 M6
  WGNW/BIL/OR WN5 ... 47 H7
  WHIT OL12 ... 28 A1
  WHTF M45 ... 54 F5
Spinningfields BOL BL1 * ... 2 A2
Spinningfield Wy HEY OL10 ... 41 G5
Spinning Jenny Wk ANC M4 * ... 7 M3
Spinning Jenny Wy LEIGH WN7 ... 66 D8
Spinning Meadow BOL BL1 ... 2 B2
Spinning Mdw BOL BL1 ... 2 B2
The Spinnings BURY BL9 * ... 24 F1
Spion Kop AIMK WN4 ... 78 E1
Spiredale Brow
  WGNNW/ST WN6 ... 31 J3
Spire Hollin GLSP SK13 ... 104 F3
Spires Cft LEIGH WN7 ... 81 L3
Spire Wk WGTN/LGST M12 * ... 88 A4
Spirewood Gdns
  MPL/ROM SK6 ... 113 K2
Spodden Fold WHIT OL12 ... 19 H3
Spodden St WHIT OL12 ... 10 A3
Spod Rd WHIT OL12 ... 27 M3
Spokeshave Wy MILN OL16 ... 28 F3
Sportside Av WALK M28 ... 69 H2
Sportside Cl WALK M28 * ... 69 H1
Sportside Gv WALK M28 ... 69 H1
Sportsmans Dr OLDS OL8 ... 75 K1
Sportsman St LEIGH WN7 ... 66 D7
Spotland Rd WHIT OL12 ... 10 B2
Spotland Tops WHIT OL12 ... 27 J1
Spreadbury St NEWH/MOS M40 ... 73 K5
Spring Av HYDE SK14 ... 102 C4
  WHTF M45 ... 55 H2
Springbank CHAD OL9 ... 58 D5
  GLSP SK13 ... 93 J7

Spring Bank GLSP SK13 * ... 104 E4
  STLY SK15 ... 91 L4
Spring Bank Av AUL OL6 ... 75 L7
  DTN/ASHW M34 ... 90 A5
Springbank Cl MPL/ROM SK6 ... 101 M6
Springbank Gdns
  NM/HAY SK22 ... 124 D4
Spring Bank La ROCH OL11 ... 27 H4
  STLY SK15 ... 76 F7
Spring Bank Pl STKP SK1 * ... 13 H6
Springbank Rd MPL/ROM SK6 ... 101 M6
Spring Bank Rd NM/HAY SK22 ... 124 E4
Springbourne
  WGNNW/ST WN6 ... 47 J2
Spring Bridge Rd
  OLDTF/WHR M16 ... 98 C2
Springburn Cl HOR/BR BL6 ... 34 A3
  WALK M28 ... 68 D6
Spring Cl AULW OL7 ... 75 K6
  OLDE OL4 ... 60 A7
  RAMS BL0 ... 18 E8
  TOT/BURYW BL8 ... 24 B6
Spring Clough WALK M28 ... 69 J2
Spring Clough Av WALK M28 ... 69 J2
Spring Clough Dr OLDS OL8 ... 59 M8
  WALK M28 ... 69 J2
Springdale Gdns
  DID/WITH M20 ... 110 D1
Springfield GLSP SK13 ... 103 M6
  RAD M26 ... 53 M6
  URM M41 ... 95 M3
Springfield Av BRAM/HZG SK7 ... 121 M1
  CHH M8 ... 72 A4
  GOL/RIS/CUL WA3 ... 94 B5
  LIT OL15 ... 21 G5
  MPL/ROM SK6 * ... 114 C5
Springfield Cl FAIL M35 ... 74 B4
  GLSP SK13 ... 93 J6
Springfield Dr WILM/AE SK9 ... 126 E7
Springfield Gdns FWTH BL4 ... 53 M6
Springfield Gdns CSLFD M3 ... 6 D1
  IRL M44 ... 94 C2
  MILN OL16 ... 29 C1
  ROY/SHW OL2 ... 42 F5
Springfield Rd ALT WA14 ... 108 A3
  ATH M46 ... 51 H8
  BOL BL1 ... 22 B5
  CHD/CHDH SK8 ... 110 E7
  DROY M43 ... 89 J1
  FWTH BL4 ... 52 D3
  FWTH BL4 ... 53 J6
  HOR/BR BL6 ... 34 A4
  MDTN M24 ... 57 J2
  RAMS BL0 ... 24 D2
  SALE M33 ... 96 E6
  WGNE/HIN WN2 ... 48 D5
  WGNNW/ST WN6 ... 47 J2
Springfield St AUL OL6 ... 76 B7
  DTN/ASHW M34 ... 90 C6
  HEY OL10 ... 40 D2
  WGN WN1 ... 47 M2
Springfield Ter NM/HAY SK22 * ... 125 M2
Spring Gdns BOLE BL2 ... 23 J8
  BRAM/HZG SK7 ... 121 M1
  CMANW M2 ... 7 G4
  GLSP SK13 ... 93 J7
  HALE/TIMP WA15 ... 108 F7
  HYDE SK14 ... 91 G8
  MDTN M24 ... 57 K2
  SLFD M6 ... 86 C1
  STKP SK1 ... 13 M5
  WGN WN1 ... 14 D3
Spring Garden St ROY/SHW OL2 ... 43 G8
Spring Gv UPML OL3 ... 61 L7
  WGN WN1 ... 15 J5
  WHTF M45 ... 55 H2
Spring Hall Cl OLDE OL4 ... 44 C8
Springhead Av DID/WITH M20 ... 98 D5
  OLDE OL4 ... 60 C7
Springhill ROY/SHW OL2 ... 43 G8
Spring La OLDE OL4 ... 60 B7
  RAD M26 ... 54 E7
Springlawn BOL BL1 ... 35 J4
Springlawns BOL BL1 ... 35 J4
Springmeadow GLSP SK13 ... 104 A5
Spring Meadow La UPML OL3 ... 61 M4
Spring Mill Wk MILN OL16 ... 28 F2
Springmount GOL/RIS/CUL WA3 ... 80 B5
Spring Mt NM/HAY SK22 ... 124 E4
Spring Pl WHIT OL12 ... 20 B2
Springpool WGNS/IIMK WN3 ... 62 E2
Spring Ri GLSP SK13 ... 104 C5
  ROY/SHW OL2 ... 43 K3
Spring Rd ALT WA14 ... 116 E2
  POY/DIS SK12 ... 129 K2
  WGNW/BIL/OR WN5 ... 46 C4
Springside HTNM SK4 ... 100 A5
Springside Av WALK M28 ... 69 H1
Springside Cl WALK M28 * ... 69 H1
Springside Gv WALK M28 ... 69 H1
Springside Rd BURY BL9 ... 25 H4
Springside Vw TOT/BURYW BL8 ... 24 F5
Springside Wk HULME M15 * ... 87 G6
Springs La STLY SK15 ... 76 C8
Springs Rd MDTN M24 ... 58 B6
The Springs ALT WA14 ... 116 D2
  ROCH OL11 ... 27 H9
Spring St BOLS/LL BL3 ... 3 H5
  BURY BL9 ... 5 G6
  FWTH BL4 ... 53 G3
  GLSP SK13 ... 104 E4
  HYDE SK14 ... 92 F7
  MOSL OL5 ... 76 F2
  OLDE OL4 ... 59 M4
  RAMS BL0 ... 18 E6
  STLY SK15 ... 91 K2
  TOT/BURYW BL8 ... 24 B5
  TOT/BURYW BL8 ... 24 D8
  UPML OL3 * ... 61 L4
  WGN WN1 ... 15 J5
  WGNS/IIMK WN3 ... 48 B8
  WGTN/LGST M12 ... 99 K3
  WILM/AE SK9 ... 126 E5
Spring Ter CHAD OL9 ... 58 D5
  MILN OL16 ... 43 L1
Spring Thyme Fold LIT OL15 ... 21 L7
Spring V BRAM/HZG SK7 * ... 122 A2
  MDTN M24 ... 57 K2
  PWCH M25 ... 71 K2
Springvale Cl AULW OL7 ... 75 J7
Spring Vale Dr TOT/BURYW BL8 ... 24 B6
Spring Vale St NM/HAY SK22 ... 125 M2
Spring Vale St TOT/BURYW BL8 ... 24 C6
Spring Vale Ter LIT OL15 * ... 21 M7
Spring Vw BURY BL9 ... 26 A7
Springville Av BKLY M9 ... 73 J5
Springwater Av RAMS BL0 ... 37 H1
Springwater Cl BOLE BL2 ... 37 H1
Spring Water Dr GLSP SK13 ... 104 B1
Springwater La WHTF M45 ... 55 H2

Springwell Cl *SLFD* M6 * 86 B2
Springwell Gdns *HYDE* SK14 ....103 H3
Springwood *GLSP* SK13 ....104 C4
  UPML OL3 ....45 H7
Springwood Av *CHAD* OL9 ....58 B4
  SWIN M27 ....70 E6
Springwood Crs
  MPL/ROM SK6 ....114 B2
Springwood Hall Rd *OLDS* OL8 ......75 K2
Springwood La *MPL/ROM* SK6 .....114 C2
Spring Wood St *RAMS* BL0 ....18 E5
Spruce Av *BURY* BL9 ....5 L4
Spruce Cl *SLFD* M6 ....86 E2
Spruce Crs *BURY* BL9 ....25 J5
Spruce Rd *WGNNW/ST* WN6 ....47 H1
Spruce St *HULME* M15 ....87 H6
  MILN OL16 * 11 H5
  RAMS BL0 ....18 D8
Sprucewood *CHAD* OL9 ....58 A4
Spurn La *UPML* OL3 ....61 L1
The Spur *OLDE* OL3 ....75 K2
Square St *RAMS* BL0 ....18 F6
The Square *DUK* SK16 * 91 J5
  HALE/TIMP WA15 ....117 L4
  HTNM SK4 ....12 C1
  SWIN M27 ....70 B7
  UPML OL3 ....61 K2
  WHTF M45 ....55 H4
Squire St *CHH* M8 ....72 C5
Squires La *TYLD* M29 ....67 H4
Squirrel Dr *ALT* WA14 ....107 M4
Squirrel's Jump *WILM/AE* SK9 ......130 E3
Stablefold *MOSL* OL5 ....76 F4
Stable Fold *RAD* M26 ....38 D8
Stablefold *WALK* M28 ....69 K7
Stableford Av *ECC* M30 ....69 K5
The Stables *DROY* M43 ....90 A1
  WHIT OL12 ....20 A3
Stable St *CHAD* OL9 ....74 D2
The Stablings *WILM/AE* SK9 ....126 E2
Stadium Wy *WGNNW/ST* WN6 ....14 B4
  WGNW/BIL/OR WN5 .....47 H3
Stafford Cl *GLSP* SK13 ....105 J3
Stafford Rd *ECC* M30 ....85 H1
  FAIL M35 ....74 D2
  SWIN M27 ....70 C4
  WALK M28 ....68 F3
Stafford St *CHAD* OL9 ....58 F8
  LEIGH WN7 ....67 G8
  NM/HAY SK22 ....124 B3
  TOT/BURYW BL8 ....25 G8
  WGNE/HIN WN2 ....48 F7
Stag Pasture Rd *OLDS* OL8 ....75 J4
Stainburn Rd *WGNNW/ST* WN6 .....30 A4
Stainburne Rd *OFTN* SK2 ....112 F6
Stainburn Rd *OP/CLY* M11 ....88 E4
Staindale *OLDE* OL4 ....60 A6
Stainer Cl *NEWLW* WA12 ....78 E7
Stainer St *WGTN/LGST* M12 ....99 K1
Stainforth Cl *GOL/RIS/CUL* WA3 .....81 G8
  TOT/BURYW BL8 ....38 C1
Stainforth St *OP/CLY* M11 ....88 C5
Stainmoor Ct *OFTN* SK2 ....113 G6
Stainmore Av *AUL* OL6 ....75 M5
Stainton Av *GTN* M18 ....89 H8
Stainton Cl *RAD* M26 ....38 C8
Stainton Dr *MDTN* M24 ....57 G1
Stainton Rd *RAD* M26 ....38 B7
Staithes Rd *WYTH/NTH* M22 ....118 F4
Stakeford Dr *CHH* M8 ....72 F4
Stakehill La *MDTN* M24 ....42 B7
Staley Cl *STLY* SK15 * 91 M2
Staley Hall Crs *STLY* SK15 ....91 M1
Staley Hall Rd *STLY* SK15 ....91 M1
Staley St *OLDE* OL4 * 59 M6
  OLDE OL4 ....60 C6
Stalham Cl *NEWH/MOS* M40 ....88 A1
Stalmine Av *CHD/CHDH* SK8 ....119 K4
Stalybridge Rd *HYDE* SK14 ....92 D8
Stalyhill Dr *STLY* SK15 ....92 B5
Stamford Av *ALT* WA14 ....107 K6
  STLY SK15 ....91 H2
Stamford Cl *STLY* SK15 ....91 H2
Stamford Dr *FAIL* M35 ....74 E7
  STLY SK15 ....91 H2
Stamford Gv *STLY* SK15 ....91 J2
Stamford New Rd *ALT* WA14 ....108 A8
Stamford Park Rd
  HALE/TIMP WA15 ....117 H1
Stamford Pl *SALE* M33 ....96 F8
Stamford Rd *ALT* WA14 ....116 E2
  BRO M7 ....71 L6
  BRUN/LGST M13 ....99 J1
  DTN/ASHW M34 ....90 A5
  MOSL OL5 ....76 F2
  OLDE OL4 ....60 C4
  PART M31 ....95 G5
  URM M41 ....95 L2
  WILM/AE SK9 ....126 E3
  WILM/AE SK9 ....130 D3
Stamford Sq *AUL* OL6 ....91 G2
Stamford St *ALT* WA14 ....108 A7
  ATH M46 ....51 H8
  HEY OL10 ....41 H3
  MILN OL16 ....11 J6
  MOSL OL5 ....76 E3
  OLDE OL4 * 60 B6
  OLDTF/WHR M16 ....87 G2
  SALE M33 ....96 D6
  STLY SK15 ....77 G8
  STLY SK15 ....91 K2
  SWIN M27 ....70 D3
Stamford St Central *AUL* OL6 ....90 F1
Stamford St East *AUL* OL6 ....90 F2
Stamford St West *AUL* OL6 ....90 E2
Stamford Wy *ALT* WA14 ....108 A7
Stampstone St *OLD* OL1 ....59 L5
Stanage Av *BKLY* M9 * 57 J8
Stanbank St *HTNM* SK4 ....100 B8
Stanbourne Dr *BOL* BL1 ....22 C8
Stanbrook St *BNG/LEV* M19 ....99 M4
Stanbury Cl *BURY* BL9 * 40 A3
Stanbury Dr *DUK* SK16 ....91 G4
Stanbury Wk
  NEWH/MOS M40 * 88 A1
Stancliffe Gv *WGNE/HIN* WN2 ......32 F6
Stancliffe Rd *WYTH/NTH* M22 ......110 B7
Stancross Rd *NTHM/RTH* M23 .....108 F4
Standish St *TYLD* M29 ....67 K4
Standish Wood La
  WGNNW/ST WN6 ....31 H5
Stand La *RAD* M26 ....54 E2

Standmoor Ct *WHTF* M45 * 55 G5
Standmoor Rd *WHTF* M45 ....55 G5
Standrick Hill Ri *STLY* SK15 ....77 G7
Standring Av *TOT/BURYW* BL8 ......38 D4
Stand Ri *RAD* M26 ....54 E4
Stanedge Cl *RAMS* BL0 ....18 F8
Stanedge Gv *WGNS/IIMK* WN3 .....63 L2
Stanford Cl *RAD* M26 * 53 M5
Stanford Hall Crs *RAMS* BL0 ....18 E8
Stanhope Av *DTN/ASHW* M34 ....55 K7
  PWCH M25 ....55 K7
Stanhope Cl *DTN/ASHW* M34 ....90 B7
  WILM/AE SK9 ....127 H4
Stanhope Ct *PWCH* M25 ....55 K6
Stanhope Rd *ALT* WA14 ....116 C2
  SLFD M6 ....71 H7
Stanhope St *AUL* OL6 * 76 A8
  BNG/LEV M19 ....99 L3
  DTN/ASHW M34 ....90 B7
  LEIGH WN7 ....66 A6
  MOSL OL5 ....76 F4
  RDSH SK5 * 100 B5
  ROCH OL11 ....10 F9
Stanhope Wy *FAIL* M35 ....74 B4
Stanhorne Av *CHH* M8 ....72 D2
Stanier Av *ECC* M30 ....85 G1
Stanier Pl *HOR/BR* BL6 ....33 M2
Stanier St *BKLY* M9 ....73 H4
Stanion Gv *DUK* SK16 ....90 F4
Stan Jolly Wk *OP/CLY* M11 ....88 F4
Stanley Av *BRAM/HZG* SK7 ....121 M1
  HYDE SK14 ....91 H8
  MPL/ROM SK6 ....114 A5
  RUSH/FAL M14 ....98 F1
Stanley Av North *PWCH* M25 ....55 K6
Stanley Av South *PWCH* M25 ....55 K6
Stanley Cl *WHTF* M45 ....55 J3
  WHTF M45 ....55 D5
Stanley Ct *BURY* BL9 ....5 G3
  OLDTF/WHR M16 ....86 F7
Stanley Dr *CHD/CHDH* SK8 ....119 M6
  HALE/TIMP WA15 ....108 D7
  LEIGH WN7 ....66 A4
  WHTF M45 ....55 J6
Stanley Gv *GTN* M18 ....88 E8
  HOR/BR BL6 ....34 A3
  HTNM SK4 ....11 G4
  URM M41 ....96 A2
  WGTN/LGST M12 ....99 H3
Stanley Hall La *POY/DIS* SK12 .....123 L5
Stanley La *WGNE/HIN* WN2 ....32 F5
Stanley Ms *BOLE* BL2 ....37 G5
Stanley Mt *SALE* M33 ....108 D1
Stanley Park Wk *BOLE* BL2 * 3 M4
Stanley Pl *WGN* WN1 ....15 K3
  WHIT OL12 ....10 D1
Stanley Rd *BOL* BL1 ....35 L3
  BRO M7 ....72 B4
  CHAD OL9 ....74 F1
  CHH M8 ....72 D8
  CSLFD M3 ....6 C4
  DTN/ASHW M34 ....100 D1
  ECC M30 ....84 F3
  FWTH BL4 ....52 B4
  HTNM SK4 ....99 L8
  OLDTF/WHR M16 ....86 F7
  OLDTF/WHR M16 ....98 B2
  RAD M26 ....38 B6
  SWIN M27 ....70 D4
  WALK M28 ....69 G2
  WGNE/HIN WN2 ....32 F6
  WGNE/HIN WN2 ....64 D1
  WHTF M45 ....55 J3
Stanley St *ATH* M46 ....66 F2
  BKLY M9 * 73 H4
  CHAD OL9 ....8 B4
  CHH M8 ....72 D8
  CSLFD M3 ....6 C4
  HEY OL10 ....41 G3
  NEWH/MOS M40 ....73 J7
  OLDE OL4 ....60 B7
  OP/CLY M11 ....89 H5
  PWCH M25 ....55 M8
  RAMS BL0 ....18 E4
  STKP SK1 * 91 J3
  STLY SK15 * 91 J3
  WGNW/BIL/OR WN5 .....14 D1
  WHIT OL12 ....10 D1
Stanley St South *BOLS/LL* BL3 ......2 C6
Stanmere Cl *EDGW/EG* BL7 ....23 L1
Stanmoor Dr *WGNE/HIN* WN2 ....32 F7
Stanmore Av *STRET* M32 ....96 E3
Stanmore Dr *BOLS/LL* BL3 ....35 M7
Stannard Rd *ECC* M30 ....84 C3
Stanneybrook Cl *MILN* OL16 ....11 K3
Stanney Cl *MILN* OL16 ....29 H7
Stanneylands Cl *WILM/AE* SK9 ....127 G2
Stanneylands Dr *WILM/AE* SK9 ....126 F2
Stanneylands Rd
  WILM/AE SK9 ....119 K8
Stanrose Cl *EDGW/EG* BL7 ....22 B3
Stansbury Pl *OFTN* SK2 ....113 H6
Stansby Gdns *WGNS/LGST* M12 ....88 B6
Stansfield Av *HALE/TIMP* WA15 ....108 F5
  RUSH/FAL M14 ....98 D3
Stansfield Dr *ROCH* OL11 ....27 H5
Stansfield Rd *BOLE* BL2 * 3 J3
  FAIL M35 ....55 J4
  HYDE SK14 ....91 H8
Stansfield St *CHAD* OL9 ....88 A8
  NEWH/MOS M40 ....74 A8
  OLD OL1 ....9 G2
  OP/CLY M11 ....89 G4
Stanstead Cl *WGNE/HIN* WN2 ......48 C2
Stanthorne Av *DID/WITH* M20 ......98 D5
Stanton Av *BRO* M7 ....71 L6
  DID/WITH M20 ....98 B8
Stanton Cl *WGNS/IIMK* WN3 ....63 L1
Stanton Gdns *HTNM* SK4 ....12 C1
Stanton St *CHAD* OL9 ....74 E1
  OP/CLY M11 ....88 F2
  STRET M32 ....97 G1
Stanway Av *BOLS/LL* BL3 * 2 B7
Stanway Cl *BOLS/LL* BL3 * 2 B7
  MDTN M24 ....57 L6
Stanway Dr *HALE/TIMP* WA15 ......117 H1
Stanway Rd *WHTF* M45 ....55 L4
Stanway St *BKLY* M9 ....73 H4
  STRET M32 ....97 G1
Stanwell Rd *NEWH/MOS* M40 ....70 B5
  SWIN M27 ....70 B5
Stanwick Av *BKLY* M9 ....56 D8
Stanworth Av *BOLE* BL2 ....37 H5
Stanworth Cl *OLDTF/WHR* M16 .....98 B1
Stanyard Ct *ORD* M5 ....86 D4
Stanycliffe La *MDTN* M24 ....57 L5
Stanyforth St *GLSP* SK13 ....93 K8
Stapleford Cl *NTHM/RTH* M23 .....109 J8
  SALE M33 ....97 H7
  TOT/BURYW BL8 ....38 D2
  WHTN BL5 ....51 K6

Staplehurst Cl *LEIGH* WN7 ....65 M2
Staplehurst Rd
  NEWH/MOS M40 ....73 K8
Stapleton Av *BOL* BL1 ....35 H4
Stapleton St *SLFD* M6 ....70 F7
  WGNE/HIN WN2 ....64 D2
Starbeck Cl *TOT/BURYW* BL8 ....38 C2
Starcliffe St *BOLS/LL* BL3 ....53 C2
Starfield Av *LIT* OL15 ....29 J2
Star Gv *BRO* M7 ....72 B6
Starkey St *HEY* OL10 ....41 G1
Starkie Rd *BOLE* BL2 ....3 K4
The Starkies *BURY* BL9 * 39 H5
Starkie St *WALK* M28 ....69 K4
Star La *HOR/BR* BL6 ....33 J4
Starling Cl *DROY* M43 ....90 A1
  WYTH/NTH M22 ....110 B6
Starling Dr *FWTH* BL4 ....52 C5
Starling Rd *RAD* M26 ....38 B4
Starmoor Dr *CHH* M8 ....72 D6
Starmount Cl *BOLE* BL2 ....37 K5
Starring La *LIT* OL15 ....21 K7
Starring Rd *LIT* OL15 ....21 J7
Starring Wy *LIT* OL15 ....21 K7
Stash Gv *NTHM/RTH* M23 ....109 H5
Statford Av *ECC* M30 ....84 F4
Statham Cl *DTN/ASHW* M34 ....101 K1
Statham Fold *HYDE* SK14 ....91 K8
Statham St *SLFD* M6 ....86 E2
Station Ap *CMANE* M1 ....7 G7
  CMANE M1 ....7 J5
  UPML OL3 ....61 J1
Station Av *WGNE/HIN* WN2 ....65 G3
  WGNW/BIL/OR WN5 .....46 A4
Station Cl *HYDE* SK14 ....101 M2
Station Cottages *TYLD* M29 * 82 F5
Stationers Entry *MILN* OL16 ....10 E4
Station La *OLDE* OL4 ....60 E7
Station Ms *AIMK* WN4 ....78 A1
Station Rd *ALT* WA14 ....106 E7
  CHD/CHDH SK8 ....120 D3
  CHF/WBR SK23 ....124 F8
  CHH M8 ....72 D3
  ECC M30 ....84 F3
  EDGW/EG BL7 ....16 F8
  EDGY/DAV SK3 ....13 H6
  FWTH BL4 ....53 J5
  GLSP SK13 ....93 K7
  HOR/BR BL6 ....33 H3
  HTNM SK4 ....111 H3
  HYDE SK14 ....102 E2
  IRL M44 ....94 B5
  LIT OL15 ....21 M7
  MILN OL16 ....29 J7
  MOSL OL5 ....77 G3
  MPL/ROM SK6 ....101 L2
  MPL/ROM SK6 ....114 C6
  MPL/ROM SK6 ....123 J3
  NM/HAY SK22 ....124 D5
  NM/HAY SK22 ....125 J2
  OLDE OL4 ....60 B2
  RDSH SK5 ....100 B2
  ROCH OL11 ....10 F7
  STRET M32 ....97 C1
  SWIN M27 ....70 C3
  TOT/BURYW BL8 ....24 C3
  UPML OL3 ....61 L4
  URM M41 ....96 A3
  WHIT OL12 ....20 B1
  WILM/AE SK9 ....126 E1
  WILM/AE SK9 ....126 F5
Station St *AUL* OL6 ....90 E3
  BOLS/LL BL3 ....2 F7
  BRAM/HZG SK7 ....121 M2
  OLDE OL4 ....60 B6
Station to Station Wk *LIT* OL15 .....29 L1
Station Vw *BNG/LEV* M19 ....99 K3
Station Yd *NM/HAY* SK22 * 124 D6
Staton Av *BOLE* BL2 ....3 M2
Staton St *OP/CLY* M11 ....88 F4
Statter St *BURY* BL9 ....39 K8
Staveleigh Ml *AUL* OL6 * 90 E1
Staveley Av *BOL* BL1 ....22 B6
  STLY SK15 ....91 K1
Staveley Cl *MDTN* M24 ....57 H3
  ROY/SHW OL2 ....44 A6
Stavesacre *LEIGH* WN7 ....81 J1
Staveton Cl *BRAM/HZG* SK7 ....121 H1
Stavordale *WHIT* OL12 ....10 D3
Staycott St *OLDTF/WHR* M16 ....87 J8
Stayley Dr *STLY* SK15 ....91 M2
Stayley Rd *MOSL* OL5 ....77 G4
Stead St *RAMS* BL0 ....18 F6
Steadway *UPML* OL3 ....61 M7
Stedman Cl *OP/CLY* M11 ....88 B3
Steele Gdns *BOLE* BL2 ....37 G7
Steeles Av *HYDE* SK14 ....102 B1
Steeple Cl *CHH* M8 ....72 C7
Steeple Dr *ORD* M5 ....86 D4
Steeple End Fold
  NM/HAY SK22 ....125 M2
Steeple Vw *ROY/SHW* OL2 ....43 G8
Stein Av *GOL/RIS/CUL* WA3 ....80 B4
Stelfox Av *HALE/TIMP* WA15 ......108 F5
  RUSH/FAL M14 ....98 D3
Stelfox La *DTN/ASHW* M34 * 90 C5
Stelfox St *ECC* M30 ....84 C4
Stella St *BKLY* M9 ....56 E8
Stelling St *GTN* M18 ....89 G7
Stenbury Cl *RUSH/FAL* M14 ....98 F1
Stenner La *DID/WITH* M20 ....110 E2
Stephens Av *DROY* M43 ....89 K3
Stephenson Rd *STRET* M32 ....97 H2
Stephenson St *FAIL* M35 ....74 D3
  HOR/BR BL6 ....33 L2
  OLDE OL4 ....60 A4
  WGNE/HIN WN2 ....64 C1
Stephens St *BOL* BL1 ....2 A5
Stephen St *CSLFD* M3 ....72 C8
  STLY SK15 ....76 D8
Stephen St South
  TOT/BURYW BL8 ....38 F3
Stephens Wy *WCNS/IIMK* WN3 .....47 J1
Stephen Wk *STKP* SK1 * 112 E4
Steps Meadow *WHIT* OL12 ....21 G8
Steptoe Dr *OLD* OL1 ....8 F1
Stern Av *ORD* M5 * 86 D4
Sterndale Av *WGNNW/ST* WN6 .....31 H2
Sterndale Rd *EDGY/DAV* SK3 ......112 B7
  MPL/ROM SK6 ....113 L3
  WALK M28 ....68 C6
Sterratt St *BOL* BL1 ....2 A5
Stetchworth Dr *WALK* M28 ....68 E5
Steuber Dr *IRL* M44 ....94 C7
Stevenson Cl *WGNS/IIMK* WN3 .....47 L7
Stevenson Dr *OLD* OL1 ....44 B7

Stevenson Pl *CMANE* M1 * 7 J4
Stevenson Rd *SWIN* M27 ....70 B4
Stevenson Sq *CMANE* M1 * 7 J4
  WHIT OL12 ....28 E1
Stevenson St *ORD* M5 * 6 A4
  WALK M28 ....68 F5
Stevens St *WILM/AE* SK9 ....130 D3
Stewart Av *FWTH* BL4 ....52 E5
Stewart Dr *WGNS/IIMK* WN3 ....63 L1
Stewart St *AULW* OL7 ....90 C2
  BOL BL1 ....36 B3
  MILN OL16 ....43 L1
  TOT/BURYW BL8 ....24 F8
Stewerton Cl *GOL/RIS/CUL* WA3 ....79 J2
Steynton Cl *BOL* BL1 ....35 J4
Stile Cl *URM* M41 ....94 F2
Stiles Av *MPL/ROM* SK6 ....114 B5
Stiles Cl *GLSP* SK13 ....93 H7
Stillwater Dr *OP/CLY* M11 ....88 D4
Stilton Dr *OP/CLY* M11 * 88 D4
Stirling Av *BRAM/HZG* SK7 ....121 M3
  DID/WITH M20 ....98 C4
  MPL/ROM SK6 ....114 C7
  WGNE/HIN WN2 ....48 D4
Stirling Cl *EDGY/DAV* SK3 ....111 M6
  LEIGH WN7 ....67 G7
Stirling Dr *AIMK* WN4 ....63 G8
  STLY SK15 ....91 K1
Stirling Gv *WHTF* M45 ....55 K4
Stirling Rd *BOL* BL1 ....22 B7
  CHAD OL9 ....58 C8
  CHAD OL9 ....49 J8
Stirling St *CHAD* OL9 ....8 D4
  OLDE OL4 ....47 L2
Stirrup Brook Gv *WALK* M28 ....68 C3
Stirrup Ga *WALK* M28 ....69 K7
Stitch La *HTNM* SK4 ....12 F1
Stitch-Mi-Lane *BOLE* BL2 ....37 J2
Stiups La *MILN* OL16 ....28 F8
Stobart Av *PWCH* M25 ....71 M2
Stockburn Dr *FAIL* M35 ....74 E5
Stock Cl *WHIT* OL12 ....28 B2
Stockdale Av *EDGY/DAV* SK3 ......112 C7
Stockdale Gv *BOLE* BL2 ....37 J3
Stockfield Rd *BKLY* M9 ....57 H8
Stockfield Mt *CHAD* OL9 ....8 B6
Stockholm Rd *EDGY/DAV* SK3 .....112 A6
Stockholm St *OP/CLY* M11 ....88 C2
Stockland Cl *BRUN/LGST* M13 * 7 J3
Stock La *CHAD* OL9 ....8 A5
Stockley Av *BOLE* BL2 ....37 H2
Stockley Dr *WGNNW/ST* WN6 ....30 B4
Stockport Rd *AULW* OL7 ....90 C4
  BNG/LEV M19 ....99 K4
  BRUN/LGST M13 ....88 C6
  CHD/CHDH SK8 ....111 D6
  DTN/ASHW M34 ....101 H3
  HALE/TIMP WA15 ....108 C7
  HYDE SK14 ....102 A5
  HYDE SK14 ....103 H3
  MOSL OL5 ....76 F2
  MPL/ROM SK6 ....113 J2
  MPL/ROM SK6 ....113 M6
  OLDE OL4 ....60 F7
  WGTN/LGST M12 ....88 B8
Stockport Rd East
  MPL/ROM SK6 ....101 J8
Stockport Rd West
  MPL/ROM SK6 ....112 F1
Stockport Village *STKP* SK1 * 13 H4
Stocksfield Dr *BKLY* M9 ....73 H1
  LHULT M38 ....52 C7
Stocks Gdns *STLY* SK15 ....91 M5
Stocksgate *WHIT* OL12 ....27 L2
Stocks La *STLY* SK15 ....91 L3
Stocks Park Dr *HOR/BR* BL6 ....34 A1
Stocks St *CHH* M8 ....72 D8
Stocks St East *CHH* M8 ....72 D8
The Stocks *GLSP* SK13 ....93 K5
Stock St *TOT/BURYW* BL8 ....25 H7
Stockton Av *EDGY/DAV* SK3 ....12 B7
Stockton Dr *TOT/BURYW* BL8 ....24 E7
Stockton Pk *OLDE* OL4 ....60 A4
Stockton Rd *CCHDY* M21 ....97 K4
  FWTH BL4 ....52 F2
  WILM/AE SK9 ....126 D8
Stockton St *LIT* OL15 ....21 L7
  OLDTF/WHR M16 ....87 H8
  SWIN M27 ....70 B4
Stockwell Cl *WGNS/IIMK* WN3 .....63 G2
Stoke Abbott Cl
  BRAM/HZG SK7 ....121 G5
Stokesay Cl *BURY* BL9 ....39 J7
  ROY/SHW OL2 ....43 K8
Stokesay Dr *BRAM/HZG* SK7 ....121 G5
Stokesay Rd *SALE* M33 ....96 B7
The Stokes Ct
  GOL/RIS/CUL WA3 ....80 A4
Stokes St *OP/CLY* M11 ....89 C4
Stoke St *MILN* OL16 ....11 K7
Stokoe Av *ALT* WA14 ....107 K6
Stonall Av *HULME* M15 ....87 G6
Stoneacre *HOR/BR* BL6 ....34 C4
Stoneacre Ct *SWIN* M27 ....70 C5
Stoneacre Rd *WYTH/NTH* M22 .....118 C2
Stonebeck Rd *NTHM/RTH* M23 ....109 J7
Stone Breaks Rd *OLDE* OL4 ....60 E5
Stonebridge Cl *HOR/BR* BL6 ....34 F6
Stonechat Cl *DROY* M43 * 89 M1
  GOL/RIS/CUL WA3 ....80 B4
  WALK M28 ....68 C4
Stonecliffe Av *STLY* SK15 ....91 K2
Stone Cl *RAMS* BL0 ....18 D8
Stoneclough Ri *RAD* M26 ....53 L4
Stoneclough Rd *FWTH* BL4 ....53 J5
Stonecrop *WGNNW/ST* WN6 ....30 A3
Stone Cross La North
  GOL/RIS/CUL WA3 ....79 M5
Stone Cross La South
  GOL/RIS/CUL WA3 ....79 M6
Stonedelph Cl *BOLE* BL2 ....38 A3
Stonefield *TYLD* M29 ....67 M3
Stonefield Dr *CHH* M8 ....72 A8
Stonefield St *MILN* OL16 ....29 J7
Stonehaven *BOLS/LL* BL3 ....51 J1
Stone Hvn *WGNS/IIMK* WN3 ....63 G2
Stonehewer St *RAD* M26 ....54 E2
Stonehill Crs *WHIT* OL12 ....27 K1
Stonehill Dr *WHIT* OL12 ....27 K1
Stonehill Rd *FWTH* BL4 ....53 G6
Stonehill Rd *WHIT* OL12 ....27 K1
Stonehouse *EDGW/EG* BL7 ....22 D1
Stonehouse Rd
  WGNW/BIL/OR WN5 .....47 G3
Stonelands Wy *OLDE* OL4 ....60 D8

Stone Lea Wy *ATH* M46 ....66 D2
Stoneleigh Av *SALE* M33 ....96 B7
Stoneleigh Dr *RAD* M26 ....53 L5
Stoneleigh Rd *OLDE* OL4 ....60 D5
Stoneleigh St *OLD* OL1 ....59 L3
Stonelow Cl *HULME* M15 ....87 J6
Stone Mead Av
  HALE/TIMP WA15 ....117 L5
Stonemead Cl *BOLS/LL* BL3 ....36 C8
Stonemead Dr *BKLY* M9 ....57 G8
Stonepail Cl *CHD/CHDH* SK8 ....110 C7
Stonepail Cottages
  CHD/CHDH SK8 * 110 D7
Stonepail Rd *CHD/CHDH* SK8 ......110 D7
Stone Pale *WHTF* M45 ....55 J5
Stone Pit Cl *GOL/RIS/CUL* WA3 .....80 C3
Stone Pits *RAMS* BL0 ....19 H1
Stone Pl *RUSH/FAL* M14 ....98 F1
Stoneridge *GLSP* SK13 ....93 J7
Stone Rw *MPL/ROM* SK6 ....114 D6
Stonesby Cl *OLDTF/WHR* M16 ....87 H8
Stonesdale Cl *ROY/SHW* OL2 ....43 H7
Stonesteads Dr *EDGW/EG* BL7 ......22 D4
Stonesteads Wy *EDGW/EG* BL7 .....22 D4
Stone St *BOLE* BL2 * 3 J1
  CSLFD M3 ....6 D7
Stoneswood Rd *MOSL* OL5 ....77 G2
Stoneswood Rd *UPML* OL3 ....61 H1
Stoney Bank *RAD* M26 ....53 M5
Stoney Bridge La
  HALE/TIMP WA15 ....108 D5
Stoneyfield *STLY* SK15 ....76 D8
Stoneyfield Cl *OLDTF/WHR* M16 ....98 C2
Stoneygate Wk *OP/CLY* M11 ....89 C1
Stoneyhurst Cl *HULME* M15 ....87 J2
Stoneyland Dr *NM/HAY* SK22 ......124 D4
Stoney La *UPML* OL3 ....45 G5
  WILM/AE SK9 ....126 D7
Stoneyroyd *WHIT* OL12 * 20 B2
Stoneyside Av *WALK* M28 ....53 H8
Stoneyside Gv *WALK* M28 ....69 H1
Stonie Heyes Av *WHIT* OL12 ....28 E2
Stonyford Rd *SALE* M33 ....96 D3
Stonyhurst Av *BOL* BL1 ....22 B7
Stonyhurst Crs
  WGNS/IIMK WN3 ....15 J8
Stonyhurst Crs
  GOL/RIS/CUL WA3 ....81 G7
Stopes Rd *BOLS/LL* BL3 ....53 L1
Stopford Av *LIT* OL15 ....21 J8
Stopford St *EDGY/DAV* SK3 ....12 F7
  OP/CLY M11 * 89 H5
  WGNE/HIN WN2 ....48 C5
Stopforth St *WGNNW/ST* WN6 ......14 B2
Stores Cottages *OLDE* OL4 * 55 M8
Stores St *PWCH* M25 ....55 M8
Store St *AULW* OL7 ....90 C2
  CMANE M1 ....7 K6
  OFTN SK2 ....112 F8
  OP/CLY M11 * 88 E5
  RAD M26 ....39 G8
  ROCH OL11 ....27 H3
  ROY/SHW OL2 ....43 M4
Storeton Cl *WYTH/NTH* M22 ....119 G2
Stortford Dr *NTHM/RTH* M23 .....109 L2
Storth Bank *GLSP* SK13 ....104 C5
Storth Meadow Rd *GLSP* SK13 .....104 D5
Storwood Cl
  WGNW/BIL/OR WN5 .....46 B7
Stothard Rd *STRET* M32 ....96 E3
Stott Dr *URM* M41 ....94 F3
Stottfield *ROY/SHW* OL2 ....58 E1
Stott La *BOLE* BL2 ....38 A4
  MDTN M24 ....41 J7
  SLFD M6 ....85 L1
Stott Milne St *CHAD* OL9 ....8 A8
Stott Rd *CHAD* OL9 ....74 B1
  SWIN M27 ....70 A6
Stott's La *NEWH/MOS* M40 ....74 A6
Stott St *FAIL* M35 ....74 A6
  MILN OL16 ....21 H8
  MILN OL16 ....29 J8
  WHIT OL12 ....10 F1
Stourbridge Av *LHULT* M38 ....52 D6
Stour Cl *ALT* WA14 ....107 M6
Stourport Cl *MPL/ROM* SK6 ....113 K3
Stourport St *OLD* OL1 * 9 M1
Stour Rd *TYLD* M29 ....67 M8
Stout St *LEIGH* WN7 ....65 M8
Stovell Av *WGTN/LGST* M12 ....99 K2
Stovell Rd *NEWH/MOS* M40 ....73 K4
Stow Cl *TOT/BURYW* BL8 ....25 H7
Stowe Gdns *LEIGH* WN7 ....66 C7
Stowell Ct *BOL* BL1 ....2 C1
Stowell St *BOL* BL1 ....36 B3
  ORD M5 ....86 B3
Stowfield Cl *BKLY* M9 ....56 E8
Stow Gdns *DID/WITH* M20 ....98 C4
Stracey St *NEWH/MOS* M40 * 88 B1
Stradbroke Cl
  GOL/RIS/CUL WA3 ....80 D5
  GTN M18 ....88 E7
Strain Av *BKLY* M9 ....57 C8
The Straits *TYLD* M29 ....67 M6
Strand Av *AIMK* WN4 ....63 L8
Strand Ct *STRET* M32 ....96 F4
The Strand *AIMK* WN4 ....63 L8
  HOR/BR BL6 ....34 A1
  ROCH OL11 ....42 C2
Strange Wy *ROY/SHW* OL2 ....59 G2
Strange Rd *AIMK* WN4 ....78 A1
Strange St *LEIGH* WN7 ....65 L8
Strangford St *RAD* M26 ....38 A8
Strang St *RAMS* BL0 ....18 F6
Stranraer Rd
  WGNW/BIL/OR WN5 .....46 F3
Stranton Dr *WALK* M28 ....69 M4
Stratfield Av *NTHM/RTH* M23 .....109 G3
Stratford Av *BOL* BL1 ....35 H4
  BURY BL9 ....25 H4
  DID/WITH M20 ....98 C7
  OLDS OL8 ....75 H1
  ROCH OL11 ....10 C9
Stratford Gdns *MPL/ROM* SK6 .....113 J1
Stratford Rd *MDTN* M24 ....57 L7
  WGNNW/ST WN6 ....16 E8
Strathblane Cl *DID/WITH* M20 ......98 E5
Strathfield Dr *OP/CLY* M11 ....88 E2
Strathmere Av *STRET* M32 ....97 G1
Strathmore Av *AIMK* WN4 ....63 K7
  CCHDY M21 ....97 L2
  DTN/ASHW M34 ....101 L2
Strathmore Cl *RAMS* BL0 ....24 F1
Strathmore Rd *BOLE* BL2 ....37 H3
Stratton Dr *WGNE/HIN* WN2 ....64 D3
Stratton Rd *OFTN* SK2 ....112 F4
  OLDTF/WHR M16 ....97 L2
  SWIN M27 ....70 C3
Strawberry Bank *SLFD* M6 * 86 E1
Strawberry Cl *ALT* WA14 ....107 L5
Strawberry HI *SLFD* M6 ....86 E1

Strawberry Hill Rd BOLE BL2 .....3 J8
Strawberry La MOSL OL5 .....61 G8
  WILM/AE SK9 .....126 C6
Strawberry Rd SLFD M6 .....86 D1
Stray St OP/CLY M11 .....89 H4
The Stray BOL BL1 .....22 E8
Streamside Cl
  HALE/TIMP 108 E8
Stream Ter STKP SK1 .....112 E3
Streetbridge OLD OL1 .....58 D2
Street Bridge Rd OLD OL1 .....58 D2
Street Elmfield BOL BL1 .....36 C2
Streetgate LHULT M38 .....52 D7
Streethouse La UPML OL3 .....61 J3
Street Kirklees TOT/BURYW BL8 .....24 C5
Street La MCFLDN SK10 .....129 H4
  RAD M26 .....38 B4
Stretford Rd HULME M15 .....87 J6
  OLDTF/WHR M16 .....86 F7
  URM M41 .....96 A3
Stretton Av DID/WITH M20 .....110 F1
  GOL/RIS/CUL WA3 * 80 A5
  SALE M33 .....96 B8
  STRET M32 .....96 D1
  WGNW/BIL/OR WN5 .....62 B7
Stretton Cl NEWH/MOS M40 .....31 H4
Stretton Rd BOLS/LL BL3 .....35 L8
  RAMS BL0 .....24 D2
Striding Edge Wk OLD OL1 * 9 L1
Strines Cl WGNE/HIN WN2 .....49 G6
Strines Rd MPL/ROM SK6 .....114 D7
Stringer Av STKP SK14 .....103 J2
Stringer Cl HYDE SK14 .....103 J1
Stringer St LEIGH WN7 .....66 C7
  STKP SK1 .....13 M5
Stroma Gdns URM M41 .....84 F7
Strong St BRO M7 .....72 B8
Strongstry Rd RAMS BL0 .....18 F2
Stroud Av ECC M30 .....84 E1
Stroud Cl MDTN M24 .....57 K7
  WGNE/HIN WN2 .....48 C3
Stuart Av IRL M44 .....94 C2
  MPL/ROM SK6 .....113 M5
  WGNE/HIN WN2 .....65 L1
Stuart Cl WGNE/HIN WN2 .....64 C3
Stuart Crs WGNW/BIL/OR WN5 .....62 A7
Stuart Rd ALT WA14 .....107 L5
  MPL/ROM SK6 .....101 G6
  STRET M32 .....97 G1
Stuart St MDTN M24 .....57 M4
  MILN OL16 .....11 J7
  OLDS OL8 .....9 G9
  OP/CLY M11 .....88 D2
Stuart St East OP/CLY M11 .....88 D2
Stuart Wk MDTN M24 .....57 J5
Stubbins Cl NTHM/RTH M23 .....109 H3
Stubbins La RAMS BL0 .....18 F4
Stubbins St RAMS BL0 .....18 F3
Stubbins Vale Rd RAMS BL0 .....18 F3
Stubbs Cl BRO M7 .....71 L4
Stubley Gdns LIT OL15 .....21 L7
Stubley La LIT OL15 .....21 K8
Stubley Mill Rd LIT OL15 .....21 K8
Studforth Wk HULME M15 * 87 J7
Studland Rd WYTH/NTH M22 .....119 H1
Studley Cl ROY/SHW OL2 .....43 K8
Studley Ct TYLD M29 .....67 H4
Sturton Av WGNS/IIMK WN3 .....63 H1
Styal Av RDSH SK5 .....100 C3
  STRET M32 .....96 D1
Styal Cl CHD/CHDH SK8 .....119 J1
Styal Rd WILM/AE SK9 .....126 E3
  WYTH/NTH M22 .....119 J4
Styal Vw WILM/AE SK9 .....126 F2
Styhead Dr MDTN M24 .....57 C1
Style St ANC M4 .....7 H1
Styperson Wy POY/DIS SK12 .....129 J1
Sudbrook Cl
  GOL/RIS/CUL WA3 * 80 B4
Sudbury Cl WGNS/IIMK WN3 .....63 L2
Sudbury Dr CHD/CHDH SK8 .....119 L5
  HOR/BR BL6 .....34 F6
Sudbury Rd BRAM/HZG SK7 .....122 A4
Sudden St ROCH OL11 .....27 M8
Sudell St ANC M4 .....7 K1
Sudley Rd ROCH OL11 .....27 M7
Sudlow St MILN OL16 .....11 L5
Sudren St TOT/BURYW BL8 .....38 C1
Suffield St MDTN M24 .....57 M4
Suffolk Av DROY M43 .....89 K1
Suffolk Cl BOLS/LL BL3 .....37 L7
  WGN WN1 .....31 L4
Suffolk Dr RDSH SK5 .....100 F6
  WILM/AE SK9 .....127 G3
Suffolk Gv LEIGH WN7 .....65 M7
Suffolk Rd ALT WA14 .....107 L8
Suffolk St CHAD OL9 .....58 E8
  ROCH OL11 .....10 E6
  SLFD M6 .....71 K7
Sugar La MCFLDN SK10 .....129 K8
  UPML OL3 .....61 K2
Sugar Mill Sq ORD M5 * 86 A2
Sugden St AUL OL6 .....91 G1
Sulby Av STRET M32 .....97 K4
Sulby St NEWH/MOS M40 .....73 K4
  RAD M26 .....53 L4
Sulgrave Av POY/DIS SK12 .....122 B8
Sullivan St WGTN/LGST M12 .....99 K1
Sullivan Wy WGN WN1 .....15 J2
Sultan St BKLY M9 .....4 E9
Sulway Cl SWIN M27 * 70 D5
Sumac St OP/CLY M11 .....89 G2
Summer Av URM M41 .....96 B2
Summer Castle MILN OL16 .....10 F5
Summercroft CHAD OL9 .....74 E1
Summercroft Cl
  GOL/RIS/CUL WA3 .....79 K5
Summerdale Dr RAMS BL0 .....24 E2
Summerfield Av DROY M43 .....89 H1
Summerfield Dr MDTN M24 .....57 M2
  TYLD M29 .....67 L4
Summerfield Pl WILM/AE SK9 * 126 E6
Summerfield Rd BOLS/LL BL3 .....36 E8
  WALK M28 .....69 K5
  WYTH/NTH M22 .....118 D3
Summerfields OLDS OL8 * 75 M1
Summerhill Vw OLDS OL8 * 45 G3
Summerlea CHD/CHDH SK8 * 120 D4
Summer Pl RUSH/FAL M14 * 98 E2
Summerseat Cl OLDE OL4 .....60 D5
  ORD M5 * 86 D4
Summerseat La RAMS BL0 .....24 D2
Summershades La OLDE OL4 .....61 G6
Summershades Ri OLDE OL4 .....61 G6
Summers St CHAD OL9 .....8 C3
Summer St MILN OL16 .....11 C5
Summerville Av BKLY M9 .....73 J1
Summerville Rd SLFD M6 .....71 H7
Summit Cl BURY BL9 .....26 C8

Summit St HEY OL10 .....40 C2
Sumner Av BOLE BL2 .....38 A3
Sumner Rd SLFD M6 .....71 G7
Sumner St ATH M46 .....66 F1
  CLSP SK13 .....104 F4
  ROY/SHW OL2 .....43 L7
  WGNE/HIN WN2 .....33 C7
Sumner Wy URM M41 .....95 M2
Sunadale Cl BOLS/LL BL3 .....35 L7
Sunbank Cl WHIT OL12 .....28 A2
Sunbank La HALE/TIMP WA15 .....117 M6
Sunbury Cl DUK SK16 .....91 J4
  WILM/AE SK9 .....127 J2
Sunbury Dr NEWH/MOS M40 .....74 A8
Sunderland Av AUL OL6 .....75 M8
Sunderland Pl
  WGNW/BIL/OR WN5 .....47 G3
Sundew Pl MDTN M24 .....58 A5
Sundial Cl HYDE SK14 .....103 C1
Sundial Rd OFTN SK2 .....113 G6
Sundown Cl NM/HAY SK22 .....124 C4
Sundridge Cl BOLS/LL BL3 .....51 K1
Sunfield Av OLDE OL4 .....44 B8
Sunfield Crs ROY/SHW OL2 .....59 H1
Sunfield Dr ROY/SHW OL2 .....59 J1
Sunfield Est UPML OL3 .....45 M8
Sunfield La UPML OL3 .....45 M8
Sunfield Rd OLD OL1 .....9 H2
Sunflower Meadow IRL M44 .....94 D3
Sunhill Cl MILN OL16 .....42 E2
Sunk La MDTN M24 .....57 K5
Sunlaws St GLSP SK13 .....104 E4
Sunlaws St GLSP SK13 .....104 E4
Sunleigh Rd WGNE/HIN WN2 .....49 H6
Sunlight Rd BOL BL1 .....35 M5
Sunningdale Av OP/CLY M11 .....88 E2
  RAD M26 .....38 A7
  SALE M33 .....109 H1
  WHTF M45 .....54 F5
Sunningdale Cl HYDE SK14 .....91 J8
  TOT/BURYW BL8 .....38 D4
Sunningdale Dr
  BRAM/HZG SK7 .....121 J5
  GLSP SK13 .....105 H3
  HEY OL10 .....41 C4
  IRL M44 .....94 C1
  PWCH M25 .....55 K7
  SLFD M6 .....70 D7
Sunningdale Gv LEIGH WN7 .....67 G5
Sunningdale Rd
  CHD/CHDH SK8 .....119 M4
  DTN/ASHW M34 .....101 L3
  URM M41 .....95 J3
Sunningdale Wk
  BOLS/LL BL3 * 35 M7
Sunning Hill St BOLS/LL BL3 .....36 A8
Sunny Av BURY BL9 .....25 J7
Sunny Bank OLDE OL4 .....60 B7
  RAD M26 .....39 K3
  WILM/AE SK9 .....126 B8
Sunny Bank Av DROY M43 .....89 J3
Sunnybank Av ECC M30 .....85 J1
  HTNM SK4 .....99 J8
Sunny Bank Rd ALT WA14 .....116 E4
  BRUN/LGST M13 .....99 H1
  BURY BL9 .....55 K1
Sunnybank Rd BOL BL1 .....35 M2
  DROY M43 .....89 J3
  TYLD M29 .....67 L6
Sunny Banks GLSP SK13 .....104 E4
Sunny Bower St
  TOT/BURYW BL8 .....24 B6
Sunny Brow Rd GTN M18 .....88 F7
  MDTN M24 .....57 H4
Sunny Dr PWCH M25 .....55 J8
  WGNW/BIL/OR WN5 .....46 C6
Sunnyfield Rd HTNM SK4 .....111 J2
  PWCH M25 .....55 M5
Sunnyfields WGNS/IIMK WN3 .....62 F2
Sunny Garth WHTN BL5 .....50 B4
Sunnylea Av BNG/LEV M19 .....99 H7
Sunnymead Av BOL BL1 .....22 C8
Sunnymede V RAMS BL0 .....24 D1
Sunnyside AULW OL7 .....75 H7
Sunnyside Ct DROY M43 * 89 J1
Sunnyside Crs AUL OL6 .....91 G2
Sunnyside Gv AUL OL6 .....91 G2
Sunnyside La DROY M43 .....74 C8
Sunnyside Rd AIMK WN4 .....63 K6
  BOL BL1 .....35 M2
  DROY M43 .....89 K1
Sunnywood Dr
  TOT/BURYW BL8 .....24 D6
Sunnywood La
  TOT/BURYW BL8 .....24 D6
Sunset Av WYTH/NTH M22 .....110 A3
Sun St MOSL OL5 .....76 F3
  RAMS BL0 .....18 E5
Sunwell Ter MPL/ROM SK6 .....123 H1
Sunbiton Rd NEWH/MOS M40 .....73 L8
Surma Cl CHAD OL9 .....8 E4
  MILN OL16 .....11 J8
Surrey Av DROY M43 .....89 J1
  LEIGH WN7 .....67 H8
  ROY/SHW OL2 .....43 J5
Surrey Cl BOLS/LL BL3 .....37 L8
Surrey Dr BURY BL9 .....5 C9
Surrey Park Cl ROY/SHW OL2 * 43 L4
Surrey Rd BKLY M9 .....73 G2
Surrey St AUL OL6 .....76 A7
  BKLY M9 * 72 F2
  CHAD OL9 .....8 B2
  GLSP SK13 .....104 F3
Surrey Wy RDSH SK5 .....100 F8
Surtees Rd NTHM/RTH M23 .....109 K2
Sussex Av BURY BL9 .....40 B3
  DID/WITH M20 .....98 B8
Sussex Cl CHAD OL9 .....8 A7
  SWIN M27 .....70 D2
  WGN WN1 .....31 L3
  WGNE/HIN WN2 .....49 K7
Sussex Dr BURY BL9 .....5 G9
  DROY M43 .....89 K1
Sussex Pl HYDE SK14 .....91 J7
  PART M31 .....106 B2
Sussex Rd EDGY/DAV SK3 .....12 A7
  PART M31 .....106 B2
Sussex St BRO M7 .....87 G1
  CMANW M2 .....6 F5
  LEIGH WN7 .....67 H8
  ROCH OL11 .....10 E6
Sutcliffe Av WGTN/LGST M12 .....99 K2
Sutcliffe St AULW OL7 .....75 J3
  BOL BL1 .....36 B2
  LIT OL15 .....21 M6
  MDTN M24 .....57 M4
  OLDS OL8 .....9 H9
  ROY/SHW OL2 .....59 K1
Sutherland Cl OLDS OL8 .....75 J3
Sutherland Gv FWTH BL4 .....52 F4

Sutherland Rd BOL BL1 .....35 K4
  HEY OL10 .....40 C3
  OLDTF/WHR M16 .....97 K1
  WGNS/IIMK WN3 .....63 K1
Sutherland St AUL OL6 .....91 H1
  ECC M30 .....84 E1
  FWTH BL4 .....52 F4
  SWIN M27 .....70 B3
  WGNE/HIN WN2 .....48 F7
  WGNW/BIL/OR WN5 .....47 J6
Suthers St CHAD OL9 .....8 C7
  RAD M26 .....54 F3
Sutton Av GOL/RIS/CUL WA3 .....81 H8
Sutton Cl TOT/BURYW BL8 .....38 E4
Sutton Dr DROY M43 .....89 H1
Sutton Dwellings SLFD M6 .....86 C1
Sutton Rd BOLS/LL BL3 .....35 J8
  GTN M18 .....99 M1
  HTNM SK4 .....111 M1
  POY/DIS SK12 .....129 L2
  WILM/AE SK9 .....130 C3
Suttons La MPL/ROM SK6 .....114 D7
Sutton Wy GLSP SK13 .....93 K3
Swailes St OLDE OL4 .....59 L6
Swaine St EDGY/DAV SK3 .....13 G5
Swainsthorpe Dr BKLY M9 .....73 H4
Swain St WHIT OL12 * 28 B3
Swalecliff Av NTHM/RTH M23 .....109 G3
Swale Cl WILM/AE SK9 .....127 J2
Swaledale Cl ROY/SHW OL2 .....43 H7
Swale Dr ALT WA14 .....107 M6
Swallow Bank Dr ROCH OL11 * 41 L1
Swallow Cl STLY SK15 .....91 M4
Swallow Dr BURY BL9 .....25 L8
  IRL M44 .....94 D1
  ROCH OL11 .....27 J5
Swallowfield Wk LEIGH WN7 .....66 C7
Swallow Fold GLSP SK13 .....104 C3
Swallow House Crs
  NM/HAY SK22 .....125 L1
Swallow House La
  NM/HAY SK22 .....125 L1
Swallow La OLDS OL8 .....75 G2
  OP/CLY M11 .....88 C3
  STKP SK1 .....13 K8
  WGTN/LGST M12 * 99 K2
Swanage Av NTHM/RTH M23 .....109 L4
  OFTN SK2 .....113 G6
Swanage Cl TOT/BURYW BL8 .....24 F5
Swanage Rd ECC M30 .....84 E1
Swanbourne Gdns
  EDGY/DAV SK3 .....111 M6
Swan Cl POY/DIS SK12 .....121 K8
Swan Ct ROY/SHW OL2 * 43 L6
Swanfield Wk
  GOL/RIS/CUL WA3 .....79 J2
Swanhill Cl GTN M18 .....89 J6
Swan La WGNE/HIN WN2 .....49 L8
Swanley Av NEWH/MOS M40 .....73 H7
Swan Meadow Rd
  WGNS/IIMK WN3 .....14 E6
Swann Gv CHD/CHDH SK8 .....120 D4
Swann La CHD/CHDH SK8 .....120 D3
Swann St WGNS/IIMK WN3 .....14 D5
Swan Rd HALE/TIMP WA15 .....108 D3
  NEWLW WA12 .....78 B8
  TOT/BURYW BL8 .....24 C2
Swansea St OLDS OL8 .....59 L8
Swan St ANC M4 .....7 G2
  AUL OL6 .....90 F1
  WILM/AE SK9 .....126 F5
Swarbrick Dr PWCH M25 .....71 J2
Swayfield Av BRUN/LGST M13 .....99 J1
Swaylands Dr SALE M33 .....108 C3
Sweetbriar Cl ROY/SHW OL2 .....43 L5
Sweet Briar La WHIT OL12 .....28 B2
Sweet Briar La WHIT OL12 .....28 B2
Sweetlove's Gv BOL BL1 .....22 B7
Sweetlove's La BOL BL1 .....22 B7
Sweetnam Dr OP/CLY M11 .....88 C2
Swettenham Rd WILM/AE SK9 .....119 M7
Swift Bank GLSP SK13 .....104 C4
Swift Cl MPL/ROM SK6 .....101 M7
Swift Rd OLD OL1 .....44 B7
  ROCH OL11 .....27 J5
Swift St AUL OL6 * 76 A7
  WGNW/BIL/OR WN5 .....14 B6
Swinbourne Gv DID/WITH M20 .....98 F5
Swinburne Av DROY M43 .....89 K1
Swinburne Gn RDSH SK5 .....100 A3
Swinburn Gv
  WGNW/BIL/OR WN5 .....62 A3
Swinburn St BKLY M9 .....73 J3
Swindells St HYDE SK14 .....91 H7
Swindon Cl GTN M18 .....89 G7
Swinfield Av CCHDY M21 .....97 J4
Swinford Gv ROY/SHW OL2 .....43 K7
Swinley Cha WILM/AE SK9 .....127 K3
Swinley La WGN WN1 .....47 M2
Swinley St WGN WN1 .....47 M2
Swinside Wy WGN WN1 .....47 M2
Swinside Cl MDTN M24 .....56 F2
Swinside Rd BOLE BL2 .....37 K4
Swinstead Av NEWH/MOS M40 .....73 H7
Swinton Crs BURY BL9 .....55 K3
Swinton Gv BRUN/LGST M13 .....87 M7
Swinton Hall Rd SWIN M27 .....70 D4
Swinton Park Rd SLFD M6 .....70 F7
Swinton St BOLE BL2 .....37 H5
  OLDE OL4 .....59 M7
Swiss Hl WILM/AE SK9 .....130 E3
Swithin Rd WYTH/NTH M22 .....119 G4
Swithland Rd ALT WA14 * 107 M3
Swythamley Ct EDGY/DAV SK3 * 111 M4
Swythamley Rd
  EDGY/DAV SK3 .....111 M4
Sybil St LIT OL15 .....21 L6
Sycamore Av ALT WA14 .....107 K7
  CHAD OL9 .....74 C1
  DTN/ASHW M34 .....101 J3
  GOL/RIS/CUL WA3 .....79 K3
  HEY OL10 .....41 H4
  MILN OL16 .....43 K1
  OLDE OL4 .....60 A4
  RAD M26 .....54 C4
  TYLD M29 .....68 A3
  WGNE/HIN WN2 .....65 J1
  WGNW/BIL/OR WN5 .....31 M3
Sycamore Ct AUL OL6 .....91 H2
Sycamore Dr BURY BL9 .....38 D2
  WGNS/IIMK WN3 .....62 E2
Sycamore Gv FAIL M35 .....74 E5

Sycamore Ldg
  BRAM/HZG SK7 * 121 H5
Sycamore Pl WHTF M45 .....55 J6
Sycamore Rd ATH M46 .....67 K1
  ECC M30 .....69 K8
  MPL/ROM SK6 .....101 K8
  NM/HAY SK22 .....125 G2
  PART M31 .....106 A1
  TOT/BURYW BL8 .....24 C7
The Sycamores GLSP SK13 .....104 C1
  MOSL OL5 .....77 H3
  OLDE OL4 .....60 C4
  RAD M26 .....53 L6
  STLY SK15 .....91 L4
Sycamore St EDGY/DAV SK3 .....12 B7
  SALE M33 .....97 H8
Sycamore Wk CHD/CHDH SK8 .....111 G6
  HOR/BR BL6 .....34 B2
Sydall St DTN/ASHW M34 .....101 J1
Syddal Cl BRAM/HZG SK7 .....120 F8
Syddal Crs BRAM/HZG SK7 .....120 F8
Syddal Gn BRAM/HZG SK7 .....120 F8
Syddal Rd BRAM/HZG SK7 .....120 F8
Syddall Av CHD/CHDH SK8 .....119 M4
Syddall St HYDE SK14 .....102 A2
Syddal Rd BRAM/HZG SK7 .....120 F7
Syderstone Cl WGNE/HIN WN2 .....49 H8
Sydney Av ECC M30 .....84 C2
  LEIGH WN7 .....81 C2
  MANAIR M90 .....118 C4
Sydney Barnes Cl ROCH OL11 .....41 L2
Sydney Jones Ct
  NEWH/MOS M40 .....73 M3
Sydney Rd BRAM/HZG SK7 .....121 H7
Sydney St FAIL M35 .....74 B5
  MOSL OL5 .....77 G4
  OFTN SK2 .....112 F5
  SLFD M6 .....86 B2
  SWIN M27 .....70 A4
  WGNE/HIN WN2 .....20 D8
Syke La WHIT OL12 .....20 D8
Syke Rd LIT OL15 .....29 M2
  WHIT OL12 .....20 D8
Sykes Av BURY BL9 .....39 L8
Sykes Cl UPML OL3 .....61 L7
Sykes Ct MILN OL16 .....11 K6
Sykes Crs WGNS/IIMK WN3 .....62 F3
Sykes Meadow EDGY/DAV SK3 .....12 D9
Sykes St BURY BL9 .....5 H2
  MILN OL16 * 11 J8
  MILN OL16 .....29 K8
  RDSH SK5 .....100 C4
Sylvan Av BURY BL9 .....39 K6
  FAIL M35 .....74 B7
  HALE/TIMP WA15 .....108 C4
  SALE M33 .....108 F1
  URM M41 .....96 A1
  WILM/AE SK9 .....126 D7
Sylvan Cl MDTN M24 .....57 J2
Sylvandale Av BNG/LEV M19 .....99 K3
Sylvan Gv ALT WA14 .....108 A7
Sylvan St CHAD OL9 .....8 D4
Sylvester Av OFTN SK2 .....112 F6
Sylvester Cl HYDE SK14 .....103 H2
Sylvia Gv RDSH SK5 .....100 B5
Symms St SLFD M6 .....71 L8
Symond Rd BKLY M9 .....57 H7
Symons Rd SALE M33 .....96 E7
Symons St BRO M7 .....72 B5
Syndall Av WGTN/LGST M12 .....88 A6
Syndall St WGTN/LGST M12 .....88 A6
Syresham St WGNE/HIN WN2 .....64 E2

T

Taberner Cl WGNNW/ST WN6 .....31 J3
Taberner St WGNE/HIN WN2 .....64 E2
Tabley Av RUSH/FAL M14 .....98 E2
Tabley Gdns MPL/ROM SK6 .....114 D8
  HALE/TIMP WA15 .....108 D4
  RDSH SK5 .....100 B5
Tabley Mere Gdns
  CHD/CHDH SK8 .....120 B1
Tabley Ms ALT WA14 .....108 A7
Tabley Rd BOLS/LL BL3 .....35 L8
  SALE M33 * 109 H2
  WILM/AE SK9 .....119 M7
Tabor St DUK SK16 .....91 H4
  MOSL OL5 .....77 G4
  SLFD M6 .....71 L7
Tabor St MDTN M24 .....57 J2
Tackler Cl SWIN M27 .....70 C5
Tadcaster Dr NEWH/MOS M40 .....73 F6
Tadman Gv ALT WA14 .....107 K6
Tadmor Cl LHULT M38 .....52 C8
Tagore Cl BRUN/LGST M13 .....88 C8
Tag Wood Vw RAMS BL0 .....18 D8
Tahir Cl CHH M8 .....72 E5
Tait Ms HTNM SK4 .....111 J2
Talavera St BRO M7 .....72 B7
Talbenny Cl BOL BL1 .....35 J4
Talbot Av BOLS/LL BL3 .....37 K8
Talbot Cl OLDE OL4 .....59 M4
Talbot Gv BURY BL9 .....25 K6
Talbot Pl OLDTF/WHR M16 .....86 E7
Talbot Rd ALT WA14 .....116 D2
  GLSP SK13 .....104 F2
  HYDE SK14 .....91 H7
  RUSH/FAL M14 .....99 H5
  SALE M33 * 97 H8
  STRET M32 .....97 J2
  WILM/AE SK9 .....130 E3
Talbot St AIMK WN4 * 64 A8
  BRAM/HZG SK7 .....113 J8
  ECC M30 .....85 H3
  GLSP SK13 .....104 F3
  GOL/RIS/CUL WA3 .....79 K4
  MDTN M24 .....57 J2
  ROCH OL11 .....10 E7
Talford Gv DID/WITH M20 .....98 D7
Talgarth Rd NEWH/MOS M40 .....72 F8
Talkin Dr MDTN M24 .....57 H7
Talland Wk BRUN/LGST M13 .....88 A7
Tallarn Cl DID/WITH M20 .....110 B4
Tallis St WGTN/LGST M12 .....99 K1
Tallow Wy IRL M44 .....94 D4
Tall Trees St ROY/SHW OL2 .....42 F8
Tall Trees Pl OFTN SK2 .....112 F6
Tallyman Wy SWIN M27 .....71 H5
Talman Gv AIMK WN4 .....63 M6
Tamar Cl FWTH BL4 .....53 L7
  WHTF M45 .....55 H5
Tama Ct HULME M15 * 87 G6
Tamar Dr NTHM/RTH M23 .....109 K8
Tamarin Cl SWIN M27 .....69 M7
Tamebank MOSL OL5 .....77 G1
Tame Barn Cl MILN OL16 .....29 K6

Tame Cl STLY SK15 .....91 M1
Tame La UPML OL3 .....44 F5
Tamer Gv LEIGH WN7 .....65 M4
Tamerton Dr CHH M8 .....72 D6
Tameside Ct DUK SK16 * 90 E5
Tame St ANC M4 .....88 A3
  DTN/ASHW M34 .....90 C5
  DTN/ASHW M34 .....90 C8
  MOSL OL5 .....77 H1
  STLY SK15 .....91 H3
  UPML OL3 .....61 L4
Tame Valley Cl MOSL OL5 .....77 H1
Tamworth Av ORD M5 .....86 E4
  WHTF M45 .....55 L5
Tamworth Av West ORD M5 * 86 D4
Tamworth Cl BRAM/HZG SK7 * 121 L4
  HULME M15 .....87 H7
Tamworth Dr TOT/BURYW BL8 .....24 F7
  WGNE/HIN WN2 .....48 C2
Tamworth Gn STKP SK1 .....112 E2
Tamworth St CHAD OL9 .....8 C8
  STKP SK1 .....112 E2
Tamworth Wk ORD M5 .....86 D4
Tandis Ct SLFD M6 * 85 K1
Tandle Hill Rd ROY/SHW OL2 .....42 E6
Tandlewood Ms
  NEWH/MOS M40 .....73 M7
Tandlewood Pk ROY/SHW OL2 .....42 E6
Tanfield Dr RAD M26 .....53 L5
Tanfield Rd DID/WITH M20 .....110 E5
Tangmere Av HEY OL10 .....41 J5
Tanhill Ct OFTN SK2 .....113 H6
Tanhill La OLDS OL8 .....75 K2
Tanhouse Av TYLD M29 .....68 A5
Tan House Dr WGNS/IIMK WN3 .....62 F3
Tan House La WGNS/IIMK WN3 .....62 F3
Tanhouse Rd URM M41 .....95 G1
Tanners Cft RAMS BL0 .....18 E6
Tanners Fold OLDS OL8 .....75 K2
Tanners Gn SLFD M6 .....86 C1
Tanner's La GOL/RIS/CUL WA3 .....79 L4
Tanners St GTN M18 * 18 E6
Tanner St HYDE SK14 .....102 A1
Tannery Wy ALT WA14 .....108 B5
Tannock Rd BRAM/HZG SK7 .....122 B3
Tanpits Rd BURY BL9 .....4 D3
Tansey Gv BRO M7 .....72 C6
Tansley Rd CHH M8 .....72 D2
Tansley Sq WGNW/BIL/OR WN5 .....47 G3
Tanworth Wk BOL BL1 * 36 B2
Tanyard Dr HALE/TIMP WA15 .....117 L6
Tanyard Gn RDSH SK5 .....100 C7
Tanyard La HALE/TIMP WA15 .....117 H7
Taper St RAMS BL0 .....18 E6
Tapley Av POY/DIS SK12 .....129 J2
Taplin Dr GTN M18 .....88 F7
Taplow Gv CHD/CHDH SK8 .....120 B2
Taplow Wk RUSH/FAL M14 .....99 H1
Tarbet Dr BOLE BL2 .....37 J6
Tarbet Rd DUK SK16 .....90 F5
Tarbolton Crs
  HALE/TIMP WA15 .....117 L1
Tariff St CMANE M1 .....7 K4
Tarleton Av ATH M46 .....50 E7
Tarleton Cl TOT/BURYW BL8 .....38 C3
Tarleton Pl BOLS/LL BL3 .....51 K1
Tarleton Wk BRUN/LGST M13 * 87 M6
Tarnbrook Cl WHTF M45 .....55 M4
Tarnbrook Dr WGNE/HIN WN2 .....32 E2
Tarn Cl AIMK WN4 .....63 L7
Tarn Dr BURY BL9 .....39 H6
Tarn Gv WALK M28 .....69 J3
Tarnrigg Cl WGNS/IIMK WN3 .....63 H1
Tarnside Cl MILN OL16 .....28 F1
  OFTN SK2 .....113 J6
Tarnside Fold GLSP SK13 .....104 D5
Tarnside Rd
  WGNW/BIL/OR WN5 .....46 B6
The Tarns CHD/CHDH SK8 .....119 K1
Tarnway Gv GOL/RIS/CUL WA3 .....80 C5
Tarporley Av RUSH/FAL M14 .....98 D4
Tarporley Cl EDGY/DAV SK3 .....111 M7
Tarran Gv DTN/ASHW M34 .....101 L3
Tarran Pl ALT WA14 .....108 B6
Tarrant Cl WGNS/IIMK WN3 .....63 G2
Tarrington Cl WGTN/LGST M12 .....88 D7
Tartan St OP/CLY M11 .....88 E2
Tarvin Av DID/WITH M20 .....98 D5
Tarvin Cl GOL/RIS/CUL WA3 .....80 B5
Tarvin Dr MPL/ROM SK6 .....101 K4
Tarvington Cl
  NEWH/MOS M40 * 72 F6
Tarvin Rd CHD/CHDH SK8 .....111 K8
Tarvin Wk BOL BL1 .....36 B2
Tasle Aly CMANW M2 .....6 F5
Tatchbury Rd FAIL M35 .....74 D5
Tate St OLDS OL8 .....59 L8
Tatham Ct BRUN/LGST M13 .....99 J1
Tatham Gv WGNS/IIMK WN3 .....63 G3
Tatham St MILN OL16 .....11 L5
Tatland Dr WYTH/NTH M22 .....119 H1
Tatlock Cl WGNW/BIL/OR WN5 .....62 B7
Tattersall Av BOL BL1 .....35 H2
Tattersall St CHAD OL9 .....8 E7
Tatton Cl BRAM/HZG SK7 .....113 J8
  CHD/CHDH SK8 .....111 K8
Tatton Dr AIMK WN4 .....63 J8
Tatton Gdns MPL/ROM SK6 .....102 A7
Tatton Gv DID/WITH M20 .....98 E6
Tatton Mere Dr DROY M43 .....89 L3
Tattonmere Gdns
  CHD/CHDH SK8 .....111 K8
Tatton Pl SALE M33 .....96 F7
Tatton Rd DTN/ASHW M34 .....101 K3
  SALE M33 .....96 F7
  WILM/AE SK9 .....120 A7
Tatton Rd North HTNM SK4 .....99 M7
Tatton Rd South HTNM SK4 .....99 M8
Tatton St HULME M15 .....87 G6
  HYDE SK14 .....102 B5
  ORD M5 .....86 A4
  STKP SK1 .....13 J4
  STLY SK15 .....91 L2
Taunton Av AULW OL7 .....75 K8
  ECC M30 .....84 E2
  LEIGH WN7 .....66 A2
  RDSH SK5 .....100 F7
  URM M41 .....95 L4
Taunton Brook La AULW OL7 .....75 M3
Taunton Cl BOL BL1 * 35 M3
  BRAM/HZG SK7 .....122 C3
Taunton Dr FWTH BL4 .....52 C3
Taunton Gn AULW OL7 .....75 M3
Taunton Hall Cl AULW OL7 .....75 L3
Taunton Lawns AULW OL7 .....75 L8
Taunton Pl AULW OL7 .....75 M3
Taunton Platting AULW OL7 * 75 L4

Taunton Rd AULW OL7 ....75 K8
  CHAD OL9 ....58 D3
  SALE M33 ....96 A8
Taunton St ANC M4 ....88 A3
Taurus St OLDE OL4 ....59 M4
Tavern Court Av FAIL M35 ....74 D5
Tavern Rd GLSP SK13 ....104 B1
Tavery Cl ANC M4 * 7 M3
Tavistock Cl HYDE SK14 ....103 H2
Tavistock Rd BOL BL1 ....2 A6
  ROCH OL11 ....42 C1
  SALE M33 ....96 A7
  WCNE/HIN WN2 ....49 K8
Tavistock St ATH M46 ....66 E1
Tawton Av HYDE SK14 ....103 H2
Tay Cl OLDS OL8 ....9 G9
Tayfield Rd WYTH/NTH M22 ...118 E2
Taylor Av ROCH OL11 ....27 J4
Taylor Green Wy OLDE OL4 ....60 C5
Taylor La DTN/ASHW M34 ....90 A8
Taylor St ALT WA14 ....107 K7
  RNFD/HAY WA11 ....78 C6
  URM M41 ....85 H5
  WCNE/HIN WN2 ....65 M1
Taylor's La BOLE BL2 ....37 L5
  WCNS/IIMK WN3 ....64 C1
Taylorson St ORD M5 ....86 B5
Taylorson St South ORD M5 ......86 D6
Taylors Pl WHIT OL12 * 10 E1
Taylor's Rd STRET M32 ....86 B8
Taylor St BOLS/LL BL3 * 2 F6
  BURY BL9 ....5 H2
  CHAD OL9 ....58 D5
  DROY M43 ....89 K3
  DTN/ASHW M34 ....90 C8
  HEY OL10 ....88 F6
  HOR/BR BL6 ....33 L1
  HYDE SK14 ....93 C7
  HYDE SK14 ....102 C1
  LEIGH WN7 ....66 A4
  MDTN M24 ....57 K4
  OLD OL1 ....59 M4
  OLDE OL4 ....60 B6
  PWCH M25 ....55 M8
  RAD M26 ....54 D1
  ROY/SHW OL2 * 43 G7
  RUSH/FAL M14 ....98 F1
  STLY SK15 ....91 J3
  WGNS/IIMK WN3 ....14 D5
  WHIT OL12 ....20 B4
  WHIT OL12 ....28 C3
Tayton Cl TYLD M29 ....67 M3
Taywood Rd BOLS/LL BL3 ....51 G2
Teak Dr FWTH BL4 ....54 A8
Teak St BURY BL9 ....5 K4
Teal Av POY/DIS SK12 ....121 J8
Tealby Av OLDTF/WHR M16 ....86 F8
Tealby Rd GTN M18 ....88 E8
Teal Cl ALT WA14 ....107 L4
  OFTN SK2 ....113 J7
  WGNS/IIMK WN3 ....46 E8
Teal Ct ROCH OL11 ....27 J5
Teal St BOLS/LL BL3 ....36 C8
Teasdale Cl CHAD OL9 ....74 B1
Tebbutt St ANC M4 ....7 K1
Tebworth Dr WGNE/HIN WN2 ...49 H8
Tedder Cl BURY BL9 ....55 L2
Tedder Dr WYTH/NTH M22 ....119 H5
Teddington Rd
  NEWH/MOS M40 ....73 M3
Ted Jackson Wk OP/CLY M11 *...88 C4
Teer St ANC M4 ....88 A2
Teesdale Av URM M41 ....84 D8
Teesdale Cl OFTN SK2 ....113 H6
Teesdale Dr LEIGH WN7 ....66 F7
Tees St MILN OL16 ....11 K7
Teignmouth Av
  NEWH/MOS M40 * 72 F8
Teignmouth St
  NEWH/MOS M40 ....72 F8
Telfer Av BRUN/LGST M13 ....99 H2
Telfer Rd BRUN/LGST M13 ....99 H2
Telford Cl DTN/ASHW M34 ....90 B5
Telford Crs LEIGH WN7 ....66 A4
Telford Ms UPML OL3 ....61 L3
Telford Rd MPL/ROM SK6 ....114 D8
Telford St ATH M46 ....66 D2
  CHH M8 ....72 F7
  HOR/BR BL6 ....33 M2
Telford Wk OLDTF/WHR M16 .....87 G8
Telford Wy ROCH OL11 ....42 D2
Tellers Cl ATH M46 ....67 G1
Tellson Cl SLFD M6 ....71 G6
Tellson Crs SLFD M6 ....71 G6
Tell St WHIT OL12 ....10 B4
Temperance St BOLS/LL BL3 ....2 C8
  HYDE SK14 * 103 K4
  WGTN/LGST M12 ....7 M8
Tempest Cha HOR/BR BL6 ....34 E8
Tempest Ct HOR/BR BL6 * 34 F7
Tempest Rd HOR/BR BL6 ....50 F1
  WILM/AE SK9 ....130 C9
Tempest St BOLS/LL BL3 ....35 L8
Temple Av GLSP SK13 ....93 M7
Temple Cl OLDE OL4 ....60 B4
Templecombe Dr BOL BL1 ....22 A6
Temple Dr BOL BL1 ....35 M1
  SWIN M27 ....70 E5
Templegate Cl
  WCNNW/ST WN6 ....31 J2
Temple Rd BOL BL1 ....35 M1
  SALE M33 ....97 G8
Temple Sq CHH M8 ....72 D7
Temple St GLSP SK13 ....93 M7
  HEY OL10 ....41 G8
  MDTN M24 ....57 L3
  OLD OL1 ....59 L5
Templeton Cl ALT WA14 ....107 L6
  WHTN BL5 ....50 H5
Templeton Rd WGNE/HIN WN2...64 E3
Ten Acre Ct WHTF M45 * 55 G5
Ten Acre Dr WHTF M45 ....55 C5
Ten Acres La NEWH/MOS M40 ...73 M4
Tenax Rd TRPK M17 ....85 L5
Tenbury Cl SLFD M6 * 86 C1
Tenbury Dr AIMK WN4 ....63 J9
  MDTN M24 ....57 M7
Tenby Av BOL BL1 ....35 K3
  DID/WITH M20 ....98 E6
  STRET M32 ....86 B8
Tenby Ct OLDTF/WHR M16 * 86 F6
Tenby Dr CHD/CHDH SK8 ....120 D3
  SLFD M6 ....71 H7
Tenby Rd EDGY/DAV SK3 ....12 A8
  OLDS OL8 ....74 E2
Tenby St WHIT OL12 ....27 M3
Tenement La BRAM/HZG SK7 ...120 F2
Tenement St WGNE/HIN WN4 ....64 C1

Teneriffe St BRO M7 ....72 A7
Ten Foot Cl GLSP SK13 ....104 E2
Tennis St BOL BL1 ....36 A2
  OLDTF/WHR M16 ....86 E8
Tennyson Av BURY BL9 ....39 J6
  DTN/ASHW M34 * 101 K5
  DUK SK16 ....91 K5
  LEIGH WN7 ....65 M4
  RAD M26 ....38 B8
Tennyson Dr WGN WN1 ....47 M1
  WGNW/BIL/OR WN5 ....62 A3
Tennyson Gdns PWCH M25 ....71 J1
Tennyson Rd CHD/CHDH SK8 ....111 J6
  DROY M43 ....89 K2
  FWTH BL4 ....52 E6
  MDTN M24 ....57 L2
  RDSH SK5 ....100 A3
  SWIN M27 ....70 A4
Tennyson St BOL BL1 ....36 B3
  BRUN/LGST M13 ....87 M7
  OLD OL1 ....59 M3
  ROCH OL11 ....11 G9
Tensing Av ATH M46 ....50 F7
  AULW OL7 ....75 L7
Tensing St OLDS OL8 ....75 K4
Tentercroft WHIT OL12 ....10 C4
Tenterden St BURY BL9 ....4 C5
Tenter Dr WCNNW/ST WN6 ....31 L5
Tenterhill La ROCH OL11 ....27 C2
Tenters St BURY BL9 ....4 C5
Tenth St TRPK M17 ....86 A6
Terence St NEWH/MOS M40 ......74 A7
Terminal Rd East MANAIR M90 ..118 D5
Terminal Rd North
  MANAIR M90 ....118 E5
Terminal Rd South
  MANAIR M90 ....118 D5
Tern Cl ALT WA14 ....107 L4
  DUK SK16 ....91 H5
  ROCH OL11 ....27 J5
Tern Dr POY/DIS SK12 ....121 K8
Ternhill Ct FWTH BL4 ....52 A7
Terrace St OLDE OL4 ....59 L5
The Terrace PWCH M25 ....71 L1
Terrington Cl CCHDY M21 ....98 B5
Tetbury Cl WGNW/BIL/OR WN5 ...47 C3
Tetbury Dr BOLE BL2 ....37 J4
Tetbury Rd WYTH/NTH M22 ......118 D3
Tetlow Gv ECC M30 ....84 F3
Tetlow La BRO M7 ....72 B4
Tetlow St CHAD OL9 * 8 F7
  HYDE SK14 * 91 H7
  MDTN M24 ....57 K4
  NEWH/MOS M40 ....73 M7
Teviot St BRUN/LGST M13 ....88 B8
Tewkesbury Av AUL OL6 ....75 J4
  DROY M43 ....89 K1
  HALE/TIMP WA15 ....117 L1
  MDTN M24 ....57 J1
  URM M41 ....85 H4
Tewkesbury Cl CHD/CHDH SK8 .120 D6
  POY/DIS SK12 ....121 M8
Tewkesbury Dr PWCH M25 ....71 M2
Tewkesbury Rd EDGY/DAV SK3...111 L6
  GOL/RIS/CUL WA3 ....79 L4
  NEWH/MOS M40 ....73 K5
Texas St AUL OL6 ....90 F2
Textile St WGTN/LGST M12 ....88 D5
Textilose Rd TRPK M17 ....85 L7
Thackeray Cl CHH M8 ....72 D6
Thackeray Gv DROY M43 ....89 K2
Thackeray Pl WGNS/IIMK WN3 ...47 K7
Thackeray Rd OLD OL1 ....59 M3
Thames Av LEIGH WN7 ....81 J3
Thames Cl BURY BL9 ....25 J5
  OP/CLY M11 ....88 E4
Thames Ct HULME M15 ....87 C6
Thames Dr WGNW/BIL/OR WN5..46 C5
Thames Rd MILN OL16 ....29 M8
Thames St MILN OL16 ....11 J7
  OLD OL1 ....9 L3
Thanet Cl BRO M7 ....72 B7
Thanet Gv LEIGH WN7 ....66 D7
Thankerton Av DTN/ASHW M34 ...90 A3
Thatcher Cl ALT WA14 ....116 E4
Thatcher St OLDS OL8 ....75 K1
Thatch Leach CHAD OL9 ....58 C7
Thatch Leach La WHTF M45 ....55 K5
Thaxmead Dr NEWH/MOS M40 ...74 A4
Thaxted Dr OFTN SK2 ....82 C3
Thaxted Pl BOL BL1 ....35 M4
Thbeechwood La STLY SK15 ....76 D3
Theatre St OLD OL1 ....9 L5
Thekla St CHAD OL9 ....8 F3
Thelma St RAMS BL0 ....18 H8
Thelwall Av BOLE BL2 ....37 G4
  RUSH/FAL M14 ....98 F3
Thelwall Cl HALE/TIMP WA15 ...108 B6
  LEIGH WN7 ....65 L8
Thelwall Rd SALE M33 ....109 H1
Theobald Rd ALT WA14 ....116 F3
Theta Cl OP/CLY M11 ....88 E2
Thetford WHIT OL12 ....10 C1
Thetford Cl TOT/BURYW BL8 ....25 G7
  WGNE/HIN WN2 ....49 H8
Thetford Dr CHH M8 ....72 E5

Thirlmere Rd GOL/RIS/CUL WA3 ..79 M3
  HOR/BR BL6 ....32 F1
  PART M31 ....94 B8
  ROCH OL11 ....27 L8
  URM M41 ....95 H1
  WCNE/HIN WN2 ....49 H7
  WGNW/BIL/OR WN5 ....46 F5
  WHTN BL5 ....51 J3
  WYTH/NTH M22 ....118 D3
Thirlmere St LEIGH WN7 ....66 B7
Thirlspot Cl BOL BL1 ....22 B6
Thirlstone Av OLDE OL4 * 44 C8
Thirsfield Dr OP/CLY M11 ....88 D2
Thirsk Av CHAD OL9 ....58 C3
  SALE M33 ....107 M1
Thirsk Cl TOT/BURYW BL8 ....24 E7
Thirsk Rd BOLS/LL BL3 ....53 K2
Thirsk St WGTN/LGST M12 ....7 L8
Thistle Bank Cl BKLY M9 ....72 F3
Thistle Cl STLY SK15 ....92 B5
Thistledown Cl ECC M30 ....84 F4
  WGNNW/ST WN6 ....47 K2
Thistle Gn MILN OL16 ....29 H5
Thistle Sq PART M31 ....106 B2
Thistleton Rd BOLS/LL BL3 ....51 J1
Thistle Wy OLDE OL4 ....60 A2
Thistlewood Dr WILM/AE SK9 ....127 H5
Thistleyfields MILN OL16 * 29 H5
Thomas Dr DTN/ASHW M34 ....90 D8
Thomas Gibbon Cl STRET M32 * ...96 F3
Thomas Henshaw Ct
  ROCH OL11 ....27 M8
Thomas Holden St BOL BL1 ....2 C3
Thomas Johnson Cl ECC M30 * 84 F3
Thomas More Cl FWTH BL4 ....53 J6
Thomasson Cl BOL BL1 ....36 B3
Thomas St ANC M4 ....7 H3
  ATH M46 ....67 G1
  BOLS/LL BL3 ....35 J8
  CHH M8 ....72 C4
  FWTH BL4 ....53 H4
  GLSP SK13 ....105 H3
  GOL/RIS/CUL WA3 ....79 K4
  HALE/TIMP WA15 ....108 B8
  MILN OL16 ....11 G2
  MPL/ROM SK6 ....113 K1
  MPL/ROM SK6 ....114 E2
  OFTN SK2 ....13 J8
  OLDE OL4 ....60 B7
  RAD M26 ....54 E1
  ROY/SHW OL2 ....43 M6
  ROY/SHW OL2 ....59 J1
  STRET M32 ....97 G1
  WCNE/HIN WN2 ....65 L1
  WHTN BL5 ....50 B1
Thomas St West OFTN SK2 ....13 J8
Thomas Telford Basin
  CMANE M1 ....7 K5
Thompson Av BOLE BL2 ....38 A5
  WHTF M45 ....55 K5
Thompson Cl DTN/ASHW M34 ....100 E1
Thompson Ct DTN/ASHW M34 ....100 E1
Thompson Dr BURY BL9 ....5 M3
Thompson Fold STLY SK15 ....91 J2
Thompson La CHAD OL9 ....58 D8
Thompson Rd BOL BL1 ....35 L3
  DTN/ASHW M34 ....100 E1
  TRPK M17 ....85 H4
Thompson St AIMK WN4 ....64 A8
  ANC M4 ....7 J2
  BOLS/LL BL3 * 87 H1
  CSLFD M3 * 87 H1
  HOR/BR BL6 ....33 K1
  LEIGH WN7 ....65 L7
  NEWH/MOS M40 ....73 J7
  WGN WN1 ....47 K8
  WGNS/IIMK WN3 ....47 K8
Thomson Rd GTN M18 ....88 F8
Thomson St BRUN/LGST M13 ......87 M6
  EDGY/DAV SK3 ....13 H7
Thoralby Cl WGTN/LGST M12 ......88 D7
Thorburn Rd
  WGNW/BIL/OR WN5 ....46 F6
Thoresby Cl RAD M26 ....37 M3
  WGNS/IIMK WN3 ....63 H1
Thoresway Rd BRUN/LGST M13 ...99 H1
  WILM/AE SK9 ....126 D7
Thor Gv ORD M5 ....86 F4
Thorley Cl CHAD OL9 ....74 B2
Thorley Dr HALE/TIMP WA15 .....108 E7
  URM M41 ....96 A2
Thorley La HALE/TIMP WA15 ....108 E6
  HALE/TIMP WA15 ....118 B3
Thorley Ms BRAM/HZG SK7 ......121 K5
Thorley St FAIL M35 ....74 C4
Thornage Dr NEWH/MOS M40 ....72 F8
Thorn Av FAIL M35 ....74 C6
Thornbank BOLS/LL BL3 ....35 M6
Thorn Bank DROY M43 * 89 J1
Thornbank Cl HEY OL10 ....41 H5
Thornbeck Dr BOL BL1 ....35 J3
Thornbeck Rd BOL BL1 ....35 J3
Thornbridge Av CCHDY M21 ....97 L4
Thornbury ROCH OL11 ....10 D7
Thornbury Av
  GOL/RIS/CUL WA3 ....80 B5
  HYDE SK14 ....103 H1
Thornbury Cl CHD/CHDH SK8 ....120 B5
Thornbury Rd STRET M32 ....86 B8
Thornbury Wy GTN M18 ....88 D5
Thornbush Cl GOL/RIS/CUL WA3 ..80 B4
Thornbush Wy MILN OL16 ....11 L3
Thorncliff Av OLDS OL8 ....75 H1
Thorncliffe Av DUK SK16 ....90 F5
  ROY/SHW OL2 ....42 F6
Thorncliffe Gv BNG/LEV M19 ....99 M3
Thorncliffe Pk ROY/SHW OL2 ......42 F6
Thorncliffe Rd BOL BL1 ....22 C7
  GLSP SK13 ....104 C1
Thorn Cl HEY OL10 ....40 E1
Thorncombe Rd
  OLDTF/WHR M16 ....98 B1
Thorn Ct SLFD M6 ....86 D2
Thorncross Cl HULME M15 ....86 F5
Thorndale Cl ROY/SHW OL2 ....43 H7
Thorndale Gv
  HALE/TIMP WA15 ....108 D7
Thorn Dr WYTH/NTH M22 ....119 J4
Thorne Av URM M41 ....95 K1
Thorneside DTN/ASHW M34 ....90 C7
Thorne St FWTH BL4 ....52 F3
Thorneycroft LEIGH WN7 ....66 F7
Thorneycroft Av CCHDY M21 ....97 M1
Thorneycroft Rd
  HALE/TIMP WA15 ....108 D7

Thornfield Crs LHULT M38 ....52 C7
Thornfield Dr SWIN M27 ....70 B5
Thornfield Gv CHD/CHDH SK8 ...120 C2
  LHULT M38 ....52 C7
Thornfield Hey WILM/AE SK9 .....127 J4
Thornfield Houses
  CHD/CHDH SK8 * 120 C2
Thornfield Rd BNG/LEV M19 ....99 H1
  HTNM SK4 ....111 K1
  TOT/BURYW BL8 ....24 A5
Thornfield St ORD M5 ....86 A3
Thorngate Rd CHH M8 ....72 D7
Thorn Gv CHD/CHDH SK8 ....120 D5
  HALE/TIMP WA15 ....117 C1
  RUSH/FAL M14 ....99 C4
  SALE M33 ....96 E8
Thorngrove Av
  NTHM/RTH M23 ....109 G5
Thorngrove Dr WILM/AE SK9 .....127 G6
Thorngrove HI WILM/AE SK9 .....127 G6
Thorngrove Rd WILM/AE SK9 ....127 G6
Thornham Ct ROY/SHW OL2 ....42 F4
Thornham La MDTN M24 ....42 B6
Thornham New Rd ROCH OL11 ....42 E4
Thornham Rd ROY/SHW OL2 ....43 C5
  SALE M33 ....108 C1
Thornholme Cl GTN M18 ....99 L1
Thornholme Rd MPL/ROM SK6 ...114 D8
Thorniley Brow ANC M4 * 7 C3
Thorn Lea ATH M46 ....67 H2
  BOLE BL2 ....23 C8
Thorn Lea Cl BOL BL1 ....35 J5
Thornlea Dr OLDS OL8 ....74 F3
Thornlea Dr ROCH OL11 ....27 L2
  SWIN M27 ....70 A6
Thornleigh Rd RUSH/FAL M14 .....98 E3
Thornley Av BOL BL1 ....35 M3
Thornley Cl OLDE OL4 ....60 D7
Thornley Crs MPL/ROM SK6 ....101 K8
  OLDE OL4 ....60 D7
Thornley La OLDE OL4 ....60 D7
Thornley La North RDSH SK5 .....100 C1
Thornley La South RDSH SK5 ....100 C1
Thornley Ms BOL BL1 * 35 M2
Thornley Park Rd OLDE OL4 ....60 D7
Thornley Rd DTN/ASHW M34 ....90 D8
  PWCH M25 ....55 M5
Thornley St HYDE SK14 ....102 B3
  MDTN M24 ....57 L3
  RAD M26 ....54 E2
Thornmere Cl SWIN M27 ....69 M2
Thorn Rd BRAM/HZG SK7 ....121 C7
  OLDS OL8 ....75 M1
  SWIN M27 ....70 B6
Thorns Av BOL BL1 ....36 A1
Thorns Cl BOL BL1 ....36 A1
Thorns Clough UPML OL3 ....45 M7
Thornsett Av EDGW/EG BL7 ....23 J5
Thornsett Cl BKLY M9 * 73 H4
Thornsgreen Rd
  WYTH/NTH M22 ....118 F4
Thorns Rd BOL BL1 ....36 A1
The Thorns CCHDY M21 ....97 L5
Thorn St BOL BL1 ....36 C2
  BURY BL9 ....4 F1
  WGNE/HIN WN2 ....49 G8
Thorns Villa Gdns WALK M28 ....68 D7
Thornton Av BOL BL1 ....35 J3
  DTN/ASHW M34 ....90 C3
  URM M41 ....95 K2
Thornton Cl AIMK WN4 ....63 J8
  BOLS/LL BL3 ....53 M2
  FWTH BL4 ....52 E5
  LEIGH WN7 ....81 J3
  WALK M28 ....68 B5
Thornton Crs PWCH M25 ....55 J7
Thornton Dr WILM/AE SK9 ....127 H1
Thornton Ga CHD/CHDH SK8 .....110 D6
Thornton Pl HTNM SK4 ....99 L8
Thornton Rd CHD/CHDH SK8 .....119 C1
  RUSH/FAL M14 ....98 D2
  WALK M28 ....68 B5
Thornton St BOLE BL2 ....3 H4
  NEWH/MOS M40 ....72 F8
  OLDE OL4 ....60 C4
  ROCH OL11 ....10 E9
Thornton St North
  NEWH/MOS M40 ....73 G8
Thorntree Cl BKLY M9 ....73 H5
Thorntree Pl WHIT OL12 ....10 E2
Thorn Vw BURY BL9 ....39 M1
Thornway BRAM/HZG SK7 ....120 E4
  MPL/ROM SK6 ....123 H5
  WALK M28 ....68 D5
Thornway Dr AULW OL7 ....90 C2
Thorn Well WHTN BL5 ....50 B5
Thornwood Av GTN M18 ....89 H8
Thorndyke Av BOL BL1 ....22 C7
Thorold Gv SALE M33 ....97 H8
Thorpe Av RAD M26 ....39 G7
  SWIN M27 ....70 B3
Thorpebrook Rd
  NEWH/MOS M40 ....73 K6
Thorpe Cl DTN/ASHW M34 ....90 C3
  OLDE OL4 ....60 D4
Thorpe Gv HTNM SK4 ....100 A6
Thorpe Hall Gv HYDE SK14 ....91 J6
Thorpe La OLDE OL4 ....60 D4
Thorpeness Sq GTN M18 ....89 C6
Thorpe St BOL BL1 ....36 A2
  GLSP SK13 ....105 L1
  MDTN M24 ....56 F5
  OLDTF/WHR M16 ....86 F8
  RAMS BL0 * 18 E7
  WALK M28 ....68 C5
Thorp Rd NEWH/MOS M40 ....73 K6
  ROY/SHW OL2 ....43 G8
Thorp St ECC M30 ....84 E4
  WHTF M45 ....55 H2
Thorp Vw ROY/SHW OL2 ....42 F7
Thorsby Av HYDE SK14 ....102 C2
Thorsby Cl EDGW/EG BL7 ....22 C4
Thorsby Rd HALE/TIMP WA15 ....108 B7
Thrapston Av DTN/ASHW M34 ....90 A3
Threadfold Wy EDGW/EG BL7 .....22 C5
Threaphurst La
  BRAM/HZG SK7 ....122 D3
Threapwood Rd
  WYTH/NTH M22 ....119 C3
Three Acre Av ROY/SHW OL2 ......43 K8
Three Acres La
  CHD/CHDH SK8 ....120 A5

Three Sisters Rd AIMK WN4 ....63 M5
Threlkeld Cl MDTN M24 ....56 F3
Threlkeld Rd BOL BL1 ....56 F3
  MDTN M24 ....56 F3
Thresher Cl SALE M33 ....109 J1
Threshfield Cl BURY BL9 ....25 J5
Threshfield Dr
  HALE/TIMP WA15 ....108 F5
Throstle Bank St HYDE SK14 ....90 F8
Throstle Gv MPL/ROM SK6 ....113 B7
  TOT/BURYW BL8 ....24 F7
Throstle Hall Ct MDTN M24 * 57 J3
Throstle Nest Av
  WGNNW/ST WN6 ....14 B1
Throstles Cl DROY M43 ....89 M1
Thrum Fold WHIT OL12 ....20 B8
Thrum Hall La WHIT OL12 ....28 B1
Thrush Dr BURY BL9 ....5 K1
Thrush St WHIT OL12 ....27 M3
Thruxton Cl OLDTF/WHR M16 ......98 B1
Thurcaston Rd ALT WA14 ....107 M3
Thurland Rd OLDE OL4 ....58 B4
Thurland St CHAD OL9 ....58 B4
Thurlby Av BKLY M9 ....64 A8
Thurlby Cl AIMK WN4 ....64 A8
Thurlby St BRUN/LGST M13 ....88 A8
Thurleigh Rd DID/WITH M20 ....98 E8
Thurlestone Av BOLE BL2 ....38 A3
Thurlestone Dr
  BRAM/HZG SK7 ....121 K2
  URM M41 ....95 M1
Thurlestone Rd ALT WA14 ....107 L6
Thurloe St RUSH/FAL M14 ....98 F1
Thurlow GOL/RIS/CUL WA3 ....80 B5
Thurlow St SALQ M50 ....86 C4
Thurlston Crs CHH M8 ....72 C5
Thurlwood Av DID/WITH M20 ....98 D5
Thurlwood Cft WHTN BL5 ....50 B3
Thurnham St BOLS/LL BL3 ....51 M1
Thursfield St SLFD M6 ....71 L7
Thursford Gv HOR/BR BL6 ....33 G3
Thurstane St BOL BL1 ....35 M2
Thurstan St WGNS/IIMK WN3 .....48 B8
Thurston Av WGNS/IIMK WN3 .....63 L1
Thurston Cl BURY BL9 ....55 K2
Thurston Clough Rd OLDE OL4 .....61 G3
Thurston Gn WILM/AE SK9 ....130 D3
Thynne St BOLS/LL BL3 ....2 F8
  FWTH BL4 ....52 F3
Tiber Av OLDS OL8 ....74 F3
Tib La CMANW M2 ....6 F5
Tib St CMANE M1 ....7 H4
  DTN/ASHW M34 ....101 J2
  RAMS BL0 * 18 E7
Tideswell Av NEWH/MOS M40 .....88 A1
  WGNW/BIL/OR WN5 ....46 D3
Tideswell Cl CHD/CHDH SK8 ......119 M4
Tideswell Rd BRAM/HZG SK7 .....122 A4
  DROY M43 ....89 H1
Tideway Cl BRO M7 ....71 J4
Tidworth Av ANC M4 ....7 L2
Tiflis St WHIT OL12 ....10 D2
Tig Fold Rd FWTH BL4 ....52 B4
Tilby Cl URM M41 ....95 H2
Tilby St OLD OL1 ....9 C2
Tildsley St BOLS/LL BL3 ....35 G2
Tile St BURY BL9 ....4 F2
Tillard Av EDGY/DAV SK3 ....12 B7
Tillerman Cl SWIN M27 ....71 G4
Tillhey Rd WYTH/NTH M22 ....118 F2
Tilney Av STRET M32 ....97 H3
Tilshead Wk BRUN/LGST M13 * 87 M6
Tilside Gv HOR/BR BL6 ....34 E6
Tilson Rd NTHM/RTH M23 ....109 J7
Tilton St OLD OL1 ....59 M2
Timberbottom BOLE BL2 ....22 F4
Timberhurst BURY BL9 ....40 A2
Times St MDTN M24 ....57 L4
Timothy Cl SLFD M6 ....85 L1
Timperley Cl OLDS OL8 ....75 K2
Timperley Fold AUL OL6 ....75 M6
Timperley La LEIGH WN7 ....81 L2
Timperley Rd AUL OL6 ....75 L6
Timperley St OP/CLY M11 * 88 E4
Timpson Rd NTHM/RTH M23 ......109 H5
Timsbury Cl BOLE BL2 ....37 J7
Timson St FAIL M35 ....74 E2
Tindall St ECC M30 ....84 E4
  RDSH SK5 ....100 C1
Tindle St WALK M28 ....69 J1
Tinkersfield LEIGH WN7 ....66 A5
Tinline St BURY BL9 ....5 J5
Tinningham Cl OP/CLY M11 ....89 H5
Tinshill Cl WGTN/LGST M12 ....88 D7
Tinsley Cl NEWH/MOS M40 ....88 B2
Tinsley Gv BOLE BL2 ....3 K2
Tin St BOLS/LL BL3 ....2 D8
Tintagel Ct RAD M26 ....37 M7
  STLY SK15 ....92 B5
Tintagel Rd WGNE/HIN WN2 ....49 K8
Tintern Av AIMK WN4 ....79 G1
  BOLE BL2 ....36 E2
  DID/WITH M20 ....98 C7
  HEY OL10 ....26 F8
  LIT OL15 ....15 J5
  TYLD M29 ....67 M5
  URM M41 ....95 K4
  WHIT OL12 ....28 B2
  WHTF M45 ....55 J3
Tintern Cl POY/DIS SK12 ....121 M7
Tintern Dr HALE/TIMP WA15 .....117 L2
Tintern Gv STKP SK1 ....112 E3
Tintern Pl HEY OL10 ....26 F8
Tintern Rd CHD/CHDH SK8 ....120 D6
  MDTN M24 ....57 J1
Tintern St RUSH/FAL M14 ....98 E2
Tinwald Pl WGN WN1 ....15 M2
Tipperary St STLY SK15 ....77 H7
Tipping St ALT WA14 ....116 F1
  WGNS/IIMK WN3 ....14 D4
Tipton Cl CHD/CHDH SK8 ....111 L8
  RAD M26 ....38 A7
Tipton Dr NTHM/RTH M23 ....109 J2
Tiree Cl BRAM/HZG SK7 ....122 B3
Tirza Av BNG/LEV M19 ....99 J5
Titanian Ri OLD OL1 ....59 M8
Titchfield Rd OLDS OL8 ....59 M8
Tithe Barn Cl WHIT OL12 * 9 H1
Tithe Barn Crs BOL BL1 ....22 E8
Tithebarn Rd
  HALE/TIMP WA15 ....117 L4
Tithe Barn Rd HTNM SK4 ....99 J8
Tithebarn St BURY BL9 ....4 F4
Tithe Barn St WHTN BL5 ....50 B3
Titherington Cl
  BNG/LEV M19 ....100 A3
Titterington Av CCHDY M21 ....97 L2
Tiverton Av LEIGH WN7 ....66 A2
  SALE M33 ....108 C1
Tiverton Cl RAD M26 ....38 A7
  TYLD M29 ....67 M5

Tiverton Dr SALE M33 108 C1
WILM/AE SK9 127 H3
Tiverton Pl AULW OL7 75 K7
Tiverton Rd URM M41 85 H8
Tiverton Wk BOL BL1 * 35 M3
Tiviot Dl STKP SK1 13 J3
Tiviot Wy RDSH SK5 112 C1
Tivoli St CSLFD M3 6 E5
Toad La WHIT OL12 10 D3
Tobermory Cl OP/CLY M11 89 G3
Tobermory Rd CHD/CHDH SK8 119 L2
Toddington La
WGNE/HIN WN2 32 E4
Todd St BRO M7 72 A6
BURY BL9 4 F1
CSLFD M3 7 G2
GLSP SK13 105 G4
HEY OL10 40 D2
MILN OL16 11 G5
Toft Rd GTN M18 88 F8
Toledo St OP/CLY M11 89 G3
Tolland La HALE/TIMP WA15 117 H4
Tollard Av NEWH/MOS M40 73 G7
Tollard Cl CHD/CHDH SK8 120 D5
Toll Bar St STKP SK1 13 K6
WGTN/LGST M12 88 B6
Tollemache Cl HYDE SK14 92 D7
Tollemache Rd HYDE SK14 92 D7
Tollesbury Cl NEWH/MOS M40 73 G8
Toll Gate Cl BRUN/LGST M13 88 B8
Tollgate Wy MILN OL16 11 L3
Tollgreen Cl WGNE/HIN WN2 49 G5
Toll St RAD M26 38 A8
WGNE/HIN WN2 64 D3
Tolworth Dr CHH M8 72 E5
Tomcroft La DTN/ASHW M34 101 G2
Tom La ALT WA14 116 A6
Tomlinson Cl OLDS OL8 9 H9
Tomlinson St HOR/BR BL6 33 L1
HULME M15 87 H6
NEWH/MOS M40 73 M1
ROCH OL11 27 M8
Tomlin Sq BOLE BL2 3 M4
Tommy Browell Cl
RUSH/FAL M14 98 D1
Tommy Johnson Wk
RUSH/FAL M14 98 D1
Tommy La BOLE BL2 37 M3
Tommy Taylor Cl
NEWH/MOS M40 * 73 M7
Tom Shepley St HYDE SK14 102 B2
Tomwood Ri GLSP SK13 103 M6
Tonacliffe Rd WHIT OL12 20 A7
Tonacliffe Ter WHIT OL12 20 A5
Tonacliffe Wy WHIT OL12 20 A6
Tonbridge Cl TOT/BURYW BL8 24 F5
Tonbridge Rd BNG/LEV M19 99 L4
RDSH SK5 100 C4
Tonge Bridge Wy BOLE BL2 3 J4
Tonge Cl WHTF M45 55 L3
Tonge Fold Rd BOLE BL2 3 L5
Tonge Gn STLY SK15 * 92 B6
Tonge Hall Cl MDTN M24 57 L4
Tonge Meadow MDTN M24 57 L4
Tonge Moor Rd BOLE BL2 3 K1
Tong End WHIT OL12 20 A2
Tonge Old Rd BOLE BL2 3 M4
Tonge Park Av BOLE BL2 36 F3
Tonge Roughs MDTN M24 58 A4
Tonge St HEY OL10 41 G2
MILN OL16 * 11 G6
WGTN/LGST M12 * 88 A5
Tongfields EDGW/EG BL7 22 C4
Tong Head Av BOL BL1 22 E8
Tong La WHIT OL12 20 A3
Tong Rd BOLS/LL BL3 37 K8
Tong St FWTH BL4 53 L7
Tonman St CSLFD M3 6 D6
Toon Crs TOT/BURYW BL8 24 F6
Tootal Dr SLFD M6 85 M1
Tootal Gv SLFD M6 85 M2
Tootal Rd ORD M5 85 M2
Toothill Cl AIMK WN4 63 L7
Topcroft Cl WYTH/NTH M22 110 B4
Topfield Rd WYTH/NTH M22 118 E1
Topgate Brow SWIN M27 71 G4
Topham St BURY BL9 5 H8
Topley St BKLY M9 72 F6
Top o' th' Brow BOLE BL2 * 23 H6
Top o' th' Gorses BOLE BL2 * 3 M8
Top o' th' Gn CHAD OL9 58 F8
Top o' th' La BOLS/LL BL3 * 37 G7
Top o' th' Meadows La
OLDE OL4 60 D3
Topping Fold Rd BURY BL9 5 M2
Toppings Gn EDGW/EG BL7 22 D5
The Toppings MPL/ROM SK6 113 K1
Topping St BOL BL1 36 B3
BURY BL9 5 G2
Topp St FWTH BL4 53 H5
Topp Wy BOL BL1 2 D3
Top Schwabe St MDTN M24 56 F4
Topside OLD OL1 59 H3
Top St MDTN M24 57 H3
OLDE OL4 60 A4
Torah St CHH M8 72 D8
Tor Av TOT/BURYW BL8 24 C3
Torbay Dr OFTN SK2 112 E5
Torbay Rd CCHDY M21 97 M4
URM M41 96 B3
Torcross Rd BKLY M9 56 E7
Tor Heg Ms TOT/BURYW BL8 24 C2
Torkington Av SWIN M27 70 C3
Torkington La BRAM/HZG SK7 122 F1
Torkington Rd BRAM/HZG SK7 122 E1
CHD/CHDH SK8 110 E7
WILM/AE SK9 127 G6
Torkington St EDGY/DAV SK3 12 E8
Torness Wk OP/CLY M11 88 E3
Toronto Av MANAIR M90 118 D5
Toronto Rd OFTN SK2 112 D6
Toronto St BOLE BL2 37 H4
Torquay Cl BRUN/LGST M13 88 A7
Torquay Dr WGNW/BIL/OR WN5 62 B4
Torquay Gv OFTN SK2 112 E8
Torra Barn Cl EDGW/EG BL7 22 B2
Torrax Cl SLFD M6 70 E6
Torre Cl MDTN M24 57 K1
Torrens St SLFD M6 71 G7
Torridon Cl WGNNW/ST WN6 31 K5
Torridon Rd BOLE BL2 37 J5
Torrin Cl EDGY/DAV SK3 112 C7
Torrington Av BKLY M9 73 K2
BOL BL1 36 B2
Torrington Dr HYDE SK14 103 G2
Torrington Rd SWIN M27 70 E6
Torrington St HEY OL10 41 H4
Torrisdale Cl BOLS/LL BL3 35 L7
Torrs Va NM/HAY SK22 124 E5
Torr Top St NM/HAY SK22 124 E4
Torrvale Rd NM/HAY SK22 124 D5
Torside Cl WGNE/HIN WN2 49 G6
Torside Wy GLSP SK13 93 K7
SWIN M27 70 C2
Torver Cl WGNS/IIMK WN3 63 K2
Torver Dr BOLE BL2 37 J4
MDTN M24 57 G2
Torwood Rd CHAD OL9 58 B3
Totland Cl WGTN/LGST M12 99 K1
Totley Ms GLSP SK13 104 A3
Totnes Av BRAM/HZG SK7 121 J2
CHAD OL9 58 C3
Totnes Rd CCHDY M21 97 M4
SALE M33 96 A7
Totridge Cl OFTN SK2 113 G7
Tottenham Dr NTHM/RTH M23 109 G5
Tottington Av OLDE OL4 60 C5
Tottington La PWCH M25 55 H7
Tottington Rd BOLE BL2 23 H7
EDGW/EG BL7 23 J2
TOT/BURYW BL8 4 A1
Tottington St OP/CLY M11 88 F2
Totton Rd FAIL M35 74 C5
Touchet Hall Rd MDTN M24 42 B8
Toulston Rd WGNNW/ST WN6 47 J2
Tours Av NTHM/RTH M23 109 K2
Towcester Cl ANC M4 88 A3
Tower Av RAMS BL0 18 D7
Tower Buildings HOR/BR BL6 * 34 D1
Tower Ct EDGW/EG BL7 16 F8
TOT/BURYW BL8 * 24 C4
Tower Gv LEIGH WN7 67 G6
Towers Av BOLS/LL BL3 35 K8
Towers Cl POY/DIS SK12 122 B7
Towers Sq BRUN/LGST M13 * 87 M6
Towers Rd POY/DIS SK12 122 B7
Towers St OLDE OL4 60 A3
Tower St DUK SK16 91 G3
EDGW/EG BL7 16 F8
HEY OL10 40 F2
HYDE SK14 102 A3
RAD M26 39 G8
Towey Cl GTN M18 89 G6
Towncliffe Wk HULME M15 * 87 G6
Towncroft DTN/ASHW M34 90 C8
Towncroft Av MDTN M24 57 J2
Towncroft La BOL BL1 35 H4
Townend St HYDE SK14 102 B2
Townfield URM M41 95 L3
Townfield Av AIMK WN4 78 E2
Townfield Gdns ALT WA14 108 A7
Townfield Rd ALT WA14 * 108 A7
Townfields AIMK WN4 78 D1
Town Fields Cl BURY BL9 4 F6
Townfield St OLDE OL4 * 59 L5
Townfield Wk HULME M15 * 87 G6
Town Fold MPL/ROM SK6 114 E5
Town Gate Dr URM M41 94 F2
Towngate Wy IRL M44 94 E3
Town Hall La CMANW M2 * 6 F5
Town House Rd LIT OL15 21 M6
Town La DTN/ASHW M34 101 G3
DUK SK16 90 F4
GLSP SK13 104 A6
Townley Fold HYDE SK14 91 L6
Townley Rd MILN OL16 29 K6
Townley St CHH M8 72 C7
MDTN M24 57 K3
OP/CLY M11 * 88 C4
Townley Ter MPL/ROM SK6 * 114 D6
Town Mdw MILN OL16 10 D5
Town Mill Brow WHIT OL12 10 D3
Townrow St HEY OL10 * 41 H2
Townscliffe La MPL/ROM SK6 114 E6
Townsend Rd SWIN M27 70 C3
Townsfield Rd WHTN BL5 50 B5
Townside Rw BURY BL9 4 F6
Townsley Gv AUL OL6 76 B7
Townson Dr LEIGH WN7 81 J3
Town St MPL/ROM SK6 114 E5
Towton St BKLY M9 73 H4
Towyn Av ORD M5 86 D2
Toxhead Cl HOR/BR BL6 33 K1
Toxteth St OP/CLY M11 89 H5
Tracey St CHH M8 72 D3
Tracks La WGNW/BIL/OR WN5 62 A1
Traders Av URM M41 85 H5
Trafalgar Av DTN/ASHW M34 89 M5
POY/DIS SK12 129 L1
Trafalgar Cl POY/DIS SK12 129 L1
Trafalgar Gv BRO M7 * 72 A7
Trafalgar Pl DID/WITH M20 98 D8
Trafalgar Rd SALE M33 96 F6
SLFD M6 85 K1
WGN WN1 14 F1
WGNE/HIN WN2 49 G7
Trafalgar Sq AULW OL7 90 C3
Trafalgar St AULW OL7 90 C3
BRO M7 72 B7
MILN OL16 11 H3
OLD OL1 9 G2
Trafford Av URM M41 96 B1
Trafford Bank Rd
OLDTF/WHR M16 * 86 F7
Trafford Bvd TRPK M17 85 G6
URM M41 84 F6
Trafford Dr HALE/TIMP WA15 108 E4
LHULT M38 52 E7
Trafford Gv FWTH BL4 53 H3
STRET M32 97 G3
Trafford Park Rd TRPK M17 85 M5
Trafford Pl OLDTF/WHR M16 87 G6
WILM/AE SK9 * 127 H6
Trafford Rd ECC M30 85 G4
SALQ M50 86 D6
WGNE/HIN WN2 48 F7
WILM/AE SK9 126 E3
WILM/AE SK9 130 D3
Trafford St CSLFD M3 6 D7
FWTH BL4 53 G3
OLDS OL8 9 H8
ROCH OL11 10 D8
Trafford Wharf Rd TRPK M17 85 M5
Tragan Cl OFTN SK2 113 G6
Tragan Dr OFTN SK2 113 G6
Trail St SLFD M6 86 B2
Tram St OP/CLY M11 88 F5
WGNE/HIN WN2 64 D3
Tramway Rd AUL OL6 90 F1
IRL M44 94 C5
Tranby Cl WYTH/NTH M22 110 C8
Tranmere Cl GTN M18 88 F7
Tranmere Dr WILM/AE SK9 127 J2
Tranmere Rd EDGY/DAV SK3 12 A6
Transvaal St OP/CLY M11 89 G3
Travis Brow HTNM SK4 12 E4
Travis St CMANE M1 7 L6
HYDE SK14 102 B2
MILN OL16 29 L8
ROY/SHW OL2 43 M5
Trawden Av BOL BL1 35 M2
Trawden Dr BURY BL9 25 H4
Trawden Gn OFTN SK2 113 G8
Traylen Wy WHIT OL12 27 K3
Traynor Cl MDTN M24 57 J3
Trecastell Cl WGN WN1 15 M2
Tredcroft St GLSP SK13 104 E4
Tredgold St HOR/BR BL6 33 M2
Tree Av DROY M43 89 K1
Tree House Av AULW OL7 75 J6
Treelands Wk ORD M5 86 E6
Treen Rd TYLD M29 67 M4
Tree Tops EDGW/EG BL7 22 F6
Treetops Av RAMS BL0 24 D1
Treetops Cl UPML OL3 * 61 J3
Trefoil Wy LIT OL15 21 K6
Tregaer Fold MDTN M24 57 M4
Tregaron Gv WGNE/HIN WN2 65 K1
Trenam Pl ORD M5 86 E2
Trenant Rd SLFD M6 71 G8
Trenchard Dr WYTH/NTH M22 119 H5
Trencherbone RAD M26 38 B7
Trencherfield Ml
WGNS/IIMK WN3 * 14 E6
Trengrove St WHIT OL12 * 27 M3
Trent Av CHAD OL9 58 B4
HEY OL10 40 D1
MILN OL16 29 K6
Trent Bridge Wk
OLDTF/WHR M16 97 K1
Trent Cl BRAM/HZG SK7 120 E6
RDSH SK5 100 F7
Trent Ct HULME M15 * 87 G6
Trent Dr BURY BL9 25 J4
WALK M28 68 E2
WGNE/HIN WN2 65 M1
Trent Gv LEIGH WN7 65 M8
Trentham Av FWTH BL4 52 F3
HTNM SK4 111 J1
Trentham Cl FWTH BL4 52 F3
Trentham Gv NEWH/MOS M40 73 K3
Trentham Lawns SLFD M6 71 K8
Trentham Rd OLDTF/WHR M16 97 K1
Trentham St FWTH BL4 52 F3
HULME M15 86 F5
SWIN M27 * 70 B3
Trent Rd AIMK WN4 64 B7
ROY/SHW OL2 43 K4
WGNW/BIL/OR WN5 46 F5
Trent St MILN OL16 * 11 J7
Trent Wk DROY M43 89 L4
Trent Wy FWTH BL4 53 L7
Tresco Av STRET M32 97 H3
Trescott Ms WGNNW/ST WN6 31 H4
Treswell Cl WGNE/HIN WN2 65 H2
Trevarrick Ct HOR/BR BL6 34 B2
Trevelyan Dr
WGNW/BIL/OR WN5 62 A3
Trevelyan St ECC M30 85 K2
Trevor Av SALE M33 108 C2
Trevor Dr NEWH/MOS M40 74 B2
Trevore Dr WGN WN1 31 M3
Trevor Gv STKP SK1 13 M6
Trevor Rd ECC M30 84 E1
SWIN M27 70 B6
URM M41 95 J1
Trevor St OP/CLY M11 89 H5
ROCH OL11 41 L1
The Triangle HALE/TIMP WA15 108 E5
Tribune Av ALT WA14 107 L5
Trident Rd ECC M30 84 C5
Trillo Av BOLE BL2 3 K7
Trimdon Cl OP/CLY M11 88 E2
Trimingham Dr
TOT/BURYW BL8 25 G6
Trimley Av NEWH/MOS M40 73 G7
Trinity Av SALE M33 97 G8
Trinity Buildings MOSL OL5 * 77 G2
Trinity Cl DUK SK16 91 H4
Trinity Ct AUL OL6 90 D1
Trinity Crs WALK M28 69 H2
Trinity Gdns AIMK WN4 63 J8
EDGY/DAV SK3 121 H1
Trinity Gn RAMS BL0 24 E2
Trinity Rd SALE M33 96 F8
Trinity St BOLS/LL BL3 2 D7
BURY BL9 4 F6
MDTN M24 * 57 J4
MPL/ROM SK6 * 114 C6
OLD OL1 9 H2
STLY SK15 91 K3
Trinity Wy CSLFD M3 6 B5
Tripland Rd ECC M30 84 C4
Tripps Ms DID/WITH M20 98 C8
Triscombe Wy OLDTF/WHR M16 98 B1
Tristam Cl BRUN/LGST M13 87 M6
Trojan Gdns BRO M7 71 M7
Troon Cl BOLS/LL BL3 51 J1
BRAM/HZG SK7 121 J5
Troon Dr CHD/CHDH SK8 119 L3
Troon Rd NTHM/RTH M23 109 J6
Trough Ga OLDS OL8 75 G2
Troutbeck Av ANC M4 7 M3
NEWLW WA12 78 B8
Troutbeck Cl TOT/BURYW BL8 23 L2
Troutbeck Dr RAMS BL0 18 F5
TYLD M29 67 K5
Troutbeck Ri
WGNW/BIL/OR WN5 46 E6
Troutbeck Rd AIMK WN4 63 M7
CHD/CHDH SK8 119 K1
HALE/TIMP WA15 109 G7
Troutbeck Wy ROCH OL11 27 L8
Trowbridge Dr
NEWH/MOS M40 73 M3
Trowbridge Rd
DTN/ASHW M34 101 K3
Trows La ROCH OL11 42 A3
Trowtree Av WGTN/LGST M12 88 B6
Troydale Dr NEWH/MOS M40 73 K6
Troy Wk ORD M5 * 86 E5
Trumpet St CMANE M1 6 E7
Truro Av AUL OL6 76 A5
RDSH SK5 100 F7
STRET M32 97 H2
Truro Cl BRAM/HZG SK7 121 H5
TOT/BURYW BL8 4 C2
Truro Dr SALE M33 96 A8
Truro Rd CHAD OL9 58 D3
TYLD M29 67 M4
Trust Rd GTN M18 99 M1
Tucana Av BRO M7 86 F1
Tucker's Hill Brow HOR/BR BL6 32 E3
Tudbury Wy CSLFD M3 6 B2
Tudor Av BKLY M9 73 H3
BOL BL1 35 L5
CHAD OL9 74 A1
FWTH BL4 52 E5
STLY SK15 92 A1
Tudor Cl MOSL OL5 77 H3
RDSH SK5 100 B5
Tudor Ct PWCH M25 71 M1
WHIT OL12 * 28 E1
Tudor Gn WILM/AE SK9 127 J3
Tudor Gv MDTN M24 57 G1
WGNS/IIMK WN3 63 H2
Tudor Hall St ROCH OL11 41 M2
Tudor Rd ALT WA14 107 L5
WILM/AE SK9 127 J3
Tudor St BOLS/LL BL3 * 35 M8
MDTN M24 57 L4
OLDS OL8 8 F8
ROY/SHW OL2 43 L5
Tuffley Rd NTHM/RTH M23 109 K8
Tugford Cl OLDTF/WHR M16 98 B1
Tuley St OP/CLY M11 88 C5
Tulip Av FWTH BL4 52 D3
FWTH BL4 53 J7
Tulip Cl CHAD OL9 58 B5
EDGY/DAV SK3 112 A7
SALE M33 95 M8
Tulip Dr HALE/TIMP WA15 108 C6
WGNNW/ST WN6 47 J1
Tulip Gv WHIT OL12 28 B1
Tulip Rd PART M31 106 B2
RNFD/HAY WA11 78 C6
Tully Pl BRO M7 72 B8
Tully St BRO M7 72 B5
Tully St South BRO M7 72 B6
Tulpen Sq CHAD OL9 8 A4
Tulworth Rd POY/DIS SK12 121 M8
Tumblewood Dr
CHD/CHDH SK8 111 H8
Tunbridge Sq ORD M5 86 D2
Tunshill La MILN OL16 29 M5
Tunshill Rd NTHM/RTH M23 109 H3
Tuns Rd OLDS OL8 75 L2
Tunstall Cl BURY BL9 39 K5
Tunstall La WGNW/BIL/OR WN5 47 G7
Tunstall Rd OLDE OL4 59 M6
Tunstall St HTNM SK4 13 H2
OP/CLY M11 * 89 H5
Tunstead Av DID/WITH M20 98 C6
Tunstead La UPML OL3 61 M7
Turbary Wk MILN OL16 29 G6
Turf Cl ROY/SHW OL2 59 H1
Turf Hill Rd MILN OL16 11 K9
Turf House Cl LIT OL15 21 K5
Turfland Av ROY/SHW OL2 59 H1
Turf La CHAD OL9 74 D1
ROY/SHW OL2 59 J1
Turf Lea Rd MPL/ROM SK6 123 K3
Turf Park Rd ROY/SHW OL2 59 J1
Turf Pit La OLDE OL4 44 C8
Turf St RAD M26 54 C1
Turf Ter LIT OL15 21 L6
Turfton Rd ROY/SHW OL2 59 J1
Turks Rd RAD M26 38 A7
Turk St BOL BL1 35 M4
Turley St CHH M8 72 E6
Turnberry BOLS/LL BL3 51 J1
Turnberry Cl TYLD M29 67 M4
Turnberry Dr WILM/AE SK9 127 H4
Turnberry Rd CHD/CHDH SK8 119 L3
Turnbull Av PWCH M25 55 M5
Turnbull Rd ALT WA14 107 L4
BRUN/LGST M13 99 J2
GTN M18 100 C1
Turnbury Cl SALE M33 96 E6
Turnbury Rd WYTH/NTH M22 110 B7
Turncliff Crs MPL/ROM SK6 114 A5
Turncroft La STKP SK1 13 M5
STKP SK1 112 E4
Turncroft Wy WALK M28 68 C5
Turnditch Cl WGNNW/ST WN6 31 K8
Turnell Wy WALK M28 69 K7
Turner Av FAIL M35 74 B6
IRL M44 94 D1
WGNE/HIN WN2 65 H3
Turner Bridge Rd BOLE BL2 3 L2
Turner Dr URM M41 96 C2
Turnerford Cl EDGW/EG BL7 22 B3
Turner Gdns HYDE SK14 91 H8
Turner La AUL OL6 75 L8
HYDE SK14 91 J8
MPL/ROM SK6 101 J6
Turner Rd MPL/ROM SK6 114 C7
Turner's Pl WHIT OL12 28 B1
Turner St ANC M4 7 H3
AUL OL6 75 L8
BOL BL1 3 H2
BRO M7 72 B5
DTN/ASHW M34 90 C7
GTN M18 89 G7
LEIGH WN7 66 D8
OLDE OL4 60 B4
OLDTF/WHR M16 86 F6
OP/CLY M11 88 F3
STKP SK1 13 J3
WGN WN1 15 J3
WHIT OL12 28 B3
WHTN BL5 50 B7
Turners Yd
WGNW/BIL/OR WN5 * 46 B6
Turnfield Cl MILN OL16 29 G1
Turnfield Rd CHD/CHDH SK8 119 L1
Turnhill Rd MILN OL16 42 E1
Turnill Dr AIMK WN4 78 E2
Turnlee Cl GLSP SK13 104 F5
Turnlee Dr GLSP SK13 104 F5
Turnlee Rd GLSP SK13 104 F5
Turn Moss Rd STRET M32 97 J4
Turnough Rd MILN OL16 29 J5
Turnpike Cl UPML OL3 45 M7
Turnpike Gn SLFD M6 * 86 C1
The Turnpike MPL/ROM SK6 114 A5
Turnpike Wk OP/CLY M11 88 C3
Turn Rd RAMS BL0 19 H4
Turnstone Av NEWLW WA12 78 F8
Turnstone Cl LEIGH WN7 66 D6
Turnstone Rd BOLE BL2 3 G7
OFTN SK2 113 K7
Turn St AUL OL6 76 A8
Turret Hall Dr
GOL/RIS/CUL WA3 80 B4
Turriff Gv WGNE/HIN WN2 65 M3
Turton Cl HEY OL10 40 D2
TOT/BURYW BL8 38 D4
Turton Ct BOL BL1 3 G2
Turton Hts BOLE BL2 22 E6
Turton La PWCH M25 55 J7
Turton Rd BOLE BL2 22 F6
TOT/BURYW BL8 24 B4
Turton St BOL BL1 2 F1
GOL/RIS/CUL WA3 79 K4
OP/CLY M11 * 89 G5
Turves Rd CHD/CHDH SK8 120 B3
Tuscan Rd DID/WITH M20 110 E4
Tuscany Vw BRO M7 71 L4
Tutbury St ANC M4 88 A3
Tuxford Wk NEWH/MOS M40 73 G7
Tweedale Av BKLY M9 56 F7
Tweedale St ROCH OL11 10 D7
Tweedale Wy CHAD OL9 74 C2
Tweed Cl ALT WA14 107 M6
OLDS OL8 9 H8
Tweedle Hill Rd BKLY M9 56 F8
Tweed St LEIGH WN7 66 E8
Tweenbrook Av
NTHM/RTH M23 118 C1
Tweesdale Cl WHTF M45 55 L3
Twelve Yards Rd ECC M30 84 A5
IRL M44 82 F8
Twigworth Rd
WYTH/NTH M22 118 E2
Twillbrook Dr CSLFD M3 * 6 D1
Twinegate WHIT OL12 28 B1
Twingates Cl ROY/SHW OL2 43 L7
Twining Brook Rd
CHD/CHDH SK8 120 D1
Twining Rd ECC M30 85 G4
Twinnies Rd WILM/AE SK9 126 F3
Twin St HEY OL10 41 H3
Twirl Hill Rd AUL OL6 76 B4
Twisse Rd BOLE BL2 37 J5
Twiss Green Dr
GOL/RIS/CUL WA3 81 H8
Twiss Green La
GOL/RIS/CUL WA3 81 H8
Twist Av GOL/RIS/CUL WA3 79 M4
Twist La LEIGH WN7 66 B8
Twoacre Av WYTH/NTH M22 109 M7
Two Acre Dr ROY/SHW OL2 43 J4
Two Acre La OLDE OL4 60 E2
Two Bridges Rd MILN OL16 43 L1
Two Brooks La
TOT/BURYW BL8 23 L2
Two Trees La DTN/ASHW M34 101 K3
Twyford Cl DID/WITH M20 110 C1
Tybyrne Cl WALK M28 68 C5
Tydden St OLDS OL8 75 J1
Tydeman Wk MILN OL16 * 29 K7
Tyldesley Ar WGN WN1 * 15 G3
Tyldesley Old Rd ATH M46 67 G2
Tyldesley Pas TYLD M29 67 J3
Tyldesley Rd ATH M46 67 G2
Tyldesley St RUSH/FAL M14 98 D1
Tyler St WILM/AE SK9 130 D3
Tymm St NEWH/MOS M40 73 M4
Tyndall Av NEWH/MOS M40 73 K3
Tyndall St OLDE OL4 59 M7
Tyne Ct WALK M28 68 F1
Tynedale Cl RDSH SK5 100 B7
Tynesbank WALK M28 68 F2
Tynesbank Cottages
WALK M28 * 68 F1
Tyne St OLDE OL4 59 M5
Tynwald St OLDE OL4 59 M5
Tyrer Av WGNS/IIMK WN3 14 A9
Tyrol Wk OP/CLY M11 88 C4
Tyrone Cl NTHM/RTH M23 109 G4
Tyrone Dr ROCH OL11 27 J7
Tyro St OLDS OL8 * 75 J1
Tyrrell Gv HYDE SK14 102 D3
Tyrrel Rd RDSH SK5 100 C3
Tysoe Gdns CSLFD M3 6 B2
Tyson St CHH M8 72 C4
Tytherington Dr
BNG/LEV M19 100 A3

U

Uganda St BOLS/LL BL3 51 M2
Ukraine Rd BRO M7 71 K6
Uldale Dr MDTN M24 57 H3
Ullesthorpe WHIT OL12 10 D3
Ulleswater Cl BOLS/LL BL3 53 J1
Ulleswater St BOL BL1 36 C2
Ullswater Av AULW OL7 75 K8
ROY/SHW OL2 43 G6
WGNW/BIL/OR WN5 46 C5
WHIT OL12 27 M3
Ullswater Dr BURY BL9 * 39 H5
FWTH BL4 52 B5
MDTN M24 57 J1
WGNE/HIN WN2 48 E5
Ullswater Gv HEY OL10 41 G4
Ullswater Rd
GOL/RIS/CUL WA3 79 M3
STKP SK1 112 E5
TYLD M29 67 K5
URM M41 84 B8
WILM/AE SK9 119 L8
WYTH/NTH M22 118 D2
Ullswater St LEIGH WN7 66 B7
Ullswater Ter STLY SK15 76 D8
Ulster Av ROCH OL11 10 D9
Ulundi St RAD M26 54 D1
Ulverston Av CHAD OL9 58 D6
DID/WITH M20 98 C5
Ulverston Rd WGNS/IIMK WN3 63 J1
Umberton Rd WHTN BL5 51 J5
Uncouth Rd MILN OL16 29 H5
Underhill MPL/ROM SK6 113 M2
Underhill Rd OLD OL1 9 H1
Underhill Wk NEWH/MOS M40 73 L8
Under La CHAD OL9 74 E1
OLDE OL4 60 E8
Underwood WHIT OL12 10 D4
Underwood Cl GTN M18 89 J6
Underwood Rd HYDE SK14 103 G1
WILM/AE SK9 130 F3
Underwood St DUK SK16 90 E4
Underwood Wy ROY/SHW OL2 44 A4
Undsworth Ct HEY OL10 * 41 G2
Unicorn St ECC M30 84 E4
Union Ar BURY BL9 4 F4
Union Buildings BOLE BL2 2 F6
Union Ct BOLE BL2 * 36 D2
Union Rd AUL OL6 75 M8
BOLE BL2 3 H1
MPL/ROM SK6 * 114 C6
NM/HAY SK22 124 D5
WHIT OL12 21 J8
Union St ANC M4 7 H3
AUL OL6 75 L8
BURY BL9 4 F4
CHAD OL9 58 E8
EDGW/EG BL7 22 A2
GLSP SK13 104 F4
GTN M18 89 H6
HYDE SK14 102 B2
LEIGH WN7 66 C7
MDTN M24 57 K3
OLD OL1 9 J6
OLDE OL4 60 B6
RAMS BL0 18 F6
ROY/SHW OL2 43 G8
RUSH/FAL M14 * 98 E1
SLFD M6 71 K8
STKP SK1 13 J7
SWIN M27 70 B4
SWIN M27 70 D4
TYLD M29 67 J3
WGNE/HIN WN2 48 D4
WGTN/LGST M12 7 M8
WHIT OL12 10 E2
WHIT OL12 20 A4

Union St West OLD8 ...... 9 C8
Union Ter BRO M7 * 72 C4
United Rd OLDTF/WHR M16 ...... 86 B7
Unity Crs HEY OL10 ...... 40 E3
Unity Dr BRO M7 ...... 72 B6
Unity St HEY OL10 ...... 40 E3
Unity Wy STKP SK1 ...... 13 L7
University Rd ORD M5 ...... 86 E2
University Rd West ORD M5 ...... 86 E2
Unsworth Av GOL/RIS/CUL WA3 ...... 80 B3
TYLD M29 ...... 67 L4
Unsworth St LEIGH WN7 ...... 66 B5
RAD M26 ...... 38 C8
Unwin Av GTN M18 ...... 89 G8
Upavon Rd WYTH/NTH M22 ...... 119 H1
Upcast La WILM/AE SK9 ...... 130 A7
Upholland Rd
WGNW/BIL/OR WN5 ...... 46 A3
LHULT M38 ...... 52 C6
Upland Dr AIMK WN4 ...... 64 A8
Upland Rd OLDS OL8 ...... 59 H8
Uplands MDTN M24 ...... 57 K5
Uplands Av RAD M26 ...... 54 C7
Uplands Rd GLSP SK13 ...... 105 G4
HYDE SK14 ...... 102 D6
URM M41 ...... 95 H4
The Uplands MOSL OL5 ...... 77 G3
Upper Brook St
BRUN/LGST M13 ...... 87 L6
STKP SK1 ...... 13 K5
Upper Camp St BRO M7 ...... 72 A7
Upper Choriton Rd
OLDTF/WHR M16 ...... 97 M1
Upper Cleminson St CSLFD M3 ...... 6 A2
Upper Cliff HI ROY/SHW OL2 ...... 43 M3
Upper Conran St BKLY M9 ...... 73 H4
Upper Dicconson St WGN WN1 ...... 15 G2
Upper Downs ALT WA14 ...... 116 E1
Upper George St TYLD M29 ...... 67 K4
WHIT OL12 ...... 10 F1
Upper Gloucester St SLFD M6 ...... 86 D1
Upper Hayes CI MILN OL16 ...... 11 L3
Upper Helena St
NEWH/MOS M40 ...... 88 B2
Upper Hibbert La
MPL/ROM SK6 ...... 114 C4
Upper Kent Rd RUSH/FAL M14 ...... 99 G1
Upper Kirby St ANC M4 ...... 7 M1
Upper Lees Dr WHTN BL5 ...... 50 D3
Upper Lloyd St RUSH/FAL M14 ...... 98 D1
Upper Mdl EDGW/EG BL7 ...... 22 C3
Upper Medlock St HULME M15 ...... 87 J6
Uppermill Dr BNG/LEV M19 ...... 111 G1
Upper Monsall St
NEWH/MOS M40 ...... 73 H6
Upper Moss La HULME M15 ...... 87 H6
Upper Park Rd BRO M7 ...... 72 B3
RUSH/FAL M14 ...... 87 M8
Upper Passmonds Gv
ROCH OL11 ...... 27 L4
Upper St Stephen St
WGNW/ST WN6 ...... 14 D3
Upper Stone Dr MILN OL16 ...... 29 C6
Upper West Gv
BRUN/LGST M13 ...... 88 A7
Upper Wharf St ORD M5 ...... 86 F3
Upper Wilton St PWCH M25 ...... 55 M8
Uppingham Dr RAMS BL0 ...... 18 E5
Upton Av CHD/CHDH SK8 ...... 120 C1
HTNM SK4 ...... 99 H8
Upton CI GOL/RIS/CUL WA3 ...... 80 A4
MDTN M24 ...... 57 K7
Upton Dr ALT WA14 ...... 108 B4
Upton La TYLD M29 ...... 67 H4
Upton Rd ATH M46 ...... 51 H8
Upton Wy TOT/BURYW BL8 ...... 24 C7
Upwood Rd GOL/RIS/CUL WA3 ...... 80 A5
Urban Dr HALE/TIMP WA15 ...... 108 B8
Urban Rd HALE/TIMP WA15 ...... 108 B8
SALE M33 ...... 96 B8
Urmston Av OLDS OL8 ...... 75 J1
Urmston Av NEWLW WA12 ...... 78 E4
Urmston La STRET M32 ...... 96 D3
Urmston Pk URM M41 ...... 96 B2
Urmston St LEIGH WN7 ...... 66 A7
Urwick Rd MPL/ROM SK6 ...... 113 L5
Usk CI WHTF M45 ...... 55 M5
Uttley St BOL BL1 ...... 36 A2
ROCH OL11 ...... 27 M8
Uxbridge Av OP/CLY M11 ...... 88 F2
Uxbridge St AUL OL6 ...... 90 D1

V

Vaal St OLDS OL8 ...... 74 F1
Valance CI WGTN/LGST M12 ...... 88 D6
Valdene CI FWTH BL4 ...... 53 L5
Valdene Dr FWTH BL4 ...... 53 L5
WALK M28 ...... 69 L4
Vale Av BURY BL9 ...... 39 G5
HOR/BR BL6 ...... 33 K1
HYDE SK14 ...... 102 D1
RAD M26 ...... 53 M5
SALE M33 ...... 97 H7
SWIN M27 ...... 70 D3
URM M41 ...... 95 H3
Vale CI BRAM/HZG SK7 ...... 113 H8
HTNM SK4 ...... 111 J2
MPL/ROM SK6 ...... 113 M3
WGNW/ST WN6 ...... 30 B4
Vale Coppice HOR/BR BL6 ...... 33 K1
RAMS BL0 ...... 24 F1
Vale Cottages LIT OL15 ...... 21 L7
Vale Crs CHD/CHDH SK8 ...... 120 B2
Vale Dr CHAD OL9 ...... 8 E7
PWCH M25 ...... 71 K2
Vale Edge RAD M26 ...... 38 D7
Vale Head WILM/AE SK9 ...... 127 H2
Vale House Dr GLSP SK13 ...... 93 K7
Vale La FAIL M35 ...... 74 D8
Valemount GLSP SK13 ...... 93 K7
Valencia Rd BRO M7 ...... 71 L6
Valentia Rd BKLY M9 ...... 57 G8
Valentine St ATH M46 ...... 66 D3
FAIL M35 ...... 74 B5
OLDE OL4 ...... 59 M6
Vale Park Wy CHH M8 ...... 72 F5
Valerie Wk HULME M15 ...... 6 F9
Vale Rd ALT WA14 ...... 116 D3
DROY M43 ...... 89 L1
HALE/TIMP WA15 ...... 108 D7
HTNM SK4 ...... 111 J3
MPL/ROM SK6 ...... 113 M3
ROY/SHW OL2 ...... 44 A6
STLY SK15 ...... 77 H3
WILM/AE SK9 ...... 126 C4
Vale Side MOSL OL5 ...... 76 F4

Vale St AULW OL7 ...... 75 K6
BOLE BL2 ...... 37 K5
EDGW/EG BL7 ...... 17 G8
HEY OL10 ...... 41 H2
MDTN M24 ...... 57 L4
OP/CLY M11 ...... 88 F2
The Vale MOSL OL5 ...... 76 E3
Vale Top Av BKLY M9 ...... 73 H5
Valetta CI RUSH/FAL M14 ...... 98 E4
Vale Vw ALT WA14 * 116 E3
Valewood Av HTNM SK4 ...... 111 K3
Valiant Rd WGNW/BIL/OR WN5 ...... 47 G4
Valletts La BOL BL1 ...... 35 M3
Valley Av TOT/BURYW BL8 ...... 24 E8
Valley CI CHD/CHDH SK8 ...... 120 A1
MOSL OL5 ...... 76 E2
Valley Dr WILM/AE SK9 ...... 127 G1
Valley Gv DTN/ASHW M34 ...... 101 L2
Valley Ms UPML OL3 ...... 61 M8
Valley MI EDGW/EG BL7 * 22 C3
Valley Mill La BURY BL9 ...... 5 H7
Valley New Rd ROY/SHW OL2 ...... 59 H1
Valley Park Rd PWCH M25 ...... 55 J7
Valley Ri ROY/SHW OL2 ...... 43 J7
Valley Rd BRAM/HZG SK7 ...... 121 H3
CHD/CHDH SK8 ...... 120 A1
GLSP SK13 ...... 104 C4
HYDE SK14 ...... 103 H4
MDTN M24 ...... 57 L2
MPL/ROM SK6 ...... 101 G8
NM/HAY SK22 ...... 125 M2
ROY/SHW OL2 ...... 59 H1
URM M41 ...... 84 A8
WGNW/BIL/OR WN5 ...... 47 G7
Valley Rd South URM M41 ...... 94 F2
Valley Vw HYDE SK14 ...... 91 K8
Valley Vw OP/CLY M11 ...... 88 C3
Valley Wy STLY SK15 ...... 91 M3
Valpy Av BOLE BL2 ...... 36 E1
Vanbrugh Gv
WGNW/BIL/OR WN5 ...... 46 E3
Vancouver Quay SALQ M50 ...... 86 C5
Vandyke Av SLFD M6 ...... 85 L1
Vandyke St WHIT OL12 ...... 27 J3
Vane St ECC M30 ...... 84 F2
Vannes Gv HYDE SK14 ...... 103 J1
Vantomme St BOL BL1 ...... 22 B8
Vant St OLDE OL4 ...... 9 M8
Varden Gv EDGY/DAV SK3 ...... 112 A7
Varden Rd POY/DIS SK12 ...... 129 J1
Vardon Dr WILM/AE SK9 ...... 127 H6
Varey St GTN M18 ...... 89 G7
Varley Rd BOLS/LL BL3 ...... 35 K8
Varley St NEWH/MOS M40 ...... 73 G8
Varna St OP/CLY M11 ...... 89 G5
Vauban Dr SLFD M6 ...... 85 L1
Vaudrey Dr BRAM/HZG SK7 ...... 122 A2
CHD/CHDH SK8 ...... 120 C2
HALE/TIMP WA15 ...... 108 D4
Vaudrey La DTN/ASHW M34 ...... 101 K2
Vaudrey Dr NTHM/RTH M23 ...... 109 J2
Vaynor WHIT OL12 ...... 10 D2
Vega St CHH M8 ...... 72 B8
Vela Wk BRO M7 ...... 86 F1
Velmere Av BKLY M9 ...... 56 D7
Velour CI CSLFD M3 ...... 6 A1
Vendale Av SWIN M27 ...... 70 A6
Venetia St NEWH/MOS M40 * 73 M7
Venice St BOLS/LL BL3 ...... 35 M8
CMANE M1 * 7 H7
Venlow Gdns CHD/CHDH SK8 ...... 120 D3
Ventnor Av BNG/LEV M19 ...... 99 M4
BOL BL1 ...... 36 C1
BURY BL9 ...... 55 J1
SALE M33 ...... 96 E6
Ventnor CI DTN/ASHW M34 ...... 101 L4
Ventnor Rd DID/WITH M20 ...... 110 F1
HTNM SK4 ...... 12 A2
Ventnor St ROCH OL11 ...... 10 E8
SLFD M6 ...... 71 L7
Ventor St BKLY M9 ...... 73 G4
Ventura CI RUSH/FAL M14 ...... 98 E4
Ventura CI NM/HAY SK22 ...... 124 F3
Venture Scout Wy GTN M18 ...... 72 C6
Venwood Rd PWCH M25 * 71 J2
Verbena Av FWTH BL4 ...... 52 D3
Verbena La PART M31 ...... 106 C1
Verdant La ECC M30 ...... 84 C4
Verdant Wy MILN OL16 ...... 42 F1
Verda St WGNE/HIN WN2 ...... 64 D4
Verdun Av SLFD M6 ...... 85 L1
Verdun Crs ROCH OL11 ...... 27 M4
Verdun Rd ECC M30 ...... 69 L8
Verdure Av BOL BL1 ...... 35 H4
SALE M33 ...... 108 F3
Verdure CI FAIL M35 ...... 74 E4
Vere St SALO M50 ...... 86 C5
Verity CI DID/WITH M20 ...... 98 E6
ROY/SHW OL2 ...... 59 G1
Vermont St BOL BL1 ...... 2 A2
Verne Av SWIN M27 ...... 70 B4
Verne Dr OLD OL1 ...... 44 B7
Verney Rd ROY/SHW OL2 ...... 59 H2
Vernham Wk BOLS/LL BL3 ...... 36 B8
Vernon Av ECC M30 * 85 J2
STKP SK1 ...... 112 D5
STRET M32 ...... 97 G3
Vernon CI CHD/CHDH SK8 ...... 120 A3
POY/DIS SK12 ...... 129 J2
Vernon Dr MPL/ROM SK6 ...... 113 M5
PWCH M25 ...... 71 K2
Vernon Gv SALE M33 ...... 97 H8
Vernon Pk HALE/TIMP WA15 ...... 108 D5
Vernon Rd BRO M7 ...... 71 M7
DROY M43 ...... 89 H2
MPL/ROM SK6 ...... 113 J1
POY/DIS SK12 ...... 129 J2
TOT/BURYW BL8 ...... 24 C3
Vernon St AUL OL6 ...... 75 M8
BKLY M9 ...... 73 H5
BOL BL1 ...... 2 C3
BRAM/HZG SK7 ...... 121 M1
BRO M7 ...... 72 A7
BURY BL9 ...... 4 F1

FWTH BL4 ...... 53 H4
HYDE SK14 ...... 102 B2
LEIGH WN7 ...... 66 C7
MOSL OL5 ...... 76 F2
OLDTF/WHR M16 ...... 86 F7
STKP SK1 ...... 13 J3
Vernon Wk BOL BL1 ...... 2 D7
Verona Dr NEWH/MOS M40 ...... 73 M8
Veronica Rd DID/WITH M20 ...... 110 F1
Verrill Av NTHM/RTH M23 ...... 109 M5
Vesper St FAIL M35 ...... 74 D4
Vesta St ANC M4 ...... 7 M2
RAMS BL0 ...... 18 E6
Vestris Dr SLFD M6 ...... 85 L1
Viaduct Rd ALT WA14 ...... 108 A5
Viaduct St CSLFD M3 ...... 6 D2
EDGY/DAV SK3 ...... 13 G5
WGTN/LGST M12 ...... 88 B4
Vicarage Av CHD/CHDH SK8 ...... 120 D4
Vicarage CI BURY BL9 ...... 25 H4
DUK SK16 ...... 91 H4
OLDE OL4 ...... 60 C5
SLFD M6 ...... 85 L1
WGNE/HIN WN2 ...... 64 D2
Vicarage Crs AUL OL6 ...... 76 A4
Vicarage Dr DUK SK16 ...... 91 H4
MILN OL16 ...... 28 F7
Vicarage Gdns EDGY/DAV SK3 * 13 G7
HYDE SK14 ...... 102 B2
Vicarage Gv ECC M30 ...... 85 J2
Vicarage La ALT WA14 ...... 116 E3
MDTN M24 ...... 58 A5
POY/DIS SK12 ...... 122 A7
WGNW/ST WN6 ...... 30 D7
Vicarage Rd AIMK WN4 ...... 78 E2
AULW OL7 ...... 75 L7
EDGY/DAV SK3 ...... 112 B6
HOR/BR BL6 ...... 33 G2
IRL M44 ...... 94 D2
SWIN M27 ...... 70 B4
URM M41 ...... 84 E8
WALK M28 ...... 52 F8
WGNE/HIN WN2 ...... 64 E3
WGNW/BIL/OR WN5 ...... 46 A8
Vicarage Rd North ROCH OL11 ...... 41 M3
Vicarage Rd South ROCH OL11 ...... 41 M3
Vicarage Rd West HOR/BR BL6 ...... 32 F2
Vicarage Sq LEIGH WN7 * 66 C7
Vicarage St BOLS/LL BL3 ...... 2 B8
OLDS OL8 ...... 74 F2
RAD M26 ...... 54 D1
ROY/SHW OL2 ...... 43 L5
Vicarage Vw ROCH OL11 ...... 42 A3
Vicar's Ga MILN OL16 ...... 10 E5
Vicar's Ga MILN OL16 ...... 10 E5
Vicars Hall Gdns WALK M28 ...... 68 C7
Vicars Hall La WALK M28 ...... 68 C7
Vicars Rd CCHDY M21 ...... 97 K4
Vicars St ECC M30 ...... 85 J2
Vicker CI SWIN M27 ...... 70 C2
Vicker Gv DID/WITH M20 ...... 98 C7
Vickerman St BOL BL1 ...... 36 A2
Vickers Rw FWTH BL4 ...... 52 E4
Vickers St BOLS/LL BL3 * 2 B8
NEWH/MOS M40 ...... 88 B1
Victor Av BURY BL9 ...... 25 H8
Victoria Av BKLY M9 ...... 56 F7
BNG/LEV M19 ...... 99 K4
BRAM/HZG SK7 ...... 122 A1
CHD/CHDH SK8 ...... 120 C2
DID/WITH M20 ...... 110 D1
ECC M30 ...... 85 J1
GLSP SK13 ...... 93 K7
HALE/TIMP WA15 ...... 108 B5
MPL/ROM SK6 ...... 113 J1
SWIN M27 ...... 70 D4
WGNE/HIN WN2 ...... 65 H3
WGNW/ST WN6 ...... 14 C1
WHTF M45 ...... 55 K4
Victoria Av East AULW OL7 ...... 90 D3
Victoria Bridge St CSLFD M3 ...... 6 E2
Victoria CI BRAM/HZG SK7 ...... 120 F6
EDGY/DAV SK3 ...... 13 H8
WALK M28 * 68 D6
WGNE/HIN WN2 ...... 32 E6
Victoria Ct AULW OL7 ...... 90 D3
FWTH BL4 ...... 52 F2
GLSP SK13 ...... 104 F4
Victoria Crs ECC M30 ...... 85 J1
WGNW/ST WN6 ...... 31 H4
Victoria Dr SALE M33 ...... 109 G1
Victoria Gdns HYDE SK14 ...... 91 J8
ROY/SHW OL2 ...... 43 L5
Victoria Gv BOL BL1 ...... 35 M3
HTNM SK4 ...... 99 M7
RUSH/FAL M14 ...... 98 F5
Victoria La SWIN M27 ...... 70 A4
WHTF M45 ...... 55 K4
Victoria Ldg BRO M7 * 71 M7
Victoria Ms BURY BL9 ...... 55 L2
Victoria Pk STKP SK1 ...... 112 F4
Victoria PI TRPK M17 ...... 86 C7
Victoria PI AIMK WN4 ...... 63 G8
ALT WA14 ...... 116 F2
BOL BL1 ...... 35 G5
DUK SK16 ...... 90 F6
ECC M30 ...... 85 H1
FWTH BL4 ...... 52 F2
HALE/TIMP WA15 ...... 108 D6
HOR/BR BL6 ...... 33 H2
IRL M44 ...... 94 C3
NEWLW WA12 ...... 78 F8
OLDTF/WHR M16 ...... 98 A2
RUSH/FAL M14 ...... 98 E4
SALE M33 ...... 109 G1
SLFD M6 ...... 70 D8
STKP SK1 ...... 112 E5
STRET M32 ...... 97 G2
URM M41 ...... 95 J2
WGNE/HIN WN2 ...... 64 D3
WILM/AE SK9 ...... 126 E6
WYTH/NTH M22 ...... 110 A4
Victoria Sq ANC M4 * 7 K2
BOL BL1 ...... 2 E5
Victoria Station Ap CSLFD M3 ...... 6 F2
Victoria St ALT WA14 ...... 108 A7
AULW OL7 ...... 90 D3
BOLE BL2 ...... 37 M3
CHAD OL9 ...... 8 C1
CSLFD M3 ...... 6 F2
DTN/ASHW M34 ...... 101 H1
DUK SK16 ...... 91 G4
FAIL M35 ...... 74 A5
FWTH BL4 ...... 52 E4
GLSP SK13 ...... 104 F4
HEY OL10 ...... 41 H3
HOR/BR BL6 ...... 33 H2
HYDE SK14 ...... 91 J8
HYDE SK14 ...... 102 B2
LEIGH WN7 ...... 66 B6

LIT OL15 ...... 21 M7
MDTN M24 ...... 57 K4
NM/HAY SK22 ...... 124 D6
OLDE OL4 ...... 9 M6
OLDE OL4 ...... 60 B6
OLDS OL8 ...... 75 J4
OP/CLY M11 ...... 88 F4
RAD M26 ...... 54 D1
ROY/SHW OL2 ...... 43 L5
STLY SK15 ...... 77 G8
STLY SK15 ...... 91 J2
TOT/BURYW BL8 ...... 4 B4
TOT/BURYW BL8 ...... 24 B5
WALK M28 ...... 68 D6
WGNE/HIN WN2 ...... 64 D2
WGNW/BIL/OR WN5 ...... 47 H6
WHIT OL12 * 10 E1
WHIT OL12 * 20 A1
WHTN BL5 ...... 50 C4
Victoria Ter ROY/SHW OL2 * 43 G7
WGNE/HIN WN2 ...... 65 J7
WGNW/LGST M12 ...... 88 D2
Victoria Wk CHAD OL9 ...... 8 C1
Victor Mann St OP/CLY M11 ...... 89 K5
Victor St CSLFD M3 ...... 6 C1
HEY OL10 ...... 41 H4
NEWH/MOS M40 ...... 72 F8
OLDS OL8 ...... 74 E3
Victory Gv DTN/ASHW M34 ...... 89 M5
Victory Rd BOL BL1 * 35 K4
RUSH/FAL M14 ...... 98 F1
Vienna Rd EDGY/DAV SK3 ...... 112 A6
Vienna Rd East EDGY/DAV SK3 ...... 112 A6
Viewlands Dr WILM/AE SK9 ...... 127 G1
View St BOLS/LL BL3 ...... 2 A9
Vigo Av BOLS/LL BL3 ...... 51 L1
Vigo St HEY OL10 ...... 41 H3
OLDE OL4 ...... 60 A7
WGNE/HIN WN2 ...... 48 C2
Viking CI OP/CLY M11 ...... 88 C3
Viking St BOLS/LL BL3 ...... 36 B8
ROCH OL11 ...... 27 M4
Villa Av WGNW/BIL/OR WN5 ...... 31 K8
Villdale Av OFTN SK2 ...... 112 F5
Villiers Ct WHTF M45 * 55 K6
Villiers Dr OLDS OL8 ...... 9 G8
Villiers St AUL OL6 ...... 91 G2
BURY BL9 ...... 5 J2
HYDE SK14 ...... 102 C1
Vinca Gv BRO M7 ...... 72 A6
Vincent Av CCHDY M21 ...... 97 K3
ECC M30 ...... 59 M4
Vincent St BOL BL1 ...... 2 A6
BRO M7 ...... 72 B5
HYDE SK14 ...... 102 C3
LIT OL15 ...... 21 L6
MDTN M24 ...... 57 K2
MILN OL16 ...... 11 H7
OP/CLY M11 ...... 88 F4
Vincent Wy
WGNW/BIL/OR WN5 ...... 47 G4
Vine Av SWIN M27 ...... 70 B4
Vine CI ROY/SHW OL2 ...... 43 L5
SALE M33 ...... 95 M7
Vine CI MILN OL16 * 11 J5
STRET M32 ...... 97 G3
Vine Fold NEWH/MOS M40 ...... 74 C3
Vine Gv OFTN SK2 ...... 112 F6
WGNS/IIMK WN3 ...... 14 F5
Vine PI ROCH OL11 * 10 D9
Vinery Gv DTN/ASHW M34 ...... 101 H1
Vine St BRAM/HZG SK7 ...... 122 A1
BRO M7 ...... 71 L4
CHAD OL9 ...... 74 E1
ECC M30 ...... 84 F3
PWCH M25 ...... 55 M7
RAMS BL0 ...... 18 D8
WGN WN1 ...... 15 J1
WGNE/HIN WN2 ...... 49 G6
Vineyard CI WHIT OL12 ...... 21 G5
Vineyard St OLDE OL4 ...... 59 L5
Viola CI WGNNW/ST WN6 ...... 31 K5
Viola St OP/CLY M11 ...... 89 G2
Violet Av FWTH BL4 ...... 52 D3
Violet St AIMK WN4 ...... 78 E2
GTN M18 ...... 89 J3
OFTN SK2 ...... 112 C6
Violet Wy MDTN M24 ...... 58 A5
Virgil St HULME M15 ...... 6 D8
Virginia Cha CHD/CHDH SK8 ...... 120 B4
Virginia CI NTHM/RTH M23 ...... 109 J4
Virginia St BOLS/LL BL3 ...... 35 L8
ROCH OL11 ...... 28 B8
Virginia Wy
WGNW/BIL/OR WN5 ...... 46 F4
Viscount Dr CHD/CHDH SK8 ...... 119 M5
MANAIR M90 ...... 118 D5
Viscount Rd
WGNW/BIL/OR WN5 ...... 47 G4
Viscount St RUSH/FAL M14 ...... 98 F1
Vista Av NEWLW WA12 ...... 78 D8
Vista Rd NEWLW WA12 ...... 78 D8
Vista Wy NEWLW WA12 ...... 78 D8
Vivian St ROCH OL11 ...... 10 D9
Vixen CI CCHDY M21 ...... 98 B5
Voltaire Av SLFD M6 ...... 85 L1
Vorlich Dr CHAD OL9 ...... 58 C4
Vulcan Dr WGN WN1 ...... 15 J5
Vulcan Rd WGNW/BIL/OR WN5 ...... 47 G4
Vulcan St OLD OL1 ...... 59 M4
Vyner Gv SALE M33 ...... 96 C6

W

Waddicor Av AUL OL6 ...... 76 B6
Waddington CI
GOL/RIS/CUL WA3 * 80 C4
TOT/BURYW BL8 ...... 38 B2
Waddington Fold MILN OL16 ...... 42 F2
Waddington Rd BOL BL1 ...... 35 H4
Waddington St CHAD OL9 ...... 8 D3
Wade Bank WHTN BL5 ...... 50 C4
Wadebridge Av
NTHM/RTH M23 ...... 109 G5

Wadebridge Dr
TOT/BURYW BL8 ...... 38 C2
Wadeford CI ANC M4 ...... 7 M2
Wade Hill La UPML OL3 ...... 61 H4
Wade Rw UPML OL3 ...... 61 H4
Wadesmill Wk BRUN/LGST M13 * 7 J9
Wadeson Rd BRUN/LGST M13 ...... 7 K9
Wade St BOLS/LL BL3 ...... 52 C1
MDTN M24 ...... 58 A6
Wadham Gdns MPL/ROM SK6 ...... 100 F8
Wadham Wy HALE/TIMP WA15 ...... 117 H3
Wadhurst Wk
BRUN/LGST M13 * 87 M7
Wadlow CI CSLFD M3 * 6 C1
Wadsley St BOL BL1 ...... 2 E2
Wadsworth CI WILM/AE SK9 ...... 127 J1
Wadsworth Dr
WGNNW/ST WN6 ...... 47 J2
Wadsworth Ms DROY M43 ...... 89 J3
Waggoners Ct SWIN M27 ...... 70 C5
Waggon Rd AULW OL7 ...... 75 L4
BOLE BL2 ...... 37 G4
MOSL OL5 ...... 76 F4
Wagner St BOL BL1 ...... 36 A1
Wagstaffe Dr FAIL M35 ...... 74 C5
Wagstaffe St MDTN M24 ...... 57 K3
Wagtail CI WALK M28 ...... 69 G4
Waincliffe Av CCHDY M21 ...... 98 A8
Wainfleet CI WGNS/IIMK WN3 ...... 63 H1
Waingap Crs WHIT OL12 ...... 20 B4
Waingap Ri WHIT OL12 ...... 20 D8
Waingap Vw WHIT OL12 ...... 20 B5
Wainhouse Brow
NM/HAY SK22 ...... 125 M1
Wainman St SLFD M6 ...... 71 L7
Wainscot CI TYLD M29 ...... 67 L5
Wainwright Av
DTN/ASHW M34 ...... 100 C1
Wainwright CI OFTN SK2 ...... 13 M9
OLDE OL4 ...... 60 D5
Wainwright Rd ALT WA14 ...... 107 L7
Wainwright St DUK SK16 ...... 91 H3
OLDS OL8 ...... 9 H8
Waithlands Rd MILN OL16 ...... 11 K6
Wakefield Crs MPL/ROM SK6 ...... 113 K3
WGNNW/ST WN6 ...... 31 K5
Wakefield Dr OLDE OL4 ...... 60 D1
SWIN M27 ...... 54 A8
Wakefield Ms EDGW/EG BL7 ...... 22 C5
Wakefield Rd STLY SK15 ...... 76 F7
Wakefield St CMANE M1 * 7 G8
GOL/RIS/CUL WA3 ...... 79 K5
OLD OL1 ...... 8 D1
Wakeling Rd DTN/ASHW M34 ...... 101 H4
Walcot PI WGNS/IIMK WN3 ...... 63 K3
Walcott CI BRUN/LGST M13 ...... 88 A7
Wald Av RUSH/FAL M14 ...... 99 H5
Waldeck St BOL BL1 ...... 35 M4
Walden Av OLDE OL4 ...... 60 A2
Walden CI RUSH/FAL M14 ...... 98 D4
Walden Crs BRAM/HZG SK7 ...... 121 L1
Walderton Av NEWH/MOS M40 ...... 73 K6
Waldon Av CHD/CHDH SK8 ...... 111 G7
Waldon CI BOLS/LL BL3 ...... 35 M8
WGNE/HIN WN2 ...... 49 J8
Waldorf CI WGNS/IIMK WN3 ...... 63 G2
Wales St OLD OL1 ...... 59 M3
Walford Rd AIMK WN4 ...... 78 F1
Walkdale Brow GLSP SK13 ...... 104 E5
Walkden Av WGN WN1 ...... 47 L2
Walkden Av East WGN WN1 ...... 47 M2
Walkdene Dr WALK M28 ...... 68 C1
Walkden Market PI
WALK M28 ...... 69 G1
Walkden Rd WALK M28 ...... 69 G3
Walkdens Av ATH M46 ...... 66 D2
Walkden St WHIT OL12 ...... 10 E1
Walker Av BOLS/LL BL3 ...... 52 C1
FAIL M35 ...... 74 E6
STLY SK15 ...... 91 M2
WHTF M45 ...... 55 K6
Walker CI FWTH BL4 ...... 53 K6
HYDE SK14 ...... 102 C2
Walker La HYDE SK14 ...... 102 C2
Walker Rd BKLY M9 ...... 57 H8
CHAD OL9 ...... 8 A8
ECC M30 ...... 69 K8
IRL M44 ...... 94 C3
Walkers CI UPML OL3 ...... 61 L4
Walkers Cft CSLFD M3 * 6 F2
Walkers Dr LEIGH WN7 ...... 66 D7
Walker's La OLDE OL4 ...... 60 D1
Walker's Rd OLDS OL8 ...... 74 F2
Walker St BOL BL1 ...... 2 B6
BURY BL9 ...... 4 E6
DTN/ASHW M34 ...... 90 B8
GLSP SK13 ...... 93 K8
HEY OL10 ...... 40 F3
MDTN M24 ...... 56 F5
MILN OL16 ...... 11 H5
OLDS OL8 ...... 8 E7
RAD M26 ...... 54 F3
STKP SK1 ...... 13 H4
WHTN BL5 ...... 50 B4
Walkerwood Dr STLY SK15 ...... 92 A2
Walkmill UPML OL3 ...... 61 J3
Walk Mill CI WHIT OL12 ...... 21 H8
Walk Mill Rd NM/HAY SK22 ...... 125 M1
The Walk ATH M46 ...... 67 G1
MILN OL16 ...... 10 E4
The Walkway BOLS/LL BL3 ...... 35 J7
Wallace Av RUSH/FAL M14 ...... 99 G2
Wallace La WGN WN1 ...... 15 K1
Wallace St OLDS OL8 ...... 59 J8
Wallasey Av RUSH/FAL M14 ...... 98 D4
Wallbank Rd BRAM/HZG SK7 ...... 121 J3
Wallbrook Av
WGNW/BIL/OR WN5 ...... 62 A3
Wallbrook Crs LHULT M38 ...... 52 C6
Wallbrook Dr BKLY M9 ...... 72 F2
The Walled Gdn SWIN M27 ...... 70 A6
Waller Av RUSH/FAL M14 ...... 98 F4
Walley St BOL BL1 ...... 36 B1
Wallgarth Av WGNS/IIMK WN3 ...... 63 G2
Wallgate WGN WN1 ...... 14 F5
Wallhead Rd MILN OL16 ...... 29 G5
Wall Hill Rd UPML OL3 ...... 61 J3
Wallingford Rd URM M41 ...... 96 F1
WILM/AE SK9 ...... 119 L7
Wallis St CHAD OL9 ...... 58 B8
NEWH/MOS M40 ...... 73 M7
Wallness La SLFD M6 ...... 86 F1
Wallshaw PI OLD OL1 ...... 9 M5
Wallshaw St OLD OL1 ...... 9 L5
Wall St OLDS OL8 ...... 8 F7
SLFD M6 ...... 86 C2
WGNNW/ST WN6 ...... 14 A1
Wall Wy GTN M18 ...... 89 H8
Wallwork CI ROCH OL11 ...... 27 H3

Wallwork Rd *TYLD* M29 .... 68 A6
Wallwork St *OP/CLY* M11 .... 89 H4
 RAD M26 .... 38 D1
 RDSH SK5 * 100 C2
Wallworth Av *GTN* M18 .... 89 G7
Wally Sq *BRO* M7 .... 72 B6
Walmer Dr *BRAM/HZG* SK7 .... 121 J3
Walmer Rd *WGNE/HIN* WN2 .... 49 K7
Walmersley Ct
 MPL/ROM SK6 * 114 C6
Walmersley Old Rd *BURY* BL9 .. 25 J2
Walmersley Rd *BURY* BL9 .... 5 G2
 NEWH/MOS M40 .... 74 B3
Walmer St *GTN* M18 .... 89 H6
 RUSH/FAL M14 .... 98 E1
Walmer St East *RUSH/FAL* M14 98 F1
Walmer St *WGNE/HIN* WN2 ...... 48 E5
Walmesley Rd *LEIGH* WN7 .... 66 B7
Walmesley St *WGN* WN1 .... 15 H5
Walmley Gv *BOLS/LL* BL3 .... 51 M1
Walmsley Av *LIT* OL15 .... 29 J1
Walmsley Gv *WALK* M41 .... 96 A2
Walmsley St *NEWLW* WA12 ...... 79 C8
 RDSH SK5 * 112 B1
 STLY SK15 .... 91 K4
 TOT/BURYW BL8 .... 24 E8
Walney Rd *WGNS/IIMK* WN3 .... 63 G2
 WYTH/NTH M22 .... 110 A8
Walnut Av *BURY* BL9 .... 5 L3
 OLDE OL4 .... 60 A4
 WGN WN1 .... 48 A2
Walnut CI *HYDE* SK14 .... 102 D2
 SWIN M27 .... 54 E4
 WILM/AE SK9 .... 127 J4
Walnut Gv *LEIGH* WN7 .... 66 C4
Walnut Rd *ECC* M30 .... 69 K8
 PART M31 .... 106 A1
Walnut St *BOL* BL1 .... 36 C1
 GTN M18 .... 89 G6
Walnut Tree Rd *EDGY/DAV* SK3 .111 K5
Walnut Wk *STRET* M32 .... 96 F1
Walpole Av *WGNS/IIMK* WN3 ... 63 J1
Walpole St *MILN* OL16 .... 11 H5
Walsall St *SLFD* M6 .... 71 K7
Walsden St *OP/CLY* M11 .... 88 F2
Walsh Av *BKLY* M9 .... 72 F2
Walshaw Brook CI
 TOT/BURYW BL8 .... 24 C8
Walshaw Dr *SWIN* M27 .... 70 C5
Walshaw La *TOT/BURYW* BL8 ... 24 C8
Walshaw Rd *TOT/BURYW* BL8 .. 24 C8
Walsh CI *NEWLW* WA12 .... 78 F7
Walshe St *BURY* BL9 .... 5 L5
Walsh St *CHAD* OL9 .... 8 B7
Walsingham Av *DID/WITH* M20 . 98 C8
 MDTN M24 .... 57 K7
Walter Scott Av *WGN* WN1 ...... 31 L8
Walter Scott St *OLD* OL1 .... 59 L4
Walters Dr *OLDS* OL8 .... 75 K1
Walters Green Crs
 GOL/RIS/CUL WA3 .... 79 K3
 BKLY M9 .... 73 C4
 GTN M18 .... 89 H6
 LEIGH WN7 .... 65 L7
 OLD OL1 .... 9 K6
 OLDTF/WHR M16 .... 86 F8
 PWCH M25 .... 55 J8
 RAD M26 .... 38 C6
 WALK M28 .... 69 G2
 WGNW/BIL/OR WN5 .... 47 G6
 WGNNW/ST WN6 .... 47 J1
Waltham Av *GOL/RIS/CUL* WA3 .81 M5
Waltham Dr *CHD/CHDH* SK8 .. 120 D6
Waltham Gdns *LEIGH* WN7 ...... 66 F4
Waltham Rd *OLDTF/WHR* M16 . 98 B3
Waltham St *OLDE* OL4 .... 59 M8
Walthew House La
 WGNW/BIL/OR WN5 .... 46 E3
Walthew La *WGNE/HIN* WN2 .... 64 D2
Walton CI *MDTN* M24 .... 56 F3
Walton Ct *BOLS/LL* BL3 .... 36 C8
Walton Dr *BURY* BL9 .... 25 H4
 MPL/ROM SK6 .... 114 A5
Walton Hall Dr *BNG/LEV* M19 .. 100 A3
Walton Houses *FAIL* M35 * 74 C4
Walton PI *FWTH* BL4 .... 53 H5
Walton Rd *ALT* WA14 .... 107 L7
 BKLY M9 .... 57 G7
 SALE M33 .... 108 C3
Walton St *ATH* M46 * 51 H8
 AULW OL7 .... 75 J7
 HEY OL10 .... 41 G4
 MDTN M24 .... 57 K2
 STKP SK1 * 13 K8
Walwyn CI *STRET* M32 .... 97 M7
Wanborough Ct *LEIGH* WN7 .... 66 C5
Wandsworth Av *OP/CLY* M11 .... 89 G2
Wansbeck CI *STRET* M32 .... 97 H3
Wansfell Wk *ANC* M4 .... 88 A2
Wansford St *RUSH/FAL* M14 .... 98 D1
Wanstead Av *BKLY* M9 .... 73 K1
Wapping St *BOL* BL1 .... 36 A2
Warbeck CI *RDSH* SK5 .... 100 D2
 WGNE/HIN WN2 .... 65 H1
Warbeck Rd *NEWH/MOS* M40 .. 74 A2
Warbreck Dr *URM* M41 .... 95 M3
Warbreck Gv *SALE* M33 .... 109 G1
Warburton CI
 HALE/TIMP WA15 .... 117 M6
 MPL/ROM SK6 .... 113 K3
Warburton Dr
 HALE/TIMP WA15 .... 117 M6
Warburton La *PART* M31 .... 106 C1
Warburton PI *ATH* M46 .... 67 G1
Warburton Rd *WILM/AE* SK9 ... 119 M8
Warburton St *BOL* BL1 .... 36 C2
 DID/WITH M20 .... 110 E1
 ECC M30 .... 85 H3
 ORD M5 .... 86 E6
Warburton Wy
 HALE/TIMP WA15 .... 108 F5
Warcock Rd *OLDE* OL4 .... 59 M5
Wardend CI *LHULT* M38 * 52 D6
Wardens Bank *WHTN* BL5 .... 50 B7
Warden St *NEWH/MOS* M40 ..... 74 A8
Warde St *HULME* M15 .... 87 H6
Ward La *POY/DIS* SK12 .... 124 A4
 UPML OL3 .... 45 M8
Wardle Brook Av *HYDE* SK14 .. 103 G3
Wardle CI *RAD* M26 .... 38 B7
 STRET M32 .... 97 J1
Wardle Edge *WHIT* OL12 .... 28 E1
Wardle Fold *WHIT* OL12 .... 28 E1
Wardle Gdns *WHIT* OL12 .... 28 F1
Wardle Rd *SALE* M33 .... 108 L1
 WHIT OL12 .... 21 G7
Wardle St *BOLE* BL2 .... 3 K8
 LIT OL15 .... 21 L6
 NEWH/MOS M40 .... 88 B1
 OLDE OL4 .... 59 L6

 HULME M15 .... 87 H6
 LEIGH WN7 .... 82 A1
 PWCH M25 .... 55 K8
 SWIN M27 .... 70 C3
 WHIT OL12 .... 28 E2
Wasdale Av *BOLE* BL2 .... 37 J3
 URM M41 .... 95 L1
Wasdale Rd *AIMK* WN4 .... 63 K4
 ROCH OL11 .... 41 M3
Wasdale Ter *STLY* SK15 .... 76 D8
Wasdale Wk *OLD* OL1 .... 9 L3
Washacre *WHTN* BL5 .... 50 C5
Washacre CI *WHTN* BL5 .... 50 C5
Washbrook *CHAD* OL9 .... 58 E8
Washbrook Av *WALK* M28 .... 68 E3
Washbrook Dr *STRET* M32 .... 96 E3
Washburn CI *WHTN* BL5 .... 50 B2
Wash Ford *TOT/BURYW* BL8 .... 24 E8
Washford Dr *NTHM/RTH* M23 .. 109 G4
Washington La *OLDE* OL4 .... 76 E2
Washington Ct *BURY* BL9 .... 5 J4
Washington St *BOLS/LL* BL3 .... 35 M6
 CHAD OL9 .... 8 D5
Wash La *BURY* BL9 .... 5 J3
 BURY BL9 .... 5 L5
 LEIGH WN7 .... 66 F7
Wash Lane Ter *BURY* BL9 .... 5 L4
Wash Ter *TOT/BURYW* BL8 .... 24 E7
Washway Rd *SALE* M33 .... 108 B3
Washwood CI *LHULT* M38 * 52 E6
Wasnidge Wk *HULME* M15 * 87 J7
Wasp Av *ROCH* OL11 .... 42 D1
Wasp Mill Dr *WHIT* OL12 .... 21 J4
Wastdale Av *BURY* BL9 .... 55 K1
Wastdale Rd *NTHM/RTH* M23 . 109 J8
Waste CI *OLD* OL1 * 9 M4
Wastwater St *OLD* OL1 * 9 L1
Watburn Rd *NM/HAY* SK22 .... 124 F3
Watchgate CI *MDTN* M24 .... 57 G1
Watchgate CI *WHTN* BL5 * 50 B2
Waterbeck CI *WGN* WN1 .... 15 M2
Waterbridge *WALK* M28 .... 68 D1
Watercroft *ROCH* OL11 .... 27 G3
Waterdale CI *WALK* M28 .... 68 E7
Waterdale Dr *WHTF* M45 .... 55 K4
Water Dr *WGNNW/ST* WN6 ...... 31 L5
Wateredge CI *LEIGH* WN7 .... 81 G1
Waterfield CI *BURY* BL9 .... 25 J5
Waterfield Ms *WALK* M35 .... 74 D6
Waterfold La *BURY* BL9 .... 5 L7
Waterfoot Cottages
 HYDE SK14 .... 92 D8
Waterford Av *DID/WITH* M20 .. 110 A1
 MPL/ROM SK6 .... 114 C3
Waterfront Quay *SALQ* M50 ..... 86 C5
Watergate *DTN/ASHW* M34 ...... 89 M4
Water Ga *UPML* OL3 .... 61 L4
Watergate Dr *WHTN* BL5 .... 51 M5
Watergate La *WHTN* BL5 .... 51 M5
Water Grove Rd *DUK* SK16 ...... 91 J5
Waterhead *OLDE* OL4 .... 60 B4
Waterhouse Av *GTN* M18 .... 89 J8
Waterhouse Rd *GTN* M18 .... 89 H8
Waterhouse St *WHIT* OL12 ...... 10 E3
Waterhouse Wy *RDSH* SK5 .... 100 B5
Water La *DROY* M43 .... 89 H3
 FWTH BL4 .... 53 H5
 HYDE SK14 .... 93 H6
 MILN OL16 .... 29 K7
 RAD M26 .... 54 C1
 RAMS BL0 .... 19 G2
 WILM/AE SK9 .... 126 E5
Water Lane St *RAD* M26 .... 54 C1
Waterloo Ct *BURY* BL9 .... 4 D8
Waterloo Gdns *AUL* OL6 .... 76 B7
Waterloo PI *STKP* SK1 * 13 K5
Waterloo Rd *AUL* OL6 .... 75 J7
 BKLY M9 .... 73 G3
 BRAM/HZG SK7 .... 121 H3
 CHH M8 .... 72 E4
 MPL/ROM SK6 .... 114 B2
 POY/DIS SK12 .... 129 L2
 STKP SK1 .... 13 K5
 STLY SK15 .... 91 K2
Waterloo St *AUL* OL6 .... 76 B7
 BOL BL1 .... 2 F1
 CHH M8 .... 72 F4
 CMANE M1 .... 7 G6
 OLD OL1 .... 9 K6
 TOT/BURYW BL8 .... 4 B4
 WGNNW/ST WN6 .... 14 B1
Watermans CI *BKLY* M9 .... 73 J4
Waterman Vw *MILN* OL16 .... 11 L2
Watermead *SALE* M33 .... 108 D3
Watermead CI *EDGY/DAV* SK3 . 112 B8
Watermede
 WGNW/BIL/OR WN5 .... 62 B1
Watermeetings La
 MPL/ROM SK6 .... 114 C2
Watermill CI *MILN* OL16 .... 29 G6
Water Mill Clough
 ROY/SHW OL2 .... 58 F2
Watermill Ct *AULW* OL7 .... 75 K7
Watermillock Gdns *BOL* BL1 .... 36 C1
Waterpark Rd *BRO* M7 .... 72 B4
Waters Edge *AUL* OL6 .... 76 B7
Waters Edge *FWTH* BL4 .... 52 D2
 MPL/ROM SK6 .... 114 C4
 WALK M28 .... 69 J2
Watersedge CI *CHD/CHDH* SK8 120 D1
Waters Edge Fold *OLD* OL1 ...... 43 M8
Watersfield CI *CHD/CHDH* SK8 120 B4
Watersheddings St *OLDE* OL4 ... 60 A3
Waterside *GLSP* SK13 .... 93 K7
 HYDE SK14 .... 103 G2
 MPL/ROM SK6 .... 114 C3
 POY/DIS SK12 .... 124 A5
 SALE M33 .... 96 F7
 TRPK M17 .... 86 C6
 UPML OL3 .... 61 M8
Waterside Av *MPL/ROM* SK6 ... 114 C2
Waterside CI *CCHDY* M21 .... 98 A8
 HYDE SK14 .... 103 G2
 OLD OL1 .... 43 M8
 RAD M26 .... 38 G8
Waterside Ct *URM* M41 * 95 G2
Waterside Dr *WGNS/IIMK* WN3 . 14 F7
Waterside La *MILN* OL16 .... 11 K3
Waterside Rd *BURY* BL9 .... 24 F2
 NM/HAY SK22 .... 124 B4
Waterside Vw *DROY* M43 .... 89 H4
Waterslea *ECC* M30 .... 84 F2
Waterslea Dr *BOL* BL1 .... 35 J5
Watersmead CI *BOL* BL1 .... 36 C1
Watersmead St *BOL* BL1 .... 36 C2
Watersmeet *STRET* M32 .... 85 M4
Waters Meeting Rd *BOL* BL1 .... 36 C1
Water's Nook Rd *WHTN* BL5 .... 50 B4
Waterson Av *NEWH/MOS* M40 .. 73 K5
Waters Reach *MOSL* OL5 .... 61 H8

 POY/DIS SK12 .... 122 B8
 TRPK M17 .... 86 C6
 SWIN WN1 .... 15 M4
Water Sreet *RAD* M26 .... 54 D1
Water St *ATH* M46 .... 67 G1
 AUL OL6 .... 90 E1
 BKLY M9 .... 73 G4
 BOL BL1 .... 2 E2
 CSLFD M3 .... 6 B7
 DTN/ASHW M34 .... 90 C5
 EDGW/EG BL7 .... 22 D7
 GLSP SK13 .... 105 H2
 HYDE SK14 .... 102 A3
 MDTN M24 .... 57 J4
 MILN OL16 .... 10 F4
 NEWLW WA12 .... 78 F8
 ROY/SHW OL2 .... 43 K8
 STKP SK1 .... 13 K1
 STLY SK15 * 91 K2
 WGN WN1 .... 15 G3
Waterton Av *MOSL* OL5 .... 76 E2
Waterton La *MOSL* OL5 .... 76 E2
Waterview CI *MILN* OL16 .... 43 L1
Waterview Pk *LEIGH* WN7 .... 66 B8
Waterworks Dr *NEWLW* WA12 .. 79 J8
Waterworks Rd *OLDE* OL4 .... 60 B3
 UPML OL3 .... 45 K6
Watford Av *RUSH/FAL* M14 ...... 98 E2
Watford Bridge Rd
 NM/HAY SK22 .... 124 F3
Watford La *NM/HAY* SK22 .... 124 F3
Watford Rd *NM/HAY* SK22 ...... 124 E2
Watkin Av *GLSP* SK13 .... 93 H8
Watkin CI *BRUN/LGST* M13 ..... 87 L6
Watkins Dr *PWCH* M25 .... 72 B1
Watkin St *CSLFD* M3 * 87 G1
 HYDE SK14 .... 91 K7
Watling St *LIT* OL15 .... 21 K7
 TOT/BURYW BL8 .... 23 J2
 TOT/BURYW BL8 .... 38 C4
Watlington CI *OLD* OL1 .... 60 A1
Watson Av *AIMK* WN4 .... 78 F1
 GOL/RIS/CUL WA3 .... 79 J3
Watson Rd *FWTH* BL4 .... 52 C4
Watson Sq *STKP* SK1 .... 13 K5
Watson St *CSLFD* M3 .... 6 E7
 DTN/ASHW M34 .... 101 L1
 ECC M30 .... 84 F2
 OLDE OL4 .... 59 M4
 RAD M26 .... 38 D8
 SWIN M27 .... 70 C3
Watson CI *SWIN* M27 * 70 C2
Watts St *BNG/LEV* M19 .... 99 L4
 CHAD OL9 .... 8 B4
 HOR/BR BL6 .... 33 J3
 OLDS OL8 .... 75 G2
 WHIT OL12 .... 10 F2
Waugh Av *FAIL* M35 .... 74 C6
Wavell Dr *BURY* BL9 .... 55 K3
Wavell Rd *WYTH/NTH* M22 .... 118 F2
Waveney Dr *ALT* WA14 .... 107 M6
 WILM/AE SK9 .... 127 H2
Waveney Rd *ROY/SHW* OL2 ..... 43 K4
 WYTH/NTH M22 .... 110 B8
Waverley *WHIT* OL12 .... 10 D2
Waverley Av *FWTH* BL4 .... 53 J6
 STRET M32 .... 97 H1
Waverley Crs *DROY* M43 .... 89 K1
Waverley Dr *CHD/CHDH* SK8 .. 120 D6
Waverley Gv *LEIGH* WN7 .... 67 G6
Waverley Rd *BKLY* M9 .... 73 J5
 BOL BL1 .... 36 B1
 DUK SK3 .... 12 D8
 GOL/RIS/CUL WA3 .... 80 A3
 HYDE SK14 .... 102 A4
 MDTN M24 .... 57 F6
 SWIN M27 .... 70 F5
 WALK M28 .... 68 E3
Waverley Rd West *BKLY* M9 ..... 73 J6
Waverley St *OLD* OL1 .... 59 L4
 ROCH OL11 .... 41 M3
Waverton Av *HTNM* SK4 .... 100 A5
Waverton Rd *RUSH/FAL* M14 ... 98 D3
Wavertree Av *ATH* M46 .... 50 E8
Wavertree Rd *BKLY* M9 .... 56 F8
Wayfarer Dr *TYLD* M29 .... 67 K4
Wayfarers Wy *SWIN* M27 .... 70 B5
Wayford Wk *WHTN* BL5 .... 51 L5
Wayland Rd *GTN* M18 .... 100 A1
Wayland Rd South *GTN* M18 ... 100 A1
Wayne CI *DROY* M43 .... 74 F8
Wayne St *OP/CLY* M11 .... 89 H4
Wayoh Cft *EDGW/EG* BL7 .... 17 G6
Wayside Dr *POY/DIS* SK12 ...... 121 L8
Wayside Gdns *BRAM/HZG* SK7 122 C2
Wayside Gv *WALK* M28 .... 53 H8
Weald CI *BRUN/LGST* M13 ...... 87 M6
Wealdstone Gv *BOLE* BL2 * 36 E2
Weardale Rd *BKLY* M9 .... 56 E7
Wearhead CI *GOL/RIS/CUL* WA3 79 K5
Wearish La *WHTN* BL5 .... 49 M6
Weaste Av *LHULT* M38 .... 52 E8
Weaste Dr *ORD* M5 .... 86 A1
Weaste La *ORD* M5 .... 86 A1
Weaste Rd *ORD* M5 .... 86 A3
Weatherall St North *BRO* M7 .... 72 C5
Weatherley CI *OLDS* OL8 .... 75 J3
Weatherley Dr *MPL/ROM* SK6 .. 114 A8
Weaver Av *WALK* M28 .... 68 D2
Weaver CI *ALT* WA14 .... 116 E3
Weaver Ct *HULME* M15 * 87 G8
Weaver Dr *BURY* BL9 .... 25 J4
Weaver Gv *LEIGH* WN7 .... 65 M8
Weaverham Ct *BRUN/LGST* M13 99 J1
Weavers Ct *BOLS/LL* BL3 .... 2 C8
 MDTN M24 .... 57 J3
Weavers Gn *FWTH* BL4 .... 53 J7
Weavers Rd *MDTN* M24 .... 57 J3
Weavers La *BRAM/HZG* SK7 .. 120 F6
Webb Gv *HYDE* SK14 .... 103 H3
Webb La *STKP* SK1 .... 13 J5
Webb St *HOR/BR* BL6 .... 33 M2
 TOT/BURYW BL8 .... 4 B4
Webdale Dr *NEWH/MOS* M40 .. 73 K5
Weber Dr *BOLS/LL* BL3 * 2 B9
Webster St *BOLS/LL* BL3 .... 3 J9
 MOSL OL5 .... 76 F2
 OLDS OL8 .... 9 H8
Wedgewood Dr
 WGNNW/ST WN6 .... 47 G1
Wedgewood St
 NEWH/MOS M40 .... 73 J8
Wedgwood Rd *SWIN* M27 .... 70 F2
Wedhurst St *OLDE* OL4 .... 59 M5
Wedneshough *HYDE* SK14 .... 92 F7
Weedall Av *ORD* M5 .... 86 D6

Weedon Av *NEWLW* WA12 .... 78 E7
Weeton St *MILN* OL16 .... 11 J3
Weeton Rd *BOLE* BL2 .... 37 J5
Weighbridge Ct *IRL* M44 .... 94 E1
Weir La *ATH* M46 .... 29 H5
Weir Rd *MILN* OL16 .... 11 J3
Weir St *FAIL* M35 .... 74 B5
Welbeck Av *CHAD* OL9 .... 74 A1
 LIT OL15 .... 21 J7
 URM M41 .... 96 B1
Welbeck CI *MILN* OL16 .... 29 H6
Welbeck Gv *BRO* M7 .... 72 B5
Welbeck Rd *AIMK* WN4 .... 63 K4
 BOL BL1 .... 35 K4
 ECC M30 .... 70 B8
 HYDE SK14 .... 102 A1
 MILN OL16 .... 28 E8
 RDSH SK5 .... 100 C4
 WALK M28 .... 69 L6
 WGNS/IIMK WN3 .... 14 A1
Welbeck St *GTN* M18 .... 89 G6
Welbeck St South *AUL* OL6 ...... 90 D2
Welburn Av *WYTH/NTH* M22 .. 119 G3
Welburn St *ROCH* OL11 .... 10 F8
Welbury Rd *NTHM/RTH* M23 .. 109 G4
Welby St *BRUN/LGST* M13 .... 88 A2
Welch Hill St *LEIGH* WN7 .... 66 B8
Welcomb CI *MPL/ROM* SK6 .... 101 M8
Welcomb St *OP/CLY* M11 .... 88 E5
Welcome Pde *OLDS* OL8 .... 75 M1
Welcroft St *STKP* SK1 .... 13 K6
Weldon Av *BOLS/LL* BL3 .... 51 K1
Weldon Crs *EDGY/DAV* SK3 ... 112 B8
Weldon Dr *BKLY* M9 .... 57 G7
Weldon Gv *WGN* WN1 .... 48 B2
Weldon Rd *ALT* WA14 .... 107 M6
Weld Rd *HYDE* SK14 .... 91 J8
Welford CI *GOL/RIS/CUL* WA3 .. 79 M5
Welford Gn *RDSH* SK5 .... 100 C7
Welford Rd *CHH* M8 .... 56 C8
Welford St *SLFD* M6 .... 71 L8
Welkin Rd *MPL/ROM* SK6 .... 112 F1
Wellacre Av *URM* M41 .... 95 G2
Welland CI *HULME* M15 * 87 G6
Welland Ct *HULME* M15 .... 87 G6
Welland Rd *AIMK* WN4 .... 64 B7
 ROY/SHW OL2 .... 43 K4
 WILM/AE SK9 .... 127 H2
Welland St *OP/CLY* M11 .... 89 G4
 RDSH SK5 .... 100 C3
The Welland *WHTN* BL5 .... 50 B4
Wellbank *PWCH* M25 * 71 J1
 STLY SK15 .... 91 M4
Wellbank Av *AUL* OL6 .... 76 B6
Wellbank CI *BOLS/LL* BL3 .... 53 L1
 OLDS OL8 .... 59 K8
Wellbank St *TOT/BURYW* BL8 .. 24 C6
Wellbank Vw *WHIT* OL12 .... 27 J3
Wellbrooke CI *AIMK* WN4 .... 78 F1
Wellbrow Ter *WHIT* OL12 .... 28 A3
Wellens Wy *MDTN* M24 .... 56 F5
Weller Av *CCHDY* M21 .... 98 A5
 POY/DIS SK12 .... 129 K2
Weller CI *POY/DIS* SK12 .... 129 K2
Wellesbourne Dr
 NTHM/RTH M23 .... 109 J5
Wellesley Av *GTN* M18 .... 89 G6
Wellesley CI *NEWLW* WA12 ..... 78 E7
 WGNW/BIL/OR WN5 .... 47 H4
Wellfield CI *BURY* BL9 .... 39 H6
Wellfield La *HALE/TIMP* WA15 . 108 F1
Wellfield PI *ROCH* OL11 * 11 G9
Wellfield Rd *BOLS/LL* BL3 .... 51 L5
 CHH M8 .... 72 C4
 COL/RIS/CUL WA3 .... 81 H8
 NTHM/RTH M23 .... 109 K5
 OFTN SK2 .... 112 F6
 WGNE/HIN WN2 .... 49 K8
 WGNNW/ST WN6 .... 31 J8
Wellfield St *ROCH* OL11 .... 11 G9
Well Ga *GLSP* SK13 .... 105 H2
Wellgate Av *BNG/LEV* M19 ...... 99 L4
Wellgreen CI *HALE/TIMP* WA15 117 L1
Well Green Ldg
 HALE/TIMP WA15 * 117 L1
Well Gv *WHTF* M45 .... 55 H1
Wellham Rd *WGNS/IIMK* WN3 .. 63 L1
Wellhead CI *HULME* M15 .... 87 J7
Wellhouse Dr *NEWH/MOS* M40 . 73 M1
Well-i-hole Rd *UPML* OL3 .... 61 J8
Welling Rd *NEWH/MOS* M40 .... 74 B4
Welling St *BOLE* BL2 .... 3 J1
Wellington Av *OLDTF/WHR* M16 . 98 A2
Wellington CI *SALE* M33 .... 96 F6
Wellington Clough *AULW* OL7 ... 75 J6
Wellington Ct *OLDS* OL8 * 59 G8
Wellington Crs
 OLDTF/WHR M16 .... 97 M1
Wellington Dr *TYLD* M29 .... 68 B4
Wellington Gv *HULME* M15 .... 87 G6
 OFTN SK2 .... 13 J9
 WGNS/IIMK WN3 .... 15 J9
Wellington Ms *EDGW/EG* BL7 .. 17 G8
Wellington PI *ALT* WA14 .... 116 F1
 MILN OL16 .... 11 H3
Wellington Rd *ATH* M46 .... 51 J7
 AUL OL6 .... 90 E1
 BRAM/HZG SK7 .... 122 D4
 BURY BL9 .... 4 F7
 CHH M8 .... 72 E4
 ECC M30 .... 85 H2
 EDGW/EG BL7 .... 17 G8
 HALE/TIMP WA15 .... 108 C6
 OLDS OL8 .... 58 F8
 OLDTF/WHR M16 .... 98 B2
 RUSH/FAL M14 .... 98 F5
 SWIN M27 .... 70 C4
 UPML OL3 .... 61 K6
Wellington Rd North
 BNG/LEV M19 .... 99 L5
 HTNM SK4 .... 12 F7
Wellington Rd South *OFTN* SK2 . 13 J8
 HTNM SK4 .... 12 F7
Wellington Sq *TOT/BURYW* BL8 . 38 C3
Wellington St *AUL* OL6 .... 90 E2
 BOLS/LL BL3 .... 2 B6
 BRAM/HZG SK7 .... 122 D4
 CHAD OL9 .... 8 A3
 CSLFD M3 .... 6 E1
 DTN/ASHW M34 .... 90 C5
 FAIL M35 .... 74 D3
 FWTH BL4 .... 53 G4
 GTN M18 .... 89 J6
 HYDE SK14 .... 101 M2
 LIT OL15 .... 21 M7
 MILN OL16 .... 29 K6
 OLD OL1 .... 9 K6
 RAD M26 .... 38 F8
 STKP SK1 .... 13 J5
 STRET M32 .... 96 F3

TOT/BURYW BL8 ....4 B6
WGN WN1 ....15 J4
WHIT OL12 ....10 F1
WHTN BL5 ....50 B2
Wellington St East BRO M7 ....72 A5
Wellington St West BRO M7 ....72 A6
Wellington Ter ORD M5 ....86 A2
Wellington Vis TOT/BURYW BL8 ....38 F3
Well i' th' La ROCH OL11 ....11 H9
Well Md MPL/ROM SK6 ....113 H1
Well La WHTF M45 ....55 J2
Wellmead Cl CHH M8 ....72 C7
Well Meadow HYDE SK14 ....91 G8
Well Meadow La UPML OL3 ....61 M4
Well Rd LEIGH WN7 ....66 A3
Well Rw HYDE SK14 ....103 K4
Wells Av CHAD OL9 ....58 D3
  PWCH M25 ....71 M2
  WGNW/BIL/OR WN5 ....62 A7
Wells Cl CHD/CHDH SK8 ....119 L5
  DROY M43 ....89 J4
  MDTN M24 ....56 F5
  TYLD M29 ....67 L5
Wells Ct DUK SK16 ....90 F6
Wells Dr DUK SK16 ....90 F6
  HTNM SK4 ....111 H2
  WGNE/HIN WN2 ....48 C2
Wells Pl WGN WN1 ....15 L3
Wells Rd OL12 ....44 B7
Wells St BURY BL9 ....4 D7
Wellstock La LHULT M38 ....52 C6
Well St BOL BL1 ....2 F4
  BOLE BL2 ....37 M3
  HEY OL10 ....41 H3
  NM/HAY SK22 ....124 D4
  ROCH OL11 ....11 H9
  TYLD M29 ....67 K4
Well St West RAMS BL0 ....18 E7
Wellwood Dr NEWH/MOS M40 ....73 K5
Wellyhole St OLDE OL4 ....60 A6
Welman Wy HALE/TIMP WA15 ....108 C8
Welney Rd OLDTF/WHR M16 ....97 L1
Welshpool Cl NTHM/RTH M23 ....109 L2
Welsh Rw MCFLDN SK10 ....130 D6
Weltdown Gdns ROY/SHW OL2 ....43 J4
Welton Av DID/WITH M20 ....110 F2
Welton Cl LEIGH WN7 ....66 F7
  WILM/AE SK9 ....126 D8
Welton Dr WILM/AE SK9 ....126 D8
Welton Gv WILM/AE SK9 ....126 D8
Welwyn Cl URM M41 ....84 F7
Welwyn Dr SLFD M6 ....70 D7
Welwyn Wk NEWH/MOS M40 ....88 A2
Wembley Gv RUSH/FAL M14 ....98 F4
Wembley Rd GTN M18 ....99 H1
Wembury St BKLY M9 ....73 H5
Wembury St North BKLY M9 ....73 H5
Wemsley Gv BOLE BL2 ....36 E3
Wem St OLD OL9 ....58 D8
Wemyss Av RDSH SK5 ....100 C3
Wendlebury Cl LEIGH WN7 ....81 H3
Wendlebury Gn ROY/SHW OL2 ....43 K7
Wendon Rd NTHM/RTH M23 ....109 L7
Wendover Dr BOLS/LL BL3 ....35 H7
Wendover Rd NTHM/RTH M23 ....108 F5
  URM M41 ....95 M3
Wenfield Dr BKLY M9 ....73 K1
Wenlock Av AULW OL7 ....75 L1
Wenlock Cl OFTN SK2 ....113 K6
Wenlock Gv WGNE/HIN WN2 ....49 G8
Wenlock Rd LEIGH WN7 ....81 H2
  SALE M33 ....108 D2
  WGNE/HIN WN2 ....49 G7
Wenlock St SWIN M27 ....70 A4
  WGNE/HIN WN2 ....49 G8
Wenlock Wy WGTN/LGST M12 ....88 D6
Wenning Cl WHTF M45 ....55 M5
Wensleydale Av
  CHD/CHDH SK8 ....110 F6
Wensleydale Cl BURY BL9 ....55 K1
  NTHM/RTH M23 ....118 B1
  ROY/SHW OL2 ....42 F7
Wensleydale Rd LEIGH WN7 ....66 F7
Wensley Dr BRAM/HZG SK7 ....121 M5
  DID/WITH M20 ....98 E7
Wensley Rd BRO M7 ....71 K3
  CHD/CHDH SK8 ....110 F6
  GOL/RIS/CUL WA3 ....80 B5
  RDSH SK5 ....100 C3
Wensley St MILN OL16 ....11 L6
Wentbridge Rd BOL BL1 ....2 B3
Wentworth Av FWTH BL4 ....52 F5
  GTN M18 ....89 H7
  HALE/TIMP WA15 ....108 D6
  HEY OL10 ....41 G4
  IRL M44 * 94 D1
  SLFD M6 ....85 M1
  TOT/BURYW BL8 ....24 E8
  WHTF M45 ....55 C5
Wentworth Cl MDTN M24 ....57 H4
  MPL/ROM SK6 ....114 C4
  RAD M26 ....38 A8
Wentworth Dr BRAM/HZG SK7 ....121 J5
  SALE M33 ....96 C7
Wentworth Rd AIMK WN4 ....63 K7
  ECC M30 ....70 C8
  RDSH SK5 ....100 C3
  SWIN M27 ....70 A6
Wenworth Av URM M41 ....95 L3
Werneth Av HYDE SK14 ....102 C4
  RUSH/FAL M14 ....98 E2
Werneth Ct BRAM/HZG SK7 ....113 H8
  DTN/ASHW M34 ....101 J2
Werneth Crs OLDS OL8 ....58 F8
Werneth Hall Rd OLDS OL8 ....8 E9
Werneth Hollow
  MPL/ROM SK6 ....101 L6
Werneth Low Rd HYDE SK14 ....102 B7
Werneth Ri HYDE SK14 ....102 C5
Werneth Rd GLSP SK13 ....104 D5
  HYDE SK14 ....102 C2
  MPL/ROM SK6 ....101 M7
Werneth St DTN/ASHW M34 ....101 J2
  STKP SK1 ....112 E1
Wescoe Cl MDTN WGNW/BIL/OR WN5 ....46 E7
Wesley Av RNFD/HAY WA11 ....78 B5
Wesley Cl WHIT OL12 ....28 E2
  WHTN BL5 ....50 B2
Wesley Ct WALK M28 * 53 G8
Wesley Dr AUL OL6 ....76 A6
  WALK M28 ....69 J4
Wesley Gn ORD M5 ....86 E4
Wesley Ms BOLE BL2 * 3 J5
Wesley Sq URM M41 ....95 K2
The Wesleys FWTH BL4 ....52 C4
Wesley St ATH M46 * 67 H1
  BOLS/LL BL3 ....35 J8
  BRAM/HZG SK7 ....122 A1
  ECC M30 ....84 F2
  EDGW/EG BL7 ....22 D4

FAIL M35 ....74 D3
FWTH BL4 ....53 H5
GLSP SK13 ....93 K7
GLSP SK13 ....105 H3
HEY OL10 ....40 F2
MILN OL16 ....29 H6
ROY/SHW OL2 ....59 H1
STKP SK1 ....13 K5
STRET M32 ....97 H1
SWIN M27 ....70 C4
TOT/BURYW BL8 ....24 B5
WGNW/BIL/OR WN5 ....47 C8
WHIT OL12 * 28 E1
WHTN BL5 ....50 B2
Wessenden Bank East
  OFTN SK2 ....113 G7
Wessenden Bank West
  OFTN SK2 ....113 G7
Wessex Cl WGN WN1 ....31 L3
Wessex Park Cl ROY/SHW OL2 ....43 L4
Wessex Rd WGNW/BIL/OR WN5 ....47 C3
Wessington Ms GLSP SK13 ....104 B3
Westage Gdns
  NTHM/RTH M23 ....109 K5
West Ashton St SALO M50 ....86 C4
West Av ALT WA14 ....107 K7
  BNG/LEV M19 ....99 J5
  CHD/CHDH SK8 ....119 L5
  FWTH BL4 ....52 E4
  GOL/RIS/CUL WA3 ....79 L3
  GTN M18 ....89 H7
  LEIGH WN7 ....81 M1
  NEWH/MOS M40 ....74 A3
  STLY SK15 ....91 K2
  WALK M28 ....68 F1
  WHTF M45 ....55 H2
West Bank OP/CLY M11 ....89 K5
  WILM/AE SK9 ....130 D4
Westbank Rd DID/WITH M20 ....99 H7
  HOR/BR BL6 ....35 C6
West Bank St ATH M46 ....66 F7
  ORD M5 ....86 F4
Westbourne Av BOLS/LL BL3 ....52 D1
  LEIGH WN7 ....66 C5
  SWIN M27 ....54 A7
  WHTF M45 ....55 C3
Westbourne Dr WILM/AE SK9 ....127 K4
  LEIGH WN7 ....66 C5
Westbourne Gv BKLY M9 ....73 C4
  DID/WITH M20 ....98 D6
  RDSH SK5 ....100 C4
  SALE M33 ....96 D8
Westbourne Pk URM M41 ....96 A1
Westbourne Range GTN M18 ....100 C1
Westbourne Rd
  DTN/ASHW M34 ....101 M2
  ECC M30 ....69 L8
  RUSH/FAL M14 ....99 G4
  URM M41 ....96 A2
Westbourne St CHAD OL9 ....8 F7
Westbridge Ms WGN WN1 ....15 C5
West Bridgewater St
  LEIGH WN7 ....66 C8
Westbrook Cl BOLE BL2 ....3 C7
  ROCH OL11 ....42 A4
Westbrook Ct BOLE BL2 * 3 C7
Westbrook Rd SWIN M27 ....70 B5
  TRPK M17 ....85 M5
Westbrook Sq WGTN/LGST M12 ....88 D6
Westbrook St BOLE BL2 ....3 H7
Westbury Av SALE M33 ....107 M3
  WGNS/IIMK WN3 ....63 G2
  WHTN BL5 ....50 D3
Westbury Dr MPL/ROM SK6 ....114 B7
Westbury Rd CHH M8 ....72 D3
Westbury St AUL OL6 ....90 F1
Westbury Wy ROY/SHW OL2 ....59 C2
Westby Cl BRAM/HZG SK7 ....121 J5
Westby Gv BOLE BL2 ....3 K3
West Canteen Rd TRPK M17 ....85 M8
West Central Dr SWIN M27 ....70 E5
West Charles St ORD M5 ....86 E3
West Church St HEY OL10 ....40 F2
Westcliffe Rd BOL BL1 ....22 C6
West Cl ATH M46 ....67 H3
Westcombe Dr
  TOT/BURYW BL8 ....24 F8
Westcott Av DID/WITH M20 ....98 D6
Westcott Cl BOLE BL2 ....23 H7
Westcott Gv WGNS/IIMK WN3 ....46 F8
Westcott Gv ROY/SHW OL2 ....43 K7
Westcourt Rd BOLS/LL BL3 ....52 A1
  SALE M33 ....96 D7
Westcraig Av NEWH/MOS M40 ....73 M1
West Craven St ORD M5 ....86 E5
West Crs MDTN M24 ....57 J5
Westcroft WGNE/HIN WN2 ....64 C7
Westcroft Rd DID/WITH M20 ....99 C8
West Crown Av ORD M5 ....86 E4
Westdale Gdns BNG/LEV M19 ....99 K7
Westdean Crs BNG/LEV M19 ....99 J7
West Dean St ORD M5 ....86 F3
West Downs Rd
  CHD/CHDH SK8 ....120 B1
West Dr BURY BL9 ....25 H7
  CHD/CHDH SK8 ....110 D8
  DROY M43 ....89 J3
  GLSP SK13 ....93 H6
  SLFD M6 ....71 H6
  SWIN M27 ....70 D5
West Duke St ORD M5 ....6 A5
West Egerton St ORD M5 ....86 E2
West End Av CHD/CHDH SK8 ....110 D6
West End St CHAD OL9 ....8 F5
Westend St FWTH BL4 ....52 E4
Westerdale OLDE OL4 ....59 M6
Westerdale Cl TYLD M29 ....67 L4
Westerdale Dr BOLS/LL BL3 ....35 K7
  ROY/SHW OL2 ....42 F7
Westerham Av ORD M5 ....86 D3
Westerham Cl TOT/BURYW BL8 ....24 E5
Wester Hill Rd OLDS OL8 ....75 K3
Westerling Wy
  OLDTF/WHR M16 ....98 B1
Western Access TRPK M17 * 85 J4
Western Av SWIN M27 ....71 C2
Western Cir BNG/LEV M19 ....99 J6
Western Rd URM M41 ....95 H3
Western St GTN M18 ....89 H6
  SLFD M6 ....86 B1
Westerton Ct BOLS/LL BL3 ....2 A8
Westfield SLFD M6 ....71 H8
Westfield Av AIMK WN4 ....63 K8
  MDTN M24 ....57 K5
Westfield Cl ROCH OL11 ....27 J3
Westfield Dr MPL/ROM SK6 ....101 M7
Westfield Gv DTN/ASHW M34 ....90 B7
  WGN WN1 ....47 L1
Westfield Rd BOLS/LL BL3 ....51 L2
  CCHDY M21 ....97 L3

CHD/CHDH SK8 ....120 B4
DROY M43 ....89 H2
Westfields HALE/TIMP WA15 ....117 H4
Westfield St BRO M7 ....72 A3
  CHAD OL9 ....8 C2
Westgate HALE/TIMP WA15 ....117 C2
  SALE M33 ....96 D8
  URM M41 ....95 J7
  WILM/AE SK9 ....126 E7
Westgate Av BKLY M9 * 72 F2
  BOL BL1 ....35 M5
  BURY BL9 ....4 D7
  RAMS BL0 ....24 C2
Westgate Dr SWIN M27 ....70 C6
  TYLD M29 ....67 M6
  WGNW/BIL/OR WN5 ....46 A7
Westgate Rd SLFD M6 ....70 E8
Westgate St AULW OL6 ....90 D3
West Gn MDTN M24 ....56 E5
West Gv BRUN/LGST M13 ....88 A7
  MOSL OL5 ....76 A4
  SALE M33 ....108 C1
  WHTN BL5 ....50 B6
Westgrove Av BOL BL1 * 22 B8
Westhead Av GOL/RIS/CUL WA3 ....80 B4
West High St BRO M7 ....86 D2
Westholm Av HTNM SK4 ....99 L5
Westholme Ct WILM/AE SK9 ....130 D2
Westholme Rd DID/WITH M20 ....98 E8
  PWCH M25 ....55 M5
West Hope St ORD M5 ....86 E3
Westhulme Av OLD OL1 ....8 E1
Westhulme St OLD OL1 ....8 E1
Westhulme Wy OLD OL1 ....58 F3
Westinghouse Cl
  WGNNW/ST WN6 ....14 C4
Westinghouse Rd TRPK M17 ....85 M7
West King St CSLFD M3 ....6 C2
Westlake Gv WGNE/HIN WN2 ....49 L8
Westland Av BOL BL1 ....35 K3
  FWTH BL4 ....52 F6
  STKP SK1 * 112 E3
Westland Dr BKLY M9 ....57 C8
Westlands WHTF M45 ....55 C8
Westlea Dr GTN M18 ....100 A1
Westleigh Dr PWCH M25 ....72 A1
Westleigh La LEIGH WN7 ....66 A2
Westleigh St BKLY M9 ....73 H3
Westlock WGNS/IIMK WN3 ....14 E8
West Malling Cl HEY OL10 ....41 J5
Westmarsh Cl BOL BL1 ....2 D1
West Marwood St BRO M7 ....72 B6
Westmead
  WGNNW/ST WN6 ....31 H4
Westmead Dr
  HALE/TIMP WA15 ....108 E5
West Meade BOLS/LL BL3 ....52 B2
  CCHDY M21 ....97 K5
  PWCH M25 ....72 A2
  SWIN M27 ....70 B6
Westmead Rd WALK M28 ....52 F7
West Meadow RDSH SK5 ....100 D3
Westmere Dr BKLY M9 ....72 F6
Westminister Cl ROY/SHW OL2 ....43 G7
Westminster Av AUL OL6 ....76 A5
  FWTH BL4 ....52 F4
  OLDTF/WHR M16 ....97 M2
  RAD M26 ....38 A8
  RDSH SK5 ....100 B5
  ROY/SHW OL2 ....42 F6
  WHTF M45 ....55 J4
Westminster Cl MPL/ROM SK6 ....114 A5
  SALE M33 ....108 A1
Westminster Dr
  CHD/CHDH SK8 ....120 D6
  LEIGH WN7 ....67 H6
  RNFD/HAY WA11 ....78 C5
  WILM/AE SK9 ....126 D8
Westminster Rd BOL BL1 ....22 B7
  ECC M30 ....85 H1
  FAIL M35 ....74 F4
  HALE/TIMP WA15 ....117 J1
  URM M41 ....85 G3
  WALK M28 ....69 G2
Westminster St BNG/LEV M19 * 99 L3
  BURY BL9 ....4 E5
  FWTH BL4 ....52 F4
  OLD OL1 ....59 L4
  ROCH OL11 ....10 A9
  SWIN M27 ....70 A3
  WGNW/BIL/OR WN5 ....47 J3
Westminster Wy DUK SK16 ....90 F6
Westmoorland St WGN WN1 ....15 K2
Westmoreland Cl ALT WA14 ....116 D4
  BURY BL9 ....39 H6
Westmorland Av AULW OL7 ....75 L8
  DUK SK16 ....91 H4
Westmorland Cl RDSH SK5 ....100 F6
Westmorland Dr RDSH SK5 ....100 E6
  WHIT OL12 ....21 H6
Westmorland Rd
  DID/WITH M20 ....110 D3
  ECC M30 ....70 D7
  PART M31 ....106 B2
  SALE M33 ....108 F2
  TYLD M29 ....67 K2
  URM M41 ....95 M3
West Mosley St CMANW M2 ....7 C5
West Mt WGN WN1 ....48 A2
  WGNW/BIL/OR WN5 ....46 C6
Westmount Cl
  NEWH/MOS M40 ....72 F6
West Oak Pl CHD/CHDH SK8 * 120 B3
Weston Av MILN OL16 ....28 E8
  NEWH/MOS M40 ....74 B3
  SWIN M27 ....54 C8
  URM M41 ....95 L3
Westonby Ct AIMK WN4 ....79 L1
Weston Dr CHD/CHDH SK8 ....111 M8
  DTN/ASHW M34 ....101 K1
Weston Gv HTNM SK4 ....99 M6
  WYTH/NTH M22 ....110 B4
Weston Pk WGNNW/ST WN6 ....47 L1
Weston Rd IRL M44 ....94 D2
  WILM/AE SK9 ....127 H6
Weston St ATH M46 ....51 H4
  BOLS/LL BL3 ....36 C8
  MILN OL16 ....29 H6
  NEWH/MOS M40 * 88 A2
  OLDE OL4 ....59 M8
  RDSH SK5 ....100 B5
Westover MPL/ROM SK6 ....113 K4
Westover Rd URM M41 ....95 H1
Westover St SWIN M27 ....70 B3
West Pk HYDE SK14 ....102 B5
West Park Av DTN/ASHW M34 ....101 J3
  POY/DIS SK12 ....121 J8
West Park Rd BRAM/HZG SK7 ....120 F2
  STKP SK1 ....112 E2
West Park St ORD M5 ....86 E5

West Pl BNG/LEV M19 ....99 J5
Westray Crs ORD M5 * 86 B3
Westree Rd BRUN/LGST M13 ....99 H2
Westrees LEIGH WN7 ....66 D5
Westridge Cha ROY/SHW OL2 ....43 G7
West Rd ALT WA14 ....116 E2
  PWCH M25 ....55 J7
  STRET M32 ....85 K8
West Rw PWCH M25 ....71 J3
West Starkey St HEY OL10 ....40 F1
West St AUL OL6 ....90 E1
  BOL BL1 ....35 M5
  CHAD OL9 ....8 E6
  DUK SK16 ....90 E3
  EDGY/DAV SK3 ....12 E5
  FAIL M35 ....74 B5
  FWTH BL4 ....53 H3
  GLSP SK13 ....93 J5
  HEY OL10 ....41 G2
  HYDE SK14 * 91 G7
  LIT OL15 ....21 M7
  MDTN M24 ....57 K2
  MILN OL16 ....11 L6
  MILN OL16 ....29 G5
  OLD OL1 ....9 H5
  OLDE OL4 ....60 B7
  OP/CLY M11 ....88 E2
  RAMS BL0 ....18 E7
  STLY SK15 ....91 J2
  WGNE/HIN WN2 ....48 D4
  WGNE/HIN WN2 ....65 L1
  WGNNW/ST WN6 ....14 D2
  WILM/AE SK9 ....130 D3
West Towers Ms
  MPL/ROM SK6 ....114 D8
West Towers St SLFD M6 ....86 C3
West V RAD M26 ....38 D7
West Vale Rd
  HALE/TIMP WA15 ....108 C7
West Vw RAMS BL0 ....18 F2
  WILM/AE SK9 * 126 C5
West View Gv WHTF M45 ....55 G3
West View Rd WYTH/NTH M22 ....110 B4
Westville Gdns BNG/LEV M19 ....99 H7
West Wk EDGW/EG BL7 ....22 C2
Westward Ho MILN OL16 ....29 J6
Westward Rd WILM/AE SK9 ....126 D6
Westway BKLY M9 ....56 D6
  ROY/SHW OL2 ....43 L6
Westway DROY M43 ....89 K5
West Wy LHULT M38 ....52 D7
Westway OLDE OL4 ....60 B7
Westwell Gv LEIGH WN7 ....66 B4
Westwell St LEIGH WN7 ....66 B4
Westwood Av BRO M7 ....72 B4
  HALE/TIMP WA15 ....108 C5
  HYDE SK14 ....102 E1
  NEWH/MOS M40 * 74 B3
  URM M41 ....96 C3
  WALK M28 ....68 D2
Westwood Cl FWTH BL4 ....53 G4
Westwood Crs ECC M30 ....69 L8
Westwood Dr CHAD OL9 ....8 E5
  OFTN SK2 ....112 E8
  STRET M32 ....96 E2
  SWIN M27 ....70 F6
Westwood La WGNS/IIMK WN3 ....15 G8
Westwood Pk WGNS/IIMK WN3 ....15 G8
Westwood Rd BOL BL1 ....35 M4
  CHD/CHDH SK8 ....119 K4
  OFTN SK2 ....112 E8
  STRET M32 ....96 E2
  WGNS/IIMK WN3 ....15 G8
Westwood St RUSH/FAL M14 ....87 J8
Westwood Ter WGNS/IIMK WN3 * 15 K9
Westwood Wy OLD OL1 * 9 M3
West Works Rd TRPK M17 ....85 M8
Westworth Cl BOL BL1 ....2 C1
Wet Gate La LYMM WA13 ....106 A8
Wetheral Cl MDTN M24 ....43 G7
Wetheral Dr BOLS/LL BL3 ....52 B1
Wetherall St BNG/LEV M19 ....99 L3
Wetherby Cl NEWLW WA12 ....78 F7
Wetherby Dr BRAM/HZG SK7 * 122 C2
  ROY/SHW OL2 ....42 F7
Wetherby St OP/CLY M11 ....89 K8
Wexham Gdns WGNE/HIN WN2 ....64 D1
Weybourne Av BKLY M9 ....73 J2
Weybourne Dr MPL/ROM SK6 ....101 J2
  WGNS/IIMK WN3 ....63 H1
Weybourne Gv BOLE BL2 ....22 E8
Weybridge Rd ANC M4 ....7 M3
Weybrook Rd BNG/LEV M19 ....99 M5
Weycroft Cl BOLE BL2 ....37 K6
Weygates Dr
  HALE/TIMP WA15 ....117 L6
Weyhill Rd NTHM/RTH M23 ....109 H3
Weylands Gv SLFD M6 ....70 C8
Weymouth Dr WGNE/HIN WN2 ....49 K8
Weymouth Rd AUL OL6 ....76 B2
  ECC M30 ....84 E1
Weymouth St BOL BL1 ....36 B2
Weythorne Dr BOL BL1 ....22 C8
  BURY BL9 ....26 C7
Whalley Av BNG/LEV M19 ....99 L2
  BOL BL1 ....35 J1
  CCHDY M21 ....97 M5
  GOL/RIS/CUL WA3 ....81 M5
  LIT OL15 ....21 L6
  OLDTF/WHR M16 ....98 A1
  SALE M33 ....96 F7
  WHTF M45 ....55 J3
Whalley Cl HALE/TIMP WA15 ....108 C4
  MILN OL16 * 29 H6
  WGNS/IIMK WN3 ....63 H1
  WHTF M45 ....55 J3
Whalley Dr TOT/BURYW BL8 ....38 C2
Whalley Gdns WHIT OL12 ....27 L3
Whalley Gv AUL OL6 ....76 B2
  LEIGH WN7 ....66 A3
  OLDTF/WHR M16 ....98 A1
Whalley Rd HALE/TIMP WA15 ....117 J2
  HEY OL10 ....41 H3
  MDTN M24 ....57 J1
  OFTN SK2 ....112 C5
  OLDTF/WHR M16 ....98 A1
  RAMS BL0 ....19 L3
  WHIT OL12 ....27 L3
Whalley St NEWH/MOS M40 ....88 A2
Wham Bar Dr HEY OL10 ....40 E2
Wham Bottom La WHIT OL12 ....20 B8
Wham La UPML OL3 ....45 G8
Wham St HEY OL10 ....40 F2
Wharfdale WHTN BL5 ....50 C2
Wharfedale Av
  NEWH/MOS M40 ....73 K3
Wharfedale Rd RDSH SK5 ....100 B4
Wharf End TRPK M17 ....86 D6
Wharf Rd ALT WA14 ....108 A5
  SALE M33 ....96 F7

Wharfside Av ECC M30 ....85 G4
Wharf St CHAD OL9 ....74 E1
  DUK SK16 ....90 F3
  HTNM SK4 ....13 H1
Wharmby Rd RNFD/HAY WA11 ....78 B6
Wharmton Ri OLDE OL4 ....61 G6
Wharmton Vw MOSL OL5 ....77 H1
  UPML OL3 ....61 K9
Wharncliffe Cl GLSP SK13 ....93 G5
Wharncliffe St
  WGNE/HIN WN2 * 49 G7
Wharton Av CCHDY M21 ....98 A5
Wharton Hall Cl TYLD M29 ....67 L3
Wharton La LHULT M38 ....52 B7
Wharton Ldg ECC M30 ....85 H1
Wheat Cl BRUN/LGST M13 ....87 M7
Wheat Cft EDGY/DAV SK3 ....112 C2
Wheatcroft GLSP SK13 ....93 H8
Wheaters St BRO M7 * 71 M8
Wheaters Ter BRO M7 ....72 A3
Wheatfield STLY SK15 ....92 B5
Wheatfield Cl BURY BL9 ....25 J3
  MPL/ROM SK6 ....101 K8
Wheatfield Crs ROY/SHW OL2 ....58 F1
Wheatfield St BOLE BL2 ....3 J3
Wheathill St MILN OL16 ....28 D8
Wheatlea Rd WGNS/IIMK WN3 ....63 J3
Wheatley Rd SWIN M27 ....70 A2
Wheatley Wk WGTN/LGST M12 ....88 C6
Wheatsheaf Wk
  WGNNW/ST WN6 ....31 G3
Wheeldale OLDE OL4 ....60 A6
Wheeldale Cl BOL BL1 ....36 B2
Wheelock Cl WILM/AE SK9 ....127 H3
Wheelton Cl TOT/BURYW BL8 ....38 D3
Wheelwright Cl MPL/ROM SK6 ....114 C4
  ROCH OL11 ....27 L8
Wheelwright Dr MILN OL16 ....28 F1
Whelan Av BURY BL9 ....39 H5
Whelan Cl BURY BL9 ....39 H5
Whelley St OP/CLY M11 ....89 G2
Whelley WGN WN1 ....48 B2
Whernside Av AUL OL6 ....75 M5
  NEWH/MOS M40 ....73 K3
Whetmorhurst Rd
  MPL/ROM SK6 ....115 H8
Whetstone Hill Cl OLD OL1 ....59 M2
Whetstone Hill La OLD OL1 ....59 M3
Whetstone Hill Rd OLD OL1 ....59 L2
Whewell Av RAD M26 ....39 C7
Whickham Cl RUSH/FAL M14 ....98 E1
Whiley St BRUN/LGST M13 ....88 C8
Whimberry Cl ORD M5 ....86 F5
Whimberry St STLY SK15 ....77 C7
Whimberry Wy DID/WITH M20 ....99 G6
Whimbrel Rd OFTN SK2 ....113 K7
  TYLD M29 ....67 H8
Whimbury Dr STLY SK15 ....77 H8
Whinberry Rd ALT WA14 ....107 L5
Whinberry Wy OLDE OL4 ....44 B8
Whinchat Av NEWLW WA12 ....78 F8
Whinchat Cl GOL/RIS/CUL WA3 ....80 B5
  OFTN SK2 ....113 K6
Whinfell Dr MDTN M24 ....56 E3
Whinfield Cl WGNNW/ST WN6 ....14 C4
Whins Av FWTH BL4 ....52 M4
Whins Crest HOR/BR BL6 ....34 F5
Whinslee Dr HOR/BR BL6 ....34 F5
Whinstone Wy OLD OL1 ....58 E3
Whipp St HEY OL10 ....40 E1
Whirley Cl HTNM SK4 ....100 A1
Whistlecroft Ct
  WGNS/IIMK WN3 ....15 M8
Whistley St WGNE/HIN WN2 ....64 E1
Whiston Rd CHH M8 ....72 E4
Whitaker St MDTN M24 ....57 J4
Whitbeam Gv WGNE/HIN WN2 ....65 H2
Whitbrook Wy MDTN M24 ....41 M7
Whitburn Av BRUN/LGST M13 ....99 H2
Whitburn Cl AIMK WN4 ....63 C8
  BOLS/LL BL3 ....35 H8
Whitburn Dr TOT/BURYW BL8 ....24 F7
Whitburn Rd NTHM/RTH M23 ....109 K8
Whitby Av HEY OL10 ....40 F1
  OLDTF/WHR M16 ....98 A2
  RUSH/FAL M14 ....98 A2
  SLFD M6 ....85 M1
  URM M41 ....96 B2
Whitby Cl CHD/CHDH SK8 ....110 F6
  POY/DIS SK12 ....121 J8
  TOT/BURYW BL8 ....38 C2
Whitby Rd OLDS OL8 ....75 M1
  RUSH/FAL M14 ....98 A4
Whitby St MDTN M24 ....57 M3
  ROCH OL11 ....11 C8
Whitchurch Dr
  OLDTF/WHR M16 ....87 C7
Whitchurch Gdns BOL BL1 ....36 B3
Whitchurch Rd DID/WITH M20 ....98 C5
Whitchurch St BRO M7 ....87 H1
Whiteacre WGNNW/ST WN6 ....30 D2
Whiteacre Rd AUL OL6 ....76 A8
Whiteacres SWIN M27 ....69 M5
White Bank Av RDSH SK5 ....100 F8
White Bank Rd OLDS OL8 ....75 J2
Whitebarn Rd WILM/AE SK9 ....130 E4
Whitebeam Cl
  HALE/TIMP WA15 ....109 H7
  MILN OL16 ....28 D1
  SLFD M6 ....86 D1
Whitebeam Ct SLFD M6 * 86 D1
Whitebeam Wk WHTN BL5 ....50 C2
White Birk Cl TOT/BURYW BL8 ....24 C2
White Brook La UPML OL3 ....61 M4
Whitebrook Rd RUSH/FAL M14 ....98 E3
Whitecar Av NEWH/MOS M40 ....74 B3
White Carr La BURY BL9 ....25 L3
Whitecarr La
  HALE/TIMP WA15 ....117 M1
Whitechapel Cl BOLE BL2 ....37 H5
Whitechapel St
  DID/WITH M20 ....110 E1
White City Wy
  OLDTF/WHR M16 ....86 D7
Whitecliff Cl RUSH/FAL M14 ....98 F1
Whitecroft Av
  GOL/RIS/CUL WA3 ....80 B3
  ROY/SHW OL2 ....59 H1
Whitecroft Dr TOT/BURYW BL8 ....38 C2
Whitecroft Gdns BNG/LEV M19 ....99 K8
Whitecroft Rd BOL BL1 ....35 K3
  MPL/ROM SK6 ....123 L2
  WGNS/IIMK WN3 ....63 K2
Whitecroft St OLD OL1 ....59 M3
Whitefield HTNM SK4 ....112 A1
Whitefield Av ROCH OL11 ....27 J4
Whitefield Rd BURY BL9 ....39 H6
  MPL/ROM SK6 ....101 K8
  SALE M33 ....96 C7

Whitegate BOLS/LL BL3 50 F2
LIT OL15 21 J8
Whitegate Av CHAD OL9 58 C8
Whitegate Cl NEWH/MOS M40 74 B3
Whitegate Dr BOL BL1 22 C7
ORD M5 86 A1
SWIN M27 70 E2
Whitegate La CHAD OL9 58 D8
Whitegate Pk URM M41 95 H2
Whitegate Rd CHAD OL9 74 A1
Whitegates Cl
HALE/TIMP WA15 108 E7
Whitegates La OLDE OL4 60 E2
Whitegates Rd CHD/CHDH SK8 111 G7
MDTN M24 41 M8
Whitehall Av WGNNW/ST WN6 30 B4
Whitehall Cl WILM/AE SK9 126 E7
Whitehall La BOL BL1 22 A6
HOR/BR BL6 33 G1
OLDE OL4 44 C8
Whitehall Rd DID/WITH M20 110 F1
SALE M33 108 E2
Whitehall St OLD OL1 9 K3
WGNS/IIMK WN3 15 K8
WHIT OL12 10 E1
White Hart Meadow
MDTN M24 57 K2
White Hart St HYDE SK14 91 G8
Whitehaven Gdns
DID/WITH M20 110 D2
Whitehaven Rd
BRAM/HZG SK7 120 E7
Whitehead Crs RAD M26 53 L5
TOT/BURYW BL8 24 F7
Whitehead Rd CCHDY M21 97 J4
SWIN M27 70 E2
Whitehead St DTN/ASHW M34 90 C5
MILN OL16 * 29 H6
ROY/SHW OL2 43 J4
WALK M28 53 G8
White Hill Cl WHIT OL12 20 B8
Whitehill Dr NEWH/MOS M40 73 K5
Whitehill St HTNM SK4 100 B8
Whitehill St West HTNM SK4 100 A8
Whiteholme Av CCHDY M21 98 A8
White Horse Gdns SWIN M27 * 69 M6
White Horse Gv WHTN BL5 50 D2
White Horse Mdw MILN OL16 * 42 F2
Whitehouse Av OLDE OL4 59 M7
White House Av PWCH M25 72 B1
White House Cl HEY OL10 41 G5
Whitehouse Dr
HALE/TIMP WA15 117 K4
NTHM/RTH M23 109 K7
Whitehouse La ALT WA14 107 G5
Whitehurst Rd HTNM SK4 99 J8
Whitekirk Cl BRUN/LGST M13 87 L6
White Lady Cl WALK M28 68 C1
Whitelake Av URM M41 95 J1
Whitelake Vw URM M41 95 H1
Whiteland Av BOLS/LL BL3 35 L7
Whitelands DUK SK16 90 F2
Whitelands Rd AUL OL6 90 F2
Whitelea Dr EDGY/DAV SK3 112 A7
White Lee Cft ATH M46 66 E1
Whitelees Rd LIT OL15 21 L7
Whitelegge St TOT/BURYW BL8 24 E8
Whiteley Dr MDTN M24 57 M5
Whiteley Pl ALT WA14 108 A6
Whiteley St CHAD OL9 58 E8
OP/CLY M11 88 E2
White Lion Brow BOL BL1 2 C5
White Lodge Dr AIMK WN4 64 B8
Whitelow Rd BURY BL9 19 H7
CCHDY M21 97 K4
HTNM SK4 111 K1
Whitemoss WHIT OL12 * 27 L2
White Moss Av CCHDY M21 97 M4
White Moss Rd BKLY M9 73 H1
Whitemoss Rd East BKLY M9 57 J8
Whiteoak Cl MPL/ROM SK6 114 B5
Whiteoak Rd RUSH/FAL M14 98 F4
Whiteoak Vw BOLS/LL BL3 37 G7
White Rd NM/HAY SK22 124 E3
Whites Cft SWIN M27 70 C4
Whiteside Av WGNE/HIN WN2 49 G5
WGNNW/ST WN6 14 B1
Whiteside Cl ORD M5 86 A2
Whiteside Fold WHIT OL12 27 K3
Whitesmead Cl POY/DIS SK12 123 M7
Whitestone Cl HOR/BR BL6 35 G6
Whitestone Wk
BRUN/LGST M13 * 88 A7
White St HULME M15 87 G6
LEIGH WN7 66 F8
SLFD M6 86 B3
TOT/BURYW BL8 38 F3
WGNW/BIL/OR WN5 46 E6
White Swallows Rd SWIN M27 70 D6
Whitethorn Av BNG/LEV M19 99 K5
OLDTF/WHR M16 98 A1
Whitethorn Cl MPL/ROM SK6 114 B5
Whitewater Dr BRO M7 71 J5
Whiteway St BKLY M9 73 H5
Whitewell Cl BURY BL9 39 G5
MILN OL16 11 L2
Whitewillow Cl FAIL M35 74 D6
Whitewood Cl AIMK WN4 63 K6
Whitfield Av GLSP SK13 104 F5
Whitfield Crs MILN OL16 43 L1
Whitfield Cross GLSP SK13 105 G5
Whitfield Dr MILN OL16 29 H7
Whitfield Pk GLSP SK13 104 F5
Whitfield Ri ROY/SHW OL2 43 K3
Whitfield St CSLFD M3 87 K1
LEIGH WN7 66 F8
Whiting Gv BOLS/LL BL3 35 H6
Whitinlea Cl WGNE/HIN WN2 65 M1
Whitland Av BOL BL1 35 J4
Whitland Dr OLDS OL8 74 E2
Whit La SLFD M6 71 K7
White Bank Rd NM/HAY SK22 124 D2
Whitledge Gn AIMK WN4 63 K7
Whitledge Rd AIMK WN4 63 K7
Whitle Rd NM/HAY SK22 124 E3
Whitley Crs WGN WN1 31 L8
WGNE/HIN WN2 64 E5
Whitley Gdns
HALE/TIMP WA15 108 F5
Whitley Pl HALE/TIMP WA15 108 E5
Whitley Rd HTNM SK4 111 L1
NEWH/MOS M40 72 F8
SKEL WN8 46 A2
Whitley St BOLS/LL BL3 53 G2
Whitley Wk GLSP SK13 104 C4
Whitlow Av ALT WA14 107 L4
GOL/RIS/CUL WA3 79 J3
Whitman St BKLY M9 73 J4
Whitmore Rd RUSH/FAL M14 98 E3
Whitnall Cl OLDTF/WHR M16 98 B1
Whitnall St HYDE SK14 * 91 G7
Whitsand Rd WYTH/NTH M22 110 B7
Whitsbury Av GTN M18 100 A1
WGNE/HIN WN2 49 G8
Whitstable Cl CHAD OL9 8 B7
Whitstable Rd
NEWH/MOS M40 * 73 M3
Whitsters Hollow BOL BL1 35 L1
Whitsundale WHTN BL5 50 C2
Whittaker Dr LIT OL15 29 J2
Whittaker La PWCH M25 55 M8
ROCH OL11 27 G3
Whittaker St AUL OL6 76 A7
CHAD OL9 8 B3
NEWH/MOS M40 73 K4
RAD M26 38 E8
ROCH OL11 * 27 H3
WGTN/LGST M12 88 A4
Whittingham Dr RAMS BL0 18 F8
Whittingham Gv OLD OL1 * 8 F2
Whittington St AULW OL7 90 D3
Whittlebrook Gv HEY OL10 41 H5
Whittle Ct WGNS/IIMK WN3 63 H2
Whittle Dr ROY/SHW OL2 44 A4
WALK M28 53 G7
Whittle Gv BOL BL1 35 L3
WALK M28 69 H1
Whittle Hl EDGW/EG BL7 22 B1
Whittle La HEY OL10 40 D7
Whittles Av DTN/ASHW M34 101 K2
Whittle's Cft CMANE M1 * 7 K5
Whittle St ANC M4 * 7 J3
LIT OL15 21 K7
SWIN M27 70 B5
TOT/BURYW BL8 4 A2
WALK M28 69 H1
Whitwell Cl WGNNW/ST WN6 31 G2
Whitwell Wy GTN M18 88 F7
Whitworth Cl AUL OL6 75 M8
Whitworth La RUSH/FAL M14 99 G3
Whitworth Rake WHIT OL12 20 B4
Whitworth Rd WHIT OL12 28 C2
Whitworth Sq WHIT OL12 20 B4
Whitworth St CMANE M1 7 J6
HOR/BR BL6 33 M2
MILN OL16 * 28 F2
MILN OL16 29 J6
OP/CLY M11 88 E5
Whitworth St East OP/CLY M11 88 F5
Whitworth St West CMANE M1 6 F7
Whixhall Av WGTN/LGST M12 88 B6
Whoolden St FWTH BL4 52 F3
Whowell Fold BOL BL1 35 M1
Whowell St BOLS/LL BL3 2 C7
Wibbersley Pk URM M41 * 95 J2
Wichbrook Rd WALK M28 68 C1
Wicheaves Crs WALK M28 68 C1
The Wicheries WALK M28 68 C1
Wicken Bank HEY OL10 41 H5
Wickenby Dr SALE M33 96 D8
Wicken St OFTN SK2 112 F5
Wickentree Holt WHIT OL12 27 K2
Wickentree La FAIL M35 74 D3
Wicker La HALE/TIMP WA15 117 K4
Wicket Gv SWIN M27 54 B8
Wickliffe Pl ROCH OL11 10 E6
Wickliffe St BOL BL1 2 D3
Wicklow Av EDGY/DAV SK3 12 A8
Wicklow Dr WYTH/NTH M22 119 G2
Wicklow Gv OLDS OL8 75 H1
Widcombe Dr BOLE BL2 37 J7
Widdop St CHAD OL9 8 E5
Widdow's St LEIGH WN7 66 E8
Widdrington Rd WGN WN1 48 A2
Widecombe Cl URM M41 * 84 E8
Widgeon Cl POY/DIS SK12 121 K8
RUSH/FAL M14 98 E4
Widgeon Rd ALT WA14 107 L5
Widnes St OP/CLY M11 * 88 F5
Wiend WGN WN1 15 G4
Wigan Investment Centre
WGNS/IIMK WN3 14 E7
Wigan La WGN WN1 15 G1
Wigan Lower Rd
WGNNW/ST WN6 30 F8
Wigan Pier WGNS/IIMK WN3 * 14 D6
Wigan Rd AIMK WN4 78 E1
ATH M46 66 C2
BOLS/LL BL3 51 H1
GOL/RIS/CUL WA3 79 L1
LEIGH WN7 65 M5
WGNE/HIN WN2 48 D1
WGNNW/ST WN6 30 E7
WGNW/BIL/OR WN5 62 C5
WHTN BL5 49 K5
Wigan Sq WGN WN1 * 14 F3
Wigan St WGNE/HIN WN2 64 D2
Wiggins Wk RUSH/FAL M14 * 98 F1
Wightman Av NEWLW WA12 78 F7
Wigley St WGTN/LGST M12 88 B5
Wigmore Rd CHH M8 72 E5
Wigmore St AUL OL6 76 A8
Wigsby Av NEWH/MOS M40 73 M5
Wigshaw Cl LEIGH WN7 81 J3
Wigwam Cl POY/DIS SK12 121 L8
Wike St TOT/BURYW BL8 4 B3
Wilbraham Rd CCHDY M21 97 L4
OLDTF/WHR M16 98 B3
RUSH/FAL M14 98 E3
WALK M28 68 C1
Wilbraham St LEIGH WN7 65 M7
WHTN BL5 50 B4
Wilburn St ORD M5 6 A6
Wilby Av BOLS/LL BL3 37 K7
Wilby Cl TOT/BURYW BL8 * 25 G7
Wilby St CHH M8 72 E6
Wilcock Cl OLDTF/WHR M16 87 H8
Wilcock Rd RNFD/HAY WA11 78 D4
Wilcock St WGNS/IIMK WN3 14 D5
Wilcott Dr SALE M33 96 B7
WILM/AE SK9 126 D8
Wilcott Rd CHD/CHDH SK8 110 D7
Wild Arum Cl
GOL/RIS/CUL WA3 80 B4
Wildbank Cha STLY SK15 92 B5
Wildbrook Cl LHULT M38 68 B1
Wildbrook Crs OLDS OL8 75 K1
Wildbrook Gv LHULT M38 68 B1
Wildbrook Rd LHULT M38 52 B8
Wildbrook Ter OLDS OL8 * 75 K1
Wild Clough HYDE SK14 102 C3
Wildcroft Av NEWH/MOS M40 73 K3
Wilders Moor Cl WALK M28 68 F4
Wilderswood Cl DID/WITH M20 98 F7
Wilde St DTN/ASHW M34 101 J1
Wildhouse La LIT OL15 29 J3
Wilding St WGNS/IIMK WN3 15 K8
Wildman La FWTH BL4 52 C4
Wildmoor Av OLDE OL4 60 B8
Wild Moor Wood Cl STLY SK15 77 G7
Wilds Pas LEIGH WN7 66 C8
Wilds Pl RAMS BL0 * 18 E7
Wild St BRAM/HZG SK7 * 121 M2
DUK SK16 91 G4
HEY OL10 41 H2
MPL/ROM SK6 113 J2
OLD OL1 9 M4
OLDE OL4 60 B6
RAD M26 39 G8
ROY/SHW OL2 43 M6
Wildwood Cl OFTN SK2 112 D7
RAMS BL0 18 D8
Wilford Av SALE M33 108 D2
Wilfred Dr BURY BL9 5 K1
Wilfred Rd ECC M30 84 D4
WALK M28 69 G2
Wilfred St BRO M7 72 B8
EDGW/EG BL7 * 22 D5
NEWH/MOS M40 73 K4
WGNW/BIL/OR WN5 47 J5
Wilfrid's Pl WGNNW/ST WN6 31 H3
Wilfrid St SWIN M27 70 C4
Wilkesley Av WGNNW/ST WN6 31 G4
Wilkes St OLD OL1 60 A1
Wilkin Cft CHD/CHDH SK8 120 A4
Wilkins La WILM/AE SK9 119 G7
Wilkinson Av BOLS/LL BL3 37 K8
Wilkinson Rd BOL BL1 22 A7
HTNM SK4 13 G2
Wilkinson St AUL OL6 90 D1
HTNM SK4 13 G2
LEIGH WN7 66 B7
MDTN M24 57 J4
SALE M33 97 G8
Wilks Av WYTH/NTH M22 119 H2
Willand Cl BOLE BL2 37 K6
Willand Dr BOLE BL2 37 K7
Willan Rd BKLY M9 56 F8
ECC M30 85 H2
Willard Av WGNW/BIL/OR WN5 62 A1
Willard St BRAM/HZG SK7 * 121 M1
Willaston Cl CCHDY M21 97 K5
Willbutts La ROCH OL11 27 M4
Willdale Cl OP/CLY M11 88 D2
Willdor Gv EDGY/DAV SK3 111 L6
Willenhall Rd NTHM/RTH M23 109 M2
Willerby Rd BRO M7 72 B7
Willesden Av BRUN/LGST M13 99 H1
Will Griffith Wk OP/CLY M11 88 B4
William Chadwick Cl
NEWH/MOS M40 87 M1
William Cl URM M41 95 M3
William Greenwood Cl
HEY OL10 40 F2
William Henry St ROCH OL11 28 D8
William Jessop Ct CMANE M1 7 L5
William Kay Cl OLDTF/WHR M16 87 H8
William Lister Cl
NEWH/MOS M40 * 74 A8
Williams Av NEWLW WA12 78 F7
Williams Crs CHAD OL9 74 C1
Williamson Av MPL/ROM SK6 101 K8
RAD M26 38 C6
Williamson La DROY M43 89 L4
Williamson St ANC M4 87 L1
AUL OL6 90 E2
RDSH SK5 100 B5
Williams Rd GTN M18 88 F7
NEWH/MOS M40 73 L5
Williams St BOLS/LL BL3 53 L1
GTN M18 88 F8
William St AULW OL7 90 D3
CSLFD M3 6 C3
DID/WITH M20 110 E1
FAIL M35 74 D3
HOR/BR BL6 33 K1
LEIGH WN7 66 D7
LIT OL15 21 L7
MDTN M24 57 L4
MILN OL16 21 H8
RAD M26 38 E8
RAMS BL0 18 F3
ROCH OL11 10 F7
STKP SK1 112 E5
WGNE/HIN WN2 49 H7
WGNS/IIMK WN3 15 J8
WGTN/LGST M12 88 A4
WHIT OL12 20 A3
Willingdon Cl TOT/BURYW BL8 24 F5
Willingdon Dr PWCH M25 55 L7
Willis Rd EDGY/DAV SK3 112 B6
Willis St BOLS/LL BL3 35 M8
Willock St BRO M7 72 B6
Willoughby Av DID/WITH M20 98 F8
Willoughby Cl SALE M33 96 D7
Willow Av CHD/CHDH SK8 120 B2
MDTN M24 57 M5
NEWLW WA12 79 G8
RDSH SK5 100 C8
TYLD M29 67 K6
URM M41 96 B2
Willow Bank CHD/CHDH SK8 120 C6
OLDE OL4 60 B4
RUSH/FAL M14 98 F4
Willowbank RAD M26 54 D4
Willowbank Av BOLE BL2 3 K7
Willow Bank Cl OFTN SK2 113 G5
Willowbrook Av
NEWH/MOS M40 73 K5
Willowbrook Dr
WGNNW/ST WN6 30 E5
Willow Cl BOLS/LL BL3 35 L8
BURY BL9 55 L2
DUK SK16 91 J5
POY/DIS SK12 129 J1
Willow Ct MPL/ROM SK6 114 C7
SALE M33 97 H7
Willow Crs LEIGH WN7 66 B4
Willowcroft Av
WGNE/HIN WN2 49 J1
Willowdale Av CHD/CHDH SK8 119 K2
Willowdene Cl EDGW/EG BL7 22 C4
NEWH/MOS M40 72 F7
Willow Dr BURY BL9 55 L2
SALE M33 108 B2
WGNE/HIN WN2 65 J1
WILM/AE SK9 127 H1
Willowfield Gv AIMK WN4 78 D2
Willowfield Rd OLDE OL4 60 A2
Willow Fold DROY M43 89 L4
Willow Gv AIMK WN4 64 B7
CHAD OL9 8 B3
DTN/ASHW M34 101 H1
GOL/RIS/CUL WA3 79 K3
GTN M18 * 89 H8
MPL/ROM SK6 114 C7
Willow Hey EDGW/EG BL7 22 F6
Willow Hill Rd CHH M8 72 D3
Willow Lawn CHD/CHDH SK8 * 120 C2
Willow Ldg WGNE/HIN WN2 64 E3
Willowmead Wy WHIT OL12 27 K2
Willowmoss Cl WALK M28 69 H3
Willow Ri LIT OL15 29 J1
Willow Rd ECC M30 69 K8
MPL/ROM SK6 123 H5
NEWLW WA12 79 H8
PART M31 106 B2
PWCH M25 55 K6
RNFD/HAY WA11 78 B5
UPML OL3 61 M5
WGNNW/ST WN6 31 J8
Willows Dr FAIL M35 74 C8
Willows End STLY SK15 92 A1
Willows La BOLS/LL BL3 35 M8
MILN OL16 29 H5
Willows Rd ORD M5 * 86 A2
The Willows BOLS/LL BL3 37 K7
CCHDY M21 97 K5
MOSL OL5 77 H3
PART M31 106 C1
Willow St ATH M46 50 F8
BURY BL9 5 L4
CHH M8 72 B8
HEY OL10 41 G2
OLD OL1 9 M4
OP/CLY M11 88 D3
SWIN M27 70 A7
WALK M28 69 M5
Willow Tree Cl WGN WN1 31 L8
Willow Tree Ms
CHD/CHDH SK8 119 K3
Willow Tree Rd ALT WA14 116 F2
Willow Wy BRAM/HZG SK7 120 E5
DID/WITH M20 110 F1
Willow Wood Cl AUL OL6 91 H1
Wilma Av BKLY M9 56 F8
Wilmans Wk GLSP SK13 93 K6
Wilmcote Cl HOR/BR BL6 35 G6
Wilmcote Rd NEWH/MOS M40 72 F8
Wilmington Rd STRET M32 * 96 E2
Wilmot Dr GOL/RIS/CUL WA3 79 J5
Wilmot St BOL BL1 35 M1
Wilmott St HULME M15 6 F9
Wilmslow Av BOL BL1 22 B7
Wilmslow Old Rd
HALE/TIMP WA15 118 B6
MCFLDN SK10 131 K1
Wilmslow Park Rd
WILM/AE SK9 127 H5
Wilmslow Rd BRAM/HZG SK7 127 M3
CHD/CHDH SK8 111 G8
DID/WITH M20 98 E8
HALE/TIMP WA15 118 B7
MCFLDN SK10 127 L8
MCFLDN SK10 128 A6
RUSH/FAL M14 87 M8
WILM/AE SK9 119 M7
WILM/AE SK9 130 D2
Wilmur Av BRO M7 72 B6
WHTF M45 55 K5
Wilpshire Av WGTN/LGST M12 99 L1
Wilsford Cl GOL/RIS/CUL WA3 79 L3
Wilsham Rd
WGNW/BIL/OR WN5 46 B7
Wilshaw Gv AULW OL7 75 L6
Wilshaw La AULW OL7 75 K7
Wilson Av HEY OL10 40 D2
SWIN M27 70 E3
WGNNW/ST WN6 47 L2
Wilson Crs AUL OL6 76 B8
Wilson Fold Av HOR/BR BL6 34 C3
Wilson Rd BKLY M9 73 G3
HTNM SK4 99 L8
Wilsons Pk NEWH/MOS M40 * 73 H7
Wilson St BOLS/LL BL3 * 2 E6
BRUN/LGST M13 87 M6
BURY BL9 5 H6
FWTH BL4 53 H4
HYDE SK14 102 B2
OLDS OL8 59 H8
OP/CLY M11 88 D4
RAD M26 38 C8
STRET M32 86 B8
UPML OL3 61 K7
WHIT OL12 10 E2
Wilson Wy OLD OL1 9 J4
Wilsthorpe Cl BNG/LEV M19 99 M6
Wilton Av CHD/CHDH SK8 119 L5
OLDTF/WHR M16 97 K1
PWCH M25 72 A2
SWIN M27 70 F5
WGNE/HIN WN2 48 C2
Wilton Ct GTN M18 89 K8
Wilton Crs WILM/AE SK9 130 C2
Wilton Dr BURY BL9 39 K7
HALE/TIMP WA15 117 L4
Wilton Gdns RAD M26 38 F7
Wilton Gv DTN/ASHW M34 89 K8
HEY OL10 41 G3
Wilton La GOL/RIS/CUL WA3 80 D7
Wilton Paddock
DTN/ASHW M34 89 K8
Wilton Pl CSLFD M3 6 A3
Wilton Rd BOL BL1 22 B7
CCHDY M21 97 L4
CHH M8 72 D2
SLFD M6 70 E8
WGNNW/ST WN6 30 D6
Wilton St AIMK WN4 63 J6
BOL BL1 36 C1
CHAD OL9 74 E1
DTN/ASHW M34 90 B8
HEY OL10 40 F2
MDTN M24 56 E5
PWCH M25 55 M8
RDSH SK5 100 C2
WGN WN1 15 H6
WHTF M45 55 J5
Wilton Ter WHIT OL12 10 C2
Wiltshire Av RDSH SK5 100 F8
Wiltshire Cl BURY BL9 5 H8
Wiltshire Dr GLSP SK13 105 J4
Wiltshire Pl
WGNW/BIL/OR WN5 46 F6
Wiltshire Rd CHAD OL9 8 B9
FAIL M35 74 C6
PART M31 106 B2
Wiltshire St BRO M7 72 B6
Wimberry Cl UPML OL3 61 L7
Wimberry Hill Rd WHTN BL5 50 A1
Wimbledon Dr EDGY/DAV SK3 111 M6
ROCH OL11 10 B9
Wimbledon Rd FAIL M35 74 E4
Wimborne Av URM M41 85 G8
Wimborne Cl CHD/CHDH SK8 111 M8
HOR/BR BL6 34 C3
Wimborne Rd
WGNW/BIL/OR WN5 46 D4
Wimbourne Av CHAD OL9 58 D3
Wimpole St AUL OL6 90 F1
OLD OL1 9 L3
Wimpory St OP/CLY M11 89 G5
Winbolt St OFTN SK2 112 F8
Winby St ROCH OL11 11 H9
Wincanton Av NTHM/RTH M23 109 G4
Wincanton Dr BOL BL1 22 A5
Wincanton Pk OLDE OL4 60 A6
Wince Cl MDTN M24 57 M6
Wincham Cl HULME M15 87 G6
Wincham Rd SALE M33 108 B2
Winchcombe Cl LEIGH WN7 81 H3
Winchester Av AIMK WN4 78 D1
AUL OL6 76 A5
CHAD OL9 58 C3
DTN/ASHW M34 101 J3
HEY OL10 40 F4
PWCH M25 71 M2
TYLD M29 67 M5
Winchester Cl ROCH OL11 27 J5
TOT/BURYW BL8 24 F5
WGNW/BIL/OR WN5 46 C5
WILM/AE SK9 126 C7
Winchester Dr HTNM SK4 12 B2
SALE M33 96 A8
Winchester Gv
WGNS/IIMK WN3 15 J8
Winchester Pk DID/WITH M20 110 C1
Winchester Rd DUK SK16 91 K5
ECC M30 70 D8
HALE/TIMP WA15 117 L3
RAD M26 38 A7
RNFD/HAY WA11 78 B3
SLFD M6 70 F8
URM M41 96 A1
WGNW/BIL/OR WN5 62 A3
Winchester Wy BOLE BL2 37 G3
Wincle Av POY/DIS SK12 129 K2
Wincombe St RUSH/FAL M14 98 E2
Windale WALK M28 68 E1
Windcroft Cl OP/CLY M11 88 C4
Winder Dr ANC M4 7 M4
Windermere Av ATH M46 51 G7
BOLS/LL BL3 37 K8
DTN/ASHW M34 100 D2
SALE M33 109 G1
SWIN M27 70 D5
Windermere Cl OP/CLY M11 88 D4
PWCH M25 55 H7
STRET M32 96 F1
Windermere Crs AULW OL7 * 75 J8
Windermere Dr BURY BL9 39 H5
RAMS BL0 18 F5
WILM/AE SK9 130 C3
Windermere Gv LEIGH WN7 66 B7
Windermere Rd DUK SK16 90 F4
FWTH BL4 52 B5
HYDE SK14 90 F7
LEIGH WN7 66 B7
MDTN M24 56 F2
MPL/ROM SK6 122 F3
ROY/SHW OL2 43 G6
STKP SK1 112 E5
STLY SK15 91 K1
URM M41 * 95 M3
WGNE/HIN WN2 48 D5
WGNE/HIN WN2 49 H7
WGNE/HIN WN2 64 E4
WGNW/BIL/OR WN5 46 C4
WILM/AE SK9 119 L8
Windermere St BOL BL1 36 C1
WGN WN1 15 K2
Winder St BOL BL1 2 E2
Winders Wy SLFD M6 71 L8
Windfields Cl CHD/CHDH SK8 120 D1
Wind Gate Ri STLY SK15 77 G8
Windham St MILN OL16 28 F1
Windle Av CHH M8 72 C1
Windle Ct OFTN SK2 113 H7
Windlehurst Dr WALK M28 68 E5
Windlehurst Old Rd
MPL/ROM SK6 123 H2
Windlehurst Rd MPL/ROM SK6 122 F4
Windleshaw St
WGNS/IIMK WN3 15 K8
Windley St BOLE BL2 3 H2
Windmill Av ORD M5 86 E5
Windmill Cl DTN/ASHW M34 100 E2
WGN WN1 15 J3
Windmill Ct MILN OL16 11 J6
Windmill La DTN/ASHW M34 100 D2
TYLD M29 67 J8
Windmill Rd SALE M33 109 J1
WALK M28 52 F7
Windmill St CMANW M2 6 E6
MILN OL16 11 J6
Windover Cl WHTN BL5 51 K5
Windover St BOLS/LL BL3 35 K8
Windrush Av RAMS BL0 24 D2
Windrush Dr BKLY M9 73 G5
WHTN BL5 50 C3
The Windrush WHIT OL12 20 A8
Windsor Av BOLS/LL BL3 53 K1
CHAD OL9 58 D8
CHD/CHDH SK8 110 C7
FAIL M35 74 E4
HEY OL10 40 E2
HTNM SK4 111 K1
IRL M44 94 E1
LHULT M38 52 E7
SALE M33 96 E6
SWIN M27 70 D2
TYLD M29 67 K6
URM M41 95 J2
WHTF M45 55 K5
WILM/AE SK9 126 D6
Windsor Cl POY/DIS SK12 121 M8
TOT/BURYW BL8 24 D3
Windsor Crs PWCH M25 72 B1
WGNE/HIN WN2 33 G7
Windsor Dr ALT WA14 108 C4
ALT WA14 116 B3
AULW OL7 75 J8
DTN/ASHW M34 90 A3
DUK SK16 91 J5
HOR/BR BL6 34 B2
MPL/ROM SK6 114 B7
RNFD/HAY WA11 78 D5
STLY SK15 91 K1
TOT/BURYW BL8 38 E4
Windsor Gv AUL OL6 75 M5
BOL BL1 35 M3
CHD/CHDH SK8 120 B4
MPL/ROM SK6 114 B2
RAD M26 53 L5
WGNE/HIN WN2 65 L1
Windsor Rd AIMK WN4 78 E2
BKLY M9 73 H5
BNG/LEV M19 99 J3
BRAM/HZG SK7 122 B2
DROY M43 89 G2
DTN/ASHW M34 100 D1
EDGW/EG BL7 22 D5
GOL/RIS/CUL WA3 79 M4
HYDE SK14 102 A5
LEIGH WN7 67 H6
MPL/ROM SK6 112 F1
NEWH/MOS M40 74 B8
OLDS OL8 8 E8
PWCH M25 72 B1
WGNW/BIL/OR WN5 62 C7

Windsor St *ATH* M46 ....67 H2
FAIL M35 ....74 D5
GTN M18 ....88 F9
NEWH/MOS M40 ....74 D8
OFTN SK2 ....112 D6
OLD OL1 ....59 K3
ORD M5 ....86 E3
ROCH OL11 ....11 C9
WGN WN1 ....15 J2
Windsor Ter *MILN* OL16 ....11 M4
MILN OL16 ....29 H6
Windybank *BKLY* M9 ....56 F7
Windy Bank Av
GOL/RIS/CUL WA3 ....80 B4
Windy Harbour La
EDGW/EG BL7 ....22 E4
Windyhill Dr *BOLS/LL* BL3 ....51 K1
Winfell Dr *NEWH/MOS* M40 ....88 A1
Winfield Av *DID/WITH* M20 ....99 G7
Winfield Dr *GTN* M18 ....89 C6
Winfield Gv *MPL/ROM* SK6 ....114 E3
Winfield St *HYDE* SK14 ....102 C2
Winford St *BKLY* M9 ....73 H4
Wingate Av *TOT/BURYW* BL8 ....38 E2
DID/WITH M20 ....110 F2
HALE/TIMP WA15 ....108 E7
WHTF M45 ....55 H3
Wingate Gv *HTNM* SK4 ....99 M8
LHULT M38 ....52 E8
Wingates Gv *WHTN* BL5 ....50 A1
Wingates La *WHTN* BL5 ....34 B8
Wingates Rd *WGN* WN1 ....31 M7
Wingates Sq *WHTN* BL5 ....50 B1
Wingate St *ROCH* OL11 ....27 G3
Wingfield Av *WILM/AE* SK9 ....126 C6
Wingfield Cl *WGNNW/ST* WN6 ....31 K8
Wingfield Dr *SWIN* M27 ....70 D6
WILM/AE SK9 ....126 C6
Wingfield Gv *GLSP* SK13 ....105 J5
Wingfield St *STRET* M32 ....86 D3
Wings Gv *HEY* OL10 ....41 G5
Winhill Rd *NM/HAY* SK22 ....124 C3
Winifred Av *BURY* BL9 ....26 C8
Winifred Rd *DID/WITH* M20 ....110 E1
FWTH BL4 ....52 D3
NEWH/MOS M40 ....73 L5
OFTN SK2 ....112 D7
URM M41 ....95 M1
Winifred St *ECC* M30 ....84 E3
HYDE SK14 ....102 B5
RAMS BL0 ....18 E7
WGNS/IIMK WN3 ....15 K8
WHIT OL12 ....27 L3
Winmarith Dr
HALE/TIMP WA15 ....117 M5
Winmarleigh Cl
TOT/BURYW BL8 ....38 C3
Winmarleigh Gdns *LEIGH* WN7 ....81 H1
Winnard St *GOL/RIS/CUL* WA3 ....79 L2
Winnats Cl *GLSP* SK13 ....105 J4
Winnie St *NEWH/MOS* M40 ....73 K4
Winnington Gn *OFTN* SK2 ....113 G7
Winnington Rd *MPL/ROM* SK6 ....114 C4
Winnipeg Quay *SALQ* M50 ....86 C5
The Winnows *DTN/ASHW* M34 ....101 G1
Winscar Rd *WGNE/HIN* WN2 ....49 G6
Winscombe Dr
NEWH/MOS M40 ....72 F8
Winser St *CMANE* M1 ....7 G7
Winsfield Rd *BRAM/HZG* SK7 ....121 M4
Winsford Cl *RNFD/HAY* WA11 ....78 C5
Winsford Dr *ROCH* OL11 ....27 J7
Winsford Gv *BOLS/LL* BL3 ....35 K7
Winsford Rd *RUSH/FAL* M14 ....98 D3
Winskill Rd *IRL* M44 ....94 D4
Winslade Cl *BRAM/HZG* SK7 ....121 J2
OLDE OL4 ....60 A3
Winslade Ms *FWTH* BL4 ....53 C3
Winsley Rd *NTHM/RTH* M23 ....109 J2
Winslow Av *HYDE* SK14 ....103 J2
Winslow Pl *BNG/LEV* M19 ....99 J6
Winslow Rd *BOLS/LL* BL3 ....50 F2
Winslow St *OP/CLY* M11 ....88 D4
Winsmoor Dr *WGNE/HIN* WN2 ....49 H8
Winstanley Pl *WGNNW/ST* WN3 ....15 K9
Winstanley Rd *AIMK* WN4 ....62 E5
NEWH/MOS M40 ....88 A1
SALE M33 ....96 A1
WGNE/HIN WN2 ....64 C4
WGNNW/BIL/OR WN5 ....62 C1
Winstanley St
WGNNW/BIL/OR WN5 ....14 A7
Winster Av *BRO* M7 ....71 L6
DID/WITH M20 ....98 B8
STRET M32 ....96 D1
Winster Cl *BOLE* BL2 ....37 J3
WHTF M45 ....55 L4
Winster Dr *BOLE* BL2 ....37 J3
MDTN M24 ....57 H2
Winster Gv *OFTN* SK2 ....112 D6
Winster Rd *ECC* M30 ....84 E4
Winston Av *BOLS/LL* BL3 ....53 M1
ROCH OL11 ....27 H6
Winston Cl *MPL/ROM* SK6 ....114 A5
RAD M26 ....38 B7
Winston Rd *BKLY* M9 ....73 J3
SALE M33 ....96 C7
Winswell Cl *OP/CLY* M11 ....88 E2
Winterbottom Gv *HYDE* SK14 ....103 J2
Winterbottom St *CHAD* OL9 ....8 F5
CCHDY M21 ....97 M8
Winterburn Av *BOLE* BL2 ....22 E6
Winterburn Gn *OFTN* SK2 ....113 H6
Winterdyne St *BKLY* M9 ....73 H5
Winterfield Dr *BOLS/LL* BL3 ....51 H9
Winterford Av *BRUN/LGST* M13 ....88 A1
Winterford Rd *BRO* M7 ....72 C5
MOSL OL5 ....77 H3
Winter Hey La *HOR/BR* BL6 ....33 L1
Winter Hill Vw *EDGW/EG* BL7 ....22 A1
Wintermans Rd *CCHDY* M21 ....98 A6
Winterslow Av
NTHM/RTH M23 ....109 G3
Winter St *BOL* BL1 ....36 A1
Winterton Cl *WHTN* BL5 ....50 D3
Winterton Rd *RDSH* SK5 ....100 D3
Winthrop Av *NEWH/MOS* M40 ....73 G7
NEWH/MOS M40 ....74 A3
Winton Av *DTN/ASHW* M34 ....90 A5
NEWH/MOS M40 ....47 G7
Winton Cl *BRAM/HZG* SK7 ....120 F3
Winton Gn *HOR/BR* BL6 ....34 C4
Winton Rd *BOLS/LL* BL3 ....35 H8
Winton St *AUL* OL6 ....90 E1
GOL/RIS/CUL WA3 ....80 B3
SLFD M6 ....71 C6
STLY SK15 ....91 L3
Winward St *BOLS/LL* BL3 ....35 K8
LEIGH WN7 ....65 L7

WHTN BL5 ....50 B3
Winwood Dr *MDTN* M24 ....57 L2
Winwood Rd *DID/WITH* M20 ....110 F4
Wirksmoor Rd *NM/HAY* SK22 ....124 D5
Wirral Cl *SWIN* M27 ....70 D2
Wirral Crs *EDGY/DAV* SK3 ....111 K4
Wirral Dr *WGNS/IIMK* WN3 ....62 F2
Wisbech Dr *NTHM/RTH* M23 ....109 J3
Wisbeck Rd *BOLE* BL2 ....3 M3
Wiseley St *OP/CLY* M11 ....88 B4
Wiseman Ter *PWCH* M25 ....55 M8
Wishaw Sq *CCHDY* M21 ....98 B6
Wisley Cl *RDSH* SK5 ....100 C4
Wistaria Rd *GTN* M18 ....88 G7
Witham Av *WYTH/NTH* M22 ....110 B7
Witham Cl *HEY* OL10 ....40 D1
WGNNW/ST WN6 ....31 G3
Witham St *AUL* OL6 ....76 B8
Withenfield Rd
NTHM/RTH M23 ....109 J4
Withens Gn *OFTN* SK2 ....113 H6
Withington Av
GOL/RIS/CUL WA3 ....81 K8
Withington Cl *AIM* M46 ....50 E8
Withington Dr *TYLD* M29 ....67 M5
Withington Gra
WGNE/HIN WN2 ....48 E2
Withington Gn *MDTN* M24 ....41 K8
Withington La *WGNE/HIN* WN2 ....1 K8
Withington Rd *CCHDY* M21 ....98 A4
OLDTF/WHR M16 ....98 A1
Withington St *HEY* OL10 ....41 H4
WHTN BL5 ....50 D2
Withinlea Cl *WHTN* BL5 ....50 D2
Withinlee Rd *MCFLDN* SK10 ....131 M6
Withins Av *RAD* M26 ....38 F7
Withins Cl *BOLE* BL2 ....37 H4
Withins Dr *BOLE* BL2 ....37 H4
Withins Gv *BOLE* BL2 ....37 H4
Withins Hall Rd *FAIL* M35 ....74 E6
Withins La *BOLE* BL2 ....37 H4
RAD M26 ....38 F7
Withins Rd *OLDS* OL8 ....9 L8
RNFD/HAY WA11 ....78 A4
Withins St *RAD* M26 ....38 F8
Withnell Cl *WGNNW/ST* WN6 ....14 B8
Withnell Dr *TOT/BURYW* BL8 ....38 D3
Withnell Rd *BNG/LEV* M19 ....111 L6
Withycombe Pl *SLFD* M6 ....71 K7
Withy Gv *ANC* M4 ....7 G3
Withypool Dr *OFTN* SK2 ....112 F7
Withy Tree Gv
DTN/ASHW M34 ....101 K2
Witley Dr *SALE* M33 ....96 A6
Witley Rd *MILN* OL16 ....11 K6
Wittenbury Rd *HTNM* SK4 ....12 A2
Witterage Cl *WGNE/LGST* M12 ....88 C6
Witton Weavers Wy *DWN* BB3 ....16 A1
Woburn Abbey *UPML* OL3 ....61 K3
Woburn Av *BOLE* BL2 ....36 F1
LEIGH WN7 ....66 A3
Woburn Cl *MILN* OL16 ....29 H6
RNFD/HAY WA11 ....78 C5
Woburn Dr *BURY* BL9 ....39 J7
HALE/TIMP WA15 ....117 K2
Woburn Rd *OLDTF/WHR* M16 ....97 K2
Woburn St *OLDTF/WHR* M16 ....98 C1
Wodens Av *ORD* M5 ....86 F5
Woking Back Gdns *BOL* BL1 ....36 B3
Woking Rd *CHD/CHDH* SK8 ....120 C6
Woking Ter *BOL* BL1 ....36 B3
Wolfenden St *BOL* BL1 ....36 B2
Wolfenden Ter *BOL* BL1 ....36 B2
Wolford Dr *TYLD* M29 ....67 M3
Wolfreton Av *SWIN* M27 ....70 D1
Wolfson Sq *AIMK* WN4 ....63 J8
Wolmer St *AIMK* WN4 ....63 K8
Wolseley Pl *DID/WITH* M20 ....98 E7
Wolseley Rd *SALE* M33 ....96 B6
Wolseley St *MILN* OL16 ....29 L8
TOT/BURYW BL8 ....4 B5
Wolsey Cl *AIMK* WN4 ....63 K7
Wolsey Dr *ALT* WA14 ....116 C3
Wolsey St *HEY* OL10 ....40 F3
RAD M26 ....38 C6
Wolstenholme Av *BURY* BL9 ....25 J6
Wolstenholme Coalpit La
WHIT OL12 ....26 E2
Wolstenholme La *WHIT* OL12 ....26 F2
Wolstenvale Cl *MDTN* M24 ....57 L3
Wolver Cl *LHULT* M38 ....52 E6
Wolverton Av *OLDS* OL8 ....75 C1
Wolverton Dr *WILM/AE* SK9 ....127 G3
Wolvesey *ROCH* OL11 ....10 D7
Wolveton St *OP/CLY* M11 ....88 C5
Woodacre *OLDTF/WHR* M16 ....98 B3
Woodacres Ct *WILM/AE* SK9 ....126 D6
Woodall Cl *SALE* M33 ....97 G8
Woodark Cl *OLDE* OL4 ....60 C7
Woodbank *BOLE* BL2 ....37 C2
Woodbank Av *MPL/ROM* SK6 ....113 H1
STKP SK1 ....112 F4
Woodbank Ct *URM* M41 ....95 L1
Woodbank Dr *TOT/BURYW* BL8 ....24 F8
Wood Bank Rd *LIT* OL15 ....29 K1
Woodbine Av *IRL* M44 ....94 A8
Woodbine Crs *OFTN* SK2 ....13 K9
Woodbine Rd *BOLS/LL* BL3 ....51 M1
MILN OL16 ....11 H8
Woodbine St East *MILN* OL16 ....11 J8
Woodbourne Rd *HTNM* SK4 ....99 M6
NM/HAY SK22 ....124 C2
SALE M33 ....108 D2
Woodbray Av *BNG/LEV* M19 ....99 H7
Woodbridge Av
DTN/ASHW M34 ....90 A5
Woodbridge Gdns *WHIT* OL12 ....27 M2
Woodbridge Gv
NTHM/RTH M23 ....109 K3
Woodbridge Rd *URM* M41 ....95 G1
Woodbrook Av *OLDE* OL4 ....60 E5
Woodbrook Dr
WGNS/IIMK WN3 ....47 C8
Wood Brook La *OLDE* OL4 ....60 E5
Woodbrook Rd *WILM/AE* SK9 ....130 E3
Woodburn Dr *BOL* BL1 ....35 L1
Woodburn Rd *WYTH/NTH* M22 ....110 A4
Woodbury Crs *DUK* SK16 ....90 E5
Woodbury Rd *EDGY/DAV* SK3 ....12 A8
Woodchurch *WGN* WN1 ....15 M1
Woodchurch Wk *CHAD* OL9 ....8 A7
ROCH OL11 ....27 J5
Woodcock Cl *DROY* M43 ....89 K1
Woodcock Dr *WGNE/HIN* WN2 ....64 E2
Woodcock Gv *GLSP* SK13 ....105 H3
Woodcock Rd *GLSP* SK13 ....105 K3
Woodcock Sq *WGN* WN1 ....14 F3
Woodcote Rd *BRAM/HZG* SK7 ....120 C3

Woodcote Rd *ALT* WA14 ....108 A3
PART M31 ....95 K8
SALE M33 ....107 K1
Woodcote Vw *WILM/AE* SK9 ....127 K3
Wood Cottage Cl *WALK* M28 ....68 C1
Woodcott Bank *BOL* BL1 ....22 A8
Woodcourt *WGNS/IIMK* WN3 ....14 E8
Wood Crs *OLDE* OL4 ....76 B1
Woodcroft *OFTN* SK2 ....113 G6
WGNNW/ST WN6 ....30 B6
Woodcroft Av *BNG/LEV* M19 ....99 H8
Wooddagger Cl
WGNE/HIN WN2 ....49 J7
Wooddeaton Cl *ROY/SHW* OL2 ....43 K8
Wooded Cl *BURY* BL9 ....25 J7
Wooddedge *AIMK* WN4 ....78 D1
Wood Edge Cl *BOLS/LL* BL3 ....52 F1
Wood End *BRAM/HZG* SK7 ....120 F2
Woodend *ROY/SHW* OL2 ....43 M3
Woodend Dr *STLY* SK15 ....92 A6
Woodend La *HYDE* SK14 ....101 M3
STLY SK15 ....92 A5
WHIT OL12 ....21 H6
Woodend Rd *EDGY/DAV* SK3 ....112 C8
WYTH/NTH M22 ....110 A8
Woodend St *OLD* OL1 ....9 H1
OLDE OL4 ....60 C7
Woodfield Av *WYTH/NTH* M22 ....118 F1
MPL/ROM SK6 ....101 K8
WHIT OL12 * 28 B2
Woodfield Cl *GLSP* SK13 ....93 J7
OLDS OL8 ....58 F8
Woodfield Ct *OFTN* SK2 * 112 D8
Woodfield Crs *AIMK* WN4 ....78 D2
MPL/ROM SK6 ....113 J2
Woodfield Dr *WALK* M28 ....69 H5
Woodfield Gv *ECC* M30 ....84 F3
FWTH BL4 ....52 F6
SALE M33 ....96 D6
Woodfield Ms *HYDE* SK14 * 102 A4
Woodfield Rd *ALT* WA14 ....107 M6
CHD/CHDH SK8 ....120 D5
CHH M8 ....72 D3
MDTN M24 ....57 H6
SLFD M6 ....71 G8
Woodfield St *BOLS/LL* BL3 ....52 D1
WGNE/HIN WN2 ....48 D1
Wood Fold *EDGW/EG* BL7 ....22 F6
Woodfold Av *BNG/LEV* M19 ....99 K2
Woodfold Rd *FAIL* M35 ....74 D4
Woodford Av *DTN/ASHW* M34 ....90 D8
ECC M30 ....84 E2
GOL/RIS/CUL WA3 ....80 A5
ROY/SHW OL2 ....44 A5
Woodford Dr *SWIN* M27 ....70 B2
Woodford Gdns
DID/WITH M20 ....110 D2
Woodford Gv *BOLS/LL* BL3 ....35 M8
Woodford La *MCFLDN* SK10 ....128 A6
Woodford Rd *BRAM/HZG* SK7 ....121 G7
POY/DIS SK12 ....121 K7
WILM/AE SK9 ....127 M4
Woodford Av *WGNE/HIN* WN2 ....49 J1
WGNW/BIL/OR WN5 ....46 E6
Wood Gdns *NM/HAY* SK22 ....125 L1
Woodgarth *LEIGH* WN7 * 65 M7
Woodgarth Av
NEWH/MOS M40 ....74 A7
Woodgarth Dr *SWIN* M27 ....70 B6
Woodgarth La *WALK* M28 ....69 J7
Woodgate Av *BURY* BL9 ....26 A8
ROCH OL11 ....27 K6
Woodgate Cl *MPL/ROM* SK6 ....113 J1
Woodgate Dr *PWCH* M25 ....55 M6
Woodgate Hill Rd *BURY* BL9 ....5 M2
BURY BL9 ....26 A8
Woodgate Rd *OLDTF/WHR* M16 ....98 B3
Woodgate St *BOLS/LL* BL3 ....52 D1
Woodgrange Cl *SLFD* M6 ....86 B2
Woodgreen Cl *WGNE/HIN* WN2 ....49 G8
Woodgreen Dr *RAD* M26 ....54 D4
Wood Gv *DTN/ASHW* M34 ....90 C8
MPL/ROM SK6 ....101 K7
WHTF M45 ....55 H1
Woodhall Av *DID/WITH* M20 ....98 D5
WHTF M45 ....55 G6
Woodhall Cl *BOLE* BL2 ....36 F1
BRAM/HZG SK7 ....128 B1
TOT/BURYW BL8 ....25 G7
Woodhall Crs *RDSH* SK5 ....100 D8
Woodhall Rd *RDSH* SK5 ....100 D8
Woodhall St *FAIL* M35 ....74 C4
Woodham Rd *NTHM/RTH* M23 ....109 J3
Woodham Wk *BOLS/LL* BL3 ....2 A8
Woodhead Cl *OLDE* OL4 ....60 B5
RAMS BL0 ....18 F8
Woodhead Dr
HALE/TIMP WA15 ....117 H3
Woodhead Gv *WGNS/IIMK* WN3 ....63 L2
Woodhead Rd *GLSP* SK13 ....93 L5
GLSP SK13 ....105 G1
HALE/TIMP WA15 ....117 J5
Woodhead St *OLDTF/WHR* M16 * 87 H8
Wood Hey Cl *RAD* M26 ....54 A1
Wood Hey Gv *DTN/ASHW* M34 ....101 K2
WHIT OL12 ....20 D8
Woodhey Rd *RAMS* BL0 ....24 D1
Woodheys *HTNM* SK4 ....111 J1
Woodheys Cottages
MPL/ROM SK6 * 103 H8
Woodheys Dr *SALE* M33 ....108 A3
Woodheys Rd *LIT* OL15 ....29 K2
Woodhill Cl *MDTN* M24 ....57 J2
WGTN/LGST M12 ....88 E8
Woodhill Dr *PWCH* M25 ....71 L2
Woodhill Fold *TOT/BURYW* BL8 ....4 C2
Woodhill Rd *TOT/BURYW* BL8 ....4 B1
Woodhill St *TOT/BURYW* BL8 ....4 B1
Woodhill V *TOT/BURYW* BL8 ....4 B2
Woodhouse Dr
WGNNW/ST WN6 ....47 H1
Woodhouse Knowl *UPML* OL3 ....45 H4
Woodhouse La *ALT* WA14 ....106 F3
SALE M33 ....107 M2
WGNNW/ST WN6 ....14 B1
WHIT OL12 ....27 G1
WYTH/NTH M22 ....110 A7
WYTH/NTH M22 ....118 F5
Woodhouse La East
HALE/TIMP WA15 ....108 E3
Woodhouse Rd *ROY/SHW* OL2 ....43 M4
URM M41 ....84 C8
WYTH/NTH M22 ....118 F4
Woodhouse St *ATH* M46 ....67 G2
GTN M18 ....89 H7
Woodhurst Dr *WGNNW/ST* WN6 ....31 G3
Wooding Cl *PART* M31 ....94 D8
Woodlake Av *CCHDY* M21 ....97 M8

Woodland Av *BOLS/LL* BL3 ....52 E2
BRAM/HZG SK7 ....122 A1
GTN M18 ....89 H8
WGNE/HIN WN2 ....65 K1
Woodland Crs *PWCH* M25 ....71 L2
Woodland Dr *WILM/AE* SK9 ....63 L7
WGNNW/ST WN6 ....31 H7
Woodland Gv *EDGW/EG* BL7 ....22 A2
WGN WN1 ....48 A2
Woodland Pk *ROY/SHW* OL2 ....42 E6
Woodland Rd *BNG/LEV* M19 ....99 K4
HEY OL10 ....41 H1
HEY OL10 ....41 H1
TYLD M29 ....67 L5
WHIT OL12 ....27 M7
Woodlands *FAIL* M35 ....74 B8
URM M41 ....95 M1
Woodlands Av *CHD/CHDH* SK8 ....120 C7
ECC M30 ....84 C4
IRL M44 ....94 D1
LEIGH WN7 ....81 J1
MPL/ROM SK6 ....101 K7
ROCH OL11 ....27 G2
STRET M32 ....97 G2
URM M41 ....94 F2
WALK M28 ....69 M6
WGNS/IIMK WN3 ....15 M8
WHTF M45 ....55 H3
Woodlands Cl *CHD/CHDH* SK8 ....120 C4
GLSP SK13 ....93 J6
HYDE SK14 ....103 J3
STLY SK15 ....92 A5
WALK M28 ....69 H5
Woodlands Dr *ATH* M46 ....101 J7
MPL/ROM SK6 ....112 F4
OFTN SK2 ....112 F4
SALE M33 ....108 F3
WGNNW/ST WN6 ....30 C8
Woodlands Gv *HYDE* SK14 ....103 J3
TOT/BURYW BL8 ....38 E1
Woodlands La
HALE/TIMP WA15 ....108 B7
Woodlands Pk *NEWLW* WA12 ....78 F6
Woodlands Park Rd *OFTN* SK2 ....113 C4
Woodlands Pkwy
HALE/TIMP WA15 ....108 B7
Woodlands Rd *ALT* WA14 ....108 B7
AUL OL6 ....76 B6
CHH M8 ....72 D4
HTNM SK4 ....111 G2
MILN OL16 ....29 H7
NM/HAY SK22 * 124 C4
POY/DIS SK12 ....123 J6
RAMS BL0 ....19 G2
SALE M33 ....96 F8
STLY SK15 ....92 A5
WALK M28 ....69 J5
WILM/AE SK9 ....126 C3
WILM/AE SK9 ....127 J1
Woodlands St *HEY* OL10 ....41 G2
WGTN/LGST M12 ....88 E7
Woodlands Wk *MILN* OL16 ....11 L3
Woodland Vw *EDGW/EG* BL7 ....22 E4
HYDE SK14 ....102 C1
Woodland Wy *MDTN* M24 ....57 J6
Wood La *AULW* OL7 ....75 L7
HALE/TIMP WA15 ....108 D2
MDTN M24 ....57 L5
MPL/ROM SK6 ....114 C4
NM/HAY SK22 ....125 M2
PART M31 ....106 A1
RAMS BL0 ....19 G2
Wood La North *MCFLDN* SK10 ....129 M4
Wood La South *MCFLDN* SK10 ....129 M4
Wood La West *MCFLDN* SK10 ....129 K4
Woodlawn Ct
OLDTF/WHR M16 ....97 M1
Woodlea *CHAD* OL9 ....58 A5
WALK M28 ....69 H4
Woodlea Av *BNG/LEV* M19 ....99 H7
Woodlea Cha *SWIN* M27 ....54 A7
Woodlea Rd *GLSP* SK13 ....104 E5
Woodleigh Ct
TOT/BURYW BL8 ....24 E7
Woodleigh Dr *DROY* M43 ....74 F8
Woodleigh Rd *OLDE* OL4 ....60 D5
Woodleigh St *BKLY* M9 ....73 J8
Woodley Av *RAD* M26 ....54 E3
Woodley Cl *OFTN* SK2 ....113 G5
Woodley Gv *LEIGH* WN7 ....66 A2
Woodman Dr *BURY* BL9 ....25 H6
Woodman St *STKP* SK1 ....13 H5
Woodmeadow Ct *MOSL* OL5 ....76 F2
Woodmere Dr *BKLY* M9 ....73 H1
Wood Mt *HALE/TIMP* WA15 ....108 E7
Woodmount Cl *MPL/ROM* SK6 ....114 B2
Woodnewton Cl *GTN* M18 ....88 F8
Woodnook Rd
WGNNW/ST WN6 ....30 B4
Woodpark Cl *OLDS* OL8 ....75 K1
Woodpecker Pl *WALK* M28 * 69 G4
Woodridge Dr *BOLE* BL2 ....36 E3
Wood Rd *HALE/TIMP* WA15 ....108 D3
OLDTF/WHR M16 ....97 M1
Wood Road La *BURY* BL9 ....24 F4
Wood Rd North
OLDTF/WHR M16 ....97 M1
Woodrow Wk *WGTN/LGST* M12 ....88 C6
Woodrow Wy *IRL* M44 ....94 C4
Woodroyd Cl *BRAM/HZG* SK7 ....120 F3
Woodroyd Dr *BURY* BL9 ....5 M2
Woodruffe Gdns
MPL/ROM SK6 ....113 K4
Woodrush Rd *WGNNW/ST* WN6 ....47 G1
Woods Ct *BOL* BL1 ....2 F4
Woodseats La *GLSP* SK13 ....103 G5
Woodseaves Cl *IRL* M44 ....94 E3
Woodsend Cir *URM* M41 ....95 G1
Woodsend Crescent Rd
URM M41 ....95 G2
Woodsend Rd *URM* M41 ....84 A8
Woodsend Rd South *URM* M41 ....95 H3
Woodshaw *WALK* M28 ....68 C4
Woodside *HTNM* SK4 ....111 J3
MILN OL16 ....29 M7
ROY/SHW OL2 ....44 A4
Woodside Av *AIMK* WN4 ....63 K4
BNG/LEV M19 ....99 K4
Woodside Cl *OLDE* OL4 ....60 B6
Woodside Dr *HYDE* SK14 ....102 B3

Woodside La *POY/DIS* SK12 ....122 A8
RAMS BL0 ....18 D7
SLFD M6 ....85 M1
Woodside Pl *BOLE* BL2 * 3 M8
Woodside Rd *OLDTF/WHR* M16 ....97 L2
RNFD/HAY WA11 ....78 B5
Woodside Sq *BOLE* BL2 ....3 M8
Woodside St *NM/HAY* SK22 ....124 D6
STLY SK15 ....91 L4
Woodside Vw *ATH* M46 ....51 H7
Wood's La *AIMK* WN4 ....63 K4
CHD/CHDH SK8 ....120 D5
UPML OL3 ....61 K3
Woods Lea *BOL* BL1 ....35 J5
Woodsley Rd *BOL* BL1 ....35 J5
Woodsmoor La *EDGY/DAV* SK3 ....112 D8
Woodsmoor Rd *SWIN* M27 ....70 A5
Wood Sorrel Wy
GOL/RIS/CUL WA3 ....80 B4
Wood Sq *DROY* M43 ....89 K4
UPML OL3 ....61 L6
Woods Rd *IRL* M44 ....94 C4
WGNE/HIN WN2 ....32 F8
Woodstock Av *CHD/CHDH* SK8 ....120 C5
RDSH SK5 ....100 C7
Woodstock Cl *HEY* OL10 ....41 H3
LEIGH WN7 ....81 H3
Woodstock Crs *MPL/ROM* SK6 ....101 L7
Woodstock Dr *BOL* BL1 ....35 K3
SWIN M27 ....70 D6
TOT/BURYW BL8 ....24 A5
WALK M28 ....69 H5
Woodstock Gn *RDSH* SK5 ....100 D7
Woodstock Rd *ALT* WA14 ....107 M4
NEWH/MOS M40 ....73 M3
OLDTF/WHR M16 ....97 L1
Woodstock St *OLDE* OL4 ....27 M3
WHIT OL12 ....27 M3
Wood St *ALT* WA14 ....108 A8
ATH M46 ....50 E8
AUL OL6 ....2 F5
BOL BL1 ....2 F5
CHD/CHDH SK8 ....111 G6
CSLFD M3 ....6 D3
CSLFD M3 ....6 D3
DTN/ASHW M34 ....90 C8
DUK SK16 ....90 D4
EDGY/DAV SK3 ....12 E6
GLSP SK13 ....104 F4
GOL/RIS/CUL WA3 ....79 L4
HOR/BR BL6 ....33 M1
HYDE SK14 ....93 G7
HYDE SK14 ....102 B2
LIT OL15 ....21 M7
MDTN M24 ....57 J3
MDTN M24 ....57 J3
MILN OL16 ....11 G6
MILN OL16 ....29 M8
NM/HAY SK22 ....124 D5
OLD OL1 ....59 L4
OP/CLY M11 ....88 E5
RAD M26 ....54 B4
RAMS BL0 ....18 E7
ROY/SHW OL2 ....43 H5
STLY SK15 ....91 J2
TOT/BURYW BL8 ....38 F1
TYLD M29 ....67 L4
WGNE/HIN WN2 ....15 G6
WGNS/IIMK WN3 ....15 G6
WGNW/BIL/OR WN5 ....14 E6
WHTN BL5 ....50 B4
Wood Ter *BOLE* BL2 ....38 A3
Woodthorpe Ct *PWCH* M25 ....72 A2
Woodthorpe Dr
CHD/CHDH SK8 ....120 C2
Woodthorpe Gra *PWCH* M25 ....72 A2
Woodtop Av *ROCH* OL11 ....27 J7
Wood Top Cl *OFTN* SK2 ....113 H5
Woodvale *ALT* WA14 ....116 E3
MDTN M24 ....41 K8
Woodvale Av *ATH* M46 ....50 E7
BOLS/LL BL3 ....52 A2
WGNE/HIN WN2 ....49 J1
Woodvale Dr *BOLS/LL* BL3 ....52 A2
GOL/RIS/CUL WA3 ....80 B3
Woodvale Gdns *BOLS/LL* BL3 ....52 A2
Woodvale Gv *BOLS/LL* BL3 ....52 A2
Woodvale Rd *RAD* M26 ....54 E3
Woodvale Wk *OP/CLY* M11 * 88 C3
Wood Vw *HEY* OL10 ....26 F8
WGNNW/ST WN6 ....30 D7
WYTH/NTH M22 ....118 B1
Woodview Av *BNG/LEV* M19 ....99 J7
Woodville Dr *MPL/ROM* SK6 ....114 B3
SALE M33 ....96 D7
STLY SK15 ....92 A1
Woodville Gv *RDSH* SK5 ....100 B4
Woodville Rd *ALT* WA14 ....107 M8
SALE M33 ....96 D7
WGNS/IIMK WN3 ....48 C3
Woodville Ter *NEWH/MOS* M40 ....73 J3
Woodward Ct *ANC* M4 ....7 M3
Woodward Pl *ANC* M4 ....7 M3
Woodward Rd *PWCH* M25 ....71 J2
Woodwards Rd *WHTN* BL5 ....50 B6
Woodward St *ANC* M4 ....7 K3
Woodwise La *NTHM/RTH* M23 ....109 H3
Woodyates St
WGNW/BIL/OR WN5 ....14 A8
Woolden St *ECC* M30 ....84 E1
WGNW/BIL/OR WN5 ....47 J6
Wooler Gv *WGNE/HIN* WN2 ....65 G2
Woollacott St *OLD* OL1 * 9 K6
Woollam Pl *CSLFD* M3 ....6 B6
Woolley Av *POY/DIS* SK12 ....129 H2
Woolley Bridge Rd *GLSP* SK13 ....93 G8
Woolley Cl *HYDE* SK14 ....93 G8
Woolley La *HYDE* SK14 ....93 F8
Woolley Mill La *GLSP* SK13 ....93 G8
Woolley St *CHH* M8 ....72 C8
Woolmore Av *OLD* OL1 ....9 H1
Woolpack Gn *SLFD* M6 * 85 M2
Wool Rd *UPML* OL3 ....61 L2
Woolston Dr *TYLD* M29 ....67 L5
Woolston Rd *RNFD/HAY* WA11 ....78 A6
Woolton Cl *AIMK* WN4 ....63 J7
Wootton St *HYDE* SK14 ....91 G4
Worcester Av *DTN/ASHW* M34 ....101 K1
RDSH SK5 ....100 F8
WGNE/HIN WN2 ....49 G1
Worcester Cl *AUL* OL6 ....76 A4
BURY BL9 ....5 J5
MPL/ROM SK6 ....113 K3
Worcester Gv *GLSP* SK13 ....105 J4

Worcester Rd *BOLS/LL* BL3 ....53 J1
  CHD/CHDH SK8 ....111 K8
  MDTN M24 ....57 J7
  SALE M33 ....108 A1
  SLFD M6 ....70 F8
  SWIN M27 ....70 A2
Worcester St *BOL* BL1 * 36 B3
  BRO M7 ....8 B8
  CHAD OL9 ....8 B8
  ROCH OL11 ....28 B8
  TOT/BURYW BL8 ....25 G8
Wordsworth Av *ATH* M46 ....51 G7
  BURY BL9 * 39 J6
  CHH M8 ....72 D6
  DROY M43 ....89 J2
  FWTH BL4 ....52 E5
  LEIGH WN7 ....66 A5
  RAD M26 ....54 B1
  WGN WN1 ....47 M1
  WGNW/BIL/OR WN5 ....46 C6
  WGNW/BIL/OR WN5 ....62 A3
Wordsworth Ct *DUK* SK16 ....91 K5
Wordsworth Crs *AULW* 75 H7
  LIT OL15 ....29 J2
Wordsworth Gdns
  PWCH M25 ....71 J1
Wordsworth Rd
  DTN/ASHW M34 ....101 K5
  LHULT M38 ....52 D7
  MDTN M24 ....57 L2
  OLD OL1 ....59 L3
  OLDTF/WHR M16 ....97 L1
  RDSH SK5 ....100 A3
  SWIN M27 ....70 A3
Wordsworth St *BOL* BL1 * 36 A2
Wordsworth Wy *ROCH* OL11 ...27 H6
Workesleigh St
  NEWH/MOS M40 ....73 M7
Works Rd *RAD* M26 * 38 D8
World Wy *MANAIR* M90 ....118 D4
Worrall St *EDGY/DAV* SK3 ....13 C8
  NEWH/MOS M40 ....73 K6
  ORD M5 ....86 F5
  WHIT OL12 ....28 A2
Worsbrough Av *WALK* M28 ......68 F2
Worsefold St
  NEWH/MOS M40 * 73 K4
Worseley Av *NEWH/MOS* M40 ...73 J3
Worsel St *BOLS/LL* BL3 ....35 M8
Worsley Av *WALK* M28 ....68 D2
Worsley Brow *WALK* M28 ....69 H6
Worsley Cl
  WGNW/BIL/OR WN5 * 46 E7
Worsley Ct *WALK* M28 ....69 G1
Worsley Crs *OFTN* SK2 ....112 E5
Worsley Gn
  WGNW/BIL/OR WN5 ....46 E7
Worsley Gv *BNG/LEV* M19 ......99 K3
  WALK M28 ....68 D2
Worsley Mesnes Dr
  WGNS/IIMK WN3 ....47 K8
Worsley Pl *ROY/SHW* OL2 ......43 K6
Worsley Rd *BOLS/LL* BL3 ....35 K8
  ECC M30 ....84 E2
  FWTH BL4 ....53 C6
  SWIN M27 ....70 A6
  WALK M28 ....69 K7
Worsley Rd North *WALK* M28 ...53 C7
Worsley St *BOLS/LL* BL3 * 2 D9
  CSLFD M3 ....6 A6
  CSLFD M3 * 6 D7
  GOL/RIS/CUL WA3 ....79 K4
  HULME M15 ....6 A8
  MILN OL16 ....11 J6
  OLDS OL8 ....59 L7
  SWIN M27 ....70 D5
  TOT/BURYW BL8 ....24 B5
  WGNW/BIL/OR WN5 ....46 E7
Worsley Ter *WGN* WN1 ....15 G2
Worston Av *BOL* BL1 ....35 J2
Worth Ct *POY/DIS* SK12 ....129 H2
Worthenbury Wk
  BRUN/LGST M13 ....99 H1
Worthing Cl *OFTN* SK2 ....113 G6
Worthing Gv *ATH* M46 ....66 E1
Worthing St *RUSH/FAL* M14 .....98 E2
Worthington Av *HEY* OL10 ......41 H5
  PART M31 ....106 C1
Worthington Cl *HYDE* SK14 * ..103 H2
Worthington Dr *BRO* M7 ....72 A3

Worthington Rd
  DTN/ASHW M34 ....101 L3
  SALE M33 ....97 H8
Worthington St *AULW* OL7 .....75 K7
  BOLS/LL BL3 ....51 M1
  NEWH/MOS M40 ....73 M4
  STLY SK15 ....91 J3
  WGNE/HIN WN2 ....49 G6
Worthington Wy
  DTN/ASHW M34 ....90 B8
  WGNS/IIMK WN3 ....63 H2
Worths La *DTN/ASHW* M34 .....101 K5
Wortley Av *SLFD* M6 ....85 M1
Wortley Gv *NEWH/MOS* M40 ....73 L2
Wotton Dr *AIMK* WN4 ....79 G1
Wragby Cl *TOT/BURYW* BL8 .....25 G7
Wrath Cl *BOLE* BL2 ....22 E7
Wraxhall Crs *LEIGH* WN7 ....66 A5
Wray Cl *WYTH/NTH* M22 ....118 F1
Wray Gdns *BNG/LEV* M19 ....99 M4
Wray Pl *MILN* OL16 ....11 L7
Wray St *WGN* WN1 ....15 L4
Wrekin Av *NTHM/RTH* M23 ....118 C1
Wren Av *SWIN* M27 ....70 E1
Wrenbury Av *DID/WITH* M20 ....98 C5
Wrenbury Cl
  WGNW/BIL/OR WN5 ....46 E7
Wrenbury Crs *EDGY/DAV* SK3 ..111 M7
Wrenbury Dr *BOL* BL1 ....22 C6
  CHD/CHDH SK8 ....111 H6
  MILN OL16 ....28 F8
Wren Cl *DTN/ASHW* M34 ....89 M2
  FWTH BL4 ....52 C4
  OFTN SK2 ....112 E8
  WGNW/BIL/OR WN5 ....46 E3
Wren Dr *BURY* BL9 ....25 J8
  IRL M44 ....83 K8
Wren Gdns *MDTN* M24 ....57 J3
Wren Gn *MILN* OL16 ....11 K6
Wren Nest Cl *GLSP* SK13 ......104 E3
Wren Nest Rd *GLSP* SK13 .....104 E3
Wren Nest Ter *GLSP* SK13 .....104 E3
Wren's Nest Av *ROY/SHW* OL2 ..43 M4
Wren St *OLDE* OL4 ....59 M6
Wrenswood Dr *WALK* M28 ......68 F4
Wren Wy *OP/CLY* M11 ....88 B4
Wrexham Cl *OLDS* OL8 ....74 E2
Wrigglesworth Cl
  TOT/BURYW BL8 ....38 C1
Wrightington St *WGN* WN1 .....14 F1
Wright Robinson Cl
  OP/CLY M11 ....88 B4
Wrights Bank North *OFTN* SK2 ..113 H7
Wrights Bank South *OFTN* SK2 ..113 G7
Wright St *AIMK* WN4 ....63 J6
  AUL OL6 ....76 A8
  CHAD OL9 ....8 A8
  DTN/ASHW M34 ....90 B4
  FAIL M35 ....74 C4
  OLD OL1 ....9 L5
  OLDTF/WHR M16 ....86 F7
  RAD M26 ....54 C1
  WGN WN1 ....15 K2
  WGNE/HIN WN2 ....64 D1
  WGNE/HIN WN2 ....64 E5
Wrigley Crs *FAIL* M35 ....74 C5
Wrigley Fold *MDTN* M24 ....40 F8
Wrigley Head *FAIL* M35 ....74 C4
Wrigley Head Crs *FAIL* M35 * ...74 C4
Wrigley La *MCFLDN* SK10 .....131 L8
Wrigley Pl *LIT* OL15 * 29 J1
Wrigley Rd *RNFD/HAY* WA11 ....78 B6
Wrigley St *AUL* OL6 ....75 L8
  OLDE OL4 ....59 L5
  OLDE OL4 ....60 C6
  OLDE OL4 ....60 E4
Wrington Cl *LEIGH* WN7 ....66 A4
Wroe St *CSLFD* M3 ....6 A4
  OLDE OL4 ....60 C6
  SWIN M27 ....70 C1
Wroe Ter *SWIN* M27 * 70 C1
Wrotham Cl *ORD* M5 ....86 D3
Wroxham Av *DTN/ASHW* M34 ...100 D1
  URM M41 ....95 L1
Wroxham Cl *TOT/BURYW* BL8 * ..25 G7
Wroxham Rd *BKLY* M9 ....72 F1
Wuerdle Cl *MILN* OL16 ....29 H1
Wuerdle Farm Wy *MILN* OL16 ..21 J8
Wuerdle Pl *MILN* OL16 * 21 J8
Wuerdle St *MILN* OL16 ....21 J8
Wyatt Av *ORD* M5 * 86 F5

Wyatt Gv *AIMK* WN4 ....79 G1
Wyatt St *DUK* SK16 ....90 F4
  HTNM SK4 ....13 G3
Wybersley Rd *MPL/ROM* SK6 ..123 J3
Wychbury St *ORD* M5 ....86 B2
Wychelm Rd *PART* M31 ....106 C1
Wycherley Rd *WHIT* OL12 ......27 L2
Wych Fold *HYDE* SK14 ....102 B5
Wych La *MCFLDN* SK10 ....129 C2
Wych St *AUL* OL6 * 90 E2
Wychwood *ALT* WA14 ....116 D3
Wychwood Cl *MDTN* M24 ....57 L5
Wycliffe Rd *RNFD/HAY* WA11 ...78 B5
  URM M41 ....95 M2
Wycliffe St *ECC* M30 ....84 F2
  HTNM SK4 ....12 F3
Wycombe Av *GTN* M18 ....89 H6
Wycombe Cl *URM* M41 ....84 F7
Wycombe Dr *TYLD* M29 ....67 L5
Wye Av *FAIL* M35 * 74 C5
Wyecroft Cl *MPL/ROM* SK6 ....101 L7
Wye St *OLDS* OL8 ....8 B7
Wykeham Cl *WGNS/IIMK* WN3 ..15 M8
Wykeham Gv *WHIT* OL12 ....27 L3
Wykeham Ms *BOL* BL1 ....35 K5
Wykeham St *RUSH/FAL* M14 ....98 D1
Wyke Pk *OLDE* OL4 ....60 A6
Wylam Wk *WGTN/LGST* M12 ...99 L1
The Wylde *BURY* BL9 ....4 E4
Wynard Av *WGN* WN1 ....15 J2
Wynchgate Rd
  BRAM/HZG SK7 ....122 C1
Wyndale Dr *FAIL* M35 ....74 C7
Wyndale Rd *OLDS* OL8 ....75 J1
Wyndcliff Dr *URM* M41 ....95 H3
Wyndham Av *BOLS/LL* BL3 .....51 K2
  SWIN M27 ....70 C2
Wyndham Cl *BRAM/HZG* SK7 ..121 G5
Wyne Cl *BRAM/HZG* SK7 ......122 C1
Wynfield Av *WYTH/NTH* M22 ..119 H5
Wynford Sq *SALQ* M50 ....86 C3
Wyngate Rd *CHD/CHDH* SK8 ..120 B3
  HALE/TIMP WA15 ....117 H4
Wynne Av *SWIN* M27 ....70 C1
Wynne Cl *DTN/ASHW* M34 .....101 J3
  OP/CLY M11 ....88 C4
Wynne Gv *DTN/ASHW* M34 ....101 J3
Wynne St *BOL* BL1 ....36 B2
  LHULT M38 ....52 D8
  SLFD M6 ....71 L8
  TYLD M29 ....67 J3
Wynnstay Gv *RUSH/FAL* M14 ...98 F4
Wynnstay Rd *SALE* M33 ....96 E7
Wynton Cl *LEIGH* WN7 ....81 H2
Wynyard Cl *SALE* M33 ....109 G2
Wynyard Rd *WYTH/NTH* M22 ..118 E1
Wyre Av *WGNE/HIN* WN2 ....64 D2
Wyre Dr *WALK* M28 ....68 E5
Wyresdale Rd *BOL* BL1 ....35 M4
Wyre St *CMANE* M1 ....7 K7
  MOSL OL5 ....76 E3
Wyrevale Gv *AIMK* WN4 ....78 F1
Wythall Av *LHULT* M38 ....52 E6
Wythburn Av *BOL* BL1 ....35 K3
  CHH M8 ....72 F6
  URM M41 ....95 L1
Wythburn Rd *MDTN* M24 ....57 H1
  STKP SK1 ....112 E5
Wythburn St *ORD* M5 ....86 B2
Wythenshawe Pk
  NTHM/RTH M23 * 109 K4
Wythenshawe Rd
  NTHM/RTH M23 ....109 H4
  SALE M33 ....97 H8
Wythens Rd *CHD/CHDH* SK8 ..119 K4
Wythop Gdns *ORD* M5 ....86 D3
Wyvern Av *HTNM* SK4 ....100 B7
Wyverne Rd *CCHDY* M21 ....98 A4
Wyville Cl *BRAM/HZG* SK7 ....122 C2
Wyville Dr *BKLY* M9 ....56 E6
  SLFD M6 ....86 C1
  SWIN M27 ....70 B6

Y

Yale Rd *GTN* M18 ....88 D2
Yarburgh St *OLDTF/WHR* M16 ..98 B1
Yardley Av *STRET* M32 ....96 D3

Yardley Cl *STRET* M32 ....96 D2
Yarmouth Dr *NTHM/RTH* M23 ..109 L3
Yarn Cft *TYLD* M29 ....67 L4
Yarnton Cl *ROY/SHW* OL2 ......43 K7
Yarrow Cl *ROCH* OL11 ....10 E9
Yarrow Pl *BOL* BL1 * 2 B1
Yarrow St *WGNE/HIN* WN2 .....48 F8
Yarwell *OLD* OL12 * 10 A2
Yarwood Av *NTHM/RTH* M23 ..109 J5
Yarwood Cl *HEY* OL10 ....41 H1
Yarwoodheath La *ALT* WA14 ..116 A4
Yarwood St *ALT* WA14 ....116 H1
  BURY BL9 * 5 H4
Yasmin Gdns *OLD* OL1 ....8 F2
Yates Dr *WALK* M28 ....68 D1
Yates Gv *WGNNW/ST* WN6 .....31 J8
Yates Rd *NM/HAY* SK22 ....124 E5
Yates St *BOLE* BL2 ....3 H1
  LEIGH WN7 ....66 B5
  MDTN M24 ....56 F5
  OLD OL1 ....9 M2
  STKP SK1 ....112 E1
  WGNS/IIMK WN3 ....14 C5
Yates Ter *TOT/BURYW* BL8 .....25 H7
Yattendon Av
  NTHM/RTH M23 ....109 G4
Yeadon Rd *GTN* M18 ....100 A1
Yea Fold *LIT* OL15 ....29 H1
Yealand Cl *ROCH* OL11 ....27 L6
Yealand Gv *WGNE/HIN* WN2 ...49 K7
Yeardsley Cl *BRAM/HZG* SK7 ..121 G1
Yeb Fold *NEWH/MOS* M40 * 73 L3
Yellow Brook Cl
  WGNE/HIN WN2 ....32 F7
Yellow Lodge Dr *WHTN* BL5 ....50 E3
Yeoford Dr *ALT* WA14 ....107 L6
Yeoman Cl *BRAM/HZG* SK7 ...121 M1
Yeoman's Cl *MILN* OL16 ....29 J5
Yeoman Wk *OP/CLY* M11 ....88 C3
Yeovil St *OLDTF/WHR* M16 .....98 C1
Yewbarrow Cl *TYLD* M29 ....67 L5
Yewbarrow Rd *OLD* OL1 ....9 L2
Yew Cl *BOLS/LL* BL3 ....35 L8
Yew Crs *OLDE* OL4 ....60 A4
Yewdale *SWIN* M27 ....70 E2
  WGNNW/ST WN6 ....30 E6
Yewdale Av *BOLE* BL2 ....37 J2
Yewdale Crs *WGN* WN1 ....47 L2
Yewdale Dr *FAIL* M35 ....74 E4
  MDTN M24 ....57 H3
Yewdale Gdns *BOLE* BL2 ....37 J2
Yew Dale Gdns *ROCH* OL11 ....27 L8
Yewdale Rd *AIMK* WN4 ....63 K5
  STKP SK1 ....112 E6
Yew Gv *WGNNW/ST* WN6 ....47 J1
Yewlands Av *BKLY* M9 ....57 G7
Yew St *BRO* M7 ....71 M6
  BURY BL9 ....5 M2
  DTN/ASHW M34 ....90 C7
  HEY OL10 ....40 E2
  HTNM SK4 ....12 B6
  HULME M15 ....87 H7
Yewtree Av *ATH* M46 ....50 F8
Yew Tree Av *BNG/LEV* M19 .....99 K3
  BRAM/HZG SK7 ....122 B4
  NEWLW WA12 ....78 D8
  RUSH/FAL M14 ....98 D1
  WYTH/NTH M22 ....110 A3
Yew Tree Cl *AULW* OL7 ....75 K6
  MPL/ROM SK6 ....114 B7
  WILM/AE SK9 ....127 H5
Yew Trees Crs *RUSH/FAL* M14 ..98 E3
Yew Tree Dr *HOR/BR* BL6 ....34 E6
  MDTN M24 ....58 A5
  MPL/ROM SK6 ....113 C1
  PWCH M25 ....55 L8
  SALE M33 ....97 H8
  URM M41 ....84 C8
  WYTH/NTH M22 ....110 A3
Yew Tree Gv *CHD/CHDH* SK8 ..119 J1
Yew Tree La *BOL* BL1 ....22 D8
  DUK SK16 ....91 K5
Yewtree La *NTHM/RTH* M23 ..109 L2
  POY/DIS SK12 ....129 K1
  WYTH/NTH M22 ....110 A3
Yew Tree Park Rd
  CHD/CHDH SK8 ....120 D6
Yew Tree Rd *DTN/ASHW* M34 ..101 H3
  EDGY/DAV SK3 ....121 H1
  MCFLDN SK10 ....129 M3

Yew Tree Wy
  GOL/RIS/CUL WA3 ....79 L5
York Av *BOLS/LL* BL3 ....53 K1
  OLDS OL8 ....59 G8
  OLDTF/WHR M16 ....97 M2
  PWCH M25 ....72 A2
  ROCH OL11 ....27 K6
  SALE M33 ....96 F7
  SWIN M27 ....70 A2
  TYLD M29 ....67 J2
York Chambers *WGN* WN1 * 14 F4
York Cl *CHD/CHDH* SK8 ....111 K7
York Crs *WILM/AE* SK9 ....127 H5
Yorkdale Rd *OLDE* OL4 ....60 A5
York Dr *ALT* WA14 ....116 F3
  BRAM/HZG SK7 ....122 C2
  MANAIR M90 ....118 B5
  RAMS BL0 ....24 D7
York Pl *AULW* OL7 ....90 D2
York Rd *AIMK* WN4 ....78 F2
  ALT WA14 ....116 E3
  CCHDY M21 ....97 L4
  CHAD OL9 ....58 C4
  DROY M43 ....89 J1
  DTN/ASHW M34 ....90 C8
  HTNM SK4 ....99 H1
  HYDE SK14 ....102 B4
  IRL M44 ....94 A7
  SALE M33 ....96 D7
  WGNE/HIN WN2 ....49 J7
York Rd East *MDTN* M24 ....57 M7
York Rd South *AIMK* WN4 ......78 F2
York Rd West *MDTN* M24 ....57 M7
Yorkshire Rd *PART* M31 ....106 B2
Yorkshire St *AULW* OL7 ....75 L8
  CSLFD M3 ....6 D3
  MILN OL16 ....10 F5
  OLD OL1 ....9 L2
  WHIT OL12 ....11 H2
Yorkshire Wy *GLSP* SK13 .....105 J4
York St *ATH* M46 ....67 G1
  AULW OL7 ....90 B4
  BNG/LEV M19 ....99 K4
  BURY BL9 ....5 H4
  CHAD OL9 ....7 G7
  CMANE M1 ....7 H9
  CMANE M1 ....7 H9
  CMANW M2 ....7 G4
  DID/WITH M20 ....110 E1
  EDGY/DAV SK3 ....13 G6
  FWTH BL4 ....53 H4
  GLSP SK13 ....105 H3
  GOL/RIS/CUL WA3 ....79 K3
  HALE/TIMP WA15 ....117 C1
  HEY OL10 ....41 G2
  LEIGH WN7 ....67 G8
  MILN OL16 ....11 K7
  RAD M26 ....39 H7
  WGNS/IIMK WN3 ....14 D5
  WHTF M45 ....55 J4
  SALE M33 * 96 D6
York Ter *GLSP* SK13 ....104 F4
  SALE M33 * 96 D6
Youd St *LEIGH* WN7 ....66 B7
Youlgreave Crs *GLSP* SK13 ....104 A3
Young St *CSLFD* M3 ....6 D5
  FWTH BL4 ....53 G5
  LEIGH WN7 ....67 H8
  RAMS BL0 ....18 E6
Yulan Dr *SALE* M33 ....95 M8
Yule St *EDGY/DAV* SK3 ....12 E6
Yvonne Cl *AIMK* WN4 ....64 A7

Z

Zama St *RAMS* BL0 * 18 D8
Zealand St *OLDE* OL4 ....59 M4
Zedburgh *WHIT* OL12 ....10 D2
Zeta St *BKLY* M9 ....73 J5
Zetland Av *BOLS/LL* BL3 ....51 L2
Zetland Av North *BOLS/LL* BL3 ..51 L1
Zetland Rd *CCHDY* M21 ....97 L4
Zetland St *DUK* SK16 ....90 F3
Zinnia Dr *IRL* M44 ....94 B4
Zion Ter *WHIT* OL12 ....27 H2
Zulu St *BOLE* BL2 ....3 K4
Zurich Gdns *BRAM/HZG* SK7 ..121 C1
Zyburn Ct *SLFD* M6 * 85 K1

Index - featured places

AA Office
  CHD/CHDH SK8 ....111 H6
Abbey College Manchester
  CMANW M2 ....6 F5
Abbey Hey Primary School
  GTN M18 ....89 H7
Abbey Lakes Sports Centre
  WGNW/BIL/OR WN5 ....46 A5
Abbey Tutorial College
  CMANE M1 ....7 G4
Abbotsford
  Preparatory School
  URM M41 ....95 K2
Abbott Primary School
  NEWH/MOS M40 ....87 M1
Abingdon Primary School
  RDSH SK5 ....100 C5
Abraham Guest High School
  WGNW/BIL/OR WN5 ....46 D6
Abraham Moss High School
  CHH M8 ....72 E4
Abram Bryn Gates
  Primary School
  WGNE/HIN WN2 ....64 C5
Abram CE Primary School
  WGNE/HIN WN2 ....64 E3
Acacias CP School
  BNG/LEV M19 ....99 J5
Acorn Business Centre
  LEIGH WN7 ....66 E8
Acorn Business Park
  EDGY/DAV SK3 ....12 F5
Acorns School
  MPL/ROM SK6 ....114 C7
Acre Hall Primary School
  URM M41 ....95 G2
Adlington Industrial Estate
  MCFLDN SK10 ....129 G3
Adlington Primary School
  MCFLDN SK10 ....129 J7
Adswood Clinic
  EDGY/DAV SK3 ....112 B7
Adswood Industrial Estate
  EDGY/DAV SK3 ....112 A7

Adswood Primary School
  EDGY/DAV SK3 ....112 A7
Adult Learning Centre
  RUSH/FAL M14 ....87 K8
Agecroft Crematorium
  SWIN M27 ....71 J4
Air & Space Museum
  SLFD M3 ....6 G6
Al-Afifah High School for Girls
  OLDTF/WHR M16 ....86 F8
Albany Trading Estate
  CCHDY M21 ....97 L3
Albert Close Trading Estate
  WHTF M45 ....55 K4
Albion Drive Clinic
  DROY M43 ....89 K1
The Albion High School
  BRO M7 ....72 A7
Albion Trading Estate
  AUL OL6 ....91 G1
  SLFD M6 ....71 K8
Alder Community
  High School
  HYDE SK14 ....103 G2
Alderley Edge CC
  WILM/AE SK9 ....130 E3
Alderley Edge Golf Club
  WILM/AE SK9 ....130 B1
Alderley Edge Hotel
  WILM/AE SK9 ....130 E4
Alderley Edge Primary School
  WILM/AE SK9 ....130 C2
Alderley Edge School for Girls
  WILM/AE SK9 ....130 D2
Alderman Kay Special School
  MDTN M24 ....57 K1
Alder Park CP School
  ECC M30 ....69 L8
Aldwyn CP School
  DTN/ASHW M34 ....89 M3
Alexander House Health Centre
  WGNE/HIN WN2 ....64 E1
Alexandra Business Centre
  UPML OL3 ....61 L5

The Alexandra Hospital
  CHD/CHDH SK8 ....111 G6
Alexandra Industrial Estate
  WHIT OL12 ....90 D8
Alexandra Park Junior School
  EDGY/DAV SK3 ....12 D9
  OLDS OL8 ....59 K8
Alexandra Retail Park
  OLDE OL4 ....9 K7
Alice Ingham RC Primary School
  MILN OL16 ....28 F2
Al-jamaiah Islamyiah-darul-Uloom
  Islamic College
  EDGW/EG BL7 ....22 D4
Alkrington Clinic Centre
  MDTN M24 ....57 K7
Alkrington Moss Primary School
  MDTN M24 ....57 L7
Alkrington Primary School
  MDTN M24 ....57 K6
All Hallows RC High School
  ORD M5 ....86 A1
Alliance Francaise
  CMANE M1 ....7 G7
Alliston House Medical Centre
  URM M41 ....96 A2
All Saints Catholic College
  DUK SK16 ....91 H8
All Saints Catholic Primary
  School
  GLSP SK13 ....105 G2
All Saints CE Primary School
  FWTH BL4 ....53 L6
  HTNM SK4 ....100 A8
  MPL/ROM SK6 ....114 D7
  NEWH/MOS M40 ....73 M7
  WHIT OL12 ....28 D3
  WHTF M45 ....55 K2
All Saints Primary School
  GTN M18 ....88 E6
All Saints RC Primary School
  GOL/RIS/CUL WA3 ....79 L4
All Souls CE Primary School
  HEY OL10 ....41 J1

All Souls RC Primary School
  ORD M5 ....86 A3
Alma Industrial Estate
  WHIT OL12 ....11 G1
Alma Lodge Hotel
  OFTN SK2 ....112 D6
Alma Park Primary School
  BNG/LEV M19 ....99 K4
Alpha Court Industrial Estate
  DTN/ASHW M34 ....100 F1
Alt Primary School
  OLDS OL8 ....76 A1
Altrincham CE Primary School
  ALT WA14 ....107 M7
Altrincham College of Arts
  HALE/TIMP WA15 ....108 D8
Altrincham Crematorium
  ALT WA14 ....107 G4
Altrincham FC
  HALE/TIMP WA15 ....117 H1
Altrincham General Hospital
  ALT WA14 ....107 M8
Altrincham Golf Club
  HALE/TIMP WA15 ....108 C7
Altrincham Grammar School
  for Boys *ALT* WA14 ......116 F2
Altrincham Grammar School
  for Girls *ALT* WA14 ......116 E1
Altrincham Ice Rink
  ALT WA14 ....108 A6
Altrincham Industrial Centre
  ALT WA14 ....107 K6
Altrincham (Kersal) RFC
  HALE/TIMP WA15 ....108 F5
Altrincham Leisure Centre
  ALT WA14 ....108 B7
Altrincham Preparatory
  School *ALT* WA14 ....116 E2
Altrincham Priory Hospital
  HALE/TIMP WA15 ....117 J4
Altrincham Retail Park
  ALT WA14 ....107 M5
Alvanley Industrial Estate
  MPL/ROM SK6 ....101 J8

Amalgamated Sports Club
  POY/DIS SK12 ....123 K6
Amberhurst Hotel
  SALE M33 ....96 D8
AMC Cinema
  CSLFD M3 ....6 E7
AMF Bowling
  WGNS/IIMK WN3 ....14 E5
Ancoats Hospital
  ANC M4 ....7 M4
Angel Trading Estate
  ANC M4 ....7 H1
Angouleme Way Retail Park
  BURY BL9 ....5 G5
Ann Street Health Centre
  DTN/ASHW M34 ....101 H1
Anson Medical Centre
  RUSH/FAL M14 ....88 A8
Aquinas College
  OFTN SK2 ....112 E1
Arcades Shopping Centre
  AUL OL6 ....90 E1
Arcadia Sports Centre
  BNG/LEV M19 ....99 K3
Arden Business Centre
  MPL/ROM SK6 ....101 H6
Arden Primary School
  MPL/ROM SK6 ....113 G1
Arlies Primary School
  STLY SK15 ....76 D7
Armitage CE Primary School
  WGTN/LGST M12 ....88 B6
Arndale Shopping Centre
  STRET M32 ....96 F3
Arrow Trading Estate
  DTN/ASHW M34 ....90 A7
Arts & Craft College
  BURY BL9 ....4 E5
Art Theatre
  NM/HAY SK22 ....124 D5
Arundale Primary School
  HYDE SK14 ....103 A1
Ashbury Meadow Primary
  School *OP/CLY* M11 ....88 C4

Ashdene Independant
  Pre School WILM/AE SK9 .... 126 D7
Ashfield Valley Primary School
  ROCH OL11 .... 28 B8
Ashgate Specialist Primary
  Support School
  WYTH/NTH M22 .... 110 C8
Ash Lea School
  ECC M30 .... 85 H1
Ashton Grange Industrial Estate
  AIMK WN4 .... 63 L6
Ashton-in-Makerfield Golf Club
  AIMK WN4 .... 78 B2
Ashton Leisure Centre
  AIMK WN4 .... 63 K8
Ashton Medical Centre
  AIMK WN4 .... 63 K7
Ashton on Mersey School
  SALE M33 .... 96 C8
Ashton Retail Park
  AUL OL6 .... 90 E1
Ashton Swimming Pool
  AUL OL6 .... 90 E1
Ashton Town AFC
  AIMK WN4 .... 64 A8
Ashton-under-Lyne Golf Club
  AUL OL6 .... 76 B5
Ashton-under-Lyne RFC
  AUL OL6 .... 75 L5
Ashton-under-Lyne Sixth Form
  College AUL OL6 .... 76 A8
Ashton United FC
  AUL OL6 .... 76 A6
Ashton upon Mersey Cricket
  & Tennis Club
  SALE M33 .... 96 B5
Ashton upon Mersey Golf Club
  SALE M33 .... 96 B5
Aspinal Primary School
  GTN M18 .... 100 B1
Aspull Church Primary School
  WGNE/HIN WN2 .... 33 H8
Aspull Clinic
  WGNE/HIN WN2 .... 32 F7
Astley Bridge CC
  BOL BL1 .... 22 A8
Astra Business Park
  TRPK M17 .... 85 J4
Astra Industrial Centre
  ROCH OL11 .... 41 M1
Atherton Industrial Centre
  ATH M46 .... 51 G8
Atherton Public Baths
  ATH M46 .... 66 F1
Atlantic Business Centre
  ALT WA14 .... 107 M5
Atlas Trading Estate
  RDSH SK5 .... 100 A1
Audenshaw Primary School
  DTN/ASHW M34 .... 89 H4
Audenshaw School
  DTN/ASHW M34 .... 90 B6
Austerlands CC
  OLDE OL4 .... 60 D4
Avenue Medical Centre
  BKLY M9 .... 57 H7
Aviation Viewing Park
  HALE/TIMP WA15 .... 118 J1
Avicenna Grammar School
  DID/WITH M20 .... 98 A4
Avondale Health Centre
  BOL BL1 .... 35 M3
Avondale High School
  EDGY/DAV SK3 .... 12 C4
Avondale Industrial Estate
  EDGY/DAV SK3 .... 12 B7
Avondale Recreation Centre
  EDGY/DAV SK3 .... 12 B8
Avro Golf Club
  BRAM/HZG SK7 .... 128 C4
Bag Lane Industrial Estate
  ATH M46 .... 50 F3
Baguley Hall Primary School
  NTHM/RTH M23 .... 109 K6
Baillie Street Health Centre
  MILN OL16 .... 10 F3
Balderstone Technology College
  ROCH OL11 .... 42 D1
Bamford Business Park
  RDSH SK5 .... 100 B8
Bamford Primary School
  ROCH OL11 .... 27 H6
Band on the Wall
  ANC M4 .... 7 H2
Bankfield Trading Estate
  HTNM SK4 .... 100 B8
Bank Meadow Primary School
  WGTN/LGST M12 .... 88 A4
Banks Lane Infant School
  STKP SK1 .... 112 E4
Bare Trees J & I School
  CHAD OL9 .... 8 A2
Baring Street Industrial Estate
  CMANE M1 .... 7 L7
Barlow Hall Primary School
  CCHDY M21 .... 97 M4
Barlow Medical Centre
  DID/WITH M20 .... 110 D1
The Barlow RC High School
  DID/WITH M20 .... 110 F2
Barrack Hill Primary School
  MPL/ROM SK6 .... 113 K2
Barrington Medical Centre
  ALT WA14 .... 108 A6
Barton Business Park
  ECC M30 .... 84 F3
Barton Clough Primary School
  STRET M32 .... 85 J8
Barton Moss Community
  Primary School
  ECC M30 .... 84 C3
Bayley Industrial Estate
  STLY SK15 .... 91 J3
BBC North
  CMANE M1 .... 7 H8
Bealey Community Hospital
  RAD M26 .... 39 G8
Bealey Industrial Estate
  RAD M26 .... 39 G7
Beal Vale Primary School
  ROY/SHW OL2 .... 43 L5
Beaumont Hospital
  HOR/BR BL6 .... 34 E4
Beaumont Primary School
  BOLS/LL BL3 .... 35 H7
Beaver Road Primary School
  DID/WITH M20 .... 110 E1
Bedford Hall Methodist
  Primary School
  LEIGH WN7 .... 81 L1
Bedford High School
  LEIGH WN7 .... 67 G8

Beech Hill Primary School
  WGNNW/ST WN6 .... 47 K1
Beech House School
  ROCH OL11 .... 10 C7
Beech Street Primary School
  ECC M30 .... 84 E3
Bee Fold Medical Centre
  AIM M46 .... 66 E2
Bee Hive Industrial Estate
  HOR/BR BL6 .... 34 B5
Beetham Tower
  CSLFD M3 .... 6 D7
Beever Primary School
  OLD OL1 .... 9 L3
Beis Rochel Girls School
  CHH M8 .... 72 C3
The Beis Yaakov Jewish High
  School BRO M7 .... 71 M4
Bel-Air Hotel
  WGN WN1 .... 31 M8
Belfield Community Primary
  School MILN OL16 .... 11 L2
Belfield Trading Estate
  MILN OL16 .... 29 G3
Belford College
  OLDS OL8 .... 58 F8
Belfry House Hotel
  WILM/AE SK9 .... 119 M6
Belle Green Industrial Estate
  WGNE/HIN WN2 .... 48 D4
Belle Vue Regional Hockey
  Centre
  WGTN/LGST M12 .... 88 D8
Benchill Primary School
  WYTH/NTH M22 .... 109 M6
Bentfield Industrial Units
  CHAD OL9 .... 8 B6
Bentinck Street Industrial Estate
  HULME M15 .... 6 A9
Best Western Cresta Court Hotel
  ALT WA14 .... 108 A7
Best Western Hotel
  Smokies Park
  OLDS OL8 .... 75 J4
Bickershaw CE Primary School
  WGNE/HIN WN2 .... 65 J4
Billinge Chapel End
  Parish Council
  WGNW/BIL/OR WN5 .... 62 B7
Billinge Chapel End Primary
  School WGNW/BIL/OR WN5 .... 62 B8
Billinge Clinic
  WGNW/BIL/OR WN5 .... 62 A8
Billinge Hospital
  WGNW/BIL/OR WN5 .... 62 A2
Birches Health Centre
  PWCH M25 .... 55 M6
Birchfields Primary School
  RUSH/FAL M14 .... 99 H3
Birch Industrial Estate
  HEY OL10 .... 40 D6
Birchinley Manor Showground
  MILN OL16 .... 29 J4
Birchley St Marys RC Primary
  School
  WGNW/BIL/OR WN5 .... 62 A8
Birch Vale Industrial Estate
  NM/HAY SK22 .... 125 J2
Birtenshaw Hall School
  EDGW/EG BL7 .... 22 E6
Birtle View Special School
  HEY OL10 .... 40 E2
Bishop Bilsborrow Memorial RC
  Primary School
  OLDTF/WHR M16 .... 98 C2
Bishop Bridgeman CE Primary
  School BOLS/LL BL3 .... 36 B8
B & L Leisure Centre
  WILM/AE SK9 .... 126 E5
Blackbrook Trading Estate
  BNG/LEV M19 .... 99 L4
Blackley Cemetery
  BKLY M9 .... 56 D8
Blackley Crematorium
  BKLY M9 .... 56 D8
Blackley Golf Club
  BKLY M9 .... 57 L8
Blackrod Church School
  HOR/BR BL6 .... 32 F2
Blackrod Primary School
  HOR/BR BL6 .... 33 H4
Blackshaw Lane CP School
  ROY/SHW OL2 .... 43 K8
Blackshaw Primary School
  BOLE BL2 .... 37 K6
Blessed Thomas Holford RC
  School
  HALE/TIMP WA15 .... 108 B8
Blue Chip Business Park
  ALT WA14 .... 107 L5
Blue Coat CE School
  OLD OL1 .... 9 K4
Bnos Yisroel Schools
  BRO M7 .... 72 B5
Boarshaw Industrial Estate
  MDTN M24 .... 57 L4
Boarshurst Business Park
  UPML OL3 .... 61 L6
Bodmin Road Clinic
  SALE M33 .... 96 A7
B of the Bang
  OP/CLY M11 .... 88 C3
Boggart Hole Clough Track
  BKLY M9 .... 73 J2
Bolholt Country Park Hotel
  TOT/BURYW BL8 .... 24 D8
Bollin CP School
  ALT WA14 .... 116 D3
Bolshaw Primary School
  CHD/CHDH SK8 .... 119 K5
Bolton Business Centre
  BOLE BL2 .... 3 G6
Bolton CC
  BOLS/LL BL3 .... 52 D2
Bolton Community College
  BOLE BL2 .... 3 G7
Bolton Gates Retail Park
  BOL BL1 .... 2 F2
Bolton Golf Club
  HOR/BR BL6 .... 34 D4
Bolton Institute
  BOLS/LL BL3 .... 2 C7
Bolton Little Theatre
  BOL BL1 .... 2 C5
Bolton Muslim Girls School
  BOLS/LL BL3 .... 36 A8
Bolton Old Links Golf Club
  BOL BL1 .... 35 G1
Bolton Open Golf Club
  BOLE BL2 .... 37 C1
Bolton Parish CE Primary School
  BOLE BL2 .... 3 J4

Bolton Road Industrial Estate
  WHTN BL5 .... 50 C3
Bolton Rugby Union FC
  BOL BL1 .... 2 A2
Bolton Running Track
  HOR/BR BL6 .... 33 M5
Bolton School (Beech House,
  Infant Department)
  BOL BL1 .... 35 L5
Bolton School (Girls Division)
  BOL BL1 .... 35 L5
Bolton School
  (Junior Boys Division)
  BOL BL1 .... 35 M5
Bolton School
  (Senior Boys Division)
  BOL BL1 .... 35 M5
Bolton Sports Arena
  HOR/BR BL6 .... 33 M5
Bolton Trophy & Sports Centre
  BOLE BL2 .... 3 L4
Bolton Wanderers FC
  (Reebok Stadium)
  HOR/BR BL6 .... 34 A5
Bond Street Industrial Estate
  WGTN/LGST M12 .... 7 L7
Bonholt Industrial Estate
  TOT/BURYW BL8 .... 24 D8
Booth Hall Hospital School
  BKLY M9 .... 73 J1
Booth House Trading Estate
  CHAD OL9 .... 8 D7
Boothstown Methodist Primary
  School WALK M28 .... 68 C6
The Borchardt Medical Centre
  DID/WITH M20 .... 98 C6
Bornmore Industrial Centre
  TOT/BURYW BL8 .... 38 E1
Borron Road Industrial Estate
  NEWLW WA12 .... 78 F8
Boundary Industrial Estate
  BOLE BL2 .... 37 K5
Boundary Trading Estate
  IRL M44 .... 83 M8
Bowdon CE Primary School
  ALT WA14 .... 116 E3
Bowdon CC
  ALT WA14 .... 116 E3
Bowdon Preparatory School
  for Girls ALT WA14 .... 116 E2
Bowdon RUFC
  HALE/TIMP WA15 .... 108 F8
Bowdon Vale CC
  ALT WA14 .... 116 E4
Bowker Bank Industrial Park
  CHH M8 .... 72 E2
Bowker Vale Primary School
  CHH M8 .... 56 C8
Bowness Primary School
  BOLS/LL BL3 .... 53 J1
Brabyns Recreation Centre
  MPL/ROM SK6 .... 114 D5
Brabyns School
  MPL/ROM SK6 .... 114 D5
Brackley Municipal Golf Club
  LHULT M38 .... 52 B6
Bradley Fold Trading Estate
  BOLE BL2 .... 37 M6
Bradley Green Primary School
  HYDE SK14 .... 91 J6
Bradley Hall Trading Estate
  WGNNW/ST WN6 .... 31 K2
Bradshaw CC
  BOLE BL2 .... 22 F7
Bradshaw Hall J & I School
  CHD/CHDH SK8 .... 120 A3
Bradshaw Trading Estate
  MDTN M24 .... 58 A7
Bramall Hall & Park
  BRAM/HZG SK7 .... 121 G3
Bramall Park Golf Club
  CHD/CHDH SK8 .... 120 E3
Bramall Park Lawn Tennis Club
  BRAM/HZG SK7 .... 120 F2
Bramall Park Tennis Club
  BRAM/HZG SK7 .... 120 F4
Bramhall Golf Club
  BRAM/HZG SK7 .... 121 H6
Bramhall Health Centre
  BRAM/HZG SK7 .... 121 G6
Bramhall High School
  BRAM/HZG SK7 .... 121 H4
Bramhall Moor
  Industrial Estate
  BRAM/HZG SK7 .... 121 K2
Bramhall Park Medical Centre
  BRAM/HZG SK7 .... 121 G2
Bramhall Village Shopping
  Centre BRAM/HZG SK7 .... 120 F6
Brandwood Primary School
  BOLS/LL BL3 .... 35 M8
Branwood Preparatory School
  ECC M30 .... 85 H1
Bredbury Clinic
  MPL/ROM SK6 .... 101 J8
Bredbury Green Primary
  School MPL/ROM SK6 .... 113 J3
Bredbury Hall Hotel
  & Country Club
  MPL/ROM SK6 .... 113 G2
Breeze Hill Comprehensive
  School OLDE OL4 .... 60 A7
Breightmet FC
  BOLE BL2 .... 37 J5
Breightmet Golf Club
  BOLE BL2 .... 37 K3
Breightmet Industrial Estate
  BOLE BL2 .... 37 J5
Brentnall Primary School
  BRO M7 .... 72 A5
Brentwood Special School
  ALT WA14 .... 108 B5
Bridge College
  OFTN SK2 .... 113 G4
Bridge Hall Primary School
  EDGY/DAV SK3 .... 112 A6
Bridge House Medical Centre
  CHD/CHDH SK8 .... 120 D1
Bridge Mills Business Estate
  SLFD M6 .... 71 J7
Bridgeside Business Centre
  MPL/ROM SK6 .... 101 G6
Bridge Trading Estate
  TOT/BURYW BL8 .... 4 B4
Bridgewater Concert Hall
  CMANE M1 .... 6 F7
Bridgewater Primary School
  LHULT M38 .... 52 F8
Bridgewater School
  WALK M28 .... 69 K6
Brighton Road Industrial Estate
  HTNM SK4 .... 12 B4

Brimrod Primary School
  ROCH OL11 .... 10 A9
Brindale Primary School
  RDSH SK5 .... 100 F8
Brindle Heath Industrial Estate
  SLFD M6 .... 71 J8
Brindle House Community
  Mental Health Centre
  HYDE SK14 .... 102 A2
Brinksway Trading Estate
  HTNM SK4 .... 12 D6
Brinnington Health Centre
  RDSH SK5 .... 100 F7
Briscoe Lane Primary School
  NEWH/MOS M40 .... 73 L7
Britannia Bridge Primary School
  WGNS/IIMK WN3 .... 15 K7
Britannia Business Park
  BOLE BL2 .... 36 E2
Britannia Mill Industrial Estate
  HEY OL10 .... 40 E2
Broadbent Fold Primary School
  DUK SK16 .... 91 K5
Broadbottom Primary School
  HYDE SK14 .... 103 J4
Broadfield Industrial Estate
  HEY OL10 .... 40 E3
Broadfield Primary School
  MILN OL16 .... 10 E5
  OLDS OL8 .... 59 J8
Broadheath Primary School
  ALT WA14 .... 107 M4
Broadhurst Primary School
  NEWH/MOS M40 .... 73 M5
Broadoak Business Park
  TRPK M17 .... 85 J5
Broad Oak High School
  PART M31 .... 106 B2
Broadoak High School
  AUL OL6 .... 75 M7
  SWIN M27 .... 69 M6
Broad Oak Primary School
  DID/WITH M20 .... 110 E4
Broadoak Sports Centre
  AUL OL6 .... 75 M6
Broadstone Hall Primary School
  HTNM SK4 .... 100 A6
Broadwalk Primary School
  SLFD M6 .... 86 D1
Broadway Business Park
  CHAD OL9 .... 58 A8
Broadway Industrial Estate
  HYDE SK14 .... 90 E7
  ORD M5 .... 86 D4
Brookburn Primary School
  CCHDY M21 .... 97 K5
Brookdale Golf Club
  FAIL M35 .... 74 E7
Brookfield Business Park
  CHD/CHDH SK8 .... 111 J7
Brookfield High School
  WGNE/HIN WN2 .... 49 H8
Brookfield Industrial Estate
  GLSP SK13 .... 104 B1
Brookhead Junior School
  CHD/CHDH SK8 .... 111 J7
Brooklands Primary School
  SALE M33 .... 108 D2
Brook Mill Medical Centre
  LEIGH WN7 .... 66 D7
Brooks Bar Medical Centre
  OLDTF/WHR M16 .... 87 G8
Brookside Business Park
  MDTN M24 .... 58 A6
Brookside Primary School
  MPL/ROM SK6 .... 123 J7
Brookway High School
  & Sports College
  NTHM/RTH M23 .... 109 H4
Broomwood CP School
  HALE/TIMP WA15 .... 109 H3
Broughton Baths
  BRO M7 .... 72 A6
Broughton CC
  BRO M7 .... 71 M6
Broughton Jewish Cassel-Fox
  Primary School
  BRO M7 .... 72 A4
Brownhill Countryside Centre
  UPML OL3 .... 61 K3
Brownhill Special School
  WHIT OL12 .... 10 D1
Brownlow Business Centre
  BOL BL1 .... 36 A3
Brownlow Fold Community
  Learning Centre
  BOL BL1 .... 36 A3
Brownlow Fold Community Primary School
  BOL BL1 .... 36 A3
Brunswick Health Centre
  BRUN/LGST M13 .... 87 L6
Bruntwood Primary School
  CHD/CHDH SK8 .... 120 A2
Buckley Road Industrial Estate
  WHIT OL12 .... 28 E2
Buckley School of Dance
  WGNNW/ST WN6 .... 47 K1
Buckstones Primary School
  ROY/SHW OL2 .... 44 A4
Buckton Vale Primary School
  STLY SK15 .... 77 J5
Buile Hill High School
  SLFD M6 .... 71 G8
Bullough Moor Primary School
  HEY OL10 .... 40 D2
Burgess Primary School
  BKLY M9 .... 73 H5
Burnage High School For Boys
  BNG/LEV M19 .... 99 J7
Burnage Rugby Club
  HTNM SK4 .... 111 H3
Burnden Industrial Estate
  BOLS/LL BL3 .... 36 E8
Burnley Brow Community
  School CHAD OL9 .... 8 C1
Burrs Country Park
  TOT/BURYW BL8 .... 25 G1
Bury Antheneum
  BURY BL9 .... 4 E5
Bury Business Centre
  BURY BL9 .... 5 J1
Bury Catholic
  Preparatory School
  BURY BL9 .... 4 D8
Bury CE High School
  BURY BL9 .... 4 C8
Bury Cemetery
  BURY BL9 .... 39 J5
Bury College
  BURY BL9 .... 4 E6

Bury County Court
  BURY BL9 .... 4 C5
Bury FC (Gigg Lane)
  BURY BL9 .... 39 J5
Bury Golf Club
  BURY BL9 .... 39 J8
Bury Grammar School (Boys)
  BURY BL9 .... 4 C5
Bury Industrial Estate
  BOLE BL2 .... 37 J4
Bury Market
  BURY BL9 .... 4 F5
Bury Sports Club
  BURY BL9 .... 4 D9
Bury & Whitefield Jewish
  Primary School
  BURY BL9 .... 55 L1
Business & Arts Centre
  HTNM SK4 .... 100 A5
Butterstile Primary School
  PWCH M25 .... 71 K2
Button Lane School
  NTHM/RTH M23 .... 109 J2
Byrchall High School
  NEWLW WA12 .... 78 E3
Byron Street Infant & Nursery
  Community School
  ROY/SHW OL2 .... 43 H8
Cadishead Primary School
  IRL M44 .... 94 A6
Cadishead Recreation Centre
  IRL M44 .... 94 A6
Caius House School
  URM M41 .... 95 M3
Caldershaw Primary School
  WHIT OL12 .... 27 J3
Camberwell Park School
  BKLY M9 .... 56 F5
Cambrian Business Park
  BOLS/LL BL3 .... 2 C9
Cambridge Industrial Estate
  BRO M7 .... 72 B8
Campanile Hotel
  ORD M5 .... 6 A7
Cams Lane Primary School
  RAD M26 .... 54 C1
Canalside Industrial Estate
  MILN OL16 .... 11 J8
Cannon Street Health Centre
  BOLS/LL BL3 .... 2 B8
Canon Burrows CE Primary
  School AULW OL7 .... 75 J7
Canon Johnson CE Primary
  School AULW OL7 .... 75 L8
Canon Sharples Primary School
  WGN WN1 .... 48 B2
Canon Slade School
  BOLE BL2 .... 22 E8
Cansfield High School
  AIMK WN4 .... 63 K8
Capital Business Centre
  BRAM/HZG SK7 .... 120 F6
Cardinal Langley RC
  High School
  MDTN M24 .... 41 M8
Cariocca Business Park
  NEWH/MOS M40 .... 88 B1
  WGTN/LGST M12 .... 88 A6
Carlton Industrial Centre
  BOLE BL2 .... 3 C6
Carrbrook Industrial Estate
  STLY SK15 .... 77 K6
Carrington Business Park
  PART M31 .... 94 F6
Castlebrook High School
  BURY BL9 .... 55 M1
Castlefield Gallery
  CSLFD M3 .... 6 D7
Castle Hawk Golf Club
  ROCH OL11 .... 41 K3
Castle Hill Primary School
  BOLE BL2 .... 36 E2
Castle Hill St Philips CE Primary
  School WGNE/HIN WN2 .... 49 J6
Castle Hill School
  RDSH SK5 .... 100 F6
Castle Leisure Centre
  BURY BL9 .... 4 D4
Castle Park Industrial Estate
  OLD OL1 .... 59 L5
Castleton Primary School
  ROCH OL11 .... 42 A2
Castleton Swimming Pool
  ROCH OL11 .... 41 M1
Cathedral Gardens
  ANC M4 .... 6 F2
Cavendish Industrial Estate
  AUL OL6 .... 90 D1
Cavendish Road Primary School
  DID/WITH M20 .... 98 D7
Central Art Gallery
  AUL OL6 .... 90 C2
Central Industrial Estate
  BOLS/LL BL3 .... 2 E9
  MDTN M24 .... 57 K4
Central Leisure Centre
  MILN OL16 .... 11 G4
Central Primary School
  DTN/ASHW M34 .... 101 H1
Central Retail Park
  ANC M4 .... 7 L4
Century Mill Industrial Estate
  FWTH BL4 .... 52 E4
CE School of the Resurrection
  OP/CLY M11 .... 88 C3
Chadderton AFC
  CHAD OL9 .... 8 A3
Chadderton Cemetery
  CHAD OL9 .... 58 D4
Chadderton Hall Junior School
  CHAD OL9 .... 58 D2
Chadderton Industrial Estate
  MDTN M24 .... 57 M7
Chadderton Sports Centre &
  Public Baths
  CHAD OL9 .... 8 B4
Chadderton Town Health Centre
  CHAD OL9 .... 8 A4
Chadkirk Industrial Estate
  MPL/ROM SK6 .... 113 L4
Chanters Industrial Estate
  ATH M46 .... 67 J2
Chantlers Primary School
  TOT/BURYW BL8 .... 38 D2
Chapelfield Primary School
  RAD M26 .... 54 F3
Chapel Medical Centre
  IRL M44 .... 94 D2
Chapel Street Primary School
  BNG/LEV M19 .... 99 L3
Charleston Industrial Estate
  AULW OL7 .... 75 L8

Charlestown Health Centre
BKLY M9 .... **73** K2
Charlestown Primary School
BKLY M9 .... **73** L1
SLFD M6 .... **71** L8
Charlesworth School
GLSP SK13 .... **103** M6
Cheadle Catholic Primary
School *CHD/CHDH* SK8 .... **120** A2
Cheadle CC
CHD/CHDH SK8 .... **110** F7
Cheadle Golf Club
CHD/CHDH SK8 .... **111** H8
Cheadle Heath Clinic
EDGY/DAV SK3 .... **111** K4
Cheadle Heath Primary School
EDGY/DAV SK3 .... **111** K5
Cheadle Heath Sports Centre
CHD/CHDH SK8 .... **111** K6
Cheadle Hulme High School
CHD/CHDH SK8 .... **120** D5
Cheadle Hulme Medical Centre
CHD/CHDH SK8 .... **120** C4
Cheadle Hulme
Recreation Centre
CHD/CHDH SK8 .... **120** C8
Cheadle Hulme School
CHD/CHDH SK8 .... **120** C4
Cheadle & Marple Sixth Form
College *CHD/CHDH* SK8 .... **120** A1
Cheadle Primary School
CHD/CHDH SK8 .... **111** G6
Cheadle Royal Business Park
CHD/CHDH SK8 .... **119** L1
Cheadle Royal Hospital
CHD/CHDH SK8 .... **119** L2
Cheadle Royal Shopping Centre
CHD/CHDH SK8 .... **119** M2
Cheadle Swimming & Recreation
Centre *CHD/CHDH* SK8 .... **111** H8
Cheadle Town FC
CHD/CHDH SK8 .... **111** H7
Cheetham CE Community School
BRO M7 .... **72** C5
Cheetham Hill CC
CHH M8 .... **72** B3
Cheetwood Community &
Sports Centre *BRO* M7 .... **72** C6
Cheetwood Primary School
CHH M8 .... **72** B8
Cherry Manor Primary School
SALE M33 .... **107** M2
Cherry Tree Hospital
OFTN SK2 .... **112** F7
Cherry Tree Primary School
FWTH BL4 .... **52** B4
Chesham Industrial Estate
BURY BL9 .... **25** K8
Chesham Primary School
BURY BL9 .... **25** K6
Chester Court Hotel
STRET M32 .... **86** C8
Chethams Library & Music School
CSLFD M3 .... **6** F2
Chichester Business Centre
MILN OL16 .... **11** H5
Child Health Clinic
MDTN M24 .... **57** J3
Chinese Medical Centre
CSLFD M3 .... **6** D6
Chorley New Road Primary
School *HOR/BR* BL6 .... **33** M2
Chorlton CE Primary School
CCHDY M21 .... **97** K4
Chorlton-cum-Hardy CC
CCHDY M21 .... **97** L6
Chorlton-cum-Hardy Golf Club
CCHDY M21 .... **97** M7
Chorlton High School
CCHDY M21 .... **97** M5
Chorlton Leisure Centre
CCHDY M21 .... **97** L3
Chorlton Park Primary School
CCHDY M21 .... **97** M5
Chorlton Shopping Centre
CCHDY M21 .... **97** K3
Chorlton Water Park
CCHDY M21 .... **97** M8
Chowbent Primary School
ATH M46 .... **67** H1
Christchurch Ainsworth CE
Primary School
BOLE BL2 .... **37** M3
Christ Church CE Primary School
CHAD OL9 .... **58** D6
UPML OL3 .... **45** G2
Christchurch CE Primary School
ECC M30 .... **84** F2
TOT/BURYW BL8 .... **24** C8
Christ Church Pennington CE
Primary School
LEIGH WN7 .... **66** C8
Christie Hospital & Holt Radium
Institute *DID/WITH* M20 .... **98** E6
Christie Street Industrial Estate
STKP SK1 .... **13** L8
Christs Church CE
Primary School
BOLE BL2 .... **37** J2
Christ the King RC
Primary School
NEWH/MOS M40 .... **73** M7
WALK M28 .... **69** H2
Christ the King School
SALE M33 .... **108** C1
Church Road Primary School
BOL BL1 .... **35** K2
Church Street Industrial Estate
MDTN M24 .... **57** K2
Cineworld
BOL BL1 .... **36** D1
DID/WITH M20 .... **111** G3
STKP SK1 .... **13** H6
WGNW/BIL/OR WN5 .... **47** H4
City Centre Campus
CSLFD M3 .... **6** C4
City College Manchester
CHH M8 .... **72** F4
DID/WITH M20 .... **98** C8
NTHM/RTH M23 .... **109** M3
NTHM/RTH M23 .... **109** J4
NTHM/RTH M23 .... **109** G4
City Course Trading Estate
OP/CLY M11 .... **88** D5
City Court Trading Estate
ANC M4 .... **7** L2
City Park Business Village
OLDTF/WHR M16 .... **86** E7
Claremont Primary School
RUSH/FAL M14 .... **98** D1
Clarendon Cottage School
ECC M30 .... **85** J1

Clarendon CP School
BOLS/LL BL3 .... **2** D9
Clarendon Fields Primary School
DUK SK16 .... **90** E4
Clarendon Industrial Estate
HYDE SK14 .... **102** B1
Clarendon Road Primary School
ECC M30 .... **85** J1
Clarendon Square Shopping
Centre *HYDE* SK14 .... **102** A2
Clarke Industrial Estate
STRET M32 .... **85** K8
Clarksfield Primary School
OLDE OL4 .... **59** M6
Claypool Primary School
HOR/BR BL6 .... **34** B3
Clayton Health Centre
OP/CLY M11 .... **88** E2
Clayton Industrial Estate
OP/CLY M11 .... **89** C5
Cleavley Athletics Track
ECC M30 .... **84** D1
Cleggs Lane Industrial Site
LHULT M38 .... **52** E6
Clevelands Preparatory School
BOL BL1 .... **35** K5
Clifton Country Park
SWIN M27 .... **54** B7
Clifton Industrial Estate
SWIN M27 .... **70** F1
Clifton Primary School
SWIN M27 .... **70** F1
Cloughside School
PWCH M25 .... **55** J7
Cloverlea Primary School
HALE/TIMP WA15 .... **108** E7
The Club Theatre
ALT WA14 .... **116** F1
Cobden Mill Industrial Estate
FWTH BL4 .... **52** E3
Coldhurst Community Centre
OLD OL1 .... **9** G3
Coldhurst Industrial Estate
OLD OL1 .... **9** H3
Coliseum Theatre
OLD OL1 .... **9** L5
College Street Health Centre
LEIGH WN7 .... **66** D7
Collegiate Medical Centre
CHH M8 .... **72** D5
Collier Brook Industrial Estate
ATH M46 .... **66** F1
Comfort Inn
WGTN/LGST M12 .... **88** D6
Commonwealth House
MANAIR M90 .... **118** D4
Community Hall
STLY SK15 .... **91** K2
Comtech Business Park
WHTN BL5 .... **50** B1
Concord Business Park
WYTH/NTH M22 .... **119** G3
Constellation Trading Estate
RAD M26 .... **38** C6
Co-operative College
ANC M4 .... **7** G2
Co-operative Museum
WHIT OL12 .... **10** D3
Copley High School
STLY SK15 .... **92** A2
Copper Beeches School
SALE M33 .... **96** C8
Coppice Industrial Estate
OLDS OL8 .... **8** E8
Coppice J & I School
OLDS OL8 .... **59** H8
Copthorne Hotel
SALQ M50 .... **86** D6
Cornbrook Estate
HULME M15 .... **6** A8
Cornerhouse Cinema
CMANE M1 .... **7** G7
Cornishway Industrial Estate
WYTH/NTH M22 .... **118** F4
Cornwall Street Industrial Estate
OP/CLY M11 .... **89** G5
Corpus Christi RC Primary School
CHAD OL9 .... **58** E8
Corpus Christi with St Anne RC
Primary School
ANC M4 .... **88** A3
Corrie Primary School
DTN/ASHW M34 .... **101** J3
Counthill School
OLDE OL4 .... **60** A2
County End Business Centre
OLDE OL4 .... **60** C5
Covenant Christian School
HTNM SK4 .... **99** M8
Crab Lane Primary School
BKLY M9 .... **56** E8
Cravenwood Primary School
CHH M8 .... **72** C4
Crescent Community High School
for Girls *RUSH/FAL* M14 .... **99** G1
The Cricketers Sports Club
WGNS/IIMK WN3 .... **14** D8
Cricket Street Business Centre
WGNW/ST WN6 .... **14** C4
Croft Industrial Estate
BURY BL9 .... **39** K7
Cromer Industrial Estate
MDTN M24 .... **57** L3
Cromford Business Park
OLD OL1 .... **59** L4
Crompton CC
ROY/SHW OL2 .... **43** L4
Crompton Fold Primary School
BOLE BL2 .... **37** H5
Crompton Health Centre
ROY/SHW OL2 .... **43** L6
Crompton House CE School
ROY/SHW OL2 .... **43** J5
Crompton Place Shopping Centre
BOL BL1 .... **2** E5
Crompton Primary School
ROY/SHW OL2 .... **43** K6
Crompton & Royton Golf Club
ROY/SHW OL2 .... **43** J2
Crompton Swimming Pool
ROY/SHW OL2 .... **43** L6
Cromwell High School
DUK SK16 .... **91** H6
Cromwell House Community
Mental Health Centre
ECC M30 .... **85** G2
Cromwell Special School
RDSH SK5 .... **100** C2
Cronshaw Industrial Estate
ROCH OL11 .... **11** G7
Crosland Industrial Estate
MPL/ROM SK6 .... **101** H8

Crossacres Primary School
WYTH/NTH M22 .... **110** C8
Crossgates Primary School
MILN OL16 .... **29** K5
Crosslee Primary School
BKLY M9 .... **57** K8
Crowcroft Park Primary School
WGTN/LGST M12 .... **99** K1
Crown Business Centre
FAIL M35 .... **74** C4
Crown Industrial Estate
ALT WA14 .... **108** B5
ANC M4 .... **7** L2
Crown Royal Industrial Park
STKP SK1 .... **13** K6
Crumpsall Lane Primary School
CHH M8 .... **72** D3
Cuba Industrial Estate
RAMS BL0 .... **18** F4
Culcheth Hall School
ALT WA14 .... **116** E1
Curzon Ashton FC
AULW OL7 .... **90** C2
Curzon Cinema
URM M41 .... **95** L1
Cutgate Shopping Precinct
WHIT OL12 .... **27** L3
Dagenham Road
Industrial Estate
RUSH/FAL M14 .... **98** F1
Daisy Nook Country Park
OLDS OL8 .... **75** H5
Dale Grove Primary School
(Bankside) *HYDE* SK14 .... **102** C3
Dale Grove Special School
OLDE OL4 .... **75** K7
The Dale Primary School
MPL/ROM SK6 .... **114** A4
Dale Street Industrial Estate
RAD M26 .... **54** D2
Dancehouse Theatre & Northern
Ballet School
CMANE M1 .... **7** G8
Dane Bank Primary School
RDSH SK5 .... **100** D2
Dane Road Industrial Estate
SALE M33 .... **96** F7
Darnhill CP School
HEY OL10 .... **40** C7
Darul Uloom Al Arabiya Al Islamia
TOT/BURYW BL8 .... **18** D8
Davaar Medical Centre
DUK SK16 .... **90** F4
Davenport Golf Club
POY/DIS SK12 .... **122** D8
David Cuthbert Business Centre
OP/CLY M11 .... **88** F5
David Lloyd Fitness Centre
BOL BL1 .... **2** B4
David Medical Centre
CCHDY M21 .... **97** M6
Davyhulme J & I School
URM M41 .... **96** A1
Davyhulme Park Golf Club
URM M41 .... **84** C8
Deakins Business Park
EDGW/EG BL7 .... **22** A2
Deane Golf Club
BOLS/LL BL3 .... **35** K7
Deane Leisure Centre
BOLS/LL BL3 .... **35** J8
Deanery CE High School
WGN WN1 .... **14** E3
Dean Lane Medical Centre
BRAM/HZG SK7 .... **121** M4
Dean Row Community Junior
School *WILM/AE* SK9 .... **127** J3
The Deans CP School
SWIN M27 .... **70** B4
Deans Road Industrial Estate
SWIN M27 .... **70** A4
Deanway Trading Estate
WILM/AE SK9 .... **127** H1
Deeplish Primary School
ROCH OL11 .... **10** F8
Delamere School
URM M41 .... **95** G2
Delph Clinic
UPML OL3 .... **45** H7
Delph & Dobcross CC
UPML OL3 .... **45** H7
Delph Primary School
UPML OL3 .... **45** H7
Delta Business Park
DTN/ASHW M34 .... **90** C4
Denton Cemetery
DTN/ASHW M34 .... **101** J4
Denton Cricket & Sports Club
DTN/ASHW M34 .... **90** A2
Denton Golf Club
DTN/ASHW M34 .... **89** L8
Denton St Lawrence CC
DTN/ASHW M34 .... **101** J2
Denton West End Primary
School *DTN/ASHW* M34 .... **100** D1
Department of Clinical
Psychology *ROY/SHW* OL2 .... **59** H2
Derby High School
BURY BL9 .... **4** C9
Derby Shopping Centre
BOLS/LL BL3 .... **2** A8
Derwent Street Trading Estate
ORD M5 .... **86** F5
The Designer Outlet
SALQ M50 .... **86** C5
De Vere Mottram Hall Golf Club
MCFLDN SK10 .... **128** A8
De Vere Mottram Hall Hotel
MCFLDN SK10 .... **128** B8
De Vere Whites Hotel
HOR/BR BL6 .... **34** A5
Devonshire Road Primary
School *BOL* BL1 .... **35** K4
Devonshire Street
Industrial Estate
WGTN/LGST M12 .... **88** A6
Dial Park Primary School
OFTN SK2 .... **113** H6
Diamond Lodge
GTN M18 .... **88** F2
Didsbury CC
DID/WITH M20 .... **110** F3
Didsbury CE Primary School
DID/WITH M20 .... **110** E1
Didsbury Golf Club
WYTH/NTH M22 .... **110** ·
Didsbury Medical Centre
DID/WITH M20 .... **98** D8
Didsbury Road Primary School
HTNM SK4 .... **111** J2
Didsbury School
DID/WITH M20 .... **98** E8

Diggle School
UPML OL3 .... **45** M7
Dinting CE Primary School
GLSP SK13 .... **104** D3
Dinting Lane Industrial Estate
GLSP SK13 .... **104** D3
Dinting Lodge Industrial Estate
GLSP SK13 .... **104** C1
Dinting Vale Business Park
GLSP SK13 .... **104** B2
Disley Golf Club
POY/DIS SK12 .... **123** L5
Disley Primary School
POY/DIS SK12 .... **123** M6
Dobson Park Industrial Estate
WGNE/HIN WN2 .... **48** D6
Dodd Lane Industrial Estate
WHTN BL5 .... **33** L8
Doffcocker Lodge Nature
Reserve *BOL* BL1 .... **35** H3
Douglas Valley Business Park
WGN WN1 .... **31** M7
Downing Street
Industrial Estate
WGTN/LGST M12 .... **7** K8
Dowry Park Industrial Estate
OLDE OL4 .... **60** B5
Dowson Primary School
HYDE SK14 .... **102** B4
Droylsden AFC
DROY M43 .... **89** K3
Droylsden High School for Girls
DROY M43 .... **89** H2
Droylsden Sports Centre
DROY M43 .... **89** H2
Droylsden Swimming Pool
DROY M43 .... **89** H2
Ducie Athletics Ground Running
Track *WGTN/LGST* M12 .... **88** E8
Ducie High School
RUSH/FAL M14 .... **87** K8
Ducie Sports Centre
HULME M15 .... **87** L8
Duke of Norfolk CE Primary
School *GLSP* SK13 .... **105** G3
Dukesgate Primary School
LHULT M38 .... **52** D7
Dukinfield Crematorium
DUK SK16 .... **91** G3
Dukinfield Golf Club
DUK SK16 .... **91** K5
Dukinfield Joint Cemetery
DUK SK16 .... **91** G3
Dunham Forest Golf & Country
Club *ALT* WA14 .... **107** J8
Dunscar Golf Club
EDGW/EG BL7 .... **22** A4
Dunscar Industrial Estate
EDGW/EG BL7 .... **22** B5
Dunstan Medical Centre
BOLE BL2 .... **3** L4
Durnford Medical Centre
MDTN M24 .... **57** J3
Eagley Infant School
EDGW/EG BL7 .... **22** D4
Eagley Junior School
EDGW/EG BL7 .... **22** E4
East Crompton St Georges CE
Primary School
ROY/SHW OL2 .... **43** M5
East Crompton St James CE
Primary School
ROY/SHW OL2 .... **43** L5
East Lancashire Railway
BURY BL9 .... **5** J7
BURY BL9 .... **25** G4
BURY BL9 .... **40** B4
RAMS BL0 .... **18** F7
East Ward Primary School
BURY BL9 .... **5** L4
Eaton Place Business Centre
SALE M33 .... **96** D8
Eccles Crematorium
ECC M30 .... **84** C4
Eccles Health Centre
ECC M30 .... **85** J2
Eccles Recreation Centre
ECC M30 .... **85** J3
Eccles Town Hall
ECC M30 .... **85** J2
Edenfield CC
RAMS BL0 .... **19** H1
Edge Fold Industrial Estate
FWTH BL4 .... **51** M3
Edgworth CC
EDGW/EG BL7 .... **17** H6
Egerton CC
EDGW/EG BL7 .... **22** A1
Egerton & Dunscar Health Centre
EDGW/EG BL7 .... **22** B2
Egerton High School
URM M41 .... **85** H8
Egerton House Hotel
EDGW/EG BL7 .... **22** B2
Egerton Park Arts College
DTN/ASHW M34 .... **90** B7
Egerton Park Community
High School
DTN/ASHW M34 .... **90** A8
Egerton Primary School
EDGW/EG BL7 .... **22** A1
Elk Mill Central Retail Park
OLD OL1 .... **58** E1
Ellenbrook Primary School
WALK M28 .... **68** E5
Ellesmere Bowling
& Tennis Club
WALK M28 .... **69** G4
Ellesmere Golf Club
WALK M28 .... **69** J3
Ellesmere Retail Park
WALK M28 .... **68** F1
Ellesmere Shopping Centre
LHULT M38 .... **68** F1
Elmridge Primary School
HALE/TIMP WA15 .... **117** L4
Elms Bank Community High
School *WHTF* M45 .... **55** J1
Elms Medical Centre
WHTF M45 .... **55** H3
Elm Wood Primary School
MDTN M24 .... **57** M4
Elsinore Business Centre
OLDTF/WHR M16 .... **86** D8
The Elton High School
TOT/BURYW BL8 .... **38** D1
Elton Primary School
TOT/BURYW BL8 .... **38** F1
Emmanuel Christian School
WHIT OL12 .... **28** B3
Emmanuel Holcombe Primary
School *TOT/BURYW* BL8 .... **18** D6

Empress Business Centre
OLDTF/WHR M16 .... **86** F6
Empress Industrial Estate
WGNE/HIN WN2 .... **15** M5
English Martyrs RC Primary
School *URM* M41 .... **95** M2
Ensor Trading Estate
NM/HAY SK22 .... **124** F6
Enterprise Trading Estate
GTN M18 .... **89** H6
TRPK M17 .... **85** K4
Esplanade Arts &
Heritage Centre
POY/DIS SK12 .... **10** D5
Estcourt Preparatory School
OLDS OL8 .... **59** G8
Etchells Primary School
CHD/CHDH SK8 .... **119** L3
Etherow Country Park
MPL/ROM SK6 .... **115** G1
Etherow Industrial Estate
HYDE SK14 .... **93** G8
Eton Hill Industrial Estate
RAD M26 .... **38** F7
Etrop Grange Hotel
MANAIR M90 .... **118** D3
Etz Chaim School
CHH M8 .... **72** D3
Europa Business Park
EDGY/DAV SK3 .... **111** L6
Europa Trading Estate
RAD M26 .... **53** L5
Ewing School
DID/WITH M20 .... **98** D7
Express by Holiday Inn
SALQ M50 .... **86** C5
Express Trading Estate
FWTH BL4 .... **53** G6
The Eye Clinic
CMANW M2 .... **6** F5
Fahay Industrial Estate
NEWH/MOS M40 .... **88** B2
Failsworth Health Centre
FAIL M35 .... **74** B5
Failsworth Industrial Estate
FAIL M35 .... **73** M6
Failsworth Shopping Centre
FAIL M35 .... **74** C4
Fairfield Community Primary
School *BURY* BL9 .... **40** A1
Fairfield General Hospital
BURY BL9 .... **26** B8
Fairfield Golf & Sailing Club
DTN/ASHW M34 .... **89** L5
Fairfield High School for Girls
DROY M43 .... **89** J4
Fairfield Road Primary School
DROY M43 .... **89** J4
Fairhill Industrial Estate
IRL M44 .... **94** C5
Fairview Medical Centre
URM M41 .... **95** L2
Fairway Primary School
OFTN SK2 .... **113** H5
Fairways Lodge
PWCH M25 .... **71** L3
Falcon Business Centre
CHAD OL9 .... **8** C2
Falinge Park High School
WHIT OL12 .... **10** B1
Fall Birch Hospital Lodge
HOR/BR BL6 .... **34** D3
Fallowfield Medical Centre
RUSH/FAL M14 .... **99** G4
Fallowfield Shopping Centre
RUSH/FAL M14 .... **99** H3
Farjo Medical Centre
CMANE M1 .... **7** H5
Farnworth Cemetery
FWTH BL4 .... **53** H3
Farnworth Leisure Centre
FWTH BL4 .... **53** G4
Farnworth Little Theatre
FWTH BL4 .... **53** G4
Farnworth Park Industrial
Estate *FWTH* BL4 .... **53** G3
Farnworth Social Circle CC
FWTH BL4 .... **52** F5
Farrowdale House School
ROY/SHW OL2 .... **43** L6
Fiddlers Lane Primary School
IRL M44 .... **94** E1
Fieldhouse CC
ROCH OL11 .... **27** H6
Fieldhouse Industrial Estate
WHIT OL12 .... **28** C2
Firbank Primary School
ROY/SHW OL2 .... **43** C5
Firgrove Business Park
MILN OL16 .... **29** G4
Firs CP School
SALE M33 .... **96** A8
Firsdale Industrial Estate
LEIGH WN7 .... **65** M6
Fir Tree Primary School
BOLE BL2 .... **100** B2
Firwood Industrial Estate
BOLE BL2 .... **36** F2
Firwood Manor Preparatory
School *CHAD* OL9 .... **8** A1
Firwood Special School
BOLE BL2 .... **36** F2
Fishbrook Industrial Estate
FWTH BL4 .... **53** J5
Fishwicks Industrial Estate
RNFD/HAY WA11 .... **78** C4
Fitton Hill Shopping Precinct
OLDS OL8 .... **75** J1
Five Fold Industrial Park
CHAD OL9 .... **8** F6
Flixton CC
URM M41 .... **95** H1
Flixton FC
URM M41 .... **95** G1
Flixton Girls High School
URM M41 .... **95** K2
Flixton Golf Club
URM M41 .... **95** K4
Flixton Health Clinic
URM M41 .... **95** J2
Flixton J & I School
URM M41 .... **95** J2
Flowery Field Primary School
HYDE SK14 .... **91** G8
Forest Gate Community Primary
School *PART* M31 .... **106** A1
Forest Park School
SALE M33 .... **96** D8
Forest School
HALE/TIMP WA15 .... **108** G4
Forge Industrial Estate
OLDE OL4 .... **59** L5

Forum Leisure Centre
  WYTH/NTH M22 .... 118 E1
Fourways Trading Estate
  TRPK M17 .... 85 K6
Fowler Industrial Estate
  HOR/BR BL6 .... 33 M2
Foyer & Coops Business Centre
  WGN WN1 .... 14 E4
Fred Longworth High School
  TYLD M29 .... 67 H3
Freehold Community Primary
  School CHAD OL9 .... 8 C8
Freetown Business Park
  BURY BL9 .... 5 H1
The Friars Primary School
  CSLFD M3 .... 6 B1
Friezland Primary School
  OLDE OL4 .... 61 H7
Fulshaw CE Primary School
  WILM/AE SK9 .... 126 D6
Furness Vale Business centre
  CHF/WBR SK23 .... 124 F8
Furrow Community School
  MDTN M24 .... 56 F1
Galleon Leisure Centre
  DID/WITH M20 .... 110 F4
The Galleries Shopping Centre
  WGN WN1 .... 14 F3
Gallery of Costume
  RUSH/FAL M14 .... 98 F2
Gallery Oldham, Library
  & Lifelong Learning Centre
  OLD OL1 .... 9 K6
Gamesley Community Primary
  School GLSP SK13 .... 104 B2
Garrett Hall Primary School
  TYLD M29 .... 68 A5
Garrick Playhouse
  ALT WA14 .... 108 A6
Garrick Theatre
  EDGY/DAV SK3 .... 13 H5
Garswood Primary School
  AIMK WN4 .... 62 B3
Garswood United FC
  AIMK WN4 .... 62 C7
Gaskell Primary School
  BOL BL1 .... 2 B2
The Gates Primary School
  WHTN BL5 .... 50 C2
The Gates Shopping Centre
  BOL BL1 .... 2 E4
Gateway Industrial Estate
  CMANE M1 .... 7 K5
Gathurst Golf Club
  WGNNW/ST WN6 .... 30 C7
Gatley Golf Club
  CHD/CHDH SK8 .... 119 K1
Gatley Health Centre
  CHD/CHDH SK8 .... 110 C4
Gatley Primary School
  CHD/CHDH SK8 .... 110 D7
Gee Cross Holy Trinity CE
  Primary School
  HYDE SK14 .... 102 C1
Gee Cross Social & Sports Club
  HYDE SK14 .... 102 B4
Gelder Wood Country Park
  ROCH OL11 .... 26 A1
George H Carnall Leisure Centre
  URM M41 .... 85 H2
George Tomlinson School
  FWTH BL4 .... 53 H6
Georgian Health Centre
  OLD OL1 .... 9 K5
Gidlow Cemetery
  WGNNW/ST WN6 .... 31 K7
Gilded Hollins Primary School
  LEIGH WN7 .... 80 F3
Gilnow Mill Industrial Estate
  BOL BL1 .... 35 M6
Gilnow Primary School
  BOL BL1 .... 35 M6
Glazebury CE Primary School
  GOL/RIS/CUL WA3 .... 81 M5
Glebe House School
  MILN OL16 .... 10 D6
Glen Trading Estate
  OLDE OL4 .... 60 A6
Globe Industrial Estate
  RAD M26 .... 54 E1
Globe Lane Industrial Estate
  DUK SK16 .... 90 E6
Globe Lane Primary School
  DUK SK16 .... 90 E6
Glodwick Health Centre
  OLDE OL4 .... 59 L6
Glodwick Infant School
  OLDE OL4 .... 59 L7
Glossopdale Community College
  GLSP SK13 .... 93 J3
  GLSP SK13 .... 104 F2
Glossop & District Golf Club
  GLSP SK13 .... 105 K4
Glossop RUFC
  GLSP SK13 .... 104 B5
Glossop Victorian
  Swimming Pool
  GLSP SK13 .... 104 F2
Gloucester House Medical
  Centre
  URM M41 .... 96 A2
GMB National College
  OLDTF/WHR M16 .... 97 M2
Godfrey Ermen Memorial CE
  Primary School
  ECC M30 .... 84 F4
Godley CP School
  HYDE SK14 .... 102 C1
Golborne Clinic
  GOL/RIS/CUL WA3 .... 79 L3
Golborne CP School
  GOL/RIS/CUL WA3 .... 79 K4
Golborne High School
  GOL/RIS/CUL WA3 .... 79 M3
Golden Tulip Hotel
  TRPK M17 .... 86 C6
Gorrells Industrial Estate
  ROCH OL11 .... 42 B1
Gorsefield Primary School
  RAD M26 .... 38 D8
Gorse Hall Primary School
  STLY SK15 .... 91 J7
Gorse Hill Health Centre
  STRET M32 .... 97 H1
Gorse Hill Primary School
  STRET M32 .... 86 B8
Gorsey Bank Primary School
  WILM/AE SK9 .... 126 D5
Gorton Brook First School
  WGTN/LGST M12 .... 88 D6
Gorton Industrial Estate
  GTN M18 .... 88 F6

Gorton Medical Centre
  GTN M18 .... 89 G7
Gorton Mount Primary School
  GTN M18 .... 99 L1
Gorton Retail Market
  GTN M18 .... 89 G7
Goshen Sports Centre
  BURY BL9 .... 39 K6
Goyt Valley Industrial Estate
  CHF/WBR SK23 .... 124 F8
Grafton House Preparatory
  School AUL OL6 .... 90 E2
Granada Studios
  CSLFD M3 .... 6 C5
Grand Arcade Shopping Centre
  WGN WN1 .... 15 G3
Grange Primary School
  WILM/AE SK9 .... 119 L8
Grange School
  CHAD OL9 .... 9 G4
  RUSH/FAL M14 .... 99 G1
Grange Valley Primary School
  RNFD/HAY WA11 .... 78 A7
Grasmere Street Health Centre
  LEIGH WN7 .... 66 B6
Grasscroft Independent School
  OLDE OL4 .... 60 F7
Greater Manchester
  Police Headquarters
  OLDTF/WHR M16 .... 86 D7
Great Lever & Farnworth
  Golf Club FWTH BL4 .... 52 A3
Great Moor Clinic
  OFTN SK2 .... 112 F7
Great Moor Infant School
  OFTN SK2 .... 112 E7
Great Northern Shopping &
  Leisure Centre
  CSLFD M3 .... 6 E6
Greave Primary School
  MPL/ROM SK6 .... 101 M8
Greenacres Primary School
  OLDE OL4 .... 59 M5
Greenbank Industrial Estate
  WGNE/HIN WN2 .... 65 K1
Greenbank School
  CHD/CHDH SK8 .... 120 B3
Greenbrow Infant School
  NTHM/RTH M23 .... 118 B1
Greencourts Business Park
  WYTH/NTH M22 .... 119 J5
Green End Junior School
  BNG/LEV M19 .... 99 H7
Greenfield CC
  UPML OL3 .... 61 L7
Greenfield Primary School
  HYDE SK14 .... 102 B3
  UPML OL3 .... 61 L6
Green Fold Special School
  FWTH BL4 .... 52 C4
Greengate Industrial Estate
  MDTN M24 .... 57 M7
Green Hall Primary School
  ATH M46 .... 51 J8
Greenheys Business Centre
  HULME M15 .... 87 K7
Greenhill Primary School
  OLDE OL4 .... 9 K8
  TOT/BURYW BL8 .... 38 C3
Green Lane Industrial Estate
  CMANE M1 .... 12 D3
Greenmount CC
  TOT/BURYW BL8 .... 24 C3
Greenmount Primary School
  TOT/BURYW BL8 .... 24 B2
Green Room Theatre
  CMANE M1 .... 6 F7
Greenside Primary School
  DROY M43 .... 89 J2
Greenside Trading Centre
  DROY M43 .... 89 K3
Greenwood Business Centre
  ORD M5 .... 86 D3
Greenwood Primary School
  ECC M30 .... 70 B8
Greswell Primary School
  DTN/ASHW M34 .... 101 H2
Greyhound & Speedway Stadium
  GTN M18 .... 88 E7
Greyland Medical Centre
  PWCH M25 .... 55 L6
Griffin Business Centre
  SLFD M6 .... 71 M7
Grosvenor Business Park
  MPL/ROM SK6 .... 101 J6
Grosvenor Industrial Estate
  AULW OL7 .... 90 D3
Grosvenor Road Primary School
  SWIN M27 .... 70 E6
Guardian Angels RC
  Primary School
  TOT/BURYW BL8 .... 38 E1
Guide Bridge Industrial Estate
  AULW OL7 .... 90 B4
Guide Bridge Theatre
  DTN/ASHW M34 .... 90 B4
Guide Bridge Trading Estate
  DTN/ASHW M34 .... 90 B4
Guinness Road Trading Estate
  TRPK M17 .... 85 J4
Hadfield Clinic
  GLSP SK13 .... 93 K7
Hadfield Industrial Estate
  GLSP SK13 .... 93 J6
Hadfield Infant School
  GLSP SK13 .... 93 J8
Hadfield St Charles RC
  Primary School
  GLSP SK13 .... 93 H7
Hague Bar Primary School
  NM/HAY SK22 .... 124 A4
Haigh Hall Country Park
  WGNE/HIN WN2 .... 32 C6
Haigh Hall Golf Complex
  WGNE/HIN WN2 .... 32 C6
Hale Barns CC
  HALE/TIMP WA15 .... 118 A4
Hale Golf Club
  HALE/TIMP WA15 .... 117 J5
Hale Preparatory School
  HALE/TIMP WA15 .... 117 L1
Halfpenny Bridge Industrial
  Estate
  MILN OL16 .... 11 G6
Hallgate Bus Station
  WGN WN1 .... 14 F3
Hall i' th' Wood Museum
  BOL BL1 .... 22 D8
Halliwell Industrial Estate
  BOL BL1 .... 36 A1
Hamer CP School
  MILN OL16 .... 28 E2

Hampson Street Trading Estate
  ORD M5 .... 6 A5
Handforth Dean
  Shopping Centre
  WILM/AE SK9 .... 120 A8
Handforth Health Centre
  WILM/AE SK9 .... 127 H1
Hanover Business Park
  ALT WA14 .... 107 L5
Harcourt Industrial Centre
  WALK M28 .... 53 C2
Hardman Fold Special School
  FAIL M35 .... 74 A3
Hardy Mill Primary School
  BOLE BL2 .... 23 J8
Hare Hill (NT)
  MCFLDN SK10 .... 131 K6
Harper Green School
  FWTH BL4 .... 52 E3
Harp Industrial Estate
  ROCH OL11 .... 42 A2
Harp Trading Estate
  TRPK M17 .... 85 K4
Harpurhey Business Centre
  BKLY M9 .... 73 G3
Harpurhey Health Centre
  BKLY M9 .... 73 G4
Harpur Mount Primary School
  BKLY M9 .... 73 G4
Harrop Fold School
  WALK M28 .... 68 E1
Harrytown Catholic High School
  MPL/ROM SK6 .... 113 K2
Hart Common Golf Club
  WHTN BL5 .... 49 L5
Hartford Industrial Estate
  CHAD OL9 .... 8 D7
Hartshead High School
  AUL OL6 .... 76 B5
Harwood Golf Club (Bolton)
  BOLE BL2 .... 23 K8
Harwood Health Centre
  BOLE BL2 .... 23 G7
Harwood Meadows Primary
  School BOLE BL2 .... 37 J1
Harwood Park Primary School
  HEY OL10 .... 41 G3
Haslam Park Primary School
  BOLS/LL BL3 .... 35 L7
Haslemere Industrial Estate
  AIMK WN4 .... 63 K4
Hathershaw Technology College
  OLDS OL8 .... 75 J2
Hattersley Health Clinic
  HYDE SK14 .... 103 H2
Hattersley Industrial Estate
  HYDE SK14 .... 103 H3
Haveley Hey Primary School
  WYTH/NTH M22 .... 109 M8
Hawkins Clinic
  MILN OL16 .... 10 F5
Hawkley Brook Trading Estate
  WGNS/IIMK WN3 .... 63 H2
Hawkley Hall High School
  WGNS/IIMK WN3 .... 63 L1
Hawksley Industrial Estate
  OLDS OL8 .... 74 F1
Hawthorns Special School
  DTN/ASHW M34 .... 90 A7
Haydock CC
  RNFD/HAY WA11 .... 78 A5
Haydock English Martyrs Catholic
  Primary School
  RNFD/HAY WA11 .... 78 A5
Haydock Lane Industrial Estate
  RNFD/HAY WA11 .... 78 B4
Haydock Medical Centre
  RNFD/HAY WA11 .... 78 A6
Haydock Park Golf Club
  NEWLW WA12 .... 79 J7
Haydock Park Racecourse
  AIMK WN4 .... 78 F3
Hayfield Primary School
  NM/HAY SK22 .... 125 L1
Hayward School
  BOLS/LL BL3 .... 51 M2
Hayward Sports Centre
  BOLS/LL BL3 .... 51 M2
Hazeldene Medical Centre
  NEWH/MOS M40 .... 74 B3
Hazel Grove Clinic
  BRAM/HZG SK7 .... 122 A1
Hazel Grove Golf Club
  BRAM/HZG SK7 .... 122 D3
Hazel Grove High School
  BRAM/HZG SK7 .... 121 L3
Hazel Grove Pools
  & Fitness Centre
  BRAM/HZG SK7 .... 121 J3
Hazel Grove Primary School
  BRAM/HZG SK7 .... 122 A1
Hazel Grove Recreation Centre
  BRAM/HZG SK7 .... 121 L4
Hazlehurst Community
  Primary School
  RAMS BL0 .... 18 D8
Heald Green Medical Centre
  CHD/CHDH SK8 .... 119 K4
Heald Place Primary School
  RUSH/FAL M14 .... 98 E1
Healey Primary School
  WHIT OL12 .... 28 B1
The Health Centre
  ALT WA14 .... 108 A7
Heap Bridge Primary School
  BURY BL9 .... 40 A3
Heathfield Primary School
  BOLS/LL BL3 .... 51 K2
Heaton CC
  BOL BL1 .... 35 K2
Heaton Cemetery
  BOL BL1 .... 35 L6
Heaton Medical Centre
  BOL BL1 .... 35 J3
Heaton Moor Golf Club
  HTNM SK4 .... 99 K7
Heaton Moor Medical Centre
  HTNM SK4 .... 99 L7
Heaton Moor Rugby Union FC
  HTNM SK4 .... 12 B1
Heaton Norris Health Centre
  HTNM SK4 .... 12 F1
Heaton Park
  PWCH M25 .... 56 B7
Heaton Park Golf Centre
  PWCH M25 .... 56 B6
Heaton Park Primary School
  WHTF M45 .... 55 L6
Heaton Special School
  HTNM SK4 .... 99 L7
Helen O'Grady Drama Academy
  ALT WA14 .... 107 M8

Hempshaw Business Centre
  STKP SK1 .... 112 E5
Henshaw Society for the Blind
  OLDTF/WHR M16 .... 86 D8
Hertford Industrial Estate
  AULW OL7 .... 90 D3
Hesketh Fletcher CE High School
  ATH M46 .... 66 F2
Hewitt Business Park
  WGNW/BIL/OR WN5 .... 46 B8
Heybrook Primary School
  WHIT OL12 .... 11 H1
Heyes Lane Infant School
  HALE/TIMP WA15 .... 108 E4
The Heys Primary School
  AUL OL6 .... 91 G1
Hey-with-Zion Primary School
  OLDE OL4 .... 60 B5
Heywood Cemetery
  ROCH OL11 .... 27 J8
Heywood Community High
  School BURY BL9 .... 40 B3
Heywood Industrial Park
  HEY OL10 .... 40 D4
Heywood Sports Complex
  HEY OL10 .... 40 E1
Higginshaw Sports Club
  OLD OL1 .... 9 L3
Highbank Trading Estate
  OP/CLY M11 .... 89 G5
Highbarn Junior School
  ROY/SHW OL2 .... 43 H7
High Birch Special School
  ROCH OL11 .... 27 L7
Higher Broughton Health Centre
  BRO M7 .... 72 B6
Higher Failsworth
  Primary School
  FAIL M35 .... 74 D4
Higher Folds Primary School
  LEIGH WN7 .... 67 G5
Higher Lane Primary School
  WHTF M45 .... 55 H4
Higher Openshaw Community
  School OP/CLY M11 .... 89 G4
Highfield Cemetery
  MPL/ROM SK6 .... 113 J2
Highfield CC
  WGNS/IIMK WN3 .... 46 F8
Highfield Hospital
  ROCH OL11 .... 10 B8
Highfield Primary School
  FWTH BL4 .... 52 D4
  URM M41 .... 96 C2
Highfield St Matthews
  CE Primary School
  WGNS/IIMK WN3 .... 46 F8
High Lane Medical Centre
  MPL/ROM SK6 .... 123 G5
High Lane Primary School
  MPL/ROM SK6 .... 123 G4
High Lawn Primary School
  BOL BL1 .... 22 B6
Highlea Secondary School
  WALK M28 .... 68 C4
Hillcrest Grammar School
  EDGY/DAV SK3 .... 112 C4
Hillgate Business Centre
  STKP SK1 .... 13 G7
Hill Top Community Primary
  School ROCH OL11 .... 42 D3
Hill Top Community Special
  School OLDE OL4 .... 44 D8
Hilton Lane Primary School
  WALK M28 .... 68 D1
Hindley All Saints CE Primary
  School WGNE/HIN WN2 .... 49 H7
Hindley Business Centre
  WGNE/HIN WN2 .... 49 G2
Hindley Green Primary School
  WGNE/HIN WN2 .... 65 L2
Hindley Hall Golf Club
  WGNE/HIN WN2 .... 49 G4
Hindley High School - Arts
  College WGNE/HIN WN2 ...... 49 J2
Hindley Leisure Centre
  WGNE/HIN WN2 .... 49 J2
Hindley Primary School
  WGNE/HIN WN2 .... 49 G2
Hindsford CE Primary School
  ATH M46 .... 67 H3
HM Prison
  CHH M8 .... 72 C8
  WGNE/HIN WN2 .... 65 H2
Hodge Clough Infant School
  OLD OL1 .... 60 A1
Hodge Clough Junior School
  OLD OL1 .... 60 A1
Holcombe Brook Primary School
  RAMS BL0 .... 24 D2
Holcombe Brook Sports Club
  RAMS BL0 .... 24 D1
Holden Clough Primary School
  AUL OL6 .... 76 A4
Holden Road Trading Estate
  LEIGH WN7 .... 66 D7
Holiday Inn
  BOL BL1 .... 2 E3
  NEWH/MOS M40 .... 73 J7
Hollingworth High School
  MILN OL16 .... 29 K6
Hollingworth Lake Activity
  Centre LIT OL15 .... 29 K2
Hollingworth Lake Country Park
  LIT OL15 .... 29 M2
Hollingworth Primary School
  HYDE SK14 .... 92 F7
Hollin Primary School
  MDTN M24 .... 57 K1
Hollins Grundy Primary School
  BURY BL9 .... 39 K7
Hollins Industrial Park
  CLSP SK13 .... 93 L7
Hollinwood Business Centre
  FAIL M35 .... 74 E4
Hollinwood Cemetery
  OLDS OL8 .... 74 F3
Hollinwood CC
  OLDS OL8 .... 74 F4
Holly Bank Industrial Estate
  RAD M26 .... 54 C1
Holly Mount RC Primary School
  TOT/BURYW BL8 .... 24 A3
Hollywood Bowl
  HOR/BR BL6 .... 34 A4
  NEWH/MOS M40 .... 74 A4
Holt Town Industrial Estate
  NEWH/MOS M40 .... 88 B2
Holy Cross & All Saints RC
  Primary School ECC M30 ..... 85 G4
Holy Cross College
  BURY BL9 .... 4 E8

Holy Family Catholic Primary
  School SALE M33 .... 97 H8
Holy Family RC Primary School
  OLDS OL8 .... 75 G4
  WGNE/HIN WN2 .... 64 D3
Holy Family RC School
  BOL BL1 .... 68 B5
Holy Family VA RC Primary
  School ROCH OL11 .... 42 D2
Holy Infant RC Primary School
  BOL BL1 .... 22 D8
Holy Name RC Primary School
  HULME M15 .... 87 K7
Holy Rosary RC Primary School
  OLDS OL8 .... 75 J2
Holy Trinity CE Dobcross School
  UPML OL3 .... 61 J2
Holy Trinity CE Primary School
  AUL OL6 .... 90 D1
  BKLY M9 .... 73 H4
  BURY BL9 .... 4 F6
Hong Sing Chinese
  Medical Centre
  BRAM/HZG SK7 .... 122 A1
Hooley Bridge Industrial Estate
  HEY OL10 .... 26 F8
Hope High School
  SLFD M6 .... 70 F8
Hope Hospital
  SLFD M6 .... 85 L2
Hope Special School
  WGNS/IIMK WN3 .... 63 J2
Hopwood Hall College
  MDTN M24 .... 41 L7
  WHIT OL12 .... 10 D4
Hopwood Medical Centre
  HEY OL10 .... 41 H3
Hopwood Primary School
  HEY OL10 .... 41 H4
Horton Mill Primary School
  OLDE OL4 .... 59 K6
Horwich Business Park
  HOR/BR BL6 .... 33 L2
Horwich Golf Club
  HOR/BR BL6 .... 34 A2
Horwich Leisure Centre
  HOR/BR BL6 .... 33 M1
Hotel Ibis
  CMANE M1 .... 7 G6
  CMANE M1 .... 7 H8
Hotel Rossetti
  CMANE M1 .... 7 J5
Houldsworth Golf Club
  RDSH SK5 .... 100 B4
Houldsworth Medical Centre
  RDSH SK5 .... 100 C5
Howe Bridge Crematorium
  ATH M46 .... 66 C3
Howe Bridge Sports Centre
  ATH M46 .... 66 E3
Hubert House Jewish Boys
  School
  BRO M7 .... 72 A4
Hulme Adult Education Centre
  HULME M15 .... 87 H6
Hulme Arch
  HULME M15 .... 87 J6
The Hulme Court Preparatory
  School OLDS OL8 .... 59 G8
The Hulme Grammar School
  for Boys
  OLDS OL8 .... 59 G8
Hulme Hall Grammar School
  CHD/CHDH SK8 .... 120 C3
Hulton Hospital
  BOLS/LL BL3 .... 51 K1
Hurstfield Industrial Estate
  RDSH SK5 .... 100 B6
Hursthead Junior School
  CHD/CHDH SK8 .... 120 E6
Hurst Knoll CE Primary School
  AUL OL6 .... 75 M8
Hurst Mills Industrial Estate
  CLSP SK13 .... 105 K3
Hyde Clarendon Sixth Form
  College HYDE SK14 .... 91 G8
Hyde CC
  HYDE SK14 .... 102 C6
Hyde Leisure Pool
  HYDE SK14 .... 102 B2
Hyde Technology School
  HYDE SK14 .... 90 F8
Hyde United FC
  HYDE SK14 .... 102 C2
IKEA Store Manchester
  AUL OL6 .... 90 D1
IMAX Cinema
  ANC M4 .... 7 G3
IMEX Business Park
  BRUN/LGST M13 .... 99 J1
Imperial War Museum North
  TRPK M17 .... 86 B5
Ince CE Primary School
  WGNE/HIN WN2 .... 48 D5
Ince Clinic & Community Centre
  WGNE/HIN WN2 .... 48 D5
Indoor Tennis Centre
  OP/CLY M11 .... 88 C2
Innes Special School
  WHIT OL12 .... 27 M3
Innkeeper's Lodge
  GOL/RIS/CUL WA3 .... 80 B6
  HTNM SK4 .... 99 M7
  OLD OL1 .... 58 E2
  WILM/AE SK9 .... 130 D1
Inscape House School
  CHD/CHDH SK8 .... 119 M1
Inscape House Special School
  WALK M28 .... 69 H3
The Instructor School
  STKP SK1 .... 13 J5
International Convention Centre
  CSLFD M3 .... 6 E6
International Swimming Pool
  WGN WN1 .... 15 G5
Iranian School of Manchester
  WGTN/LGST M12 .... 99 L1
Irlam & Cadishead Community
  High School IRL M44 .... 94 B5
Irlam CP School
  IRL M44 .... 94 B3
Irlam Endowed Primary School
  IRL M44 .... 94 D2
Irlam Industrial Estate
  IRL M44 .... 94 B5
Irlam Swimming Pool
  IRL M44 .... 94 D3
James Brindley Primary School
  WALK M28 .... 68 F3
The Jeff Joseph Sale Moor
  Technology College
  SALE M33 .... 109 G2

Jewish Museum *CHH* M8 ... 72 D8
Jewish Senior Boys School *BRO* M7 ... 72 A5
John Rylands Library *CSLFD* M3 ... 6 E5
Johnson Fold Community Primary School *BOL* BL1 ... 35 J1
John Street Medical Centre *GOL/RIS/CUL* WA3 ... 79 K4
Joseph Adamson Industrial Estate *HYDE* SK14 ... 101 M2
Joseph Rayner Independent School *AULW* OL7 ... 75 K5
Jumbles Country Park *BOLE* BL2 ... 23 G3
Jurys Inn *CMANE* M1 ... 6 E7
Kaskenmoor School *OLDS* OL8 ... 74 E3
Kassim Darwish Grammar School for Boys *OLDTF/WHR* M16 ... 98 B3
Kayley Industrial Estate *AULW* OL7 ... 90 C1
Kearsley West Primary School *FWTH* BL4 ... 53 H5
Kenmore Medical Centre *WILM/AE* SK9 ... 126 E6
Kentmere Primary School *WHIT* OL12 ... 28 C1
Kenyon Business Park *BOLS/LL* BL3 ... 2 D8
Kershaw Business Centre *BOLS/LL* BL3 ... 2 B8
Kiely Business Park *BURY* BL9 ... 5 H1
Kilhey Court Hotel *WGN* WN1 ... 31 M2
King David Junior & High School *CHH* M8 ... 72 C3
Kingfisher Community Special School *CHAD* OL9 ... 58 C7
The King of Kings School *ANC* M4 ... 7 H1
Kingsdown High School *WGNW/BIL/OR* WN5 ... 46 F5
Kingshill School *TYLD* M29 ... 67 J4
Kings Road Primary School *OLDTF/WHR* M16 ... 97 K1
King Street Remedial Clinic *DUK* SK16 ... 90 E3
Kingsway CP School *URM* M41 ... 85 H8
Kingsway Retail Park *MILN* OL16 ... 29 G5
Kingsway School *CHD/CHDH* SK8 ... 110 F8
Kingsway Secondary School *CHD/CHDH* SK8 ... 110 F7
Kingsway West Business Park *MILN* OL16 ... 11 K8
Kirkfield Hotel *NEWLW* WA12 ... 79 H8
Kirkless Industrial Estate *WGNE/HIN* WN2 ... 48 D2
Knoll Street Industrial Park *BRO* M7 ... 72 A5
Knowsley Junior School *OLDE* OL4 ... 60 D5
Kratos Industrial Estate *URM* M41 ... 85 J7
Lacey Green Primary School *WILM/AE* SK9 ... 126 E3
Lady Barn House School *CHD/CHDH* SK8 ... 119 M1
Ladybarn Primary School *DID/WITH* M20 ... 99 G6
Ladybridge High School *BOLS/LL* BL3 ... 35 J8
Ladybridge Primary School *BOLS/LL* BL3 ... 35 J7
CHD/CHDH SK8 ... 111 L7
Ladybrook Primary School *BRAM/HZG* SK7 ... 121 H5
Ladysmith Shopping Centre *AUL* OL6 ... 90 E1
Ladywell Hospital Lodge *SALQ* M50 ... 85 K2
Ladywood School *BOLS/LL* BL3 ... 37 L8
Lamberhead Green Community Primary School *WGNW/BIL/OR* WN5 ... 46 D5
Lamberhead Industrial Estate *WGNW/BIL/OR* WN5 ... 46 E7
Lancashire CCC (Old Trafford) *STRET* M32 ... 97 J1
Lancasterian School *DID/WITH* M20 ... 98 B7
Lance Burn Health Centre *SLFD* M6 ... 86 D2
Landgate Industrial Estate *AIMK* WN4 ... 63 K4
The Landgate School *AIMK* WN4 ... 63 K5
Lane End Primary School *CHD/CHDH* SK8 ... 120 E2
Langley Primary School *MDTN* M24 ... 57 H1
Langworthy Clinic *SLFD* M6 ... 86 C2
Langworthy Road Primary School *SLFD* M6 ... 86 C1
La Pergola Hotel *UPML* OL3 ... 44 E1
Lark Hill Primary School *EDGY/DAV* SK3 ... 12 D6
SLFD M6 ... 86 C2
Last Drop Village Hotel *EDGW/EG* BL7 ... 22 D3
The Last Drop Village *EDGW/EG* BL7 ... 22 D3
Lavenham Business Centre *CHAD* OL9 ... 8 D7
Law Courts *BOL* BL1 ... 2 D5
Lawn Cemetery *ALT* WA14 ... 107 G4
Lawnhurst Trading Estate *CHD/CHDH* SK8 ... 111 L7
Leigh Business Park *LEIGH* WN7 ... 81 L1
Leigh CC *LEIGH* WN7 ... 81 H2
Leigh CE Infant School *LEIGH* WN7 ... 66 C7
Leigh CE Junior School *LEIGH* WN7 ... 66 C7

Leigh Central Primary School *LEIGH* WN7 ... 66 C7
Leigh Centurions RLFC *LEIGH* WN7 ... 66 B6
Leigh County Court *LEIGH* WN7 ... 66 C7
Leigh FC *LEIGH* WN7 ... 66 B6
Leigh Golf Club *GOL/RIS/CUL* WA3 ... 81 G8
Leigh Infant & Primary School *HYDE* SK14 ... 102 B2
Leigh Infirmary *LEIGH* WN7 ... 66 D5
Leigh Rangers ARLFC *LEIGH* WN7 ... 67 G8
Leigh RUFC *LEIGH* WN7 ... 81 H3
Leigh Street Primary School *HYDE* SK14 ... 102 C2
Lemon Park Industrial Estate *HEY* OL10 ... 41 H3
Levenshulme Baths *BNG/LEV* M19 ... 99 L3
Levenshulme Health Centre *BNG/LEV* M19 ... 99 L3
Levenshulme High School *BNG/LEV* M19 ... 99 K5
Levenshulme Trading Estate *BNG/LEV* M19 ... 99 M2
Lever Edge Primary School *BOLS/LL* BL3 ... 52 A2
Leverhulme Park Athletics Stadium *BOLS/LL* BL3 ... 37 G6
Lever Park School *HOR/BR* BL6 ... 33 M1
Light Oaks Junior School *SLFD* M6 ... 70 L8
Lily Lane J & I School *NEWH/MOS* M40 ... 73 K4
Limehurst Primary School *OLDS* OL8 ... 75 G4
Limeside Primary School *OLDS* OL8 ... 74 F3
The Limes School *AULW* OL7 ... 75 K8
Lime Tree Primary School *SALE* M33 ... 109 H1
Linden Road Primary School *DTN/ASHW* M34 ... 101 K1
Lindow Primary School *WILM/AE* SK9 ... 130 A1
Linguard Business Park *MILN* OL16 ... 11 G5
Linkway Industrial Estate *MDTN* M24 ... 57 L1
Linnyshaw Industrial Estate *FWTH* BL4 ... 53 H6
Littleborough CC *LIT* OL15 ... 21 M6
Littleborough Primary School *LIT* OL15 ... 21 M5
Little Heaton VC CE Primary School *MDTN* M24 ... 56 F5
Little Hulton Skills Centre *WALK* M28 ... 52 D8
Little Lever School Specialist Language College *BOLS/LL* BL3 ... 53 H1
Littlemoor Primary School *OLDE* OL4 ... 59 M4
Littlemoss Business Park *DROY* M43 ... 89 M1
Littlemoss High School *DROY* M43 ... 74 F8
Little Theatre *TYLD* M29 ... 67 J4
Livingstone Primary School *MOSL* OL5 ... 76 E4
L & M Business Park *ALT* WA14 ... 107 L6
Lobden Golf Club *WHIT* OL12 ... 20 C5
Local Studies Library *OLD* OL1 ... 9 K6
Lockett Business Park *AIMK* WN4 ... 63 M7
Lockside Medical Centre *STLY* SK15 ... 91 L2
Longdendale Community Language College *HYDE* SK14 ... 92 F7
Longdendale Recreation Centre *HYDE* SK14 ... 103 J1
Longford Park Special School *STRET* M32 ... 97 J2
Longford Trading Estate *STRET* M32 ... 97 G1
Longshoot Health Centre *WGN* WN1 ... 15 J2
Longsight CC *WGTN/LGST* M12 ... 99 K1
Longsight Health Centre *WGTN/LGST* M12 ... 88 C8
Longsight Industrial Estate *WGTN/LGST* M12 ... 88 C8
Lords College *BOLE* BL2 ... 3 G7
Loreto Grammar School *ALT* WA14 ... 107 M4
Lostock College *STRET* M32 ... 96 D1
Lostock Hall Primary School *POY/DIS* SK12 ... 128 F1
Lostock Industrial Estate *HOR/BR* BL6 ... 34 B5
Lostock Primary School *HOR/BR* BL6 ... 34 F6
Lower Broughton Health Centre *BRO* M7 ... 72 A8
Lowercroft Primary School *TOT/BURYW* BL8 ... 38 B2
Lower Kersal Primary School *BRO* M7 ... 71 L6
Lower Park Primary School *POY/DIS* SK12 ... 121 L8
Lowerplace Primary School *MILN* OL16 ... 28 E8
Lowes Park Golf Club *BURY* BL9 ... 25 K6
Low Hall Community Primary School *WGNE/HIN* WN2 ... 64 D1
The Lowry Hotel *CSLFD* M3 ... 6 D3
The Lowry *TRPK* M17 ... 86 B5
Lowton Business Park *GOL/RIS/CUL* WA3 ... 80 D4
Lowton Community Sports College *GOL/RIS/CUL* WA3 ... 80 E4
Lowton J & I School *GOL/RIS/CUL* WA3 ... 80 D5

Lowton St Marys CE Primary School *GOL/RIS/CUL* WA3 ... 80 E4
Lowton West Primary School *GOL/RIS/CUL* WA3 ... 79 M4
Ludworth Primary School *MPL/ROM* SK6 ... 114 D4
Lum Head Primary School *CHD/CHDH* SK8 ... 119 K1
The Lyceum Musical Theatre *OLD* OL1 ... 9 J6
Lyme Community Primary School *NEWLW* WA12 ... 78 C8
Lyndhurst Primary School *DUK* SK16 ... 90 F3
OLDS OL8 ... 75 G1
Lyntown Trading Estate *ECC* M30 ... 85 G2
Lyon Industrial Estate *ALT* WA14 ... 107 L5
Lyon Road Industrial Estate *FWTH* BL4 ... 53 H7
Mabs Cross Primary School *WGN* WN1 ... 15 H1
Macdonald Norton Grange Hotel *ROCH* OL11 ... 41 M5
Macdonald Road Medical Centre *IRL* M44 ... 94 B4
Mackenzie Industrial Estate *CHD/CHDH* SK8 ... 111 L6
Magda House Medical Centre *OFTN* SK2 ... 113 J7
Malbern Industrial Estate *DTN/ASHW* M34 ... 89 M8
The Mall Shopping Centre *ECC* M30 ... 85 J2
Malmaison Hotel *CMANE* M1 ... 7 J5
Mancentral Trading Estate *ORD* M5 ... 6 B4
Manchester Academy *NEWH/MOS* M40 ... 87 K8
Manchester Airport Hotel *MANAIR* M90 ... 118 E5
Manchester Airport World Freight Terminal *MANAIR* M90 ... 118 D7
Manchester Aquatics Centre *BRUN/LGST* M13 ... 7 J9
Manchester Arndale Shopping Centre *CMANE* M1 ... 7 G3
Manchester Art Gallery *CMANE* M1 ... 7 G5
Manchester (Barton) Airfield *ECC* M30 ... 84 B5
Manchester Business Park *MANAIR* M90 ... 118 E4
Manchester Business School *HULME* M15 ... 87 K6
Manchester Cathedral *CSLFD* M3 ... 6 F3
Manchester Cathedral Visitor Centre *CSLFD* M3 ... 6 F3
Manchester Central *CSLFD* M3 ... 6 E7
Manchester Central Library *CMANW* M2 ... 6 F6
Manchester Centre for the Deaf *BRUN/LGST* M13 ... 7 L6
Manchester Centre for Vision *BRUN/LGST* M13 ... 87 L7
Manchester City FC (City of Manchester Stadium) *OP/CLY* M11 ... 88 C3
Manchester City Museum & Tour *OP/CLY* M11 ... 88 C2
Manchester College of Arts & Technology *CSLFD* M3 ... 6 C5
WGTN/LGST M12 ... 88 A3
CMANE M1 ... 7 J4
OP/CLY M11 ... 88 E5
Manchester Conference Centre & Hotel *CMANE* M1 ... 7 J7
The Manchester Crematorium *CCHDY* M21 ... 97 M6
Manchester Golf Club *MDTN* M24 ... 41 M6
Manchester Grammar School *BRUN/LGST* M13 ... 99 H2
Manchester High School for Girls *RUSH/FAL* M14 ... 98 F3
Manchester Industrial Centre *CSLFD* M3 ... 6 B6
Manchester International Airport *MANAIR* M90 ... 118 D7
Manchester Islamic High School for Girls *CCHDY* M21 ... 97 K4
Manchester Junior Girls School *BRO* M7 ... 72 A3
Manchester Mesivta High School *PWCH* M25 ... 71 L1
Manchester Mesivta School *PWCH* M25 ... 71 L1
Manchester Metropolitan University *BRUN/LGST* M13 ... 87 M8
CMANE M1 ... 7 G8
CMANE M1 ... 7 H6
DID/WITH M20 ... 110 C1
DID/WITH M20 ... 110 E2
HULME M15 ... 87 K6
OLDTF/WHR M16 ... 98 C2
RUSH/FAL M14 ... 98 F1
Manchester Metropolitan University Institute of Education Didsbury *DID/WITH* M20 ... 110 E2
Manchester Museum *BRUN/LGST* M13 ... 7 J9
Manchester Road Primary School *DROY* M43 ... 89 H3
Manchester Royal Infirmary *BRUN/LGST* M13 ... 87 M7
Manchester RUFC *CHD/CHDH* SK8 ... 120 C6
Manchester School of Management *BRUN/LGST* M13 ... 87 K4
Manchester Southern Cemetery *CCHDY* M21 ... 98 A6
Manchester United FC (Old Trafford) *OLDTF/WHR* M16 ... 86 C7
Manchester United Museum & Tour Centre *TRPK* M17 ... 86 B7
Manchester University *BRUN/LGST* M13 ... 87 M7
Manchester Victoria & Albert Hotel *CSLFD* M3 ... 6 B5
Manchester Youth Theatre *HULME* M15 ... 87 J7

Mandelay Health Centre *BOL* BL1 ... 22 B6
Manley Park Junior School *OLDTF/WHR* M16 ... 97 M2
Manley Park Primary School *OLDTF/WHR* M16 ... 97 M2
Manor Golf Club *FWTH* BL4 ... 53 L8
Manor Green Primary School *DTN/ASHW* M34 ... 101 K4
Manor High School *SALE* M33 ... 95 M7
Manor House Surgery *GLSP* SK13 ... 105 G3
Manway Business Park *ALT* WA14 ... 108 B5
The Maples Medical Centre *NTHM/RTH* M23 ... 109 J8
Marcliffe Industrial Estate *BRAM/HZG* SK7 ... 122 B3
Marjory Lees Health Centre *OLD* OL1 ... 9 K4
Marketgate Shopping Centre *WGN* WN1 ... 14 F3
Market Place Shopping Centre *BOL* BL1 ... 2 E4
Market Street Athletics Track *BURY* BL9 ... 4 F7
Market Street Medical Centre *WGNE/HIN* WN2 ... 49 G6
Markland Hill Primary School *BOL* BL1 ... 35 J4
Marland Hill Primary School *ROCH* OL11 ... 27 M1
Marland Park Golf Club *ROCH* OL11 ... 27 K7
Marlborough Road Primary School *BRO* M7 ... 72 C6
Marple Clinic *MPL/ROM* SK6 ... 114 C6
Marple Golf Club *MPL/ROM* SK6 ... 123 G1
Marple Hall School *MPL/ROM* SK6 ... 113 M5
Marriott Hotel *HALE/TIMP* WA15 ... 118 A5
Marriott Worsley Park Hotel & Country Club *WALK* M28 ... 69 H5
Marsh Green CP School *WGNW/BIL/OR* WN5 ... 47 G4
Marsh Green Health Centre *WGNW/BIL/OR* WN5 ... 47 G3
Marsh Lane Trading Estate *NM/HAY* SK22 ... 124 F5
Marsland Street Industrial Centre *BRAM/HZG* SK7 ... 121 M2
Marston Bentley Industrial Estate *WGNE/HIN* WN2 ... 48 E2
Martland Mill Business Park *WGNW/BIL/OR* WN5 ... 47 G2
Martland Mill Industrial Estate *WGNW/BIL/OR* WN5 ... 46 F2
Marus Bridge Health Centre *WGNS/IIMK* WN3 ... 63 J2
Marus Bridge Primary School *WGNS/IIMK* WN3 ... 63 H2
Masefield Primary School *BOLS/LL* BL3 ... 37 L8
Mason Street Industrial Estate *WGNS/IIMK* WN3 ... 14 D5
Maternity & Child Welfare Clinic *WGNE/HIN* WN2 ... 48 F7
Mather Street Primary School *FAIL* M35 ... 74 A4
Matthew Moss High School *HEY* OL10 ... 27 K8
Mauldeth Medical Centre *DID/WITH* M20 ... 99 G5
Mauldeth Road Primary School *RUSH/FAL* M14 ... 99 H5
Mayfield Industrial Park *IRL* M44 ... 94 F1
Mayfield Primary School *OLD* OL1 ... 59 L4
Mayflower Brewery *WGN* WN1 ... 15 G2
Maypole Farm Estate *PART* SK1 ... 95 G6
Maypole Industrial Estate *WGNE/HIN* WN2 ... 64 F5
Meade Hill School *CHH* M8 ... 56 C8
Meadowbank Primary School *ATH* M46 ... 50 F8
CHD/CHDH SK8 ... 111 J7
Meadow Industrial Estate *FAIL* M35 ... 74 A6
STKP SK1 ... 13 K1
The Meadows School *BKLY* M9 ... 57 J8
Meadway Health Centre *SALE* M33 ... 108 B2
Meanwood Primary School *WHIT* OL12 ... 27 M3
Mechinoh School *BRO* M7 ... 72 B3
Medlock Infant School *BRUN/LGST* M13 ... 7 K9
Medlock Leisure Centre *DROY* M43 ... 89 L1
Medlock Primary School *BRUN/LGST* M13 ... 7 L9
Medlock Valley Community School *OLDS* OL8 ... 75 K1
Megabowl *BURY* BL9 ... 39 L6
OLDTF/WHR M16 ... 86 D7
Melland High School *GTN* M18 ... 100 A2
Mellor Primary School *MPL/ROM* SK6 ... 115 H6
Mellor Sports Club *MPL/ROM* SK6 ... 115 G6
Mellor & Towncliffe Golf Club *MPL/ROM* SK6 ... 115 G7
MEN Arena *CSLFD* M3 ... 6 F1
Mental Health Centre *BOLE* BL2 ... 37 J3
Mere Oaks School *WGN* WN1 ... 31 L7
Mereside Educational Trust *SALE* M33 ... 109 G1
Meridian Clinic *BURY* BL9 ... 4 D5
Mersey Drive Primary School *BURY* BL9 ... 55 M2
Mersey Road Industrial Estate *FAIL* M35 ... 74 E3
Mersey Trading Estate *HTNM* SK4 ... 111 J3

Mersey Vale Primary School *HTNM* SK4 ... 111 K3
Merseyway Centre *STKP* SK1 ... 13 H3
Mesne Lea Primary School *WALK* M28 ... 69 H3
Methodist Cemetery *BOLE* BL2 ... 23 H8
Metro Cinema *AUL* OL6 ... 90 E2
Micklehurst All Saints Primary School *MOSL* OL5 ... 77 H3
Micklehurst CC *MOSL* OL5 ... 77 H3
Middlebrook Retail & Leisure Park *HOR/BR* BL6 ... 34 A4
Middleton Cemetery *MDTN* M24 ... 57 M2
Middleton Crematorium *MDTN* M24 ... 57 M2
Middleton CC *MDTN* M24 ... 57 J2
Middleton Parish Church School *MDTN* M24 ... 57 J2
Middleton Public Baths *MDTN* M24 ... 57 K4
Middleton Shopping Centre *MDTN* M24 ... 57 J4
Middleton Technology School *MDTN* M24 ... 57 L4
Midland Hotel *CMANW* M2 ... 6 F6
Miles Platting Pool *NEWH/MOS* M40 ... 88 A1
Milking Green Industrial Estate *OLDE* OL4 ... 60 D7
Mill 5 Belgrave Industrial Estate *OLDS* OL8 ... 75 K1
Millbrook Business Centre *NTHM/RTH* M23 ... 109 H6
Millbrook Industrial Estate *NTHM/RTH* M23 ... 109 H6
Millbrook Primary School *STLY* SK15 ... 77 H7
WGNW/ST WN6 ... 30 E6
Mill Gate Shopping Centre *BURY* BL9 ... 4 F5
Millingford Industrial Estate *GOL/RIS/CUL* WA3 ... 79 L4
Mills Hill Primary School *CHAD* OL9 ... 58 B4
Mill Street Industrial Estate *BOL* BL1 ... 3 G4
Millwood Primary Special School *BURY* BL9 ... 39 J6
Milnrow CC *MILN* OL16 ... 29 J7
Milnrow CE Aided Primary School *MILN* OL16 ... 29 J6
Milnrow Health Centre *MILN* OL16 ... 29 J7
Milo Industrial Park *DROY* M43 ... 89 L2
Milton St Johns CE Primary School *MOSL* OL5 ... 76 F2
Minden Medical Centre *BURY* BL9 ... 5 G4
Moat House School *HTNM* SK4 ... 112 B1
Monde Trading Estate *TRPK* M17 ... 85 K6
Montague Business Park *OLDTF/WHR* M16 ... 86 D7
Monton Bowling Club *ECC* M30 ... 70 B8
Monton CC *ECC* M30 ... 70 B8
Monton Green Primary School *ECC* M30 ... 70 B8
Monton House Hotel *ECC* M30 ... 85 G1
Monton Medical Centre *ECC* M30 ... 69 M8
Montrose School *WGNW/BIL/OR* WN5 ... 47 G5
Moor Allerton School *DID/WITH* M20 ... 98 C8
Moorfield Community Primary School *IRL* M44 ... 94 D1
Moorfield Primary School *BRAM/HZG* SK7 ... 121 L3
Moorgate Primary School *BOLE* BL2 ... 3 K2
Moorgate Retail Park *BURY* BL9 ... 5 G3
Moorhouse Primary School *MILN* OL16 ... 29 H6
Moorlands Junior School *SALE* M33 ... 97 H7
Moor Lane Bus Station *BOL* BL1 ... 2 D5
Moorside High School *SWIN* M27 ... 70 A5
Moorside Leisure Centre *SWIN* M27 ... 70 A5
Moorside Primary School *DROY* M43 ... 89 L3
SWIN M27 ... 70 A5
Moravian College *DROY* M43 ... 89 K4
Mornington High School *WGNE/HIN* WN2 ... 49 J7
Morris Green Business Park *BOLS/LL* BL3 ... 35 M8
Moses Gate Country Park *FWTH* BL4 ... 53 H2
Moses Park Country Park *BOLS/LL* BL3 ... 37 G8
Moss Field Community Primary School *FWTH* OL10 ... 40 F1
Mossfield CP School *SWIN* M27 ... 70 C3
Moss Hey Primary School *BRAM/HZG* SK7 ... 120 E7
Moss Industrial Estate *GOL/RIS/CUL* WA3 ... 80 G3
MILN OL16 ... 11 K8
Moss Lane Industrial Estate *ROY/SHW* OL2 ... 59 K1
Mossley AFC *MOSL* OL5 ... 76 F3
Mossley Health Centre *MOSL* OL5 ... 76 F3
Mossley Hollins High School *MOSL* OL5 ... 77 H3
Moss Park J & I School *STRET* M32 ... 96 F2
Moss Side Health Centre *RUSH/FAL* M14 ... 87 K4
Moss Side Leisure Centre *HULME* M15 ... 87 J4

Moss View Primary School PART M31 ... 106 D1
Moston Fields Primary School NEWH/MOS M40 ... 73 K3
Moston Indoor Market NEWH/MOS M40 ... 73 J4
Moston Lane Primary School BKLY M9 ... 73 H4
Mottram CE Primary School HYDE SK14 ... 103 K1
Mottram St Andrew Primary School MCFLDN SK10 ... 131 L2
Mount Carmel RC Junior School BKLY M9 ... 73 K3
Mount Carmel RC Primary School BKLY M9 ... 73 K3
Mountheath Industrial Park PWCH M25 ... 71 L4
Mount Pleasant Business Centre OLDE OL4 ... 59 L6
Mount St Joseph Business & Enterprise College BOLS/LL BL3 ... 52 C2
The Museum of Science & Industry in Manchester CSLFD M3 ... 6 B6
Museum of the Manchester Regiment AUL OL6 ... 90 C4
Museum of Trade Union History CMANE M1 ... 7 G6
Museum of Transport CHH M8 ... 72 D6
The Music School CHH M8 ... 72 D4
Mytham Primary School BOLS/LL BL3 ... 53 L1
Nasmyth Business Centre ECC M30 ... 84 F2
National Cycling Centre (Velodrome) OP/CLY M11 ... 88 D7
National Industrial Estate AULW OL7 ... 90 C4
National Squash Centre OP/CLY M11 ... 88 C2
National Trading Estate BRAM/HZG SK7 ... 121 L1
Natural History Museum CHAD OL9 ... 8 D9
Navigation Primary School ALT WA14 ... 108 A6
Navigation Trading Estate NEWH/MOS M40 ... 73 J4
Nelson Business Centre DTN/ASHW M34 ... 90 C8
Nether Alderley Mill MCFLDN SK10 ... 130 D7
Nether Alderley Primary School MCFLDN SK10 ... 130 D6
Neville Street Industrial Estate CHAD OL9 ... 8 C5
Nevill Road Infant School BRAM/HZG SK7 ... 121 J4
Newall Green High School NTHM/RTH M23 ... 109 J8
Newall Green Primary School NTHM/RTH M23 ... 109 L8
New Ardwick Sports Centre WGTN/LGST M12 ... 88 A6
New Bridge School OLDS OL8 ... 74 E4
Newbridge Special School OLDS OL8 ... 75 L2
Newbrook School DID/WITH M20 ... 98 B7
Newby Road Industrial Estate BRAM/HZG SK7 ... 121 M2
New Croft Community High School SLFD M6 ... 86 C1
New Harvest Learning Centre CSLFD M3 ... 6 D3
Newhaven Business Park ECC M30 ... 85 H3
Newhey Community Primary School MILN OL16 ... 29 K8
New Kingsway Health Centre BNG/LEV M19 ... 99 G8
Newlands Medical Centre BOL BL1 ... 35 K5
New Mills FC NM/HAY SK22 ... 124 F4
New Mills Golf Club NM/HAY SK22 ... 124 C3
New Mills Leisure Centre & Swimming Pool NM/HAY SK22 ... 124 E4
New Mills Primary School NM/HAY SK22 ... 124 D4
New Mills School & Sixth Form Centre NM/HAY SK22 ... 124 E4
New Moston Primary School NEWH/MOS M40 ... 74 B2
New Museum OLD OL1 ... 9 H3
New North Manchester Golf Club MDTN M24 ... 57 G4
New Springs Holy Family RC Primary School WGNE/HIN WN2 ... 48 D3
Newton Bank Preparatory School NEWLW WA12 ... 79 H8
Newton Business Park HYDE SK14 ... 91 K7
Newton Health Clinic NEWLW WA12 ... 78 E8
Newton-le-Willows Community High School NEWLW WA12 ... 79 G7
Newton-le-Willows High School NEWLW WA12 ... 79 G7
Newton-le-Willows Sports Club NEWLW WA12 ... 78 F8
Newton Moor Industrial Estate HYDE SK14 ... 91 H7
Newton Street Police Museum CMANE M1 ... 7 G4
Newton Westpark Primary School LEIGH WN7 ... 65 M4
Newtown Primary School NM/HAY SK22 ... 124 D6
Nicholas Varley Community School NEWH/MOS M40 ... 73 H8
Nicholls Sixth Form Centre WGTN/LGST M12 ... 88 A6
Nicol Mere School AIMK WN4 ... 63 K7
Norbury Hall Primary School BRAM/HZG SK7 ... 122 A3

Norden Community Primary School WHIT OL12 ... 27 J2
Norden CC WHIT OL12 ... 27 H2
Norley Hall CC WGNW/BIL/OR WN5 ... 46 E5
Norris Bank Medical Centre HTNM SK4 ... 12 C4
Norris Bank Primary School HTNM SK4 ... 12 B1
Nortex Business Centre BOL BL1 ... 35 M4
Northbank Industrial Park IRL M44 ... 94 B6
North Cestrian Grammar School ALT WA14 ... 107 M7
North Chadderton School CHAD OL9 ... 58 D2
North Cheshire Jewish Primary School CHD/CHDH SK8 ... 119 K2
Northenden Golf Club WYTH/NTH M22 ... 110 B2
Northenden Primary School WYTH/NTH M22 ... 110 A3
Northern A & O Medical Centre BURY BL9 ... 4 F4
Northern Cemetery SWIN M27 ... 71 J5
Northern Moor Clinic NTHM/RTH M23 ... 109 J3
North Grecian Street Primary School BRO M7 ... 71 M6
North Heaton Primary School HTNM SK4 ... 99 M6
North Manchester General Hospital CHH M8 ... 72 F3
North Manchester High School for Boys BKLY M9 ... 73 L1
North Manchester High School for Girls NEWH/MOS M40 ... 73 K2
North Quarry Business Park WGNNW/ST WN6 ... 30 A3
North Quays Business Park ALT WA14 ... 108 B3
North Reddish Health Centre RDSH SK5 ... 100 B3
North Reddish J & I School RDSH SK5 ... 100 C3
North Trafford College STRET M32 ... 86 C8
North Walkden Primary School WALK M28 ... 52 F7
Novotel CMANE M1 ... 6 F6
Novotel WALK M28 ... 69 H7
Nugent House School WGNW/BIL/OR WN5 ... 62 A8
Oakdale Special School DUK SK16 ... 91 G6
Oakenclough Primary School WILM/AE SK9 ... 127 H3
Oakfield Primary School HYDE SK14 ... 91 H7
Oakfield Trading Estate HALE/TIMP WA15 ... 108 B7
Oakgrove School CHD/CHDH SK8 ... 119 L5
Oakhill Trading Estate WALK M28 ... 52 E7
Oaklands Infant School WILM/AE SK9 ... 127 J3
Oakleigh Medical Centre CHH M8 ... 72 E3
The Oaks Business Park NTHM/RTH M23 ... 109 G5
The Oaks Primary School BOL BL1 ... 22 C6
Oakwood High School CCHDY M21 ... 97 L1
SLFD M6 ... 70 F7
Octagon Theatre BOL BL1 ... 2 E5
Odeon Cinema ROCH OL11 ... 28 B8
Offerton Green Clinic OFTN SK2 ... 113 J7
Offerton Health Centre OFTN SK2 ... 112 E4
Offerton High School OFTN SK2 ... 113 H5
Offerton Industrial Estate STKP SK1 ... 112 E5
Old Boston Trading Estate RNFD/HAY WA11 ... 78 D4
Oldfield Brow Primary School ALT WA14 ... 107 J7
Old Hall Clinic CHD/CHDH SK8 ... 110 E6
Old Hall Drive Primary School GTN M18 ... 89 G8
Old Hall Primary School TOT/BURYW BL8 ... 24 E5
Oldham Athletic FC (Boundary Park) ROY/SHW OL2 ... 59 G2
Oldham Broadway Business Park CHAD OL9 ... 58 B4
Oldham Business Centre OLD OL1 ... 9 H7
Oldham Central Industrial Park OLD OL1 ... 9 M3
Oldham Central Trading Park OLD OL1 ... 9 M2
Oldham College CHAD OL9 ... 8 F5
Oldham County Court OLD OL1 ... 9 G4
Oldham Crematorium OLDS OL8 ... 74 F3
Oldham CC OLD OL1 ... 59 M3
Oldham Golf Club OLDE OL4 ... 60 C8
Oldham RUFC OLDS OL8 ... 75 J4
Oldham Sixth Form College OLDS OL8 ... 9 G7
Oldham Sports Centre OLD OL1 ... 9 J5
Oldham West Business Centre CHAD OL9 ... 8 B5
Old Mill Hotel RAMS BL0 ... 18 E5
Old Moat J & I School DID/WITH M20 ... 98 D5
Old Rectory Hotel DTN/ASHW M34 ... 101 K5
Old Trafford Community School OLDTF/WHR M16 ... 86 F6
Oldwood Primary School WYTH/NTH M22 ... 118 D2

Olympia Trading Estate HULME M15 ... 6 D8
Olympic House MANAIR M90 ... 118 E5
Open University CCHDY M21 ... 97 L3
Opera House CSLFD M3 ... 6 D5
The Operating Theatre STRET M32 ... 97 H1
Orchard House Day Hospital ROY/SHW OL2 ... 43 H8
Orchard Industrial Estate SLFD M6 ... 71 K8
Orchard Trading Estate SLFD M6 ... 71 J7
Ordsall Hall Museum ORD M5 ... 86 E6
Ordsall Health Centre ORD M5 ... 86 E4
Ordsall Recreation Centre ORD M5 ... 86 D5
Oriel Bank High School OFTN SK2 ... 112 C7
Oriental Arch CMANE M1 ... 7 G5
Orion Business Park EDGY/DAV SK3 ... 111 M7
Orion Trading Estate TRPK M17 ... 85 K4
Orrell Clinic WGNW/BIL/OR WN5 ... 46 B5
Orrell Holgate Primary School WGNW/BIL/OR WN5 ... 46 B7
Orrell Newfold Community Primary School WGNW/BIL/OR WN5 ... 46 A8
Orrell RUFC WGNW/BIL/OR WN5 ... 46 B7
Orrell Water Park WGNW/BIL/OR WN5 ... 46 B8
Orrishmere Primary School CHD/CHDH SK8 ... 120 C1
Osborne Trading Estate CHAD OL9 ... 8 D3
Oswald Road Primary School CCHDY M21 ... 97 K3
Oulder Hill Community Language College ROCH OL11 ... 27 L5
Our Lady Immaculate Catholic Primary School WALK WN4 ... 63 G6
Our Lady of Grace RC Primary School PWCH M25 ... 55 K6
Our Lady of Lourdes Catholic Primary School PART M31 ... 106 B1
Our Lady of Lourdes RC Primary School FWTH BL4 ... 52 D4
TOT/BURYW BL8 ... 24 F6
Our Lady of Mount Carmel RC Primary School AUL OL6 ... 76 A8
Our Lady of the Rosary RC Primary School URM M41 ... 84 F8
Our Lady RC Primary School WGNE/HIN WN2 ... 32 F7
Our Lady & St Anselms RC Primary School WHIT OL12 ... 20 B2
Our Lady & St Pauls RC Primary School HEY OL10 ... 40 B2
Our Ladys Catholic Primary School EDGY/DAV SK3 ... 13 G7
Our Lady's RC High School BKLY M9 ... 57 G6
Our Ladys RC High School ROY/SHW OL2 ... 59 G1
Our Ladys RC Primary School OLDE OL4 ... 60 B1
OLDTF/WHR M16 ... 98 A1
Our Lady & the Lancashire Martyrs RC Primary School WALK M28 ... 68 D1
Outwood Primary School CHD/CHDH SK8 ... 119 L5
Overdale Crematorium BOL BL1 ... 35 K6
Overdale School MPL/ROM SK6 ... 113 J3
Owl Business Centre OLDE OL4 ... 60 A4
Oxford Grove Primary School BOL BL1 ... 35 M3
OYY Lubavitch Girls School BRO M7 ... 72 A3
Padfield Primary School GLSP SK13 ... 93 L7
Pagefield Industrial Estate WGNNW/ST WN6 ... 14 A2
Palace Cinema STLY SK15 ... 91 K2
The Palace Hotel CMANE M1 ... 7 G7
Palace Theatre CMANE M1 ... 7 G7
Palm Business Centre CHAD OL9 ... 8 A5
Paragon Business Park HOR/BR BL6 ... 34 B4
Paragon Industrial Estate LIT OL15 ... 29 J1
Parish Church CE Junior School OLD OL1 ... 9 J3
Park Business Centre WGNE/HIN WN2 ... 49 G8
Parker International Estate DUK SK16 ... 90 E5
Parkfield Industrial Estate MDTN M24 ... 57 H4
Parkfield Primary School MDTN M24 ... 57 H3
Park Industrial Estate AIMK WN4 ... 78 B1
Parklands High School WYTH/NTH M22 ... 118 E1
Park Mill Industrial Estate MOSL OL5 ... 61 G8
Park Parade Industrial Estate AUL OL6 ... 90 D2
Park Road CP School SALE M33 ... 96 D6
Park Road Primary School ALT WA14 ... 108 B4
Park School NTHM/RTH M23 ... 109 J4
Parkside Industrial Estate ROY/SHW OL2 ... 43 H8

Parkview Centre OLDS OL8 ... 9 K8
Parkway Business Centre OLDTF/WHR M16 ... 98 C3
Parkway Four Industrial Estate TRPK M17 ... 85 K5
Parkway Trading Estate STRET M32 ... 85 K7
Parochial CE Primary School AUL OL6 ... 90 F1
WHTN BL5 ... 50 B4
Parrenthorn High School PWCH M25 ... 55 M6
Parrs Wood Technology College DID/WITH M20 ... 111 G3
Parsonage Retail Park LEIGH WN7 ... 66 B6
Partington CP School PART M31 ... 106 C1
Partington Health Centre PART M31 ... 106 C1
Partington Shopping Centre PART M31 ... 106 C1
Partington Sports Centre PART M31 ... 106 C1
Peacefield Primary School MPL/ROM SK6 ... 114 B7
Peacock CP School GTN M18 ... 88 F6
Peacock Primary School HULME M15 ... 6 C9
Pearlbrook Industrial Estate HOR/BR BL6 ... 33 L1
Pear New Mill Industrial Estate MPL/ROM SK6 ... 112 F2
Peel Brow Primary School RAMS BL0 ... 19 G6
The Peel Centre STKP SK1 ... 13 L3
Peel Hall CP School LHULT M38 ... 68 C1
Peel Hall Primary School WYTH/NTH M22 ... 119 H1
Peel Health Centre BURY BL9 ... 4 F6
Peel Moat Recreation Centre HTNM SK4 ... 99 L7
Peerglow Industrial Estate ALT WA14 ... 108 B4
Pemberton Business Centre WGNW/BIL/OR WN5 ... 46 F6
Pemberton Clinic WGNW/BIL/OR WN5 ... 47 G6
Pendleton College SLFD M6 ... 85 M1
Pendleton Medical Centre SLFD M6 ... 86 D2
Pennant Industrial Estate OLD OL1 ... 59 L4
Pennine Business Park HEY OL10 ... 40 E4
Pennington Flash Country Park LEIGH WN7 ... 80 F2
Pennington Golf Club LEIGH WN7 ... 80 F1
Pepper Mill Business Park WGN WN1 ... 15 H5
Peterloo Medical Centre MDTN M24 ... 57 H4
Philips High School WHTF M45 ... 55 H4
Phoenix Industrial Estate FAIL M35 ... 74 D4
Phoenix Medical Centre STKP SK1 ... 13 K7
Phoenix Park Industrial Estate HEY OL10 ... 41 G9
Piccadilly Trading Estate CMANE M1 ... 7 M6
Pictor Special School SALE M33 ... 96 C8
Pike Fold Primary School BKLY M9 ... 72 F1
Pikes Lane Primary School BOLS/LL BL3 ... 2 A7
Pilot Industrial Estate BOLS/LL BL3 ... 36 E8
Pilsworth Industrial Estate BURY BL9 ... 39 L6
Pinfold J & I School HYDE SK14 ... 103 H3
Pinnacle Business Centre HTNM SK4 ... 13 H1
Pioneer Industrial Estate WGNW/BIL/OR WN5 ... 47 H6
Piper Hill School NTHM/RTH M23 ... 109 L2
Plantation Industrial Estate AUL OL6 ... 90 F2
Plant Hill High School BKLY M9 ... 56 F8
Plasman Industrial Centre BNG/LEV M19 ... 99 K3
Platt Bridge Clinic WGNE/HIN WN2 ... 64 D2
Players Theatre UPML OL3 ... 45 H8
Playhouse Theatre ORD M5 ... 86 D2
Plodder Lane Primary School FWTH BL4 ... 52 E3
Plymouth Court Business Centre BRUN/LGST M13 ... 87 M7
Plymouth Grove Primary School BRUN/LGST M13 ... 88 B7
The Point Retail Park MILN OL16 ... 11 G4
Poland Industrial Estate ANC M4 ... 7 L2
Portland Basin Museum AULW OL7 ... 90 D3
Portland Industrial Estate BURY BL9 ... 25 K8
Portwood Trading Estate STKP SK1 ... 13 M2
Potters House School BURY BL9 ... 25 J6
Pownall Green Primary School BRAM/HZG SK7 ... 121 G8
Pownall Hall School WILM/AE SK9 ... 126 D1
Poynton Clinic POY/DIS SK12 ... 122 A8
Poynton High School & Performing Arts College POY/DIS SK12 ... 129 J2
Poynton Leisure Centre POY/DIS SK12 ... 129 K2
Poynton Sports Club POY/DIS SK12 ... 122 A8
Premier Travel Inn AIMK WN4 ... 78 E2
ALT WA14 ... 108 B3
ALT WA14 ... 108 A5
CCHDY M21 ... 98 A7
CHAD OL9 ... 74 B2
CHD/CHDH SK8 ... 119 L2
CHH M8 ... 56 C8
CMANE M1 ... 6 F6
DTN/ASHW M34 ... 100 F1
GOL/RIS/CUL WA3 ... 79 L5
HOR/BR BL6 ... 34 C4
HULME M15 ... 6 E9
HYDE SK14 ... 103 H1
MDTN M24 ... 56 E5
MILN OL16 ... 29 K8
OFTN SK2 ... 112 D6
PWCH M25 ... 55 K7
SALE M33 ... 96 A6
SALQ M50 ... 86 D5
STKP SK1 ... 13 K4
SWIN M27 ... 70 B6
SWIN M27 ... 70 F5
TRPK M17 ... 85 G6
WGNNW/ST WN6 ... 30 E3
WGNS/IIMK WN3 ... 63 J3
WGNW/BIL/OR WN5 ... 46 C5
WILM/AE SK9 ... 127 H1
WILM/AE SK9 ... 126 C5
WILM/AE SK9 ... 130 D4
WYTH/NTH M22 ... 119 J4
Premier Travel Inn (Manchester Trafford Centre) URM M41 ... 85 G5
Prestolee Primary School RAD M26 ... 53 L4
Prestwich Arts College PWCH M25 ... 55 L7
Prestwich Golf Club PWCH M25 ... 71 K3
Prestwich Health Centre PWCH M25 ... 55 K7
Prestwich Hospital PWCH M25 ... 55 J6
Prestwich Industrial Estate ATH M46 ... 50 E8
Prestwich Preparatory School PWCH M25 ... 55 M7
Priestnall School HTNM SK4 ... 111 J1
Prince of Wales Business Park OLD OL1 ... 59 M4
Princess on Portland CMANE M1 ... 7 G6
The Printworks Leisure Complex ANC M4 ... 7 G2
Priorsleigh Medical Centre POY/DIS SK12 ... 122 A8
Propps Hall Primary School FAIL M35 ... 74 B6
Prospect House Medical Centre WGNW/BIL/OR WN5 ... 46 D6
Prospect Industrial Estate WGNE/HIN WN2 ... 49 G7
Prospect Vale Primary School CHD/CHDH SK8 ... 119 K3
Pump House People's History Museum CSLFD M3 ... 6 C4
The Quadrangle Business Centre WGNE/HIN WN2 ... 49 L8
Quality Hotel WGN WN1 ... 15 H3
Quality Hotel (Altrincham) ALT WA14 ... 116 F2
Quarry Bank Mill & Styal Estate (NT) WILM/AE SK9 ... 126 C2
Queen Elizabeth Hall OLD OL1 ... 9 H5
Queen Elizabeths School MDTN M24 ... 41 J8
Queensbridge Primary School FWTH BL4 ... 52 F4
Queensgate Primary School BRAM/HZG SK7 ... 121 G8
Queens Road Primary School CHD/CHDH SK8 ... 120 C1
Rack House Primary School NTHM/RTH M23 ... 109 K3
Radcliffe Borough AFC RAD M26 ... 38 B8
Radcliffe CC RAD M26 ... 38 B8
Radcliffe Hall CE Methodist Primary School RAD M26 ... 38 F8
Radcliffe Hall CE Primary School RAD M26 ... 38 B8
Radcliffe Riverside School RAD M26 ... 54 C1
Radcliffe Tower (Remains of) RAD M26 ... 55 G1
Radclyffe Athletics Centre CHAD OL9 ... 58 C5
Radclyffe Primary School ORD M5 ... 86 D5
The Radclyffe School (Lower) CHAD OL9 ... 58 C6
The Radclyffe School (Upper) CHAD OL9 ... 58 C5
Radisson SAS Hotel MANAIR M90 ... 118 D5
Raikes Lane Industrial Estate BOLS/LL BL3 ... 36 E8
Railway Street Industrial Estate GTN M18 ... 88 F6
Ralph Williams Clinic WHIT OL12 ... 28 F1
Ramada Hotel HOR/BR BL6 ... 33 K5
Ramillies Hall School CHD/CHDH SK8 ... 120 E2
Ramsbottom Cemetery RAMS BL0 ... 18 D8
Ramsbottom Cottage Hospital RAMS BL0 ... 18 F7
Ramsbottom Health Centre RAMS BL0 ... 18 E6
Ramsbottom Swimming Pool RAMS BL0 ... 18 F5
Rassbottom Industrial Estate STLY SK15 ... 91 J2
Ravensbury Community School OP/CLY M11 ... 88 D2
Ravensfield Industrial Estate DUK SK16 ... 90 D3
Ravenside Retail Park BOLE BL2 ... 2 F7
Rectory CE Primary School AIMK WN4 ... 63 G7
Reddish Vale Golf Club RDSH SK5 ... 100 D6
Reddish Vale Technology College RDSH SK5 ... 100 C5

Red Lane Community School
BOLE BL2 .... 37 J3
Red Rose Retail Centre
ORD M5 .... 86 E3
Reebok Museum
HOR/BR BL6 .... 34 A4
Regal Industrial Estate
WGTN/LGST M12 .... 88 C5
Regent Cinema
MPL/ROM SK6 .... 114 C6
Regent Park Golf Course
HOR/BR BL6 .... 34 E5
Regent Trading Estate
ORD M5 .... 6 A4
The Regimental Museum of the
Lancashire Fusiliers
TOT/BURYW BL8 .... 38 E3
Reliance Trading Estate
NEWH/MOS M40 .... 73 M5
Renaissance Hotel
CSLFD M3 .... 6 E3
Ribble Drive Primary School
WHTF M45 .... 55 K3
Richmond Medical Centre
AUL OL6 .... 90 F1
Richmond Park Athletics
Stadium *AULW* OL7 .... 75 H8
Richmond Park School
WGTN/LGST M12 .... 88 B7
Richmond Primary School
CHAD OL9 .... 8 F6
The Ridge College
MPL/ROM SK6 .... 114 B7
Ridge Danyers College
CHD/CHDH SK8 .... 120 A1
Ridgmont Cemetery
HOR/BR BL6 .... 34 A1
Ringway Golf Club
HALE/TIMP WA15 .... 117 L3
Ringway Primary School
WYTH/NTH M22 .... 118 F4
Ringway Trading Estate
WYTH/NTH M22 .... 119 G4
Riverside Business Park
WILM/AE SK9 .... 126 F5
R L Hughes Primary School
AIMK WN4 .... 61 D1
Roaches Industrial Estate
MOSL OL5 .... 61 H8
Robin Park Arena
WGNW/BIL/OR WN5 .... 14 A3
Robin Park Sports Centre
WGNW/BIL/OR WN5 .... 47 J4
Rochdale AFC
(Spotland Stadium)
ROCH OL11 .... 27 M4
Rochdale Cemetery
ROCH OL11 .... 27 L5
Rochdale Crematorium
ROCH OL11 .... 27 L5
Rochdale Cricket, Lacrosse &
Squash Club
ROCH OL11 .... 10 A4
Rochdale Curtain Theatre
WHIT M16 .... 10 D7
Rochdale Golf Club
ROCH OL11 .... 27 K4
Rochdale Healthcare
WHIT OL12 .... 21 H7
Rochdale Industrial Centre
ROCH OL11 .... 10 A6
Rochdale Infirmary
WHIT OL12 .... 10 E1
Rodney House School
BNG/LEV M19 .... 99 J4
Roe Cross Industrial Park
HYDE SK14 .... 92 D7
Roker Industrial Estate
OLD OL1 .... 59 L4
Rolls Crescent Primary School
HULME M15 .... 87 H7
Roman Fort
CSLFD M3 .... 6 C7
Romiley Golf Club
MPL/ROM SK6 .... 114 A1
Romiley Health Centre
MPL/ROM SK6 .... 113 M2
Romiley Primary School
MPL/ROM SK6 .... 114 A2
Roscow Fold Primary School
BOLE BL2 .... 37 H4
Rose Bridge High School
WGN WN1 .... 15 M3
Rosedale Shopping Centre
NEWH/MOS M40 .... 73 M7
Rosehill Methodist Community
Primary School
AUL OL6 .... 76 C6
Rosehill Methodist Community
School *AUL* OL6 .... 76 C7
Rose Hill Primary School
MPL/ROM SK6 .... 114 B6
Ross Business Centre
WGNW/BIL/OR WN5 .... 47 G7
Rossendale School
RAMS BL0 .... 19 J5
Roundthorn Industrial Estate
NTHM/RTH M23 .... 109 H6
Roundthorn Primary School
OLDE OL4 .... 59 M7
Roundwood School
WYTH/NTH M22 .... 109 M5
Roxy Cinema
OLDS OL8 .... 74 D3
Royal Albert Edward Infirmary
WGN WN1 .... 47 M2
Royal Bolton Hospital
FWTH BL4 .... 52 C3
Royal Exchange Clinic
CMANW M2 .... 6 F4
Royal Exchange Shopping
Centre
CMANE M1 .... 6 F3
MILN OL16 .... 10 D4
Royal Exchange Theatre
CSLFD M3 .... 6 F4
Royal Manchester Childrens
Hospital *SWIN* M27 .... 70 E5
Royal Northern College of Music
HULME M15 .... 87 K6
Royal Oak Industrial Estate
STKP SK1 .... 13 K7
Royal Oak Primary School
NTHM/RTH M23 .... 109 K5
Royal Oldham Hospital
OLD OL1 .... 8 F1
Royal Pennine Trading Estate
ROCH OL11 .... 41 L1
Royce Trading Estate
TRPK M17 .... 85 J5
Royle Pennine Trading Estate
ROCH OL11 .... 42 A1

Royton & Crompton School
ROY/SHW OL2 .... 43 K8
Royton Medical Centre
ROY/SHW OL2 .... 43 G8
Royton Public Baths
ROY/SHW OL2 .... 43 H8
Rugby Road Industrial Estate
WHIT OL12 .... 11 G1
Rumworth School
BOLS/LL BL3 .... 35 J7
Rushcroft Primary School
ROY/SHW OL2 .... 43 L4
Russell Scott Primary School
DTN/ASHW M34 .... 90 B8
Rycroft Park Sports Club
CHD/CHDH SK8 .... 120 B3
Rydings Special School
WHIT OL12 .... 20 F8
Ryecroft Business Park
WHIT OL12 .... 90 C3
The Ryleys School
WILM/AE SK9 .... 130 C3
Sacred Heart Catholic Primary
School *WGNE/HIN* WN2 .... 65 L1
Sacred Heart RC Infant School
GTN M18 .... 88 F8
Sacred Heart RC Junior School
GTN M18 .... 88 F8
Sacred Heart RC Primary
School *ATH* M46 .... 67 H3
LEIGH WN7 .... 66 B7
MILN OL16 .... 11 L6
NTHM/RTH M23 .... 109 J4
OLD OL1 .... 59 M2
WGNNW/ST WN6 .... 47 J2
WHTN BL5 .... 50 C3
Saddleworth Business Centre
UPML OL3 .... 45 J8
Saddleworth Golf Club
UPML OL3 .... 61 K4
Saddleworth Museum &
Art Gallery
UPML OL3 .... 61 K4
Saddleworth Preparatory School
OLDE OL4 .... 60 F4
Saddleworth School
UPML OL3 .... 61 L3
Saddleworth Swimming Pool
UPML OL3 .... 61 L5
St Aelreds RC Technology College
NEWLW WA12 .... 79 G8
St Agnes CE Primary School
BRUN/LGST M13 .... 99 J1
OLDE OL4 .... 60 D7
St Aidan & Oswalds RC Primary
School *ROY/SHW* OL2 .... 59 G1
St Aidans Catholic Primary
School
NTHM/RTH M23 .... 109 L3
St Aidans CE Primary School
WGNW/BIL/OR WN5 .... 62 B7
St Aidans RC Primary School
WGNS/IIMK WN3 .... 63 G2
St Alphonsus RC Primary School
OLDTF/WHR M16 .... 86 F7
St Ambrose Barlow RC High
School & Salford College
SWIN M27 .... 70 C5
St Ambrose Barlow RC Primary
School *TYLD* M29 .... 67 K7
St Ambrose College
HALE/TIMP WA15 .... 117 K3
St Ambrose RC Primary School
CCHDY M21 .... 98 A3
EDGY/DAV SK3 .... 112 A7
St Andrews CE Junior School
GLSP SK13 .... 93 J8
St Andrews CE Primary School
BNG/LEV M19 .... 99 L1
RAD M26 .... 38 B6
RAMS BL0 .... 18 E7
WALK M28 .... 68 D7
WGNNW/ST WN6 .... 47 J2
WHTN BL5 .... 51 K4
St Andrew's CE Primary School
WHIT OL12 .... 21 J8
St Andrews CE School
ECC M30 .... 85 H3
St Andrews Medical Centre
ECC M30 .... 85 H2
St Andrews Methodist Primary
School *WALK* M28 .... 68 E1
St Annes CE Lydgate Primary
School *OLDE* OL4 .... 60 F6
St Annes CE Primary School
ROY/SHW OL2 .... 59 H1
SALE M33 .... 96 F8
WGNNW/ST WN6 .... 47 G1
St Annes Ear Nose & Throat
Hospital *ALT* WA14 .... 116 E1
St Annes Primary School
DTN/ASHW M34 .... 90 D8
St Annes RC High School
HTNM SK4 .... 100 A8
St Annes RC Primary School
CHH M8 .... 72 D4
DTN/ASHW M34 .... 89 K5
OLDE OL4 .... 59 M5
St Anns RC Primary School
STRET M32 .... 97 G2
St Anthonys RC Primary School
WYTH/NTH M22 .... 118 F3
St Antonys Catholic College
STRET M32 .... 96 C2
St Augustine of Canterbury RC
School *OLDS* OL8 .... 75 G1
St Augustines CE Primary School
NEWH/MOS M40 .... 73 H7
SWIN M27 .... 70 E4
St Barnabas CE Primary School
OP/CLY M11 .... 88 E4
St Bartholomews CE Primary
School *WHIT* OL12 .... 20 A4
St Bede CE Primary School
BOLS/LL BL3 .... 51 M2
St Bede's Preparatory School
OLDTF/WHR M16 .... 98 B1
St Benedicts Catholic Primary
School *WGNNW/ST* WN6 .... 48 F6
St Benedict's Catholic Primary
School *WILM/AE* SK9 .... 127 J1
St Bernadettes Catholic Primary
School *WGNNW/ST* WN6 .... 30 D6
St Bernadettes RC Primary
School *RDSH* SK5 .... 100 B8
WHTF M45 .... 55 J2
St Bernard CE Primary School
BOLS/LL BL3 .... 35 H7
St Bernard's RC Primary School
BNG/LEV M19 .... 99 J6
St Boniface RC Primary School
BRO M7 .... 71 M6

St Brendan RC Primary School
BOLE BL2 .... 23 H7
St Brigids RC Primary School
OP/CLY M11 .... 88 D3
St Catharines CE Primary School
WGN WN1 .... 15 K4
St Catherines CE Primary School
HOR/BR BL6 .... 33 L1
St Catherines Preparatory
School
MPL/ROM SK6 .... 114 E5
St Catherines RC Primary
School *DID/WITH* M20 .... 110 F1
GOL/RIS/CUL WA3 .... 80 B4
St Chads CE Primary School
UPML OL3 .... 61 M3
St Chads RC Primary School
CHH M8 .... 72 D7
St Charles RC Primary School
SWIN M27 .... 70 A4
St Christophers RC Primary
School
AUL OL6 .... 76 B6
RAD M26 .... 113 K2
St Chrysostoms CE Primary
School
BRUN/LGST M13 .... 87 M7
St Clares RC Primary School
BKLY M9 .... 56 F7
St Clement (Egerton) CE Primary
School
ORD M5 .... 86 E4
St Clement's CE Primary School
OP/CLY M11 .... 89 H5
St Columbas RC Primary School
BOLE BL2 .... 22 F8
St Cuthberts RC High School
MILN OL16 .... 42 E3
St Cuthberts RC Primary School
DID/WITH M20 .... 98 F7
WGNW/BIL/OR WN5 .... 47 G6
St Damians RC High School
AUL OL6 .... 76 B5
St Davids CE Primary School
WGNE/HIN WN2 .... 32 K5
St Dunstans RC Primary School
NEWH/MOS M40 .... 73 K4
St Edmund Arrowsmith Catholic
High School
AIMK WN4 .... 78 D2
St Edmunds RC Primary School
LHULT M38 .... 52 E8
NEWH/MOS M40 .... 73 H6
St Edwards CE Primary School
ROCH OL11 .... 41 L2
St Edwards RC Primary School
OLDE OL4 .... 60 B5
RUSH/FAL M14 .... 98 E2
St Elisabeths CE Primary School
RDSH SK5 .... 100 B4
St Elizabeth RC Primary School
WYTH/NTH M22 .... 119 G1
St Ethelbert RC Primary School
BOLS/LL BL3 .... 35 L7
St Gabriels CE Primary School
MDTN M24 .... 57 M5
St Gabriels Medical Centre
PWCH M25 .... 72 A2
St Gabriels RC High School
TOT/BURYW BL8 .... 4 B6
St Gabriels RC Primary School
LEIGH WN7 .... 67 H5
ROCH OL11 .... 42 A3
St Georges Central CE Primary
School *TYLD* M29 .... 67 K3
St Georges CE Primary School
ATH M46 .... 50 E8
HYDE SK14 .... 102 A3
MOSL OL5 .... 76 A3
NM/HAY SK22 .... 124 E4
OFTN SK2 .... 112 C6
SLFD M6 .... 71 K7
WHTN BL5 .... 50 A5
St Georges Craft Centre
BOL BL1 .... 2 E3
St Georges RC High School
WALK M28 .... 68 F2
St Gilberts RC Primary School
ECC M30 .... 84 D2
St Gregory RC Primary School
FWTH BL4 .... 53 H4
St Helens Community College
NEWLW WA12 .... 78 E8
St Herberts RC Primary School
CHAD OL9 .... 58 D5
St Hilarys School
WILM/AE SK9 .... 130 D3
St Hildas CE Primary School
OLD OL1 .... 9 G3
PWCH M25 .... 55 M8
St Hugh of Lincoln RC Primary
School *STRET* M32 .... 96 C1
St Hughs Catholic Primary
School *HALE/TIMP* WA15 .... 108 C3
St Hughs CE Primary School
OLDE OL4 .... 76 A1
St James Catholic High School
CHD/CHDH SK8 .... 120 B5
St James Catholic Primary
School *HYDE* SK14 .... 103 G2
WGNW/BIL/OR WN5 .... 46 A8
St James CE Primary School
AUL OL6 .... 90 F1
FWTH BL4 .... 52 E5
GTN M18 .... 89 G6
RUSH/FAL M14 .... 99 G2
WGNS/IIMK WN3 .... 14 A9
WHIT OL12 .... 21 G6
St James CE School
GLSP SK13 .... 104 E4
St James CE Secondary School
FWTH BL4 .... 52 D4
St James (Daisy Hill) CE Primary
School *WHTN* BL5 .... 50 C7
St James Primary School
RNFD/HAY WA11 .... 78 B6
St James School
HTNM SK4 .... 13 G1
St James's RC School
SLFD M6 .... 86 C1
St John Bosco RC Primary School
BKLY M9 .... 57 J8
St John CE Primary School
FWTH BL4 .... 53 H4
St John Fisher Catholic High
School *WGNNW/ST* WN6 .... 47 J1
St John Fisher RC Primary
School *DTN/ASHW* M34 .... 101 L3
St John Fisher & St Thomas
More RC Primary School
WYTH/NTH M22 .... 110 A8

St John RC Primary School
MILN OL16 .... 10 F6
St John Rigby College
WGNW/BIL/OR WN5 .... 46 C2
St Johns Cathedral
CSLFD M3 .... 6 A3
St Johns CE Infant School
FAIL M35 .... 74 C4
LEIGH WN7 .... 66 C6
St Johns CE Junior School
FAIL M35 .... 74 D5
St Johns CE Primary School
BRUN/LGST M13 .... 88 B8
HTNM SK4 .... 111 H2
MDTN M24 .... 42 B6
RAD M26 .... 54 D3
SLFD M6 .... 70 F6
STLY SK15 .... 91 H4
WGNE/HIN WN2 .... 65 L1
WGNW/BIL/OR WN5 .... 46 E6
St Johns Industrial Estate
OLDE OL4 .... 60 B6
St Johns Medical Centre
ALT WA14 .... 116 E1
St Johns Mosley Common CE
Primary School
WALK M28 .... 68 C4
St Johns RC Primary School
CCHDY M21 .... 97 K3
St Johns with St Marks CE
Primary School
BURY BL9 .... 25 H8
St John the Evangelist RC
Primary School
EDGW/EG BL7 .... 22 C5
St John Vianney School
HTNM SK4 .... 12 A3
St John Vianney Upper School
OLDTF/WHR M16 .... 97 L2
St Josephs & St Bedes RC Primary
School *BURY* BL9 .... 25 L8
St Josephs Catholic Primary
School
WGNNW/ST WN6 .... 30 C1
St Josephs RC High School
HEY OL10 .... 40 F4
St Josephs RC Infant School
RDSH SK5 .... 100 B4
St Josephs RC Junior School
RDSH SK5 .... 100 B4
St Josephs RC Primary School
BOL BL1 .... 35 M2
BRUN/LGST M13 .... 88 B8
HEY OL10 .... 40 F3
LEIGH WN7 .... 66 D8
LHULT M38 .... 52 D7
MOSL OL5 .... 76 F3
ORD M5 .... 86 E4
RAMS BL0 .... 18 C6
ROY/SHW OL2 .... 43 K7
SALE M33 .... 96 E8
STKP SK1 .... 13 J4
St Josephs RC School
HOR/BR BL6 .... 34 B3
St Josephs the Worker RC
Primary School
IRL M44 .... 94 D1
St Judes Catholic
Primary School
WGNS/IIMK WN3 .... 47 J7
St Judes CE Primary School
ANC M4 .... 7 L3
St Kentigerns RC Primary School
RUSH/FAL M14 .... 98 D3
St Lukes CE Primary School
BRUN/LGST M13 .... 88 B7
BURY BL9 .... 4 F9
CHAD OL9 .... 58 D5
GLSP SK13 .... 104 F3
GOL/RIS/CUL WA3 .... 80 B5
HEY OL10 .... 41 G1
St Lukes RC Primary School
SLFD M6 .... 70 F7
St Lukes with All Saints CE
Primary School
ORD M5 .... 86 A3
St Malachys RC Primary School
NEWH/MOS M40 .... 72 F7
St Margaret Marys RC Primary
School *NEWH/MOS* M40 .... 74 A1
St Margarets CE Primary School
HEY OL10 .... 40 D3
OLDS OL8 .... 74 F2
OLDTF/WHR M16 .... 98 A2
PWCH M25 .... 56 A4
St Margarets RC Primary School
GLSP SK13 .... 104 A4
St Margaret Ward RC Primary
School *SALE* M33 .... 107 M2
St Maries RC Primary School
BURY BL9 .... 4 F6
WGNNW/ST WN6 .... 31 H2
St Marks CE Primary School
MPL/ROM SK6 .... 101 K8
NEWH/MOS M40 .... 88 A1
WALK M28 .... 69 J6
WGNW/BIL/OR WN5 .... 47 J5
St Marks RC Primary School
SWIN M27 .... 70 D2
St Martins CE Primary School
OLDS OL8 .... 75 L2
St Martins School
SALE M33 .... 96 B7
St Mary CE Primary School
BOLS/LL BL3 .... 35 J8
St Mary RC Primary School
HOR/BR BL6 .... 34 A2
St Mary's Catholic Cemetery
WALK M28 .... 69 L4
St Marys Catholic Junior School
NEWLW WA12 .... 78 E8
St Marys Catholic School
NEWLW WA12 .... 78 F8
St Marys CE J & I School
WGNS/IIMK WN3 .... 47 J4
St Marys CE Primary School
DROY M43 .... 89 K3
NEWH/MOS M40 .... 73 M3
OLDTF/WHR M16 .... 87 H8
PWCH M25 .... 55 K7
RDSH SK5 .... 100 C6
ROCH OL11 .... 28 D8
ROY/SHW OL2 .... 43 J4
TOT/BURYW BL8 .... 23 L2
UPML OL3 .... 61 M8
St Marys CE Primary School
SALE M33 .... 96 C8
St Mary's Hospital
BRUN/LGST M13 .... 87 M8
St Marys Medical Centre
OLD OL1 .... 9 K5

St Marys RC High School
TYLD M29 .... 67 K8
St Marys RC Primary School
BNG/LEV M19 .... 99 K4
DTN/ASHW M34 .... 101 H1
DUK SK16 .... 91 H6
FAIL M35 .... 74 B6
GLSP SK13 .... 105 G4
HTNM SK4 .... 13 G2
MDTN M24 .... 57 H2
MPL/ROM SK6 .... 114 D5
NM/HAY SK22 .... 124 D4
RAD M26 .... 38 D8
SWIN M27 .... 70 C4
St Mary's RC Primary School
ECC M30 .... 85 H3
LIT OL15 .... 21 L6
St Marys & St Johns RC Primary
School *WGN* WN1 .... 15 H2
St Matthew CE Primary School
BOL BL1 .... 2 D1
BOL BL1 .... 36 B3
BOLS/LL BL3 .... 53 K1
St Matthews CE Infant School
OLD OL1 .... 58 C2
St Matthews CE Primary School
EDGY/DAV SK3 .... 13 G7
STRET M32 .... 96 F4
St Matthews RC High School
NEWH/MOS M40 .... 73 M2
St Maxentius CE Primary School
BOLE BL2 .... 23 G7
St Michael CE Primary School
BOLS/LL BL3 .... 52 E1
St Michaels CE Aided Primary
School *URM* M41 .... 95 J3
St Michaels CE Primary Howe
Bridge School
ATH M46 .... 66 E2
St Michaels CE Primary School
HEY OL10 .... 26 E5
MDTN M24 .... 57 K7
WHTF M45 .... 55 L3
St Monicas RC High School
PWCH M25 .... 71 M1
St Monicas RC Primary School
URM M41 .... 95 G3
St Nathaniels CE Primary School
WGNE/HIN WN2 .... 64 E1
St Osmunds & St Andrews
Primary School
BOLE BL2 .... 37 G5
St Oswalds RC J & I School
AIMK WN4 .... 78 E1
St Patrick's Catholic High School
ECC M30 .... 84 C2
St Patricks RC Primary School
ANC M4 .... 87 M1
CHAD OL9 .... 8 F7
WGN WN1 .... 15 J4
St Patricks VA RC Primary School
WHIT OL12 .... 28 D3
St Paul CE Primary School
BOL BL1 .... 36 C1
St Pauls Catholic High School
NTHM/RTH M23 .... 109 L8
St Pauls Catholic Primary School
POY/DIS SK12 .... 129 J2
St Paul's Cemetery
BOL BL1 .... 35 M2
St Pauls CE Primary School
BRO M7 .... 71 L4
BURY BL9 .... 5 K1
DID/WITH M20 .... 98 E6
ORD M5 .... 86 E3
RDSH SK5 .... 100 B4
ROY/SHW OL2 .... 58 F1
STLY SK15 .... 91 M2
WALK M28 .... 69 H2
WGNS/IIMK WN3 .... 63 J1
St Pauls Peel CE Primary School
LHULT M38 .... 52 C7
St Pauls RC Primary School
HYDE SK14 .... 91 J8
St Pauls Trading Estate
STLY SK15 .... 91 M2
St Peter CE Primary School
FWTH BL4 .... 53 G5
St Peter & St John Primary School
CSLFD M3 .... 6 B2
St Peter & St Paul RC Primary
School *BOLS/LL* BL3 .... 2 E4
St Peters Catholic High School
WGNW/BIL/OR WN5 .... 46 C5
St Peters Catholic Primary
School *BRAM/HZG* SK7 .... 121 M3
NTHM/RTH M23 .... 118 C1
STLY SK15 .... 91 L3
St Peters CE Infant School
LEIGH WN7 .... 65 M7
St Peters CE Junior School
LEIGH WN7 .... 65 M7
St Peters CE Primary School
AIMK WN4 .... 63 J6
AULW OL7 .... 90 D3
BURY BL9 .... 39 H6
SWIN M27 .... 70 A8
WGNE/HIN WN2 .... 48 F7
St Peter's CE Primary School
NEWLW WA12 .... 79 G8
St Peters RC High School Upper
School *DROY* M43 .... 89 H4
St Peter's RC Primary School
MDTN M24 .... 57 K5
St Peters VC CE Primary School
MILN OL16 .... 11 K9
St Philip Howard Catholic School
GLSP SK13 .... 104 E3
St Philips Catholic Primary School
OFTN SK2 .... 113 H6
St Philips CE Primary School
ATH M46 .... 67 H1
HULME M15 .... 87 J3
St Philips RC Primary School
PWCH M25 .... 71 M3
St Philips School
CSLFD M5 .... 6 A4
St Raphaels Catholic Primary School
STLY SK15 .... 77 K7
St Richards RC Primary School
WGTN/LGST M12 .... 99 L1
St Saviour Primary School Ringley
RAD M26 .... 53 M5
St Sebastians RC Primary School
SLFD M6 .... 71 K7
St Simons Catholic
Primary School
BRAM/HZG SK7 .... 122 A1
St Stephen & All Martyrs
CE Primary School
BOLE BL2 .... 3 L7

St Stephens & All Martyrs Infant
School *OLD* OL1 .... 9 K3
St Stephens CE Primary School
DTN/ASHW M34 .... 90 B4
FWTH BL4 .... 53 K6
OFTN SK2 .... 113 J8
TOT/BURYW BL8 .... 38 E3
TYLD M29 .... 67 L6
St Stephens RC School
DROY M43 .... 89 K2
St Teresa RC Primary School
BOLS/LL BL3 .... 53 K1
St Teresas RC Primary School
IRL M44 .... 94 B4
OLDTF/WHR M16 .... 97 K1
St Thomas Aquinas
RC High School
CCHDY M21 .... 97 M5
St Thomas CE Primary School
AIMK WN4 .... 78 F1
BOL BL1 .... 36 A2
BURY BL9 .... 5 K6
GOL/RIS/CUL WA3 .... 79 L3
HTNM SK4 .... 99 M6
LEIGH WN7 .... 66 E8
MILN OL16 .... 29 L8
OLDS OL8 .... 9 C8
STKP SK1 .... 13 K6
WHTN BL5 .... 50 E3
St Thomas Leesfield CE Primary
School *OLDE* OL4 .... 60 B7
St Thomas Moorside CE (VA)
Primary School
OLD OL1 .... 44 B8
St Thomas More Catholic High
School
WGNW/BIL/OR WN5 .... 14 A6
St Thomas More RC College
DTN/ASHW M34 .... 101 J2
St Thomas More
RC Primary School
MDTN M24 .... 57 K7
St Thomas of Canterbury RC
Primary School
BOL BL1 .... 35 K4
BRO M7 .... 72 B6
St Thomas Primary School
CHH M8 .... 72 C7
St Thomas's Hospital
EDGY/DAV SK3 .... 13 H8
St Vincent RC Infant School
HALE/TIMP WA15 .... 108 B7
St Vincents RC Primary School
WHIT OL12 .... 27 K3
St Wilfrids Catholic Primary
School *AIMK* WN4 .... 64 A8
St Wilfrids CE Primary School
NEWH/MOS M40 .... 74 A7
WGNNW/ST WN6 .... 31 J3
WYTH/NTH M22 .... 110 B4
St Wilfrids RC Primary School
HULME M15 .... 87 H6
St William RC Primary School
BOLS/LL BL3 .... 52 B1
St Williams RC Primary School
WGNE/HIN WN2 .... 48 C1
St Willibrords RC Primary School
OP/CLY M11 .... 88 F1
St Winifreds RC Primary School
HTNM SK4 .... 111 K2
SS Simon & Jude CE Primary
School *BOLS/LL* BL3 .... 52 C1
Sale CC
SALE M33 .... 97 G7
Sale Golf Club
SALE M33 .... 97 J7
Sale Grammar School
SALE M33 .... 108 F1
Sale Leisure Centre
SALE M33 .... 96 F7
Sale Water Park
SALE M33 .... 97 H6
Salford City Academy
ECC M30 .... 84 C3
Salford City Reds RLFC
(The Willows) *ORD* M5 .... 86 A2
Salford College
ECC M30 .... 84 D2
SALQ M50 .... 86 D5
SLFD M6 .... 71 L8
SWIN M27 .... 69 M2
WALK M28 .... 69 G3
Salford County Court
ORD M5 .... 86 D3
Salford Medical Centre
SLFD M6 .... 86 B1
Salford Museum & Art Gallery
ORD M5 .... 86 F2
Salford Shopping City
SLFD M6 .... 86 D1
Salford University Business Park
SLFD M6 .... 71 L8
Samuel Laycock Special School
AUL OL6 .... 76 D8
Sandbrook Community Primary
School *ROCH* OL11 .... 42 B1
Sandilands Primary School
NTHM/RTH M23 .... 108 F4
Saviour CE Primary School
NEWH/MOS M40 .... 72 F7
Savoy Cinema
HTNM SK4 .... 111 K1
Saxon Hall Leisure Centre
MILN OL16 .... 11 L3
Scholes Shopping Precinct
WGN WN1 .... 15 J3
School Street Industrial Estate
BRAM/HZG SK7 .... 122 A2
Scot Lane End CE
Primary School
HOR/BR BL6 .... 33 H4
Scot Lane Industrial Estate
HOR/BR BL6 .... 33 H4
Seaford Industrial Estate
SLFD M6 .... 71 L4
Sedgley Park Community
Primary School
PWCH M25 .... 71 M2
Sedgley Park RUFC
WHTF M45 .... 55 G6
Sedgley Park Trading Estate
PWCH M25 .... 71 L2
Seedley Primary School
SLFD M6 .... 86 B2
Sett Valley Medical Centre
NM/HAY SK22 .... 124 E4
Seven Brooks Medical Centre
ATH M46 .... 67 G1
Severnside Trading Estate
TRPK M17 .... 85 L7
Seymour Park Primary School
OLDTF/WHR M16 .... 86 E8

Seymour Road Primary School
OP/CLY M11 .... 89 G3
Shakerley CE Primary School
TYLD M29 .... 67 K2
Shandon Clinic (Europe)
HULME M15 .... 87 K7
Sharples Primary School
BOL BL1 .... 22 D7
Shawclough Community
Primary School
WHIT OL12 .... 28 B1
Shawclough Trading Estate
WHIT OL12 .... 28 A1
Shawgrove School
DID/WITH M20 .... 98 C6
Shaw Heath Health Centre
EDGY/DAV SK3 .... 13 H8
Shay Lane Medical Centre
HALE/TIMP WA15 .... 117 L3
Shepherd Cross Industrial Estate
BOL BL1 .... 35 M2
Shepley North Industrial Estate
DTN/ASHW M34 .... 90 D5
Shepley South Industrial Estate
DTN/ASHW M34 .... 90 D6
Sherborne Trading Estate
CHH M8 .... 72 C7
Sherwood Business Park
ROCH OL11 .... 42 A2
Shevington Community Primary
School
WGNNW/ST WN6 .... 30 C6
Shevington High School
WGNNW/ST WN6 .... 30 E5
Shevington Vale Primary School
WGNNW/ST WN6 .... 30 B4
Shire Hill Hospital
GLSP SK13 .... 105 H1
Shiv Lodge Medical Centre
BRUN/LGST M13 .... 99 J1
The Shopping Centre
CHD/CHDH SK8 .... 120 C2
Showcase Cinemas Belle Vue
GTN M18 .... 88 E7
Siddal Moor Sports College
HEY OL10 .... 41 G5
Simmondley Primary School
GLSP SK13 .... 104 D4
Skylink Walkway
MANAIR M90 .... 118 C5
Slough Industrial Estate
ORD M5 .... 86 F4
Smallbridge Health Centre
WHIT OL12 .... 28 F1
Smallbridge Industrial Park
MILN OL16 .... 28 F2
Smedleylane Junior School
CHH M8 .... 72 E6
Smithills School
BOL BL1 .... 35 L1
Smithy Bridge Primary School
LIT OL15 .... 29 J1
The Smithy Surgery
HYDE SK14 .... 93 G7
Snipe Retail Park
AULW OL7 .... 90 A4
South Chadderton School
OLD OL1 .... 74 C2
Southern Cross School
CCHDY M21 .... 97 M7
South Failsworth Primary
School *FAIL* M35 .... 74 B7
Southfield Industrial Estate
TRPK M17 .... 85 M7
Southgate Industrial Estate
HEY OL10 .... 41 J3
South Lancashire Industrial
Estate *AIMK* WN4 .... 63 L6
Southlink Business Park
OLD OL4 .... 9 M6
South Manchester High School
WYTH/NTH M22 .... 118 F1
Southmoor Business Park
NTHM/RTH M23 .... 109 H5
Southmoor Industrial Estate
NTHM/RTH M23 .... 109 H5
South Oldham Business Park
CHAD OL9 .... 8 D2
South Reddish Medical Centre
RDSH SK5 .... 100 C8
Southside Industrial Park
ATH M46 .... 50 E8
South Trafford College
ALT WA14 .... 108 A4
South West Manchester CC
CCHDY M21 .... 97 M3
Sovereign Business Park
WGN WN1 .... 15 J6
Spa Road Industrial Estate
BOL BL1 .... 2 B5
Spindle Point Primary School
FWTH BL4 .... 53 L7
The Spindles Shopping Centre
OLD OL1 .... 9 H6
Spinning Gate Shopping Centre
LEIGH WN7 .... 66 C7
Sport City
OP/CLY M11 .... 88 C2
Sports Injury Centre
MDTN M24 .... 57 K5
Spotland Bridge Industrial Centre
ROCH OL11 .... 27 M4
Spotland Primary School
WHIT OL12 .... 10 B2
Springbank Industrial Estate
WGNE/HIN WN2 .... 64 E1
Spring Brook School
CHAD OL9 .... 58 C5
Springfield Business Centre
CSLFD M3 .... 6 E1
Springfield Hotel
MPL/ROM SK6 .... 114 C5
Springfield House
Medical Centre *OLD* OL1 .... 59 M4
Springfield Industrial Estate
FAIL M35 .... 74 B4
Springfield Primary School
SALE M33 .... 96 E8
Springhead Community Infant
& First School
OLDE OL4 .... 60 C6
Springhill High School
MILN OL16 .... 11 L9
Springside CP School
BURY BL9 .... 25 H5
Spring View CC
WGNE/HIN WN2 .... 64 D1
Springwood Primary School
MPL/ROM SK6 .... 114 B1
Spurley Hey High School
BNG/LEV M19 .... 99 L2

Stag Industrial Estate
ALT WA14 .... 107 L6
Stakehill Industrial Estate
MDTN M24 .... 42 A8
Stalybridge Celtic AFC
STLY SK15 .... 91 M4
Stalybridge CC
DUK SK16 .... 91 H4
Stalybridge Millbrook CC
STLY SK15 .... 77 G8
Stalybridge St Pauls CC
DUK SK16 .... 91 J5
Stalyhill Infant School
STLY SK15 .... 92 B5
Stalyhill Junior School
STLY SK15 .... 92 A5
Staly Industrial Estate
STLY SK15 .... 91 L2
Stamford Golf Club
STLY SK15 .... 77 H5
Stamford High School
AUL OL6 .... 76 B8
Stamford Park Junior School
HALE/TIMP WA15 .... 117 G1
Standish Clinic
WGNNW/ST WN6 .... 31 H4
Standish Community High
School
WGNNW/ST WN6 .... 30 F2
Standish Court Golf Club
WGNNW/ST WN6 .... 31 J3
Standish CC
WGNNW/ST WN6 .... 31 H4
Stanley Green Industrial Estate
CHD/CHDH SK8 .... 120 A6
Stanley Green Retail Park
WILM/AE SK9 .... 120 A8
Stanley Grove Primary School
WGTN/LGST M12 .... 88 C8
Stanley Road Primary School
CHAD OL9 .... 58 E8
Stanneylands Hotel
WILM/AE SK9 .... 126 F2
Star Industrial Estate
OLDS OL8 .... 9 J8
Station Approach Business
Estate *ROCH* OL11 .... 10 E7
Staveleigh Medical Centre
STLY SK15 .... 91 K2
Stella Maris School
HTNM SK4 .... 111 H2
Stepping Hill Hospital
OFTN SK2 .... 112 E8
Stirling Industrial Estate
HOR/BR BL6 .... 33 M2
Stockport Air Raid Shelter
STKP SK1 .... 13 H4
Stockport Art Gallery
EDGY/DAV SK3 .... 13 H6
Stockport Bus Station
HTNM SK4 .... 13 G5
Stockport CC
EDGY/DAV SK3 .... 112 C6
Stockport College
HTNM SK4 .... 99 L6
Stockport College of Further
& Higher Education
EDGY/DAV SK3 .... 13 H7
Stockport County Court
STKP SK1 .... 13 H5
Stockport County FC & Sale
Sharks RUFC (Edgeley Park)
EDGY/DAV SK3 .... 13 G9
Stockport Crematorium
OFTN SK2 .... 13 M9
Stockport Golf Club
OFTN SK2 .... 113 L7
Stockport Grammar School
OFTN SK2 .... 112 E7
Stockport Mega Bowl
STKP SK1 .... 13 H6
Stockport RUFC
BRAM/HZG SK7 .... 121 H4
Stockport School
OFTN SK2 .... 112 E7
Stockport Trading Estate
HTNM SK4 .... 12 A6
Stone Cross Business Park
GOL/RIS/CUL WA3 .... 79 L5
Stone Hill Industrial Estate
FWTH BL4 .... 52 F5
Stoneleigh Primary School
OLDE OL4 .... 59 L2
The Strand Medical Centre
ROCH OL11 .... 42 C2
Stretford Grammar School
STRET M32 .... 97 H3
Stretford High School Community
Language College
STRET M32 .... 86 B8
Stretford Leisure Centre
STRET M32 .... 86 C8
Stretford Memorial Hospital
OLDTF/WHR M16 .... 97 L1
Stubbins Primary School
RAMS BL0 .... 19 G3
Styal Country Park (NT)
WILM/AE SK9 .... 126 C1
Styal Golf Club
WILM/AE SK9 .... 119 J7
Styal Primary School
WILM/AE SK9 .... 119 G8
Sudden Health Centre
ROCH OL11 .... 27 M8
Sudell Street Trading Estate
ANC M4 .... 7 K1
Sugden Sports Centre
CMANE M1 .... 7 H9
Summersales Industrial Estate
WGNS/IIMK WN3 .... 46 E8
Summerseat Methodist Primary
School *BURY* BL9 .... 25 G2
Summerville Primary School
SLFD M6 .... 71 G7
Sunning Hill Primary School
BOLS/LL BL3 .... 36 A8
Sunnybank Clinic
BURY BL9 .... 55 K1
Sunny Bank Primary School
BURY BL9 .... 55 K1
Sunset Business Centre
FWTH BL4 .... 53 M7
Swan Meadow Industrial Estate
WGNS/IIMK WN3 .... 14 D7
Swinton Cemetery
SWIN M27 .... 70 B2
The Swinton County High
School
SWIN M27 .... 70 B3
Swinton Industrial Estate
SWIN M27 .... 70 D4

Swinton Leisure Centre
SWIN M27 .... 70 C4
Swinton Park Golf Club
SWIN M27 .... 70 D6
Talmud Torah Chinuch Norim
School
BRO M7 .... 72 A5
Tameside Business Development
Centre *DTN/ASHW* M34 .... 101 J1
Tameside Business Park
DUK SK16 .... 90 E5
Tameside College
AUL OL6 .... 91 G1
HYDE SK14 .... 102 A5
Tameside County Court
AUL OL6 .... 90 F2
Tameside General Hospital
STLY SK15 .... 76 C8
Tame Valley Primary School
RDSH SK5 .... 100 T5
Tandle Hill Country Park
ROY/SHW OL2 .... 42 D6
Tanfield Special School
WGNE/HIN WN2 .... 49 J7
Tashbar School
BRO M7 .... 72 B3
Tavistock Industrial Estate
OP/CLY M11 .... 89 G6
Taylors Sports Club
ECC M30 .... 85 H3
Temple Primary School
CHH M8 .... 72 E6
Ten Acres Sports Complex
NEWH/MOS M40 .... 73 K7
Thames Industrial Estate
WGTN/LGST M12 .... 88 A5
Thames Trading Centre
IRL M44 .... 94 C5
Thistle Hotel
CMANE M1 .... 7 F3
RNFD/HAY WA11 .... 78 E4
WILM/AE SK9 .... 119 M7
Thomasson Memorial Special
School *BOL* BL1 .... 35 L5
Thorn Grove Primary School
CHD/CHDH SK8 .... 120 C4
Thornham CC
MDTN M24 .... 42 A5
Thornham St James CE Primary
School *ROY/SHW* OL2 .... 43 G4
Thornleigh Salesian College
BOL BL1 .... 22 B4
Thornsett Primary School
NM/HAY SK22 .... 125 G1
Thornsett Trading Estate
NM/HAY SK22 .... 125 G2
Thorp Primary School
ROY/SHW OL2 .... 42 F7
Three Sisters Racing Circuit
AIMK WN4 .... 63 M5
Times Retail Park
HEY OL10 .... 40 F2
Timperley Health Centre
HALE/TIMP WA15 .... 108 D5
Tintwistle CE Primary School
GLSP SK13 .... 93 K5
Tithe Barn Primary School
HTNM SK4 .... 111 K1
Tonacliffe Primary School
WHIT OL12 .... 20 A6
Tonge Bridge Industrial Estate
BOLE BL2 .... 3 J3
Tonge CC
BOLE BL2 .... 36 F1
Tonge Fold Health Centre
BOLE BL2 .... 3 L5
Tonge Moor Health Centre
BOLE BL2 .... 36 F3
Tonge Moor Primary School
BOLE BL2 .... 3 L1
Tootal Drive CP School
ORD M5 .... 85 M2
Top o' th' Brow Primary School
BOLE BL2 .... 37 H2
Torkington Primary School
BRAM/HZG SK7 .... 122 C2
Tottington Health Centre
TOT/BURYW BL8 .... 24 B5
Tottington High School
TOT/BURYW BL8 .... 24 C6
Tottington Primary School
TOT/BURYW BL8 .... 24 C7
Towers Business Park
DID/WITH M20 .... 110 E3
Townfield Industrial Estate
OLDE OL4 .... 59 L5
Towngate Business Centre
LHULT M38 .... 52 B7
Town Hall & Albert Halls
BOL BL1 .... 2 E4
Town Square Shopping Centre
OLD OL1 .... 9 J5
Trafalgar Business Park
CHH M8 .... 72 B8
Trafford Athletics Track
CCHDY M21 .... 97 J3
Trafford Centre
TRPK M17 .... 85 G2
Trafford Centre
Leisure Complex
TRPK M17 .... 84 E6
Trafford FC
URM M41 .... 95 K3
Trafford General Hospital
URM M41 .... 95 K1
Trafford Healthcare
SALE M33 .... 109 G1
Trafford Retail Park
URM M41 .... 84 F7
Trafford Water Sports Centre
SALE M33 .... 97 H6
Trans Pennine Trading Estate
ROCH OL11 .... 42 A1
Travelodge
ANC M4 .... 7 J3
BURY BL9 .... 39 L5
CHAD OL9 .... 58 B8
CSLFD M3 .... 6 E3
DID/WITH M20 .... 111 G3
HEY OL10 .... 40 E8
MCFLDN SK10 .... 129 G4
RNFD/HAY WA11 .... 78 B5
Trent Industrial Estate
ROY/SHW OL2 .... 43 L4
The Triangle
ANC M4 .... 6 F7
Trinity CE High School
HULME M15 .... 87 K4
Trinity Retail Park
BOLE BL2 .... 3 H7
Trinity School
STLY SK15 .... 91 J3

Tudor Industrial Estate
DUK SK16 .... 90 D6
Tulip Inn Hotel
URM M41 .... 84 F6
Tulketh Street Industrial Estate
BKLY M9 .... 73 J4
Tunshill Golf Club
MILN OL16 .... 29 M6
Turton & Edgworth CE/Methodist
Primary School
EDGW/EG BL7 .... 17 H7
Turton Golf Club
EDGW/EG BL7 .... 22 D2
Turton High School
EDGW/EG BL7 .... 22 E5
Turton Leisure Centre
EDGW/EG BL7 .... 22 D2
Turton Tower
EDGW/EG BL7 .... 22 F1
Tweed Street Industrial Estate
LEIGH WN7 .... 66 E8
Twelve Apostles RC
Primary School
LEIGH WN7 .... 66 A4
Twine Valley Country Park
& Fishery
RAMS BL0 .... 19 K4
Twiss Green Primary School
GOL/RIS/CUL WA3 .... 81 H8
Two Porches School
ATH M46 .... 67 G1
Two Porches Special School
ATH M46 .... 50 F8
Two Trees High School
DTN/ASHW M34 .... 101 L3
Tyldesley Cemetery
TYLD M29 .... 68 A4
Tyldesley Primary School
TYLD M29 .... 67 L5
Tyldesley Swimming Pool
ATH M46 .... 67 H3
Tyntesfield CP School
SALE M33 .... 108 B3
UCI Cinema
TRPK M17 .... 85 G6
Union Mill Industrial Estate
MOSL OL5 .... 77 G1
United Trading Estate
OLDTF/WHR M16 .... 86 C7
University College Salford
CSLFD M3 .... 6 A2
University Dental Hospital
of Manchester
HULME M15 .... 87 K6
University of Bolton
BOLS/LL BL3 .... 2 C7
University of Bolton Chadwick
Campus *BOLE* BL2 .... 3 J6
University of Manchester
ANC M4 .... 7 K1
BRUN/LGST M13 .... 87 K7
CMANE M1 .... 7 K5
CMANE M1 .... 7 J7
ECC M30 .... 84 A6
HULME M15 .... 87 L7
RUSH/FAL M14 .... 98 F1
RUSH/FAL M14 .... 99 G3
University of Manchester Institute
of Science & Technology
CMANE M1 .... 7 J9
University of Salford
ECC M30 .... 85 H2
ORD M5 .... 86 F2
SLFD M6 .... 71 L8
SLFD M6 .... 86 E1
Unsworth Medical Centre
BURY BL9 .... 55 M1
Unsworth Primary School
BURY BL9 .... 55 K2
Urbis
CSLFD M3 .... 6 F2
Urmston Grammar School
URM M41 .... 95 M1
Urmston J & I School
URM M41 .... 95 L2
Urmston Leisure Centre
URM M41 .... 95 L2
Urmston Town FC
URM M41 .... 95 J3
Vaishali Medical Centre
CCHDY M21 .... 97 L3
Vale Park Industrial Estate
CHH M8 .... 72 F5
The Valley Community School
BOL BL1 .... 36 C2
The Valley Leisure Centre
BOL BL1 .... 36 D1
Valley Special School
BRAM/HZG SK7 .... 120 E7
Varley Street Clinic
NEWH/MOS M40 .... 73 G8
Varna Street Primary School
OP/CLY M11 .... 89 G6
Vaughan Street
Industrial Estate
WGTN/LGST M12 .... 88 C5
Vauxhall Industrial Estate
RDSH SK5 .... 100 C8
RDSH SK5 .... 100 B6
Vernon Industrial Estate
STKP SK1 .... 13 K3
STKP SK1 .... 13 M2
The Vernon Infant School
POY/DIS SK12 .... 129 J1
The Vernon Junior School
POY/DIS SK12 .... 129 J1
Vernon Park Museum
STKP SK1 .... 112 E2
Vernon Park Primary School
STKP SK1 .... 13 L4
Vernon Road Medical Centre
TOT/BURYW BL8 .... 24 D3
Victoria Avenue Primary School
BKLY M9 .... 57 G7
Victoria Industrial Estate
ANC M4 .... 88 A3
LEIGH WN7 .... 66 B6
Victoria Medical Centre
ANC M4 .... 96 A2
Victoria Park Infant School
STRET M32 .... 97 G2
Victoria Park Junior School
STRET M32 .... 97 G2
Victoria Trading Estate
CHAD OL9 .... 74 E1
Victory Trading Estate
BOLS/LL BL3 .... 3 G9
The Village Hotel & Leisure Club
HYDE SK14 .... 90 F6
Village Medical Centre
LIT OL15 .... 21 M7

VIP Centre Industrial Estate
 OLD OL1 .... 59 M3
Vue Cinema
 BURY BL9 .... 39 L6
 HOR/BR BL6 .... 34 A4
 SALQ M50 .... 86 C5
Wadsworth Industrial Park
 BOLS/LL BL3 .... 36 B8
Walkden High School
 WALK M28 .... 69 H2
Walmersley Golf Club
 BURY BL9 .... 25 L4
Walmsley CE Primary School
 EDGW/EG BL7 .... 22 B3
Walshaw Sports Club
 TOT/BURYW BL8 .... 24 C7
Walton Park Leisure Centre
 SALE M33 .... 108 D2
Wardle High School
 WHIT OL12 .... 21 H7
Wardley CE Primary School
 SWIN M27 .... 70 B2
Wardley Industrial Estate
 WALK M28 .... 69 M3
Warren Wood Primary School
 OFTN SK2 .... 113 K7
Warrington Road Industrial
 Estate
 WGNS/IIMK WN3 .... 47 H7
Warth Park Industrial Estate
 BURY BL9 .... 38 F5
Washacre Primary School
 WHTN BL5 .... 50 C5
Washway Road Medical Centre
 SALE M33 .... 96 D8
Waterfold Business Park
 BURY BL9 .... 5 L6
The Watergate Clinic
 MILN OL16 .... 10 F4
Waterloo Industrial Park
 BOL BL1 .... 3 C2
 STKP SK1 .... 13 K5
Waterloo Primary School
 AULW OL7 .... 75 J7
The Water Place
 BOL BL1 .... 2 E6
Waters Edge Business Park
 ORD M5 .... 86 E6
Watersheddings Primary School
 OLD OL1 .... 59 M3
Waterside Business Park
 GLSP SK13 .... 93 J6
The Waterside Hotel
 CHD/CHDH SK8 .... 111 G8
Waterside Industrial Park
 BOLS/LL BL3 .... 52 F1
Waterside Trading Estate
 LEIGH WN7 .... 66 E8
Watersports Centre
 SALQ M50 .... 86 C5
Watford Bridge Industrial
 Estate NM/HAY SK22 .... 124 E3
Waybridge Industrial Estate
 SALQ M50 .... 86 A4
Weaste Trading Estate
 ORD M5 .... 86 A2
Welfare Clinic
 MDTN M24 .... 57 G2
Welkin Road Industrial Estate
 STKP SK1 .... 112 E1
Wellacre Technology College
 URM M41 .... 95 G2
Wellfield Infant School
 SALE M33 .... 96 C6
Wellfield Junior School
 SALE M33 .... 96 C6
Wellfield Medical Centre
 CHH M8 .... 72 C4
Well Green Primary School
 HALE/TIMP WA15 .... 117 K2
Wellington Road Industrial
 Estate AUL OL6 .... 90 D1

Wellington School
 HALE/TIMP WA15 .... 108 C6
Wentworth High School
 ECC M30 .... 70 C8
Werneth Cricket Bowling &
 Tennis Club
 OLDS OL8 .... 9 G9
Werneth Golf Club
 OLDS OL8 .... 75 H3
Werneth J & I School
 OLDS OL8 .... 59 G8
Werneth Low Country Park
 HYDE SK14 .... 102 E5
Werneth Low Golf Club
 HYDE SK14 .... 102 E6
Werneth School
 MPL/ROM SK6 .... 113 J2
Wesley Methodist Primary
 School
 RAD M26 .... 38 B7
Westbrook Trading Estate
 TRPK M17 .... 86 A5
Westbury Street Industrial
 Estate HYDE SK14 .... 90 F7
West Croft Industrial Estate
 MDTN M24 .... 56 F5
West End Medical Centre
 AULW OL7 .... 90 C3
West End Primary School
 AULW OL7 .... 90 C2
West End Trading Estate
 SWIN M27 .... 70 C3
Westernlea Clinic
 DTN/ASHW M34 .... 90 B7
Westfield Community School
 WCNW/BIL/OR WN5 .... 46 F6
 WCNW/BIL/OR WN5 .... 47 H5
West Gorton Medical Centre
 WGTN/LGST M12 .... 88 C6
West Hill School
 STLY SK15 .... 91 J2
Westhoughton CC
 WHTN BL5 .... 50 B4
Westhoughton Clinic
 WHTN BL5 .... 50 B4
Westhoughton Golf Club
 WHTN BL5 .... 50 A3
Westhoughton High School &
 Specialist Technology College
 WHTN BL5 .... 50 C3
Westhoughton Industrial Estate
 WHTN BL5 .... 50 B2
Westhoughton Primary School
 WHTN BL5 .... 50 C3
Westinghouse Industrial Estate
 TRPK M17 .... 86 A7
Westleigh CC
 LEIGH WN7 .... 66 A7
West Leigh House School
 LEIGH WN7 .... 65 M7
Westleigh Methodist Primary
 School
 LEIGH WN7 .... 66 A3
Westleigh St Pauls CE Primary
 School
 LEIGH WN7 .... 66 B4
Westmorland Primary School
 RDSH SK5 .... 100 F6
West One Retail Park
 SALQ M50 .... 85 K3
Westpoint Medical Centre
 BNG/LEV M19 .... 99 J3
Westwood Business Centre
 CHAD OL9 .... 8 E6
Westwood Cemetery
 WCNS/IIMK WN3 .... 15 H9
Westwood Industrial Estate
 CHAD OL9 .... 8 D5
Westwood Park Primary School
 ECC M30 .... 84 E1
Westwood Primary School
 CHAD OL9 .... 8 E5

Westwood Trading Estate
 MPL/ROM SK6 .... 114 A7
Whalley Range FC
 CCHDY M21 .... 98 A3
Whalley Range High School
 OLDTF/WHR M16 .... 98 C4
Wharfside Business Centre
 TRPK M17 .... 86 C6
Wharton Primary School
 LHULT M38 .... 52 B6
Wheatfield Industrial Estate
 ROY/SHW OL2 .... 59 G1
Wheatlea Industrial Estate
 WGNS/IIMK WN3 .... 63 J2
Wheatsheaf Industrial Estate
 SWIN M27 .... 70 E3
Wheatsheaf Shopping Centre
 MILN OL16 .... 10 F3
Whelley Hospital
 WGN WN1 .... 48 B2
White City Retail Park
 OLDTF/WHR M16 .... 86 D7
Whitefield Community
 Primary School
 WHTF M45 .... 55 K4
Whitefield Golf Club
 WHTF M45 .... 55 H5
Whitefield Medical Centre
 WHTF M45 .... 55 H4
Whitegate End Primary School
 CHAD OL9 .... 74 B1
Whitehill Industrial Estate
 HTNM SK4 .... 100 B7
Whitehill Primary School
 HTNM SK4 .... 100 B8
White Swan Industrial Estate
 OLD OL1 .... 59 M4
Whitley Road Medical Centre
 NEWH/MOS M40 .... 72 F8
Whittaker Moss Primary School
 ROCH OL11 .... 27 G3
The Whitworth Art Gallery
 HULME M15 .... 87 L8
Whitworth Community High
 School WHIT OL12 .... 20 A4
Whitworth Football & CC
 WHIT OL12 .... 20 A3
Whitworth Park School
 RUSH/FAL M14 .... 87 K8
Whitworth Swimming Pool
 WHIT OL12 .... 20 B2
The Wiend Centre
 WGN WN1 .... 15 G4
Wigan Athletic FC
 & Wigan Warriors RLFC
 (The JJB Stadium)
 WGNW/BIL/OR WN5 .... 14 A3
Wigan Borough Cemetery
 WGNS/IIMK WN3 .... 48 A7
Wigan Crematorium
 WGNS/IIMK WN3 .... 48 A8
Wigan Golf Club
 WGN WN1 .... 32 A2
Wigan & Leigh College
 LEIGH WN7 .... 66 B7
 WGN WN1 .... 14 E2
 WGNNW/ST WN6 .... 47 L2
Wigan & Leigh College &
 Community Sixth Form
 College LEIGH WN7 .... 81 H1
Wigan Little Theatre
 WGN WN1 .... 15 H3
Wigan Magistrates Court
 WGN WN1 .... 15 H5
Wigan Pier
 WGNS/IIMK WN3 .... 14 D6
Wigan RUFC
 WGN WN1 .... 32 A7
Wilbraham Primary School
 RUSH/FAL M14 .... 98 D3
Wild Bank Community School
 STLY SK15 .... 92 A2

Willan Industrial Estate
 ORD M5 .... 86 C3
William Andrews Swimming
 Baths DUK SK16 .... 91 G5
William Hulmes Preparatory
 School OLDTF/WHR M16 .... 98 C3
William Wroe Municipal Golf
 Course URM M41 .... 95 K2
Willow Bank Hotel
 RUSH/FAL M14 .... 98 F4
Willow Grove Cemetery
 RDSH SK5 .... 100 D7
Willow Grove School
 AIMK WN4 .... 64 D7
The Willows Primary School
 HALE/TIMP WA15 .... 108 C6
 WYTH/NTH M22 .... 118 E2
Wilmslow Albion FC
 WILM/AE SK9 .... 126 E1
Wilmslow Grange Community
 Primary School
 WILM/AE SK9 .... 119 M7
Wilmslow Health Centre
 WILM/AE SK9 .... 126 E6
Wilmslow High School
 WILM/AE SK9 .... 126 F6
Wilmslow Leisure Centre
 WILM/AE SK9 .... 126 F6
Wilmslow Preparatory School
 WILM/AE SK9 .... 126 F5
Wilmslow RFC
 WILM/AE SK9 .... 126 D3
Wilmslow Road Medical Centre
 RUSH/FAL M14 .... 98 F1
 WILM/AE SK9 .... 119 M8
Wind in the Willows Hotel
 GLSP SK13 .... 105 J4
Windlehurst School
 MPL/ROM SK6 .... 123 H2
Windmill Lane
 Industrial Estate
 DTN/ASHW M34 .... 100 F2
Wingates Industrial Estate
 WHTN BL5 .... 50 A1
Winstanley College
 WCNW/BIL/OR WN5 .... 62 B1
Winstanley Medical Centre
 WGNS/IIMK WN3 .... 63 G1
Winstanley Primary School
 WGNS/IIMK WN3 .... 62 F2
Withington Bowling Club
 RUSH/FAL M14 .... 98 F5
Withington Girls School
 RUSH/FAL M14 .... 98 E4
Withington Golf Club
 DID/WITH M20 .... 110 C2
Withington Hospital
 DID/WITH M20 .... 98 C6
Withington Swimming Baths
 DID/WITH M20 .... 98 E6
Withins High School
 BOLE BL2 .... 37 H2
Wolfenden Primary School
 BOL BL1 .... 36 B2
Woodbank CC
 TOT/BURYW BL8 .... 25 G8
Woodbank Park Athletics Track
 OFTN SK2 .... 112 F3
Woodbank Primary School
 TOT/BURYW BL8 .... 25 G8
Woodend Mills Industrial Estate
 OLDE OL4 .... 60 C7
Woodfield Primary School
 WGN WN1 .... 31 M8
Woodfields Retail Park
 BURY BL9 .... 4 E3
Wood Fold Primary School
 WGNNW/ST WN6 .... 31 G4
Woodford Aerodrome
 BRAM/HZG SK7 .... 128 D3
Woodford CC
 BRAM/HZG SK7 .... 128 C2

Woodhey High School
 RAMS BLO 24 D1
Woodheys Primary School
 SALE M33 .... 108 B2
Woodhouse Primary School
 URM M41 .... 84 D8
Woodhouses Voluntary
 Controlled Primary School
 FAIL M35 .... 74 F6
Woodlands Hospital
 WALK M28 .... 52 C8
Woodlands Industrial Estate
 NEWLW WA12 .... 78 F6
Woodley Health Centre
 MPL/ROM SK6 .... 101 K7
Woodley Primary School
 MPL/ROM SK6 .... 101 L7
Woodley Sports Centre
 MPL/ROM SK6 .... 101 K6
Woodsend Primary School
 URM M41 .... 94 F1
Woods Hospital
 GLSP SK13 .... 104 E1
Woolfold Industrial Estate
 TOT/BURYW BL8 .... 24 E8
Woolworths Sports Club
 ROCH OL11 .... 41 M1
Worsley Business Park
 TYLD SK7 .... 68 C4
Worsley Golf Club
 ECC M30 .... 69 M8
Worsley Mesnes Primary School
 WGNS/IIMK WN3 .... 47 K8
Worsley Road Industrial Estate
 FWTH BL4 .... 52 F6
Worsley Trading Estate
 LHULT M38 .... 52 B7
Worthington Lakes Business
 Park WGN WN1 .... 31 M4
Worthington Primary School
 SALE M33 .... 97 J8
Worth Primary School
 POY/DIS SK12 .... 129 K1
Wrightington Hospital
 WGNNW/ST WN6 .... 30 B3
Wrightington Hotel & Country
 Club WGNNW/ST WN6 .... 30 C1
Wright Robinson Sports College
 GTN M18 .... 89 J6
The Wycliffe Hotel
 EDGY/DAV SK3 .... 12 C8
Wythenshawe Hall Country Park
 NTHM/RTH M23 .... 109 L4
Wythenshawe Hospital
 NTHM/RTH M23 .... 109 J8
Wythenshawe Park Track
 NTHM/RTH M23 .... 109 K4
Xaverian Sixth Form College
 RUSH/FAL M14 .... 98 F1
Yeargate Industrial Estate
 BURY BL9 .... 40 A2
Yeshivah Ohr Torah School
 BRO M7 .... 72 A4
Yesoiday Hatorah School
 PWCH M25 .... 71 L2
Yew Tree Community School
 CHAD OL9 .... 58 C8
Yew Tree Primary Community
 School DUK SK16 .... 91 G5
Yew Tree Trading Estate
 RNFD/HAY WA11 .... 78 A4
YMCA Leisure Centre
 CSLFD M3 .... 6 C6

Acknowledgements

Schools address data provided by Education Direct

Petrol station information supplied by Johnsons

Manchester transport information provided by GMPTE © 2007

Garden centre information provided by:

Garden Centre Association   Britains best garden centres

Wyevale Garden Centres

The statement on the front cover of this atlas is sourced, selected and quoted
from a reader comment and feedback form received in 2004